THE
ALL ENGLAND
LAW REPORTS
1984

Volume 2

Editor
PETER HUTCHESSON LL M
Barrister, New Zealand

Assistant Editor
BROOK WATSON
of Lincoln's Inn, Barrister
and of the New South Wales Bar

Consulting Editor
WENDY SHOCKETT
of Gray's Inn, Barrister

London
BUTTERWORTHS

ENGLAND	Butterworth & Co (Publishers) Ltd, 88 Kingsway, **London** WC2B 6AB
AUSTRALIA	Butterworths Pty Ltd, **Sydney, Melbourne, Brisbane, Adelaide, Perth, Canberra** and **Hobart**
CANADA	Butterworth & Co (Canada) Ltd, **Toronto** and **Vancouver**
NEW ZEALAND	Butterworths of New Zealand Ltd, **Wellington** and **Auckland**
SINGAPORE	Butterworth & Co (Asia) Pte Ltd, **Singapore**
SOUTH AFRICA	Butterworth Publishers (Pty) Ltd, **Durban** and **Pretoria**
USA	Butterworth Legal Publishers, **Seattle**, Washington, **Boston**, Massachusetts, **Austin**, Texas and **St Paul**, Minnesota D & S Publishers, **Clearwater**, Florida

©

Butterworth & Co (Publishers) Ltd

1984

ISBN 0 406 85151 4

Typeset by CCC, printed and bound in Great Britain by William Clowes Limited, Beccles and London

REPORTERS

House of Lords

Mary Rose Plummer Barrister

Privy Council

Mary Rose Plummer Barrister

Court of Appeal, Civil Division

Mary Rose Plummer Barrister
Frances Rustin Barrister
Diana Procter Barrister

Diana Brahams Barrister
Patricia Hargrove Barrister
Sophie Craven Barrister

Carolyn Toulmin Barrister

Court of Appeal, Criminal Division

N P Metcalfe Esq Barrister
Dilys Tausz Barrister

April Weiss Barrister
Raina Levy Barrister

Martine Kushner Barrister

Chancery Division

Jacqueline Metcalfe Barrister
Evelyn M C Budd Barrister
Hazel Hartman Barrister
Vivian Horvath Barrister

Queen's Bench Division

David Bartlett Esq Barrister
M Denise Chorlton Barrister

J M Collins Esq Barrister
K Mydeen Esq Barrister

Family Division

Bebe Chua Barrister

Admiralty

N P Metcalfe Esq Barrister

Revenue Cases

Rengan Krishnan Esq Barrister
Clare Mainprice Barrister

Courts-Martial Appeals

N P Metcalfe Esq Barrister

SUB-EDITOR

Radhika Edwards Barrister

MANAGER

John W Wilkes Esq

House of Lords

The Lord High Chancellor: Lord Hailsham of St Marylebone

Lords of Appeal in Ordinary

Lord Diplock
Lord Fraser of Tullybelton
Lord Keith of Kinkel
Lord Scarman
Lord Roskill

Lord Bridge of Harwich
Lord Brandon of Oakbrook
Lord Brightman
Lord Templeman

Court of Appeal

The Lord High Chancellor

The Lord Chief Justice of England: Lord Lane
(President of the Criminal Division)

The Master of the Rolls: Sir John Francis Donaldson
(President of the Civil Division)

The President of the Family Division: Sir John Lewis Arnold

The Vice-Chancellor: Sir Robert Edgar Megarry

Lords Justices of Appeal

Sir John Frederick Eustace Stephenson
Sir Frederick Horace Lawton
Sir George Stanley Waller
Sir James Roualeyn Hovell-Thurlow-
    Cumming-Bruce
Sir Edward Walter Eveleigh
Sir Desmond James Conrad Ackner
Sir Robin Horace Walford Dunn
Sir Peter Raymond Oliver
Sir Tasker Watkins VC
Sir Patrick McCarthy O'Connor
Sir William Hugh Griffiths

Sir Michael John Fox
Sir Michael Robert Emanuel Kerr
Sir John Douglas May
Sir Christopher John Slade
Sir Francis Brooks Purchas
Sir Robert Lionel Archibald Goff
Sir George Brian Hugh Dillon
Sir Stephen Brown
Sir Roger Jocelyn Parker
Sir Nicolas Christopher Henry Browne-
    Wilkinson

Chancery Division

The Lord High Chancellor

The Vice-Chancellor

Sir John Norman Keates Whitford
Sir Ernest Irvine Goulding
Sir Raymond Henry Walton
Sir John Evelyn Vinelott
Sir Martin Charles Nourse
Sir Douglas William Falconer

Sir Jean-Pierre Frank Eugene Warner
Sir Peter Leslie Gibson
Sir David Herbert Mervyn Davies
Sir Jeremiah LeRoy Harman
Sir Donald James Nicholls
Sir Richard Rashleigh Folliott Scott

Queen's Bench Division

The Lord Chief Justice of England

Sir Joseph Donaldson Cantley
Sir Hugh Eames Park
Sir Bernard Caulfield
Sir William Lloyd Mars-Jones
Sir Ralph Kilner Brown
Sir Peter Henry Rowley Bristow
Sir Hugh Harry Valentine Forbes
Sir David Powell Croom-Johnson
Sir Leslie Kenneth Edward Boreham
Sir Alfred William Michael Davies
Sir John Dexter Stocker
Sir Kenneth George Illtyd Jones
Sir Haydn Tudor Evans
Sir Peter Richard Pain
Sir Kenneth Graham Jupp
Sir Ralph Brian Gibson
Sir Walter Derek Thornley Hodgson
Sir James Peter Comyn
Sir Anthony John Leslie Lloyd
Sir Frederick Maurice Drake
Sir Brian Thomas Neill
Sir Michael John Mustill
Sir Barry Cross Sheen
Sir David Bruce McNeill
Sir Harry Kenneth Woolf

Sir Christopher James Saunders French
Sir Thomas Patrick Russell
Sir Peter Edlin Webster
Sir Thomas Henry Bingham
Sir Iain Derek Laing Glidewell
Sir Henry Albert Skinner
Sir Peter Murray Taylor
Sir Murray Stuart-Smith
Sir Christopher Stephen Thomas Jonathan
  Thayer Staughton
Sir Donald Henry Farquharson
Sir Anthony James Denys McCowan
Sir Iain Charles Robert McCullough
Sir Hamilton John Leonard
Sir Alexander Roy Asplan Beldam
Sir David Cozens-Hardy Hirst
Sir John Stewart Hobhouse
Sir Michael Mann
Sir Andrew Peter Leggatt
Sir Michael Patrick Nolan
Sir Oliver Bury Popplewell
Sir William Alan Macpherson
Sir Philip Howard Otton
Sir Paul Joseph Morrow Kennedy
Sir Michael Hutchison

Family Division

The President of the Family Division

Sir John Brinsmead Latey
Sir Alfred Kenneth Hollings
Sir Charles Trevor Reeve
Dame Rose Heilbron
Sir Brian Drex Bush
Sir Alfred John Balcombe
Sir John Kember Wood
Sir Ronald Gough Waterhouse

Sir John Gervase Kensington Sheldon
Sir Thomas Michael Eastham
Dame Margaret Myfanwy Wood Booth
Sir Anthony Leslie Julian Lincoln
Dame Ann Elizabeth Oldfield Butler-Sloss
Sir Anthony Bruce Ewbank
Sir John Douglas Waite
Sir Anthony Barnard Hollis

CITATION

These reports are cited thus:

[1984] 2 All ER

REFERENCES

These reports contain references to the following major works of legal reference described in the manner indicated below.

Halsbury's Laws of England

The reference 26 Halsbury's Laws (4th edn) para 577 refers to paragraph 577 on page 296 of volume 26 of the fourth edition of Halsbury's Laws of England and the reference 37 Halsbury's Laws (3rd edn) 135, para 239 refers to paragraph 239 on page 135 of volume 37 of the third edition.

Halsbury's Statutes of England

The reference 5 Halsbury's Statutes (3rd edn) 302 refers to page 302 of volume 5 of the third edition of Halsbury's Statutes of England.

The Digest

References are to the green band reissue volumes and the blue band replacement volumes of The Digest (formerly the English and Empire Digest), and to the continuation volumes.

The reference 36(2) Digest (Reissue) 764, 1398 refers to case number 1398 on page 764 of Digest Green Band Reissue Volume 36(2).

The reference 47 Digest (Repl) 781, 25 refers to case number 25 on page 781 of Digest Blue Band Replacement Volume 47.

The reference Digest (Cont Vol E) 640, 2392a refers to case number 2392a on page 640 of Digest Continuation Volume E.

Halsbury's Statutory Instruments

The reference 20 Halsbury's Statutory Instruments (4th reissue) 302 refers to page 302 of the fourth reissue of volume 20 of Halsbury's Statutory Instruments; references to other reissues are similar.

Cases reported in volume 2

Digest of cases reported in volume 2

CRIMINAL LAW

CORRIGENDA

[1984] 1 All ER

p 729. **Clough Mill Ltd v Martin.** Lines *f*5 and *f*6 should read '. . . until he has *been* paid for them in full . . .'

p 1045. **Freeman v Home Office.** Solicitors for the plaintiff should read '*Gamlens*, agents for *George E Baker & Co*, Guildford'.

p 1066. **Barclays Bank Ltd v TOSG Trust Fund Ltd.** Line *a*5 should read '. . . Barclays and the *irrevocable* duty to employ that sum . . .'

[1984] 2 All ER

p 105. **IRC v Stannard.** Date of hearing and judgment should read '6 February 1984'.

p 258. **Re a debtor (No 26 of 1983).** Lines *d*6 and *d*7. Omit the words 'as from 16 November 1983'.

p 344. **Grand Champion Tankers Ltd v Norpipe A/S.** First line should read '. . . the vessel's navigational charts was brought to their managing director's notice . . .' Page 350. Lines *c*5 and *c*6 should read '. . . The Lord Justice continued as follows (at 164):'

p 390. **Chief Constable of Hampshire v A.** Solicitors for the defendants should read '*Hancock & Willis*, agents for *Faithfull & Bowker*, Winchester'.

p 591. **Thames Guaranty Ltd v Campbell.** Line *j*1 should read '. . . the first Defendant [Mr Campbell] to the . . .'

p 680. **R v Foster.** Lines *b*1 and *b*2 should read '. . . appeal against conviction would be *allowed* for reasons to be given later.'

Vickerman (Inspector of Taxes) v Mason's Personal Representatives

CHANCERY DIVISION
SCOTT J
10 FEBRUARY 1984

Income tax – Assessment – Mistake, defect or omission not invalidating assessment – Mistake – Error in computation of tax due – Further assessment to recover tax lost – Further assessment stated to be made pursuant to statutory provision inapplicable in circumstances – Validity of assessment – Whether 'assessment to tax' including error in computation of tax – Taxes Management Act 1970, s 29(3)(b)(c).

The inspector of taxes assessed the taxpayer to income tax under Sch E. The assessment however contained an arithmetical error in the calculation of tax due with the result that part of the sum on which the taxpayer was assessed was not subjected to tax. To recover the tax on that sum the inspector made a further assessment, stating incorrectly that it was made under s 29(3)(c)[a], instead of s 29(3)(b), of the Taxes Management Act 1970. The taxpayer appealed, contending (i) that the inspector had had no power to make the further assessment to correct the arithmetical error in the original assessment and (2) that since in making the assessment the inspector had purported to rely on s 29(3)(c), which was not applicable in the circumstances, the assessment was not valid. The Crown contended that the further assessment was in fact valid under s 29(3)(b) and accordingly should be confirmed. The General Commissioners determined that the Revenue had made the further assessment under s 29(3)(c) and, since that subsection was not the correct legal provision under which they could act to recover the tax undercharged, the assessment should be discharged. The Crown appealed.

Held – The appeal would be allowed for the following reasons—

(1) The validity of an assessment to tax once made was a question of law and could be established by the Crown as a matter of law without regard to the erroneous reasons given when making the assessment. Thus the fact that the inspector had notified the taxpayer that he was relying on s 29(3)(c) for making the assessment did not preclude him from justifying it by reference to another statutory provision (see p 4 *d* to *f* and p 5 *d g*, post).

(2) The expression 'assessment to tax' in s 29(3)(b) covered all stages leading up to the calculation and statement of the amount of tax due. An arithmetical error in the computation of tax due was therefore covered by that expression and accordingly where the tax assessed was insufficient by reason of such an error the Revenue had power to correct that error under s 29(3)(b) (see p 4 *g* to p 5 *d* and *g*, post); *Hallamshire Industrial Finance Trust Ltd v IRC* [1979] 2 All ER 433 applied.

Notes

For the Revenue's power to raise further assessments where there has been an undercharge to tax, see 23 Halsbury's Laws (4th edn) paras 1576–1577, and for cases on the subject, see 28(1) Digest (Reissue) 546–553, 1984–2016.

For the Taxes Management Act, s 29, see 34 Halsbury's Statutes (3rd edn) 1274.

---

a   Section 29(3) is set out at p 4 *c*, post

Cases referred to in judgment

Cenlon Finance Co Ltd v Ellwood (Inspector of Taxes) [1962] 1 All ER 854, [1962] AC 782,   **a**
[1962] 2 WLR 871, HL.
Hallamshire Industrial Finance Trust Ltd v IRC [1979] 2 All ER 433, [1979] 1 WLR 620.

Case also cited

Olin Energy Systems Ltd v Scorer (Inspector of Taxes) [1982] STC 800.

b

Case stated

1. At a meeting of the Commissioners for the General Purposes of the Income Tax for
the division of St Margaret and St John, Westminster, held on 28 July 1982 at Caxton
Hall, Westminster, the personal representatives of I H M Mason deceased (the taxpayer)
appealed against an additional assessment to tax under Sch E for the year 1979–80 made
on the taxpayer on 22 January 1982 pursuant to s 29(3)(c) of the Taxes Management Act   **c**
1970.

2. The additional assessment was made in respect of the same item of income as the
first assessment to tax under Sch E for the year 1979–80 made on the taxpayer on 20
March 1981 in the sum of £11,111.

3. The question for the commissioners' determination was whether the additional
assessment was validly made.   **d**

4. The personal representatives of the taxpayer were represented at the hearing by Mr
K Wilson, chartered accountant. The inspector of taxes conducted the case on behalf of
the Crown.

[Paragraph 5 listed the documents admitted before the commissioners.]

6. The commissioners found the following facts proved: (i) there was an arithmetical
error in the assessment made on 20 March 1981; (ii) the additional assessment was made   **e**
in order to correct the arithmetical error; (iii) in notifying Mr Wilson by letter dated 6
January 1982 that an additional assessment would be made, the inspector stated that it
was made pursuant to s 29(3)(c) of the Taxes Management Act 1970; (iv) there was no
reference to s 29(3)(b) of the 1970 Act in any correspondence or document sent by the
inspector to either Mr Wilson or the taxpayer; (v) the manner of completion of the
additional assessment did not constitute an error or mislead the accountant.   **f**

7. It was contended on behalf of the personal representatives that: (i) there was no
power available to the inspector to correct an arithmetical error in an assessment to tax
which had been charged and paid, s 29(1)(a) of the 1970 Act being satisfied; (ii) the
inspector's express exercise of powers of correction under s 29(3)(c) was void as the
provision concerned was inapplicable as it only enabled the inspector to raise an
assessment where error relating to 'relief' was discovered; (iii) in the circumstances   **g**
reference to s 29(3)(b) of the 1970 Act in a mere telephone conversation was irrelevant
when throughout the correspondence s 29(3)(c) had been referred to; (iv) the further
assessment dated 22 January 1982 was invalid as in the form 'Copy of Notice of Further
Assessment and Statement of tax unpaid or overpaid' it expressly failed to state the
amount of the gross income on which the further assessment was raised.

8. It was contended by the inspector that: (i) the additional assessment was validly   **h**
made under s 29(3) of the 1970 Act; (ii) accordingly the additional assessment should be
confirmed.

9. The commissioners were referred to one authority, namely *Cenlon Finance Co Ltd v
Ellwood (Inspector of Taxes)* [1962] 1 All ER 854, [1962] AC 782.

10. The commissioners who heard the appeal found on the evidence before them that
the appeal succeeded on the grounds that, in their opinion, the Revenue had raised the   **j**
further assessment under s 29(3)(c) of the 1970 Act which they did not consider to be the
correct legal provision under which the Revenue could act to recover the undercharged
tax. They therefore discharged the further assessment.

11. Immediately on being informed of the determination of the appeal, the Crown
declared its dissatisfaction therewith as being erroneous in point of law, and on 6 August

1982 required the commissioners to state a case for the opinion of the High Court
pursuant to s 56 of the Taxes Management Act 1970.

12. The question of law for the opinion of the court was whether on the evidence
before the commissioners the additional assessment was validly made.

Robert Carnwath for the Crown.
The personal representatives did not appear.

SCOTT J. In this appeal the Crown appeals against a finding by the General
Commissioners, the result of which was that an arithmetical error made in the original
assessment against the taxpayer was not permitted to be corrected by a further assessment.
The point can, I think, be briefly demonstrated from the copy notice of assessment
admitted before the commissioners. The notice shows a net amount chargeable to tax of
£11,111. It then, in Pt III, shows the rates of tax applicable to the various slices of that
taxable income. It shows as taxable under the 30% rate a sum of £4,927 crossed out and
with the sum of £4,297 inserted in its place. It then shows as taxable under the 50%
bracket the sum of £434. The error in these figures is that the sum of £630, which
represents the difference between the £4,927 and the £4,297, ought to have been, but
was not, included under the 50% bracket; so that the figure of £434 ought correctly to
have been £1,064. On the basis of the figures in the assessment the tax payable was
calculated. That assessment was not appealed, and the tax due under it has, as I understand
it, been paid. Following that assessment, it came to the attention of the Revenue that the
mistake I have referred to had been made. Correspondence took place between the
Revenue and Mr Wilson, the professional accountant acting on behalf of the personal
representatives of the taxpayer, whereby the Revenue suggested the mistake could be
informally adjusted; Mr Wilson declined to accept that. The Revenue then made a
further assessment correcting the arithmetical error which had been made in the
calculation of the tax due under the original assessment. In the correspondence with Mr
Wilson they purported to be acting under a particular section of the Taxes Management
Act 1970, namely s 29(3)(c). Mr Wilson by letter asserted that that statutory provision
did not permit the further assessment to be made. Counsel for the Crown before me
today accepts that the assertion was right. The further assessment was, however, made.
It contained nothing on its face to say under what statutory provision it was made; it
simply purported to correct the arithmetical calculation of tax due in respect of the
amount chargeable to tax, that is to say the £11,111. Since the error in the original
assessment was the omission of £630 from the 50% tax bracket, it is not surprising to
find that the additional tax payable under this further assessment is the sum of £315.
The personal representatives of the taxpayer refused to accept that the further assessment
was correctly made and the matter came before the General Commissioners.

There were two main points taken before the General Commissioners. The first was
the question whether there was any power in the Revenue to make any additional
assessment at all to correct the arithmetical error in the original assessment. The second
point was whether it mattered that, in the correspondence leading up to the further
assessment, the Revenue had purported to act under s 29(3)(c) or whether the Revenue
could justify the further assessment under whatever legal provision might be available
for that purpose. In the event, it was s 29(3)(b) that the Revenue relied on before the
commissioners. The question for the commissioners was whether the Revenue were
entitled so to justify the further assessment, or whether they were caught by their
original reliance, expressed in the correspondence, on para (c). The commissioners on
that point decided against the Revenue; they did not purport to decide the first point,
that is to say the question whether there was any power for the Revenue to correct the
error by a further assessment. That point is alive for me to deal with. It is, as I see it,
simply a question of law, and I ought, therefore, to decide it; there is no need to send the
matter back to the commissioners for that purpose.

I must refer to the relevant statutory provisions which bear on the point I have to decide. Section 29(1) of the Taxes Management Act 1970 requires the assessment of tax to be made. Section 29(6) provides:

'After the notice of assessment has been served on the person assessed, the assessment shall not be altered except in accordance with the express provisions of the Taxes Acts.'

That provision produces the result that once the assessment has been served, subject to any appeal and the result of any appeal and subject to any mitigating effect that express statutory provisions may produce, the assessment is final as between the Revenue and the taxpayer. Section 29(3) deals with errors. It provides as follows:

'If an inspector or the Board discover—(a) that any profits which ought to have been assessed to tax have not been assessed [I interpose that that does not apply in the present case], or (b) that an assessment to tax is or has become insufficient [that is the provision which, as I have said, is relied on by the Revenue], or (c) that any relief which has been given is or has become excessive [that is the provision which in the correspondence was relied on but, it is now accepted, is not relevant to the present case], the inspector or, as the case may be, the Board may make an assessment in the amount, or the further amount, which ought in his or their opinion to be charged.'

The first question is whether the Crown must fail because, in the correspondence leading up to the further assessment, the Revenue relied on and sought to justify the further assessment by reference to a statutory provision on which reliance could not, for the purpose of this particular assessment, be placed. In my judgment, the validity of this assessment once made is a matter of law and it is a point of irrelevance what justification prior to the assessment may or may not have been given by the Revenue in order to explain the assessment they were proposing to make. This is not a case in which the discretion of the Revenue to make the additional assessment has been challenged. In sub-s (3) the power to make an additional assessment is permissive, not mandatory; there is, therefore, a discretion, but the exercise of the discretion has not been challenged. That being so, the validity of the assessment is, in my judgment, simply a question of law and may be established by the Crown as a matter of law without regard to the erroneous reasons put forward in the correspondence that preceded the assessment. Accordingly, in my judgment, the only real point in the case is whether the Revenue do have power under s 29(3)(b) to correct the arithmetical error. I will read the relevant provision again:

'If an inspector or the Board discover ... (b) that an assessment to tax is ... insufficient ... the inspector or, as the case may be, the Board may make an assessment in the amount, or the further amount, which ought in his or their opinion to be charged.'

Simply as a matter of language, it seems to me that that provision covers, inter alia, an arithmetical error in the computation of tax. In such a case, I would have thought, the situation would be one where the assessment to tax was insufficient by reason of that error. It has been suggested by Mr Wilson, in a note which he passed to counsel for the Crown and which counsel very properly referred me to, that the reference to 'assessment to tax' in para (b) should be read as a reference to the assessment of the amount which is liable to tax, and since there was no insufficiency in the taxable sum, that is to say the £11,111, the power to correct the error under para (b) does not arise. I do not think that that argument is consistent with the language of the section. The section refers, in its final lines, to 'an assessment in the amount, or the further amount, which ought ... to be charged'.

The reference to 'assessment' in that passage is plainly a reference to an assessment of the tax to be charged, and it would seem to me to be odd to give 'assessment' in one part of the section a meaning different from that which the word should bear in another part of the section. But the point has been dealt with conclusively by Browne-Wilkinson J in *Hallamshire Industrial Finance Trust Ltd v IRC* [1979] 2 All ER 433, [1979] 1 WLR 620. In

that case the Crown was seeking to argue the same point Mr Wilson has sought to put
a before me today, namely that 'assessment to tax' means assessment of the amount that is
amenable to tax, rather than assessment of the tax. Browne-Wilkinson J, in his judgment,
said that was wrong and that the expression 'assessment to tax' covered all the various
stages leading up to the calculation and statement of the amount of tax due. In my
judgment that decision decides the point against Mr Wilson's contention. I have also
been referred to a decision of the House of Lords in *Cenlon Finance Co Ltd v Ellwood*
b *(Inspector of Taxes)* [1962] 1 All ER 854, [1962] AC 782. That case concerned the
correction of an error of law made in an assessment. It was held that a new assessment in
order to correct that error of law was justified under a statutory provision not materially
different from that in s 29(3)(b). There is a statement of principle by Viscount Simonds
(see [1962] 1 All ER 854 at 859, [1962] AC 782 at 794) which I would also pray in aid in
justifying the power of the Revenue in the present case to correct the arithmetical error.
c   I turn, therefore, to the contentions of the taxpayer's personal representatives as set out
in para 7 of the case stated. The first contention was that there was no power available to
the inspector to correct an arithmetical error in an assessment to tax which had been
charged and paid. In my judgment there is such a power and it is to be found in s 29(3)(b)
of the 1970 Act.
The second contention was that, the inspector having expressed his reliance on
d s 29(3)(c), it was not open to him to raise an assessment and justify it by a reference to
another statutory provision. In my judgment that contention is wrong in law.
Thirdly, reliance was placed on the irrelevance of a certain telephone conversation in
which it is said the Revenue mentioned s 29(3)(b) as justifying a further assessment. I
agree that that matter is irrelevant. It does not matter, in my judgment, what power
previous to the assessment the Revenue purported to be relying on. Perhaps I should add
e that it was found, as a matter of fact, by the commissioners that Mr Wilson was not
misled by the Revenue's shift of ground from their argued reliance on para (c) to their
eventual, and as I find successful, reliance on para (b). Even if Mr Wilson had been, in
some degree, misled, it would not, in my judgment, have affected the legal result; but it
would, no doubt, have justified him in asking for an adjournment, if he had conceived
he required one, in order to be able to deal properly before the commissioners with the
f actual case which was being put forward.
Finally, the point was taken, and is set out in para 7(iv) of the case stated that the
further assessment was invalid on the ground, as a point of form, that it failed to state the
amount of gross income on which the further assessment was raised. The amount of
income on which tax was being raised, the £11,111, is set out in the further assessment,
and it is clear on the face of the assessment that it was raised in order to correct the
g arithmetical error to which I have referred. In those circumstances I do not find there is
any inadequacy of form. If there had been any inadequacy of form it would have been
cured by s 114(1) of the 1970 Act.
For those reasons I allow the appeal.

Appeal allowed.

Solicitors: *Solicitor of Inland Revenue.*

Clare Mainprice   Barrister.

Alcom Ltd v Republic of Colombia   *a*
(Barclays Bank plc and another, garnishees)

HOUSE OF LORDS
LORD DIPLOCK, LORD FRASER OF TULLYBELTON, LORD KEITH OF KINKEL, LORD ROSKILL AND LORD
TEMPLEMAN
22, 26 MARCH, 12 APRIL 1984   *b*

*Constitutional law − Foreign sovereign state − Immunity from suit − Enforcement proceedings −
Exceptions − Commercial transactions − Default judgment obtained against foreign sovereign
state in respect of claim for sale of goods − Plaintiff obtaining garnishee orders nisi to attach
moneys in foreign state's accounts at London banks − Ambassador certifying that accounts used or
intended for use in day-to-day running expenses of embassy in London − Whether funds used for*   *c*
*such running expenses constituting funds used for commercial transactions − Whether bank
accounts 'property' − Whether foreign state entitled to claim immunity from enforcement in
respect of accounts − State Immunity Act 1978, ss 13(2)(b)(4), 17(1).*

In May 1982 the plaintiffs issued a writ against the defendant, a friendly foreign sovereign
state with an accredited diplomatic mission in the United Kingdom, claiming a sum of   *d*
money in respect of goods sold and delivered. In December the plaintiffs obtained
judgment in default of notice of intention to defend, and subsequently sought to levy
execution against moneys in bank accounts held to the credit of the foreign state's
embassy in London. In September 1983 the plaintiffs obtained garnishee orders nisi
against the respective accounts. The foreign state applied to the High Court to discharge
the orders, claiming immunity from execution under the provisions of the State   *e*
Immunity Act 1978. By s 13(2)(b)[a] of the 1978 Act the property of a state could not be
'subject to any process for the enforcement of a judgment'. However, by s 13(4) a state
was not immune from the enforcement of a judgement against 'property which is for
the time being in use or intended for use for commercial purposes', which by s 17(1)[b]
were defined as being the purposes of commercial transactions. In claiming immunity,
the foreign state's ambassador certified that the funds in the bank accounts were not used   *f*
or intended for use for commercial purposes but to meet the expenditure necessarily
incurred in the day-to-day running of the diplomatic mission. Under s 13(5) such a
certificate was sufficient evidence that the property against which enforcement was
sought was not used for commercial purposes unless the contrary was proved. The judge
held, inter alia, that a bank account used for an embassy was prima facie non-commercial
and he discharged the garnishee orders nisi. The plaintiffs appealed to the Court of   *g*
Appeal, which held that funds in bank accounts used for the day-to-day expenditure of
an embassy were used or intended for use for 'commercial transactions' and therefore
property against which execution could be levied. The foreign state appealed to the
House of Lords.

                                                                        h

Held − The foreign state's appeal would be allowed for the following reasons—
  (1) Although the amount standing to the credit of a diplomatic mission in a current
account at a commercial bank was capable of being 'property' for the purposes of s 13(2)(b)
and (4), it was not 'property . . . in use or intended for use for commercial purposes'
within s 13(4) unless the judgment creditor who was seeking to attach the credit balance
by garnishee proceedings was able to show that the bank account was earmarked by the   *j*
foreign state solely for the settlement of liabilities incurred in commercial transactions,

---

a   Section 13, so far as material, is set out at p 11 *d* to *g*, post
b   Section 17(1), so far as material, is set out at p 11 *c*, post

eg for issuing documentary credits in payment for goods sold to the state. Accordingly,
a where the bank account of a foreign state was used to meet the day-to-day running
expenses of a diplomatic mission it fell outside the scope of s 13(4), since it was indivisible
and would be used not only to settle liabilities incurred under contracts for the supply of
goods or services to the mission but also in the exercise by the state of its sovereign
authority. That immunity from process was in accordance with the rule of public
international law that neither the executive nor the legal branch of government in a
b receiving state was entitled to act in any manner which obstructed a diplomatic mission
in carrying out its functions (see p 9 *e f*, p 12 *b c*, p 13 *a* to *d* and *h* and p 14 *f* to *j*, post).

(2) It was for the plaintiffs to show that the funds in the foreign state's bank accounts
were used solely to meet liabilities incurred in commercial transactions, and since the
ambassador's certificate was, in the circumstances, conclusive on that issue, the bank
accounts were immune from the levying of execution (see p 13 *d e h* and p 14 *f* to *j*, post).
c Decision of the Court of Appeal [1984] 1 All ER 1 reversed.

Notes
For sovereign and diplomatic immunity from suit, see 8 Halsbury's Laws (4th edn) para
410 and 18 ibid para 1548, and for cases on the subject, see 1(1) Digest (Reissue) 54–59,
358–382.
d For the State Immunity Act 1978, ss 13, 17, see 48 Halsbury's Statutes (3rd edn) 96, 99.

Cases referred to in opinions
I Congreso del Partido [1981] 2 All ER 1064, [1983] 1 AC 244, [1981] 3 WLR 328, HL.
Philippine Admiral (owners) v Wallem Shipping (Hong Kong) Ltd, The Philippine Admiral [1976]
1 All ER 78, [1977] AC 373, [1976] 2 WLR 214, PC.
e *Trendtex Trading Corp v Central Bank of Nigeria* [1977] 1 All ER 881, [1977] 1 QB 529,
[1977] 2 WLR 356, CA.

Interlocutory appeal
The defendant, the Republic of Columbia, appealed with leave of the Court of Appeal
f against the decision of that court (Sir John Donaldson MR, May and Dillon LJJ) ([1984] 1
All ER 1, [1983] 3 WLR 906) on 24 October 1983 allowing an appeal by the plaintiffs,
Alcom Ltd, against the judgment of Hobhouse J dated 21 October 1983 whereby he
ordered to be set aside the garnishee orders nisi made by Master Topley on 27 September
1983 ordering Barclays Bank plc and the First National Bank of Boston to attach such
sum standing to the credit of the defendant as would satisfy the judgment of £41,690·56
and £147·50 costs obtained by the plaintiffs on 10 December 1982. The facts are set out
g in the opinion of Lord Diplock.

Anthony Thompson QC and *Timothy Saloman* for the appellant.
Richard Slowe for the respondents.
Simon D Brown and *Rosalyn Higgins* as amici curiae.

h Their Lordships took time for consideration.

12 April. The following opinions were delivered.

LORD DIPLOCK. My Lords, the diplomatic mission of the Republic of Colombia in
j the United Kingdom, like the diplomatic missions of most other foreign sovereign states,
maintains at a London branch of a commercial bank a current account on which it draws
for the purpose of meeting expenditure incurred in the day-to-day running of the
mission. The question of law in this appeal is whether the English High Court has
jurisdiction in garnishee proceedings to order the attachment of the whole or part of the
balance standing to the credit of the foreign state in such an account, in order to satisfy a

judgment for a sum of money that has been validly obtained against that state by a
judgment creditor.　　　　　　　　　　　　　　　　　　　　　　　　　　　　*a*

Since, under RSC Ord 49, a garnishee order is in the first instance made ex parte and
operates forthwith to freeze the bank account to the extent of the amount specified in
the order, the grant by the court of such an order for a substantial sum can gravely
hamper and may soon temporarily prevent the day-to-day running of the diplomatic
mission. So the question that falls to be determined by your Lordships is one of
outstanding legal importance not only nationally but also internationally.　　　　*b*

The answer to this question depends on the true construction of s 13(2)(*b*) and (4) of
the State Immunity Act 1978. The Act, as its short title indicates, deals primarily with
relations between sovereign states, though its provisions are capable of extension by
Order in Council to relations between the United Kingdom and the constituent territories
of federal states. Accordingly, its provisions fall to be construed against the background
of those principles of public international law as are generally recognised by the family　*c*
of nations. The principle of international law that is most relevant to the subject matter
of the Act is the distinction that has come to be drawn between claims arising out of
those activities which a state undertakes jure imperii, ie in the exercise of sovereign
authority, and those arising out of activities which it undertakes jure gestionis, ie
transactions of the kind which might appropriately be undertaken by private individuals
instead of sovereign states.　　　　　　　　　　　　　　　　　　　　　　*d*

The particular aspect of public international law dealt with by Pt I of the 1978 Act,
comprising ss 12 to 17, is the immunity of foreign states from the jurisdiction of courts
of law in any part of the United Kingdom. The distinction between the jurisdiction of
national courts to decide, and to authorise the execution of remedies for the enforcement
of, claims made against foreign states arising out of the exercise of jus imperii and those
arising out of transactions entered into in the exercise of jus gestionis obtained growing　*e*
recognition in European countries as sovereign states began increasingly to engage, either
directly or through separate entities that were emanations of the executive government
of the state, in commercial and trading transactions with private citizens of other states.
Under what came to be termed the 'restrictive' theory of sovereign immunity the
jurisdiction of national courts was exercised over foreign states in claims against them
that arose out of commercial or trading transactions into which they had entered with　*f*
private individuals. The United States of America had clung longer than several European
states to the 'absolute' theory of sovereign immunity, under which its courts declined to
entertain any claims against foreign states even where these arose out of commercial or
trading transactions. Following a change of policy by the executive branch of government
this practice was abandoned in 1952 by the United States courts which then adopted the
'restrictive' theory; and the matter has since 1976 been regulated in the United States by　*g*
an Act of Congress, the Foreign Sovereign Immunities Act.

In England the jurisdiction of its courts of justice over claims against foreign sovereign
states was governed by the common law. Although the courts' refusal to exercise
jurisdiction over foreign sovereigns was originally attributed in the eighteenth century
to the acceptance of the law of nations as part of the common law of England, the English
courts during the twentieth century were slow to recognise and give effect to the change　*h*
that had been taking place in public international law over the last 50 years, whereby,
among the great majority of trading nations, the restrictive theory of sovereign immunity
had replaced the absolute theory. That recognition first occurred in a judgment of the
Privy Council in *Philippine Admiral (owners) v Wallem Shipping (Hong Kong) Ltd, The
Philippine Admiral* [1976] 1 All ER 78, [1977] AC 373 delivered in November 1975,
though this in its terms was limited to actions in rem. It was the seminal judgment of　*j*
Lord Denning MR in *Trendtex Trading Corp v Central Bank of Nigeria* [1977] 1 All ER
881, [1977] 1 QB 529 that marked the definitive absorption by the common law of the
restrictive theory of sovereign immunity.

Lord Denning MR's statement in the *Trendtex* case as to what had become the revised
common law rule as to the immunity of foreign sovereign states from the jurisdiction of

a the English courts before the passing of the State Immunity Act 1978 received the seal of approval of this House in *I Congreso del Partido* [1981] 2 All ER 1064, [1983] 1 AC 244. Although the speeches in *I Congreso del Partido* were delivered after the 1978 Act had come into force they dealt with matters that had occurred before the Act was passed and to which s 23(3) prevented it from being applicable. So as respects the immunity of foreign states from the jurisdiction of national courts the critical distinction drawn by the existing law, English common law and public international law alike, was between

b what a state did in the exercise of its sovereign authority and what it did in the course of commercial or trading activities. The former enjoyed immunity; the latter did not.

The functions of a diplomatic mission that are recognised in public international law are set out in art 3 of the Vienna Convention on Diplomatic Relations of 1961 (Cmnd 1368) as follows:

c   '1. The functions of a diplomatic mission consist *inter alia* in: (a) representing the sending State in the receiving State; (b) protecting in the receiving State the interests of the sending State and of its nationals, within the limits permitted by international law; (c) negotiating with the Government of the receiving State; (d) ascertaining by all lawful means conditions and developments in the receiving State, and reporting thereon to the Government of the sending State; (e) promoting friendly relations between the sending State and the receiving State, and developing their economic, d   cultural and scientific relations . . .'

If one were seeking for prototypes of things done in the exercise of its sovereign authority by one state within the territory of another it would be difficult to find examples more striking than those included in this list; and the Convention by art 25 goes on to provide:

e   'The receiving State shall accord full facilities for the performance of the functions of the mission.'

Transposed into its negative form: neither the executive nor the legal branch of government in the receiving state, and enforcement of judgments of courts of law is a combined operation of both these branches, must act in such manner as to obstruct the mission in carrying out its functions.

f   On the specific question whether international law prohibits the attachment by legal process of moneys standing to the credit of a current bank account of a diplomatic mission that is used to defray the expenses incurred in performance of the functions of the mission, your Lordships have been referred to a comprehensive and closely reasoned judgment of the Constitutional Court of the German Federal Republic of 13 December 1977, which decisively rejected the claim of a judgment creditor of the Philippine

g Republic to distrain on a current bank account maintained by the diplomatic mission of that sovereign state for the purpose of defraying the expenses incurring in the day-to-day running of the mission. It was thus a case which was closely parallel to that with which this House is now concerned; and the judgment is particularly helpful inasmuch as the question was decided by that distinguished court by reference to public international law which, by the Federal Constitution Act, is incorporated ipso jure as part of German

h Federal Law.

My Lords, I find the reasoning of the German Constitutional Court in the *Philippine Republic* case wholly convincing that immunity from legal processes of execution was required by public international law to be accorded to the current bank account of a diplomatic mission used for defraying the expenses of running the mission at the date when the State Immunity Act 1978 was passed by the Parliament of the United Kingdom.

j   Of itself, however, the fact that under public international law, including the Vienna Convention to which the United Kingdom is a party, the bank account of the Colombian diplomatic mission that the respondent sought to make the subject of garnishee proceedings would have been entitled to immunity from attachment, at the date of the passing of the State Immunity Act 1978, is not sufficient to answer the question with which your Lordships are confronted in the instant appeal. It makes it highly unlikely that Parliament intended to require United Kingdom courts to act contrary to international law unless the clear language of the statute compels such a conclusion; but **a** it does not do more than this.

The State Immunity Act 1978, whose long title states as its first purpose to make *new* provision with respect to proceedings in the United Kingdom by or against other states, purports in Pt I to deal comprehensively with the jurisdiction of courts of law in the United Kingdom both (1) to adjudicate on claims against foreign states (adjudicative jurisdiction) and (2) to enforce by legal process (enforcement jurisdiction) judgments **b** pronounced and orders made in the exercise of their adjudicative jurisdiction. But, although comprehensive, the 1978 Act in its approach to these two aspects of the jurisdiction exercised by courts of law does not adopt the straightforward dichotomy between acta jure imperii and acta jure gestionis that had become familiar doctrine in public international law, except that it comes close to doing so in s 14(2) in relation to the immunity conferred on 'separate entities that are emanations of the State'. Instead, as **c** respects foreign states themselves the Act starts by restating in statutory form in s 1(1) the general principle of absolute sovereign immunity, but makes the principle subject to wide-ranging exceptions for which the subsequent sections in Pt I of the Act (ss 2 to 17) provide.

In creating these exceptions, for which it has recourse to a somewhat convoluted style of draftsmanship providing for exceptions to exceptions which have the effect of restoring **d** in part an immunity which some other subsection would appear to have removed, the Act nevertheless draws a clear distinction between the adjudicative jurisdiction and the enforcement jurisdiction of courts of law in the United Kingdom. Sections 2 to 11 deal with adjudicative jurisdiction. Sections 12 to 14 deal with procedure and of these, ss 13(2) to (6) and 14(3) and (4) deal in particular with enforcement jurisdiction. (Admiralty jurisdiction in rem, with which your Lordships in the instant case are not concerned, **e** may be regarded for the purposes of the 1978 Act as hybrid; exceptions to immunity from such suits is dealt with in s 10; immunity of ship or cargo from arrest, detention and sale, whether before or after judgment, is dealt with in s 13(2)(b) and (4).)

Of the various exceptions to immunity from adjudicative jurisdiction created by ss 2 to 11, a brief reference is needed to s 2, which deals with voluntary submission by a foreign state to the adjudicative jurisdiction of United Kingdom courts. Section 13(3), **f** which I shall be setting out verbatim later, makes it clear that such submission does not of itself imply any submission to the enforcement jurisdiction of the courts. Separate consent to that is needed. Before coming to s 3 itself brief mention may be made of s 4 which deals with contracts of employment, s 5 which deals with liability in tort for personal injury or injury to property, s 7 which deals with patents, trade marks and intellectual property, s 8 which deals with liabilities arising out of membership of **g** corporate and unincorporated bodies, and s 11 which deals with liability for value added tax and rates. Section 10, as already mentioned, deals with Admiralty proceedings and withdraws adjudicative immunity from ships and cargo used or intended for use for commercial purposes. To the relevance to the instant appeal of s 6 dealing with immovable property I shall be reverting later.

Section 3 is not only the section under which the respondents obtained judgment in **h** default of appearance (which has since been set aside) against the Republic of Colombia for a liability alleged to have been incurred by the republic under a contract for the supply of goods. The definition of 'commercial transaction' in sub-s (3) is relied on by the respondents as subjecting to the enforcement jurisdiction of the High Court the bank account sought to be attached by garnishee proceedings. This section accordingly merits citation in full: **j**

'(1) A State is not immune as respects proceedings relating to—(a) a commercial transaction entered into by the State; or (b) an obligation of the State which by virtue of a contract (whether a commercial transaction or not) falls to be performed wholly or partly in the United Kingdom.

(2) This section does not apply if the parties to the dispute are States or have otherwise agreed in writing; and subsection (1)(b) above does not apply if the contract (not being a commercial transaction) was made in the territory of the State concerned and the obligation in question is governed by its administrative law.

(3) In this section 'commercial transaction' means—(a) any contract for the supply of goods or services; (b) any loan or other transaction for the provision of finance and any guarantee or indemnity in respect of any such transaction or of any other financial obligation; and (c) any other transaction or activity (whether of a commercial, industrial, financial, professional or other similar character) into which a State enters or in which it engages otherwise than in the exercise of sovereign authority; but neither paragraph of subsection (1) above applies to a contract of employment between a State and an individual.'

The particular importance attaching to sub-s (3) is, that in s 17, which serves, inter alia, as a definition section for Pt I of the Act, it is provided:

'(1) In this Part of this Act . . . "commercial purposes" means purposes of such transactions or activities as are mentioned in section 3(3) above . . .'

I turn next to the relevant provisions of s 13 that relate to enforcement jurisdiction. On the meaning of these provisions read in conjunction with those of ss 3 and 17 that I have just quoted your Lordships' decision in the instant appeal will depend:

'(2) Subject to subsections (3) and (4) below—(a) relief shall not be given against a State by way of injunction or order for specific performance or for the recovery of land or other property; and (b) the property of a State shall not be subject to any process for the enforcement of a judgment or arbitration award or, in an action in rem, for its arrest, detention or sale.

(3) Subsection (2) above does not prevent the giving of any relief or the issue of any process with the written consent of the State concerned; and any such consent (which may be contained in a prior agreement) may be expressed so as to apply to a limited extent or generally; but a provision merely submitting to the jurisdiction of the courts is not to be regarded as a consent for the purposes of this subsection.

(4) Subsection (2)(b) above does not prevent the issue of any process in respect of property which is for the time being in use or intended for use for commercial purposes . . .

(5) The head of a State's diplomatic mission in the United Kingdom, or the person for the time being performing his functions, shall be deemed to have authority to give on behalf of the State any such consent as is mentioned in subsection (3) above and, for the purposes of subsection (4) above, his certificate to the effect that any property is not in use or intended for use by or on behalf of the State for commercial purposes shall be accepted as sufficient evidence of that fact unless the contrary is proved . . .'

My Lords, I would accept that the expression 'property' in sub-ss (2)(b) and (4) is broad enough to include as being the property of a banker's customer the debt owed to him by the banker which is represented by the total amount of any balance standing to the customer's credit on current account. It is erroneous and misleading to confuse the legal nature of this property with the legal nature of property that consists of cash or currency notes belonging to a customer and physically lodged in a safe deposit at the bank. For the purposes of execution by attachment in garnishee proceedings by a judgment creditor, the customer's right to withdraw his credit balance is a single not a composite chose in action and the superadded contractual obligations in respect of cheques drawn on the account in favour of third parties are irrelevant to the liability of the whole credit balance on current account to attachment in the exercise of the enforcement jurisdiction of the court.

The crucial question of construction for your Lordships is whether a debt which has

these legal characteristics falls within the description contained in s 13(4) of 'property
which is for the time being in use or intended for use for commercial purposes'. To speak   *a*
of a debt as 'being used or intended for use' for any purposes by the creditor to whom the
debt is owed involves employing ordinary English words in what is not their natural
sense, even if the phrase 'commercial purposes' is given the ordinary meaning of jure
gestionis in contrast to jure imperii, that is generally attributed to it in the context of
rights to sovereign immunity in public international law, though it might be permissible
to apply the phrase intelligibly to the credit balance in a bank account that was earmarked   *b*
by the state for exclusive use for transactions into which it entered jure gestionis. What
is clear beyond all question is that, if the expression 'commercial purposes' in s 13(4) bore
what would be its ordinary and natural meaning in the context in which it there appears,
a debt representing the balance standing to the credit of a diplomatic mission in a current
bank account used for meeting the day-to-day expenses of running the mission would
fall outside the subsection.   *c*

'Commercial purposes', however, is given by s 17(1) the extended meaning which
takes one back to the comprehensive definition of 'commercial transaction' in s 3(3).
Paragraph (a) of this tripartite definition refers to *any* contract for the supply of goods or
services, without making any exception for contracts in either of these two classes that
are entered into for purposes of enabling a foreign state to do things in the exercise of its
sovereign authority either in the United Kingdom or elsewhere. This is to be contrasted   *d*
with the other paragraph of the definition that is relevant to the instant case, para (c),
which on the face of it would be comprehensive enough to include all transactions into
which a state might enter, were it not that it does specifically preserve immunity from
adjudicative jurisdiction for transactions or activities into which a state enters or in which
it engages in the exercise of sovereign authority, other than those transactions that are
specifically referred to either in para (a) or in para (b), with the latter of which the instant   *e*
appeal is not concerned.

The prima facie breadth of the definition of 'commercial transaction' in s 3(3) and thus
of 'commercial purposes' in s 13(4) is, however, considerably narrowed not only by the
express exclusion from that definition of contracts of employment, which is to be found
in s 3(3) itself, but also by the fact that separate provision is made by other sections of Pt I
of the Act to remove, subject to detailed and sometimes convoluted exceptions, the   *f*
immunity of foreign states from adjudicative jurisdiction as respects liabilities incurred
in relation to other transactions and activities. Apart from contracts of employment
themselves the most significant of these are to be found in s 6, particularly s 6(1) read in
conjunction with s 16(1)(b). The former reads:

'(1) A State is not immune as respects proceedings relating to—(a) any interest of
the State in, or its possession or use of, immovable property in the United Kingdom;   *g*
or (b) any obligation of the State arising out of its interest in, or its possession or use
of, any such property.'

There is no exception here, or elsewhere in s 6 itself, for immunity in relation to
immovable property that is occupied by a state for purposes that are not commercial
purposes; but the special status of the state's diplomatic mission is recognised in a later   *h*
section, s 16(1)(b), which provides:

'(1) This Part of this Act does not affect any immunity or privilege conferred by
the Diplomatic Privileges Act 1964 or the Consular Relations Act 1968; and . . . (b)
section 6(1) above does not apply to proceedings concerning a State's title to or its
possession of property used for the purposes of a diplomatic mission.'   *j*

My Lords, the decisive question for your Lordships is whether in the context of the
other provisions of the Act to which I have referred, and against the background of its
subject matter, public international law, the words 'property which is for the time being
in use or intended for use for commercial purposes', appearing as an exception to a
general immunity to the enforcement jurisdiction of United Kingdom courts accorded

by s 13(2) to the property of a foreign state, are apt to describe the debt represented by
a the balance standing to the credit of a current account kept with a commercial banker
for the purpose of meeting the expenditure incurred in the day-to-day running of the
diplomatic mission of a foreign state.

Such expenditure will, no doubt, include *some* moneys due under contracts for the
supply of goods or services to the mission, to meet which the mission will draw on its
current bank account; but the account will also be drawn on to meet many other items
b of expenditure which fall outside even the extended definition of 'commercial purposes'
for which ss 17(1) and 3(3) provide. The debt owed by the bank to the foreign sovereign
state and represented by the credit balance in the current account kept by the diplomatic
mission of that state as a possible subject matter of the enforcement jurisdiction of the
court is, however, one and indivisible; it is not susceptible of anticipatory dissection into
the various uses to which moneys drawn on it might have been put in the future if it had
c not been subjected to attachment by garnishee proceedings. Unless it can be shown by
the judgment creditor who is seeking to attach the credit balance by garnishee
proceedings that the bank account was earmarked by the foreign state solely (save for de
minimis exceptions) for being drawn on to settle liabilities incurred in commercial
transactions, as for example by issuing documentary credits in payment of the price of
goods sold to the state, it cannot, in my view, be sensibly brought within the crucial
d words of the exception for which s 13(4) provides.

The onus of proving that the balance standing to the credit of the diplomatic mission's
current bank account falls within the exception created by the crucial words in s 13(4)
lies on the judgment creditor. By s 13(5) the head of the mission's certificate that property
is not in use or intended for use by or on behalf of the state for commercial purposes is
sufficient evidence of that fact unless the contrary is proved. In the instant case the
e Colombian ambassador gave a certificate in the following terms:

'3 Hans Crescent
London SW1X 0LR

CERTIFICATION

f The undersigned Ambassador Extraordinary and Plenipotentiary of the Republic of
Colombia to the Court of St. James's hereby certifies that:

The funds deposited by the Colombian Embassy in its bank accounts at the First
National Bank of Boston in London are not in use nor intended for use for
commercial purposes but only to meet the expenditure necessarily incurred in the
day to day running of the Diplomatic Mission.

g   [Signed]

Augusto Espinosa
Ambassador

7th October 1983'

h   For the reasons I have given this certificate in my opinion is conclusive that the bank
account referred to falls outside s 13(4). It is thus also conclusive that the Republic of
Colombia is entitled to succeed in this appeal.

Although it does not affect the question of law involved in this appeal it needs to be
said, in fairness to the Republic of Colombia, that this is not a case in which that state is
seeking to escape from satisfying a judgment on the merits, given against it, on a cause
j of action for breach of a contract which, if the existence of such a contract were
established, would fall within the adjudicative jurisdiction of a United Kingdom court
under s 13 of the 1978 Act as a commercial transaction. What happened was that,
through a series of mischances and misunderstandings as to the new procedure for service
of writs on foreign states that had been introduced by s 12 of the State Immunity Act
1978, the Republic of Colombia failed to enter an appearance timeously and judgment

in default of appearance was obtained against it by the respondent company. The
garnishee proceedings to attach the debt represented by the credit balance of the *a*
diplomatic mission in its current bank account with a London branch of the First
National Bank of Boston were brought ex parte to obtain satisfaction of the default
judgment. Master Topley without the advantage of adversarial argument but having
been shown the ambassador's certificate got the answer right; he refused to make an
order nisi; but an appeal from this refusal was allowed by Hodgson J who laboured under
the same disadvantage. After the Republic of Colombia had belatedly repaired its failure *b*
to enter an appearance the matter came before Hobhouse J on an application to set the
order aside. That judge, after hearing adversarial argument by both parties, set aside the
garnishee order. An appeal from this decision was brought to the Court of Appeal by the
respondent company. That court was informed that the Republic of Colombia intended
to apply to set aside the default judgment and to contest the case on the merits, but by
agreement between the parties, in view of the importance of the point of law involved, *c*
the appeal against the order of Hobhouse J was proceeded with forthwith; it was not
postponed to await the result of the intended application to set the default judgment
aside. The Court of Appeal reversed the order of Hobhouse J but gave leave to appeal
from its decision to this House.

Since the date when leave to appeal was granted, the default judgment has been set
aside and with it the garnishee order which was dependent on the existence of the default *d*
judgment has gone; so the only financial consequences to the parties which can result
from the success or failure of this appeal will depend on the order which your Lordships
are disposed to make as to the costs incurred in the garnishee proceedings. These, to the
discredit of our legal system, your Lordships were told, already exceeded the amount of
the judgment debt even before the appeal reached this House.

Your Lordships do not encourage appeals of which the only financial consequences are *e*
limited to costs; but the question of law which is involved in the appeal is of outstanding
international importance, although more so to the appellant sovereign state than it is to
the respondent company. It was however the respondent company who persisted in
appealing to the Court of Appeal from the order of Hobhouse J which I understand all
your Lordships accept as having been right in law. Justice would, I think, be done to
both parties if each side bore its own costs of the garnishee proceedings here and below. *f*
I would so order.

LORD FRASER OF TULLYBELTON. My Lords, I have had the advantage of
reading the speech of my noble and learned friend Lord Diplock, and I agree with his
reasoning and his conclusion. For the same reasons I would allow this appeal. I agree that
each party should bear its own costs of the garnishee proceedings here and below.

g

LORD KEITH OF KINKEL. My Lords, I have had the benefit of reading in draft the
speech of my noble and learned friend Lord Diplock. I agree with it, and for the reasons
he gives I too would allow the appeal.

LORD ROSKILL. My Lords, I have had the advantage of reading in draft the speech
of my noble and learned friend Lord Diplock. I agree with it and for the reasons he gives *h*
I would allow the appeal.

LORD TEMPLEMAN. My Lords, I agree with the speech of my noble and learned
friend Lord Diplock, and for the reasons he gives I too would allow the appeal.

Appeal allowed.   *j*

Solicitors: *Boodle Hatfield & Co* (for the appellant); *William T Stockler* (for the respondents);
Treasury Solicitor.

Mary Rose Plummer   Barrister.

Oswald Hickson Collier & Co (a firm) v Carter-Ruck

COURT OF APPEAL, CIVIL DIVISION
LORD DENNING MR, KERR AND MAY LJJ
20 JANUARY 1982

Restraint of trade by agreement – Partnership – Solicitors – Restriction on practice in event of partner ceasing to be a partner – Deed of partnership providing that outgoing partner not to solicit or act for clients of firm except for 'any client introduced to the firm' by him – Defendant partner joining sole practitioner practising under name of firm – Other partner dying leaving defendant in sole practice – Defendant later joined by other partners – Whether clients for whom defendant acted in sole practice clients 'introduced to the firm' by defendant – Whether defendant entitled to continue to act for clients for whom he had acted while in sole practice.

Solicitor – Client – Fiduciary relationship – Entitlement to act for client – Clause in partnership deed precluding outgoing partner of firm acting for client in future – Whether clause contrary to public policy.

In December 1943 the defendant entered into partnership with a solicitor who until then had practised on his own account under a firm name. In January 1944 the other partner died leaving the defendant in sole practice under the firm name. In August 1944 the defendant was joined in partnership by another solicitor and thereafter the partnership grew to eight partners. Clause 24 of the deed of partnership under which the partnership was conducted in 1975 provided that an outgoing partner was not to 'approach solicit or act' for any clients of the firm for a period of two years from his leaving the firm except for, inter alios, 'Any client introduced to the firm' by the partner whom he elected to retain as a client. In 1981 the defendant decided to quit the partnership and commence practice on his own account. However, the defendant wished to continue acting for a Lloyd's syndicate which had been a client of his since the time when he was in sole practice. The remaining partners in the firm applied for an injunction restraining the defendant from acting for the client, on the ground that the client was a 'client of the firm' within cl 24 of the deed of partnership and that therefore the defendant was not entitled to act for that client within two years of leaving the firm. At the hearing of the application, the defendant gave an undertaking that, inter alia, until judgment in the action he would not solicit or act for the Lloyd's syndicate. The defendant appealed, seeking an order releasing him from the undertaking.

Held – Since there had not been a 'firm' practising as solicitors under the name of the plaintiff firm at the time when the defendant was in sole practice from January to August 1944, any clients for whom the defendant then acted were to be taken as clients 'introduced to the firm' by him when he was joined in partnership by another solicitor in August 1944 and as such were outside the scope of the restrictive covenant in the deed of partnership. The defendant was therefore entitled to continue to act for the Lloyd's syndicate for whom he had acted while in sole practice. The appeal would accordingly be allowed and the defendant released from his undertaking (see p 17 e to j and p 18 d to j, post).

Per curiam. Since the relationship between a solicitor and his client is a fiduciary relationship it is contrary to public policy for a solicitor to be precluded from acting for a client when that client wants him to act, especially in pending litigation. A clause in a partnership deed preventing one of the partners from acting for a client in the future is accordingly contrary to public policy because there is a fiduciary relationship between them and the client ought reasonably to be entitled to the services of such solicitor as he wishes (see p 18 a to c and g to j, post).

Notes

For restraint of trade, see 47 Halsbury's Laws (4th edn) paras 9–67, and for cases on the subject, see 45 Digest (Repl) 441–510, 252–984.

Interlocutory appeal

The defendant, Peter Frederick Carter-Ruck, appealed, seeking to be discharged and *a* released from the undertakings given to the plaintiffs, Oswald Hickson Collier & Co (the firm), at the hearing of an application before Jupp J on 11 November 1981 for, inter alia, injunctions restraining, inter alios, Mr Carter-Ruck from representing to any clients or former clients of the firm that Mr Carter-Ruck was entitled to solicit or act for any client or former client of the firm other than a client introduced to the firm by Mr Carter-Ruck whom he elected to retain as a client. The undertakings given were (i) that until after the *b* earliest of judgment in the action, further order in the mean time or 18 December 1983 Mr Carter-Ruck would not whether by himself or by his servants or agents represent to clients or former clients of the firm or to any persons in the employment of the firm or to any banker or professional adviser to the firm or to any other person or persons that Mr Carter-Ruck was entitled to solicit or, after 18 December 1981, to act for any client of the firm other than a client introduced to the firm by Mr Carter-Ruck whom he elected *c* to retain as a client and (ii) that from 18 December 1981 until the earliest of judgment in the action, further order in the mean time or 18 December 1983 Mr Carter-Ruck would not solicit or act for the client, a Lloyd's syndicate, whose name appeared in the notice of election to retain clients dated 20 October 1981 and served by Mr Carter-Ruck on the firm. The facts are set out in the judgment of Lord Denning MR.

d

T L G Cullen QC and *Hazel Williamson* for Mr Carter-Ruck.
Robert Wright QC and *David Mabb* for the firm.

LORD DENNING MR. The late Mr Oswald Hickson was a well-known solicitor. He carried on business, largely in libel work, for many years. There is now a dispute amongst the successors to his firm. *e*

Until very recently there were eight partners. The senior partner was Mr Peter Carter-Ruck. The others joined later. The partnership has now come to an end. Various disputes have gone to arbitration. But they do not concern us today.

The question before us is the extent to which Mr Carter-Ruck is to be restrained from acting for previous clients of the firm, in particular one client, the Frank Barber syndicate of Lloyd's. It all depends on the interpretation of cl 24 of the deed of partnership made *f* on 10 June 1975. That says:

> 'In the event of retirement or determination [it is 'retirement' in this case] any Partner retiring or in respect of whom the Partnership with the firm shall not be renewed shall not either in his own name alone or as Managing Clerk to or as Agent for or on behalf of or in Partnership with any other person or persons for a period of two years from such retirement or determination or non-renewal approach solicit *g* or act for any clients of the firm except (a) In connection with business appertaining to relations by blood or marriage or business concerns in which the Partner had or there is a family interest or (b) Any client introduced to the firm by such Partner whom he elects by notice in writing to the other Partners to retain as a client of his . . .'

h

For the determination of this case it is necessary to interpret the meaning of the words 'Any client introduced to the firm by such Partner'. Especially the word 'firm'.

For this purpose I must relate the history of Oswald Hickson Collier & Co. It is well shown by the various applications which were made under the Registration of Business Names Act 1916. It is clear that Mr Oswald Hickson started the business himself in 1919. He was joined later on by Mr Collier. Mr Collier died in June 1930. Then Mr Thirlby *j* entered the partnership. On 29 April 1941 the partnership was dissolved. From that date the business was carried on by Mr Oswald Hickson himself alone.

The important date is 29 April 1941. From that date there was not a 'firm' or 'partnership' in point of law. Mr Oswald Hickson himself was carrying on his own individual business or practice. He did it under the name of Oswald Hickson Collier & Co, but it was himself alone.

He carried on alone until 30 December 1943. On 30 December 1943 Mr Oswald
Hickson was joined by Mr Peter Carter-Ruck. Mr Peter Carter-Ruck had worked for
Oswald Hickson Collier & Co just before the war; but not as a partner. He had gone to
the war. When he came back, a partnership was formed by Mr Oswald Hickson and Mr
Peter Carter-Ruck. That was on 30 December 1943. That partnership did not last very
long. Within nine days of its being formed Mr Oswald Hickson died. So that partnership
came to an end. That was on 9 January 1944.

Under a clause in the deed of partnership Mr Peter Carter-Ruck bought up the interest
of Mr Oswald Hickson. So, from 9 January 1944, Mr Peter Carter-Ruck was the sole
person running the business. There was no firm or partnership for eight months.

On 21 August 1944 Mr Peter Carter-Ruck formed a partnership with Mr John Gow.
That was duly registered. So from that date onwards Mr Peter Carter-Ruck and Mr John
Gow carried on business as partners in the firm of Oswald Hickson Collier & Co, which
was now a firm. That firm continued operating over the years with partners going out
and partners coming in until the deed of partnership was entered into in 1975 which
contained the clause I have read.

I now turn to the meaning of the word 'firm' in cl 24. In construing it, I note that cl
25 of the deed says: 'The firm name shall be registered pursuant to the *Registration of
Business Names Act 1916 . . .*' It is quite plain from s 1 of the 1916 Act that the word 'firm'
applies when two or more persons are in partnership. The meaning of the word 'firm' is
to be found in s 4(1) of the Partnership Act 1890, which says:

> 'Persons who have entered into partnership with one another are for the purposes
> of this Act called collectively a firm, and the name under which their business is
> carried on is called the firm-name.'

Applying that meaning to the word, it seems to me that during the time when Mr
Oswald Hickson worked alone there was no firm. There was a firm for a short time from
30 December 1943 until 9 January 1944. Then there was no firm again until Mr Gow
became a partner of Mr Peter Carter-Ruck on 21 August 1944. For the period from
January 1944 until August 1944 the sole individual running the business was Mr Peter
Carter-Ruck. There was no firm during that time.

In those circumstances it seems to me that the 'firm', within the meaning of the deed
of partnership, started in August 1944. It started when Mr Gow joined Mr Peter Carter-
Ruck and carried on business in partnership with him under the name of Oswald
Hickson Collier & Co. That was the 'firm' referred to in the deed of partnership.

That brings me back to cl 24(b):

> 'Any client introduced to the firm by such Partner whom he elects by notice in
> writing to the other Partners to retain as a client of his.'

When the firm started in August 1944, Mr Peter Carter-Ruck brought in his clients
whom he had had when he was carrying on business alone in the name of Oswald
Hickson Collier & Co by himself from January 1944 until August 1944. They were his
clients for whom he had paid by the payments he had made to the executors of Mr
Oswald Hickson. They were his clients whom he introduced into the firm in August
1944. No doubt Mr Gow introduced his own clients into the firm at that time.

The particular client in dispute in this case is one of Lloyd's syndicates. That client is
one which Mr Peter Carter-Ruck introduced into the firm in August 1944. He elected
by notice to retain that client as his. Therefore Mr Peter Carter-Ruck, in regard to that
client, is not caught by the restrictions contained in the deed of partnership.

It seems to me, having read the judgment of Jupp J, that this point was not submitted
to him. He said: 'After Oswald Hickson's death the partnership continued, being joined
by Gow in 1944 . . .' I am afraid that was an error, because, on Mr Oswald Hickson's
death, the previous partnership came to an end, and the firm did not start again until
August 1944. It seems to me that, on the meaning of the word 'firm' in the deed of
partnership, Mr Peter Carter-Ruck did not break any of the provisions at all by continuing
to act for the Lloyd's syndicate. They were his clients.

One or two other points were raised in this case. One point which was discussed here
was not taken in the court below. That was the introduction into cl 24 of the words   *a*
'approach solicit or act for any clients of the firm'. It was submitted by counsel for Mr
Carter-Ruck that, as the relationship between a solicitor and his client is a fiduciary
relationship, it would be contrary to public policy that he should be precluded from
acting for a client when that client wanted him to act for him, especially in pending
litigation. It seems to me that that submission is right. I cannot see that it would be
proper for a clause to be inserted in a partnership deed preventing one of the partners   *b*
from acting for a client in the future. It is contrary to public policy because there is a
fiduciary relationship between them. The client ought reasonably to be entitled to the
services of such solicitor as he wishes. That solicitor no doubt has a great deal of
confidential information available to him. It would be contrary to public policy if the
solicitor were prevented from acting for him by a clause of this kind.

I think the words 'or act' are too wide. Counsel for Mr Carter-Ruck agreed that they   *c*
were severable. Those words ought to be struck out of the undertaking which was made.
Counsel went further and said that there was no need to make an order about soliciting.
He said that would be sufficiently covered by the rules of the profession as to etiquette.
But I would leave it at that. I do not think it is proper to go into the various cases which
were submitted to us. Mr Carter-Ruck admitted that he made a mistake in one case,
quite innocently, in approaching a particular individual. I think the more satisfactory   *d*
position is to strike out the words 'or act' in the first undertaking. The whole of the
second undertaking should be struck out.

There was a further point about the family interest. That was a difficult point on
construction, which I do not think it is necessary to go into in view of the matters which
I have already mentioned.

I would be in favour of allowing the appeal. The second undertaking should go. As to   *e*
the first undertaking, I think it would be proper to strike out the words 'or act'. We could
make an order to that effect, but, if Mr Carter-Ruck wishes, he can give an undertaking
in place of the injunction.

I am very sorry to hear of all the other proceedings which have been going on between
these very reputable solicitors. I only wish they could be resolved amicably, but I do not
think there is anything more we can do about it or about the pending litigation.   *f*

I would allow the appeal in the circumstances which I have mentioned.

KERR LJ. I agree. In fact, the orders at the moment take the form of an undertaking
and not of an injunction; so, if the reference to 'or act' in part 1 is struck out and the
whole of part 2 is struck out, that would produce the result which Lord Denning MR has
indicated and with which I respectfully agree.   *g*

I would only add that while I respectfully agree with the reasons which Lord Denning
MR has given, I do so on the basis that, although this is perhaps going to be the ultimate
end of this particular bit of this unfortunate dispute, we are not of course deciding these
points finally if the plaintiffs should wish to take them on to the trial. Nor are we
deciding that a one-man practice can never be a 'firm' in any context, eg in an agreement
for the valuation of goodwill, but only in the present context and on the basis of these   *h*
interlocutory proceedings. However, my present inclination is entirely on the lines of
what has been said by Lord Denning MR on the merits of the points which have been
argued, and I would in any event modify the order in the way in which he has indicated
on the grounds of convenience. I therefore agree.

MAY LJ. I also agree and, although we are differing from the judge below, I do not   *j*
think that I can add anything useful in this matter other than to agree with the judgments
which have been delivered and the order proposed.

Appeal allowed.

Solicitors: *P F Carter-Ruck; Oswald Hickson Collier & Co.*

Diana Procter   Barrister.

a

Deacons (a firm) v Bridge

PRIVY COUNCIL

LORD FRASER OF TULLYBELTON, LORD WILBERFORCE, LORD SCARMAN, LORD ROSKILL AND LORD
TEMPLEMAN

13, 14, 15 FEBRUARY, 26 MARCH 1984

b *Restraint of trade – Partnership – Solicitors – Restriction on practice in event of partner ceasing*
to be partner – Firm of solicitors divided into self-contained departments – Partnership agreement
containing restrictive covenant preventing partner from acting for any client of firm if he ceased
to be a partner – Goodwill put in at nominal figure in partnership agreement – Whether
restrictive covenant too wide – Whether covenant should only apply to department of firm in
which outgoing partner employed – Whether firm entitled to protect goodwill when only nominal
c *amount paid for it.*

The plaintiff was a large and well-established firm of solicitors in Hong Kong. The firm
had 27 partners and 49 assistant solicitors and was divided into specialist departments
which were largely self-contained. One such department was the intellectual property
and trade marks department, which dealt with about 10% of the files in the firm and was
d responsible for billing about 4·5% of the firm's fees. The defendant joined the firm in
1967 as an assistant solicitor. In 1973 he became a salaried partner and in 1974 a full
capital partner in charge of the intellectual property and trade marks department. The
defendant only dealt with those clients of the firm who used his department. Under the
terms of the partnership agreement which the defendant entered into when he became a
partner he received a 5% share in the partnership business and its assets, including
e goodwill which was put in at a purely nominal amount in the agreement. The partnership
agreement also contained a restrictive covenant which stated that if a partner ceased to be
a partner he was not to act as a solicitor in Hong Kong for a period of five years for any'
client of the firm or any person who had been a client in the three years preceding his
departure from the firm. In 1982 the defendant resigned from the firm and received a
substantial payment for his share of the partnership although only a nominal amount
f was stated to be for goodwill. Very soon after his resignation the defendant set up a
practice in Hong Kong on his own account in the course of which he commenced acting
for former clients of the plaintiff firm, which consequently sought an injunction to
enforce the restrictive covenant in the partnership agreement. The defendant claimed (i)
that the scope of the restraint was unreasonable in so far as it restricted the defendant
from acting for the 90% of the firm's clients with whom he had had no connection or
g dealings while with the firm and in respect of whom he was no different from any other
solicitor in seeking to attract their business, (ii) that because the plaintiff firm had paid
only a nominal amount for his share of the goodwill it was not entitled to protect it by
the restrictive covenant, and (iii) that the duration of the restraint was unreasonable. The
judge granted the plaintiff firm the injunction sought and on appeal the injunction was
upheld by the Hong Kong Court of Appeal. The defendant appealed to the Privy Council.

h

Held – Applying the principle that the plaintiff firm was entitled to protect its legitimate
interests by means of a restraint of trade imposed on outgoing partners, and having
regard to the nature of the firm's business and the defendant's position in it, the scope
and duration of the restraint of trade sought by the firm was not unreasonable. The firm
was a single practice for the mutual benefit of all the partners, who shared the profits and
j the losses. The partnership agreement applied equally to all partners, and the defendant
himself while he was a partner had had the benefit of the goodwill which the firm
wished to protect by means of the restrictive covenant in the agreement. It was
reasonable, as between the parties, for the firm to protect itself against the appropriation
by the defendant of any part of the firm's goodwill, notwithstanding the division of the
firm's practice into self-contained departments. The fact that the defendant had received
only a nominal sum for goodwill when he resigned in 1982 was irrelevant, since the
defendant's share of the goodwill passed back to the firm not by a sale for a cash

consideration but as part of the partnership contract made with the defendant in 1974
under which he was charged only a nominal sum for goodwill at that date. Furthermore, *a*
the protection of the firm's goodwill was in the public interest since by facilitating
younger people being taken into partnership it encouraged the entry of younger people
into the profession and it also tended to secure continuity in a solicitor's practice which
was beneficial to clients. The defendant's appeal would therefore be dismissed (see p 22 *f*
to *h*, p 23 *g* to *j*, p 24 *a* to *c* and *e* to *j*, p 25 *c* to *j* and p 26 *j*, post.

Dictum of Lord Reid in *Esso Petroleum Co Ltd v Harper's Garage (Stourport) Ltd* [1967] 1 *b*
All ER at 709 applied.

Dictum of Lord Denning MR in *Oswald Hickson Collier & Co v Carter-Ruck* [1984] 2 All
ER at 18 not followed.

Notes
For goodwill and the protection of it by restraint of trade, see 47 Halsbury's Laws (4th *c*
edn) paras 5, 9 et seq.

Cases referred to in judgments
British Reinforced Concrete Engineering Co v Schelff [1921] 2 Ch 563, [1921] All ER Rep 202.
Edwards v Worboys (18 March 1983, unreported), Ch D; *affd* 127 SJ 287, CA.
Esso Petroleum Co Ltd v Harper's Garage (Stourport) Ltd [1967] 1 All ER 699, [1968] AC
269, [1967] 2 WLR 871, HL. *d*
Fitch v Dewes [1921] 2 AC 158, [1921] All ER Rep 13, HL.
Geraghty v Minter (1979) 142 CLR 177, Aust HC.
Leather Cloth Co v Lorsont (1869) LR 9 Eq 345.
Lynch v Bailey (1949) 90 NYS 2d 359; *affd* 300 NY 615.
Mitchel v Reynolds (1711) 1 P Wms 181, [1558–1774] All ER Rep 26, 24 ER 347.
Morris (Herbert) Ltd v Saxelby [1916] 1 AC 688, [1916–17] All ER Rep 305, HL. *e*
Nordenfelt v Maxim Nordenfelt Guns and Ammunition Co Ltd [1894] AC 535, [1891–4] All
ER Rep 1, HL.
Oswald Hickson Collier & Co v Carter-Ruck [1984] 2 All ER 15, CA.

Appeal
The defendant, Robin M Bridge, appealed against the decision of the Court of Appeal of *f*
Hong Kong (Leonard V-P, Cons and Fuad JJA) given on 3 May 1983 dismissing the
defendant's appeal from the decision of the High Court of Hong Kong (Hunter J) on 1
March 1983 ordering, on the application of the plaintiff, Deacons (a firm), that the
defendant be restrained from acting as a solicitor, notary, trade mark or patent agent in
the Colony of Hong Kong for any person, firm or company who was at the time the
defendant ceased to be a partner in the plaintiff firm, or who had during the period of *g*
three years prior to the defendant ceasing to be a partner, been a client of the plaintiff
firm. Prior to issuing a writ on 4 February 1983 seeking the injunction the plaintiff firm
sought an undertaking from the defendant that he would not act for clients of the
plaintiff firm but that undertaking was refused. The facts are set out in the judgment of
Lord Fraser.

h

Sir Patrick Neill QC and *Paul Smith* for the defendant.
Leonard Hoffmann QC and *R G B McCombe* for the plaintiff.

26 March. The following judgment of the Board was delivered.

LORD FRASER OF TULLYBELTON. The question in this appeal is whether a *j*
restrictive covenant in a partnership agreement between the partners in a firm of
solicitors is enforceable against one of their number who has ceased to be a partner, or
whether it is unenforceable as being in unreasonable restraint of trade.

The respondent (the plaintiff) is Deacons, one of the oldest and largest firms of solicitors
in Hong Kong. The appellant (the defendant) Mr Bridge was a full (capital) partner in
the firm from 1 April 1974 until he retired from the firm at 31 December 1982. The
partnership agreement contained a clause (cl 28(a)) whereby a partner who ceased to be a

a partner was restricted for a period of five years thereafter from acting as solicitor in Hong Kong for any client of the firm's, including any person who had been a client during a period of three years immediately before he ceased to be a partner. The plaintiff is seeking to enforce the restriction by injunctions against the defendant. The defendant contends that the restriction is not enforceable against him as being in unreasonable restraint of trade.

b The judge (Hunter J) granted injunctions substantially in the terms sought by the plaintiff. Before the appeal to the Court of Appeal was heard, the defendant gave undertakings in accordance with two subsidiary injunctions ordered by the judge, respectively against soliciting clients and against inducing employees of the firm to break their contracts of employment with the plaintiff. The appeal was limited to the central issue of the enforceability of the restriction against the defendant's acting for clients of the firm. The parties agreed that the interlocutory order by Hunter J which was under appeal should be treated as having been in the form of a permanent injunction as if made

c at trial. The Court of Appeal (Leonard V-P, Cons and Fuad JJA) dismissed the appeal against that order.

The clause imposing the restriction is in the following terms:

d '28(a) Except on dissolution, no partner ceasing to be a partner for any reason whatsoever shall for a period of 5 years thereafter act as a solicitor, notary, trade mark or patent agent or in any similar capacity in the Colony of Hong Kong whether as principal, clerk or assistant for any person, firm or company who was at the time of his ceasing to be a partner or had during the period of 3 years prior thereto been a client of the partnership Provided however that this Clause shall not apply to a partner acting in any such capacity in the course of employment with Government or any public body or with any company or organisation which is not

e itself engaged in professional practice in any of the above fields.'

It is well-established law that covenants in restraint of trade are unenforceable unless they can be shown to be reasonable in the interests of the parties and in the public interest. The classic statement of the law is in the well-known passage in the speech of Lord Macnaghten in *Nordenfelt v Maxim Nordenfelt Guns and Ammunition Co Ltd* [1894]

f AC 535 at 565, [1891–4] All ER Rep 1 at 18, which is as follows:

'The public have an interest in every person's carrying on his trade freely: so has the individual. All interference with individual liberty of action in trading, and all restraints of trade of themselves, if there is nothing more, are contrary to public policy, and therefore void. That is the general rule. But there are exceptions: restraints of trade and interference with individual liberty of action may be justified

g by the special circumstances of a particular case. It is a sufficient justification, and indeed it is the only justification, if the restriction is reasonable—reasonable, that is, in reference to the interests of the parties concerned and reasonable in reference to the interests of the public, so framed and so guarded as to afford adequate protection to the party in whose favour it is imposed, while at the same time it is in no way injurious to the public,'

h In *Herbert Morris Ltd v Saxelby* [1916] 1 AC 688 at 707, [1916–17] All ER Rep 305 at 316 Lord Parker explained that—

'for a restraint to be reasonable in the interests of the parties it must afford *no more than* adequate protection to the party in whose favour it is imposed.'

j While Lord Macnaghten referred to restraints which might be justified by 'the special circumstances of a particular case', it has come to be accepted that certain types of contract which impose a measure of interference with the freedom of trade are treated as not being within the field of restraint of trade, provided that the degree of interference does not exceed the accepted standard. One such type is what Lord Wilberforce in *Esso Petroleum Co Ltd v Harper's Garage (Stourport) Ltd* [1967] 1 All ER 699 at 731, [1968] AC 269 at 335 called 'the well-known type of case where a man sells his business and its goodwill and accepts a limitation on his right to compete'. The justification for the

limitation in that type of case is that it enhances the price which the vendor can obtain for his business: see *Mitchel v Reynolds* (1711) 1 P Wms 181, [1558–1774] All ER Rep 26. **a**
Even in contracts of this type it is necessary to consider whether the restrictions on the vendor of the goodwill are fairly and properly ancillary to the sale; if they exceed that limit the doctrine of restraint of trade may be applied: see *Leather Cloth Co v Lorsont* (1869) LR 9 Eq 345. The other type of contract which has some relevance to this appeal is that in which restrictions are imposed on former employees. In cases of this type only much more limited restrictions are normally enforceable, and if their effect will merely be to **b**
protect the employer from competition from his former employee they will be invalid, unless the circumstances are unusual, as in *Fitch v Dewes* [1921] 2 AC 158, [1921] All ER Rep 13. The reasons for the restrictions being treated differently in the two types of cases are familiar and they were explained, for example, in *Herbert Morris Ltd v Saxelby* [1916] 1 AC 688 at 713–714 [1916–17] All ER Rep 305 at 313, where Lord Shaw said:

> 'When a business is sold, the vendor, who, it may be, has inherited it or built it **c**
> up, seeks to realize this piece of property, and obtains a purchaser upon a condition without which the whole transaction would be valueless. He sells, he himself agreeing not to compete; and the law upholds such a bargain, and declines to permit a vendor to derogate from his own grant. Public interests cannot be invoked to render such a bargain nugatory: to do so would be to use public interest for the destruction of property. Nothing could be a more sure deterrent to commercial **d**
> energy and activity than a principle that its accumulated results could not be transferred save under conditions which would make its buyer insecure. In the case of restraints upon the opportunity to a workman to earn his livelihood a different set of conditions comes into play. No actual thing is sold or handed over by a present to a future possessor. The contract is an embargo upon the energy and activities and labour of a citizen; and the public interest coincides with his own in preventing **e**
> him, on the one hand, from being deprived of the opportunity of earning his living, and in preventing the public, on the other, from being deprived of the work and service of a useful member of society.'

The agreement, in the present case, being one between partners, does not conform exactly to either of the types to which reference has just been made, although it has some **f**
resemblance to both. Their Lordships are of opinion that a decision on whether the restrictions in this agreement are enforceable or not cannot be reached by attempting to place the agreement in any particular category, or by seeking for the category to which it is most closely analogous. The proper approach is that adopted by Lord Reid in the *Esso Petroleum* case [1967] 1 All ER 699 at 709, [1968] AC 269 at 301, where he said:

> 'I think it better to ascertain what were the legitimate interests of the appellants **g**
> which they were entitled to protect, and then to see whether these restraints were more than adequate for that purpose.'

What were the plaintiff's legitimate interests will depend largely on the nature of its business, and on the position of the defendant in the firm. Their Lordships therefore turn to consider the evidence on these matters. **h**
The plaintiff is a large firm established in Hong Kong in 1860, though not under its present name. At the time these proceedings began it had 27 partners and employed 49 assistant solicitors. Its main office is in Hong Kong itself, and it has a small branch in Kowloon. The defendant began his connection with the plaintiff firm on 1 May 1967 when he entered its employment as an assistant solicitor. He had recently completed his articles of clerkship in England but he had not actually been admitted as a solicitor in **j**
England. He had not previously practised as a solicitor in Hong Kong. He became a salaried partner in the plaintiff firm on 1 July 1973, and was admitted a full capital partner on 1 April 1974. He was then aged about 31. He resigned from the firm at 31 December 1982. After starting work with the firm he worked generally for several of the partners, but fairly soon he began working for one partner, a Mr Turnbull, and he developed a growing interest in intellectual and industrial property law and in the law relating to trade marks. That was an area of the plaintiff's practice which had been

a growing during the 1960s. The growth continued and accelerated during the 1970s partly because industrial design copyright became actionable in Hong Kong in 1973. The defendant's invitation to join the firm as a salaried partner was given in the expectation, which was fulfilled, that Mr Turnbull would, in the following year, become senior partner and that the defendant would then become the partner responsible for this part of the practice, which had by then been, or was about to be, recognised as a separate department.

b An important feature of the case, which distinguishes it from any of the reported cases on partnership agreements that were brought to their Lordship's attention, and which was strongly relied on by counsel for the defendant, is that the plaintiff's office is divided into a number of departments, largely separate from each other. This division has occurred as a result of the great expansion in the plaintiff's practice over approximately the last 20 years. The division is emphasised by the fact that each file in their office is specifically assigned to the partner who remains ultimately responsible for it and who c reads all incoming correspondence and signs all outgoing correspondence relating to it. Consequently, each partner's knowledge of the firm's business tends to be concentrated on his own department.

So far as the defendant personally was concerned, the industrial property department was moved about July 1981 to a separate suite of offices on a different floor, and served d by different lifts, from the firm's other departments. He was thus physically, to some extent, cut off from the other departments. The evidence was that he had only acted for those clients of the firm who made use of the intellectual and industrial property department.

In 1981 the total of delivered bills of the plaintiff was approximately $HK132m of which only about $HK6m was attributable to that department, that is about 4·5%. The number of files in the office as a whole was disputed but it seems that something of the e order of 10% of the total was marked as being the responsibility of the defendant. Thus the defendant had no connection or dealings with the great majority (over 90%) of the plaintiff's clients, and, as he claimed, he had no advantage over any other solicitor in seeking to attract their business.

Counsel for the defendant maintained that, in these circumstances, the plaintiff was f not entitled to protection against the defendant's acting for clients of the firm for whom he had never acted while he was a partner. The plaintiff was only entitled to protect such part of its goodwill as would be threated by the defendant if he were to set up practice on his own account, and that part, on the evidence which was filed, consisted only of the business which he was advantageously placed to attract because it came from clients for whom he had acted and to whom he was known.

g Their Lordships do not accept that submission. In their view it is necessary to recall that the partners in the plaintiff firm, as constituted from time to time, are the owners of the firm's whole assets, including its most valuable asset, goodwill. The defendant had owned a share of the assets while he was a partner, but he transferred this share to the continuing partners when he ceased to be a partner. Thereafter the continuing partners owned the whole of the assets: see 8(a) of the agreement which provides:

h   'The assets of the partnership including goodwill and all furniture, safes, boxes, equipment, fittings, fixtures, stores and books held or used for or in connection with the practice . . . belong to the partners in proportion to their respective shares.'

The question is whether it was reasonable, as between the parties, for the plaintiff to obtain protection against appropriation by the defendant of any part of the goodwill, j notwithstanding the 'departmentalisation' of the practice.

Their Lordships consider that it was reasonable, provided (which is not suggested here) that the protection did not extend beyond the plaintiff's practice: see *British Reinforced Concrete Engineering Co v Schelff* [1921] 2 Ch 563, [1921] All ER Rep 202. On this question the mutuality of the contract is a most important consideration. The contract applied equally to all the partners. None of them could tell whether he might find himself in a position of being a retiring partner subject to the restriction in cl 28, or of a continuing partner with an interest to enforce the restriction. It was at least as favourable to the defendant as to the more senior partners; by cl 22 of the agreement every partner is obliged to retire on 31 December immediately following his sixtieth birthday, and the probability therefore was rather that the restriction would apply first against the more senior partners than the more junior ones. Moreover, if any of the senior partners had retired soon after the defendant joined the firm, he might well have been able to take many more of the firm's clients with him than could the defendant. Their Lordships agree with Mason J in the Australian case of *Geraghty v Minter* (1979) 142 CLR 177 at 198 (notwithstanding that he dissented on the facts of that case) that—

> 'The fact that the covenant is entered into by each of the partners and may become binding on any of them, depending upon the events which happen, is a factor which is to be taken into account in assessing whether it is reasonable between the parties.'

It was suggested on behalf of the defendant that a restriction which would have been reasonable between the parties would have been one restricting a retiring partner from acting for clients for whom he had personally acted or for whose work he was generally responsible by, for instance, files of the plaintiff having been opened bearing reference to his name, But a restriction on those lines might well be difficult to apply, particularly in the case of a client who had sought advice from several partners at different times on a variety of matters. Moreover, it might work very unfairly in the case of a partner who for some reason had acted only for a small number of clients, perhaps one or two very large clients, whose business took up practically his whole time, or even for no clients at all, if he were in charge of office administration, as compared with another partner which a large number of relatively small clients. And what of the partner who led an active social life and was instrumental in introducing a number of clients whose business did not fall within the scope of his department? Such possible unfairness illustrates what in their Lordships' view is the fundamental error in this part of the argument for the defendant. It overlooks the fact that the firm had one single practice in which each of the partners had an interest. Each was bound to give a just and faithful account of all transactions relating to the partnership (cl 17(c)) and each was entitled at all times to have free access to, and to inspect, books of account and all records and letters concerning the partnership (cl 11). They shared in the profits and losses of the partnership, and each stood to benefit to some extent from the success of each of the others in attracting clients. It may be possible that a partnership could exist in which the partners' interests were so separated as to make an agreement such as that in the present case unreasonable, but this is not shown to be such a case.

As regards the five-year period of restriction, and the application of the restriction to persons who had been clients within three years before the particular partner retired, counsel for the defendant complained that there was no evidence to justify these periods of time. Their Lordships consider that these are matters which are hardly susceptible of proof by specific evidence. The inclusion of persons who have been clients within the previous three years appears to be perfectly reasonable, having regard to the intermittent nature of a solicitor's employment by any particular client; there must be many regular clients of a solicitor's firm who do not have occasion to employ the firm even as often as once every three years. The five years' limitation also impresses their Lordships as being in no way unreasonable. They have in mind that there appears to be no reported case where a restriction which was otherwise reasonable has been held to be unreasonable solely because of its duration. They have also in mind that some weight should be given to the fact that the restriction is found in a partnership agreement which has evidently been carefully drafted and which must be taken to represent the views of experienced solicitors who would be well aware that an unduly severe restriction would be unenforceable. It must be assumed that they considered the five-year period to be reasonable and their Lordships are not prepared to differ from that view.

One further argument against the reasonableness of the restriction, as between the parties, turns on the alleged inadequacy of the consideration provided for in cl 23 of the agreement. Clause 23(b) provides:

> 'The continuing or surviving partners shall, subject as provided in Clause 25 hereof, and if more than one in the proportions in which they are entitled on the

a expiry date to share in the profits of the partnership, succeed to the share of the outgoing, retiring or deceased partner in the partnership and all the assets and goodwill thereof including the partnership name and shall pay to the outgoing or retiring partner . . . in respect of such share in the manner hereinafter provided: (1) The amount at which the share of the outgoing, retiring or deceased partner stands in the balance sheet . . . and (2) A due proportion of the sum not appearing in the balance sheet and from time to time agreed between the partners for the purposes

b of this Agreement as the value of the following items, namely, goodwill, library, office equipment, furniture, fixtures and fittings (which sum is for convenience hereinafter referred to as "the agreed value of the office assets"). Until otherwise agreed, the agreed value of the office assets shall be [HK$1,000,000, as amended by a supplemental agreement dated 24th April, 1979].'

c Taking the fixed value of $1m for all the 'office assets' it can be shown that only some $60,000 (say £6,000) is attributed to goodwill. That merely nominal amount is in no way related to its real value, having regard to the large profits earned by the firm. From that state of facts two conclusions were said to follow. First, this is not a case like the sale of a business where protection against competition by the vendor can be justified because it will enhance the price he receives for the business. That is plainly correct and

d distinguishes their restriction to some extent from the vendor and purchaser type of restriction. Second, it was said that because the defendant's share of the goodwill had not in any real sense been sold by him to the plaintiff, the plaintiff was not entitled to protect it. Their Lordships were unable to agree with this conclusion. It may well be that the defendant's share of the goodwill was not sold for its market value in cash, but that is immaterial. It passed to the continuing partners not by a sale for a cash consideration in

e 1983, but as part of the contract made in 1974.
The adequacy of the consideration and the reasonableness of the contract as between the parties must be judged in 1974. At that date the defendant received a 5% share in the partnership business and all its assets, including goodwill. In return he agreed to various conditions one of which was that he would transfer his share in the business, including goodwill, to the continuing partners when he retired, and would thereafter not compete

f with them. The value placed on goodwill in 1974 and in 1984 may have been only nominal but there were good reasons for treating it in that way. One reason was to avoid the need to value it on each occasion, and thus to avoid much trouble and expense. Another reason was that, when a new capital partner joins a large firm, he is not normally in a position to pay the full market value of his share of the goodwill, and the only practical system is to charge him a nominal sum. Provision was made in cl 14(b) of the

g contract for a new partner paying for his share in the partnership by applying his share of the profits after deducting a limited amount of drawings for his current use. It is therefore reasonable that when a partner retires, he should receive only a nominal sum for his share of the business. Their Lordships accordingly find no reason to consider that the restriction was unreasonable between the parties by reason of the consideration paid to the defendant having been inadequate.

h On the question of reasonableness in the public interest, their Lordships are of opinion that there is a clear public interest in facilitating the assumption by established solicitors' firms of younger men as partners. It benefits clients by tending to secure continuity in the practice. It also tends to encourage the entry of younger men into the profession. Their Lordships accept the evidence on this matter from Mr Wimbush (the senior partner) in his first addidavit dated 5 February 1983 to the effect that the continuing

j partners in the plaintiff firm would only feel able to take on new capital partners if they knew that in doing so they would not run the risk that the new partners would acquire a connection with clients of the firm and then depart with that part of the plaintiff's goodwill. Conversely, the new capital partners in the plaintiff firm are required to purchase their share of its goodwill, but they could not reasonably be expected to do that if a retiring partner could freely remove part of the goodwill. Accordingly, the restriction was in their Lordships' opinion reasonable in the public interest.
One recent English case must be briefly noticed because certain obiter dicta of Lord

Denning MR seem to have been relied on to some extent in argument before the court in Hong Kong. Before this Board counsel for the defendant declined (rightly in their Lordships' view) to rely on these dicta. The case is *Oswald Hickson Collier & Co v Carter-Ruck* [1984] 2 All ER 15, decided in the (English) Court of Appeal on 20 January 1982. It was a case of a solicitors' partnership. Lord Denning MR, referring to a provision that a retired partner should not 'act for any clients of the firm', said (at 18):

> 'It was submitted by counsel for [the appellant] that, as the relationship between a solicitor and his client is a fiduciary relationship, it would be contrary to public policy that he should be precluded from acting for a client when that client wanted him to act for him, especially in pending litigation. It seems to me that that submission is right. I cannot see that it would be proper for a clause to be inserted in a partnership deed preventing one of the partners from acting for a client in the future. It is contrary to public policy because there is a fiduciary relationship between them. The client ought reasonably to be entitled to the services of such solicitor as he wishes. That solicitor no doubt has a great deal of confidential information available to him. It would be contrary to public policy if the solicitor were prevented from acting for him by a clause of this kind.

Kerr and May LJJ agreed with Lord Denning MR. If these dicta were intended to state a general rule, their Lordships must respectfully but emphatically decline to agree with it. It is unsupported by authority, and appears to have been made without any reference to the fact that it was directly contrary to a considerable volume of authority including a decision of the House of Lords in *Fitch v Dewes* [1921] 2 AC 158, [1921] All ER Rep 13. It also seems to be unjustified in principle. For one thing a solicitor is always (except to some extent in legal aid cases) entitled to refuse to act for a particular person, and it is difficult to see any reason why he should not be entitled to bind himself by contract not to act in future for a particular group of persons. For another thing, the relationship of solicitor and client is not unique in being confidential; the relationship of medical men with their patients and of many other professional men with their clients are also confidential. If there were a general rule that they could not bind themselves not to act for former clients of the firm after they had retired from a partnership, the results would be very far reaching. It must be remembered that the clients are clients of the firm, rather than of an individual partner. These and other objections to treating the dicta in the *Carter-Ruck* case as being of general application were pointed out by Walton J in *Edwards v Worboys* (18 March 1983, unreported). When *Worboys* reached the Court of Appeal (see (1983) 127 SJ 287) Dillon LJ and Sir John Donaldson MR both treated the obiter dicta in *Carter-Ruck* as not being of general application. Their Lordships agree with that view.

Their Lordships' attention was also drawn to the American case of *Lynch v Bailey* (1949) 90 NYS 2d 359 where the Appellate Division of the Supreme Court, New York County held that a very severe restriction applicable to a retiring partner from an accountancy practice was against public policy and void for lack of mutuality and consideration. In the circumstances of that case their Lordships, if they may respectfully say so, have no difficulty in accepting the reasons for the decision. But, with the utmost respect, their Lordships doubt whether it justifies the proposition in the American Law Institute Restatement (2nd) on Contracts, § 188(h):

> 'A rule similar to that applicable to an employee or agent applies to a partner who makes a promise not to compete that is ancillary to the partnership agreement . . .'

In any event such is not yet the law of Hong Kong.

For these reasons their Lordships will humbly advise Her Majesty that this appeal should be dismissed with costs.

Appeal dismissed.

Solicitors: *Herbert Smith & Co* (for the defendant); *Lovell White & King* (for the plaintiff).

Mary Rose Plummer   Barrister.

a
R v Chief Registrar of Friendly Societies, ex parte New Cross Building Society

COURT OF APPEAL, CIVIL DIVISION
SIR JOHN DONALDSON MR, GRIFFITHS AND SLADE LJJ
12, 13, 15, 16, 21 DECEMBER 1983, 10, 12 JANUARY 1984

b
Building society – Chief registrar – Powers of chief registrar – Power of revocation of designation – Extent of registrar's discretion to revoke designation of building society and to prohibit it from taking in deposits – Whether registrar's powers limited until actual failure by building society to comply with statutory requirements – House Purchase and Housing Act 1959, s 1 – Building Societies Act 1962, s 48.

c
Building society – Advances – Special advances – Debts of any description (whether immediately repayable or not) – Unpaid interest and insurance premiums – Whether 'debts of any description (whether immediately repayable or not)' including unpaid interest and insurance premiums – Whether unpaid interest and insurance premiums to be taken into account when determining whether advance a special advance – Building Societies Act 1962, s 21(2).

d
Procedure – Hearing – Hearing in camera – Circumstances in which hearing will be conducted in camera.

By s 1[a] of the House Purchase and Housing Act 1959 the Chief Registrar of Friendly Societies was empowered, if he was satisfied that a building society fulfilled certain requirements prescribed by Treasury regulations, to designate the society for the purposes
e
of s 1 thereby qualifying it for government loans and trustee investment. Section 1 also gave the registrar an implied power to revoke such designation, and by s 48[b] of the Building Societies Act 1962 the registrar was empowered to order a building society not to accept investments or deposits from the public if he considered that such a prohibition was expedient in the interests of the investors or depositors. In August 1983 the chief registrar made an order under s 1 of the 1959 Act revoking the designation of the
f
applicant building society and an order under s 48 of the 1962 Act prohibiting it from receiving deposits and investments from the public, on the grounds, inter alia, (i) that the society had failed to maintain the minimum reserves specified in the Treasury regulations, (ii) that its policy of rapid expansion would result in a diminution of its reserve ratio and a risk of the society having inadequate reserves in relation to the structure of its assets and the nature of its business, and (iii) that it had exceeded its
g
powers to make 'special advances', ie advances to borrowers which exceeded the lending limit in force for the time being. By s 21(2)[c] of the 1962 Act an advance became a special advance if the amount lent, together with 'all other debts of any description (whether immediately payable or not)' owed to the society, exceeded a specified limit. The society applied for judicial review of the registrar's decision seeking certiorari to quash his orders revoking the society's designation and prohibiting it from taking in deposits. The society
h
contended (i) that the registrar was only entitled to make an order revoking the society's designation or prohibiting it from taking in deposits if the society failed to comply with the statutory requirements or if he reasonably perceived actual loss to investors if no order was made, and (ii) that the registrar had wrongly taken into account arrears of

---

a   Section 1, so far as material, is set out at p 32 *h* to p 33 *b*, post
j
b   Section 48 is set out at p 33 *e* to *j*, post
c   Section 21(2), so far as material, provides: '. . . the amount by which a person is indebted to a building society after the making of an advance shall be ascertained so as to take into account both that advance and all other debts of any description (whether immediately repayable or not) in which he is indebted to the society, and shall be so ascertained both—(*a*) immediately after the making of the advance, and (*b*) at the end of a period of three months beginning with the date of the advance or (if sooner) at the end of the financial year in which the advance was made.'

interest and unpaid insurance premiums in determining whether loans by the society
were to be treated as special advances. The registrar contended, inter alia, that his *a*
discretion to revoke a society's designation or prohibit it from taking in deposits was very
wide and extended to all matters relevant to whether the society was a suitable repository
for trust funds. The judge quashed the registrar's orders on the grounds that he had acted
beyond the powers conferred on him by s 1 of the 1959 Act and s 48 of the 1962 Act.
The registrar appealed.

Held – The appeal would be allowed for the following reasons—   *b*
   (1) Having regard to the intention of Parliament in enacting the 1959 and 1962 Acts,
namely that the public should have a high degree of protection when investing in any
building society, the chief registrar had very wide discretionary powers to revoke the
designation of a society and prohibit it from taking in deposits if he considered it
expedient to do so in the interests of present or future investors and depositors. In
particular, the registrar was not limited to waiting until there was an actual failure by a *c*
society to comply with the statutory requirements; instead, he was entitled to take into
account all factors which he considered relevant when granting a designation and also to
act when he apprehended a risk of loss rather than waiting until actual loss was virtually
certain (see p 35 *a* to *c h j*, p 41 *j*, p 43 *a* to *c* and *g* to p 44 *b g h*, p 45 *j*, p 46 *c d h j*, p 47 *b*
to *d* and *f* to *h*, p 48 *d e* and p 55 *c*, post).
   (2) On the true construction of s 21(2) of the 1962 Act 'debts of any description *d*
(whether immediately repayable or not)' included unpaid interest and insurance
premiums relating to existing loans made by a building society, so that an existing loan
which had not been a 'special advance' when made could become a special advance if the
total indebtedness of the borrower, including unpaid interest and insurance premiums,
later exceeded the financial limits relating to special advances (see p 40 *f* to *h*, p 41 *b c j*,
p 44 *j*, p 45 *j*, p 49 *d e h j*, p 50 *b* to *g* and p 55 *c*, post).   *e*
   Per curiam. It is a general rule that courts should conduct their proceedings in public
and it is only if, in wholly exceptional circumstances, the presence of the public or public
knowledge of the proceedings is likely to defeat the paramount object of the courts to do
justice in accordance with the law that the court is justified in proceeding in camera.
Every application for privacy must be considered on its merits, and the applicant must
satisfy the court that nothing short of total privacy will enable justice to be done; it is not *f*
sufficient that a public hearing will merely create embarrassment for some or all those
concerned. In the case of an application by a building society to challenge an order made
by the Chief Registrar of Friendly Societies that would effectively cause the society to
cease to carry on business, the society's vulnerability to the risk of abnormal levels of
withdrawal if there is a loss of confidence on the part of its customers is a sufficient reason
for hearing the society's application in camera, since a public hearing would effectively *g*
deprive the society of any relief to which it might be entitled (see p 30 *a b*, p 31 *b* to *g*,
p 41 *j* and p 45 *j*, post).

Notes
For designation of building societies, see 4 Halsbury's Laws (4th edn) para 1510.
   For special advances and limitations on special advances, see ibid paras 1659–1660. *h*
   For the House Purchase and Housing Act 1959, s 1, see 16 Halsbury's Statutes (3rd
edn) 315.
   For the Building Societies Act 1962, ss 21, 48, see 3 ibid 330, 351.

Cases referred to in judgments
Associated Provincial Picture Houses Ltd v Wednesbury Corp [1947] 2 All ER 680, [1948] 1 *j*
   KB 223, CA.
R v Registrar of Building Societies, ex p a building society [1960] 2 All ER 549, [1960] 1 WLR
   669, DC and CA.
Scott v Scott [1913] AC 417, [1911–13] All ER Rep 1, HL.
Secretary of State for Education and Science v Tameside Metropolitan Borough [1976] 3 All ER
   665, [1977] AC 1014, [1976] 3 WLR 641, CA and HL.

Stock v Frank Jones (Tipton) Ltd [1978] 1 All ER 948, [1978] 1 WLR 231, HL.
a   Webb v Stenton (1883) 11 QBD 518, [1881–5] All ER Rep 312, CA.

Appeal
The Chief Registrar of Friendly Societies appealed against the order of Webster J made
on 1 December 1983 whereby he granted the applications of the New Cross Building
Society (the society) for orders of certiorari to quash (i) the order dated 17 August 1983
b   made by the chief registrar applying to the society s 48(2) of the Building Societies Act
1962, and (ii) the order dated 17 August 1983 made by the registrar revoking the
designation of the society for the purposes of s 1 of the House Purchase and Housing Act
1959. The hearing was held in camera. Judgment was delivered in camera on 21
December 1983 and published on 12 January 1984 following a statement read by Sir
John Donaldson MR. The facts are set out in the judgment of Sir John Donaldson MR.

c
John Mummery for the chief registrar.
T L G Cullen QC and J Patrick Powell for the society.
Timothy Lloyd for the Woolwich Equitable Building Society (on 10, 12, 17 January 1984).

Cur adv vult

d
12 January. **SIR JOHN DONALDSON MR** read the following statement. The full
title of these proceedings is *R v Chief Registrar of Friendly Societies, ex p New Cross Building
Society*, but it has previously been listed simply as 'Re a society'. The members of the
court concerned are Griffiths and Slade LJJ and myself. Griffiths LJ is unable to be present
at this particular sitting.
e   On 17 August 1983 the Chief Registrar of Friendly Societies made orders under the
House Purchase and Housing Act 1959 and the Building Societies Act 1962, the effect of
which was to revoke the designation of the New Cross Building Society as a trustee
investment and to prevent the society accepting money from the public. The orders were
stayed when the society applied for judicial review. Webster J quashed the orders and the
chief registrar appealed to this court. By judgments delivered on 21 December 1983 this
f   court allowed the appeal and restored the chief registrar's orders. We refused leave to
appeal to the House of Lords, but stayed the operation of the chief registrar's orders until
the hearing of a petition to the House of Lords for leave to appeal which was expected to
be heard on 19 January 1984. In reaching this decision, we took account of the fact that,
in the absence of a stay, any leave to appeal which might be given by the House of Lords
would be wholly valueless to the society, since the damage to its credit which would
g   occur as soon as the orders took effect would be irremediable.
On 10 January 1984 we were informed that the society had on the previous day
reached a conditional agreement with the Woolwich Equitable Building Society for a
transfer to that society of it engagements and that accordingly the society would not
proceed with its petition to the House of Lords. We were, however, asked to continue
the stay until midnight on Monday–Tuesday, 16–17 January 1984, that is next week, in
h   order to facilitate the proposed transfer of engagements. This application was supported
by the Woolwich Building Society and by the chief registrar. It was accordingly granted.
Thus far the whole of the proceedings before Webster J and in this court, including
the judgments delivered here and below, have been in camera. Our reasons, and those of
Webster J, for adopting this highly unusual course were the same, namely that publication
would prevent any effective challenge to the validity of the orders. However, when the
j   society abandoned its intention to apply for leave to appeal to the House of Lords, a
different situation obtained. Publication would no longer frustrate the course of justice,
since the society no longer wished to challenge our decision that the chief registrar's
orders were valid. Accordingly, when we sat on 10 January, we had to decide whether to
publish full details of the proceedings at once or to accede to the society's application that
publication be postponed until the stay was removed.
It was common ground between the society, the Woolwich Equitable Building Society

(who then appeared) and the chief registrar that publication before the orders took effect would adversely affect the proposed transfer of engagements because skilled staff would have to be diverted to dealing with questions from depositors, borrowers and others instead of proceeding with the arrangements for the transfer. We had to balance this consideration against the public interest in all court proceedings either being in public or, if that were not possible, being published at the earliest possible moment. We concluded that, whilst the considerations urged on us by the society would not have justified us in closing the court to the public if the proceedings had not hitherto been in camera, the position was different where, as here, these have been in camera since 12 September 1983 and we were only being asked to postpone publication for one week until 17 January 1984, at which time the members of the society could be informed of the position at the same time as the public and both would have the benefit of a white paper now being prepared by the Treasury.

Accordingly we indicated that we would sit on 17 January in open court and would on that occasion give copies of our judgments and that of Webster J to the press. At the same time we would give such further directions as might be necessary concerning such matters as money which has been lodged in court pursuant to orders made during the hearing before this court.

At lunch-time today the court was told that the chief registrar wished to apply as a matter of urgency for the removal of the stay on his orders and for leave to make those orders and these proceedings public. We heard the application at 3·30 pm, and it was not opposed. The basis of the application was that there was reason to believe that confidentiality could no longer be maintained, and it was thought to be contrary to the best interests of the New Cross Building Society and its members, and of other building societies, that they should be the subject of uninformed or partially informed rumours. All concerned were agreed that the stay should be removed from midnight tonight. The only problem was whether publication should take place tonight or at the sitting of the court tomorrow. Our view was that publication should take place this evening but that it should be delayed until the branches of the society had closed business at 5.00 pm.

We have not given any further directions as to the money in court or similar matters because they are the subject of discussions between the parties, and it would be premature to do so. There will, however, be liberty to all parties to apply.

Griffiths LJ, as I have said, is unable to be present on this occasion, but I want to make it clear that he took part in the hearing earlier this afternoon and he had of course been a partly to all our previous decisions and knew of the statement which I have just made.

Subject to allowing counsel to make any submissions they wish to make, we will now make available copies of the judgment which Webster J gave on 1 December 1983 and of our own judgments which were given on 21 December 1983.

21 December. The following judgments were delivered in camera.

SIR JOHN DONALDSON MR. Building societies are an essential part of the fabric of British life in the twentieth century. They provide a repository for the funds of small savers. They provide the primary source of money for house purchase. They are a success story which is the envy of other countries and the key to their success is to be found in public confidence in their financial probity and stability. Investment in building society accounts is believed to be, and usually is, 'as safe as houses'.

This happy and necessary state of affairs does not come about by accident. The societies are and have always been subject to strict statutory control and currently are regulated by the requirements of the Building Societies Act 1962. Equally important, they are subject to the supervisory jurisdiction of the Chief Registrar of Friendly Societies.

In the present appeal it is the exercise by the chief registrar of his supervisory powers which is called in question. On 17 August 1983 he made two orders. By the first he revoked the designation of the society under s 1(1) of the House Purchase and Housing Act 1959, thereby causing it to cease to be an acceptable repository for most trust funds. By the second he applied s 48(2) of the 1962 Act to the society thereby in effect preventing it accepting money for investment from the public.

a The society sought to have these orders quashed by judicial review and on 1 December 1983 it succeeded before Webster J. The chief registrar now appeals.

Hearing in camera

The whole of the proceedings before Webster J were conducted in camera and they were listed simply as 'Re a society'. When he gave judgment, he did so in camera and accordingly the members of the society and the public generally are unaware that the b registrar made these orders or that they have been quashed by the High Court or why they have been quashed.

In this highly unusual situation, the first question which we had to ask ourselves was whether and to what extent it would be right that the proceedings in this court should also be in camera. It is fundamental to British justice as we know it, and as our forbears have known it, that the Queen's courts are open to all. And when I say that they are open c to all I do not limit this to those who have business in the courts. The judges administer justice in the Queen's name on behalf of the whole community. No one is more entitled than a member of the general public to see for himself that justice is done. Nevertheless it is well settled that occasions can arise when it becomes the duty of the court to close its doors.

This problem was considered in depth by the House of Lords in *Scott v Scott* [1913] AC d 417, [1911–13] All ER Rep 1. The guidance which I get from their Lordships' speeches can be summarised as follows. The general rule that the courts shall conduct their proceedings in public is but an aid, albeit a very important aid, to the achievement of the paramount object of the courts, which is to do justice in accordance with the law. It is only if, in wholly exceptional circumstances, the presence of the public or public knowledge of the proceedings is likely to defeat that paramount object that the courts e are justified in proceeding in camera. These circumstances are incapable of definition. Each application for privacy must be considered on its merits, but the applicant must satisfy the court that nothing short of total privacy will enable justice to be done. It is not sufficient that a public hearing will create embarrassment for some or all of those concerned. It must be shown that a public hearing is likely to lead, directly or indirectly, to a denial of justice.

f The instant case provides a good example of such exceptional circumstances. When the matter came before Webster J, all that was known was that the chief registrar had made orders which would effectively cause the society to cease to carry on business and that the society challenged the validity of the orders. Assuming, as Webster J has held, that the orders should never have been made, the society is entitled not only to have them quashed but to continue in business. However, the judge was told and accepted g that, if the society had to publicise the chief registrar's actions in the process of getting the orders quashed, the loss of public confidence in the society would be such that, whether or not the orders were quashed, the society would be forced to close. In other words, a public hearing would effectively have deprived the society of the relief to which in law and justice it was or might be entitled. Accordingly Webster J was entirely justified in hearing the society's application in camera.

h Before this court the position might be thought to be a little different. No longer was it simply the case that the registrar had made the orders and that the society was seeking to have them quashed. By that time a judge of the High Court had investigated the matter and had ordered that they be quashed. We therefore invited argument on why we should not hear the appeal in public or subject to an order under s 4(2) of the Contempt of Court Act 1981 that reports of the proceedings be postponed until after we j had given judgment or subject to there being no reference to the identity of the society.

As a result of substantial argument, we were satisfied that it would be right to hear the appeal in camera. Building societies, like banks, are always subject to the risk of abnormal levels of withdrawal due to a loss of confidence on the part of their customers. However, building societies are much more vulnerable than banks for by the very nature of their business they are compelled to borrow short and lend long. The society is convinced that public knowledge that the chief registrar had ever made these orders would be sufficient to force it to close, even if it were also known that Webster J had held that the orders should never have been made. The society is even convinced that it could not survive   *a* publication of the fact that these proceedings had taken place, even if it were known that it had been successful in this court as well as before Webster J. The chief registrar was slightly more optimistic as to the society's chances of survival, but he agreed that very serious damage would be suffered by the society and that it might have to suspend payment for a time.

The decision to hear the appeal in camera still left two problems. The first was how we   *b* should give judgment. The considerations which led us to hear argument in camera would apply equally to any judgment which upheld the decision of Webster J to quash the chief registrar's orders. On the other hand, the appeal turns in large measure on questions of statutory construction and the interests of justice require that the decision of this court on such a matter should be published. We decided provisionally, and informed the parties, that if we upheld the decision of Webster J that the chief registrar's   *c* orders should be quashed we would either frame our judgment in such a way as to prevent identification of the society or would authorise the publication of an edited version, the full judgments being available for the confidential use of the parties.

We had also to consider the position which would arise if we allowed the appeal and the chief registrar's orders took effect. In such a situation, subject to any further appeal, there would be no objection to our judgment being published and identifying the   *d* society. However, it seemed to us that depositors, who had paid money to the society whilst the appeal was being heard which they would not have done if the proceedings had been in open court, might have a legitimate grievance which we should seek to remedy. A similar situation arose in previous proceedings in relation to a different building society: see *R v Registrar of Building Societies, ex p a building society* [1960] 2 All ER 549, [1960] 1 WLR 669. There an order was made requiring the society to pay into   *e* court all moneys deposited with it during the course of the proceedings. This put the court in a position in which it could return this money to the depositors if, as happened in that case, the registrar's orders were upheld. In the instant appeal the society undertook to pay into court day by day a sum equal to the total amount deposited with the society during the previous day.

The powers of the chief registrar   *f*

The chief registrar has acted in purported exercise of powers contained in s 1 of the House Purchase and Housing Act 1959 and s 48 of the Building Societies Act 1962. I would add in parenthesis that he would also have made an order under s 51 of the 1962 Act, which gives him power to control advertising by a building society, had the society not given him certain undertakings, but as he did not in fact make any order under that section we are not concerned with his right to do so. The primary issue between the   *g* parties is without doubt the extent of the chief registrar's powers under these sections.

The 1959 Act enables the chief registrar to designate a building society for the purposes of the Act and thereupon it qualifies for government loans and as a 'narrower-range investment' under s 1 of and Pt II of Sch 1 to the Trustee Investments Act 1961. Section 1 of the 1959 Act, so far as it is material, originally provided as follows:

h

'(1) Where the Chief Registrar of Friendly Societies (in this section referred to as the Registrar) is satisfied that a permanent building society fulfils such requirements as to its assets and liabilities, liquid funds, reserves, and other matters, as the Treasury may by regulations prescribe, he may designate the society for the purposes of this section; and where a society has been so designated and the designation has not been revoked—(a) the powers of a trustee under section one of the Trustee Act, 1925, or   *j* section ten of the Trusts (Scotland) Act, 1921, shall include power to invest funds of trusts in his hands by depositing with the society amounts not exceeding five thousand pounds for any one trust; and (b) the Minister may make advances to the society in accordance with the provisions of section two of this Act.

(2) Where the officer appointed to perform in Northern Ireland the functions of registrar of friendly societies (in this section referred to as the Registrar for Northern

Ireland) is satisfied that a society incorporated under the Building Societies Acts (Northern Ireland), 1874 to 1940, which is a permanent society within the meaning of those Acts fulfils the requirements prescribed under subsection (1) of this section, he may designate the society for the purposes of paragraph (a) of that subsection; and where a society has been so designated and the designation has not been revoked, that paragraph shall apply in relation to it as it applies in relation to a permanent building society within the meaning of this Act.

(3) The Registrar or, as the case may be, the Registrar for Northern Ireland, shall publish in the London, Edinburgh and Belfast Gazettes, a notice of every designation made by him under this section and of any revocation of such a designation . . .'

Paragraph (a) of sub-s (1) was superseded by provisions contained in the Trustee Investments Act 1961, but there is no suggestion that this change in any way affected the power of the chief registrar to revoke a designation under the section.

The regulations referred to in sub-s (1) have been changed from time to time and those currently in force are the Building Societies (Designation for Trustee Investment) Regulations 1972, SI 1972/1577. There are three requirements which must be fulfilled before a society can be designated: see reg 2(1) of the 1972 regulations. They are that—

'(a) the society's annual return for its last financial year shows that at the end of that year the requirements set out in the Schedule to these Regulations were fulfilled [these requirements relate to the amount of the society's assets, liabilities, liquid funds and reserves]; (b) the society's debts in respect of deposits, loans and overdrafts are unsecured; and (c) the society is empowered to make special advances in its current financial year up to the limit specified in section 22(3) of the Building Societies Act 1962 . . .'

There is an issue as to the definition of 'special advances', but that is not material to the nature and extent of the chief registrar's powers.

Section 48 of the 1962 Act is in the following terms:

'(1) If, with respect to any building society, the Chief Registrar considers it expedient to do so in the interests of investors and depositors, he may, by an order made with the consent of the Treasury, apply subsection (2) of this section to the society.

(2) Subject to the provisions of this section, while this subsection applies to a building society, the society shall not—(a) accept the deposit of, or otherwise borrow, any money, or (b) accept any payment representing the whole or any part of the amount due by way of subscription for a share in the society, other than a payment which fell due before the making of the order applying this subsection to the society.

(3) This section shall not make it unlawful for a building society to borrow from a banking or finance company, or from a director or other officer of the society, if the society has obtained the consent in writing of the Chief Registrar.

(4) If a building society contravenes the provisions of subsection (2) of this section, it shall be liable on conviction on indictment or on summary conviction to a fine which, on summary conviction, shall not exceed [the prescribed sum under the Magistrates' Courts Act 1980, s 32]; and every officer of the society who is in default shall be liable—(a) on conviction on indictment, to a fine, or to imprisonment for a term not exceeding two years, or to both, or (b) on summary conviction, to a fine not exceeding [the prescribed sum under the Magistrates' Courts Act 1980, s 32], or to imprisonment for a term not exceeding three months, or to both.

(5) References in this section to the amount due by way of subscription for a share in a building society do not include amounts due in respect of a share which represent interest on, or the repayment of, an advance made to the holder of the share.

(6) In this and the next following section "investors and depositors", in relation to a building society, means persons who have invested or deposited or may invest or deposit, money with the society.'

It is common ground that the chief registrar has some power to revoke the designation of a society under s 1 of the 1959 Act. Indeed, it is obvious from the terms of sub-s (3). *a* The controversy concerns the extent of the power.

The starting point for the argument is, and must be, the initial power to designate. The section makes clear that it only arises if and when a society fulfils the requirements of the regulations. It also makes clear that even when those requirements are fulfilled the chief registrar has a discretion whether or not to designate: 'he may designate' (see s 1 of the 1959 Act). The necessity for this discretion is obvious. Designated status as a suitable *b* repository of trust funds is a long-term concept, but in some circumstances a society may meet the requirements in one year but not in the next. The chief registrar therefore needs to be satisfied that the society will be able to retain its status before he designates it. This much is common ground. However, counsel for the society submits that this is the limit of the chief registrar's discretion. The chief registrar takes a wholly different view and in this he is at one with his predecessors. Counsel for the chief registrar submits that, *c* before he exercises his discretion to designate a society, he has to be satisfied not only that the society fulfils the requirements of the regulations and is likely to continue to fulfil them in the foreseeable future, but also that 'the society is efficiently managed in compliance with the 1962 Act and is pursuing sensible policies, that there is provision for the continuance of the society on a stable basis and that the society is in control of its own destiny'. *d*

The same difference of approach is then applied to the power to revoke designated status. Whilst it is common ground that a failure to fulfil all the requirements of the regulations on an isolated occasion would not of itself justify the chief registrar in revoking the designation, the society submits that he has no such power unless and until there is a failure to fulfil some of the requirements of the regulations and that if this occurs his discretion is exercisable solely on a consideration of how likely this failure is to *e* be maintained. The chief registrar on the other hand takes the view that the power of revocation arises wherever a situation exists in which, if the society were applying for designation, he would in the exercise of this discretion refuse the application. In exercising his discretion, whether or not to exercise that power, he considers 'it proper . . . to look not only at the 1972 regulations (or their predecessors or successors) but also at other matters relevant to the question of whether the society is a suitable home for *f* trust funds'.

Webster J thought that the difference between these two approaches could be illuminated by labelling the society's contention as being that the chief registrar had a power of revocation exercisable subject to a discretion, whereas the chief registrar's contention was that he had a discretionary power. With all respect to the judge, I do not find this supposed contrast illuminating. Indeed, I find it positively misleading. The *g* power is without doubt discretionary. The problem lies in defining the parameters within which the chief registrar can properly decide to exercise or not to exercise it. This depends entirely on the width of the discretion which Parliament has conferred on the chief registrar.

In upholding the view of the society that the registrar could never revoke a designation unless there had been a failure to fulfil some of the requirements of the 1972 regulations, *h* the judge seems to have been oppressed by the thought that any other view might lead to the registrar taking action when a society was pursuing policies, for example in relation to investment, which he considered unwise, notwithstanding that a respectable body of opinion would have regarded them as wholly sensible and appropriate. He also seems to have been concerned that, if failure to fulfil the requirements of the 1972 regulations were not a condition precedent to the exercise of the power, a society could be exposed to *j* the risk of revocation of its status without warning prior to receiving notice inviting it to show cause why a revocation order should not be made. In his view—

> 'a power to revoke on a ground other than a failure to comply with a statutory requirement would rarely if ever be necessary to achieve the purposes of the 1962 Act in any particular case because in most if not all cases those purposes could be secured in the case of any given society by its fulfilling the statutory requirements.'

a I must most respectfully disagree. The logical consequence of this view, as the judge recognised, is that, even if a situation arose in which the registrar could properly make an order under s 48 of the 1962 Act which would effectively prevent the society carrying on business, he would have no power to revoke its designated status as a suitable repository for trust funds unless, coincidentally, there was a failure to meet the requirements of the 1972 regulations. This cannot possibly have been the intention of Parliament. Parliament intended that the public should have a high degree of protection

b when investing in any building society and the 1962 Act is intended to achieve this end. Designated status as a suitable repository for trust funds necessarily contemplates an even higher degree of security and any construction which removes the lower status whilst leaving the higher status intact must be wrong.

The legislative purpose of s 1 of the 1959 Act is to accredit some building societies as suitable for the investment of trust funds. Such suitability must of its very nature be

c affected by many and varied factors which are not and probably could not be fully reflected either by the 1962 Act or by the 1972 regulations. An obvious way of achieving that legislative purpose and that which I am confident that Parliament intended to adopt is to give the chief registrar a discretionary power of revocation. All discretionary powers have to be used with discretion and abuse will involve exceeding the power. It is this consideration and not that proposed by the society and supported by the judge which

d provides such protection as is necessary if the registrar were considering revoking a society's status without adequate notice of his anxieties or on the basis that whilst secure and reputable societies adopted different policies the chief registrar favoured one rather than the other.

A similar difference of view between the society, supported by the judge, and the chief registrar arises in the context of s 48(1) of the 1962 Act. For the society it was contended

e that s 48(1) empowers the chief registrar to apply sub-s (2) only when he 'perceives an actually foreseeable loss'. By this is meant loss in the more or less immediate future. The power having then arisen, the registrar has to exercise a discretion as to its use. For the chief registrar it was contended that s 48(1) gives him a discretionary power to apply sub-s (2) if and when he considers it expedient to do so in the interests of existing and future investors and depositors. Plainly the power is intended to avoid risk of loss and, in the

f absence of such a risk, its exercise can never be justified. But in the chief registrar's submission such a risk can arise in many different ways and it is nothing to the point, particularly in relation to future investors and depositors, that the risk of loss may not be immediate if it is clear. Indeed, the power would have very limited value if it could only be exercised when a loss was immediately in prospect. The immediacy or otherwise of the loss foreseen by the chief registrar would only be relevant to a decision whether to

g exercise the power or to make representations to the society giving it an opportunity to take remedial action.

The judge held:

'Section 48(1) of the 1962 Act, properly construed, confers on the registrar a power to make an order where a society has broken or failed to comply with an

h express or implied requirement of the 1962 Act or where the registrar perceives actually foreseeable loss to investors or depositors if no order is made. In my view the risk of such a loss is only relevant to the exercise of his discretion where he has a power to make an order by virtue of a failure to comply with the 1962 Act.'

I am quite unable to accept this construction, which involves writing words into the subsection. In my judgment, the chief registrar has been given a discretionary power to

j apply sub-s (2) if and whenever he considers it expedient to do so in the interests of present and future investors and depositors. The power involves the exercise of a high degree of discretion because it is draconian and in the absence of strong countervailing considerations it can never be expedient in the interests of present and future investors and depositors to make an order which will have the effect of putting a building society out of business. However, the chief registrar occupies a highly responsible position and I see no reason whatsoever for concluding that Parliament did not mean to confer on him a discretionary power in accordance with the plain meaning of the words of s 48(1), such power to be exercised only with the concurrence of the Treasury.

The role of the court

It is common ground that the decisions of the chief registrar are amenable to judicial review, notwithstanding the subjective wording of s 48(1) of the 1962 Act and the absence of any expressed criteria governing the exercise of his discretion under s 1 of the 1959 Act. It is also common ground that on the society's application for judicial review it is not for the court to consider whether the chief registrar's decisions were 'right' or 'wrong', or to entertain an appeal from them or to substitute the court's discretion for his. The role of the court is to consider whether the chief registrar has exceeded his powers. His good faith is not in question and accordingly the court is concerned to consider whether he has misdirected himself as to the scope of his powers either expressly or by necessary implication from the absence of facts or findings which could justify the making of the orders.

The decision-making procedure

Section 49 of the 1962 Act contains provisions supplementary to s 48 which require the chief registrar to give not less than 14 days' notice to the society that he proposes to make an order under s 48 and to specify the considerations which have led him to conclude that it would be in the interests of investors and depositors to make the order. The society has to be given not less than 14 days in which to make representations. The chief registrar has then to consider these representations and, if the society so requests, afford it an opportunity of being heard within the period for making representations. Finally, on making the order the chief registrar must serve on the society a notice specifying the considerations which have led him to conclude that it is expedient to make the order and he is only empowered to make the order if all the considerations so specified were those, or were amongst those, which were specified in the notice of his proposal to make an order.

No similar provisions have been enacted in relation to a proposal to make a revocation order under s 1 of the 1959 Act or to the making of such an order. Accordingly, the only procedural fetter would be that provided by the rules of natural justice, but the chief registrar decided, and rightly decided, to apply the provisions of s 49 of the 1962 Act mutatis mutandis to his proposal to make an order under s 1 of the 1959 Act.

A report dated 17 August 1983, which accompanied the decision to make the orders, specified considerations all of which were amongst those specified in the original notices served on the society. It is a formidable and closely reasoned document of 88 pages containing self-directions as to law and a review of the facts as the chief registrar found them. Whether or not his decisions should be set aside, it was a wholly admirable document and a model of its kind.

The approach of Webster J

The chief registrar relied on eleven grounds or considerations for making the two orders. Six of them related to statutory requirements and, of these six, five related directly or indirectly to the making of special advances under s 21 of the 1962 Act. The judge, having decided, wrongly as I think, that considerations relating to statutory requirements were, so to speak, the key which unlocked the safe containing the chief registrar's powers and that other considerations were only relevant to whether he should take the powers from the safe and use them, examined all the grounds and considerations seriatim on their merits and then put on one side any which did not have a statutory basis. It was clearly his intention to bring them back into account when reviewing the chief registrar's exercise of this discretion, applying the test of whether a reasonable chief registrar could have exercised it in the way in which he did. However, counsel for the chief registrar complains that in some respects he failed to reconsider those discretionary matters which he had put on one side. Suffice it to say that, when the judge came to examine the chief registrar's exercise of discretion, he concluded that the chief registrar had failed to take account of two matters of which, in the judge's view, he should have taken account and that, in the absence of so doing, no reasonable chief registrar could have made the orders.

The judge's decision is in my judgment invalidated by this approach of first considering whether the power had been activated and then whether, as a matter of discretion, it should have been exercised. For the reasons which I have already expressed, I do not think that there is any such dichotomy. The registrar has been given discretionary powers and the sole question was whether in all the circumstances he was entitled to exercise them. Furthermore, I think that the judge's approach led him into the error of in the end substituting his own discretion for that of the chief registrar. We have therefore to examine the application for judicial review de novo.

The background to the chief registrar's action

The society was established in 1866 and designated under the 1959 Act. However it remained a relatively small society having, as late as 1974, assets of about £6m and reserves of £300,000. In 1977 the board formulated a five-year plan for controlled growth. There was certainly growth and by the end of the period the society's assets were £103m and its reserves £4·235m. However, the chief registrar has become concerned about the control. Thus at the end of 1979 and again at the end of 1981 the adjusted reserve ratio of the society was allowed to fall below the minimum of 2·5% prescribed by the 1972 regulations. The figures were 1·62% at the end of 1979 and 2·21% at the end of 1981. Furthermore there was some doubt whether the society might not have exceeded its power to make what are known as 'special advances'.

This led the chief registrar in April 1982 to serve formal notice proposing to revoke the society's trustee designation. This in turn led to extensive consultation both with the society and with the Building Societies Association. In the end the chief registrar accepted certain assurances from the society and notice of the proposed revocation was withdrawn in October 1982.

The chief registrar's anxieties returned in the early months of 1983 for more than one reason. The accounts for 1982 showed a continued rapid expansion of the society's business and the society in March 1983 decided to increase interest rates independently of the members of the Building Societies Association. This was, of course, likely to accelerate the rate of expansion and whilst expansion may well be desirable it is a process which, in the chief registrar's view, has to be carefully monitored and controlled by the management of the society. This was followed by the receipt of a signed copy of the annual report of the society which stated the 'ascertained proportion' in relation to special advances to have been 12·09% at 31 December 1982. If this was correct, the society would for a third time in four years have ceased to fulfil the requirements of the 1972 regulations. Another disturbing feature was a decision to raise £10m through the wholesale money market, coupled a little later by the disclosure of a budget calling for an expansion of assets to £166m by the end of the year: an increase of over 50% within 12 months.

The proposal to take action under s 1 of the 1959 Act and s 48 of the 1962 Act

Close contact was maintained between the registry and the society during the first six months of 1983 and on 27 June the chief registrar reached the provisional conclusion that he should make orders under these sections. In notifying the society that he proposed to take this course, the chief registrar followed the procedure laid down in s 49 of the 1962 Act. He specified the considerations which had led him to conclude that orders should be made and fixed a time within which the society could make representations. This time was later extended until 2 August, on which day there was an oral hearing at which the society was represented by counsel.

The chief registrar has stated in his report of 17 August that—

'I have followed the guidance of the Court of Appeal in a previous case relating to a statutory order made by the Chief Registrar: I have neither sought nor taken into account additional information between the last hearing and making this decision, apart from obtaining material to verify some points made on behalf of the society in representations.'

This decision to adhere strictly to the closing date for the submission of new material has been criticised by the society. On 3 August the secretary of the society told registry staff that a mistake had been made in calculating what is known as 'the ascertained proportion' (a term defined in s 22(3) of the 1962 Act) in that two accounts had been wrongly included. The society say that the chief registrar should have taken this correction into account.

I have no doubt that in the exercise of his discretion he could have done so. Where the exercise of statutory powers involves putting forward proposals, receiving representations and then confirming, varying or abandoning these proposals, it is a rule of general application that the decision-maker should not allow himself to be influenced by considerations which are unknown to those who may be affected by his decision and on which they might wish to comment. This rule does not rest on any particular Court of Appeal decision given in the context of a building society. It is rooted in 'natural justice', the lawyer's term for 'fair play'. The rule, as I have formulated it, would not have been infringed if the chief registrar had had regard to the two disputed accounts, because the society knew of the point and quite clearly had no need to comment further. A better ground on which to exclude consideration of the society's allegation that there was some inaccuracy in the figures would have been that it put the contention forward too late. It may seem hard to exclude something which is only 24 hours too late, but there had already been a number of extensions in the time limited for making representations and finality has to be reached at some stage.

Strictly speaking the chief registrar was not required to give any reasons for deciding to revoke the designation of the society under s 1 of the 1959 Act and was only obliged to state the 'considerations' which had led him to conclude that it was expedient to make an order under s 48 of the 1962 Act. This could have been done, and was in fact done, on two sheets of paper. It is very greatly to his credit that in a separate document he set out in full every stage of his reasoning and informed the society of it. This has given the society an opportunity of making far more detailed criticisms than would otherwise have been the case. There is no harm and much good in this, provided always that it does not lead the court into the classic error in proceedings for judicial review of thinking that it is, or at least behaving as if it were, hearing an appeal from the decision-maker or, even worse, substituting its own views for his. The correct approach is to regard the explanations which accompany a decision as painting a picture of the decision-making process. Such a picture may properly be only an outline sketch or it may be a detailed and finished work of art. But either way it is the same picture which must be looked at as a whole. The details may alter the whole picture, but they are not to be looked at in isolation.

If I were to reproduce the whole of the document giving the chief registrar's reasons, I should unduly extend this judgment. On the other hand, as the hearing has been in camera, I feel that it is more necessary than usual to refer fully to those reasons. The scheme of the chief registrar's document involved dealing with various general matters, such as the nature of his powers and the procedure adopted and then (a) to set out each of the considerations which he had specified in the notice accompanying his proposal to make the orders, (b) to record and comment on matters which had subsequently come to his notice, including any representations by the society, and (c) to record his conclusions. I think that for present purposes I can omit (b) and that it will suffice if I set out (a) and (c)[1].

As counsel for the chief registrar has pointed out, counsel for the society has not alleged that the chief registrar has taken account of any irrelevant matters or that he has failed to take account of any relevant matters, other than the society's request that the ascertained proportion for 31 December 1982 be further revised by the exclusion of two accounts. The burden of the society's complaint has been twofold, viz: (a) that certain facts or conclusions were not established on the evidence and (b) that the chief registrar misdirected himself in law in deciding what is and what is not a 'special advance'.

As to (a) it is important to remember that it is for the chief registrar and not for the courts to establish the facts and to draw conclusions from those facts. Whilst in theory it

---

1   The registrar's decision, so far as material, is set out at pp 55–64, post

may be possible to challenge factual findings on the basis that there was no evidence to
support them, in practice this is unlikely to be possible. I say that because the chief
registrar is entitled to take account of the accumulated experience of the registry and of
his own experience and he is in day-to-day contact with the society, other societies and
the Building Societies Association. The judge lost sight of this fact when he held that,
without a valuation of the mortgage book or evidence as to the availability of a possible
purchaser of it at a particular price and without evidence of an assurance that the
association would make up any deficiency between assets and liabilities on a sale of the
mortgage book, there was insufficient evidence to justify a finding that investors would
be repaid 100p in the pound. This was based on assertions by the society, but neither the
society nor the judge could know what evidence the chief registrar had and the chief
registrar was under no obligation to tell them, either when making the decision or in the
course of the proceedings. Were it otherwise, all the conclusions of the chief registrar
would be open to challenge and he would be required to justify each one by setting out
the evidence on which it was based. This is not the nature of judicial review.

A similar argument was addressed to us in relation to the chief registrar's finding that
there were deficiencies in the board's direction and management of the society. In
particular it was submitted that the chief registrar had misconstrued the society's 'Board
Procedures'. Like the judge, I am unable to accept that there was any misdirection.
Whether or not the board's direction and management of the society was in fact
satisfactory is a pure question of fact to which the society's written 'Board Procedures'
were only relevant to the extent that they were operated in practice.

The complaint that the chief registrar misdirected himself on what is and what is not
a 'special advance' requires more detailed consideration, both because it affects ground 1
(ascertained proportion at 31 December 1982) (see p 55 g to p 56 a, post), consideration
(a) (previous failures on designation requirements) (see p 56 a to d, post), consideration
(c) (investors protection scheme) (see p 56 j to p 57 b, post), ground 2 (statutory and
regulatory requirements) (see p 59 e to g, post) and 'The further consideration in relation
to the 1962 Act' (see p 64 c to e, post) and because the definition of 'special advance' is of
general interest and application. However, for reasons which I must now set out, in my
judgment the chief registrar did not misdirect himself.

Special advances

Section 21 of the 1962 Act defines what is a 'special advance' and s 22 provides
limitations on the extent to which a building society may make special advances.

Section 22(1) of the 1962 Act requires a building society so to conduct its business as to
secure that special advances are not made except as authorised by the section. Section
22(2) requires a society at the end of each financial year to ascertain (a) the total amount
of outstanding advances together with any arrears of interest and (b) the proportion of
that sum which is in respect of advances made to a person who, at that time, 'is indebted
to the society (taking into account any kind of debts, whether immediately repayable or
not)' in an amount exceeding £37,500.

By sub-ss (3), (4) and (5) this 'ascertained proportion' fixes the proportion of special
advances out of the total advances which can be made in the following financial year. If
the 'ascertained proportion' does not exceed 10%, the society in the following year may
make special advances not exceeding 10% of the whole of the advances made in that year.
If it exceeds 10% but does not exceed 25%, the society can make special advances not
exceeding 2½% of the whole. If it exceeds 25%, the society can make no special advances
in the following year. Failure to comply with the requirements of this section constitute
a criminal offence (see s 22(7)). One of the conditions which must be fulfilled by a
building society seeking to be designated under the 1959 Act as fit for the deposit of
trustee funds is that it is a society whose ascertained proportion enables it to make up to
10% of its total advances in the form of special advances.

Section 21(1) of the 1962 Act contains three different descriptions of advance in
separate lettered paragraphs and provides that if any advance made by a building society
falls within one of these descriptions it is a 'special advance'. Paragraph (a) consists of an

advance to a body corporate. Paragraph (*b*) consists of an advance to an individual, where the amount of the advance exceeds £37,500. Both these descriptions are clear and create no problem. The problem arises in relation to para (*c*), which, like para (*b*), relates to advances to individuals. Here the amount of the advance is not initially relevant, save that if it exceeds £37,500 it is a special advance anyway by virtue of para (*b*). A para (*c*) advance becomes a special advance if the advance, when added to 'all other debts of any description (whether immediately repayable or not) in which he is indebted to the society' exceeds £75,000 immediately after the advance is made or exceeds £37,500 at the end of a period of three months from the date of the advance or at the end of the society's financial year, whichever be the sooner.

No doubt the prime purposes of this somewhat complicated provisions are (i) to prevent a society avoiding the special advance limitations by making a series of advances none of which itself exceeds £37,500 and so falls within para (*b*) and (ii) to enable a building society to make short-term bridging loans. Counsel for the society submits that the section should be construed in such a way as to give effect to these prime purposes or to remedy the 'mischief', but no wider. However, the 'mischief' to which the statutory provisions are directed is only relevant if the words used are ambiguous. If they are clear, as I think that they are, and if they are wider than is necessary to remedy the 'mischief', the proper conclusion is that Parliament intended to do more than simply remedy that 'mischief'. A similar point arises under s 22(2)(*b*).

The particular bone of contention is whether 'all other debts of any description (whether immediately repayable or not)' in s 21(2) and 'is indebted to the society (taking into account any kind of debts, whether immediately repayable or not)' in s 22(2)(*b*) includes arrears of interest and unpaid insurance premiums.

Arrears of interest

As interpreted by the parties this refers to interest which is payable but unpaid. The argument for the society is that (a) where the statute intends to refer to arrears of interest, it does so in terms (see ss 22(2)(*a*) and 24(2)(*b*)) and that arrears of interest are 'payable', not 'repayable'. Accordingly the parenthetic reference to 'whether immediately repayable or not' in s 21(2) and 'whether immediately repayable or not' in s 24(2)(*b*) shows that 'all other debts of any description' and 'any kind of debts' is limited to advances since these alone are debts which are repayable as contrasted with being payable. I do not accept this submission. Section 22(2)(*a*) is contrasting 'arrears of interest' with 'advances' and s 24(2)(*b*) is contrasting 'arrears of interest' with 'the amount of the mortgage debt'. Neither is contrasting 'arrears of interest' with a 'debt of any description' or 'any kind of debts'. I agree that 'repayable' is not a particularly apt term to apply to arrears of interest, but I think that this is not sufficient to cause a court to refrain from giving 'all other debts of any description' and 'any kind of debts' their natural meaning as including arrears of interest. Although it is not directly material, since neither party considered anything other than interest which was payable but unpaid, I think that interest which has been earned, but is not yet payable, is also within the description, since 'a debt' has been defined as 'a sum of money which is now payable or *will become payable in the future by reason of a present obligation*' (my emphasis) (see per Lindley LJ in *Webb v Stenton* (1883) 11 QBD 518 at 527, [1881–5] All ER Rep 312 at 316). This is to be contrasted with sums of money which may never become payable, because there is no present obligation.

Insurance premiums

The society insures all mortgaged property by declarations under a master policy, the premium for which is payable on 1 February annually. The mortgagee's obligation under the mortgage deed is—

'to pay punctually to the Society all premiums necessary for effecting and maintaining any insurance against fire and such other risks as the Society thinks fit in the full replacement value of the property'.

The society submits that there is no repayable debt due from the borrower to the
a society until the society has paid the bulk premium on 1 February. The chief registrar
submits that insurance premiums due from the borrower become 'debts' when payment
is demanded by the society. In my judgment the chief registrar is more right than the
society. A 'debt of any description' or 'any kind of debts' does not have to be 'repayable'
as contrasted with 'payable'. My own view is that a 'debt of any description' and 'any kind
of debts' arise as soon as the property has been declared under the master policy, whenever
b the premium may be payable.

Earlier in this judgment, when considering the period when the society was making
representations to the chief registrar, I recorded a complaint that he had refused to take
account of a suggestion by the society that it had erred in including two accounts while
calculating its 'ascertained proportion' on 31 December 1982. The society attaches great
importance to this point, because the exclusion of the two accounts would reduce the
c ascertained proportion from 10·19% to 9·96%. The significance of this is that if the figure
does not exceed 10% the society becomes a '10% society' in terms of the amount of special
advances which it can make in 1983 and being a '10% society' is a statutory requirement
for designation under the 1959 Act.

In my judgment there is nothing in this point. The chief registrar was faced with a
situation in which the society had stated in its annual return that its ascertained
d proportion was 12·09% and it was seeking to say that this was wrong. The chief registrar
investigated and came to the conclusion that, even if it was given the benefit of the doubt
on various points, the asscertained proportion was still over 10% and that he could not
get it below 10·09%. If the two accounts had been excluded, he would have had to
reconsider the doubtful points and, if he had correctly directed himself in law, he would
have resolved most of those doubts against the society and the figure would still have
e been above 10%.

Although this exclusion of consideration of the two accounts might appear critical
because of its knock-on effect on considerations (a) and (c) (see p 56 a to d and j to p 57 b,
post), it does not really have this importance even if, contrary to my view, the exclusion
of the two accounts would have led the chief registrar to conclude that the ascertained
proportion in December 1982 was just below 10%. I say this because it has no bearing on
f the consideration that in 1982 the society made special advances of 11·61% after having
made special advances of 11·53% in 1981, thus in successive years breaching one of the
most important requirements of the 1962 Act that such advances shall in no circumstances
exceed 10% of the total. It is, of course, true that these breaches may have occurred due
to a failure to appreciate what is a special advance, but this goes to show lack of criminality
on the part of the management rather than to showing a less serious breach. Further it
g has no bearing on the consideration that the society itself appeared not to know what was
its 1982 figure for the ascertained proportion and so what level of special advances was
permissible in 1983. Last, but by no means least, it has no bearing on the chief registrar's
complaints of the quality of the managerial control of the society, and indeed the whole
spectacle of a society returning a figure exceeding 12%, carrying on business on the
supposition that this was the correct figure and then seeking retrospectively to argue that
h it was not is a grave reflection on the managerial control of the society.

I can find no grounds whatsoever for quashing the chief registrar's orders and I would
allow the appeal accordingly.

This leaves over the question of when our judgment should be published and in what
form. If my brethren agree that the appeal should be allowed, this can be discussed in
court when this judgment is delivered.

j **GRIFFITHS LJ.** I agree that, for the reasons given by Sir John Donaldson MR, it was
necessary to hear this appeal in camera.

The registrar has given his reasons for acting against the building society in great detail
and lucidity in a masterly document of 88 pages. This fact has resulted in very detailed
consideration of these reasons by the judge and they have been subject to much closely

reasoned analysis by counsel for the society during the course of this appeal. I think that
this has at times led to the danger of the court losing sight of the nature of these   *a*
proceedings and of that which the building society must establish in order to succeed. I
propose therefore for a moment to go back to first principles.

The building society is not appealing against the decision of the registrar, much as it
would like to do so. It is given no right of appeal: the registrar's decision is final. The
building society is asking the High Court to review the registrar's decision and to grant a
writ of certiorari to quash it. In order to obtain this relief it must satisfy the court that   *b*
either the registrar had no power to make the orders he did, ie that he has misconstrued
the powers given to him by the relevant statutes, or alternatively that he has abused the
power that Parliament has given him, ie that he has used the power in a way that
Parliament cannot have intended.

The first challenge involves the court in the construction of the relevant statutes. The
second challenge involves a consideration of the reasons for the decision to see if they can   *c*
be challenged on what have come colloquially to be referred to as 'Wednesbury principles':
see *Associated Provincial Picture Houses Ltd v Wednesbury Corp* [1947] 2 All ER 680, [1948]
1 KB 223. But in carrying out this exercise it is of importance to bear firmly in mind that
the court is looking to see if there has been an abuse of power and not whether the court
considers it would have been wiser to have exercised the power differently: the wisdom
of the decision is for the registrar to decide, not the court.   *d*

The court must take a broad view of the decision and not allow itself to be bogged
down in minutiae, or led into the error of taking over the role of a fact finding tribunal.

The court must not allow the tests proposed in the *Wednesbury* decision to be erected
into immutable propositions of law. Take as an example the proposition that the decision
must take into account relevant considerations and leave out of account irrelevant
considerations. In a decision involving the weighing of many complex factors it will   *e*
always be possible to point to some factors which should arguably have been taken into
account or left out of account; even if they should have been, the court should not
intervene unless it is convinced that this would have resulted in the decision going the
other way. The same applies to an error of law on the face of the record: if the error is
fundamental to the decision the court should intervene; but certiorari is a discretionary
remedy and not every error of law will justify quashing the decision. And, finally,   *f*
particular care must be taken before stigmatising a decision as one at which no reasonable
person could have arrived, for this is coming dangerously close to the court substituting
its own discretion for that of the tribunal. With these warnings in mind I now turn to
the particular circumstances of this appeal.

The construction of the Acts   *g*
The first question that has to be considered is the nature and scope of the powers
conferred by Parliament on the Chief Registrar of Friendly Societies for the purpose of
exercising control over the operations of building societies, under both the House
Purchase and Housing Act 1959 and the Building Societies Act 1962.

The 1959 Act   *h*
Section 1 of the 1959 Act gives a power to the registrar to confer what I will call 'trustee
status' on a building society. If the registrar confers this status, trustees may so long as
that status is not revoked invest their funds in the society. Before the registrar can
exercise this power he must be satisfied that the building society 'fulfils such requirements
as to its assets and liabilities, liquid funds, reserves and other matters, as the Treasury may
by regulations prescribe'. But, even if a building society does fulfil all these requirements,   *j*
the registrar is not obliged to confer trustee status on it. The 1959 Act says 'he may', not
'he must', do so. Parliament has vested a discretion in the registrar to decide whether or
not the building society is fit to receive trustee status.

What is the width of this discretionary power? There are no words in the section that
limit the discretion, but the society says that it must have been Parliament's intention

that the discretion should only be exercised in respect of matters prescribed by Treasury

a regulations. I cannot agree. To my mind the manifest purpose of the power is to give, through the registrar, protection to trustees so that they may feel confident that they are depositing their funds in safe hands. Suppose that although a building society was complying to the letter with all Treasury regulations it had now fallen into the hands of a man with a long record of financial fraud. Can it be though that in such circumstances Parliament intended that a registrar should designate it as a safe haven for trustees' funds?

b But such would be the result of accepting the society's argument. By s 1 of the 1959 Act Parliament has placed its trust in the registrar to exercise a wise discretion for the protection of trustee funds leaving him free to take into account any matters that might reasonably bear on the question of whether or not the building society is a safe home for trustee funds.

Now comes the question of revocation. Although not expressly stated, it is implicit in

c the wording of the section that the registrar may revoke trustee status. The judge concluded that, although the registrar could take into account matters other than those contained in Treasury regulations when deciding to grant trustee status, he was nevertheless confined to consideration of the Treasury regulations when revoking trustee status. With the utmost respect to him, this seems to me to be an untenable position. Neither logic nor reason can support construing the discretion differently when granting

d the designation and when revoking it. It would produce the absurd result that the registrar could prevent a fraudsman ever acquiring trustee status but could do nothing to thwart the fraudsman who acquired control of a building society which had trustee status. It was the recognition of this difficulty that, as I understood his argument, led counsel for the society to seek to restrict the discretion to grant trustee status to matters directly related to Treasury regulations and thus to produce consistency between the

e power to grant and the power to revoke. In my view the registrar has the same discretion to revoke as he has to grant. That which he can give he can also take away.

I should add that, although I have used the example of a fraudsman to show the necessity for a wide discretionary power to be vested in the registrar, there is no suggestion of dishonesty against anyone concerned with the affairs of this society. Nevertheless such factors as the lack of proper documentary control, lax board procedures,

f the relationship between explosive growth and reserves and ineligibility to take advantage of an investor's protection scheme are all matters which the registrar is entitled to take into consideration in the course of the exercise of his discretion, because they are all relevant to the central issue: is this a safe home for trustee funds?

The 1962 Act

g Section 48(1) of the 1962 Act gives a power to the registrar to stop a building society from accepting deposits or borrowing or accepting subscriptions for shares. The registrar may exercise this power if he 'considers it expedient to do so in the interests of investors and depositors', which includes past and future investors and depositors.

The judge placed a very restricted construction on this power: he said it only arises either when the society has broken or failed to comply with an express or implied

h requirement of the 1962 Act or where the registrar perceives actually foreseeable loss to investors or depositors if no order is made. This construction means that, if the registrar is satisfied that there is a serious risk of loss to investors or depositors if he does not act, he cannot intervene because the point has not yet been reached when the risk has moved to the point of virtually certain loss if no action is taken.

Such a construction would place the registrar in an impossible position.

j To draw the line between serious risk and actually foreseeable loss would be very difficult, and whilst the registrar was trying to make up his mind on which side of the line the case fell actual loss might supervene; experience has shown how swiftly financial nemesis can overtake any institution.

This section was enacted in the aftermath of the collapse of the State Building Society, which had pointed to the necessity for some further control of building societies in order

to protect those who entrusted their savings to them. In my view the wording of the
section points to the intention of Parliament to put its trust in the registrar to provide
this protection. The words clearly indicate that it is to be left to the judgment of the
registrar to decide whether the time has come to act in protection of the saving public;
and it is to be remembered that this includes not only those who have invested in the
building society but also all those who may be induced to do so in the future.

The judge was much impressed by the following argument against a wide construction:

'... a registrar would be entitled to revoke a designation (or to make an order
under s 48(1) of the 1962 Act) whenever in his bona fide opinion either a society's
valuation policy or its investment policy or its management policy or its accounting
procedures exposed investors and depositors to risk, even though in each case the
policy or procedure accorded with that approved by one reputable school of thought,
provided that the registrar's opinion accord with another reputable school of thought
...'

I am not moved by this argument. In the first place, it seems to me a highly improbable
scenario: I cannot think it likely that the registrar would condemn an approved and
reputable school of thought. On the other hand, I can foresee a risky practice insidiously
spreading and being adopted by a number of societies until it gained an apparent
respectability, in which case there is a real need for a truly independent person to put an
end to it.

I do not attempt to put any gloss on the words of the section; they are clear enough
and they are backed by the provisions of s 49 of the 1962 Act, which provides that the
registrar shall specify the considerations which have led him to conclude that he should
make an order and gives the building society the chance to answer them and thus seek to
persuade the registrar to change his mind. It goes without saying that these considerations
must be relevant to the purpose for which the power is given, namely to protect the
investing public. But subject to this, if the registrar forms the view that for relevant
considerations it is expedient to act, the court should not impede him by introducing a
fetter on this discretion in order to limit his power. Parliament has placed its trust in the
registrar and so should the court.

I would also add that I find nothing surprising in Parliament placing this degree of
trust in the registrar. The office of Chief Registrar of Friendly Societies has existed now
for almost a century, he is backed by a large skilled staff well versed in the affairs of
societies and he places an annual report before Parliament. In these circumstances he
seems to be the natural choice to protect those who do not wish to speculate but to find a
safe place for their savings. The effect of these two Acts is to appoint the registrar as a
public watchdog to protect the investor and especially the small investor who places his
savings in a building society. To discharge his task effectively he must be given a wide
discretion and not be placed in a judicial strait-jacket.

It will of course still be open to challenge the order of the registrar on the grounds that
there has been an improper exercise of the power under *Wednesbury* principles. But for
the reasons I have endeavoured to state the judge in my opinion wrongly construed both
Acts and interpreted the registrar's powers too narrowly.

Has the registrar abused his power?

The first line of attack was directed to the registrar's construction of s 21 of the 1962
Act which he set out in his decision. I think that this is a difficult point of construction
and I have considerable sympathy for the argument of counsel for the society that
s 21(1)(b) stands on its own, and that interest is not to be added to a single advance for the
purpose of calculating special advances. I have however in the end been persuaded, for
the reasons given by the judge and by Sir John Donaldson MR and Slade LJ, that the
registrar's construction is to be preferred and that his decision cannot be impugned on
this ground.

It is therefore not necessary to decide whether if the registrar's construction had been
wrong the court should have quashed his order. But I very much doubt if it would have

a been right to do so. On any view of the figures, the society was sailing very close to the wind and adopting a very different policy from that of the majority of building societies, who on average made special advances of 2·8% as a proportion of the total yearly advances in 1982. The registrar's investigation demonstrated the unreliability of the society's figures and that their auditors could not in all cases be relied on to correct them. In these circumstances the registrar would, in my view, be entitled to regard the society's conduct of its business with great concern, particularly when it is remembered that making

b special advances above the prescribed limit is a criminal offence. Even if the building society had not exceeded the special advance limit on this occasion, the registrar could well have taken the view that it was more by luck than judgment.

The attack on the registrar's construction of ss 21 and 22 of the 1962 Act has always been put in the forefront of the society's argument; once it has been disposed of, there is little left. It is not submitted that any of the other considerations taken into account by

c the registrar were irrelevant; the principal complaint has been that the registrar attached too much weight to them because it is said they were all capable of being put right by the society. Questions of weight and possible remedial action are matters for the registrar and not the court; they are the very stuff on which the exercise of discretion depends.

I should also say a word about the way in which the judge expressed himself on the view of the registrar that depositors would be repaid pound for pound, albeit that there

d might have to be a temporary freeze on withdrawals. The judge held that without a valuation of the mortgage book or an assurance from the Building Societies Association that they would make up any shortfall in the assets after the sale of the mortgage book there was insufficient evidence to justify the registrar's view, and that on the material before the registrar it was an inevitable inference that there would be a loss to the depositors. Now the first observation I have to make is that the judge did not know what

e evidence was before the registrar. In making his inquiries the registrar is not conducting an adversarial inquiry in which two sides lay out before him all the evidence they wish him to take into account. The registrar makes his own inquiries and he has extensive powers and a large department at his disposal to do so. The registrar is engaged in an inquisitorial, not an adversarial, process. It is true that he is required to give the building society notice of the considerations that may lead him to act against the society so that

f the society may have an opportunity to answer them and to persuade the registrar to change his mind, and no doubt considerations of natural justice would require him to put to the society any particularly damaging evidence so that the society has the chance to refute it if it can. But this is very far from a requirement that the registrar should on judicial review be required to file affidavits setting out all the evidence that he has collected during the course of the inquiry and which has contributed to his decision.

g Such a requirement would alter the whole nature of the inquiry, turning it from a review into an appeal.

The registrar is not bound to accept the view of Mr Rowland, the chairman of the society, of the value of the mortgage book, and with all the expertise available to him within his department and from constant contact with all the building societies in this country it is a judgment which he is far better fitted to form than a judge who has to rely

h only on the affidavit of the building society. The same considerations apply to the judgment the registrar formed about the probability of help being available from the Building Societies Association if it becomes necessary. In my view the registrar was entitled to form the judgments he did, and he was not required to justify them by filing affidavit evidence on an application for judicial review.

I can find no grounds for holding that the registrar abused his powers, and for these

j reasons and those more fully set out in the judgments of Sir John Donaldson MR and Slade LJ I would allow this appeal.

SLADE LJ. I agree that this appeal should be allowed and with the reasons explained by Sir John Donaldson MR why it was necessary to hear it in camera. It is not necessary to recapitulate the facts. I will begin by dealing with the disputed questions of statutory

construction, which are of crucial importance in this case. This will explain some of the
principal reasons why I find myself in respectful disagreement with the judge.   *a*

Section 1 of the House Purchase and Housing Act 1959

Under the terms of s 1(1) of the 1959 Act the chief registrar's power to designate any
given society for the purposes of the section does not arise unless the one condition
specified in the subsection is fulfilled. The condition is that he must be satisfied that the
society fulfils 'such requirements as to its assets and liabilities, liquid funds, reserves and   *b*
other matters, as the Treasury may by regulations prescribe'. I will call these requirements
'the prescribed requirements'. They are currently embodied in the Building Societies
(Designation for Trustee Investment) Regulations 1972, SI 1972/1577.

However, even where in any instance he is so satisfied, he still has a discretion whether
to give or to withhold designation. This is made quite plain by the use of the permissive
word 'may' which appears in sub-s (1), instead of the mandatory word 'shall'. Furthermore,   *c*
the wording of the section places no restriction on the exercise of (or refusal to exercise)
the discretion in any case where the power has arisen.

I therefore agree with the judge's conclusion that, in considering whether or not to
exercise his discretion to designate a society in the first place, the chief registrar is at
liberty to take into account other matters in addition to the society's fulfilment of the
prescribed requirements.   *d*

It is common ground that the chief registrar has a power to revoke a designation after
it has been given. The provisions of s 1(3), which require that he shall publish notice of
'any revocation of such a designation', make it plain beyond argument that Parliament
intended him to have, and assumed the existence of, such a power. The problems of
construction involved in the section arise principally because the legislature, by an
extraordinary omission, failed in express terms to give him the contemplated power to   *e*
revoke a designation, and correspondingly failed expressly to specify the limits of any
such power. The dispute in the present context concerns the extent of the limits of the
power of revocation which has to be read into the section.

The judge thought that, as a matter of principle, he should read into the section a
power of revocation only to the extent necessary to achieve the purposes of the 1959 Act
and that he should not read into it a power which would produce 'injustice, absurdity,   *f*
anomaly or contradiction'. Thus far I would agree with him. With great respect to him,
however, I think he erred in the application of this principle.

He considered that the power to revoke which should be read into the section is more
narrowly circumscribed than the power to designate and only arises 'where there is a
failure to comply with one or more of the requirements of the 1972 regulations'. As I
follow his reasoning, he considered that any broader power than this might expose   *g*
societies to injustice, because the non-statutory criteria, which the chief registrar would
apply in deciding whether or not to exercise his powers of revocation—

> 'are likely to be unspecific, may well be unknown to the society until it is given
> an opportunity to make representations that its designation should not be revoked
> (there is no formal procedure provided by the 1959 Act) and would be difficult and
> sometimes impossible to challenge, even though the policies and proceedings of the   *h*
> society in question accorded with one recognised school of thought.'

I see the force of this point, but am not convinced by it. The principal purpose of the
section appears to be to provide appropriate machinery for the designation of building
societies as suitable repositories for the investment of trust funds. To this end the
legislature has seen fit to confer on the chief registrar the discretionary power to designate   *j*
or withhold designation, and it has imposed only the one condition on the exercise of
such power, that being the condition relating to fulfilment of the prescribed
requirements. There are a number of matters beyond the prescribed requirements which
the chief registrar will naturally wish to take into account in deciding whether or not to
designate. As appears from *Wurtzburg and Mills on Building Society Law* (14th edn, 1976)
p 67, the matters which (in my view properly) he takes into account under his current

practice in considering whether or not to confer designation (even though they are not
a dealt with by the 1972 regulations), are the following:

> '(i) Efficient management; (ii) Compliance with the 1962 Act, as amended; (iii)
> Sensible policies; (iv) Basis for continuance in a stable manner; (v) Independence of
> outside control or influences (such as too close links with a particular insurance
> company, or with particular firms of estate agents, accountants or solicitors).'

b   On the judge's view, however, as supported by counsel for the society in argument in
this court, the chief registrar has no right to take into account any of these matters in
considering whether or not to exercise his powers to *revoke* a designation, save perhaps
where they are relevant to the likelihood of continued compliance with the prescribed
requirements in the immediate future.
      I cannot agree with this view. If it were correct, it would mean that the chief registrar
c could find himself obliged to permit a society's designation to continue, solely because
for the time being it fulfilled the prescribed requirements, even though he would
without hesitation have refused (and justifiably refused) designation in the first place.
Such a result cannot, in my opinion, have been the intention of the legislature in enacting
a section which was clearly intended to ensure that a designated society should be, and
remain, a suitable receptacle for the investment of trust funds. Indeed I think that it
d would produce absurdity and anomaly.
      In considering whether the contrary construction, supported by the chief registrar,
would expose societies to possible injustice, I merely wish to say this. The legislature has
displayed sufficient confidence in the holder of that office to place no express fetters on
his discretionary power to withhold designation from a society in the first place. No
doubt it has taken this course having regard both to the nature of the qualifications likely
e to be possessed by the holder of this important position and to the fact that any abuse of
his powers would be open to the process of judicial review. Of course, a theoretical risk
of injustice must exist in any case where an official is entrusted with such a wide
discretion. However, I cannot see any sufficient reason why fears of possible injustice
could justify the court in implying fetters on the chief registrar's discretion to revoke a
designation which do not apply to his discretion to designate.
f   In short, I conclude that on the true construction of s 1 of the 1959 Act the chief
registrar has an unfettered discretion to revoke the designation of a society, whether or
not for the time being it fulfils the prescribed requirements, but that, in an appropriate
case, the court can investigate the exercise of his discretion by the process of judicial
review, to which subject I will revert.

Section 48 of the Building Societies Act 1962
g   Much the same comments as those which I have made in relation to s 1 of the 1959
Act apply in relation to s 48 of the 1962 Act. Under the terms of s 48(1) the power of the
chief registrar to apply s 48(2) to a society does not arise until the one condition specified
in the section is fulfilled. The condition is that he 'considers it expedient to do so in the
interests of investors and depositors'. The phrase 'investors and depositors' is defined in
s 48(6) in terms wide enough to include both the present and future investors and
h depositors.
      He must not actually exercise the power until the consent of the Treasury has been
obtained. Subject to these two fetters, however, the wording of the section places no
express restrictions on the power or its exercise.
      The judge's view was that the subsection properly construed—

j   'confers on the registrar a power to make an order where a society has broken or
      failed to comply with an express or implied requirement of the 1962 Act or where
      the registrar perceives actually foreseeable loss to investors or despositors if no order
      is made.'

He considered that, unless and until one or other of these alternative conditions is
fulfilled, the chief registrar's power does not arise and correspondingly no question of the
exercise of his discretion arises.

In reading words into the section by a process of implication, the judge appears to have been particularly influenced by two points. First, he considered that to construe the *a* section without such implication would attract the same comments as he had made on the wider power under the 1959 Act for which the chief registrar had contended and which he had rejected, that is to say, in his view, the meaning would produce injustice. In this context he referred to Lord Wensleydale's 'golden rule', as expressed by Lord Simon in *Stock v Frank Jones (Tipton) Ltd* [1978] 1 All ER 948 at 952, [1978] 1 WLR 231 at 235, which may permit a court to depart from the natural and ordinary meaning of *b* words used in a statute, if a more literal construction would produce 'injustice, absurdity, anomaly or contradiction'.

Second, in his view, such construction of the section would produce a serious anomaly in that—

'If s 48(1) bears the wider meaning for which [counsel for the chief registrar] contends, but if the power of revocation under the 1959 Act extends no further than *c* I have decided, the registrar would have power in certain circumstances ... to prevent the society from accepting the deposit of, or otherwise borrowing, any money but not to prevent it from being the depository of trustee funds.'

If my construction of the power of revocation conferred by the 1959 Act is correct, there is no substance in the anomaly point relied on by the judge. As to the 'injustice' *d* point, much the same comments apply in the present context as those which I have made in relation to the power of revocation under the 1959 Act.

In referring to 'actually foreseeable loss', the judge, as I understand him, was referring to immediately foreseeable loss. His construction of the subsection would thus mean that in many cases the chief registrar would have no power to intervene for the protection of investors and depositors until it was too late. In my judgment, with great respect to him, *e* there are no sufficient grounds for departing from the plain natural and ordinary meaning of the words used in s 48(1). This meaning is that, subject to obtaining Treasury consent, the chief registrar has an unfettered discretion to apply s 48(2) to a society if he considers it expedient to do so in the interests of present or future investors and depositors. Once again, however, the actual exercise of his discretion will be open to investigation by the court through the process of judicial review, in appropriate cases. *f*

Sections 21 and 22 of the 1962 Act: (A) mortgage interest

I now turn to the provisions of ss 21 and 22 of the 1962 Act, dealing with 'special advances'. The general purpose of these provisions is described with masterly clarity by the chief registrar in paras 4.1 ff of his decision. In referring to 'the prescribed sum', I mean the sum for the time being prescribed under s 21: see s 21(1)(c). At the times material for the purposes of this case it was £37,500. *g*

In a number of cases the society has made first advances of the full sum of £37,500 to borrowers. Interest has then accrued on such transactions and has remained unpaid at the end of the financial year in which the loan was made. The first question that arises in the context of ss 21 and 22 is whether arrears of interest accrued and unpaid at the end of a financial year in respect of these advances should (as the chief registrar thought) properly be taken into account for the purposes of the calculations required by ss 21(3)(b) *h* and 22(2)(b). The answer to this question must turn on the meaning of the phrase 'all other debts of any description (whether immediately repayable or not)' in s 21(2) and 'any kind of debts, whether immediately repayable or not' in s 22(2)(b). It is common ground that these two phrases must bear the same meaning and at this stage I will concentrate my attention on s 21(2) and (3)(b).

The subsection which leads into these two subsections is s 21(2)(c). By virtue of that *j* subsection the phrase 'special advance' includes an advance of any amount by a building society on the security of freehold or leasehold estate—

'to a person other than a body corporate, being a person who, after the advance is made to him, is indebted to the society in an amount exceeding the limit in force for the purposes of this paragraph.'

It should be particularly noted that s 21(1)(c) uses the phrase 'after the advance is made
a   to him' rather than 'immediately after the advance is made to him'. The reason is that
s 21(2) provides in effect that the process of ascertaining whether the 'limit in force' for
the purposes of s 21(1)(c) has been exceeded in respect of any give advance has to be gone
through on two occasions, that is to say once on the making of the advance itself and
once at the end of a period of three months beginning with the date of the advance or (if
sooner) at the end of the financial year of the society in which the advance is made.
b   One effect of s 21(2)(b) is that, if an advance is made and is followed by a bridging loan,
the bridging loan will not have to be taken into account in considering whether the
'limit in force' has been exceeded in relation to the advance, unless the bridging loan is
still outstanding at the end of three months from the date of the advance or (if sooner) at
the end of the current financial year of the society. In any other case, however, s 21(2)(b)
will cause any further advance, even if only a bridging loan, to be taken into account for
c   the last-mentioned purpose. It is therefore by no means merely a dispensing provision,
designed to give exemption to bridging loans, as I think the society has suggested.
    Section 21(3) sets out the relevant criteria for the purposes of determining whether the
amount of a person's indebtedness to a society exceeds the 'limit in force'. As one would
expect, different criteria are to be applied at the two different times specified in s 21(2).
    The clear combined effect of s 21(1)(c), read in conjunction with s 21(2)(b) and (3)(b), is
d   in my opinion that an advance made to a person, which is not a 'special advance' at the
time when it was made, may *become* a special advance, if its effect is that at the end of
three months beginning with the date of the advance, or (if sooner) the end of the
society's financial year in which the advance was made, the amount of the indebtedness
of the borrower, taking into account 'both that advance and all other debts of any
description (whether immediately repayable or not) in which he is indebted to the
e   society' exceeds the 'limit in force'.
    However, as his primary submission in this context on this appeal, counsel for the
society has contended that s 21(1)(c) has no application to a *first* advance made to a person
who is not already indebted to the society. Correspondingly, he has contended that, even
if the reference to debts in s 21(2) includes interest, a first advance made to an individual
of the prescribed sum or less at a time when he is not already indebted to the society can
f   never thereafter *become* a special advance by reason of s 21(2)(b) and (3)(b). On any other
construction, he has submitted, anomalous results would ensue. It was Parliament's
intention, it is said, to allow for a further loan to a borrower already indebted, without
involving the creation of a special advance, provided that the further loan and existing
loan do not together exceed twice the prescribed sum and the excess over the prescribed
sum is repaid within a period of three months (or, if sooner, the end of the society's
g   financial year). On the other hand, if s 21(1)(c) is capable of applying to a 'first-time'
advance, and the debts referred to in s 21(2) include interest, the mere default of a
borrower in paying interest in this three-month period could result in a first-time advance
becoming a 'special advance'. Such a conclusion, it is submitted, would be quite contrary
to the intention of the legislature. Furthermore, it would mean that the mere default of
a borrower in paying interest could expose a society to criminal liability, since s 22
h   imposes limits on the amounts of special advances which a building society may make
and renders the failure to observe those limits a criminal offence.
    I am not persuaded by these submissions. There is nothing in the wording of s 21 of
the 1962 Act to exclude first-time advances from s 21(1)(c). This wording is plainly wide
enough to catch them; and I can see no sufficient justification for restricting its ambit by
a process of implication. The interpretation of the section which I consider the correct
j   one does mean that a society which makes a first-time advance of an amount equal or
very near to the 'limit in force' cannot be certain at the time of making it whether it will
or not become a special advance by virtue of the combined operation of s 21(1)(c), (2)(b)
and (3)(b), when both that advance and 'all other debts of any description (whether
immediately repayable or not)' are taken into account in the calculation which will fall
to be made at the end of the three-month period or the earlier expiration of the society's
financial year. However, the solution to this problem will lie in the society's own hands.

If it wishes to be sure to avoid making a special advance in any given case, it should restrict itself to lending an amount sufficiently below the 'limit in force' that, at the time *a* when it is made, it can be ascertained with confidence that it will never become a special advance.

There was a second and alternative reason why counsel for the society submitted that interest which had accrued due from borrowers but was unpaid should not be taken into account for the purpose of the calculations required by ss 21(3)(*b*) and 22(2)(*b*). This was that the phrase 'all other debts of any description (whether immediately repayable or *b* not)' in s 21(2) and the phrase 'any kind of debts, whether immediately repayable or not' in s 22(2)(*b*), in their context, are confined to debts in the category of advances and are not apt to include arrears of interest, which, it is said, involve no element of 'repayment'.

I cannot accept this very restricted construction of the two phrases. The general words 'all other debts of any description' and 'any kind of debts', read on their own, are plainly wide enough to include accrued debts of any category, whether in respect of mortgage *c* advances, interest, insurance premiums or anything else. The purpose of the words in the parenthesis 'whether immediately repayable or not' is not so much to restrict the generality of the words which immediately precede it as to extend it, by making it clear that an accrued debt will fall to be included, even if the obligation to pay it has not yet arisen. If the legislature had intended nothing but debts in the category of advances to be included, the use of the phrases 'all other debts of any description' and 'any kind of debts' *d* would have been an extraordinary use of language; a simple reference to all other advances would have sufficed.

Counsel for the society referred to certain other provisions in the 1962 Act relating to special advances, namely ss 21(7), 22(2)(*a*) and 24(2)(*b*), which in his submission showed that the draftsman was aware of the differences between payment and repayment and that he expressly referred to interest when he intended a reference to debts to include it. *e* These, however, were all section where the reference to interest followed a reference to an 'advance' or a 'mortgage debt'. The express reference to interest was therefore necessary, or clearly advisable for the avoidance of doubt, if interest was intended to be included. I can find nothing in these three sections to justify the exclusion of interest from the very different, much wider general phrases used in ss 21(2) and 22(2)(*b*). Indeed, s 21(7) seems to me to support the contention that arrears of interest are to be taken into *f* account in making the calculations envisaged by that section.

For all these reasons I conclude that the judge was right to conclude that arrears of interest accrued and unpaid at the end of a financial year should properly be taken into account for the purposes of the calculations required by ss 21(3)(*b*) and 22(2)(*b*).

(B) *Insurance premiums*   *g*

The chief registrar, in calculating 'the ascertained proportion' referred to in s 22 of the 1962 Act as at 31 December 1982, took into account, inter alia, insurance premiums, payment of which had been demanded but which remained unpaid as at 31 December 1982. The society submitted that he should not have taken them into account and the judge upheld this submission.

The arrangements relating to the payment of insurance premiums have been *h* summarised in the judgment of Sir John Donaldson MR. As the judge said, the particular premiums referred to above give rise to a question of construction on cl 3(*c*) of the standard form of mortgage deed used by the society, by which the borrower covenants with the society—

> 'To pay punctually to the Society all premiums necessary for effecting and *j* maintaining any insurance against fire and such other risks as the Society thinks fit in the full replacement value of the property.'

It is the use of the word 'punctually' which gives rise to the problems of construction in the present context. The judge summarised the issue as being whether cl 3(*c*) is to be construed as meaning, on the one hand, 'to pay punctually on demand to the society all premiums necessary' or, on the other hand, 'to pay punctually on it becoming necessary a for the society to pay all premiums necessary for . . .' He preferred the latter construction and, in doing so, relied particularly on the absence of an express provision equivalent to one which is to be found in the subsequent cl 4(c) of the mortgage deed, requiring moneys to be paid punctually 'on demand'.

There is, however, a third possible construction of the clause to which the judge did not advert. This is to read the word 'punctually' as referring to the point of time on which the insurance of a particular property, or the renewal of such insurance, takes
b effect. This, in my view, is the correct construction of the clause. The practice is that, on the making of an advance, the society calculates the premium from the date of the advance until 31 January in the following year and debits the borrower's account with the premium. Since, as I understand the arrangements, the borrower will enjoy the benefit of cover from the date of the advance, there arises on that date a corresponding indebtedness on his part to the society, which falls to be taken into account in calculating
c the 'ascertained proportion' in accordance with s 22(2)(b). The mere fact that the society, by arrangements made between itself and the underwriters, does not itself have to pay the premiums until the following February does not affect this conclusion. The construction favoured by the judge appears to involve the proposition that the borrower can enjoy the benefit of insurance arranged by the society, while at the same time there is no accrued indebtedness to the society on the part of the borrower in respect of the
d premium for such insurance. With great respect to the judge, I do not think that this proposition can be or is correct.

The limits of judicial review in the present case

At this point it will be convenient to consider the limits within which the court can control the exercise of the two relevant statutory powers of the chief registrar in any
e given case.

Section 1 of the 1959 Act and s 48 of the 1962 Act are both drafted in subjective form: they are expressed to be exercisable if the chief registrar 'is satisfied' or 'considers' and, on the face of them, are concerned only with his state of mind. However, the recent decision of the House of Lords in *Secretary of State for Education and Science v Tameside Metropolitan Borough* [1976] 3 All ER 665, [1977] AC 1014 well illustrates that the use of subjective
f language in sections of this nature does not necessarily preclude the intervention of the court under ordinary *Wednesbury* principles: see *Associated Provincial Picture Houses Ltd v Wednesbury Corp* [1947] 2 All ER 680, [1948] 1 KB 223. The court may intervene if the official concerned is shown in a material respect to have misdirected himself in law in exercising his discretion or to have taken into account matters which, on the true construction of the statute, he should not have taken into account or to have failed to
g take into account matters which he should have taken into account (see, for example, [1976] 3 All ER 665 at 681–682, 695–696, [1977] AC 1014 at 1047, 1064–1065 per Lord Wilberforce and Lord Diplock).

If the chief registrar could be shown to have misdirected himself in any such manner in exercising either of the statutory powers in the present case, the court could, in my opinion, intervene by way of judicial review, though no doubt in practice it would afford
h this discretionary remedy only if it was satisfied that the relevant error had, or might have, materially influenced the chief registrar's decision. Likewise, it could, in my opinion, intervene if the chief registrar were shown to have acted in bad faith or in breach of the requirements of natural justice, or to have made a decision which no reasonable person in his position could have made. Bad faith is not, of course, alleged in the present case. Nor is a breach of the requirements of natural justice.

j In my opinion, however, these are the limits of the powers of the court to interfere. It is not at liberty merely to substitute its own opinion for that of the chief registrar (see the *Tameside* case [1976] 3 All ER 665 at 695, [1977] AC 1014 at 1064 per Lord Diplock); nor is it at liberty to act as an appellate court from the chief registrar's decision on questions of fact. If the society were in a position to prove by compelling evidence that a particular finding of crucial fact by the chief registrar was clearly wrong, this might give the court power to intervene. Subject to this, however, on this application for judicial review, the society is not, in my opinion, entitled to call on the chief registrar to justify his findings of fact by evidence or to expect the court to reverse findings of fact made by the chief *a* registrar, for the purpose of upsetting the exercise of his discretionary powers.

The 'ascertained proportion'

Since the judge had concluded that the chief registrar's power to revoke a designation under the 1959 Act only arises where there is a failure to comply with one or more of the requirements of the 1972 regulations, he appears to have considered that the onus fell on *b* the chief registrar affirmatively to prove such failure. This point is well illustrated by the judge's approach to the crucial matter of 'the ascertained proportion' (referred to in s 22(2) and (3) of the 1962 Act) as at 31 December 1982.

In the case of any building society, this 'ascertained proportion' is of great importance because, among other reasons, it determines the proportion of 'special advances' which a society can properly make in the next financial year. If the ascertained proportion at the *c* end of a financial year does not exceed 10%, the society may make special advances in the next following financial year up to 10% of the total amount of all advances: see s 22(3). If the ascertained proportion is more than 10% but does not exceed 25%, the society is limited to a figure of 2½% in making special advances in the next financial year: see s 22(4). If it is more than 25%, the society can make no special advances in the next financial year: see s 22(5). Furthermore, unless a society is empowered to make special *d* advances in its current financial year up to the limit specified in s 22(3), it does not comply with the requirements of reg 2(1)(c) of the 1972 regulations and is thus in danger of losing its 'trustee status' by an exercise of the chief registrar's power to revoke a designation under the 1959 Act.

The chief registrar had decided that the society did not fulfil the requirement set out in reg 2(1)(c) of the 1972 regulations in that it only had power to make advances up to *e* the limit specified in s 22(4), and not up to the higher limit specified in s 22(3). He found that the ascertained proportion on 31 December 1982 was at least 10·09%. These findings were referred to as 'Item 1' in the judge's judgment.

In the forefront of the society's attack on the chief registrar's decision, both before the judge and in this court, was the contention that this figure was in fact less than 10%, so that the last-mentioned ground for the chief registrar's decision was ill-founded. *f*

In response to this challenge, the judge said this: 'To make out this ground it was necessary for the registrar to be satisfied that the ascertained proportion on 31 December 1982 exceeded 10%.' He then proceeded to find on the facts that the true figure was not 10·09%, but either 9·7% or 9·96%.

In view of what I have said in relation to the construction of s 1 of the 1959 Act and to judicial review of any exercise of the chief registrar's powers under that section, I do not *g* think that the onus fell on the chief registrar to prove that the ascertained proportion 'exceeded 10%'. On the contrary, so far as the society's attack is based on this figure, I think it is incumbent on it to show by compelling evidence that the chief registrar was clearly wrong in his finding that the ascertained proportion on 31 December 1982 was over 10%.

In my judgment, the society has not come near to establishing this point. I can *h* summarise my reasons briefly as follows. The judge found that, subject to what is said below in regard to two particular accounts, the ascertained proportion on 31 December 1982, including unpaid interest and unpaid insurance premiums (both of which I think ought to be included), would have been 10·09%. There were, however, two accounts representing a total of 0·13% which, for the reasons given in his judgment, he thought should have been excluded in the chief registrar's final calculation of the above-mentioned *j* figure of 10·09%. The deduction of 0·13% from the latter figure left only 9·96%. The judge therefore concluded that the chief registrar had erred in his final reckoning of the 'ascertained proportion'.

This reasoning might have had some force if the registrar had made a positive finding that the 'ascertained proportion' was 10·09% (no more and no less). His finding, however, was merely that 'the proportion was more than 10%: I estimate 10·09%' (see para 5.24(ii)

of his decision). In earlier paragraphs of his decision he made it plain that, for the
a purposes of his calculations, he had given the society the benefit of the doubt by not
including in the calculation certain other items of indebtedness, referred to in paras 5.16
to 5.19 of his decision. In particular, he had not included those cases where the society
had failed to send out a request for payment of insurance premiums until after 31
December. Such cases alone would have added 0·83% to the ascertained proportion,
making a total of 10·79% when added to 9·96%. Counsel for the registrar has submitted,
b and I accept, that this figure of 0·83% could and should properly have been taken into
account in calculating the 'ascertained proportion' in accordance with s 22(2) and (3) of
the 1962 Act. For this reason if no other (though in my opinion there are further reasons),
I do not think the society has established that the chief registrar was clearly wrong in
finding that the ascertained proportion on 31 December 1982 was over 10%, and that the
society did not fulfil the requirement set out in reg 2(1)(c) of the 1972 regulations, in that
c it only had power to make advances up to the limit specified in s 22(4) of the 1962 Act.

Further findings of the chief registrar

It is not surprising that in his submissions on the facts counsel for the society directed
a good deal of our attention to the matter of the 'ascertained proportion'. For if, as is my
view, it cannot be shown that the chief registrar manifestly went wrong on this important
d point (the judge's 'Item 1') the obstacles facing the society in challenging his decision
become all the more formidable.

The chief registrar's further findings of fact included, inter alia, the following. (1) The
society had failed to comply with the provisions of s 22(3) of the 1962 Act for the years
respectively ending 31 December 1981 and 31 December 1982 in that it had made
special advances in excess of 10% of the total amount of all advances made by the society
e during those respective years. (2) The society's current policies run a distinct risk of the
society having inadequate reserves in relation to the structure of its assets and the nature
of its business. (3) The arrangements for the direction and management of the society
were inappropriate and unsatisfactory for a number of separate reasons set out in the
chief registrar's decision. (4) The society had conducted its affairs in such a way as to have
repeatedly put into question its continued eligibility for designation for trustee
f investment under the 1972 regulations. (5) The society had actually failed to meet the
requirements of reg 2(1)(a) of the 1972 regulations on the basis of the figures shown in
its annual returns for the years ended 31 December 1979 and 31 December 1980 in that
the society did not meet the minimum requirements for reserves set out in para 4 of the
schedule to those regulations. (6) The society's failure to ensure that it complied with the
requirements set out in reg 2(1) of the 1972 regulations resulted in it being ineligible to
g join the Investors Protection Scheme promoted by the Building Societies Association and
denied its investors the full protection available under that scheme.

The judge's decision

The judge in effect held that it could not be said that any of these listed findings were
findings which, on the evidence, no reasonable chief registrar could have reached. And,
h indeed, in the case of some of them he affirmatively held that they had been established
on the evidence.

If the society's attack on the chief registrar's construction of ss 21 and 22 of the 1962
Act had been established, then conceivably (I put it no higher) it might have been able to
show that some at least of these findings were manifestly erroneous and unsustainable.
This was why the points of construction arising on the two sections assumed such
j importance. As things are, however, despite counsel's valiant argument on its behalf, I
think that the society has not come near to demonstrating that any of these findings were
clearly wrong or ones which no reasonable chief registrar could have reached on the
evidence before him.

The process of reasoning which led the judge to grant the society's application, while
accepting more or less all the chief registrar's findings of fact, other than that relating to
the 'ascertained proportion', was briefly as follows. He considered that the only grounds

relied on by the chief registrar which empowered him to make an order under s 48(1) of
the 1962 Act and to revoke the society's trustee designation under the 1959 Act were the   *a*
society's failure to comply with the provisions of s 22(3) of the 1962 Act for the years
1981 and 1982, which he described as 'statutory grounds'. He considered that those 'non-
statutory' grounds relied on by the chief registrar which he had upheld conferred no
power on the chief registrar to make such an order in the absence of a finding that there
was 'an actually foreseeable loss to investors or depositors unless an order was made'.

He then proceeded to consider whether, in deciding to make the orders, the chief   *b*
registrar exercised his discretion properly. He pointed out that the chief registrar had
treated the risk to investors and depositors as a factor relevant to the exercise of his
discretion and accepted that he was perfectly entitled so to treat it. Rightly, in my
opinion, he rejected a contention that the chief registrar had failed to exercise his
discretion properly on the grounds that the society had made it clear that the board were
ready to take any further steps which he reasonably required to effect changes in its   *c*
board. The point on which the judge ultimately fastened was as follows.

As appears from paras 15.4 and 15.5 of his decision, the chief registrar had attached
importance to the facts that, at present, the society's assets would in his view suffice to
permit it to make a full pound in the pound payment to investors and depositors, while
there would no longer be a certainty that it would be in a position to do so in future
years, if its present management and existing policies continued. The judge concluded   *d*
that there was 'insufficient evidence to justify a finding that investors and depositors
would be repaid a pound in the pound'. He said:

> 'In my view on the material before the registrar, there was an inevitable inference
> that there would be a loss to them, if the orders were made, of an uncertain amount.
> As against that certain loss to present investors and depositors there is said to be no
> more than the risk of a loss, within a few years, to present and future investors and   *e*
> depositors of an unspecified and unspecifiable amount. In these circumstances in
> my view the decision by the registrar to exercise his discretion to make the orders
> was a decision which no registrar, acting reasonably on the material before him, or
> which ought to have been before him, would have made.'

The judge, in reaching his final decision, thus attached the greatest importance to a   *f*
supposed erroneous conclusion on the part of the chief registrar as to the financial
consequences to investors and depositors of the orders made by the chief registrar.
However, with great respect to the judge, I do not think it was open to him to go behind
such conclusion, unless the society had shown that this was clearly wrong.

Though certain passages in an affidavit sworn on 28 October 1983 by the society's
chairman attempt to cast doubts on its correctness, I do not think they come near to   *g*
establishing this. The chief registrar apparently considered it unnecessary to answer these
passages by further evidence and in my view rightly so; as I have already pointed out, he
is under no general obligation to justify his findings of fact on an application for judicial
review.

While the judge, in considering the exercise of the chief registrar's discretion, thus
attached much weight to what he supposed to be the insolvency of the society, he did not   *h*
apparently take into account, in this context, the individual or cumulative effect of the
findings of the chief registrar, which I have listed above under the heading 'Further
findings of the chief registrar'. Nor did he take into account the fact that (in his view
wrongly, but in my view unassailably) the chief registrar had found that the society's
ascertained proportion as at 31 December 1982 exceeded 10%, and accordingly that it
did not fulfil the requirement set out in reg 2(1)(c) of the 1972 regulations.   *j*

Conclusions

In my judgment, all these findings taken together make it quite impossible for the
society to establish either that the chief registrar was acting beyond his powers or that he
abused his powers in any way in making the two relevant orders. It cannot, in my view,
be said that on the basis of these findings no reasonable person in his position could

reasonably have made them. He volunteered a large number of hostages to fortune in setting out in his decision, so fully and comprehensively, the considerations of fact and law which led him to make the orders. But I cannot find any point which both is clearly shown to have demonstrated error on his part and can conceivably have affected his final decision. The orders are of a drastic character and must have caused him anxiety, as they have caused this court anxiety, because it seems to be common ground that, if they are affirmed and published, the society cannot survive; and there are different views as to the effect which this will have on present investors and depositors. Counsel for the society submitted very persuasively that the society should have been, and should be, given a second chance so as to put its affairs in order. However, I come back to the point where I began. On the face of his two orders the chief registrar has acted wholly intra vires. As to the exercise of his discretions, these have been conferred by the statute on him, not on the court. I can see no grounds on which the court is entitled to interfere with his exercise of these discretions in the present case.

For these reasons, and the further reasons given by Sir John Donaldson MR and Griffiths LJ, I conclude that the chief registrar's orders must be permitted to stand and I would accordingly allow this appeal.

Appeal allowed. Leave to appeal to the House of Lords refused. Stay pending petition to House of Lords.

17 January. The Court of Appeal approved an agreed order that all moneys paid into court by the society on and after 12 December 1983 pursuant to its undertaking (see p 32 e, ante) be paid out to the society together with interest thereon and that all such moneys and interest should be dealt with in accordance with the terms of a schedule to the order. That schedule provided that on receipt of the moneys paid out of court the society should pay them into an account with a London clearing bank to be operated jointly by the society and the Woolwich Equitable Building Society. The schedule also dealt in detail with the rights of depositors under the order.

Solicitors: *Treasury Solicitor; Stephenson Harwood* (for the society); *Prestons*, Woolwich (for the Woolwich Equitable Building Society).

Diana Procter   Barrister.

EXTRACTS FROM CHIEF REGISTRAR'S DECISION REFERRED TO IN JUDGMENT OF SIR JOHN
DONALDSON MR

The proposal to revoke designation under s 1 of the 1959 Act

5. *Ground 1: Ascertained proportion on 31 December 1982*

'On the basis of the figures shown in Part 6, section C of its annual return for 1982, it appears that the society does not fulfil the requirement set out in reg 2(1)(c) of the Building Societies (Designation for Trustee Investment) Regulations 1972, SI 1972/1577, in that it is not empowered to make special advances in its current financial year up to the limit specified in s 22(3) of the Building Societies Act 1962 by virtue of the fact that it may only make advances up to the limit specified in s 22(4) of the 1962 Act.'. . .

5.24 I therefore conclude that: (i) the 'ascertained proportion' was less than indicated by the society's annual return for 1982: Part 6(C) of that return should be correct; (ii) the proportion was nevertheless more than 10%: I estimate 10·09%; (iii) the society is therefore limited in 1983 to making special advances of not more than 2½% of total advances by virtue of s 22(4) of the 1962 Act; (iv) the society therefore failed to meet the requirement specified in reg 2(1)(c) of the 1972 regulations; (v) the margin by which the ascertained proportion exceeded 10% was slight, but there is no power to temper the provisions of s 22 or of the regulations; (vi) the society could readily have avoided the position by either (a) making advances marginally less than the £37,500 limit, rather than of that amount, (b) monitoring the position, maintaining its accounts in a way

which both made this possible during the year and facilitated the proper calculation at
the end of the year; (vii) the ground is therefore substantiated.

6. *Consideration a: previous failures on designation requirements*

'On the basis of the figure shown in its annual returns for the years ended 31 December
1979 and 31 December 1981 the society did not fulfil the requirement set out in
reg 2(1)(a) of the 1972 regulations in that the society did not meet the minimum
requirement for reserves set out in para 4 of the schedule to those regulations. Thus, on
three occasions in the last four years the society has failed to meet the requirements of
the said regulations.'. . .

6.8 I therefore conclude that: (i) the society failed to meet the reserves requirement
specified in the 1972 regulations at the end of 1979: its reserves ratio, adjusted as
prescribed in those regulations, was 1·62% as compared with 2·5% specified for a society
of its then size; (ii) the society again failed to meet the reserves requirement at the end of
1981: its reserves ratio, similarly adjusted, was 2·21% compared with the 2·5% specified
for a society of its then size; (iii) the second, and probably the first, failure could have
been readily avoided by adjusting growth to the availability of reserves and by adopting
a more appropriate policy for the investment of liquid funds; (iv) the society has rebuilt
its reserves position, and has also met all, or all but one, of the assurances which it gave to
me after the failure to meet the requirement at the end of 1981; (v) I can properly take
these failures, and the action to correct them, into account in so far as the recent track
record of the society is relevant to the prospect for investors in it.

7. *Consideration b: special advances in 1982*

'On the information provided by the society in the chairman's letter of 27 May 1983
(as amended by the chairman's letter of 15 June 1983) it appears that the society has: (i)
failed to comply with the provisions of s 22(3) of the 1962 Act for the year ended 31
December 1982 in that it has made special advances in excess of 10% of the total amount
of all advances made by the society during that year; (ii) incorrectly completed Part 9,
section A of its annual return for the year ended 31 December 1982 with the result that
it did not disclose the excess of special advances made in that year; and (iii) for the
purposes of s 82(2)(b) of the 1962 Act, given wrong figures in its directors' report for the
year ended 31 December 1982 with the same result. As a consequence of (i) above, the
society and those officers in default have rendered themselves liable to prosecution for a
criminal offence under s 22(7) of the 1962 Act and have also, by virtue of s 22(8) of the
1962 Act, rendered the society liable to be the subject of a petition for winding up under
the Companies Act 1948 by the chief registrar.'. . .

7.28 I therefore conclude that: (i) the society was permitted by s 22 of the 1962 Act to
make advances of not more than 10% of its total advances in 1982; (ii) it made 11·61%,
and so failed to meet the requirement that it should so conduct its business as to secure
that special advances are not made except as authorised by that section; (iii) this compared
with the proportion of special advances of 8·54% which the society reported in its
directors' report to members and potential investors and in its annual return to the
registry; (iv) it is not necessary to include in the consideration the references to
prosecution and winding up: the consideration should be restricted in this respect; (v)
the failure by the society to comply with one of the most important provisions of the
1962 Act is indicative of the way in which the society is managed, and so directly relevant
to a decision on revocation.

8. *Consideration c: investors protection scheme*

'The society's failure to ensure that it complied with the requirements set out in
reg 2(1) of the 1972 regulations resulted in it being ineligible to join the investors
protection scheme promoted by the Building Societies Association and so denied its
investors the full protection available under that scheme.'. . .

8.11 I therefore conclude that: (i) the society was not eligible to join the building
societies investors protection scheme when it was set up in the spring of 1982 because at

a the end of 1981 the society had failed to meet the reserves requirement, equivalent to that in the 1972 regulations; (ii) investors in the society would have gained materially greater protection if the society had joined the scheme; I understand that the board wished to do so; (iii) however, the failure of the society to keep the ascertained proportion not more than 10% at the end of 1982 meant that the society was still not eligible; it cannot now join before the spring of 1984 at the earliest; (iv) this is directly relevant to the suitability of the society to hold trust funds.

b 9. *Consideration d: future growth and reserves*
'The society's budget for the year ending 31 December 1983 as received by the registry on 25 May 1983 forecast a rate of asset growth and a resulting diminution of the reserve ratio and so showed, in the opinion of the chief registrar, that the society's current policies run a severe risk of the society again having inadequate reserves in relation to the structure of its assets and the nature of its business.'. . .

c 9.25 I therefore conclude: (i) the adequacy of the reserves in relation to the circumstances of a particular society, and not just the comparison of the reserves with the minimum specified in the 1972 regulation, can be relevant to the continued designation of that society; (ii) the nature of the assets of the society is such that, if anything, a higher reserve ratio is appropriate than for the generality of societies; in particular this is because

d of (a) the higher proportion of loans outside the traditional type of advances secured on owner-occupied property made to finance the purchase or improvement of that property; (b) the relatively bad arrears position, (c) the new practice of making 'interest only' loans without the assignment of an endowment policy; the somewhat unconventional mortgage policy is not undesirable in itself, but it points to a need for higher than normal reserves; (iii) in 1982 the society was able by a combination of its actions and external events to rebuild its reserves position; its proposed growth of 60% in total assets in 1983

e is likely to dissipate this; (iv) its own projection of the reserve ratio at the end of 1983 would give it a ratio, allowing for the difference in accounting policies, which is about half of the average ratio at the end of 1982 of societies of broadly comparable size; (v) moreover, it is prudent to budget for a reserve ratio above the minimum considered acceptable; (vi) I therefore consider that, on present policies there is a distinct risk of the society having inadequate reserves in relation to its type of business at the end of 1983;

f (vii) the potential weakness of the reserve position is directly relevant to the suitability of the society to take money from the public, and particularly trust moneys; (viii) the consideration should stand, except that it should be restricted by substituting 'distinct' for 'severe'.

10. *Consideration e: special advances in 1981*

g 'On the basis of documents produced and information furnished by the society, it appears that the society failed to comply with the provisions of s 22(3) of the 1962 Act, also for the year ended 31 December 1981 in that it made special advances in excess of 10% of the total amount of all advances made by the society during that year, with similar consequences to those set out in relation to consideration (b)(i) to (iii) in the said notice dated 27 June 1983.'. . .

h 10.9 I therefore conclude: (i) the society was authorised by s 22 of the 1962 Act to make special advances of not more than 10% of total advances in 1981; (ii) it made 11·53% and so failed to meet the requirement that it should so conduct its business as to secure that special advances are not made except as authorised by that section; (iii) this compared with the proportion of special advances of 9·66% which the society reported in its directors' report to members and potential investors and in its annual return to the

j registry; (iv) as with the similar breach in 1982, the failure to comply with one of the most important provisions of the 1962 Act is an indication of the way in which the society is managed, and so directly relevant to a decision on revocation.

11. *Consideration f: direction and management*
(i) and (ii) *Board procedures*
'On the basis of documents produced and information furnished by the society, in the

opinion of the chief registrar the arrangements for direction and management of the society are, or have been, inappropriate and unsatisfactory for the society in that: (i) it appears that important decisions have been taken without full discussion and formal approval by the board; (ii) the board has not laid down in writing a formal procedural framework to govern the manner in which it performs its functions so as to establish and maintain its collective authority; (iii) in the opinion of the chief registrar, the society has not available to it adequate and comprehensive documentation of its systems of control and inspection.'. . .

11.42 I therefore conclude that: (i) the society is now one of substance, growing rapidly and pursuing somewhat unorthodox policies; for all these reasons effective board control in the interests of investors and other members is vital; (ii) the executive structure in the society is unusual for a building society, because there is no chief executive separate from the chairman; the chairman, Mr Rowland, is effectively chief executive. Another director, Mr Tombs, is also an executive. There are two general managers who are not directors; these four form the 'executive', or 'policy committee'; there are four non-executive directors; (iii) one recent decision, that to vary the rates paid to the generality of the society's investors independently of any general move in building society interest rates, was of sufficient importance to merit a board decision based on consideration of papers setting out alternatives: it was merely put to the non-executive directors over the telephone, with only the policy committee's recommendation being described; (iv) a more fundamental policy decision, that to take an amount equivalent to 10% of the society's total funds from the wholesale money markets, was taken and implemented by the chairman after consultation with only one other director; it was reported at the next board meeting, although it would appear from the representations that the potential implications, including the need for the society to refinance that amount in a very short period in a year's time, were not brought out; (v) there has been no systematic or comprehensive documentation of the respective powers of the board and the executives; a recent board minute gave such wide delegation to Mr Rowland and Mr Tombs, severally or jointly, to make it possible for them to make the collective authority of the board ineffective, were they to wish to do so; (vi) the new board manual submitted with the representations includes comparable delegations which would enable Mr Rowlands and Mr Tombs to render the collective role of the board ineffective if they so wished; the manual does not 'establish and maintain the board's collective authority'; (vii) the board of a financial institution has to be collectively in a position to discharge its fiduciary duty to those who have placed money with it; it is therefore essential for the procedures of the board of a building society to include checks and balances between the executive and the non-executive directors; the latter have a particular duty to the investing members; if there are not such checks and balances, power can pass effectively into the hands of an individual or small group; cases of failure of building societies, banks and insurance companies over the last decade have brought out the dangers when this happens; (viii) the society's representations, and revised procedures, show a disturbing lack of awareness of these dangers; this is particularly disturbing because of the clear positive guidance from the registry; there are other ways of securing flexibility and speed of response than through blanket delegations, or by proceeding by bilateral oral discussions; (ix) therefore the society's practice and procedures fail to achieve the effective collective control of the board over policy which is necessary for the proper protection of members interests, including the security of their funds; (x) both of the first two part of this consideration are therefore substantiated, and are relevant to the future suitability of this society to take trust funds.

12. *Consideration f: direction and management*
(iii) *Documentation of systems of control and inspection*
'On the basis of documents produced and information furnished by the society, in the opinion of the chief registrar the arrangements for direction and management of the society are, or have been, inappropriate and unsatisfactory for the society in that: (iii) in

the opinion of the chief registrar the society has not available to it adequate and
a comprehensive documention of its system of control and inspection.'. . .

12.44 I therefore conclude that: (i) the adequacy of documentation of inspection
should be regarded as 'not proven' and the reference to inspection in the consideration
should be deleted; (ii) the society's documentation of its control systems is incomplete,
inadequate for the areas it does cover and fragmented; in particular it does not specify
sufficiently *who* is responsible and *how* the operation of controls should be evidenced; (iii)
b this does not necessarily mean that the control systems are at present inadequate, but it
makes it exceedingly difficult for the society or its auditors to satisfy themselves that the
controls are complete and adequate, particularly in respect of those aspects where they
have a statutory duty to do so, respectively under ss 76 and 87 of the 1962 Act; (iv) even
if the control systems are complete and effective at present, the absence of adequate
documentation makes it most difficult to maintain them, particularly in a society which
c is expanding and so has new staff and reallocation of duties of existing staff; (v) the board's
failure to devote attention to this aspect of the society's activities, particularly in a rapidly
expanding society, risks at best administrative failure and at worst the failure of financial
management and control; the latter can create an opportunity for fraud or financial
mismanagement; it is not a risk which ought to be taken by the board of a building
society; (vi) the society's readiness to bring in consultants to review the society's systems
d is welcome; it would have been better two years ago, after my predecessor's letter of 19
August 1981 called for the work to be done as a matter of urgency; (vii) the consideration
is well founded, except that the word 'inspection' should be deleted; the consideration is
directly relevant to the safety of money placed with the society, including by trustees.

13. *Ground 2: statutory and regulatory requirements*
e 'The society has so conducted its business that it has failed to ensure that it complies
with the statutory and regulatory requirements which apply to it.'. . .

13.11 I therefore conclude that: (i) the society in 1981 and 1982 broke the special
advance provision of s 22 of the 1962 Act, one of the main provisions introduced by the
1962 Act; (ii) it also broke the requirements for the directors' reports and annual returns
for those two years by showing the wrong figures, so potentially misleading investors;
f (iii) the breaches of the law were almost certainly due to giving too little attention to
ensuring that the society complied with the law, rather than to a deliberate decision to
flout the law; (iv) the statutory framework and supervisory framework for building
societies intended to protect investors is built up on the presumption that boards will
take care to comply with the law and to report accurately to their members and to the
registry; this society has singularly failed to do so, and thereby cast serious doubt on its
g suitability to continue to take investors' money, including trust moneys.

14. *Ground 3: the interests of members*
'The society has conducted its business recklessly and in such a way as to: (i) be contrary
to the interest of its members; and (ii) the essential confidence of the public in the society
and in building societies generally.'. . .
h 14.7 I therefore consider that the ground, restricted to read as follows, is well
established and that it should be a major consideration in the decision: 'The society has
conducted its business imprudently and in such a way as to be contrary to the interests of
its members.'

15. *Proposal to revoke designation: summing up*
j 15.1 It is clear to me, on the basis of these grounds and considerations, that, if the
society did not already have designation, met the minimum requirements in the 1972
regulations on 31 December 1983 and then applied to me for designation, I would not
be justified in granting that designation. The application would be refused. The society
does not measure up to the criteria specified by my predecessors for societies which are
to be allowed to take investments by trustees of beneficiaries' funds under the Trustee
Investment Act 1961.

15.2 However, that is not a sufficient test for revocation. I have to take account of the implications for the society, particularly its investing members, of the act of revocation, as well as of the implications for investors, particularly beneficiaries of trusts, if I were to allow designation to continue.

15.3 It was represented on behalf of the society that the society was solvent and that the only thing which would cause a loss to investors would be if I took this step. I do not accept either limb of the latter proposition.

15.4 I accept that, if I do revoke designation, there would almost certainly be a run on the society. The effect would not be confined to investment by trustees. The loss of 'trustee status' would affect the confidence of other investors. If there were a run, the society would have to impose a temporary freeze on withdrawals. At present, to the best of my knowledge, the assets are sufficient to permit a full payment to investors, a pound in the pound. I am confident that on the basis of their past performance, the Building Societies Association would seek to help the board of the society in the reordering of its affairs so that such repayment in full, with interest, would be a matter of months, rather than years, and part-payment would probably be possible fairly quickly. (As there would be no loss, the situation would not come within the scope of the investors protection scheme.) I would also hope that the present board and management would now act in the best interests of the members to mitigate the consequences of the statutory action.

15.5 The alternative would be to allow the society to retain its designation and to continue as it is. In my view, if the society continued with its present management and existing policies, there would be a distinct risk of the society overreaching itself, either in terms of business policies or administration, and that this would lead, within a few years, to such problems that there would be some form of crisis. If that happened, in my view there would no longer be the certainty that the society would be able to pay its investors a pound in the pound. Also, in that event, the delay in repayment to investors would affect substantially more investors and substantially larger sums, because of the growth of the society in the mean time.

15.6 In cases such as this, the prudential supervisor inevitably faces the dilemma of setting the immediate and virtually certain consequences of his action for existing investors against the longer term risks to existing and future investors of his not acting. It can be an onerous judgment. But, in this case, the immediate consequence for investors will in most cases be inconvenience, if anything at all. The risk of substantive damage later is real.

15.7 Also, in this particular case, it is a judgment which cannot readily be postponed further by, say, accepting assurances from the board in the way which I did last year. The society's latest failure to meet the requirements of the 1972 regulations is already in the public domain. But it is not yet widely known because it is only available on the annual returns, or indirectly to those who inquire about the society's position in relation to the investors protection scheme. However, the position on special advances must soon be known more widely. The errors in the figures for special advances in the directors' reports for 1981 and 1982 are sufficiently material in a statement required by statute for it to be necessary for them to be corrected, if investors are not to be further misled. The corrections will have to be public and brought to the attention of members and investors. The publication will inevitably raise the question of what action the chief registrar proposes to take in respect of the breaches of s 22 of the 1962 Act, one of the more important provisions in that Act which carries severe penal sanctions. If I did not act on these breaches now, I would be saying tacitly, and quite possibly explicitly, that the underlying position of the society was sufficiently sound for me to condone publicly the breaches in that and other regulatory requirements, and to continue the society's designation and authorisation. I therefore have to decide now, one way or the other.

15.8 I am satisfied that, if I did not revoke designation, there would be a distinct risk of more substantial damage to existing and future investors, and particularly to investments by trustees.

15.9 I therefore conclude that the right course is to revoke designation.

a 15.10 Finally, counsel for the society submitted that sufficient doubt had been cast on the provisions of ss 21 and 22 of the 1962 Act, relating to special advances and the ascertained proportion, and to the extent of the power to revoke designation under s 1 of the 1959 Act for it to be wrong for me to go ahead with either statutory act without establishing the law on these points. He pointed out that it was for the court, not the chief registrar, to determine the law.

b 15.11 I entirely accept that the determination of the law is a matter for the court. If there were a serious doubt about the interpretation of the law, and if that were critical to a decision, there would be a good case for seeking clarification of the law before I proceeded.

15.12 I do not, however, think that there is a sufficient doubt about the interpretation of ss 21 and 22 of the 1962 Act to justify such a reference to the court by me. I have considered carefully the alternative constructions put forward as hypotheses by counsel.

c But, for the reasons I have set out, I do not consider that they create a serious doubt about these provisions. The view which I am taking has been that generally accepted and accords with the advice which I have received, taking account of the points made in representations. It is not sufficient for a society just to put forward alternative constructions, which are not sufficiently convincing to cast serious doubt on that interpretation, to give cause for me to take the initiative in having the law clarified by

d the court. In a situation such as this, I consider that it is incumbent on me to take a view on the best advice which is available to me, and then to act on it.

15.13 As far as s 1 of the 1959 Act is concerned, I am also satisfied that, on the basis of the best advice, I have the discretion to revoke in the way which I have considered. Indeed, as I have explained above, the actions of the society have placed on me publicly the duty to decide whether to exercise that discretion or not. And I am satisfied that the

e right thing in the interests of the beneficiaries of potential trustee investors is to revoke designation.

15.14 However, I must clearly regard very seriously a point which puts in question my powers to do something. I feel the more confident in going ahead on the basis of my present best advice in that, if I did not do so, the end result would be much the same. As will become clear later in this decision, the s 48 order would, in my view, be justified

f even if there were not the power to revoke trustee designation in this way. The practical outcome for the society and investors of a s 48 order alone would be virtually the same as that of the combination of revocation and the order.

15.15 I have therefore decided that the correct course is to revoke designation. However, I consider that it would be in the best interests of members of the society if the board and management had an opportunity to consider, before the revocation becomes

g public, what is now the best course in the interests of members. I therefore propose to make the revocation so that it takes effect two weeks after making it, to defer publication in the Gazettes until it takes effect, and to take no initiative in publicising the notice of revocation until after the close of business on the day preceding that on which revocation becomes effective.

h   *The proposal for an order under s 48 of the 1962 Act*
16. *Considerations already reviewed*
16.1 Most, but not all, of the considerations cited in the original and supplementary notices for the proposed s 48 order were put in virtually identical wording, but in a different order, in the original and supplementary notices for the proposal to revoke designation. They, and the representation by the society on them, have been reviewed

j earlier in this decision in relation to that proposal.

16.2 So I review them here again briefly, partly because the criterion for a s 48 order is slightly different. In the case of revocation of designation the criterion is the suitability of the society to take funds from trustees tempered by the practical consequences for investors in the society if I removed the status conferred by designation. In the case of the s 48 order, I have to be satisfied before making it that the order would be in the interests of investors and depositors, including both those who have invested and those who may invest.

a

Consideration 1

'On information provided by the society in the chairman's letter of 27 May 1983 (as amended by the chairman's letter of 15 June 1983) it appears that the society has so conducted its business that it has failed to ensure that it complies with the statutory and regulatory requirements which apply to it in that: (i) the society has failed to comply *b* with the provisions of s 22(3) of the 1962 Act for the year ended 31 December 1982 in that it has made special advances in excess of 10% of the total amount of all advances made by the society during that year; (ii) the society had incorrectly completed Part 9, section A of its annual return for the year ended 31 December 1982 with the result that it did not disclose the excess of special advances made in that year; and (iii) the society has wrongly stated the figures required to be included by virtue of s 82(2)(*b*) of the 1962 Act *c* in its directors' report for the year ended 31 December 1982 with the same result.'

16.3 My findings as to fact on special advances and my view on the legal construction of ss 21 and 22 of the 1962 Act are set out in Part 7 of this decision. My view of the importance of this and the consequential breaches of law are set out in Part 12.

16.4 In brief: (a) the society made special advances in 1982 amounting to 11·6% of its total advances in the year, compared with the 10% limit appropriate to it under s 22 of *d* the 1962 Act; (b) it gave materially lower figures for this in its directors' report to members and in its annual return; this could well mislead the type of investor which the society seeks to attract; (c) I do not consider that there was a conscious decision to flout the law; but the society gave insufficient attention to ensuring that it complied with a part of building society law to which Parliament had attached particular significance; (d) the society thus accorded insufficient attention to keeping within the framework which *e* Parliament has established to protect investors in building societies. In so doing it did not conform to the standards which the public rightly expects of building societies entrusted with other people's funds.

Consideration 2 (except para (iii))

'The society has conducted its business recklessly and in such a way as to be contrary to *f* the interests of members and undermine the essential confidence of the public in the society and in building societies generally in that: (i) by failing to comply with the provisions of s 22(3) of the 1962 Act for the year ended 31 December 1982 the society and those officers in default have rendered themselves liable to prosecution under s 22(7) of the Act and have also, by virtue of s 22(8) of the Act, rendered the society liable to be the subject of a petition for winding up under the Companies Act 1948 by the chief *g* registrar; and (ii) the society's budget for the year ending 31 December 1983 as received by the registry on 25 May 1983 forecast a rate of business growth and resulting diminution of reserves ratio which showed, in the opinion of the chief registrar, that the society's current policies run a severe risk of the society again having inadequate reserves in relation to the structure of its assets and the nature of its business.' [(iii) This is reviewed in Part 17.]

h

16.5 The preamble to this consideration repeats ground 3 of the notice of proposed revocation, but restricts it to three specific points. The first is part of consideration (b) of that notice reviewed in Part 7 above. The second is identical to consideration (d) reviewed in Part 9 above. The third is additional and is discussed in Part 17.

16.6 I accepted in Part 13 that the word 'recklessly' might be too strong for the generality of actions of the society cited in relation to that ground for the proposed *j* revocation order. It is certainly arguable that it is nevertheless appropriate to some of the actions in sub-paragraphs (ii) and (iii) of the consideration. But I do not press the point: here again I will restrict the ground by substituting the word 'imprudently'.

16.7 I also agreed to the omission of 'and undermine the essential confidence of the public in the society and in building societies generally'.

16.8 On sub-para (i), I accepted in Part 7 that it was not necessary to include references
a to possible prosecution or winding up. The substantive point about the implications of
the breaches in the law for the way in which the society has been managed is sufficient
in itself; I have summarised that in para 16.4 in relation to consideration 1. Sub-
paragraph (i) of the second consideration should be deleted.

16.9 Sub-paragraph (ii) is identical to consideration (d) reviewed in Part 9. I agreed to
substitute 'distinct risk' for 'severe risk'. But subject to that marginal change the substance
b of the ground stands. As I concluded in para 9.24: 'I do consider that the society's policies
as they stand show an intention to grow at a very rapid rate, without due regard to the
need to maintain the reserves position: there is a distinct risk that if persisted with, in the
way in which the society has persisted with its growth objectives in the past, the society
would not have adequate reserves by the end of the year.'

c *Consideration 3*
'On the basis of documents produced and information furnished by the society it
appears to him that the society failed to comply with the provisions of s 22(3) of the 1962
Act also for the year ended 31 December 1981, in that it made special advances in excess
of 10% of the total amount of all advances made by the society during that year, with
similar consequences to those set out in consideration 1(ii) and (iii) in the notice dated 27
d June 1983 in relation to its annual return for the year ended 31 December 1981 and its
directors' report for that year.'

16.10 The breach of the special advances provisions was reviewed in Part 10 above. I
concluded that it was well founded.

16.11 In brief: (a) the society made special advances in 1981 amounting to 11½% of
total advances compared with the statutory limit of not more than 10%; (b) it gave
e materially lower figures in its directors' report and annual return; this could well mislead
the type of investors which the society seeks to attract; (c) my conclusions on the
significance of this are that it reinforces what was said about the 1982 breach in para 16.4
above.

f *Consideration 4*
'On the basis of documents produced and information furnished by the society it
appears to him that the arrangements for direction and management of the society are,
or have been, inappropriate and unsatisfactory for the society in that: (i) it appears that
important decisions have been taken without full discussion and formal approval by the
board of the society; (ii) the board has not laid down in writing a formal procedural
framework to govern the manner in which it performs its functions so as to establish and
g maintain its collective authority; and (iii) in the opinion of the chief registrar, the society
has not available to it adequate and comprehensive documentation of its systems of
control and inspection.'

16.12 This consideration was reviewed in Parts 11 and 12 above, the former dealing
with board procedures, the latter with documention of control systems. I accepted that,
as a result of representations, the reference to 'inspection' in sub-para (iii) should be
h omitted.

16.13 In brief, on board procedures: (a) one important policy decision was taken
recently without giving the four non-executive directors a proper opportunity for
discussion; (b) a far more fundamental decision, on the taking of substantial funds from
a new source, the wholesale money markets, was taken by the chairman, in consultation
with only one other director. It was merely reported orally to the board, and then
j apparently with an incomplete explanation of the full implications; (c) both were
apparently permitted by the existing procedures; the new codification will do nothing to
re-establish the collective authority of the board; (d) instead it would permit a situation
in which effective power could pass into the hands of an individual or a small group, a
situation which has proved disastrous in some other financial institutions; the non-
executive directors would lack the entrenched rights to ensure that they can act as

guardians of the interests of members; (e) the society's representations show a disturbing lack of awareness of this risk; the need to have adequate checks and balances is the greater *a* in a rapidly expanding and innovating society such as this.

16.14 On documentation: (a) the society's documentation of its control systems is incomplete, inadequate for the areas it does cover and fragmented; (b) this makes it hard to establish the adequacy of the present system or to maintain its effectiveness at a time of rapid change; such adequacy is an essential protection for investors; (c) the board's lack of attention to this exposes the society to a number of risks, risks at least administrative *b* failure, at worst opening the door to fraud or financial mismanagement; indeed, the way in which the money market decision was taken can only be described as financial mismanagement.

17. *The further consideration*

17.1 The new element in the notice of intention to make a s 48 order is: *Consideration 2 (iii)* *c*

'The society has conducted its business imprudently and in such a way as to be contrary to the interests of members in that: (iii) the society has conducted its affairs in such a way as to have repeatedly put into question its continued eligibility for designation for trustee investment under the 1972 regulations, on the grounds cited in the notice served on the society with this notice, proposing the revocation of designation under s 1 of the House Purchase and Housing Act 1959.'... *d*

17.9 I therefore conclude that: (i) the board of a society which is designated has a duty to its members to avoid the potential consequences for them of revocation of designation; (ii) the board of this society has singularly failed to do this: it allowed the society to fail to meet the requirements of the 1972 regulations in three out of the last four years, in ways which should have been readily avoidable, particularly if the society had been readier to adjust its rate of growth ... *e*

Conclusion

19. *Decision*

19.1 I therefore conclude that the correct course is to proceed with both the proposed revocation of designation and the proposed s 48 order.

19.2 I do so with regret. The use of statutory powers is always the supervisor's last *f* resort. But in this case the regret is the greater because the society has sought to be innovative in a number of respects, particularly in the ways in which it was prepared to offer mortgages. It has widened the range of consumer choice. But a society which does innovate, particularly if it also seeks to grow rapidly, needs to be certain that it is protecting the interests of investors sufficiently, by keeping its growth to what can be justified by its reserves, by making sure that it has effective management systems which *g* can take the strain of that growth, by making sure that it complies with the statutory and prudential framework and by ensuring that its board structures are such that non-executive directors can, where necessary, exercise a controlling hand over the natural enthusiasm of the executive, and generally discharge their fiduciary duty as holders of other people's money. All these the New Cross Building Society has failed to do to a *h* greater or lesser extent.

19.3 I therefore decide that: (i) I should issue an order revoking the designation of the New Cross Building Society for the purposes of s 1 of the House Purchase and Housing Act 1959; (ii) I should seek Treasury consent for an order applying s 48(2) of the Building Societies Act 1962 to the New Cross Building Society; (iii) the effective date of each should be two weeks after the making of the orders to permit time for the board to consider what action would now be in the best interests of members; (iv) publication in *j* the Gazettes should be delayed until the orders come into effect, and the registry should not take the initiative in publicising the existence of the orders until after the close of normal business on the day before the orders come into effect.

a # Harvela Investments Ltd v Royal Trust Co of Canada (CI) Ltd and others

CHANCERY DIVISION

PETER GIBSON J

19–21, 24–26 OCTOBER, 29 NOVEMBER 1983

b

Contract – Implied term – Bids – Sealed bids – Contract for sale of shares – Invitation to make sealed competitive bids for shares – Bid of '$101,000 in excess of any other offer' – Whether implied term in invitation to bid excluding bids framed by reference to other bids.

Contract – Offer and acceptance – Invitation to treat – Contract for sale of shares – Invitation to
c *make bids for shares – Party inviting bids stating that it bound itself to accept highest bid – Whether invitation to bid an offer or invitation to treat – Whether submission of bid providing sufficient consideration to found contract.*

Interest – Sale of shares – Interest on unpaid purchase money – Delay in completion of contract – Delay through fault of vendor – Vendor not entitled to interest under contract – Whether vendor
d *entitled to equitable interest.*

The plaintiff and the second defendant were rival offerors for a parcel of shares which would give effective control of a company to the plaintiff or to the second defendant and his family, whichever was the successful offeror. The parcel of shares was held by the first defendants, the trustees of a settlement, which invited both parties to submit by
e sealed offer or confidential telex a 'single offer' for the whole parcel by 3 pm on 16 September 1981. The trustees stated in the invitation to bid that 'we bind ourselves to accept [the highest] offer'. The invitation to bid further stated that interest at the rate of 4% over prime rate was to be payable by the purchaser in the event of delay in completing the purchase, unless the delay was caused by the trustees. The plaintiff tendered a bid of $2,175,000. The second defendant tendered a bid of 'C$2,100,000 or C$101,000 in excess
f of any other offer . . . which is expressed as a fixed monetary amount, whichever is the higher'. The trustees accepted the second defendant's bid, as being a bid of $2,276,000, and entered into a contract with the second defendant for the sale of the parcel of shares. The trustees also informed the plaintiff of the terms of the second defendant's bid, whereupon the plaintiff commenced proceedings against the trustees and the second defendant contending that the second defendant's bid was invalid because (i) it was not a
g 'single offer' within the terms of the invitation to bid, and (ii) it was an implied term of the invitation to bid that referential bids (ie bids framed by reference to other bids) would be excluded from the bidding. The plaintiff accordingly sought a declaration that there was a binding contract between the trustees and the plaintiff for the sale of the shares for the sum of $2,175,000 and specific performance of that contract. The second defendant counterclaimed for specific performance of the contract for the sale of shares
h to him for $2,276,000.

Held – (1) The second defendant's bid was a 'single offer' within the terms of the trustees' invitation to bid even though it was in two parts, because at the time of the closing of bids it was possible, by reference to the plaintiff's bid, to say which part constituted the second defendant's bid, which, at that stage, became a single offer (see p 71 *e* to *g*, post).
j (2) It was, however, an implied term of an invitation to make sealed competitive bids that bids which were framed by reference to another bid would be excluded, because a referential bid in whatever form it was made was inconsistent with the purpose and essential nature of sealed competitive bidding, namely that each bidder should make an independent bid of the maximum amount (rather than the maximum increment over another bid) he was prepared to pay. Accordingly, the trustees' invitation to bid contained an implied term excluding referential bids and the second defendant's bid was therefore

invalid as being inconsistent with that term (see p 73 *h* to p 74 *a*, p 75 *c* and p 76 *a* to *d*, post); *Liverpool City Council v Irwin* [1976] 2 All ER 39 applied; *South Hetton Coal Co v Haswell Shotton and Easington Coal and Coke Co* [1898] 1 Ch 465 and.*SSI Investors Ltd v Korean Tungsten Mining Co Ltd* (1982) 449 NYS 2d 173 considered.

(3) A contract for the sale of the parcel of shares by the trustees to the plaintiff was completed at the time of the closing of bids because the terms of the invitation to bid, in particular that the trustees bound themselves to accept the highest offer, were such that the invitation to bid constituted an offer rather than a mere invitation to treat and the plaintiff's bid, being the only valid bid and therefore the highest bid, was an acceptance of that offer. Furthermore, the mere fact of making the bid, which was the performance of the act invited by the trustees and the benefit which it wanted, was sufficient consideration on the part of the plaintiff to found the contract. It followed that there was a valid contract made between the plaintiff and the trustees prior to the trustees concluding the contract with the second defendant and accordingly the plaintiff, rather than the second defendant, would be granted specific performance of its contract (see p 76 *j* to p 77 *c*, p 78 *b* to *e* and p 79 *a b*, post); *Spencer v Harding* (1870) LR 5 CP 561 and *Carlill v Carbolic Smoke Ball Co* [1891–4] All ER Rep 127 applied.

(4) The trustees were entitled neither to contractual interest on the purchase money payable by the plaintiff, because the trustees themselves had occasioned the delay in completion of the contract by an erroneous belief that they were bound to accept the second defendant's bid, nor to equitable interest on the purchase money, because only in very special circumstances would the court impose on a purchaser of shares an equitable obligation to pay interest when he was not bound to do so under the contract by which the parties had agreed the circumstances in which the purchaser would and would not pay interest. Furthermore, applying the same rules regarding payment of equitable interest on a contract for the sale of land, where the delay in completion was occasioned by the vendor and the equitable interest claimed greatly exceeded the interim dividends paid on the shares during the period of the delay equity would not give the vendor any interest on the purchase money, since to do so would enable him to profit by his own delay. Instead, the vendor would be left in possession of the interim dividends, and accordingly the trustees were entitled to retain and receive all dividends on the shareholding in respect of the period from the date fixed for completion to the actual date of completion (see p 79 *j* and p 80 *a* to *j*, post); *Esdaile v Stephenson* (1822) 1 Sim & St 122 applied.

Notes

For implied terms in a contract, see 9 Halsbury's Laws (4th edn) paras 351–362, and for cases on the subject, see 12 Digest (Reissue) 750–757, 5390–5425.

For offer and acceptance generally and for the difference between an offer and an invitation to treat, see 9 Halsbury's Laws (4th edn) paras 226–230, and for cases on the subject, see 12 Digest (Reissue) 63–66, 328–338.

For what amounts to consideration, see 9 Halsbury's Laws (4th edn) paras 316–328, and for cases on the subject, see 12 Digest (Reissue) 223–235, 1430–1569.

For interest on purchase money in proceedings for specific performance, see 44 Halsbury's Laws (4th edn) paras 541–545.

Cases referred to in judgment

Bartlett v Barclays Bank Trust Co Ltd (No 2) [1980] 2 All ER 92, [1980] Ch 515, [1980] 2 WLR 430.

Carlill v Carbolic Smoke Ball Co [1893] 1 QB 256, [1891–4] All ER Rep 127, CA.

Daulia Ltd v Four Millbank Nominees Ltd [1978] 2 All ER 557, [1978] Ch 231, [1978] 2 WLR 621, CA.

Esdaile v Stephenson (1822) 1 Sim & St 122, 57 ER 49.

Hewitt's Contract, Re [1963] 3 All ER 419, [1963] 1 WLR 1298.

Hillas & Co Ltd v Arcos Ltd (1932) 147 LT 503, [1932] All ER Rep 494, HL.

Liverpool City Council v Irwin [1976] 2 All ER 39, [1977] AC 239, [1976] 2 WLR 562, HL.

Saltzberg and Rubin v Hollis Securities Ltd (1964) 48 DLR (2d) 344.

South Hetton Coal Co v Haswell Shotton and Easington Coal and Coke Co [1898] 1 Ch 465, CA.
a   Spencer v Harding (1870) LR 5 CP 561.
SSI Investors Ltd v Korean Tungsten Mining Co Ltd (1982) 449 NYS 2d 173.

Action

By a writ issued on 4 February 1983 the plaintiff, Harvela Investments Ltd (Harvela) a
Newfoundland company sought (1) as against the first and second defendants, Royal
b   Trust Co of Canada (CI) Ltd (Royal Jersey) and Sir Leonard Outerbridge (a) a declaration
that Royal Jersey were contractually bound to transfer to Harvela 825 common shares,
311 6% voting preference shares and 24,337 non-voting redeemable preferences shares
in the capital of the third defendants, A Harvey & Co Ltd (Harveys), at the price of
$Can2,175,000 in accordance with the terms and conditions contained in telexes sent on
15 and 16 September 1981 by Royal Jersey's solicitors to Harvela's agents, Chalker Green
c   & Rowe of Newfoundland, (b) in the alternative a declaration that Sir Leonard held any
interest in those shares which he might have obtained from Royal Jersey on trust for
Harvela or, in the further alternative, subject to an obligation to assign and transfer his
interest therein to Harvela on payment by the latter of the sum of $Can2,175,000; (c) in
the further alternative an order setting aside any transfer of the shares whether legal or
equitable by Royal Jersey to Sir Leonard, (d) damages, (e) an injunction restraining Royal
d   Jersey and Sir Leonard or either of them whether by themselves, their respective servants
or agents or otherwise from presenting to Harveys for registration any transfer of the
shares or any of them and (f) any necessary and consequential directions, accounts and
inquiries, (2) as against Royal Jersey (a) specific performance of the contract referred to in
(1)(a) above and (b) an injunction restraining Royal Jersey whether by themselves, their
servants or agents or otherwise from doing the following acts or any of them, namely
e   parting with or disposing of any of the shares or any document of title or certificate
relating thereto otherwise than to Harvela until after the trial of the action or further
order, (3) as against Harveys an injunction restraining them whether by themselves, their
servants or agents or howsoever from taking any step whatever relating to the registration
of any transfer of any of the shares by Royal Jersey to Sir Leonard, and (4) as against all
the defendants further or other relief and costs. Sir Leonard counterclaimed for specific
f   performance of an alleged valid contract for the sale of the shares by Royal Jersey to
himself and joined as defendants to the counterclaim, in addition to Harvela and Royal
Jersey, Royal Jersey's London-based associated company, Royal Trust of Canada (Royal
London).   The facts are set out in the judgment.

Michael Essayan QC and Michael Driscoll for Harvela.
g   Edward Nugee QC and Oliver Weaver for Royal Jersey and Royal London.
Leolin Price QC and James Denniston for Sir Leonard Outerbridge and Harveys.

Cur adv vult

29 November. The following judgment was delivered.
h

PETER GIBSON J. In this action the plaintiff, Harvela Investments Ltd, a
Newfoundland company, seeks specific performance of what it claims is a contract for
the sale to it by the first defendant, the Royal Trust Company of Canada (CI) Ltd (Royal
Jersey), of certain shares in the third defendant, A Harvey & Co Ltd (Harveys). Royal
Jersey, a Jersey company, has since about April 1979 been the registered holder of those
j   shares on behalf of the trustees for the time being of a Scottish settlement made by Mrs
Lillian Campbell in 1962. The second defendant, Sir Leonard Outerbridge, who is Mrs
Campbell's brother and a nonagenarian, denies the existence of the contract claimed by
Harvela. He claims that there is a valid contract for the sale of the same shares by Royal
Jersey to himself. By his counterclaim he seeks specific performance of the contract and
he has joined as defendants to that counterclaim not only Harvela and Royal Jersey but
also Royal Jersey's London-based associated company, the Royal Trust Co of Canada
(Royal London) which is now the sole trustee of Mrs Campbell's settlement. In his

original defence and counterclaim Sir Leonard had claimed that there was a prior option
agreement for the same of some of those shares to him and that he had duly exercised   *a*
that option; accordingly in his counterclaim he claimed in the alternative specific
performance of the contract brought into being by the exercise of the option. But that
part of the defence and counterclaim was abandoned at the start of the fourth day of the
hearing before me, before any oral evidence had been heard. As a result this action has
been fought on the basis of documentary evidence alone.

Harveys is a Newfoundland company. It owns 11 acres of the waterfront of St John's,   *b*
Newfoundland, and has several subsidiaries engaged in transportation, warehousing and
distribution activities. Its history is that it was formed as the successor to the business of
a partnership carried on by two members of the Harvey family and an Outerbridge. The
partners had succeeded to the business founded by a Harvey over 100 years ago. For
many years the issued share capital in Harveys was held as to one-half by a member or
members of the Harvey family and as to the other half by a member or members of the   *c*
Outerbridge family. But in the early 1960s some shares owned by a Harvey were
purchased by Sir Leonard and the Outerbridges then, between them, held the majority
of the shares in Harveys. Mrs Campbell is an Outerbridge and when she transferred to
her settlement some of her Harvey shares the votes of such of the Harvey shares so
transferred as were voting shares were exercised by an Outerbridge acting as proxy for
the trustee or trustees of her settlement. If one leaves aside the votes on the shares   *d*
comprised in Mrs Campbell's settlement, the Outerbridges control between them only
about 40% of the Harveys votes. Harvela is a company owned and controlled by Mrs
Susan Pattern, who is a Harvey, and it has approximately 43% of the issued share capital
of Harveys. The Harveys shares comprised in Mrs Campbell's settlement are 825
common shares with voting rights, 311 6% voting preference shares and 24,337 non-
voting redeemable preference shares. The voting shares control about 12% of the Harveys   *e*
votes. Thus if Harvela were to acquire those shares it would have voting control of
Harveys. If Sir Leonard were to acquire those shares, so long as the other Outerbridge
shareholders voted with him he would have control of Harveys. In the circumstances the
minority holding comprised in Mrs Campbell's settlement is a crucial holding which
determines whether Harveys is controlled by Mrs Patten through Harvela or whether
control rests with Sir Leonard and other members of the Outerbridge family as long as   *f*
they act together.

Mrs Campbell made her settlement on 21 September 1962 in discretionary form for
the benefit of herself, her children and remoter issue and the respective spouses and
widows and widowers of her children and issue. Royal London was until 4 April 1979
the sole trustee of the settlement.

On 30 October 1978 Mrs Patten and her husband called on Royal London to inquire   *g*
whether it was prepared to consider a sale of the 825 common and 311 6% preference
shares in Harveys. They were told by a trust officer of Royal London that it might be
prepared to consider a sale, but he indicated to them that there were various matters to
be considered, including the probable necessity of referring the matter to the Campbell
family. A Newfoundland lawyer, Mr Chalker, made a written offer on 8 November 1978
on behalf of Harvela. The total sum offered was $443,600 (I add in parenthesis that   *h*
references to dollars in this judgment are references to Canadian dollars) made up of
$500 per common share and $100 per 6% preference share. Royal London calculated
that there would be a substantial capital gains tax liability if it sold the shares to Harvela
and it sought ways to avoid or defer that liability. Early steps which it took to that end
were to appoint, on 4 April 1979, as additional trustees Royal Jersey and two officials
from that company, to transfer the administration of the settlement to Jersey and to   *j*
cause all the Harveys shares held for the settlement to be vested in Royal Jersey. Harvela
improved its offer in May 1979 so that, subject to certain safeguards reserved for itself,
the price for the common shares would be increased to the amount stated by independent
valuers to be the value of those shares. Initially Harvela required Royal London to keep
its offer secret, but on the trustees' insistence Mrs Campbell and Sir Leonard were
consulted about the offer. This prompted Sir Leonard to make an offer in June 1979
amounting to $526,000 for the common and 6% preference shares: $600 per common

share and $100 per 6% preference share. Mrs Campbell and her adult children and
a grandchildren all informed the trustees that they supported Sir Leonard's offer and
Harvela's offer was rejected. However, whilst the trustees explored various tax-saving
schemes no binding contract to sell the shares to Sir Leonard was concluded. In October
1980 Mr Patten discussed with Royal London the possibility of Harvela making a further
offer for the settlement's Harveys shares and in January 1981 Mr Chalker on behalf of
Harvela offered $856,100 made up of $1,000 per common share and $100 per 6%
b preference share.

In June 1981 the trustees took the advice of Chancery leading counsel. Mr Nugee
advised that the trustees had a duty to accept the highest offer they could obtain for the
shares. On 17 August 1981 both Harvela and Sir Leonard were invited by the trustees to
submit further offers for the shares and they were told that this was only an invitation to
treat and that no offer received would be regarded as binding. In response Harvela offered
c $1,742,612 payable in two tranches. That sum was made up of $2,025 for each common
share, $150 for each 6% preference share and $1 for each non-voting preference share.
Sir Leonard offered $1,741,942 made up of $2,000 for each common share, $100 for each
6% preference share and $2·50 for each non-voting preference share. The trustees then
decided that they should invite both Harvela and Sir Leonard to submit revised offers on
identical terms and conditions. They sent a telex (the invitation telex) to each of Harvela
d and Sir Leonard asking each to continue its or his existing offer to 3 pm on 16 September
1981 and containing (so far as material) the following terms and conditions:

'We have before us two similar offers but subject to differing terms and conditions
and value. Accordingly we invite you to submit to [Royal Jersey] any revised offer
which you may wish to make by sealed tender or confidential telex to be submitted
to our London solicitors, Messrs. Bischoff and Co. ... by 3 p.m. London time
e Wednesday 16th September 1981, attention J. Jowitt who has undertaken not to
disclose any details of any revised offer to any party before that time . . . Tenders are
to be submitted on the following terms:—1. That tenders are a single offer for all
shares held by us . . . 5. In the event that closing shall not take place within 30 days
interest shall be payable by the purchaser on the full purchase price at a rate higher
by 4 per cent. than the Bank of Montreal prime rate from time to time for Canadian
f dollar loans. We hereby agree subject to acceptance by us of any offer made by
you:— . . . C) We confirm that if any offer made by you is the highest offer received
by us we bind ourselves to accept such offer provided that such offer complies with
the terms of this telex.'

Two amendments to those terms were made by the trustees by a telex dated 16
g September 1981 and sent to each of Harvela and Sir Leonard before either had responded
to the invitation telex. I need refer only to the amendment to term 5, the words 'other
than by reason of any delay on our part' being inserted after the words 'within 30 days'.
Further on 16 September Royal Jersey orally confirmed to Sir Leonard and Harvela that
the promise in para C to accept the highest offer was not qualified by the words 'subject
to acceptance by us of any offer made by you'.

h   Thus each of Harvela and Sir Leonard knew that the other had already bid a sum of an
amount similar to its or his bid of $1¾m without knowing which of the earlier bids was
the higher. Each knew that it was likely that it or he would have to increase its or his
previous bid to be successful but each had the assurance that the trustees were promising
to be bound to accept the highest offer made in accordance with the terms of the
invitation telex.

j   On 16 September 1981 before 3 pm Mr Chalker telexed to Mr Jowitt Harvela's revised
offer; this was in the sum of $2,175,000. Also on 16 September before 3 pm the London
solicitors of Sir Leonard sent his written revised offer to Mr Jowitt. That offer was
expressed as follows:

'The amount of our client's tender is C$2,100,000 or C$101,000 in excess of any
other offer which you may receive which is expressed as a fixed monetary amount,
whichever is the higher.'

At 4.47 pm the same afternoon Mr Broughton, the assistant manager of Royal Jersey's
trust department, telexed Mr Chalker that Harvela's tender was unsuccessful. Royal   *a*
London however decided not to notify Sir Leonard of acceptance of his offer unless Mr
Nugee advised that the offer was valid and satisfied the conditions of Royal Jersey's
invitation and that Royal Jersey was bound to accept. Mr Nugee advised orally on 22
September and in writing on 29 September. Whilst confessing to a feeling of unease
regarding the form of the offer, Mr Nugee advised that Sir Leonard's offer was a valid
offer of $2,276,000 which Royal Jersey was bound to accept. Mr Nugee further advised   *b*
that Royal Jersey should advise both parties of the tenders which it had received, that it
proposed to complete with Sir Leonard and that if Harvela wished to dispute the validity
of Sir Leonard's offer it would have to do so by proceeding against both Royal Jersey and
Sir Leonard. On 18 September Mr Chalker asked that the details of the successful tender
should be telexed to him and that request was repeated on 27 September. On 29
September Royal Jersey in accordance with advice from Mr Jowitt telexed each of Sir   *c*
Leonard and Harvela, giving the details of each bid, and concluded:

> 'In the circumstances our clients are bound to accept and do hereby accept the
> offer received from Sir Leonard Outerbridge and give notice that they propose and
> require the purchase of the shares to be completed on the 15th October next.'

Harvela was thus put on notice of the view taken by Royal Jersey which of the two   *d*
bidders had made the highest offer in accordance with the invitation telex and of Royal
Jersey's intention to complete with Sir Leonard on 15 October. On 12 October 1981
Harvela commenced proceedings in Jersey against Royal Jersey and Sir Leonard and
obtained ex parte injunctions restraining Royal Jersey and Sir Leonard from presenting
to Harveys any transfer of the shares for registration, restraining Royal Jersey from
disposing of the shares and restraining Harveys from registering any transfer of the   *e*
shares. On 23 October 1981 those injunctions were confirmed at an inter partes hearing
on Harvela giving a cross-undertaking as to damages. The parties thereafter proceeded
with pleadings and discovery, but on 1 October 1982 Sir Leonard's and Harveys' London
solicitors suggested that the proceedings be, in effect, transferred to the English High
Court on the footing that the proper law of the contracts claimed by Harvela and Sir
Leonard respectively was English. Harvela agreed, but Royal Jersey did not give its   *f*
consent. Nevertheless on 4 February 1983 this action was commenced in the Chancery
Division. Leave was given by the master to serve Royal Jersey out of the jurisdiction, but
Royal Jersey applied to set aside that order. At the hearing of that application, on Harvela
undertaking to the court to abide by any order made by the court as to damages in case
the court was of opinion that Royal Jersey had sustained any by reason of the injunctions
on 12 and 23 October 1981 of the Jersey Court and on Royal Jersey undertaking not to   *g*
seek to have the injunctions discharged, no order was made.

By its statement of claim, Harvela claims a declaration that Royal Jersey is contractually
bound to transfer the shares to Harvela for $2,175,000, an order for specific performance
of that contract and damages. Sir Leonard in his defence denies any such contract and
asserts that there is a valid contract between Royal Jersey and himself for the sale of the
shares to him for $2,276,000 and he counterclaims for a declaration that Royal Jersey is   *h*
contractually bound to transfer the shares to him and for an order for specific performance
of that contract and for damages. Royal Jersey in its defence to Harvela's claim and in its
defence to Sir Leonard's counterclaim adopts a neutral attitude as between Harvela and
Sir Leonard, but it indicates that if Harvela obtains an order for specific performance
Royal Jersey will claim from Harvela interest on the purchase moneys from 16 October
1981 till payment by way of equitable relief at a specified rate which is lower than the   *j*
rate specified in the invitation telex. It further indicates that if Harvela fails to obtain
such order Royal Jersey will claim interest from Harvela pursuant to the undertaking in
damages given to the court and if Sir Leonard succeeds in obtaining an order for specific
performance, Royal Jersey will claim interest from him by way of equitable relief.
Harveys in its defence to Harvela's claim states that it seeks to take no active part in the
proceedings. Royal London in its defence to Sir Leonard's counterclaim adopts a stance
similar to that of Royal Jersey, that is to say that it takes no part in the proceedings but

a claims interest by way of equitable relief from Sir Leonard if he succeeds in obtaining an order for specific performance.

The primary question that arises for decision is whether Harvela or Sir Leonard made the highest offer in accordance with the terms of the invitation telex. Depending on the answer to that question are various consequential questions, including which of Harvela and Sir Leonard should obtain an order for specific performance, whether the successful purchaser should be required to pay interest and if so at what rate and whether an inquiry
b as to damages should be ordered.

I start with that primary question. It is common ground between counsel for Harvela and counsel appearing for Sir Leonard that this question turns on the true construction of the invitation telex. Counsel for Sir Leonard submits that there can be no doubt as to that construction: at 3 pm on 16 September 1981 it was apparent that the second limb of Sir Leonard's offer could take effect because Harvela's offer was for a fixed monetary amount and was higher than the first limb and so constituted his offer; at that time it
c was also apparent that his offer was the highest offer because it exceeded Harvela's offer by $101,000; Royal Jersey had made no stipulation as to the form of the offer other than that it was to be a single offer for all the shares and that stipulation was obeyed; the certain and unambiguous nature of Sir Leonard's offer was demonstrated by the fact that within two hours of 3 pm on 16 September Royal Jersey rejected Harvela's bid, and
d counsel for Sir Leonard describes as Gilbertian any conclusion that Harvela's offer constituted the highest offer.

Counsel for Harvela submits first that Sir Leonard's bid was not a single offer as required by the invitation telex and, second, that it was not the highest offer as an invitation to bid by sealed competitive tender is one which impliedly excludes bids framed by reference to other bids.

e The first point of counsel for Harvela rests on the basis that the two limbs of Sir Leonard's bid constituted separate offers. But it seems to me that the short answer to that point is that on the plain wording of Sir Leonard's bid there was only one offer by Sir Leonard, that is to say the higher of the amounts specified in the two bids. True it is that at the time the bid was received it was not possible for Royal Jersey to say which of the two limbs was higher or indeed whether the second limb could have any application, but
f that is irrelevant. What is relevant is whether at 3 pm on 16 September there was a single certain bid by Sir Leonard. At that time there was no difficulty, still less any impossibility, in quantifying the amount indicated in the second limb of Sir Leonard's bid as manifestly Harvela's bid was of a fixed monetary amount. Royal Jersey, having then received Harvela's bid, could immediately perceive that Sir Leonard's offer was one of $2,276,000, and only an offer of that sum as being higher than $2,100,000. In my judgment therefore
g Sir Leonard's offer was a single offer.

Counsel for Harvela's second point raises an important question of principle in relation to sealed competitive bidding: is it open to a bidder to make a bid by reference to the bid of another? More specifically on the facts of the present case the question for determination is whether it is open to any bidder to make a bid in the form of the higher of a fixed amount and an amount exceeding by a stated sum a rival bid expressed as a
h fixed monetary amount. I say that because, as was pointed out in course of argument, referential bids may take one of several forms and different considerations may apply to each. The discussion of the various form of bid proceeded on the footing, which is plainly correct, that if a particular form of bid is open to one bidder it is open to every bidder.

The crudest form of referential bid is that of an amount greater by a stated sum than the bid of a rival bidder. If more than one bidder bids in that form, it is obvious that
j bidding would be frustrated as there would be an infinite ascension as bid exceeded bid. Counsel for Sir Leonard submitted that such frustration was no different from that produced by two or more bidders chancing on the same amount which was the highest amount bid. Whilst it is of course right that such coincidence of bids would frustrate that round of bids, I cannot accept that it is right to treat the two possibilities of frustration as being on a par with each other. The risk of a coincidence of the amounts of bids is inevitable but, I would apprehend, slight. The risk of a referential bid frustrating the bidding is, I apprehend, more substantial. Despite the hazards involved in making a

referential bid where the bidder will not know how much he is bidding till he knows the amount of the rival bid, many a bidder, I would think, would not be content to bid *a* only a fixed amount knowing that one's rival could succeed simply by wording his bid in terms of an amount, however small, in excess of one's own bid. Even before considering counsel for Harvela's fundamental objection to referential bids, I would have thought that this practical objection to referential bids of this first type was a formidable one.

Another form of bid is one expressed as the higher or highest of more than one limb. *b* If one such limb is in the referential form already discussed, the same objection would of course apply to such a bid. To avoid that objection the referential limb might be in the form of an amount greater by a stated amount than the fixed element in another bid. I have had the benefit of much learned disputation as to the rival bidding theories if this form of bid were permissible. Counsel for Sir Leonard, and also counsel for Royal Jersey and Royal London fortified by his junior's mathematical skills, argued in favour of the *c* permissibility of such bidding and allowing the market to regulate this matter. Counsel for Harvela on the other hand pointed out the paradoxical results if such bidding were allowed. Thus the bidder (who would do well to consult a senior wrangler) might find it to his advantage to pitch the amount of his fixed amount limb as low as possible, so as not to boost the bid of his rival bidding in like form, and to pitch the increment in his referential limb as high as possible. *d*

To avoid the difficulties inherent in the other forms of referential bid which I have discussed, the referential limb might be couched in the form which Sir Leonard has used in the present case, that is to say referential only to a rival bid expressed as a fixed monetary amount. Counsel for Sir Leonard submitted that if Harvela had bid in the same form, the referential limb of each bid could not apply as the other's bid was not expressed as a fixed monetary amount. Although counsel for Harvela did not accept this, *e* I think that counsel for Sir Leonard was plainly right in this, having regard to the word 'expressed'. Thus, in such a situation the outcome of the bidding would have been determined by the fixed amount bid by each. Whatever else one may say about this form of bidding two matters are self-evident: first, that the utility of this formula depends on other bidders not using a referential formula themselves (I have already commented on the likelihood that if referential bids are possible, many would want to employ a formula *f* incorporating a referential limb); second, if more than one person were to adopt the same formula so that the referential limb could not apply, the result would be that the vendor would not have obtained from each bidder the highest bid that each bidder was prepared to make: each by the terms of his bid has indicated that he would have been prepared to go higher.

This leads me to counsel for Harvela's fundamental objection to all referential bids in *g* whatever form in sealed competitive bidding. He submits that all such bids are inconsistent with the very essence of such bidding and that the general law requires a term to be implied into an offer or invitation to treat, in each case inviting competitive bids, that is to say that a bid is invalid if it is expressed by reference to the bid of another. Before I consider the merits of that submission, I shall first discuss the circumstances in which terms will be implied. I have not been shown any authority which relates to the *h* implication of a term in an offer or an invitation to treat, as distinct from a contract, but counsel for Sir Leonard has not contended that it is impossible for a term to be so implied. He submits that the fact that it is only an offer or an invitation to treat into which the court is asked to imply a term is a relevant consideration for the court to take into account, it being open to the vendor unilaterally to put whichever term he wishes into his offer or invitation. I agree that there is in principle no impossibility inherent in the *j* implication of a term into an offer or an invitation to treat. The term which the law will imply in appropriate circumstances into a contract will have been present sub silentio in the offer the acceptance of which constitutes the contract and, it may be, in any invitation to treat before this. The question that I must determine is whether it is appropriate in the circumstances of the present case to imply such a term. Both counsel for Harvela and counsel for Sir Leonard are agreed that the principles stated in *Liverpool City Council v Irwin* [1976] 2 All ER 39, [1977] AC 239 govern the test to be applied in this case. That

authority establishes that there are various categories of implied term. One such category
a is where there is a relationship between the parties (eg landlord and tenant, master and
servant) which demands by its nature and subject matter certain obligations. Those
obligations will be implied by the general law, not by reference to tests such as what the
officious bystander, still less what a party, would have said if asked about such obligations,
but because they are legal incidents of that relationship. Those obligations must be
necessary terms required by that relationship. It is not enough that they are reasonable.
b However, what is necessary must, I think be determined by a broad consideration of the
relationship and the subject matter thereof, and a term may be implied even though it is
possible to envisage circumstances in which the absence of the term would not frustrate
the contract between the particular parties. For example, in the *Liverpool* case it was held
that there was an implied obligation on the landlord to take reasonable care to keep in
reasonable repair the lifts and other means of access to flats let to tenants in a 15-storey
c tower block. If one postulates as tenant a pregnant woman with a young child living on
the fifteenth floor (see [1976] 2 All ER 39 at 50, [1977] AC 239 at 262 per Lord Salmon)
the necessary implication of a term relating to the lifts is obvious. It is less so if one
postulates as tenant on that floor a fit mountaineer with athletic children, or indeed a
tenant on the first floor in normal health. In the present case the relationship relied on
by counsel for Harvela is that of vendor and bidder in sealed competitive bidding as well
d as the relationship between bidder and bidder in that situation. Counsel for Sir Leonard
submitted that there was no reason why the law should intervene by implying a term in
relation to sealed competitive bidding and he contrasted the relationship relied on by
counsel for Harvela with the two relationships providing the established examples of this
type of implied term (namely landlord and tenant, and master and servant). But I do not
see why the categories of relationship need be so limited and provided that I can be
e satisfied that the term contended for is a term required by the relationships relied on, I
would be prepared to imply that term. I should also refer to one further point taken by
counsel for Sir Leonard. He has stressed the facts, which are accepted by counsel for
Harvela, first, that it would be easy for a vendor inviting sealed competitive bids to insert
a term which made clear that referential bids are excluded, and second, that such a term
is sometimes to be found. But whilst it is right for the court to take these facts into
f account, they are not in themselves conclusive. It would be easy to include in contracts
for tenancies of flats in high-rise blocks terms such as those which the court implied in
the *Liverpool* case, nor would it be in the least surprising if such provisions were found in
some contracts.

In my judgment the question that I must determine is whether in sealed competitive
bidding a bid framed by reference to another's bid is excluded as a necessary incident of
g the relationship between vendor and bidder and between bidder and bidder. A vendor is
free to choose the method by which he sells his property, but a vendor who opts for
sealed competitive bidding must be presumed to have done so deliberately. It will be
noted that in the present case the trustees had in 1979 insisted on Harvela's earlier secret
bid being referred to Sir Leonard. It is pertinent to ask: what can be taken to have been
the purpose of a vendor in choosing to sell by means of inviting sealed competitive bids?
h Counsel for Sir Leonard says that the purpose is simply to get the best price. No doubt
every vendor wants that, but the vendor who has opted for sealed bids has plainly chosen
not to proceed by way of open bids and the difference between the two methods is that
in sealed bidding the bidder does not know what any other bidder has bid or is bidding,
whereas in open bidding (of which the prime example is an auction) the bidder does
know and, save for the opening bid (which is not expected to be the maximum bid), he
j pitches his bid by reference to, and so as to surpass, the previous bid. In making a sealed
bid when only a single bid is possible, the bidder is expected by vendor and competitor
alike to bid the maximum amount that the bidder is prepared to pay. If referential
bidding is possible, the bidder does not bid the maximum amount that he is prepared to
pay: he bids the maximum increment over the bid of another. In this respect it seems to
me that referential bids in whatever form are inconsistent with the purpose and essential
nature of sealed bids. I do not lose sight of the points made by counsel for Sir Leonard as
to the ease with which referential bids may be excluded by appropriate language and to

the use of such language in practice. Nevertheless unless compelled by authority to a
contrary conclusion I would be prepared to imply a term into the invitation telex   *a*
excluding referential bids as being a term required by the relationship between vendor
and bidder and between bidder and bidder.

There are only two reported cases bearing on the point. The first is the decision of the
Court of Appeal in *South Hetton Coal Co v Haswell Shotton and Easington Coal and Coke Co*
[1898] 1 Ch 465. In that case the defendant company was the lessee of two coal measures
(which I shall call A and B). The A coal measures were valuable but there was a   *b*
considerable liability in respect of the B coal measures. There were two prospective
purchasers for the A coal measures: the plaintiff company and the second defendant Mr
Barwick. The liquidator of the defendant company asked the plaintiff and Mr Barwick
to submit sealed tenders by a specified date and indicated to both that 'the highest net
money tender I receive (all other things being equal and satisfactory) that tender I will at
once accept'. The tenders by arrangement were handed in and opened in the presence of   *c*
all parties. Mr Barwick's tender was for £31,100 plus the acceptance of the assignment
of, and the giving of an indemnity in respect of, the B coal measures. The plaintiff's
tenders was such a sum as would exceed by £200 the amount offered by Mr Barwick,
coupled with a transfer of the B coal measures if Mr Barwick's offer was on that footing.
There was no doubt therefore that the plaintiff's bid was, at the time it was made, one in
a definite sum of £31,000. The liquidator declined to recognise the plaintiff's tender and   *d*
acepted Mr Barwick's tender. The plaintiff claimed specific performance of his alleged
contract. The defendants applied to strike out the statement of claim and North J did so
on the ground that the condition as to all other things being equal and satisfactory was
not satisfied. The plaintiff appealed and it was argued that the plaintiff's bid was the
highest net money tender and that it was immaterial to the liquidator that the offer was
made in such a form as to give the plaintiff an advantage over its competitor. That   *e*
argument received short shrift in the Court of Appeal. Without calling on counsel for
the defendants Lindley MR (with whom Rigby and Vaughan Williams LJJ concurred)
said (at 468–469):

> 'But now we have to consider whether [the liquidator] was bound to accept [the
> plaintiff's offer]. That raises two questions. Does the offer fairly answer the
> description of what the liquidator had bound himself to accept—in other words,   *f*
> does it answer the description of being "the highest net money tender I receive"? It
> appears to me obviously not. Whether it was a tender at all depended entirely not
> upon the construction of the letter, but upon whether other people tendered. That
> is not what the liquidator wanted, and that is not what he bound himself to accept.
> He says "Send me your highest net money tender, and I will consider it." This [and
> I pause to say 'This' must be the plaintiff's offer] is merely illusory. It does not   *g*
> answer the description in a business sense, and it does not answer the description in
> a legal sense. I do not think that the liquidator was under the slightest obligation to
> accept this, although he might have accepted it. That is not the ground to which
> North J. attached most importance, but to my mind it is decisive. I think that we
> should be encouraging trickery and making a very bad precedent if we held that
> this was, in any fair sense of the word, the highest net money tender which the   *h*
> liquidator had bound himself to accept. I do not accuse these gentlemen of trickery;
> but if we said that this letter answered the description of the highest net money
> tender, we should open the door to gross fraud, not only on purchasers, but on
> vendors also.'

He then went on to the question which North J had determined in the defendants'   *j*
favour and held that on that ground, too, the appeal failed.

The decision of the Court of Appeal was, as counsel for Sir Leonard rightly points out,
based on the particular words of the invitation made by the liquidator inviting bids. The
words 'the highest net money tender' are more precise than 'the highest offer' even
though every offer received by Royal Jersey would, if not of a fixed sum, have to be
reduced to money terms. As I read the remarks of Lindley MR the words of invitation
used in the *South Hetton* case were construed as requiring the tender to state a monetary

sum and this excluded a bid by reference to the amount offered by a competitor. I doubt
a if the words in the present case 'the highest offer' can as a matter of construction be read
in the same way. Counsel for Sir Leonard also pointed to the fact that the referential
formula used in the *South Hetton* case was different. It was in what might be described as
the crudest referential form, viz a bid only of an amount expressed as greater than the
other bid, as distinct from the more sophisticated form of Sir Leonard's bid. But in
condemning as Lindley MR did the form of the bid in terms of fraud and trickery, in
b my judgment he was going beyond merely holding that as a matter of construction the
referential bid failed to answer the particular words used. It is clear that he thought
referential bids tricky and highly undesirable. The force of that criticism must apply to
every form of referential bid. It is to be noted that the gross fraud to which he said the
court would be opening the door was not only on purchasers (ie rival bidders) but also
on vendors. In my judgment those observations give some support to the approach urged
c by counsel for Harvela, that in the relationship between vendor and bidder in sealed
bidding, as well as between bidder and bidder, the law should require the exclusion of
referential bids.

A similar view was expressed by the majority of the New York Court of Appeal in *SSI
Investors Ltd v Korean Tungsten Mining Co Ltd* (1982) 449 NYS 2d 173. In that case pursuant
to an invitation to submit sealed competitive bids a bid was made of $US556,000 'and/or
d $1 more than the highest bidding price you have received'. The ratio of the decision of
all six of the judges whose views are briefly reported in the memorandum of judgment
was that the purported bid was too uncertain because of the words 'and/or' in the absence
of words such as 'whichever is the higher'. Five of the six judges, however, went on to
say (at 174):

> 'Even if it were to be concluded that this deficiency was remedied by necessary
e implication, however the "one-dollar-more" alternative, standing alone, was
> indefinite and meaningless without reference to the bid or bids of other bidders.
> Although in some circumstances a bid which by itself is incomplete may properly
> be made definite and certain by reference to external objective facts, in the context
> of sealed competitive bidding the necessary certainty cannot be imported by cross
> reference to the bids of others participating in the same competitive bidding over
f the objection of the owner or another bidder.'

I have some doubts whether the language used, if capable of being remedied and if
remedied in the way suggested, would in English law be held too uncertain. But it is the
following passage that is material to the present case (at 174–175):

> 'The very essence of sealed competitive bidding is the submission of independent,
g self-contained bids, to the fair compliance with which not only the owner but the
> other bidders are entitled. As the Appellate Division observed, to give effect to this
> or any similar bidding practice in which the dollar amount of one bid was tied to
> the bid or bids of another or others in the same bidding would be to recognize
> means whereby effective sealed competitive bidding could be wholly frustrated. In
> the context of such bidding, therefore, a submission by one bidder of a bid
h dependent for its definition on the bids of others is invalid and unacceptable as
> inconsistent with and potentially destructive of the very bidding in which it is
> submitted. On the only other occasion a similar ploy appears to have received
> judicial attention, over 80 years ago, it was likewise rejected . . .'

Reference was then made to the *South Hetton* case.

Again the formula used in the *SSI Investors Ltd* case is not exactly the same as that used
j by Sir Leonard, but again the sentiments expressed are consistent with and support the
view that I have formed. Counsel for Sir Leonard relied on the opinion expressed by
Judge Fuchsberg, who, whilst concurring in the decision that the referential bid failed as
being too uncertain, dissented on the question of the validity of the referential bid. He
said (at 175):

> 'Nor do I see any reason, in the absence of illegality, and in the context of a private
> sector business transaction in our relatively free enterprise society, to concern

ourselves with the possible or potential effect of appellant's novel offer on commercial
competitive bidding. This problem, if it turns out to be one, could easily be abated   *a*
by appropriate conditions imposed by those who invite bids or, if the Legislature
thought it of sufficient general interest, by statutory enactment.'

But, as I have already indicated, the fact that it is easy to exclude referential bids by
express terms does not in itself prevent the implication of a term. Nor, to my mind, does
the possibility that the legislature would choose to intervene prevent a term being   *b*
implied. No doubt Parliament could easily have legislated to impose on landlords the
obligations relating to common parts of tower blocks which the House of Lords in the
Liverpool case was prepared to imply.

Accordingly the authorities seem to me to be not inconsistent with the conclusion that
referential bids are necessarily excluded from sealed competitive bidding and indeed to
provide support for that conclusion. I would add that I am happy to base my decision on
a broad ground covering all forms of referential bid. I would not have thought it right   *c*
for the law to imply a term excluding some forms of referential bidding, leaving more
sophisticated forms open to the ingenious bidder.

It follows that I must treat Sir Leonard's bid as inconsistent with the implied term
excluding referential bids and that Harvela's, and not Sir Leonard's, bid was the highest
offer in accordance with the terms of the invitation telex. I am therefore parepared to   *d*
make the declaration sought by Harvela.

I turn next to the consequences flowing therefrom. The question that then arises is
whether any enforceable contract between Royal Jersey and Harvela was created at 3 pm
on 16 September 1981. Counsel for Harvela submits that a contract for the sale by Royal
Jersey of the shares to Harvela came into existence at that time, the invitation telex
constituting an offer to sell and the making by Harvela of the bid in response constituting
the acceptance which took effect as soon as Harvela was seen to have made the highest   *e*
offer. Alternatively, if the invitation telex and Harvela's bid did not itself constitute a
contract, he submits that the invitation telex was an offer to enter into a contract, which
offer was accepted by Harvela's bid and the contract thereby created to enter into a
contract is in law treated as itself the contract for sale of the shares. Counsel for Harvela
has yet a third string to his bow, that is to say that if the contract to enter into a contract
should not be treated as itself a contract for sale but as a distinct contract, that contract is   *f*
specifically enforceable. Counsel for Sir Leonard takes two points: first, that the invitation
telex was no more than an invitation to treat and Harvela's bid was an offer which has
never been accepted and, second, that no consideration has been provided by Harvela for
the alleged contract.

The first point of counsel for Sir Leonard turns on the construction of the invitation
telex. He relies on the wording of that telex using as it does, terms usually indicative of   *g*
an invitation to treat. Thus, it refers first to the previous 'offers' of Harvela and Sir
Leonard (each of which can only have been an offer and not the acceptance of an offer)
and invites a revised 'offer'. Prima facie 'offer' would bear the same meaning throughout
the telex and it is the term invariably used in relation to what each of Harvela and Sir
Leonard was invited to do. Further, Royal Jersey's part was to 'accept' the highest offer.
In its original form, with the promise by Royal Jersey to be bound to accept the highest   *h*
offer being expressly made subject to acceptance by Royal Jersey, there would in my view
have been much to be said for the submission of counsel for Sir Leonard that this was an
invitation to treat. But the removal of that qualification 'subject to acceptance' in my
judgment was very significant. It is trite law that the true character in law of a document
is not determined merely by the label or description given to it by the parties: one must
look at all the provisions of the document to see whether it has been accurately labelled   *j*
or described by the parties. In the present case I must look at all the terms of the
invitation telex as modified to determine whether it amounted to an offer. In contrast to
Royal Jersey's invitation on 17 August 1982 in which it was expressly stated that that
communication was an invitation to treat and that the trustees did not bind themselves
to accept the highest or any offer, the invitation telex as modified contained an
unequivocal promise to be bound to accept the highest offer. The word 'offer' in an

a

appropriate context can mean no more than 'bid' and that to my mind is its plain meaning here. Whether that bid is intended to be only an offer or an acceptance for the purposes of the law of contract will depend on all the circumstances; and where as here the person inviting the bid indicates clearly that he binds himself to accept the highest bid, that invitation goes beyond being a mere invitation to treat and is itself an offer capable of being accepted by a bid in response to that invitation.

b

I accept the submission of counsel for Harvela that the present case is an example of a unilateral contract, in the sense of a contract brought into existence by the act of one party in response to a conditional promise by another. Royal Jersey by the invitation telex promised to accept Harvela's bid if that were the highest offer in accordance with the terms of the invitation telex, and Harvela by responding thereto by making the highest bid brought the contract into existence. Counsel for Harvela referred me to the remarks of Willes J in *Spencer v Harding* (1870) LR 5 CP 561 at 563 which were approved

c

in *Carlill v Carbolic Smoke Ball Co* [1893] 1 QB 256, [1891–4] All ER Rep 127. It is sufficient to read a passage from the judgment of Bowen LJ in which he refers to those remarks as well as discussing the nature of the offer by the defendants in the *Carlill* case in their advertisement to pay £100 to any person who contracted influenza after having used one of their smoke balls. He said ([1893] 1 QB 256 at 268–269, [1891–4] All ER Rep 127 at 133–134):

d

'It is an offer made to all the world; and why should not an offer be made to all the world which is to ripen into a contract with anybody who comes forward and performs the condition? It is an offer to become liable to anyone who, before it is retracted, performs the condition, and, although the offer is made to the world, the contract is made with that limited portion of the public who come forward and perform the condition on the faith of the advertisement. It is not like cases in which

e

you offer to negotiate, or you issue advertisements that you have got a stock of books to sell, or houses to let, in which case there is no offer to be bound by any contract. Such advertisement are offers to negotiate—offers to receive offers—offers to chaffer, as, I think, some learned judge in one of the cases has said. If this is an offer to be bound, then it is a contract the moment the person fulfils the condition. That seems to me to be sense, and it is also the ground on which all these advertisement cases

f

have been decided during the century; and it cannot be put better than in Willes, J.'s judgment in *Spencer v. Harding* (LR 5 CP 561 at 563). "In the advertisement cases," he says, "there never was any doubt that the advertisement amounted to a promise to pay the money to the person who first gave information. The difficulty suggested was that it was a contract with all the world. But that, of course, was soon overruled. It was an offer to become liable to any person who before the offer should

g

be retracted should happen to be the person to fulfil the contract, of which the advertisement was an offer or tender. That is not the sort of difficulty which presents itself here. If the circular had gone on, 'and we undertake to sell to the highest bidder,' the reward cases would have applied, and there would have been a good contract in respect of the persons." As soon as the highest bidder presented himself, says Willes, J., the person who was to hold the vinculum juris on the other side of

h

the contract was ascertained, and it became settled.'

The second point of counsel for Sir Leonard was that there was no consideration moving from Harvela. He said that Harvela merely did what it was invited to do, that is to say it made a bid and paid no money with the bid. He referred me to a case in the Nova Scotia Supreme Court, *Saltzberg and Rubin v Hollis Securities Ltd* (1964) 48 DLR (2d)

j

344. In that case a vendor invited bids for the purchase of the vendor's property and informed the bidders that the highest offer would be accepted. Patterson J held that on the true construction of the invitation it was only an invitation to treat and not an offer. I say nothing about that part of the decision which relates to the construction of the invitation in the particular circumstances of that case. But the judge briefly commented that there was no consideration for the promise that the highest tender would be accepted. That comment, if I may respectfully say so, was correct if he was confining himself to the position before the bids were made pursuant to the invitation. But what

the judge does not appear to have considered (no doubt because of the conclusion that he
reached on the construction of the invitation) was whether the performance of the act   *a*
which the vendor had invited, that is to say the submission of the bid, constituted
consideration moving from the bidder to the vendor for the contract claimed by the
bidder. On the face of the report, cases like *Spencer v Harding* and the *Carlill* case were not
considered. In the *Carlill* case it was argued by the defendant company that there was no
consideration for the contract claimed by the plaintiff. But the Court of Appeal held that
the act of the plaintiff in responsing to the invitation in the advertisement, that is to say   *b*
the use of the smoke ball, was in itself sufficient consideration. In my judgment similarly,
Harvela provided consideration when it did what Royal Jersey invited it to do, that is to
say it submitted the highest bid. The consideration moving to Royal Jersey was the
performance of that act. That was the benefit to Royal Jersey which it wanted. If further
consideration were needed, it can be found in the detriment suffered by Harvela in
having gone to the expense of making its bid through its lawyers.   *c*
    In my judgment therefore there was an enforceable contract at 3 pm on 16 September
1981 between Royal Jersey and Harvela. It matters not whether one treats the contract
that came into existence then as a contract for the sale of the shares or, as I am inclined to
think, a contract whereby Royal Jersey bound itself to accept Harvela's bid, which
amounts to a contract to enter into a contract. As Lord Wright said in *Hillas & Co Ltd v
Arcos Ltd* (1932) 147 LT 503 at 515, [1932] All ER Rep 494 at 505:   *d*

> 'A contract *de præsenti* to enter into what, in law, is an enforceable contract, is
> simply that enforceable contract, and no more and no less . . .'

Even if these first two ways in which counsel for Harvela puts his case were wrong and
the contract entered into at 3 pm on 16 September 1981 must be treated as a contract
distinct from the contract for the sale of shares, it is still a specifically enforceable contract   *e*
conferring on Harvela an interest in the shares: see *Daulia Ltd v Four Millbank Nominees
Ltd* [1978] 2 All ER 557 at 563, [1978] Ch 231 at 241 per Goff LJ.
    The next question that arises is whether Sir Leonard entered into a contract with Royal
Jersey for the purchase of the shares at a price of $2,276,000. His counsel says that Sir
Leonard did. Counsel for Royal Jersey and Royal London says that he did not, there never
having been any consensus ad idem between Sir Leonard and Royal Jersey for the sale of   *f*
the shares to Sir Leonard other than as the winner of the contest between him and
Harvela to make the highest bid in accordance with the invitation telex. The owner of
property who has bound himself contractually to sell it to A may of course enter into a
binding contract to sell the same property to B, and if authority were needed for that it
can be found in the *South Hetton* case [1898] 1 Ch 465 at 468 where Lindley MR said:

> 'I have not the slightest doubt that if the liquidator had thought fit to accept the   *g*
> plaintiffs' offer it would have been open to him to do so, and the plaintiffs would
> have been bound by that acceptance. I say nothing as to the right of [the defendant]
> to object, but, as between the liquidator and the plaintiffs I do not doubt that the
> liquidator might have accepted that offer.'

    As a contract between Royal Jersey and Harvela came into existence on 16 September   *h*
1981 by virtue of Harvela having made the highest offer, Royal Jersey could not enter
into a contract for the sale of the shares without a further act by Royal Jersey accepting
Sir Leonard's bid. On 29 September 1981 Royal Jersey did indicate to Sir Leonard its
acceptance of that bid and prima facie a contract between Royal Jersey and Sir Leonard
for the sale of the shares to him then came into existence. In Royal Jersey's defence to the
counterclaim of Sir Leonard it has not been pleaded that there was any mistake vitiating   *j*
any such contract. Let me nevertheless deal with counsel for Royal Jersey and Royal
London's point that there was such a mistake. Plainly there was a mistake on the part of
Royal Jersey in accepting Sir Leonard's bid in that it thought that it was bound by the
terms of the invitation telex to do so. But whether that was a unilateral mistake (and
counsel for Royal Jersey and Royal London referred me to various passages in *Chitty on
Contracts* (25th edn, 1983) paras 330 ff, on unilateral mistake) or, as I think a mutual
mistake to which Sir Leonard, too, was a party, I agree with counsel for Sir Leonard that

the mistake was one of law rather than of fact. The mistake related to the effect in law of
a Sir Leonard's bid, and both Royal Jersey and Sir Leonard on the view that I have formed
made a mistake of law. Accordingly as the law now stands, that mistake would not
prevent the formation of the contract between Royal Jersey and Sir Leonard.

Which contract should the court now enforce, given that each of Harvela and Sir
Leonard seeks specific performance of contracts for the sale of the same shares to it or
him? The answer to that question is simple. The court will not order specific performance
b of Sir Leonard's contract as that would necessitate a breach of Royal Jersey's prior contract
with Harvela. In my judgment Harvela is entitled to an order for specific performance
of its contract.

The next question relates to interest on the purchase moneys to be paid by Harvela.
Royal Jersey claims that as a term of the order for specific performance, Harvela should
be required to pay interest to Royal Jersey by way of equitable relief. Counsel for Royal
c Jersey and Royal London in putting forward that claim submitted that while Royal Jersey
would have been entitled to interest at the contractual rate specified in term 5 of the
invitation telex, ie at the rate of 4% above the Bank of Montreal prime rate for Canadian
dollar loans, he was only asking for interest at a lower rate. He said that Royal Jersey
might have asked for interest at the short term investment account rate (cf *Barlett v
Barclays Bank Trust Co Ltd (No 2)* [1980] 2 All ER 92 at 98, [1980] Ch 515 at 547) but he
d was content to limit his claim to a rate equal to the one-month fixed Canadian dollar
LIBOR (London Inter-Bank Offered Rate) quoted at 11 am London time on 16 October
1981 and each renewal date thereafter. Despite the seeming moderation of Royal Jersey's
demands, and even without the compounding of interest claimed by Royal Jersey, the
interest from the completion date (16 October 1981) to 15 November 1983 amounts to a
little over $650,000. In marked contrast, the income received by the trustees from the
e shares is limited to $1,866 per annum on the 311 6% preference shares. The 24,337 non-
voting preference shares are entitled to no dividend and no dividends have been paid in
or in respect of the period since 16 October 1981 on the common shares. There is no
evidence before me to indicate what dividends (if any) Harveys might yet properly
declare on its common shares in respect of that period.

The general rule in equity as to the payment of interest on unpaid purchase moneys
f on a sale of land where there is a delay in completion and the vendor remains in
occupation was stated by Leach V-C in *Esdaile v Stephenson* (1822) 1 Sim & St 122 at 123,
57 ER 49 at 50 quoted with approval by Wilberforce J in *Re Hewitt's Contract* [1963] 3 All
ER 419 at 422, [1963] 1 WLR 1298 at 1302. Leach V-C said:

> 'Where there is no stipulation as to interest, the general rule of the Court is that
> the purchaser, when he completes his contract after the time mentioned in the
g > particulars of sale, shall be considered as in possession from that time, and shall from
> thence pay interest at £4 per cent. taking the rents and profits. If, however, such
> interest is much more in amount than the rents and profits, and it is clearly made
> out that the delay in completing the contract was occasioned by the vendor there, to
> give effect to the general rule would enable the vendor to profit by his own wrong;
> and the Court therefore gives the vendor no interest, but leaves him in possession of
h > the *interim* rents and profits.'

There are two points of distinction that leap to the eye. First, the rule was expressed in
relation to the sale of land and we are here concerned with the sale of shares. Counsel for
Sir Leonard, in his submissions on the footing that interest was sought against Sir
Leonard if he obtained an order for specific performance, suggested that the court should
j not apply to contracts for the sale of shares the same rules as applied to the sale of land.
But in the absence of special circumstances justifying a different rule it seems to me that
the same principle should apply. I do not understand counsel for Harvela to take any
point on this distinction. The second point of distinction lies in the fact that Leach V-C
prefaced his comments with the words, 'Where there is no stipulation as to interest',
whereas here the parties did specifically agree that interest at a specified rate should be
paid save in one particular circumstance, that is to say where there has been delay on the
part of Royal Jersey. Counsel for Royal Jersey and Royal London says that even, if

contrary to his submission, Royal Jersey could not rely on the contractual term as to interest, all that means is that the contractual term has no application and the court is *a* free to do equity by applying its ordinary rules. I accept that if Harvela is not obliged by term 5 of the invitation telex to pay interest the court is not precluded in the exercise of its discretion from requiring Harvela to pay interest, but in my judgment the existence of the contractual terms and the exemption of Harvela thereunder (if that can be shown) would be very material matters for the court to take into consideration in the exercise of its discretion. In my judgment, where the parties have considered and agreed the *b* circumstances in which interest will or will not be payable by the purchaser, it would require very special circumstances for the court to interfere and impose on the purchaser who is not required to pay interest under the contract an obligation to pay interest in order to obtain the vendor's performance of the contract.

I shall therefore consider first whether Harvela is, under the contract, liable to pay interest. It can only escape that liability if the delay in completion is on the part of the *c* trustees. Counsel for Royal Jersey and Royal London submits that the delay cannot be so described. I cannot agree. It is to be noted that the relevant delay is not qualified in the contract in any way such as one sometimes finds: for example, where it is stipulated that the delay must have been caused by the wilful default of the vendor. The delay in completion was certainly not on the part of Harvela which, Royal Jersey accepts, was willing to complete on 16 October 1981. Though I cannot avoid feeling some sympathy *d* with Royal Jersey and its advisers, faced as they were with an awkward problem of law, the simple fact of the matter is that they erroneously thought that Royal Jersey was bound to accept Sir Leonard's offer; it was for that reason that Royal Jersey did not complete what can now be seen to have been its contract to sell to Harvela. True it is that, had Royal Jersey indicated an intention to complete with Harvela, Sir Leonard would have been likely to have obtained an injunction pending such completion; but in that *e* event, no doubt, Royal Jersey would have obtained the comfort of a cross-undertaking in damages from Sir Leonard. That is not what happened. Royal Jersey it was which refused to complete with Harvela and in my judgment it is clear beyond argument that the delay in completion was on the part of Royal Jersey. Accordingly Royal Jersey has no contractual right to interest.

Ought the court nevertheless to require interest to be paid on the basis of the equitable *f* rules applicable to delays in completing contracts where there is no contractual term as to interest? I can see no special circumstances which would require the court as a matter of equity to improve in Royal Jersey's favour on the terms of its contract with Harvela. Indeed, as counsel for Harvela pointed out, the two conditions laid down by Leach V-C in *Esdaile v Stephenson* appear to be satisfied in that the interest greatly exceeds the income from the property sold and the delay has been occasioned by the vendor, Royal Jersey. *g* The riposte of counsel for Royal Jersey and Royal London to that was that this would be to ignore the basis of the rule, which is to prevent a vendor from profiting by his own wrong, and that, he says, is not an apt description of his client. But, in its context, Leach V-C's remark seems to me to be directed simply to the vendor who commits a wrong in the sense of breaking his contractual obligation to complete timeously, yet profits by receiving more by way of interest from the innocent purchaser than the purchaser would *h* have received by way of income from the property. Having regard to the fact that the delay was occasioned by Royal Jersey and not by Harvela, to the very great disparity between the interest claimed and the dividends received, and to the contractual terms as to interest, I am far from satisfied that equity requires the imposition of a term on Harvela as to interest at the rate claimed or indeed any other rate. Counsel for Harvela submitted that he should be allowed to keep the dividends too, because they were paid *j* after the shares belonged in equity to Harvela; but on this I propose to apply by analogy the rule as stated in *Esdaile v Stephenson* and not to allow Harvela both freedom from interest as well as the retention of the dividends. I think that it would be equitable to direct specific performance on the terms that Royal Jersey is entitled to retain and receive all dividends paid and to be paid on any of the shares in respect of the period from 16 October 1981 to completion.

That leaves only the claims by each of Harvela and Sir Leonard for damages. Harvela

claim damages for the failure by Royal Jersey to complete on the contractual completion
a date and it asks for an inquiry as to damages. It is conceded by counsel for Royal Jersey
and Royal London that Harvela, owning as it pleaded and has been admitted 43% of the
Harveys shares, would have had control of Harveys had completion of its contract duly
occurred and that some damage to Harvela has resulted such that it is appropriate for
there to be an inquiry as to damages. I therefore make that order. Sir Leonard's claim for
damages is on a different footing. That claim is a claim for damages in lieu of specific
b performance. Counsel for Sir Leonard, in asking for an inquiry as to damages, accepts
that he must show that Sir Leonard has suffered some damage even though the amount
thereof cannot yet be quantified. He says that it is obvious that Sir Leonard has suffered
damage through not receiving the shares. He relies on two matters. First, he says that
the shares which Sir Leonard contracted to buy were worth more than what Harvela bid
for them as is demonstrated by the fact that he was willing to pay $101,000 more than
c any bid by Harvela. But Sir Leonard would have had to establish that he suffered loss by
Royal Jersey not selling the shares to him for $2,276,000, a price which in a letter dated
29 September 1981 to Mrs Campbell he described as crippling. There is no evidence
before me of such loss. Second, counsel for Sir Leonard says that the failure of Royal
Jersey to transfer the shares to Sir Leonard has deprived Sir Leonard of control of Harveys.
But it is accepted by counsel that Sir Leonard alone would not have control of Harveys
d even if the shares in the settlement were transferred to him, because he would need the
consent of other Outerbridge shareholders to exercise such control. It is not alleged that
he has any right to such control. It is, of course, well established that damages may in an
appropriate case be awarded notwithstanding that it is only in respect of a loss of a chance
subject to contingencies. But no facts have been put before me from which I can safely
infer that Sir Leonard has suffered any damage. In the circumstances I shall award Sir
e Leonard nominal damages of £2 only and I refuse the request for an inquiry.

Judgment accordingly.

Solicitors: *Slaughter & May* (for Harvela); *Bischoff & Co* (for Royal Jersey and Royal
London); *McKenna & Co* (for Sir Leonard Outerbridge and Harveys).

f   Vivian Horvath   Barrister.

Government of Denmark v Nielsen

g HOUSE OF LORDS
LORD DIPLOCK, LORD KEITH OF KINKEL, LORD ROSKILL, LORD BRIDGE OF HARWICH AND LORD
BRIGHTMAN
6, 7, 8 MARCH, 12 APRIL 1984

Extradition – Committal – Evidence – Fugitive criminal accused of extradition crime – Evidence
h *to be considered by magistrate – Evidence of substantive criminal law of foreign state –*
Admissibility – Magistrate required to consider whether evidence justifying, according to English
law, committal of accused if crime committed in England – Whether magistrate also required to
consider foreign law – Whether question of double criminality to be considered – Extradition Act
1870, s 10, Sch 1.

j The appellant was accused in Denmark under s 280 of the Danish Criminal Code of
fraudently abusing his position as a controlling shareholder of a Danish company of
which he was a director. It was alleged that he had caused the company to purchase
shares from a second company, which he also controlled, at an inflated price and on
onerous terms and to advance loans to that company without security with the aim of
rescuing that company from severe financial difficulties. It was further alleged that the
loans had not been repaid and that the capital invested in the purchase of the shares had
been lost. The Danish government sought extradition of the appellant, who was arrested

and brought before a metropolitan stipendiary magistrate on a provisional warrant issued under s 8(2) of the Extradition Act 1870. The warrant stated that the appellant was *a* suspected and accused in Denmark of the crime of 'Fraud by a director of a company'. Shortly afterwards the provisional warrant was superseded by an order to proceed made by the Secretary of State under s 7 of the 1870 Act. The order described the crimes of which the appellant was accused and for which surrender was sought as 'theft, procuring the execution of valuable securities by deception, publishing misleading, false or deceptive statements and false accounting'. By virtue of the appellant's office as a director *b* of the Danish company those crimes fell within the provisions of the Theft Act 1968 and item 8ᵃ of the list of extradition crimes set out in Sch 1 to the 1870 Act (which was reproduced in art I of the principal extradition treaty of 1873 between Denmark and the United Kingdom), namely 'Fraud by a . . . director, or member . . . of any company made criminal by any Act for the time being in force'. At the hearing before the metropolitan magistrate expert evidence was called on behalf of the Danish government as to the *c* wording and practice regarding prosecutions under s 280 of the Danish Criminal Code in order to show that the offence of which the appellant was accused was not only a criminal offence under Danish law but also a crime substantially similar to one or more of the English crimes set out in Sch 1 to the 1870 Act. The magistrate confined himself to considering the description of the Danish offence in s 280 of the Danish Criminal Code, although there were other sections in the code which corresponded to the offences *d* referred to in the Secretary of State's order to proceed, and concluded that the two laws were not substantially similar in concept because the Danish offences were narrower in ambit than the corresponding English offences. He therefore discharged the appellant. The Danish government applied to the Divisional Court of the Queen's Bench Division for judicial review of the magistrate's order. The court quashed the magistrate's order and ordered him to continue with the hearing of the proceedings against the appellant *e* in accordance with s 10ᵇ of the 1870 Act, which provided that in the case of a 'fugitive criminal accused of an extradition crime' the magistrate was required to commit him to prison to await extradition if evidence was produced which 'would, according to the law of England, justify the committal for trial of the prisoner if the crime of which he is accused had been committed in England'. The appellant appealed to the House of Lords.

f

Held – On the true construction of s 10 of the 1870 Act a magistrate considering an application for extradition of a fugitive under a treaty which incorporated the whole of the list of extradition crimes set out in Sch 1 to the 1870 Act was only required to determine whether the conduct or acts of the accused constituted, under English law, a crime so that he would be committed for trial if he had committed such acts or conduct in England provided that the crime was one of the crimes listed in Sch 1 to the 1870 Act and in the relevant extradition treaty. In considering whether the fugitive's acts or *g* conduct would amount to a crime in England the magistrate was not required to consider any question of foreign law, since comparison of English and foreign law was only necessary if the extradition treaty contained limitations on surrender or if extradition was being sought on the basis of a conviction already obtained in the foreign state and the foreign certificate or judicial documents merely stated the fact of the conviction *h* without reciting the facts on which the conviction was based. Since the conduct of which the appellant had been accused in Denmark was covered by English crimes contained in the list of extradition crimes set out in Sch 1 to the 1870 Act and incorporated without modification into the 1873 treaty between England and Denmark it followed that the magistrate had exceeded his jurisdiction in considering whether there was double criminality based on a comparison of s 280 of the Danish Criminal Code and relevant *j*

---

a   Item 8, so far as material, is set out at p 85 *j*, post

b   Section 10, so far as material, provides: 'In the case of a fugitive criminal accused of an extradition crime, if the foreign warrant authorising the arrest of such criminal is duly authenticated, and such evidence is produced as (subject to the provisions of this Act) would, according to the law of England, justify the committal for trial of the prisoner if the crime of which he is accused had been committed in England, the police magistrate shall commit him to prison, but otherwise shall order him to be discharged . . .'

English offences. The appeal would therefore be dismissed (see p 88 g to p 89 d and p 90
a j to p 91 e and j to p 92 d, post).
Re Bellencontre [1891] 2 QB 122 and Re Arton (No 2) [1896] 1 QB 509 considered.
Dictum of Griffiths J in R v Governor of Pentonville Prison, ex p Budlong [1980] 1 All ER
at 712 disapproved.

Notes
b For extradition to a foreign state, see 18 Halsbury's Laws (4th edn) paras 203–229, and
for cases on the subject, see 24 Digest (Reissue) 1118–1142, 11910–12158.
For the Extradition Act 1870, ss 7, 8, 10, Sch 1, see 13 Halsbury's Statutes (3rd edn)
254, 255, 257, 266.
For the Theft Act 1968, see 8 ibid 782.

Cases referred to in opinions
c Arton, Re, (No 2) [1896] 1 QB 509, DC.
Bellencontre, Re [1891] 2 QB 122, DC.
Government of the Federal Republic of Germany v Sotiriadis [1974] 1 All ER 692, [1975] AC
1, [1974] 2 WLR 253, HL.
R v Governor of Pentonville Prison, ex p Budlong [1980] 1 All ER 701, [1980] 1 WLR 1110,
DC.
d
Appeal
Jan Niels Bonde Nielsen appealed with leave of the Divisional Court of the Queen's Bench
Division against the decision of that court (Robert Goff LJ and Mann J) on 12 May 1983
allowing an application for judicial review by way of orders of certiorari and mandamus
by the government of Denmark and quashing the order of the Chief Metropolitan
e Stipendiary Magistrate sitting at Bow Street Magistrates' Court dated 30 September 1982
discharging the appellant in extradition proceedings and directing that the magistrates
should hear the evidence and determine in accordance with s 10 of the Extradition Act
1870 whether the evidence justified the committal of the appellant for trial of the crime
of which he was accused had it been committed in England. The Divisional Court
certified under s 1(2) of the Administration of Justice Act 1960 that a point of law of
f general public importance (set out at p 88 c to e, post) was involved in the decision. The
facts are set out in the opinion of Lord Diplock.

John Mathew QC and Clive Stanbrook for the appellant.
Clive Nicholls QC and R Alun Jones for the respondent.

Their Lordships took time for consideration.

g 12 April. The following opinions were delivered.

LORD DIPLOCK. My Lords, the appellant, Nielsen, is a Danish national for whose
extradition from the United Kingdom requisition has been made by the government of
Denmark, pursuant to the Extradition Acts 1870 to 1935.
The 1870 Act prescribes the procedure to be followed when a requisition for the
h surrender of a fugitive criminal is made by a foreign state to which that Act has been
made applicable by an Order in Council under s 2. Except where otherwise indicated
any subsequent reference that I make to a numbered 'section' should be understood as
referring to that section in the 1870 Act.
The Extradition Acts 1870 to 1935 have been made applicable to Denmark by Orders
in Council dated respectively 26 June 1873 and 30 April 1936, which recite the terms of
j arrangements made pursuant to s 2 of the 1870 Act. These take the form of treaties
between the two countries providing for the extradition by each country of persons
accused or convicted of crimes committed in the other country. The 1873 treaty (the
principal treaty) was entered into before the Extradition Act 1873 had added to the list
of extradition crimes listed in Sch 1 to the 1870 Act (the 1870 list) any of the crimes that
have been added to that list by the schedule to the 1873 Act or by any later Extradition
Act. It is the 1870 list that is reproduced verbatim in the English language version of the
principal treaty to describe the crimes for which extradition is to be granted of persons,

other than British nationals, accused or convicted of having committed any of those
crimes in Denmark; and it is with conduct that is alleged to constitute a crime or crimes   *a*
described in the 1870 list that the instant case is concerned.

The 1936 treaty (the supplementary treaty) has the effect of adding to the 1870 list of
crimes for which extradition is to be granted between the United Kingdom and
Denmark; but it leaves the 1870 list in the principal treaty untouched, and such additions
as it makes to extradition crimes are made in qualified terms to which it will be necessary
to advert later.   *b*

It is, however, appropriate at this juncture to draw attention to the fact that, when one
is describing crimes committed in a foreign state that are regarded in the United
Kingdom as serious enough to warrant extradition of an offender by whom they have
been committed, one is describing the way in which human beings have conducted
themselves and their state of mind at the time of such conduct. Since conduct of that
kind consists of wicked things that people do in real life it is possible to describe it either   *c*
in broad generic terms and using popular language, or in varying degrees of specificity,
as had been done in minute detail, nine years before the 1870 Act itself was passed, in the
five Acts that had been passed in 1861, consolidating and amending the statute law of
England relating to criminal offences of larceny, malicious injuries to property, forgery,
coinage and offences against the person respectively. These Acts condescended to minute
detail of their descriptions of numerous distinct offences included within the broad genus   *d*
of crimes with which, as their titles indicate, each Act dealt. Between them the five Acts
ran into 380 sections.

The 1870 list uses the former technique. It describes each of the list of 19 'extradition
crimes' in general terms and popular language, irrespective of whether (as the
introductory words of Sch 1 to the 1870 Act make clear) the conduct described is rendered
criminal by common law or by statute *made before or after the passing of the 1870 Act.* So   *e*
the 1870 list covered all offences under the five consolidating and amending Acts of 1861
that fell within any of the 19 genera of conduct described in the list, and also any criminal
offence created by any subsequent statute but only if it fell within a described genus. The
1870 list would not extend to offences created by any of the 1861 Acts which did not fall
within any of those generic descriptions. The list in the schedule to the 1873 Act as well
as adding two additional genera to the list of extradition crimes (viz 'Kidnapping and   *f*
false imprisonment' and 'Perjury, and subornation of perjury, whether under common
or statute law') filled these lacunae by adding to the list any indictable offence under any
of the five 1861 consolidation and amending Acts (or any Act amending or substituted
for the same) 'which is not included in the first schedule to the [1870] Act'.

The list in the 1873 Act has been subsequently amended by replacing the reference to
the Larceny Act 1861 by a reference to the Theft Acts 1968 and 1978, and adding   *g*
references to the Criminal Damage Act 1971 and the Sexual Offences Act 1956.

The introductory words to both the 1870 list and the later list provide that the list of
crimes is to be construed according to the law existing in England at the date of the
alleged crime. So in order to determine whether conduct constitutes an 'extradition
crime' within the meaning of the Extradition Acts 1870 to 1935, and thus a *potential*
ground for extradition if that conduct had taken place in a foreign state, one can start by   *h*
inquiring whether the conduct if it had taken place in England would have fallen within
one of the 19 generic descriptions of crimes in the 1870 list. If it would have so fallen the
inquiry need proceed no further where, as in the case of the principal treaty with
Denmark, the extradition treaty with the foreign state demanding the surrender of a
person as a fugitive criminal incorporates the whole of the 1870 list in the descriptions of
crimes for which surrender may be required and makes no modification to those   *j*
descriptions.

The conduct of which Nielsen, who is not a British subject, was accused in Denmark is
stated succinctly in the judgment in the instant case delivered by Robert Goff LJ in the
Divisional Court:

'... Nielsen fraudulently abused his position as controlling shareholder of a
company called Gredana A/S to rescue another company under his control, called

a   Egtofte Industri A/S, from financial difficulties. The means alleged to have been employed by him for this purpose were to cause Gredana (1) to purchase certain shares from Egtofte at an inflated price and on onerous terms, the total purchase price being nearly 100m kroner, and (2) to advance loans to Egtofte, without security, in a sum of about 13m kroner. In the outcome, it is alleged, the loan has not been repaid, and Gredana has lost the whole of the capital invested in the purchase of the shares.'

b   This brief description of the conduct of which Nielsen is accused is sufficient to identify the point of law that is raised by this appeal.

My Lords, in my speech in *Government of the Federal Republic of Germany v Sotiriadis* [1974] 1 All ER 692, [1975] AC 1, I undertook an analysis, which received the express approval of Lord Wilberforce and Lord Simon, of the procedure laid down in the Extradition Acts 1870 and 1873 for the extradition of persons accused or convicted of
c   crimes committed within the jurisdiction of a foreign state with which the United Kingdom had entered into an extradition treaty. I refer to, but will not take up space by repeating, that analysis, except to draw attention to the facts (1) that the Extradition Acts 1870 to 1935, from which alone is derived the jurisdiciton of the Bow Street magistrate to make orders under s 10 committing a fugitive criminal to prison to await surrender to the person authorised to receive him on behalf of the foreign state, extend only to
d   those foreign states which have entered into an extradition treaty with the United Kingdom to which the Acts have been made applicable by Order in Council and (2) that the magistrate's jurisdiction and powers under the Acts are subject to such limitations, restrictions, conditions, exceptions and qualifications as may be provided for in the extradition treaty with the particular foreign state. The jurisdiction conferred on the Bow Street magistrate by the Extradition Acts 1870 to 1935 is the widest that he may
e   lawfully exercise on applications for extradition of fugitive criminals from foreign states. His jurisdiction cannot be extended beyond that maximum but it may be limited, in the case of fugitive criminals from a particular foreign state, by the terms of the extradition treaty with that state. The *Sotiriadis* case involved an example of an additional limitation imposed by the relevant extradition treaty with the German Federal Republic.

While the Extradition Acts 1870 to 1935 apply to persons convicted, as well as those
f   accused, of having committed an extradition crime within the jurisdiction of a foreign state, your Lordships in the present appeal are concerned only with the extradition of an accused person (which I shall call 'an accusation case') and not with the extradition of a convicted person (which I shall call 'a conviction case'). Your Lordships are likewise not concerned in the instant case with alleged political offences.

Nielsen was first arrested under a provisional warrant issued on 27 July 1981 under
g   s 8(2) by a metropolitan magistrate in the form set out in Sch 2 to the 1870 Act. Nielsen was stated in the provisional warrant to be suspected and accused of the commission of the crime in Denmark of 'Fraud by a director of a company'. The provisional warrant, however, was shortly afterwards superseded by an order to proceed made by the Home Secretary under s 7, in the form set out in Sch 2 to the 1870 Act. This described the crime of which Nielsen was accused and for which his surrender was sought by the government
h   of Denmark as 'obtaining property by deception'. Shortly before the opening of the hearing of the case against Nielsen by the Chief Metropolitan Stipendiary Magistrate under ss 9 and 10, this order to proceed was supplemented by a further order to proceed which described offences of which Nielsen was accused of having committed in Denmark as: 'theft, procuring the execution of valuable securities by deception, publishing misleading, false or deceptive statements and false accounting'. In view of Nielsen's office
j   as director of the Danish company Gredana A/S these are particular species of crimes dealt with in ss 1(1), 15(1), 17(1)(a), 19(1) and 20(2) of the Theft Act 1968, which fall within the genus described in item 8 of the 1870 list and reproduced in art I of the principal treaty as 'Fraud by a . . . director, or member . . . of any company made criminal by any Act ['law' in the principal treaty] for the time being in force'.

The Extradition Acts 1870 to 1935 do not themselves provide that an arrangement made with a foreign state under s 2 of the 1870 Act for the surrender by the United

Kingdom to that foreign state of fugitive criminals accused or convicted of criminal *a* conduct committed within its jurisdiction must provide for reciprocity of surrender by the foreign state to the United Kingdom of persons accused or convicted of similar criminal conduct committed in this country. In practice, extradition treaties do provide for a substantial degree of reciprocity, but the surrender by a foreign state of a fugitive criminal from the United Kingdom who is found in the territory of that foreign state is not governed by English law at all, but solely by the law of the foreign state that is party to the treaty. If the foreign state fails to comply with its treaty obligations as respects *b* surrender, this is a matter for the Secretary of State: it has nothing to do with the English magistrate.

Likewise the Extradition Acts 1870 and 1873 do not themselves lay down what documents, if any, must be sent to the Secretary of State by the foreign state together with the requisition for the surrender of a fugitive criminal. That is a matter that is left to be dealt with by the extradition treaty. At the hearing of the extradition proceedings *c* by the magistrate under ss 9 and 10 there must be produced in an accusation case a duly authenticated warrant authorising the arrest of the accused person and issued by a judge, magistrate or officer of the foreign state by which the requisition was made; and, except in so far as their use may be restricted by the extradition treaty under which the application for surrender was made, depositions, statements on oath and affirmations taken in the foreign state are admissible in evidence at the hearing, as well as any *d* additional oral evidence that is called before the magistrate himself.

The principal treaty provides by art II that the requisition by Denmark for the surrender of a fugitive criminal other than a British national accused of having committed an extradition crime in that country shall be—

'accompanied by (1) a warrant or other equivalent judicial document for the arrest of accused, issued by a Judge or Magistrate duly authorized to take cognizance of *e* the acts charged against him in Denmark, (2) duly authenticated depositions or statements taken on oath before such Judge or Magistrate, clearly setting forth the acts on account of which the fugitive is demanded; and (3) a description of the person claimed, and any other particulars which may serve to identify him.'

By art III, provisions in identical terms apply to requisitions by the United Kingdom government for the surrender by Denmark of a fugitive criminal, other than a Danish *f* national, accused of having committed an extradition crime in the United Kingdom. What is significant in these provisions is, *first*, that the treaty refers to the *acts* charged against the accused and on account of which his surrender is demanded, that is to say the conduct of the accused that is alleged to constitute an extradition crime included in the list contained in art I of the principal treaty which, as already mentioned, merely reproduces verbatim the 1870 list, *second*, that the treaty does not require that the warrant *g* of arrest should specify the particular provision of the Danish Criminal Code for the infringement of which the warrant of arrest was issued.

Under Danish criminal practice it would appear that a warrant of arrest does specify the section of the Danish Criminal Code which creates the crime which the Danish judge who issues the warrant of arrest considers that the evidence before him constitutes reasonable cause for suspecting that the person whose arrest is applied for has committed. *h* In the instant case, the section of the Danish Criminal Code referred to in the Danish warrant for the arrest of Nielsen was s 280. The terms of the section are set out in the judgment of the Divisional Court but I see no reason for referring to them because, for reasons which will appear, I do not think that, on the true construction of the Extradition Acts 1870 to 1935, they had any relevance to any question that the magistrate or the Divisional Court had jurisdiction to decide. *j*

My Lords, the definitions of 'extradition crime', 'fugitive criminal', 'fugitive criminal of a foreign state' and 'warrant' in s 26 of the Extradition Act 1870, read in conjunction with the introductory words of Sch 1 which require the description of each listed crime to be construed according to the law existing in England at the date of the alleged crime, are all important. They are:

'The term "extradition crime" means a crime which, if committed in England or

a   within English jurisdiction, would be one of the crimes described in the first
     schedule to this Act . . . The term "fugitive criminal" means any person accused or
     convicted of an extradition crime committed within the jurisdiction of any foreign
     state who is in or is suspected of being in some part of Her Majesty's dominions;
     and the term "fugitive criminal of a foreign state" means a fugitive criminal accused
     or convicted of an extradition crime committed within the jurisdiction of that state
     . . . The term "warrant," in the case of any foreign state, includes any judicial
b   document authorising the arrest of a person accused or convicted of crime.'

Important too are the forms set out in Sch 2 to the 1870 Act the use of which, or of forms
as near thereto as circumstances admit, is authorised by s 20 of the Act. The form of
order to proceed issued by the Secretary of State to the police magistrate pursuant to s 7
contains a space in which the Secretary of State specifies the crime (which, ex hypothesi,
for the list so requires, must be described in terms of a crime according to the laws of
c   England) as being the crime for which the magistrate is required to issue his warrant for
the apprehension of the fugitive criminal under s 8. Likewise, the form of warrant of
apprehension addressed to the constables of the police area in which the fugitive criminal
is, or is suspected of being, recites the Secretary of State's specification of the crime for
which he is to be apprehended; so does the form of warrant of committal of the fugitive
criminal to prison to await surrender that is issued by the magistrate under s 10, if at the
d   hearing under s 9 such evidence is produced as would according to the law of England
justify his committal for trial if the crime of which he is accused had been committed in
England.

The expression 'the crime of which he is accused' in s 10 thus means the crime specified
in an order by the Secretary of State to the magistrate to proceed to issue his warrant for
the apprehension of the fugitive criminal to show cause why he should not be surrendered
e   for that crime pursuant to the Extradition Acts 1870 to 1935. The magistrate has no
jurisdiction under s 10 to issue his warrant for committal of the fugitive criminal for any
crime other than one so specified in an order to proceed.

Under the principal treaty, the documents accompanying the requisition for the
surrender of a fugitive criminal in an accusation case will state the 'acts' on account of
which the fugitive is demanded by the Danish government. It is for the Secretary of State
f   to make up his mind what crime those acts would have amounted to according to the
English law in force at the time they were committed if they had been committed in
England. In the instant case, this meant identifying the offences which those acts would
have amounted to under the relevant criminal statute in force in England at the relevant
date (viz in the instant case the Theft Act 1968) had they been done by Nielsen in
England. This was what the Secretary of State did in the orders to proceed, to which I
g   have previously referred.

At the hearing before the Chief Metropolitan Stipendiary Magistrate, which lasted for
several days, the Director of Public Prosecutions representing the Danish government
produced evidence, including statements made on oath taken before the Danish judge
who had issued the foreign warrant for Nielsen's arrest, directed to establishing a prima
facie case that Nielsen had done the acts that are summarised in the passage from the
h   judgment of the Divisional Court that I have already quoted. Pursuant to a practice
which has apparently been followed at Bow Street in extradition cases since the judgment
of a Divisional Court in Re Arton (No 2) [1896] 1 QB 509, evidence of Danish criminal
law was called on behalf of the Danish government and, in particular, expert evidence as
to the wording of, and practice followed in prosecutions under, s 280 of the Danish
Criminal Code, which was the offence referred to in the Danish warrant of arrest as being
j   the crime committed in Denmark in respect of which that warrant was issued.'

On this expert evidence of Danish law the magistrate apparently took the view that,
although there were other sections in the Danish Criminal Code which corresponded to
the English offences referred to in the Secretary of State's orders to proceed, the Danish
offence created by s 280 involved a *narrower* concept than was involved in any of the
specified English offences. He regarded himself as bound by authority to discharge an
accused unless 'the offences in English law and . . . Danish law are substantially similar in

concept' and he took the view that for the purpose of determining whether there was the necessary similarity he was compelled to confine himself to the description of the Danish offence contained in the single section of the Danish Criminal Code, viz s 280, that was referred to in the Danish warrant of arrest as being the offence in respect of which it had been issued.

On this ground, in response to a submission made by counsel on behalf of Nielsen, he ordered Nielsen to be discharged, although at that stage there was further evidence which the Danish government had intended to adduce of the acts done by Nielsen on which the claim for his surrender was based.

The Danish government thereupon applied to the Divisional Court for judicial review of the magistrate's order that Nielsen should be discharged. The Divisional Court in a judgment by Robert Goff LJ, for which I should wish to record my respectful admiration, quashed the magistrate's order and ordered him to continue with the hearing of the proceedings against Nielsen in accordance with s 10 of the 1870 Act. Leave to appeal to this House was granted and the following point of law of general public importance was certified as being involved:

> 'In the case of a fugitive criminal accused of an extradition crime (not being the case of one who claims that the requisition for his surrender was made with a view to his trial or punishment for an offence of a political character) are the only functions of a police magistrate under section 10 of the Extradition Act 1870 to determine i. whether the foreign warrant authorising the arrest is duly authenticated and ii. whether with reference as a matter of practice to the extradition crime or crimes specified in the order of the Secretary of State made under section 7 of the Act the evidence produced to the magistrate is sufficient according to the Law of England to justify the fugitive criminal being committed for trial on a crime described in Schedule 1 to the Act as amended had the conduct described in that evidence been committed in England.'

My Lords, the certified question is confined to the functions of the police magistrate under ss 9 and 10, since it was his functions only that were in issue in the application for judicial review. The question is couched in terms so general as to preclude a categorical answer Yes or No, since it contains no reference to the extradition treaty between the United Kingdom and the particular foreign state by which the surrender of the fugitive criminal is sought. As has been pointed out, the effect of ss 1 and 5 is that such a treaty when embodied in an Order in Council may impose limitations, restrictions, conditions and qualifications on the provisions of the Act; and these may include restrictions on the list of crimes in Sch 1 to the 1870 Act as amended. If they do so, the magistrate, in the exercise of the statutory jurisdiction conferred on him by ss 9 and 10, must give effect to them.

In the principal treaty with Denmark, the list of crimes in respect of which surrender of fugitive criminals will be granted is confined to those contained in the 1870 list, and it was for crimes within this list alone that the Secretary of State's orders to proceed in the instant case was made. That is the reason why the magistrate had not, in my view, any jurisdiction in the instant case to make any findings of fact as to Danish substantive criminal law or to hear expert evidence about it.

It would have been otherwise if the conduct of which Nielsen was accused in Denmark had not been covered by any description of an English crime in the 1870 list but had been added to the list of extradition crimes by later Extradition Acts. For, in that event, it would only have been brought into the list of extradition crimes applicable to fugitive criminals from Denmark by the supplementary treaty of 1936 of which the relevant provision is the addition to art I of the principal treaty of the words:

> 'Extradition may also be granted at the discretion of the High Contracting Party applied to in respect of any other crime or offence for which, according to the laws of *both* of the High Contracting Parties for the time being in force, the grant may be made.' (My emphasis.)

Had it been necessary for the Danish government to rely on the supplementary treaty it would have been necessary for the magistrate to hear evidence of Danish law in order to

satisfy himself that the conduct of the accused, in addition to constituting in English law
a an extradition crime included among those subsequently added to the 1870 list, also
constituted an offence that was treated as an extradition crime in Denmark.

Whether in an accusation case the police magistrate has any jurisdiction to make
findings as to the substantive criminal law of the foreign state by which the requisition
for surrender of a fugitive criminal is made will depend on the terms of the arrangement
made in the extradition treaty with that state. Some treaties may contain provisions that
b limit surrender to persons accused of conduct that constitutes a crime of a particular kind
(for example, one that attracts specified minimum penalties) in both England and the
foreign state. Accusation cases arising under extradition treaties that contain this kind of
limitation I shall call 'exceptional accusation cases'. In an exceptional accusation case it
will be necessary for the police magistrate to hear expert evidence of the substantive
criminal law of that foreign state and make his own findings of fact about it.

c In conviction cases, too, if the foreign certificates or judicial documents stating the fact
of conviction issued in accordance with the procedure followed by that state do not recite
the facts on which the conviction was based but only give the name of the crime or the
article of the criminal code of the foreign state of which the fugitive criminal was
convicted, expert evidence of what under the law of that foreign state constitute the
kinds of conduct and state of mind of a person that make him guilty of that particular
d offence will be admissible before the magistrate in order to enable him to decide whether
that kind of conduct and state of mind would constitute in English law a crime described
in the list in the Extradition Acts 1870 to 1935 as amended.

The practice adopted at Bow Street in accusation cases since Re Arton (No 2) in 1896,
however, has not been to confine the calling of evidence of foreign law to exceptional
accusation cases only. So far as living memory stretches it appears to have been the
e invariable practice of the requisitioning foreign government in all accusation cases to call
expert evidence of its own criminal law in order to prove that what the fugitive criminal
is accused of having done, within the jurisdiction of its courts, is not only criminal under
its domestic law but is also a crime that is 'substantially similar' (or 'similar in concept')
to one or more of the English crimes of which descriptions are included in the 1870 list
or later lists as currently amended and reproduced in the English language version of the
f extradition treaty with that state.

This is the first time that this House has had occasion to examine the origin and
justification of this practice. Its origin would appear to be not so much what was said as
what was done in the two late nineteenth century cases of Re Bellencontre [1891] 2 QB 122
and Re Arton (No 2) [1896] 1 QB 509. Both were decisions of a Divisional Court in
proceedings to discharge an order nisi for habeas corpus and both were concerned with
g extradition to the French Republic pursuant to an extradition treaty entered into in 1876,
ie after the 1873 Act had made the additions to the list of extradition crimes in Sch 1 to
the 1870 Act, to which I have already drawn attention.

The curious feature of the judgments in each of these two cases is that in neither of
them was there any reference to the terms of those sections of the Acts which were the
sole source of the jurisdiction of the magistrate to make the committal order that was the
h subject of attack by habeas corpus. The extradition treaty embodied in the Order in
Council under s 2 of the 1870 Act which made the Acts applicable to France does not
appear to have incorporated any provisions rendering the operation of the Acts as respects
the surrender of fugitive criminals from France who were not of British nationality
subject to any limitations, restrictions, conditions, exceptions or qualifications additional
to those contained in the Acts themselves; and, so far as was relevant, the descriptions in
j the English language version of the treaty of the crimes for which the United Kingdom
undertook to surrender fugitive criminals to the French government were in the identical
words appearing in Sch 1 to the 1870 Act.

Following the lead given by the Solicitor General in his opening argument, as reported,
Cave and Wills JJ in Re Bellencontre, apparently without the benefit of any expert evidence
of French criminal law, confined their judgments to construing for themselves art 408
of the French Code Pénal which was cited in the French warrant for Bellencontre's arrest
as the French crime of which he was accused, and comparing the terms of this article

with s 76 of the Larcency Act 1861. They came to the conclusion that the conduct with
which Bellencontre was charged as having committed in France fell both within that   *a*
particular article of the Code Pénal and within that particular section of the English
statute. I have been unable to extract from either of the judgments any clear statement
of the reasons why it was thought that the 1870 and 1873 Acts made necessary this kind
of investigation of comparative French and English criminal law.

In *Re Arton (No 2),* following a similar lead that had been given in the argument, this
time by the Attorney General, a similar exercise in comparative French and English   *b*
criminal law was undertaken by Lord Russell CJ, but on this occasion the Divisional
Court was assisted by expert evidence of French law adduced before it on affidavit which,
however, had not been before the magistrate. This evidence was directed to the
correspondence between art 147 of the French Code Pénal, on the one hand, and s 83 of
the 1861 Act and s 1 of the Falsification of Accounts Act 1875, on the other. The expert
evidence of French criminal law showed that the conduct of which Arton was accused   *c*
was a crime against that article of the Code Pénal, that such crime fell within the
description of one item in the list of extraditable crimes in the French language version
of the treaty, and that, although it did not fall within the item bearing the same number
in the list, as it did in the English language version, it did fall within an item that bore
another number in the English language version. This the Divisional Court held to be
sufficient to justify Arton's committal for surrender under the 1870 and 1873 Acts.   *d*

There are two passages in the judgment of Lord Russell CJ in this case which appear to
be intended to express the principles on which the decision of the court was based. The
first is equivocal ([1896] 1 QB 509 at 513):

> 'The conditions of extradition, the fulfilment of which we have in this case to
> consider, are the following: (1.) the imputed crime must be within the treaty; (2.) it
> must be a crime against the law of the country demanding extradition; (3.) it must   *e*
> be a crime within the English Extradition Acts, 1870 and 1873; and (4.) there must
> be such evidence before the committing magistrate as would warrant him in
> sending the case for trial, if it were an ordinary case in this country.'

If by 'imputed crime' is meant the conduct which the fugitive criminal whose
surrender is sought is accused of having committed in the foreign state demanding   *f*
extradition, I have no quarrel with this as a statement of principle. But in the penultimate
paragraph of the judgment there is a further statement which also appears to be intended
as one of principle (at 517):

> 'The English and French texts of the treaty are not translations of one another.
> They are different versions, but versions which, on the whole, are in substantial
> agreement. We are here dealing with a crime alleged to have been committed   *g*
> against the law of France; and if we find, as I hold that we do, that such a crime is a
> crime against the law of both countries, and is, in substance, to be found in each
> version of the treaty, although under different heads, we are bound to give effect to
> the claim for extradition.'

This double comparison between the substantive criminal law of England and of the
foreign state and between the versions in the English and the foreign language versions   *h*
of the list of extraditable crimes in the treaty, which appears to have become an invariable
practice in all extradition cases since *Re Arton (No 2),* was first given the sobriquet of
'double criminality' by Griffiths J in *R v Governor of Pentonville Prison, ex p Budlong* [1980]
1 All ER 701, [1980] 1 WLR 1110. After discussion of the cases in which the practice had
been followed, Griffiths J summarised it thus ([1980] 1 All ER 701 at 712, [1980] 1 WLR
1110 at 1122–1123):   *j*

> '... double criminality in our law of extradition is satisfied if it is shown: (1) that
> the crime for which extradition is demanded would be recognised as substantially
> similar in both countries, and (2) that there is a prima facie case that the conduct of
> the accused amounted to the commission of the crime according to English law.'

My Lords, I can find no justification whatever in the 1870 Act for adducing at the
hearing before the magistrate, under ss 9 and 10, evidence of foreign law directed to

satisfying Griffiths J's proposition (1) in an accusation case in which the surrender of a
a fugitive criminal is requisitioned by the Danish government under the principal treaty
which, in contradistinction to the supplementary treaty, does not give rise to any
exceptional accusation cases.

The jurisdiction of the magistrate is derived exclusively from the statute. It arises
when a person who is accused of conduct in a foreign state which if he had committed it
in England would be one described in the 1870 list (as added to and amended by later
b Extradition Acts) has been apprehended and brought before the magistrate under a
warrant issued pursuant to an order made by the Secretary of State under s 7 or confirmed
by him under the last paragraph of s 8.

At the hearing, ss 9 and 10 require that the magistrate must first be satisfied that a
foreign warrant (within the definition in s 26 that I have already cited) has been issued
for the accused person's arrest and is duly authenticated in a manner for which s 15
c provides. Except where there is a claim that the arrest was for a political offence or the
case is an exceptional accusation case, the magistrate is not concerned with what provision
of foreign criminal law (if any) is stated in the warrant to be the offence which the person
was suspected of having committed and in respect of which his arrest was ordered in the
foreign state.

The magistrate must then hear such evidence, including evidence made admissible by
d ss 14 and 15, as may be produced on behalf of the requisitioning foreign government,
and by the accused if he wishes to do so; and at the conclusion of the evidence the
magistrate must decide whether such evidence would, *according to the law of England*,
justify the committal for trial of the accused for an offence that is described in the 1870
list (as added to or amended by subsequent Extradition Acts) provided that such offence
is also included in the extraditable crimes listed in the English language version of the
e extradition treaty. In making this decision it is English law alone that is relevant. The
requirement that he shall make it does not give him any jurisdiction to inquire into or
receive evidence of the substantive criminal law of the foreign state in which the conduct
was in fact committed.

Reliance was placed by Nielsen on the second paragraph of s 9, viz:

f 'The police magistrate shall receive any evidence which may be tendered to show
that the crime of which the prisoner is accused or alleged to have been convicted is
an offence of a political character or is not an extradition crime.'

If only English law were relevant to determining whether the conduct of the accused
amounted to an extradition crime this, it was argued, would not be a matter for evidence
whereas foreign law would. But the answer to this is that, under an extradition treaty in
such terms as give rise to what I have called exceptional accusation cases and in some at
g any rate of conviction cases, evidence of foreign law may be relevant to a decision
whether particular conduct constitutes an extradition crime, and for these kinds of cases
s 9 had to make provision. In an ordinary accusation case, such as arises on a requisition
by the Danish government for surrender of a fugitive criminal under the principal
treaty, s 3(2) of the Act supplies the safeguard for the person who is surrendered. It
h provides:

'A fugitive criminal shall not be surrendered to a foreign state unless provision is
made by the law of that state, or by arrangement, that the fugitive criminal shall
not, until he has been restored or had an opportunity of returning to Her Majesty's
dominions, be detained or tried in that foreign state for any offence committed
prior to his surrender other than the extradition crime proved by the facts on which
the surrender is grounded.'

j So it is the facts proved before the magistrate at the hearing of committal proceedings
against the fugitive criminal under ss 9 and 10, and not whatever section of the Danish
Criminal Code that may be referred to in the original Danish warrant for arrest, that
determine the only crime or crimes under Danish law for which the fugitive criminal
who has been surrendered can be tried in Denmark without being given an opportunity
of returning to the United Kingdom.

In my opinion, therefore, there being no claim that any political offence was involved

and no dispute as to the authenticity of the Danish warrant for Nielsen's arrest, the
magistrate in the instant case, which was not an exceptional accusation case, had no   *a*
jurisdiction to enter on any question of Danish criminal law. The evidence of Danish
law, adduced though it was on behalf of the Danish government in accordance with the
long prevailing practice, was irrelevant. It should not have been admitted by the
magistrate. I would therefore uphold the order of the Divisional Court setting aside the
magistrate's order for Nielsen's discharge and remitting the case to the magistrate to
continue hearing the as yet unfinished evidence which the Danish government wish to   *b*
produce.

LORD KEITH OF KINKEL. My Lords, I have had the benefit of reading in advance
the speech of my noble and learned friend Lord Diplock, and for the reasons he gives I
too would dismiss the appeal.

LORD ROSKILL. My Lords, I have had the advantage of reading in draft the speech   *c*
of my noble and learned friend Lord Diplock. I agree with it and for the reasons he gives
I would dismiss the appeal.

LORD BRIDGE OF HARWICH. My Lords, for the reasons given in the speech of
my noble and learned friend Lord Diplock, with which I agree, I would dismiss the
appeal.   *d*

LORD BRIGHTMAN. My Lords, I am in agreement with the speech of my noble
and learned friend Lord Diplock, and would dismiss the appeal.

Appeal dismissed.

Solicitors: *Memery Crystal & Co* (for the appellant); *Director of Public Prosecutions.*   *e*

Mary Rose Plummer   Barrister.

Di Palma v Victoria Square Property Co Ltd and others   *f*

CHANCERY DIVISION
SCOTT J
8, 9, 12, 21 DECEMBER 1983

Landlord and tenant – Forfeiture of lease – Arrears of rent – County court action – Relief against   *g*
forfeiture – Jurisdiction of High Court – Lessee 'barred from all relief' if lessee failing to pay
arrears of rent specified in possession order made by county court – Whether lessee merely barred
from seeking further relief in county court – Whether jurisdiction of High Court to grant relief
against forfeiture ousted – County Courts Act 1959, s 191(1)(c).

In August 1978, when the lessee of a flat failed to pay the service charge, the lessor
commenced proceedings in the county court against the lessee for arrears of service   *h*
charge and possession of the premises. The lease contained a provision in the usual form
giving the lessor the right to re-enter and forfeit the lease in the event of the tenant
failing to pay the rent or observe the covenants of the lease. On 9 February 1981 the
county court judge made a possession order requiring the lessee to pay arrears of rent
amounting to £299·36 to the registrar of the court by 7 April failing which the lessee
was to give up possession of the premises to the lessor. The lessee failed to pay the amount   *j*
stated in the order or take any other action despite a number of warnings, and on 29
March 1982 on the instructions of the lessor the lessee was evicted from the flat by
bailiffs. The lessee then issued an originating summons in the High Court seeking relief
against forfeiture. On the hearing of the summons the question arose whether the court
had jurisdiction to grant relief, since s 191(1)(c)[a] of the County Courts Act 1959 provided

---

a   Section 191(1), so far as material, is set out at p 95 *e f*, post

that if the lessee did not pay into court the arrears of rent and costs within the period
a specified in the possession order the order could be enforced in the prescribed manner
and 'the lessee shall be barred from all relief'. The lessor contended that s 191(1)(c) barred
all relief whatsoever including relief from forfeiture granted by the High Court. The
lessee contended that s 191(1)(c) merely meant that no further relief could be granted by
the county court and that the power of the High Court to grant relief was not excluded.

b **Held** – On the true construction of s 191(1)(c) of the 1959 Act the phrase 'be barred from
all relief' was, by necessary implication from the statutory predecessors of s 191(1)(c),
intended to bar all relief whatsoever, including the equitable jurisdiction of the High
Court to grant relief from forfeiture for non-payment of rent, whenever a possession
order had been made by a county court under s 191. It followed that the plaintiff's
summons would be dismissed (see p 104 *b* to p 1015 *a* and *d*, post).

c

Notes

For relief from forfeiture for non-payment of rent, see 27 Halsbury's Laws (4th edn) para
442, and for cases on the subject, see 31(2) Digest (Reissue) 827–832, 6863–6891.

For the County Courts Act 1959, s 191, see 7 Halsbury's Statutes (3rd edn) 417.

d **Cases referred to in judgment**

Howard v Fanshawe [1895] 2 Ch 581, [1895–9] All ER Rep 855.
IRC v Joiner [1975] 3 All ER 1050, [1975] 1 WLR 1701, HL.
Lovelock v Margo [1963] 2 All ER 13, [1963] 2 QB 786, [1963] 2 WLR 794, CA.
Newbolt v Bingham (1895) 72 LT 852, CA.
Sanders v Pope (1806) 12 Ves 282, 33 ER 108, LC.
e *Standard Pattern Co Ltd v Ivey* [1962] 1 All ER 452, [1962] Ch 432, [1962] 2 WLR 656.
Thatcher v C H Pearce & Sons (Contractors) Ltd [1968] 1 WLR 748.

Cases also cited

Anisminic Ltd v Foreign Compensation Commission [1969] 1 All ER 208, [1969] 2 AC 147,
f   HL.
Bowser v Colby (1841) 1 Hare 109, [1835–42] All ER Rep 478.
Cullen v Rogers [1982] 2 All ER 570, [1982] 1 WLR 729, HL.
Davis v West (1806) 12 Ves 476, 33 ER 180.
Farrell v Alexander [1976] 2 All ER 721, [1977] AC 59, HL.
Gill v Lewis [1956] 1 All ER 844, [1956] 2 QB 1, CA.
Hill v Barclay (1811) 18 Ves 56, 34 ER 238, LC.
g *Kingswood Estate Co Ltd v Anderson* [1962] 3 All ER 593, [1963] 2 QB 169, CA.
Pyx Granite Co Ltd v Ministry of Housing and Local Government [1959] 3 All ER 1, [1960]
    AC 260, HL.
R v Paddington Valuation Officer, ex p Peachey Property Corp Ltd [1965] 2 All ER 836,
    [1966] 1 QB 380, CA.
h *Wadman v Calcraft* (1804) 10 Ves 67, 32 ER 768.
Wolmer Securities Ltd v Corne [1966] 2 All ER 691, [1966] 2 QB 243, CA.

Originating summons

The plaintiff, Margarita di Palma, applied by originating summons dated 28 July 1982
for an order that she be granted relief against forfeiture in respect of the premises at 25
j Churchdale Court, Harvard Road, London W4. The defendants to the summons were
Victoria Square Property Co Ltd, Northumberland and Durham Property Trust Ltd and
Stoll Construction Ltd. The facts are set out in the judgment.

Anthony Speaight for the plaintiff.
Gerald Rabie for the defendants.

Cur adv vult

21 December. The following judgment was delivered.

SCOTT J. In this case the plaintiff, Margarita di Palma, seeks relief from forfeiture of a *a* lease. There are two issues; first, whether, on the merits, this is a case in which it would be right to grant relief; second, whether the court has jurisdiction to grant relief. I will relate the background to the plaintiff's claim and then return to these two issues.

The property in question is a flat, 25 Churchdale Court, Harvard Road, London W4. The lease in respect of which relief from forfeiture is sought was dated 2 July 1975. It *b* granted a 99-year term from 29 September 1974 and reserved an annual rent of £10 per annum together with a service charge.

Prior to the grant of this lease the plaintiff was occupying the flat as a tenant enjoying protection under the Rent Acts. She was thereby enabled to purchase the lease on very favourable terms. She told me that she had used her savings to provide the purchase price for the lease.

The lease was granted to her by Alliance Property Co Ltd, the then freeholder. A term *c* of 99 years was granted. Clause 2 of the lease contained, inter alia, covenants by the plaintiff to pay the rent and service charge. Clause 4(ii) of the lease contained a right for the lessor to re-enter and forfeit the lease in the event of failure by the tenant to pay rent or observe the tenant's covenants. This provision was in normal form.

Following on the grant of the lease there were disputes between the lessor and the *d* plaintiff regarding the amount of the service charge and the quality of certain external painting which had been carried out by the lessor and charged to the various tenants of Churchdale Court as part of the service charge.

At the end of 1977 or early 1978 the freehold passed from the original lessor, Alliance Property Co Ltd, to Victoria Square Property Co Ltd, the first defendant, which was registered as proprietor of the freehold title on 6 January 1978. Victoria Square Property *e* Co Ltd inherited the dispute between the plaintiff and the original lessor regarding the service charge. I am not concerned with the merits of this dispute or whether the plaintiff's complaints were justified. It is accepted for the purposes of this case that the plaintiff believed her complaints to be justified.

On account of these complaints she withheld payment of the service charge due under the terms of the lease. Accordingly, on 31 August 1978 the first defendant commenced *f* proceedings against the plaintiff in the Brentford County Court. By the particulars of claim, the first defendant claimed a sum on account of arrears of service charge and possession of the premises. The claim to possession was an assertion of the right of re-entry contained in cl 4 of the lease. However, it has been the law for very many years that such a claim for possession in the county court could be met by payment of what was due. I shall return later to examine in more detail the relevant legislation. For the *g* moment it is appropriate to observe that the real dispute between the first defendant as plaintiff and the plaintiff, Miss di Palma, as defendant in the Brentford County Court concerned her liability to pay the service charge that had been demanded and concerned the amount of the service charge that could be justified against her by the lessors.

The county court proceedings pursued at first a distinctly desultory course. The plaintiff put in a home-made handwritten defence challenging the service charge. She *h* made later certain payments on account. In due course the issue of what was due in respect of service charge was referred to the county court registrar. The registrar held a hearing and on 3 July 1980 determined the amount of the service charge still owed by the plaintiff at £299·36. The case then came on for hearing in the county court and on 9 February 1981 his Honour Judge Main QC made an order that the plaintiff pay the sum of £299·36 on or before 7 April 1981. The order was in the Form 136 used in county *j* courts for cases where landlords claim possession for non-payment of rent. It provided as follows:

'IT IS ADJUDGED that [the first defendant] is entitled to recover against [the plaintiff] possession of the land mentioned in the particulars annexed to the summons in this action, that is to say 25 Churchdale Court, Harvard Road, London, W.4, the rent of the said land amounting to £299·36, being in arrear, and [the first defendant] having a right of re-entry or forfeiture in respect thereof; AND IT IS ADJUDGED that a [the first defendant] do recover against [the plaintiff] the sum of £299·36 for the arrears of rent aforesaid; and it is further ordered that [the plaintiff] do pay [the first defendant's] costs on and after 20th March 1979, to be taxed on Scale II.'

The order goes on:

b 'AND IT IS ORDERED that [the plaintiff] shall pay the said sum of £299·36 to the registrar of this court on or before 7th April 1981. AND IT IS FURTHER ORDERED that unless payment of the said sum is made by the said date, [the plaintiff] shall thereupon give possession of the land to [the first defendant]. Dated 9th February 1981.'

I should at this point refer to s 191(1) of the County Courts Act 1959. That subsection reads:

c 'Where a lessor is proceeding by action in a county court (being an action in which a county court has jurisdiction), to enforce against a lessee a right of re-entry or forfeiture in respect of any land for non-payment of rent, the following provisions shall have effect:—(a) If the lessee pays into court not less than five clear days before the return day all the rent in arrear and the costs of the action, the action shall cease, and the lessee shall hold the land according to the lease without any new lease [I interpose to observe that that did not happen in this case.] (b) If the action does not d cease as aforesaid and the court at the trial is satisfied that the lessor is entitled to enforce the right of re-entry or forfeiture, the court shall order possession of the land to be given to the lessor at the expiration of such period, not being less than four weeks from the date of the order, as the court thinks fit, unless within that period the lessee pays into court all the rent in arrear and the costs of the action . . .'

e The order made by Judge Main on 9 February 1981 followed the requirements of that statutory provision. Section 191(1) continues:

'(c) if within the period specified in the order, the lessee pays into court all the rent in arrear and the costs of the action, he shall hold the land according to the lease without any new lease, but if the lessee does not, within the said period, pay into court all the rent in arrear and the costs of the action, the order shall be enforced in f the prescribed manner, and so long as the order remains unreversed the lessee shall be barred from all relief . . .'

There then follows a proviso that I need not read.

Accordingly, para (c) enables the tenant by payment of the requisite sum before the expiry of the specified period to avoid giving up possession; but in lieu of such payment g within the specified period, possession is required to be given according to the order. Form 136 reflects this statutory provision.

The effect of failure by a tenant to pay the requisite sum by the date specified in a Form 136 order has been mitigated by s 23 of the Administration of Justice Act 1965, which gave power to the county court to extend the period for payment. Subsection (1) is in these terms:

h 'Where a lessor is proceeding by action in a county court in England or Wales to enforce against the lessee a right of re-entry or forfeiture in respect of any land for non-payment of rent, and the court by order made in pursuance of section 191(1)(b) of the County Courts Act 1959 orders possession of the land to be given to the lessor at the expiration of a period fixed by the court unless within that period the lessee pays into court all the rent in arrear and the costs of the action, the court may extend j that period at any time before possession of the land is recovered in pursuance of the order.'

Accordingly, until the lessor has recovered possession under the court order the tenant retains the right to ask for an extension of time for payment and by payment to avoid forfeiture of the lease.

At the hearing before Judge Main, the plaintiff appeared in person. There was evidence that at some stage in 1980 she had consulted a solicitor, but she was not represented when

Judge Main made his order. The order of 9 February 1981 was duly served on the
plaintiff. I am satisfied that she read it. She is literate and capable of understanding it. *a*
Unfortunately she does not seem to have been able to have brought herself to believe it.
Acting in person, she drew up and served a notice of appeal against Judge Main's order.
She was, in the notice of appeal, still disputing her obligation to pay the amount in
respect of service charge that she had been adjudged liable to pay. In the summer of 1981
she once more sought advice from a solicitor, a different solicitor from the solicitor that
she had consulted in 1980. I infer that she placed the order of 9 February 1981 before the *b*
solicitor whom she instructed. She seems not to have placed any more value on this
solicitor's advice and services than she had placed on the advice and services she had
received in 1980, for she was very soon once more acting in person.

In November 1981 occurred an important incident as to which there has been a good
deal of evidence and some dispute of detail. It is common ground that the plaintiff
attended on a date in November at the offices of the Brentford County Court. It is *c*
common ground that she was there handed a document purporting to be an order dated
9 February 1981 ordering her to pay £299·36 to the first defendant by 23 February 1981.
This order is in Form 133, the form used in county courts for simple money judgments.
It is inappropriate and not used for a case in which possession for non-payment of rent is
to be ordered. This is obvious, for the order contains no reference whatever to possession.

The plaintiff says that she went to the county court offices because she was not sure *d*
what current order was in force against her, that she asked to be supplied with the latest
order made against her, that she received the document I have referred to and that she
consequently assumed that there was not a current possession order against her. I should
read the operative parts of this document:

> 'It is adjudged that [the first defendant] do recover against [the plaintiff] the sum
> of £299·36 for debt and his costs of this action to be taxed on Scale II as from 20th *e*
> March 1979, and it is ordered that [the plaintiff] do pay the sum of £299·36 to the
> Registrar of this Court on 23rd February 1981 and do pay the amount of the said
> costs when taxed to the Registrar of this Court three days after taxation.'

There then follows a provision regarding default in payment that I need not trouble
with.   *f*

This document is dated 9 February 1981. The person in the county court offices who
dealt with the plaintiff gave evidence. He was a Mr Withers, an executive officer at the
Brentford County Court. He told me that when first asked about the incident he could
not recall the details, but that when he realised that the plaintiff was the person involved
his recollection was prompted. He said he remembered her, remembered dealing with
her query and remembered the conversation he had had with her. He said her query was *g*
as to the full amount of the monetary order made against her. He said he had no doubt
she knew a possession order had been made because he had advised her to apply for a stay
of execution. He said she had asked him for a written record of the money judgment
part of the order of 9 February 1981, and he had therefore inserted those details into an
order in the Form 133 applicable to money judgments.

I do not think that in the end much, if anything, turns on this conflict, but I must *h*
make clear how I find the incident and my view of the two witnesses who testified about
it. Mr Withers was a reliable witness, although I was not wholly satisfied that his
recollection of the incident was quite as clear as he believed it to be. I base this slight
reservation about his recollection on two matters. First, I am satisfied after an inspection
of the various copies of the Form 133 document that the original document handed to
the plaintiff bore an official Brentford County Court stamp over the space provided for a *j*
seal on the form. There is to my mind no other credible explanation for the appearance
of that stamp on some of the copies. But Mr Withers had no recollection of how the
stamp had been placed on the document and testified, incorrectly as I think, that when
he handed the document to the plaintiff it bore no stamp. Second, the document handed
to the plaintiff contained an error on its face. The date for payment of the judgment debt
of £299·36 was given as 23 February 1981 instead of 7 April 1981. This mistake suggests
that Mr Withers dealt with the plaintiff in some haste. He could not have made this error

if he had carefully read the master card which he testified was the source of his
information about the order made. However, despite these reservations, I accept Mr
Withers's evidence as to the broad outline of what took place and what was said during
the plaintiff's visit to the county court offices in November 1981. I do not, however,
accept his conclusion from it that the plaintiff 'knew a possession order was in force'.

Having seen and heard the plaintiff in the witness box, I conclude that she is a person
who cannot, where difficult decisions are to be made and difficult situations are to be
faced, bring herself to accept reality. I think she regarded the dispute between herself
and her landlords as being a dispute about money. She regarded references to possession
in the particulars of claim and in the eventual court order, and, indeed, in the two letters
later sent to her by Mr Samson of the first defendant's solicitors, as being merely threats
to induce her to pay the sum the first defendants wanted her to pay. She did not believe
an order for possession could be made against her and used to evict her, and she continued
in this wholly unreasonable belief even after the order of 9 February 1981 had been
made. She indicated in the witness box that she still does not regard the possession order
as having provided lawful justification for her eviction. She has not, since at least
February 1981, been willing to face the fact that failure to pay the lessors what she owed
by the date fixed for such payment risked eviction and the loss of her flat. In the witness
box, when asked a question which she found difficult, her answers simply avoided the
question. In these circumstances, while I acquit her of any conscious intention to mislead
or evade, I find myself unable to place any reliance on her accurate recollection of past
events.

Accordingly, as I have said, I accept Mr Withers's broad outline of what took place at
the county court offices in November 1981. She was on that occasion given by Mr
Withers a document, the Form 133 order, which was on its face inaccurate in detail and
misleading as a résumé of what had been in fact ordered on 9 February 1981. It was an
error for Mr Withers to have given her such a document, an error which he frankly
acknowledged in the witness box. The effect of the plaintiff receiving this erroneous
order was, I think, to reinforce her unreasonable and self-induced belief that she was not
at risk of being deprived of possession of her flat.

Following the November 1981 incident, the plaintiff consulted yet another firm of
solicitors, Messrs Parmenter & Co. To these solicitors she took, no doubt with other
documents, both the original and the incorrect orders of 9 February 1981. She then, on
3 February 1982, withdrew her appeal against Judge Main's order. It is a fair inference
that she did so in consequence of advice that she had received from Parmenter & Co.

At this stage, therefore, there was a final order, not subject to appeal, for her to pay the
£299·36 and taxed costs by 7 April 1981, a date long passed, failing which the first
defendants were entitled to possession of the flat. The amount in question, £299·36, was
no longer in dispute. Her appeal had been withdrawn. Yet she did not pay it. Nor did
she seek any extension of time for such payment so that the threat of loss of her flat
might be averted.

The lessors had been quiescent for some time. They had taken no step to enforce their
judgment of 9 February 1981. But, once the appeal had been withdrawn, they naturally
endeavoured to recover the money owing to them. On 1 February 1982 Mr Samson,
solicitor to the first defendant, wrote to the plaintiff in these terms:

'As you have now withdrawn your appeal the amount of the judgment should be
paid forthwith, as failing this I shall have to proceed with the forfeiture of the lease.
I am also instructed to point out that there are estimated service charges for the half
years ended respectively 30th September 1981 and 31st March 1982 totalling £185,
which also has to be paid. Will you kindly deal with this matter immediately to
avoid further action.'

If ever a letter should have sounded a warning bell, this was such a letter. The plaintiff
did not need to go back to the county court and seek from it an extension of time to pay.
The first defendants were by this letter offering her such an extension. What did she do?
Virtually nothing. She told me that she made two telephone calls to her solicitors,
Parmenter & Co, but that the line was engaged on both occasions. So she did nothing.

She told me she had 'flu. There was shown to me a medical statement suggesting that she had suffered for some time from ill-health. I do not find that *any* of this explains her astonishing inaction. But there it is; she did nothing. Mr Samson then wrote a further letter on 24 February 1982, three weeks later, as follows:

> 'Not having heard from you with reference to my letter of the 1st instant, I have to inform you that unless this matter is dealt with forthwith I intend instructing the bailiffs to take possession of the above premises.

Again the plaintiff did nothing save, she said, to make two further unsuccessful attempts to communicate by telephone with her solicitors. She did not reply to Mr Samson. She did not pay what she owed. She did nothing. Yet she stood to lose a valuable flat worth many thousands of pounds. Her inaction is to my mind incomprehensible and is to be explained, if that is the right verb, by her inability to bring herself to face up to her difficulties and recognise the reality of the situation confronting her.

Notwithstanding the terms of the letter of 24 February, the first defendant did not send in the bailiffs until over a month later. On 26 March 1982 a notice from the bailiffs was received by the plaintiff. It indicated that they would be taking possession on 29 March 1982. On that day the bailiffs attended, the plaintiff was evicted in execution of the order of Judge Main made on 9 February 1981 and the first defendants resumed possession of the flat. The plaintiff has since remained and remains out of occupation. She has continued to pay rates, and as I understand it some of her furniture is still in the flat. In view of the litigation which followed the eviction and which has culminated in this hearing, the lessors have not put anyone else into occupation or sought to relet.

I can recite quite quickly the remaining material events. When the bailiffs arrived on 29 March the plaintiff offered then and there to pay the £299·36. The bailiffs had no authority to accept that offer and did not do so. On 1 April 1982 she paid into court £314·26. That sum comprised the judgment debt and £15 in respect of the bailiffs' costs. That sum has been taken out of court by the first defendants in satisfaction of the judgment debt and those costs. The costs of the proceedings before Judge Main have still not been taxed.

Also on 1 April 1982, the plaintiff, acting in person, applied to the county court to re-enter her flat. That application was heard on 5 April 1982 by his Honour Judge Barr and dismissed. The plaintiff then instructed her present solicitors. These solicitors did two things. First, on 14 May 1982 they entered an appeal against Judge Barr's dismissal of the plaintiff's application for leave to re-enter the flat. That appeal is still pending. Second, on 18 May 1982 they made an application in the Brentford County Court for relief from forfeiture. That application was heard by his Honour Judge Main on 14 June 1982. I have been shown an approved note of the judgment of the judge. He dismissed the application on the ground that he had no jurisdiction to grant such relief. He expressed the view that if he had had jurisdiction he would have been inclined to exercise it in favour of the plaintiff.

On 23 June 1982 notice of appeal against that decision of Judge Main was served on behalf of the plaintiff and is still pending.

And, finally, on 28 July 1982 the originating summons which is now before me and by which the plaintiff seeks from the High Court relief from forfeiture was issued. In the meantime, Churchdale Court has changed hands and the registration of the leasehold title to the flat at Her Majesty's Land Registry has been closed. On 4 February 1983 the first defendants applied to close the said leasehold title. On 15 February 1983 the second defendants contracted at auction to purchase Churchdale Court (including no 25). I need not trouble with the detail, but, in effect, the second defendants contracted to purchase subject, inter alia, to whatever rights in no 25 the plaintiff might still have. On 15 March 1983 the plaintiff's leasehold title was closed. Also on 15 March the second defendants completed their purchase and agreed to sell Churchdale Court to the third defendants on terms, inter alia, that the third defendants would grant a lease back to the second defendants of no 25 on the same terms as those contained in the plaintiff's lease. In effect the third defendant was agreeing to take the property subject to and with the benefit of either the plaintiff's lease, if she should succeed in her litigation, or an identical lease to

be held by the second defendant if the plaintiff should fail. This litigation is, therefore,
a of commercial consequence only to the second defendant and, of course, to the plaintiff.
The contract between the second defendant and the third defendant was completed on
15 April 1983. The registered proprietor remains the first defendant, but an application
to Her Majesty's Land Registry for the registration of the third defendant as proprietor
of the freehold has been made.

Questions as to the effect of this conveyancing history on the plaintiff's rights were, at
b one time, raised, but the position before me is that the defendants, who all appear by Mr
Rabie, very properly accept that if the plaintiff is entitled to relief from forfeiture, she is
so entitled against each and every one of them. It follows that if she is so entitled the
defendants accept that the register must be rectified so as to revive her leasehold title.

I now come to the two issues in the case. I propose to deal first with the merits.
Assuming that I have power to grant the plaintiff relief from forfeiture, would it be
c right, on the facts of this case, that I should do so? In my opinion, it would.

It has been many times stated, and is well settled, that the purpose of including in a
lease a right of re-entry for failure by the tenant to pay rent is to secure the payment of
the rent. In *Sanders v Pope* (1806) 12 Ves 282 at 289, 33 ER 108 at 110 Lord Erskine LC
expressed the point thus:

d
> 'The obvious intention is to secure the payment of the rent; that the landlord may
> not be put to his action of debt, coming from time to time against an insolvent
> estate; but may be enabled to recover possession of the premises.'

In *Howard v Fanshawe* [1895] 2 Ch 581 at 588, [1895–9] All ER Rep 855 at 859 Stirling J
made the same point. He said:

e
> 'These authorities appear to me to establish that the ground on which Courts of
> Equity formerly gave relief was that the proviso for re-entry was in the eye of the
> Court simply a security for the rent; and, on principle, I cannot see that it makes
> any difference whether the lessor avails himself of such security with or without the
> assistance of a court of law.'

This passage was cited with approval by Simon P in *Thatcher v C H Pearce & Sons*
f *(Contractors) Ltd* [1968] 1 WLR 748 at 754.

I start, therefore, with this: the lessor's right of re-entry was intended to provide
security for payment by the lessee, the plaintiff, of rent and service charge due under the
lease. She has, albeit very belatedly, paid the outstanding rent and service charge. She
paid into court the requisite sum on 1 April 1982 and it has been taken out by the lessor
entitled thereto. So the proviso for re-entry has served the purpose for which it was
g invoked. Why, in these circumstances, should it be right that the lessee, the plaintiff,
should lose her lease worth many thousands of pounds?

There are two possible cumulative reasons put forward by counsel for the defendants
why this question should be answered in a sense adverse to the grant of relief.

First, he invites me to notice the conduct of the plaintiff. As to this, I think the epithets
he used to describe her conduct were broadly justified. I think that in the period between
h Judge Main's order of 9 February 1981 and the execution of the order for possession by
the bailiffs on 29 March 1982 she exhibited by any objective standard a reckless and
astonishing disregard for her own interests. I would doubt whether in fact she had any
clear understanding of the risk she was incurring by her failure either to pay the
judgment debt or to obtain an extension of the time for payment. It is said on her behalf
that she was misled by the substitute and erroneous order that she was handed by Mr
j Withers in November 1981 into believing that there was no order for possession that
could be enforced against her. But that particular belief seems to have been present
before the November 1981 incident and to have survived to this day notwithstanding
the advice she has no doubt received from her present solicitors and counsel. I think that
during the period I have mentioned she just shut her eyes to that which she did not wish
to be true.

But I cannot conclude that this behaviour should disentitle her to relief. The landlords
have received all the rent and service charge due to them. They can be compensated for

any additional expense to which they have been put by her behaviour. What factor in
the history of the case can justify a result by which, in addition, they recover and she _a_
loses an asset worth, on her view, £30,000 and on any view many thousands of pounds?
I need not labour this point, since it was, as I understood it, conceded by counsel for the
defendants that had the case been one in which the landlords had obtained their order
for possession in the High Court and recovered possession under that High Court order,
the plaintiff's present application for relief from forfeiture would have been entitled to
succeed. _b_

Counsel's second reason, which he adds to his points based on the plaintiff's conduct,
is based on s 191(1) of the 1959 Act, as amended by s 23(1) of the 1965 Act. Both those
statutory provisions I have read. There is set out in s 191(1) of the 1959 Act, as amended,
a statutory scheme which a lessee faced with a claim for forfeiture of his lease for non-
payment of rent can use. This scheme was available to be used by the plaintiff. She failed
to use it. If the High Court has jurisdiction, submitted counsel, it should exercise such _c_
jurisdiction in cases where the applicant has failed to use the statutory county court
procedure only in exceptional circumstances. I am not satisfied that this is the right
approach. Failure to avert the forfeiture by means of the statutory scheme would be a
factor to be taken into account. But it seems to me to be no more than a factor, to be
weighed up with the other factors in the case, among which, in particular, are the relative
positions of lessor and lessee. _d_

In the present case the lessor, the first defendant, has obtained payment of what was
due. The first defendant has sold the property to the second defendant, who purchased
with full knowledge of the dispute and expressly subject to the plaintiff's rights in the
legal proceedings that were pending. The third defendant's position is not affected in
substance one way or the other whether the forfeiture stands or whether relief is granted.
The plaintiff, on the other hand, stands to lose a very valuable asset. I regard such a loss _e_
as a wholly disproportionate penalty for her to suffer for her delayed payment of the
judgment debt and, in effect, for her inability to take reasonable steps to protect and
preserve her asset.

My opinion that this is a case in which it would be right to grant relief from forfeiture
is fortified by authority. In _Sanders v Pope_, to which I have already referred, and following
the passage I have already cited, Lord Erskine LC continued (12 Ves 282 at 289, 33 ER _f_
108 at 110):

'. . . equity is in the constant course of relieving the tenant, paying the rent and
all expences, and placing his landlord in exactly the same situation: and in that case
it is not necessary, that the failure in paying the rent should arise from accident, the
miscarriage of a letter with a remittance, insolvency or disease: but even against
negligence, the tenant being solvent, and not prevented by any accidental _g_
circumstance, equity interferes; and upon payment of the rent and all expenses will
not permit the tenant to be turned out of possession; considering, that in the one
case frequently great hardship might be the consequence; in the other, the party
being placed in the same situation, there is in general no hardship.'

In _Newbolt v Bingham_ (1895) 72 LT 852 at 854 Rigby LJ said this: _h_

'It was the settled practice of a court of equity to grant relief against forfeiture for
non-payment of rent on payment of all rent in arrear and costs. Of course, the court
was not absolutely bound by its practice where it would not do justice, and if some
new interest had been created before the application, the court would refuse to
interfere. That was not done to put the landlord in a better position, but because the
rights of third parties had intervened. I know of no case where a court of equity has _j_
refused relief because actions had had to be brought on previous occasions to recover
the rent.'

In the present case it is accepted that the second and third defendants acquired their
respective interests with notice of the plaintiff's claim for relief. There are here no third
party rights of the sort contemplated by Rigby LJ.

In _Thatcher v C H Pearce & Sons (Contractors) Ltd_ the question at issue was whether in a
case of peaceable re-entry by the landlord the tenant's application for relief from forfeiture

had necessarily to be brought within six months of the date of re-entry; a strict analogy
was sought to be drawn with the case where the landlord has re-entered under a High
Court order, in which case, under the Common Law Procedure Act 1852, the application
for relief is required to be brought within six months of the re-entry. Simon P said
([1968] 1 WLR 748 at 756):

> 'I think that a court of equity (and it is such jurisdiction that I am exercising now)
> would look at the situation of the plaintiff to see whether in all the circumstances he
> acted with reasonable promptitude. Naturally it would also have to look at the
> situation of the defendants to see if anything has happened, particularly by way of
> delay on the part of the plaintiff, which would cause a greater hardship to them by
> the extension of the relief sought than by its denial to the plaintiff.'

In the present case the plaintiff has brought her application for relief with reasonable
promptitude after her ejectment. The balance of hardship referred to by Simon P comes
down firmly, in my view, on the side of the plaintiff. Accordingly, if I have power to
grant her relief from forfeiture I would do so.

The second and, therefore, critical issue is whether on the facts of this case I, as a judge
of the High Court, have such power. Counsel for the defendants submits that I do not,
and he bases his submission on the wording of s 191(1)(c) of the 1959 Act. I will read this
crucial provision again:

> 'if within the period specified in the order, the lessee pays into court all the rent
> in arrear and the costs of the action, he shall hold the land according to the lease
> without any new lease, but if the lessee does not, within the said period, pay into
> court all the rent in arrear and the costs of the action, the order shall be enforced in
> the prescribed manner, and so long as the order remains unreversed the lessee shall
> be barred from all relief . . .'

'All relief', counsel submits, means what it says. It includes in its natural language
relief from forfeiture granted by the High Court. The statutory language on which
counsel relies is, I readily accept, capable of bearing the meaning for which he contends.
The consequences of such a construction are, however, stark. Section 191(1) provides a
scheme whereby a tenant may escape a forfeiture for non-payment of rent by payment
of the sum due in accordance with the provisions of the subsection. The statutory
provisions allow for no element of discretion in the county court judge. He cannot, as a
matter of discretion, withhold relief if the outstanding rent and costs are duly paid. He
cannot, under this subsection, relieve the tenant who fails to pay by the specified date.
The full rigour of this provision was mitigated, as I have said, by s 23(1) of the 1965 Act,
which gives the county court discretion to extend the period for payment 'at any time
before possession of the land is recovered in pursuance of the order'. However, there is
no discretion to extend the period or provide relief from forfeiture once possession under
the order has been obtained.

Section 191(3) deals with the case where the landlord has peaceably re-entered. Here,
the county court judge is given all the powers of the High Court to grant relief from
forfeiture provided the application for relief is made within six months from the date of
re-entry. As may be seen from *Thatcher v C H Pearce & Sons (Contractors) Ltd*, the power
of the High Court to grant relief in such a case is not so limited. Accordingly, there
might well be a case falling within the county court jurisdiction where peaceable re-
entry has been taken by the landlord and the tenant is out of time for making a claim for
relief under s 191(3) of the 1959 Act. In such a case the High Court would nevertheless
have power to grant relief from forfeiture.

How, then, should I approach the words 'barred from all relief' in s 191(1)(c)? Do these
words simply make clear that no further relief can be granted by the county court but
leaving the tenant still able to apply for relief to the High Court, as can be done in a case
falling under sub-s (3)? Or do the words, as counsel for the defendants contends, exclude
also the power of the High Court to grant relief?

My instinctive inclination is to read these words, if I can, as leaving intact the High
Court jurisdiction and as applying only to the powers of the county court. That this

would be the right approach to construction of the statutory provision is supported by authority. The principle is shortly expressed in 44 Halsbury's Laws (4th edn) para 907:   *a*

> 'Unless they do so by express words or necessary implication, statutes should not be construed so as to take away the jurisdiction of superior courts . . .'

The cases cited in the footnote amply support that well-known principle, 'Express words or necessary implication'. The High Court jurisdiction is not taken away by any express words in s 191(1)(c). There is no express mention of the High Court powers. Is   *b* the jurisdiction taken away by necessary implication?

The 1959 Act is expressed to be 'An Act to consolidate, with corrections and improvements' the previous enactments relating to county courts.

In *IRC v Joiner* [1975] 3 All ER 1050, [1975] 1 WLR 1701 the House of Lords gave guidance as to the proper approach to construction of a consolidating Act. Lord Diplock said ([1975] 3 All ER 1050 at 1059–1060, [1975] 1 WLR 1701 at 1711):   *c*

> 'So the primary rule of construction of a consolidation Act is to examine the actual language used in the Act itself without reference to any of the statutes which it has repealed. If this examination leads to the conclusion that, when read in the context of other provisions of the Act, the language in which a general description of some factual situation is expressed is more apt to include than to exclude the particular factual situation found to exist in the case of a decision or vice versa, the duty of the   *d* court is to ascribe to that language the more apt meaning and to give effect to it accordingly. It is only where such an examination of the actual language of the general description has led to the conclusion that it is no more apt to include than to exclude the particular factual situation, that it is permissible for a court of construction to have recourse to the repealed legislation in order to see if its meaning was clearer, and, if it was, to ascribe to the corresponding provision of the   *e* consolidation Act a meaning which would not involve an alteration in the previous law.'

After reading s 191(1)(c) of the 1959 Act I am left uncertain whether it was or was not intended to exclude High Court jurisdiction. In my view I am therefore entitled, and ought, to have recourse to the statutory predecessors of sub-s (1)(c) to see if the meaning   *f* of the phrase becomes clearer.

County courts are creatures of statute and have the powers bestowed on them by statute. The first relevant empowering Act for me to notice is 9 & 10 Vict c 95 entitled 'An Act for the more Easy Recovery of Small Debts and Demands in *England*'. This statute was enacted in 1846. Section 58 expressly provided that the county courts established under the Act should have no jurisdiction in ejectment. At that time actions in ejectment were required to be brought in the courts of common law; applications for   *g* relief from forfeiture were required to be made in the courts of Chancery, and, where necessary, injunctions were issued by the Chancery courts to restrain ejectment proceedings in the common law courts.

Section 122 of the 1846 Act did, however, give the county court jurisdiction to entertain claims for possession of certain premises where a tenancy had determined by   *h* effluxion of time or by notice to quit. At this stage, therefore, county courts could not entertain actions for possession for non-payment of rent.

In 1856 the County Courts Acts (Amendment) Act was enacted. Section 50 reproduced s 122 of the 1846 Act. Section 52 gave the county court for the first time a jurisdiction to deal with claims by lessors for possession on the ground of non-payment of six months' rent. Its provisions are, broadly, comparable with the provisions of s 191(1) of the 1959   *j* Act. It enabled the tenant to defeat the claim for possession by payment of the rent in arrear into court within a specified time before the return day of the summons. It empowered the county court to order possession to be given to the lessor unless within a specified period not being less than four weeks the tenant paid into court the rent in arrear and costs. And it provided as follows:

> '. . . and if such Order be not obeyed and such Rent and Costs be not so paid, the Registrar shall . . . issue a Warrant authorizing and requiring the High Bailiff of the

a
Court to give Possession of such Premises to the Plaintiff, and the Plaintiff shall from the Time of Execution of such Warrant hold the Premises discharged of the Tenancy, and the Defendant, and all Persons claiming by, through, or under him, shall so long as the Order of the Court remains unreversed, be barred from all Relief in Equity or otherwise.'

This is the statutory predecessor of s 191(1)(c) of the 1959 Act.

b
The 1856 Act gave no general jurisdiction in equity to county courts. That jurisdiction was not given to the county courts until 1865. In 1856 the reference to the tenant being 'barred from all Relief in Equity' could not refer to any county court power. It must, in my judgment, by necessary implication have referred to the power of the Chancery courts, administering equity, to grant relief from forfeiture for non-payment of rent. In my judgment, that statutory provision did bar the jurisdiction of the Chancery courts to grant relief from forfeiture in cases which fell within that section.

c
It is relevant to note in this review of the relevant legislation that ss 210, 211 and 212 of the Common Law Procedure Act 1852 regulated the procedure regarding ejectment actions for non-payment of rent where the rent was at least six months in arrear. These sections restricted the tenant's right to apply for relief from forfeiture to a period of six months after possession had been recovered pursuant to a court order. The six-month limitation period had no application where possession was peaceably recovered (see

d
Howard v Fanshawe [1895] 2 Ch 581, [1895–9] All ER Rep 855 and *Lovelock v Margo* [1963] 2 All ER 13, [1963] 2 QB 786) nor where possession had been taken under a court order based on non-payment of rent for less than six months (see *Standard Pattern Co Ltd v Ivey* [1962] 1 All ER 452, [1962] Ch 432). In such cases the inherent jurisdiction of the court to grant relief from forfeiture remained, albeit that in its exercise the six-month period prescribed under the Common Law Procedure Act 1852 would be taken as a

e
guide (cf *Thatcher v C H Pearce & Sons (Contractors) Ltd* [1968] 1 WLR 748).

In 1860, by s 1 of 23 & 24 Vict c 126 entitled 'An Act for the further Amendment of the Process, Practice, and Mode of Pleading in and enlarging the Jurisdiction of the Superior Courts of Common Law at *Westminster*', the power to grant relief in equity from forfeiture for non-payment of rent was vested in a common law court before which ejectment proceedings based on the non-payment were being brought. A claim for relief

f
where re-entry had been peaceable and no ejectment proceedings had been brought still had to be sought from the Chancery courts.

The courts of law and equity were fused by the Supreme Court of Judicature Act 1873. Thereafter the jurisdiction of the Chancery courts to grant relief from forfeiture was exercisable by the High Court.

In the mean time, s 1 of the County Courts Equitable Jurisdiction Act 1865 had granted

g
to the county courts for the first time specified equitable jurisdiction. This section was the predecessor of s 52 of the County Courts Act 1959. The section did not, however, confer on the county courts any equitable jurisdiction to grant relief from forfeiture.

The county court enactments were consolidated by the County Courts Act 1888. Section 67 conferred on county courts the jurisdiction in equity provided by the 1865 Act. Sections 56 and 59 conferred on the county courts a limited jurisdiction in ejectment.

h
Section 138 of the 1888 Act conferred on the county courts jurisdiction to entertain claims for possession by a lessor where the term of the lease had expired by effluxion of time or notice to quit. And s 139 conferred jurisdiction on the county courts to entertain claims for possession by a lessor on the ground of non-payment of rent. The scheme contained in s 139 was the same as the scheme contained in s 52 of the 1856 Act. Section 139 concluded thus:

j
'. . . and if such order be not obeyed and such rent and costs are not so paid, the registrar shall . . . at the instance of the plaintiff, issue a warrant authorising and requiring the bailiff of the court to give possession of such premises to the plaintiff, and the plaintiff shall, from the time of execution of such warrant, hold the premises discharged of the tenancy, and the defendant and all persons claiming by, through, or under him shall, so long as the order of the court remains unreversed, be barred from all relief.'

The difference between that provision and the corresponding provision in the 1856 Act is confined to the difference between the phrase 'be barred from all relief in equity' and the phrase 'be barred from all relief'.

I have already held that the comparable phrase in the 1856 Act, 'be barred from all relief in equity', excluded by necessary implication the jurisdiction of the Chancery courts. The 1888 Act was enacted after the fusion of law and equity and after the creation of the High Court. The 1888 Act conferred no equitable jurisdiction on county courts to grant relief from forfeiture. Construed against that background, the phrase in s 139, 'be barred from all relief', must, in my judgment, by necessary implication, have been intended, in cases falling within the section, to bar the equitable jurisdiction of the High Court to grant relief from forfeiture for non-payment of rent.

The 1888 Act was replaced by the County Courts Act 1934, which in turn was replaced by the County Courts Act 1959. Section 180 of the 1934 Act replaced s 139 of the 1888 Act and was in its turn replaced by s 191(1)(c) of the 1959 Act. Both these successive sections incorporate the same statutory phrase '. . . be barred from all relief'.

Accordingly, in my judgment, the phrase in s 191(1)(c) has the same effect as its predecessor in s 139 of the 1888 Act in a case falling within the subsection, namely that the jurisdiction of the High Court to grant relief in equity from forfeiture for non-payment of rent is ousted.

By s 52(3) of the 1934 Act, the county courts were, inter alia, given the jurisdiction provided by s 146 of the Law of Property Act 1925 to grant relief from forfeiture for breach of covenant not being a covenant for the payment of rent. This jurisdiction is now conferred by s 52(3) of the 1959 Act. It is to be noted that this jurisdiction is expressly granted.

Section 74 of the 1959 Act (following s 71 of the 1934 Act) empowers the county court to give effect to any equitable defence or counterclaim. Prima facie, that section would, as it seems to me, have enabled the county courts to exercise the jurisdiction of the High Court to grant relief from forfeiture for non-payment of rent. It has been suggested that the words in s 191(1)(c), 'be barred from all relief', may have been intended to prevent an application for such relief in a case caught by the subsection from being made in the county courts. I am not persuaded that that was the intention of the provision. First, its legislative antecedents as I have set them out indicate that it was intended to deal with High Court jurisdiction to grant relief. There was under the 1856 and 1888 Acts no such power granted to county courts as is now granted by s 74 of the 1959 Act, and the comparable phrase in those Acts, 'barred from all relief in equity' and 'be barred from all relief', could not have been aimed at the then non-existent county court jurisdiction. Second, the mandatory wording of sub-s (1)(b) of s 191 of the 1959 Act suggests that the possibility of a claim for possession by a lessor being met by a counterclaim by the lessee for relief from forfeiture was not being contemplated by the legislature. As it seems to me, the only relief that the statutory provision could be contemplating was the relief which the High Court might otherwise grant under its equitable jurisdiction.

Counsel for the plaintiff has argued that the whole of sub-s (1) is subject to a condition precedent, namely 'where a lessor is proceeding in a county court'. At that date of, and at all times since, the plaintiff's application to the High Court for relief, namely 28 July 1982, the lessor, he says, was not proceeding in a county court. The county court proceedings had come to an end, and accordingly, the argument proceeds, the subsection does not apply and the High Court can grant relief.

In my judgment, that argument is based on a misconstruction of the subsection. The phrase at the end of para (c), 'be barred from all relief', bites only after a final order for possession has been made. The proceedings are necessarily at an end. The continuance of the county court proceedings cannot sensibly be regarded as a condition precedent to the application of the provision. In my judgment, on the true construction of the subsection the statutory provision applies whenever county court proceedings for possession on the ground of non-payment of rent have led to an order for possession being made.

In the result, therefore, I hold that by reason of s 191(1)(c) of the 1959 Act, and in the events which have happened in this case, the jurisdiction of the High Court to grant the plaintiff relief against forfeiture for non-payment of rent is ousted, and that I am unable to grant her the equitable relief which I would otherwise have thought it right to grant.

a I reach this conclusion with no pleasure at the state of the law. I can see no good reason why county court judges, who exercise a like discretion to grant relief from forfeiture in cases which fall within s 146 of the Law of Property Act 1925 to that exercised by High Court judges, should not be trusted with the same discretion as High Court judges in cases of forfeiture for non-payment of rent. I think it is clear that cases like the present, where the lessee's failure to take the simple steps available and necessary to save her lease

b has been inexplicable on any rational basis, must be few and far between. But it is common ground that if the proceedings for possession in the instant case had been brought and the order for possession made in the High Court, the plaintiff would have been able to remedy the ejectment she suffered on 29 March 1982 by making her application for relief on 28 July 1982 (see s 210 of the Common Law Procedure Act 1852). Counsel for the defendants accepts that, in that event, on authority it would have

c been right to grant the relief sought. As I have said, I would have granted her application if I had had power to do so. The fact that the value of the land brought the case within county court jurisdiction and that the lessor elected to bring the proceedings in the county court means that she cannot be granted relief and has lost her lease. This difference in result seems to me to lack rational justification and to be unjust to the plaintiff however much she may be the author of her own misfortune.

d In the event, however, I dismiss her application.

Application dismissed.

Solicitors: *Prynn-Miller Sandhu & Co*, Gravesend (for the plaintiff); *Dickinson Dees* Newcastle upon Tyne (for the defendants).

e

Jacqueline Metcalfe Barrister.

f # Inland Revenue Commissioners v Stannard

CHANCERY DIVISION
SCOTT J
6 FEBRUARY 1984

g *Capital transfer tax – Liability for tax – Persons liable as executor or trustee – Immunity from suit – Executor resident abroad – Testator dying resident and domiciled in England – Executor resident in Jersey – Whether executor immune from suit in England to recover capital transfer tax arising on death of testator.*

Capital transfer tax – Liability for tax – Persons liable as executor or trustee – Capital transfer
h *tax arising on death – Executor's liability to pay tax arising on death – Whether executor personally liable – Finance Act 1975, s 27.*

The defendant, who was resident in Jersey, was the executor of the testator, who died on 19 September 1976 resident and domiciled in England. The defendant received from the Revenue a notice of determination to capital transfer tax arising on the testator's death.

j The defendant did not appeal against the notice within the prescribed time limit and the notice became conclusive against him. On 25 July 1980 the Revenue issued a writ against him claiming the amount of capital transfer tax remaining unpaid together with interest thereon. On 14 October the defendant served a defence which merely denied liability. The Revenue sought summary judgment under RSC Ord 14 and on 31 December the master made an order for payment in the de bonis testatoris form, under which execution could issue only against the estate of the deceased and not against the defendant personally for the tax due. The Crown appealed against the order, claiming that the order should be

in the de bonis propriis form, under which the defendant's liability would be personal
and not representative. The defendant appealed against the finding of liability. The   *a*
judge allowed the defendant's appeal and gave him unconditional leave to defend the
action. At the trial the issues of law before the court were (i) whether the defendant was
immune from suit because of his residence in Jersey and (ii) whether the defendant
was, as the Crown claimed, personally liable for the unpaid tax and interest.

Held – (1) The court had jurisdiction to deal with the claim for capital transfer tax arising   *b*
on the death of a person who died resident and domiciled in England and accordingly
the defendant was not immune from suit notwithstanding that he was resident in Jersey
(see p 108 *g* and p 109 *d*, post); *IRC v Stype Investments (Jersey) Ltd, Re Clore (decd)* [1982]
3 All ER 419 applied.

   (2) A charge to capital transfer tax which arose on death was not and could never have
been a liability of the deceased but was an original liability of his personal representative.   *c*
Although s 27*ᵃ* of the Finance Act 1975 limited that liability to the amount which the
personal representative had received, or might have received but for his neglect or
default, from the deceased's estate, that did not affect the character of the liability but
only its extent (see p 110 *c* to *f* and *h*, post).

   (3) Accordingly the defendant was personally liable for the sum claimed and the
Crown was entitled to an order against him for payment in the de bonis propriis form   *d*
(see p 110 *j*, post); *Berry v Gaukroger* [1900–3] All ER Rep 166 applied.

Notes

For actions against personal representatives generally, see 17 Halsbury's Laws (4th edn)
paras 1580–1585, and for cases on the subject, see 24 Digest (Reissue) 1075–1105, 11437–
11779.   *e*

   For the liability of personal representatives for capital transfer tax following a
chargeable transfer on death, see 19 Halsbury's Laws (4th edn) para 835.

   For the Finance Act 1975, s 27, see 45 Halsbury's Statutes (3rd edn) 1808.

Cases referred to in judgment

Berry v Gaukroger [1903] 2 Ch 116, [1900–3] All ER Rep 166, CA.   *f*
IRC v Stype Investments (Jersey) Ltd, Re Clore (decd) [1982] 3 All ER 419, [1982] Ch 456,
   [1982] 3 WLR 228, CA; *rvsg* [1981] 2 All ER 394, [1981] Ch 367, [1981] 3 WLR 426
   and *affg* [1982] Fam 113, [1982] 2 WLR 314.

Action

By a notice of determination dated 14 January 1980, the Inland Revenue Commissioners   *g*
determined that, of the capital transfer tax chargeable on the transfer of value on the
death of Hans Erwin Hock (the deceased), a balance of £60,672 was still outstanding and
that the defendant, Michael Richard Stannard, as executor of the deceased, was liable for
that sum together with interest thereon until the date of payment. The defendant did
not appeal against the notice within 30 days and the notice became conclusive against
him under para 6(5) of Sch 4 to the Finance Act 1975. On 25 July 1980 the commissioners   *h*
issued a writ against the defendant claiming the unpaid tax together with interest
thereon. The facts are set out in the judgment.

John Mummery for the Crown.
The defendant did not appear.

                                                                                              j

SCOTT J. In this action the Commissioners of Inland Revenue sue to obtain payment
from the defendant of capital transfer tax and interest. The defendant is resident in Jersey
in the Channel Islands and is in the statement of claim expressed to be sued as executor
of Hans Erwin Hock (deceased).

---

a Section 27, so far as material, is set out at p 110 *b*, post

The proceedings commenced with an order made on 21 July 1980 by Master Waldman
a under RSC Ord 11, r 1(o), giving leave for service of the writ and statement of claim out
of the jurisdiction of the court. That order was clearly justified under the terms of para
(o) and the contrary has not been suggested.

Following that order, on 25 July 1980 a writ and statement of claim were issued and
served. The main paragraph of the statement of claim reads as follows:

b   'The plaintiffs' claim is against the Defendant as Executor of Hans Erwin Hock
        deceased (who died on 19 September 1976) for £74,313·33 Capital Transfer Tax and
        Interest thereon payable by virtue of Section 22 of the Finance Act 1975.'

Then follow particulars showing how the sum claimed is made up and referring in
particular to a notice of determination issued by the Capital Taxes Office to the defendant
under para (6) of Sch 4 to the Finance Act 1975 on 14 January 1980.
c   An appearance was entered on behalf of the defendant to the writ. The solicitors who
entered an appearance are still on the record, although they have taken no part in this
hearing.

On 14 October 1980 a defence was served on behalf of the defendant. It was a very
short document, in effect doing no more than denying liability as claimed. Not
surprisingly, on receipt of such a defence, the Crown sought to obtain summary
d judgment, and on 31 December 1980 an Ord 14 summons for that purpose was issued.
That summons came before Master Bickford Smith on 10 March 1981 and he made an
order for payment of the sum claimed in what is known as the de bonis testatoris form.
The Crown had asked him to make the order in the de bonis propriis form. He had
refused to do so and said that in his view the statement of claim should be amended in
order to make clear that the defendant was sued in a representative capacity only.
e   The Crown, for its part, had not intended to sue the defendant in a representative
capacity only. It had intended to sue him, and had supposed that it had sued him, in a
personal capacity.

The explanation for the difference between the two types of order is this. An order
which is made in the de bonis testatoris form is appropriate where a personal
representative is being sued for a liability of the deceased. His, the personal representative's,
f liability is purely representative. Execution under such an order can issue only against
the estate of the deceased and not against the personal representative's own goods. If
there are insufficient assets in the estate to satisfy the order made in the de bonis testatoris
form, then, if plene administravit has been raised as a defence and established or accepted,
there is no way in which the deficiency can be recovered against the personal
representative personally. If, however, plene administravit has not been raised as a
g defence, then, if the assets of the estate are insufficient to satisfy the judgment, the
creditor can claim the balance from the personal representative personally, who may not
at that stage raise plene administravit.

On the other hand, an order in the de bonis propriis form enforces a personal liability
of the personal representative. Such an order can be enforced by execution only against
the personal assets of the personal representative and not against assets held by the
h personal representative in trust.

Master Bickford Smith, as I have mentioned, said that in his view the order in favour
of the Crown should be made in the de bonis testatoris form. It is relevant to notice the
consequence if this had been right. No plea of plene administravit had been made by the
defendant. So he would be taken to have admitted assets. If the assets of the estate, taken
by way of execution in satisfaction of the judgment debt, turned out to be insufficient,
j his own assets would have been liable to be taken. It does not, I think, arise as an essential
matter for me to decide, but it seems to me that if the de bonis testatoris order made by
Master Bickford Smith was correct the order ought conveniently to have been made in
the form de bonis testatoris et si non de bonis propriis. I can see no sense whatever, in a
case which has, by pleading or otherwise, established that a plene administravit defence
is not available, in requiring a second action to be brought in order to enable the creditor
to have the full value of what he has established by his action.

In all events, Master Bickford Smith made the order against the defendant in the de bonis testatoris form. Both the Crown and the defendant appealed, the Crown appealing against the making of the order in that form as opposed to the de bonis propriis form and the defendant appealing against the finding of liability as such.

On 29 October 1981 the appeals came before Tudor Evans J. He allowed the defendant's appeal and gave him unconditional leave to defend the action. In the process, necessarily, he dismissed the Crown's appeal as well. But he did not need to and did not adjudicate on the question whether the order, if it had been an order which the commissioners were entitled to hold at an Ord 14 stage, should have been in the de bonis testatoris form or should have been, as the Crown contended, in the de bonis propriis form.

Following the leave to defend, the defendant, on 21 November 1981, served an amended defence. In his amended defence he raised two substantive points by way of defence. First, he contended that his liability was simply de bonis testatoris and not de bonis propriis. He contended that this was so, first, as a matter of construction of the notice of determination, which had been served on him on 14 January 1980, and, second, as a matter of construction of the relevant provisions of the Finance Act 1975.

Second, the defendant contended that his Jersey residence made him immune from suit. The paragraph raising this defence is in these terms:

'. . . the defendant is an inhabitant of Jersey and is thereby entitled to the immunities from process in this Honourable Court and from taxation in aid of the Crown that have been granted by the Crown to the inhabitants of Jersey, which immunities date back to time immemorial and/or are expressed in or granted by the Charters of 4 Elizabeth I and of 3 James II.'

The defendant, as I have said, has not been represented before me today. Accordingly, the Crown must strictly prove its case. However, on the pleadings all the factual issues are admitted by the defendant. Counsel for the Crown identified five such issues. (1) The testator, Hans Erwin Hock, died on 19 September 1976. I interpose that his death on that date was after the introduction of capital transfer tax. (2) The defendant is the executor of Mr Hock. (3) Notice of determination as pleaded in the statement of claim was served on the defendant. (4) That notice of determination is conclusive against the defendant. (5) The amount of capital transfer tax fixed by that notice was £367,259·55, of which payments of capital transfer tax of £306,887·55 have been made.

The statement of claim sets out also the amounts of interest due and paid respectively, and the arithmetic and figures generally in the statement of claim are all admitted by the defence. The pleaded issues that are left are therefore simply the two issues of law to which I have referred. I will deal first with the second issue, immunity as a Jersey resident, which is claimed by the defendant.

This point is settled against the defendant by the recent decision of the Court of Appeal in *IRC v Stype Investments (Jersey) Ltd, Re Clore (decd)* [1982] 3 All ER 419, [1982] Ch 456. In that case Stype Investments was a Jersey corporation and it was alleged to be liable in respect of capital transfer tax consequent on the death of Sir Charles Clore. Leave to serve the proceedings out of the jurisdiction was given by Dillon J but was set aside by Goulding J (see [1981] 2 All ER 394, [1981] Ch 367). On appeal it was argued on behalf of Stype Investments that it, Stype Investments, was entitled to immunity from suit by virtue of its character as a Jersey corporation. For the purposes of this argument, which was not dealt with by Goulding J, who decided the case on another point, reliance was placed by counsel for Stype Investments on the same two charters relied on by the defendant in para 8 of his defence. The argument of counsel for Stype Investments was as follows ([1982] Ch 456 at 463):

'As a result of Royal charters giving immunity from process in England, the defendant company as an inhabitant of Jersey is naturally and properly accountable in Jersey for the monies now in a Jersey bank . . . A matter arising in Jersey cannot be the subject of a writ or other process arising otherwise than in Jersey . . . The account can only be taken in Jersey because to allow otherwise would be contrary to the privileges granted by Royal charter.'

This argument was dealt with by Templeman LJ, who gave the judgment of the court
a ([1982] 3 All ER 419 at 427, [1982] Ch 456 at 471):

> 'We can deal summarily with the submission made on behalf of Stype Investments
> that this court has no jurisdiction over Stype Investments, which is a Jersey company,
> or, alternatively, that this court should not exercise jurisdiction over Stype
> Investments because by doing so the English court would flout the privileges and
> the immunities granted by the Crown to the courts and inhabitants of Jersey. The
> *b* Jersey courts have jurisdiction over causes of action which arise in Jersey. The
> English courts have jurisdiction over causes of action which arise in England. In the
> present case Stype Investments voluntarily came to England, accepted a conveyance
> of English land as nominee for Sir Charles and, if the Inland Revenue are correct,
> incurred personal liabilities to the Crown for capital transfer tax which became
> payable as the result of the death of Sir Charles. In these circumstances, the English
> *c* court has power to determine the dispute between the Inland Revenue and Stype
> Investments over capital transfer tax. The exercise by the English court of its powers
> will not cause any affront to the courts or the inhabitants of Jersey.'

It is plain from that that there is nothing in the defendant's point pleaded in para 8 of
his defence. The High Court has jurisdiction to deal with the claim for capital transfer
d tax raised by the Revenue in consequence of the death of somebody who died, as I am
told, resident and domiciled in this country, and I therefore reject that pleaded defence.

That leaves the other point that I mentioned. It follows from my rejection of the
constitutional immunity defence that the Crown is entitled to an order against the
defendant for payment of the claimed tax and interest. Is it, however, entitled to that
order in the de bonis propriis form, as counsel for the Crown contends, or simply in the
e de bonis testatoris form, which would limit execution to execution against the assets of
the estate, subject, of course, to any consequences of the failure of the defendant to plead
plene administravit?

Liability to capital transfer tax arises under the Finance Act 1975. Section 22(1) is the
charging section:

f
> 'On the death of any person after the passing of this Act tax shall be charged as if,
> immediately before his death, he had made a transfer of value and the value
> transferred by it had been equal to the value of his estate immediately before his
> death, but subject to the following provisions of this section.'

Section 25 sets out the provisions as to the persons on whom liability for capital transfer
tax falls, and s 25(5) deals with the case of capital transfer tax falling due on account of
g the death of a person. Subsection (5) reads as follows:

> 'Where the chargeable transfer is (under section 22 of this Act) made on the death
> of any person, the persons liable are, subject to subsection (7) below,—(a) so far as
> the tax is attributable to the value of property which either—(i) was not immediately
> before the death comprised in a settlement; or (ii) was so comprised and consists of
> *h* land in the United Kingdom which devolves upon or vests in the deceased's personal
> representatives, the deceased's personal representatives . . .'

It is para (a)(ii) which imposes liability on the defendant in the instant case. I will go on,
however, to refer to some of the other provisions of sub-s (5) because they bear, as it
seems to me, on the proper meaning to be attributed to the provision I have just read.
j Subsection (5) continues:

> '(b) so far as the tax is attributable to the value of property which, immediately
> before the death, was comprised in a settlement, the trustees of the settlement;
> (c) so far as the tax is attributable to the value of any property, any person in whom
> the property is vested (whether beneficially or otherwise) at any time after the death
> or who at any such time is beneficially entitled to an interest in possession in the
> property; (d) so far as the tax is attributable to the value of any property which,

immediately before the death, was comprised in a settlement, any person for whose benefit any of the property or income from it is applied after the death . . .'

a

Section 27 of the 1975 Act provides for limitation of liability to which the persons on whom liability is imposed under ss 22 and 25 might otherwise be exposed. It provides, so far as relevant to the present case:

'(1) A person shall not be liable under section 25(5)(a) of this Act for any tax as a personal representative of a deceased person, except to the extent of the following assets, namely—(a) so far as the tax is attributable to the value of any property . . . the assets . . . which he has received as personal representative or might have so received but for his own neglect or default . . .'

b

And so, even if the Crown is right in saying that the liability is personal and that the order which reflects the liability should be an order de bonis propriis, nevertheless the extent of the liability of a defendant from whom capital transfer tax is sought is limited to the extent of the assets he has received or which he ought to have received.

c

It is plain, in my view, from s 25(5) that the liability in respect of capital transfer tax for which a personal representative becomes liable is not and could never have been a liability of the deceased. It is necessarily an original liability which is in terms imposed on the personal representative. There is nothing in the statutory scheme which in express terms limits the liability of the personal representative to assets of the estate except in so far as such limitation is found in s 27 of the 1975 Act, which I have just read. There is, in my judgment, nothing in s 25(5) which justifies limiting the liability of a personal representative to liability in a representative capacity only. The relevant limitation is that limitation which is provided by s 27 and which goes to the extent of the liability, not its character. There is no basis, as it seems to me, for distinguishing between the liability of personal representatives imposed under para (a) and the liability of trustees imposed under para (b). Both incur original liability, both are plainly designated as persons liable, and in respect of neither is there any indication apt to render liability anything other than personal liability.

d

e

The position in respect of capital transfer tax so far as the liability of personal representatives is concerned seems to me, from the authorities and references that counsel for the Crown has put before me, to be on all fours with the position that used to pertain in regard to death duties before the introduction of capital transfer tax. In *Dymond's Death Duties* (15th edn 1973) vol 1, p 927 under the heading 'Enforcement of Liability—Personal Liability' the text proceeds thus:

f

'Every person who is made accountable for Estate Duty becomes a Crown debtor, and his goods and estate are accordingly liable to satisfy the debt . . .'

g

Reference is then made to *Berry v Gaukroger* [1903] 2 Ch 116, [1900–3] All ER Rep 166 and the text continues:

'Thus, if an administrator dies intestate while duty payable by him is outstanding, *his* administrator, although not in the chain of representation to the first intestate, is liable for the unpaid duty. So also is the executor or administrator of one of several trustees, notwithstanding that other trustees survive.' (My emphasis)

h

In my judgment, the same is true in respect of capital transfer tax.

Accordingly, in my judgment, the appropriate order where the Crown establishes liability to capital transfer tax against a personal representative is an order in the de bonis propriis form. An order in the de bonis testatoris form seems to me only to be justified where the liability of the executor which is being reflected in the order is a liability transmitted from the deceased whose liability it originally was. This can never be true of capital transfer tax except in the case where the deceased was liable for the tax.

j

Accordingly, in my judgment, the order which the Crown is entitled to in this action is an order in the de bonis propriis form. I have been supplied with calculations of the

interest to date from which the indebtedness as at today appears to be £91,472·96. It
seems to me appropriate, therefore, to make an order for payment of that sum. The
Crown is also entitled to costs.

Order accordingly.

Solicitors: *Solicitor of Inland Revenue.*

b

Clare Mainprice   Barrister.

Re Koeppler's Will Trusts
Barclays Bank Trust Co plc v Slack and others

CHANCERY DIVISION
PETER GIBSON J
16, 17, 18, 21 NOVEMBER, 21 DECEMBER 1983

*Charity – Will – Gift to institution known as 'Wilton Park' – No entity by name of Wilton Park
– Expression 'Wilton Park' used to describe conferences organised by testator for persons capable
of influencing public opinion in Western countries – Purposes of conference formation of informed
international public opinion and promotion of greater co-operation in Europe and West – Whether
gift for charitable purposes – Whether gift for educational purposes or purposes beneficial to
community – Whether gift for political purposes – Whether gift too vague and uncertain –
Whether charitable means of achieving non-charitable purposes of gift making gift charitable.*

*Will – Gift – Gift over – Condition precedent for gift over to take effect – Exact event on which
gift over to take effect not occurring – Rule that gift over to take effect if it must have been intended
to take effect in event that happened – Application of rule contradicting express terms of condition
precedent for gift over – Whether rule applying – Whether gift over taking effect.*

By his will dated 12 January 1972 the testator left a substantial portion of his estate to
'the Warden and the Chairman of the Academic Advisory Council . . . of the institution
known as Wilton Park . . . for the benefit at their discretion of the said institution as long
as Wilton Park remains a British contribution to the formation of an informed
international public opinion and to the promotion of greater co-operation in Europe and
the West in general . . .' The will further provided that in the event of Wilton Park
ceasing to exist by the date of the testator's death there was to be a gift over to a named
Oxford college. At the time the testator made his will and when he died in 1979 the
expression or name 'Wilton Park' was used to describe a series of conferences for a broad
range of persons, such as politicians, academics, civil servants, industrialists and journalists,
who were capable of influencing opinion in member states of the Organisation for
Economic Co-operation and Development, that organisation being a grouping of most
western nations. The conference enabled participants from member nations of the OECD
and other major Western organisations to exchange views on political, economic and
social issues of common interest. The conferences were private and unofficial and not
intended to conform to a particular party political line. They were financed by fees paid
by conference participants and by a subvention from the Foreign Office, which also
provided premises and facilities for the conference. The small academic staff who
organised the conferences were civil servants on the Foreign Office establishment. The
conferences were the brainchild of the testator, who was himself an academic. Until 1977

he organised the conferences himself and described himself as 'Warden of Wilton Park' but thereafter the conferences were organised by the 'Director' and his staff. At the testator's death there was neither an entity by the name of 'Wilton Park' nor a 'Warden' of Wilton Park. The gift was bound to fail unless it was charitable. Accordingly, the questions arose (i) whether the bequest in favour of Wilton Park was valid as being a charitable gift, (ii) if not, whether the gift over to the named Oxford college took effect, and (iii) if not, whether the bequest devolved to the next-of-kin on an intestacy.

Held – (1) The condition attached to the bequest, namely 'as long as Wilton Park remains a British contribution to the formation of an informed international public opinion' etc, was not a temporal condition which required Wilton Park to continue in being for the specified purposes but was instead merely a condition which was required to be satisfied at the date of the testator's death (see p 119 c d and f to h, post).

(2) Since Wilton Park was not an entity but only an activity or process and since the designated trustees could not take the gift beneficially for themselves but only for the benefit of Wilton Park, the gift could only be valid if it was a gift for the purposes of Wilton Park and if those purposes were charitable. The twin purposes of Wilton Park were (a) the formation of an informed international public opinion and (b) the promotion of greater co-operation in Europe and the West in general, neither of which was charitable because they were too vague and uncertain for the court to be able to control the application of Wilton Park's assets and activities by reference to those purposes. Furthermore, the promotion of greater co-operation in Europe and the West was neither an educational purpose nor a purpose beneficial to the community but a political purpose. Although it could be described as a purpose of public utility it did not benefit persons in any material way which the law recognised as being charitable (see p 120 b c and g to j, p 121 a to d and j, p 122 e to j, p 123 d e, p 124 a to c and j and p 125 c d, post); *Income Tax Special Purposes Comrs v Pemsel* [1891–4] All ER Rep 28, *Anglo-Swedish Society v IRC* (1931) 16 TC 34 and *Buxton v Public Trustee* (1962) 41 TC 235 applied; *Re Strakosch (decd)*, *Temperley v A-G* [1949] 2 All ER 6 and *McGovern v A-G* [1981] 3 All ER 493 considered; *Re Harwood* [1935] All ER Rep 918 doubted.

(3) The Wilton Park process could itself be described as educational because (a) the concept of education was wide enough to cover the intensive discussion process adopted by Wilton Park, (b) although the selection of participants was restricted to those capable of influencing opinion in their own countries the selection was widely drawn and was not from a private class, and (c) there was a public benefit in persons who were capable of influencing public opinion attending educational courses. However, the Wilton Park process was not the purpose of Wilton Park but merely a means of achieving the purposes of Wilton Park, and the testator had not limited the means to that process. Furthermore, the mere fact that a gift for a non-charitable purpose was to be achieved by charitable means did not endow the gift with different and charitable purposes. Accordingly, the gift for the benefit of Wilton Park was not exclusively charitable and therefore failed (see p 121 c d, p 125 g h and p 126 a to d and f g, post); dictum of Collins MR in *Smith v Kerr* [1902] 1 Ch at 779 and *Gilmour v Coats* [1949] 1 All ER 848 distinguished.

(4) On the strict construction of the express terms of the gift over to the named Oxford college the condition precedent for the gift over, namely that Wilton Park had ceased to exist in a particular form at the date of the testator's death, had not been fulfilled. Furthermore, the gift over did not fall within the rule that if the exact event on which the gift over was to take effect did not occur the gift over was nevertheless to be allowed to take effect if it must have been intended to take effect in the event that had in fact happened, because to apply that rule merely because the gift to Wilton Park failed by operation of law would involve contradicting the express terms of the condition precedent for the gift over. Since both the bequest to Wilton Park and the gift over failed the bequest devolved to the next-of-kin on an intestacy (see p 128 c to j, post); *Re Bailey (decd)*, *Barrett v Hyder* [1951] 1 All ER 391 applied; *Jones v Westcomb* (1711) Prec Ch 316, *Hall v Warren* (1861) 9 HL Cas 420 and *Re Fox's Estate* [1937] 4 All ER 664 distinguished.

Notes

a   For the requirement that a charity be for the public benefit, see 5 Halsbury's Laws (4th edn) paras 505–507, and for cases on the subject, see 8(1) Digest (Reissue) 238–240, 6–10.

For trusts for political purposes, see 5 Halsbury's Laws (4th edn) para 558, and for cases on the subject, see 8(1) Digest (Reissue) 301–302, 425–427.

For trusts for educational purposes, see 5 Halsbury's Laws (4th edn) paras 522–527, and for cases on the subject, see 8(1) Digest (Reissue) 256–266, 112–118.

b
Cases referred to in judgment

A-G v National Provincial and Union Bank of England [1924] AC 262, [1923] All ER Rep 123, HL.

Anglo-Swedish Society v IRC (1931) 16 TC 34.

Bailey (decd), Re, Barrett v Hyder [1951] 1 All ER 391, [1951] Ch 407, CA.

c   Barralet v A-G [1980] 3 All ER 918, sub nom Re South Place Ethical Society [1980] 1 WLR 1565.

Bonar Law Memorial Trust v IRC (1933) 17 TC 508.

Bowman v Secular Society Ltd [1917] AC 406, [1916–17] All ER Rep 1, HL.

Buxton v Public Trustee (1962) 41 TC 235.

Davies v Perpetual Trustee Co Ltd [1959] 2 All ER 128, [1959] AC 439, [1959] 2 WLR 673,

d   PC.

Dingle v Turner [1972] 1 All ER 878, [1972] AC 601, [1972] 2 WLR 523, HL.

Finger's Will Trusts, Re, Turner v Ministry of Health [1971] 3 All ER 1050, [1972] Ch 286, [1971] 3 WLR 775.

Fox's Estate, Re [1937] 4 All ER 664.

Gilmour v Coats [1949] 1 All ER 848, [1949] AC 426, HL.

e   Hall v Warren (1861) 9 HL Cas 420, 11 ER 791; varying sub nom Warren v Rudall (1858) 4 K & J 603, 70 ER 250.

Harwood, Re, Coleman v Innes [1936] Ch 285, [1935] All ER Rep 918.

Hopkins's Will Trusts, Re, Naish v Francis Bacon Society Inc [1964] 3 All ER 46, [1965] Ch 669, [1964] 3 WLR 840.

Hopkinson (decd), Re, Lloyd's Bank Ltd v Baker [1949] 1 All ER 346.

f   Income Tax Special Purposes Comrs v Pemsel [1891] AC 531, [1891–4] All ER Rep 28, HL.

IRC v McMullen [1980] 1 All ER 884, [1981] AC 1, [1980] 2 WLR 416, HL.

Jackson v Phillips (1867) 96 Mass 539.

Jones v Westcomb (1711) Prec Ch 316, 24 ER 149.

McDougall (Arthur) Fund, Re Trusts of the, Thompson v Fitzgerald [1956] 3 All ER 867, [1957] 1 WLR 81.

g   McGovern v A-G [1981] 3 All ER 493, [1982] Ch 321, [1982] 2 WLR 222.

Neville Estates Ltd v Madden [1961] 3 All ER 769, [1962] Ch 832, [1961] 3 WLR 999.

Oppenheim v Tobacco Securities Trust Co Ltd [1951] 1 All ER 31, [1951] AC 297, HL.

Royal Choral Society v IRC [1943] 2 All ER 101, CA.

Shaw's Will Trusts, Re, National Provincial Bank Ltd v National City Bank Ltd [1952] 1 All ER 49, [1952] Ch 163.

h   Smith v Kerr [1902] 1 Ch 774.

Strakosch (decd), Re, Temperley v A-G [1949] 2 All ER 6, [1949] Ch 529, CA.

Tribune Press, Lahore (Trustees) v Income Tax Comr, Punjab, Lahore [1939] 3 All ER 469, PC.

Vernon's Will Trusts, Re [1971] 3 All ER 1061, [1972] Ch 300, [1971] 3 WLR 786.

Cases also cited

j   Camile and Henry Dreyfus Foundation Inc v IRC [1954] 2 All ER 466, [1954] Ch 672.

Whicker v Hume (1858) 7 HL Cas 124, [1843–60] All ER Rep 450.

Wing v Angrave and Tulley (1860) 8 HL Cas 183, 11 ER 397.

Originating summons

By an originating summons dated 22 September 1982 the plaintiff, Barclays Bank Trust Co plc sought, inter alia, the determination of the court on question 1 of the summons,

namely whether on the true construction of the will dated 12 January 1972 of Sir
Heinrich Koeppler deceased and in the events which had happened the gift of 20/36ths   *a*
of the capital and income of the testator's residuary estate to the Warden and the
Chairman of the Academic Advisory Council for the time being of the institution known
as Wilton Park (a) was a valid charitable gift, or (b) was a valid gift for the purposes of
Wilton Park, or (c) failed with the result that the subject matter of the gift was to be held
on trust (i) for the third defendant or (ii) for the next-of-kin of the testator on a partial
intestacy, or (d) was to be held on some other and, if so, what trusts. The defendants to   *b*
the summons were Timothy Willatt Slack, sometime Director of Wilton Park, Joanne
Capper, the testator's sister and next-of-kin, the president and scholars of the College of
St Mary Magdalen in the University of Oxford and Her Majesty's Attorney General. The
facts are set out in the judgment.

Roger Cooke for Barclays Bank Trust Co plc.
Leolin Price QC and *James K S Denniston* for Mr Slack.   *c*
Kenneth Farrow for Mrs Capper.
David Unwin for Magdalen.
Christopher McCall for the Attorney General.

                                                                            Cur adv vult

21 December. The following judgment was delivered.   *d*

PETER GIBSON J. By his will dated 12 January 1972 Sir Heinrich (better known as
Sir Heinz) Koeppler left a share of his residuary estate as follows:

'As to twenty thirty-sixth parts of both capital and income thereof for the Warden
and the Chairman of the Academic Advisory Council for the time being of the
institution known as Wilton Park now housed at Wiston House Steyning Sussex of   *e*
which I am the Founder Director for the benefit at their discretion of the said
institution as long as Wilton Park remains a British contribution to the formation
of an informed international public opinion and to the promotion of greater co-
operation in Europe and the West in general but in the event of the said institution
having ceased to exist in such form at the date of my death the Company shall hold
this legacy upon trust for the President and Scholars of the College of St. Mary   *f*
Magdalen in the University of Oxford to be utilised so far as practicable for the
assistance of undergraduates or post-graduates (but not for established scholars) who
have left their own country for political racial or religious reasons.'

Although the will was for the most part professionally drawn, that bequest was worded
by Sir Heinz himself. He died on 1 April 1979 and the plaintiff, Barclays Bank Trust Co
plc, is the sole executor and trustee of his will. The first defendant, Mr Slack, was at the   *g*
date of the originating summons the director of Wilton Park, there being no one then
with the title of warden nor was there then a chairman of the Academic Advisory
Council. Mr Slack has been joined to argue in favour of the validity of the gift for Wilton
Park. It is common ground that its validity depends on the question whether the gift is
charitable. If it is not charitable, then the gift to Wilton Park fails. There then arises the   *h*
question whether the gift to the third defendant, Magdalen College, Oxford, expressed
as that gift is conditionally, takes effect. If it does not, the 20/36ths share of the residuary
estate is undisposed of by the will and goes to Sir Heinz's next of kin, his sister the second
defendant, Mrs Capper. Quite understandably she, though joined to argue in favour of
intestacy, does not accept that role with any great enthusiasm, as she had made clear in
her affidavit, but her counsel has nevertheless very properly presented full arguments on   *j*
her behalf. These then are the parties. I should add that there are obvious capital transfer
tax consequences turning on whether Sir Heinz made an effective charitable gift. If he
did, the 20/36ths share is worth about £107,500. If he did not, that share is worth only
about £62,500. The Commissioners of Inland Revenue were invited to become a party
to the originating summons but they declined to do so, as was their right.

a I must now give some details of Sir Heinz's life and work and attempt to describe what he called the institution known as Wilton Park. Sir Heinz was born in 1912 in Prussia. He was brought up in Germany and attended German universities as an undergraduate before he came to this country and to Magdalen in 1933 as a post-graduate student. He obtained a degree as Doctor of Philosophy in 1936 and the following year he was appointed lecturer in modern history and senior demy of Magdalen. But his main academic interest lay in medieval history and shortly before the war he spent some

b formative months in Italy. He was particularly interested in that early part of the Renaissance that had its flowering in northern Italy, the academic institutions of which attracted scholars from all over Europe. Mr Alan Hughes, the deputy director of Wilton Park, who has been connected with its work since 1972 and who knew Sir Heinz well, said this in his first affidavit:

c 'Heinz Koeppler admired the "studium generale" concept that typified the schools of Bologna, which for him emphasised the interaction of contemporary problems; from this came his espousal of generalism and the global view, and his distrust of people who studied blindly and compartmentally.'

d During the 1939–45 war Sir Heinz served the British government in the Political Warfare Executive. In 1943, in response to Mr Winston Churchill's request for creative ideas about post-war Germany, he suggested setting up a centre at which Germans in public life might discuss and examine mutual problems in an intellectually invigorating atmosphere. Participants, most of whom had never experienced or practised democracy, would learn by seeing and hearing Britain and the British doing just that. Every issue would concern everyone; experts would be challenged by laymen, and specialists be made to think generally. Sir Heinz's ideas were supported by the Foreign Office and on

e 12 January 1946 the first conference assembled at Wilton Park in Buckinghamshire. Wilton Park gave its name to the conferences even though from 1950 onwards the conferences have been held at Wiston House, Steyning, West Sussex in premises and with facilities, such a library, provided for Wilton Park by the Foreign Office. The first persons to attend such conferences were volunteers from among former German prisoners of war, but the range of persons attending was quickly extended and since 1957 such

f persons have been drawn from all the countries which are for the time being member states of the Organisation for Economic Co-operation and Development (OECD). Sir Heinz took the title of Warden of Wilton Park and in that capacity was exclusively responsible for the organisation of the conferences, the choice of themes, the selection of speakers and participants and the management of staff. Sir Heinz acted as warden from 1946 to 1977. Thereafter the warden's functions have been performed by a person with the title of 'director'. The director, the deputy director and all the academic staff (who are

g now five in number) are civil servants on the Foreign Office establishment. Till Sir Heinz's death there was no need to consider whether or not the purposes of Wilton Park were charitable as there were no assets held for those purposes. A fee is charged to each participant attending a conference but this does not cover all the Wilton Park expenditure; the balance is met by the Foreign Office.

h An Academic Advisory Council was established for Wilton Park in 1949. There is a chairman of such council and about 20 other members of whom three are members ex-officio, being nominees of the Royal Institute of International Affairs (better known as Chatham House), the Confederation of British Industry (CBI) and the Trades Union Congress (TUC). The other members are drawn from the academic world, politics (for example, the council includes a Conservative, a Labour and a Liberal member of

j Parliament) and various other international bodies, such as the International Institute for Strategic Studies, the Commission of the EEC and the European Movement. The council affords advice and assistance in connection with the running of Wilton Park. When a new member of the council is required, the council is consulted and makes recommendations, but the Foreign Office makes the appointment. A further advisory body was set up in 1959, the International Advisory Council. The members of that

council are 24 ambassadors and high commissioners of member states of the OCED, the
European Economic Community (EEC), the European Free Trade Association (EFTA)   *a*
and the North Atlantic Treaty Organisation (NATO) and a senior Foreign Office official.
Mr Slack in his affidavit describes the mode of operation of Wilton Park as follows:

'(1) Wilton Park operates by conferences organised and conducted at (since 1950)
Wiston House and attended by members drawn from the member states of OECD
and from the central staffs of OECD, EEC, EFTA, NATO, and the Council of Europe.
(2) 10–12 conferences are normally held in each year. Each conference is now   *b*
usually of one week's duration. Members participating in any one conference may
be as many as 40. During the conference they live at Wiston House, where the
facilities for study and research include a well furnished library.
(3) Each (one-week) conference consists of 8–10 plenary sessions. At a typical
session there is an initial address or paper from an authoritative or specialist speaker
followed by open discussion—in which all members can and do participate—of the   *c*
subject of the address or paper.
(4) The discussion is continued in smaller discussion groups, each concerned to
develop some specific topic or aspect of, or connected with, the subject. The
academic staff of Wilton Park are available to guide, supervise and underpin
discussions in these groups, but the high quality of members selected to attend by
and from the various countries ensures that the educational process involved is not   *d*
wholly dependent on the academic staff and the direction taken in any particular
discussion group is not, in any sense, controlled by the academic staff.
(5) Often one plenary session is designated as a Round Table; this is held near the
end of a conference, and several participants are invited to form a panel with whom
the remaining members can debate fresh ideas not hitherto expressed. Alternatively,
the Round Table occasionally allows a representative from each discussion group to   *e*
report on conclusions reached during the week.
(6) At Wilton Park conferences there are 3 official languages: English, French and
German. Members are expected to have an adequate command of at least one of
these. There are facilities for simultaneous translation. There is no recording of
discussions and verbatim reports of the conferences are not prepared or published.   *f*
But articles are published containing reports of or commenting on addresses and
papers delivered by distinguished speakers; and the Wilton Park Journal is published
regularly and sent to many of the people throughout the world who have attended
Wilton Park conferences.
(7) At a Wilton Park conference each person attending is not only educated, but
contributes to the education of the others; and this is a continuing process which
does not end at the end of the conference. There is throughout the world an ever-   *g*
widening membership. Some members attend more than one conference. Many
participate in the selection of new members from their own countries or
organisations.'

In those passages and elsewhere in Mr Slack's affidavit, as well as in other affidavits put in
on behalf of Wilton Park by Lord Beloff, Professor Hoggart and Professor Seton Watson,   *h*
the deponent expresses the view that the purposes and work of Wilton Park were
educational. But I must say at once, without intending any disrespect to those
distinguished deponents, that in my judgment the question whether those purposes and
that work were educational for the purposes of the law of charity is a question of law on
which the opinions even of such eminent educationalists as them do not assist. It is quite
another matter when they give factual evidence such as of what occurred at Wilton Park   *j*
conferences.
Mr Slack exhibited, inter alia, a number of conference programme previews which
gave those considering whether to, or intending to, attend conferences an outline of the
programme of the conference. Each such preview commences with the following
statement:

'Wilton Park is a British contribution to the formation of an informed international public opinion. To promote greater cooperation in Europe and the West in general, it offers those influencing opinion in their own countries an opportunity of exchanging views on political, economic and social questions of common interest.'

In the next paragraph there are statements as to what happens at a conference:

'*Every Wilton Park conference deals with a broad range of these problems.* Within this framework some sessions of each conference are devoted to a specific aspect which, however, does not dominate the conference since Wilton Park avoids narrow specialisation.'

There then follows a statement of what the specific aspect of that conference would be, and on the following page, which gives details of the timetable of the conference, under the heading 'The Scope of the Conference' there is the following statement:

'Every Wilton Park conference deals with a broad range of common problems. Within this framework some sessions of each conference are devoted to a specific aspect. But Wilton Park avoids narrow specialisation and the specific aspect does not dominate the conference.'

The type of specific aspects of such conferences can be seen from those of the four conferences prior to the date of Sir Heinz's will and from those of the four conferences prior to Sir Heinz's death, namely: (1) an inquiry into the 'Quality of Life,' ecology and the environment; participation in government and industry; tensions in free societies; (2) Europe and the emergent patterns of superpower relationships; (3) the unification of Europe: a balance sheet; (4) the requirements of western defence and the possibilities of arms control; (5) the European Community and its external relations; (6) the media, public opinion and the decision-making process in government; (7) security issues as a factor in domestic and international politics; (8) labour and capital and the future of industrial society.

Those specific themes are self-evidently matters on which persons of differing political persuasions may have differing views, and some of the speakers invited to speak at plenary sessions of the conferences were politicians, but it is clear that Wilton Park has taken pains to avoid inculcating any particular political viewpoint. Thus if a speaker at one session was a politician putting forward a Conservative view on a theme, in the course of the same conference there would be a Labour politician as a speaker at another session putting forward the Labour view on that theme. The speakers at each plenary session are drawn from a variety of sources. In addition to politicians they include academics, civil servants, industrialists and journalists. The speaker is described in each conference preview as opening the discussion. He speaks for about half an hour and then there follows a 1½-hour period of discussion, the speaker as well as the participants being expected to take part. But, as Mr Slack said in his affidavit, each conference includes sessions at which the participants, divided into groups, discuss issues among themselves; and members of the academic staff of Wilton Park are present at each session to help stimulate discussion. It is a strict rule (no doubt, to encourage a full and frank exchange of views by speakers and participants alike) that there is no attribution outside the conference of any view expressed at the conference to the person who has put forward that view without that person's consent. The Wilton Park Journal to which Mr Slack referred is published twice a year; this records what has occurred at the conferences and reports some of the speeches. The journal is sent to each participant for a year after he or she has attended a conference and thereafter if the participants so request. There is some evidence of the journals going to certain libraries for the past four or five years. Mr Hughes mentioned Chatham House and the British Library, but, as I understood him, his knowledge was derived from persons writing in to Wilton Park and saying that they had seen the journal in such a library.

The evidence how participants are selected was somewhat imprecise. Mr Slack in the passage that I have cited from his affidavit refers to 'members selected to attend by and from the various countries'. It appeared from Mr Hughes's oral evidence that Wilton Park received applications from persons wanting to attend and the warden or director had the final say as to whether such person would be accepted. Further, many of the applicants will have been through a selection process in their own country before their application is made. By far the greater part of the English participants (who amounted to one-sixth to one-fifth of those attending conferences) were nominated by various bodies with whom Wilton Park had strong links, such as government departments, local authorities, police forces and certain companies. Abroad the position varies from country to country. Some countries like Switzerland and Finland have selection committees to select persons suitable for attending such conferences. In some countries there are associations of persons who have attended Wilton Park and indeed in the United States of America there is an active association which holds conferences on the lines of Wilton Park. Some of those attending Wilton Park conferences are persons who have attended before but by far the greater proportion consists of those attending Wilton Park for the first time. From the brief description of the participants attending specific conferences that I have seen, it is apparent that there is a fairly broad range of persons drawn from various quarters but falling within the broad classification of persons influencing opinion in their own western countries who attend the conferences.

After the death of Sir Heinz in 1979, the question whether the bequest in favour of Wilton Park was charitable arose. A declaration of trust in a form settled by leading Chancery counsel was executed in May 1982 by the then chairman and vice-chairman of the Academic Advisory Council, by Mr Slack, Mr Hughes and one other intended trustee. That deed contains two recitals in the following form:

'(F) Wilton Park has been established and it and its work have been and are carried on for the purpose of promoting for the public benefit the advancement of education about and by and as part of such advancement the expansion and improvement of public knowledge and understanding of and concerning world affairs and the influence upon national and international policies of the diverse cultures historical perspectives governmental structures and powers political assumptions and attitudes of the people and nations of the world And that purpose (hereinafter called 'the Wilton Park Purpose') has at all times been and is based on the belief that international peace is served and preserved by such knowledge and understanding.

(G) The mode of operation of Wilton Park in promoting the Wilton Park Purpose has been primarily by the organisation of regular conferences attended by persons from the various countries of the world with a view to the expansion and improvement of their knowledge and understanding as aforesaid by study and discussion and through them the constant enlargement of such public knowledge and understanding throughout the world.'

The originating summons now before me was taken out on 22 September 1982. There are three questions which arise. (1) Is the gift in favour of Wilton Park charitable? (2) If so, is the subject matter of the gift liable at any future date to cease to be held on charitable trust? (3) If the gift is not charitable, does Magdalen take the gift over or is there an intestacy?

On the first question, counsel appearing for Mr Slack and counsel appearing for the Attorney General submit that the gift is charitable. Counsel appearing for Mrs Capper submits that the gift is not charitable. Counsel appearing for Magdalen, on instructions refrained from presenting argument on this question but made submissions on the meaning of the condition attached to the gift in favour of Wilton Park.

The gift in favour of Wilton Park is charitable if, but only if, the property is given for exclusively charitable purposes. The first question can be divided into two issues: (i) what are the purposes of the gift; (ii) are those purposes charitable?

To ascertain the purposes of the gift I look in the first place to the will. As counsel for the Attorney General pointed out, the will must be construed to try to give effect to all

its terms and if and so far as necessary it must be construed with regard to the principle
a   of benignancy, that is to say that if the will is equally capable of two constructions on one
of which the gift lapses and on the other of which the gift is effective, the latter
construction is to be preferred (see *IRC v McMullen* [1980] 1 All ER 884 at 890, [1981]
AC 1 at 14 per Lord Hailsham LC). That is a general principle not confined to gifts to
charity or gifts by will and is simply the application of the maxim ut res magis valeat
quam pereat. But the principle is not applicable if the will is not equally capable of two
b   constructions, for example if one construction is to be preferred to the other.

There are three obvious features of the gift. First, the gift is on its face to persons
holding office in relation to what is said to be an institution for the benefit of that
institution. Plainly therefore the gift is to those persons as trustees and the gift will not
fail merely because there is no such person for the time being. Second, the gift is for the
benefit of Wilton Park, the intended beneficiary. Third, that gift is subject to the
c   condition introduced by the words 'as long as'.

It is convenient at this point to consider the meaning of that condition. Counsel for
Mr Slack submitted that 'as long as' should not be construed in a purely temporal sense.
He said that it has a well-recognised secondary meaning: 'provided that' or 'if'. He further
submitted that the condition is one to be satisfied at the time of the death. Although the
verb 'remains' in conjunction with 'as long as' prima facie supports a temporal meaning,
d   it is not inconsistent with the meaning for which counsel for Mr Slack contends. Further,
as counsel for Magdalen points out, the terms of the gift were not drawn professionally.
Sir Heinz in the bequest used language which indicated that he was wording his gift at
the date of the will (as witness the present tense in 'I am the Founder Director'). The
words of the condition, while looking to the future, make sense as a reference to the
future viewed from the date of the will rather than the date of death and it would have
e   been illogical for Sir Heinz to have intended the condition to apply beyond the date of
death, the date at which the condition attached to the gift to Magdalen had to be satisfied.
The condition attached to the gift over is linked to the condition attached to the gift for
the benefit of Wilton Park: compare the words 'as long as Wilton Park remains' with the
words 'in the event of the said institution having ceased to exist in such form at the date
of my death'. This is a gift of part of the residuary estate and it seems to me improbable
f   that Sir Heinz would have intended to introduce a gap between the condition attached
to the gift for Wilton Park and the condition attached to the gift to Magdalen. I therefore
construe the condition attached to the gift for Wilton Park as one requiring Wilton Park
to remain at the date of Sir Heinz's death a British contribution as there stated. So far as
Sir Heinz was concerned, the gift for Wilton Park would take effect if at his death Wilton
Park could be described as a British contribution as there stated. What he was guarding
g   against was the possibility of a change such that Wilton Park might have ceased to exist
in that form or at all by the time of his death. In that event he wanted Magdalen, not
Wilton Park, to take. But it follows from this construction that, if Wilton Park ceased to
exist in that form or at all at any time after the death of Sir Heinz (and in Sir Heinz's eyes
that must have been a possibility), Sir Heinz made no provision that the gift should go
away from Wilton Park to Magdalen or indeed anyone else.

h   That leads me to consider what in law was and is the intended beneficiary, Wilton
Park. It was described by Sir Heinz as an institution and that is convenient nomenclature.
But that term is suggestive of Wilton Park having some form of corporate or quasi-
corporate existence. It is not a body corporate or even an unincorporated association in
the ordinary sense of that term, that is to say an association of persons bound together by
identifiable rules and having an identifiable membership. Until Sir Heinz's gift there
j   was no property held for Wilton Park which might have given rise to the question
whether the purposes of Wilton Park were charitable. All that there was at the time of
Sir Heinz's death, and earlier at the date of his will, and indeed since 1946, was an activity
and a consistently repeated expression of what Wilton Park existed to do. The activity,
that of organising and holding conferences of a particular type and in a particular
manner, had been carried on by certain Crown servants with the material assistance of
the Crown, which had provided the premises and the staff and had met the balance of

expenditure not recouped by way of conference fees. The statements as to what Wilton
Park existed to do had appeared in every conference preview. But those carrying on that   *a*
activity were not bound by any constitution or rules which committed them or the
Crown to continue that activity in that form or at all, and, as I read the condition attached
by Sir Heinz to the gifts in favour of Wilton Park and Magdalen, he was well aware of
the fact that there was nothing immutable about Wilton Park.

There being no entity by the name of Wilton Park which itself could receive the gift
beneficially, and as the trustees designated in the will also cannot take the gift beneficially,   *b*
counsel for the Attorney General submitted that the gift must be construed as a gift for
the purposes of Wilton Park. For this submission he referred me to *Re Finger's Will
Trusts, Turner v Ministry of Health* [1971] 3 All ER 1050, [1972] Ch 286 in which Goff J,
following a dictum of Buckley J in *Re Vernon's Will Trusts* [1971] 3 All ER 1061, [1972]
Ch 300, held that a gift to an unincorporated association which was conceded to have
charitable purposes was a gift for those purposes. In the present case it is very much in   *c*
issue whether Wilton Park does have charitable purposes. But I accept that the gift, if it
is to take effect at all, should be construed as a gift for the purposes of Wilton Park.
However the changeable nature of Wilton Park as recognised by Sir Heinz must be borne
in mind. I shall come back to this point later. In the mean time I shall follow the course
adopted by counsel before me of first seeking to identify the purposes of Wilton Park at
the date of the will and Sir Heinz's death (it is common ground that no material change   *d*
occurred between those dates) and then considering whether those purposes are charitable.

The will and the conference previews are obvious sources of evidence of the purposes
of Wilton Park. Counsel for Mr Slack submitted that in addition the recitals in the
declaration of trust should be taken into account. However on this counsel for Mrs
Capper submitted (and counsel for the Attorney General agreed with him) that the court
could derive little assistance from the recitals in a deed drawn after the death of Sir Heinz   *e*
and after it had become apparent that there was a dispute whether Wilton Park had
charitable purposes. He said that the contemporary documentary evidence was the
evidence on which the court should place chief weight. I agree, but in so doing I would
make it clear that I do not doubt that the recitals constituted the conscientious attempt
by the parties to the deed to record what they believed to be the position. But it seems to
me that what I am primarily concerned to ascertain is what Sir Heinz, the founder and   *f*
warden for so many years, including at the time when he made his will, conceived to be
the purposes of Wilton Park. In effect his purposes for Wilton Park were the purposes of
Wilton Park. On this his own words are the most cogent evidence. I have the evidence
of the gift in the will couched as it is in his own language and the evidence of the very
similar language used in the conference previews, which I infer to be Sir Heinz's language
again. Further I bear in mind that Mr Hughes in cross-examination accepted that the   *g*
statement in the conference previews was a pithy summary of what Sir Heinz was trying
to achieve.

The gift in the will in favour of Wilton Park is conditional on Wilton Park remaining
a British contribution to two ends: the formation of an informed international public
opinion (the formation end) and the promotion of greater co-operation in Europe and
the West in general (the promotion end). The first sentence of every conference preview   *h*
states that Wilton Park is a British contribution to the formation end. The second
sentence states, in effect, that to achieve the promotion end, Wilton Park offers those
influencing opinion in their own countries an opportunity of exchanging views on
political, economic and social questions of common interest.

Counsel for Mr Slack submitted that the purpose of Wilton Park was the formation
end to be achieved by the work carried on at Wilton Park. But he submitted that the   *j*
promotion end was not a purpose but a by-product of the realisation of the formation
end. The submission of counsel for the Attorney General was that the purpose of Wilton
Park was education in the form of offering those influencing opinion in their own
countries an opportunity of exchanging views on political, social and economic questions
of common interest. Counsel for the Attorney General described the formation end and
the promotion end as 'ultimate aims', thereby, I think, consciously referring to certain

a remarks made by the Court of Appeal in *Re Strakosch (decd), Temperley v A-G* [1949] 2 All ER 6, [1949] Ch 529 to which I must refer shortly. Counsel for Mrs Capper submitted that the formation end and the promotion end were the purposes of Wilton Park.

Looking at both the will and the conference previews, I find it impossible to say that the promotion end is not a purpose but the formation end is a purpose. Either they are both purposes or neither is. In the second sentence of the conference preview the promotion end is clearly, to my mind, worded as a purpose, the means of achieving that

b purpose being what may be termed the Wilton Park process, that is to say, what counsel for the Attorney General has submitted to be the educational purpose of Wilton Park. In the will the gift for Wilton Park is conditional on Wilton Park remaining a British contribution to both the formation end and the promotion end. On this wording, if Wilton Park ceased to be such a contribution to either, then the gift for Wilton Park would not have effect. Again unaided by authority and looking only at Sir Heinz's own

c language in the will and conference previews, I find it difficult to accept both counsel for the Attorney General's elevation of the Wilton Park process to the purpose of Wilton Park as distinct from the means to achieve the promotion end, and possibly the formation end as well, and also his relegation of the formation end and the promotion end to the remote distance of 'ultimate aims'. Sir Heinz thought those ends important enough to make his gift for Wilton Park subject to a condition framed by reference to them. He

d said nothing about the Wilton Park process other than what is implicit in the gift being for the benefit of Wilton Park. But the conference preview supports the view that the Wilton Park process is the means rather than the purpose, the purpose again being the formation end and the promotion end.

Before I leave this point I should refer to *Re Strakosch (decd), Temperley v A-G* [1949] 2 All ER 6, [1949] Ch 529. In that case a testator directed that part of his residuary estate

e should be held by his trustees on trust to be applied to a fund for any purpose which in their opinion was designed to strengthen the bond of unity between the Union of South Africa and this country and which incidentally would conduce to the appeasement of racial feeling between the Dutch and English-speaking sections of the South African community. The Court of Appeal held that the bequest was not a good charitable gift, the very wide and vague scope of the gift and the unrestricted latitude of application

f which its language permitted making it impossible for the court to find that it fell within the spirit and intendment of the preamble to the Statute of Elizabeth I (43 Eliz 1 c 4, the Charitable Uses Act 1601), that is to say that it was charitable in the same sense as the recited purposes in that preamble are charitable. The Court of Appeal referred to Viscount Haldane's remarks in *A-G v National Provincial and Union Bank of England* [1924] AC 262 at 267, [1923] All ER Rep 123 at 126 distinguishing between benefiting a cause

g (for example, patriotism) which would not be a charitable object and a charitable object benefiting people who would otherwise not have benefited. The appeasement of racial feeling was said to be such a cause ([1949] 2 All ER 6 at 9, [1949] Ch 529 at 538). After referring to certain opinions expressed by a deponent on the proper educational methods for the appeasement of racial feeling, Lord Greene MR said this ([1949] 2 All ER 6 at 9, [1949] Ch 529 at 538):

h   'It is unfortunate if, as may well be, these methods were in the testator's mind that he did not seek to constitute a trust which might well have been valid as an educational trust notwithstanding that the education had the ultimate aim as set out in the will.'

Those remarks were obiter and, as was said by Plowman J in *Buxton v Public Trustee* (1962)

j 41 TC 235 at 242–243 in relation to those remarks, all depends on the language used describing the objects of the trust. On the language used by Sir Heinz in his will and in the conference previews, I reach the conclusion that the purpose of Wilton Park at the date of the will and at his death were the formation end and the promotion end. The evidence to the contrary contained in the affidavits put in on behalf of Wilton Park and in the recitals to the declaration of trust seems to me to be of lesser weight than the contemporaneous words of Sir Heinz.

Are those purposes charitable? Counsel for Mr Slack submitted that the formation end is an exclusively educational purpose, further or alternatively a purpose falling within the fourth head of Lord Macnaghten's classification of charitable purposes in *Income Tax Special Purposes Comrs v Pemsel* [1891] AC 531 at 583, [1891–4] All ER Rep 28 at 55, that is to say a purpose other than the relief of poverty, education and religion, which is beneficial to the community. He also submitted that the promotion end falls within the fourth head.

Counsel for Mr Slack referred me to a number of cases where gifts have been held to be educational for the purpose of the law of charity: *Royal Choral Society v IRC* [1943] 2 All ER 101, *Re Shaw's Will Trusts, National Provincial Bank Ltd v National City Bank Ltd* [1952] 1 All ER 49, [1952] Ch 163, *Re Trusts of the Arthur McDougall Fund, Thompson v Fitzgerald* [1956] 3 All ER 867, [1957] 1 WLR 81, *Re Hopkins's Will Trusts, Naish v Francis Bacon Society Inc* [1964] 3 All ER 46, [1965] Ch 669, *IRC v McMullen* [1980] 1 All ER 884, [1981] AC 1 and *Barralet v A-G* [1980] 3 All ER 918, sub nom *Re South Place Ethical Society* [1980] 1 WLR 1565. These cases illustrate the broad and evolving concept of education in the law of charity, but in none was language used bearing any close similarity to that of the purpose in the present case.

Counsel for Mr Slack also referred me to *Tribune Press, Lahore (Trustees) v Income Tax Comr, Punjab, Lahore* [1939] 3 All ER 469, in which the Privy Council held that a gift of the stock and goodwill of a newspaper had the object of supplying the province of Lahore with an organ of educated public opinion and that it should, prima facie, be held to be an object of general public utility and as such exempt from tax under an Indian taxing Act. Whilst there is some similarity between such an object and the formation object, the purpose of the gift in that case was far more limited in scope than the formation object. I was also referred to *Re Harwood* [1936] Ch 285, [1935] All ER Rep 918, in which it was accepted, apparently without argument to the contrary, that gifts to peace societies were charitable gifts. The purposes with which I am concerned are differently worded and in any event it seems to me at least strongly arguable that the purposes of a peace society are political and not charitable.

In my judgment the short answer to the submissions of counsel for Mr Slack was provided by counsel for the Attorney General, who accepted that the formation end and the promotion end were not amenable to the control of the court, being too vague and uncertain to be valid charitable objects. The requirement of certainty must be satisfied in relation to a charitable as well as any other type of trust. The court must be able to control the application of a charity's assets and its activities by reference to its purposes. If the purposes are couched in vague language, the court cannot do so. I have already referred to the remarks of the Court of Appeal in *Re Strakosch (decd), Temperley v A-G* [1949] 2 All ER 6, [1949] Ch 529, in which the court in holding that a gift was not charitable referred to the very wide and vague scope of the gift.

Even if that be wrong, there are other objections as well. I doubt if the formation end can be limited to an exclusively educational purpose, wide thought the concept of education is in the law of charity, and, whilst it may be a purpose of public utility, I doubt if it is of a kind which the law regards as charitable so as to bring it within the fourth head of Lord Macnaghten's classification. But I need not express any final conclusion in respect of that purpose. There are to my mind clearer objections to the promotion end. In my judgment that purpose cannot be said to be an educational purpose. Again it may be described as of public utility, but not in my judgment in a manner which the law regards as charitable. It is well established that not every object of public utility falls within the spirit and intendment of the Statute of Elizabeth. The law has developed empirically, case by case, and the decided cases seem to me to point away from, rather than to support, such an object being charitable.

Counsel for Mrs Capper drew my attention to two cases, *Anglo-Swedish Society v IRC* (1931) 16 TC 34 and *Buxton v Public Trustee* (1962) 41 TC 235. The earlier case related to an unincorporated association under the rules of which it had as its objects the promotion of a closer and more sympathetic understanding between the English and Swedish peoples, to secure which object it was proposed as a first measure to afford opportunities

for Swedish journalists to visit the United Kingdom and to study at first hand British
a modes of thought and British national institutions. Rowlatt J held that whilst that object
might be thought a useful public object it was not charitable within the analogy of the
Statute of Elizabeth. He said (16 TC 34 at 38):

> 'Now what is this? It is a trust really to promote an attitude of mind, the view of
> one nation by another; that is all really that it is. There may be many trusts to
> influence general opinion the results of which influence may be very good, but
b > where the immediate trust is only to influence general opinion in favour of some
> theory or aspiration, or whatever it may be, I cannot myself see that the statute of
> Elizabeth is looking to that sort of thing at all. Education and relief of poverty and
> all these things seem to me to materialise, if I may use the expression, in some fairly
> proximate way. Perhaps the least one says about it the better, because, as I said this
> morning, as Lord Haldane said, it is much easier to say that a certain case does not
c > come within the doctrine than to define the limits of the doctrine affirmatively. I
> must say I think in this case that I cannot see where this case touches the area which
> one may consider to be marked out by the analogy of the statute of Elizabeth; it
> seems to me outside it and on a different plane altogether.'

The reference to Lord Haldane I take to be a reference to his speech in *A-G v National*
d *Provincial and Union Bank of England* [1924] AC 262, [1923] All ER Rep 123 to another
part of which I have referred in relation to *Re Strakosch (decd), Temperley v A-G* [1949] 2
All ER 6, [1949] Ch 529. So too in the present case it can be said that the promotion end
is a cause and, as such, too nebulous a purpose and is not seen to benefit persons in any
material way analogous with what is contained in the preamble to the Statute of
Elizabeth.

e Even closer, to my mind, is the decision of Plowman J in *Buxton v Public Trustee* (1962)
41 TC 235. In that case there was a trust the purposes of which were expressed as 'To
promote and aid the improvement of international relations and intercourse by', and
then there are set out four lettered sub-paragraphs of which sub-para (*a*) was 'Educating
or informing public opinion' by certain methods there specified and sub-para (*e*) was
'Employing or following any other methods which in the opinion of the Trustees may
f conduce to the attainment of the above-mentioned objects and purposes'. It was conceded
on behalf of the Attorney General in that case that the trusts were not exclusively
charitable. The question that arose was whether the trusts were validated by the
Charitable Trusts (Validation) Act 1954 as being for objects such that the property could
be used exclusively for charitable purposes but could nevertheless be used for purposes
which were not charitable. It was argued on behalf of the Revenue that the only objects
g were the improvement of international relations and intercourse and that those objects
were political objects containing no element of charity. It was argued for the Attorney
General that sub-para (*a*) represented a charitable (that is to say educational) method of
application such that the 1954 Act applied to the trusts. Plowman J rejected the Attorney
General's argument. He drew a distinction between the objects of the trusts ('To promote
and aid the improvement of international relations and intercourse') and the methods set
h out in the lettered sub-paragraphs which he said were not ends but means. He then asked
himself the question whether the purposes of the trusts comprehended a charitable
educational purpose and answered that question by saying that the objects of the trusts
had nothing to do with charity. He cited extensively from *Anglo-Swedish Society v IRC*
(1931) 16 TC 34 and *Re Strakosch (decd), Temperley v A-G* [1949] 2 All ER 6, [1949] Ch 529
and said (41 TC 235 at 242):

j
> 'So here it seems to me that the objects of this trust are really public utility or
> political. The only element of education which might be said to be comprehended
> in those objects appears to me to be education for a political cause, by the creation of
> a climate of opinion and that is not, in my judgment, education of a kind which is
> charitable. As Mr. Stamp [counsel for the Revenue] said, it is really no more than
> propaganda.'

There is an obvious similarity between promoting and aiding the improvement of international relations and intercourse and the promotion of greater co-operation in Europe and the West in general. Indeed, if the objects in *Buxton v Public Trustee* are political, a fortiori the promotion end can be described as political, the co-operation referred to being limited to Europe and the West and therefore excluding the remainder of the world and in particular the East with its connotation of a different political system from that enjoyed in Europe and the West.

Counsel for Mr Slack submitted that I should follow *Re Harwood* [1936] Ch 285, [1935] All ER Rep 918 rather than *Buxton v Public Trustee* (1962) 41 TC 235. I decline to do so. In *Buxton v Public Trustee* the point was fully argued and, as I have said, the language of the purpose is similar language to that used in the present case. In *Re Harwood* it was accepted without argument that a peace society was charitable, and I have indicated my doubts whether the court was right in that acceptance. Unless therefore it can be shown that Plowman J was wrong, it seems to me that I should, by analogy with that case, hold that the formation end is political and of public utility without being charitable, even though counsel for Mrs Capper confined his submissions to the latter point.

Counsel for the Attorney General submitted that *Buxton v Public Trustee* (1962) 41 TC 235 was distinguishable. It is true that it related to the application of the 1954 Act with which I am not concerned, but the ratio of the case was that the object of the trust in that case was not charitable and to that extent that authority has direct relevance to the present case. Counsel for the Attorney General also submitted that Plowman J went too far in his comments on education for a political cause. He said that the mere fact that the donor has a political aim or that political consequences may flow from the gift does not cause the gift to be for a political purpose and so not charitable. Counsel for the Attorney General referred me to *McGovern v A-G* [1981] 3 All ER 493, [1982] Ch 321 in which Slade J considered various authorities relating to trusts for political purposes. The classic statement on this subject is that by Lord Parker in *Bowman v Secular Society Ltd* [1917] AC 406 at 442, [1916–17] All ER Rep 1 at 18 to the effect that trusts for the alteration of the law are political objects and invalid not as being illegal but because the court has no means of judging whether a proposed change in the law will or will not be for the public benefit. Slade J recognised that there are other trusts which are not directed at a change in the law but which the court will nevertheless regard as political and within the spirit of Lord Parker's remarks. Slade J summarised his conclusions in relation to trusts for political purposes thus ([1981] 3 All ER 493 at 508–509, [1982] Ch 321 at 340):

'(1) Even if it otherwise appears to fall within the spirit and intendment of the preamble to the Statute of Elizabeth, a trust for political purposes falling within the spirit of Lord Parker's pronouncement in *Bowman's* case can never be regarded as being for the public benefit in the manner which the law regards as charitable. (2) Trusts for political purposes falling within the spirit of this pronouncement include (inter alia) trusts of which a direct and principal purpose is either—(i) to further the interests of a particular political party, or (ii) to procure changes in the laws of this country, or (iii) to procure changes in the laws of a foreign country, or (iv) to procure a reversal of government policy or of particular decisions of governmental authorities in this country, or (v) to procure a reversal of government policy or of particular decisions of governmental authorities in a foreign country.'

But Slade J made clear that his categorisation was not intended to be exhaustive, nor in my view was it exhaustive. For example, trusts to oppose a particular change in the law or a change in a particular law would not in my view be charitable (see eg *Re Hopkinson (decd), Lloyds Bank Ltd v Baker* [1949] 1 All ER 346 at 350), as I think counsel for the Attorney General accepted. Further, in my judgment, trusts aimed at securing better international relations, including co-operation in a particular part of the world, can properly be called political causes and within the spirit of Lord Parker's pronouncement, because the court cannot pronounce on the public benefit of such causes. Whether there should be better relations and co-operation and, if so, how it should be achieved and with whom are matters for government decision, not for the court. Counsel for the Attorney

General submitted, rightly in my view, that educational trusts are charitable
a notwithstanding that there may be political consequences therefrom. Thus in *McGovern
v A-G* [1981] 3 All ER 493, [1982] Ch 321 Slade J would have held that the objects of
Amnesty International, which are limited to research into human rights and the
dissemination of the results of that research, would have been charitable had they not
been tainted by the political objects to which they were held to be adjuncts. Again,
counsel for the Attorney General referred me to the approval given by Slade J to the
b celebrated American case, *Jackson v Phillips* (1867) 96 Mass 539, in which the object was
to create a public sentiment to put an end to negro slavery in America. In that case it was
held that only lawful and not political means were to be used to achieve an object falling
within the spirit and almost the letter of many clauses in the Statute of Elizabeth. It is of
course necessary to consider each case on its own facts to ascertain the purposes of a gift.
A trust to provide education for a political aim would in my judgment not be charitable
c notwithstanding that the means may be charitable (cf *Bonar Law Memorial Trust v IRC*
(1933) 17 TC 508). In the present case having regard to the language used by Sir Heinz, I
cannot escape the conclusion that in the formation end the gift has a political purpose. In
any event, though of public utility, in my judgment it is a cause which does not come
within the spirit and intendment of the preamble to the Statute of Elizabeth.

Counsel for the Attorney General further submitted that even if the purposes were not
d charitable, the only method prescribed by Sir Heinz of achieving those purposes was the
Wilton Park process. That method, he submitted, was charitable as being educational
and the gift was therefore valid. Counsel for Mr Slack also submitted that the work of
Wilton Park was educational. Counsel for Mrs Capper argued to the contrary. Let me
consider first whether the Wilton Park process can properly be described as educational.
Counsel for the Attorney General submitted, and I accept, that the following salient
e points emerged from the evidence: (i) the conference sought to improve the minds of
participants, not necessarily by adding to their factual knowledge but by expanding their
wisdom and capacity to understand; (ii) the subjects discussed at conferences were
recognised academic subjects in higher education; (iii) the conferences operated by a
process of discussion designed to elicit an exchange of views in a manner familiar in
places of higher education; (iv) the conferences were designed to capitalise on the
f expertise of participants who were there both to learn and to instruct.

Counsel for Mrs Capper took several points. First, he submitted that the process was
merely an exchange of views and that, he said, was not educational. He referred me to
Smith v Kerr [1902] 1 Ch 774 at 779, where Collins MR made certain observations that
suggest that he would not have accepted that the mutual interchange of the views of
novice law students in debate was educational. But there is no clear statement of principle
g on this point by the Master of the Rolls and in any event the position here is different. In
my judgment the concept of education is now wide enough to cover the intensive
discussion process adopted by Wilton Park in relation to a somewhat special class of
adults, persons influencing opinion in their own countries, designed (as I was told Sir
Heinz put it) to dent opinions and to cross-fertilise ideas. Second, counsel for Mrs Capper
submitted that the selection process meant that the benefits of Wilton Park were not
h available to the public but were only available to a narrow class, an elite, those influencing
opinion in their own countries. He referred me to *Oppenheim v Tobacco Securities Trust Co
Ltd* [1951] 1 All ER 31, ['1951] AC 297 and *Dingle v Turner* [1972] 1 All ER 878, [1972]
AC 601; to which counsel for the Attorney General added *Davies v Perpetual Trustee Co
Ltd* [1959] 2 All ER 128, [1959] AC 439. Those cases establish that the benefits of a
charity (other than for the relief of poverty) must be for a sufficient section of the
j community and the beneficiaries must not be a private class qualifying by reason of some
relationship unconnected with the charitable purpose. But in the present case the
participants appear to have been widely drawn and cannot properly be described as a
private class. Though the participants are selected, selectivity is common in higher
education.

Third, counsel for Mrs Capper submitted by reference to *Gilmour v Coats* [1949] 1 All
ER 848, [1949] AC 426 that the gift must promote a public benefit and there is no

evidence of such a benefit having been promoted. The present case is on its facts far removed from the case of the community of cloistered and contemplative nuns which was the subject of *Gilmour v Coats*. In my judgment the law is entitled to assume a benefit from those who attend an educational course, just as it can from attendance at a place of worship by those who live in the world and mix with their fellow citizens (see *Neville Estates Ltd v Madden* [1961] 3 All ER 769 at 781, [1962] Ch 832 at 853 per Cross J; see also *Re Shaw's Will Trusts, National Provincial Bank Ltd v National City Bank Ltd* [1952] 1 All ER 49 at 53–54, [1952] Ch 163 at 169). This is the more so when those attending the educational course are selected as persons influencing opinion in their own country and who can be expected to pass on the benefits of the Wilton Park process.

I would therefore hold that the Wilton Park process can be described as educational.

However I have difficulty in accepting the submissions of counsel for the Attorney General based thereon. First, I cannot accept that Sir Heinz had limited the means of attaining the promotion end and the formation end to the Wilton Park process. Though I suspect that is what he may have had in mind, the will is silent on this point. Second, although counsel for Mrs Capper was prepared to concede the point, I do not see how a gift for a non-charitable purpose but by charitable means becomes a valid charitable gift. A gift is charitable because it has charitable purposes. If a gift has non-charitable purposes, the charitable means do not in my judgment endow the gift with different purposes. Accordingly I cannot accept that the charitable nature of the Wilton Park process makes the gift valid.

Finally I must revert to the point to which I referred earlier, that is to say the changeable nature of Wilton Park. I do not doubt that it is possible for a donor to make a gift to persons carrying on an activity for a particular purpose albeit under no fixed rules in such a way as to fix the purpose of the gift by reference to that activity and the purpose for which it is for the time being carried on. In the present case Sir Heinz, whilst recognising that Wilton Park might not remain in the particular form defined by reference to purposes that it had in his eyes at the date of the will, nevertheless did not make his gift to Wilton Park conditional on its remaining in that form after his death. Given that Wilton Park had no immutable form, his gift if valid would not have prevented those running Wilton Park from changing its form, including its purposes, after his death. In such circumstances, on this ground too I think that the gift in favour of Wilton Park cannot be said to be for exclusively charitable purposes.

For all these reasons I reach the conclusion that the gift for the benefit of Wilton Park is not exclusively charitable and it therefore fails.

The second question, conditional as it is on the gift to Wilton Park taking effect as a charitable bequest, does not arise.

The third question relates to the gift to Magdalen. At first blush the answer to that question would seem obvious. The gift was subject to a condition precedent that Wilton Park should have ceased to exist in 'such form', ie as a British contribution to the formation end and the promotion end. It is common ground that whatever else might be said about Wilton Park, there was no material change between the date of the will and the date of death. It is well established that as a general principle, where there is a gift over upon a certain contingency, it will not take effect unless the exact contingency happens (see *Theobald on Wills* (14th edn, 1982) p 655). The primary example given in *Theobald* is a gift to A with a gift over if he dies in the testator's lifetime and A dies simultaneously with the testator. In such a case the gift over does not take effect. There are two distinct and independent events on which the gift to A will lapse, death in the testator's life-time and death simultaneously with the testator, one of which the testator has contemplated and the other not. It is pointed out in *Theobald* that no doubt it might be said that the gift over might be read as equivalent to 'if A does not survive me, to B,' but this would be making a will for the testator, since the event that happened did not include the event contemplated and it cannot be said that if the gift over was to take effect if A died in the testator's lifetime, a fortiori it was to have effect if A died simultaneously with the testator.

Counsel for Magdalen submitted that the present case falls within a well-recognised

exception to that principle. It is known as the rule in *Jones v Westcomb* (1711) Prec Ch
a 316, 24 ER 149. Its origin appears to be of even more respectable, indeed remarkable,
antiquity. In *Hall v Warren* (1861) 9 HL Cas 420 at 429–430, 11 ER 791 at 795 Lord
Campbell LC referred to their Lordships' House being well aware of what was the leading
case. That was a Roman case of 68 BC reported by no less a reporter than Cicero. The rule
is applicable where, although the exact event on which the gift over is to take effect does
not occur, the gift over must a fortiori have been intended to take effect in the event that
b happens (see *Theobald* p 656). Thus if there is a gift to a child of which the testator
supposed his wife to be pregnant and there is a gift over if the child dies under 21, or if
there is a gift to a class of children with a gift over if they all die under 21, and the wife is
not pregnant or there never are any children of the class, the gift over nevertheless takes
effect. Of the two cases cited to me by counsel for Magdalen, one, *Re Fox's Estate* [1937]
4 All ER 664, is an illustration of the application of the rule in similar circumstances,
c though in fact the point appears to have been conceded. In that case there was a bequest
of a share in an estate to the testator's daughter Anne for life and after her death for her
children equally, and there was a direction that any legacy which by the death of any
person should lapse should go to another daughter. Anne survived the testator but died
without ever having children and her share lapsed for that reason. What was said to be
the real argument in that case was as to the meaning of 'lapse', it being contended that it
d should bear its technical meaning of death in the lifetime of the testator. That contention
was rejected and the Court of Appeal held that 'lapse' in the will included death before
the legacy vested in possession. On that construction it was not disputed that the rule in
Jones v Westcomb (1711) Prec Ch 316, 24 ER 149 applied. There is little difficulty in cases
of this sort. The testator by the condition attached to the gift over indicates that he
assumes the beneficiary under the previous conditional limitation will come into
e existence. If that beneficiary never exists, it can be inferred that the testator intended the
gift over to take effect not only, as he has expressly provided, if the beneficiary fails to
perform the condition but also if the beneficiary never exists. The greater includes the
less.

Counsel for Magdalen placed chief reliance on *Hall v Warren* (1861) 9 HL Cas 420, 11
ER 791, reported in the court below as *Warren v Rudall* (1858) 4 K & J 603, 70 ER 250.
f In that case a testator devised a house in Bayswater to the inhabitants of Bayswater for a
specific charitable purpose. He directed that his executors should call a meeting of local
inhabitants to appoint a committee and trustees to carry out the scheme, but in the event
of the inhabitants not appointing a committee or not being willing to carry out the
scheme there was a gift over. The charitable gift failed as offending the Statute of
Mortmain, the Charitable Uses Act 1735. No meeting of the local inhabitants took place.
g Page Wood V-C held that the rule in *Jones v Westcomb* (1711) Prec Ch 316, 24 ER 149
applied. He said that there was no difference in principle between a gift to a nonentity
followed by a gift over if that nonentity failed to satisfy a condition and a gift to a charity
which by operation of law could not take followed by a gift over if that charity omitted
to perform a specified act. His decision on this point was affirmed by the House of Lords
(9 HL Cas 420, 11 ER 791). Lord Campbell LC, while saying that the rule applied,
h expressed himself more broadly. He held that the testator, ignorant of the Statute of
Mortmain, intended that the failure, from whatever cause, of the foundation of the
charity was the contingency on which he intended the gift over to take effect. Lord
Cranworth pointed out that the condition on which the gift over was to take effect had
in fact been satisfied as there never had been a meeting to appoint a committee.
Accordingly he said that there was no room for the application of the rule in *Jones v*
j *Westcomb*. However, he went on to say that if the inhabitants had met and appointed a
committee and trustees (that is to say if the very opposite to the condition for the gift
over had occurred), and the charity had failed by reason only of the Statute of Mortmain,
he was inclined to think that the rule would apply (see 9 HL Cas 420 at 431–432, 11 ER
791 at 796). Lord Wensleydale expressed very considerable doubt and stated the general
principle of giving effect to a particular condition but did not dissent from the remainder
of the House. Lord Kingsdown said that the gift over took effect whether by the precise

language of the condition or the general intention of the testator. Despite the diversity of views expressed in it, *Hall v Warren* is therefore an instance of the operation of the rule **a** in *Jones v Westcomb* in circumstances where by operation of law the limitation prior to the gift over fails. So, counsel for Magdalen says, it provides a close analogy with the present case.

I state the obvious when I say that the true construction of each will must be ascertained from the language of that will. A rule of construction like that of *Jones v Westcomb* is merely an aid to ascertain what the testator intended. In *Hall v Warren* Lord Campbell **b** was able to find from the language of the will that the testator intended the gift over to take effect however the previous limitation failed. In the present case Sir Heinz limited Magdalen to taking only if at his death Wilton Park ceased to exist in the form he specified, and not if that cesser occurred at any time after the death. Whatever the law says about the existence of Wilton Park as an institution, viewed from the armchair of Sir Heinz Wilton Park had an existence as an institution at the date of the will and indeed **c** since 1946 and nothing changed before the time of his death when Wilton Park had as much existence as it ever had. It still continued to operate as it had done before. To treat the gift over as taking effect because the gift for the benefit of Wilton Park fails by operation of law therefore involves contradicting the express terms of the condition for the gift over. Counsel for Mrs Capper submitted that none of the authorities, including *Hall v Warren*, goes so far as that, and that it cannot be said in such circumstances that **d** the gift over must a fortiori have effect.

I agree with counsel for Mrs Capper. The general rule of construction of a conditional gift requires the condition to be strictly observed. The rule in *Jones v Westcomb* is but a limited exception, operating where, from the condition attached to the gift, it is possible to infer that the testator must have intended the gift over to take effect on another event not express but implicit in the condition. To extend the rule in *Jones v Westcomb* to a case **e** such as the present would involve a contradiction of the express terms of the gift over and would be tantamount to holding that, in a case where a previous gift fails only by operation of law, the gift over must take effect whatever the terms of the condition. I do not think that is justified. The only support for applying the rule in such circumstances is the tentative obiter dictum of Lord Cranworth to which I have referred, and I am not persuaded that I should follow it. I should add that after the conclusion of the argument **f** in this case I have found in the judgments of the Court of Appeal in *Re Bailey (decd)*, *Barrett v Hyder* [1951] 1 All ER 391, [1951] Ch 407 support for the view that I had already formed that the rule in *Jones v Westcomb* should not be made to apply to circumstances which would involve a contradiction of the condition for the gift over.

Therefore despite counsel for Magdalen's attractive argument, I must hold that there was an intestacy as to the 20/36ths share. **g**

I confess that I have reached these conclusions on the first and third questions with considerable regret. The work of Wilton Park, being the work of Sir Heinz's lifetime, seems to me to be admirable and worth while. Plainly Sir Heinz would have liked Wilton Park and, failing that, Magdalen to benefit, and by using somewhat different language in his will I believe he could have achieved that result. But I cannot rewrite Sir Heinz's will for him even under the benignancy principle. I am glad to note from Mrs Capper's **h** affidavit that in the event of the bequest failing she intends to honour her brother's memory in some other way.

In the result I answer question 1 of the amended originating summons in sense c(ii). Question 1(a) does not arise.

Gift for benefit of Wilton Park failed; gift over failed; legacy passed on a partial intestacy to **j** *testator's next of kin.*

Solicitors: *J E Dell & Loader*, Brighton (for Barclays Bank Trust Co plc); *Akerman & Co*, Storrington (for Mr Slack); *Sears Tooth & Co* (for Mrs Capper); *Grangewoods* (for Magdalen); *Treasury Solicitor*.

Vivian Horvath   Barrister.

a
Gewiese and another v Mackenzie
(Case 24/83)

COURT OF JUSTICE OF THE EUROPEAN COMMUNITIES
JUDGES MERTENS DE WILMARS (PRESIDENT), KOOPMANS, BAHLMANN, GALMOT (PRESIDENTS OF
CHAMBERS), PESCATORE, LORD MACKENZIE STUART, O'KEEFFE, BOSCO, DUE, EVERLING AND

b
KAKOURIS
ADVOCATE GENERAL SIR GORDON SLYNN
1, 15 DECEMBER 1983, 14 FEBRUARY 1984

European Economic Community – Fishing rights – Conservation – National measures –

c
Consultation – Re-enactment of national measure – Re-enactment without substantive amendment
– Re-enactment to cure technical defect – Original measure made after consultation and with
approval of EC Commission – Re-enacted measure notified to but made without consultation of
Commission – Validity of re-enacted measure – Whether fresh consultation of Commission required
before re-enactment – West Coast Herring (Prohibition of Fishing) Order 1981.

d
The masters of two German fishing vessels were convicted in a sheriff court of fishing for
herring off the west coast of Scotland on 10 July 1981 contrary to the West Coast Herring
(Prohibition of Fishing) Order 1981. They appealed to the High Court of Justiciary,
contending that the 1981 order was not in conformity with Community law because,
although its making had been notified to the EC Commission, it had been made without
prior consultation of the Commission. The 1981 order was a re-enactment of a 1978

e
order the proposed making of which had been notified to the Commission and the
making of which had been approved by the Commission so far as it was a national
conservation measure. The 1981 order, which was not materially different from the
1978 order, had been made after the 1978 order had been held by a court in England to
be invalid to the extent that it included in the prohibited area certain waters adjacent to
Northern Ireland. The re-enactment of the 1978 order in the 1981 order was designed to

f
cure that defect. The High Court of Justiciary referred to the Court of Justice of the
European Communities the question of the absence of express Commission approval of
a re-enactment of a national conservation measure which had been made and maintained
in conformity with Community law.

g
Held – Although the notification of new national measures for the conservation of
fishery resources continued to be necessary in order that the EC Commission might be
accurately informed of the state of the law in force in the various member states, no fresh
consultation of the Commission was required in the case of the re-enactment, without
substantive amendment, of a measure which had previously been adopted in conformity
with the procedural and substantive conditions laid down by Community law (see p 135

h
b c h and p 136 *a*, post).
EC Commission v UK Case 804/79 [1981] ECR 1045 distinguished.

Notes
For fishing rights in the European Economic Community, see 18 Halsbury's Laws (4th

j
edn) para 608.

Cases cited
Dunkley v Evans [1981] 3 All ER 285, [1981] 1 WLR 1522, DC.
EC Commission v UK Case 804/79 [1981] ECR 1045.
R v Tymen Case 269/80 [1981] ECR 3079.

Reference

The High Court of Justiciary, Scotland, referred a question (set out at p 134 *c d*, post) as   *a*
to the re-enactment without substantive amendment, of a national conservation measure
to the Court of Justice of the European Communities under art 177 of the EEC Treaty.
The question arose following the conviction on 13 July 1981 in the Sheriff Court at
Stornoway, on the complaint of Colin Scott Mackenzie, the Procurator Fiscal, Stornoway,
of Manfred Mehlich and Wolfgang Gewiese of contravening the West Coast Herring
(Prohibition of Fishing) Order 1981, SI 1981/585, on 10 July 1981, for which they were   *b*
admonished and their catches confiscated. The convictions were brought under review
by the High Court of Justiciary by way of stated case on the ground, inter alia, that the
1981 order was invalid under Community law. The United Kingdom, the Procurator
Fiscal, the government of the Federal Republic of Germany and the Commission of the
European Communities submitted observations to the court. The language of the case
was English. The facts are set out in the opinion of the Advocate General.   *c*

The Solicitor General for Scotland (Peter Fraser QC) for the Procurator Fiscal and the United
    Kingdom.
Martin Seidel for the government of the Federal Republic of Germany.
Richard Wainwright for the EC Commission.

    d

15 December. **The Advocate General (Sir Gordon Slynn)** delivered the following
opinion. My Lords, the masters of two German fishing vessels, the Hannover and the
Kiel, were found fishing for herring off the west coast of Scotland on 10 July 1981. They
were arrested and prosecuted for an offence under the West Coast Herring (Prohibition
of Fishing) Order 1981, SI 1981/585, which was made under the Sea Fish (Conservation)   *e*
Act 1967 (as amended) and which prohibited fishing in the area where the vessels were
found. On 13 July 1981, after trial, the masters were convicted and admonished, their
catch being confiscated. They appealed to the High Court of Justiciary on the ground
that the 1981 order infringed Community law. That court has referred to the Court of
Justice under art 177 of the EEC Treaty the following question:

> 'Where, after 1 January 1979, a Member State notifies the Commission of a re-   *f*
> enactment, without substantive amendment, of a national conservation measure
> which was itself made and maintained in conformity with Community law, does
> the measure so re-enacted remain made and maintained in conformity with
> Community law in the absence of express Commission approval?'

The question arises in this way. On 16 June 1978, following a recommendation by the   *g*
International Council for the Exploration of the Sea, in the light of then depleted herring
stocks, the Commission proposed that in a zone including the area in question (and
known as ICES Division VI(a)) no herring fishing should be allowed as from 1 July 1978.
The United Kingdom government, following the practice agreed in the Hague Resolution
of 3 November 1976, notified the Commission on 3 July 1978 of an order which it
proposed to make, with effect from 6 July 1978, forbidding the fishing of herring in the   *h*
relevant area. After querying the omission of one area from the scope of the order, which
was satisfactorily explained, the Commission approved the order, the West Coast
(Prohibition of Fishing) Order 1978, SI 1978/930, on 22 December 1978.

By a judgment given on 15 April 1981, the High Court in London held that the 1978
order was invalid to the extent that it included certain waters adjacent to Northern
Ireland (since they were excluded from the 1967 Act referred to and included in the   *j*
Fisheries Act (Northern Ireland) 1966 (as amended) but was otherwise valid (see *Dunkley
v Evans* [1981] 3 All ER 285, [1981] 1 WLR 1522). The Northern Ireland waters comprise
0·8% of the total area covered by the 1978 order.

Separate orders were then made to cover the waters respectively included in each of
the statutes referred to, the order made under the 1967 Act, under which the prosecution

a   in this case was brought, the 1981 order, being made on 6 April 1981, to come into operation on 1 May 1981. The two orders together dealt with the whole area covered by the 1978 order, but only that area, and, apart from dividing the area, were in no material way different from it. The two new orders were notified to the Commission by letter of 4 May 1981 with the explanation that 'it has been necessary to correct a minor technical error' in the 1978 order. On 1 July 1982 the United Kingdom government, in reply to a question from the Commission dated 27 May, explained the reasons why these two

b   orders had been made following the High Court's decision.

The principal point of law taken on behalf of the two defendants was that the Commission should have been asked to approve the 1981 order before it was made. It was not asked in advance.

On 1 January 1979, after the 1978 order had been made, the six-year transitional period provided for in art 102 of the Act of Accession (1972) expired. The court has held

c   in *EC Commission v UK* Case 804/79 [1981] ECR 1045 that thereupon the Community had exclusive powers in respect of fishery conservation matters, and that conservation measures in existence at that time should not be altered by member states, save in a limited way as required by biological or technical developments, and not in any event so as to change the policy. The Commission was to be consulted about, and its approval sought of, conservation measures by member states. In fact, the Council maintained the

d   national conservation measures which were in force on 31 December 1978 by decisions relating to the years 1979 and 1980. On 27 March 1981, though no final agreement had by then been reached by the Council as to what should happen in 1981, the Council noted that certain steps were to be taken by member states. In the English version, this minute reads: '. . . would take conservation measures similar to those which had been taken in previous years.' The German text is capable of a different meaning. The sense

e   may be rather that of taking measures appropriate to the need to avoid disturbance rather than measures corresponding to those taken in previous years; on the other hand, the French text is: '. . . des mesures de conservation analogues à celles qu'ils avaient déjà prises durant les années précédentes.'

On 5 May 1981 the ICES Herring Working Group, in the light of the current stock position, recommended to the ICES Advisory Committee on Fishery Management

f   (ACFM) that a total allowable catch of 62,500 tonnes should be permitted in area ICES VI(a). The Commission adopted this suggestion in a proposal to the Council made on 12 June. Thereafter, on 29 June the two masters were licensed by the government of the Federal Republic of Germany to fish in that area. On 3 July the ACFM recommended that the figure be increased to 65,000 tonnes and that figure was in turn recommended by the Commission to the Council on 24 July. On 27 July the Council met but was

g   unable to reach agreement, and on 28 July the Commission issued a formal declaration (to be found in (1981) OJ C224, p 1) calling on member states to carry out the Commission's 'existing proposals', which the Commission considered 'in the present situation as being legally binding upon the Member States and which the Commission intended to do all in its power to enforce'. The next day the Commission, having cited the proposals made to the Council, told the United Kingdom government that it could

h   not approve the 1981 orders 'as they are not now justified by the requirements of conservation'. Nor could analogous provisions to those in the 1978 order 'continue to have the approval of the Commission as they [stood]'. The United Kingdom government was asked not to apply those measures, to repeal them as necessary and to replace them with measures compatible with the new proposals. The 1981 order was in fact revoked with effect from 11 August, the Northern Ireland order three days later.

j   The prosecution in the case, supported by the United Kingdom government and the Commission, contends that on 10 and 13 July the 1981 order was valid. All that had happened is that the 1978 order had been re-enacted following an error, and no substantive changes were made. The position was just the same, so far as the relevant waters were concerned, as if the partially valid 1978 order had been left untidily in existence, or amended so as to delete the Northern Ireland waters. The 1978 order had been approved and its complete equivalent did not need the Commission's approval since no change was made.   *a*

The government of the Federal Republic contends that all measures, whether involving changes of substance or not, require the approval of the Commission; if they do not get it prior to enactment, they are automatically invalid. At the least they must be submitted prior to adoption. Moreover, in the present case, it was well known even prior to the April–May meeting of the ICES Working Group that herring spawn stocks far exceeded the minimum of 200,000 tonnes which justified the reintroduction of fishing. That   *b* knowledge and in particular the proposals made on 5 May produced such a substantial difference that the 1981 order could not lawfully re-enact the 1978 order. The logic of the argument compelled the German government to say that the 1978 order should have been replaced in any event at the latest once these proposals of the ICES Herring Working Group were made. It goes further and contends that the 1978 order was defective because it was not limited in time, since review of the position should take place on an annual   *c* basis. Above all, once the Commission made its proposals on 12 June, the 1981 order ceased to be valid so that on 10 July no offence was committed. This latter point is not covered by the express terms of the question referred, apparently by deliberate decision of the national court. It is, however, convenient to deal with it briefly to test the strength of the argument as to the position at the time the 1981 order was made.

I can see nothing in the EEC Treaty, in EEC Council Regulation 101/76 of 19 January   *d* 1976, laying down a common structural policy for the fishing industry, or in the court's judgments in *EC Commission v UK* Case 804/79 [1981] ECR 1045 or *R v Tymen* Case 269/80 [1981] ECR 3079 which require that approved national measures have to be limited in time or fixed on an annual basis. It is sufficient that as and when Community policy changes they should be replaced or amended. Nor does it seem to me to be the law that when the facts change, here that herring stocks had increased, national measures cease to   *e* be valid and cannot lawfully be re-enacted. A recommendation of the ICES Herring Working Group to the ACFM and the latter's recommendations to the Commission are no doubt of great importance in the formulation of Community policy, but those bodies are not composed exclusively of the member states and they are not organs of the Commission. Their reports did not accordingly invalidate the 1978 order or mean that the situation had so changed that, subject to the procedural argument, the 1981 order   *f* could not re-enact it. It seems to me that the High Court of Justiciary was right to pose its question on the basis that the 1978 order was not only lawfully made, but also lawfully 'maintained'. The contrary result would lead to uncertainty and diversification and seems wrong in principle, since it presupposes that national provisions become invalid without the intervention of any Community institution.

Nor does it seem to me that the terms of the Council minute of 27 March 1981,   *g* whichever version is accepted, change the position so far as the validity of the 1978 order was concerned. If fishing was to be permitted, in my view it had to be permitted on a clearer basis than a mere note of member states' intentions. The Commission's proposals of 12 June and its amended proposals of 24 July were clearer. There was, however, not least in view of the history of attempts to reach agreement, no certainty that they would be adopted, and indeed on 12 June the Commission reserved the right to change the   *h* proposals, as it in fact did. These proposals were subsequent to the making of the 1981 order; they could not have made it invalid at the time it was made, and since they remained as proposals subject to further amendment, they could not in my view render the order invalid, once they were made, so as to exclude a prosecution for a breach of the order in respect of the events of 10 July. If this is correct, the suggestion that the order was invalid before the Commission's proposals of 12 June is even weaker.   *j*

I assume for present purposes that the Commission's declaration of 27 July and its letter of 28 July produce the necessary certainty and clarity, but the United Kingdom government complied with them. They cannot affect the validity of the order as of 10 July 1981.

The German government also relies on the minutes of a Council meeting on 15, 16 and 17 December 1980 noting that member states in carrying out their fishing would

take account of the total allowable catches (TAC) for 1981 submitted by the Commission
a on 18 November and 16 December 1980. Those proposals were, however, for a negative
TAC and the minute cannot be read as imposing an obligation on member states to
comply with whatever proposals that Commission subsequently made.

There were thus, in my view, no substantive grounds which invalidated the 1978
order so as to prevent its re-enactment in 1981, or so as to make the latter invalid by 13
July 1981. The position would, as I see it, have been different if the Commission's
b declaration had been made prior to the making of the 1981 order.

So far as the procedural argument is concerned, it is obviously desirable that measures
should be submitted to the Commission in advance as otherwise the risk is taken that
substantive changes may have been made inadvertently. It may also be necessary in law,
as the Commission contends, for amendments which extend the period of a measure
which is limited in time to be submitted in advance. Where, however, a measure which
c is not limited in time is re-enacted, or is re-enacted during its life and for no longer than
the period prescribed, without any change of substance being made, it does not seem to
me that it is invalidated because it is not submitted to the Commission for prior
authorisation. It produced no change in law and nothing in the court's judgments seems
to me to require that it should be so submitted as a prerequisite of validity, even though
as a matter of administrative efficiency it is right that it should be notified. There was in
d substance nothing for the Commission to assess or supervise; in no way can it be said that
it breached the government's duties 'as a trustee of the common interest' or that it showed
a lack of collaboration with the Commission.

Finally, it is submitted by the Federal Republic that if the measure was valid the court
should rule that a person who commits what would otherwise be an offence as a result of
an unavoidable mistake cannot be convicted of an offence in relation to that act. This
e point does not seem to me to be raised on the present reference, and is, in my view, in
any event a matter for the High Court of Justiciary to deal with under national law in the
first place if the point is taken.

I conclude that the question referred should be answered on the following lines:
'Where after 1 January 1979 a member state notifies the Commission of a re-enactment,
without substantive amendment, of a national fishery conservation measure which was
f itself made and maintained in conformity with Community law, that re-enacted measure
is made in conformity with Community law even though made without express
Commission approval, and remains in conformity with Community law in the absence
of a decision by the Council or the Commission requiring that measure to be repealed or
amended in order to conform with the conservation policy of the Community.'

In so far as the Procurator Fiscal has incurred separate costs of the reference, these fall
g to be dealt with by the High Court in the main proceedings. The Commission and the
governments of the United Kingdom and the Federal Republic of Germany should, in
my view, bear their own costs.

14 February. **THE COURT OF JUSTICE** delivered its judgment which, having
summarised the facts, procedure and submissions of the parties, dealt with the law as
h follows.

1. By order of 1 February 1983 the High Court of Justiciary, Scotland, submitted a
question for a preliminary ruling under art 177 of the EEC Treaty on the interpretation
of the provisions of Community law relating to the conservation of fishery resources.

2. The question is submitted in the context of proceedings instituted against two
j German fishermen by the United Kingdom authorities following the confiscation on 10
July 1981 of their herring catches taken, in contravention of the relevant United
Kingdom legislation, in the area to the west of Scotland designated Division VI(a) by the
International Council for the Exploration of the Sea (hereinafter referred to as 'ICES
Division VI(a)').

3. The national legislation under which the two German fishermen were convicted
was the West Coast Herring (Prohibition of Fishing) Order 1981, SI 1981/585, which was

brought into force on 1 May 1981. There was also in force at the material time the North
Coast (Prohibition of Herring Fishing) Regulations (Northern Ireland) 1981, SR 1981/ *a*
100, which related to an adjoining maritime zone. These two measures are hereinafter
referred to as 'the 1981 measures'. According to the order making the reference for a
preliminary ruling the two measures re-enacted, without substantive amendment, the
provisions of the West Coast Herring (Prohibition of Fishing) Order 1978, SI 1978/930,
solely in order to correct a procedural irregularity by which the latter order was partially
invalidated since it covered a small area of sea, not relevant to the present case, which fell *b*
to be dealt with under a statute applicable to Northern Ireland.

4. After they had been convicted of a contravention of the 1981 order by the Sheriff
of Grampian, Highlands and Islands at Stornoway, the fishermen brought their
convictions under review by the High Court of Justiciary, Scotland, claiming that the
order was not in conformity with Community law. The national court requests the
Court of Justice to give a ruling on the following question: *c*

'Where, after 1 January 1979, a Member State notifies the Commission of a re-
enactment, without substantive amendment, of a national conservation measure
which was itself made and maintained in conformity with Community law, does
the measure so re-enacted remain made and maintained in conformity with
Community law in the absence of express Commission approval?'
d

5. It must be borne in mind that by virtue of art 102 of the Act concerning the
Conditions of Accession and the Adjustments to the Treaties (1972), the power to adopt
measures for the protection of the biological resources of the sea has since 1 January 1979
been vested exclusively in the Council, acting on a proposal from the Commission.

6. The legal context of the main proceedings has to be viewed in the light of the
situation created by the fact that the Council did not lay down for 1981 the conservation *e*
measures provided for in art 102 of the Act of Accession.

7. Although, as the court made clear in its judgment of 5 May 1981 (see *EC Commission
v UK* Case 804/79 [1981] ECR 1045) the member states may, in the case of inaction by
the Council, bring into force interim conservation measures, they must, within the
framework of the general task of supervision which art 155 of the EEC Treaty entrusts
to the Commission, comply with the procedural and substantive conditions laid down *f*
by the Council in Annex VI to the Hague Resolution of 3 November 1976 which were
confirmed by the Council Declaration of 31 January 1978.

8. It follows from the terms of the above-mentioned resolution and declaration, taken
together, that as regards the procedural rules the member states concerned must not
bring national conservation measures into force until it has sought in good faith the
approval of the Commission, which has to be consulted at all stages of the procedure. *g*

9. It is not in dispute that the 1981 order, which entered into force on 1 May 1981,
was not notified to the Commission until 4 May 1981 and that therefore that condition
was not satisfied.

10. It thus appears that the national court is asking the Court of Justice whether the
obligation to consult the Commission and seek its approval before bringing national
conservation measures into force is absolute and whether, consequently, that obligation *h*
extends to the adoption of every national measure, including the re-enactment, without
substantive amendment, of measures approved at the appropriate time by the
Commission.

11. The binding force of the procedural rules laid down in the above-mentioned
resolution and declaration must be judged in the light of the objectives pursued by the
Community. *j*

12. In that respect, it should be emphasised that the procedural rules in question are
intended to ensure compliance with the substantive conditions which were laid down by
the Council in the said documents, and which are binding on the member states, in a
situation marked by the failure to implement a common policy regarding the
conservation of fishery resources.

13. As the Court acknowledged in the above-mentioned judgment of 5 May 1981 (*EC*
a *Commission v UK* Case 804/79), the requirements inherent in the safeguarding by the
Community of the common interest and of the integrity of its own powers impose on
the member states in such circumstances the obligation not to lay down national
conservation measures in the face of objections, reservations or conditions which might
be formulated by the Commission.

14. It follows, on the other hand, from the foregoing consideration that in principle
b no fresh consultation of the Commission is required in the case of the re-enactment by a
member state, without substantive amendment, of a national measure for the conservation
of fishery resources which was adopted previously in conformity with the procedural
and substantive conditions laid down by Community law. The notification of new
national measures nevertheless continues to be necessary, in order that the Commission
may be accurately informed of the state of the law in force in the various member states.

c 15. It is important to note that in its statement of 27 March 1981, which was annexed
to the minutes of its meeting, the Council noted that out of a desire to avoid serious
disruptions the member states would take for 1981 measures similar to those which they
had taken in previous years.

16. By EEC Regulation 754/80 of 26 March 1980 the Council fixed, for 1980, the total
allowable catch for herring in ICES Division VI(a) at zero; on 18 November and 16
d December 1980 the Commission proposed that the total allowable catch for herring in
the same division for the year 1981 should be zero.

17. It was not until after the bringing into force of the 1981 measures that, on 12 June
and 24 July 1981, the Commission amended its initial proposals for a total allowable
catch of zero for that year, proposals which had not yet been adopted by the Council,
and, on 27 July 1981, notified the member states that its latest proposal for a total
e allowable catch of 65,000 tonnes of herring should be regarded as binding on them (see
(1981) OJ C224, p 1).

18. According to the observations submitted to the court by the government of the
Federal Republic of Germany, a situation may arise in which a national conservation
measure previously adopted in compliance with Community law cannot be retained
without substantive amendment, that is to say where the trend revealed by the relevant
f available scientific data shows that the earlier protection measures are no longer strictly
necessary for the management and conservation of the fishery resources. It is therefore
for the national authorities to take the initiative by amending their rules, in conformity
with the procedural and substantive conditions referred to above, in order to adapt them
to the new situation.

19. That argument cannot be upheld. It fails to take account of the power vested in
g the Community since 1 January 1979 to adopt measures for protection of the biological
resources of the sea. The determination that the former rules on protection are no longer
appropriate in the light of scientific information newly available and the adoption of the
measures called for by that situation are therefore matters exclusively for the Community
authorities.

20. In view of the foregoing considerations, the answer to be given to the national
h court should be that no fresh consultation of the Commission is required in the case of
the re-enactment, without substantive amendment, of a national measure for the
conservation of fishery resources, which was previously adopted in conformity with the
procedural and substantive conditions laid down by Community law.

Costs
j 21. The costs incurred by the United Kingdom and the Procurator Fiscal, Stornoway,
the government of the Federal Republic of Germany and the Commission of the
European Communities, which have submitted observations to the court, are not
recoverable. Since these proceedings are, so far as the parties to the main proceedings are
concerned, in the nature of a step in the proceedings pending before the national court,
the decision on costs is a matter for that court.

On those grounds, the court, in reply to the question referred to it by the High Court
of Justiciary, Scotland, by order of 1 February 1983, hereby rules: no fresh consultation　*a*
of the Commission is required in the case of the re-enactment, without substantive
amendment, of a national measure for the conservation of fishery resources, which was
previously adopted in conformity with the procedural and substantive conditions laid
down by Community law.

Agents: *W H Godwin*, Treasury Solicitor's Department, *W G Chalmers*, Crown Agent,
Edinburgh and *A C Normand*, Assistant Solicitor, Crown Office, Edinburgh (for the　*b*
Procurator Fiscal and the United Kingdom); *Martin Seidel*, Ministerialrat, Federal Ministry
for the Economy, *Rudolf Illing*, Ministerialrat, Federal Ministry of Food, Agriculture and
Forests and *Jochim Sedemund*, Rechtsanwalt, Cologne (for the government of the Federal
Republic of Germany); *Richard Wainwright*, Legal Service of the EC Commission (for the
Commission).

Mary Rose Plummer　Barrister.　*c*

R v Tweedie

COURT OF APPEAL, CRIMINAL DIVISION　　　　　　　　　　　　　　　　　　　　　*d*
LAWTON LJ, DRAKE AND HOBHOUSE JJ
19, 27 JANUARY 1984

*Criminal law – Corruption – Transaction by agent – Agent knowingly using with intent to deceive
principal a document containing false statement intended to mislead principal – Ingredients of
offence – Accounting document containing false entry – Document intended for use by principal
only – Whether offence committed – Prevention of Corruption Act 1906, s 1(1).*　　　　　*e*

The defendant, who was employed as a metal dealer by a company which bought and
sold precious metals, had to enter each deal that he made on a trading sheet, which he
then had to submit to the company's accounting staff so that they could prepare the
appropriate accounting documents. On one occasion the company instructed him to sell
some silver and palladium. He did not do so, but made three false entries on the trading　*f*
sheet indicating that he had done so. He handed the sheet to the accounting staff, who
subsequently discovered what he had done. He was charged with, and convicted of,
knowingly using, with intent to deceive his principal, a document which contained a
false statement which was intended to mislead his principal, contrary to s 1(1)[a] of the
Prevention of Corruption Act 1906, which provided, inter alia, that an agent who
knowingly used with intent to deceive his principal 'any receipt, account, or other　*g*
document in respect of which the principal is interested' and which contained any
statement which was false in any material particular and which to his knowledge was
intended to mislead the principal was guilty of an offence. The appellant appealed against
his conviction, contending that he could not be guilty of such an offence because s 1(1)
did not cover a document, like the trading sheet, which was intended for use only by the
principal.　　　　　　　　　　　　　　　　　　　　　　　　　　　　　　　　　　　*h*

Held – On its true construction s 1(1) of the 1906 Act applied only to documents which
were intended to pass between a principal and a third party and did not cover documents,
like the trading sheet, which were never intended to go to a third party. The appeal
would accordingly be allowed and the conviction quashed (see p 139 *f* to *j*, post).

Notes　　　　　　　　　　　　　　　　　　　　　　　　　　　　　　　　　　　　　　*j*
For corruption relating to agents, see 11 Halsbury's Laws (4th edn) para 1285, and for
cases on the subject, see 15 Digest (Reissue) 1397–1398, 12230–12235.
　　For the Prevention of Corruption Act 1906, s 1, see 8 Halsbury's Statutes (3rd edn) 236.

a　Section 1(1), so far as material, is set out at p 138 *g*, post

Cases referred to in judgment

a *R v Terry* [1984] 1 All ER 65, [1984] 2 WLR 23, HL.
   Sage v Eicholz [1919] 2 KB 171, [1918–19] All ER Rep 424, DC.
   Welham v DPP [1960] 1 All ER 805, [1961] AC 103, [1960] 2 WLR 669, HL.

Cases also cited
   DPP v Anderson [1978] 2 All ER 512, [1978] AC 964, HL.
   R v Payne [1965] Crim LR 543, CCA.

b

Appeal
On 8 October 1982 in the Central Criminal Court before his Honour Judge Wickham
and a jury, the appellant, Brian Gordon Tweedie, was convicted on count 2 of an
indictment charging corruption, contrary to s 1(1) of the Prevention of Corruption Act
1906, the particulars of the charge being that the appellant, an agent of Gerald Metals
c Ltd, on 23 September 1980 with intent to deceive his principal knowingly used a
document in respect of which the principal was interested, namely a daily trading sheet
which contained a statement which was false in a material particular and which to the
appellant's knowledge was intended to mislead the principal. He was sentenced to nine
months' imprisonment, suspended for two years, and a criminal bankruptcy order for
£170,000 was made against him. He appealed against conviction and sentence by leave
d of Wood J. The facts are set out in the judgment of the court.

John Black (assigned by the Registrar of Criminal Appeals) for the appellant.
R Alun Jones for the Crown.

Cur adv vult

e 27 January. The following judgment of the court was delivered.

LAWTON LJ. The judgment I am about to read is the judgment of the court.
Hobhouse J has seen it and approved it, but he is unable to be here today.
   On 8 October 1982 at the Central Criminal Court the appellant was convicted of
corruption contrary to s 1(1) of the Prevention of Corruption Act 1906 (count 2) and was
f sentenced to nine months' imprisonment suspended for two years. A criminal bankruptcy
order was made in the sum of £170,000. He was acquitted on two counts of false
accounting. Count 2 was put by the prosecution as an alternative to the first of the false
accounting counts. He now appeals against both conviction and sentence by leave of the
single judge.
   The prosecution on count 2 was based on a seldom used paragraph in s 1(1) of the 1906
g Act. We have had to construe this paragraph and apply our construction to the facts of
this case.
   The appellant was employed as a senior metal dealer by Gerald Metals Ltd, who bought
and sold precious metals, including palladium and silver. Each day when the appellant
made a deal he had to enter the transaction on his trading sheet. After he had made up
his trading sheet, which was normally at the end of each day's trading, he handed it to
h his employers' accounting staff so that the appropriate documents required for accounting
could be made out. One would be a memorandum of contract confirming what had
been bought and sold, which was sent to the other party to the deal. If there had been a
sale, an invoice would be made out. When there had been a series of buying and selling
transactions with one customer, dealing accounts would be made out by one party or the
other and balances agreed.
j On 23 September 1980 the appellant was told by one of his employers' directors to sell
silver and palladium before the close of trading. This director thought that the market
was likely to start falling before long. He was right. It started to fall the next day and
went on doing so for some months. The appellant did not do as he had been told; but he
made three false entries on his trading sheet purporting to show that he had sold to
Johnson Matthey 3,000 troy ounces of palladium and 16,000 troy ounces of silver. He

handed this trading sheet to a member of the accounting staff. The accounting procedure
started. As there had been no such sales it was inevitable that queries would arise and   *a*
they did. On 6 October 6 1980, when asked how a large payment from Johnson Matthey
which had been received should be allocated, he said that it was in respect of the sales
which had not been made on 23 September. More queries followed and in so far as they
were made to him he avoided answering. On 5 January 1981 he confessed to the director
who had given him instructions to sell that he had not done so. As a result of what the
appellant did his employers suffered a loss of £170,000.   *b*

After a long investigation it was decided to charge the appellant with false accounting
in respect of what he had done on 23 September and 6 October and with an offence of
corruption based on the third paragraph of s 1(1) of the 1906 Act. The Attorney General
gave his fiat for such a charge. As far as is known this was the first time such a charge had
been preferred in respect of a false entry made by an employee in a document which was
to be used only in the employer's business.   *c*

In order to prove the two charges of false accounting, the prosecution had to satisfy the
jury in respect of each that the appellant had dishonestly and with a view to gain for
himself or another or with intent to cause loss to another produced documents required
for an accounting purpose. They failed to do so. The jury returned verdicts of not guilty.

In the grounds of appeal which counsel drafted for the appellant he stated that an
intent to make a profit or the making of a profit was a constituent element of the third   *d*
limb of s 1(1) of the 1906 Act. He had been encouraged to put that ground forward by
what had been set out in two textbooks, one published in 1907 and the other in 1920.
He did not pursue that point in this court. It would have been impossible for him to do
so having regard to the decisions of the House of Lords in *Welham v DPP* [1960] 1 All ER
805, [1961] AC 103 and *R v Terry* [1984] 1 All ER 65, [1984] 2 WLR 23. The submission
which he made was that when the third paragraph was construed in its context this court   *e*
should infer that Parliament intended that paragraph only to apply in respect of
accounting documents passing or intended to pass between a principal and a third party.

We turn now to consider the context in which the third paragraph comes. The 1906
Act is short. Its title is 'An Act for the Better Prevention of Corruption'. Section 1(1), as
printed by the King's Printer, is in three paragraphs. Each deals with the differing
circumstances which can amount to an offence under the Act. The first paragraph,   *f*
broadly stated, deals with the corrupt acceptance of bribes, the second with the corrupt
giving of bribes. The third is in these terms:

> 'If any person knowingly gives to any agent, of if any agent knowingly uses with
> intent to deceive his principal, any receipt, account, or other document in respect of
> which the principal is interested, and which contains any statement which is false
> or erroneous or defective in any material particular, and which to his knowledge is   *g*
> intended to mislead the principal'

he shall be guilty of an offence. The word 'or' comes at the end of the first and second
paragraphs. The word 'agent' in s 1(1) includes any person employed by or acting for
another and the word 'principal' includes an employer (see s 1(2)).

As was pointed out in *Sage v Eicholz* [1919] 2 KB 171 at 175, 177, [1918–19] All ER   *h*
Rep 424 at 428, 429, the word 'corruptly' is omitted from the third paragraph. In that
case, which seems to be the only one fully reported, A T Lawrence J said ([1919] 2 KB
171 at 177; cf [1918–19] All ER Rep 424 at 429):

> 'In the case before us I do not think that [counsel for the accused] has sufficiently
> explained the absence of the word "corruptly" from the third branch of this   *j*
> subsection. The word "corruptly" is used in the first and second branches, and, as
> [Bray J] has pointed out, is deliberately omitted from the third. That omission is to
> my mind readily explained by the fact that it is frequently found impossible to
> prove that an agent has been corrupted; and in view of that difficulty it was thought
> sufficient, in order to establish an offence on the part of the giver, to prove that he
> knowingly gave to an agent a document which contained a statement that was false,

a   erroneous, or defective, intending it to mislead the principal, to prove that the agent,
     knowing that the document was false, used it with intent to deceive his principal.'

We accept and adopt what was said in that case.

In this court counsel for the appellant accepted first that there was evidence that the
appellant knowingly used the trading sheet which to his knowledge contained a false
statement intended to mislead his employers with intent to deceive them, and second
that the jury were properly directed as to intent to deceive and mislead. Nevertheless, he
b   submitted that a document of this kind, which was intended only for use within Gerald
Metals Ltd's business, did not come within the ambit of the third paragraph.

Counsel for the Crown submitted that it did. Parliament would have appreciated that
in some cases there might be difficulty in proving that an employee had acted corruptly;
but there might be evidence from which his dishonesty could be inferred. There would
be evidence of dishonesty if the prosecution were able to prove that an employee in a
c   position of trust had knowingly used with intent to deceive and mislead his employers a
document which he knew contained a false statement. As the law stood in 1906 it might
have been difficult to bring such conduct within the ambit of the criminal law. A charge
of forgery would not have been appropriate if the employee had done nothing more than
put false entries in a document which was otherwise genuine. He submitted that we
should infer that Parliament intended to fill such a gap in the criminal law by the
d   provisions in the third paragraph. The use of the word 'or' at the beginning of this
paragraph shows that an employee can be guilty without anyone else being so. This
argument has much force.

If this paragraph had stood by itself as a separate section creating an offence, the
argument might have had more force; but it does not. It is part of one subsection which
deals in the first two paragraphs with dishonest conduct, either as a fact or in
e   contemplation, between an employee and a third party. It would be odd drafting for the
last part of this subsection to create an offence which made an employee criminally liable
for using a document which did not have any connection with a third party or was not
intended to go to a third party. As Hobhouse J pointed out in the course of argument,
the words 'receipt' and 'account' in the third paragraph, as a matter of the ordinary use of
English, refer to documents inter partes either in creation or use. A receipt is made out
f   to someone who has paid a debt. An account is rendered by one person to another. The
words 'or other document' should, in our judgment, be construed as meaning a document
which would pass inter partes. Such documents are capable of being *given* by a third
party and then *used* by an employee. Both or one or other can be guilty of the offence
created by the third paragraph if there is proof of the knowledge and intent specified. All
the words following 'intent to deceive his principal' are words common to the definition
g   of an offence by a third party or an employee.

In this case the document relied on by the Crown was one which was to be used for
accounting purposes by the employers. It was never intended to go to a third party. It
had none of the characteristics of an inter partes document. It did not acquire these
characteristics merely because its existence started the procedure by which later inter
partes documents would come into existence.
h   If the Crown's contention were right, the third paragraph would apply to any false
document knowingly used by an employee with intent to deceive or mislead his
employers. An employee who put a false entry on his time sheet would be guilty of an
offence under the 1906 Act. Parliament could not have intended that this should be so.
We adjudge that the third paragraph did not apply to the facts of this case.

The appeal will be allowed. The conviction will be quashed and the criminal
j   bankruptcy order discharged.

Appeal allowed. Conviction quashed and criminal bankruptcy order discharged.

Solicitors: *Director of Public Prosecutions.*

Martine Kushner   Barrister.

Seven Seas Transportation Ltd v Pacifico Union Marina Corp
The Oceanic Amity

COURT OF APPEAL, CIVIL DIVISION
OLIVER AND ROBERT GOFF LJJ
19, 20, 21 DECEMBER 1983, 7 FEBRUARY 1984

Shipping – Time charterparty – Exceptions – Loss or damage arising from negligent navigation – Vessel chartered for lightening operations – Charterparty purporting to incorporate US Carriage of Goods by Sea Act – US Act exempting owners of chartered vessel from liability for 'loss or damage arising or resulting from . . . neglect . . . in navigation' – Chartered vessel causing damage to charterers' vessel because of negligent navigation – Whether owners of chartered vessel liable for damage – Whether US Act applying to charterparties – Whether US Act only applying in respect of carriage to or from US ports – Whether US Act applying to exempt owners from liability for damage – Carriage of Goods by Sea Act 1936 (US), § 4(2)(a).

Shipping – Time charterparty – Exceptions – Negligent navigation – Errors of navigation – Charterparty exempting shipowners from liability for 'errors of navigation' – Whether 'errors of navigation' including negligent navigation.

The appellants, who were the owners of a vessel in which they had carried a cargo of grain to a port in India, chartered another vessel owned by the respondents for the purpose of lightening their own vessel, which was too deeply laden to enter port. On three separate occasions during the lightening operations damage was caused to the appellants' vessel as a result of negligent navigation by the master of the respondents' vessel. Clause 24 of the charterparty under which the respondents' vessel was chartered incorporated the Carriage of Goods by Sea Act 1936 of the United States of America, which by § 4(2)(a)^a exempted the carrier (the respondents) from liability for 'loss or damage arising or resulting from [the] Act, neglect, or default of the master . . . or the servants of the carrier in the navigation or in the management of the ship'. Clause 16 of the charterparty further exempted the owners (the respondents) from liability for 'errors of Navigation'. The appellants contended that they were entitled to damages arising out of the negligent navigation of the respondents' vessel. The dispute was referred to a sole arbitrator, who found that, although the respondents had been negligent, they were exempted from liability by cl 24, which, he held, validly incorporated § 4(2)(a) of the US Act in the charterparty. On appeal by the appellants the judge held (i) that cl 24 of the charterparty was effective in incorporating into the charterparty the US Act, which applied notwithstanding that the Act had not been intended to apply to charterparties, and (ii) that the damage to the appellants' vessel was 'loss or damage arising or resulting from' the negligent navigation of the respondents' vessel and accordingly § 4(2)(a) applied to exempt the respondents from liability for the physical damage caused to the appellants' vessel. The appellants appealed, contending (i) that although cl 24 was effective to incorporate the US Act into the charter, on its true construction § 4 of that Act was not incorporated into the charter in relation to the adventure as contemplated and performed, and (ii) even if § 4 was so incorporated, the damage suffered by their vessel was not 'loss or damage arising or resulting from . . . [the] Act, neglect, or default of the master [of the respondents' vessel]' within § 4(2) because (a) the damage was not 'in relation to the loading, handling, stowage, carriage, custody, care [or] discharge of [the] goods' as provided by § 2^b of the US Act and (b) the damage suffered by the appellants by reason of

a   Section 4(2), so far as material, is set out at p 144 *f*, post
b   Section 2 is set out at p 144 *d e*, post

the damage to their vessel was not suffered by them in their capacity as charterers of the
a respondents' vessel and such damage did not therefore fall within the protection of § 4(2)
of the US Act as incorporated into the charter.

Held – The appeal would be dismissed for the following reasons—
(1) In the same way that the geographical restrictions in the US Act did not apply when
the Act was incorporated in a bill of lading which was not restricted to a contract of
b carriage of goods covering a range of ports outside the United States, so, when the Act
was stated by a charterparty to be incorporated therein, those parts of the Act which were
inappropriate to charterparties (such as § 5, which stated that the Act was not applicable
to charterparties) likewise did not apply to exclude those parts of the Act which were
applicable, including § 4 and the immunities thereby given to the shipowner. It followed
therefore that the charterparty between the appellants and the respondents had effectively
c incorporated the US Act and § 4 was accordingly applicable to the contractual adventure
as contemplated and performed (see p 147 *d* to *h*, p 148 *a* and p 151 *g* and *j*, post);
Adamastos Shipping Co Ltd v Anglo-Saxon Petroleum Co Ltd [1958] 1 All ER 725 applied.
(2) Since the reason the appellants had chartered the respondents' vessel under the
charterparty was to lighten grain from a mother ship, it followed that loading grain from
the mother ship was a contractual activity to be performed by the respondents' vessel
d under the charterparty, and there was no reason why, in principle, the benefit of the
immunities contained in § 4 of the US Act should not be available to the respondents in
respect of damage caused to the appellants in performance of that activity, even though
that damage did not fall within any of the range of activities specified in § 2 of the US
Act (see p 149 *e*, p 150 *c* to *j* and p 151 *b e* to *g* and *j*, post); *Adamastos Shipping Co Ltd v
Anglo-Saxon Petroleum Co Ltd* [1958] 1 All ER 725 and *Australian Oil Refining Pty Ltd v R
e* *W Miller & Co Pty Ltd* [1968] 1 Lloyd's Rep 448 applied.

Per curiam. A clause in a charterparty exempting a shipowner from liability for loss
or damage arising out of 'errors of navigation' does not provide exemption in respect of
negligent navigation (see p 151 *g* to *j*, post); *Industrie Chimiche Italia Centrale SpA v Nea
Ninemia Shipping Co SA, The Emmanuel C* [1983] 1 All ER 686 approved.

Decision of Staughton J [1983] 1 All ER 672 affirmed.

f **Notes**
For exemption of a shipowner from liability for loss or damage, see 43 Halsbury's Laws
(4th edn) para 760, for immunity of a shipowner in respect of the navigation or
management of a ship, see ibid para 779, and for cases on exemption of a shipowner for
negligence, see 43 Digest (Reissue) 165–182, 7700–7786.
g The US Carriage of Goods by Sea Act 1936, §§ 2, 4(2)(*a*) correspond to the Carriage of
Goods by Sea Act 1971, Sch, arts II, IV(2)(*a*). For arts II, IV(2)(*a*) of the schedule to the
1971 Act, see 41 Halsbury's Statutes (3rd edn) 1318, 1323.

Cases referred to in judgment
Adamastos Shipping Co Ltd v Anglo-Saxon Petroleum Co Ltd [1958] 1 All ER 725, [1959] AC
133, [1958] 2 WLR 688, HL; rvsg [1957] 2 All ER 311, [1957] 2 QB 233, [1957] 2
h WLR 968, CA; rsvg [1957] 1 All ER 673, [1957] 2 QB 233, [1957] 2 WLR 509.
Australian Oil Refining Pty Ltd v R W Miller & Co Pty Ltd [1968] 1 Lloyd's Rep 448, Aust
HC.
Hadley v Baxendale (1854) 9 Exch 341, [1843–60] All ER 461, 156 ER 145.
Heron II, The, Koufos v C Czarnikow Ltd [1967] 3 All ER 686, [1969] 1 AC 350, [1967] 3
WLR 1491, HL.
j *Industrie Chimiche Italia Centrale SpA v Nea Ninemia Shipping Co SA, The Emmanuel C* [1983]
1 All ER 686.
Polemis and Furness Withy & Co Ltd, Re [1921] 3 KB 560, [1921] All ER Rep 40, CA.

Interlocutory appeal
The appellants, Seven Seas Transportation Ltd, by a time charter dated 26 June 1975
chartered the vessel Oceanic Amity owned by the respondents, Pacifico Union Marina

Corp, for the purpose of lightening the appellants' own vessel, the Satya Kailash, which
was too deeply laden to enter port at Tuticorin, India. On 7, 12 and 14 July 1975 the
vessels were damaged when they came into contact with each other during the lightening
operations. Pursuant to an agreement dated 9 March 1977 the parties agreed to refer the
dispute over liability to John Franklin Willmer QC as sole arbitrator. The arbitrator held
that the respondents were exempted from liability by cl 24, but not by cl 16, of the time
charter. At the request of the parties the arbitrator stated a special case for the decision of
the High Court pursuant to s 21(1)(a) of the Arbitration Act 1950 for the determination
of the question whether on the true construction of the time charterparty the respondents
were exempt by reason of the provisions of either cl 16 or cl 24 thereof from liability for
physical damage to the appellants' vessel Satya Kailash and consequential loss caused by
the negligence of their master in the navigation or management of the Oceanic Amity
while coming alongside or departing from the Satya Kailash. On 11 June 1982
Staughton J ([1983] 1 All ER 672) answered the question asked in the case stated in the
affirmative by reason of cl 24 although not by reasons of cl 16. The appellants appealed
to the Court of Appeal. The facts are set out in the judgment of the court.

Kenneth Rokison QC and *John Thomas* for the appellants.
Nicholas Phillips QC and *Jonathan Sumption* for the respondents.

Cur adv vult

7 February. The following judgment of the court was delivered.

ROBERT GOFF LJ. There is before the court an appeal from a decision by Staughton J
([1983] 1 All ER 672) on a consultative case stated by an arbitrator, Mr John Franklin
Willmer QC. The appellants, Seven Seas Transportation Ltd, who were the claimants in
the arbitration, were the charterers of a vessel called Oceanic Amity from the respondents,
Pacifico Union Marina Corp, who were the respondents in the arbitration.

The matter arises in the following way. The appellants were the owners of another
vessel called Satya Kailash. That vessel had carried a cargo of grain from the United States
to India. She was due to discharge her cargo at an Indian port, Tuticorin; but she was too
deeply laden to enter the port. So the appellants chartered the Oceanic Amity from the
respondents for the purpose of lightening the Satya Kailash to enable her to enter
Tuticorin. The Oceanic Amity was chartered under a time charter in the New York
Produce Exchange form, dated 26 June 1975. We will refer to the relevant terms of that
charter in a moment. It is enough to record at present that it was for a period of '20/40
days lightening operation in Charterers' option', and that it was stated in the charter that
'it is understood Charterers intend use vessel to lighten grain from mother ship to Indian
ports'.

The lightening operation took place as planned. But, in the course of coming alongside,
and during the lightening operation, the two vessels came into contact on a number of
occasions. We are concerned with three of these occasions, in the course of which both
vessels suffered damage. This damage led to claims and counterclaims which were the
subject of an ad hoc arbitration before Mr Willmer. We need not go into the full details
of the arbitration. For present purposes, it is enough to record the arbitrator's conclusion
that, on each of the three relevant occasions, the contact between the two vessels was
caused by negligent navigation by the master of the Oceanic Amity. There then arose
the question whether the respondents were exempted from liability for the damage so
caused to the Satya Kailash. There were two provisions of the charterparty on which the
respondents relied: cl 16, a mutual exceptions clause, and cl 24, a clause paramount. The
arbitrator indicated that, in his opinion, the respondents were not protected by cl 16 but
were protected by cl 24. He then posed the following question for the opinion of the
court:

> 'Whether, upon the true construction of the time charterparty dated the 26th
> June, 1975, the Respondents are exempt by reason of the provisions of either clause

a
16 or clause 24 thereof from liability for physical damage to the Claimants' vessel "SATYA KAILASH" and consequential loss caused by the negligence of their master in the navigation or management of the "OCEANIC AMITY" while coming alongside or departing from the "SATYA KAILASH".'

Staughton J, in agreement with the view of the arbitrator, answered this question: not exempt by virtue of cl 16, but exempt by virtue of cl 24 (see [1983] 1 All ER 672 at 686).

b
From his decision that the respondents are exempt by virtue of cl 24, the appellants now appeal to this court; the respondents cross-appeal in order to challenge the judge's decision that they are not exempt by virtue of cl 16.

So on this appeal we are concerned with the construction and effect of these two clauses, set in their context in the charterparty. We shall now set out the text of these two clauses. They are both printed clauses, and read as follows:

c
'16 . . . The Act of God, enemies, fire, restraint of Princes, Rulers and People, and all dangers and accidents of the Seas, Rivers, Machinery, Boilers and Steam Navigation, and errors of Navigation throughout this Charter Party, always mutually excepted . . .

24. It is also mutually agreed that this Charter is subject to all the terms and provisions of and all the exemptions from liability contained in the Act of Congress

d
of the United States approved on the 13th day of February, 1893, and entitled "An Act relating to Navigation of Vessels; etc." in respect of all cargo shipped under this charter to or from the United States of America. It is further subject to the following clauses, both of which are to be included in all bills of lading issued hereunder:

U.S.A. Clause Paramount

e
This bill of lading shall have effect subject to the provisions of the Carriage of Goods by Sea Act of the United States, approved April 16, 1936, which shall be deemed to be incorporated herein, and nothing herein contained shall be deemed a surrender by the carrier of any of its rights or immunities or an increase of any of its responsibilities or liabilities under said Act. If any term of this bill of lading be

f
repugnant to said Act to any extent, such term shall be void to that extent, but no further . . .'

There was then a 'Both-to-Blame Collision Clause' in the printed form, forming part of cl 24; that was deleted in the present charter, but a new both-to-blame collision clause was incorporated elsewhere in the charter, by a typed clause, cl 40.

There are very few other provisions of the charter which are relevant. We have already

g
recorded that the charter was a time charter in the New York Produce Exchange form. It contained a London arbitration clause; it is common ground that the charter is governed by English law. The only other clause we need set out is cl 39, which provides as follows:

'The vessel on delivery and during Charter Party is classed B.V., fully seaworthy, ready, clean and suitable to receive and carry food grains. The ship's holds/tweendeck shall also be free from loose scale.'

h
Before the judge four issues were canvassed. The first three issues related to cl 24 and the fourth to cl 16. These issues, and the judge's decision on them, were as follows. (1) Was the Carriage of Goods by Sea Act 1936 of the United States effectively incorporated in the charterparty? The judge held that it was. (2) If so, was its effect confined to voyages to and from United States ports? The judge held that it was not. (3) Did the

j
damage to the Satya Kailash fall within the exception of 'loss or damage' arising from act neglect or default of the master in the navigation of the ship within § 4(2) of the United States Act? The judge held that it did. (4) Were the respondents exempted from liability for the damage to the Satya Kailash by reason of the exception of errors in navigation in cl 16? The judge held that they were not.

On the appeal before this court counsel for the appellants advanced two submissions. First, while accepting that cl 24 was effective to incorporate the United States Act into a charter in this form, nevertheless he submitted that, on a true construction, § 4 of the Act (on which the respondents relied for protection) was not incorporated into this charter in relation to the adventure as contemplated and performed. Second, if (contrary to his first submission) § 4 was so incorporated, nevertheless the damage suffered by the Satya Kailash was not 'loss or damage' arising or resulting from the act, neglect or default of the master in the navigation of the ship within § 4(2) of that Act, because (1) the damage was not 'in relation to the loading, handling, stowage, carriage, custody, care [or] discharge of the goods' as provided in § 2 of the Act, and (2) the damage suffered by the appellants by reason of the damage to the Satya Kailash was not suffered by them in their capacity as charterers of the Oceanic Amity, and such damage did not therefore fall within the protection of § 4(2) of the Act as incorporated into the charter.

In order to consider these submissions, we must first refer to the relevant provisions of the United States Act. This is, of course, the Act of Congress which, to the extent there provided, incorporated the Hague Rules into the law of the United States. In the preamble to the Act, it is provided—

> '. . . every bill of lading or similar document of title which is evidence of a contract for the carriage of goods by sea to or from ports of the United States, in foreign trade, shall have effect subject to the provisions of this Act.'

Section 1 then sets out the definitions in art I of the Hague Rules. Section 2 provides, as in art II:

> 'Subject to the provisions of section 6, under every contract of carriage of goods by sea, the carrier in relation to the loading, handling, stowage, carriage, custody, care, and discharge of such goods, shall be subject to the responsibilities and liabilities and entitled to the rights and immunities hereinafter set forth.'

Section 3 then sets out (as in art III) the responsibilities and liabilities of the carrier; and § 4 (as in art IV) his rights and immunities. Section 4(2), which contains 17 immunities in paragraphs lettered (a) to (q), provides in respect of para (a):

> 'Neither the carrier nor the ship shall be responsible for loss or damage arising or resulting from—(a) Act, neglect, or default of the master, mariner, pilot, or the servants of the carrier in the navigation or in the management of the ship . . .'

The only other section of the Act to which we need refer is § 13, which provides as follows:

> 'This Act shall apply to all contracts for carriage of goods by sea to or from ports of the United States in foreign trade . . . Nothing in this Act shall be held to apply to contracts for carriage of goods by sea between any port of the United States or its possessions, and any other port of the United States or its possessions: Provided, however, That any bill of lading or similar document of title which is evidence of a contract for the carriage of goods by sea between such ports, containing an express statement that it shall be subject to the provisions of this Act, shall be subjected hereto as fully as if subject hereto by the express provisions of this Act: Provided further, That every bill of lading or similar document of title which is evidence of a contract for carriage of goods by sea from ports of the United States, in foreign trade, shall contain a statement that it shall have effect subject to the provisions of this Act.'

We turn then to the first submission of counsel for the appellants. This was that § 4 of the Act (including, of course, the exception in § 4(2)(a)) was not effectively incorporated into this charter as contemplated and performed. The argument ran as follows. The New York Produce Exchange form is nowadays probably the most widely used form of time charter. It is a form approved by the United States government. Clause 24 is intended to give effect to relevant applicable United States legislation, viz the Harter Act of 13 February 1983 and the United States Carriage of Goods by Sea Act 1936. Strikingly, however, the latter Act is made applicable as such; it is not just the Hague Rules which

are incorporated. Furthermore, whereas the Harter Act is rendered applicable 'in respect
a of all cargo shipped under this charter to or from the United States of America', no such
express limitation is made in the case of the latter Act. The reason, submitted counsel, is
not far to seek. It is that by virtue of § 13 the latter Act only applies to contracts for the
carriage of goods by sea to or from ports of the United States in foreign trade; so that, by
incorporating the Act (as opposed to just incorporating the Hague Rules), the effect was
in any event only to render the provisions of the Act applicable to carriage of goods by
b sea to or from ports of the United States, and it was unnecessary expressly so to provide
in the charter. So construed, the incorporation both of the Harter Act and of the Carriage
of Goods by Sea Act was effective in relation to similar voyages. It followed, therefore,
that § 4 of the United States Carriage of Goods by Sea Act had no application to this
charter, which was only concerned with a lightening operation off an Indian port.

In considering this argument, we have the benefit of guidance from the decision of
c the House of Lords in *Adamastos Shipping Co Ltd v Anglo-Saxon Petroleum Co Ltd* [1958] 1
All ER 725, [1959] AC 133. In that case a tanker was chartered under a charter for as
many consecutive voyages as the vessel could tender for loading within a period of 18
months. Trading was to be worldwide. The charter contained, in cl 1, an express
warranty of seaworthiness. However, there was attached to the charter a typed slip, in
the following terms:

d
 'Paramount clause. This bill of lading shall have effect subject to the provisions of
the Carriage of Goods by Sea Act of the United States ... 1936, which shall be
deemed to be incorporated herein, and nothing herein contained shall be deemed a
surrender by the carrier of any of its rights or immunities or an increase of any of
its responsibilities or liabilities under said Act. If any term of this bill of lading be
repugnant to said Act to any extent, such term shall be void to that extent, but no
e   further.'

As a result of the incompetence of the engineroom staff on the vessel, she broke down on
her approach voyage to her first loading port. There were other similar breakdowns; and
in consequence no less than 106 days were lost. The incompetence of the engineroom
staff rendered the ship unseaworthy. However, it was held that the owners had exercised
f due diligence in the selection of the engineroom staff; and they sought to escape
responsibility for the delay which had occurred by relying on the immunity in § 4(1) of
the United States Act, restricting liability for unseaworthiness to cases where it is caused
by want of due diligence on the part of the owners.

This submission led to a remarkable division of judicial opinion. The case came first
before Devlin J (see [1957] 1 All ER 673, [1957] 2 QB 233). He concluded (1) that, despite
g the use of the words 'this bill of lading . . .' in the clause paramount, nevertheless the
clause should be regarded as having been incorporated into the charterparty, on the
principle of falsa demonstratio non nocet, (2) that the immunities conferred on carriers
by the United States Act should not, in the particular charter, be limited to cargo-carrying
voyages to or from ports in the United States, but should extend to other cargo-carrying
voyages contemplated under the charter, but (3) that the immunity did not extend to
h non-cargo-carrying voyages. The Court of Appeal rejected the whole clause paramount
as insensible (see [1957] 2 All ER 311, [1957] 2 QB 233). The House of Lords held
unanimously that, by the attachment of the typed slip to the charter, the parties had
agreed that their rights and liabilities under the charter were subject to the provisions of
the United States Act. By a majority of three to two, they also held that the provisions of
the Act affected the parties' rights and liabilities in connection with voyages other than
those to or from United States ports, and both cargo-carrying and non-cargo-carrying
j voyages; the two dissentients both considered that the Act only applied to voyages to or
from United States ports.

Now it is to be observed that, in that case, the owners had to surmount a number of
obstacles before they could successfully invoke the due diligence provision in § 4(1) of
the Act. First, they had to overcome the initial difficulty that the typed clause paramount
referred not to 'this charterparty' but to 'This bill of lading'. Second, there was the

difficulty that the preamble to the Act expressly makes its provisions applicable to bills
of lading or other similar documents of title, and that § 5 provides that the provisions of
the Act shall not be applicable to charterparties. Third, there was the difficulty that the
Act is, by the preamble and § 13, expressly applicable only to the carriage of goods by sea
to or from ports of the United States in foreign trade. Fourth, there was the difficulty
that the Act, being (like the Hague Rules) expressly designed for contracts for the carriage
of goods under bills of lading or similar documents of title, was directed towards forms
of activity performed by shipowners under such contracts, and not to the wider range of
activities performed by shipowners under charterparties.

The House of Lords were unanimous that, on the facts of the case before them, the
first of these obstacles could be overcome. As Viscount Simonds put it ([1958] 1 All ER
725 at 731, [1959] AC 133 at 154):

'I can entertain no doubt that the parties, when they agreed, by cl. 52 of the
charterparty, that the "Paramount Clause . . . as attached" should be incorporated in
their agreement and proceeded physically to attach the clause which I have set out,
had a common meaning and intention which compels me to regard the opening
words "This bill of lading" as a conspicuous example of the maxim "falsa
demonstratio non nocet cum de corpore constat".'

Having gone thus far, their Lordships (again unanimously) concluded that the provision
in § 5 of the Act that its provisions should not be applicable to charterparties should not
defeat this contractual intention.

It was at the next stage that their Lordships were acutely divided. It was recognised by
the majority that there was much in the Act which was inapplicable to a charterparty
and must therefore be disregarded. The majority decided that the provision in the
preamble and in § 13 of the Act, confining its application to the jurisdictional limits of
the United States, must be regarded as inapplicable. Again, to quote Viscount Simonds
([1958] 1 All ER 725 at 732, [1959] AC 133 at 155):

'The contract between the parties is of world-wide scope; the area of state
jurisdiction is necessarily limited, and, because it is limited, the Act is given a
restricted operation. No reason has been suggested, nor, as far as I am aware, could
be suggested, why a similar restriction should be imported into the contract. On the
contrary, to do so would, from the commercial point of view, make nonsense of it.
I find it easy, therefore, as did the learned judge, to construe this contract as making
the substituted standard of obligation coterminous with the enterprise."

Lord Keith said ([1958] 1 All ER 725 at 748, [1959] AC 133 at 180):

'Very good reasons can be seen for the United States legislature limiting its Act to
goods carried under a bill of lading to or from United States ports. They seem quite
inapposite when the Act is introduced contractually into a charterparty covering a
very wide range of ports outside the United States.'

And Lord Somervell said ([1958] 1 All ER 725 at 752, [1959] AC 133 at 185):

'. . . once one has come to the conclusion that the "Act" is being incorporated in a
contract to which it does not as an Act apply, one prima facie rejects the limitations
which are imposed in these various Acts necessitated by the limits of the legislative
jurisdiction of the country concerned. One takes the geographical limits from the
contract.'

The majority went on to hold that the application of the Act should not be confined to
cargo-carrying voyages. In reaching this conclusion, they were much influenced by the
consideration that no sensible distinction could be drawn for this purpose between cargo-
carrying and ballast voyages. As Viscount Simonds put it ([1958] 1 All ER 725 at 732,
[1959] AC 133 at 156):

'. . . it is, I think, permissible in a consideration of this commercial transaction to
ask what possible difference it makes to the charterers whether the delay, to which

a   their loss is due, occurs when the ship is in ballast or is loaded with a cargo of oil or water. It matters not for this purpose whether the charterparty was for a single voyage, as the original document seemed to contemplate, or for a number of consecutive voyages. The contractual subject-matter was the whole period during which the vessel was under charter and it is, in my opinion, to this whole period that the parties agreed that the statutory standard of obligation and immunity should relate.'

b

This decision was, not surprisingly, much relied on by counsel for the respondents in the present case. Of course, here he had no difficulty in surmounting the first two obstacles which faced the owners in the *Adamastos* case. For cl 24 of the New York Produce Exchange form expressly provides that the *charter* is subject to the United States clause paramount, which has to be included in all bills of lading issued thereunder. On c   the appeal before this court, it was not suggested by the appellants that a provision in these terms was not effective to render a charter in this form subject to the Act; their submission was that this particular charter was not subject to the Act, because the Act relates only to voyages to or from ports in the United States, and this charter was concerned only with a lightening operation off an Indian port. We are unable to agree with this submission. It is accepted that cl 24 shows an intention to render the United d   States Act applicable to charterparties in this form, notwithstanding that the Act is so drawn as to be applicable not to charterparties but to bill of lading contracts. From this it follows that the intention was to render applicable to such charterparties standards of performance applicable under United States law to certain bills of lading; and so, inevitably, the Act, to be made so applicable, must be subject to the process described by Viscount Simonds in the *Adamastos* case, whereby those parts of the Act which are e   inappropriate to charterparties must be disregarded. It also follows that, by making the Act applicable to charterparties in this form, the intention cannot have been to give effect to the law of the United States which is in terms not applicable to charterparties. Furthermore, the New York Produce Exchange form of charter is a form of time charter; it is not a form of voyage charter, though it is no doubt used on occasions as a time charter for the period of a particular voyage. It will normally be used for a contract f   whereby the services of a ship, her master and her crew are made available for a particular period of time, no doubt with named delivery and redelivery ports, and no doubt also within specified trading limits. But a voyage or voyages will not as such normally be specified. In these circumstances, it would be most surprising if the intention was that, over that period of time, the standards of performance provided for in the United States Act should only be applicable where the charterer ordered the ship to sea on a voyage to g   or from a United States port. No sensible reason can be given for any such distinction, once it is recognised that, by rendering the Act applicable to charterparties as such, there can be no intention to give effect to the law of the United States. In these circumstances, exactly the same considerations as impelled the majority of the House of Lords in the *Adamastos* case to reject the geographical restrictions in the United States Act persuade us that they should likewise be rejected in a case of a charter incorporating the Act by this h   form of clause; so to import the restrictions would, as Viscount Simonds said, make nonsense of the contract from the commercial point of view.

Counsel for the appellants placed reliance on cl 39 of the charter, which was a typed clause imposing, in the respects there provided, an absolute warranty of seaworthiness; the same point was made in respect of cl 52. But, in our judgment, these clauses cannot affect the construction to be placed on cl 24 as such. The most that could be said of these j   clauses is that, as typed clauses, they might be given precedence over the printed clause paramount in cl 24 so as to override pro tanto the provisions of § 4(1) of the United States Act as incorporated into the charter. We cannot see that the fact that the parties have thought fit to provide for an absolute warranty of seaworthiness in these clauses can otherwise affect the incorporation of the United States Act into the charter by cl 24. If anything, their presence presupposes that the qualified seaworthiness obligation under §§ 3(1) and 4(1) of the United States Act would otherwise be applicable.

For these reasons, we agree with the conclusion of the judge, and of the umpire before him, that the charterparty does effectively incorporate the United States Act, and that its effect is not confined to voyages to and from United States ports, so that § 4 of the Act becomes applicable to the contractual adventure as contemplated and performed.

We turn then to the second submission of counsel for the appellants, which was that, if § 4 of the United States Act was incorporated into the charter, nevertheless the damage suffered by the Satya Kailash was not 'loss or damage' arising or resulting from the act, neglect or default of the master in the navigation of the ship within s 4(2) so that the respondents could not invoke the immunity in that subsection in the present case. There were two limbs to this argument. The first was based on § 2 of the Act, which provides:

'Subject to the provisions of section 6, under every contract of carriage of goods by sea, the carrier in relation to the loading, handling, stowage, carriage, custody, care, and discharge of the goods, shall be subject to the responsibilities and liabilities and entitled to the rights and immunities hereinafter set forth.'

Counsel submitted that the damage suffered by the Satya Kailash did not occur in relation to any of these matters, so that such damage did not fall within the 'loss or damage' in respect of which the respondents were entitled to immunity under § 4. Counsel further submitted, however, that the respondents were only entitled to the benefit of such immunities in respect of loss or damage suffered by the appellants in their capacity as charterers, and that, since the damage to the Satya Kailash did not fall within that category of loss or damage, the respondents could not rely on § 4(2) in respect of it.

Of course, when the United States Act is incorporated into an ordinary bill of lading contract, it is unlikely that problems of this kind will arise; for in such a case a claim by the bill of lading holder will naturally arise in relation to one of the matters specified in § 2, the typical case being concerned with a claim for damage to cargo shipped under the bill of lading. But where, as here, the Act is incorporated into a charterparty, difficulties arise because of the more extended range of obligations imposed on the shipowner under what is after all a contract of services. These will generally include an obligation to proceed to a place specified in the charter or as ordered to load cargo. In the present case, however, the cargo was not to be loaded at a specified place, but from a mother ship; and the question on this part of the case is whether the respondents can invoke the immunities in § 4 not in respect of damage to the goods but in respect of damage to the mother ship.

On this point, we have the assistance of two authorities. Once again, we have the benefit of guidance from the House of Lords in the *Adamastos* case; but we can also derive assistance from the decision of the High Court of Australia in *Australian Oil Refining Pty Ltd v R W Miller & Co Pty Ltd* [1968] 1 Lloyd's Rep 448.

We turn again to the *Adamastos* case. It will be recalled that the damages claimed by the charterers in that case were damages in respect of delay resulting in a shorter period of use of the ship under the charter, such delay having arisen from the unseaworthiness of the ship, ie incompetence of the engineroom staff. Before Devlin J the consultative case posed one restricted question directed to the character of the loss or damage claimed by the charterers: this was simply whether 'loss or damage' in § 4(1) and (2) of the United States Act relates only to the physical loss of or damage to the goods (see [1957] 1 All ER 673 at 676, [1957] 2 QB 233 at 247). Devlin J held that the words did not bear such a restricted meaning (see [1957] 1 All ER 673 at 680, [1957] 2 QB 233 at 253). He considered that the 'loss or damage' must, having regard to § 2, arise in relation to the 'loading, handling, stowage, carriage, custody, care, and discharge of such goods', but was subject to no other limitation. Pressed by counsel, he went on to express the opinion that, though phrases like 'in relation to' and 'in connection with' are very wide, nevertheless the character of the compensation claimed must bear some relation to the goods, and that relation must not be too remote. From what he understood of the loss or damage claimed, it seemed unlikely to him that § 4 would apply to it.

Before the House of Lords, the question of law was amended to insert the words 'and in so far as they are in breach are not protected from loss or damage of the kind claimed resulting therefrom' (see [1958] 1 All ER 725 at 734, [1959] AC 133 at 139, 159).

Viscount Simonds was of the opinion that the contractual subject matter was the whole
a period during which the vessel was under charter, and that it was to that whole period
that the parties agreed that the statutory standard of obligation and immunity should
relate (see [1958] 1 All ER 725 at 732, [1959] AC 133 at 156). On the specific question
relating to loss or damage, he agreed with Devlin J that the words 'loss or damage' in
§ 4(1) and (2) did not relate only to physical loss or damage to the goods (see [1958] 1 All
ER 725 at 733, [1959] AC 133 at 157). Finally he expressed his conclusion that the parties
b intended to introduce as a term governing their relationship as owners and charterers the
limited measure of responsibility prescribed by the American Act; and he then answered
the amended question of law in such a way as to decide that the owners had (except in
relation to one matter) the benefit of the protection of § 4(1) and (2) of the United States
Act (see [1958] 1 All ER 725 at 734, [1959] AC 133 at 158–159). Lord Keith could see no
reason for limiting the loss or damage for which immunity might be claimed to physical
c loss of or damage to goods (see [1958] 1 All ER 725 at 749, [1959] AC 133 at 181).
Furthermore, he proceed on the view that the subject matter of the contract was voyages,
and loss of voyages naturally fell under the words 'loss or damage'. He agreed that the
question of law should be answered in the manner proposed by Viscount Simonds, with
whom he appears to have substantially agreed. Lord Somervell took a slightly different
view (see [1958] 1 All ER 725 at 752–753, [1959] AC 133 at 186–187). He agreed that
d 'loss or damage' in the Act was not limited to physical damage to the goods. However, he
considered that the claim in the case before him was a claim in relation to loading and
carriage of goods, and so fell within § 2. On that basis, he agreed that the question of law
should be answered as proposed.

In so far as a ratio decidendi is discernible on this part of the case, it is, in our judgment,
to be found in the speeches of Viscount Simonds and Lord Keith; so that, where the
e subject matter of the contract is not merely the carriage of goods by sea but is voyages,
the immunities in § 4 are, despite the express words of § 2, to be read as relating to the
contractual voyages.

We turn next to the Australian case of *Australian Oil Refining Pty Ltd v R W Miller & Co
Pty Ltd* [1968] 1 Lloyd's Rep 448. That case was concerned with a voyage charter, under
which the charterers chartered the owners' tanker to proceed to Botany Bay and there
f load a cargo of oil in dock for carriage to a discharging port. The charterers had an oil
refinery on the southern side of Botany Bay; and cl 30 of the charter expressly
contemplated that the vessel might load at the charterers' own wharf, because it provided
in cl 30 that, whenever the vessel was about to proceed to a berth at the charterers' wharf
or submarine terminal in Botany Bay, the owners should instruct the master to engage a
pilot for the purpose of directing or advising the master as to such berthing. The charter
g also included a clause (cl 33) which excluded any absolute warranty of seaworthiness and
conferred on the owners the rights and immunities in the Hague Rules as enacted in the
country of shipment, viz the Australian Sea-Carriage of Goods Act 1924. In addition, by
cl 15, it was provided that the owners should not be responsible for loss or damage arising
or resulting from 'Act, Neglect or Default of the Master, mariner, pilot or the servants of
the Owners in the navigation or in the management of the vessel', ie the exception in art
h IV(2)(a) of the Hague Rules was expressly incorporated into the charter. The vessel was
ordered to load oil from the charterers' wharf, and, while endeavouring to berth, there
collided with the wharf and damaged it. This was held to be due to the negligence of the
pilot. The charterers claimed damages from the owners who, whilst conceding that cl 33
did not avail them, invoked the exception in cl 15. The High Court of Australia, by a
majority of three to two, held that the owners could rely on that exception. Of the
j majority Owen J (with whom Barwick CJ agreed) considered that, but for cl 30, cl 15
should be given the same construction as would have been placed on the same words as
used in art IV(2) and so would read as limited to loss or damage 'in relation to the loading,
handling, stowage, carriage, custody, care and discharge' of the cargo. However, cl 30
contemplated that the vessel would load at the charterers' wharf or submarine terminal,
and he could see no reason why the general words of cl 15 should be read so as to exclude
from its operation loss or damage which might occur to any property of the charterers

which the parties intended to be used by the owners for the purposes of loading the contractual cargo. While agreeing with Owen J, Barwick CJ had this to say (at 451–452):

> 'Consideration of the cases which confine the unlimited expression "loss or damage" in a charter-party to loss or damage in relation to the handling, stowage, etc., of the goods the subject of carriage leads me to think that the conclusion that this was the proper construction of those expressions in such a contract was reached because of the relationship in which the parties stood and of the extent of the rights and obligations of the contract they had made. In this case, in my opinion, the limitation of the generality of the expression "loss or damage" in Clause 15 must similarly be found in the relationship of the parties and the nature and extent of the rights and obligations exacted and given by each to the other rather than in the attribution to them of an intention to use the expression in their contract regulating their mutual rights and obligations in a sense which is traditionally appropriate to the more limited relationship and to the more limited contractual obligation.'

The third member of the majority, Kitto J, delivered a judgment to the same effect.

In the light of these authorities, we approach the matter as follows. Section 2 of the United States Act specifies the activities in relation to which the carrier, under any contract of carriage of goods by sea, shall be subject to the responsibilities and liabilities and entitled to the rights and immunities set forth in the Act. This range of activities is very comprehensive, and comprehends the full range of activities under the ordinary bill of lading contract to which the Act applies; so that, under any such contract, the carrier will be able, in respect of any such activities, to invoke the immunities in § 4. However, under a charterparty (whether a time or a voyage charterparty) the owner is required to perform a wider range of activities than those specified in § 2; for example, under a time charter there will be ballast voyages to be performed, and under a voyage charter the vessel will be required to proceed to a loading port as specified in the charterparty or as ordered by the charterers. The question arises: if the United States Act is incorporated into a charterparty, is the owner entitled to invoke the immunities in § 4 in respect of this wider range of activities? The answer given to that question by the majority of their Lordships in the *Adamastos* case is, in our judgment, in the affirmative, because of the wider subject matter of the contract: in a consecutive voyage charterparty, as in the *Adamastos* case, the subject matter being 'voyages'. This approach is consistent with that expressed in the passage from Barwick CJ's judgment in the *Miller* case which we have just quoted. It appears, however, that the majority of the High Court of Australia was adopting a somewhat more strict approach than the majority of the House of Lords in the *Adamastos* case; for they appear to have proceeded on the basis that the owners' concession that they were not entitled to the protection of the general incorporation (in cl 33) of s 4 of the Australian Act was correct. In our judgment, on the approach of the majority of the House of Lords in the *Adamastos* case, even such general words of incorporation can be effective to given an owner the protection of the statutory immunities in respect not merely of those matters specified in § 2, but also of other contractual activities performed by him under the charter.

It follows that we are unable to accept the first limb of the submission of counsel for the appellants on this point. Under the charterparty, the Oceanic Amity was chartered to lighten grain from a mother ship. It follows that loading grain from the mother ship was a contractual activity to be performed by the Oceanic Amity under the charter; and we can see no reason why, in principle, the benefit of the immunities contained in § 4 of the United States Act should not be available to the respondents in respect of damage caused to the appellants in performance of this activity, even though such damage did not fall within any of the range of activities specified in § 2.

The present case is very similar to the *Miller* case; but there are points of difference. In the present case, the vessel damaged the appellants' mother ship while coming alongside to load; in the *Miller* case, the vessel damaged the charterers' wharf. This of itself does not seem to be a material distinction. However, in the *Miller* case, it was expressly contemplated in the charterparty that the vessel would load at the charterers' wharf; whereas in the present case there was nothing in the charterparty to indicate that the

mother ship was or might be owned by the appellants. This was plainly a point which
a influenced the majority of the High Court of Australia in reaching their decision; and
their opinion is reflected in the second limb of the submission of counsel for the
appellants that, since the damage to the Satya Kailash did not result in loss or damage
suffered by the appellants in their capacity as charterers, the respondents were not entitled
to the benefit of the immunities in § 4(2) of the United States Act in respect of the
damage to the Satya Kailash.

b   We do not, however, regard this distinction as material. Reasonable contemplation, at
the time of contracting, that damage of a certain type is not unlikely to result from a
breach of contract is essential before a contractual party can be held liable for such
damage, on the principle in *Hadley v Baxendale* (1854) 9 Exch 341, [1843–60] All ER Rep
461, as explained in *The Heron II, Koufos v C Czarnikow Ltd* [1967] 3 All ER 686, [1969] 1
AC 350. We are, however, here not concerned with liability for damage, but with the
c scope of a contractual immunity. In that connection, there is indeed a line to be drawn.
This can be illustrated by two contrasting examples. Suppose that charterers' cargo is
loaded on board a chartered ship and, while the ship so loaded is proceeding to her
discharging port, she collides on the high seas with another ship which coincidentally
happens to be owned by the charterers. In such circumstances, the owners of the
chartered ship could not, we consider, invoke the immunity in § 4(2)(*a*) of the United
d States Act, if incorporated into the charterparty, in respect of the damage suffered by the
charterers' ship. But if, on the other hand, the chartered ship collided with a wharf
owned by the charterers while performing her contractual obligation under the
charterparty to berth at that wharf in order to load or discharge cargo, we can see no
reason why the owners should not invoke that immunity in respect of such damage. The
crucial difference between these two contrasting examples, it seems to us, is that, in the
e latter case, the property of the charterers which was damaged was property which was
exposed to risk by reason of the charterers' involvement in the contractual adventure. To
us it is of no relevance that, in the present case, it was not stated in the charterparty that
the mother ship was, or might be, owned by the appellants. The point is simply that, by
contracting in the terms of the present charterparty, the appellants were expressly
conferring on the respondents the benefit of the relevant immunities in respect of their
f contractual activities, and the appellants must be taken to have recognised that, if any of
their property involved in the adventure was at risk from such activities, the respondents
should be entitled to the benefit of such immunities in respect of loss or damage suffered
by the appellants in consequence.

It follows that we are unable to accept the second limb of the second submission of
counsel for the appellants. For these reasons, having rejected both submissions advanced
g by the appellants, we would dismiss the appeal.

Finally, we must briefly mention the respondents' cross-appeal against the decision of
the judge that, if unprotected by the United States Act, they could not escape liability by
relying on the exception of 'errors of Navigation' in cl 16 of the charterparty. The basis
of the judge's conclusion was that, on their true construction, the words 'errors of
Navigation' in cl 16 referred only to non-negligent errors, and were not wide enough to
h embrace negligent errors. In reaching that conclusion, the judge invoked the authority
of the decision of this court in *Re Polemis and Furness Withy & Co Ltd* [1921] 3 KB 560,
[1921] All ER Rep 40, in which the court gave a similar limited construction to an
exception of 'fire', holding that the exception did not embrace fires negligently caused.
Furthermore, in the recent case of *Industrie Chimiche Italia Centrale SpA v Nea Ninemia
Shipping Co SA, The Emmanuel C* [1983] 1 All ER 686 the point on 'errors of Navigation'
j was reargued, apparently more fully, before Bingham J, who reached the same conclusion
as the judge in the present case. We find it sufficient to say that we agree with both these
judgments. We would, therefore, dismiss the cross appeal.

Appeal dismissed. Leave to appeal to the House of Lords refused.

Solicitors: *Richards Butler & Co* (for the appellants); *Ince & Co* (for the respondents).

Carolyn Toulmin   Barrister.

Hendy Lennox (Industrial Engines) Ltd v   *a*
Grahame Puttick Ltd

QUEEN'S BENCH DIVISION AT WINCHESTER
STAUGHTON J
9, 12, 13, 16 SEPTEMBER 1983

b

Sale of goods – Passing of property – Vendor retaining property in goods – Goods supplied to company on credit terms – Clause reserving vendor's title to goods until goods paid for – Company going into receivership before goods paid for – Goods sold on to company's customers but not paid for at time of receivership – Effect of reservation of title clause.

The plaintiffs supplied a number of diesel engines to the defendants on credit terms   *c* under contracts which stipulated (i) by cl 10, that 'all goods . . . shall be and remain the property of the [plaintiffs] until the full purchase price thereof shall be paid' and that the plaintiffs had the right to retake possession in the event of default, (ii) by cl 12, that the plaintiffs had the right to terminate the contract immediately if the defendants went into receivership, and (iii) that payment was to be made monthly on the first day of the month following the expiry of one month from delivery of an invoice, so that in effect   *d* the defendants were always given between one and two months' credit. The engines were used by the defendants as a major component of diesel generating sets, which were assembled and then sold to customers. The engines remained readily identifiable by a serial number once they were used in the generators sets and could be disconnected from the generators relatively easily. On 6 November 1980 the defendants went into receivership owing some £728,000 to their bank, who held a charge on their assets. At   *e* that time the defendants had sold and delivered a number of generators to customers but had not yet received payment for them and also had on their premises three engines, two of which had been incorporated into generators while the third had not. All three engines were later delivered to customers of the defendants as part of generators sold to them. The plaintiffs brought an action against the receiver claiming (i) part of the proceeds of sale of the three engines on the defendants' premises at the time the   *f* defendants went into receivership, on the basis that prior to the delivery to the defendants' customers the plaintiffs had been entitled to assert a proprietary right to those engines by virtue of their power of repossession under cl 10 and had not waived that proprietary right, and (ii) the proceeds of sale of the engines incorporated into generators that were already sold and delivered to the defendants' customers at the time of the receivership.

g

Held – (1) Although the plaintiffs retained, by virtue of cl 10, all proprietary rights in the engines until they were paid in full or until the property in the engines passed to the defendants' customers and although those rights were not affected when the engines were wholly or partially incorporated into generator sets, nevertheless the plaintiffs' right to retake possession under cl 10 arose only on default of payment, which was only after the period of credit expired or delivery up was sought by the plaintiffs, whichever was   *h* the later, and if the property in the engines passed to the defendants' customers before that date the plaintiffs were not entitled to maintain their proprietary title. On the facts, the property in two of the engines on the defendants' premises at the time of the receivership had passed to the defendants' customers by the time the credit period had expired and the plaintiffs had demanded delivery up, while the property in the third engine had not. The plaintiffs were therefore entitled to the proceeds of sale of the third   *j* engine (see p 158 *a b*, p 159 *h j* and p 160 *b* to p 161 *c*, post); *Aluminium Industrie Vaassen BV v Romalpa Aluminium Ltd* [1976] 2 All ER 552, *Re Bond Worth Ltd* [1979] 3 All ER 919, *Borden (UK) Ltd v Scottish Timber Products Ltd* [1979] 3 All ER 961 and *Re Peachdart Ltd* [1983] 3 All ER 204 considered.

(2) There could not be implied in the contracts between the plaintiffs and the defendants a term that the proceeds of sales of generators containing engines supplied by the plaintiffs were to be kept separate from other sales and that those proceeds were to

a belong wholly or in part to the plaintiffs, because the credit arrangements between the
parties did not support such an inference and the express provision of a remedy in respect
of the goods themselves, namely the right to retake possession, was to be taken as
excluding any implied remedy in respect of the proceeds of sale. In the absence of such
an implied term the plaintiffs were not entitled to maintain any direct claim against the
proceeds of the sale of engines in generators to the defendants' customers regardless of
when the generators were sold and delivered to the customers (see p 163 c to j, post);
b dicta of Jessel MR in Re Hallett's Estate [1874–80] All ER Rep at 796, of Lord Upjohn in
Boardman v Phipps [1966] 3 All ER at 758, of Roskill LJ in Aluminium Industrie Vaassen BV
v Romalpa Aluminium Ltd [1976] 2 All ER at 564 and of Buckley LJ in Borden (UK) Ltd v
Scottish Timber Products Ltd [1979] 3 All ER at 974 applied.

Notes

c For retention of title clauses in contracts for the sale of goods, see 41 Halsbury's Laws (4th
edn) paras 707, 731.

Cases referred to in judgment

Aluminium Industrie Vaassen BV v Romalpa Aluminium Ltd [1976] 2 All ER 552, [1976] 1
   WLR 676, QBD and CA.
d Boardman v Phipps [1966] 3 All ER 721, [1967] 2 AC 46, [1966] 3 WLR 1009, HL.
Bond Worth Ltd, Re [1979] 3 All ER 919, [1980] Ch 228, [1979] 3 WLR 629.
Borden (UK) Ltd v Scottish Timber Products Ltd [1979] 3 All ER 961, [1981] Ch 25, [1979] 3
   WLR 672, CA.
Coomber, Re, Coomber v Coomber [1911] 1 Ch 723, CA.
Hallett's Estate, Re, Knatchbull v Hallett (1880) 13 Ch D 696, [1874–80] All ER Rep 793,
e   CA.
Henry v Hammond [1913] 2 KB 515.
Lewis v Andrews & Rawley Pty Ltd (1937) 73 WN (NSW) 670.
Peachdart Ltd, Re [1983] 3 All ER 204, [1983] 3 WLR 878.

Cases also cited

McEntire v Crossley Bros Ltd [1895] AC 457, [1895–9] All ER Rep 829, HL.
f South Australian Insurance Co v Randell (1869) LR 3 PC 101, PC.

Action

On 24 November 1980 the plaintiffs, Hendy Lennox (Industrial Engines) Ltd (the sellers),
issued a writ against the defendants, Grahame Puttick Ltd (the buyers), seeking, inter
alia, (1) a declaration that certain goods covered by 15 invoices issued by the plaintiffs
g were the property of the plaintiffs except in so far as title had passed to a bona fide
purchaser for value from the defendants, (2) delivery up of the goods, (3) further or
alternatively, a declaration that the proceeds of sale of the goods were held by the
defendants in a fiduciary capacity and/or as trustees for the plaintiffs, and (4) an order
that the defendants pay the proceeds of sale to the plaintiffs. The facts are set out in the
judgment.

h
Leslie Joseph QC and J Norman Rudd for the sellers.
John E A Samuels QC and Richard King for the buyers.

Cur adv vult

j 16 September. The following judgment was delivered.

STAUGHTON J. This action has been tried at the Winchester Crown Court in
September. It raises legal issues of some difficulty. Despite the efforts of counsel and the
court staff, it has not been possible to obtain all the books that might have been desirable.
In the circumstances it is, perhaps, to be regretted with hindsight that an application to
transfer the case to the Commercial Court in London was opposed, and was refused.
   The plaintiffs, whom I shall call the sellers, are main dealers of the Ford Motor Co. In
the autumn of 1980 they supplied a number of diesel engines and some spare parts to

the defendants (the buyers). It was contemplated by both parties to the transaction that the buyers would incorporate each engine in a diesel generating set, which they would then sell to one of their customers (the sub-buyers). The process of incorporation would not in any way alter or destroy the substance of the engine. It would remain identified by the serial number which the sellers or the Ford Motor Co had given it; it would be attached by bolts to the generator and by various other connections to items such as a fuel tank and a radiator for coolant. (I should add that the radiator is apparently not part of the engine.) But the engine would not physically be changed; the connections could be undone and the engine removed within a period described in the evidence as 'several hours'. I was told that this vague expression was used by agreement so that it would be unnecessary to resolve a minor dispute between the parties as to the actual period of time required.

The buyers have not paid the agreed price of the engines and spares to the sellers. It is agreed that the sellers would be entitled to judgment against the buyers for the price, amounting to £46,355·79. But that remedy may be of little or no value to them. On 6 November 1980 the buyers went into receivership. They had an overdraft of £728,435 with Barclays Bank Ltd, who held a charge on the buyers' assets.

It is now agreed that the sellers' standard conditions of sale formed part of the contracts pursuant to which the engines and spares were supplied to the buyers. Those conditions included the following:

'10. *Payment.* (i) The terms of payment specified overleaf or as stated on the official quotation and/or acknowledgment of order shall apply and if none be specified then payment in full shall be made at the time when the goods are ready for delivery. Unless the company shall otherwise specify in writing all goods sold by the company to the purchaser shall be and remain the property of the company until the full purchase price thereof shall be paid to the company. In the case of default in payment by the purchaser, the company shall have the right to retake possession of and permanently retain any unpaid for goods and to revoke all liability of the company to the purchaser on the contract of sale and delivery of such goods . . .

12. *Termination.* The company shall have the right immediately to terminate the contract at any time upon occurrence of any of the following events:—(i) if the purchaser commits any act of bankruptcy or compounds or makes any arrangements with his creditors or executes a bill of sale on his goods or any of them or if any execution or distress is levied upon the goods of the purchaser. (ii) If the purchaser being a company is wound up either compulsorily or voluntarily or a receiver of its assets is appointed. (iii) If the purchaser fails to take delivery of any of the goods subject to the contract. Upon any such termination of the contract the company shall have the right either (a) to require the purchaser to take over and pay for at the then current price such materials as the company shall have allocated to the contract including labour and other expense incurred by the company in relation to such materials or (b) to dispose of the said materials at its discretion without being liable to account to the purchaser for the proceeds of such disposal.'

It was argued that others of the conditions were relevant; but I do not myself see that they are of any assistance in solving the problems in this action. What is important, however, is the agreed term as to credit. It was 'net monthly account'. That meant, as is agreed, that the buyers were bound to pay for the engines and spares on the first day of the month following the expiry of one month from the date of delivery of the invoice. So credit was allowed for a minimum of one month, and possibly for two months.

When these proceedings began on 17 November 1980 by ex parte application, the sellers were claiming delivery up of engines and spares which had not been paid for by the buyers, or alternatively payment of the proceeds of resale of those goods to sub-buyers. After certain interlocutory proceedings which I shall presently relate, the action continued as a claim against the proceeds of sale only. But the point that it was in origin also a claim for delivery of goods is, in some respects, of importance.

Fifteen invoices formed part of the claim indorsed on the writ of summons. Mercifully

eleven of those have been removed from the area of dispute, by concession on one side or
a the other. I shall mention what I was told or believe to have been the motive for those
concessions, not by way of finding or because it is directly relevant, but in order to
illustrate the boundaries of the dispute that does remain alive.

(1) Of the fifteen, six invoices were for small quantities of spares at a total price of
£545·37. Those goods remained unused on the buyers' premises at the time of the
receivership. The receiver wanted to use them. So he paid the price to the sellers.

b   (2) Another group comprised three invoices for engines and two for spares. According
to my calculator, these totalled £16,822·39, although counsel proposed a slightly different
figure. Most of those goods had been delivered to sub-buyers, and all had been paid for
by them, before the receivership. The money had disappeared into the maw of the
buyers' overdraft at Barclays Bank. It had sunk without trace. The sellers abandoned
their claim in respect of those goods and the proceeds of resale.

c   (3) A third group comprises two invoices in respect of engines (invoices nos 68952
and 68953). It is agreed that the property in those engines had passed to sub-buyers at
the time of the receivership. For the most part they had also been delivered to sub-
buyers. But the price was not paid until April 1981, some months later. It amounted to
£24,693·94, and has been preserved in a joint deposit account of the parties' solicitors.
The sellers do not assert that they now have, or that they have had at any time during the
d currency of these proceedings, a proprietary title to those engines. That is because they
accept that the buyers were able to pass title in the goods up to the time of the
receivership, and that the buyers did so. The sellers' claim in respect of those goods is in
respect of the proceeds of sale alone.

(4) The last group comprises two invoices for engines (invoices nos 68954 and 68981).
The three engines covered by those invoices were still on the buyers' premises on 12 and
e 13 November 1980, when the sellers' representative went there to see what he could find.
(In fact there was also a fourth, but that was covered by one of the invoices included in
group (2) above, because it had already been paid for. No claim is made in respect of it.)
The three engines were of course identifiable by their serial numbers. The sellers'
representative was also able to learn in some way the destination for which each engine
was intended by the buyers. I do not know how this occurred. The destination may have
f been written on each engine, or he may have been told it by an employee of the buyers,
or he may have observed it in a document. The evidence is silent on that point. I do not
find it proved that, on those facts alone, there had been an appropriation of each engine
to a particular sub-sale by the buyers with the assent of their sub-buyers (see the Sale of
Goods Act 1979, s 18, r 5(1)). In two cases the incorporation of the engine into a generator
set was complete; in the third it was not. The details are as follows:

g

Invoice no	Sub-buyers	Proceeds of sale claimed
68954	Holliday Hall & Co	£1,820·42
68981	W W Martin (Thanet) Ltd	} £2,473·65
68981	Sands & Toner (Newry) Ltd	
	Total	£4,294·07

h

In the case of the generator set intended for W W Martin (Thanet) Ltd, incorporation was
not complete on 12 and 13 November 1980. That generator set was not yet in a
deliverable state so far as a resale to sub-buyers was concerned (see r 5(1)). The engines
comprised in this group were, between 2 and 4 December 1980, delivered to sub-buyers.
j The sums which I have inserted into the column headed 'Proceeds of sale claimed' were
paid, as parts of larger sums, by the sub-buyers to the receiver; and for the most part were
paid by him into the joint deposit account already mentioned.

The sellers allege in respect of this group that initially they were entitled to claim, and
did claim, delivery up of the engines. That claim, they say, became transformed in the
course of interlocutory proceedings, by agreement or by order of the court or both, into
a claim against the proceeds of sale. If that claim fails, they allege in the alternative that
they have a direct claim against the proceeds of sale, as in the case of group (3).

The issues which require to be determined are thus as follows. (a) Did the sellers once have a valid proprietary claim in these proceedings to the engines in group (4), that is to say those that were still on the buyers' premises on 12 and 13 November 1980? (b) If so, has that claim been transferred into a claim against the proceeds of sale? (c) In any event, do the sellers have a direct claim for the proceeds of sale of the engines in both groups (3) and (4)? The amount in dispute on issues (a) and (b) is £4,294·07, and on issue (c), £28,988·01.

At one time there was a further issue. The buyers alleged that there had been under-payments by sub-buyers in respect of the generator sets which included the engines in group (4). Although the sums actually received from sub-buyers were, as one might expect, well in excess of the sums due to the sellers for the engines, the buyers claimed that the underpayments should be apportioned, so as to fall pro rata on themselves and the sellers. This contention was later abandoned. It appeared to me that there might not in reality have been any underpayment, or if there was the buyers might be unable to explain the reason for it. But that I do not now have to consider. I mention the argument about apportionment because it explains why something less than the whole amount listed as 'Proceeds of sale claimed' was paid into the joint deposit account. The effect of the concession now made is, I think, that the whole amount should have been paid into that account; but that is of course without prejudice to the question who is now entitled to it, which these proceedings must decide.

One last preliminary consideration before I come to the interlocutory proceedings, and then to the issues which I have to decide. There was some discussion in the course of the argument as to what answer would accord with the merits, or with equity, or with justice. I do not know any of the details of the receivership. But I am prepared to assume, from the fact that these proceedings are being contested, that if the sellers' claim fails they will receive nothing or little as unsecured creditors. Equally I assume, and I was given to understand, that, if the sellers' claim succeeds, still the receiver will not go away empty-handed from his office. From what I was told it follows that the claims of employees for wages and of the revenue authorities for taxes will be met, whatever I decide. But that consideration applies only on the facts of this case; it might not apply in other cases. Otherwise I can discern no preponderance of merit or equity, or justice, on either side. The dispute is simply as to which of the sellers and Barclays Bank is entitled to salvage £28,988·01 from the wreck of the buyers' affairs, and must be decided according to law. I have considerable sympathy with the sellers, in that that they have become embroiled in expensive and protracted litigation in a field where the law is unclear. But I cannot award them compensation, as such, for that misfortune.

Interlocutory proceedings

The receiver was appointed, as I have said, on 6 November 1980, and the sellers' representative visited the buyers' premises on 12 and 13 November. On 14 November the sellers' solicitors completed a pro forma summons. It claimed an injunction restraining the buyers from purporting to sell or parting with possession of the goods covered by the 15 invoices. This was put before Stocker J ex parte on 17 November. The judge granted an injunction until the hearing of a summons returnable on 1 December or further order.

On 24 November the writ was issued. It claimed (1) a declaration that the goods covered by the 15 invoices were the property of the sellers, except in so far as title might have passed to a bona fide purchaser for value from the buyers, (2) delivery up of the goods, (3) further or alternatively, a declaration that the proceeds of sale of the goods were held by the buyers in a fiduciary capacity and/or as trustees for the sellers, (4) an order that the buyers pay the proceeds of sale to the sellers, (5) various other remedies.

On 1 December 1980 Stocker J made an order which is in the following terms:

'Upon hearing counsel for the parties and upon reading the affidavits of John Herbert Cuff and the affidavit of Malcolm John London, it is ordered and directed that the order made on 17th December 1980 be and hereby is discharged upon the defendant undertaking (until 15th December 1980 or further order) (a) so soon as it

receives payments for the generator units into which the goods referred to in invoice
a   nos. 68954, 68981, 68982 are incorporated, it will pay into a joint solicitors account
the invoice price of the goods referred to in the said invoices.'

Those, I should say, are the invoices in group (4), plus one from group (2). The order
continues:

'(b) within 14 days of the date thereof to pay the plaintiff the sum of £545·37,
being invoice price of goods referred to in invoice nos. 50848, 51019, 51079, 51126,
b   51166 and 51023.'

Those, I should say, are the invoices in group (1). The order continues:

'Costs reserved. And it is ordered and directed ex parte until 15th December or
further order, the defendant shall, so soon as it receive payment for the generator
units into which goods referred to in invoice nos. 68952 and 68953 are incorporated,
c   paid into a joint solicitors account the invoice price of the goods referred to in the
said invoices.'

Both counsel sought to tell me what happened at the hearing before Stocker J, with a
view to assisting me in the interpretation of the order that he made. As there seemed to
be some dispute, I ruled that I would act on the terms of the order alone, unless and until
d   evidence was put before me in proper form. In the event I was not furnished with any
such evidence.

*Issue (a): Did the sellers once have a valid proprietary claim in these proceedings to the engines
in group (4), that is to say those which were still on the buyers' premises on 12 and 13 November
1980?*

This turns on the words of cl 10(i) in the sellers' conditions: 'all goods . . . shall be and
e   remain the property of the company until the full purchase price thereof shall be paid
. . .' There has been much recent case law on retention of title clauses. In the present case
counsel for the sellers does not contend that those words have their full literal effect;
counsel for the buyers does not contend that they have no effect at all. So I can narrow
the gap by stating the maximum which the sellers ask for and the minimum which the
buyers concede.

f   The sellers' case is that the engines remained their property, whether or not
incorporated into generator sets, until either (i) they were paid for in full or (ii) the
property in the engines passed to sub-buyers. They acknowledged, in para 7(a) of the
statement of claim, an implied term in their contracts with the buyers that the buyers
were entitled to sell the goods or any of them in advance of paying the price thereof to
the sellers.

g   The sellers argue that means of enforcing their title were available both under cl 10(i)
of the conditions and under cl 12. Their rights under cl 10(i), to retake possession of and
retain permanently any unpaid for goods, were, they admitted, only exercisable when
the buyers were in default of payment, ie when the period of credit had expired but the
price had not been paid. But their rights under cl 12 to terminate the contract could be
exercised, for example, if a receiver were appointed of the buyers' assets, and if exercised
h   would entitle them to retake possession of goods not yet paid for, even before the period
of credit had expired.

The buyers, on the other hand, admitted only that the sellers had the right to retake
possession of and retain the engines after (but not before) the period of credit had expired,
until either (i) they were paid for in full or (ii) the property in the engines passed to sub-
buyers or (iii) the engines (or spares) were incorporated into generator sets.

j   On either view the sellers retained for the time being some rights of a real or
proprietary nature. Scholars in jurisprudence may wish to argue whether they retained
the full rights of ownership, subject to certain personal or contractual restrictions, or
whether they retained only some of the rights of ownership, and transferred the
remainder to the buyers. My own view is that the former answer is correct. The contract
said that the goods should 'be and remain the property of the company'. Sections 16 and
17 of the Sale of Goods Act 1979 provide, in effect, that the property passed when it was
intended to pass. I do not see why the plain words of the contract should not mean what

they say. The sellers retain the full rights of ownership, subject to contractual terms limiting the exercise of those rights and regulating how they might be transferred to others. But in truth I do not see why it is necessary to decide the question at all, since both parties agree that, in one way or another, each was to some extent restricted in the exercise of full dominion over the goods. What I do need to decide, because the contrary view was argued by counsel for the buyers, is that the buyers did not 'confer' any proprietary rights in the goods on the sellers. In my judgment it was the sellers who *retained* proprietary rights: either all (as I think) or some of them.

There is nothing surprising in the concession that the sellers were entitled to retake the engines themselves, so long as they were not incorporated in generator sets, in the circumstances which I have set out. It accords with the view of the Court of Appeal in *Aluminium Industrie Vaassen BV v Romalpa Aluminium Ltd* [1976] 2 All ER 552, [1976] 1 WLR 676. The point was, however, conceded in that case: see the judgment of Mocatta J at first instance ([1976] 2 All ER 552 at 555, [1976] 1 WLR 676 at 680):

> '. . . it is admitted that the plaintiffs are the owners of the remaining unsold aluminium foil held by the receiver, and that they are entitled to an order for its delivery up to them.'

The fact that there was an appeal against that conclusion (see [1976] 2 All ER 552 at 561, [1976] 1 WLR 676 at 687 per Roskill LJ) must, I think, be explained by the dispute whether the sellers' conditions were incorporated at all, and not by any argument as to their effect on foil remaining in the buyers' possession, if they were incorporated. A similar concession was made in *Re Peachdart Ltd* [1983] 3 All ER 204 at 209, [1983] 3 WLR 878 at 884, where Vinelott J said:

> 'In the instant case counsel for the receiver concedes that the property in the unused stock of leather which came into the hands of the receiver when he was appointed remained with Freudenbergs.'

There are passages in the judgments of the Court of Appeal in *Borden (UK) Ltd v Scottish Timber Products Ltd* [1979] 3 All ER 961, [1981] Ch 25 which, if taken out of context, might suggest that an unpaid seller cannot lawfully retain proprietary rights in goods delivered to a buyer, whether or not those goods have been used or altered in a manufacturing process. But the whole dispute in that case was about chipboard, or the proceeds of sale of chipboard; it was not about the resin which the plaintiffs had sold to the defendants and which the defendants had used to make chipboard. The passages I have mentioned must be understood in that context.

Counsel for the buyers relied heavily on *Re Bond Worth Ltd* [1979] 3 All ER 919, [1980] Ch 228, decided by Slade J. That case was indeed concerned both with the actual goods sold (Acrilan fibre), as well as with yarn made from the fibre, carpets made from the yarn, and proceeds of sale of the carpets. It was held that the retention of title clause, in respect of all four categories of assets, amounted to the grant by the buyers of a floating equitable charge to the sellers, which was unregistered and therefore void against the other creditors of the buyers. However, the clause in question there provided that the risk in the goods should pass to the buyers, but that 'equitable and beneficial ownership' should remain with the sellers until full payment had been received. If those words had occurred in a document prepared by commercial men, one might perhaps have concluded that they simply meant ownership. But they occurred in a document which evidently had a legal provenance, and Slade J accordingly held that the legal title or property in the fibre passed to the buyers on delivery.

That case is readily distinguishable from the present case, where the contract provided that the goods should 'be and remain the property of the company'. Indeed I do not think that counsel for the buyers intended to rely on the decision in the *Bond Worth* case in relation to this part of the argument, as otherwise he would not have conceded as much effect for the retention of title clause as he did. Furthermore, when he later argued that the clause was an unregistered charge, he expressly limited that argument to its effect on the proceeds of sale, and not on the engines and spares themselves.

I have spent some time in explaining why I consider that the concessions made by

counsel for the buyers, at the least, were rightly made, for two reasons. First, this area of
a   the law is presently a maze if not a minefield, and one has to proceed with caution for
every step of the way. Second, the argument on those points which I do have to decide is
to some extent elucidated by what has already been conceded.

The first major difference between the parties in this part of the case is whether the
sellers did or did not retain any proprietary rights once the engines had been wholly or
in part incorporated into generator sets. If they did not, issue (a) must inevitably be
b   answered No, since two of the engines had been wholly incorporated, and one partially,
before the sellers made any claim to them in these proceedings.

I have already stated the facts as to how incorporation would be effected. It was a
question of doing up bolts and other connections, which could later be undone. Indeed
there was evidence, which I accept, that the engine in a generator set may in practice be
changed from time to time, for example if it is worn out or has broken down. In an
c   emergency, removal and replacement may have to be effected quickly and efficiently.

Some guidance on the law is to be found in *Crossley Vaines on Personal Property* (5th
edn, 1973). The preface describes the book as basically a students' textbook but continues
that it may—

> 'be of use to practitioners with regard to such questions of title as quite often arise
> in county court cases, not only at short notice but where collections of more detailed
d   > books are inaccessible to the advocate.'

For my part I consider that it deserves a greater accolade than the author claimed for it.
In the book there is this passage (p 430):

> '*Alteration and accession*—According to Bracton and Blackstone when a thing is
> changed into a different species, as by making wine, oil, bread or malt out of the
e   > grapes, olives, wheat or barley of another, the operator becomes the new owner
> thereof and is only liable (in damages) to the former proprietor for the value of the
> materials he has so converted. Similarly, says Halsbury when the goods of one man
> are affixed to the land or chattel, e.g., a ship, of another, they may become part of it
> and so accrue to the owner of the principal thing.'

f   The footnote to the reference to Halsbury reads:

> '*Halsbury's Laws of England* (3rd edn, vol 29 (1960) para 747, p 378). But this
> statement has been discounted in so far as it applies to attachment to chattels ((1935)
> 9 ALJ 50 (G Sawer), approved in *Lewis v. Andrews and Rowley Pty. Ltd.* (1937) 73 WN
> (NSW) 670 at 671; (1960) 39 ALJ 408 (J A Nicholson)).'

g   None of the authorities there mentioned have been available to me. I am aware that until
very recently the radio and radar apparatus on a ship was commonly hired by the
shipowner rather than bought by him. No doubt it was attached to the ship; but I do not
suppose that it thereby became the property of the shipowner or his mortgagee. Nor in
my judgment would an engine which was the property of A become the property of B
merely because B incorporated it in a generator set otherwise composed of his own
h   materials.

Those reflections and the facts of this case persuade me that the proprietary rights of
the sellers in the engines were not affected when the engines were wholly or partially
incorporated into generator sets. They were not like the Acrilan which became yarn and
then carpet (the *Bond Worth* case), or the resin which became chipboard (*Borden's* case), or
the leather which became handbags (the *Peachdart* case), or the grapes, olives, wheat and
j   barley mentioned by *Crossley Vaines*. They just remained engines, albeit connected to
other things.

The next sub-issue is whether the sellers were entitled to demand the return of their
engines, pursuant to cl 12 of their conditions, when the buyers went into receivership,
even if there was then no default of payment, or whether that remedy was only available
under cl 10(i), on payment becoming overdue. This point is significant because invoice
no 68981 (the engines for W W Martin (Thanet) Ltd and Sands & Toner (Newry) Ltd)
was issued on 2 October 1980. It did not become overdue until after 1 December 1980.

By contrast, invoice no 68954 (the engine for Holliday Hall & Co) was issued on 5 September 1980; it became overdue after 1 November 1980, but before the various *a* interlocutory proceedings that I have mentioned.

This is a short question of construction, on which at most the sum of £2,473·65 depends. As I read cl 12 of the conditions, it is concerned with termination of the two main outstanding obligations of the parties, ie the obligation of the sellers to deliver future engines and spares, and of the buyers to pay for them. It deals specifically with materials allocated for future performance. I do not consider that it touches at all on the *b* buyers' obligation to pay for goods already delivered, or in the sellers obligation (if it could really be so described) to leave those goods with the buyers until either payment or default of payment should occur. In my judgment the remedy of retaking goods is exclusively dealt with in cl 10(i), and there it is provided only on default of payment. Were it otherwise, the sellers might terminate under cl 12(iii) on the ground of a failure by the buyers to take delivery of the last engine or parcel of spares, and then retake all *c* engines and spares previously delivered under that contract, even if incorporated in generator sets, provided that they had not been paid for and notwithstanding the period of credit expressly allowed. That does not seem to me a very plausible construction.

The parties are agreed that the sellers had no right to retake the engines after the property in them had passed to sub-buyers. The third sub-issue is whether the property in the engines had passed to sub-buyers before the material date. In the light of my *d* conclusion on the previous sub-issue, that the sellers could not acquire a right to retake the engines by terminating the contract but only when payment became overdue, the 'material date' means the later of (i) the date when payment became overdue and (ii) the date when delivery up was first sought from the buyers.

Payment became overdue in respect of invoice no 68981 on 2 December 1980, which is the material date in respect of that invoice. In the case of invoice no 68984 payment *e* became overdue on 2 November 1980; but I have no evidence of any claim for delivery up before 17 November 1980, when the sellers applied ex parte to Stocker J. So 17 November is the material date in respect of that invoice.

Had the property in the engines passed to sub-buyers before 2 December and 17 November 1980 respectively? I have already held that whatever process of marking or identification enabled the sellers' representative to discover the destination of the engines, *f* on 12 and 13 November, that was not in itself an appropriation of each generator set to a contract of sale to sub-buyers with the assent of the sub-buyers. Furthermore, one of the generator sets was not then in a deliverable state. However, invoices and delivery notes were sent to the sub-buyers by the buyers. These stated the serial numbers of the generator sets to be delivered. When those invoices or delivery notes were received by the sub-buyers there did occur, in my judgment, an appropriation with the assent of the *g* sub-buyers, if the goods were in a deliverable state and if appropriation had not occurred earlier.

It is necessary to set out the dates in a table:

Sellers' invoice no	Sub-buyers	Date of invoice or delivery note to sub-buyers
68954	Holliday Hall & Co	6 October 1980
68981	W W Martin (Thanet) Ltd	2 December 1980
68981	Sands & Toner (Newry) Ltd	12 September 1980

Accordingly I find that property passed to the sub-buyers on the following dates. (i) *Holliday Hall & Co*: not later than 13 November 1980. It is known that the goods were *j* then in a deliverable state, and the serial number had been communicated to the sub-buyers some time before. (ii) *W W Martin (Thanet) Ltd*: 2 December 1980. That was the date when the goods were delivered to the sub-buyers. Before that it is not proved that the serial number had been communicated to the sub-buyers, although there is an affidavit which suggests that the generator set was in a deliverable state by 28 November 1980. (iii) *Sands & Toner (Newry) Ltd*: not later than 13 November 1980, for the reasons set out in (i) above.

It is therefore apparent that the sellers had no right to retake the engines in cases (i)
and (iii) when they first sought to do so on 17 November 1980: the property in the
engines had passed to sub-buyers. Case (ii) is more difficult. On 17 November 1980 the
sellers had no right to retake that engine because payment was not overdue. On 2
December it became overdue; but on the same day the property passed to sub-buyers. It
is a fine point. But I suppose I must decide that the price became due at the first moment
of 2 December, before the property passed, since delivery must have occurred later in the
day.

So I answer issue (a) in this way: the sellers had a valid proprietary claim in these
proceedings in respect of the engine delivered to W W Martin (Thanet) Ltd, for a few
hours on the morning of 2 December 1980.

By way of appendix I would add that counsel for the sellers sought to rely on cl 7 of
the buyers' conditions, which were included in their contracts of resale. That clause read:

'*Terms of payment*—Payment in respect of any goods or services shall be made in
accordance with the terms specifically stated in our offer. If not so specifically stated
10 per cent. of the amount of the payment shall be deemed to be due on placement
of order and the remainder due on notification by us that goods have been tested
under condition 4 or that they are ready for despatch. Any liability on our part is
subject to the terms of payment and all your other obligations to us under the
contract being strictly observed.'

In my judgment the clause did not touch on the passing of property. No argument was
addressed to me whether the buyers reserved the right of disposal within s 19 of the 1979
Act.

*Issue (b): Has the sellers' proprietary claim been transformed into a claim against the proceeds of
sale?*

This depends on the meaning and effect of the undertaking and order of Stocker J on
1 December 1980. Specifically, it depends on the first part of that document, since it is
now a live issue only in relation to invoice no 68981.

Counsel for the sellers argued that the intention of the undertaking and order was to
replace any claim which the sellers might have against the goods by a claim against the
proceeds of sale. That would enable the ex parte order to be discharged, and the receiver
to proceed with the realisation of the buyers' assets for whom it might concern.

Counsel for the buyers argues that the ex parte order had been wrongly made and was
discharged. In return the sellers were content to accept an undertaking which would
enable any direct claim which they might have against the proceeds of sale to be enforced
at a later date.

In my judgment counsel for the sellers is entitled to succeed on this point. In the
ordinary way the aim of a judge on such an application is to preserve as best he can the
status quo, without deciding the rights and wrongs of the dispute to any greater extent
than is absolutely necessary. It seems to me improbable that Stocker J decided, or that
the parties agreed, that the sellers had no claim to retake any of the goods. It is more
likely that that issue was left to be decided at the trial. It was therefore an implied term
of the undertaking that the sellers should have a *derivative* claim against the proceeds of
sale in substitution for any direct claim they might have to retake the goods.

There remains the difficulty that the sellers did not have, on 1 December 1980 when
the order was made and the undertaking given, a presently enforceable claim to retake
any of the engines. They acquired such a claim, in respect of one engine only, at midnight
on 1–2 December. Nevertheless I think that their inchoate claim was covered by the
term which I have found to be implied in the undertaking. Spelt out in full, the
implication was that, if the sellers had, *or thereafter acquired*, a right to retake any of the
goods, they should have a derivative claim against the proceeds of sale in substitution for
that right.

Accordingly I answer issue (b) as follows: the proprietary claim which the sellers had,
on the morning of 2 December, to retake the engine later delivered to W W Martin
(Thanet) Ltd was transformed into a claim for £1,236·82, part of the proceeds of sale of
the generator set in which that engine was incorporated. I have taken that figure because

it is half the amount of the sellers' invoice no 68981, which related to two engines. Counsel must correct me if I am wrong.

It was argued that, if I found any such claim to exist, it was a charge which should have been registered and was therefore void against the creditors of the buyers. I do not consider that it was a charge at all. A chose in action was created when that sum was paid into the solicitors' joint deposit account. I have to decide who is the beneficial owner of that chose in action. I hold that the sellers are the beneficial owners, absolutely and not by way of charge, to the extent of £1,236·82.

*Issue (c): Do the sellers have a direct claim for the proceeds of sale of the engines in both groups (3)
and (4)?*

This is a more difficult and more important issue than any other in the case. It involves two questions. (i) Have the parties in their contracts used language appropriate to create such a right, expressly or by implication? (ii) Is the right nevertheless one which the law will not countenance, either because it is an unregistered charge or for any other reason? To answer both questions one must begin with an examination of the *Romalpa* case [1976] 2 All ER 552, [1976] 1 WLR 676, which was decided by the Court of Appeal and by which I am bound. In that case such a right was recognised and enforced. But it is argued that there are at least three points of distinction between the present case and *Romalpa*. First, the parties have used different language in their contracts; second, the proceeds of sale in *Romalpa* were of the selfsame goods as the sellers had supplied to the buyers, without any addition or annexation; third, a concession was made in *Romalpa* (that the buyers were bailees) which has not been made in this case.

The ratio of the *Romalpa* case is, I think, set out in the judgment of Roskill LJ ([1976] 2 All ER 552 at 564, [1976] 1 WLR 676 at 690):

> 'It seems to me clear . . . that to give effect to what I regard as the obvious purpose of cl 13 one must imply into the first part of the clause not only the power to sell but also the obligation to account in accordance with the normal fiduciary relationship of principal and agent, bailor and bailee. Accordingly, like the learned judge, I find no difficulty in holding that the principles in *Re Hallett's Estate* (1880) 13 Ch D 696, [1874–80] All ER Rep 793, to which I have already referred, are of immediate application . . .'

The principles which Roskill LJ referred to are contained in the passages cited by Mocatta J at first instance (see [1976] 2 All ER 552 at 561, [1976] 1 WLR 676 at 687). Particularly relevant is this quotation from the judgment of Jessel MR in *Re Hallett's Estate* 13 Ch D 696 at 709, [1874–80] All ER Rep 793 at 796:

> 'Has it ever been suggested, until very recently, that there is any distinction between an express trustee, or an agent, or a bailee or a collector of rents, or anybody else in a fiduciary position? I have never heard, until quite recently, such a distinction suggested.'

If thereby it was decided that every agent selling his principal's goods, and every bailee selling his bailor's goods, was necessarily a fiduciary, two results would have followed. First, the *Romalpa* case could have been decided very shortly indeed: the buyers were admitted to be bailees, and found to be agents; there was no need to consider any implied term as to their obligations; they were bound to account as a fiduciary. Second, *Henry v Hammond* [1913] 2 KB 515 must have been wrongly decided. There it was held that the defendant, a shipping agent who was employed to sell the cargo of a vessel in distress, was not bound to keep the money thereby realised separate from other moneys; accordingly he was not a trustee of the money, but merely a debtor.

Notwithstanding an earlier passage in the judgment of Roskill LJ which might suggest otherwise, it is, I think, implicit in the reasoning of the Court of Appeal in the *Romalpa* case that some bailees and some agents do not occupy a fiduciary position, although there may well be a presumption that they do ('the normal fiduciary relationship'). With that reasoning, if I may say so, I respectfully agree.

Since preparing this judgment, I have obtained a copy of *Bowstead on Agency* (14th edn,

1976) and I find this passage cited (at p 126) from the speech of Lord Upjohn in *Boardman*
v Phipps [1966] 3 All ER 721 at 758, [1967] 2 AC 46 at 127:

> 'The facts and circumstances must be carefully examined to see whether in fact a
> purported agent and even a confidentail agent is in a fiduciary relationship to his
> principal. It does not necessarily follow that he is in such a position (see *Re Coomber*,
> *Coomber v. Coomber* ([1911] 1 Ch 723)).'

One therefore has to examine the relationship in each individual case to see whether it
is of a fiduciary nature. That the Court of Appeal did, by considering what term should
be implied. As Templeman LJ observed in *Borden's* case [1979] 3 All ER 961 at 973,
[1981] Ch 25 at 45, Roskill LJ in refusing leave to appeal to the House of Lords in
Romalpa referred to 'a rather simple contract, not altogether happily expressed in the
English language, but [which] could not govern any other case'.

In the present case, it seems to me that there are four grounds for suggesting a different
answer to the inquiry as to what term should be implied from that reached by the Court
of Appeal in the *Romalpa* case. First, the express terms here referred only to the actual
goods supplied; there was no attempt to deal with mixed or manufactured objects, such
as occurred in *Romalpa* and was considered important by the Court of Appeal. Second,
there was here no express obligation on the buyers if required to store the goods in such
a way that they were clearly the property of the sellers. Third, there was no mention in
any other part of the clause of the expression (derived from the Dutch) 'fiduciary owner';
that too had been considered important by the Court of Appeal. Fourth, the implied
term contended for here would have to relate to the proceeds of sale of the generator sets,
which comprised more than the goods supplied by the sellers, or at any rate to part of
those proceeds; whereas the implied term found in *Romalpa* related, as I see it, only to
the proceeds of sale of the actual goods supplied by the sellers.

Here I do reach a different conclusion. Of course I must start with the presumption of
a fiduciary relationship. That to my mind is neutralised by the agreement between the
parties that the buyers should have credit for at least one month, and possibly two
months. It is not easy to reconcile that with an obligation to keep the proceeds of resale
in a separate account. A similar argument was described by Roskill LJ as 'formidable' in
Romalpa [1976] 2 All ER 552 at 563, [1976] 1 WLR 676 at 689, although the Court of
Appeal there found other considerations which overcame it.

Next I direct myself in accordance with the observations of Buckley LJ in *Borden's* case
[1979] 3 All ER 961 at 974, [1981] Ch 25 at 46:

> 'If any term is to be implied, that must be a term which is necessary to give the
> contract business efficacy, but it must also be a term which the court can see
> unambiguously to be a term which the parties would have inserted into their
> contract had they thought it appropriate to express it.'

By that test I cannot find in the contracts between the parties to this case a term that the
proceeds of sale must be kept separate and would belong wholly or in part to the sellers.
In the express terms they had concerned themselves only with the property in the goods.
They provided expressly for a remedy in respect of the goods: the power to retake
possession and retain them permanently. On the principle that the expression of one is
an exclusion of the other, that militates against the suggested implication. Viewing these
transactions as a whole, I do not find it implied that the buyers were to occupy a fiduciary
position in respect of the proceeds of sale.

That conclusion makes it unnecessary for me to hold whether the buyers were or were
not bailees, by virtue of what might be called a bailment in the earlier stages of a contract
of sale (see Benjamin *Sale of Goods* (2nd edn, 1981) para 57), or a bailment with a
superimposed contract of sale (see *Re Peachdart Ltd* [1983] 3 All ER 204 at 210–211,
[1983] 3 WLR 878 at 886 per Vinelott J). Nor need I decide whether an agreement which
rendered the buyers a fiduciary in respect of the proceeds of sale would have been a
charge which ought to have been registered. There were interesting and sustained
arguments on both points; but however tempted I might be to consider them in this
judgment, I do not think that it would be right for me to do so.

The answer to issue (c) is that the sellers do not have a direct claim for the proceeds of sale of the engines in groups (3) and (4). There will accordingly be a declaration that the sellers are entitled to payment of £1,236·82 and any interest accrued thereon out of the joint deposit account, but no more. I shall hear counsel on whether I am asked to order judgment on the sellers' admitted monetary claim against the buyers.

Judgment accordingly.

Solicitors: *Moore & Blatch*, Southampton (for the sellers); *Durrant Piesse* (for the buyers).

K Mydeen Esq   Barrister.

R v Young

COURTS-MARTIAL APPEAL COURT

STEPHEN BROWN LJ, KILNER BROWN AND RUSSELL JJ

31 JANUARY, 16 FEBRUARY 1984

Drugs – Dangerous drugs – Unlawful possession – Defence – Lack of knowledge – Absence of belief, suspicion or reason to suspect substance a controlled drug – Self-induced intoxication making accused unable to hold belief or register suspicion – Whether self-induced intoxication affording defence – Whether test of knowledge objective in regard to all three states of mind covered by defence – Whether concept of reasonable sober man relevant – What is proper direction to jury on defence – Misuse of Drugs Act 1971, s 28(3)(b).

When considering whether a person accused of being in possession of a controlled drug with intent to supply it, contrary to s 5(3) of the Misuse of Drugs Act 1971, has made out the exculpatory defence available under s 28(3)(b)[a] of that Act that 'he neither believed nor suspected nor had reason to suspect' that the substance in question was a controlled drug, although the test whether he 'believed' or 'suspected' the substance was a controlled drug is subjective the third limb of the defence, ie that the accused had no 'reason to suspect' that the substance was a controlled drug, introduces the concept of reasonableness so that the test of whether the accused had no 'reason to suspect' the substance was a controlled drug is objective and not subjective, and because the third limb is an integral part of the defence under s 28(3)(b) it follows that self-induced intoxication which makes the accused unable to hold a belief or register a suspicion is irrelevant in considering whether the defence as a whole is made out. Accordingly, where a defence under s 28(3)(b) is put forward it is sufficient for the trial judge to direct the jury that the accused's self-induced intoxication is irrelevant to the decision whether he had the necessary knowledge. Moreover, it is an unnecessary gloss for the judge to introduce into his direction the concept of the reasonable sober man (see p 167 e to g, post).

R v Woods (1982) 74 Cr App R 312 applied.

Jaggard v Dickinson [1980] 3 All ER 716 considered.

DPP v Majewski [1975] 3 All ER 296 distinguished.

Notes

For effect of drink on the commission of a crime generally, see 11 Halsbury's Laws (4th edn) para 28, and for cases on the subject, see 14(1) Digest (Reissue) 49, 50, 232–240.

For the defence of lack of knowledge in proceedings for unlawful possession of controlled drugs, see 11 Halsbury's Laws (4th edn) para 1097.

For the Misuse of Drugs Act 1971, ss 5, 28, see 41 Halsbury's Statutes (3rd edn) 884, 905.

---

a   Section 28(3), so far as material, is set out at p 165 j, post

Cases referred to in judgment

a   *DPP v Majewski* [1975] 3 All ER 296, [1977] AC 443, [1975] 3 WLR 401, HL.
    Jaggard v Dickinson [1980] 3 All ER 716, [1981] QB 527, [1981] 2 WLR 118, DC.
    R v Woods (1982) 74 Cr App R 312, CA.

Appeal

On 1 June 1983 before a district court-martial at Soest, West Germany (Assistant Judge

b   Advocate General Canner) the appellant, Signalman Robert Gordon Young, was convicted
    of possessing a controlled drug, lysergide, with intent to supply it, contrary to s 5(3) of
    the Misuse of Drugs Act 1971. He was sentenced to eight months' detention and
    dismissed the service. He appealed against conviction. The grounds of the appeal were
    that the conviction was unsafe and unsatisfactory because the assistant judge advocate
    general misdirected the court (1) on the question of the defence under s 28(3)(b) of the

c   1971 Act by directing the court that they need only be satisfied that the appellant knew
    he was in possession of something which turned out to be or to contain the controlled
    drug in question and (2) on the question whether drunkenness negated the appellant's
    belief, suspicion or reason for suspicion that what he possessed was a controlled drug, by
    further directing the court that the applicable test was that of the belief or suspicion of a
    reasonable and sober person. The facts are set out in the judgment of the court.

d   *John Bishop* (assigned by the Registrar of Courts-Martial Appeals) for the appellant.
    Michael Hucker for the Crown.

                                                                              Cur adv vult

e   16 February. The following judgment of the court was delivered.

KILNER BROWN J. The appellant, a signalman in 22 Signal Regiment, appeals by
leave of the single judge against a conviction by a district court-martial at Soest in West
Germany on 1 June 1983. He was convicted of possessing a controlled drug (lysergide or
LSD) with intent to supply and was sentenced to eight months' detention and to be
dismissed from the service.

f   The facts were simple. The case for the Crown was that, after a previous transaction
between the appellant and a German by name of Wunsch in which the appellant had
sold a small quantity of lysergide, a meeting was arranged outside a disco bar for 27
January 1983. As they were negotiating for a further sale police, who had previously
been alerted and stationed close by, moved in and the appellant was arrested. The
evidence clearly established that the appellant did have some lysergide which he

g   swallowed as the police approached and some was found in the vomit which he was
    induced to produce. He had obviously been drinking, but the first witness who said he
    was very drunk was his German girlfriend, who was called as a witness for the Crown.
    The others called for the Crown put him as slightly tipsy or as affected, but not drunk.
    There was strong evidence from the defence that he was seriously affected by drink and
    was almost incapable.

h   His condition was an important issue. There was really no defence available other than
    the statutory defence provided by s 28 of the Misuse of Drugs Act 1971. The relevant
    parts read as follows:

        '(2) Subject to subsection (3) below, in any proceedings for an offence to which
        this section applies it shall be a defence for the accused to prove that he neither knew
        of nor suspected nor had reason to suspect the existence of some fact alleged by the

j   prosecution which it is necessary for the prosecution to prove if he is to be convicted
        of the offence charged.
            (3) ... the accused ... (b) shall be acquitted thereof—(i) if he proves that he
        neither believed nor suspected nor had reason to suspect that the substance or
        product in question was a controlled drug ... .'

The first ground of appeal alleges a misdirection by the assistant judge advocate general
in indicating that the court need only be satisfied that the appellant knew that he was in

possession of something which turned out to be or to contain the controlled drug in question. In our judgment this did not amount to a misdirection. It was a proper and *a* helpful interpretation and application of the words in the statute which served to indicate to the court what had to be established once the statutory defence was raised. The submission is rejected.

There is considerably more force in the second ground, which introduces a difficult, interesting and, as far as we are aware, hitherto unexplored aspect of the effect of self-induced intoxication. The misdirection alleged is the application of the test of a reasonable *b* sober man and the withdrawal of the consideration of the inability of the accused, caused by drink, to hold a belief or to register suspicion.

He began the relevant part of his direction, to which reference in full will later be made, by relating the effect of self-induced intoxication to the burden on the prosecution to prove knowledge of possession as well as intent to supply. He treated the two matters together. No doubt he had in mind the decision in *DPP v Majewski* [1975] 3 All ER 296, *c* [1977] AC 443, with reference to the irrelevance of the effect of drink as to primary intent. We have doubts whether the same criterion applies when knowledge as distinct from intent is under consideration. However, in the circumstances of this case it matters little if at all. There was no need to analyse the burden on the Crown as to establishing knowledge once the primary facts as to his conduct in swallowing the portion of drug was proved to the satisfaction of the court. Prima facie knowledge of possession is the *d* only reasonable inference to be drawn. The introduction of the effect of drink at this stage was unnecessary. It was not, however, a misdirection because the attention of the court was properly drawn to the statutory defence on which the appellant relied and in this context the effect of self-induced intoxication was a relevant, indeed the only relevant, factor.

The directions by the assistant judge advocate general on the whole of this matter was *e* as follows:

'So, your conviction of the accused, even of the lesser and basic offence of unlawful possession, requires you to be satisfied as to the accused's knowledge of possession of something which turns out to be the controlled drug averred in the charge particulars. When, therefore, you come to decide the matter of such knowledge you *f* should, again, have due regard to the evidence of the drink he had taken. For, depending on the view you take of the accused's evidence on other matters, that evidence of his drinking and its effect on him is as relevant and as important to this question of his knowledge of possessing lysergide, or what proved to be or to contain lysergide, as to any intent on his part to supply it to another. In other words, it is in the light of the evidence of his drinking that you may have to ask yourselves *g* whether the accused had this requisite knowledge. Remember once again, it is not for the accused to prove he was so drunk he didn't have that knowledge, but for the prosecution to satisfy you beyond reasonable doubt that whatever his drinking the accused did have such knowledge. However, if you are so satisfied, that is to say that he did have such knowledge, you will then have to ask yourselves, in the light of the evidence as to the drink this accused had taken, whether on the balance of *h* probabilities, which is not such an onerous burden, the accused has proved that because of his drinking he neither believed nor suspected, nor had reason to suspect, what he had was a controlled drug. Pausing there for a moment, I have to tell you that you should reach your decision as to this in the light of what a reasonable and sober person would in the particular circumstances have believed, or suspected, and whether a reasonable and sober person would have reason to suspect what he had in *j* his possession was a controlled drug. A controlled drug, I hasten to say, the prosecution, need I remind you, doesn't have to satisfy you the accused suspected or had reason to suspect it was lysergide. I remind you again that the test you apply, or have to apply, in deciding this question is that of an ordinary reasonable and sober man. Accordingly, you should understand that in this respect, as opposed to the other matters I've already dealt with, the accused's drunkenness, if any, and voluntary, does not avail him. For a person who voluntarily consumes so much *a*   alcohol that he makes it impossible for him to appreciate what would have been apparent to him but for the drink or what a reasonable sober man would in all the other circumstances have believed, suspected or had reason to suspect cannot pray in aid his voluntary drunkenness.'

For the appellant it is submitted that this was a misdirection. It is contended that the three requirements are to be read as one, all of which require consideration of the effect of alcohol on the appellant's actual personal ability to believe, suspect or have reason to *b*   suspect. In other words, the subjective approach applies throughout and the introduction of the test of the reasonable sober man is not appropriate. For the Crown it is submitted that the words 'nor had reason to suspect' introduce the concept of that which is reasonable and this affects the belief and suspicion also. That being so, it is said that it was correct to introduce the objective test of the reasonable sober man.

We were referred to various authorities. In support of the Crown's case the most recent *c*   authority is *R v Woods* (1982) 74 Cr App R 312. That laid down that a defendant's self-intoxication was not a relevant consideration which a jury were entitled to take into account on a charge of rape in deciding whether there were reasonable grounds for his belief that the woman in question was consenting to sexual intercourse. We would not require authority for that proposition. It is clearly the law that, when reasonable grounds for belief are canvassed, self-intoxication will not avail.

d   For the appellant it is contended that 'had reason to suspect' is not the same thing as 'reasonable grounds for belief'. Reliance is place on the decision of the Divisional Court in *Jaggard v Dickinson* [1980] 3 All ER 716, [1981] QB 527. That is authority not binding on this court, but nevertheless persuasive for the proposition that, where there is an exculpatory statutory defence of honest belief, self-induced intoxication is a factor which must be considered in the context of a subjective consideration of the individual state of *e*   mind. The objective test of a reasonable sober man is irrelevant. Accepting and applying this decision as we do, it would lead to the conclusion that, in so far as the belief and suspicion are concerned, there would have been a misdirection in the instant case. But it leaves untouched the problem created by the introduction of the third limb, which is an integral part of the exculpatory defence. The remaining question is whether a reason is something entirely personal and individual, calling for an entirely subjective *f*   consideration, or involves the wider concept of an objective rationality. We are of the opinion that it is the latter. It follows therefore that, in our judgment, it was a correct direction that the self-induced intoxication did not avail. Moreover, it was an unnecessary gloss to introduce the concept of the reasonable sober man. Nevertheless, this gloss did not vitiate the fundamental direction that the self-intoxication was no defence. The drunkenness relied on could not assist in considering whether or not the accused had no *g*   reason to suspect. The effect of this conclusion is that self-induced intoxication is not a relevant consideration in the exercise of this statutory defence. The appeal is dismissed.

Appeal dismissed.

4 May. The Courts-Martial Appeal Court (Lawton LJ, Kilner Brown and Beldam JJ) *refused leave to appeal to the House of Lords but certified, under s 39(2) of the Courts-Martial (Appeals) Act 1968, that the following point of law of general public importance was involved in the decision: if because of self-induced intoxication a defendant did not believe or suspect, nor have reason to do so, that a substance or product was a controlled drug when he would have done so had he been sober, can he establish a defence under s 28(3)(b)(i) of the Misuse of Drugs Act 1971?*

Solicitors: *Director of Army Legal Services* (for the Crown).

N P Metcalfe Esq   Barrister.

Cadogan v Dimovic and others   *a*

COURT OF APPEAL, CIVIL DIVISION
WALLER, FOX AND ROBERT GOFF LJJ
12, 13 JANUARY, 8 FEBRUARY 1984

Landlord and tenant – Relief against forfeiture – Underlessee – Business premises – Forfeiture of   *b*
underlease in consequence of forfeiture of superior lease – Underlessee applying for vesting order
granting him new lease of premises – Contractual term of underlease expiring before application
heard – Landlord not terminating underlease in accordance with Landlord and Tenant Act 1954
– Whether jurisdiction to make vesting order – Whether 'term' of underlease including period
during which sublease continues prior to termination under 1954 Act – Whether 'term' of
underlease limited to term specified in sublease – Law of Property Act 1925, s 146(4) – Landlord   *c*
and Tenant Act 1954, s 24(1).

The tenants under a superior lease of premises for a term expiring in 1995 granted an
underlease of the basement of the premises to C Ltd for a term expiring on 31 December
1982. C Ltd carried on a business in the basement. On 7 July 1981 the landlord under
the superior lease served a writ on the tenants claiming possession of the premises and
forfeiture of the superior lease because of a breach of the repairing covenants in the lease.   *d*
On 12 October 1981 the landlord obtained judgment in default of defence against the
tenants so that both the superior lease and C Ltd's underlease were forfeited as from 7
July 1981. The landlord did not however re-enter the premises and furthermore took no
steps to terminate C Ltd's underlease under the provisions of Pt II of the Landlord and
Tenant Act 1954 (relating to the termination of business tenancies). In September 1982
C Ltd applied, as an underlessee claiming an interest in the property comprised in the   *e*
headlease, for an order under s 146(4)[a] of the Law of Property Act 1925 vesting the
basement in C Ltd on such terms and conditions as the court thought fit. The application
was heard on 31 October 1983 when it was dismissed for want of jurisdiction on the
grounds that (i) s 146(4) precluded the court from vesting in C Ltd a lease for a longer
term than its original sublease, which had expired on 31 December 1982, and (ii) s 24(1)[b]   *f*
of the 1954 Act, which provided that a business tenancy could only be terminated in
accordance with Pt II of the 1954 Act, did not apply because s 24(1) was subject to s 24(2)
which provided that s 24(1) did not prevent a business tenancy coming to an end by
forfeiture. C Ltd appealed.

Held – The appeal would be allowed for the following reasons—   *g*
    (1) On the true construction of s 146(4) of the 1925 Act the restriction preventing the
grant of a new lease to an underlessee for 'any longer term than he had under his original
sub-lease' following the forfeiture of his underlease as the result of the forfeiture of the
superior lease referred to the term the underlessee would have had but for the forfeiture,
which in the case of a business tenancy was, by virtue of s 24(1) of the 1954 Act, the
period which would elapse before the tenancy could be terminated in accordance with Pt   *h*
II of the 1954 Act following the expiry of the term stated in the underlease. Accordingly,
although the term of the underlease had expired on 31 December 1982 the underlease
itself was still continuing at the time C Ltd's application was heard because it had not yet
been terminated in accordance with Pt II of the 1954 Act. Accordingly, the judge had
been wrong to decline jurisdiction to consider C Ltd's application for a vesting order (see
p 172 *d* to p 173 *d* and *j* to p 174 *c* and p 175 *a b*, post); *Factors (Sundries) Ltd v Miller*   *j*
[1952] 2 All ER 630 considered.
    (2) Furthermore, s 24(2) of the 1954 Act did not operate to prevent s 24(1) from
applying to C Ltd's business tenancy, because s 24(2) only applied where there had been

a   Section 146(4) is set out at p 170 *f* to *h*, post
b   Section 24, so far as material, is set out at p 170 *j*, post

a   absolute 'forfeiture' of a lease and not where relief against forfeiture could be granted by
     way of a vesting order under s 146(4) of the 1925 Act (see p 173 b to d and p 175 a b, post).

     Notes
     For an underlessee's right to relief against forfeiture, see 27 Halsbury's Laws (4th edn)
     para 441.
       For the continuation of business tenancies, see ibid para 483.
b   For the Law of Property Act 1925, s 146, see 27 Halsbury's Statutes (3rd edn) 563.
       For the Landlord and Tenant Act 1954, Pt II, s 24, see 18 ibid 555, 557.

     Cases referred to in judgments
     Bradshaw v Pawley [1979] 3 All ER 273, [1980] 1 WLR 10.
     Chelsea Estates Investment Trust Co Ltd v Marche [1955] 1 All ER 195, [1955] Ch 328,
         [1955] 2 WLR 139.
c   *Factors (Sundries) Ltd v Miller* [1952] 2 All ER 630, CA.
     Meadows v Clerical Medical and General Life Assurance Society [1980] 1 All ER 454, [1981]
         Ch 70, [1980] 2 WLR 639.
     Roberts v Church Comrs for England [1971] 3 All ER 703, [1972] 1 QB 278, [1971] 3 WLR
         566, CA.

d   **Cases also cited**
     Brikom Investments Ltd v Seaford [1981] 2 All ER 783, [1981] 1 WLR 863, CA.
     Ewart v Fryer [1901] 1 Ch 499, CA; *affd* [1902] AC 187, HL.

     Interlocutory appeal
     By a writ issued on 17 June 1981 the plaintiff, the Hon Charles Gerald John Cadogan,
e   Viscount Chelsea, the freehold owner of premises known as 28, 29 and 30 Cadogan Place,
     London SW3, claimed against the defendants, Nebojsa George Dimovic and Jack
     Grenville Riley, the tenants of the premises under a headlease, in respect of a breach of
     the repairing covenants in the lease, possession of the premises, forfeiture of the lease,
     mesne profits, damages and costs. On 12 October 1981 the plaintiff obtained judgment
     against the defendants in default of defence but the plaintiff did not re-enter the premises.
f   In July 1982 Mr Riley's application for relief from forfeiture was dismissed. On 14
     September 1982 Chesham Property Overseas Ltd (Chesham), the underlessee of part of
     the basement of the premises under a sublease made between them and the defendants,
     and who carried on a business in the part of the basement sublet to them, applied for an
     order under s 146(4) of the Law of Property Act 1925 vesting that part of the basement
     in them on such terms and conditions as the court thought fit and for an order if
g   necessary adding them as a defendant to the action. On 21 October 1983 Sir Neil Lawson,
     sitting as a judge of the High Court, dismissed Chesham's application, holding that he
     had no jurisdiction under s 146(4) to entertain the application because under the terms
     of the sublease Chesham's subtenancy had come to an end on 31 December 1982 and the
     court could not under s 146(4) make a vesting order granting Chesham a new lease for
     any longer term than they had had under the original terms of their sublease, and
h   furthermore that, by virtue of s 24(2) of the Landlord and Tenant Act 1954, s 24(1) of
     that Act did not prevent the sublease coming to an end by the forfeiture of the headlease.
     Chesham appealed pursuant to leave granted by the judge. The facts are set out in the
     judgment of Fox LJ.

     J G Boggis for Chesham.
j   *William Poulton* for the plaintiff.

                                                                          Cur adv vult
     8 February. The following judgments were delivered.

     FOX LJ (giving the first judgment at the invitation of Waller LJ). This case is concerned
     with an application by a sublessee for relief from forfeiture consequent on the forfeiture

of the superior lease. It raises a question as to the effect, in relation to business premises, of s 146(4) of the Law of Property Act 1925.

By a lease dated 26 April 1950 and made between Earl Cadogan of the first part, Cadogan Settled Estates Co of the second part and Chesham Property Co Ltd of the third part, Earl Cadogan and the Cadogan Settled Estates Co demised to the lessee 28, 29 and 30 Cadogan Place and 8 and 10 Cadogan Lane, London, for 48¾ years from 25 March 1947 at a rental of £1,200 per year. The lease contained convenants by the lessee for the repair and maintenance of the premises with a proviso for re-entry in the event of any breach of any of the covenants.

Subsequently, the reversion expectant on the determination of the term created by the lease became vested in the plaintiff; and the term itself became vested in the defendants, Messrs Dimovic and Riley.

By an agreement dated 14 January 1976, and made between the defendants of the one part and Chesham Property Overseas Ltd (Chesham) of the other part, a portion of the basement of the Cadogan Place premises was sublet to Chesham for seven years commencing 1 January 1976, and expiring on 31 December 1982. The underlease contained an option to renew for a further term of five years. That option was never exercised.

On 17 June 1981 the plaintiff instituted the present action against the defendants for forfeiture of the lease by reason of breach of the repairing covenants.

On 12 October 1981 the plaintiff obtained judgment for possession of the property comprised in the lease. In July 1982 an application by the second defendant, Mr Riley, for relief from forfeiture was dismissed.

On 14 September 1982 Chesham issued a summons for an order under s 146(4) of the 1925 Act, vesting the basement in Chesham on such terms and conditions as the court should think fit. At all times since 17 June 1981 Chesham has been in possession of the basement and has conducted a business there.

At this point it will be convenient if I refer to the relevant statutory provisions. Section 146(4) of the 1925 Act, states:

'Where a lessor is proceeding by action or otherwise to enforce a right of re-entry or forfeiture under any covenant, proviso, or stipulation in a lease, or for non-payment of rent, the court may, on application by any person claiming as under-lessee any estate or interest in the property comprised in the lease or any part thereof, either in the lessor's action (if any) or in any action brought by such person for that purpose, make an order vesting, for the whole term of the lease or any less term, the property comprised in the lease or any part thereof in any person entitled as under-lessee to any estate or interest in such property upon such conditions as to execution of any deed or other document, payment of rent, costs, expenses, damages, compensation, giving security or otherwise, as the court in the circumstances of each case may think fit, but in no case shall any such under-lessee be entitled to require a lease to be granted to him for any longer term than he had under his original sub-lease.'

Section 24 of the Landlord and Tenant Act 1954 states:

'(1) A tenancy to which this Part of this Act applies shall not come to an end unless terminated in accordance with the provisions of this Part of this Act; and, subject to the provisions of section twenty-nine of this Act, the tenant under such a tenancy may apply to the court for a new tenancy—(a) if the landlord has given notice under section 25 of this Act to terminate the tenancy, or (b) if the tenant has made a request for a new tenancy in accordance with section twenty-six of this Act.

(2) The last foregoing subsection shall not prevent the coming to an end of a tenancy by . . . surrender or forfeiture or by the forfeiture of a superior tenancy . . .'

Section 25 states:

a

'(1) The landlord may terminate a tenancy to which this Part of this Act applies by a notice given to the tenant in the prescribed form specifying the date at which the tenancy is to come to an end (hereinafter referred to as "the date of termination"): Provided that this subsection has effect subject to the provisions of Part IV of this Act as to the interim continuation of tenancies pending the disposal of applications to the court.

b

(2) Subject to the provisions of the next following subsection, a notice under this section shall not have effect unless it is given not more than twelve nor less than six months before the date of termination specified therein.

(3) In the case of a tenancy which apart from this Act could have been brought to an end by notice to quit given by the landlord . . . (a) . . . on the date of the giving of the notice under this section . . .'

c

Section 26 deals with a tenant's request for a new tenancy.

Section 64 states:

d

'(1) In any case where—(a) a notice to terminate a tenancy has been given under Part I or Part II of this Act or a request for a new tenancy has been made under Part II thereof, and (b) an application to the court has been made under the said Part I or the said Part II, as the case may be, and (c) apart from this section the effect of the notice or request would be to terminate the tenancy before the expiration of the period of three months beginning with the date on which the application is finally disposed of, the effect of the notice or request shall be to terminate the tenancy at the expiration of the said period of three months and not at any other time.'

e

Chesham's application for relief under s 146(4) of the 1925 Act was heard by Sir Neil Lawson sitting as a judge of the Queen's Bench Division on 31 October 1983. He dismissed the application. It was submitted on behalf of Chesham that because Chesham continued to occupy the premises for business purposes down to 31 December 1982, and the plaintiff had not by that date re-entered, the 1954 Act applied, and Chesham were entitled to a new lease.

f

The judge rejected that contention. He held that s 146(4) of the 1925 Act prevents the grant of a lease for a longer term than the applicant originally had under the sublease, and that term had already expired on 31 December 1982.

He held further that the provisions of the 1954 Act did not assist Chesham in view of the provisions of s 24(2) of that Act, that s 24(1) shall 'not prevent the coming to an end of a tenancy by . . . forfeiture of a superior tenancy'. The judge also rejected an argument based on the decision of Sir Robert Megarry V-C in *Meadows v Clerical Medical and General Life Assurance Society* [1980] 1 All ER 454, [1981] Ch 70 on the ground that *Meadows* was the case of a tenancy (not a subtenancy) which had been forfeited so that the tenant had the right to apply for relief by way of restoration of the *old* tenancy, whereas Chesham (being a subtenant) could only apply for a vesting order of what is, in fact, a *new* tenancy; Chesham had no right to ask for its old tenancy back. The old tenancy therefore had come to an end and there was nothing on which the 1954 Act could operate.

h

Section 146(4) of the 1925 Act in the case of the forfeiture of an underlease in consequence of the superior lease having been forfeited, confers on the court jurisdiction to make an order vesting—

g

j

'for the whole of the term of the lease [ie the superior lease] or any less term, the property comprised in the lease or any part thereof in any person entitled as an under-lessee . . . but in no case shall any such under-lessee be entitled to require a lease to be granted to him for any longer term that he had under his original sublease.'

It is evident from these provisions that the new sublease is not merely a restoration of the old one. It is a new grant. The parties, the term and the other provisions may be different from those of the forfeited sublease (see *Chelsea Estates Investment Trust Co Ltd v Marche* [1955] 1 All ER 195, [1955] Ch 328). The new lease is therefore a quite distinct piece of property from the old, and in this respect the position of a sublessee is different from that of a lessee under s 146(2) of the 1925 Act.

It is settled law that a lease, as a grant, takes effect only from the date of delivery (see *Roberts v Church Comrs for England* [1971] 3 All ER 703 at 704, 707, [1972] 1 QB 278 at 282, 285 per Russell and Stamp LJJ). If, for example, a lease of 1 January 1984 is expressed to grant a term of years from 30 June 1983, the document is inoperative to create any term in respect of the period prior to 1 January 1984.

Section 146(4) of the 1925 Act prohibits the grant of any longer term than the sublessee 'had under his original sublease'. If that refers to the contractual term specified in the sublease, the court, in my view, has no jurisdiction to make any vesting order in this case since the original term expired on 31 December 1982 and the court cannot grant a term in respect of any period prior to the date of the order. But, in any event, it is difficult to see how the court could make an order vesting property which, at the date of the order, neither exists nor is capable of existing, ie a term which ended in December 1982. I should add that by s 9 of the 1925 Act, a vesting order operates to convey a legal estate in the same manner as if the order had been a conveyance.

That, however, is not the end of the matter. The fundamental question is the meaning in s 146(4) of the words 'any longer term than he had under his original sub-lease'. In my opinion the words refer to the position immediately before forfeiture. At that time, it seems to me, Chesham did not merely have a term which came to an end on 31 December 1982. Chesham had a tenancy on which was superimposed by law the provisions of Pt II of the 1954 Act. Those provisions conferred rights which Chesham held at the date of forfeiture. The core of the rights conferred by the 1954 Act is the provision in s 24(1) that a tenancy within Pt II of the Act shall not come to an end unless terminated in accordance with the provisions of the Act. At the time of the forfeiture, the tenancy granted by the original sublease had not been terminated in accordance with the provisions of the 1954 Act. The result is that, immediately before the forfeiture, Chesham was entitled to a tenancy which would not determine on 1 December 1982, but which would continue until brought to an end under the provisions of the 1954 Act.

It is said, as I understand it, that the 'term' which Chesham 'had under [its] original sub-lease' has now come to an end and that all that could exist if there had been no forfeiture is a 'tenancy' created by the statute. But what the 1954 Act provides is that the 'tenancy' shall not come to an end save under the provisions of the Act. The 'tenancy' must mean the tenancy created by the original sublease. If that tenancy had not come to an end it seems to me to be quite unreal to say that the 'term' has come to an end and that there is nothing on which s 146(4) could now operate. The fact is that the estate created by the original sublease would, but for the forfeiture, be continued under the provisions of the 1954 Act for a period which is clearly identified by those provisions. There would, therefore, be still in existence something which could fairly be called a term; in s 146(4) the word is, I think, used merely to indicate duration. There are not two terms, one created by the original grant, and on the expiry of that, a new one created by the statute. The effect of the statute is that there is simply a continuing term. I do not think that *Factors (Sundries) Ltd v Miller* [1952] 2 All ER 630 is inconsistent with that view. The present question did not arise: the case was concerned with a monthly tenancy and the court made an order under s 146(4) of the 1925 Act creating a tenancy for one month.

On behalf of Chesham some reliance was placed on the decision in *Meadows v Clerical Medical and General Life Assurance Society*. That again did not raise the issue in the present case. It was concerned with a forfeiture of a sublease by the sublessor and the question was whether, pending determination of an application for relief, the sublessee could properly issue a summons under Pt II of the 1954 Act against the superior landlord for the grant of a new lease under the Act.

The result, in my view, is that, but for the forfeiture, the tenancy would have continued under the 1954 Act until it came to an end under the provisions of that Act.

In my view, therefore, the court has jurisdiction under s 146(4) of the 1925 Act to make
a a vesting order for a new term of appropriate duration but within the limits of the
extension imposed by the 1954 Act. I do not reach that result with any regret. The
contrary result could, I think, only have been the consequence of a lacuna in the
legislation. I see no reason, in principle, to suppose it could have been intended. In
general the purpose of s 146(4) must be to enable the court, if it thinks fit, to restore the
sublessee to his position before the forfeiture; that position included the protection given
b by the 1954 Act without which his situation would be wholly changed.

I do not at all lose sight of the provisions of s 24(2) of the 1954 Act. But the references
there to forfeiture must mean an absolute forfeiture against which relief has not been
given.

The question of jurisdiction being decided, there remains the question whether the
court should exercise its discretion under s 146(4) to make a vesting order. The judge did
c not consider that in view of his decision as to jurisdiction. We shall therefore have to
consider the question of discretion after hearing argument on it.

ROBERT GOFF LJ. I agree that, for the reasons given by Fox LJ, the appeal should be
allowed; and I only desire to express my conclusion in my own words because we are
differing from the judge.
d On 7 July 1981 the plaintiff served on the tenants under the headlease a writ claiming
possession of the demised premises. On 12 October 1981, judgment was entered (in
default of defence) for possession, mesne profits, damages and costs. In these circumstances,
the headlease was forfeited as from the date of service of the writ; and in consequence, as
from the same date, the sublease to Chesham was also forfeited. The question in this case
is whether Chesham can obtain a vesting order under s 146(4) of the Law of Property Act
e 1925, which has the effect of granting them a new lease. They can only do it if (1) the
court has jurisdiction, in the circumstances of the present case, to make a vesting order
and (2) if so, the court can be persuaded to exercise its discretion to do so.

The judge held that the court had no jurisdiction to make a vesting order in favour of
Chesham. According to the note of his judgment which has been agreed by counsel and
approved by him, his reasoning was as follows. (1) Section 24(1) of the Landlord and
f Tenant Act 1954 (which provides that tenancies to which Pt II of that Act applies shall
not come to an end unless terminated in accordance with the provisions of Pt II) did not
prevent the sublease from coming to an end by reason of the forfeiture of the headlease,
because s 24(2) provides that sub-s (1) shall not prevent the coming to an end of a tenancy
by, inter alia, the forfeiture of a superior tenancy. (2) Although Chesham could apply for
a vesting order under s 146(4) of the 1925 Act, the court had no power to make a vesting
g order granting a new lease for any longer term than Chesham had under their original
sublease, viz after 31 December 1982. (3) The court could not, after 31 December 1982,
make a vesting order granting a new lease to Chesham.

I, for my part, agree that Chesham's subtenancy came to an end on the forfeiture of
the headlease, ie on 7 July 1981. It is to be observed that, under s 146(4), the court's
jurisdiction, in respect of subtenancies, is not to grant relief against forfeiture (cf its
h jurisdiction under s 146(2)) but to grant a new lease, no doubt because one of the parties
to the new lease will be a person who was not a party to the original headlease, and
because the demised premises, the term of the lease and the conditions on which it is
held, may also be different: see *Chelsea Estates Investment Trust Co Ltd v Marche* [1955] 1
All ER 195, [1955] Ch 328. I also agree that, under s 146(4), a lease cannot be granted for
any longer term than the sublessee had under his original sublease; and that if, in the
j present case, that term is to be identified as the contractual term which would have
expired on 31 December 1982, the court would have had no power, after that date, to
grant a new lease to Chesham, because a tenancy 'cannot take effect as such before the
date of execution and delivery that it bears': see *Roberts v Church Comrs for England* [1971]
3 All ER 703 at 705, [1972] 1 QB 278 at 282 per Russell LJ, and see also *Bradshaw v Pawley*
[1979] 3 All ER 273 at 276–277, [1980] 1 WLR 10 at 14 per Sir Robert Megarry V-C.

But the crucial question in this case is: what was, for the purposes of s 146(4), the term

which Chesham had under their original sublease? This must mean the term which
would have existed, but for the forfeiture. In ascertaining that term, I do not consider   *a*
that it would be right to ignore the effect of s 24(1) of the 1954 Act. For the effect of
s 24(1) was that the *tenancy* of Chesham would not come to an end unless terminated in
accordance with the provisions of Pt II of the 1954 Act. It must follow, in my judgment,
that at the date of forfeiture the term which Chesham had under their original sublease
was the term specified in the sublease (viz until 31 December 1982) plus such further
period as might elapse until the tenancy was brought to an end in accordance with the   *b*
provisions of Pt II of the 1954 Act. That term had not expired at the date when the judge
made his order in the matter; and it follows that, at that date, there was no bar to the
judge exercising his discretion, if he thought it right to do so, to make a vesting order
under s 146(4), the effect of which was to grant a new lease to Chesham as from that date.
    In his powerful argument, counsel for the plaintiff submitted that this was not correct.
He argued that the 'term' under the original sublease must be a term for a fixed period.   *c*
But *Factors (Sundries) Ltd v Miller* [1952] 2 All ER 630 shows (although the point in the
present case was not there in issue) that the court is prepared to make a vesting order
under s 146(4) in the case of a periodic tenancy, although the relevant period (there one
month) had expired at the date of the order, and the tenancy would (but for the forfeiture)
have continued indefinitely until determined by notice of the relevant length. Indeed,
the effect of s 24(1) of the 1954 Act on the subtenancy in the present case was to produce   *d*
a term not materially different from a contractual term for a fixed period and thereafter
until determined by notice of a specified length; and we were told that leases in that
form were fairly common. Counsel for the plaintiff also submitted that the term which
Chesham had under their original sublease was simply the term specified in the sublease
itself, viz that which expired on 31 December 1982. But in my judgment that submission
ignores the express effect of s 24(1) of the 1954 Act, that the *tenancy* (here Chesham's   *e*
tenancy under their sublease) shall not come to an end unless terminated in accordance
with the provisions of Pt II of that Act.
    In the course of his argument, counsel for Chesham placed reliance on a passage in the
judgment of Sir Robert Megarry V-C in *Meadows v Clerical Medical and General Life
Assurance Society* [1980] 1 All ER 454, [1981] Ch 70. In that case Sir Robert Megarry V-C
was concerned with the position of a tenant pending the hearing of his application for   *f*
relief against forfeiture under s 146(2) of the 1925 Act. It is well settled that, if a tenant
is granted relief under s 146(2), the effect will be as though the lease was never forfeited.
However, in the course of his judgment, Sir Robert Megarry V-C said ([1980] 1 All ER
454 at 459, [1981] Ch 70 at 76–77):

> 'I do not think that it matters much whether the form that any relief would take
> would be the restoration of the old lease or the grant of a new lease on the terms of   *g*
> the old: in either case the relief would relate back to the date of the forfeiture and so
> produce a tenancy which was within the Act when the originating summons was
> issued.'

    Sir Robert Megarry V-C was not, however, concerned to consider the problem in the
present case; and I do not think that, had he done so, he would have concluded that a   *h*
vesting order made under s 146(4) of the 1925 Act relates back to the date of forfeiture.
For the vesting order has the effect that a new lease is granted to the former subtenant,
and on the authorities which I have already referred to, the vesting order cannot take
effect to create an interest in land subsisting before the date on which the order is made.
    I wish to add that I am glad to be able to reach the conclusion which I have reached in
this case. To hold otherwise would have been to defeat the manifest intention of the   *j*
legislature. Indeed, the spectacle of a subtenant promptly issuing his application for a
vesting order under s 146(4), and pursuing his application with all due diligence, but
being deprived of the benefit of Pt II of the 1954 Act simply because, for reasons beyond
his control, the matter was not dealt with by the court before the expiry of the term
specified in the sublease, is not one which commends itself; yet such could have been the
effect of counsel for the plaintiff's argument, if we had felt compelled to accept it. Of

course, if a subtenant does not act promptly in relation to his application, this may be a
a matter which can be taken into account by the court in exercising its discretion under
s 146(4); we are not however concerned with any question of discretion at this stage, only
with jurisdiction, and nothing which I have said in this judgment should be understood
as affecting the exercise by the court hereafter of its discretion in the present case.

WALLER LJ. I agree.
b

Appeal on jurisdiction allowed.

15 February. The Court of Appeal ordered that the question whether the court should
exercise its discretion under s 146(4) in favour of Chesham be remitted to a judge in
chambers.
c

Solicitors: *Lieberman Leigh & Co* (for Chesham); *Lee & Pembertons* (for the plaintiff).

Sophie Craven   Barrister.

d

Northern Regional Health Authority v Derek Crouch Construction Co Ltd
Northern Regional Health Authority v Derek Crouch Construction Co Ltd and another
e

COURT OF APPEAL, CIVIL DIVISION
f SIR JOHN DONALDSON MR, DUNN AND BROWNE-WILKINSON LJJ
30, 31 JANUARY, 1, 2, 6, 7, 17 FEBRUARY 1984

*Arbitration – Stay of arbitration – Action and arbitration proceedings side by side – Overlap of
issues – Whether arbitration should be stayed.*

g *Building contract – Sub-contractors – Nominated sub-contractor – Right to arbitrate disputes with
building owner – Sub-contractor entitled to arbitrate in name of main contractor against building
owner – Whether sub-contractor should be restrained from arbitrating because action and
arbitration between building owner and main contractor raising same issues.*

*Building contract – Architect – Architect's certificate – Arbitrator – Official referee – Jurisdiction
h – Arbitrator having jurisdiction under contract to open up and review architect's certificates and
opinions – Whether official referee having same jurisdiction to open up and review architect's
discretion.*

In December 1977 a health authority (the building owner) entered into a building
contract with the main contractor to build a hospital. The contract was in the standard
j Joint Contracts Tribunal (JCT) form, which provided that the building owner, acting by
its architect as agent, had the right to nominate, and give directions to, any specialist sub-
contractors required but that nothing in the contract was to render the building owner
in any way liable to a nominated sub-contractor. The JCT form also provided for
arbitration of disputes between the building owner and the main contractor and that the
arbitrator was to be entitled 'to open up, review and revise any certificate, opinion,
decision, requirement or notice' given by the building owner's architect, while the form

of sub-contract provided (i) for arbitration of disputes between the main contractor and
the sub-contractor and (ii) that if the sub-contractor wished to arbitrate disputes with the   *a*
building owner over certain matters, including extensions of time, it was entitled to use
the main contractor's name to do so. In May 1978 the building owner's architect
instructed the main contractor to enter into a sub-contract with a particular sub-
contractor for the installation of mechanical services, including boilers. Serious delays
occurred in making the boilers operational, giving rise to disputes between all parties
regarding the cause of the delay and who should bear the blame. The building owner's   *b*
architect granted an extension of time until 24 June 1983 for completion of the boiler
plant under both the main contract and the sub-contract but there were further delays
giving rise to further disputes. In September 1982 the main contractor issued a writ
against the building owner seeking declarations as to its entitlement to extensions of
time and reimbursement of loss and expenses incurred up to 31 July 1982. The sub-
contractor was not a party to that action, which was still pending. On 4 November 1983   *c*
the main contractor referred to arbitration under the main contract its dispute with the
building owner as to the reasons and responsibility for the delays in connection with the
boiler plant, and its entitlement to further extensions of time beyond 24 June 1983. On
30 November 1983 the sub-contractor, using the main contractor's name, referred to
arbitration its dispute with the building owner's architect regarding his failure to issue
necessary instructions regarding the boiler plant or to extend the time for completing   *d*
the work. The same arbitrator was appointed under both references. The building owner
applied to the High Court for injunctions restraining both arbitrations, on the grounds
that both would involve investigating and deciding responsibility for delays, which issue
was already before the court by virtue of the main contractor's pending action against
the building owner, and that such an overlap might give rise to issue estoppel or result
in the duplication of issues and the possibility of conflicting decisions. The building   *e*
owner further contended that in any event the sub-contractor's arbitration should be
stayed because its claim in reality arose under the terms of the main contract and was
therefore subsumed into the main contractor's claim. The official referee refused to grant
the injunctions, on the ground that the precise scope of the arbitrations could be left to
the arbitrator and accordingly if there was an overlap of issues the arbitrator could avoid
deciding matters which were also the subject of the action. The building owner appealed   *f*
contending, inter alia, that the arbitrator was bound to decide all the matters referred to
him and to comply with the strict terms of the references and therefore might be forced
to decide issues which were before the court in the pending action.

Held – The building owner's appeal would be dismissed for the following reasons—
    (1) (Per Dunn and Browne-Wilkinson LJJ) There was no rule of law that an arbitrator   *g*
must decide all matters in dispute between the parties and nor was there any inherent
objection to an action and an arbitration proceeding side by side. Accordingly, if any
overlap of issues occurred the arbitrator, who would be in the best position to decide
whether that was so, would be entitled to refuse to decide any issues which overlapped
with the High Court proceedings. Alternatively (per Sir John Donaldson MR), although
an arbitrator was under a primary duty to decide all matters referred to him, he was   *h*
entitled to indicate whether he was being asked to decide issues which were concurrently
before the court thereby giving the parties an opportunity to apply to the court to
exercise its supervisory jurisdiction over arbitrators by giving directions whether to
proceed with the arbitration (see p 181 *g* to *j*, p 184 *j*, p 185 *j* to p 186 *b*, p 187 *j*, p 191 *g*
to *j* and p 192 *h*, post). *Wrightson v Bywater* (1838) 3 M & W 199 and *Lloyd v Wright*
[1983] 2 All ER 969 applied.   *j*
    (2) Since the sub-contractor could not sue the building owner direct because there was
no privity of contract between them and since the building owner knew of the terms of
the sub-contract and directed the main contractor to enter into it with the sub-contractor,
it would be unjust if the sub-contractor was to be prevented by an injunction from
pursuing its only direct remedy against the building owner, namely bringing arbitration
proceedings against the building owner using the name of the main contractor which

a
was in effect a conduit between the building owner and the sub-contractor (see p 183 g to j, p 184 j, p 185 c to f, p 187 j and p 191 j to p 192 a c d and h, post).

(3) The High Court, and thus an official referee, did not have the power which the arbitrator had to open up and review the exercise of the architect's discretion, since the court's jurisdiction was limited to determining and enforcing the contractual rights of the parties and did not extend to substituting its own discretion simply because it would have reached a different conclusion, since to do so would interfere with the agreement of

b
the parties. The arbitrator on the other hand, because the parties' agreement expressly gave him such power, was entitled to modify the parties' contractual rights by substituting his own discretion for that of the architect if he disagreed with the architect's certificates and opinions. Accordingly, if the parties chose to litigate rather than arbitrate the court would not have the same powers as an arbitrator to open up and revise the architect's opinions and certificates. It followed that it would unjust if the sub-contractor

c
was to be prevented by an injunction from insisting on arbitration and was forced to have its rights determined by litigation to which it had never agreed under a jurisdiction which would probably be more limited than that of the arbitrator (see p 184 g to j, p 186 g to p 187 e and j, p 189 b to d and g to j, p 191 b c and p 192 c d and h, post); dictum of Lord Wilberforce in *P & M Kaye Ltd v Hosier & Dickinson Ltd* [1972] 1 All ER at 132 applied; *Neale v Richardson* [1938] 1 All ER 753, *Prestige & Co Ltd v Brettell* [1938] 4 All

d
ER 346 and *Sudbrook Trading Estate Ltd v Eggleton* [1982] 3 All ER 1 distinguished.

Notes
For injunctions restraining arbitration proceedings, see 2 Halsbury's Laws (4th edn) para 518, and for cases on the subject, see 3 Digest (Reissue) 95–98, 484–500.

For powers of arbitrators generally, see 2 Halsbury's Laws (4th edn) para 577.

e
Cases referred to in judgments
Brodie v Cardiff Corp [1919] AC 337, HL.
Compagnie Nouvelle France Navigation SA v Compagnie Navale Afrique du Nord, The Oranie and The Tunisie [1966] 1 Lloyd's Rep 477, DC and CA.
Crouch (Derek) Construction Co Ltd v Northern Regional Health Authority (unreported, 30 March 1983), QBD.

f
East Ham BC v Bernard Sunley & Sons Ltd [1965] 3 All ER 619, [1966] AC 406, [1965] 3 WLR 1096, HL; *affg in part* [1965] 1 All ER 210, [1965] 1 WLR 30, CA.
Kaye (P & M) Ltd v Hosier & Dickinson Ltd [1972] 1 All ER 121, [1972] 1 WLR 146, HL.
Lloyd v Wright [1983] 2 All ER 969, [1983] QB 1065, [1983] 3 WLR 223, CA.
Neale v Richardson [1938] 1 All ER 753, CA.
Prestige & Co Ltd v Brettell [1938] 4 All ER 346, CA.

g
Robins v Goddard [1905] 1 KB 294, CA.
Sudbrook Trading Estate Ltd v Eggleton [1982] 3 All ER 1, [1983] 1 AC 444, [1982] 3 WLR 315, HL.
Wrightson v Bywater (1838) 3 M & W 199, 150 ER 1114.

Cases also cited
Abu Dhabi Gas Liquefaction Co Ltd v Eastern Bechtel Corp [1982] 2 Lloyd's Rep 425, CA.

h
Anisminic Ltd v Foreign Compensation Commission [1969] 1 All ER 208, [1969] 2 AC 147, HL.
Cap Bon, The [1967] 1 Lloyd's Rep 543.
Gilbert-Ash (Northern) Ltd v Modern Engineering (Bristol) Ltd [1973] 3 All ER 195, [1974] AC 689, HL.
Piggott v Townsend (1926) 27 SR(NSW) 25.

j
Taunton-Collins v Cromie [1964] 2 All ER 332, [1964] 1 WLR 633, CA.
Tradax Internacional SA v Cerrahogullari TAS, The M Eregli [1981] 3 All ER 344, DC.
Trollope & Colls Ltd v North West Metropolitan Regional Hospital Board [1973] 2 All ER 260, [1973] 1 WLR 601, HL.

Appeal
By an amended notice of appeal dated 9 January 1984 the plaintiffs, the Northern

Regional Health Authority, appealed against the order of his Honour Judge Smout QC
sitting as an official referee on 12 December 1983 whereby he dismissed the health   *a*
authority's applications for (i) an injunction restraining the first defendant, Derek Crouch
Construction Co Ltd (Crouch), from seeking an arbitration award in respect of certain
matters set out in the terms of reference proposed by the first defendant in a request to
the President of the Royal Institute of British Architects for the appointment of an
arbitrator, and (ii) an injunction restraining Crouch and the second defendant, Crown
House Engineering Ltd (Crown), from seeking an arbitration award in respect of the   *b*
reference to arbitration made by Crown in the name of Crouch in a request to the
President of the Royal Institute of British Architects for the appointment of an arbitrator.
The facts are set out in the judgment of Dunn LJ.

Swinton Thomas QC and *David Blunt* for the health authority.
Rupert Jackson for Crouch.   *c*
Colin Reese for Crown.

Cur adv vult

17 February. The following judgments were delivered.

DUNN LJ (giving the first judgment at the invitation of Sir John Donaldson MR). This   *d*
is an appeal from a judgment of his Honour Judge Smout QC sitting as an official referee
on 12 December 1983 whereby he dismissed the plaintiff's applications for injunctions
restraining the defendants from seeking awards in two references to arbitration dated
respectively 4 and 30 November 1983. The dispute arises in relation to the construction
of a hospital at Barrow-in-Furness, and in particular to the installation and commissioning
of the boilers. The plaintiff's (the health authority) were the building owner or employer,   *e*
the first defendant (Crouch) was the main contractor and the second defendant (Crown)
was one of a number of nominated sub-contractors. The contractual arrangements are
contained in three relevant contracts. The first in point of time was an agreement dated
3 November 1977 (the warranty agreement) between the health authority and Crown
made under cl 27(c) of the standard form of building contract issued by the Joint
Contracts Tribunal (JCT) (1963 edn). The second contract (the main contract) was dated   *f*
22 December 1977 between the health authority and Crouch made on the standard form
of building contract issued by JCT (1963 edn). The third contract (the sub-contract) was
dated 15 May 1978, and was made as the result of an instruction by the architect to
Crouch dated 9 December 1977 to enter into a sub-contract with Crown for the
installation of the mechanical services. Pursuant to that instruction the sub-contract was
made on the standard form for use where the sub-contractor is nominated under the   *g*
main contract.

Crouch took possession of the site on 13 February 1978 and the completion date for
the whole of the main contract works was 10 November 1981. The sub-contract provided
for the boilers to be operational by 5 October 1980, for Crown to complete the installation
by 19 April 1981, and for a six months' commissioning period until 18 October 1981. It
is common ground that the main contract works were very substantially delayed, the   *h*
causes of which are in dispute. However, on 10 May 1983 the architect issued an
instruction in accordance with cl 23(e) of the main contract stating that in his opinion
the works had been delayed, and extending the contract completion date to 24 June. On
12 May 1983 the architect consented to an extension of time for completion of the sub-
contract works down to the same date.

The sub-contract specification required the installation of three 'Cochrane Coalmaster'   *j*
boilers, which were delivered to the site in May 1980, but for various reasons were not
brought into operation until December 1982. It was then found that the coal handling
plant was incapable of dealing with the specified coal, 'Maryport smalls', because the
aperture at the bottom of the bunker was too small, and the coal compressed in the
bunker neck and blocked the system. On 21 February 1983 the architect issued an
instruction (no 861) requiring the use of a different coal, 'Bickershaw singles'. It was not

possible for Cochrane to adjust the boilers so that the heat output required by the
a specification was achieved with Bickershaw singles, and on 14 June the architect notified
Crouch by letter that—

> 'Boilers should be set to work at the optimum burning rate for the fuel, referred
> to in Architect's Instruction No. 861 [ie the Bickershaw singles] commensurate with
> obtaining complete combustion of the fuel in the boilers.'

b Following receipt of that letter, tests were carried out during July and on 30 September
the architect wrote to inform Crouch (a) that the contents of the letter of 14 June did not
amend his instruction no 861, and (b) on the basis of the results of the tests with
Bickershaw singles the boilers as installed were not acceptable, and Crouch's proposals for
remedying the situation were required. On 28 October the architect notified Crouch
that the consulting engineers had advised them that the boiler installation was practically
c complete. The boiler house was handed over on 25 November and the final phase of the
main contract was complete on 12 January 1984.

Meanwhile on 21 September 1982 Crouch issued a writ against the health authority
claiming declarations as to entitlement to extensions of time, and reimbursement of loss
and expense under the main contract by reason of matters occurring down to 31 July
1982. In those proceedings Crouch referred to claims which Crown had made against it,
d but Crown was not a party to the proceedings and took no part in them. The health
authority withdrew an application to stay the proceedings under s 4 of the Arbitration
Act 1950, which had been opposed by Crouch on the ground, inter alia, that resolution
of the very substantial claims by Crown and another sub-contractor, coupled with a claim
by Crouch itself, would only be possible if one tribunal heard all matters. The proceedings
had been transferred to the official referee and an application for an interim payment
e was refused by his Honour Judge Sir William Stabb QC on 30 March 1983. A date for
the hearing has been fixed for February 1985.

On 27 July 1983 Crouch wrote to the health authority in the following terms:

> 'Please accept this letter as our formal notice of reference to arbitration under
> Clause 35 of the contract between us on the following grounds. (1) Your expressed
> intention to deduct damages. (2) Your Architect's failure to issue meaningful
f > instructions to facilitate the completion of the Boiler House which is in our opinion
> an essential prerequisite to the practical completion of the contract. (3) Your
> Architect's refusal to grant further extensions of time in relation to item No. 2 and
> various other valid matters.'

It was agreed that that dispute should be referred to Mr Norman Royce FRIBA, a most
g experienced arbitrator in this field, and it was also agreed that the terms of reference
should expressly exclude the issue as to the boilers. As a result of that exclusion, Crown
took no part in the reference, which was settled between the health authority and Crouch
on 22 November 1983. One of the terms of the settlement was that there should be a
further arbitration in relation to the boilers (the boiler house dispute).

By letter dated 4 November 1983 Crouch applied under the contract to the president
h of the Royal Institute of British Architects for an arbitrator to be appointed for the boiler
house dispute, and on 10 November the president appointed Mr Royce as arbitrator in
that arbitration (which I shall call the 'Crouch arbitration'). The terms of reference were
contained in a telex from Crouch dated 27 October and were as follows:

> '(1) For what reason or reasons is the boiler plant inoperable in accordance with
> the conditions of the contract between the parties dated 22 December 1977, and the
j > responsibility therefor?
> (2) Was the boiler-house practically complete on 24th June 1983 and if not in
> what respect?
> (3) If the answer to '2' is No, did the works in the boiler house achieve practical
> completion at any time thereafter, and if so, when?'

The health authority agreed that paras (2) and (3) should be referred to Mr Royce, but disputed the reference of para (1). On 30 November the health authority issued an originating summons seeking an injunction restraining Crouch from seeking an award in relation to any of the matters set out in para (1) of the telex.

Meanwhile Crown wished to commence its own arbitration in relation to the boiler house dispute, and on 14 October 1983 Crouch notified Crown that it was free to proceed in Crouch's name in accordance with the terms of the sub-contract. On 10 November 1983 solicitors for Crown wrote to the health authority in the following terms:

'In conclusion, we think it would be convenient to set out the matters of dispute or difference which exist between [Crown] and the Authority. They are:—A. The boilers *can* achieve the contractually specified outputs and efficiencies using "Maryport Smalls" but the coal handling plant cannot deliver that fuel. The boilers *cannot* achieve those outputs and efficiencies using "Bickershaw Singles" but the coal handling plant is able to deliver the fuel. Accordingly, the design team must decide which of the two alternatives they wish the sub-contractor to achieve. The design team's requiring "experiments" to be carried out using "Bickershaw Singles" without their then accepting the results by unequivocally amending the sub-contract specification is improper and unacceptable. Accordingly, the sub-contractor requires that the arbitrator should issue one or other of the following instructions—(1) An instruction confirming that the sub-contractually specified requirements as to boiler outputs and efficiencies have been varied to those achievable using "Bickershaw Singles" as the fuel. Any such instruction must be given on appropriate terms bearing in mind the fact that this was not the intended fuel for these boilers. (2) An instruction to modify the fuel handling plant to some revised design which will enable "Maryport Open Cast Smalls" to be conveyed to the boilers and to make the necessary re-adjustments to the boilers to enable them to achieve the contractually specified outputs and efficiencies with that fuel. B. A full extension of time for completion of the sub-contract works up to the following dates: (1) If an instruction under A(1) above is to be issued there should be an extension of time up to the date on which the boilers are accepted as complete in their present tested state. (2) If an instruction under A(2) above is issued there should be an extension of time up to a date which allows a reasonable time for the works to be carried out after the necessary detailed instructions have been issued.'

On 1 December 1983 the president of the RIBA appointed Mr Royce as arbitrator in that arbitration (which I shall call the 'Crown arbitration') with terms of reference substantially as set out in the letter of 10 November. On 6 December the health authority issued an originating summons seeking an injunction restraining Crouch from seeking an award in relation to any of the matters set out in those terms of reference.

In an affidavit sworn on 5 December Mr Robson, solicitor to the health authority, stated:

'. . . there is no dispute as to the cause of the problem, namely that the coal-handling plant as a consequence of design defect would not operate with Maryport Smalls.'

Both summonses were heard together by the official referee and he dismissed them both. It is accepted that he directed himself properly in accordance with authority (*Compagnie Nouvelle France Navigation SA v Compagnie Navale Afrique du Nord, The Oranie and The Tunisie* [1966] 1 Lloyd's Rep at 477 at 487 per Sellers LJ) and that he asked himself the correct questions, namely: (1) would a stay of the references cause injustice to either of the claimants? and (2) would the continuance of the references be oppressive or vexatious to the health authority or an abuse of the process of the court? What is said on behalf of the health authority is that the official referee in answering those questions in favour of Crouch and Crown misdirected himself as to the issues of fact between the parties, and that in exercising his discretion as he did he was plainly wrong.

The health authority submit, and it is accepted by Crouch, that the use of the word 'responsibility' in para (1) of the telex would necessarily involve an investigation in the

Crouch arbitration not only as to whether Crouch was entitled under cl 23 of the main
a contract to a further extension of time after 24 June 1983, but also whether Crouch was
entitled to loss and expense under cl 24. The health authority submit that those issues
would involve opening up the causes of delay from inception of the works under the
main contract, which it claims was largely the fault of Crouch, and would not confine
the arbitration simply to the events relevant to the boilerhouse after 24 June. The health
authority submit that those issues, at any rate down to 21 September 1982 when Crouch
b issued its writ, are properly before the court in Crouch's action, and could easily be
brought up to date by the issue of a new writ and consolidation of the two sets of
proceedings. If the Crouch arbitration is allowed to continue with the inclusion of para
(1) of the telex in its terms of reference, then the health authority submit that there will
be duplication or overlapping of many issues of fact which may, if the arbitration
proceeds, give rise to issue estoppel in the action.

c   Crouch submits that further instructions with regard to the boiler house must be
given, since the boiler is admittedly not in accordance with the specification due to a
design defect. Once that instruction is given, the architect must grant an extension of
time under cl 23(e) or (f) until such time as Crouch is able to comply with the instruction,
and the instruction stating that the works ought reasonably to have been completed on
24 June 1983 must be set aside. If the arbitrator decides that an extension of time should
d be granted, he should also be empowered to decide, in principle, that Crouch is entitled
to loss and expense under cl 11(6) or cl 24(1) of the main contract. These issues can be
decided now in the arbitration, and it will not be necessary to pursue all the other
arguments and counter arguments concerning the health authority's entitlement to
damages for delay. If the arbitration goes forward, the issues in the action will be
correspondingly reduced.

e   Similar issues arise in the Crown arbitration, but since the date of the judgment Crown
has delivered particulars of claim which seek not only a decision in principle whether or
not Crown is entitled to loss and expense, but also an investigation of the amount of loss
and expense actually suffered. Counsel for Crown admitted that these issues did not arise
in terms on the present reference, but indicated that it would be his intention, if the
arbitration proceeds, to refer them to the arbitrator and invite him to deal with them.
f The health authority have delivered points of defence alleging that any delay has been
caused by the default of Crouch and to some extent of Crown, and opening up many of
the issues which are the subject of the action.

The official referee took the view that the precise scope of the arbitration could be left
to the arbitrator, that on the face of it there was no overlap with the action, but if there
was he cautioned the arbitrator to tread carefully and seek to avoid any duplication of
g issues. The health authority submitted that in approaching the matter in that way the
official referee erred in law, since the arbitrator was bound to decide the disputes referred
to him and to comply strictly with the terms of the references (see Russell on Arbitration
(20th edn, 1982) p 218).

I cannot accept that submission. There is no rule of law that an arbitrator must decide
all matters in dispute between the parties. It is a matter of construction of the reference
and the intention of the parties (see Wrightson v Bywater (1838) 3 M & W 199 at 206, 150
h ER 1114 at 1117–1118 per Parke B). In this case the parties have agreed that some
matters will be litigated and others arbitrated. There has already been one arbitration
which resulted in a settlement. The health authority accept that there will be another
arbitration to decide what, if any, further instructions are necessary in relation to the
boiler plant. The sole issue is where the line should be drawn between the action and the
j arbitration. The arbitrator is in at least as good a position as a court to decide that issue so
as to avoid any overlap, and to identify any genuine areas of overlap. There is no inherent
objection to an action and an arbitration proceeding side by side (see Lloyd v Wright
[1983] 2 All ER 969, [1983] QB 1065).

On well-established principles an issue estoppel will arise from issues decided as the
fundamental basis of an award in the Crouch arbitration, which will bind both Crouch
and the health authority in the action. I do not see that the health authority will be

prejudiced by this any more than Crouch. But the position in the Crown arbitration may be different. As I shall show, although under the sub-contract Crown proceed in the name and with the consent of Crouch, the issues may be different to the issues in the Crouch arbitration, and the proceedings will be in the interest of Crown and not in the interest of Crouch. Although issues which are common to both arbitrations and fundamental to both awards would in my judgment raise an issue estoppel as between Crouch and the health authority, there may be other issues relating only to Crown which would not raise an estoppel as against Crouch. But again I do not see any prejudice likely to be suffered by the health authority on this account.

One of the health authority's grounds of appeal is that the official referee erred in law in finding no objection to two separate references to arbitration. It was said that only disputes between Crouch and the health authority could be referred to arbitration, since any claim for a further instruction was a claim under the main contract and any claim for loss and expense suffered by Crown was subsumed in Crouch's claim for loss and expense. Accordingly the Crown arbitration should in any event be stayed.

This ground of appeal gave rise to a most interesting and able argument by counsel for Crown, which I gratefully accept. The argument may be summarised as follows. Although it is accepted that there is no privity of contract between the employer and the sub-contractor under the standard form of building contract and sub-contract issued by the JCT (indeed cl 27(f) of the main contract expressly provides that nothing in the main contract shall render the employer in any way liable to any nominated sub-contractor), there are in the sub-contract elaborate arbitration provisions (cll 7(2), 8(b) and 11(d)) which are complementary to the arbitration clause, cl 35, in the main contract, and by cl 1 of the main contract the sub-contractor is deemed to have notice of all the provisions of the main contract. The reason for these elaborate provisions is that although there may be a dispute between the main contractor and the sub-contractor, which would be referred to arbitration under cl 24 of the sub-contract, there may also be a dispute between the sub-contractor and the employer arising out of a decision of the architect as to the sub-contract work, with which the main contractor is not at all concerned.

Take as an example one of the relevant clauses in this case, cl 8(b) of the sub-contract:

'Upon it becoming reasonably apparent that the progress of the Sub-Contract Works is delayed, the Sub-Contractor shall forthwith give written notice of the cause of the delay in the progress or completion of the Sub-Contract Works or any section thereof to the Contractor, who shall inform the Architect thereof and of any representations made to him by the Sub-Contractor as to such cause as aforesaid. If on receipt of such information and representations as aforesaid the Architect is of the opinion that the completion of the Sub-Contract Works is likely to be or has been delayed beyond the periods or period stated in Part II of the Appendix hereto or beyond any extended periods previously fixed under this Clause, (i) by reason of any of the matters specified in Clause 7(1) of this Sub-Contract or by any act or omission of the Contractor, his sub-contractors his or their respective servants or agents; or (ii) for any reason (except delay on the part of the Sub-Contractor) for which the Contractor could obtain an extension of time for completion under the Main Contract then the Contractor shall, but not without the written consent of the Architect, grant a fair and reasonable extension of the said period or periods for completion of the Sub-Contract Works or each section thereof (as the case may require) and such extended period or periods shall be the period or periods for completion of the same respectively and this clause shall be read and construed accordingly. PROVIDED always that if the Sub-Contractor shall feel aggrieved by a failure of the Architect to give his written consent to the Contractor granting an extension of the said period or periods for completion of the Sub-Contract Works, then, subject to the Sub-Contractor giving to the Contractor such indemnity and security as the Contractor may reasonably require, the Contractor shall allow the Sub-Contractor to use the Contractor's name and if necessary will join with the Sub-Contractor as plaintiff in any arbitration proceedings by the Sub-Contractor in respect of the said complaint of the Sub-Contractor.'

The main contractor is required by cl 27(a)(v) and (d)(i) of the main contract to enter into a sub-contract which contains a clause similar to cl 8(b). Under cl 8(b) if the work is delayed the sub-contractor gives the main contractor written notice of the cause of the delay, and the main contractor is bound to inform the architect thereof and of any representations made by the sub-contractor. But it is the architect who has to form an opinion as to the delay and the reason for it. If he is of the opinion that the delay warrants an extension of time and consents to such extension, then the contractor is bound to grant the extension, even though the delay may have been caused by the contractor himself. The contractor cannot grant an extension without the written consent of the architect. By the proviso, if the sub-contractor is aggrieved by a failure of the architect to give his consent then the contractor is bound to allow the sub-contractor to use his name in arbitration proceedings against the employer under the main contract.

Similar provisions apply mutatis mutandis to variations (cl 7) and certificates of payment (cl 11). In each case the procedure is the same. The decision is made by the architect: the obligation of the contractor is confined to transmitting information from the sub-contractor to the architect, and carrying out the architect's decisions vis-à-vis the sub-contractor by delivering instructions or variations (cl 7), granting extensions of time (cl 8) and making payments under certificates (cl 11). So far as those clauses are concerned, the contractor acts as no more than a conduit pipe between the architect and the sub-contractor, and exercises no independent judgment of his own.

The reasons for these provisions arise out of the unique contractual relationships developed over many years by the JCT and their predecessors in the standard forms of building contracts and sub-contracts. The scheme enables the building owner to deal with one main contractor instead of making separate contracts with specialists. But he has the right to decide which specialist the main contractor is to engage, and retains control through the architect over the amount paid to the specialist for his work. The main contractor, having on instructions entered into a sub-contract with a nominated specialist, is required to pay the sums identified as having been included in the certificates issued to him by the architect in respect of the specialist's work. The main contractor is protected against claims for liquidated damages by the owner if the contract work as a whole is delayed by the specialist sub-contractor's failures. The architect is given power to control variations, the granting of extensions of time, and certificates of payment of the sub-contract work. The main contractor has no power to do any of these things.

Counsel for Crown was unable to put any jurisprudential label on the relations of the building owner, the main contractor and the sub-contractor. As I have said, there is no privity of contract between the owner and the sub-contractor, and save in two respects (cl 30(4) of the main contract and cl 11(h) of the sub-contract) the main contractor is not a trustee for either of them. But properly understood the scheme has the effect, while identifying the sub-contractor with the main contractor for certain purposes, of recognising a separate identity in the sub-contractor for other purposes, and enabling him when he is in dispute with the decision of the architect to use the name of the main contractor in arbitration proceedings against the building owner.

Given the contractual arrangements in this case, in my judgment serious injustice would be caused to Crown were it enjoined from proceeding with its arbitration. Its dispute is with the architect, as agent of the health authority. It cannot sue the health authority direct in contract since there is no privity. Its only remedy at law would be to sue Crouch (with whom it has no dispute) for declaratory relief under cl 12 of the sub-contract requiring Crouch to obtain rights or benefits of the main contract applicable to the sub-contract. Crouch would then have to join the health authority in a dispute in which it was not or might not be concerned. This is a cumbersome procedure, and ignores the special arbitration machinery to which I have referred which was designed to deal with it.

Accordingly, in my judgment the judge was right to hold that as a matter of law Crown had an independent right to use Crouch's name in arbitration proceedings against the health authority, and that such proceedings were not an abuse of the process of the court.

That is sufficient to dispose of this appeal but in the course of the hearing a further point arose which, if right, would further reinforce the view of the official referee. The point, put shortly, is that the court has no power to open up, review, or revise any certificate, opinion or decision of the architect, since the parties have agreed by cl 35(3) of the main contract that that power shall be exercised exclusively by the arbitrator. A decision on the point is, as I have indicated, not necessary for the determination of this appeal, but in deference to the full arguments we have heard on it I feel that I should deal with it. And if it is right it means that the court in the action would not be able to open up the architect's decisions, since the only way that could be done would be by arbitration.

Perhaps surprisingly there is no direct authority on the point which is binding on us, and we were told that it is common practice for official referees to open up and review certificates and other decisions of architects, a practice supported by the textbook writers on grounds of expediency and convenience. There are dicta of high authority either way. It was accepted in this court that the court retains ultimate control in seeing that the architect acts properly and honestly and in accordance with the contract (see *P & M Kaye Ltd v Hosier & Dickinson Ltd* [1972] 1 All ER 121 at 132, [1972] 1 WLR 146 at 157 per Lord Wilberforce), but reliance was placed on his obiter dictum ([1972] 1 All ER 121 at 132, [1972] 1 WLR 146 at 158):

'Had the matter gone to arbitration the position would no doubt have been different; this is because cl 35 of the contract confers very wide powers on arbitrators to open up and review certificates which a court would not have.'

Reliance was also placed on *East Ham BC v Bernard Sunley & Sons Ltd* [1965] 3 All ER 619 at 623–624, 628, [1966] AC 406 at 424, 432 per Lord Dilhorne and Lord Cohen, whose obiter dicta reached the same result as Lord Wilberforce in *P & M Kaye Ltd v Hosier & Dickinson*.

On the other side it was said that in order to give business efficacy to the contract there must be an implied term that if the parties litigate rather than arbitrate then the court shall have the same powers as the arbitrator (see *East Ham BC v Bernard Sunley & Sons Ltd* [1965] 3 All ER 619 at 638, [1966] AC 406 at 447 per Lord Pearson). Reliance was also placed on the judgment of Judge Stabb QC in the instant case given on 30 March 1983 when he held, following *Neale v Richardson* [1938] 1 All ER 753 and *Prestige & Co Ltd v Brettell* [1938] 4 All ER 346, that the court is invested with the same power as the contract bestows on the arbitrator, including the power to award any sum which ought to have been the subject of a certificate. In *Neale v Richardson* the arbitrator (who was also the architect) had simply refused to arbitrate or issue a certificate, and it was held that the court could decide the amount due notwithstanding the absence of a certificate. It seems to me that this is an example of the court controlling the contract, and since the arbitrator had acted improperly the court assumed jurisdiction.

In my judgment it is not necessary to imply the term suggested in cl 35. The contract gives the architect wide discretionary powers as to the supervision, evaluation and progress of the works. The parties have agreed that disputes as to anything left to the discretion of the architect should be referred to arbitration, and cl 35 gives wide powers to the arbitrator to review the exercise of the architect's discretion and to substitute his own views for those of the architect. Where parties have agreed on machinery of that kind for the resolution of disputes, it is not for the court to intervene and replace its own process for the contractual machinery agreed by the parties.

I am reinforced in my view by the relevant statutory provisions. By s 11 of the Arbitration Act 1950 the parties may agree that the reference shall be made to an official referee, and the practice is set out in RSC Ord 36, r 5. If that course were taken, then the official referee would have all the powers of an arbitrator under cl 35.

BROWNE-WILKINSON LJ. I agree that these appeals should be dismissed.

This court can only overturn the decision of the official referee not to exercise his discretion to stay the arbitration proceedings if the health authority demonstrate that the official referee misdirected himself or reached a wholly wrong conclusion. The health

authority seeks to do this by showing that it is impossible for the arbitration to go
forward without considering the reasons and responsibility for delays which occurred
before 24 June 1983 and that accordingly the arbitrator will be bound to make decisions
on these points which are the very points at issue in the High Court litigation. They say
that, unless findings made in the arbitration give rise to an issue estoppel, this possibility
of the same points being considered by separate adjudicators may lead to conflicting
decisions. Moreover, they reasonably wish to have the matter decided in the High Court
proceedings since only in such proceedings can they make third party claims against, for
example, the architect.

These are formidable submissions and if the matter arose simply for decision as
between Crouch and the health authority they might well have succeeded: Crouch itself
started the High Court proceedings and resisted the health authority's application to stay
such proceedings; it is on weak ground in now insisting on arbitration which may raise
overlapping issues.

But the issue does not arise solely between the health authority and Crouch. As Dunn
LJ has demonstrated, these contractual provisions place Crown in a most unusual position.
As sub-contractor Crown has no direct legal rights as against the health authority:
Crown's rights are against Crouch alone. Yet to the knowledge and at the instigation of
the health authority the terms of the sub-contract are such that Crouch is a mere conduit
between the health authority and Crown. Crown is in fact largely controlled by the
decisions and directions of the agent of the health authority, namely the architect.
Although there is no way in which Crown can litigate directly against the health
authority (since it has no legal right directly enforceable) the sub-contract provides
machinery for a number of relevant disputes between Crown and the health authority to
be decided by arbitration under the main contract by the device of Crown arbitrating in
the name of Crouch. Since the health authority knew the terms of the sub-contract and
directed Crouch to enter into it, the health authority cannot be heard to object to Crown
arbitrating in Crouch's name pursuant to the provisions of the sub-contract.

The position, therefore, as between the health authority and Crown is quite different
to that between the health authority and Crouch. Standing back from the technicalities
of privity of contract, Crown in its own right has an overwhelming case to be allowed to
go forward with its own arbitration. Only by such arbitration can it directly establish its
rights against the health authority, and Crown, as opposed to Crouch, has never sought
to have any of the issues litigated as opposed to arbitrated.

However, the technicalities of privity of contract cannot be ignored. Since, for some
reason, the parties have chosen to cloak the reality of their commercial relationship in a
particular legal guise, the court can only give effect to the legal relationships they have,
to my mind unwisely, chosen to adopt, ie that Crown's 'rights' against the health
authority can only be established through Crouch. How far is it proper to treat Crown as
having rights to arbitrate separate from those of Crouch? Can Crown have any better
right than Crouch as against the health authority? As regards issues of fact or law decided
in an arbitration at the instigation of Crown, will there be issue estoppel in the High
Court action as between Crouch and the health authority? If there is no such issue
estoppel, the same matters may have to be litigated twice at great expense and with the
risk of two inconsistent decisions on each issue.

These questions (which flow entirely from the unusual nature of the contractual
arrangements the parties have adopted) are extremely difficult to answer in a way which
gives effect both to the legal structure and to the commercial realities. In the event I find
it unnecessary to reach any concluded view on them since in my view there are two
factors which demonstrate that the official referee's conclusion was right.

First, I am not satisfied that there will necessarily be any overlap between the issues in
the arbitration and the issues in the High Court proceedings. Crouch and Crown
maintain that all questions of delay before 24 June 1983 are irrelevant to the claims they
are seeking to arbitrate; the health authority contend that such earlier delays must
directly arise. It is quite impossible to reach a concluded view on this point until the facts
are known. But I am satisfied that Crown and Crouch have an arguable case that earlier

delays are irrelevant. If they are right, the arbitration issues will not overlap and there is
no reason why the arbitration should not continue. If, on the other hand, it emerges that
the health authority are correct and that the earlier delays are relevant, I agree with Dunn
LJ and the official referee that in law the arbitrator is entitled to refuse to decide any
issues which overlap with the High Court proceedings and that he is in the best position
to decide whether such overlap does exist.

The second point was not considered by the official referee and only arose in the course
of the hearing of this appeal. It is a point of general importance, namely will the High
Court in the action have the same wide powers of reopening and revising the opinions
and certificates of the architect which are conferred on the arbitrator by cl 35(3) of the
main contract? This is of direct importance to all the parties, but in particular to Crown.

The importance of the point to Crown arises in the following way. It is a necessary
part of its case that the correctness of certain certificates given and opinions expressed by
the architect should be investigated and revised or amended. It is common ground that
an arbitrator appointed under cl 35 of the main contract has power to do this: cl 35(3)
expressly provides that the arbitrator has power—

> 'to open up, review and revise any certificate, opinion, decision, requirement or
> notice and to determine all matters in dispute which shall be submitted to him in
> the same manner as if no such certificate, opinion, decision, requirement or notice
> had been given.'

If in any litigation the official referee also has such power, there is no problem. But, if
the official referee does not have such power, any injunction restraining the continuation
of the arbitration proceedings would deprive Crouch (and, through Crouch, Crown) of
rights which it enjoys under the contract. So much is common ground.

What then are the powers of the official referee? It appears that there are two separate
types of proceedings which may come before the official referee. First, the parties may
by an arbitration agreement appoint the official referee as arbitrator under s 11 of the
Arbitration Act 1950. If this is done, the official referee plainly has all the powers
conferred on the arbitrator by the agreement of the parties. We were told that such a
procedure is nowadays very rare. Second (and this is the normal case such as the present),
one of the parties having started ordinary High Court proceedings, the court may refer
the matter to the official referee. In such a case the powers of the official referee are
regulated by RSC Ord 36, r 4, which, in effect, confers on him all the powers of the court
making the reference.

Accordingly, although the official referee's business is regarded as a special category of
business and in practice official referees treat themselves as having jurisdiction to exercise
all the powers conferred on an arbitrator by the standard form of building contract, the
official referee can in fact have no wider powers than a judge of the Queen's Bench
Division if an action relating to the building contract were to be heard by him.

In principle, in an action based on contract the court can only enforce the agreement
between the parties: it has no power to modify that agreement in any way. Therefore, if
the parties have agreed on a specified machinery for establishing their obligations, the
court cannot substitute a different machinery. So, in this contract the parties have agreed
that certain rights and obligations are to be determined by the certificate or opinion of
the architect. In an action questioning the validity of an architect's certificate or opinion
given or expressed under cl 22 or cl 23 of the main contract, in my judgment the court's
jurisdiction would be limited to deciding whether or not the certificate or opinion was
legally invalid because it was given, for example, in bad faith or in excess of his powers.
In no circumstances would the court have power to revise such certificate or opinion
solely on the ground that the court would have reached a different conclusion, since to
do so would be to interfere with the agreement of the parties.

The powers conferred on the arbitrator are of a different kind. Under cl 35(3) he has
power not merely to determine disputes on legal rights under the earlier provisions of
the contract (including the consequences flowing from certificates or opinions of the
architect). In addition, he is given power to modify those contractual rights by varying
the architect's certificates and opinions if he disagrees with them by substituting his own

discretion for that of the architect. The arbitrator has power not only to enforce the
a contractual obligations but to modify them. His modifying power is by agreement
conferred on a specified person, ie the person appointed as arbitrator by agreement or by
the president or vice-president of the Royal Institute of British Architects. In many cases
such arbitrator would be an architect or engineer having specialist knowledge. The
parties have never agreed to vest in the court power to vary their contractual obligations
even if they could validly so agree.

b Of course, the parties cannot by agreement oust the jurisdiction of the court to
determine those matters within the court's jurisdiction, ie the enforcement of the
contractual rights of the parties. But this does not mean that, if the court asserts its
jurisdiction, it thereby assumes all the powers of the arbitrator including the power to
modify the contractual obligations. The court is asserting the court's jurisdiction, not
assuming the jurisdiction of the arbitrator. The court's jurisdiction does not include a
c right to modify contractual rights.

Therefore as a matter of principle I reach the conclusion that if this matter were to be
litigated in the High Court (whether before the official referee or a judge) the court
would not have power to open up, review and revise certificates or opinions as it thought
fit since so to do would be to modify the contractual obligations of the parties. The limit
of the court's jurisdiction would be to declare inoperative any certificate or opinion given
d by the architect if the architect had no power to give such certificate or opinion or had
otherwise erred in law in giving it. The court could not (as an arbitrator could) substitute
its discretion for that of the architect.

The position might well be different if the machinery in cl 35 had broken down and
was incapable of operating. In such a case the agreement of the parties on a matter of
machinery (as opposed to substantive obligation) having been frustrated, the court could
e and would substitute different machinery. But so long as the agreed machinery is
workable, I can see no ground on which the court can alter the agreed machinery for
establishing the contractual obligations.

These views accord with the approach and reasoning of the House of Lords in *Sudbrook
Trading Estate Ltd v Eggleton* [1982] 3 All ER 1, [1983] 1 AC 444, where the problem,
though not the same as in the instant case, was analogous. The lessees had exercised an
f option to purchase at a price to be established by valuers, one of whom had to be
appointed by the lessor. The lessor refused to appoint a valuer and contended that as the
price could not be ascertained, the exercise of the option had merely produced an
unenforceable agreement to agree. The House of Lords held that the substantive
obligation was to sell at a fair and reasonable price and that the provisions as to fixing
that price were mere machinery. One party having wrongfully failed to operate the
g machinery, the court could substitute a different machinery to ascertain what was the
fair and reasonable price. Lord Diplock plainly considered that the court could only use
its own machinery to fix the price if the parties either could not insist, or were not
insisting, on the agreed machinery being operated (see [1982] 3 All ER 1 at 7, [1983] AC
444 at 479). Lord Fraser also was confining the cases in which the court could substitute
different machinery to those where the contractually agreed machinery had broken
h down (see [1982] 3 All ER 1 at 10, [1983] AC 444 at 484).

The judgments of Sir John Donaldson MR and Dunn LJ demonstrate that there is no
authority directly in point (apart from the decision of his Honour Judge Sir William
Stabb QC) which shows that the view I have adopted is wrong. Indeed the weight of
judicial dicta supports me in the view that I have formed.

I therefore reach the view that there are overwhelming reasons why Crown should not
j be prevented from pursuing its arbitration. If Crown is to arbitrate these points, in order
to avoid difficult questions of issue estoppel it is obviously desirable that Crouch also
should be free to arbitrate the same points before the same arbitrator. Accordingly, I do
not think it has been demonstrated that the official referee in this case erred in principle
in refusing a stay of the arbitration proceedings. The appeals should be dismissed.

SIR JOHN DONALDSON MR. This appeal started as an appeal against a discretionary
decision of his Honour Judge Smout QC and it finished as such an appeal. But on the

way it raised three questions of more than passing interest to those concerned with JCT building contracts, namely (a) what is the status of a nominated sub-contractor who uses the name of the main contractor to make claims in arbitration against the building owner or, alternatively, that of the main contractor whose name is so used, (b) to what extent is the court entitled to exercise the powers granted to the arbitrator appointed under the main contract arbitration clause and (c) to what extent is an arbitrator entitled to refrain from deciding issues referred to him? It also drew attention to the enormous workload of official referees and the consequent inevitable delays in disputes with which they are concerned.

The decision of his Honour Judge Smout QC
   The background to this dispute has been fully set out in the judgment of Dunn LJ and I need do no more than summarise the reasons which the judge gave for refusing, in the exercise of his discretion, to grant a stay of either arbitration. These were: (i) there might well be no conflict between the two sets of proceedings, since the litigation as at present constituted concerned events prior to September 1982, whilst the delays complained of in the two arbitrations were later in date; (ii) if any application were made to up-date the litigation to take account of later events, the court could and would ensure that it did not enable the parties to reopen any issues already decided by Mr Royce in the arbitrations; (iii) he had every confidence that Mr Royce would seek to avoid any overlap between the matters with which he was concerned and those which were the subject-matter of the litigation; (iv) Mr Royce was fully capable of rephrasing para 1 of the terms of reference of the Crouch telex arbitration in order to make it clear that the issue was not who was responsible for the boiler plant being inoperable, but whether Crouch was so responsible.
   Although he did not say so in terms, I think that it is a legitimate inference from the judge's judgment that he also took account of the fact that Mr Royce was able to give the parties an appointment for a combined hearing or hearings in the middle of this month whereas, as I have already noted, the courts would consider the rights of Crouch at the earliest in 1985. He must also have taken account of the fact that Crown had at no time asked the courts to interest themselves in its claims, but instead had relied exclusively on its contractual right to arbitration.

The extent of the potential conflict between the litigation and the arbitrations
   I fully accept that the litigation as at present constituted cannot be concerned with events after September 1982 and, so far as such events are concerned, there can be no conflict. I also accept that if any attempt were made to up-date the litigation, either by amendment or by the issue of a further writ followed by an application to consolidate, the official referee would have ample discretionary power to ensure that no attempt was made to reopen issues already decided by Mr Royce or indeed to explore issues which were under consideration by him.
   I am less confident that the Crouch arbitration and also the Crown arbitration, if it were extended on the lines indicated in the pleading which they have delivered, might not involve an examination of events prior to September 1982. It is possible that the health authority might be minded to contend that there were two reasons why the boiler plant is inoperable. The first reason is likely to be that there was an error in design, but a second reason which might be put forward is failures by Crouch which had delayed the performance of the contract and so had prevented the failure of design being detected and remedied at an earlier date.
   Accordingly I examine the judge's decision on the footing that some conflict is possible. This raises several issues. (1) Is the jurisdiction of the official referee coextensive with that of the arbitrator? (2) Could there be issue estoppel arising out of decisions by the arbitrator in (a) the Crouch arbitration and (b) the Crown arbitration which would affect the action before the official referee? (3) To what extent could this be avoided by restraint on the part of the arbitrator? (4) Can Crown litigate its claims separately from Crouch?

What is the jurisdiction of the official referee?
   Under JCT contracts the architect, who is the agent of the building owner, is a key figure in deciding such matters as what extensions of time should be granted for the

performance of the contract, whether and to what extent contractors and sub-contractors
a are responsible for delay, how much each should be paid and when they should be paid
and whether and when the works have been completed. These are very personal decisions
and, within limits, different architects might reach slightly different conclusions. Despite
the fact that the architect is subject to a duty to act fairly, these powers might be regarded
as draconian and unacceptable if they were not subject to review and revision by a more
independent individual. That process is provided for by the arbitration clause. It is,
b however, a rather special clause. Arbitration is usually no more and no less than litigation
in the private sector. The arbitrator is called on to find the facts, apply the law and grant
relief to one or other or both of the parties. Under a JCT arbitration clause (cl 35) the
arbitrator has these powers but he also has power to 'open up, review and revise any
certificate, opinion, decision, requirement or notice'. This goes far further than merely
entitling him to treat the arbitrator's certificates, opinions, decisions, requirements and
c notices as inconclusive in determining the rights of the parties. It enables, and in
appropriate cases requires, him to vary them and so create new rights, obligations and
liabilities in the parties. This is not a power which is normally possessed by any court and
again it has a strong element of personal judgment by an individual nominated in
accordance with the agreement of the parties.

This, of course, raises the vexed question of what happens if, instead of arbitrating, (a)
d one of the parties resorts to the courts and the application of the other party for a stay is
refused or (b) both parties agree to waive their rights under the arbitration clause and to
submit their dispute to the jurisdiction of the courts.

Somewhat surprisingly this has only once been the subject matter of decision by the
courts. This was in an earlier round in the conflict between the health authority and
Crouch in connection with the same contract when Crouch sought an interim payment:
e *Derek Crouch Construction Co Ltd v Northern Regional Health Authority* (unreported). The
decision was that of his Honour Judge Sir William Stabb QC and was given on 30 March
1983. He held, on the authority of *Neale v Richardson* [1938] 1 All ER 753, that—

'if the parties, as in this case, are able to choose the court as a forum for litigation
rather than an arbitrator for arbitration, the court is invested with the same powers
f as the contract bestows on the arbitrator and the court, after determining the issue,
can give judgment for the payment of any money which that determination shows
to be due.'

It should be added that this also reflects the practice of official referees.

In this appeal this issue has been much more fully argued and I am indebted to all
g counsel and, in particular, to counsel for Crown for the assistance which I have received.

In principle the exercise by a court of the powers conferred by the JCT contract on the
arbitrator appointed for the purposes of that contract seems to me to involve the exercise
of a completely novel jurisdiction. The function of the courts is to determine facts and to
declare and enforce the contractual rights of the parties. It may be retorted that the same
comment can be made about the functions of an arbitrator, and this I would accept.
h However the truth of the matter is, I think, that the 'arbitrator' appointed under a JCT
contract has a double function. He has first the right and the duty to review the architect's
decisions (in which I include certificates, opinions, requirements and notices) and, if
appropriate, to substitute his own. Second, he has to declare the rights of the parties on
the basis of the situation produced by his own revising activity. The latter is truly an
arbitrator's function. The former is not.
j All this would be nothing to the point if the matter were governed by authority, but I
do not think that it is. *Neale v Richardson* is, I think, distinguishable. There the issue of
the final certificate was a condition precedent to payment and the architect refused to
issue the certificate. He was also the arbitrator under a straightforward arbitration clause
reading, 'In all cases arising out of this contract the decision of the architect shall be
binding on all parties' but he refused to act as such. The court, on the authority of *Brodie
v Cardiff Corp* [1919] AC 337, decided that the issue of a certificate by the architect as
being a condition precedent to payment was subject to any decision by an arbitrator as to

the rights of the parties. As the architect refused to act and neither party had taken any step to have another arbitrator appointed, the court was free to determine the rights of the parties without regard to the absence of a certificate. This seems to me to be very different from deciding that the court can substitute itself for the architect or exercise the powers of an arbitrator under a clause such as the JCT clause. The court in *Neale v Richardson* was merely performing its normal function, uninhibited by the absence of the certificate.

A similar example of the court's substituting its own machinery for contractual machinery which has broken down is provided by *Sudbrook Trading Estate Ltd v Eggleton* [1982] 3 All ER 1, [1983] 1 AC 444. But this is wholly different from assuming a jurisdiction to take over and operate the contractual machinery which is not designed for use by a court.

Prestige & Co Ltd v Brettell [1938] 4 All ER 346, to which the judge also referred, is another example of the court applying *Brodie's* case and holding that as arbitration had been claimed, the refusal by the architect to issue a certificate was not fatal to the contractor's claim. That has no bearing on the question of whether special powers given to the arbitrator can be exercised by the court.

While, as I have said, the point does not appear to be governed by authority, it was considered in *East Ham BC v Bernard Sunley & Sons Ltd* [1965] 3 All ER 619, [1966] AC 406, HL; *affg in part* [1965] 1 All ER 210, [1965] 1 WLR 30, CA and in *P & M Kaye Ltd v Hosier & Dickinson Ltd* [1972] 1 All ER 121, [1972] 1 WLR 146, HL.

In the *East Ham* case the court was concerned with the conclusiveness of a final certificate by the arbitrator but also considered arguments based on cl 27, the arbitration clause, which, it was contended, rendered the final certificate inconclusive. Salmon LJ appears to have accepted, although it was not necessary for the decision, that a court would not be able to use the powers of the arbitrator under cl 35 (cl 27 in that contract), saying ([1965] 1 All ER 210 at 220, [1965] 1 WLR 30 at 43–44):

'... in an action (should the parties prefer litigation to arbitration) the judge would be bound by the final certificate, since on no view could the impact of cl. 24 [the final certificate clause] be removed save by the powers conferred by cl. 27 on the arbitrator and only on the arbitrator. I do not consider that *Robins* v. *Goddard* ([1905] 1 KB 294) decides anything to the contrary.'

In the House of Lords Viscount Dilhorne did not find it necessary to deal directly with the point but did comment that *Robins v Goddard* was not authority for the proposition that 'if special powers are given to an arbitrator, they devolve on the court should there be litigation' (see [1965] 3 All ER 619 at 623, [1966] AC 406 at 424). Lord Cohen (dissenting in the result) said ([1965] 3 All ER 619 at 630, [1966] AC 406 at 434):

'It was suggested in argument that if the matter came before the court the judge would have all the powers that an arbitrator would have under cl. 27 and that therefore on the construction which I have placed on the contract it is impossible to give any meaning to cl. 24. This argument was based on the decision in *Robins* v. *Goddard*, but I agree with SALMON, L.J., that at a trial in court the judge would be bound by the final certificate since on no view could the impact of cl. 24 be removed save by the powers conferred on an arbitrator and only on the arbitrator. *Robins* v. *Goddard* does not, in my opinion, decide anything to the contrary.'

Lord Pearson expressed the view that there might be a contractual implication, in order to avoid absurdity, that the court has the same powers in an action as the arbitrator would have in an arbitration under cl 27 but did not decide whether there was such an implication saying only that if there was not and one party brought an action, there would be very strong grounds for granting a stay of that action (see [1965] 3 All ER 619 at 638, [1966] AC 406 at 447).

In *P & M Kaye Ltd v Hosier & Dickinson Ltd* the question in issue was the evidential effect of a final certificate in relation to High Court proceedings begun before that

certificate was issued. Lord Morris said ([1972] 1 All ER 121 at 128, [1972] 1 WLR 146
at 153):

> 'It is understandable that as the parties had contracted to refer disputes to
> arbitration they would not give to a final certificate issued while arbitration
> proceedings were proceeding or pending the attribute of being "conclusive
> evidence". But they have not agreed that a final certificate issued while court
> proceedings are pending should not have the attribute.'

And Lord Wilberforce said ([1972] 1 All ER 121 at 132, [1972] 1 WLR 146 at 158):

> 'Had the matter gone to arbitration the position would no doubt have been
> different; this is because cl 35 of the contract confers very wide powers on arbitrators
> to open up and review certificates which a court would not have.'

I respectfully agree with Lord Wilberforce's dictum, but I should stress that my view
relates only to the exercise by the official referee of his normal jurisdiction. Under s 11
of the Arbitration Act 1950—

> 'Where an arbitration agreement provides that the reference shall be to an official
> referee, any official referee to whom application is made shall . . . hear and determine
> the matters agreed to be referred.'

RSC Ord 36, r 5(2) and (3) also refers to this power. However, in the present case there
was no such arbitration agreement which must, of course, be in writing: see s 32 of the
1950 Act.

Could there be issue estoppel arising out of decisions by the arbitrator?

In the case of the Crouch arbitration there can be no argument but that there can be
issue estoppel which would affect the proceedings before the official referee.

In the case of the arbitration initiated by Crown in the name of Crouch, the same is
true. Crown has no contractual rights under the main contract and is forced to claim in
the name of Crouch under the rights given to it by cll 8(b) and 11(d) of the sub-contract.
Its claims are therefore those of Crouch and issue estoppel could accordingly result. It
was submitted that the status of Crown suing in the name of Crouch might be sui generis
and that no estoppel would result, but I can see no basis for such a submission. Were it
so, Crown would be suing in its own name under the main contract.

To what extent can the arbitrator refuse to decide issues?

This problem only arises in the unusual situation of concurrent overlapping
proceedings before the court and before an arbitrator. The primary duty of an arbitrator
is to decide all issues referred to him. However, an arbitrator is subject to the supervision
of the court and it is well settled that the court has jurisdiction to restrain an arbitrator
from deciding issues which are being litigated before the court. If, therefore, an arbitrator
has reason to believe that he is being asked to decide issues which the court concurrently
has under consideration, he should ask himself whether the court, if asked, would be
likely to enjoin him from proceeding. If the answer is Yes, he should indicate his view
and give the parties an opportunity of applying to the court for a mandatory injunction
requiring him to proceed. If the answer is No, he should indicate his view and give the
parties an opportunity of applying to the court for a prohibitory injunction restraining
him from proceeding. This is analogous to the duty of an arbitrator when his jurisdiction
is challenged. This does not mean that, whatever his view, the arbitration will grind to a
halt. The arbitrator may be able to proceed with matters which create no risk of conflict
or, if this is impossible and he thinks that the court would wish the arbitration to proceed,
he can do so and only refrain from issuing his award until the wishes of the court are
known.

Can Crown litigate its claims separately from Crouch?

There is no way in which Crown can litigate any claims under the main contract in its
own name. Its only right is either to make claims against Crouch under the sub-contract,

leaving it to Crouch to pass its claims on under the main contract, or to seek to use Crouch's name to claim under the main contract. The latter claim will be Crouch's claim and every conceivable complication will arise if Crouch disagrees with the case which Crown wishes to submit in its name.   *a*

Conclusion

All parties concerned with the construction of this hospital, the health authority, Crouch and Crown, agreed to a system of disputes settlement which involved the   *b* appointment of an arbitrator under the main contract with special powers and, if necessary, the appointment of an arbitrator, who would probably be the same individual, under the sub-contract. It is not surprising that problems are likely to arise if two of those parties, Crouch and the health authority, first decide to abandon this system and litigate instead, then decide to revert to arbitration on a limited front, settle that arbitration while starting another and then fall out as to the scope of that other. While it is a free   *c* country and they are entitled to do this, the one party thoroughly deserving of protection is Crown, which is entitled to insist on arbitration and to be protected from having its rights adversely affected by litigation, to which it has never agreed, under a jurisdiction which is probably more limited than that of an arbitrator. Against this background I should expect the arbitrator, Mr Royce, to proceed with the arbitration with all expedition and the court, in the form of the official referee, to stand aside and leave him to do so.   *d* This clearly was in the mind of the official referee when he refused this application. The matter was one for his discretion and I can detect no error in the way in which he exercised it. I would go further and say that if I had to exercise the same discretion, which I do not, I would do exactly what he has done.

The state of the official referee's list   *e*

The delays in disposing of business before the official referees is, through no fault of theirs, wholly unacceptable. It may be that the indications which we have given that, in the absence of a written submission to arbitration, they do not have jurisdiction to exercise the powers of an arbitrator under cl 35, or its equivalent in other standard forms of contract, will reduce the length of the lists. I say this because our view, if accepted, will virtually give any party a right of veto on any attempt to bypass the arbitration   *f* clauses. They will be able to point out that they are thereby being deprived of the benefit of the special powers of the arbitrator under those clauses and they will accordingly have a very strong claim to a stay under s 4 of the 1950 Act unless they voluntarily join in a submission to the official referee as an arbitrator. If this reduction in the length of the lists does not occur or seems unlikely to occur, urgent consideration should be given to conferring upon the official referees a power analogous to that contemplated by s 92 of   *g* the County Courts Act 1959 to enable the official referees, whether sitting as such or as arbitrators, to refer, or sub-refer, the 'nuts and bolts' of the suit to a suitably qualified arbitrator for enquiry and report. This would result in the official referees becoming, in effect, the construction industry court, having the same relationship to the construction industry as the Commercial Court has to the financial and commercial activities of the City of London. It could decide questions of principle which are of general interest,   *h* leaving it to the individual arbitrators to apply those principles to the details of individual disputes.

For the reasons which I have sought to express, I would dismiss this appeal.

Appeals dismissed. Leave to appeal to the House of Lords refused.

Solicitors: *Ingledew Botterell Roche & Pybus*, Newcastle upon Tyne (for the health authority); *McKenna & Co* (for Crouch); *Bristows Cooke & Carpmael* (for Crown).

Diana Procter   Barrister.

a
R v Clerkenwell Metropolitan Stipendiary Magistrate, ex parte Director of Public Prosecutions

QUEEN'S BENCH DIVISION
b ROBERT GOFF LJ AND FORBES J
22, 29 JULY 1983

Magistrates – Jurisdiction – Trial of information – Validity of information – Laying of information – Time limit – Informations when laid not accompanied by proper certificate of compliance with time limit – Informations in fact laid within time limit – Proper certificate not produced until
c *after expiry of time limit – Magistrate declining jurisdiction to hear informations – Whether magistrate entitled to decline jurisdiction – Gas Act 1972, s 43(2).*

Judicial review – Availability of remedy – Magistrate declining jurisdiction to hear information – Whether appropriate remedy application for judicial review or appeal by way of case stated.

d On 17 August 1982 four informations were laid against the defendants alleging that more than six months previously they had committed certain offences against the Gas Safety Regulations 1972. The informations were accompanied by a certificate stating that it was only on 28 May 1982 that evidence justifying the prosecution had come to the Secretary of State's knowledge. By virtue of s 43(2)[a] of the Gas Act 1972 summary proceedings in respect of an offence under the 1972 regulations could be brought either
e within the six-month time limit prescribed by s 127(1)[b] of the Magistrates' Courts Act 1980 or within three months from the date on which evidence sufficient in the opinion of the Secretary of State to justify a prosecution for the offence came to his knowledge, whichever was the longer, and a certificate purporting to be signed by the Secretary of State as to the date on which such evidence came to his knowledge was conclusive. Summonses were issued to the defendants. The prosecutor subsequently discovered that
f the certificate was not a valid one because it had not been signed by the Secretary of State himself, as required by s 43(2). Accordingly, on 14 December, when the informations came on for hearing before the magistrate, the prosecutor produced a fresh certificate, duly signed by the Secretary of State. The magistrate declined jurisdiction and dismissed the informations on the ground that they had not been validly laid in time because, when they were laid, they had not been accompanied by a valid certificate. At the request of the prosecutor, the magistrate stated a case for the opinion of the High Court. Before
g the case was lodged, the prosecutor was advised that, since the magistrate had declined jurisdiction, the appropriate remedy was by way of an application for judicial review. He accordingly sought an order of certiorari to quash the magistrate's decision.

Held – (1) On the true construction of s 43(2) of the 1972 Act, the validity of the
h informations depended not on whether they were accompanied by a valid certificate but on whether they were in fact laid within one of the time limits prescribed by s 43(2), and the certificate was merely one of the means by which the prosecutor could prove that the informations had been so laid. It followed that, since the magistrate had had a valid certificate before him proving that the informations against the defendants had been laid within three months of the relevant evidence coming to the knowledge of the Secretary
j of State, he had erred in declining jurisdiction and dismissing the informations (see

---

a   Section 43(2) is set out at p 195 *d* to *f, post*
b   Section 127(1), so far as material, provides: '. . . a magistrates' court shall not try an information . . . unless the information was laid . . . within 6 months from the time when the offence was committed . . .'

p 197 *e* to p 198 *a* and *j* to p 199 *a* and p 202 *h*, post); *Price v Humphries* [1958] 2 All ER
725 considered.

(2) As the magistrate had merely declined jurisdiction and as there was no question of
the defendants having been acquitted after having been put in jeopardy, there was no
bar to the court granting orders of certiorari and mandamus, although the more
appropriate means of challenging a refusal of jurisdiction was an appeal by way of case
stated. Since the magistrate had already stated a case, the application for judicial review
would be dismissed, the prosecutor would be given leave for the case stated to be lodged
out of time and the hearing of the application would be treated as the hearing of the case
stated. In view of the exceptional circumstances, however, the matter would not be
remitted to the magistrate for hearing (see p 199 *d e*, p 200 *f* and p 201 *j* to p 202 *c* and
g h, post); *R v Carden* (1879) 5 QBD 1 and *R v Wisbech Justices* (1890) 54 JP 743 followed;
R v Middlesex Justices, ex p DPP [1952] 2 All ER 312 and *R v Dorking Justices, ex p
Harrington* [1983] 3 All ER 29 distinguished; *Pratt v AA Sites Ltd* [1938] 2 All ER 371 not
followed.

Per curiam. If an information is laid alleging an offence under s 42(1) of the 1972 Act
or any regulation made under that Act, then, if the ordinary time limit under s 127 of
the 1980 Act has expired, the clerk to the justices should not issue a summons unless
evidence of the date when the relevant evidence came to the knowledge of the Secretary
of State is produced, such date being no more than three months before the laying of the
information (see p 198 *g h* and p 202 *h*, post).

Notes

For limitation of time in laying informations, see 29 Halsbury's Laws (4th edn) para 291.

For offences against regulations made under the Gas Act 1972, see 19 ibid para 465.

For the Gas Act 1972, ss 42, 43, see 42 Halsbury's Statutes (3rd edn) 503, 504.

For the Magistrates' Courts Act 1980, s 127, see 50(2) ibid 1552.

For the Gas Safety Regulations 1972, see 10 Halsbury's Statutory Instruments (4th
reissue) 17.

Cases referred to in judgments

Pratt v AA Sites Ltd [1938] 2 All ER 371, [1938] 2 KB 459, DC.
Price v Humphries [1958] 2 All ER 725, [1958] 2 QB 353, [1958] 3 WLR 304, DC.
R v Carden (1879) 5 QBD 1, DC.
R v Dorking Justices, ex p Harrington [1983] 3 All ER 29, [1983] QB 1076, [1983] 3 WLR
370, DC.
R v Middlesex Justices (1877) 2 QBD 516, DC.
R v Middlesex Justices, ex p DPP [1952] 2 All ER 312, [1952] 2 QB 758, DC.
R v Wisbech Justices (1890) 54 JP 743, DC.
Wakefield Local Board v West Riding Rly Co (1866) 30 JP 628.

Application for judicial review

On 14 December 1982, J Denis Purcell Esq, a metropolitan stipendiary magistrate sitting
at Clerkenwell Magistrates' Court, declined jurisdiction to hear, and dismissed, four
informations which had been preferred by Detective Chief Inspector Humphries, on
behalf of the applicant, the Director of Public Prosecutions, against the respondents,
James Martin (Contractors) Ltd, alleging that they had committed certain offences under
the Gas Safety Regulations 1972, SI 1972/1178. At the request of the Director of Public
Prosecutions, the magistrate stated a case for the opinion of the High Court. Before the
case stated was lodged, the Director of Public Prosecutions was advised that, since the
magistrate had declined jurisdiction to hear the informations, his proper course was not
to appeal by way of case stated but to apply for a judicial review. Accordingly he applied,
with the leave of Woolf J granted on 4 March 1983, for an order of certiorari to bring up

a and quash the magistrate's order of 14 December 1982. The facts are set out in the judgment of Robert Goff LJ.

Andrew Collins for the Director of Public Prosecutions.
Donald Broatch for the respondents.

Cur adv vult

b 29 July. The following judgments were delivered.

ROBERT GOFF LJ. There is before the court an application by the Director of Public Prosecutions for judicial review of an order made by the stipendiary magistrate for Clerkenwell, on 14 December 1982, whereby he purported to dismiss four informations laid by the applicant against the respondents, James Martin (Contractors) Ltd, in respect of offences alleged to have been committed by them contrary to the Gas Safety Regulations 1972, SI 1972/1178.

The application raises for decision a question of construction of s 43(2) of the Gas Act 1972. It will be convenient if I set out at once the terms of sub-ss (1) and (2) of that section. They read as follows:

d '(1) Proceedings for an offence under section 42(1) above or any regulation made under this Act shall not in England and Wales be instituted except by or with the consent of the Secretary of State or by the Director of Public Prosecutions.

(2) In England and Wales, any proceedings before a court of summary jurisdiction—(a) for an offence against any regulations made under section 31 above, or for aiding, abetting, counselling or procuring the commission of such an offence,

e may, notwithstanding any enactment prescribing the time within which proceedings may be brought, be brought either within the time so prescribed or within three months from the date on which evidence sufficient in the opinion of the Secretary of State to justify a prosecution for the offence comes to his knowledge, whichever is the longer; and for the purposes of this subsection a certificate purporting to be signed by the Secretary of State as to the date on which such evidence comes to his

f knowledge shall be conclusive evidence thereof.'

The facts of the matter, as appear from the evidence before the court, are as follows. On 6 October 1981 there was a serious explosion at a sixth-floor flat known as 26 Richbell House, Boswell Street, London WC1, which caused extensive damage to the block of flats and also injured the lady who was the tenant of flat 26. The respondents had been awarded a contract by North Thames Gas to provide a new gas supply system to the flats

g in Richbell House. This work included the fitting of new service pipes externally, extending them into the flats, installing a meter-controlled tap and fitting new meters. The work had continued for several weeks before 6 October 1981. On that date fitters from the respondents were working on the site, and it was alleged that, to test the system, they opened the main service valve in the pavement outside the block, so causing gas to

h flow through the whole system. The tenant of flat 26 smelt gas in her flat. It was alleged that there was at that time no cap on the end of the meter control, as required by reg 16(d) of the 1972 regulations. The explosion then occurred. It was also alleged that the respondents had failed to cap several of the other meter controls, pending the connection of meters to them.

After the explosion, the Gas Standards Branch of the Department of Energy were

j informed by the police, who were investigating the case. The police agreed to keep the Gas Standards Branch informed of the progress of their investigation. By April 1982, there having been no record of the police having communicated further with the Gas Standards Branch, officials then communicated with the police and, on 27 April 1982, they discovered that the police were not taking any action themselves. The Gas Standards Branch, therefore, carried out their own investigation. As a result, they made a

submisssion to the Secretary of State, on or about 27 May 1982. This they did for the
purpose of s 43(2) of the 1972 Act.

Under s 127 of the Magistrates' Courts Act 1980 a magistrates' court shall not try an
information unless it is laid within six months from the time when the offence was
committed. Here, the alleged offences had been committed some time before the date of
the explosion, so that the six-month period expired some time before 6 April 1982. It
was, therefore, necessary for the department to take advantage of the extended limitation
period permitted under s 43(2) of the 1972 Act.

On 28 May 1982 there came to the knowledge of the Secretary of State for Energy
evidence sufficient, in his opinion, to justify a prosecution of the respondents. Then,
unfortunately, an error of procedure was made in the department.

Previously, on 11 January 1982, the Secretary of State had signed a document
purporting to authorise a Mr Boreham, an assistant secretary in the department
responsible for gas standards, to sign certificates for the purposes of s 43, that is to say
certificates which should be conclusive evidence of the dates on which evidence, sufficient
in the opinion of the Secretary of State to justify prosecution for the offences in question,
came to his knowledge. In pursuance of this authority, on 9 August 1982, Mr Boreham
signed a certificate in the present case specifying 28 May 1982 as the relevant date in
respect of the offences alleged against the respondents arising out of events at Richbell
House.

Thereafter, on 17 August 1982, Detective Chief Inspector Humphries, on behalf of the
Director of Public Prosecutions, laid informations alleging four offences by the
respondents, contrary to the 1972 regulations, in which he stated that the Secretary of
State had signed a certificate pursuant to s 43(2) of the 1972 Act. Attached to the
informations was a copy of the Secretary of State's authority, dated 11 January 1982, and
Mr Boreham's certificate, dated 8 August 1982.

As a result, the chief clerk at the Clerkenwell Magistrates' Court caused summonses to
be issued to the respondents, also dated 17 August 1982. The defect in this procedure
was that, on a true construction of s 43(2) of the 1972 Act, as indeed was in due course
accepted by the department and by the Director of Public Prosecutions, only the Secretary
of State himself could sign the relevant certificate, so that the purported authority to Mr
Boreham to do so was ultra vires and the certificate signed by him and annexed to the
informations was not a valid certificate.

Thereafter, the matter proceeded as follows. The first hearing in the Clerkenwell
Magistrates' Court took place on 21 October 1982. On that occasion, a representative of
the Director of Public Prosecutions handed to a representative of the defence a copy of
the informations, dated 17 August 1982. That was the first occasion on which the defence
had sight of the informations.

The next hearing was on 11 November 1982. On that occasion, counsel for the
respondents made known to a representative of the Director of Public Prosecutions that
an issue was going to be raised as to the jurisdiction of the magistrates' court, and that the
validity of the certificate under s 43 of the 1972 Act was going to be raised as a
preliminary issue. The case was put over for argument until 14 December 1982. No
doubt in response to that communication, on 9 December 1982, a further certificate was
signed by the Secretary of State himself under s 43(2) of the 1972 Act, to the effect that
28 May 1982 was the date on which there came to his knowledge evidence sufficient in
his opinion to justify a prosecution of the respondents in respect of the offences alleged
to have been committed by them.

On 14 December 1982 the matter came before Mr Purcell, a metropolitan stipendiary
magistrate, sitting at Clerkenwell Magistrates' Court. On that occasion, the prosecution
produced the new certificate of the Secretary of State, dated 9 December. For the
respondents, however, it was contended that the matter in dispute was one of jurisdiction
and not merely of form, that the last paragraph of the information contained an error of
fact, in that it stated, contrary to the facts, that the Secretary of State had then issued a
certificate pursuant to s 43(2) of the 1972 Act and that it was this error which had

procured the issue of the summonses. Having been referred to *Price v Humphries* [1958]
a   2 All ER 725, [1958] 2 QB 353, the magistrate formed the opinion that the informations
should have been accompanied by a certificate duly signed by the Secretary of State when
they were initially laid, and he purported to dismiss the informations.

Following the magistrate's decision, the applicant requested the magistrate to state a
case for the opinion of the court. This he did on 11 February 1983. In the case stated,
after setting out the material facts, he posed the question for the opinion of the court:

b   '. . . whether, after an information has been laid for an offence under Regulations
made under the Gas Act, 1972, the prosecution may produce a fresh certificate
pursuant to Section 43(2) Gas Act, 1972, in order to cure a defect in a certificate
before the Court when the information was laid.'

However, following representations by the solicitors acting for the respondents, on 9
c   February 1983 the applicant was advised that, since the magistrate had decided that he
had no jurisdiction to hear the information, the proper course was to seek judicial review
of the magistrate's decision. So the present proceedings were launched, seeking an order
of certiorari to remove into this court and quash the magistrate's order dated 14 December
1982.

Finally, I should record that there is before the court an affidavit of Mr Dawson, the
d   solicitor acting for the respondents, which not only sets out the course of events before
the magistrate and takes the point on the certificate and certain other points, but also
complains of the delay in the matter and of the fact that, at the date of his affidavit (31
March 1983), no explanation had been given why the matter was not put before the
Secretary of State until 28 May 1982, and indeed that much of the investigation was not
carried out until after that date. It was after receipt of this affidavit that the applicant, on
e   27 May 1983, explained that the delay was due to a failure of communication between
the department and the police.

Having heard the submissions of counsel, I am satisfied that the magistrate erred in
law in making his decision on 14 December 1982. Under s 43(2) of the 1972 Act, it is
necessary to draw a distinction between two matters, first, the date when, in relation to
the time when proceedings are brought before a court of summary jurisdiction, the
f   relevant evidence comes to the knowledge of the Secretary of State and, second, the
certificate which shall be conclusive evidence of such date for the purposes of s 43(2). The
first matter is a question of fact. The second is a means whereby, by an appropriate
certificate, the first act may be conclusively proved. If the relevant evidence has come to
the knowledge of the Secretary of State not more than three months before the time
when proceedings are brought, then, notwithstanding that such proceedings are brought
g   outside the time prescribed by any enactment (here, outside the six-month period
prescribed by s 127 of the Magistrates' Courts Act 1980), nevertheless, they may be
brought by virtue of s 43(2) of the 1972 Act.

Let it be supposed that proceedings are brought outside the six-month period, but
within three months after the date when the relevant evidence comes to the knowledge
of the Secretary of State, in the form of an information laid before magistrates. In such
h   circumstances, the magistrates cannot decline jurisdiction on the ground that the
proceedings are out of time. Of course, the magistrates or their clerk may properly, on
observing that the six-month period prescribed in s 127 of the 1980 Act has expired,
decline to issue a summons unless evidence is produced that the case falls within s 43(2)
of the 1972 Act. If so, production of an appropriate certificate will provide the requisite
evidence in conclusive form. In such circumstances, the person laying the information
j   may well anticipate that such evidence will be required by the magistrates or their clerk,
in which event he may attach the certificate to the information. Even so, the prerequisite
of the proceedings being validily brought beyond the six-month period is not the
certificate, but the fact of the proceedings being brought within three months of the
relevant evidence coming to the knowledge of the Secretary of State. The certificate
remains no more than evidence of that fact, which, because it is conclusive, provides the

prosecution with a convenient method of proof. In theory at least, the fact could be
proved by other means, without production of any certificate, though it is difficult to
imagine circumstances in which this could be done.

Counsel for the respondents submitted that this was not so. I am unable, however, to
accept his submission that any other conclusion can be reached as a matter of construction
of the 1972 Act. Before this court, as before the magistrates, he relied on *Price v Humphries*
in support of a submission that the certificate must be in existence at the time when
proceedings are brought, ie, here, when the informations were laid.

Price v Humphries was concerned with informations laid under the National Insurance
Act 1946, under which proceedings could not be brought except by, or with, the consent
of the minister, or of an inspector, or other officer, duly authorised. The point was taken
by the defence, after the prosecution had closed their case before the justices, that the
prosecution had failed to prove the requisite consent and that, therefore, there was no
case to answer. The justices upheld the submission and dismissed the information.

On an appeal by way of case stated, this court allowed the appeal of the prosecution.
Devlin J said ([1958] 2 All ER 725 at 727–728, [1958] 2 QB 353 at 358–359):

> 'It is the duty of the clerk to the justices, or whoever issues the summons, to see
> that it is not issued unless the consent or the authority is produced, and there is a
> presumption which, indeed, is merely a facet of the wider maxim omnia
> praesumuntur rite et solemniter esse acta that the clerk has discharged his duty in
> that respect. Accordingly, prima facie the position was that the summons had been
> properly issued and there was no need for the prosecution to take any further step
> unless objection was taken. If objection were taken then they must be in a position
> to prove it . . .'

However, he continued:

> '. . . if the prosecution is allowed without objection to close its case, then the
> prosecution has done all that is necessary and the summons is presumed to be a good
> one and properly authorised. If the defence wants to challenge that and take
> objection, they should take their objection before the prosecution case is closed, and,
> having taken their objection, the burden will pass to the prosecution to produce
> what evidence they have which shows that the proceedings were duly authorised.
> For these reasons, I think that the decision of the justices was wrong, the appeal
> should be allowed, and that the case should go back to the justices in order that they
> may proceed with the hearing of it.'

As I understand the judgment of Devlin J, he was saying that, if the information was
laid without producing evidence of the requisite consent or authority, the justices, or
their clerk, should not issue the summons unless such evidence was produced to them.
In my judgment, exactly the same principle is applicable in the present case. If an
information is laid alleging an offence under s 42(1) of the 1972 Act, or any regulation
made under that Act, then, if the ordinary time limit has expired (here, the six-month
time limit under s 127 of the 1980 Act), the clerk to the justices should not issue a
summons unless evidence is produced of the date when the relevant evidence came to
the knowledge of the Secretary of State, such date being no more than three months
before the laying of the information. Of course, ordinarily an appropriate certificate
which is conclusive evidence of that date will be furnished with the information.

It follows that *Price v Humphries* does not require that this court should depart from
the construction of s 43(2) of the 1972 Act, which I have already set out, under which a
distinction must be drawn between the fact of proceedings being brought within three
months of the date on which the relevant evidence has come to the knowledge of the
Secretary of State and a certificate, which is conclusive evidence of that fact. Furthermore,
the facts that the informations in this case inaccurately stated that an appropriate
certificate had been issued and that the ultra vires certificate of Mr Boreham was attached
to the informations should not, in my judgment, affect our decision in the present case

a because, as was conclusively proved before the magistrate on 14 December 1982, at the time the point was taken before him, by the later certificate signed by the Secretary of State, dated 9 December 1982, the proceedings had in fact been brought within the three-month period.

I now turn to the course of action which this court should take in the light of our conclusion that the magistrate erred in law.

b In this connection, counsel, for the Director of Public Prosecutions very properly drew our attention to the decision of this court in *R v Middlesex Justices, ex p DPP* [1952] 2 All ER 312, [1952] 2 QB 758, recently applied in *R v Dorking Justices, ex p Harrington* [1983] 3 All ER 29, [1983] QB 1076. Under these decisions this court will not, on proceedings for judicial review, interfere with a decision of an inferior court to dismiss a charge against a respondent where he has been in jeopardy and has been acquitted, even though there has in fact been no trial on the merits. However, I am satisfied that this line of *c* authority provides no bar to this court interfering with the decision of the magistrate in the present case.

Although the magistrate is recorded as having dismissed the charges against the respondents, in fact what he did was to decline jurisdiction on the ground that the informations had not been laid in time. Strictly speaking, what he must have done was to hold that there was no certificate, as required by s 43(2) of the 1972 Act, and that, since *d* the informations were not laid within six months from the time when the alleged offences were committed, the magistrates' court could not try the informations. In these circumstances, it seems to me that there is no question of the respondents having been acquitted when they were in jeopardy. There was simply a refusal to hear the matter at all and, in those circumstances, certiorari will lie to quash the decision and mandamus may be issued to order the inferior tribunal to proceed with the hearing of the matter. If *e* authority is needed for this proposition, it is to be found in the judgment of Cockburn CJ in *R v Carden* (1879) 5 QBD 1 at 5, when he said:

> 'In cases where a magistrate has authority to hear and determine a matter, but refuses to do so to the frustration of justice, we have undeniably jurisdiction in the exercise of our mandatory authority to direct him to hear and determine.'

f There is, however, another matter which has been drawn to our attention. I have already recorded the fact that, after the magistrate had, at the request of the prosecution, stated a case for the opinion of the court, the solicitors for the respondents suggested to the prosecution that this was not an appropriate case for a case stated, and the prosecution then launched instead the present application for judicial review. The respondents' solicitors, when they made this suggestion to the prosecution, referred to the decision of *g* this court in *Pratt v AA Sites Ltd* [1938] 2 All ER 371, [1938] 2 KB 459. In that case it was held that, where justices had decided that they had no jurisdiction to hear the relevant complaints, they had no power to state a case because they had not made any order or determination disposing of the matters raised by the case. Lord Hewart CJ said ([1938] 2 KB 459 at 461–462; cf [1938] 2 All ER 371 at 372–373):

> *h* 'Whatever else may be doubtful in this case it seems to be perfectly clear that the justices expressed the view that they had no jurisdiction to hear the complaints which were before them. That being so, the position is the same as that disclosed in *Wakefield Local Board* v. *West Riding Ry. Co.* ((1866) 30 JP 628 at 629), where Blackburn J., addressing counsel for the appellants, said: "Your proper course seems rather to have been to apply for a rule by way of *mandamus*, calling on the justices to hear the case, for they have not heard it yet. I think there has never been an instance *j* where the justices declined to hear the case for want of jurisdiction and then stated a case for the opinion of the superior Court." In his judgment Blackburn J. said (at 629): "I think nothing can be clearer than that the justices made a mistake in granting the case, as the statute 20 and 21 Vict. c. 43 [the Summary Jurisdiction Act, 1857], does not apply. The justices, when the question of jurisdiction was raised before them, decided, rightly or wrongly, that they had no jurisdiction. If they were

right, then the parties can only go and renew the information before other justices
who are not interested. If they were wrong, then the remedy is to apply for a rule
under Jervis's Act, commanding them to hear and determine the case." In the
present case the justices have stated in language which is quite free from ambiguity
that they had no jurisdiction to hear the complaints, and, in my opinion, this appeal
should be dismissed on the preliminary point taken on behalf of the respondents.'

Humphreys J said ([1938] 2 KB 459 at 462–463; cf [1938] 2 All ER 371 at 373):

'By the Summary Jurisdiction Act, 1857, s. 2: "After the hearing and determination
by a justice or justices of the peace of any information or complaint, which he or
they have power to determine in a summary way . . . either party to the proceeding
before the said justice or justices may, if dissatisfied with the said determination as
being erroneous in point of law, apply . . . to the said justice or justices, to state and
sign a case setting forth the facts and the grounds of such determination, for the
opinion thereon of one of the Superior Courts of Law . . . ." Those provisions were
somewhat amended by s. 33 of the Summary Jurisdiction Act, 1879, which provides:
"Any person aggrieved who desires to question a conviction, order, determination,
or other proceeding of a court of summary jurisdiction, on the ground that it is
erroneous in point of law, or is in excess of jurisdiction, may apply to the court to
state a special case setting forth the facts of the case and the grounds on which the
proceeding is questioned, and if the court decline to state the case, may apply to the
High Court of Justice for an order requiring the case to be stated." In my view, the
later statute does not extend to get rid of the rule which existed long before it was
passed—namely, that this Court will not hear a case stated except to dispose of the
matters raised by the case. Where justices have not heard and determined the
question before them, but have merely said: "We decline jurisdiction in this matter
and we have no power to adjudicate," this Court leaves the party aggrieved to his
remedy. He is not without remedy.'

As counsel for the Director of Public Prosecutions has submitted, this decision is by no
means without difficulty. First of all, it is inconsistent with *R v Wisbech Justices* (1890) 54
JP 743, an earlier decision of this court under the same section of the same statute (s 33
of the Summary Jurisdiction Act 1879). In that case, there was before the court not a case
stated but an application for mandamus, the preferred remedy of the Divisional Court in
Pratt v AA Sites Ltd. Yet the court refused to make the order, on the ground that there
was available to the applicant a more convenient remedy, in the form of a case stated.
The following exchange is recorded as having taken place between counsel for the
applicant and the court:

'*Cooper* showed cause on the part of the defendant, and contended that the
magistrates had not declined jurisdiction, but on the authority of *R. v. Justices of
Middlesex* ((1877) 2 QBD 516), had heard and determined the case by deciding the
preliminary point of law raised by Arthur Ollard on behalf of the defendant, and
which was rightly decided. But even if the decision arrived at by the justices was
erroneous in law, the remedy of the prosecutor was to get a case stated for the
opinion of the court, and not to apply to a *mandamus*.

Colam, in support of the rule, on behalf of the prosecutor contended that the
magistrates were wrong in their decision of the point of law as to the lapse of time,
and that a calendar month had not elapsed before the information, and that the
justices had not heard and determined the case, but had wrongly allowed a technical
objection to their jurisdiction.

HAWKINS, J.—It was not a technical point at all. The defendant appears before the
court, and through his solicitor says, I submit myself to the court, and plead not
guilty; and the solicitor then very properly says, I have an objection to take to the
very initial stage of the proceedings, viz, the information, which I contend was not
laid in time, and is, therefore, bad; and the justices hear the argument on the point

a
raised, and decide the objection is good. You should have asked for a "case" to raise the question. You have been negligent, and ought not to be allowed to recommence the litigation.

Colam.—It was difficult, from the nature of the case, to discover the offence, and in fact the magistrates were wrong in their view of the law.

STEPHEN, J.—Why did you not ask for a case to be stated?

Colam.—The seven days had elapsed.

b
STEPHEN, J.—That was the fault of the prosecutor.

HAWKINS, J.—If the magistrates decide wrongly, the remedy is to apply to them to state a case, and not apply for a *mandamus*, which is both expensive and vexatious. The magistrates heard and decided the case.

Per Curiam.—There was no ground for this application, as the magistrates had in fact heard and decided the case.'

c
I can for myself see no way of reconciling these two decisions. It cannot possibly be said that Hawkins and Stephen JJ in the earlier case did not have in mind the provisions of s 33 of the Summary Jurisdiction Act 1879, especially as it was being asserted by counsel for the defence that there had been a determination of the matter by the magistrates. Furthermore, it is important to observe that the decision of this court in *Wakefield Local Board v West Riding Rly Co* (1866) 30 JP 628, on which Lord Hewart CJ

d
relied in *Pratt v AA Sites Ltd*, was made under s 2 of the old Summary Jurisdiction Act 1857, which was in different terms from s 33 of the 1879 Act. Section 2 of the 1857 Act commences with the words:

'After the hearing and determination by a Justice or Justices of the Peace of any information or complaint . . .'

e
It comes as no surprise that Blackburn J considered that these words were inapt to describe circumstances where justices had refused to hear and determine an information, on the ground that they had no jurisdiction to do so. However, s 33 of the 1879 Act commences with the words:

f
'(1.) Any person aggrieved who desires to question a conviction, order, determination, or other proceedings of a court of summary jurisdiction, on the ground that it is erroneous in point of law, or is in excess of jurisdiction . . .'

These words are certainly different from the opening words of s 2 of the 1857 Act, and I must confess that I, for my part, can see no reason why a decision of a magistrate, erroneous in point of law, to decline jurisdiction in a matter, should not be a 'determination . . . of a court of summary jurisdiction' which is 'erroneous in point of

g
law', within the meaning of those words in s 33. Such a reading is entirely consistent with the approach of Hawkins and Stephen JJ in *R v Wisbech Justices*. I cannot help thinking that this is the view which they must have formed of the construction of the section.

I feel bound to say, with all due respect, that I do not find the reasoning of this court in *Pratt v AA Sites Ltd* persuasive. Lord Hewart CJ simply cited the decision under the

h
earlier statute, without considering the different wording of the two statutes. Humphreys J simply stated, without reasons, that 'the later statute does not extend to get rid of the rule which existed long before it was passed'. Faced with two inconsistent decisions of this court, it is open to this court, having heard full argument on the point, to hold that the later decision, made by a court to which the earlier decision was not cited, was made per incuriam. In my judgment, the appropriate conclusion in the

j
circumstances of the case is not to follow the decision of the court in *Pratt v AA Sites Ltd* but to prefer the decision in *R v Wisbech Justices*.

In these circumstances, it is necessary to consider the course to be taken in the present case. Having regard to the influence of *Pratt v AA Sites Ltd* on the course of action adopted by both parties, it would, I consider, be open to this court, exceptionally, to exercise its discretion to proceed by way of judicial review and make an order for certiorari.

However, it so happens that the magistrate has in fact stated a case for the opinion of the court, though that case has not been proceeded with. In those circumstances, there being no prejudice to the respondent in so proceeding, I consider that the appropriate course is to give leave to the applicant to set down the case stated for hearing out of time and to treat this hearing as being the hearing of the case stated.

On this basis, the application for judicial review should be dismissed and the question posed for the opinion of the court in the case stated, viz 'whether, after an information has been laid for an offence under Regulations made under the Gas Act, 1972, the prosecution may produce a fresh certificate pursuant to Section 43(2) Gas Act, 1972, in order to cure a defect in a certificate before the Court when the information was laid', should be answered in the affirmative.

Finally, I turn to consider whether the court should remit the matter to the magistrate to continue with the hearing of the informations. The circumstances of the case are, in my opinion, exceptional. Nearly two years have elapsed since the time of the commission of the offences charged in the informations. Over two years will, in all probability, have elapsed before they are heard, if they are now remitted to the magistrate. Prima facie, the time within which informations should be laid before a magistrate is six months from the commission of the offence, in the present case by early March 1982. In fact, since the explosion occurred in 1981, the informations could, I have no doubt, have been laid within the six-month period and, if the relevant procedures had been properly complied with, the hearing could have taken place not long after. But there were a number of delays.

First, there was the failure of communication between the department and the police, which resulted in the six-month limitation period being allowed to elapse, and the evidence not being placed before the Secretary of State until late May 1982. Then, the informations were not laid until 17 August 1982, and it was not until 21 October 1982, on the occasion of the first hearing before the magistrates' court, that the defence had a sight of the informations. Further delay was then caused by the fact that the certificate attached to the information, purporting to have been issued under s 43(2) of the 1972 Act, was ultra vires. True, that matter was corrected by a new certificate, dated 9 December 1982, and the decision of the magistrate to decline to accept that new certificate has been held to be erroneous. But, in all reality, it has to be recognised that the point was not free from difficulty, and that the origin of the delay resulting from the need to come to this court lay in the ultra vires certificate itself. That delay has, moreover, to some extent been prolonged by the change in the procedure adopted by the Director of Public Prosecutions, very understandably, on the authority of *Pratt v AA Sites Ltd*, a case which, after argument, I have concluded should not be followed.

I recognise, of course, the seriousness of the charges made against the respondents, but it seems to me that, in the somewhat exceptional circumstances of this case, the delay and the causes of that delay are such that, in the exercise of its discretion, this court should not remit the matter back to the magistrate for hearing.

For these reasons, apart from dismissing the application for judicial review and answering the question in the case stated in the affirmative, I would make no further order in the matter, save for any order as to costs which may be appropriate.

FORBES J. I agree.

Application dismissed. Leave to set down case stated for hearing out of time granted. Hearing of application for judicial review treated as hearing of case stated. Question for opinion of the court in the case stated answered in affirmative. Applicant's costs to be paid out of central funds. Order as to costs below quashed.

Solicitors: *Director of Public Prosecutions; Underwood & Co* (for the respondents).

N P Metcalfe Esq   Barrister.

a # R H & D International Ltd v IAS Animal Air Services Ltd

QUEEN'S BENCH DIVISION (COMMERCIAL COURT)
NEILL J
21 OCTOBER, 10 NOVEMBER, 6 DECEMBER 1983

b

Carriers – Contract – Carriage by road – Freight – Claim for freight – Set-off – Counterclaim for loss caused by delay in delivery – Whether right of set-off for counterclaim for delay maintainable in carrier's claim for freight – Carriage of Goods by Road Act 1965, Sch, arts 32(4), 36.

c The well-established rule of common law that a carrier's claim for freight is to be paid in full on delivery of the cargo and cannot be subject to any deduction or abatement by way of a set-off counterclaiming against the carrier in respect of the cargo, whether the counterclaim be for loss or damage to the cargo or for delay in delivery, is not confined to contracts of carriage by sea but extends to claims for freight for the carriage of goods by road which are subject to the Convention on the Contract for the International Carriage of Goods by Road (CMR) as set out in the schedule to the Carriage of Goods by
d Road Act 1965, notwithstanding that arts 32(4)[a] and 36[b] of the CMR contemplate that a counterclaim against the carrier may be exercised by way of set-off. Accordingly, where a carrier claims for freight under a contract which is subject to the CMR it is not open to the consigner to counterclaim by way of set-off for losses suffered because of delay in delivery (see p 205 h j and p 206 a to e, post).

e *Aries Tanker Corp v Total Transport Ltd* [1977] 1 All ER 398 and dictum of Roskill LJ in *A/S Gunnstein & Co K/S v Jensen, The Alfa Nord* [1977] 2 Lloyd's Rep at 436 applied.

Notes

For the carriage of goods by road generally, see 5 Halsbury's Laws (4th edn) paras 417–418.
f   For actions for freight, see ibid para 445.

For remedies against carriers, see ibid paras 452–455.

For the Carriage of Goods by Road Act 1965, Sch, arts 32, 36, see 28 Halsbury's Statutes (3rd edn) 455, 456.

Cases referred to in judgment

g *Aries Tanker Corp v Total Transport Ltd* [1977] 1 All ER 398, [1977] 1 WLR 185, HL.
A/S Gunnstein & Co K/S v Jensen, The Alfa Nord [1977] 2 Lloyd's Rep 434, CA.
Concorde Express Transport Ltd v Lecalite Contracts Ltd (7 March 1978, unreported), QBD.
Fleetview Ltd v Hart (29 March 1983, unreported), QBD.
Italmondo v SIP Industrial Products Ltd (20 January 1978, unreported), QBD.
M & S Shipping Ltd v Simon International Haulage Ltd (1 November 1977, unreported),
h QBD.
Seawheel Ltd v Henry G Collins & Co Ltd (8 May 1979, unreported), QBD.
Silver Wind v Wood Shipping (27 April 1977, unreported), QBD.

Summons for final judgment

By a writ indorsed with statement of claim issued on 3 August 1983 the plaintiffs,
j R H & D International Ltd, claimed against the defendants, IAS Animal Air Services Ltd, the total sum of £3,643·60 for freight charges in respect of the carriage of goods from England to Verona, Italy and from Verona to Bristol. By a summons dated 15 September 1983 the plaintiffs applied for final judgment in the action under RSC Ord 14 in respect of £2,643·60 of the amount claimed. The summons was heard in chambers but

---

a   Article 32(4) is set out at p 205 c, post
b   Article 36 is set out at p 205 d, post

judgment was given by Neill J in open court at the request of the parties. The facts are
set out in the judgment.   *a*

David Mildon for the plaintiffs.
Austin Allison for the defendants.

                                                                          Cur adv vult
                                                                                      b

6 December. The following judgment was delivered.

NEILL J. This matter was heard in chambers, but at the request of the parties and also
in accordance with my own inclination I am giving judgment in open court.

Before the court is a summons for judgment under RSC Ord 14. The plaintiffs,
R H & D International Ltd, carry on business as haulage contractors. In the middle of   *c*
December 1982 the plaintiffs agreed to transport a quantity of cartons from Sunbury-on-
Thames to Verona in Italy. The total weight of the consignment was about 19 tons. The
goods were carried in two trailers. The first part of the plaintiffs' claim is the charge for
freight for this consignment, amounting to £1,850. The claim in respect of one trailer is
£850, and in respect of the other trailer it is £1,000.

The second part of the plaintiffs' claim is in respect of three loads of penning equipment   *d*
transported by the plaintiffs on the instructions of the defendants from addresses in Italy
to England. The invoices in respect of these loads amount to £1,793·60.

The total claim is therefore for £3,643·60. It is common ground that the relevant
contracts of carriage were subject to the Convention on the Contract for the International
Carriage of Goods by Road (CMR) which is set out in the schedule to the Carriage of
Goods by Road Act 1965.   *e*

The defendants seek to resist the plaintiffs' claim by means of arguments on the
following lines: (1) that it was an express term of the contract for the delivery of the
goods to Verona that they should be delivered at Verona airport not later than noon on
15 December 1982 so that they could be loaded on to an aircraft for Lagos and Accra;
that only 5½ tons of the goods were delivered in time; and that as a result the defendants
suffered loss in excess of £8,000; (2) that it was an express term of the contracts for the   *f*
transportation of the penning equipment from Italy to England that the equipment
should be delivered in time to be used on a flight from Bristol on 18 January 1983; that
none of the equipment was delivered in time; and that as a result the defendants suffered
loss in excess of £2,000; (3) that the defendants are entitled to set off against the plaintiffs'
claim their counterclaim in respect of these losses, though it is conceded that under art
23.5 of the CMR the counterclaim is limited to the amount of the freight; (4) that this   *g*
set-off can be maintained despite the rule in *Aries Tanker Corp v Total Transport Ltd* [1977]
1 All ER 398, [1977] 1 WLR 185 because (a) the breaches by the plaintiffs were
repudiatory so that the rule has no application, (b) the rule does not apply to contracts for
international carriage by road which are governed by the CMR, (c) the rule does not
apply to contracts governed by the CMR where the counterclaim is in respect of loss
caused by delay; (5) that the sum of £850 was the agreed charge for the whole 19 tons   *h*
transported from Sunbury-on-Thames to Verona.

I propose to deal with these arguments under three headings. Before I do so, however,
I should mention that the plaintiffs accept that there is a triable issue whether the freight
for the journey to Verona should include charges for two trailers rather than one.
Accordingly the sum for which the plaintiffs now seek summary judgment is reduced to
£2,643·60.   *j*

Repudiation
Counsel argued on behalf of the defendants that the underlying purpose of all the
contracts was that the goods should be delivered in time to be taken by air to the specified
destinations and that the late deliveries were in the circumstances repudiatory breaches.
He conceded that repudiation had not been pleaded in the draft points of defence but
submitted that the facts pleaded were sufficient to raise an arguable case of fundamental

breach. The difficulty about this argument, however, as counsel for the plaintiffs pointed
out, is that, even if any breach by the plaintiffs was repudiatory, the repudiation was
never accepted by the defendants. I see no answer to counsel for the plaintiffs' objection
to a possible defence of repudiation. There is no evidence that the defendants elected to
rescind the contracts by accepting a repudiation by the plaintiffs.

The application of the CMR

Counsel for the defendants submitted that the rule in *The Aries* should not be extended
to claims for freight for the carriage of goods by road; it was an anomalous rule, which
should be limited to carriage by sea. Furthermore, he said, there were clear indications
in the CMR itself that the right to set off a counterclaim was recognised. He drew my
attention to paragraphs in two articles set out in the schedule to the Carriage of Goods by
Road Act 1965. Article 32, which is in Ch V dealing with 'Claims and Actions', provides
in para 4:

> 'A right of action which has become barred by lapse of time may not be exercised
> by way of counter-claim or set-off.'

And art 36, which is in Ch VI dealing with 'Provisions relating to carriage performed by
successive carriers', provides:

> 'Except in the case of a counter-claim or a set-off raised in an action concerning a
> claim based on the same contract of carriage, legal proceedings in respect of liability
> for loss, damage or delay may only be brought against the first carrier, the last carrier
> or the carrier who was performing that portion of the carriage during which the
> event causing the loss, damage or delay occurred; an action may be brought at the
> same time against several of these carriers.'

Counsel for the defendants submitted that art 32(4) plainly contemplated that a right of
action that was *not* barred by lapse of time *could* be exercised by way of counterclaim or
set-off, and that, as some of the periods of limitation prescribed in art 32(1) applied to
claims by consignees, the article read as a whole suggested that a claim by a consignee
which was not barred by lapse of time could properly be exercised by way of set-off.
Moreover, art 36 was concerned in terms with legal proceedings 'in respect of liability
for loss, damage or delay' and therefore the opening words of the article, which were by
way of an excepting provision, were also wholly consistent with there being a right to set
off a claim in respect of such liability against a claim for freight.

Counsel for the plaintiffs, on the other hand, argued that the rule in *The Aries* did apply
to contracts subject to the CMR. He referred me to six unreported cases at first instance
and provided me with notes of the judgments in five of them. The cases date from 1977
and are as follows: *Silver Wind v Wood Shipping* (27 April 1977, unreported) Donaldson J;
M & S Shipping Ltd v Simon International Haulage Ltd (1 November 1977, unreported)
Forbes J; *Italmondo v SIP Industrial Products Ltd* (20 January 1978, unreported) Donaldson
J; *Concorde Express Transport Ltd v Lecalite Contracts Ltd* (7 March 1978, unreported)
Parker J; *Seawheel Ltd v Henry G Collins & Co Ltd* (8 May 1979, unreported) Mustill J;
Fleetview Ltd v Hart (29 March 1983, unreported) Lawson J.

In each of these six cases the plaintiffs obtained summary judgment for unpaid freight
due for carriage of goods under the CMR despite the fact that the defendants made
counterclaims for damage to or loss of the goods. In each case the court applied the
principle in *The Aries* on the basis that it was of general application to all claims for
freight, though Donaldson J suggested that there might be an overriding discretion if
there was a real risk that a counterclaim if successful would be valueless. According to
the notes I have seen, however, in only one of these cases was any express reference made
to arts 32 and 36. In the *Seawheel* case Mustill J said:

> 'I should mention the argument of the defendant relating to arts 32 and 36 of
> CMR, namely that counterclaims can be the subject of a set-off. It may be that this
> was in the contemplation of the draftsman. It seems to me that he has done no more
> than contemplate the possibility of a set-off. I find it impossible to transfer that into

a contractual right of set-off when it would not otherwise have existed. There will accordingly be judgment for the plaintiff.'

For my part I see some force in the argument of counsel for the defendants based on arts 32(4) and 36, but I am quite satisfied that, even if I had been fully persuaded by his argument, it would be wrong for me as a judge of first instance to introduce uncertainty into this branch of the law by reaching a decision in conflict with the earlier decisions to which I have been referred and which now extend over a period of 6½ years. I have also in mind the fact that in *The Aries* [1977] 1 All ER 398 at 404, [1977] 1 WLR 185 at 190 itself Lord Wilberforce (in a passage on which Donaldson J relied in *The Silver Wind* case) said this in relation to the rule of deduction or abatement:

'There is no case of its having been extended to contracts of any kind of carriage. The rule against deduction in cases of carriage by sea is, in fact, as well settled as any common law rule can be.'

Delay

Counsel for the defendants further argued that, even if the rule in *The Aries* had to be extended to the CMR cases where goods had been lost or damaged, it would be wrong to extend the rule to cases of delay. I find myself unable to draw this suggested distinction between cases of delay and cases of damage or loss. It is sufficient for me to refer to the judgment of Roskill LJ in *A/S Gunnstein & Co K/S v Jensen, The Alfa Nord* [1977] 2 Lloyd's Rep 434 at 436, where he said:

'We have to apply the well-established principle that there is no right of set off for claims for damages for breach of charter, whether for loss of or damage to goods or for alleged failure to prosecute a voyage with reasonable despatch or otherwise, against a claim for freight.'

Accordingly I am satisfied that if the rule in *The Aries* has to be applied to carriage under the CMR no right of set-off exists even where the cross claim relates to delay.

Finally, I should mention a further argument which counsel for the plaintiffs put forward in relation to the alleged counterclaim concerning the voyage to Verona in December 1982. He conceded that there was a triable counterclaim in respect of the journeys to England in 1983, but he submitted that the counterclaim for loss on the journey to Verona could not be sustained because no written 'reservation' had been sent to the plaintiffs within the 21-day time limit imposed by art 30(3) of the CMR. Counsel for the defendants sought to counter this argument by reliance on a telex from the plaintiffs dated 29 December 1982, which was not exhibited to any affidavit but which I looked at without any objection by counsel for the plaintiffs. Counsel for the defendants argued that the effect of this telex, in which a detailed explanation was given of the circumstances which caused the delay, amounted to a waiver by the plaintiffs of the necessity for a written reservation. On the evidence at present before me I am unable to accept that argument. The telex could only be treated as a waiver if it amounted to a representation by the plaintiffs that they would not seek to rely on the time limit and if it could be shown that the defendants acted on the strength of that representation. Had it been necessary for me to reach a conclusion on this point for the purpose of the Ord 14 proceedings, I would therefore have been disposed to hold that the counterclaim in respect of the first consignment had little prospect of success. In view of my conclusion about the application of the rule in *The Aries*, however, it is unnecessary for me to say any more about this part of the case. At the trial, further relevant evidence may be forthcoming.

In these circumstances, for the reasons which I have endeavoured to outline, there will be judgment for the plaintiffs for £2,643·60, and the defendants will have unconditional leave to defend for the balance of £1,000.

Judgment for plaintiffs for £2,643·60. Leave to defend for balance of claim of £1,000.

Solicitors: *Boodle Hatfield & Co*, Southampton (for the plaintiffs); *Coole & Haddock*, Worthing (for the defendants).

K Mydeen Esq   Barrister.

Leal v Dunlop Bio-Processes International Ltd

COURT OF APPEAL, CIVIL DIVISION
STEPHENSON, MAY AND SLADE LJJ
30, 31 JANUARY, 13 FEBRUARY 1984

Practice – Service out of the jurisdiction – Writ – Leave – Service without leave – Validity of writ and limitation period for action expired – Whether failure to get leave for service out of jurisdiction rendering service of writ a nullity or merely an 'irregularity' which can be cured – Whether if irregularity court having power to cure by granting leave for service out of jurisdiction retroactively – Whether if court having that power it should exercise it – Whether improper for court to grant retroactive leave for service out of jurisdiction if improper for court to exercise discretion to renew writ because action statute-barred – RSC Ord 2, r 1, Ord 11, r 1, Ord 12, rr 7, 8.

On 20 May 1981, just within the limitation period, the plaintiff (without obtaining the leave of the court) issued a writ claiming damages for negligence against the defendants, a company whose registered office was outside the jurisdiction. On 18 May 1982, just before the 12-month period of the writ's validity expired but after the expiry of the limitation period for the action, the plaintiff's solicitors purported to serve the writ on the defendant out of the jurisdiction without first obtaining the leave of the court pursuant to RSC Ord 11, r 1*a*. The defendants, who were aware of the failure to obtain the court's leave for service out of the jurisdiction, acknowledged the service of the writ and then applied, under RSC Ord 12, r 8*b*, to set aside the service by reason of the irregularity therein caused by the failure to obtain the court's leave (the irregularity not having been waived by the acknowledgment of service by virtue of Ord 12, r 7*c*). The defendants also applied to dismiss the action on the ground of the failure to obtain the court's leave to serve the writ out of the jurisdiction. On 12 July the plaintiff cross-applied for an order under RSC Ord 6, r 8(2) for the renewal of the writ and for leave under Ord 11, r 1 to serve the renewed writ out of the jurisdiction. On 30 July the registrar dismissed the defendants' applications and in effect gave the plaintiff leave retroactively to serve the original writ out of the jurisdiction. The defendants appealed to the judge, who held that, although the service of the writ out of the jurisdiction without the court's leave was not a nullity but merely an irregularity in the service, it would be a wrong exercise of his discretion under Ord 2, r 1*d* to rectify the irregularity if he were to give leave under Ord 11, r 1 retroactively to serve the writ out of the jurisdiction. Accordingly, he refused to cure the irregularity in service by retroactively granting leave. He also refused the plaintiff's alternative application for an extension of the validity of the writ and for leave to serve the writ out of the jurisdiction, on the ground that to grant that application would infringe the general rule that the validity of a writ ought not to be extended if to do so would deprive a defendant of a defence under a statute of limitation unless there were exceptional circumstances, which he held did not exist in the circumstances. The plaintiff appealed to the Court of Appeal, submitting that the failure to obtain the court's leave to serve the writ out of the jurisdiction was a mere irregularity which the court could and should cure by exercising its power under Ord 2, r 1.

Held – (1) Having regard to the wide wording of RSC Ord 12, rr 7 and 8 and of Ord 2, r 1, a failure to get the court's leave to serve a writ out of the jurisdiction in accordance with Ord 11, r 1 was an 'irregularity' in the service of the writ within Ord 12, r 7 and an 'irregularity' within Ord 2, r 1 which the court had power to cure under Ord 2, r 1 by

---

a   Rule 1, so far as material, is set out at p 211 *g*, post
b   Rule 8, so far as material, is set out at p 212 *e*, post
c   Rule 7 is set out at p 212 *d*, post
d   Rule 1, so far as material, is set out at p 211 *d* to *f*, post

retroactively giving leave under Ord 11, r 1 to serve the writ out of the jurisdiction (see p 210 *j*, p 212 *g h*, p 213 *f* to *h* and p 215 *d e*, post).   *a*

(2) However, in the circumstances it would be a wrong exercise of the court's power under Ord 2, r 1 retroactively to grant the plaintiff leave to serve the writ out of the jurisdiction because (a) the procedure under Ord 11 was an exceptional enlargement of the pre-existing jurisdiction of the English courts, any misuse of which procedure the courts should restrain, and (b) it would have been an improper exercise of the registrar's discretion for him to have extended the validity of the plaintiff's writ under Ord 6, r 8   *b* for the purpose of enabling service of the renewed writ out of the jurisdiction with leave, since there were no special circumstances to justify the renewal of the writ when the action was statute-barred, and accordingly it would also be an improper exercise of the court's discretion to cure the irregularity in the service of the writ by means of an order under Ord 2, r 1 giving leave retroactively to serve the writ out of the jurisdiction. The appeal would therefore be dismissed (see p 210 *f g* and *j* to p 211 *a*, p 213 *a* to *h*,   *c* p 215 *d f* to *h* and p 216 *a*, post); *Heaven v Road and Rail Wagons Ltd* [1965] 2 All ER 409 applied; *Bernstein v Jackson* [1982] 2 All ER 806 explained.

Per May and Slade LJJ. Only in an exceptional case should the court, in the exercise of its power retroactively to make good irregular service of a writ out of the jurisdiction, validate after the event the purported service out of the jurisdiction without leave of process issued by an English court (see p 213 *g h* and p 215 *j*, post).   *d*

Notes

For service of a writ out of the jurisdiction with leave and for applications for leave, see 37 Halsbury's Laws (4th edn) paras 172, 190, and for cases on the subject, see 37(2) Digest (Reissue) 326–336, 2026–2092.

For disputing jurisdiction for irregularity in service of process, see 37 Halsbury's Laws   *e* (4th edn) paras 209–210, and for cases on the subject, see 37(2) Digest (Reissue) 341, 2123–2127.

For the effect of non-compliance with the Rules of the Supreme Court and the power to rectify irregularities, see 37 Halsbury's Laws (4th edn) paras 36–39, and for cases on the subject, see 37(2) Digest (Reissue) 205–217, 1355–1412.   *f*

Cases referred to in judgments

Afro Continental Nigeria Ltd v Meridian Shipping Co SA, The Vrontados [1982] 2 Lloyd's Rep 241, CA.

Bernstein v Jackson [1982] 2 All ER 806, [1982] 1 WLR 1082, CA.

Chappell v Cooper, Player v Bruguire [1980] 2 All ER 463, [1980] 1 WLR 958, CA.   *g*

Evans v Bartlam [1937] 2 All ER 646, [1937] AC 473, HL.

Harkness v Bell's Asbestos and Engineering Ltd [1966] 3 All ER 843, [1967] 2 QB 729, [1967] 2 WLR 29, CA.

Heaven v Road and Rail Wagons Ltd [1965] 2 All ER 409, [1965] 2 QB 355, [1965] 2 WLR 1249.

Pritchard (decd), Re [1963] 1 All ER 873, [1963] Ch 502, [1963] 2 WLR 685, CA.   *h*

Tsai v Woodworth (1983) Times, 30 November, CA.

Tyne Improvement Comrs v Armement Anversois SA, The Brabo [1949] 1 All ER 294, [1949] AC 326, HL.

Interlocutory appeal

The plaintiff, Robert Frederick Thomas Leal, appealed from the order of Neill J made on   *j* 12 November 1982 allowing the appeal of the defendants, Dunlop Bio-Processes International Ltd (Dunlop), whose registered office was out of the jurisdiction, in Jersey, from the order of the district registrar in Newport, Isle of Wight, District Registry refusing to set aside the service out of the jurisdiction without leave of the writ in an action by the plaintiff against Dunlop claiming damages for negligence and refusing to dismiss the plaintiff's action for failure to get that leave. Neill J set aside the service of the

writ and refused to extend the validity of the writ. The facts are set out in the judgment
of Stephenson LJ.

David Tucker for the plaintiff.
Edwin Glasgow for Dunlop.

Cur adv vult

13 February. The following judgments were delivered.

STEPHENSON LJ. This is an appeal by the plaintiff against an order of Neill J made
on 12 November 1982, by leave of the judge granted on 17 December 1982, setting aside
the service of a writ on the defendants (to whom I refer as 'Dunlop') and refusing to
extend the validity of the writ.

Dunlop's registered office is in the Channel Island of Jersey, which is admittedly
outside the jurisdiction. The plaintiff's writ was issued out of the Newport district
registry in the Isle of Wight on 20 May 1981, just in time to avoid being statute-barred,
claiming damages for personal injuries alleged to have been sustained by the negligence
of Dunlop, in the course of the plaintiff's employment by them under a contract in
writing expressed to be subject to English law, in Malaya on 27 May 1978. It was issued,
without leave of the court, after correspondence thinly spread by the plaintiff's solicitors
and Eagle Star, Dunlop's insurers, over more than two years. On 8 March 1979 the
plaintiff's solicitors wrote to Dunlop to notify them that a claim for damages was being
made. On 27 May 1981 Dunlop's insurers, whose replies to the plaintiff's solicitors had
been unhelpful, wrote informing the plaintiff's solicitors that they wished the proceedings
to be served on Dunlop direct.

Nearly a year later, on 18 May 1982, the plaintiff's solicitors' agents in Jersey purported
to serve the writ on Dunlop in Jersey, the day before the writ expired, again without
leave of the court.

If the writ was 'to be served out of the jurisdiction' the plaintiff required the leave of
the court to issue it. There is some doubt whether this writ was to be served out of the
jurisdiction, because a writ against a foreign defendant, and Dunlop are admittedly a
foreign defendant, can be marked 'Not to be served out of the jurisdiction' and no one
can tell us whether this writ or any copy of it was so marked. But there is no doubt that
the plaintiff required the leave of the court (and I find it hard to avoid the use of the word
'required') to serve the writ out of the jurisdiction in Jersey: see Ord 11, r 1.

Dunlop's solicitors knew this. On 9 June 1982 they returned an acknowledgment of
service on the newly prescribed form accompanying the writ as required by Ord 10,
r 1(6), and on 10 June they took out a summons under Ord 12, r 8 in the Newport district
registry applying to set aside the purported service of the writ and to dismiss the action
on the ground that the plaintiff had failed to obtain, pursuant to Ord 11, leave to serve it
out of the jurisdiction. On 19 July the plaintiff's solicitors took out a cross-summons
applying for an order that the writ be renewed under Ord 6, r 8(2) and for leave to serve
the renewed writ out of the jurisdiction under Ord 11, r 1.

On 30 July the registrar dismissed Dunlop's application. He did not give the plaintiff
leave to serve the writ out of the jurisdiction, nor did he extend the validity of the writ.
He simply dismissed Dunlop's application, but the judge rightly treated the real intention
of his order to be the grant of leave to serve the writ out of the jurisdiction ex post facto,
so that there was no need to renew the writ.

The principal argument of counsel for the plaintiff before the registrar and the judge,
ably repeated before this court, is that the failure to obtain the leave of the court to serve
the writ in Jersey was an irregularity, due to a mistake by the plaintiff's solicitors and
counsel, which could and should be put right by the exercise of the court's power under
Ord 2, r 1. That argument prevailed with the registrar, but not with the judge, who said
in an approved note of his reserved judgment that he was satisfied (1) 'that the service of
a writ out of the jurisdiction for which the leave of the court has not been obtained is not

a nullity' and (2) 'that the court cannot then given leave retroactively under Ord 11 by exercising the general power in Ord 2, r 1'. He added:

'It may be that such a power does exist in theory, but I am satisfied that in the light of the decision of the Court of Appeal in *Bernstein v Jackson* [1982] 2 All ER 806, [1982] 1 WLR 1082 it would be a wrong exercise of discretion for me to seek to cure this irregularity by exercising such a power.'

He expressed his conclusion thus:

'. . . I cannot or at any rate should not cure the irregularity of the service in Jersey by purporting to grant leave to serve out of the jurisdiction ex post facto.'

The second argument of counsel for the plaintiff was likewise rejected by the judge, who disposed of it in this way:

'He submitted that even if it were not permissible to cure the irregularity of service ex post facto the same result could be achieved by extending the validity of the writ and then giving leave to [the plaintiff] to issue a concurrent writ for service outside the jurisdiction on Dunlop in Jersey. The difficulty about this argument, however, is that the claim by [the plaintiff] is wholly or at any rate mainly in respect of personal injuries and is therefore subject to a three-year period of limitation prescribed by s 11 of the Limitation Act 1980. On this point I was referred by [counsel] on behalf of Dunlop to the decision of Megaw J in *Heaven v Road and Rail Wagons Ltd* [1965] 2 All ER 409, [1965] 2 QB 355. In the light of this decision and the more recent decision of the Court of Appeal in *Chappell v Cooper* [1980] 2 All ER 463, [1980] 1 WLR 958 I do not consider that there are any special circumstances in the present case which would justify me in granting leave to extend the validity of the original writ. In respect of any claim for damages for personal injuries the period of limitation expired at the end of May 1981. In my judgment no good or sufficient reason has been put forward on behalf of [the plaintiff] to entitle me to extend the validity of the writ ex post facto for any further period. It is true that the present case is distinguishable from *Bernstein v Jackson*, where the court could not in any event have extended the validity of the writ because more than 12 months had elapsed from the date of its expiry. Nevertheless there is a general and well-established rule that a writ will not be extended so as to deprive a defendant of a limitation defence except for some good reason. I see no such reason in the present case.'

I fully agree with that paragraph, with only one reservation. I agree that the present case is distinguishable from *Bernstein v Jackson*, but not for the reason given by Neill J. In that case the writ expired in December 1978, but in 1981, when it would have needed more than one extension, first the registrar and then the judge dispensed with non-renewal and the judge cured it as an irregularity under Ord 2, r 1. This court decided that he was wrong. Dunn LJ gave two reasons: (1) no jurisdiction ('I do not think that the judge *could* have extended the writ . . .' (my emphasis)); and (2) wrong exercise of discretion ('assuming that it [sic] could') (see [1982] 2 All ER 806 at 812, [1982] 1 WLR 1082 at 1089). Slade LJ agreed that the appeal should be allowed for the reasons given by Dunn LJ and said ([1982] 2 All ER 806 at 812, [1982] 1 WLR 1082 at 1089–1090): '. . . I do not think that [the judge] could have properly extended its validity for the reasons already given by Dunn LJ.'

If Dunn LJ meant to say that the judge had no power to extend the validity of the writ under Ord 6, r 8(2), even if an application to extend had been made, I respectfully consider that he was ignoring the terms of Ord 6, r 8(2); if he meant to say that the judge had no power to treat the failure to extend the writ as an irregularity under Ord 2, r 1, again I have to disagree with him, for the reasons I give later. So I would prefer to regard *Bernstein v Jackson* as decided on the ground, apparently preferred by Slade LJ, that there was an improper exercise of the judge's powers. It has long been a principle of the exercise of the court's discretion to renew a writ or to extend its validity, as the heading

of Ord 6, r 8 and the rule itself variously describe it, that the discretion should not be
a exercised retrospectively after the period of 12 months prescribed by the rules has expired
so as to deprive the defendant of a defence under a statute of limitation unless there are
exceptional circumstances. That principle has survived new rules (see *Heaven v Road and
Rail Wagons Ltd* [1965] 2 All ER 409, [1965] 2 QB 355) and new statutes of limitation (see
Chappell v Cooper [1980] 2 All ER 463, [1980] 1 WLR 459). To those cases may now be
added *Afro Continental Nigeria Ltd v Meridian Shipping Co SA, The Vrontados* [1982] 2
b Lloyd's Rep 241. The plaintiff's application to renew the writ, which expired on 20 May
1982, was made on 19 July 1982; but there was nothing exceptional in the mistake made
by the plaintiff's legal advisers, however serious, if incurable, its effect on his claim might
be. Though Dunlop were in fact aware that they were to be pursued in the courts when
the plaintiff's writ was served on 18 May 1982, uncertainty as to that matter is only one
of the factors listed by Megaw J in *Heaven's* case [1965] 2 All ER 409 at 416, [1965] 2 QB
c 355 at 366 on which he based the requirement that exceptional circumstances are
necessary to justify depriving a defendant of his statutory defence (see [1965] 2 All ER
409 at 413, [1965] 2 QB 355 at 361).

The main argument of counsel for the plaintiff has given me more difficulty. Has the
court the power to rectify the plaintiff's mistake in purporting to serve the writ without
getting the court's leave? And if it has the power, should it exercise it to validate the
d service on Dunlop? The argument for the plaintiff is that the court can and should under
Ord 2, r 1, which is headed 'Non-compliance with rules' and provides:

> '(1) Where, in beginning or purporting to begin any proceedings or at any stage
> in the course of or in connection with any proceedings, there has, by reason of any
> thing done or left undone, been a failure to comply with the requirements of these
> rules, whether in respect of time, place, manner, form or content or in any other
e > respect, the failure shall be treated an an irregularity and shall not nullify the
> proceedings, any step taken in the proceedings, or any document, judgment or
> order therein.
> (2) Subject to paragraph (3), the Court may, on the ground that there has been
> such a failure as is mentioned in paragraph (1), and on such terms as to costs or
> otherwise as it thinks just, set aside either wholly or in part the proceedings in which
f > the failure occurred, any step taken in those proceedings or any document, judgment
> or order therein or exercise its powers under these rules to allow such amendments
> (if any) to be made and to make such order (if any) dealing with the proceedings
> generally as it thinks fit . . .'

Order 11 r 1(1) provides that, except in some Admiralty actions—

g
> 'service of a writ out of the jurisdiction is permissible with the leave of the Court
> in the following cases, that is to say . . . (*f*) if the action begun by the writ is brought
> against a defendant not domiciled or ordinarily resident in Scotland . . . to recover
> damages . . . in respect of the breach of a contract . . . which . . . (iii) is by its terms
> . . . governed by English law . . .'

h Order 11, r 4 provides:

> '(1) An application for the grant of leave under Rule 1 or 2 must be supported by
> an affidavit stating the grounds on which the application is made and that, in the
> deponent's belief, the plaintiff has a good cause of action, and showing in what place
> or country the defendant is, or probably may be found.
> (2) No such leave shall be granted unless it shall be made sufficiently to appear to
j > the Court that the case is a proper one for service out of the jurisdiction under this
> Order . . .'

Here, submits counsel for the plaintiff, there has, by reason of a thing left undone,
namely the obtaining of leave of the court, been a failure to comply with the requirement
of Ord 11, r 1 that leave of the court must be obtained. That failure shall be treated as an
irregularity and shall not nullify the proceedings purporting to be begun by the plaintiff's

writ: see Ord 2, r 1(1). The court may, on the ground that there has been that failure, exercise its powers under the Rules of the Supreme Court to allow such amendments (if *a* any) to be made and to make such order (if any) dealing with the proceedings generally as it thinks fit: see Ord 2, r 1(2). And the order for which he asks is an order that leave to serve the writ on Dunlop in Jersey be granted, or be treated as having been granted, before the service of the writ on 18 May 1982. The cap fits exactly, whether or not it is measured by the comment of Lord Denning MR in *Harkness v Bell's Asbestos and Engineering Ltd* [1966] 3 All ER 843 at 845–846, [1967] 2 QB 729 at 735–736:   *b*

> 'This new rule does away with the old distinction between nullities and irregularities. Every omission or mistake in practice or procedure is henceforward to be regarded as an irregularity which the court can and should rectify so long as it can do so without injustice. It can at last be asserted that "it is not possible . . . for an honest litigant in Her Majesty's Supreme Court to be defeated by any mere *c* technicality, any slip, any mistaken step in his litigation." That could not be said in 1963; see *Re Pritchard (decd.)* ([1963] 1 All ER 873 at 879, [1963] Ch 502 at 518); but it can be in 1966. The new rule does it.'

But the question whether this omission to get leave is to be treated as an irregularity by this rule is now answered by the rules themselves. Order 2, r 2 provides generally for applications to set aside for irregularity in proceedings. The new rr 7 and 8 of Ord 12 *d* provide:

> '**7.** The acknowledgment by a defendant of service of a writ shall not be treated as a waiver by him of any irregularity in the writ or service thereof or in any order giving leave to serve the writ out of the jurisdiction or extending the validity of the writ for the purpose of service.
> **8.**—(1) A defendant who wishes to dispute the jurisdiction of the court in the *e* proceedings by reason of any such irregularity as is mentioned in rule 7 or on any other ground shall give notice of intention to defend the proceedings and shall, within 14 days thereafter, apply to the Court for—(a) an order setting aside the writ or service of the writ on him . . .'

What Dunlop did on 10 June 1982 was to apply under Ord 12, r 8 to set aside the *f* service of the writ by reason of an irregularity mentioned in r 7, an irregularity in the service of the writ, which they had by virtue of r 7 not waived by acknowledging service of it. The note headed 'Dispute as to Irregularity in Issue or Service of Writ' in *The Supreme Court Practice 1982* vol 1, p 133, para 12/7–8/10 takes the same view as Dunlop did. So, I think, did the judge in holding that the service of the writ was not a nullity and in referring to a defendant being 'irregularly served' and to the 'irregularity' of the service *g* more than once.

I accordingly do not share the judge's doubt whether the failure to get the court's leave to serve this writ out of the jurisdiction is an irregularity which the court has the power to cure. It is a failure to comply with a requirement of Ord 11, r 1. Leave of the court for permission to serve a writ out of the jurisdiction is as clearly a requirement of Ord 11, r 1 as leave of the court for the issue of a writ which is to be served out of the jurisdiction is *h* a requirement of Ord 6, r 7. Each rule requires the leave of the court in different language. I have come to the conclusion that Ord 2, r 1 gives the court the power to make good the service of the writ and the judge *could* have given leave retroactively.

That, however, does not decide the appeal in the plaintiff's favour because the question remains: *should* he have exercised his discretion in the plaintiff's favour? He concluded that that would be a wrong exercise of his discretion in the light of the decision in *j* *Bernstein v Jackson* [1982] 2 All ER 806, [1982] 1 WLR 1082. We can only interfere with his exercise of his discretion in that way if satisfied that it was plainly wrong; for counsel for the plaintiff has not been able to point to any of those specific errors which entitle this court to interfere, or to claim that the judge's decision will result in injustice being done to the plaintiff: see *Evans v Bartlam* [1937] 2 All ER 646 at 650, [1937] AC 473 at 480. For it is common ground that this case is another instance of the game played between

defendants' insurance companies and solicitors' insurance companies which Ormrod LJ
a deplored in *Chappell v Cooper* [1980] 2 All ER 463 at 470, [1980] 1 WLR 958 at 967.

For my part I am not satisfied that the judge's decision was wrong. I am not sure that I
should have made the same decision myself, but I probably would and that anyhow is
not the question raised by an appeal of this kind. The mistake which required correction
was serious. True it was not always the law that the court's leave was required *before*
service of a writ out of the jurisdiction; ss 18 and 19 of the Common Law Procedure Act
b 1852 allowed service of the writ to be followed by the grant of liberty to proceed.
However, the procedure for which Ord 11 provides is an exceptional enlargement of our
courts' jurisdiction: see, for example, *Tyne Improvement Comrs v Armement Anversois SA,
The Brabo* [1949] 1 All ER 294 at 298, [1949] AC 326 at 338 per Lord Porter. The court's
restraining hand is an important restriction on the misuse of the procedure, and r 4(2)
underlines its importance. It is, as counsel for Dunlop pointed out, by no means certain
c that the plaintiff would in all the circumstances, including his delay, have surmounted
the barrier of r 4(2) in May 1981. Purporting to bypass the restriction, even by accident,
was what Dunn LJ in *Bernstein's* case [1982] 2 All ER 806 at 812, [1982] 1 WLR 1082 at
1089 called 'such a fundamental defect in the proceedings that the judge should not have
exercised his discretion to make an order under Ord 2, r 1'. I share the opinion of Slade
LJ that, if it is wrong to allow the plaintiff to continue these statute-barred proceedings
d by extending the validity of his writ under Ord 6, r 8 to enable the plaintiff to apply to
issue a concurrent writ for service out of the jurisdiction under Ord 6, r 6, it must be
wrong to allow him to continue them by giving him leave to serve it out of the
jurisdiction under Ord 11, r 1. Order 2, r 1 should not be invoked to allow either course.
The mistake has not resulted in real prejudice to Dunlop, but it was not an irregularity
fit to be cured under Ord 2, r 1 like the mistake in *Tsai v Woodworth* (1983) Times, 30
e November.

That was the view of the mistake which commended itself to the judge and in spite of
the persuasive submissions of counsel for the plaintiff it commends itself now to me. I
would therefore dismiss the appeal.

MAY LJ. I too would dismiss this appeal for the reasons given by Stephenson LJ.
f However I confess that I have changed my mind more than once about the correct
answer to the questions, first, whether the issue and purported service of a writ out of the
jurisdiction without prior leave of the court can be treated as an irregularity and must
not be considered a nullity, and, second, whether the court has power under the Rules of
the Supreme Court to grant such leave retroactively. In the end, I have come to the
conclusion that the wording of Ord 2, r 1 and Ord 12, rr 7 and 8 is now so wide that the
g answer to both these questions must be in the affirmative. Nevertheless I hope and expect
that it will only be in the exceptional case that the court will validate after the event the
purported service in a foreign country without leave of process issued by an English
court. In the present case I respectfully think that the judge was right to set aside the
service of the writ and to refuse to extend its validity.

h **SLADE LJ.** Subject to one reservation, I respectfully agree with the judgments of
Stephenson and May LJJ. The reservation relates to the observations of Stephenson LJ
concerning the decision in *Bernstein v Jackson* [1982] 2 All ER 806, [1982] 1 WLR 1082,
to which I was a party with Dunn LJ.

The facts of that case were unusual. The plaintiffs had obtained a monetary judgment
in South Africa against the first defendant. On 7 December 1977 they issued a writ in
j England against the first defendant claiming the money in her account with an English
building society and joining the society as second defendant. The first defendant was
then resident in South Africa. The plaintiffs obtained leave to serve the notice of the writ
out of the jurisdiction, but service was not effected. The writ ceased to be valid for service
after 6 December 1978, 12 months from the date of its issue. It was never renewed in
accordance with RSC Ord 6, r 8. On 28 January 1981, after the first defendant had
returned to live in England, the district registrar, on the plaintiffs' application, made a

most unusual order. Even though no application to renew the writ was before him, he
gave the plaintiffs leave to serve notice of the writ on the first defendant by substituted   *a*
service by serving a copy of the notice on the building society. He made no order for the
renewal of the writ. Proceedings were handed by the society to the first defendant, who
did not acknowledge service or effect an appearance. Thereupon judgment in default
was signed against her. She then applied to set aside the order for substituted service, and
the judgment, for irregularity.

Lawson J, who heard her application on 23 November 1981, accepted that the order of   *b*
28 January 1981 was irregular, because he considered that it was a condition precedent
of obtaining an order for substituted service of notice of a writ that there must be a writ
valid for service. He held that the writ was not valid for service because it had not been
renewed in accordance with the provisions of Ord 6, r 8. But he accepted the plaintiffs'
argument based on Ord 2, r 1, saying this:

> 'Finally he relies on the provisions of Ord 2, r 1 as his longstop, and I take the   *c*
> view that he is entitled to rely on the provisions of Ord 2, r 1, and that,
> notwithstanding the irregularity caused by the non-renewal of the writ and the
> irregularity of the order made on 28 January 1981, I should uphold the validity of
> that order.'

(See [1982] 2 All ER 806 at 812, [1982] 1 WLR 1082 at 1089.)   *d*

He proceeded to order that the first defendant should have liberty to defend the action
on condition that she filed a memorandum of appearance or acknowledgment of service
within 14 days.

The plaintiffs then appealed from this order. The principal judgment of this court was
delivered by Dunn LJ. The ratio of his decision to allow the appeal is to be found in the
following passage ([1982] 2 All ER 806 at 812, [1982] 1 WLR 1082 at 1089):   *e*

> 'I do not think that the judge could have extended the writ under Ord 6, r 8 and,
> that being the case, I think that there is great force in the submission that Ord 6, r 8
> provides a compendious code for extension and renewal of writs, and that it is not
> the type of irregularity which it was envisaged could be dealt with by the provisions
> of Ord 2, r 1. But, assuming that it could, in my view this was such a fundamental   *f*
> defect in the proceedings that the judge should not have exercised his discretion to
> make an order under Ord 2, r 1. Accordingly, I would allow the appeal and I would
> set aside the writ under the provisions of Ord 2, r 1(2) and also the order for
> substituted service on the ground of the plaintiffs' failure to comply with the
> requirements of Ord 6, r 8(2).'

In a short judgment, I agreed that the appeal should be allowed for the reasons given   *g*
by Dunn LJ. I quoted the passage from the judgment of Lawson J, cited above, and said
([1982] 2 All ER 806 at 812, [1982] 1 WLR 1082 at 1089–1090):

> 'The judge did not explicitly state what he meant by the phrase "uphold the
> validity of that order". However, it was necessarily implicit in his judgment that he
> thought it right, notwithstanding all the previous irregularities, to treat the writ as   *h*
> a writ which had been validly renewed. If a specific application to renew the writ
> had been before him, I do not think that he could have properly extended its validity
> for the reasons already given by Dunn LJ. Correspondingly, I do not think that the
> plaintiffs can be in a better position than they would have been if such a specific
> application had been before the judge.'

While, of course, I cannot speak for Dunn LJ, I think that the principal points which I   *j*
had in mind in agreeing with his judgment and saying what I did say were these.
(1) Lawson J himself had said, correctly in my opinion, that it was a condition precedent
to obtaining an order for substituted service that there must be a writ valid for service.
(2) Accordingly, in upholding the order for substituted service made by the district

registrar on 28 January 1981, Lawson J must have been implicitly treating the writ as
a one which had been renewed so as to be valid for service on 28 January 1981. (3) If,
however, a specific application to renew the writ had been before him on 23 November
1981, he could not have renewed it beyond 5 December 1979 (see [1982] 2 All ER 806 at
810, [1982] 1 WLR 1082 at 1086 per Dunn LJ). For, though Ord 6, r 8 gives the court
power in its discretion to entertain an application for the renewal of a writ after the
period of its validity has expired, it only gives it power to extend its validity for a period
b not exceeding 12 months at a time (that is to say on any one application) and that period
must begin on the day next following the day of its expiry. (4) I considered (without
deciding the point) that there was force in the submission that Ord 2, r 1 on its true
construction does not even give the court jurisdiction to treat a writ as having been
renewed, when it has not in fact been renewed pursuant to the machinery specifically
provided for by Ord 6, r 8. (5) However, even if Ord 2, r 1 conferred such jurisdiction, I
c considered that the judge, in making the order of 23 November 1981, should not have
exercised it so as implicitly to treat the validity of the writ as having been extended up to
28 January 1981, when he could not have properly made an order to this effect on a
specific application under Ord 6, r 8.

Having had the advantage of reading the judgment of Stephenson LJ, I am now
persuaded that the judge in *Bernstein v Jackson* would have had the jurisdiction under
d Ord 2, r 1 to treat the failure to extend the writ as an 'irregularity' within the meaning
of Ord 2, r 1 and to waive it accordingly. The width of the wording of the rule, in my
opinion, compels this conclusion. Nevertheless, I adhere to my view that it would not
have been a proper exercise of his discretion so to do.

Having read the judgment of Stephenson LJ, I am similarly persuaded that the
wording of Ord 2, r 1, on its true construction, would be wide enough to give the court
e jurisdiction to cure the irregular service (and irregular issue, if any) of the writ in the
present case by giving retroactive leave for its service out of the jurisdiction. So far as the
plaintiffs' case rests on Ord 2, r 1, the matter therefore resolves itself to a question of
discretion.

The facts of the present case are distinguishable from *Bernstein v Jackson* in the sense
that the writ which had been irregularly served on Dunlop on 18 May 1982 had not
f become invalid for service by that date. This particular point, therefore, would have
presented no obstacle to the plaintiffs in the instant case in putting before the registrar
on 30 July 1982 an application to extend the validity of the writ. Nevertheless, as
Stephenson LJ has pointed out, it is a long-established principle that the court will not
exercise its discretion so as retrospectively to extend the validity of a writ beyond the
period of 12 months allowed for its service, unless there are exceptional circumstances
g sufficient to justify such extension. I agree that no such exceptional circumstances have
been shown in the present case. Accordingly, in my opinion, in response to the plaintiff's
application under Ord 6, r 8, the registrar could not in the proper exercise of his discretion
have extended the validity of the writ.

Likewise, in my opinion, it would have been an improper exercise of the registrar's
discretion under Ord 2, r 1 to make good the irregular service of the writ retroactively in
h this case, where he could not properly have renewed the writ under Ord 6, r 8. When
seeking the indulgence of the court under Ord 2, r 1, in circumstances such as the
present, a plaintiff cannot, in my opinion, expect the court to exercise its discretion more
favourably than it would be prepared to exercise it on an application under Ord 6, r 8. If
he cannot properly enter through the front door of Ord 6, r 8, he should not be allowed
to enter through the back door of Ord 2, r 1. Essentially, therefore, I regard this case as
j being on all fours with *Bernstein v Jackson*, so far as it relates to the exercise of the court's
discretion, and I think that Neill J was right so to regard it.

Finally, and more generally, I would specifically express my agreement with May LJ's
view that only in the exceptional case should the court, in the exercise of the discretion
which we have held to exist, validate, after the event, the purported service in a foreign
country without leave of process issued by an English court. In most cases breaches of

the requirements of Ord 6, r 7 or Ord 11, r 1, relating to the leave of the court, are not in
my opinion likely to be breaches which can be lightly disregarded.

    For these reasons, I too would dismiss this appeal.

Apoeal dismissed. Leave to appeal to House of Lords refused.

Solicitors: *Hewitt Woollacott & Chown*, agents for *Robinson Jarvis & Rolf*, Newport, Isle of
Wight (for the plaintiff); *C A Norris*, Ringwood (for Dunlop).

Diana Brahams   Barrister.

Attorney General's Reference (No 2 of 1982)

COURT OF APPEAL, CRIMINAL DIVISION
WATKINS AND KERR LJJ
4, 5, 6 OCTOBER, 24 NOVEMBER 1983

*Criminal law – Theft – Dishonesty – Consent of owner – Appropriation of property belonging to
company – Whether director and shareholder in total control of company can commit offence of
theft from company – Whether consent of director and shareholder in total control of company to
appropriation necessarily involving company's consent to appropriation – Whether fact that
defendant's acts intra vires company relevant to his defence of honest belief that he was entitled to
deprive company of property – Theft Act 1968, ss 1(1), 2(1)(a)(b).*

*Company – Director – Appropriation of company's property – Whether director and shareholder
in total control of company capable of committing theft of company's property – Theft Act 1968,
ss 1(1), 2(1)(a)(b).*

The two defendants, who were the shareholders and directors of various companies
engaged in property development and money lending, were each charged, either
individually or jointly, with theft from the companies, contrary to s 1[a] of the Theft Act
1968. It was alleged that, with each other's consent, they appropriated the companies'
funds for their own private use by drawing cheques on the companies' bank accounts.
At their trial the judge ruled at the end of the Crown's case that they had no case to
answer and directed an acquittal, on the ground that because they were the only
shareholders and directors their consent to the appropriations was to be taken as being
the consent of the companies to the appropriations, which had therefore not been made
'dishonestly' within s 1(1), and that therefore there was no theft from the companies.
The Attorney General referred to the Court of Appeal for its opinion the questions
whether a person in total control of a limited company by reason of his shareholding and
directorship was capable of stealing the company's property and whether two persons in
total control of a company were while acting in concert capable of jointly stealing the
company's property. At the hearing of the reference the defendants submitted that,
although the ingredients of theft under s 1(1) had otherwise been prima facie satisfied,
they had been entitled to believe that the companies would have consented to the
appropriations and therefore, under s 2(1)(b)[b] of the 1968 Act, their appropriation of the
companies' funds could not be regarded as being dishonest. The defendants also relied
on the fact that the acts of appropriation were intra vires the wide objects clause in the
memoranda of association of the companies.

---

a   Section 1 is set out at p 220 f, post
b   Section 2(1), so far as material, is set out at p 220 g, post

Held – (1) Where all the shareholders and directors of a company acted illegally or
a dishonestly in relation to the company their knowledge of, or consent to, the illegal or
dishonest acts was not to be imputed to the company. Accordingly, the issue of whether
the defendants had 'dishonestly' appropriated funds from the companies should have
been left to the jury (see p 223 *h j*, post); *Belmont Finance Corp Ltd v Williams Furniture Ltd*
[1979] 1 All ER 118 applied.

(2) Since the essence of the defendant's defence was that they and the company were
b one and the same, so that their consent was the same as the company's consent to the
appropriations, it was not open to the defendants to rely on s 2(1)(*b*) of the 1968 Act by
way of a defence, because it was not possible to regard the company as the 'other' person
whose consent would be given. Moreover, even if s 2(1)(*b*) was available to the defendants
as a defence, that would not have precluded the jury from finding that the defendants
had acted dishonestly if they were satisfied that the defendants had not had an honest
belief that the company would have consented to the appropriation and that the
c company's consent had not been its true consent honestly obtained. Furthermore, unless
the defendants had had an honest belief that they had been entitled to appropriate the
companies' funds, they could not have honestly believed that the company had truly
consented to the appropriation (see p 222 *h* to p 223 *a*, p 224 *b c* and *f* to *j* and p 225 *a* to
c, post); dicta of Megaw LJ in *R v Lawrence* [1970] 3 All ER at 936 applied.

d Per curiam. Where the shareholders and directors of a company which they wholly
own are charged with theft of the company's property, the appropriate defence to the
charge is that provided by s 2(1)(*a*) of the 1968 Act, namely that the defendants honestly
believed that in law they had the right to deprive the other, ie the company, of the
property. Furthermore, although the vires of a company may be of evidential relevance
on the issue of a defendant's honesty, the fact that the transaction was intra vires the
e company is not conclusive of the issue (see p 224 *j* to p 225 *a* and *d e*, post).

Notes
For theft, see 11 Halsbury's Laws (4th edn) paras 1262–1270, and for cases on theft by an
officer of a company, see 15 Digest (Reissue) 1317–1318, 11354–11372.
For the Theft Act 1968, ss 1, 2, see 8 Halsbury's Statutes (3rd edn) 783, 784.

f **Cases referred to in judgment**
Bell Houses Ltd v City Wall Properties Ltd [1966] 2 All ER 674, [1966] 2 QB 656, [1966] 2
    WLR 1323, CA.
Belmont Finance Corp Ltd v Williams Furniture Ltd [1979] 1 All ER 118, [1979] Ch 250,
    [1978] 3 WLR 712, CA.
Lawrence v Comr of Police for the Metropolis [1971] 2 All ER 1253, [1972] AC 626, [1971] 3
g   WLR 225, HL; *affg* sub nom *R v Lawrence* [1970] 3 All ER 933, [1971] 1 QB 373,
    [1970] 3 WLR 1103, CA.
Multinational Gas and Petrochemical Co v Multinational Gas and Petrochemical Services Ltd
    [1983] 2 All ER 563, [1983] Ch 258, [1983] 3 WLR 492, CA.
R v Bonner [1970] 2 All ER 97, [1970] 1 WLR 838, CA.
R v Davies [1954] 3 All ER 335, [1955] 1 QB 71, [1954] 3 WLR 664, CCA.
h *R v Kohn* (1979) 69 Cr App R 395, CA.
R v McDonnell [1966] 1 All ER 193, [1966] 1 QB 233, [1965] 3 WLR 1138, Assizes.
R v Mainwaring, R v Madders (1981) 74 Cr App R 99, CA.
Salomon v A Salomon & Co Ltd [1897] AC 22, [1895–9] All ER Rep 33, HL.
Tesco Supermarkets Ltd v Nattrass [1971] 2 All ER 127, [1972] AC 153, [1971] 2 WLR
    1166, HL.
j
Cases also cited
Belmont Finance Corp Ltd v Williams Furniture Ltd (No 2) [1980] 1 All ER 393, CA.
Horsley & Weight Ltd, Re [1982] 3 All ER 1045, [1982] Ch 442, CA.
R v Arthur [1967] Crim LR 298, CA.
R v Painter [1983] Crim LR 189, CA.

R v Sinclair [1968] 3 All ER 241, [1968] 1 WLR 1246, CA.
Selangor United Rubber Estates Ltd v Cradock (a bankrupt) (No 3) [1968] 2 All ER 1073,   *a*
    [1968] 1 WLR 1555.
Tarling v Government of the Republic of Singapore (1978) 70 Cr App R 77, HL.

Reference

In June 1982 in the Crown Court at Winchester before his Honour Judge Blaker QC and
a jury the defendants, X and Y, the sole directors and shareholders of certain companies,   *b*
pleaded not guilty to an indictment containing a number of counts of theft from the
companies. At the end of the Crown's case the trial judge ruled, after hearing legal
argument, that the defendants had no case to answer. The Attorney General referred,
under s 36 of the Criminal Justice Act 1972, the following point of law to the Court of
Appeal, Criminal Division for its opinion: whether a man in total control of a limited
liability company (by reason of his shareholding and directorship) is capable of stealing   *c*
the property of the company; and whether two men in total control of a limited liability
company (by reason of their shareholdings and directorships) are (while acting in concert)
capable of jointly stealing the property of the company. The facts are set out in the
opinion of the court.

Alan Rawley QC and *Philip Mott* for the Attorney General.   *d*
John Gorman QC and *Andrew Baillie* for the defendants.

Cur adv vult

24 November. The following opinion of the court was delivered.

KERR LJ. On this reference by the Attorney General under s 36 of the Criminal Justice   *e*
Act 1972 the court is asked to give its opinion on the following point of law:

> 'Whether a man in total control of a limited liability company (by reason of his
> shareholding and directorship) is capable of stealing the property of the company;
> and whether two men in total control of a limited liability company (by reason of
> their shareholdings and directorships) are (while acting in concert) capable of jointly
> stealing the property of the company.'   *f*

In June 1982 two defendants pleaded not guilty before his Honour Judge Blaker QC
and a jury in the Crown Court at Winchester to an indictment which included a number
of counts of theft from companies wholly owned and controlled by them. At the end of
the case for the Crown, followed by several days of legal argument in the absence of the
jury, the judge directed the jury to acquit both defendants after delivering a short   *g*
judgment to which we refer later. In view of rr 3 and 6 of the Criminal Appeal (Reference
of Points of Law) Rules 1973, SI 1973/1114, we will refer to the defendants as X and Y, as
they are in the reference, although their identity has already been mentioned in a
number of legal publications.

The counts of theft were specimen counts alleging the appropriation by the defendants
for their own private purposes of funds of various companies of which they were the sole   *h*
shareholders and directors. The total amounts involved ran into millions. Some of the
counts related to X alone, some to Y alone, and in some of them they were charged
jointly. However, it is common ground that, in relation to all of them, each acted with
the consent of the other; indeed, all the alleged thefts appear to have been carried out by
means of cheques drawn on various accounts of the companies concerned and signed in
each case by X and Y jointly. There is no question of X or Y having been the victim of the   *j*
dishonesty of the other, as, for instance, in the case of theft of partnership property by
one of the partners: see *R v Bonner* [1970] 2 All ER 97, [1970] 1 WLR 838. It was therefore
common ground that on the facts of this case the two parts of the point of law must stand
or fall together. We will so treat them although, in relation to the first part, it should be
borne in mind that a private company with limited liability must in any event have at
least two shareholders: see s 1 of the Companies Act 1948.

For present purposes it is unnecessary to go through all the relevant counts on which
this point of law arises. It is sufficient to quote some extracts from the reference
summarising the evidence for the Crown and to deal with one of the specimen counts as
an illustration. By way of background it should be explained that all the funds in question
appear to have been supplied on overdraft facilities by one finance company, and that the
indictment also included two counts of corruption contrary to s 1 of the Prevention of
Corruption Act 1906 against both X and Y in relation to an employee of that company.
This part of the indictment proceeded to trial, but the defendants were acquitted on both
these counts.

The following are extracts from the reference of the evidence for the Crown, first by
way of background:

'Between 1970 and 1974 X and Y traded as property developers and speculators
borrowing vast sums of money from various financial institutions. The principal
lender was a merchant bank called H & P. The borrowing was on X and Y's own
accounts and on the accounts of a large number of companies controlled by one or
both of them. They operated 55 bank accounts with H & P. By the end of 1974
their indebtedness exceeded £7m of which £5·8m was owed to H & P. By that time
the property market had collapsed and inevitably the security held by H & P was
well below the level of borrowing. In respect of seven companies whose affairs were
specifically analysed, the deficiency as regards creditors was over £2·5m. X and Y
themselves went bankrupt with gross liabilities of £4·8m and £3·5m respectively.
Throughout the period under consideration both X and Y lived extravagantly. In
one year the wife of X spent over £27,000 at an exclusive West End couturier. Not
only was money spent on cars, yachts, hotels and restaurants, but also large sums of
money were spent on improvements to the homes of X and Y and on silver and
antiques to put in them, all of which eventually found its way into their wives'
names. From the seven companies whose bank accounts were analysed X drew out
for personal expenditure about £577,167 net and Y £215,217 net. The word "net"
is used to indicate that X and Y also paid sums into those companies but the sources
of the payments in were often traced to unauthorised drawings from other
companies controlled by one or both of them or by circular payments ...
Throughout the period X and Y were advised by an accountant. He on a number of
occasions, both orally and in writing, informed X and Y that it was illegal to borrow
or take money from the companies for their private purposes. One reason was that
it would be treated by the Inland Revenue as a distribution and would be subject to
tax, but the prohibition was expressed in much wider terms by the accountant.'

We then turn to the Crown's evidence concerning four specimen counts against X
which is summarised in the reference as follows:

'All charge X with stealing moneys from F Ltd, a company wholly under his
control. F Ltd was incorporated on 27 July 1970; its directors were X and his wife;
the company records revealed massive drawings by X for jewellery, antiques,
household effects, holiday travel for X and his associates and family, alterations and
renovations to his home and those of his family and his secretary at the time. At
liquidation it had large liabilities mostly owed to H & P. There were no assets. The
company had only participated in one minor transaction during its existence but it
borrowed very heavily and most of the borrowed money was spent by X in
transactions which could not in any way be classed as company expenditure. By 30
May 1973 the account with H & P was £487,065 in debit. On that day £400,000
was credited to the F Ltd account at H & P reducing the overdraft to £87,065. X
paid off this £400,000 by borrowing on his own personal account at H & P on the
same day. This switching of borrowing was done because X had been frequently
told by his accountant that he was not entitled to borrow from F Ltd; and the object
was to put the situation right. Thereafter X's personal overdraft soared to £519,556.

Nevertheless X continued to draw on F Ltd and on 12 June 1974 when the last cheque was honoured its overdraft had increased from £87,065 to £220,817.'   *a*

It is only necessary to refer to one of these specimen counts, count 4. This charged X with theft of a sum £5,600 belonging to F Ltd contrary to s 1(1) of the Theft Act 1968. The reference summarises the evidence in relation to this count as follows, and counsel for the Attorney General pointed out that the alleged facts concerning this count occurred after and notwithstanding the events summarised in the previous extract:

b

'Count 4 related to a cheque paid to travel agents. Between 1 November 1970 and 28 February 1974 X used £25,869 of F Ltd's money to pay various travel bills at the travel agents. X spent a great deal on travel and hotels, some £60,000 in five years. This count relates to a holiday he and his family spent in Switzerland. This holiday was preceded immediately by a Christmas cruise; the total cost of both was about £15,000. The sum charged, £5,600, is only part of the story. The date of the cheque was 7 February 1974.'   *c*

For present purposes it is unnecessary to go into any of the other counts. They were all of a similar, often more complex, nature, charging X or Y, or both of them jointly, with theft from various companies which were wholly owned and controlled by them. The counts were originally charged as thefts of the sums of money obtained by means of the cheques signed by X and Y, as already mentioned, but by consent all these counts were amended by including a charge of theft of a thing in action pursuant to s 4(1) of the Theft Act 1968. Having regard to this amendment and to the decision of this court in *R v Kohn* (1979) 69 Cr App R 395, and since all the relevant company accounts were at all material times in debit within the overdraft facilities granted by H & P, it was common ground that there was no issue as to the subject matter of the thefts which were charged.   *d*

We must next set out the relevant provisions of the Theft Act 1968 on which the issues mainly turn, as follows: *e*

'**1.** *Basic definition of theft.*—(1) A person is guilty of theft if he dishonestly appropriates property belonging to another with the intention of permanently depriving the other of it; and "thief" and "steal" shall be construed accordingly.

(2) It is immaterial whether the appropriation is made with a view to gain, or is *f* made for the thief's own benefit.

(3) The five following sections of this Act shall have effect as regards the interpretation and operation of this section (and, except as otherwise provided by this Act, shall apply only for purposes of this section).

2. *"Dishonestly".*—(1) A person's appropriation of property belonging to another is not to be regarded as dishonest—(a) if he appropriates the property in the belief *g* that he has in law the right to deprive the other of it, on behalf of himself or of a third person; or (b) if he appropriates the property in the belief that he would have the other's consent if the other knew of the appropriation and the circumstances of it . . .

(2) A person's appropriation of property belonging to another may be dishonest notwithstanding that he is willing to pay for the property.   *h*

3. *"Appropriates".*—(1) Any assumption by a person of the rights of an owner amounts to an appropriation, and this includes, where he has come by the property (innocently or not) without stealing it, any later assumption of a right to it by keeping or dealing with it as owner . . .

4. *"Property".*—(1) "Property" includes money and all other property, real or personal, including things in action and other intangible property . . .   *j*

5. *"Belonging to another".*—(1) Property shall be regarded as belonging to any person having possession or control of it, or having in it any proprietary right or interest (not being an equitable interest arising only from an agreement to transfer or grant an interest).

(2) Where property is subject to a trust, the persons to whom it belongs shall be

a   regarded as including any person having a right to enforce the trust, and an intention to defeat the trust shall be regarded accordingly as an intention to deprive of the property any person having that right.

(3) Where a person receives property from or on account of another, and is under an obligation to the other to retain and deal with that property or its proceeds in a particular way, the property or proceeds shall be regarded (as against him) as belonging to the other . . .

b   **6.** *"With the intention of permanently depriving the other of it".*—(1) A person appropriating property belonging to another without meaning the other permanently to lose the thing itself is nevertheless to be regarded as having the intention of permanently depriving the other of it if his intention is to treat the thing as his own to dispose of regardless of the other's rights; and a borrowing or lending of it may amount to so treating it if, but only if, the borrowing or lending is for a period

c   and in circumstances making it equivalent to an outright taking or disposal . . .'

Although there was no transcript of the several days' legal argument before the trial judge, we were told by counsel, who had also appeared below, that the arguments presented to us were in all respects similar to those presented at the trial. We can begin by putting these compendiously as follows. We will take F Ltd as an example and refer

d   to it for convenience as 'the company', and, since they acted jointly, we will refer to 'the defendants' throughout, as did the judge.

Following the classic decision of the House of Lords in *Salomom v A Salomon & Co Ltd* [1897] AC 22, [1895–9] All ER Rep 33, it was of course common ground that the company is a legal entity separate from the defendants, albeit that they were its sole shareholders and directors, and that the things in action or moneys alleged to have been

e   stolen were its property and not that of the defendants. The case for the Crown was accordingly that on the evidence summarised above there was a case to go to the jury, since the evidence alleged all the necessary ingredients to support a charge of theft against the defendants. The subject matter was 'property belonging to another', the company, within s 5(1) of the 1968 Act. In relation to the defendants' position as directors it was also submitted that s 5(2) and (3) applied, but it is unnecessary to consider this aspect

f   further. Second, it was submitted that the defendants' acts constituted an appropriation within ss 1(1) and 3(1). All that remained in issue was therefore whether or not the defendants had acted 'dishonestly' and that was an issue which should have been left to the jury. Further, it was submitted that the effect of ss 1 to 6 of the 1968 Act is that the offence of theft compendiously replaces the whole of the more complex series of offences comprised in the Larceny Act 1916, including fraudulent conversion.

g   Under s 20(1)(ii) of the 1916 Act it was a specific offence for directors, members or officers of any company fraudulently to take or to apply the company's property for their own use, and this provision also applied to private companies: see *R v Davies* [1954] 3 All ER 335, [1955] 1 QB 71. The Crown accordingly submitted that Parliament had not intended that such acts should cease to be criminal, but that they were now comprised within the new offence of theft under the 1968 Act. Admittedly, the defendants could

h   have been charged with conspiracy, but it was felt that the trial would be shortened and made simpler for a jury by simply charging theft. They could also have been charged with fraudulent trading under ss 330 and 332 of the Companies Act 1948, but in view of the gravity of the offences and the limited penalties imposed by these provisions at that time it was decided to proceed under the Theft Act 1968. On behalf of the defendants much of this was unchallenged. In particular, it was conceded that, with the exception

j   of 'dishonestly', all the ingredients of the definition of 'theft' were prima facie satisfied, viz the definitions of 'appropriates' under s 3, of 'property' under s 4 and of 'belonging to another' under s 5. (No issue was raised on 'with the intention of permanently depriving the other of it', presumably since this was clearly covered by s 6(1).) However, it was submitted that this failed to take account of the relationship between the defendants and the companies, and it was pointed out that, even in relation to the offence of fraudulent conversion under s 20(1)(ii) of the 1916 Act, there was no reported case where the defendants were the sole shareholders and directors of the company in question, as here.

It was submitted that since the defendants were the sole owners of the company and, through their shareholding, the sole owners of all its property, they could not, in effect, be charged with stealing from themselves. In particular, it was submitted that there was no issue to go to the jury on the ingredient of 'dishonestly'. The defendants were the sole will and directing mind of the company. The company was therefore bound to consent to all to which they themselves consented. In the light of the decision of the House of Lords in *Lawrence v Comr of Police for the Metropolis* [1971] 2 All ER 1253, [1972] AC 626 it was conceded that one ingredient of the former offence of larceny, 'without the consent of the owner', was no longer a necessary ingredient of the new offence of theft, and that the judge had erred in referring to this aspect, as mentioned below. However, it was said that the defendants were in any event bound to succeed under s 2(1)(b) of the 1968 Act, since consent to the appropriations by the defendants necessarily involved consent by the company for the purposes of this provision. Further, the defendants relied on the wide 'objects' clauses of the memorandum of association of the various companies concerned and submitted that the defendants' acts were covered by these and were accordingly intra vires. Thus the principal object of the company which we have taken by way of illustration was to act as 'financiers and industrial brokers to loan and advance money'. We comment on this aspect at the end of this judgment.

As already mentioned, at the conclusion of the legal argument before him, Judge Blaker directed an acquittal on the theft charges and gave a short judgment, of which the material extract is as follows:

'We are faced as I see it with this situation. We know from *R v Kohn* (1969) 69 Cr App R 395 that a director can steal from the company. The problem is: can two directors steal, one or two directors, I shall say two throughout, steal from the companies of which they are in complete control? *Salomon v A Salomon & Co Ltd* [1897] AC 22, [1895–9] All ER Rep 33 is authority for saying that, if all shareholders know of fraud on the company, there is no fraud. X and Y when they wrote the cheques as directors, can it be said they did so without the consent of the company? I take the view, having considered carefully *Tesco Supermarkets Ltd v Nattrass* [1971] 2 All ER 127, [1972] AC 153 and the opinions of the noble Lords therein set out, that they are the company, and therefore they cannot steal from it. They gave consent to the writing of the cheques and the drawing of the money, and therefore, in my view, there is in law no theft . . . In addition I was urged that the case should be stopped by reason of the prejudice, bearing in mind the other offences of dishonesty which might have been committed. I do not agree that would have prejudiced the jury in coming to a correct verdict had I seen fit to leave it to them, but I do not consider that any jury properly directed would regard, according to the ordinary standards of reasonable and honest people, it to be dishonest for two directors who were also the shareholders to draw money from their own companies to pay private bills. I do not think I need say any more.'

In our view the judge clearly erred in taking this course. As was ultimately accepted on behalf of the defendants, on the case for the Crown all the ingredients of the definition of theft were present and satisfied in relation to the defendants' conduct, subject only to the ingredient 'dishonestly' and the terms of s 2(1)(b) of the 1968 Act. Honesty or dishonesty must however always be a question for the jury, and the present type of case is no exception. In our view, this elementary principle itself provides an affirmative answer to the question posed on this reference. The basic fallacy in the submission on behalf of the defendants is the contention that, in effect, in a situation such as the present a jury is bound to be directed that, when all the members and directors of a company act in concert in appropriating the property of their company, they cannot, as a matter of law, be held to have acted dishonestly, or that, on such facts, any reasonable jury is bound to reach this conclusion. We entirely disagree with both these propositions. In our view,

for the reasons explained below, they derive no support from s 2(1)(b) of the 1968 Act or
a from the cases to which the judge referred.

We deal first with the authorities. The speeches in the House of Lords in *Tesco
Supermarkets Ltd v Nattrass* merely illustrate that in situations like the present the
defendants 'are' the company in the sense that any offences committed by them in
relation to the affairs of the company would be capable of being treated as offences
committed by the company itself. The decision has no bearing on offences committed
b against the company. Similarly, we do not consider that anything in *Salomon v A Salomon
& Co Ltd* assists the defendants. One of the issues decided in that case can be summarised
as follows. Where a solvent company enters into a transaction (in that case with one of
the shareholders) with the knowledge and consent of all the shareholders and directors,
all acting honestly, and then becomes insolvent, the liquidator cannot subsequently seek
to have the transaction set aside on the ground that it was a fraud on the company, or the
c shareholder, or the company's creditors. A similar conclusion was recently reached by a
majority of the Civil Division of this court in *Multinational Gas and Petrochemical Co v
Multinational Gas and Petrochemical Services Ltd* [1983] 2 All ER 563, [1983] Ch 258. It was
held that in such a case the liquidator cannot maintain an action for negligence or breach
of fiduciary duty against the shareholders or directors in relation to their conduct of the
company's affairs: their knowledge of, and consent to, the decisions alleged to have been
d taken negligently or in breach of duty were the decisions of the company itself, and, the
transactions being intra vires the company's memorandum, there was no basis for any
claim by the liquidator.

However, neither *Salomon's* case nor the *Multinational Gas* case were concerned with
allegations that the shareholders and directors had acted illegally or dishonestly in relation
to the company. Where this is alleged the position is different, as illustrated by the
e decision of the Civil Division of this court in *Belmont Finance Corp Ltd v Williams Furniture
Ltd* [1979] 1 All ER 118, [1979] Ch 250. In that case it was alleged by the receiver of the
company that its shareholders and directors had unlawfully and dishonestly conspired to
use the company's funds to purchase shares in another company for an excessive price,
and also to give financial assistance to the shareholders of that other company to purchase
its shares in contravention of s 54 of the Companies Act 1948. Foster J dismissed the
f receiver's claims for damages, breach of trust and misfeasance, on the ground that in
these circumstances the company must itself have been a party to the alleged conspiracy,
with the result that the receiver could not maintain the action in its name. His decision
was, however, unanimously reversed. Buckley LJ said and Orr and Goff LJJ agreed with
him ([1979] 1 All ER 118 at 125–126, 132–133, [1979] Ch 250 at 261, 270–271):

> 'It may emerge at a trial that the facts are not as alleged in the satatement of claim,
g > but if the allegations in the statement of claim are made good, the directors of the
> plaintiff must then have known that the transaction was an illegal transaction. But
> in my view such knowledge should not be imputed to the plaintiff, for the essence
> of the arrangement was to deprive it improperly of a large part of its assets. As I
> have said, the plaintiff was a victim of the conspiracy. I think it would be irrational
> to treat the directors, who were allegedly parties to the conspiracy, notionally as
h > having transmitted this knowledge to the plaintiff; and indeed it is a well-recognised
> exception from the general rule that a principal is affected by notice received by his
> agent that, if the agent is acting in fraud of his principal and the matter of which he
> has notice is relevant to the fraud, that knowledge is not to be imputed to the
> principal. So in my opinion the plaintiff should not be regarded as a party to the
> conspiracy, on the ground of lack of the necessary guilty knowledge.'

j
So far as the authorities in the realm of the civil law are concerned, this decision
directly contradicts the basis of the defendants' argument in the present case. There can
be no reason, in our view, why the position in the criminal law should be any different.
This is also the view expressed in Glanville Williams *Textbook of Criminal Law* (2nd edn,
1983) pp 746–747, 811 and by G R Sullivan 'Company Controllers, Company Cheques

and Theft' [1983] Crim LR 512 at 514–515, both of which criticise the decision which
has given rise to the present reference.

We accordingly turn to the 1968 Act and the definition of 'theft'. We have already
stated that, on the facts alleged by the Crown, all the ingredients of this definition are
satisfied other than the issue as to the defendants' honesty or dishonesty, and that this,
together with the truth or otherwise of all the facts alleged, must always be a matter for
the jury. In our view there is no substance whatever in the submission that s 2(1)(b)
would preclude a jury from concluding, as a matter of law, that the defendants had acted
dishonestly in these cases. Nor can we accept for one moment that any jury would be
bound to conclude, on the facts alleged, that dishonesty had not been established.

First, a defendant's 'belief that he would have the other's consent' under s 2(1)(b) must
itself be an honest belief, and it must be an honest belief in a true consent, honestly
obtained. In giving the judgment of this court in *R v Lawrence* [1970] 3 All ER 933 at
936, [1971] 1 QB 373 at 377 Megaw LJ said:

> 'Of course, where there is true consent by the owner of property to the
> appropriation of it by another, a charge of theft under s 1(1) must fail. This is not,
> however, because the words "without consent" have to be implied in the new
> definition of theft. It is simply because, if there is such true consent, the essential
> element of dishonesty is not established. If, however, the apparent consent is
> brought about by dishonesty, there is nothing in the words of s 1(1), or by reason of
> any implication that can properly be read into those words, to make such apparent
> consent relevant as providing a defence. The prosecution have to prove the four
> elements already mentioned, and no more. No inference to the contrary is to be
> drawn from the words of s 2(1)(b), already quoted. That reference does no more
> than show that the essential element of dishonesty does not exist if the defendant
> when he appropriates the property believes that the owner would consent if he
> knew the circumstances. "The circumstances" are, of course, all the relevant
> circumstances. "The belief" is an honest belief. That paragraph does not give rise to
> the inference that an appropriation of property is not theft when there is a
> "consent"—if it can be rightly so described—which is founded on the dishonesty of
> the defendant.'

We can see nothing in the speech of Viscount Dilhorne in the House of Lords in that
case (see *Lawrence v Comr of Police for the Metropolis* [1971] 2 All ER 1253, [1972] AC 626),
with which the other members of the House agreed, to cast any doubt on the correctness
of that passage. But the essence of the defendants' argument in the present case is that,
their consent must necessarily involve consent by the company. It must then follow that
unless they themselves had an honest belief that they were entitled to appropriate the
company's funds, they could not honestly believe that the company had truly consented
to the appropriations in question.

Second, we do not consider that in circumstances such as those alleged in the present
case s 2(1)(b) has any application or that it can provide the basis for any defence. The
essence of the defendants' argument is the alleged identity, in all respects, and for every
purpose, between the defendants and the company. It is said, in effect, that their acts are
necessarily the company's acts, that their will, knowledge and belief are those of the
company and that their consent necessarily implies consent by the company. But how
then can the company be regarded as 'the other' for the purposes of *this* provision? One
merely has to read its wording to see that it cannot be given any sensible meaning in a
context such as the present, where the mind and will of the defendants are also treated in
law as the mind and will of 'the other'. It is for this reason that in such cases there can be
conspiracy between the directors and shareholders on the one hand and the company on
the other: see *R v McDonnell* [1966] 1 All ER 193, [1966] 1 QB 233.

However, it does not by any means follow that the members and directors of a
company which is wholly owned by them cannot properly be charged with theft of the
company's property, or that the defendants cannot rely on s 2 of the 1968 Act in answer
to such a charge. Their appropriate defence in such cases is provided by s 2(1)(a), the

a belief of a defendant, which must of course be an honest belief, 'that he has in law the right to deprive the other [the company] of it [the property]'.

In effect, the defendants' answer to the charges in the present case, assuming that the Crown establishes the facts alleged, would have been: 'We honestly believed that we were entitled to do what we did. They were our companies, and we honestly believed that we were entitled to draw all the cheques and expend all the moneys which are now charged as acts of theft.' This is the defence provided by s 2(1)(a). To obtain a conviction, the

b Crown would have had to establish the contrary to the satisfaction of the jury. A direction to the jury on these lines would be simple, and would follow the ordinary direction in all cases where a defendant's state of mind, and his honesty or dishonesty, is an essential ingredient of the offence in question. We can see no difficulty whatever in leaving to the jury the issues concerning the ingredient 'dishonestly' of the offence of theft charged in this case, and that is what should have been done at the trial. Accordingly, our answer to

c the question posed on this reference is Yes.

Before concluding, however, we must briefly refer to a discussion in the course of the arguments before us whether it was relevant to consider whether the acts charged as thefts were in themselves intra or ultra vires the company concerned on the true construction of its memorandum of association. Thus, in the context of s 2(1)(b) counsel for the defendants rightly conceded that a company cannot consent to anything which is

d ultra vires its constitution and powers. Similarly, in the context of s 2(1)(a) there was some discussion in this connection about the effect of the words 'that he has in law the right . . .' In our view the vires of the company may be of evidential relevance to, but not determinative of, the crucial issue as to the defendants' honesty or dishonesty. Of course, in asserting an honest belief in his right to act as he did, a defendant may wish to refer to the objects for which the company was constituted, and to the terms of its memorandum,

e to assist him in his defence that he had acted honestly.

In R v Mainwaring, R v Madders (1981) 74 Cr App R 99 the defendants were charged with theft from a number of persons, who had made payments to them in their capacity as directors of a company, on the ground that they applied these moneys to various purposes other than the purpose for which they had been received: see s 5(3) of the 1968 Act. One of the defences raised was that the moneys had been used for purposes covered

f by the company's memorandum. In that connection Lawton LJ, giving the judgment of this court, said (at 108):

'But, as Bristow J. pointed out in the course of [counsel for the appellant Mainwaring's] submission, a good deal depends upon the state of mind of the directors of the company when they decide to conduct a separate activity. Clearly if they do so honestly the decision cited above [namely Bell Houses Ltd v City Wall

g Properties Ltd [1966] 2 All ER 674, [1966] 2 QB 656] protects them from the suggestion that they acted ultra vires, but if their decision to conduct some other activity is not made honestly the criminal law intervenes.'

The converse equally applies to the case for the Crown. Thus, although the Crown may seek to prove by reference to the company's memorandum that on its true

h construction the acts charged were ultra vires, the Crown will not thereby inevitably establish that the defendant had acted dishonestly. The defendant would of course be perfectly entitled to assert that in all the circumstances, and especially because he at all times believed his acts to be intra vires, he had not acted dishonestly. Whether or not the defendant had acted ultra vires is a matter which the jury would then be entitled to take into account, giving it such weight as they thought proper in deciding the ultimate

j question, namely: has the Crown proved that the defendant had acted dishonestly?

Opinion accordingly.

Solicitors: Director of Public Prosecutions; Lamport Bassitt & Hiscock, Southampton (for the defendants).

N P Metcalfe Esq   Barrister.

UBAF Ltd v European American Banking Corp

COURT OF APPEAL, CIVIL DIVISION
ACKNER AND OLIVER LJJ
1, 2 NOVEMBER, 9 DECEMBER 1983

Company – Signature – Agent, officer or employee – Signature of duly authorised agent of company – Signature of officer or employee of company acting in the course of his duties – Whether signature of company.

Misrepresentation – Fraudulent misrepresentation – Company – Signature of company – Fraudulent misrepresentation made in letter signed by assistant secretary of company – Whether misrepresentation 'signed' by company – Statute of Frauds Amendment Act 1828, s 6.

Limitation of action – When time begins to run – Actions in tort – Accrual of cause of action – Negligent misrepresentation – Plaintiff induced to lend money by defendant's negligent misrepresentation – Security for loan proving inadequate – Whether plaintiff suffering damage and cause of action accruing when misrepresentation made or when security becoming inadequate – Limitation Act 1980, s 2.

Limitation of action – Concealment of right of action by fraud – Continued concealment – Defendant under fiduciary duty to inform plaintiff if security for loan becoming insufficient – Whether defendant's continuing failure to inform plaintiff a continuing breach of defendant's fiduciary duty – Whether continuing breach of duty preventing time from running – Limitation Act 1980, s 32(1)(b).

The defendant, a New York banking corporation, invited the plaintiff, an English bank, to participate in a syndicate loan to two companies in a Panamanian shipping group, and under cover of a letter signed by the defendant's assistant secretary supplied the plaintiff with information about the loans and a study of the shipping group. The plaintiff later made a loan of $US500,000 to each company. As a result of the deteriorating shipping market the shipping group got into financial difficulties and the two companies defaulted on the loans, leaving the sum of $US880,000 owing to the plaintiff. The plaintiff brought an action against the defendant claiming damages alleging (i) deceit in fraudulently misrepresenting that the intended loans were 'attractive financing of two companies in a sound and profitable group', (ii) misrepresentation under s 2(1) of the Misrepresentation Act 1967 and (iii) negligent misrepresentation in connection with the information provided to the plaintiff. The plaintiff obtained leave under RSC Ord 11, r 1 to serve the writ on the defendant outside the jurisdiction. The defendant applied to have the leave set aside, on the grounds that (i) the claim in deceit and under the 1967 Act were precluded by s 6[a] of the Statute of Frauds Amendment Act 1828 because the signature of the defendant's assistant secretary could not in law be the defendant company's signature because he could not have had the requisite authority to sign any representation, which accordingly had not, for the purposes of s 6, been 'signed by the Party to be charged' with making it, and (ii) the claim of negligent misrepresentation was barred by s 2[b] of the Limitation Act 1980 because the plaintiff's claim that it would not have entered into the contract if it had known that the defendant's representations were inaccurate implied that it had suffered damage when it had entered into the contract, which was when any cause of action arose and which was more than six years before the writ was issued. The defendant further contended that the plaintiff could not rely on s 32(1)(b)[c] of the 1980

---

a   Section 6 is set out at p 229 h, post
b   Section 2 is set out at p 234 g, post
c   Section 32(1), so far as material, is set out at p 236 a, post

Act to prevent time running on the ground that relevant matters were deliberately
a   concealed, because any duty of disclosure related to the defendant's fraudulent
misrepresentations, which was a cause of action barred by s 6 of 1828 Act. The judge
upheld the defendant's contentions and set aside the leave to serve the writ on the
defendant outside the jurisdiction, on the ground that the plaintiff was precluded by law
from bringing its action. The plaintiff appealed.

b   **Held** – (1) For the purposes of s 6 of the 1828 Act a representation signed on behalf of a
limited company by a duly authorised agent acting within the scope of his authority or
by an officer or employee of the company acting in the course of his duties in the business
of the company constituted a representation made by the company and signed by it (see
p 230 f g and p 234 e, post); *Swift v Jewsbury* (1874) LR 9 QB 301 and *Hirst v West Riding
Union Banking Co Ltd* [1900–3] All ER Rep 782 explained.
c   (2) Since it was not inevitable that the plaintiff had suffered damage at the time it
entered into the contract because it was possible that the chose in action which it acquired
in return for the loan might at that time have equalled or exceeded the money lent, it
could not be assumed that the plaintiff's cause of action arose when it entered into the
contract. The plaintiff's claim based on negligent misrepresentation was therefore not
necessarily barred by s 2 of the 1980 Act. In any event, the plaintiff's loan was part of a
d   syndicate loan organised by the defendant, which was under a fiduciary duty to inform
all participants in the syndicate, including the plaintiff, if at any time it acquired
knowledge that the security for the loan was insufficient. The defendant's continued
failure to so inform members of the syndicate would constitute a continuing breach of ·
the defendant's fiduciary duty which would, for the purposes of s 32(1)(b) of the 1980
Act, prevent time from running until the plaintiff discovered the concealment or could
e   with reasonable diligence have discovered it (see p 234 j to p 235 a and p 236 j, post);
Forster v Outred & Co (a firm) [1982] 2 All ER 753 distinguished.
(3) The judge had been wrong to set aside the leave given to the plaintiff to serve the
writ on the defendant outside the jurisdiction, since the plaintiff was not precluded by
law from bringing its action and a trial would be necessary to determine the issues (a)
whether the defendant company's assistant secretary had acted within the scope of his
f   authority when signing the letter to the plaintiff, (b) whether, if at all, the plaintiff's
cause of action had accrued when the plaintiff advanced the loan and (c) whether, and if
so when, the defendant was in breach of its fiduciary duty to the plaintiff to inform it
that the security for the syndicate loan was or had become inadequate. Accordingly, the
plaintiff's appeal would be allowed (see p 230 j, p 234 g h and p 237 a b, post).

g   **Notes**
For a company's liability in tort for its agent's acts, see 7 Halsbury's Laws (4th edn) para
721, and for cases on the subject, see 9 Digest (Reissue) 696–698, 4137–4145.
For time limits for actions founded on tort, see 28 Halsbury's Laws (4th edn) paras
679, 690, and for cases on the subject, see 32 Digest (Reissue) 709–715, 5174–5200.
For the Statute of Frauds Amendment Act 1828, s 6, see 7 Halsbury's Statutes
h   (3rd edn) 7.
For the Limitation Act 1980, ss 2, 32, see 50(1) ibid 1255, 1285.

Cases referred to in judgment
Baker v Ollard & Bentley (a firm) (1982) 126 SJ 593, CA.
Banbury v Bank of Montreal [1918] AC 626, [1918–19] All ER Rep 1, HL; affg [1917] 1 KB
j   409, CA.
Barwick v English Joint Stock Bank (1867) LR 2 Exch 259, [1861–73] All ER Rep 194, Ex
Ch.
Cow v Casey [1949] 1 All ER 197, [1949] 1 KB 481, CA.
Diamond v Bank of London and Montreal Ltd [1979] 1 All ER 561, [1979] QB 333, [1979] 2
WLR 228, CA.
Forster v Outred & Co (a firm) [1982] 2 All ER 753, [1982] 1 WLR 86, CA.

Hirst v West Riding Union Banking Co Ltd [1901] 2 KB 561, [1900–3] All ER Rep 782, 70
   LJKB 828, CA.   *a*
National Enterprises Ltd v Racal Communications Ltd [1974] 3 All ER 1010, [1975] Ch 397,
   [1974] 2 WLR 733.
Swift v Jewsbury (1874) LR 9 QB 301, Ex Ch.
Williams v Mason (1873) 28 LT 232.

Cases also cited   *b*
Dove v Banhams Patent Locks Ltd [1983] 2 All ER 833, [1983] 1 WLR 1436.
Howell v Young (1826) 5 B & C 259, [1824–34] All ER Rep 377.
Lennard's Carrying Co Ltd v Asiatic Petroleum Co Ltd [1915] AC 705, [1914–15] All ER Rep
   280, HL.
Pirelli General Cable Works Ltd v Oscar Faber & Partners (a firm) [1983] 1 All ER 65, [1983]
   2 AC 1, HL.   *c*

Interlocutory appeal
The plaintiff, UBAF Ltd, appealed against the order made by Leggatt J in chambers on
14 April 1983 whereby the judge set aside, pursuant to RSC Ord 12, r 8, (1) an order of
Parker J dated 18 December 1981 giving leave to the plaintiff to issue and serve out of
the jurisdiction a concurrent writ on the defendant, European American Banking Corp,   *d*
a corporation organised and incorporated under the laws of the State of New York, USA,
and (2) an order of Staughton J dated 8 October 1982 giving leave to the plaintiff to issue
and serve a second concurrent writ on the defendant out of the jurisdiction. The grounds
of Leggatt J's decision were that the plaintiff had not shown a good arguable case against
the defendant justifying service out of the jurisdiciton under RSC Ord 11, r 1 because
the plaintiff's action against the defendant in which it claimed damages for fraudulent   *e*
misrepresentation and/or misrepresentation under s 2(1) of the Misrepresentation Act
1967 was by virtue of s 6 of the Statute of Frauds Amendment Act 1828 not maintainable
and was time barred by s 2 of the Limitation Act 1980. The facts are set out in the
judgment of the court.

Kenneth Rokison QC and *Timothy Charlton* for the plaintiff.   *f*
Leonard Hoffmann QC and *Richard Siberry* for the defendant.

                                                                                              Cur adv vult

9 December. The following judgment of the court was delivered.

ACKNER LJ. The plaintiff, who is the appellant, is an English banking corporation,   *g*
and the defendant, the respondent, is a New York banking corporation. The defendant
has had a history of dealing with the Colocotronis group of shipping companies.
Apparently, in September 1974, the defendant approached the plaintiff and requested it
to take a participation in two loans which the defendant was intending to make to two
Panamanian corporations in the Colocotronis group, namely Marcresta Armadora SA
(Marcresta) and Astrocamino Armadora SA (Astrocamino), which corporations owned   *h*
respectively the m t Illustrious Colocotronis and the m t Pacific Colocotronis.
   Under cover of a letter dated 12 September 1974 and signed by Francios Macheras as
assistant secretary of the defendant, there was sent to the plaintiff (a) two 'term' sheets
prepared by the defendant to give information to prospective participants about the loans
to Macresta and Astrocamino, (b) a study of the Colocotronis group prepared by the
defendant and dated April 1974, (c) a copy of a letter dated 20 August 1974 from   *j*
H Clarkson & Co Ltd to the defendant giving valuations of the vessels Pacific Colocotronis
and Illustrious Colocotronis.
   In its points of claim the plaintiff alleges that, in so doing, the defendant represented
to it that the intended loans to Marcresta and Astronocamino were 'attractive financing
of two companies in a sound and profitable group'. In support of this allegation the
plaintiff relies, inter alia, on the following matters. First, that the purpose of the loans to

a the two companies was the refinancing of their tankers, to repay the defendant's existing financing loan and to make down payments on the building of certain tankers; second, that the collateral for the loan to each of the companies would be a first preferred mortgage on their respective vessels, which had an appraised value as at 20 August 1974 of $US18m and $US20m; and that, by way of further collateral for the loans, there would be assignments of charter hire due under a transportation agreement with Petrofina SA and that the cash flow to be expected from the vessels was more than enough in each case

b to meet total debt service requirements of the two companies under the loans. The plaintiff also relied on representations contained in the Colocotronis group study and in the very letter of 12 September to which reference has already been made.

In reliance on these representations the plaintiff lent $US500,000 to each company.

In detailed particulars in its pleadings the plaintiff contends that a number of the representations referred to, and others, are untrue, in particular as to the purposes of the

c loan, the value of the vessels, the transportation agreement and the financial position of the Colocotronis group.

Following the deterioration in the shipping market in 1975–76, the Colocotronis group got into difficulties, the two companies defaulted and $US880,000 remains outstanding. The plaintiff's claim is in the sum of $US900,000 plus interest. It pleads three separate causes of action: (1) deceit, the representations being alleged to be untrue

d to the knowledge of the defendant, (2) misrepresentations under s 2(1) of the Misrepresentation Act 1967, and (3) negligence in and about the presentation to the plaintiff of the transactions in which it was inviting the plaintiff to participate.

It is common ground that the representations were made in England and, accordingly, there was no objection raised to the jurisdiction of the English courts, nor was it contended that England was not the appropriate forum. The defendant, however,

e contended that the plaintiff does not have a good arguable case for two reasons. (1) As regards the claim in deceit, it says first that any such claim is precluded by the provisions of s 6 of the Statute of Frauds Amendment Act 1828 (Lord Tenterden's Act), and, second, that that equally rules out any claim under s 2(1) of the Misrepresentation Act 1967. (2) As regards any claim in negligence, it says that it is statute-barred, the writ having been issued more than six years after the cause of action (if any) arose.

f On this basis it sought and obtained from Leggatt J the appropriate orders to set aside the service out of the jurisdiction which had been permitted by Staughton J on 8 October 1981.

The appeal thus raises only two issues, it being well established that the court will not seek at this stage to decide disputed questions of fact, but that in relation to issues of law it will, however, refuse leave, even though the point raised may be of some difficulty, if

g satisfied that the plaintiff is bound to fail (see *Cow v Casey* [1949] 1 All ER 197, [1949] 1 KB 481, a case concerning RSC Ord 14, but where the principle is essentially the same).

1. *The Statute of Frauds Amendment Act 1828, s 6*

Section 6 provides:

h 'No Action shall be brought whereby to charge any Person upon or by reason of any Representation or Assurance made or given concerning or relating to the Character, Conduct, Credit, Ability, Trade, or Dealings of any other Person, to the Intent or Purpose that such other Person may obtain Credit, Money, or Goods upon, unless such Representation or Assurance be made in Writing, signed by the Party to be charged therewith.'

j
The following propositions are common ground.

(1) The section applies to fraudulent misrepresentations only (see *Banbury v Bank of Montreal* [1918] AC 626, [1918–19] All ER Rep 1). Accordingly, the section has no application to the alleged innocent but negligent misrepresentations; hence the second issue referred to hereafter. However, the representations alleged to give rise to liability under s 2(1) of the Misrepresentation Act 1967 are also within Lord Tenterden's Act,

because the person making the representation is liable only if he 'would be liable to damages in respect thereof had the misrepresentation been made fraudulently'.   *a*

(2) The word 'person' in the section includes a corporation (see *Banbury v Bank of Montreal*, approving *Hirst v West Riding Union Banking Co Ltd* [1901] 2 KB 561, [1900–3] All ER Rep 782).

(3) In order to be within the section the representations on which the action is based must relate in some way to the credit or creditworthiness of a person (see *Diamond v Bank of London and Montreal Ltd* [1979] 1 All ER 561, [1979] QB 333).   *b*

The two matters on which the parties are at issue, however, are (a) whether the signature of Mr Macheras could, as a matter of law, constitute the signature of the party to be charged within the meaning of the section, and (b) whether, even assuming against the plaintiff that it could not, the representations relied on in this case were in fact representations as to the credit or creditworthiness of a person so as to entitle the defendant to rely on the section.   *c*

The judge considered that the first of these two issues was concluded against the plaintiff by authorities which were binding on him and which counsel for the defendant submits are equally binding on this court. Essentially, the question is whether Mr Macheras, the defendant's assistant secretary, who signed the alleged misrepresentations, either had or could have had the requisite authority from the defendant which would even render it arguable that his signature was the signature of 'the Party to be charged'   *d* within the meaning of the section.

The judge seems to have started from the assumption that the only case capable of being raised from the affidavits was that the document containing the representations was one which was signed by Mr Macheras in the course of his ordinary duties as an assistant secretary of the defendant and that the document was one of a type which it was within Mr Macheras's general authority to sign. Making that assumption, he considered   *e* that he was bound by authority, albeit, as he put it, only 'indirectly' bound, to hold that the defendant was entitled to the protection of the 1828 Act. It does not appear that, in reaching this conclusion, he was accepting a proposition that a corporation as such cannot sign a document and is, therefore, always protected by the section, no matter who signs a representation on its behalf. Indeed, it is difficult to see how that proposition could reasonably be sustained, for a corporation cannot sign a document save by some human   *f* agency and, once it is established, as it is on the authorities referred to above, that the section applies to a corporation, the signature of some person must be sufficient for the purposes of the Act. Otherwise, one is compelled to the absurd conclusion that, although a company being a 'person' is entitled to claim the protection of the Act, it is never capable of losing that protection because, as a legal abstraction, it cannot literally and physically 'sign' anything. Counsel for the defendant did not feel able to embrace so   *g* unattractive a conclusion. He did, however, contend both before Leggatt J and before us that, in order to cause a corporate person to lose protection of the section, the signature must be that of a person who is the corporation's 'alter ego', a description which, with respect, we find largely meaningless, save as an indication of some very wide but undefined authority, and he ultimately felt compelled to accept (and we think rightly) that, at least if Mr Macheras had been specifically authorised by a resolution of the board   *h* to sign the representations, then the defendant would have been bound. But we do not know whether or not the board did so resolve. The judge appears to have assumed that the fact that Mr Macheras was and signed as assistant secretary of the company necessarily indicated no specific authority, but merely the authority which might normally have been thought to be vested in an assistant secretary, which he equated with that of a branch manager of a bank. But we are not here concerned with an ostensible authority,   *j* but with an actual authority, and we do not know any detail concerning the terms of Mr Macheras's actual authority in relation to this transaction. Nor do we know with any precision what is involved in the defendant company in the status 'assistant secretary'. Thus, the short answer to the first question is that evidence is required to determine this issue and, accordingly, the matter must be allowed to proceed.

There is, however, a longer answer which, despite the temptation, we do not think we *a* should avoid giving. It involves dealing with the important question raised by counsel for the plaintiff in the court below and decidedly adversely to the plaintiff, namely whether a representation signed on behalf of a limited company by a properly authorised officer or employee acting in the course of his duties in the business of the company constitutes the company's signature for the purposes of s 6. Since an affirmative answer makes to us such obvious commercial sense, we would view with respectful surprise any authority which obliged us to take the contrary view. Leggatt J, however, concluded that

b *Hirst v West Riding Union Banking Co Ltd* [1901] 2 KB 561, [1900–3] All ER Rep 782 presented an insuperable obstacle to his accepting this proposition. With respect, we do not share that view.

The headnote to that case reads as follows ([1901] 2 KB 561):

c
> 'The word "person" in the 6th section of 9 Geo. 4, c. 14 [ie the 1828 Act], includes a corporation; and an incorporated company is, under the terms of that section, not liable for a false representation of the kind contemplated by the section, made in a letter written and signed by their agent.'

d The action was against the defendants, a banking company incorporated under the Companies Acts, to recover damages for a statement alleged to be a misrepresentation, made by the manager of one of their branches, within the scope of his employment and in their interests, with regard to the credit and position of a certain trading company, who were customers of the defendants, acting on the faith of which misrepresentation the plaintiff had incurred loss. The representation complained of was contained in letter signed by the defendants' before-mentioned manager, which was written by him in answer to a letter of inquiry addressed to the defendants by the plaintiff's bankers on behalf of the plaintiff. The jury found a verdict for the plaintiff and judgment was

e entered accordingly.

The issue which was raised by this appeal, as appears from the reported arguments, was whether the 1828 Act extended to affording protection to a corporation and in particular whether *Swift v Jewsbury* (1874) LR 9 QB 301, which related not to a corporation but to a copartnership, decided this issue. The plaintiff (the respondent) took the point that the protection of the Act was not available to the defendants since a company was

f not a 'person' within s 6, basing his argument, so it appears, on the proposition that, since a corporation could not personally sign a document, it could not, as a matter of construction, be the sort of 'person' contemplated by the section.

In rejecting this argument, A L Smith MR and Vaughan Williams LJ were content simply to say that the provisions of the section applied to an incorporated company and that the defendants' application succeeded. Stirling LJ, however, in delivering a

g concurring judgment, gave fuller reasons for his decision. The question whether the word 'person' in the 1828 Act included a corporation must, he said, be judged by considering the context and the object of the enactment. The meaning of s 6 had, he observed, been very clearly stated by Bramwell B in *Swift v Jewsbury* LR 9 QB 301 at 316 when he said:

h
> 'In my opinion the effect of the statute is this, that a man should not be liable for a fraudulent representation as to another person's means unless he puts it down in writing, and acknowledges his responsibility for it by his own signature. He is neither to have the words proved by word of mouth, nor the authority given to an agent for whose act it is sought to make him responsible proved by word of mouth.'

j Stirling LJ continued ([1901] 2 KB 560 at 563):

> 'It is now argued that the protection given by this enactment must be taken to be limited to "persons" who are capable of signing a representation, and therefore a corporation is not within it. That argument is based on the context: but I do not think that the true construction of the enactment supports it. It could not be argued that a human being, who by reason of some disease was incapacitated from signing a document, ought to be deprived of the protection of the Act, which he might need

more than other persons. Nor do I think that there is anything in the object of the
Act to exclude a corporation from the benefit of it.'   *a*

He concluded that a corporation under the Companies Acts was equally entitled to the
protection of the 1828 Act.

Hirst's case thus did not purport to decide that a company cannot sign by a properly
authorised officer or employee acting in the course of his duties in the business of the
corporation, although it does seem to have been assumed both by counsel and by the
court that that was the case. This is odd, since Lord Coleridge CJ had said in *Swift's* case   *b*
LR 9 QB 301 at 312–313:

> '... I apprehend that there can be no doubt that a different set of principles
> altogether arises where an agent of a joint stock company, in conducting the business
> of the joint stock company, does something of which the joint stock company take
> advantage, and by which they profit, or by which they may profit, and it turns out   *c*
> that the act which is so done by their agent is a fraudulent act. Justice points out,
> and authority supports justice in maintaining, that where a corporation takes
> advantage of the fraud of their agent, they cannot afterwards repudiate the agency
> and say that the act which has been done by the agent is not an act for which they
> are liable. If parliament should so enact, well and good, but parliament not having
> so enacted, the Courts have held what seems to me, if I may venture to say so,   *d*
> exceeding good sense as well as justice, and which in no manner conflicts with the
> judgment I am pronouncing to-day.'

Leggatt J, basing himself on the report of *Hirst's* case referred to above, concluded that
Mr Tindal Atkinson KC, for the plaintiff, had accepted as unarguable the proposition that
a signature by the bank manager in that case to the representation could not be considered   *e*
to be the signature of the banking company, and that he had, accordingly, confined
himself to the argument that the word 'person' in s 6 of the 1882 Act meant a natural
person and did not include an artificial person such as a corporation. Counsel for the
defendant has, however, drawn our attention to the report in the Law Journal (70 LJKB
828 at 829), where Mr Tindal Atkinson's argument is more fully reported. He contended:

> 'Moreover, the present case is outside the scope of section 6 of the Act of 1828.   *f*
> Here the defendants' manager, acting within the scope of his authority, has made a
> fraudulent representation in their interest, and they have taken benefit of it.'

He was thus, it seems, seeking to pray in aid, as demonstrating that the signature of
the bank manager bound the defendants, the principle established by *Barwick v English
Joint Stock Bank* (1867) LR 2 Exch 259, [1861–73] All ER Rep 194 and referred to by Lord   *g*
Coleridge CJ in the passage above quoted. The application of that principle to the facts of
Hirst's case was thus, by necessary implication, rejected by the court in arriving at the
conclusion at which it did arrive, but it does not appear to us that the point urged by
counsel for the plaintiff was ever taken by Mr Tindal Atkinson, and this accounts for the
absence of any reference to it in the judgment. *Hirst's* case does not, therefore, involve
the insuperable difficulty that the judge thought it posed, for counsel's concession or his   *h*
omission to argue a point do not constitute an authority. If the court does not address
its mind to the point, or pronounce on it, it cannot constitute a binding precedent (see
National Enterprises Ltd v Racal Communications Ltd [1974] 3 All ER 1010 at 1014, [1975]
Ch 397 at 406). It is, perhaps, worth noting that, in the more recent case of *Banbury v
Bank of Montreal* [1917] 1 KB 409, when the appeal was heard in the Court of Appeal,
Scrutton LJ did not cite *Hirst's* case as to the nature of the signature of the corporation   *j*
required to satisfy the Act. He said (at 431):

> '... it has been held in *Swift* v. *Jewsbury* that where the defendant is a company,
> as a banking company, the signature of an agent such as a branch manager will not
> suffice; there must be the seal of the company.'

It is, of course, common ground that *Swift's* case decided no such thing. Indeed, the

seal itself is not a signature. In addition to the seal there are, of course, accompanying
a signatures, but their function is, generally speaking, merely to authenticate the seal.

Of course, it does not follow that, because it was assumed by the court and counsel that
Swift's case had conclusively established that the signature of a duly authorised agent does
not constitute the corporation's signature for the purpose of the section, that assumption
may not have been right. It is, therefore, necessary to examine *Swift*'s case to see exactly
what it did decide. The first point to note is that, although the facts were very similar to
b *Hirst*'s case, it did not concern a corporation at all but a partnership, which does not, as
such, have any separate legal personality apart from the partners themselves. The partners
were carrying on a banking business pursuant to a statutory authority which relaxed the
banking monopoly of the Bank of England in relation to partnerships of more than six
persons so long as they did not carry on business within 65 miles of London and which
provided convenient means by which such partnerships could sue and be sued, but there
c was nothing otherwise extraordinary about the partnership which invested it with any
legal personality apart from its constituent partners. Thus, the case was concerned with
the simple question of the liability of an individual, or rather a number of individuals,
for a false representation contained in a document which none of them had signed. It
had already been decided in *Williams v Mason* (1873) 28 LT 232 that a non-signing
partner, even if he had ratified the act of the signing partner, was entitled to the
d protection afforded by s 6, because the statute in express terms requires the signature of
the party to be charged and no one else, and the signature of a copartner is not his
partner's signature. The signature of an agent who is not also a partner would, therefore,
not be an a fortiori case. Moreover, quite apart from the pure question of construction,
there is good reason for such a provision in the case of an individual, aptly summarised
by Lord Coleridge CJ in this passage from his judgment (LR 9 QB 301 at 311–312):
e
> 'It may be remarked further, that there is very good ground antecedently for the
> observation, because the subject of s. 6 is the charging of a person for an act of fraud,
> and it may well be—and, without diving very deep for motives, one cannot help
> seeing that there was an excellent motive for that enactment—that a person should
> not be proved fraudulent without the matter which is the evidence of his fraud
f > resting on his own signature to a document to be produced,—that it should not rest,
> as before that time it might have rested, on the conflict of evidence as to oral
> communications. If you mean to charge a person with a fraudulent act, whereby
> you have been damnified in respect of the conduct of another, you shall not charge
> that person unless you can produce his own handwriting for the statement of fraud
> by which you say you have been misled.'

g None of this, however, appears in the least appropriate to the case of a corporation
which is incapable of signing any document at all save by some human agency, and not
only does the case not purport to decide the question of corporate responsibility but, in
fact, it goes on expressly, in the passage already quoted, to explain that the basis of the
corporate responsibility of a joint stock company rests on a different set of principles
altogether. In addition to that passage, there is a further passage in the judgment of
h Bramwell B, where he recognises that, even in the case of a partnership, different
considerations may apply where the act of the agent relied on is one necessary for the
carrying on of business. He observed (at 316):

> 'It seems to me that Mr. Day's argument [for the plaintiff] is, that there must be a
> sort of exception put in the statute to meet the necessity of the case. If this were a
j > necessary thing for the purpose of the banking company carrying on their business,
> it might be otherwise . . .'

It seems to us clear from the judgments that the court in *Swift*'s case did not have in
mind at all the question of the application of the section to a corporate entity which,
indeed, they seem to have been prepared to assume, counsel having submitted that it was
covered by *Barwick*'s case. What they were dealing with and rejecting was his submission

that the same principle applied by analogy to a partnership which he submitted was a 'quasi-corporation' (at 309).

In our judgment, therefore, *Swift's* case does not, in fact, provide any support for the assumption that the court was prepared to make in *Hirst's* case.

In any event, even if 80 years ago or so it was assumed that the signature of a duly authorised officer or employee, acting in the course of his duties in the business of the company, was not the signature of the company, then it must also be recalled that it was not until *Barwick's* case in 1867 that it was finally decided that the doctrine of vicarious liability extended to the fraudulent act of the agent of the company committed in the course of its business and for its benefit. The law relative to corporate activities has developed considerably over the years and cannot be taken to have stood still all this time. Parliament is continually placing the obligation on corporate bodies to serve notices in writing of one kind or another and, in the case of local authorities, has expressly provided for such documents to be signed by the proper officer (see s 234(2) of the Local Government Act 1972). Since a company, not being a physical entity, can only act in relation to the outside world by its agents, no one nowadays would question that the signature of the duly authorised agent of the company, acting in the course of the company's business, is the signature of the company. Take as a simple, yet frequent, example the statutory notice of termination of a tenancy given by a company landlord under s 25 of the Landlord and Tenant Act 1954. While there may always be questions as to the authority of the agent who purported to sign the notice, given that he had the company's authority to give such notices and was doing so in the course of his duties in the business of the company, no one would nowadays question that his signature is to be taken as the signature of the company.

We do not, therefore, find any impediment in authority against deciding, and we think that it should now be decided, that the signature on behalf of a company of its duly authorised agent acting within the scope of his authority is, for the purpose of s 6 of the 1828 Act, the signature of the company.

Having concluded that the 1828 Act does not preclude the plaintiff from pursuing its claims in fraud, there is no need for us to consider the subsidiary points raised by the plaintiff in answer to the defence raised by the Act, namely the intent or purposes for which the representations were made or whether they or some of them did or did not relate to the creditworthiness of the borrower.

2. *Are the claims based on negligent but innocent misrepresentations barred by s 2 of the Limitation Act 1980?*

Section 2 provides: 'An action founded on tort shall not be brought after the expiration of six years from the date on which the cause of action accrued.'

The defendant successfully contended before Leggatt J that the accrual of the cause of action occurred when the plaintiff parted with its money and acquired instead claims for repayment of money lent against borrowers, whose ability to repay was, contrary to the alleged representations, a matter of considerable doubt. Again, there is a short answer to this question: it depends on the facts as found at the trial. The plaintiff does not assert that it is entitled to damages to be measured by the difference in the value of the chose in action which it acquired by making this loan as compared with the value it would have had if the representations had been accurate, as in a claim for breach of warranty. Its case is that, if it had known the respects in which the representations were inaccurate, it would not have entered into the contract. Accordingly, it is argued by the defendant that, at the very moment of entering into that contract, the plaintiff must have suffered damage. In our judgment, this bare proposition is not self-evident. The plaintiff is suing in tort, the tort of negligence. To establish a cause of action it must establish not only a breach of duty, but that that breach of duty occasioned it damage. This is axiomatic. It is possible, although it may be improbable, that, at the date when the plaintiff advanced its money, the value of the chose in action which it then acquired was, in fact, not less than the sum which the plaintiff lent, or indeed even exceeded it.

This must depend on the evidence. The mere fact that the innocent but negligent

misrepresentations caused the plaintiff to enter into a contract which it otherwise would
a not have entered into does not inevitably mean that it had suffered damage by merely
entering into the contract. To take and somewhat modify an example canvassed during
the course of argument. A tells B that he wishes to sell his vintage Bentley which he
innocently but negligently represents is a blue label long chassis. It is, in fact, a red label
short chassis. If A had known, he would not have agreed to buy the Bentley, because he
only collects blue label long chassis Bentleys. Assume, however, that the red label short
b chassis Bentleys were at all material times significantly the more valuable cars so that he
was able to resell at a profit. He has then no cause of action.

Our attention was directed to the recent case of *Forster v Outred & Co (a firm)* [1982] 2
All ER 753, [1982] 1 WLR 86, a decision of this court. The facts are important and we
take them from the headnote ([1982] 1 WLR 86). On 8 February 1973 the plaintiff
executed a mortgage in the presence of the defendants, who were acting as her solicitors.
c The mortgage charged her freehold property as security for a loan made by a company
to her son, who subsequently went bankrupt. Following a demand under the mortgage
on 21 January 1975 the plaintiff repaid the loan. By a specially indorsed writ dated 7
January 1977 the plaintiff claimed damages for negligence and/or breach of contract by
the defendants in failing properly to advise her when the mortgage was executed. In
February 1980 the defendants applied to dismiss the action for want of prosecution, and
d on 25 March 1980 the plaintiff's solicitors, who attributed the delay to pressure of other
work, issued another writ. The issue was whether or not the limitation period in relation
to the plaintiff's cause of action in negligence had expired by the date of the defendants'
summons to dismiss the action for want of prosecution and/or by the date of the plaintiff's
second writ issued on 25 March 1980. The court held that her cause of action accrued in
February 1973, notwithstanding that she did not actually become liable for the repayment
e of the loan until the demand was made and, accordingly, the second writ was issued
outside the six years' limitation period and the action begun by the first writ was rightly
dismissed.

It is clear from the judgments (see in particular [1982] 2 All ER 753 at 764, 765, [1982]
1 WLR 86 at 98, 100 per Stephenson and Dunn LJJ) that the court accepted the
defendants' contention that the plaintiff suffered actual damage when she signed the
f mortgage deed, thereby encumbering her freehold interest and reducing the value of her
property and subjecting herself to liability to discharge her son's debts under the
mortgage deed. Such a loss was a quantifiable loss. Equally, in *Baker v Ollard & Bentley (a
firm)* (1982) 126 SJ 593, a case in this court, damage was suffered and the cause of action
accrued when the plaintiff's solicitors negligently failed to carry out their obligations to
secure for her security of tenure in her occupation of the first floor of certain premises so
g that she could freely dispose of her interest. By negligently advising and procuring the
conveyance of the house to her and another family on the trusts for sale described in the
judgment instead of as joint tenants followed by the grant of a long lease to her, the
plaintiff suffered damage because she there and then received an interest of less value
than that which the defendants were under a duty to procure for her.

These two cases are dealing with a different situation. In the former, it was self-evident
h that the plaintiff, when she signed the mortgage deed, suffered some damage. In the
latter, it was pleaded that building societies would not lend on the security of a freehold
of the first floor and, therefore, purchasers would not purchase at a reasonable price. If,
however, the solicitors had done their duty and procured the grant of a long lease, then
building societies would have been prepared to lend on the security of that long lease.
The damage sustained by the plaintiff was the difference in value between the unsaleable
j freehold and the saleable long lease. Those allegations had to be assumed by the court to
be correct when hearing the application to strike out.

Even, however, if we are wrong in concluding that evidence is required to establish
whether or not the plaintiff's alleged cause of action accrued when it advanced the loan,
there is a further matter to consider. In answer to the defendant's Limitation Act plea,
the plaintiff seeks to rely on s 32(1)(b) of the Limitation Act 1980. It is necessary to set
out both paras (a) and (b) of s 32(1), which provides:

'Subject to subsection (3) below, where in the case of any action for which a period of limitation is prescribed by this Act, either—(a) the action is based upon the fraud *a* of the defendant; or (b) any fact relevant to the plaintiff's right of action has been deliberately concealed from him by the defendant . . . the period of limitation shall not begin to run until the plaintiff has discovered the fraud [or] concealment . . . or could with reasonable diligence have discovered it.'

In dealing with this aspect of the case, Leggatt J said: *b*

'According to [counsel for the plaintiff's] argument the affidavits show that relevant matters were deliberately concealed, with the result that the plaintiff had no inkling of any problem or, indeed, of any misrepresentation until after December 1975. He therefore contends that, even if the plaintiff was prima facie statute-barred, it would be saved by s 32 of the Limitation Act 1980. But, as [counsel for the defendant] retorts, in relation to negligent representations, with which alone *c* this part of the argument is concerned, the representations must be assumed to have been made innocently. The allegation made is that it ought to have been known that the representations were untrue. If it was known, why then reliance, as in relation to the first two classes of misrepresentation, could be placed on Lord Tenterden's Act. But this is not a sphere in which the allegations of deliberate concealment can live.'   *d*

In our view, this shows a confusion of thought. Section 32(1)(a) and s 32(1)(b) are alternatives and it does not at all follow that, because a representation may in fact have been made fraudulently, a plaintiff is compelled to rely on s 32(1)(a) alone in repelling a defence of limitation. In the case of a claim in negligence, it is not so much that, as the judge put it, 'the representations must be assumed to have been made innocently' as that *e* whether they were made innocently or otherwise is irrelevant to the cause of action, which is based simply on the breach of a duty to take reasonable care to see that they were true. The plaintiff's case, which is adequately supported in the affidavits for the purpose of these interlocutory proceedings, is that it will be possible to demonstrate at the trial that the falsity of the representations was, at a time between the date when they were made and the date on which a cause of action based on them might otherwise have *f* been barred, known to the defendant and that the relevant facts were then concealed. Counsel for the defendant, in seeking to uphold the judge's decision on this point, links the concealment of the facts with the making of the representations in this way. In order to rely on a non-disclosure, he submits that there must first be established a duty to disclose and that that duty arose and was broken when the defendant first knew of the falsity which, he submits, was when the representations were made, on the plaintiff's *g* own case. Thus, the fraudulent non-disclosure relied on is, in fact, the making of the representation with knowledge of its falsity, a cause of action precluded by the 1828 Act, and one cannot escape from that by dressing up what is essentially a fraudulent misrepresentation as a fraudulent non-disclosure that the misrepresentation was fraudulent. Now, we see the force of this argument if, as counsel for the defendant submits, it is right to say that there was never any independent and continuing duty of *h* disclosure apart from that which was broken on the making of the representations themselves.

The difficulty that he has to face, however, is that the facts appear to be against him. The transaction into which the plaintiff was invited to enter, and did enter, was that of contributing to a syndicate loan where, as it seems to us, quite clearly the defendant was acting in a fiduciary capacity for all the other participants. It was the defendant who *j* received the plaintiff's money and it was the defendant who arranged for and held, on behalf of all the participants, the collateral security for the loan. If, therefore, it was within the defendant's knowledge at any time while it was carrying out its fiduciary duties that the security was, as the plaintiff alleges, inadequate, it must, we think, clearly have been its duty to inform the participants of that fact and its continued failure to do so would constitute a continuing breach of its fiduciary duty. Whether the plaintiff will

be able to establish such a breach of duty as a matter of fact is a question on which we
a   express no opinion, but the material conditions in which such a breach of duty could be
found clearly existed here. The validity of a claim to rely on s 32(1)(b) depends, therefore,
on an analysis of the evidence and this can only be decided at trial.

For the reasons given above, this appeal should be allowed and the summons to set
aside the service of the writ dismissed.

b   *Appeal allowed. Defendant to enter a new acknowledgment of service within 28 days with liberty
to apply. Leave to appeal to the House of Lords refused.*

Solicitors: *Clifford-Turner* (for the plaintiffs); *Freshfields* (for the defendants).

Mary Rose Plummer   Barrister.

c

d

Moore v Ball

FAMILY DIVISION
SIR JOHN ARNOLD P AND HOLLIS J
e   30 JANUARY 1984

*Affiliation – Affiliation order – Variation – Jurisdiction of magistrates – Order varied so that
payments under it to be made to Secretary of State rather than to mother – Complaint by Secretary
of State requesting order be further varied by increasing amount payable – Whether magistrates
can entertain complaint – Whether complaint can be made by person who was not a party to
f   original order – Supplementary Benefits Act 1976, s 19(5) – Magistrates' Courts Act 1980, s 60.*

On the true construction of s 60[a] of the Magistrates' Courts Act 1980, where an affiliation
order has been varied under s 19(5)[b] of the Supplementary Benefits Act 1976 so that
payments under it are to be made to the Secretary of State instead of to the mother, the
Secretary of State is entitled to make a complaint under s 60 to a magistrates' court for an
order that the affiliation order be further varied by increasing the amount payable under
g   it, even though the Secretary of State was not the beneficiary under the original order
(see p 239 *f* to *j*, post).

Notes
For affiliation orders and recovery of expenditure on supplementary benefit, see 33
Halsbury's Laws (4th edn) paras 830–831.
h   For the Supplementary Benefits Act 1976, s 19, see 46 Halsbury's Statutes (3rd edn)
1063.
For the Magistrates' Courts Act 1980, s 60, see 50(2) ibid 1492.

Case stated
j   Thomas Martin Moore (an officer duly appointed by and on behalf of the Secretary of
State for Social Services) appealed, by way of case stated by justices for the county of
Cumbria, acting for the petty sessional division of Maryport, in respect of their

---

a   Section 60 is set out at p 238 *j*, post
b   Section 19(5), so far as material, provides: 'Any affiliation order . . . may . . . be varied so as to
provide for the making of payments, or part thereof, [to the Secretary of State] . . .'

adjudication as a domestic court sitting at Workington on 6 July 1982, whereby they
dismissed his application under s 60 of the Magistrates' Courts Act 1980 for an order   *a*
increasing the amount payable by the respondent under an affiliation order, which had
already been varied on 6 July 1982 by the justices so that payments under it were made
payable to the Secretary of State and not to the mother. The question for the opinion of
the High Court was whether the justices were wrong in law in determining that, when
an affiliation order was varied under s 19(5) of the Supplementary Benefits Act 1976 so
as to provide that payments under the order should be made to the Secretary of State, the   *b*
Secretary of State had no right to apply under s 60 of the 1980 Act for the order to be
further varied by an order increasing the amount of the payments. The facts are set out
in the judgment of Sir John Arnold P.

Simon D Brown for the appellant.   *c*
Henry Globe for the respondent.

SIR JOHN ARNOLD P. This is a point which is raised by the case stated by the   *d*
Cumbrian justices which, surprisingly, seems never to have been considered before. The
case is simplicity itself.

Under the provisions of s 19 of the Supplementary Benefits Act 1976, provision is
made for the transfer of the benefit of an affiliation order to the Secretary of State for
Social Services, in his capacity as the manager of supplementary benefit, in certain
circumstances. The provisions are in this form.

In a case in which supplementary benefit is paid to meet requirements, which include   *e*
those of an illegitimate child, certain provisions are made in the subsequent subsections
of s 19 to enable the Secretary of State to obtain from the person who ought under the
law to meet those requirements the amount required to do so, and two cases are dealt
with. One is the case of the existence of an affiliation order obtained by the mother, and
the other is the case dealt with first in the section, where no such order has been obtained.
In that second case, by sub-s (2), if there is no affiliation order in force the Secretary of   *f*
State may, subject to certain restrictions, make application for one. Then, in that case and
in the case of another statutory provision which has rather fallen into desuetude, the
order may be made in such a way that the payments under it are made to the Secretary
of State. That is sub-s (4), but sub-s (5) is the one which deals with the state of things
where there is an affiliation order in existence.

Under sub-s (5) an affiliation order may, on the application of the Secretary of State, be   *g*
varied so as to provide for the making of the payments to the Secretary of State, in effect,
that being enacted by reference to sub-s (4). Subsection (6) is also worthy of notice,
because there one finds the opposite case in a sense, where it is the mother who desires to
reduce the right of receipt into her hands from those of the Secretary of State. That says:

> 'Any affiliation order which provides for the making of payments [in effect to the   *h*
> Secretary of State] may, on the application of the mother ... be varied so as to
> provide that the payments shall be made to the mother ...'

What has happened in this case is that the procedures in sub-s (5) for causing the right
of receipt to devolve on the Secretary of State have been gone through and the Secretary
of State, being in that position, seeks to employ the provisions of s 60 of the Magistrates'
Courts Act 1980 so as to secure an increase in the amount payable to him under the   *j*
conjoint effects of the original affiliation order and the order of transfer made under
s 19(5) of the 1976 Act. Section 60 provides:

> 'Where a magistrates' court has made an order for the periodical payment of
> money, the court may, by order on complaint, revoke, revive or vary the order.'

What has happened is that the magistrates have said that the court may not receive a complaint under s 60 for a variation (or presumably for any other purpose), because such a complaint can be made only by a person who was the beneficiary of the original order.

The way that is put in the case is this:

'In the absence of a definition of the word "complainant" in relation to [an application under s 60] and because our powers sprang from statute, "complainant" ought to be construed narrowly, and we felt unable to extend the definition to encompass anyone other than a party to the original order (or person acting on their behalf) or someone specifically authorised by statute.'

The only issue on this appeal by way of case stated is whether that construction is correct.

It is perfectly true, so far as the extensive researches of counsel on both sides and those who have assisted them have gone, that there is no definition of 'complainant' or, more precisely, of 'complaint' in terms of who can make one, but equally there is no jurisprudence, common law, by statute or otherwise, which provides a guide as to whether it is sufficient to sustain a right to make a complaint, where a complaint is authorised, that the legitimate class of complainants is limited by reference to either, on the one hand, such right as is given by a party to the order about which complaint is sought to be made or, on the other hand, by a person having the benefit of that order for himself or herself. So the case resolves itself into what are the principles by which the court should be guided in supplying that definition which is absent from statutory enactment.

The Secretary of State says that, since he is the person to whom, by an order of the court, the sum payable under the original order is directed to be enjoyed by him beneficially, then logic dictates that he should be the person who has the right to take advantage of such statutory provisions as there may be to regulate the amount of the payment, namely s 60 of the 1980 Act. He supports that partly, as it seems to me, by pointing to an equal illogicality, if there be absent a power by the mother, who has reduced into her power the right to receive the relevant payments beneficially, where the original order was made under s 19(2) of the 1976 Act for payment to the Secretary of State, a power given to the mother by sub-s (6) of the same section; and he says, that being the logic of the matter, it is the function of the court to flesh out that which is not provided for one way or the other by the relevant statute in the sense of logical desirability.

Nowhere is a power given to such a person as the Secretary of State in this situation, or the mother in the hypothesised situation, to make such a complaint or take advantage of such a provision as that in s 60, so that the argument which is often available in this sort of case, that in effect inclusio unius est exclusio alterius, is simply not available or relevant. In the absence of any such indication and of any other indication elsewhere in the jurisprudence, my conclusion is that logic should dictate that this word 'complaint' in s 60 should be seen and construed to be a complaint made by any person at least, who has the right to recover for his own benefit the amount payable under the order in relation to which the quantum is sought to be varied. It is not necessary to go beyond that in this case, and so far I would go. I would therefore allow the appeal.

HOLLIS J. I agree with the judgment delivered by Sir John Arnold P and have nothing to add.

Appeal allowed. Case remitted to magistrates to be dealt with on its merits.

Solicitors: *Solicitor to the Department of Health and Social Security; Brockbank Tyson & Co,* Whitehaven (for the respondent).

Bebe Chua   Barrister.

South West Water Authority v Rumble's   *a*

COURT OF APPEAL, CIVIL DIVISION
ACKNER AND O'CONNOR LJJ
27 FEBRUARY, 12 MARCH 1984

Water supply – Charges – Power of water authority to make charges – Charges for services   *b*
performed – Liability of person who has not received services – Power of water authority to make
such charges for services performed, facilities provided or rights made available by them as they
think fit – Sewerage services – Roof drainage – Occupier of shop – Shop not connected to public
sewers – Occupier not receiving sewerage services – Surface water from roof on hereditament
above occupier's shop draining into water authority's sewer – Whether water authority having
power to impose charge on occupier for sewerage and drainage services provided by authority –   *c*
Water Act 1973, s 30(1) (1A).

The respondent was the tenant and occupier of a ground floor shop situated in the area
of the appellant water authority. There was no water, no sink, no toilet or draining
facilities laid on to the premises, which formed a separate hereditament within the   *d*
meaning of s 2 of the Water Charges Act 1976. There was a separate hereditament above
the respondent's premises containing facilities connected to the main sewer, and above
which was a roof from which surface water was drained into the water authority's sewer.
The water authority sought to charge the respondent £196·84 for water services under s
30ᵈ of the Water Act 1973 but the respondent refused to pay. The registrar held that the
respondent was liable for the water charges, but on appeal the judge held that it was not.   *e*
The water authority appealed, contending (i) that the removal of surface water from the
roof was removal of water from the building and constituted, for the purposes of
s 30(1)(a), a service performed or facility provided for the occupiers of the building as a
whole, including the respondent, (ii) that the drainage of water by a sewer from the
building as a whole constituted, for the purposes of s 30(1)(b) and (1A)(a), drainage from a
hereditament since the respondent's shop was an integral part of the building, and (iii)   *f*
that the drainage of water falling on the roof of the premises above the shop amounted
to the 'use, for the benefit of the hereditament, of facilities which drain to a sewer' for
the purposes of s 30(1)(b) and (1A)(b).

Held – The appeal would be dismissed for the following reasons—   *g*
    (1) Since no water went into or out of the respondent's premises the respondent was
not a person who availed himself of the services, facilities and rights of the water
authority and therefore it was not liable under s 30(1)(a) of the 1973 Act to pay the water
charges (see p 243 a to c and p 244 b and e, post); dictum of Viscount Dilhorne in *Daymond
v South West Water Authority* [1976] 1 All ER at 50 applied.
    (2) In the absence of clear and unambiguous language to the contrary, s 30(1)(b) did   *h*
not create a liability for water charges merely because a hereditament which was not
itself drained formed part of a building which was drained into a public sewer (see p 243
d to f and p 244 b and e, post).
    (3) Any benefit which the respondent received from the drainage of water from the
roof of the premises above its shop was merely an indirect result of the use of the drainage
system by the owner or occupier of the hereditament which included the roof. Since that   *j*
owner or occupier used the drainage primarily for his own benefit and he alone had
control of it and could modify or disconnect it the respondent did not have the 'use' of it
for the purposes of s 30(1)(b) and (1A)(b) (see p 243 b j and p 244 a b and e, post).

---

a   Section 30, so far as material, is set out at p 242 d to h, post

Notes

a For the power of a water authority to make charges for services performed, facilities provided or rights made available, see Supplement to 39 Halsbury's Laws (3rd edn) para 918A(6).

For the Water Act 1973, s 30(1) and (1A) (as substituted by the Water Charges Act 1976, s 2(1)), see 46 Halsbury's Statutes (3rd edn) 2099.

b **Case referred to in judgments**
Daymond v South West Water Authority [1976] 1 All ER 39, [1976] AC 609, [1975] 3 WLR 865, HL.

Cases also cited
Prosser (A) & Son Ltd v Levy [1955] 3 All ER 577, [1955] 1 WLR 1224, CA.
c *Woodspring DC v Taylor* (1982) Times, 15 May.

Appeal
The South West Water Authority appealed against the decision of his Honour Judge Chope given on 25 August 1983 in the Truro County Court where he allowed an appeal by the defendant, A B & P J Rumble trading as Rumble's, against an order of Mr Registrar
d Lyne dated 9 June 1983 that the defendant pay to the water authority the sum of £196·84 in respect of water charges levied pursuant to s 30 of the Water Act 1973, as amended by s 2 of the Water Charges Act 1976, on the defendant's shop at 5 Fore Street, Newquay. The facts are set out in the judgment of Ackner LJ.

Roger Toulson for the water authority.
e Mr Rumble appeared in person.

Cur adv vult

12 March. The following judgments were read.

ACKNER LJ. The occupier, a partnership trading under the name Rumble's, the
f respondent to this appeal, is the tenant of a shop in Newquay, situated on the ground floor of 5 Fore Street. There is no water, no sink, no toilet or draining facilities laid on to the premises. It is a unit of property which is shown as a separate item in the valuation list and is thus an hereditament within the meaning of s 2 of the Water Charges Act 1976.

Above the shop is another separate hereditament consisting of two floors of residential
g accommodation which has toilet and washing facilities which are connected to the main sewer. Above that residential accommodation is a roof, the surface water of which runs off and goes down a downpipe, into a gulley and then into the South West Water Authority's, the appellants', sewer. The water authority are seeking to charge the occupier £196·84 for water services which they allege they provide to it. This charge is calculated by reference to the rateable value of its shop (£930) as a specified rate in the pound, plus
h an annual standing charge. We have not been given the precise figure charged on the residential premises, but it is probably less than that charged on the shop. The occupier, very understandably, says that as there is no water supply to the shop and there are no appliances inside the shop which drain to a sewer it should be charged nothing, or a great deal less than it is in fact being charged.

The registrar of the Truro County Court found in favour of the water authority, but
j his Honour Judge Chope on 25 August 1983 allowed the occupier's appeal, holding that the water authority were not entitled to make any charge but, if he was wrong about that, the basis of the charge seemed to him to be so unfair as to discriminate unduly against those who have no sewerage and no drainage other than the benefit of having a rain-water downpipe which they cannot control from a roof which they do not own, and this was thus contrary to s 30(5) of the Water Act 1973.

Section 30(1) of the 1973 Act provided as follows:

> 'Subject to the provisions of this Act, a water authority shall have power to fix, *a* and to demand, take and recover such charges for the services performed, facilities provided or rights made available by them . . . as they think fit.'

In *Daymond v South West Water Authority* [1976] 1 All ER 39, [1976] AC 609 the House of Lords held by a majority that s 30(1) did not give power to a water authority to require payment of sewer charges from those whose premises were not connected to public *b* sewers. In the words of Viscount Dilhorne ([1976] 1 All ER 39 at 50, [1976] AC 609 at 640):

> 'The natural inference to be drawn from a provision which only says that a statutory body can demand, take and recover such charges for the services it performs, the facilities it provides and the rights it makes available, as it thinks fit, is, in my opinion, that it can charge only those who avail themselves of its services, *c* facilities and rights.'

It was as a result of that decision that the Water Charges Act 1976 was enacted, which provided for the refund by water authorities of charges for sewerage and sewage disposal levied in 1974–75 and 1975–76 on properties not connected to public sewers and which also contained provisions to clarify the water authorities' charging powers. Section 2(1) *d* substituted new subsections for s 30(1) of the 1973 Act. It provided, so far as is material to this case, as follows:

> '**2.** *Water authorities' power to charge.*—(1) The following subsections shall be substituted for section 30(1) of the Water Act 1973—
>
> "(1) Subject to the provisions of this Act, a water authority shall have power to fix such charges for the services performed, facilities provided or rights made *e* available by them (including separate charges for separate services, facilities or rights or combined charges for a number of services, facilities or rights) as they think fit, and to demand, take and recover such charges—(a) for services performed, facilities provided or rights made available in the exercise of any of their functions, from persons for whom they perform the services, provide the facilities or make the rights available, and (b) without prejudice to paragraph *f* (a) above,—(i) for services performed, facilities provided or rights made available in the exercise of functions under section 14 above, from persons liable to be rated in respect of hereditaments to which this sub-paragraph applies, and (ii) for services performed, facilities provided or rights made available in the exercise of functions specified in subsection (1B) below, from all persons liable to be rated in respect of hereditaments in their area or *g* particular classes of such persons.
>
> (1A) Subsection (1)(b)(i) above applies to a hereditament if—(a) it is drained by a sewer or drain connecting, either directly or through an intermediate sewer or drain, with a public sewer provided for foul water or surface water or both, or (b) the person liable to be rated in respect of the hereditament has the use, for the benefit of the hereditament, of facilities which drain to a sewer or *h* drain so connecting, or (c) it is subject to special rating . . .".'

The water authority make three separate submissions as to their entitlement to charge the occupier, only the third of which was argued before the county court judge. I will deal with them seriatim.

j
Section 30(1)(a)

The water authority submit that the removal of surface water from *the building* by means of the public sewerage system and/or the maintenance of the public sewerage system so that it continues to serve that function constitutes a service performed and/or a facility provided for the occupiers of the *building as a whole*, including the occupier's

premises, and not merely for the occupier of the uppermost part of the building. It is
a accordingly submitted that the occupier is therefore liable to charge under this subsection
of the amended s 30 of the 1973 Act.

However, the words of s 30(1)(a) are essentially the same words as those contained in
the original s 30(1), namely that the water authority may demand, take and recover
charges 'for services performed, facilities provided or rights made available'. A natural
inference to be drawn from this provision, as quoted earlier in this judgment from the
b speech of Viscount Dilhorne in the *Daymond* case, is that the authority can only charge
those who *avail* themselves of the authority's service, facilities and rights. The occupier is
not, in my judgment, availing itself of the services, facilities or rights. No water comes
into its premises and no water goes out of them, let alone into the water authorities'
sewerage system. If water did in fact drain out of the occupier's premises into a soakaway
in the garden of the building, then no one could argue that it was availing itself of the
c water authority's facilities. When no water at all comes out of its premises, it is an a
fortiori case. I accordingly cannot accept this submission.

Section 30(1)(b)(i), by virtue of sub-s (1A)(a)
For this submission the water authority submit that they are seeking to recover charges
from the occupier, who is a person liable to be rated in respect of the shop, which is a
d hereditament within the meaning of the 1976 Act (see s 3(3)). I have already confirmed
that the shop is a hereditament within the meaning of the Act. The water authority next
argue, relying on the words of s 30(1A), that the hereditament (the shop) is drained by a
sewer or drain connecting with a public sewer, inasmuch as the building as a whole is so
drained, and the occupier's shop is an integral part of that building. Accordingly, the
service is performed or the facility is provided in the exercise of their functions under
e s 14 of the 1973 Act. However, in my judgment, it cannot be said that its hereditament
is drained by a sewer etc. There is no water coming out of it. If Parliament had intended
that there should be liability where the hereditament, although not itself drained, forms
part of a building which is drained into a public sewer, it could and should have been so
stated. It is well established that all charges on citizens of this country must be imposed
by clear and unambiguous language. Subsection (1A)(a) of s 30 has, therefore, no
f application.

Section 30(1)(b)(i), by virtue of sub-s (1A)(b)
The water authority in this submission rely on sub-s (1A)(b) and contend that the
occupier being 'the person liable to be rated in respect of the hereditament [the shop] has
the use, for the benefit of the hereditament, of facilities which drain to a sewer, or drain
g so connecting' because it has the benefit of the drainage system which collects water from
the roof over the building in which its shop is situate and this discharges into a public
sewer. This was the submission made to the county court judge. He said this:

> '. . . I find it extremely difficult to find the [occupier] has the use of the facility of
> the sewerage. There is a roof, the landlord is obliged to repair it, but it is not a
> facility of which the [occupier] has the use. No doubt the occupiers of the premises
h > above have the use but it seems to me quite unreal for the [water authority] to say
> that there is a facility of which the [occupier] in its self-contained shop has the use.
> There is a facility for water to be directed into the public sewer. [It] cannot use it,
> [it] has no control over it and is it for [its] benefit? Is it to be said that any property
> which avoids flooding because surface water from a separate property is directed
> into or finds its way into a public sewer is using the facility of the drainage for its
j > own benefit? If the [water authority's] construction is applied, it would mean that
> because somewhere in the vicinity of a property there was a public sewer into which
> surface water might find its way, without being directed by the occupier of that
> property, that occupier was liable as using a facility for the benefit of his property.'

I am prepared to accept that it may be of *benefit* to the occupier that the water falling on the roof over the premises above it is effectively drained away from the building, but that does not mean that it has the *use* of that drainage system. It is the owner or occupier of the hereditament which includes the roof who uses it, i e avails himself of that drainage system, primarily for his own benefit, but maybe indirectly for the benefit of other occupants of the building. It is that owner or occupier who has the control of the drainage system who can disconnect it from the sewage system, or otherwise alter it at his will. The occupier can do no more than take note of the fact that, for the present, that is the method of draining the roof, a purely passive role. Counsel for the water authority, with characteristic frankness, was prepared to accept that his third point was the weakest and that sub-s $1(A)(b)$ appeared to be designed for the case of a person who is liable to be rated, having the use in some other premises of a facility which benefits his hereditament, e g the use of a lavatory in other premises which drains to a sewer. I therefore reject this submission.

I would, therefore, dismiss this appeal. As regards the suggestion that the charge, if it could have been validly made, was excessive, and therefore amounted to undue discrimination within the meaning of s 30(5) of the 1973 Act, I would have accepted counsel for the water authority's submission that, while the judge in his discretion was entitled to allow the point, although apparently not argued before the registrar, to be taken and to set aside the registrar's decision, he ought to have ordered a trial of this issue, because there was insufficient material on which to make a decision. It seems quite clear that the water authority had not come prepared to deal with what is a complex question and, understandably, Mr Rumble, who has acted throughout in person, was unaware of the technical problems involved.

O'CONNOR LJ. I agree this appeal should be dismissed for the reasons given by Ackner LJ.

Appeal dismissed. Leave to appeal to the House of Lords granted on terms that the water authority pay the respondent's costs of the appeal to the House of Lords in any event.

Solicitors: *I A D Todd*, Exeter (for the water authority).

Carolyn Toulmin   Barrister.

Procedure Direction

HOUSE OF LORDS

House of Lords – Leave to appeal – Petition for leave to appeal – Criminal appeals – Oral hearing of petition – Fee allowed on taxation.

The Appeal Committee of the House of Lords have made the following amendment to Direction no 11 as to Procedure applicable to Criminal Appeals (Form of Appeal, Directions as to Procedure (the Red Book, 1982) p 9):

Direction 11(i) is amended by leaving out in line 8 the words 'unless a Legal Aid Order provides otherwise'.

12 April 1984

JOHN SAINTY
Clerk of the Parliaments.

a

Darch v Weight

QUEEN'S BENCH DIVISION
ROBERT GOFF LJ AND MANN J
24 NOVEMBER 1983

b *Criminal law – Harbouring escaped prisoner – Ingredients of offence – Necessary to prove accused carried out some positive act to provide shelter for escapee – Lodger in house which escapees entered and stayed in overnight engaging them in conversation – Whether lodger carried out positive act to provide shelter – Whether necessary for an accused to have an interest in the property in which shelter provided to constitute offence – Criminal Justice Act 1961, s 22(2).*

c The appellant was a lodger in G's house. On her return to the house one day she found three men with G and was told that they were escapees from prison. The appellant and G spent some time talking to the men and discussing prison conditions, the circumstances of their escape etc. The following day the men left. The appellant was subsequently charged with knowingly harbouring persons who had escaped from prison, contrary to s 22(2)[a] of the Criminal Justice Act 1961. The magistrates held that by entertaining the escapees by way of conversation she had assisted and encouraged the commission of an *d* offence under s 22(2) of the 1961 Act and convicted her. The appellant appealed, contending (i) that she was a lodger with no right to admit or exclude persons from the house and was therefore unable to 'harbour' the men, and (ii) that she had not knowingly 'harboured' escaped prisoners since she had not carried out any positive act to assist or provide support or shelter for the prisoners.

e **Held** – A person knowingly 'harboured' an escapee from prison for the purposes of s 22(2) of the 1961 Act only if it was proved that he carried out some positive act to provide shelter, in the sense of providing a refuge, for the escapee. However, if the accused did carry out a positive act to provide shelter for an escapee he could be guilty of 'harbouring' the escapee notwithstanding that he had no interest in the property in which he gave shelter but was, for example, a mere lodger there or even a trespasser. *f* Accordingly, where the only activity of a lodger in a house which escapees from prison entered and stayed in overnight was to engage the escapees in conversation regarding their prison conditions, the circumstances and reasons for their escape and their future plans, the lodger was not guilty of harbouring the escapees because she had not carried out any positive act to provide them with shelter. The appeal would therefore be allowed (see p 247 *d* to *h* and p 248 *a* to *d* and *h*, post).

g *R v Mistry* [1980] Crim LR 177 applied.

Notes
For harbouring an escaped prisoner, see 11 Halsbury's Laws (4th edn) 970.
For the Criminal Justice Act 1961, s 22, see 25 Halsbury's Statutes (3rd edn) 862.

h **Case referred to in judgments**
R v Mistry [1980] Crim LR 177, CA.

Cases also cited
R v Singh (Amar Jit) [1973] 1 All ER 122, [1972] 1 WLR 1600, CA.
R v Clarkson [1971] 3 All ER 344, [1971] 1 WLR 1402, C-MAC.
j

Case stated
On 14 December 1982 the appellant, Diana Darch, was convicted by the justices for the petty sessional division of Weymouth and Portland, sitting as a magistrates' court at

---

a Section 22(2), so far as material, is set out at p 246 *e*, post

Weymouth, of knowingly harbouring three persons who had escaped from Her Majesty's
Prison, The Verne, Portland, Dorset, contrary to s 22 of the Criminal Justice Act 1961
and was sentenced to one month's imprisonment suspended for two years. The appellant
appealed against the conviction by way of a case stated by the magistrates for the opinion
of the High Court dated 4 March 1983. The question for the opinion of the High Court
in the case stated was 'whether a person may in law be convicted of the offence of
knowingly harbouring escaped prisoners under section 22 of the Criminal Justice Act
1961, where the evidence shows that such a person had not carried out any positive act
to assist or provide support or shelter for any prisoner'. The facts are set out in the
judgment of Robert Goff LJ.

David Fish for the appellant.
Michael Parroy for the respondent.

ROBERT GOFF LJ. There is before the court an appeal by way of case stated by the
appellant from a decision by the Weymouth magistrates when they convicted the
appellant on 14 December 1982 of a charge that she, between 19 and 23 October 1982,
at Weymouth, did knowingly harbour three persons, namely Peter Randall, John Randall
and Sonny Duke, who had escaped from Her Majesty's Prison, The Verne, Portland,
Dorset, contrary to s 22 of the Criminal Justice Act 1961.
    Section 22 of the 1961 Act, so far as material, provides:

    '. . . (2) If any person knowingly harbours a person who has escaped from a prison
    or other institution to which the said section thirty-nine [of the Prison Act 1952]
    applies, or who, having been sentenced in any part of the United Kingdom or in any
    of the Channel Islands or the Isle of Man to imprisonment or detention, is otherwise
    unlawfully at large, or gives to any such person any assistance with intent to prevent,
    hinder or interfere with his being taken into custody, he shall be liable [and it states
    the relevant penalties] . . .'

    The facts set out by the magistrates in the case are as follows. They are quite brief so I
shall set them out in full:

    '(a) The Appellant lodged with Mrs. Jill Grant at 111 Corporation Road,
    Weymouth, although on what terms or basis we are uncertain. (b) On the evening
    of the twentieth of October, the Appellant returned home to find three men in the
    house as were Mrs. Grant and her daughter Esther. (c) The Appellant was told that
    the men had arrived, one asking for her or for another woman and that they were
    escapees from the Verne. (d) The Appellant and Mrs. Grant spent some time
    entertaining the men in conversation discussing prison conditions, the circumstances
    and reasons for their escape and their plans for the future. (e) The next morning,
    the twenty first of October, the men were still in the house when Mrs. Grant and
    the Appellant left to go shopping. When they returned at about twelve thirty in the
    afternoon the escapees were still there. They left at about one thirty after a discussion
    as to where they might go.'

    The magistrates dismissed the submission of no case to answer and the appellant
elected to give no evidence. A submission was made on behalf of the appellant that she
was a lodger with no right to admit or exclude and was therefore unable to harbour these
men.
    The magistrates then expressed the following opinion in the case:

    'We were of the opinion that prima facie the escapees were as much the guests of
    the Appellant as of any other occupier of that house. That in any case the Appellant
    had done far more than stand idly by. In entertaining the escapees by way of
    conversation during the evening and the next afternoon she was assisting and
    encouraging the commission of the offence in a way she knew to be wrong and she

a was rightly charged as a principal. Accordingly we convicted the Appellant and after adjourning for reports on the 7th January we sentenced her to one month's imprisonment, suspended two years.'

The magistrates posed the following question for the opinion of the court:

b '... whether a person may in law be convicted of the offence of knowingly harbouring escaped prisoners under Section 22 of the Criminal Justice Act 1961, where the evidence shows that such a person had not carried out any positive act to assist or provide support or shelter for any prisoner.'

In considering this case I think I should first record the fact that we have been told, very helpfully, by counsel for the respondent, that Mrs Jill Grant, who was charged and convicted at the same time as the appellant, subsequently appealed to the Crown Court, and her conviction was then quashed but no reasons were given on that occasion why c her conviction was quashed.

The question of law in this case is concerned with the problem whether a person can be convicted of the relevant offence where the evidence shows that that person had not performed any positive act to assist, provide support or shelter for any prisoner. In this connection we are addressing our minds, of course, to the offence created by the first part d of s 22(2) of the 1961 Act and not with that created by the second part. The second part is concerned with persons who give assistance to escapees with a specified intent. The first part is concerned with persons who harbour escapees knowingly.

I am of the opinion that the word 'harbour' in this context means to shelter a person, in the sense of giving refuge to that person. This is an ordinary dictionary meaning of the word. We have been referred to the Oxford English Dictionary and we can see, at e no 3 under the heading of the word 'harbour', that it means 'to give shelter to, to shelter'. This appears to me to be the natural meaning of the word in its context in this particular statute and I am fortified in this opinion by a case which has been cited to us by counsel for the appellant, a transcript having been provided by counsel for the respondent. This is *R v Mistry* [1980] Crim LR 177, which was decided by the Court of Appeal, Criminal Division, on 8 November 1979. It was concerned with an appeal under a different statute, f the Immigration Act 1971. Section 25(2) of that Act is concerned with a person knowingly harbouring anyone whom he knows or has reasonable cause for believing to be either an illegal entrant or a person who has committed certain specified offences.

Roskill LJ, who delivered the judgment of the Court of Appeal on that occasion, regarded the word 'harbouring' in that statute as meaning 'giving shelter to'. I for myself can see no material distinction between the use of the word 'harbouring' in that statute and the use of the word 'harbours' in the present statute. Indeed Roskill LJ in the course g of his judgment did refer to the present statute.

I would add that, in a passage towards the end of his judgment, Roskill LJ referred to the fact that a person can harbour another person within the meaning of the section of the 1971 Act, and I would say also within the meaning of s 22(2) of the 1961 Act, even though such a person may have no interest in the land in question and even though he h may have no right to be on the land in question.

I refer to the transcript of Roskill LJ's judgment in *R v Mistry*, where he says:

j 'Anybody who is in a position to provide shelter to an illegal immigrant is, by reason of the fact that he provides that shelter with knowledge that that person is an illegal immigrant is guilty of the offence. It does not matter whether he did it as a freeholder, a lessee, a licensee, a person with only temporary accommodation or, as Ormrod LJ said, even a squatter in a squat. The question is not in what capacity he is doing it, but what he is doing as between himself and the illegal immigrant. If he offers the illegal immigrant shelter for him or her, then whatever his right or lack of right in those premises, whatever his title or interest or lack of it, he is in our view plainly guilty.'

With that guidance we can see that it is necessary in each case to consider whether the accused person has given shelter to a person within the category specified in the statute, bearing in mind that he may be able to give shelter to such a person even though he has no interest in the relevant place and even if in fact he himself is a trespasser in that relevant place. To give an example raised in the course of argument before us, if a man looked after the key to his neighbour's house while he was away, and used a garden shed in his neighbour's garden to give shelter to an escaped prisoner, it is difficult to see why that man should not in those circumstances be harbouring the escapee, even though he was trespassing himself on the shed when he made it available to the escapee.

Such being, in the light of the authorities, the meaning of the word 'harbours' within this section, I turn to the question of law in the case, which is whether a person may in law be convicted of the relevant offence where the evidence shows that such a person has not carried out any positive act to assist or to provide support or shelter for any prisoner. In my judgment, of those three words the only relevant word for the purposes of this part of s 22(2) of the 1961 Act is the word 'shelter'. Merely to assist or to provide support (in the sense in which I read it as being exclusive of shelter) would not be enough to commit the offence; there has to be a provision of shelter in the sense of providing a refuge for an escapee before there can be a conviction on the offence charged under the first part of s 22(2). Furthermore, if a person has not carried out any positive act to provide shelter for an escapee, I do not see how that person can be guilty of the offence in question. I would answer the question of law as posed to this court in the negative.

It was drawn to our attention, however, by counsel for the respondent that in the passage where the magistrates expressed their opinion it appears that the magistrates may have been looking at the matter on the basis that the appellant was assisting and encouraging the commission of an offence by another person, the landlady, Mrs Jill Grant.

The only finding of fact regarding the activity of the appellant was that she simply engaged the escapees in conversation on two occasions: in the evening, when she herself came back to the premises, and on the following afternoon. In those circumstances the magistrates may have been of the opinion that, by engaging the escapees in conversation, the appellant was encouraging the commission of the offence by Mrs Jill Grant. However, we now know that Mrs Grant's conviction has been quashed, and therefore she has been held not guilty as a principal. On those bare facts, we do not think it would be possible to approach this case on the basis that the appellant could herself be guilty of encouraging the commission of an offence by another person, when that person has been held to be not guilty of the offence. There may be very special cases where a person can be guilty of encouraging the commission of an offence by another when that person has been held not to be guilty. It has been suggested this may be so where some special defence is open to that other person, but there are no facts of that kind before this court. All we know is that Mrs Grant's conviction has been quashed, and, on the material before us, we cannot say that the appellant herself could properly be convicted of the offence as having encouraged or assisted in the commission of the offence by Mrs Grant.

In those circumstances, I myself would answer the question of law in the negative, and I would allow the appeal.

MANN J. I agree.

Appeal allowed.

Solicitors: *Turner Kenneth Brown*, agents for *Hollowell & Bollam*, Weymouth (for the appellant); *Sharpe Pritchard & Co*, agents for *Michael J Davies*, Dorchester (for the respondent).

Dilys Tausz   Barrister.

a # R Walker & Son (a firm) and others v British Railways Board (Lancashire County Council, third party) and another

CHANCERY DIVISION
b GOULDING J
15 FEBRUARY 1984

Railway – Accommodation works – Duty of railway authority to maintain works – Fencing separating land acquired for railway from adjoining agricultural land – Railway authority required to maintain fencing 'at all times thereafter' – Railway closed down, track and railway
c *equipment removed and land sold to third party – Fencing not maintained – Cattle straying from adjoining land through fencing onto site of disused railway – Whether railway authority under duty to maintain fencing in perpetuity – Whether cesser of use of land for railway terminating railway authority's obligation to maintain fence – Railways Clauses Consolidation Act 1845, s 68.*

In 1845 a railway company acquired under a special Act which incorporated the Railways
d Clauses Consolidation Act 1845 land (the railway land) for the purpose of constructing a railway on it. Pursuant to its obligations under s 68[a] of the 1845 Act the railway company constructed a fence along the boundary between the railway land and adjoining agricultural land and thereafter, pursuant to s 68, maintained the fence. The railway company's rights and obligations became vested in the British Railways Board, which in the exercise of its general powers closed down the railway in the early 1970s, removed
e the railway tracks and other railway equipment from the railway land and conveyed the land to the local county council in 1974. The conveyance required the county council to perform the board's obligations in regard to accommodation works such as fencing and to indemnify the board against liability in respect of such works. The plaintiffs, who had been the occupiers of the adjoining agricultural land since 1964, alleged that since 1976 the fence dividing their land from the railway land had not been maintained and in
f consequence had become dilapidated and was no longer stockproof. The plaintiffs brought an action against the board seeking specific performance of the board's obligation under s 68 to maintain the fence and/or damages. The board brought third party proceedings against the county council claiming indemnification against the plaintiffs' claim. On the application of the board and the county council a preliminary issue was ordered to be tried in the action and third party proceedings, namely whether on the
g true construction of s 68, which required a railway authority to make and 'at all times thereafter maintain' fences for the accommodation of the occupiers of adjoining land, the board was liable to maintain the fence in perpetuity notwithstanding the abandonment of the railway, cesser of use of the railway land for railway purposes, the removal of the track and railway equipment from the railway land and the sale of that land to the county council.
h

Held – Although s 68 of the 1845 Act imposed a duty on a railway authority, once it had made accommodation works, to maintain accommodation works such as fencing 'at all times thereafter' that duty ceased if the purpose of the particular accommodation work became extinct. However, the fact that a railway adjoining agricultural land had been
j abandoned and ceased to exist so that the need to protect cattle straying from the adjoining land onto the railway no longer existed did not necessarily mean that the purpose for which fencing dividing the railway from the adjoining land was constructed had become extinct, because the purposes for which fencing was to be constructed under

---

a Section 68, so far as material, is set out at p 252 d to f, post

s 68 included not only the protection of cattle from straying onto the railway but also the
separation of land taken for the railway from adjoining land and the protection of   *a*
adjoining land from trespass. Accordingly, on the true construction of s 68 the board's
obligation to maintain the fence 'at all times thereafter' had not been terminated merely
by reason of the abandonment of the railway, the removal of track and equipment from
the railway land and the sale of that land to the county council (see p 253 g to j, p 254 g
to j and p 256 b c, post).

Midland Rly Co v Gribble [1895] 2 Ch 827 applied.   *b*

Simpson v Caledonian Rly Co (1878) 5 R (Ct of Sess) 525 and Cairns Bros v Canadian
National Rly [1937] 2 DLR 537 considered.

Notes

For the obligation of a railway undertaker to maintain accommodation works, see 38
Halsbury's Laws (4th edn) para 871, and for cases on accommodation works by way of   *c*
fencing, see 38 Digest (Reissue) 201–212, 1258–1379.

For the Railways Clauses Consolidation Act 1845, s 68, see 26 Halsbury's Statutes (3rd
edn) 766.

Cases referred to in judgment

Cairns Bros v Canadian National Rly [1937] 2 DLR 537.   *d*
Cooper v Rly Executive (Southern Region) [1953] 1 All ER 477, [1953] 1 WLR 223.
Dixon v Great Western Rly Co [1897] 1 QB 300, CA.
Midland Rly Co v Gribble [1895] 2 Ch 827, CA.
Moore v Rawson (1824) 3 B & C 332, [1824–34] All ER Rep 173, 107 ER 756.
Simpson v Caledonian Rly Co (1878) 5 R (Ct of Sess) 525.

e

Preliminary issue

By a writ issued on 7 November 1980 the plaintiffs, R Walker & Son (a firm), John Ernest
Dawson and Frederick Robert Dawson, who claimed to have been in occupation of land
forming part of Lina Laithe Farm, Earby, near Colne in Lancashire, as tenants or owners
since 1964, claimed against the defendants, the British Railways Board, specific
performance of the board's statutory obligation to maintain a fence along the boundary   *f*
between the plaintiffs' land and adjoining land forming part of a former, disused, railway
between Colne and Skipton, damages in addition to or in lieu of specific performance,
and further or other relief. By a third party notice dated 29 April 1981 the board claimed
against Lancashire County Council as third party indemnification against the plaintiffs'
claim on the grounds that by a conveyance made in 1974 the board conveyed the relevant
part of the site of the disused railway to the West Riding County Council, the predecessors   *g*
in title of Lancashire County Council, and the conveyance provided that West Riding
County Council should perform the board's obligations relating to fencing or other
accommodation works for the benefit of the owners or occupiers of land adjoining the
railway and should indemnify the board against liability in respect thereof. The board
and Lancashire County Council applied, by summonses dated 9 and 24 January 1984, for
an order that the following preliminary issue be determined pursuant to RSC Ord 33,   *h*
r 3, namely whether on the true construction of s 68 of the Railways Clauses Consolidation
Act 1845 (i) the board's obligations to maintain fences pursuant to s 68 remained in
perpetuity on the board in respect of the site of the disused railway notwithstanding (a)
the board's cesser of user of the site for running trains, (b) the board's cesser of user
thereof for railway purposes, (c) the removal of the railway track and other equipment
from the site and (d) the sale of the site in 1974 to West Riding County Council; and if   *j*
not (ii) whether cesser of the board's statutory obligations under s 68 occurred on the date
of any of the above-mentioned events (a) (b) or (c) (d) and if so on which one or occurred
on some other date and if so which date. By an order dated 27 January 1984 Master
Barratt ordered the trial of the preliminary issue in the action and third party proceedings.
The facts are set out in the judgment.

Martin Buckley for the plaintiffs.
a   *Timothy Jennings* for the board.
Peter W Smith for Lancashire County Council.

GOULDING J. I have to determine a question arising in an action between a number of persons as plaintiffs and the British Railways Board (to which I will refer as 'the board') as defendant, whereto the Lancashire County Council has been brought in by third party
b   proceedings. The plaintiffs claim that they are, or have been, in occupation of certain land near Colne in Lancashire, either as owners or tenants. I say they so claim, because their title is not admitted by the board until discovery has been given. Under an 1845 special railway Act a certain railway company, the Leeds and Bradford, acquired land adjoining that occupied more recently by the plaintiffs. The land was acquired for the purpose of constructing part of a railway running from Colne to Skipton, which railway
c   was in due course completed and for many years operated. The special Act incorporated two public Acts passed shortly before it, namely the Railways Clauses Consolidation Act 1845 and the Lands Clauses Consolidation Act 1845, with certain immaterial exceptions. The railway company constructed a fence along the boundary of what became the plaintiffs' land, and it is not in dispute that that fence was constructed and afterwards maintained pursuant to the provisions of s 68 of the Railways Clauses Consolidation Act
d   1845, a section to which I shall have to refer. The rights and obligations of the railway company, by virtue of divers intermediate enactments and assurances, have become vested in the board. In or about 1970 the board ceased to operate the railway for the purpose of running trains, and in or about 1972 the board caused the railway tracks and other equipment relating to the railway to be removed from its land. Later, by a conveyance of 1974, the board conveyed the site of the disused railway (so far as regards
e   the part now in question) to the West Riding County Council, and subsequently the rights and obligations of the West Riding County Council became vested in the Lancashire County Council, which is sued by the board, as I have said, as third party. The conveyance of 1974 by the board to the predecessor county council has not been put in evidence, but it is common ground that it contained provisions for the grantee (the county council) to perform any obligations relating to fencing or other accommodation
f   works for the benefit of the owners or occupiers of adjoining land and to indemnify the board against any liability in respect thereof.

The plaintiffs claim (and these facts are not admitted and will have to be established, unless later admitted, at the trial) that the fence dividing the former railway property from the plaintiffs' land has not been maintained since about 1976, has become dilapidated and is no longer stock proof. The plaintiffs say that they have thereby suffered
g   and will continue to suffer damage and expense. The claims are made in respect of labour expended in pursuing and bringing back stock that has escaped from the plaintiffs' land, across the broken-down fence to the former railway land, and also, in the case of two of the plaintiffs, for the value of a lamb drowned in an uncovered drain or cesspool on the former railway land. As I say, the condition of the fence and the alleged damage are not admitted. The plaintiffs claim against the board specific performance of the obligation
h   arising under the Railways Clauses Consolidation Act 1845, and also damages.

Master Barratt made an order on 27 January 1984, directing the trial of a preliminary question in this action and in the third party proceedings. The question is framed as follows:

j   'Whether on the true construction of Section 68 of the Railways Clauses Consolidation Act 1845 (i) the obligations of the Defendants to maintain fences pursuant to such Section remain in perpetuity on the Defendants in respect of "the Railway land" in the Statement of Claim mentioned notwithstanding (a) cesser of user by the Defendants thereof for the running of the trains (b) cesser of user by the Defendants thereof for railway purposes (c) physical removal of railway track and other equipment therefrom and (d) sale thereof by the Defendants on 18th March

1974 and (if not) (ii) did the cesser of such statutory obligations upon the Defendants occur on the date of any of the events (a) (b) or (c) (d) above-mentioned and if so which one or on some other date and if so which date.'

a

It is to be noted (and my whole judgment relies on this) that no party has alleged any provisions of any legislation governing the discontinuance or abandonment of railways. So I proceed on the footing that the closing down of the railway, the removal of the track and the sale of the land were simply done by the board in exercise of its general powers.

As is the way with preliminary questions and preliminary issues, close argument and the submissions of counsel suggest that the question when answered may not have so general an application in this and other cases as at first sight appeared. Before I express my views on it I must first read the relevant parts of the Railways Clauses Consolidation Act 1845. I should mentioned first the definition of the expression 'the railway' contained in s 3 of the Act. By that section:

b

c

'... unless there be something in the subject or context repugnant to such construction ... The expression "the railway" shall mean the railway and works by the special Act authorized to be constructed ...'

Then I come to s 68. That section consists of some opening words, followed by four paragraphs and a final proviso. All parts of the section have been referred to in argument, but it will be sufficient for my purpose if I read in extenso the opening words and the second paragraph. The opening words are these:

d

'The company shall make and at all times thereafter maintain the following works for the accommodation of the owners and occupiers of lands adjoining the Railway; (that is to say,) ...'

And then the second of the four paragraphs which follow is in these terms:

e

'Also sufficient posts, rails, hedges, ditches, mounds, or other fences, for separating the land taken for the use of the railway from the adjoining lands not taken, and protecting such lands from trespass, or the cattle of the owners or occupiers thereof from straying thereout, by reason of the railway, together with all necessary gates, made to open towards such adjoining lands, and not towards the railway, and all necessary stiles; and such posts, rails, and other fences shall be made forthwith after the taking of any such lands, if the owners thereof shall so require, and the said other works as soon as conveniently may be.'

f

Counsel for the plaintiffs takes his stand firmly on the literal interpretation of the opening words of the section 'The company shall make and at all times thereafter maintain the following works ...' and the words '... at all times thereafter ...' mean perpetually, forever, and that is good sense, says counsel for the plaintiffs, because, as the facts alleged by the plaintiffs (but not yet admitted) will show and establish, the need for accommodation works, such as a fence of the railway land, continues to exist, notwithstanding that the railway itself may have physically disappeared and dissolved in memory into the mists of history. He cited two reported cases in support of that submission. One of them does not require any lengthy comment. That is *Dixon v Great Western Rly Co* [1897] 1 QB 300, a decision of the Court of Appeal. It is true that, in that case, the judgments contain expressions, particularly by Lopes LJ, which, taken out of context, are of assistance to counsel for the plaintiffs' argument. The judge said of s 68 ([1897] 1 QB 300 at 304):

g

h

j

'That section, in my view, creates an absolute and permanent obligation upon the railway company to make and maintain certain accommodation works, and amongst them a sufficient fence for separating the land taken by them from the adjoining land not taken, and protecting such lands from trespass and the cattle upon them from straying thereout by reason of the railway.'

Later in his judgment, he said (at 305):

> '. . . as I have already said, I think that section creates a permanent obligation upon the company to make and maintain a fence.'

The previous judgment by Lord Esher MR contained a similar expression (at 303):

> '. . . s. 68 remains without any limitation of time, and puts on the company the obligation to make and maintain fences which will prevent the cattle of people who have lands adjoining the railway from straying.'

In spite of that language, in my opinion the judgments do not assist me in the present case, because nothing was further from the minds of the members of the Court of Appeal than a question arising from discontinuance or abandonment of a railway. The point they were dealing with was taken on s 73 of the Railways Clauses Consolidation Act 1845, where there was a provision that the company should not be compelled to make any further or additional accommodation works after five years from the opening of the railway. They were using the expressions I have cited to repel the suggestion that after those five years an adjoining owner could not complain of any neglect of the company to fence or to maintain a fence. So it would be wholly unfair to the defendant and the third party and indeed to the judges who used that language to read it in a context to which it was never intended to apply.

The other case, however, does something to help counsel for the plaintiffs' argument. It is a case in the Court of Session in Scotland, an appeal from a sheriff court in 1878, *Simpson v Caledonian Rly Co* (1878) 5 R (Ct of Sess) 525. That was a case where a railway had been constructed under an 1826 Act, which required the company—

> '. . . after any land shall be taken for the use of the said railway, to divide and separate, and keep constantly divided and separated, the same from the lands or grounds adjoining to such railway.'

The reasoning by which the Court of Session decided in favour of the respondent in that case, who was the adjoining landowner, is not necessarily applicable to the plaintiffs here, but the Lord Justice-Clerk (Moncreiff), with whom the other members of the court agreed, clearly interpreted the requirement that the company should keep their land constantly divided and separated from the adjoining property as a perpetual one. He said (at 526):

> 'That they were bound to do that whether they used their railway or not I think there can be no question. The fact that they have ceased to use this part of the line may, no doubt, limit to some extent their obligation to the public; but their obligation to the proprietor and the tenant of the land was to keep up that fence in all time coming.'

So that case is of some persuasive authority, as showing that a statutory obligation, like that contained in s 68 to maintain a fence at all times, is not terminated by the abandonment of the railway line.

Counsel who has argued the case for the Lancashire County Council (the third party) and is supported by counsel for the board, divides his submissions as I understand them, essentially into two propositions. The first proposition is that the duty to maintain a fence or any other accommodation works required by s 68 ceases when the purposes of the works is extinct. The second proposition (again in my own wording) is that in the present case the purpose of the fence was to protect cattle from the railway and that purpose has wholly ceased, or, to use my previous words, is now extinct.

The first proposition, in my judgment, is correct, and it is supported by an authority cited by counsel for the third party from the Court of Appeal, that of *Midland Rly Co v Gribble* [1895] 2 Ch 827. There a railway was made through the land of a certain landowner and a level crossing was provided under s 68 as an accommodation work. By the conveyance of the land to the railway company, a right of way over the level crossing

was reserved to the landowner and his successors in title and the company convenanted
to maintain the level crossing. Afterwards the landowner sold the land on one side only
of the railway to a third party. He did not grant the purchaser any right of way over his
own retained land nor did he reserve any right of way over the land sold so that, from a
practical point of view, the level crossing was no good to anybody. It is to be noticed that
the railway company was not a party to that severance of the landowner's retained land.
The Court of Appeal were unanimous in holding that the railway company was at liberty
to stop maintaining the level crossing. Lindley LJ, after citing the language of s 68, not
the part I have read, but the first of the four paragraphs (which dealt with the situation
under which a means of communication was to be provided between the parts of land
cut in half by the railway), continued ([1895] 2 Ch 827 at 830):

> 'The words "shall at all times maintain" do not mean that the company must
> maintain it at all times if he [ie the person through whose lands the railway passes]
> does not want it. Having asked for this accommodation and got it, he could if he
> chose release it; and if he chose to release it there would be an end of the statutory
> obligation to maintain it. The maintenance of it is not a public duty; it is a duty to
> him privately, and, of course, to those claiming under him.'

Then after reciting what had happened, Lindley LJ said (at 831):

> 'That appears to me to be a clear and distinct abandonment of his right of way
> over the railway. It was no longer of any use to him; and when he severed the land
> without any reservation of any right of way there was an end of the right of way
> over the railway—he abandoned his easement. It was perfectly competent to him
> to do so in point of law. Ever since the great case of *Moore* v. *Rawson* ((1824) 3 B & C
> 332, [1824–34] All ER Rep 173) with regard to ancient lights the law as to
> abandonment of easements has been perfectly well settled. It was not an
> abandonment for a month or a year, but a distinct final abandonment without any
> intention to reserve this right of way. To my mind, upon the conveyance to Mr.
> Plowman without any express reservation, there was an end of the statutory right.'

Lopes LJ, after stating that the level crossing was an accommodation work under s 68,
said (at 832):

> 'That accommodation work is made by the railway company for a special purpose,
> that special purpose being to maintain a communication between the lands of the
> same owner or occupier which have been intersected by the railway; and, in my
> judgment, as soon as that special purpose is at an end, and when, as Mr. Bridgeman
> [counsel for the appellant claiming a right of way over the level crossing] has
> admitted, it is practically impossible now to use the work for that purpose, the
> accommodation being no longer required, the obligation to afford it also ceases.'

Rigby LJ agreed.

Accordingly I accept the first proposition put forward by counsel for the third party,
that, although the section in terms requires maintenance at all times, the duty can cease
if and when the purpose of the particular accommodation work is extinct.

The second proposition, that the purpose of the fence in this case was to protect cattle
from the railway and that purpose is now extinct, I cannot accept. The language of the
second paragraph in s 68 is not expressed solely with reference to straying cattle. There
are three separate purposes mentioned: separating the land taken for the use of the
railway from the adjoining lands, protecting the adjoining lands from trespass, protecting
the cattle of the owners or occupiers of the adjoining lands from straying thereout by
reason of the railway. Whether those words 'by reason of the railway' ought to be applied
simply to that third purpose or also to the others or perhaps the second and third, I do
not find it necessary to determine. What is clear is that the need of the adjoining lands
for a fence for those purposes does not obviously and automatically cease when the
railway is abandoned.

Counsel for the third party referred to two authorities on this aspect of his case. One

of them was *Cooper v Rly Executive (Southern Region)* [1953] 1 All ER 477, [1953] 1 WLR
223, where he cited a passage from Devlin J showing that the real or paramount purpose,
as I think was submitted, was to keep cattle from straying on a railway. What the judge
said was this ([1953] 1 WLR 223 at 228; cf [1953] 1 All ER 477 at 479):

> 'That involves a consideration of the true construction of the Act as it had been
> construed in the authorities. It is, of course, an absolute obligation in this sense, that
> the Railway Executive is absolutely bound to maintain a fence, and it is no answer
> to say that some accident or act of a trespasser has made the fence defective. But the
> question is: what is the quality of the fence which it is absolutely bound to maintain?
> The Act says that it is to be such a fence as will protect "the cattle of the owners or
> occupiers thereof from straying thereout." It is important not to ignore those words
> "from straying thereout", because those are the words which give a clue to the sort
> of fence which the Railway Executive shall be obliged to maintain. It is protection
> against straying, and all the cases which have been cited to me have been cases in
> which the cattle have, in the ordinary sense of the word, strayed through a gap in
> the fence, or something of that sort.'

That is, of course, perfectly correct when read in the context, which was a question
whether the railway executive had maintained a sufficient fence having regard to the
fact that certain very anxious cows, whose calves were on the other side of the railway
line, had been strong and persistent enough to break through it. But it cannot be applied
to the question I have to decide, because again nothing of the sort was in the judge's
mind.

However, the second case has got more to do with the question of an abandoned
railway. It is *Cairns Bros v Canadian National Rly* [1937] 2 DLR 537 before the railways
board sitting in the province of Ontario. There, unfortunately, the report does not set
out verbatim the full section of the statute in question. The paragraph that contains some
mention of it, in the judgment of Chief Commissioner Guthrie, with which the two
other commissioners concurred, is as follows (at 538–539):

> 'It is to be noted that the requirement for fencing is that the company shall erect
> and maintain fences *upon the railway* . . . Where abandonment of operation has been
> authorized and has taken place, the right of way through which the railway is
> operated ceases to be used for railway purposes and is held by the company, not as
> part of its *railway* qua railway company, but in the same way as land is held by
> private individuals, subject to any provincial or municipal laws in respect of fencing
> which may be in force in the particular district. It is to be further noted that the
> principal, if not the sole, reason for the fencing requirement in the Railway Act is to
> prevent cattle from getting upon railway lands and being killed or injured by
> railway operation. Where complete abandonment of a line of railway takes place,
> the necessity for fencing the line largely disappears, and the section does not apply.'

So he concluded that the board had no authority under the terms of the Railway Act to
order the company to maintain fences on the sides of its abandoned railway as the other
party sought, though an arrangement for an order for obstructing the termini of the
abandoned railway was in the end made.

That case, which in any event would only be a persuasive authority so far as I am
concerned, is, I think, entirely distinguishable. First of all, the section so far as considered
by the railway board was for one purpose only, that of protecting cattle on the adjoining
lands from railway operation, not for three purposes like the relevant paragraph in s 68
of the English Act. Secondly, the words which were greatly relied on, 'maintain fences
upon the railway' do not appear in the English Act. The grammatically, somewhat
obscurely, placed words 'by reason of the railway' in the second paragraph of s 68, do not,
to my mind, have an equivalent effect. Thirdly, the Chief Commissioner was merely
expressing an opinion on a matter of fact when, having referred to the protection of
cattle as the principal or sole object, he said: 'Where complete abandonment of a line of
railway takes place the necessity for fencing the line largely disappears . . .' If at the trial

the plaintiffs' allegations here prove well founded, it may very likely appear that the complete abandonment of the Skipton to Colne railway did not, so far as adjoining *a* agricultural occupiers are concerned, cause the necessity for fencing to disappear.

Accordingly, I do not think that the Canadian case can persuade me to agree with counsel for the third party's second proposition.

Having regard to the first proposition, at one time I wondered whether this preliminary question ought to share the fate that most preliminary questions and preliminary issues deserve, of being stood over to be decided at the trial, but I think I can, with some slight *b* alteration of wording, properly make a declaration as follows:

> 'On the true construction of s 68 of the Railways Clauses Consolidation Act 1845 the obligations of the defendants at all times to maintain fences pursuant to such section have not been determined in respect of "the railway land" in the statement of claim mentioned by reason only of the following facts or any of them, [and then the facts (a), (b), (c) and (d) exactly as drawn by the master, ending] 18 March 1974.' *c*

Declaration accordingly.

Solicitors: *Ellis & Fairbairn* (for the plaintiffs); M G *Baker* (for the board); *Norton Rose Botterell & Roche*, agents for *Brian Hill*, Preston (for Lancashire County Council). *d*

Evelyn M C Budd   Barrister.

Practice Direction

e

FAMILY DIVISION

Divorce – Financial provision – Consent order – Application – Evidence – Agreed statement of means of parties – Registrar to be satisfied that claimant consents where claim for periodical payments is dismissed – Wife acting in person required to attend before registrar where claim is dismissed – Matrimonial Causes Act 1973, s 25. *f*

The decision of the Court of Appeal in *Jenkins v Livesey* (*formerly Jenkins*) (1983) Times, 22 December is a reminder that in all cases where application is made for financial provision or property adjustment order the court is required to have before it an agreed statement of the general nature of the means of each party signed by the parties or their solicitors. *g* If affidavits of means have been filed it will be sufficient if the statement is in the form of a certificate that there has been no change of substance since the date of the affidavit or, if there has, what changes there have been. If no such evidence has been filed the statement should include a summary of the amount or value of the capital and income resources of each of the spouses (and, if relevant, of any minor child) and any special *h* features which require to be considered under s 25 of the Matrimonial Causes Act 1973.

Where a spouse's claim for periodical payments is being dismissed the registrar will need to be satisfied that it is appropriate that the parties should be financially independent and that the claimant consents to dismissal. In all cases where a wife is acting in person and her claim for periodical payments is being dismissed, the wife's attendance before the registrar is required save in exceptional circumstances.

This direction should be read in conjunction with the Registrar's Direction of 10 April *j* 1974 ([1974] 2 All ER 1120, [1974] 1 WLR 937).

Issued with the concurrence of the Lord Chancellor.

B P TICKLE
13 April 1984   Senior Registrar.

Re a debtor (No 26 of 1983)
Re a debtor (No 72 of 1982)

CHANCERY DIVISION
SIR ROBERT MEGARRY V-C AND PETER GIBSON J
30, 31 JANUARY 1984

Bankruptcy – Practice – Adjournment of bankruptcy proceedings – Discretion to adjourn – Conditions attached to adjournment – Registrar repeatedly adjourning petitions because of possibility of debtor firm returning to solvency – Registrar making adjournment subject to condition that debtor firm and partner pay into court specified amount to be held on trust for creditors – Whether registrar properly exercising discretion to adjourn bankruptcy proceedings – Bankruptcy Act 1914, s 109(2).

Bankruptcy notice – Service – Substituted service – Whether substituted service required to be effected within two months of issue of notice – Bankruptcy Rules 1952, rr 140, 154(1).

Bankruptcy – Bankruptcy notice – Issue – Leave of court – Proceedings against partnership – Petition founded on judgment debt – Whether leave of court required before issue of notice against firm – Whether bankruptcy notice 'execution to enforce judgment' – RSC Ord 81, r 5(1)(4).

In related proceedings two judgment creditors of a partnership and of an individual partner in the firm respectively petitioned for the bankruptcy of the firm and for the bankruptcy of the partner. Because personal service of the bankruptcy notice on the partner could not be effected and the judgment creditor petitioning against the partner had to get an order for substituted service under r 154(1)ᵃ of the Bankruptcy Rules 1952, the bankruptcy notice against the partner, although issued on 8 September 1982, was not served until 8 November, ie after the expiry of the period of two months from the issue of the notice prescribed by r 140ᵇ of the 1952 rules for service of a bankruptcy notice. Furthermore, the judgment creditor petitioning against the firm did not obtain the court's leave under RSC Ord 81, r 5(4)ᶜ to issue the bankruptcy notice against the firm. The registrar, purporting to exercise the court's discretion under s 109(2)ᵈ of the Bankruptcy Act 1914 to adjourn bankruptcy proceedings on such terms as the court thought fit, granted successive adjournments of the petitions at the request of the firm, because he took the view that the firm should be allowed to continue trading since it was probable that it would become solvent and be able to pay the creditors in full. The last such adjournment was granted on 16 November 1983, when the registrar adjourned the petitions until 22 March 1984 on condition that the firm and the individual partner pay into court a specified sum of money to be held in trust for the benefit of all the creditors. The judgment creditors appealed from the adjournment order made on 16 November 1983, submitting that the registrar ought not to have granted a further adjournment on that date but should instead have made receiving orders on the petitions. On the hearing of the appeals two further questions arose, namely (i) whether the substituted service of the notice on the individual partner after the expiry of the two months' period prescribed

---

a Rule 154 is set out at p 264 c d, post
b Rule 140, so far as material, is set out at p 264 b, post
c Rule 5, so far as material, provides:
   '(1) Where a judgment is given ... against a firm, execution to enforce the judgment ... may ... issue against any property of the firm within the jurisdiction ...
   (4) Where a party who has obtained a judgment ... against a firm claims that a person is liable to satisfy the judgment ... as being a member of the firm, and the foregoing provisions of this rule do not apply in relation to that person, that party may apply to the Court for leave to issue execution against that person, the application to be made by summons which must be served personally on that person ...'
d Section 109(2) is set out at p 262 d e, post

in r 140 of the 1952 rules was invalid and (ii) whether the leave of the court under Ord 81, r 5(4) ought to have been obtained before issuing the bankruptcy notice against the firm.

Held – The appeals would be allowed for the following reasons—

(1) The registrar had wrongly exercised his discretion under s 109(2) of the 1914 Act in granting the further adjournment on 16 November 1983 because—

(a) in doing so he gave insufficient weight to the prima facie right of a petitioning creditor to obtain a receiving order on a duly presented petition and to the importance of avoiding or minimising delay once bankruptcy proceedings had been instituted. Delay negated the primary purpose of bankruptcy proceedings, which was to enable an independent person, namely the Official Receiver or the trustee in bankruptcy, to make orderly and comprehensive provision for the satisfaction of the creditors (see p 263 a to p 264 a and p 266 g, post); *Re a debtor (No 452 of 1948), ex p the debtor v M R Le Mee-Power* [1949] 1 All ER 652 followed;

(b) there was no statutory procedure for directing, as a condition of an adjournment, that money should be paid into court and held in trust for the firm's creditors and such an arrangement gave rise to problems as to who was the trustee of the money and who precisely were the beneficiaries of the trust (see p 263 h to p 264 a and p 266 g, post);

(c) there was no evidence before the registrar on 16 November to justify his view that the grant of a further adjournment until 22 March 1984 would probably enable the judgment creditors to be paid in full by that date (see p 262 h to p 263 a and j to p 264 a and p 266 g, post).

(2) Since the registrar had wrongly exercised his discretion the court was entitled to substitute its own discretion in the matter by ordering that receiving orders be made as from 16 November 1983 (see p 262 fg, p 264 a and p 266 g, post).

(3) The time limit for service of a bankruptcy notice prescribed in r 140 of the 1952 rules applied (subject to any extension of time granted under s 109(4)[e] of the 1914 Act) to service of the notice by whatever means and therefore applied to substituted service of a bankruptcy notice, which thus had to be effected within two months from the issue of the notice. Rule 154(1) dealt merely with the manner of substituted service and not with the time within which the substituted service had to be effected. It followed that the substituted service on the individual partner on 8 November 1982 had been out of time. However, in all the circumstances, it was appropriate to grant an extension of time under s 109(4) so as to validate the bankruptcy notice. Alternatively, the service of the notice out of time would be treated as a mere defect or irregularity which, by virtue of s 147(1)[f] of the 1914 Act, did not invalidate the proceedings against the individual partner, since substantial injustice had not been caused to her by the late service of the notice (see p 264 f to j, p 265 a d e and p 266 g, post).

(4) Leave to issue a bankruptcy notice against the firm under RSC Ord 81, r 5(4) had not been required because the issue of a bankruptcy notice founded on a judgment debt against a firm, as distinct from a member of the firm, was not 'execution' to enforce the judgment within Ord 81, r 5(1) and (4) (see p 265 h j and p 266 b to g, post); *Ex p Ide, re Ide* (1886) 17 QBD 755 distinguished.

Per Sir Robert Megarry V-C. The grant of repeated adjournments of a bankruptcy petition coupled with payments into court under some form of trust is a wholly irregular substitute for the normal process of bankruptcy or schemes of arrangement (see p 266 g to j, post).

---

e   Section 109(4) provides: 'Where by this Act, or by general rules, the time for doing any act or thing is limited, the court may extend the time either before or after the expiration thereof, upon such terms, if any, as the court may think fit to impose.'

f   Section 147(1) provides: 'No proceeding in bankruptcy shall be invalidated by any formal defect or by any irregularity, unless the court before which an objection is made to the proceeding is of opinion that substantial injustice has been caused by the defect or irregularity, and that the injustice cannot be remedied by any order of that court.'

Notes

a For the adjournment of bankruptcy proceedings, see 3 Halsbury's Laws (4th edn) para 343, and for cases on the subject, see 4 Digest (Reissue) 162–165, 1441–1463.

For the time for service of a bankruptcy notice, see 3 Halsbury's Laws (4th edn) para 270, and for cases on the subject, see 4 Digest (Reissue) 105–107, 927–941.

For leave to issue execution against a partner in the case of judgment against the partnership, see 3 Halsbury's Laws (4th edn) para 262, and for cases on the subject, see 4 b Digest (Reissue) 95, 838–839.

For the Bankruptcy Act 1914, ss 109, 147, see 3 Halsbury's Statutes (3rd edn) 136, 149.

For the Bankruptcy Rules 1952, rr 140, 154, see 3 Halsbury's Statutory Instruments (4th reissue) 246, 250.

Cases referred to in judgments

c Debtor (No 4 of 1942), Re a [1943] 1 All ER 125, DC.

Debtor (No 452 of 1948), Re a, ex p the debtor v M R Le Mee-Power [1949] 1 All ER 652, CA.

Debtor (No 36 of 1952), Re a, ex p the debtor v J T Richardson Rymer Bros Ltd [1953] 1 All ER 776, [1953] Ch 144, [1953] 2 WLR 561, DC.

Debtor (No 12 of 1970), Re a, ex p the Official Receiver v the debtor [1971] 2 All ER 1494, [1971] 1 WLR 1212, CA; affg [1971] 1 All ER 504, [1971] 1 WLR 261, DC.

d Ide, Ex p, re Ide (1886) 17 QBD 755, CA.

Lovell & Christmas v Beauchamp [1894] AC 607, [1891–4] All ER Rep 1184, HL; varying sub nom Re Beauchamp Bros, ex p Beauchamp [1894] 1 QB 1, CA.

Warburg, Ex p, re Whalley (1883) 25 Ch D 336, CA.

Appeals

e In separate but related bankruptcy proceedings against the respondents, Mrs Pearl J Clifford and P J Clifford & Sons (a firm), the appellants, Mumford Leasing Ltd, the petitioning creditor against Mrs Clifford, and Drygrass Ltd, the petitioning creditor against the firm, appealed from an order made on 16 November 1963 by the registrar of Plymouth County Court adjourning both petitions until 22 March 1984. The facts are set out in the judgment of Peter Gibson J.

f

John Vallat for the appellants.
Florence O'Donoghue for the respondents.

PETER GIBSON J (delivering the first judgment at the invitation of Sir Robert Megarry V-C). These are two related appeals. One is an appeal in proceedings against Pearl Joan Clifford (Mrs Clifford), the appellant being the petitioning creditor Mumford
g Leasing Ltd (Mumford). The second appeal is in proceedings against a partnership, P J Clifford & Sons, of which Mrs Clifford, Clare Clifford, Philip Clifford and Peter Clifford are partners. The appellant in that appeal is the petitioning creditor Drygrass Ltd (Drygrass). The appeals are from an order made by Mr Registrar Trayhurn in the Plymouth County Court on 16 November 1983 whereby he ordered, inter alia, that the
h petitions of Mumford and Drygrass be adjourned to 22 March 1984. Mr Vallat appears for Mumford and Drygrass and Mr O'Donoghue for Mrs Clifford and the partnership.

Mumford obtained judgment against Mrs Clifford on 18 August 1982 in the Plymouth district registry of the High Court for £6,091·80, including costs. On 8 September 1982 Mumford issued a bankruptcy notice addressed to Mrs Clifford for that sum but had to obtain an order on 4 November 1982 for substituted service. That order was to the effect
j that recorded delivery post addressed to Mrs Clifford at Cansford Farm, Camelford, Cornwall, should be deemed to be good and sufficient service on the day following such posting. Counsel for the appellants told us that his instructing solicitors only received the order on 8 November by post; and that it was sent by post appears from the court file. Counsel for the appellants told us that the solicitors promptly complied with the order by posting it, by recorded delivery post, to Mrs Clifford on the same day. Thus the deemed effect of the order, according to its terms, was that it was served on 9 November

1982, that is to say two months and one day after the issue of the bankruptcy notice. The failure by Mrs Clifford to comply with the bankruptcy notice before 20 November 1982 was the act of bankruptcy relied on by Mumford in its petition, which was presented on 21 November 1982.

The first hearing of the petition was on 23 February 1983, when Mr Registrar Carder adjourned the hearing for one month to 23 March 1983 to enable Mrs Clifford to settle the debt due to Mumford. On 23 March 1983 there was a second adjournment, this time for just over a month to 27 April 1983, the registrar recording that Mrs Clifford would probably be solvent at the end of this period.

For the hearing on 27 April 1983 the partners swore a joint affidavit. They referred to other proceedings in the Launceston County Court against them in which mortgagees of Cansford Farm had sued for possession of that farm and obtained a warrant for possession. That warrant was stayed to enable the farm to be sold by auction on 8 June 1983. The partners had arranged for a further sale that is to say, a sale of the live and dead stock on 10 June 1983. The partners undertook that within eight weeks of the sale of the farm and of the sale of the stock they would pay into court Mumford's debt and costs. They referred in the affidavit to advice which they had received from well-known chartered surveyors that the farm should fetch £250,000 and that there should be a reserve price at the auction of £225,000. They said that their joint assets exceeded their joint debts by a very considerable margin, conservatively expressed at not less than £25,000. They also referred to negotiations for a sale and leaseback of the farm which, if carried through, they expected would improve their cash flow dramatically by substituting for the interest payable to the mortgagees in a sum of about £34,000 rent of only £10,000. They said that they were about to start their summer trade in the farm shops which they operated and the provision of cream teas, and they said that this was the most prosperous time of the year for them. In the light of that evidence the registrar granted a further adjournment on 27 April to 16 May 1983.

The hearing on 16 May 1983 was before Mr Registrar Trayhurn. The evidence put before him was an affidavit by Mrs Clifford to which she exhibited certain other affidavits in other proceedings commenced against her or the partnership by other creditors. She set out a list of creditors and it is clear from her affidavit that that was intended to be a comprehensive list. The unsecured creditors apart from Mumford, she stated, totalled 24 and her debts amounted to just under £13,500. She said that there were no less than eight of those creditors who had issued bankruptcy notices, one of whom was Drygrass.

Drygrass had obtained judgment in the Birmingham district registry of the Queen's Bench Division against the partnership on 23 May 1980 for £2,418·30, including costs. On 13 January 1983 it served a bankruptcy notice based on that judgment debt and presented a petition on 3 May 1983. Both the bankruptcy notice and the petition were against the partnership. The petition was based on the non-compliance by the partnership before 8 February 1983 with the bankruptcy notice. The petition was served on Peter Clifford on 9 May 1983. In her affidavit of 16 May 1983 Mrs Clifford again referred to the possibility of a sale and leaseback of the farm, the sale to be at £190,000 and the lease to be for five years at £10,000 per annum with an option to repurchase the farm at the end of that period. The proceeds of sale were to be used to discharge the debts owed to the secured creditors, and again she referred to the savings on net outgoings. Amongst the affidavits exhibited by Mrs Clifford to her affidavit was one sworn by the partners and dated 5 May 1983 in other proceedings in the Bodmin County Court, in which the partners said that they were coming into what for them was the most prosperous time of the year. They said that what they desperately needed was a fairly short breathing-space. On that evidence the registrar granted a fourth adjournment of the petition presented by Mumford to 22 June 1983, when the first hearing of the Drygrass petition took place. The reason given by the registrar was the likelihood of payment.

For the joint hearings of the two petitions on 22 June there was a further affidavit by Mrs Clifford. She revealed that the farm had been withdrawn from auction on 8 June 1983 and the live and dead stock had also been withdrawn from auction on 10 June a   1983; instead an agreement had been entered into for the sale of the farm for £190,000, the purchaser being a Mr Hawkins. There was to be an option granted to repurchase Cansford Farm after five years, and there was to be a partnership agreement between Mr Hawkins and Philip Clifford, Peter Clifford and Mrs Clifford for five years. Under that agreement Mr Hawkins was to receive the first £14,400 of the profits of that partnership, but no rent was to be paid for the use of the farm and the Cliffords were to take the remaining profits. The live and dead stock were to be contributed by the Cliffords as

b   capital, and there was provision that in the event of the bankruptcy of a partner that person should cease to be a partner. I interpose to say that in the event the farm was purchased by Mrs Hawkins, who became the partner instead of Mr Hawkins. The Cliffords have retained the farm shops and are continuing the partnership between the members of the family in running the farm shops. Mrs Clifford in her June affidavit claimed that, in selling the farm on this arrangement with Mr Hawkins, they were acting

c   in the best interests of all the creditors, secured and unsecured. But it is to be noted that whereas the sale by auction of the farm and stock, according to the earlier evidence, would have raised more than was needed to pay off all the creditors, the Cliffords had entered into an arrangement whereby they deprived themselves of the means of paying the unsecured creditors except out of trading profits.

    In an affidavit of 14 June 1983 sworn by Mrs Clifford in the Bodmin County Court

d   proceedings, but exhibited by her to her June affidavit in the bankruptcy proceedings, she set out the sum which she stated would be available for the unsecured creditors during the months from June to October 1983. Those sums, she stated, were computed on a conservative basis. Those sums were set out month by month and totalled nearly £22,000, and she said that those sums would be paid to her solicitors. She then estimated the sums that were owed to the unsecured creditors of herself and the partnership as

e   totalling approximately £20,000. She said that by the end of October all the unsecured creditors would be paid in full. On the basis of that evidence Mr Registrar Trayhurn again granted an adjournment of both petitions to 11 August 1983 and again expressed his reason as the likelihood of payment.

    By the time of the hearing on 11 August 1983 two further petitions had been presented by other creditors: one against Mrs Clifford and the other against the partnership. Mrs

f   Clifford swore another affidavit on 8 August, and, although on 22 June there had been no hint of trading difficulties in the farm shops, in her August affidavit she said that during June and early July the holiday season had been very bad indeed and only with the advent of good weather did things begin to look up. She said that the holiday trade was then very good indeed. She said that nearly £6,500 had been paid to her solicitors towards what was owing to the unsecured creditors. On that evidence the registrar

g   granted a further adjournment of all the petitions, again on the ground of likelihood of payment.

    The adjournment this time was for three months to 16 November 1983. For the hearing on that date of the four petitions there was a further affidavit by Mrs Clifford. She added another five creditors to the list of unsecured creditors but referred to one previously listed as having been paid since, except for costs. She referred to the sums that

h   were, or were about to be, put into the hands of her solicitors as increasing to £10,000. She also referred to negotiations for a loan of £20,000. The weather was again blamed in part for the failure to pay the unsecured creditors. This time it was the excellence of the weather in August and September that had kept customers on the beaches and away from the farm shops. It is noticeable that in that affidavit she was less firm in her forecast when creditors would be paid.

j   At the hearing on 16 November 1983, in addition to the four petitions, Mr Registrar Trayhurn had before him no less than nine warrants of execution obtained by other creditors. The registrar ordered that the four petitions be adjourned to 22 March 1984 because of the likelihood of payment in full. He also suspended the nine warrants of execution in the interim. Further, he directed that Mrs Clifford and the partnership should pay into court sums totalling just under £10,000, all such moneys to be held for

the benefit of all creditors pursuant to the Trustee Act 1925. On 13 December 1983 each
of Mumford and Drygrass served notices of appeal against that part of the registrar's *a*
order that adjourned the petitions.

Finally, I should record that we have seen two further affidavits. In one by Peter
Clifford and dated 24 January 1984, he says that a further £1,000 is expected to be paid
into court shortly, which would make a total of nearly £11,000 so paid. In the other
affidavit, that sworn by Mrs Clifford, she names five more unsecured creditors to be
added to her list. No explanation is given by her as to the lateness of these additions, nor *b*
indeed had there been any explanation of the lateness of the earlier addition to that list,
and this does not leave me confident that all the creditors of Mrs Clifford and the
partnership have been identified.

In their notices of appeal both Mumford and Drygrass say that the registrar should not
have granted a further adjournment of their respective petitions but should have made a
receiving order. In addition, the bankruptcy clerk to this court has drawn to the attention *c*
of the court, and to the attention of counsel, what might be described as a technical point
in relation to the bankruptcy notice in each case; and we have heard argument on each
of those points. In describing the points as technical I do not intend to denigrate them:
bankruptcy is indeed a technical subject and a technical point may be a good point on
appeal. I shall discuss those two points after dealing with the issue raised by the notice of
appeal.   *d*

The registrar in adjourning the petition was, as counsel for the appellant accepts,
exercising a discretion conferred on him by s 109(2) of the Bankruptcy Act 1914. That
subsection provides:

> 'The court may at any time adjourn any proceedings before it upon such terms, if
> any, as it may think fit to impose.'   *e*

That provision must be read with r 173(1) of the Bankruptcy Rules 1952, SI 1952/2113,
which provides:

> '. . . no adjournment of the hearing of a petition shall be allowed except for such
> reason as the court thinks sufficient.'

On an appeal to this court, the court's power to interfere with the exercise of the *f*
discretion of the registrar is limited. If the registrar directed himself correctly the mere
fact that the court might have exercised the discretion differently does not entitle the
court to allow the appeal. But if the court is satisfied that the registrar has erred in law or
otherwise exercised his discretion wrongly, such as by giving no, or no sufficient, weight
to relevant considerations, then the court can and should substitute its own discretion for
that of the registrar: see, for example, *Re a debtor (No 12 of 1970), ex p the Official Receiver* *g*
v the debtor [1971] 1 All ER 504 at 507, [1971] 1 WLR 261 at 265 per Stamp J. One of the
difficulties in the present case is that all that the court knows of the reasoning of the
registrar is contained in the bare statement of his ground for the adjournment, 'because
of the likelihood of payment in full' and from what can be inferred from the other orders
that he made at the same time.

In my judgment, the registrar's decision is open to criticism on four grounds. First, *h*
having regard to the history of the matter and the numerous opportunities already
afforded by the successive adjournments, the registrar seems to me to have been
unjustifiably optimistic in making his assessment of the probability of payment in full.
In my judgment, no prospect of payment in full by the time of the adjourned hearing in
March was revealed by the evidence before him in November. As I have already stated,
since June 1983 the only hope of unsecured creditors being paid in full has been out of *j*
trading profits. There was evidence before the registrar that in November the period
until the ensuing summer would be a less profitable time for the partnership. The
affidavits put in by Mrs Clifford and the partnership have emphasised that it is during
the summer that the farm shops obtain most trade and cream teas can be sold. On any
objective appraisal of the facts deposed to by Mrs Clifford and the partners, a good deal of
scepticism as to their forecasts seems to me unavoidable. In November the evidence, in

a my judgment, was simply not sufficient to enable the registrar to say that there was a likelihood of payment in full such as would justify yet another adjournment, and this time for the longest period of all, that is to say four months.

Second, in my judgment, the registrar does not appear to have given any or sufficient weight to the prima facie right of a petitioning creditor to obtain a receiving order on a duly presented petition. In *Re a debtor (No 452 of 1948)*, *ex p the debtor v M R Le Mee-Power* [1949] 1 All ER 652 at 655 Cohen LJ said:

b   'In my opinion, the short ground on which this appeal fails is that the petitioning creditor has a *prima facie* right to an order unless the debtor has established some very special circumstances which justify the court in departing from its usual practice.'

The facts of that case differ, as counsel for the respondents rightly pointed out, from the present case. But, as I see it, the statement of principle by Cohen LJ is no less applicable to this as to any other case where an adjournment of a petition is under consideration. Counsel for the respondents in supporting the registrar's decision referred the court to the passage in *Williams and Muir Hunter on Bankruptcy* (19th edn, 1979) p 61 on the principles applicable in respect of the adjournment of petitions. But that passage contains nothing to suggest that a debtor in the circumstances of Mrs Clifford and the partnership, d who at present have no realisable assets with which to pay their creditors, will be allowed by means of adjournments of petitions against them to go on trading in the hope that the profits will eventually be sufficient to pay their creditors.

Third, there is no indication that the registrar attached any or sufficient weight to the importance in bankruptcy proceedings of the court ensuring that delays are avoided or minimised once bankruptcy proceedings have been instituted. A primary purpose of e such proceedings is to enable an independent person (the Official Receiver and subsequently the trustee) to ascertain and preserve all the assets of the debtor and to ascertain who are the creditors and in what amounts, with a view to the fair distribution of the assets to the creditors and the payment, so far as possible, of the sums owing to them, pari passu. The longer the delay through adjournments the greater the difficulties and anomalies. Thus in the present case, at least one creditor has, it appears, been paid f since the presentation of Mumford's petition, whilst the remainder have been kept waiting for payment of their debts.

Further, there are particular statutory provisions that render it desirable to avoid delays. Under s 37 of the Bankruptcy Act 1914, the bankruptcy is deemed to relate back to, and to commence at, the act of bankruptcy. I do not overlook s 45, which affords protection to creditors dealing with the debtor bona fide and without notice; but the g longer the delay the greater the difficulty for all concerned to establish whether or not that section applies. Further, the trustee in bankruptcy may need to investigate past transactions of the debtor in case such transactions can be avoided under s 42, relating to voluntary settlements, or s 44, relating to fraudulent preferences. It would have required quite exceptional circumstances to justify seven adjournments over a period of more than a year in the case of the petition presented by Mumford, and three adjournments h over a period of nine months in the case of the petition presented by Drygrass. In my judgment, no such exceptional circumstances can be shown.

Fourth, in my judgment the registrar was wrong to give the direction that money should be paid into court to be held in trust for all creditors. As I see it, he must have taken that direction into account in deciding on the adjournments. Such a direction gives rise to a number of problems. Who is the trustee? Who are the creditors? Who are the j beneficiaries? And how are they to be ascertained? There is no statutory procedure prescribed for such an arrangement, in contrast to the elaborate provisions under the Bankruptcy Act 1914 relating to advertisement for creditors and the lodging of proofs.

In my judgment, the registrar misdirected himself in giving such a direction and in taking that into account in granting the adjournment. I would add that the making of a receiving order does not prevent the debtor from putting forward a scheme of arrangement under s 16 of the 1914 Act. For these reasons, which are in effect what

counsel for the appellants urged on the court, I am satisfied that the registrar did go
wrong in the exercise of his discretion. In my judgment, had he directed himself   *a*
properly he would have been bound to refuse any further adjournment. Subject to the
technical point on each of Mumford's and Drygrass's petitions, in my judgment he
would have been bound to make a receiving order.

I turn then to the point on Mumford's petition, that is to say that the bankruptcy
notice in the proceedings filed against Mrs Clifford was served more than two months
after the issue of the bankruptcy notice. Rule 140 of the Bankruptcy Rules 1952, as   *b*
recently amended by SI 1982/441, is in this form:

> 'Subject to the power of the court to extend the time, a bankruptcy notice to be
> served in England shall be served within two months from the issue of the notice
> ...'

Rule 154, as applied to bankruptcy notices by r 141, provides: *c*

> '(1) If the court is satisfied by affidavit or other evidence on oath that prompt
> personal service cannot be effected because the debtor is keeping out of the way to
> avoid service of the petition or any other legal process, or for any other cause, it may
> order substituted service to be effected in such manner as it thinks fit.
> (2) Where any such order has been carried out, the petition shall be deemed to
> have been duly served on the debtor.'   *d*

Counsel for the appellant takes two points on the construction of those rules. First, he
says that r 154 stands by itself and the time limit of r 140 has no application thereto. He
submits that the words 'in such manner' in r 154(1) enable the court to make orders as to
time which are not affected by r 140. He referred the court to *Ex p Warburg, re Whalley*
(1883) 25 Ch D 336, in which it was held by the Court of Appeal that the time limit   *e*
prescribed by the rules for the personal service of a debtor's summons did not apply to
the predecessor of r 154 relating to substituted service. The debtor's summons was, of
course, the precursor of the bankruptcy notice. But the Bankruptcy Rules 1883 then in
force differ, as counsel for the appellants very properly acknowledged, in an important
respect. Instead of a rule in general form, as one now finds r 140, there was a rule (r 59)
to the effect that a debtor's summons should be personally served within 21 days from   *f*
the date of the summons. In my judgment, as r 140 is now worded it applies to service
by whatever means of the bankruptcy notice, and it prescribes the time for such service
subject to extensions. Rule 154 deals with the manner, not the time, of substituted
service.

Counsel for the appellants' second point of construction was that for the purpose of the
1952 rules service was effected when the order for substituted service was carried out.   *g*
That, he says, Mumford carried out when by its solicitors it posted the bankruptcy notice
to Mrs Clifford. Indeed there is no more, he said, that Mumford could do. That is, of
course, true. But I cannot see that it helps him to establish that service was effected within
two months from the issue of the notice when the order for substituted service on which
he relies is explicit in deeming service to be effected the day after posting.

Counsel for the appellants takes two further points which are, in my judgment, of   *h*
greater substance. The first is that s 109(4) of the 1914 Act expressly allows the court to
extend time even after the expiration of time fixed by the rules (and there is a similar
provision in r 389 for the extension of time for good cause shown). The second point is
that under s 147 of the 1914 Act no proceeding in bankruptcy is to be invalidated by a
formal defect or by any irregularity, unless the court is of opinion that substantial
injustice has been caused by the defect or irregularity, and that the injustice cannot be   *j*
remedied by any order of the court. There is a similar provision in r 388 in respect of
non-compliance with the rules. Counsel for the appellants says that this is a case where
the court should extend time, and further or alternatively that no substantial injustice
has been caused by the defect or irregularity.

Counsel for the respondents addressed the court on the questions whether it was
appropriate to treat this matter as a mere defect or irregularity, and whether we should
extend the time. He drew our attention to one authority, *Re a debtor (No 36 of 1952), ex*

a
p the debtor v J T Richardson Rymer Bros Ltd [1953] 1 All ER 776, [1953] Ch 144, which turned on the construction of r 389. That case establishes that a mere error on the part of a party's solicitor is not 'good cause shown' for the purpose of r 389. I do not think it materially assists the court in considering counsel for the appellants' two further points.

In my judgment, counsel for the appellants is entitled to succeed on both of the further points that he has advanced. On the face of the bankruptcy notice it should have been obvious to Mrs Clifford that the bankruptcy notice had not been served within two

b
months of its issue, and she could have applied to set aside the bankruptcy notice if she thought she had a grievance: consider the remarks of Lord Clauson in Re a debtor (No 4 of 1942) [1943] 1 All ER 125 at 126. Counsel for the respondents said that there was some doubt whether Mrs Clifford had solicitors at the time the bankruptcy notice was served; on whether or not that is so there is no evidence before us. It is quite clear that she and the partners have had two firms of solicitors acting for them since the commencement

c
of the proceedings. Yet no point was taken in respect of the bankruptcy notice, despite the many opportunities afforded by the frequent hearings before the registrar, until the matter was drawn to the attention of counsel on this appeal. The service of the bankruptcy notice was only just outside the two months' period. Counsel for the respondents says that the extension shortly before the bankruptcy notice was served of the requisite period of one month to two months was all the more reason why the court should not permit

d
any extension in the present case. But, given the circumstances, in my judgment this is an appropriate case in which to grant the extension of time so as to make valid the bankruptcy notice. I do not think that any hardship has been caused to Mrs Clifford. Even if I were wrong on that, I would hold that, under s 147, the service of the bankruptcy notice was not invalidated by the failure to serve it within the two months, there being no substantial injustice caused by that late service. It would to my mind be deplorable if, at this very late stage, Mumford could not rely on its bankruptcy notice. I

e
therefore see nothing in the way of Mumford obtaining the relief it seeks by this appeal.

The technical point in the proceedings by Drygrass against the partnership is what is said to be the failure by Drygrass to obtain the leave of the court under RSC Ord 81, r 5 to issue the bankruptcy notice. As I understand the point, the reasoning in support of it proceeds thus. The ultimate purpose of bankruptcy proceedings against a firm is a

f
receiving order against the firm which will operate as if it were a receiving order against the individual partners (see r 285 of the 1952 rules), and separate orders of adjudication against each individual partner; for an order of adjudication cannot be made against the firm but must be made against the individual partners (see r 288 of the 1952 rules). Therefore the proceedings commenced by the bankruptcy notice were proceedings to enforce a judgment against the partners personally. The judgment cannot be enforced

g
by the issue of a bankruptcy notice unless RSC Ord 81, r 5 is complied with, and under that rule, so far as material, execution on a judgment given against a firm cannot be enforced against an individual partner unless that partner is a person to whom r 5(2) applies (and it is not suggested in the present case that r 5(2) is applicable) or the leave of the court is obtained under r 5(4). No leave was obtained in the present case.

The chain of reasoning seems to me to break down in relation to RSC Ord 81, r 5. I

h
cannot accept that the issue of a bankruptcy notice is 'execution to enforce the judgment' within the meaning of the rule. One thinks of execution in terms of the enforcement of a judgment by a public officer under writs of fieri facias and the like. It may be that it would extend to other procedures, such as attachment of debts and garnishee proceedings, but whether or not that is right I cannot see any justification for extending its meaning to comprehend the issue of a bankruptcy notice.

j
The suggestion that it does appears to be based on the decision of the Court of Appeal in Ex p Ide, re Ide (1886) 17 QBD 755. In that case the creditor had obtained judgment against a firm. The creditor purported to issue a bankruptcy notice based on that judgment against an individual partner. Under the statutory predecessor of s 1(1)(g) of the 1914 Act it was a condition for the validity of a bankruptcy notice founded on a final judgment or a final order that execution had not been stayed thereon. The Court of Appeal held that, on the true construction of the subsection, in order to entitle a creditor to issue a bankruptcy notice he must be in a position to issue execution on his judgment

at the time when he issued the bankruptcy notice. Thus in addition to there being no
stay on the judgment there must be no other impediment to issuing execution on the *a*
judgment; and the predecessor rule to RSC Ord 81, r 5(4), requiring the leave of the
court to issue execution, was held to be such an impediment. That case therefore turned
on the true construction of the subsection in circumstances where a creditor issued a
bankruptcy notice not against the firm but against one partner, that notice being founded
on a judgment against the firm.

In the present case the position, as it seems to me, is different. The judgment was duly *b*
obtained against the firm. Omitting immaterial words, RSC Ord 81, r 5(1) provides:

> 'Where a judgment is given or order made against a firm, execution to enforce
> the judgment or order may . . . issue against any property of the firm within the
> jurisdiction.'

There was therefore no need for leave to issue execution against the firm. There was no *c*
stay of the judgment. The bankruptcy notice was issued against the firm and not against
any individual partner. Section 119 of the 1914 Act permits proceedings against a firm
in the firm's name. The bankruptcy notice was therefore properly issued against the
firm. Had it been against the partners individually then, of course, *Ex p Ide, re Ide* would
have applied. Indeed a petition can be issued against a firm in the firm name subject to
complying with the requirements of r 148 as to information about the partners. *d*

In my judgment, therefore, there is nothing in the 1914 Act or in the rules made
thereunder, or in the Rules of the Supreme Court, and there is no authority, to show that
leave must be obtained before the issue of a bankruptcy notice against a firm, as distinct
from one against an individual partner.

We were told by counsel for the appellants that on this point there appears to have
been a recent change of practice by the registrars of the High Court. Hitherto the position *e*
that appears to have been adopted was that a bankruptcy notice against a firm did not
require leave, and we were referred to *Lovell & Christmas v Beauchamp* [1894] AC 607,
[1891–4] All ER Rep 1184, reported in the Court of Appeal as *Re Beauchamp Bros, ex p
Beauchamp* [1894] 1 QB 1, where the point might have been taken but was not. Counsel
for the appellants tells us that there are other reported cases where, again, the point might
have been, but was not, taken. For my part I can see no justification for the change of *f*
practice.

I would therefore hold that this technical point does not prevent the making of a
receiving order founded on the bankruptcy notice by Drygrass in the present case.

For these reasons, therefore, for my part I would allow the appeal in each case. I can
see no ground for refusing to make a receiving order and I would make that order.

g

SIR ROBERT MEGARRY V–C. I agree. I propose merely to add a few words on the
point of substance.

The effect of the registrars' orders in this case has been to set up some sort of process of
repeated adjournments, coupled with payments into court in support of some form of
trust, to be used as a substitute for the normal processes of bankruptcy or schemes of
arrangement. The effect of this is to allow the debtor to continue in control of his assets *h*
and attempt to trade out of his insolvency, merely paying over what he considers to be
the surplus from his trading for the purposes of the trust that is being set up. This seems
to me to be a wholly irregular substitute for bankruptcy or schemes of arrangement,
with their machinery for making orderly and comprehensive provision for the satisfaction
of creditors. I wish to make it quite clear that in my judgment there is not, and must not
be, any future for any process of this kind. *j*

Appeals allowed.

Solicitors: *Bond Pearce*, Plymouth (for the appellants); *Pethybridges & Best*, Torrington (for
the respondents).

Vivian Horvath   Barrister.

a   # Archer v Brown

QUEEN'S BENCH DIVISION
PETER PAIN J
5, 6, 28 OCTOBER 1983

b   *Misrepresentation – Damages – Deceit – Fraudulent misrepresentation contrasted with deceit –
Plaintiff induced to enter contract through defendant's fraud – Defendant conceding that plaintiff
entitled to rescission of contract for misrepresentation – Whether defendant's concession precluding
plaintiff from recovering damages for deceit.*

*Damages – Exemplary damages – Deceit – Whether exemplary damages can be awarded for
deceit – Whether criminal punishment of deceiver only reason for not awarding exemplary*
c   *damages.*

*Damages – Aggravated damages – Deceit – Whether aggravated damages can be awarded in
deceit to compensate for injured feelings.*

The plaintiff was the victim of a fraud perpetrated on him by the defendant, who sold
d   him the share capital in a company for £30,000 when he had already sold the same shares
several times over to other unsuspecting victims. The defendant was later convicted and
imprisoned on charges arising out of the fraud and also on other charges. The plaintiff
financed the purchase of the shares by borrowing some £30,000 from a bank. The
plaintiff also entered into a service agreement with the company whereby he was to be a
joint managing director of the company, with the defendant, at a salary of £16,750 per
e   annum. On discovering the fraud the plaintiff brought an action against the defendant
claiming the return of the £30,000, all damage resulting from the defendant's deceit,
including interest of £13,528 on the bank loan, and damages for deceit or breach of
contract and also exemplary damages. The defendant conceded that the plaintiff was
entitled to rescission of his contract with the defendant and the return of the £30,000
but disputed the claims for bank interest and damages, contending, inter alia, that the
f   plaintiff was restricted to claiming remedies for rescission, and that the bank interest had
been caused by the plaintiff's impecuniosity rather than the defendant's conduct.

Held – (1) It was not open to the defendant by making a concession that the plaintiff was
entitled to rescission thereby to deprive the plaintiff of the right to damages in deceit,
since the plaintiff was entitled to recover damages under whatever head he chose provided
g   he did not duplicate his claim. In any event, even if the plaintiff was restricted to
claiming relief for misrepresentation, he was entitled to damages as well as rescission
because the misrepresentation was fraudulent, but even if it had been innocent the
plaintiff would still have been entitled to damages under s 2 of the Misrepresentation Act
1967 (see p 275 c to f and h, p 277 e f and p 284 g, post); dicta of Lord Denning MR in
Doyle v Olby (Ironmongers) Ltd [1969] 2 All ER at 122 and of Lord Denning MR in *Esso*
h   *Petroleum Co Ltd v Mardon* [1976] 2 All ER at 16 applied; *Redgrave v Hurd* [1881–5] All
ER Rep 77 distinguished; *F & H Entertainments Ltd v Leisure Enterprises Ltd* (1976) 120 SJ
331 considered.
    (2) The plaintiff was entitled to recover the bank interest of £13,528 because the
defendant had known how the plaintiff proposed to raise the money and it must have
been plain to the defendant that he was putting the plaintiff in a position where he could
j   not repay the bank immediately and would have to pay interest until he did. Moreover,
the defendant's deceit had placed the plaintiff at the mercy of the bank and in so far as
the plaintiff was impecunious it was by reason of the defendant's deceit (see p 276 d to g,
p 277 b e f and p 284 g, post); *The Edison* [1933] All ER Rep 144 distinguished.
    (3) Although the plaintiff was not entitled to damages for loss of what he would have
earned with the company, since his prospective earnings depended on the success of the

company, he was entitled to damages of £2,500 for loss of employment and £1,000 representing his expenses incurred in seeking new employment after his discovery of the fraud (see p 283 h j and p 284 a to c and g, post).

(4) There was no reason in logic or justice why aggravated damages could not be awarded in deceit to compensate the plaintiff for his injured feelings. However, such an award was required to be moderate and therefore the plaintiff would be awarded £500 aggravated damages (see p 283 e to g and p 284 g, post); dicta of Lord Denning MR and Stephenson LJ in *Jarvis v Swans Tours Ltd* [1973] 1 All ER at 74, 77 applied; *Ichard v Frangoulis* [1977] 2 All ER 461 and dictum of Bristow J in *Shelley v Paddock* [1978] 3 All ER at 136 considered.

(5) The plaintiff was not entitled to exemplary damages, even if they could be awarded in deceit, because under the principle that a man was not to be punished twice for the same offence it would be wrong to award exemplary damages when the defendant had already spent a considerable time in gaol for the fraud perpetrated on the plaintiff (see p 281 e f, post); dicta of Lord Devlin in *Rookes v Barnard* [1964] 1 All ER at 410–411, of Sachs and Widgery LJJ in *Mafo v Adams* [1969] 3 All ER at 1406–1407, 1410–1411 and of Lord Hailsham LC and Lord Diplock in *Cassell & Co Ltd v Broome* [1972] 1 All ER at 830–831, 873–874 considered.

Notes

For the action of deceit, see 31 Halsbury's Laws (4th edn) paras 1090–1092.

For the distinction between exemplary and aggravated damages, see 12 ibid para 1186, and for cases on the subject, see 17 Digest (Reissue) 80–83, *11–17.*

For the Misrepresentation Act 1967, s 2, see 22 Halsbury's Statutes (3rd edn) 676.

Cases referred to in judgment

Anglia Television Ltd v Reed [1971] 3 All ER 690, [1972] 1 QB 60, [1971] 3 WLR 528, CA.
Bailey v Bullock [1950] 2 All ER 1167.
Cassell & Co Ltd v Broome [1972] 1 All ER 801, [1972] AC 1027, [1972] 2 WLR 645, HL.
Dodd Properties (Kent) Ltd v Canterbury City Council [1980] 1 All ER 928, [1980] 1 WLR 433, CA.
Doyle v Olby (Ironmongers) Ltd [1969] 2 All ER 119, [1969] 2 QB 158, [1969] 2 WLR 673, CA.
Esso Petroleum Co Ltd v Mardon [1976] 2 All ER 5, [1976] QB 801, [1976] 2 WLR 583, CA.
F & H Entertainments Ltd v Leisure Enterprises Ltd (1976) 120 SJ 331.
Hamlin v Great Northern Rly Co (1856) 1 H & N 408, 156 ER 1261.
Heywood v Wellers (a firm) [1976] 1 All ER 300, [1976] QB 446, [1976] 2 WLR 101, CA.
Hobbs v London and South Western Rly Co (1875) LR 10 QB 111, [1874–80] All ER Rep 458.
Ichard v Frangoulis [1977] 2 All ER 461, [1977] 1 WLR 556.
Jackson v Horizon Holidays Ltd [1975] 3 All ER 92, [1975] 1 WLR 1468, CA.
Jarvis v Swans Tours Ltd [1973] 1 All ER 71, [1973] QB 233, [1972] 3 WLR 954, CA.
Liesbosch, Dredger (owners) v Edison (owners) [1933] AC 449, [1933] All ER Rep 144, HL.
McNally v Welltrade International Ltd [1978] IRLR 497.
Mafo v Adams [1969] 3 All ER 1404, [1970] 1 QB 548, [1970] 2 WLR 72, CA.
Perry v Sidney Phillips & Son (a firm) [1982] 3 All ER 705, [1982] 1 WLR 1297, CA.
Redgrave v Hurd (1881) 20 ChD 1, [1881–5] All ER Rep 77, CA.
Rookes v Barnard [1964] 1 All ER 367, [1964] AC 1129, [1964] 2 WLR 269, HL.
Shelley v Paddock [1978] 3 All ER 129, [1979] QB 120, [1978] 2 WLR 877; affd [1980] 1 All ER 1009, [1980] QB 348, [1980] 2 WLR 647, CA.
Wilkes v Wood (1763) Lofft 1, 98 ER 489.

Cases also cited

Cullinane v British 'Rema' Manufacturing Co Ltd [1953] 2 All ER 1257, [1954] 1 QB 292, CA.
Drane v Evangelou [1978] 2 All ER 437, [1978] 1 WLR 455, CA.
Hadley v Baxendale (1854) 9 Exch 341, [1843–60] All ER Rep 461, 156 ER 145.

a
Victoria Laundry (Windsor) Ltd v Newman Industries Ltd [1949] 1 All ER 997, [1949] 2 KB 528, CA.

Action

b
By a writ issued on 7 April 1981 and a statement of claim served on 4 August 1981 the plaintiff, Dennis John Archer, claimed against the defendant, Kevin Brown, rescission of agreements made between the plaintiff and the defendant on or about 27 February and 24 March 1981 for the sale of shares in a company, Mantec Personnel Services Ltd, to the plaintiff, repayment of the sum of £30,000 paid by the plaintiff for the shares, damages for deceit or alternatively for breach of contract, and interest. The facts are set out in the judgment.

c
Kenneth Hamer for the plaintiff.
Donald Broatch for the defendant.

Cur adv vult

28 October. The following judgment was delivered.

d
PETER PAIN J. This case arises out of a swindle practised on the plaintiff by the defendant. The case has taken a course such that I have heard evidence only from the plaintiff's side. My findings are, of course, based on that evidence. I understand that the defendant, who is at present in prison, is appealing against his conviction next month. From what counsel tell me, I do not see how any of the findings which I make can have any bearing on the appeal, but by way of caution I emphasise that they are made on
e
limited evidence and should not be referred to in that appeal. Had I thought otherwise I might have adjourned this case until after that appeal, although such adjournment would have worked further hardship on the plaintiff; but I was fortified in my decision to go ahead by counsel for the defendant. He told me that he had considered asking for an adjournment but concluded that it would not be right to do so.

I will deal with the facts.

f
The initial negotiations

The plaintiff, who had been employed by the Italian Hospital as an accountant, parted company with his employers on 31 October 1980 by mutual consent. His final salary was £11,000 per annum. He was a man in his early fifties who had wearied of working for employers and wanted to set up business with a partner on his own account.

g
Soon after he left, the plaintiff saw an advertisement inserted in a paper by the defendant and contacted him. Discussions began. He also had two other irons in the fire: a business in Slough which did not seem very promising, and a garage business in Leicester which was interesting but did not attract him as much as the defendant's business.

The plaintiff met the defendant in December. The defendant said that he was the
h
owner of an employment agency, Mantec Personnel Services Ltd (Mantec). He wanted to expand it into an insurance and holiday travel business. He wanted a partner who would introduce £20,000 and he and his partner would share fifty-fifty.

The defendant produced audited accounts for the years 1979–80 and 1980–81. He helped the plaintiff to prepare an estimate for the year ending 28 February 1982. The accounts appeared satisfactory. The plaintiff had a company search made; this showed by
j
the annual return for 1980 that Mantec had a capital of 100 £1 shares, of which 99 were held by the defendant and one by Mrs Jackson (the defendant's sister). No changes of shareholding were shown. The annual return was signed by the defendant and his sister.

The plaintiff sought advice from solicitors, Messrs Titmuss Sainer & Webb, but before any drafting work was done he changed solicitors and went to Mr Swayne, who was with him at one of the interviews with the defendant and who told me that everything appeared to be in order.

The plaintiff went to Barclays Bank, Kettering, where he had had an account for about twenty years. The bank was prepared to advance the plaintiff £20,000 for the purchase *a* of half the shares in Mantec, but it wanted security. The security was to be a first charge on the plaintiff's son's house at 101 Barton Road and a second mortgage on the plaintiff's house in Warkton Lane. The plaintiff and his wife had originally lived with their son at Barton Road. When they moved to Warkton Lane they conveyed the Barton Road property to their son for £16,000 and lent him that sum on second mortgage. There was already a first mortgage for £6,000 which the son took over. By February 1980 *b* approximately £6,000 was due by way of interest on the second mortgage, the son having paid no interest by that date. The arrangement made with the bank was that the advance of £20,000 was placed in a separate loan account. The bank paid off the first mortgage on the son's house, thereby becoming first mortgagees. The £6,000 so paid was treated as a loan by the bank to the son. The second mortgage held by the plaintiff and his wife was postponed to the bank's mortgage. The whole arrangement was made *c* on the basis that the property would be put up for sale.

In the course of discussions the plaintiff told the defendant that he was borrowing £20,000 from the bank. Mr Swayne was instructed to draw up an agreement between the plaintiff and the defendant by which the plaintiff would purchase 50 shares from the defendant for £20,000, and service agreements between the plaintiff and Mantec, and the defendant and Mantec, by which each would be employed by Mantec at an annual *d* salary of £16,750 as joint managing directors.

The sale agreement recited that (1) Mantec was a private company incorporated in England on 3 December 1975 with limited liability under the Companies Act 1948 and had an authorised share capital of £100 divided into 100 ordinary shares of £1 each all of which had been issued and were fully paid and accredited as fully paid, (2) the vendor was the beneficial owner of all such ordinary shares, (3) the vendor and the purchaser had *e* agreed to be equal shareholders in the company and to run the business of the company henceforth as equal partners on the basis as set out in that agreement. The defendant warranted with the plaintiff that the statements contained in the first and the second recitals were true and accurate in all respects and that no person had any right to call for the issue of any shares in the capital of the company. The defendant also warranted that none of the shares was subject to any charge, lien, encumbrance or option, and that the *f* company had not any outstanding debts, liabilities, contracts or engagements otherwise than in the ordinary and proper course of its trading business.

Completion took place on 27 February 1981. The agreement provided that the £20,000 should be paid as to £15,000 forthwith and as to £5,000 on 1 March 1982. The plaintiff made out two cheques: one to the defendant for £15,000 and one to the company for £5,000. The latter was to be held by the company and paid to the defendant *g* on 1 March 1982.

The course of business

Almost immediately things began to go wrong. The cheque for £5,000 was paid by the defendant into his own account. There was not the number of staff that the defendant had said there were. The defendant asserted that £5,000 was due to him for arrears of *h* salary. There was a dispute about the assets. By 15 March the plaintiff had drawn up an agenda of complaints for discussion and was most dissatisfied with the defendant's replies.

The defendant then suggested that the company be wound up. The plaintiff was flabbergasted. It appeared to him that the defendant was determined that he could not work with the plaintiff, so he proposed that the defendant should buy back the plaintiff's shares. The defendant suggested that the plaintiff should buy the rest of the shares for a *j* further £10,000. The plaintiff saw no option but to agree. The defendant took the plaintiff to the New Bridge Street branch of Barclays Bank, where the company and he banked. The bank made an unsecured loan of £10,000 to the plaintiff. Mr Swayne drew up a supplemental agreement to which I must refer.

The agreement provided that the defendant would sell and the plaintiff would purchase 50 ordinary shares of the company from the defendant free from all charges or

liens or other incumbrances and with all rights attaching thereto. The total consideration
a payable by the plaintiff for the shares was to be £10,000 payable in cash. Completion of
the sale and purchase of the shares was to take place on 24 March 1981 at the offices of
the company, when against delivery to the purchaser of the deed of transfer duly executed
by the vendor in favour of the purchaser in respect of the shares, accompanied by the
share certificate relating thereto, the purchaser should pay to the vendor the sum of
£10,000. The vendor warranted and undertook with the purchaser that the provisions
b of cll 4 and 5 of the principal agreement (i e the original sale agreement) remained true
and accurate in every respect and that the provisions of sub-cll (a) and (b) of cl 4 were true
in respect of the shares which formed the basis of that agreement with the exception of
the period from 1 March to 20 March 1981. The defendant further undertook with the
plaintiff that he would, out of the sum of money paid to him, discharge all debts and
other amounts owing by the company up to and including the close of business on 20
c March 1981 and that he would forthwith reimburse the company in the sum of £3,500
received on the sale of the word processor machine belonging to the company.

In fact, of the £10,000 which the plaintiff paid, £3,500 went into a special account.
The plaintiff was very confused in his evidence about this, and eventually said, despite
what the agreement provides, that the £3,500 was in respect of both outstanding debts
and the word processor. The word processor was an asset which the defendant had sold
d and put the proceeds in his own pocket. It was suggested to the plaintiff in cross-
examination that he had had the balance of this account, but it then transpired that some
had been used to pay debts and the balance had been recovered by the defendant in
garnishee proceedings.

Completion was on 24 March 1981. On completion the plaintiff was given a share
certificate signed by the defendant for 99 shares and Mrs Archer (the plaintiff's wife) was
e given a similar certificate for one share.

The true position emerges

The plaintiff then attended at the office to try to pull the business together. After a
few days he met a Mr Bree, who asked what he was doing. Mr Bree said that he was a
director and shareholder and had put £10,000 into the business by way of purchase of
f shares the previous November.

The plaintiff then inquired into the position and suffered a dreadful shock. It appeared
from documents that came to light that the defendant had sold the shares time and again.
I have in the agreed bundle: (a) three share certificates dated 24 December 1979 each
stating that the capital of the company was £300, for 100 shares for the defendant, 100
shares for a Mr Gawish and 100 shares for a Mr Park; each of these is signed by the
g defendant as secretary; (b) a share certificate dated 11 August 1980 stating the capital as
£100 for 50 £1 shares for a Mr Cheesman; this is signed by the defendant as a director
and as secretary; (c) a share certificate dated 22 July 1980 stating the capital as £100 for
50 shares for a Mr McConnell; this is signed by the defendant as a director and as
secretary; (d) a share certificate dated 4 November 1980 stating the capital as £100 for 30
shares for Mr Bree; this is signed by the defendant as director and as secretary, together
h with a transfer form signed by the defendant.

I have no evidence how these documents and other documents tending to show that
the defendant had purported to sell shares to these gentlemen had come into existence.
In view of the course this case took it was unnecessary for me to inquire into this. But it
is small wonder that the plaintiff took the view that the defendant had no shares to sell
to him.

j

The course of proceedings

On 3 April 1981 the plaintiff obtained a Mareva injunction as to £30,000 of the
defendant's bank account at the New Bridge Street branch of Barclays Bank. On 7 April
1981 he issued his writ in these proceedings.

By June 1982 criminal proceedings had been launched against the defendant. The
defendant made application to have the proceedings now before me stayed till after the

criminal trial but this application was dismissed. In August and September 1982 he
applied to have the Mareva injunction lifted but this application too was dismissed.   *a*

In November 1982 the defendant was tried at the Old Bailey and after a 3½-week trial
was convicted on five counts. Two of those counts relate to this matter. On count 10 he
was convicted of fraudently inducing the investment of money, contrary to s 13(1)(*a*) of
the Prevention of Fraud (Investment) Act 1958, and the particulars of the offence were:

'[The defendant] on 27th February 1981 fraudulently induced [the plaintiff] to
enter into an agreement for acquiring 50 shares at a total purchase price of £20,000   *b*
in Mantec Personnel Services Ltd. by stating that (1) the company was then a
profitable and expanding concern; (2) the trading results of the company had not on
a comparative basis deteriorated since 28th February 1980; (3) [the defendant] was
the beneficial owner of all 100 £1 ordinary shares which comprised the company's
authorised share capital, all such shares being issued and fully paid; (4) the company
was absolutely entitled to all the assets described in the balance sheet as at 28th   *c*
February 1980; (5) there had been no material change in the position or prospects of
the company since 28th February 1980 which had not been disclosed to [the
plaintiff] during the course of negotiations; (6) since 28th February 1980 there had
been no reduction in the aggregate respective net assets position of the company as
represented by the balance sheet; (7) the company had purchased a word processor
which was then on hire realising some £60 per week income; (8) the tax returns of   *d*
the company had at all times been correct and kept on a proper basis and were not
the subject of any back duty claim or other dispute with the Revenue authorities;
(9) the company was not engaged in any litigation or arbitration proceedings and
that no such proceedings were pending or threatened and [the defendant] knew of
no facts or matters likely to give rise thereto; and (10) all debts of any substance then
owing to the company would be met by the debtor or debtors concerned; all of   *e*
which statements [the defendant] then knew to be misleading, false or deceptive.'

He was also convicted on the count 12 of the indictment for a similar offence, the
particulars in that case being that the defendant—

'on 24th March 1981, fraudulently induced [the plaintiff] to enter into an
agreement for acquiring 50 shares at a total purchase price of £10,000 in Mantec   *f*
Personnel Services Ltd. by stating that (1) the acquisition of the said 50 shares would
then ensure that [the plaintiff] held the entire share holding of the company, no
other person owning or having a beneficial interest in any share or shares of the
company; (2) the company's assets were then realistically valued at £25,490 and that
the list of the said assets compiled by [the defendant] was true and accurate in all
material particulars; (3) there had been no material change in the position as to the   *g*
potential profitability or property of the company since 21st March 1981 and in
particular no change had occurred or was pending with regard to the company's
contracts for the placement of staff; (4) it was then his [the defendant's] intention to
discharge all debts and other amounts owing by the company up to and including
the close of business on 20th March 1981 from the sum of money paid to him by
[the plaintiff] under the terms of the said agreement; all of which statements [the   *h*
defendant] then knew to be misleading, false or deceptive.'

In the course of the criminal trial certain information emerged as to the defendant's
assets. As a result of this the plaintiff made a further application to the court and obtained
an order from Jupp J on 15 December 1982 freezing all the defendant's bank accounts,
four accounts being named specifically, preventing him from disposing of his flat,   *j*
freezing the interest accruing on the account to which the original order related and
ordering him to disclose to the plaintiff the identity and whereabouts of any other bank
account or building society account maintained by him or in his name.

The defendant did not obey the order as to disclosure. The plaintiff applied again to
the court and obtained orders from Master Hodgson on 13 July 1983 that he—

a 'must identify and make full disclosure of (1) all his assets within and outside the jurisdiction up to the present date and as at 7th April 1981; (2) the present whereabouts and manner of any changes in disposals; (3) all documents relevant to the value, distribution, disposals or change between 7th April 1981 and the date of the order, within 28 days, to be verified by affidavit, time to run in the vacation.'

Once again the defendant did not obey the order of the court, and on 12 September 1981 it was ordered that—

b 'the defendant's defence be struck out for failure to comply with the orders for discovery and disclosure dated 18th July 1983, and that the plaintiff be at liberty to enter judgment.'

The plaintiff duly entered judgment.

The relief which the plaintiff seeks is defined in this way in the amended statement of
c claim: (1) rescission of the agreements made on 27 February and 24 March 1981 for the sale of shares in Mantec to the plaintiff; (2) repayment of the sum of £30,000; (3) damages for deceit; (4) alternatively damages for breach of contract; (5) exemplary damages; (6) interest paid to Barclays Bank at the rates charged by the bank to the plaintiff in respect of the loan on current account, alternatively at the commercial rate of interest; (7) interest on the remainder of the sum for such period as the court may deem
d just; (8) an injunction restraining the defendant from removing, disposing or otherwise dealing with any moneys forming an account in the name of the defendant maintained at the New Bridge Street branch of Barclays Bank, and a declaration that the moneys presently standing to the credit of the bank account are held by the defendant.

What the plaintiff did after the truth came out
e The plaintiff immediately sought advice from his solicitors. He left the company's premises, but he retained possession of a car which the company had on hire purchase. He agreed in evidence that as at March 1981 £2,300 was a reasonable valuation for the car. There was correspondence with the hire-purchase finance company and the car was retained with their consent. In January 1983 Mrs Archer paid the finance company £600 which was the amount outstanding and the car became her property. I have no evidence
f as to the instalments which the company paid either before or after March 1981 or as to the value of the car in January 1983.

The loan of £20,000 had been made on the understanding that 101 Barton Road would be sold. It was not sold until about July 1982. The price was £30,000 but after deduction of the various costs this was reduced to £28,823·85.

By arrangement with the bank, £6,000 of the sale price was used to extinguish the
g son's loan account. The rest was placed in a security realisation account. This account earned interest at about 9% as a deposit account (the rate of interest varied according to deposit account interest rates). Meanwhile interest was accruing to the bank on the loan account at a rate of about 12% (and again, of course, that rate varied from time to time). The interest earned by the security realisation account was applied in partial extinction of the interest due on the loan account.

h On the face of it, it would appear more sensible to use the security realisation account to pay off the loan in whole or in part; but by this time the plaintiff's current account, which had been in the black in March 1981, was running deeply into the red. I do not have the account before me but am told that it is by now about £17,000 in deficit. In the nature of things a large part of this must have arisen in the early months after the disaster when the plaintiff had no job. Mr Hansford, the Kettering bank manager, who gave
j evidence, was cross-examined to show that the arrangement made was unduly favourable to the bank. He insisted that it was for the benefit of the customer. I do not have figures to show whether what was realised on sale was sufficient then to pay off the loan account having regard to the fact that some 16 months' interest would have accrued by then, but I think it improbable that it was. I am quite satisfied that Mr Hansford would not have agreed to any other disposal. The plaintiff was really at the bank's mercy.

The position as to interest as at the date of trial is that £9,071 is owing on the Kettering loan account, £4,457 is owing on the New Bridge Street loan account, which has been *a* transferred to Fleet Street.

I am satisfied that the plaintiff was very deeply upset when the truth emerged. He had put himself deeply into debt, his ambition to become self-employed was frustrated, what appeared to be a promising development had gone up in smoke and he was unemployed in a difficult market. There is no evidence that he was actually ill, but I am satisfied by Mrs Archer's evidence that he lived through a nightmare and was deeply affected by it. *b*

He did not sit down under his troubles but made vigorous efforts to obtain employment. He has drawn up a schedule of the expenses incurred during his search for work and these show that he made almost a full-time job of looking for work. Nor was he too proud to accept rather inferior jobs. He worked for Transalpina on a temporary basis from early August to mid-October 1981 at a rate of £10,000 per annum. This job ended and in the latter part of November he found another temporary job with Old *c* Court Clinic, again at £10,000 per annum. Then in January 1982 he went to a permanent job with the Advertising Association initially at £10,000 per annum.

Counsel for the defendant did not criticise the plaintiff's estimate of his expenses at £1,126 save that he suggested £3 per day for lunch was too much because the plaintiff would have had to have lunch wherever he was. I think there is force in this submission; that it is only the extra cost which can legitimately be regarded as an expense and that *d* the plaintiff's estimate could fairly be reduced to the round figure of £1,000.

The main issue

The plaintiff's case is simple. He says that he can recover all the damage which flows from the defendant's deceit: this is the original £30,000 which he paid for nothing, the two sums of interest of £9,071 and £4,457 which he owes to the bank, his solicitors' *e* expenses, the cost of realising Barton Road, his loss of earnings and his expenses while looking for a new job. He also claims exemplary damages, alternatively aggravated damages, in respect of the disappointment that he has undergone.

The plaintiff relied on *Doyle v Olby (Ironmongers) Ltd* [1969] 2 All ER 119, [1969] 2 QB 158 and referred me to a passage in the judgment of Lord Denning MR ([1969] 2 All ER 119 at 122, [1969] 2 QB 158 at 167): *f*

'The object of damages is to put the plaintiff in as good a position, as far as money can do it, as if the promise had been performed. In fraud, the defendant has been guilty of a deliberate wrong by inducing the plaintiff to act to his detriment. The object of damages is to compensate the plaintiff for all the loss he has suffered, so far, again, as money can do it. In contract, the damages are limited to what may reasonably be supposed to have been in the contemplation of the parties. In fraud, *g* they are not so limited. The defendant is bound to make reparation for all the actual damage directly flowing from the fraudulent inducement. The person who has been defrauded is entitled to say: "I would not have entered into this bargain at all but for your representation. Owing to your fraud, I have lost not only all the money I paid you, but, what is more, I have been put to a large amount of extra expense as well and suffered this or that extra damages."' *h*

It is of some significance that, although of course each case depends on its own facts, *Doyle v Olby (Ironmongers) Ltd* was a case of a plaintiff who had been induced fraudulently to invest money in a business.

That decision was followed by the Court of Appeal in *Esso Petroleum Co Ltd v Mardon* [1976] 2 All ER 5, [1976] QB 801, when, again, Lord Denning MR referred specifically *j* to *Doyle's* case and said ([1976] 2 All ER 5 at 16, [1976] QB 801 at 820):

'Mr Mardon [the defendant] is not to be compensated here for "loss of a bargain". He was given no bargain that the throughput *would* amount to 200,000 gallons a year. He is only to be compensated for having been induced to enter into a contract which turned out to be disastrous for him. Whether it be called breach of warranty *a*   or negligent misrepresentation, its effect was *not* to warrant the throughput, but only to induce him to enter the contract. So the damages in either case are to be measured by the loss he suffered.' (Lord Denning MR's emphasis.)

Counsel for the defendant said that his client conceded that the plaintiff was entitled to rescission and the return of his £30,000. He also conceded that the plaintiff was entitled to interest at the rate provided for by the Rules of the Supreme Court from 14 days after the service of the writ. But he insisted that the plaintiff was entitled to nothing *b*   more. He said that by his calculations, interest pursuant to the Rules of the Supreme Court would amount to £6,525 on both loan accounts (this was counsel's calculation, not an agreed figure).

To decide the case on this reasoning would work a gross injustice and I am happy to find that the law does not require it of me. It seems to me that this argument is quite fallacious on three grounds. (1) Judgment has been given against the defendant for the *c*   relief sought in the writ. The defendant applied to set this judgment aside but abandoned his application. It is not open to him to say now that he concedes rescission for misrepresentation and that this precludes the plaintiff claiming damages for deceit. The plaintiff can recover damages under whichever head of claim he chooses, provided he does not duplicate his claim. He is entitled to the return of his £30,000 by way of *d*   damages for deceit as much as damages for rescission. (2) Counsel for the defendant said that the defendant conceded that the plaintiff was entitled to rescission for misrepresentation. When I asked him, 'What misrepresentation?' he would not commit himself. He suggested that I need not go into this. The reason is plain. If the position is examined on the evidence before me, the conclusion is really inescapable that the defendant knew perfectly well that he was not entitled to sell the plaintiff the shares that he purported to sell. His conduct was fraudulent and I so find. In cases of fraudulent *e*   misrepresentation the plaintiff has always been entitled to damages as well as rescission. (3) In cases of innocent misrepresentation a plaintiff was entitled to rescission only until recently. This was considered to work injustice and the Misrepresentation Act 1967 was passed to put this matter right. Even if the defendant's misrepresentation had been innocent the plaintiff would in my opinion have been entitled to claim damages as well as rescission by virtue of s 2 of that Act.

f   Counsel for the defendant relied on several authorities. First he referred me to a passage in *Snell's Principles of Equity* (28th edn, 1982) p 606, where, under the heading 'Effect of rescission', he read this:

g   'A person who rescinds a contract is entitled to be restored to the position he would have been in had the contract not been *made*. Hence, property must be returned, possession given up, and accounts taken of profits or deterioration. But no damages are recoverable, since the purpose of damages is to place the party recovering them in the same position (so far as money can do it) as he would have been in, had the contract been *carried out*.' (*Snell's* emphasis.)

I was a little puzzled by this passage because it does not present the law as I understand it. But on reading the chapter in which it occurs I find that counsel has made the familiar *h*   mistake of taking a passage out of context. This passage is simply describing the effect of rescission. The law as it stands today is set out earlier (at pp 601–602), making it clear that in a case like this the plaintiff would be entitled to damages as well as to rescission. To use this passage as counsel does, does an injustice to the editors of *Snell*.

Counsel then referred me *Redgrave v Hurd* (1881) 20 Ch D 1, [1881–5] All ER Rep 77. In my view this case helps him not at all. That was a case, back in the last century, where *j*   damages were not awarded because the misrepresentation was not proved to be fraudulent. It does not represent the law since the Misrepresentation Act 1967.

He also referred to *Anglia Television Ltd v Reed* [1971] 3 All ER 690, [1972] 1 QB 160. This was a case in contract where the issue was whether damages could be recovered in respect of expenses incurred before the contract was entered into. It has no bearing, as I see it, on the present case.

F & H Entertainments Ltd v Leisure Enterprises Ltd (1976) 120 SJ 331 is a good deal nearer the mark. Walton J was reported as saying:　　　　　　　　　　　　　　　　　　　*a*

> 'On the question of damages . . . no case had been made out that the defendants had reasonable grounds to believe that the representation was true and they did not, therefore, come within the proviso to s 2 of the Misrepresentation Act 1967 . . . So the measure of damages under s 2 was clearly the same as in an action for damages for deceit. The defendants sought to shelter behind a letter stating that the plaintiffs *b* had been allowed into occupation at their own risk, pending completion, but his lordship would not accept that. It was the misrepresentation which induced the plaintiffs to enter into the whole contract, containing the provisions under which they had acted to their ultimate disadvantage. Their acts were directly attributable to the misrepresentation. Alternatively s 3 of the 1967 Act entitled the court to disallow any exempting provisions of the agreement. The proper measure of damages covered all expenditure properly and not prematurely or extravagantly *c* incurred.'

Counsel sought to put a gloss on this last sentence by adding the words 'at the date of the rescission'. To my mind there is no justification for that. Certainly, Walton J's mind can hardly have been directed to that, as he was considering expenditure which had already been incurred and he ordered an inquiry as to damages. His decision is no *d* authority for the proposition that a liability already incurred to the knowledge of the defendant could be excluded because it did not require payment until after rescission.

I accept, of course, that the plaintiff is confined to expenses reasonably and properly incurred. In this case the defendant assisted the plaintiff, knowing how the first loan had been raised. He cannot be heard to say that liability to interest was not properly incurred. Further, as to the arrangements which were made at Kettering after the true position was *e* known, I do not think the plaintiff had any choice. The defendant's deceit had placed him at the mercy of the bank. Accordingly I find that the interest at the bank was reasonably and properly incurred on both loans. I will deal with the other heads of damage later.

An alternative way in which the defendant puts his case is to say that the plaintiff should have paid off the loans so that the bank interest did not arise. The fact that he did *f* not do so was due to his impecuniosity and not the defendant's deceit. The defendant relies on the decision of the House of Lords in *Dredger Liesbosch (owners) v Edison (owners)* [1933] AC 449, [1933] All ER Rep 144. This is a brazen argument. In so far as the plaintiff was impecunious it was by reason of the defendant's deceit. I find assistance in the analysis of the *Liesbosch* case by Donaldson LJ in *Dodd Properties (Kent) Ltd v Canterbury City Council* [1980] 1 All ER 928 at 940, [1980] 1 WLR 433 at 458–459:　　　　　*g*

> 'The Edison fouled the Liesbosch's moorings, carried her out to sea and sank her. The ordinary measure of damage was the cost of buying another similar vessel, the cost of getting her to the Liesbosch's old moorings and any loss of profit consequent on the disruption of commercial operations whilst the substitute vessel was being obtained and delivered. However, the plaintiffs contended for a different and special *h* measure of damage. Substitute dredgers were available for purchase but the plaintiffs could not afford to buy them. Instead they hired another dredger, the Adria, which was larger than the Liesbosch, more expensive to operate and for which they had to pay a very high rate of hire. Eventually the port authority, for whom the plaintiffs were working, bought the Adria and resold her to the plaintiffs under a credit sale contract. The plaintiffs claimed the cost of hiring the Adria until the port authority bought and resold her to them, the cost of purchasing the Adria and the excess cost *j* of working her as compared with the Liesbosch together with unrecovered overhead charges and lost profit whilst they were without any dredger. The ordinary measure of damage is based on market rates. The measure of damage claimed by the plaintiffs was quite different, namely, one based on their actual loss and expenditure. As I understand Lord Wright's speech, he took the view that, in so far as the plaintiffs in

a fact suffered more than the loss assessed on a market basis, the excess loss flowed directly from their lack of means and not from the tortious act, or alternatively it was too remote in law. In modern terms, I think that he would have said that it was not foreseeable.'

I observe that that decision was followed by the Court of Appeal in *Perry v Sidney Phillips & Son (a firm)* [1982] 3 All ER 705, [1982] 1 WLR 1297.

b Accepting the reasonable foreseeability test, it must have been plain to the defendant that his deceit was putting the plaintiff in a position where he could not repay the bank. This was quite different from the *Liesbosch* case, where the parties were complete strangers before the accident which gave rise to the claim.

The main issue has been confused by the way in which counsel for the plaintiff put his case. In opening he appeared to be claiming damages for deceit. But, when he arrived at the point of his argument for exemplary or, alternatively, aggravated damages, he began
c to veer, because he felt that his claim might be stronger in contract. It seemed to me that he had a choice how he would put his claim but that he could not apply the measure for breach of contract to one item and the measure for tort to another. I therefore called on him to elect before counsel for the defendant addressed me. Counsel for the plaintiff would not do so, an attitude which I found unhelpful. He should by that stage have been sufficiently master of his case to be able to make a choice. Counsel for the defendant
d suggested that I should compel counsel for the plaintiff to elect on pain of being non-suited, but I could not do that because the plaintiff had already recovered judgment. Eventually I indicated that I would deal with the matter in deceit. It seemed to me essential that defendant's counsel, who had called no evidence, should know what case he had to meet.

Having reflected on the matter I am satisfied that this was a non-issue. While it is true
e that the measure of damages is different in tort and in contract, it makes no difference which measure one applies in this case: the damages are the same. The damages which flow from the defendant's deceit are no different from what must have been in the reasonable contemplation of the parties at the time of the contract. The defendant knew that the money had been borrowed from the bank. He must have appreciated, if he put his mind to it, (a) that the plaintiff would have to pay interest at bank rates until the loan
f was repaid, (b) that the plaintiff would find it difficult, if not impossible, to repay, certainly impossible to repay immediately, (c) that the plaintiff would be deeply distressed and (d) that the plaintiff would have to find a job, would have expenses looking for a job and would have nothing but unemployment benefit till he found one.

Exemplary damages
g The plaintiff asserted that this was a case in which exemplary damages should be awarded and rested his case in the first place what was said by Lord Devlin in the well-known case of *Rookes v Barnard* [1964] 1 All ER 367 at 410–411, [1964] AC 1129 at 1226–1228 when he came to deal with exemplary damages. In dealing with the second category of cases in which exemplary damages might be awarded (and it is plain that this case could only come in that category) Lord Devlin said:

h   'Cases in the second category are those in which the defendant's conduct has been calculated by him to make a profit for himself which may well exceed the compensation payable to the plaintiff. [He referred to earlier cases and continued:] It is a factor also that is taken into account in damages for libel; one man should not be allowed to sell another man's reputation for profit. Where a defendant with a cynical disregard for a plaintiff's rights has calculated that the money to be made
j   out of his wrongdoing will probably exceed the damages at risk, it is necessary for the law to show that it cannot be broken with impunity. This category is not confined to moneymaking in the strict sense. It extends to cases in which the defendant is seeking to gain at the expense of the plaintiff some object,—perhaps some property which he covets,—which either he could not obtain at all or not obtain except at a price greater than he wants to put down. Exemplary damages can

properly be awarded whenever it is necessary to teach a wrongdoer that tort does
not pay ... I wish now to express three considerations which I think should always *a*
be borne in mind when awards of exemplary damages are being considered. First,
the plaintiff cannot recover exemplary damages unless he is the victim of the
punishable behaviour. The anomaly inherent in exemplary damages would become
an absurdity if a plaintiff totally unaffected by some oppressive conduct which the
jury wished to punish obtained a windfall in consequence. Secondly, the power to
award exemplary damages constitutes a weapon that, while it can be used in defence *b*
of liberty, as in the *Wilkes* case [*Wilkes v Wood* (1763) Lofft 1, 98 ER 489], can also be
used against liberty. Some of the awards that juries have made in the past seem to
me to amount to a greater punishment than would be likely to be incurred if the
conduct were criminal; and moreover a punishment imposed without the safeguard
which the criminal law gives to an offender. I should not allow the respect which is
traditionally paid to an assessment of damages by a jury to prevent me from seeing *c*
that the weapon is used with restraint ... Thirdly, the means of the parties,
irrelevant in the assessment of compensation, are material in the assessment of
exemplary damages. Everything which aggravates or mitigates the defendant's
conduct is relevant. Thus a case for exemplary damages must be presented quite
differently from one for compensatory damages; and the judge should not allow it
to be left to the jury unless he is satisfied that it can be brought within the categories *d*
I have specified. But the fact that two sorts of damage differ essentially does not
necessarily mean that there should be two awards. In a case in which exemplary
damages are appropriate, a jury should be directed that if, but only if, the sum
which they have in mind to award as compensation (which may of course be a sum
aggravated by the way in which the defendant has behaved to the plaintiff) is
inadequate to punish him for his outrageous conduct, to mark their disapproval of *e*
such conduct and to deter him from repeating it, then they can award some larger
sum. If a verdict given on such direction has to be reviewed on appeal, the appellate
court will first consider whether the award can be justified as compensation, and, if
it can, there is nothing further to be said. If it cannot, the court must consider
whether or not the punishment is in all the circumstances excessive. There may be
cases in which it is difficult for a judge to say whether or not he ought to leave to *f*
the jury a claim for exemplary damages. In such circumstances, and in order to save
the possible expense of a new trial, I see no objection to his inviting the jury to say
what sum they would fix as compensation and what additional sum, if any, they
would award if they were entitled to give exemplary damages.'

Then in a further passage he stated ([1964] 1 All ER 367 at 412, [1964] AC 1129 at 1230):
g
'This conclusion will, I hope, remove from the law a source of confusion between
aggravated and exemplary damages which has troubled the learned commentators
on the subject. Otherwise, it will not, I think, make much difference to the substance
of the law or rob the law of the strength which it ought to have. Aggravated
damages in this type of case can do most, if not all, of the work that could be done
by exemplary damages. In so far as they do not, assaults and malicious injuries to *h*
property can generally be punished as crimes, whereas the objectionable conduct in
the categories in which I have accepted the need for exemplary damages are not,
generally speaking, within the criminal law and could not, even if the criminal law
was to be amplified, conveniently be defined as crimes. I do not care for the idea
that in matters criminal an aggrieved party should be given an option to inflict for
his own benefit punishment by a method which denies to the offender the protection *j*
of the criminal law.'

Conflict of views has arisen whether damages could properly be given in cases of
deceit. I refer next to *Mafo v Adams* [1969] 3 All ER 1404, [1970] 1 QB 548. It was a case
in which a landlord had deceitfully induced a tenant to leave protected premises. The
county court judge had awarded the aggrieved tenant £100 by way of 'ordinary' damages

(if I may so call them) and £100 by way of exemplary damages. Sachs LJ said ([1969] 3
a All ER 1404 at 1406–1407, [1970] 1 QB 548 at 554–555):

'Alternatively, in regard to the award of exemplary damages for the deceit,
[counsel for the landlord] contends that even if that cause of action was established,
no such award should have been made; and, in addition, he asserts that the sums of
£100 for compensatory and exemplary damages were each excessive. The tenant
cross-appeals against the dismissal of his claim for wrongful eviction and trespass.
b Having regard to the course of proceedings in this court and the concessions made
for counsel, it is convenient to deal first with the action for deceit, which is here a
realistic cause of action on which . . . all the relevant heads of damage can be dealt
with. The first question is to decide whether a cause of action in deceit was
established. It appears to me quite clear that, once the fraud was proved, the cause
of action became complete on it being shown that the landlord secured by means of
c that fraud something of value, that is to say, possession of the flat at no. 10, Duncan
Road, by fraudulently inducing the tenant to surrender it. Possession of rent-
protected premises is, of course, valuable property. Thus the first point taken on
apppeal fails. Once it is shown that the cause of action is complete, the next question
is what is the measure of damages proper to compensate this particular tenant for
that fraud. The loss flowing from the fraud which can be taken into account in
d accordance with the principles recently enunciated in this court in *Doyle* v. *Olby*
(Ironmongers), Ltd. ([1969] 2 All ER 119, [1969] 2 QB 158) includes, of course, the
loss of the protected tenancy. The tenant apparently still has not got a tenancy with
an equally sure protection, and for that he is entitled to compensation. In addition,
he is entitled on accepted principles to compensation for the *physicial inconvenience*
suffered when put in the position to which I have already adverted [Sachs LJ's
e emphasis]. Counsel for the landlord has submitted that, in those circumstances, the
sum of £100 for compensation is excessive. As he has conceded that the matters to
be taken into account are those already related, it is sufficient in a case of this sort
simply to say that to my mind the sum of £100 is a reasonable quantification of the
damages due by way of compensation . . . Next one comes to a considerably more
difficult question; that is, whether this is a case in which exemplary damages are
f recoverable, and whether, if so, the sum of £100 was a correct assessment. [He
referred to various authorities and then said:] When, however, counsel for the
landlord opened the present case he was minded to concede that, in actions for
deceit, such damages could now be awarded, and, after considering the matter
carefully, he in fact did make this concession. He did so, basing himself on that
sentence in LORD DEVLIN's speech [in *Rookes v Barnard* [1964] 1 All ER 367 at 411,
g [1964] AC 1129 at 1227] which states: "Exemplary damages can properly be awarded
whenever it is necessary to teach a wrongdoer that tort does not pay." That passage
he interpreted as applying to all actions of tort. So far as this case is concerned, there
is thus inter partes agreement on that matter. In the upshot, however, it has in any
event become unnecessary to decide the point, having regard to the view held by
my brethren and myself, that, on the findings of the judge, such a claim cannot be
h supported on the particular facts of the case. I state the position carefully in this
way, because had that concession not been made, it would have been necessary to
have considerably further argument on the point and to consider that argument
with care. I would, indeed, need to be persuaded, despite the generality of the phrase
already quoted, that this speech which sought so drastically to limit the circumstances
in which exemplary damages can be awarded, was by reason of that phrase or
j otherwise either intended to, or on its proper construction did, enlarge considerably
the number of causes of action in which claims to such damages can be maintained.'

Widgery LJ took a different view ([1969] 3 All ER 1404 at 1410–1411, [1970] 1 QB 548
at 558–559):

'The position with regard to exemplary damages is perhaps a little more difficult.

I think counsel for the landlord was entirely right in accepting that LORD DEVLIN's
dicta as to exemplary damages apply to the tort of deceit. As I understand LORD   *a*
DEVLIN's speech, the circumstances in which exemplary damages may be obtained
have been drastically reduced, but the range of offences in respect of which they
may be granted has been increased, and I see no reason since *Rookes* v. *Barnard* why,
when considering a claim for exemplary damages, one should regard the nature of
the tort as excluding the claim. If the circumstances are those prescribed by LORD
DEVLIN, it seems to me that the fact that the tort was one which did not formerly   *b*
attract exemplary damages is a matter of no consequence. On the other hand, I am
firmly of opinion that, since it is now clear that exemplary damages are punitive
only and all cases of aggravation which result in additional injury to the plaintiff are
to be dealt with by aggravated damages, then it follows that the circumstances in
which exemplary damages are awarded should be exceptional indeed. It is not the
function of civil courts to punish. In the past, in my judgment, much confusion has   *c*
been caused because judges awarding compensation to plaintiffs for ruffled feelings
have sometimes said they were awarding exemplary damages. It is clear now that
that kind of case does not come under the exemplary heading at all, and, in my
judgment, the number of cases hereafter where exemplary damages are properly to
be awarded will in fact be very few. First of all it must be shown that the case comes
within the categories prescribed by LORD DEVLIN; and, secondly, it must be shown   *d*
that it is one of those special cases in which the punishment of the offender is
justified; and it is, I think, implicit in what LORD DEVLIN said that exemplary
damages are in the main awarded in cases where the defendant realises that he is
breaking the law, realises that damages may be awarded against him, but nevertheless
makes what has been described as a cynical calculation of profit and loss, and says
that he will flout the powers of the court because on a purely cash basis he can show   *e*
a profit.'

In the circumstances of that case, of course, what was said in the Court of Appeal was
obiter. There are also certain obiter observations to which I ought to refer in *Cassell & Co
Ltd v Broome* [1972] 1 All ER 801 at 830–831, [1972] AC 1027 at 1078–1079, where Lord
Hailsham LC dealt with the matter:
                                                                                      f
'When one comes to the second category [ie Lord Devlin's second category], we
reach a field which was more exhaustively discussed in the case before us. It soon
became apparent that a broad rather than a narrow interpretation of Lord Devlin's
words was absolutely essential, and that attempts to narrow the second category by
a quotation out of context of one sentence from the passage wherein it is defined
simply will not do. [He then referred to various cases, and continued:] Even a casual   *g*
reading of the above passage shows that the sentence: "Where a defendant with a
cynical disregard for a plaintiff's rights has calculated that the money to be made
out of his wrongdoing will probably exceed the damages at risk, it is necessary for
the law to show that it cannot be broken with impunity" is not intended to be
exhaustive but illustrative, and it is not intended to be limited to the kind of
mathematical calculations to be found on a balance sheet. The sentence must be   *h*
read in its context. The context occurs immediately after the sentence ending: "one
man should not be allowed to sell another man's reputation for profit", where the
word "calculation" does not occur. The context also includes the final sentence:
"Exemplary damages can properly be awarded whenever it is necessary to teach a
wrongdoer that tort does not pay." The whole passage must be read sensibly as a
whole, together with the authorities on which it is based.'   *j*

I refer also to passages in Lord Diplock's speech ([1972] 1 All ER 801 at 873–874, [1972]
AC 1027 at 1130–1131):

'I have no similar doubts about the retention of the second category. It too may
be a blunt instrument to prevent unjust enrichment by unlawful acts. But to restrict

a   the damages recoverable to the actual gain made by the defendant if it exceeded the loss caused to the plaintiff, would leave a defendant contemplating an unlawful act with the certainty that he had nothing to lose to balance against the chance that the plaintiff might never sue him or, if he did, might fail in the hazards of litigation. It is only if there is a prospect that the damages may exceed the defendant's gain that the social purpose of this category is achieved—to teach a wrongdoer that tort does not pay ... on this aspect of the case I would express my agreement with the view

b   that *Rookes v Barnard* was not intended to extend the power to award exemplary or aggravated damages to particular torts for which they had not previously been awarded, such as negligence and deceit. Its express purpose was to restrict, not to expand, the anomaly of exemplary damages.'

I ought also to mention, without reading a lengthy passage, that Lord Hailsham LC, in his speech, also expressed the view, after referring to *Mafo v Adams*, that exemplary

c   damages could not be awarded in an action for deceit, but could not claim that the matter had been finally determined.

It seems to me, therefore, that the door, on the authorities, is open but there are other considerations which make it unnecessary for me to decide whether to plunge through it.

I do not think that the argument that the defendant could not make a profit here

d   defeats the plaintiff's claim. It seems to follow from what Lord Diplock said in *Cassell & Co Ltd v Broome* that the wrongdoer may be caught if he weighs the risk of loss against the chance of getting away with it. In this case, as one sees from the course of proceedings, the defendant could well have got away with it against a less determined plaintiff.

But what seems to put the claim under this head out of court is the fact that exemplary damages are meant to punish and the defendant has been punished. Even if he wins his

e   appeal he will have spent a considerable time in gaol. It is not surprising that there is no authority whether this provides a defence, since there is no direct authority whether exemplary damages can be given in deceit. I rest my decision on the basic principle that a man should not be punished twice for the same offence. Since he has undoubtedly been punished, I should not enrich the plaintiff by punishing the defendant again.

f   *Damages for injured feelings*

As a student I was taught that damages are not recoverable for injured feelings. But the law has moved a long way since then. In *Bailey v Bullock* [1950] 2 All ER 1167 damages were awarded for inconvenience but not for emotional injury. The passage I have already quoted from Lord Devlin's speech in *Rookes v Barnard* plainly allowed for aggravated damages where the defendant had behaved badly, not by way of punishment, but by

g   way of compensation to the plaintiff for the additional injury caused.

In recent years, damages for injured feelings have been awarded in a number of cases sounding in contract: see *Jarvis v Swans Tours Ltd* [1973] 1 All ER 71 at 74, [1973] QB 233 at 237–238, a case in which the plaintiff had not received a holiday that he had paid for, where Lord Denning MR in his judgment said:

h   'What is the right way of assessing damages? It has often been said that on a breach of contract damages cannot be given for mental distress. Thus in *Hamlin v Great Northern Railway Co* (1856) 1 H & N 408 at 411, 156 ER 1261 at 1262 Pollock CB said that damages cannot be given "for the disappointment of mind occasioned by the breach of contract". And in *Hobbs v London & South Western Railway Co* (1875) LR 10 QB 111 at 122, [1874–80] All ER Rep 458 at 463 Mellor J said that—". . . for

j   the mere inconvenience, such as annoyance and loss of temper, or vexation, or for being disappointed in a particular thing which you have set your mind upon, without real physical inconvenience resulting, you cannot recover damages." The courts in those days only allowed the plaintiff to recover damages if he suffered physical inconvenience, such as having to walk five miles home, as in *Hobbs's* case; or to live in an overcrowded house: see *Bailey v Bullock* [1950] 2 All ER 1167. I think that those limitations are out of date. In a proper case damages for mental distress can be recovered in contract, just as damages for shock can be recovered in tort. One *a* such case is a contract for a holiday, or any other contract providing entertainment and enjoyment. If the contracting party breaks his contract, damages can be given for the disappointment, the distress, the upset and frustration caused by the breach. I know that it is difficult to assess in terms of money, but it is no more difficult than the assessment which the courts have to make every day in personal injury cases for loss of amenities.'

Stephenson LJ also dealt with the matter when he said ([1973] 1 All ER 71 at 77, [1973] QB 233 at 240–241):

'The learned judge in assessing the loss also underestimated the inconvenience to the plaintiff, perhaps because he followed the distinction drawn by Mellor J in *Hobbs*'s case and disallowed any inconvenience or discomfort that was not physical, *c* insofar as that can be defined. I agree that, as suggested in McGregor on Damages (13th edn, 1972) p 45, para 68 there may be contracts in which the parties contemplate inconvenience on breach which may be described as mental: frustration, annoyance, disappointment; and, as counsel for the defendants concedes that this is such a contract, the damages for breach of it should take such wider inconvenience or discomfort into account.' *d*

Similarly in *Heywood v Wellers (a firm)* [1976] 1 All ER 300, [1976] QB 446 damages were awarded for vexation, anxiety and distress suffered by a wife when a solicitor's clerk negligently failed to obtain an injunction against a harassing husband.

I now have to ask myself: is there any reason why these damages should sound in breach of contract and not in deceit? Certainly there is nothing in what Lord Devlin said *e* to confine them in this way: in fact, if anything, his speech tended to the contrary, although he did not really envisage the giving of them as a separate head of damage. In *Doyle v Olby (Ironmongers) Ltd* [1969] 2 All ER 119 at 123–124, [1969] 2 QB 158 at 167– 168 Winn LJ suggested that they might be recoverable. In *McNally v Welltrade International Ltd* [1978] IRLR 497 Sir Douglas Frank QC awarded damages for considerable worry and inconvenience in a case in which he found that the plaintiff was entitled to *f* succeed in tort.

In *Ichard v Frangoulis* [1977] 2 All ER 461, [1977] 1 WLR 556 I awarded damages in tort for loss of enjoyment of a holiday, but not as a separate item. It was a case in which, as the result of a motor accident in Yugoslavia, due to the negligence of the plaintiff, the defendant's holiday had been ruined. I said ([1977] 2 All ER 461 at 462, [1977] 1 WLR 556 at 558): *g*

'We have had some discussion at the Bar whether I ought to take into account at all the fact that the defendant had his holiday ruined. Counsel for the plaintiffs has helpfully referred me to a couple of cases in contract, *Jarvis v Swans Tours Ltd* [1973] 1 All ER 71, [1973] QB 223 and *Jackson v Horizon Holidays Ltd* [1975] 3 All ER 92, [1975] 1 WLR 1468 where damages were given in contract for loss of enjoyment of a holiday where the tour operator had let the customer down (to put it shortly) but *h* he said, and counsel for the defendant agreed, there is no authority for that being treated as a head of damage in tort, and it was, I think, common ground between counsel that one applied the ordinary test in tort whether the damages were reasonably foreseeable by the negligent party. This accident took place during the holiday period between two cars both driven by tourists in an area which one knows is much frequented by tourists, and I cannot doubt that if anyone had asked *j* Monsieur Ichard whether, if he drove into another tourist and injured him, that tourist would have suffered a particular loss thereby, Monsieur Ichard would have given a Gallic shrug of the shoulders and regarded the thing as perfectly obvious. It may be that this is why this matter has hitherto never figured in the reports. I regard it not as a separate head of damage but as one of the factors to be taken into a account when assessing general damages, and as a factor which would lead me to give rather more by way of general damages than I otherwise would do.'

In *Shelley v Paddock* [1978] 3 All ER 129, [1979] QB 120 Bristow J awarded damages for mental suffering caused by the defendant's fraud. The case turned on another point and it was not contested by the defendant's counsel that such damages would be proper if the plaintiff were otherwise entitled to succeed. It is helpful to read what the judge said ([1978] 3 All ER 129 at 136, [1979] QB 120 at 131):

b
'Counsel for the defendants, again very candidly and realistically says that this being an action in fraud, there is no principle which prevents [the plaintiff] from recovering damages for mental and physical suffering which the fraud may have caused. The plaintiff says: "Here I was moving myself, lock, stock and barrel to Spain. Selling up in England, putting the money into a house in Spain. I have been
c defrauded of the money. I have never had a house since—I have got nothing to buy a house with—and I have been living ever since in greatly reduced circumstances, and this has caused me considerable anguish." She says: "I put in £500 as the appropriate figure when I brought my action in 1974, and I have been living in reduced circumstances ever since and I regard my claim of £500 as very moderate." There is, of course, no medical evidence before me about any particular injury to
d her health, but on principle as it seems to me, and this is a principle illustrated also in the law of libel where your right to the integrity of your reputation has been infringed, she is entitled to recover damages under that head and I shall award the £500 which she claims.'

I find nothing in the passages which I have quoted from the speeches of Lord Hailsham LC and Lord Diplock in *Cassell & Co Ltd v Broome* which should extend their doubts
e whether exemplary damages should be awarded for deceit to aggravated damages for deceit. I cannot help wondering whether the close relationship between contract and deceit mentioned by Lord Hailsham LC is the reason why exemplary damages have not been awarded in deceit. Sachs LJ's reference to the Theft Act 1968 in his judgment in *Mafo v Adams* [1969] 3 All ER 1404 at 1407, [1970] 1 QB 548 at 555 leads me to ask whether the true reason why there is no reported case where damages have been given
f for deceit is that most deceits are punishable by the criminal law and that it would therefore be inappropriate to award exemplary damages. If this be so, then it is no reason for refusing to award damages which are compensatory for injured feelings.

I can see no reason in logic or justice why such damages should not be awarded in deceit on the same basis as in contract. The authorities make it plain that the sum awarded should be moderate. In the light of the findings of fact which I have already
g made I think a sum of £500 would be appropriate under this head.

Items of damage

I now propose to run through the items of damage claimed in the statement of claim: (a) the sum of £30,000 will be awarded as damages for deceit; (b), (c) and (d) the plaintiff's contract of employment was with Mantec. He cannot claim anything under that. But in
h my view he has suffered damage by reason of the defendant's deceit in respect of his employment. Were it not for this he would have had a job at £16,750 a year with Mantec. His loss is not what he would have earned with that company, because his earnings depended on the success of that company and, sanguine though the plaintiff may have been, there must be a query whether it could have provided salaries for both the plaintiff and the defendant at that rate. I take account also of the fact that the plaintiff
j did not have a job to go when he left the Italian Hospital.

The loss which the defendant's deceit has caused is that instead of having a job with Mantec the plaintiff had to look elsewhere for employment and take what he could find. In the light of what the plaintiff discovered there must be considerable doubt whether the defendant ever had authority to act on behalf of Mantec in making a contract of service with the plaintiff. If he did, then the contract technically subsisted in April 1981,

but it was plainly worthless in the light of what had occurred and the plaintiff did right
to accept his solicitor's advice and cut his losses and get out.   *a*

The plaintiff was without a job for four months. Then he took a temporary job and
was out of work for a further five weeks before he found another temporary job, which
he left for a permanent job. When employed, his earnings were in the £10,000–£11,000
level. While out of work he received £942·20 by way of unemployment benefit and he
must give credit for that. In addition I have to allow for the fact that he would have
suffered deductions for income tax and national insurance had he been in work.   *b*

Since these are general damages it would not be appropriate to make a precise
calculation even if it were possible. But, bearing in mind all these factors, I think an
appropriate sum under this head would be £2,500.

The plaintiff only got this employment because he searched for it with the greatest
vigour. As I have already found, this involved him in considerable expense: £1,000. I
hold that this sum is recoverable under head (g).   *c*

The plaintiff claims in head (f) for the cost of selling the Barton Road property. I hold
that this damage does not flow from the defendant's deceit. When the plaintiff raised the
original loan, it was part of the agreement with the bank that this house should be sold.
The plaintiff would have had this expense even if the defendant had been thoroughly
honest. The house was not worth its sale price, but only the sale price less the cost of sale.

As to the solicitor's expenses, the plaintiff was so vague as to what he had paid Mr   *d*
Swayne that Mr Swayne had to be called as a witness. It then appeared that Mr Swayne
regarded himself as having been instructed by Mantec and did not look to the plaintiff
for his costs. So, Mr Swayne's costs are not recoverable.

Messrs Titmuss Sainer & Webb were instructed by the plaintiff at an early stage. They
gave general advice some time before the plaintiff had made the bargain with the
defendant. The plaintiff would have needed such advice before he made a bargain with   *e*
anyone. But they did nothing towards the execution of the agreement. I hold that this
damage is too remote.

There remains the question whether the plaintiff should give credit for any benefit he
received. He drew one month's pay from Mantec, but he worked for this. This was not
therefore a benefit and is allowed for by the fact that his claim for loss of a job would be
higher without it.   *f*

There is also the question of the car. I have set out the facts. It may well be that, if the
full facts were gone into, it would be shown that the plaintiff or his wife had some benefit
here. But the evidence is far too vague to justify any firm conclusion. I do not think I
should take this into account.

The plaintiff is therefore entitled (if my mathematics are correct) to judgment for:
£30,000, £13,528 as interest payable to bank, £500 for injury of feelings, £2,500 for   *g*
loss of employment and £1,000 for costs incurred in seeking new employment, making
a total of £47,528.

I leave open to argument by counsel the question whether on the three last items there
ought to be an award of interest.

Judgment for the plaintiff accordingly.   *h*

Solicitors: *Lawrence & Co* (for the plaintiff); *Awtar Singh & Co* (for the defendant).

K Mydeen Esq   Barrister.

a

Re Cherrington (deceased)

FAMILY DIVISION
BUTLER-SLOSS J
17, 31 JANUARY 1984

b   *Will – Executor – Appointment – Testator bequeathing all his estate to his wife – Testator's sons to be executors if she 'predeceased' him – Marriage dissolved before testator's death – Devise to wife lapsing in consequence – Lapse – Wife still alive at testator's death – Whether appointment of sons as executors effective – Wills Act 1837, s 18A(1)(b).*

By cl 3 of his will dated 8 August 1966 the testator bequeathed all his estate to his wife and directed that, if she 'predeceased' him, other clauses, including cl 4 by which he
c   appointed his sons as executors, were to take effect. The marriage was dissolved on 28 January 1983. The testator died on 28 March 1983 and was survived by his sons and former wife. By s 18A(1)(b)ª of the Wills Act 1837 after a decree of dissolution of marriage any devise to a former spouse was to 'lapse except in so far as a contrary intention appears in the will'. The question arose whether, in view of s 18A(1)(b), the appointment by cl 4
d   of the testator's sons as executors took effect even though his former wife was still alive.

Held – On the true construction of s 18A(1)(b) of the 1837 Act, where a devise to a former spouse 'lapsed' on the dissolution of a marriage, that spouse was to be treated as having predeceased the testator. Accordingly, the devise to the testator's former wife lapsed under s 18A(1)(b), with the effect that, in accordance with the intention of the testator, his
e   sons became the executors of his estate by virtue of cl 4 of the will (see p 287 *b* and *f g*, post).

Notes

For dissolution or annulment of the marriage of a testator who dies on or after 1 January 1983, see 50 Halsbury's Laws (4th edn) para 281.
f   For the Wills Act 1837, s 18A (as inserted by the Administration of Justice Act 1982, s 18(2)), see 52 Halsbury's Statutes (3rd edn) 1972.

Cases referred to in judgment

Last (decd), Re [1958] 1 All ER 316, [1958] P 137, [1958] 2 WLR 186.
Sanford, Re, Sanford v Sanford [1901] 1 Ch 939.

g
Motion

The applicant, Christopher Cherrington, the son of Piotr Cherrington deceased (the testator) by his marriage to Thelma Joyce Cherrington, which was dissolved by decree absolute made on 28 January 1983, sought the determination of the court on the following questions: (1) whether, on the true construction of s 18(2) of the Administration
h   of Justice Act 1982 and in the events which had happened, the appointment in the testator's last will, dated 8 August 1966, of the applicant, Anthony Cherrington and Thomas Bailey, as executors and trustees took effect, the appointment being expressed by the will to take effect in the event of the testator's wife predeceasing him; (2) in the event of question (1) being answered in the negative, whether on the true construction of s 18(2) of the 1982 Act and in the events which had happened, the applicant and Anthony Cherrington were entitled to a grant of letters of administration to the estate of the
j   testator (with will annexed) as residuary legatees; (3) in the event of question (2) being

---

a   Section 18A(1), so far as material, provides: 'Where, after a testator has made a will, a decree of a court dissolves ... his marriage ... (b) any devise or bequest to the former spouse shall lapse, except in so far as a contrary intention appears by the will.'

answered in the negative, whether on the true construction of s 18(2) of the 1982 Act
and in the events which had happened, the applicant was entitled to a grant of letters of
administration to the estate of the testator (with will annexed) as sole next of kin entitled
thereto on the testator's intestacy. The facts are set out in the judgment.

Geoffrey Jaques for the applicant.

Cur adv vult

31 January. The following judgment was delivered.

BUTLER-SLOSS J. This is a motion seeking the court's decision as to the proper
person or persons to obtain a grant of probate of, or letters of administration to, the estate
of Piotr Cherrington deceased: (1) whether the appointment of Anthony Cherrington,
Christopher Cherrington (the applicant), and a solicitor, Thomas Bailey, should take
effect; or (2) whether Anthony and Christopher Cherrington are entitled to a grant of
letters of administration to the estate of the testator of the will annexed as residuary
legatees; or (3) whether Christopher Cherrington, as sole next of kin, is entitled to a grant
of letters of administration with the will annexed on the residue of the estate falling into
intestacy.

The testator married on 26 June 1954 Thelma Joyce Cherrington, by whom he had
one son, the applicant, born on 29 July 1955. The testator and his wife informally
adopted a son, Anthony Cherrington, born in 1950. The testator executed his last will on
8 August 1966. On 28 January 1983 the marriage was dissolved, and on 28 March 1983
the testator died, survived by Anthony, Christopher and his former wife.

By his will, the testator appointed, in cl 2, Thelma Cherrington to be the sole executrix.
In cl 3, he gave his entire estate to his wife in the following terms:

'I GIVE DEVISE AND BEQUEATH all my estate real and personal whatsoever and
wheresoever unto my wife the said Thelma Joyce Cherrington PROVIDED that if my
said wife shall predecease me then I DIRECT that the following clauses of this my will
shall take effect.'

There follow cll 4 and 5. In cl 4 he appoints Christopher, Anthony and the solicitor to be
executors. In cl 5 he leaves the residue of his estate to Anthony and Christopher equally.

By operation of the Administration of Justice Act 1982, the Wills Act 1837 is amended
in various ways. Section 18(2) of the 1982 Act provides a new s 18A of the 1837 Act to
deal with the effect of dissolution or annulment of marriage on wills. By s 18A(1)(a), after
such a decree of dissolution or annulment, the will shall take effect as if any appointment
of the former spouse as an executor or as the executor and trustee of the will were
omitted, and by s 18A(1)(b), any devise or bequest to the former spouse shall lapse, except
in so far as a contrary intention appears by the will.

The section draws a distinction between the appointment of the executor being
omitted, and the devise or bequest lapsing. It is clearly intended that such a distinction
should be observed. In my judgment, cl 2 of the will, appointing the wife as executrix,
must be omitted. The problem then arises as to who should take the grant and whether
it should be the executors under the contingency envisaged in cl 3, or is there now no
appointment under the will of an executor?

In order to ascertain the proper person to take a grant, I must essay at least a preliminary
interpretation of the construction of the proviso to cl 3 of the will in the light of the
interpretation of s 18A(1)(b).

It is a small estate, and to adjourn it to the Chancery Division when the division of the
estate has, I understand, been agreed, and the only issue is who should take a grant, would
be unduly onerous on the estate. I am fortified in this view by the decision in *Re Last*
(decd) [1958] 1 All ER 316, [1958] P 137, in which Karminski J said during argument
([1958] P 137 at 140):

a
'... although the modern view as to the function of the Probate Court is that the court should interfere in questions of construction as little as possible, I have come to the conclusion that it would be proper to determine the question of the construction of the will as a matter of convenience in order to avoid any further depletion of the assets of a small estate if reference to the Chancery Division had to be made.'

b
The devise to the wife must lapse under s 18A(1)(b), but does the effect of the lapse bring into effect the proviso under cl 3 of the will, since she is still alive? Counsel for the applicant, in his admirable submission, urged me to equate lapse with predecease. In order for cll 4 and 5 of the will to take effect, the word 'lapse' in s 18A(1)(b) requires to be considered as if intended to refer to predeceasing the testator.

The section in *Jarman on Wills* (8th edn, 1951) vol 1, p 438 dealing with the doctrine of lapse shows that the general principle assumes lapse to refer to predecease.

c
In the new s 33 of the Wills Act 1837, substituted by s 19 of the Administration of Justice Act 1982, which deals with gifts to children who predecease the testator, the section is referred to in the note at the side as, 'Gifts to children or other issue who leave issue living at the testator's death shall not lapse', and the word is used as meaning death before the testator.

d
Section 18A(3) is somewhat difficult to follow if lapse is intended to refer to predecease, since the second part of the subsection will be unnecessary, but it is probable that it is set out for avoidance of doubt.

The alternative possibility is that lapse means 'shall be of no effect'. The effect of that interpretation, in the present will, would cause a residual intestacy and defeat the purpose of the testator, and is likely to do so in many other wills.

e
In *Re Sanford* [1901] 1 Ch 939 at 944 Joyce J said:

'... if the terms of the codicil be ambiguous ... there is not wanting authority to shew that in a case of obscurity or ambiguity ... weight may be given to the consideration that it is better to effectuate than to frustrate the testator's intention.'

f
Although not strictly relevant, *Tristram and Coote's Probate Practice* (26th edn, 1983) p 41 refers to the Law Reform Committee's majority view that, in respect of gifts to a former spouse, the will should be treated as if the spouse had predeceased the testator (see 22nd Report of the Law Reform Committee on the Making and Revocation of Wills (Cmnd 7902 (1980)) paras 20(3)(ii) and 27(7)).

g
For the purposes of simplicity, certainty, and to give effect to the intentions of the testator, I propose to interpret s 18A(1)(b) of the 1982 Act as referring to the former spouse predeceasing the testator and hold, therefore, that the proviso to cl 3 of the will takes effect. In those circumstances, the appointment of the executors under cl 4 takes effect, and the answer to the first question of the motion is in the affirmative.

Determination accordingly.

Solicitors: *Colin Bell & Co*, Bournemouth (for the applicant).

Bebe Chua   Barrister.

Practice Note   *a*

QUEEN'S BENCH DIVISION
LORD LANE CJ, MUSTILL AND OTTON JJ
15 MAY 1984

Costs – Taxation – Review of taxation – Procedure – Queen's Bench Division – RSC Ord 62,   *b*
r 35.

LORD LANE CJ gave the following direction at the sitting of the court. As from 10
May 1984 the Practice Direction issued on 10 October 1960 ([1960] 3 All ER 448, [1960]
1 WLR 1226) by Lord Parker CJ in relation to applications in the Queen's Bench Division
under RSC Ord 62, r 35 is revoked. On and after the aforementioned date that Practice
Direction will be replaced by the following.   *c*

1. Every application in the Queen's Bench Division under RSC Ord 62, r 35 to review
a taxing officer's decision in respect of the taxation of a bill of costs shall be made to one
of the judges nominated for this purpose by the Lord Chief Justice.
2. Every application shall be made by summons to be served within three days after
issue and returnable on a day to be appointed.   *d*
3. Every summons must contain full particulars of the item or items or the amount
allowed in respect of which the application to review is made.
4. The summons retained by the court will be sent to the Chief Clerk of the Supreme
Court Taxing Office, who will arrange for the necessary documents to be lodged, for the
appointment of assessors, if required, and for the date of hearing of the summons; and
he will notify the assessors and the parties of the date fixed.   *e*

April Weiss   Barrister.

Prior (Valuation Officer) v Sovereign Chicken Ltd

COURT OF APPEAL, CIVIL DIVISION
LAWTON, OLIVER AND DILLON LJJ
13 FEBRUARY 1984

Rates – Exemption – Agricultural buildings – Buildings used for keeping or breeding of livestock – Poultry processing factory – Building occupied by 'persons' who are the 'occupiers' qualifying for rating relief – Whether 'persons' and 'occupiers' in plural also including singular – Whether a limited company qualified – General Rate Act 1967, s 26(4)(b)(i) – Rating Act 1971, s 4(2)(b)(ii).

The respondent company was the occupier for rating purposes of a processing factory where broiler chickens were killed and prepared for dispatch to retail outlets for consumption as food. The processing factory, although used in connection with agricultural operations, was described in the valuation list as a 'factory and premises' and valued as such for rating purposes. The respondent company claimed that the factory qualified for relief from rating because it was a building used in connection with agricultural operations which was occupied by 'persons' who were the 'occupiers' of the land within s 26(4)(b)(i)[a] of the General Rate Act 1967 and s 4(2)(b)(ii)[b] of the Rating Act 1971. The respondent company contended that the terms 'persons' and 'occupiers' in the relevant sections were, by virtue of s 6[c] of the Interpretation Act 1978, to be taken as including the singular and therefore could refer to the respondent company. The Lands Tribunal upheld that contention and deleted the hereditament from the valuation list. The valuation officer appealed.

Held – The terms 'occupiers' in s 26(4)(b)(i) of the 1967 Act and 'persons' in s 4(2)(b)(ii) of the 1971 Act specifically referred to a multiplicity of occupiers or persons and did not include a singular occupier or person, because the purpose of the relevant sections was to extend rating relief to farming co-operatives. Accordingly, the respondent company, being a single occupier or person, was not entitled to rate relief as the occupier of an agricultural building. The valuation officer's appeal would accordingly be allowed (see p 291 e, p 293 f to j, p 294 a to c e f and h j and p 295 g to j, post).

Farmers' Machinery Syndicate (11th Hampshire) v Shaw (Valuation Officer) [1961] 1 All ER 285 considered.

Notes

For exemption from rating of agricultural land and buildings, see 39 Halsbury's Laws (4th edn) para 62, and for cases on the subject, see 38 Digest (Reissue) 335–338, 2296–2307.

For the General Rate Act 1967, s 26, see 27 Halsbury's Statutes (3rd edn) 106.

For the Rating Act 1971, s 4, see 41 ibid 1171.

For the Interpretation Act 1978, s 6, see 48 ibid 1299.

Cases referred to in judgments

Farmers' Machinery Syndicate (11th Hampshire) v Shaw (Valuation Officer) [1961] 1 All ER 285, [1961] 1 WLR 393, CA.
Farrell v Alexander [1976] 2 All ER 721, [1977] AC 59, [1976] 3 WLR 145, HL.

Cases also cited

DPP v Schildkamp [1969] 3 All ER 1640, [1971] AC 1, HL.

---

a   Section 26(4) is set out at p 291 c d, post
b   Section 4 is set out at p 292 f to h, post
c   Section 6, so far as material, is set out at p 290 g, post

Eastwood (W & J B) Ltd v Herrod (Valuation Officer) [1970] 1 All ER 774, [1971] AC 160,
    HL.
Floor v Davis (Inspector of Taxes) [1979] 2 All ER 677, [1980] AC 695, HL.
Sin Poh Amalgamated (HK) Ltd v A G of Hong Kong [1965] 1 All ER 225, [1965] 1 WLR 62,
    PC.

Appeal

Anthony Basil Prior (the valuation officer) appealed by way of case stated against a
decision of the Lands Tribunal (president C R Mallett) dated 16 September 1982
dismissing two appeals by the valuation officer and allowing one appeal by the ratepayer,
Sovereign Chicken Ltd (formerly Golden Produce Ltd), from decisions of the Hampshire
(South) Local Valuation Court given on 28 January 1981 arising out of proposals dated
20 March 1979 and 11 August 1980 made by the ratepayer and a proposal dated 15
September 1980 made by the valuation officer for the alteration of the valuation list in
respect of a poultry processing factory at Bridge Yard, Lymington, occupied by the
ratepayer. The Lands Tribunal determined that the factory qualified for exemption from
rating as an agricultural building under s 26 of the General Rate Act 1967, as amended
by the Rating Act 1971, and therefore that all three entries in the valuation list relating
thereto should be deleted from the valuation list. It was agreed that if the hereditament
was held not to be exempted from rating it should be included in the valuation list with
the following descriptions in relation to the respective appeals: factory and premises,
£11,100; factory and premises (damaged by fire), £2,000; factory and premises, £18,250.
The facts are set out in the judgment of Dillon LJ.

Alan Fletcher for the valuation officer.
David Widdicombe QC and *Guy Roots* for the ratepayer.

DILLON LJ (delivering the first judgment at the invitation of Lawton LJ). This is an
appeal from a decision of the Lands Tribunal given on 16 September 1982 which is
concerned with the exemption from rating of agricultural buildings.
      The question formulated by the Lands Tribunal in the case stated, on which the
decision of this court is desired, is put thus: whether on a true construction of s 26 of the
General Rate Act 1967 and ss 1, 2 and 4 of the Rating Act 1971 the word 'persons' in
s 4(2)(b)(ii) of the 1971 Act includes the singular 'person'. A similar question arises on the
word 'occupiers' in s 26(4)(b)(i) and (ii) of the 1967 Act. In each case the question turns on
whether or not s 6 of the Interpretation Act 1978 applies. That section states: 'In any Act,
unless the contrary intention appears . . . (c) words in the singular include the plural and
words in the plural include the singular.'
      The appellant in this court is the valuation officer; the respondent is the occupier of
the building in question. The respondent is a company which, at the time of the hearing
in the Lands Tribunal, was called Golden Produce Ltd but is now called Sovereign
Chicken Ltd. Its business is the production of chickens for consumption as food. It is the
occupier for rating purposes of a number of broiler farms (I think 17) to which batches
of day-old chicks are transferred from hatcheries belonging to the respondent. In the
broiler farms the chicks are kept for their period of growth and fattening until they are
ready for killing. They are then transferred to a processing factory for killing, plucking,
eviscerating, dressing, packing and blast freezing ready for despatch to retail outlets. The
particular processing factory with which this appeal is concerned is at Lymington in
Hampshire and is not in a wholly agricultural area. (The relevance of that will become
apparent when I come to the wording of the 1971 Act.) It appears that the respondent
has two other processing factories for other broiler farms. These other processing factories
are in appropriately rural situations and, therefore, quality for rating relief.
      The current statutory provision for relief from rating of agricultural land and
agricultural buildings is to be found first in s 26 of the 1967 Act, sub-s (1) of which
provides:

'No agricultural land or agricultural buildings shall be liable to be rated or be included in any valuation list or in any rate.'

Subsection (2) is irrelevant for the purposes of this appeal. Subsection (3) contains a definition of the expression 'agricultural land'. This is primarily defined to mean any land used as arable, meadow, or pasture ground only, land used for a plantation, or a wood or for the growth of saleable underwood, land exceeding 0·10 hectare used for the purposes of poultry farming and various cottage gardens, market gardens, nursery grounds, orchards, and so forth. I would observe in passing that land used for the purposes of poultry farming does not include the site of a broiler house.

Section 26(4) contains the definition of 'agricultural buildings':

'In this section, the expression "agriculture buildings"—(a) means buildings (other than dwellings) occupied together with agricultural land or being or forming part of a market garden, and in either case used solely in connection with agricultural operations thereon; and (b) includes a building which is used solely in connection with agricultural operations carried on on agricultural land which is occupied either—(i) by the occupiers of all that land; or (ii) by individuals who are appointed by the said occupiers for the time being to manage the use of the building and of whom each is an occupier of some of the land or a member of the board of directors or other governing body of such an occupier who is a body corporate, where the number of occupiers of all the said land does not exceed twenty-four (two or more persons occupying jointly being counted as one, but as a separate person from any of them who are occupying any of the land severally).'

It is plain on the legislative history that whatever else it may cover s 26(4)(b), which was originally included in the Rating and Valuation Act 1961, was introduced to cover certain varieties of agricultural co-operative as a result of the decision of this court in *Farmers' Machinery Syndicate (11th Hampshire) v Shaw (Valuation Officer)* [1961] 1 All ER 285, [1961] 1 WLR 393. Several points had become clear from that case in relation to the law as it previously stood. One was that where several individual farmers occupied their own several farms and they combined together to acquire machinery for the use of all of them (in that particular case a grain-dryer) it could not be said that the grain-dryer was occupied together with the individual farms, or used solely in connection with the agricultural operations thereon. It also appeared from that case that there were cases where the rateable occupation of a co-operative venture was in some form of committee selected by the co-operators whose individual farms were serviced by it and that there were possibilities of difficulty where a member of the committee was a director of a company which owned one of the farms and not himself actually the owner of the farm. That, therefore, was the reason for the introduction of what became para (b) of s 26(4).

The other thing that needs to be stated in relation to s 26 was that it was held that it did not cover buildings used for factory farming, such as broiler houses and buildings for other forms of intensive production of meat and food: it was concerned with farming the land and with buildings which were used for farming the land.

It was in particular as a result of the decision that buildings used for factory farming were not covered that the Rating Act 1971 was enacted. Section 1(1) of that Act provides that in s 26 of the General Rate Act 1967 (which is referred to as the 'principal section')—

'(a) the expression "agricultural buildings" shall include any building which is an agricultural building by virtue of section 2, 3 or 4 of the 1971 Act; and (b) the expression "agricultural land" shall include land occupied with and used solely in connection with the use of one or more such buildings.'

There is then a provision in sub-s (3) that 'livestock' includes any mammal or bird kept for the production of food or wool or for the purpose of its use in the farming of land. Livestock would thus include chickens kept for the production of food.

Section 2(1) of the 1971 Act provides:

'Subject to subsections (2) to (4) of this section, each of the following is an *a*
agricultural building by virtue of this section—(*a*) any building used for the keeping
or breeding of livestock [I interject that that would clearly include a broiler house];
(*b*) any building (other than a dwelling) which is occupied together with one or
more buildings falling within paragraph (*a*) above and is used in connection with
the operations carried on in that building or those buildings.'

(Again, prima facie, that would include a processing plant for processing the chickens *b*
which have been bred in a broiler house.) However, s 2(4) of the 1971 Act provides:

'A building is not an agricultural building by virtue of this section unless it is
surrounded by or contiguous to an area of agricultural land (as defined in the
principal section) which amounts to not less than two hectares; but [and there is
then a proviso that] in determining for the purposes of this subsection—(*a*) whether *c*
a building is contiguous to or surrounded by an area of agricultural land; or (*b*)
whether an area contiguous to or surrounding a building is an area of agricultural
land and what is the size of such an area; there shall be disregarded any road, railway
or watercourse, any agricultural building (as defined in the principal section or [in
the 1971 Act] and, if occupied together with the first mentioned building, also any
other building and any land which is not agricultural land.' *d*

It is because of this two hectares limitation that the respondent cannot claim rating relief
in respect of its Lymington processing plant under s 2 of the 1971 Act, though it can in
respect of its other plants. The limitation is strange in this respect, that it is not required
that the area of not less than two hectares should belong to, or be in the occupation of,
the occupier of the building which is claimed as an agricultural building. It has to be *e*
agricultural land but it does not matter whose land it is.

Section 3 of the 1971 Act gives an exemption for buildings used in connection with
the keeping of bees and is immaterial for present purposes. Section 4 then provides:

'(1) Subject to subsection (3) of this section, a building other than a dwelling, is an
agricultural building by virtue of this section if—(*a*) it is used in connection with
agricultural operations carried on on agricultural land (as defined in the principal *f*
section); and (*b*) it is occupied by a body corporate any of whose members are, or are
together with the body, the occupiers of the land.
(2) Subject to subsection (3) of this section, a building, other than a dwelling, is
also an agricultural building by virtue of this section if—(*a*) it is used in connection
with the operations carried on in one or more buildings which, being used for the
keeping or breeding of livestock, are agricultural buildings by virtue of section 2 of *g*
this Act; and (*b*) it is occupied either—(i) by a body corporate any of whose members
are, or are together with the body, the occupiers of that building or those buildings,
or (ii) by persons who would satisfy the requirements of subsection (4)(*b*)(i) or (ii) of
the principal section if the other building were agricultural land as defined in that
section.
(3) A building used as mentioned in either of the preceding subsections is not an *h*
agricultural building by virtue of this section unless that use, or that use together
with the use mentioned in the other of those subsections, is its sole use.'

It is to be noted that sub-ss (1) and (2) of s 4 of the 1971 Act are directed to rather
different objects. Section 4(1)(*b*) picks up sub-s (4)(*b*) of s 26 of the 1967 Act (the principal
section); s 4(1)(*a*) echoes the opening words of sub-s (4)(*b*) in the principal section in *j*
referring to a building which is used in connection with agricultural operations carried
on on agricultural land and what is done by s 4(1) of the 1971 Act is to extend the
exemptions granted to co-operatives by sub-s (4)(*b*) of the principal section to the case
where the co-operative building is occupied by a body corporate, any of whose members
are or are together with the body the occupiers of the agricultural land. That is, therefore,
dealing with a possible variant in agricultural co-operatives. There may be something

a that is in the nature of an unincorporated partnership of individual farmers, or there
may be rateable occupation by a committee of individuals who are appointed by the
occupiers of the several farms, or there may be a body corporate.

Section 4(2) starts off in para (a) by referring to a building which is used in connection
with the operations carried on in one or more of the buildings which, being used for the
keeping or breeding of livestock, are agricultural buildings by virtue of s 2 of the 1971
Act. That echoes s 2(1)(b), the buildings used in connection with operations carried on in
b the building, referred to in s 2(1)(a), used for the keeping or breeding of livestock; and
s 4(2) grants exemption in respect of such a building if it is occupied either (i) by a body
corporate, any of whose members are or are together with the body the occupiers of that
building or those buildings, which echoes what we have had in s 4(1)(b) of the 1971 Act,
or (ii) 'by persons who would satisfy the requirements of subsection (4)(b)(i) or (ii) of the
principal section'. What we have, therefore, essentially in s 4(2) is exemption in respect
c of the particular type of building referred to in para (a) if it is occupied by someone
within s 26(4)(b)(ii) of the 1967 Act or within s 4(1) of the 1971 Act.

In the present case the respondent company cannot satisfy s 4(2)(b)(i) of the 1971 Act
since its members are not the occupiers of the relevant building and the respondent
company therefore has to rely on s 4(2)(b)(ii) of the 1971 Act.

No problem arises under s 4(3) of the 1971 Act. It is common ground that with the
d processing plant in question the condition is satisfied that its use in connection with the
operations carried on in the broiler factories is its sole use.

The question, therefore, for consideration in the application of the Interpretation Act
1978 is in relation to s 4 of the 1971 Act whether the word 'persons' in s 4(2)(b)(ii) can
include a single person (the respondent company), and, in relation to the principal
section, s 26(4) of the 1967 Act, whether the word 'occupiers' in sub-s (4)(b)(i) can mean a
e single occupier and again in sub-s (4)(b)(ii).

So far as the 1971 Act is concerned, if it is right, as the respondent contends, that a
single owner can satisfy the word 'persons' in s 4(2)(b)(ii) and the 1978 Act does require
the plural to include the singular in the principal section also, there is the anomalous
result that exemption can be obtained under s 4 in respect of any building for which no
exemption is available under s 2 because of the two hectares restriction in s 2(4). It is
f difficult to suppose that Parliament had it mind that s 4 would have that effect whatever
purpose Parliament may have had in mind in imposing the two hectares restriction.

When I turn back to s 26 of the 1967 Act and look at para (b) of sub-s (4), again it seems
to me that it is difficult to suppose that Parliament intended that the plural could include
the singular. For this I see two reasons. First, the case of the single owner of the building
occupied together with agricultural land used solely in connection with agricultural
g operations thereon is covered by sub-s (4)(a) and there is no need to bring it under sub-s
(4)(b), although there was need to bring in under sub-s (4)(b) the case of the building
which was used for the purposes of a co-operative or syndicate. Then, second, in sub-s
(4)(b)(ii), where what is in mind is occupation not by all the occupiers of the agricultural
land but by individuals who are appointed by those occupiers, the wording goes on 'to
manage the use of the building and of whom each is an occupier of some of the land or a
h member of the board of directors or other governing body of such an occupier who is a
body corporate'. It is plain, it seems to me, that the instance of occupation by such
individuals envisages necessarily several individuals and each of those individuals must
be an occupier of some of the land which necessarily envisages that there must be more
than one occupier of all the land.

I do not take the view, which counsel for the respondent has urged on us, that the
j wording of para (b)(ii) is merely machinery in the event of a plurality of occupiers. I
think it is of the substance of the enactment.

The member of the Lands Tribunal reached the opposite conclusion and held in favour
of the respondent on the view that s 26 contained so many words used in the singular or
the plural interchangeably or where the singular would include the plural, as in the
references to buildings or a building, that there was not enough to justify holding that a
plural is to be construed strictly as a plural.

For the reasons I have endeavoured to give, viewing the matter as one of construction of s 26(4)(b) I do not agree with him. I read the words 'by the occupiers of all that land' in para (b)(i) as referring only to a plurality of occupiers and to the individuals in para (b)(ii), who were appointed by the said occupiers, as referring to a plurality of individuals and occupiers. Then, when I turn across to s 4 of the 1971 Act, in view of the anomaly which I have mentioned, which would otherwise follow in comparing s 2(4) with s 4 in relation to the two hectares restriction, I read the word 'persons' in s 4(2)(b)(ii) as referring necessarily again only to a plurality of persons as it does under s 26.

I would therefore allow this appeal. It is agreed between the parties that the consequences of allowing the appeal are that the building in question should be included in the rating lists as a rateable hereditament at the values given in the narrative part of the decision of the member of the Lands Tribunal.

OLIVER LJ. I agree. The statutory provisions with which this appeal is concerned are not, on any analysis of the matter, models of legislative clarity, but the short question is whether, in s 4(2)(b)(ii) of the Rating Act 1971 the word 'persons' and in s 26(4)(b) of the General Rate Act 1967 the word 'occupiers' are, in the context in which those words appear, sensibly capable of bearing a singular as well as plural connotation, or, to put it another way, whether there appears from the sections a contrary intention which would exclude the provisions of s 6 of the Interpretation Act 1978 that words in the plural include the singular.

It is certainly true that, as the tribunal pointed out, the definition of agricultural land contained in s 26(3)(a) contains admixtures of the plural and singular without reason or any logical distinction between them. Perhaps the most striking example is to be found in the definition of a cottage garden, previously referred to in the plural by reference to occupation by a person (singular) of the labouring classes (plural). So far as I know, no reported case has yet enshrined the judicial identification of this social phenomenon. Nevertheless, for the reasons which Dillon LJ has given, I cannot for my part make sense of the provisions of the two sections referred to if, as the respondent contends, the provisions of s 6 of the 1978 Act are applied to them so that occupiers and persons fall to be read as meaning also a singular occupier, or person.

The key section is, as the tribunal pointed out, s 26 of the 1967 Act and there is a clear distinction between paras (a) and (b) of sub-s (4). Subsection (4)(a) defines what an agricultural building means and sub-s (4)(b) goes on to tell us what that meaning includes, so that straightaway one is looking for something which, prima facie and without express mention, might not be thought to fall within the primary meaning which has just been set out.

The meaning for which the respondent contends would have the result that agricultural holdings in sub-s (4)(b)(i) would, in the case of a single occupier, both of the buildings and the agricultural land, have exactly the same meaning (although slightly differently expressed) as the meaning in sub-s (4)(a). This anomaly is even more apparent when one comes to the 1971 Act for there one finds, as Dillon LJ has pointed out, that the results would be that Parliament, having restricted the exemption in s 2(4) to the particular case of a building surrounded by or contiguous to a particular area of agricultural land, then goes on to enact in the next but one section a provision which effectively dispenses with that restriction. In my judgment therefore, and for the reasons which Dillon LJ has given, I agree that this appeal should be allowed.

LAWTON LJ. I, too, agree. Counsel for the respondent, in the course of his submissions accepted, as one would have expected him to do, that if the word 'persons' in s 4(2) of the Rating Act 1971 should be construed in the singular, at once an anomaly arises under the provisions of s 2(4) of the same Act. He also accepted that, when the court comes to construe s 26(4)(b) of the General Rate Act 1967, there is some difficulty about the use of the language in the second part of sub-para (ii) of sub-s (4)(b). He submitted, however, that in the circumstances of these two statutes, there being so many anomalous situations arising under their provisions, the court ought not to pay too much a   attention to the fact that the construction which he asked the court to give to these two words, 'persons' and 'occupiers', is not strong enough to overcome the provisions of the Interpretation Act 1978.

There being some force in that submission, the court is entitled to look at the litigious and legislative history of s 26 of the 1967 Act and s 4 of the 1971 Act. All through this case I have kept in mind what Lord Wilberforce said in *Farrell v Alexander* [1976] 2 All ER 721 at 725–726, [1977] AC 59 at 72–73. He criticised the practice when construing

b   consolidating Acts, and the General Rate Act 1967 is a consolidating Act, of looking back to the past and analysing in detail what words meant and were construed to mean in earlier statutes. He said:

c   'But unless the process of consolidation, which involves much labour and careful work, is to become nothing but a work of mechanical conveniences, I think that this tendency should be firmly resisted; that self-contained statutes, whether consolidating previous law, or so doing with amendments, should be interpreted, if reasonably possible, without recourse to antecedents, and that the recourse should only be had when there is a real and substantial difficulty or ambiguity which classical methods of construction cannot resolve.'

d   As there is a difficulty of construction in this case and a series of anomalies arising out of the operation of s 26 of the 1967 Act and s 4 of the 1971 Act, it seems to me that clarity is achieved by looking at what has happened.

In *Farmers' Machinery Syndicate (11th Hampshire) v Shaw (Valuation Officer)* [1961] 1 All ER 285 at 289, [1961] 1 WLR 393 at 398 Donovan LJ said:

e   'In my opinion it is going to be very difficult for any combination of farmers working separate farms to obtain exemption from rating in circumstances like the present, in respect of a common grain drying machine, short of an alteration of the law, and particularly in respect of the definition of an "agricultural building".'

And Lord Evershed MR said:

f   '. . . Parliament may think fit to revise the present language of s. 2(2) of the Rating and Valuation (Apportionment) Act, 1928; but until it is done, for the reasons which my Lords have given, I do not think that the so-called syndicate can say that they are the occupiers, even if that were to get over all the difficulties in the case.'

The next year Parliament, in the Rating and Valuation Act 1961, did alter the law. It is interesting to see that it did so in Sch 4, which was described in s 25 as making 'minor amendments'. Parliament clearly, in my view, intended to bring the co-operative situation within the derating provisions of the then rating law. One finds the paragraph

g   in Sch 4 which did make this minor amendment to enable co-operatives of farmers to get the benefit of agricultural derating being followed almost word for word in the 1967 Act. There were some textual variations of no significance at all and it is important to remember that the 1971 Act was intended to be an extension of the derating provisions of the 1967 Act. The two Acts are bound together by the terms of the 1971 Act in which the 1967 Act is described as 'the principal Act'.

h   I have been conscious all through this case that marginal notes are not usually to be relied on as having any significance at all, and certainly not sure guides for the construction of statutes; nevertheless, having regard to the legislative history, I find comfort, if not support, for my construction of s 4 by the marginal note in the 1971 Act, which reads as follows: 'Buildings occupied by bodies corporate and certain associations.'

j   I have no doubt that s 4 was intended to remedy the gap in the law which the *Farmers' Machinery* case had revealed. I, too, would allow the appeal.

Appeal allowed.

Solicitors: *Solicitor of Inland Revenue; Lovell White & King* (for the ratepayer).

Mary Rose Plummer   Barrister.

R v Berry

COURT OF APPEAL, CRIMINAL DIVISION
DUNN LJ, STOCKER AND JUPP JJ
26 MARCH 1984

Explosives – Offence – Making or possessing explosive under suspicious circumstances – Making explosive for unlawful object – Explosive manufactured with object of using outside jurisdiction – Whether offence can be committed if object of manufacture is to use explosive outside jurisdiction – Whether lawfulness of object can be tested only by reference to whether object is to use explosive within jurisdiction in breach of English law – Explosive Substances Act 1883, s 4(1).

Because there is a well-established presumption that an offence-creating section of an Act of Parliament is not, in the absence of clear and specific words in the section to the contrary, intended to apply to conduct outside the jurisdiction, s 4(1)[a] of the Explosive Substances Act 1883 (which makes it an offence to make or possess explosive substances in such circumstances as to give rise to a reasonable suspicion that they are not made or possessed for a lawful object) does not apply to a case where an explosive substance is manufactured in England but with the object of using it outside the jurisdiction, because whether the substance was made for a 'lawful object' within s 4 can be determined only by reference to whether the accused knew that someone into whose hands the substance would pass intended to use it within the jurisdiction in breach of the law of England and cannot be determined by reference to objects which those concerned hoped to achieve outside the jurisdiction. Where, therefore, the evidence against an accused charged with committing an offence against s 4(1) is that he manufactured in England timers for time bombs with the object that the timers should be used in bombs which were to be exploded abroad, it is a misdirection for the judge to direct the jury to consider the purpose for which the timers were to be used abroad and to direct them that it does not matter whether the explosions were to take place in the United Kingdom or abroad (see p 300 *h* to p 301 *c* and p 303 *c* to *g*, post).

Dictum of Lord Reid in *Treacy v DPP* [1971] 1 All ER at 113 and *Air-India v Wiggins* [1980] 2 All ER 593 applied.

Notes
For making explosive substances for an unlawful object, see 18 Halsbury's Laws (4th edn) para 109.

For the Explosive Substances Act 1883, s 4, see 8 Halsbury's Statutes (3rd edn) 221.

Cases referred to in judgment
Air-India v Wiggins [1980] 2 All ER 593, [1980] 1 WLR 815, HL.
Board of Trade v Owen [1957] 1 All ER 411, [1957] AC 602, [1957] 2 WLR 351, HL.
R v El-Hakkaoui [1975] 2 All ER 146, [1975] 1 WLR 396, CA.
R v Hallam [1957] 1 All ER 665, [1957] 1 QB 569, [1957] 2 WLR 521. CCA.
R v Hornett [1975] RTR 256, CA.
Treacy v DPP [1971] 1 All ER 110, [1971] AC 537, [1971] 2 WLR 112, HL.

Appeal
On 24 May 1983 in the Crown Court at Chelmsford before his Honour Judge Greenwood and a jury, the appellant, John Rodney Francis Berry, was convicted by a majority verdict of making explosive substances contrary to s 4 of the Explosive Substances Act 1883. The jury was discharged from returning a verdict on a second count of being knowingly concerned in the evasion of the prohibition on exporting military appliances contrary to

---

a   Section 4, so far as material, is set out at p 299 *g*, post

s 68(2) of the Customs and Excise Management Act 1979. On 25 May 1983 in the same
a court the appellant was sentenced to eight years' imprisonment. He appealed with the
leave of the single judge against conviction and sentence. The facts are set out in the
judgment of the court.

Roy Amlot and Nigel Sweeney (assigned by the Registrar of Criminal Appeals) for the
appellant.
b David Cocks QC and Henry Green for the Crown.

DUNN LJ delivered the following judgment of the court. On 24 May 1983 in the
Crown Court at Chelmsford before his Honour Judge Greenwood and a jury the appellant
was convicted (by a majority of ten to one) of making explosives and on the following
day was sentenced to eight years' imprisonment. He now appeals against conviction and
c sentence by leave of the single judge who granted him bail.
    The background to the case is that the appellant and his co-accused, Jeffrey Smith, were
charged in an indictment containing two counts. The jury were discharged from
returning a verdict on count 2, which was a count of being knowingly concerned in the
evasion of the prohibition on exportation of military appliances contrary to s 68(2) of the
Customs and Excise Management Act 1979. That count had been added after committal
d for trial by way of a voluntary bill some weeks before the trial started. The jury was
unable to reach a verdict in respect of Smith and at his subsequent trial a verdict of not
guilty was returned by direction of the trial judge, McCullough J.
    The Crown alleged that between January and December 1981 the appellant made a
quantity of electronic timers designed for use by terrorists in the construction of time
bombs. The appellant was in the business of exporting various electrical appliances and
e had contacts in Lebanon and Syria. The timers were produced by a company owned and
managed by Smith under a contract between him and the appellant dated 15 January
1981 which contained a specification of the timers.
    In October 1981 the appellant approached a Mr Aspin, a licensed arms dealer, who said
that they discussed the sale of detonating and transmitting equipment for export. Mr
Aspin said that the appellant produced one of the timers to him. The timer gave him
f cause for concern and after taking legal advice he handed it to the police. The timer was
sent to Woolwich, where it was examined by Mr Feraday, a scientific officer with a long
experience of terrorist devices. He examined the timer with care and expressed the view
that he had considered many possible military and civilian uses for the device but had
come to the conclusion that it had been designed for use in a terrorist operation, namely
attachment to an explosive device. He said in evidence that he could find no military or
g civilian use for the timer. He said he had seen similar timers and devices used by
terrorists in several countries, including Northern Ireland.
    The appellant was first seen by the police on 20 October 1981 and he told them that
the timer had numerous applications, for example for runway lighting and garage doors.
He was interviewed again on 16 November 1981 and he made a statement. In the
statement he said that the timers were first discussed in Beirut while he was there
h transacting other business with government officials. As a result he supplied 1,000 of the
devices and he added that on a subsequent visit he saw the timers in the government's
possession.
    On 11 December 1981 the appellant was again interviewed and expanded on his
statement. He said that in early January 1981 he and Smith were in Beirut and were
introduced to some businessmen who were interested in buying equipment. A timer
j was discussed and an order placed but it was never discussed what they would be used
for. He was asked whether there was ever any mention of the timers being used for
aircraft landing lights and he replied, 'No.' Mr Feraday said in evidence that the timers
were not suitable for that use.
    The appellant gave evidence at his trial. He said that in 1976 he had formed a company
to import electrical goods and began to trade in security devices. He formed several

contacts in the Middle East, his main one being a Mr Monzer. He said that in September 1980 he went to Damascus and discussed various matters at a government building in Mr Monzer's presence. In December of that year he went to Beirut with Smith to discuss certain difficulties experienced in the operation of some hovercraft. They went to Damascus and during the course of discussions, at which Mr Monzer was present, a timer was produced, although no mention was made of its purpose. It was agreed that Smith would manufacture the timers and that the appellant would sell them to Mr Monzer.

The appellant described how the timers were eventually delivered and said that on 29 March 1981 while in Beirut again he understood from Mr Monzer that most of the timers had been returned to him because they were defective. He said that he had never knowingly dealt with terrorists and that so far as he was aware the timers were not made for any terrorist purpose. He added that he had brought 12 of the devices back to England and subsequently showed some to Mr Aspin, although he was not aware that the timers had been handed to the police.

Mr Monzer gave evidence. He said that the timers were delivered to the Syrian government but were returned to him because they were not satisfactory. He said he did not inquire what they were being used for but that he thought there had been mention of landing lights.

A scientific consultant, Dr Hanka, who examined the timers was also called as a witness for the defence. He said the timers were of poor quality and inaccurate and that there was nothing in their design which led him to the conclusion that they had been produced to detonate explosives. He was of the opinion that they could be used to operate airstrip lights although it would be a very cumbersome system. But in cross-examination he said that he did not disagree with anything that Mr Feraday had said.

Count 1 of the indictment was a count charging making explosives contrary to s 4 of the Explosive Substances Act 1883. The particulars of the offence were that the appellant and Smith—

'on a day between the 1st of January and 11th December 1981 made an explosive substance, namely a quantity of electronic timers, in such circumstances as to give rise to a reasonable suspicion that they had not made them for a lawful object.'

The defence made a request for particulars of the circumstances giving rise to the suspicion that the timers were not made for a lawful object. That request was refused and at the outset of the trial counsel for the appellant made an application for those particulars. In the course of the discussion counsel for the Crown said that the Crown's submission 'is that once the manufacture takes place at all, it matters not where the unlawful object is to be carried out, later, like manufacturing a bomb which in due course is to explode in the Lebanon, and exporting it to the Lebanon, that is sufficient'.

The judge refused the application for particulars of the count and in the course of his ruling said:

'What the Crown say, from reading the papers and from what [counsel for the Crown] said, is that these things were going to the Lebanon, maybe some were and some were not, we simply do not know, but what we are saying is that there is evidence to satisfy a jury here that these electronic timers were going to be used for terrorism, terrorist purposes, and they were manufactured in this country, and we cannot with certainty say where they were going to be used, and therefore it would not be right to give further and better particulars and to state whether they were for the Lebanon, where the only evidence for the prosecution is coming from the defendants, and one cannot be certain, with no documentary evidence on the papers to support such a suggestion.'

So the case proceeded on that basis. The case was opened by counsel for the Crown, the evidence for the Crown was called and at the conclusion of the Crown's case the application for particulars was renewed and coupled with a submission that if the unlawful object was one that was to be fulfilled abroad then on the true construction of

s 4 the court had no jurisdiction, because the object is confined to an unlawful object in
this country. After considerable argument, the judge rejected that submission.

Counsel put the case for the Crown in this way. He said once the Crown proves that
there are suspicious circumstances of manufacture, as it has in this case in the form of Mr
Feraday, so that the reasonable suspicion arises from those circumstances, 'Then I submit
the offence is complete and it matters not whether the object was the commission of
activity abroad or here'. At that point the judge stopped counsel and gave his reasons in a
short judgment in which he said:

> 'The offence, in my respectful view, is the manufacturing of the article, as I shall
> call it, the explosive substance, under certain circumstances. Once the Crown have
> proved that the defendant manufactured an article which turns out to be an
> explosive substance (which is a matter for the jury) under certain circumstances,
> those being to give rise to a reasonable suspicion that he is not making it for a lawful
> object, then, subject to his having the statutory defence, the actual object of where
> that device is going to be used, be it in this country or abroad, I shall tell the jury, is
> immaterial. It can be used in either.'

The judge did indeed leave the question to the jury in that way in his directions as to
the law. He put it in these words:

> 'So what have the prosecution to prove in a nutshell? This is the way the Crown
> have put their case in this court from beginning to end: that both the accused were
> making these timers, not making them in the sense that [the appellant] was putting
> them physically together, or necessarily that Mr Smith was, but that they were
> responsible for their being produced. That is sufficient; indeed no possible point has
> been taken on that by the defence in this case. The case for the prosecution is that
> both the accused were making these timers to be used for the setting off of detonators
> to explode bombs for terrorist purposes. [Then comes this material sentence and
> direction:] It matters not where those explosions were going to take place, whether
> it be in this country or elsewhere.'

Counsel for the Crown has conceded that if the judge was wrong in that direction then
the conviction could not be upheld.

The question, therefore, which arises in this appeal is the question of law as to the true
construction of s 4 of the Explosive Substances Act 1883. I say at once that it is an unusual
section. It is difficult to construe because it is expressed in a negative form. The section is
in the following terms, so far as material:

> 'Any person who makes . . . any explosive substance, under such circumstances as
> to give rise to a reasonable suspicion that he is not making it . . . for a lawful object,
> shall, unless he can show that he made it . . . for a lawful object, be guilty of [an
> offence] . . .'

Section 9, which is the definition section, provides, so far as material:

> '(1) . . . The expression "explosive substance" shall be deemed to include any
> apparatus, machine . . . or materials used, or intended to be used, or adapted for
> causing, or aiding in causing, any explosion in or with any explosive substance . . .'

The timers were capable of falling within that definition and no complaint is made by
the appellant of the necessary inferential finding of the jury that in fact the timers did
fall within the definition of 'explosive substance'.

So the Crown had to prove not only that the appellant made the timers but also that
he did so under such circumstances as to give rise to a reasonable suspicion that he was
not making them for a lawful object. That is plain from the wording of the section itself.
It is made clear beyond a peradventure by the judgment of the Court of Criminal Appeal
in *R v Hallam* [1957] 1 All ER 665 esp at 666, [1957] 1 QB 569 esp at 573, where Lord
Goddard CJ said:

'We think the proper direction to give to a jury in this case [this was a charge of possession under the same section] is that they must first of all be satisfied that he had the substance in his possession. Secondly, they must be satisfied that it was in his possession in circumstances such as to give rise to a reasonable suspicion that he had it in his possession not for a lawful object . . .'

Once the Crown has established that, then the onus shifts to the defendant to prove on a balance of probabilities that he made the substance for a lawful object. The question in this case is what is meant by the words 'lawful object' and whether the court has jurisdiction if the object is to use the explosive substance abroad.

Counsel for the appellant first submitted that s 4, in its ordinary natural meaning, was confined to an object to use the explosive substance within the United Kingdom. He drew our attention, first, to s 3 of the Act, which deals with attempting to cause an explosion with intent to endanger life or property. He pointed out that that section applied to any British subject who without Her Majesty's dominions did any of the prohibited acts with the intention of causing an explosion within the United Kingdom.

Counsel for the appellant drew our attention also to s 5, which deals with accessories, and once again applies to British subjects without Her Majesty's dominions who aid or abet any crime under the Act, that is to say any offence within the United Kingdom.

He also drew our attention to s 7(3), which (prior to its repeal by the Criminal Law Act 1967) provided:

'For all purposes of and incidental to arrest, trial, and punishment, a crime for which a person is liable to be punished under this Act, when committed out of the United Kingdom, shall be deemed to have been committed in the place in which such person is apprehended or is in custody.'

So he submitted that in their original form in 1883 there was a distinction between the offences under ss 3 and 5, which caught British subjects outside the United Kingdom intending to commit or be accessory to crimes within the United Kingdom, and s 4, which has no such extension.

Counsel for the appellant then referred us to the amendment made by s 7 of the Criminal Jurisdiction Act 1975, whereby two sections were substituted for ss 2 and 3 of the 1883 Act. Section 2 made it an offence for 'A person . . . in the United Kingdom or (being a citizen of the United Kingdom and colonies) in the Republic of Ireland' to cause an explosion. Similarly under s 3, the attempt section, it was made an offence for a citizen of the United Kingdom to do any act with intent to cause an explosion either in the United Kingdom or in the Republic of Ireland. Counsel submitted that it was significant that although those two sections have been amended so as to achieve some extra-territorial effect, that is to say to extend their ambit to acts of United Kingdom citizens in the Republic of Ireland, no such amendment was made to s 4.

Finally, on this part of his argument, counsel for the appellant referred us to s 4 of the Suppression of Terrorism Act 1978, which amends ss 2 and 3 so as to extend those offences to cover acts of persons whether United Kingdom citizens or not in a convention country as defined by the 1978 Act. But once again, as counsel pointed out, there was no amendment of s 4.

Counsel for the appellant submitted that that was of particular significance because of the well-known presumption that in the absence of clear and specific words to the contrary Parliament does not intend an offence-creating section (such as s 4) to apply to conduct outside the United Kingdom.

It is not necessary to cite more than one authority in support of that well-known proposition. I refer only to the most recent, a decision of the House of Lords in *Air-India v Wiggins* [1980] 2 All ER 593 at 596, [1980] 1 WLR 815 at 819, where Lord Diplock said:

'My Lords, in construing Acts of Parliament there is a well-established presumption that, in the absence of clear and specific words to the contrary, an "offence-creating section" of an Act of Parliament . . . was not intended to make conduct taking place

a   outside the territorial jurisdiction of the Crown an offence triable in an English
criminal court.'

Counsel for the appellant submitted that there were no such words in s 4 and that it
was of significance that ss 2 and 3 had been amended in the way which has been described
so as to give them some extra-territorial effect. Counsel submitted that it would have
been the easiest thing in the world to amend s 4 in a similar way if that had been the

b   intention of Parliament, and that in the absence of such clear words the presumption
remains. Accordingly, if the object of the manufacture was to use these devices outside
the jurisdiction, albeit for some terrorist purpose or some purpose that would be unlawful
by English law, that was not a matter over which this court had any jurisdiction, and
such manufacture would not be an offence under the section.

Counsel for the Crown accepted the presumption as a matter of principle, but he

c   submitted that the fact that a crime may be intended outside the jurisdiction does not
prevent it being justiciable here, provided that the act or conduct prohibited takes place
within the jurisdiction. He submitted that what had to be done in any particular case
was to look at the necessary elements of the offence, and if all those elements were proved
to have taken place in this country, so that the offence could be said to have been
completed in this country, then the English courts would have jurisdiction notwithstand-

d   ing that some criminal consequences might follow abroad. He referred the court to two
authorities in support of that proposition.

The first of those authorities was R v Hornett [1975] RTR 256. That was a case in which
there were a count of conspiracy to forge documents with intent to defraud and counts
of conspiracy to utter forged documents with intent to defraud and deceive. It was held
that, although the conspiracies involved defrauding persons abroad, none the less both

e   offences were complete within the jurisdiction because the forgery and the uttering had
taken place in this country. The fact that the intention was that the documents should
be used abroad in order to defraud or deceive persons there was irrelevant.

The other authority was R v El-Hakkaoui [1975] 2 All ER 146, [1975] 1 WLR 396. That
was a case in which the appellant had been charged under s 16 of the Firearms Act 1968
with having in his possession a firearm with intent to endanger life. The facts were that

f   he had the firearm in his possession in this country with the intention to endanger life
abroad. Browne LJ, giving the judgment of the court, said ([1975] 2 All ER 146 at 150,
[1975] 1 WLR 396 at 400):

'In our view there are only two elements which have to be proved to establish an
offence under s 16: (a) that the defendant had a firearm in his possession in the

g   United Kingdom, and (b) that at the time when he had it in his possession in the
United Kingdom he intended by means thereof to endanger life. If these elements
are proved the offence is complete. It is quite irrelevant whether or not the intention
was carried out.'

Then, having referred to Board of Trade v Owen [1957] 1 All ER 411, [1957] AC 602,

h   Browne LJ said ([1975] 2 All ER 146 at 154, [1975] 1 WLR 396 at 405):

'We have thought it right to refer to that judgment at some length because it
seems to us to be relevant and conclusive in the present case. We can see no
distinction between the intent to defraud or deceive in R v Hornett and the intent to
endanger life in the present case. In both cases the intent was present in England
and the offence was complete here, and the fact that the persons who would or

j   might suffer from the carrying out of that intent were abroad was and is irrelevant.'

So counsel for the Crown said that in this case the unlawful object was determined on
in this country. The manufacture of the timers took place in this country. The fact that
the unlawful object might be carried out abroad was irrelevant. If those two elements
were established to the satisfaction of the jury and if the appellant failed to prove on a

balance of probabilities that the timers were manufactured with a lawful object, then the offence was complete. Effectively, said counsel for the Crown, there was no distinction between an intent to defraud or deceive or endanger life and the manufacture of a device with an unlawful object.

The difficulty that the court feels about that submission is that in *R v Hornett* and *R v El-Hakkaoui* the relevant statute required a specific intent to be proved, and if the intent was formed in the United Kingdom then the fact that the act pursuant to the intent was to be carried out abroad was irrelevant. But in this case the section does not require any specific intent to be proved. It refers to an unlawful object and at once raises the question: by what law is the object to be judged if it is to be carried out abroad? This was the difficulty which McCullough J felt in the retrial of the co-accused Smith when he upheld submissions by counsel for Smith, who made a similar submission to that which has been made by counsel on behalf of the appellant today.

Having referred to *R v Hornett* and *R v El-Hakkaoui* McCullough J said this:

'Whether or not life is to be endangered or persons are to be defrauded are questions of fact which an English court is as well able to consider, whether the potential victims are in this country or another. However, an unlawful object is not capable of the same relatively simple consideration. The question arises and it cannot be escaped: unlawful according to what law? There can only be three possible answers: first, unlawful under English law; second, unlawful under the law of the country where the object was to be achieved; and, third, unlawful under both such systems of law. There are obvious difficulties about the first. Acts which take place outside the jurisdiction are not, with rare exceptions, amenable to English law and, therefore, could not be unlawful according to English law. One might sensibly ask whether an act committed abroad would have been unlawful under English law if it had been committed in England, but had it been Parliament's intention that this test should be applied we would have expected to find in s 4 of the Explosive Substances Act 1883 some such provision as is found in s 70(2) of the Army Act 1955, namely: "In this Act the expression 'civil offence' means any act or omission punishable by the law of England or which, if committed in England, would be punishable by that law . . ." For example, and I quote [and McCullough J there is, I think, suggesting appropriate words which could have been inserted into s 4]: "'Lawful object' means any act or omission which, if achieved in England, would be lawful by that law." However, the 1883 Act contains no such expression. This, it seems to me, places a considerable obstacle in the way of accepting possibilities 1 and 3. [Counsel for the Crown] did not argue for one. He argued, if I understood him correctly, for 2, or, alternatively, 3. Possibilities 2 and 3 would both necessitate an examination of the law or laws of the foreign country or countries in question. Matters of foreign law are questions of fact which, since s 15 of the Administration of Justice Act 1920, are to be decided by the judge, but, so far as I have been able to discover, they were, prior to that date, matters of fact for the jury and this would have been so in 1883, when the relevant Act was passed, when, presumably, if such a question arose, a jury would have had to hear the evidence of an expert claiming knowledge of the law or laws in question; indeed, they might have been asked to choose between the evidence of two such witnesses. I find it difficult to believe that Parliament, in 1883, should have intended to saddle a jury deciding a criminal case with such a task. Had this been their intention I should have expected to find clear words to that effect and there are none. As Lord Reid said in his dissenting speech in *Treacy v DPP* [1971] 1 All ER 110 at 113, [1971] AC 537 at 551: "It has been recognised from time immemorial that there is a strong presumption that when Parliament, in an Act applying to England, creates an offence by making certain acts punishable, it does not intend this to apply to any act done by anyone in any country other than England."'

Then later the judge went on to say:

'The 1883 Act is an Act with penal consequences, some potentially very severe, and, in the absence of clear indications, which I cannot find, I am not prepared to hold that the lawfulness of the object or objects referred to in s 4 is to be tested by reference to the law of any country other than our own. I find each of the three possible tests which I numbered 1, 2 and 3 to be unsatisfactory. I do not believe that Parliament intended any of them to be applied. I am led to the conclusion that, in its reference to a "lawful object" in s 4, Parliament did not intend to refer to objects which those concerned hoped to achieve outside the jurisdiction. I do not see the conclusion to which I have come as drawing attention to any gap in the law: there is none. The Secretary of State has power to prohibit the export of explosive substances without a licence.'

The judge accordingly ruled that a correct direction would have been that the lawfulness of the object shall be determined by reference to whether the defendant knew that someone into whose hands the timers would pass intended to use them within the jurisdiction in breach of the law of England. It is significant that counsel for the Crown did not invite the judge to deal with the case on the basis that some, at any rate, of the timers were to be used for an unlawful object in England.

Counsel for the Crown in this court submitted, as I understood him, that it was a necessary inference from *R v Hornett* and particularly *R v El-Hakkaoui* that the English court was to decide not only the fact of the specific intent but that the carrying out of that intent in the foreign country would be an offence under English law, and that by analogy s 4 should be construed so as to apply English law to the object to be achieved in the foreign country.

We do not feel able to accept that submission. We respectfully agree with the ruling of McCullough J and the reasons that he gave for it. It may be that this case could have been put before the jury in a way which would have enabled them to consider only the use to be made of such timers as they found had been retained within the jurisdiction of this court. But the case was never put in that way. In so far as the judge invited the jury to consider the purpose for which the timers were to be used abroad we are of the opinion that he fell into error, and in particular we are of opinion that he fell into error in saying that 'It matters not where those explosions were going to take place, whether it be in this country or elsewhere'. It may be that this section should be looked at in the proper place, but that is not a matter for us. Like McCullough J, we are of opinion that there are statutory provisions which would effectively prohibit the manufacture of explosives in this country for use abroad. In our judgment, s 4 of the 1883 Act is not one of them and accordingly this appeal must be allowed and the convictions quashed.

Appeal allowed. Conviction quashed.

The court refused leave to appeal to the House of Lords but certified, under s 33(2) of the Criminal Appeal Act 1968, that the following point of law of general public importance was involved in the decision: whether, on a true construction of s 4 of the Explosive Substances Act 1883, the lawful object specified therein was confined to an object taking place in the United Kingdom the lawfulness of which was to be defined by English law.

10 May. The Appeal Committee of the House of Lords granted the Crown leave to appeal.

Solicitors: *Director of Public Prosecutions.*

Raina Levy   Barrister.

Balsamo v Medici and another

a

CHANCERY DIVISION
WALTON J
10, 11, 12, 21 OCTOBER 1983

Negligence — Cause of action — Damage — Plaintiff requesting agent or bailee to enter car in auction and account to him for proceeds — Agent or bailee delegating performance to third party — Third party negligently paying proceeds to wrong person — Whether plaintiff entitled to sue agent or bailee in contract and third party in tort in respect of same damage — Whether plaintiff having direct cause of action against third party.

b

The plaintiff, an Italian resident, wished to sell a car at a classic car auction in England. He arranged with the first defendant for him to transport the car to England, enter it in the auction, receive the proceeds and pay them to a relative of the plaintiff who resided in England and had a bank account there. The first defendant sought and obtained the assistance of a friend in England, the second defendant, regarding the entry of the car into the auction. The second defendant was unaware of the plaintiff's existence and throughout thought he was acting solely on behalf of the first defendant. The car was duly sold but the first defendant had to return to Italy before the whole of the proceeds were paid over by the auctioneer. The first defendant accordingly instructed the second defendant to collect the money and telephone the plaintiff's relative to arrange for her to collect it. Shortly afterwards, the second defendant lost the telephone number of the plaintiff's relative and thereafter had no means of contacting or identifying her. The second defendant was later contacted by an imposter claiming to be the person who was to receive the money on behalf of the plaintiff and, without making any effort to check her identity, the second defendant handed over the money to the imposter's representative. The plaintiff brought an action against the first defendant alleging that the first defendant had received money on behalf of the plaintiff and was accountable accordingly. The plaintiff later added a claim against the second defendant alleging that the second defendant was bound to account for the proceeds as a sub-agent or had been negligent in handing over the money to the imposter. The first defendant did not serve a third-party notice on the second defendant and the question arose whether in those circumstances the plaintiff could bring a direct action against the second defendant based on the latter's negligent handling of the money, causing it to be lost.

c

d

e

f

Held — Although (as in the case of a sub-bailment) knowledge of the plaintiff's identity by the second defendant was not an essential prerequisite to the plaintiff suing the second defendant in negligence, nevertheless in the absence of privity between the two and having regard to the fact that the plaintiff was pursuing his action in contract against the first defendant, the plaintiff had no direct cause of action against the second defendant despite the latter's undoubted negligence, because the plaintiff's only right, and only cause of action, was against the first defendant to account for the proceeds of the sale of the car and that right and cause of action remained unaffected by the second defendant's negligence. The plaintiff could only have a cause of action against the second defendant as a co-contractor or joint tortfeasor with the first defendant and could not, as he was attempting to do, pursue the first defendant in contract and the second defendant in tort in respect of the same damage. The plaintiff's action against the second defendant would therefore be dismissed (see p 309 *f* and p 310 *j* to p 311 *b* and *h* to p 312 *b* and *d* to *j*, post).

g

h

Dicta of Lord Reid in *Home Office v Dorset Yacht Co Ltd* [1970] 2 All ER at 297, of Lord Wilberforce in *Anns v Merton London Borough* [1977] 2 All ER at 498 and *Junior Books Ltd v Veitchi Co Ltd* [1982] 3 All ER 201 considered.

j

Notes

For when a cause of action arises in negligence, see 34 Halsbury's Laws (4th edn) para 5, and for cases on the subject, see 36(1) Digest (Reissue) 36–39, *104–114.*

Cases referred to in judgment

a *Anns v Merton London Borough* [1977] 2 All ER 492, [1978] AC 728, [1977] 2 WLR 1024,
   HL.
   Bart v British West Indian Airways [1967] 1 Lloyd's Rep 239.
   Home Office v Dorset Yacht Co Ltd [1970] 2 All ER 294, [1970] AC 1004, [1970] 2 WLR
   1140, HL.
   Junior Books Ltd v Veitchi Co Ltd [1982] 3 All ER 201, [1983] AC 520, [1982] 3 WLR 477,
b HL.
   Lee Cooper Ltd v C H Jeakins & Sons Ltd [1965] 1 All ER 280, [1967] 2 QB 1, [1965] 3 WLR
   753.
   Lockwood v Abdy (1845) 14 Sim 437, 60 ER 428.
   M'Alister (or Donoghue) v Stevenson [1932] AC 562, [1932] All ER Rep 1, HL.
   Morris v C W Martin & Sons Ltd [1965] 2 All ER 725, [1966] 1 QB 716, [1965] 3 WLR
c 276, CA.
   Moukataff v British Overseas Airways Corp [1967] 1 Lloyd's Rep 396.
   National Employers' Mutual General Insurance Association Ltd v Elphinstone [1929] WN 135.

Action

By a writ dated 21 January 1981 and amended in November 1981 the plaintiff, Carlo
d Saverio Balsamo, claimed against the first defendant, Guiseppe Medici, an account of
money received by the first defendant on behalf of the plaintiff in respect of the sale of a
Frazer-Nash BMW Motor car, and against the second defendant, Peter Morris, inter alia
damages for negligence. The facts are set out in the judgment.

Michael Lerego for the plaintiff.
e *David Ashton* for Mr Morris.
The first defendant did not appear.

Cur adv vult

21 October. The following judgment was delivered.
f

WALTON J. The plaintiff, who, I gather, was, before titles were abolished in Italy, a
marquis, is an Italian resident in Italy. He collects vintage cars. He had a car in his
collection, a 1937 Frazer-Nash BMW 328, of which he wished to dispose. He had bought
the car in Switzerland, and it had English, not Italian or Swiss, number plates. In
consequence it could not be driven on Italian roads, so that when he came to sell it
g England appeared to be the natural place of sale. He had a friend, Mr Medici, the first
defendant, who was a dealer in cars and also, I gather, earth-moving machinery. Mr
Medici thought that he would be able to arrange the transport of the car to England on a
return journey of one of the lorries or transporters which brought him some earth-
moving machinery, and this was indeed duly accomplished.

Mr Medici had a friend here, Mr Morris (the second defendant) who is, or was at the
h relevant time, a tug-boat captain with an interest in old cars. Mr Medici used his friend
as his man of business in England, since he apparently had a number of dealings in cars
which involved this country, and Mr Morris was accustomed to carry out any instructions
he received from Mr Medici. He was not rewarded by any payments in cash, but from
time to time Mr Medici provided him with holidays in Italy, sometimes for himself
alone and sometimes with his wife, free of expense. Until a late stage in the story, the
j plaintiff had never heard of and knew nothing of Mr Morris.

The plaintiff's instructions to Mr Medici were simple. He was to have the car entered
into an auction of vintage and other cars in England, with a reserve price of £12,500.
The plaintiff realised that there would be certain expenses to come off the price realised,
including in all probability some remuneration for Mr Medici himself, and the plaintiff's
instructions as regards the remainder was, eventually, that it should be paid, by cheque,
to a Mrs Zecchi, who was in fact his mother-in-law. The reason for choosing Mrs Zecchi

as the recipient of the proceeds of sale was that she was partly resident here, and had a
bank account here, which the plaintiff himself did not. He gave Mr Medici Mrs Zecchi's   *a*
telephone number, in London, at which she could be contacted when the time was ripe.

Mr Medici sought and obtained Mr Morris's assistance in dealing with the car once it
had reached England, its storage, its entry into the auction, and assistance with auction
particulars. And so the car was entered in the auction held by Mike Carter Sales Ltd at
Alexandra Palace on 22 November 1980. The car was sold to a company called Coys.
Coys were rather slow in paying up the auction price in full, because they alleged there   *b*
was something wrong with the engine of the car which ought to have been disclosed.
Ultimately, there was a meeting on 5 December, at the Cunard Hotel where another
auction of cars was taking place, between Mr Medici, Mr Morris and Mr Carter, the man
behind the auctioneers. Mr Medici, who of course had instructions from the plaintiff as
to the disposal of the balance of the auction moneys, had expected to have been in
England when the money was received, but he was now in the position that he wished   *c*
or was obliged to return to Italy without having been able to fulfil that expectation. So
what was arranged was that Mr Morris should collect a cheque for the balance of the
money from Mr Carter (which he did four or five days later), and, having done so, should
telephone Mrs Zecchi and arrange for her to come and collect the money from him. To
that end, Mr Medici gave Mr Morris Mrs Zecchi's name and telephone number.

There arises at this point one of the extremely few conflicts of fact which I have to   *d*
resolve. The plaintiff's instructions to Mr Medici were, as I have already indicated, to pay
the balance to Mrs Zecchi by cheque. Mr Morris, on the other hand, is adamant that his
instructions from Mr Medici were to pay the money to Mrs Zecchi in cash. Mr Medici
has not attended or taken any part in the hearing of these proceedings before me,
although at an earlier stage a defence on his part was put in, and so I do not have his
evidence on anything. But what I do have is a statement which he made to the police (in   *e*
circumstances which will hereafter appear) as a witness to a crime on 22 December 1980,
under the usual conditions rendering him liable to prosecution if he has stated wilfully
anything which he knew to be false or did not believe to be true. This statement was put
in by counsel for Mr Morris, pursuant to a notice under the Civil Evidence Act 1968,
dated 1 September 1983.

In this statement (which admittedly does not square on a number of points with Mr   *f*
Morris's evidence) Mr Medici states that he told Mr Morris to give Mrs Zecchi a cheque,
or, failing that, to send her the cheque by post. Of course Mr Medici's evidence has not
been tested by cross-examination; but I ask myself what conceivable reason could Mr
Medici have had for translating the plaintiff's instructions to pay Mrs Zecchi by cheque
into instructions to Mr Morris to pay her in cash? It makes no sense whatsoever. It turns
a perfectly safe operation into a potentially risky one (nobody carries about large sums in   *g*
cash if it can be avoided) and it entailed Mr Morris actually having to make a journey to
his bank to draw out the cash, and retain it until somebody came to collect it.

Therefore, I am reluctantly forced to believe that Mr Morris has forgotten what
actually took place, which I think will appear later. I am, however, of opinion that
nothing, at the end of the day, turns on this point. My decision would be the same
whatever be the true version of events.   *h*

So, having given the instructions, Mr Medici returned to Italy. But, almost before the
instructions were given, Mr Morris had lost them. He cannot remember when he lost
them. He had in fact scribbled down Mrs Zecchi's name (misspelt) on an auction
catalogue, together with her telephone number; but he never thereafter had that
catalogue. The inference is, I think, that he lost the piece of paper on which he had
written those instructions virtually as soon as he had written them. And this is consistent   *j*
with the fact that somebody astutely picked up the facts that there was a sum of money
arising out of the sale of a car which Mr Morris was to pay to a Mrs Zecchi. Had the
auction catalogue with the vital instructions on been lost casually later on, it is unlikely
in the extreme that any such information would have been available to the person who
found the catalogue, even if anybody had bothered to pick it up.

a   Mr Medici then returned to Italy, and told the plaintiff that he had had to return without paying the money over to Mrs Zecchi, but that he had arranged that this should be dealt with by Mr Morris and he gave the plaintiff Mr Morris's name and telephone number. The plaintiff told Mr Medici that this was in order as Mr Morris was somebody he knew, but he telephoned Mr Carter to find out what Mr Carter knew about Mr Morris. The report was favourable.

b   However, on 16 December the plaintiff telephoned Mr Morris direct from Italy (the one and only time this happened), and was informed that Mr Morris had given the money to somebody sent by Mrs Zecchi to collect it. And, of course, the plaintiff was perfectly satisfied with this, and courteously thanked Mr Morris.

  What had happened was in fact vastly different. Looked at perfectly objectively, once Mr Morris had lost Mrs Zecchi's telephone number he was wholly unable to comply with the request which had been made to him. His only means of identification of Mrs Zecchi

c   was through that telephone number, and, once lost, he had no sure means of either finding or identifying her whatsoever. He did not know that Mrs Zecchi was the plaintiff's mother-in-law; in fact at this stage he knew nothing of the plaintiff at all. He thought, but had no sure means of knowledge, that Mrs Zecchi was a girlfriend of Mr Medici.

  However, somebody purporting to be Mrs Zecchi telephoned him, and inquired about

d   payment over of the money. Mr Morris says that a very large number of telephone calls were made, something like ten, by or on behalf of the person purporting to be Mrs Zecchi over the period between 4 and 15 December. The cheque of Mike Carter Auctions Ltd was in fact slow in being cleared, and it took this time before Mr Morris was able to draw out the cash for payment to Mrs Zecchi. I deduce that it was in fact in the course of these telephone conversations that the soi-disant Mrs Zecchi managed to suggest that there should be payment in cash. Ultimately it was arranged on the telephone between

e   Mr Morris and a man saying he was speaking on her behalf that the man would come to collect the money, bearing evidence of identification. The man was apparently called Julian.

  As arranged, on December 15 Julian duly called, bearing, as evidence of identification, one of Mr Medici's trade cards, on the back of which was written: 'This man Mr. Julian

f   is acting on my behalf to collect one envelope containing money for Fraser Nash B.M.W.'

  In fact, the card itself appears to be a forgery; it is not one of Mr Medici's cards, although an extremely good imitation. I do not think that anybody could be blamed for taking it to be a genuine card. However, all that the writing on the reverse side does, if it does anything at all, is to link up Mr Julian with the person who had spoken to Mr Morris calling herself Mrs Zecchi. Beyond that it does not go at all. However, on the faith of

g   that card, the money was handed over (actually by Mr Morris's wife, but nothing turns on that) to Mr Julian, who counted it, signed a receipt for it, and, at any rate so far as the parties are concerned, has never been seen again.

  In spite of strenuous arguments to the contrary by counsel for Mr Morris, it is as plain as a pikestaff that, if he owed any duty at all to look after the money, Mr Morris's course of conduct was from first to last about as negligent as could possibly be imagined, in that

h   he took no steps at any stage to check the identity of the soi-disant Mrs Zecchi. It hardly requires stating that, if the only certain identification you have for a particular person is that she is to be found at the end of a telephone at a particular number, the only certain means of finding her is to ring that number and ask to speak to her. Of course, it is quite possible even then that you will not be put through to the right person: she may be being held hostage at gunpoint. But, to put it no higher, it is a step in the right direction and if

j   somebody purporting to be Mrs Zecchi had spoken at the end of the correct telephone number nobody could possibly have dubbed the person who accepted that person as being the real Mrs Zecchi as being in any way negligent. But from first to last Mr Morris did not make any efforts whatsoever to check her true identity. Nor, indeed, given the mode of description, could he possibly have done so once he had lost the telephone number which alone identified her. There would have been no difficulty in getting the number from Mr Medici again; if the expense of a telephone call to Italy was too much, an express letter would have done the trick very swiftly.

Moreover, the negligence was doubly compounded in that payment was made in this manner in cash. If a cheque is given, then it can be drawn in such a way that it would at any rate have to be paid into an account in the name of a Mrs Zecchi, which at any rate would have afforded some, although not total, protection against the money falling into wrong hands. But if cash is being paid over, there can never be the slightest possibility of establishing where it has gone thereafter. So that, if anything, identification is even more important than otherwise.

There is another small conflict of evidence at this point, on which I think nothing at all really turns, namely whether, in telling the plaintiff, of course falsely, that the money had been paid to Mrs Zecchi, Mr Morris mentioned the name Julian. He thinks he did. The plaintiff is certain he did not. I prefer on this, as on all other matters, the evidence of the plaintiff.

Having thus received the joyful but inaccurate news, the plaintiff telephoned Mrs Zecchi. She was then in England, according to the plaintiff. Mrs Zecchi told him that she had in fact not had the money. The fat was then, of course, in the fire. Now it is not only the plaintiff who says that the telephone call to which I have last referred was made when Mrs Zecchi was in England: she herself gave corroborative evidence to that effect. Neither of them was seriously challenged in cross-examination on this point. But what was said by counsel for Mr Morris was that Mrs Zecchi had returned to Italy, leaving London on 9 December 1980. The importance of this point from counsel's point of view was that he used that as the foundation of a claim of contributory negligence on the part of the plaintiff, assuming that the plaintiff had a cause of action against the defendant in negligence.

But I am quite satisfied that the conversation to which both the plaintiff and Mrs Zecchi deposed did take place; and that it must have taken place in any event *after* the money had been paid away by Mr Morris is self-evident. The plaintiff and Mrs Zecchi, being confronted with the suggestion of this alleged contributory negligence at the very last moment, were not in a position to deal with it by documentary evidence (Mrs Zecchi's diaries might have been very helpful) save by means of a cheque given by Mrs Zecchi which was dated 12 December 1980. On examination, all that can properly be gleaned from the cheque is that it was paid into the payee's bank on 9 December so that the cheque must have been given (undated, because it appears to have been dated by the bank) at some time on or before 9 December. This therefore does not assist. But the analysis of the contents of the phone call and the fact that both the plaintiff and Mrs Zecchi recall that she was in London when it was made and received puts the matter beyond all doubt.

Quoad ultra, the suggestion that failure to inform Mr Morris that it had become impossible to carry out his instructions amounted to contributory negligence will not bear the slightest examination. The negligence in the present case consists in giving money away to the wrong person, a person whose identity you have not checked. How can any difficulty or even, as here, impossibility (if the allegation were correct) in finding the right person have any bearing on giving the money away in this fashion? The suggestion is wholly untenable.

Thereafter, the police were informed; statements were made to them. I do not think that they carry the matter any further. Naturally the police, having very little to go on, have made no progress with the case.

The present proceedings were commenced by writ on 21 January 1981. Originally there was only one defendant, Mr Medici, the claim being the simple one that he had received the money on behalf of the plaintiff (of course through the instrumentality of Mr Morris) and was accountable accordingly. A defence was put in on his behalf, and all that it did was to deny the receipt of the purchase price, and deny that he owed any duty of care to the plaintiff, I gather on the ground that he was merely a gratuitous agent. There is of course nothing in these allegations whatsoever, and in one sense it is hardly

surprising that Mr Medici, who by this date was acting in person, did not appear at the
a trial. What is surprising, of course, is that he never sought to bring Mr Morris into the
proceedings, nor, after Mr Morris had been made a party, to serve a third-party notice on
him, to which, so far as I can see, there could not have been any answer, accordingly.

In November 1981 the writ and statement of claim were amended so as to add Mr
Morris as the second defendant; basically, the claim against Mr Morris was grounded on
allegations that Mr Morris was bound to account to the plaintiff for the proceeds of sale
b as sub-agent, or, alternatively was liable to the plaintiff in negligence for having parted
with his money in the manner I have already indicated. The first ground was not pursued
by counsel for the plaintiff; and, indeed, having regard to a well-settled line of authority,
of which the most frequently cited case is *Lockwood v Abdy* (1845) 14 Sim 437, 60 ER 428,
it could not possibly have succeeded. It was the claim in negligence which formed the
whole thrust of counsel for the plaintiff's argument. Mr Morris's original case as pleaded
c was that he was never acting as the plaintiff's sub-agent, was never liable to account to
the plaintiff, and that if he was a sub-agent he was not in breach of any duty (in particular
the duty not to be negligent) owed to the plaintiff. By a late amendment he added an
allegation of contributory negligence on the part of the plaintiff, in that he alleged that
Mrs Zecchi had returned to Italy on 9 December 1980, that that fact was known to the
plaintiff and not communicated by him to Mr Morris. This I have incidentally dealt with
d already.

Interestingly enough, Mr Morris did serve a contribution notice on the first defendant,
Mr Medici, on the basis that there was some negligence on the part of that defendant
which contributed to the non-receipt of the money by the plaintiff. Not surprisingly, at
no stage has this matter been pursued any further.

I now therefore turn to the plaintiff's case against the first defendant, Mr Medici.
e Here, there are no difficulties and there can be no real argument. The final proceeds of
the sale of the car, £13,062·50, were received from Mike Carter Auctions Ltd. It is
perfectly true that, having regard to the arrangements between the two defendants, they
were received by the second defendant, Mr Morris, by means of the cheque from the
auction company, but it is trite law that, for the purpose of accountability in respect of
the receipt of money, receipt by a sub-agent is the same as receipt by the agent himself:
f see *National Employers' Mutual General Insurance Association Ltd v Elphinstone* [1929] WN
134. It is quite clear that neither the agent nor the sub-agent has accounted to the plaintiff
in respect of this money. Accordingly, he is entitled to recover the amount thereof as
against the agent, the first defendant, by way of damages for breach of contract. If the
plaintiff's instructions had been carried out, the money would have been accounted for
by, at latest, 15 December 1980. Hence that sum must carry interest from that date until
g today's date, and I would think it appropriate that the rate should follow the rate from
time to time awarded on judgment debts.

I now turn to the plaintiff's case against the second defendant, Mr Morris. It was
conceded by counsel for the plaintiff that no case could be made out in contract, because
there never was at any stage any privity of contract between the plaintiff and Mr Morris.
The case he seeks to make is a case in tort, for negligence, in having lost the plaintiff's
h money in the manner already described. Of course, there is no such thing as negligence
in the abstract, and, although I have already indicated in the earlier part of my judgment
that Mr Morris was negligent in his handling of the money, that was, of course, on the
unspoken assumption that he was handling the money of some third party for which he
would, in some shape or form, be accountable.

It is one of the unfortunate circumstances of this case that Mr Medici never served a
j contribution notice on Mr Morris, because had such a notice been served I can see no
possible answer to it. Mr Morris did not comply with the instructions he received from
Mr Medici; such non-compliance was negligent non-compliance, and it seems to me
quite clear that, as between the two of them, Mr Morris must pay Mr Medici the sum he
was directed to pay to Mrs Zecchi.

In a sense, the question in this action is whether this process can be short-circuited by means of a direct action between the plaintiff and Mr Morris, based simply on the latter's negligent handling of the money, whereby it has been lost. So far as the plaintiff's case under this head is concerned, it is desirable to bear in mind just how far the modern law as to negligence has been carried. I cite two very well known passages, in fact collected in *Junior Books Ltd v Veitchi Co Ltd* [1982] 3 All ER 201 at 210–211, [1983] AC 520 at 541– 542. First, Lord Reid said in *Home Office v Dorset Yacht Co Ltd* [1970] 2 All ER 294 at 297, [1970] AC 1004 at 1026:

> 'In later years there has been a steady trend towards regarding the law of negligence as depending on principle so that, when a new point emerges, one should ask not whether it is covered by authority but whether recognised principles apply to it. *Donoghue v Stevenson* ([1932] AC 562, [1932] All ER Rep 1) may be regarded as a milestone, and the well-known passage in Lord Atkin's speech (see [1932] AC 562 at 580, [1932] All ER Rep 1 at 11) should I think be regarded as a statement of principle. It is not to be treated as if it were a statutory definition. It will require qualification in new circumstances. But I think that the time has come when we can and should say that it ought to apply unless there is some justification or valid explanation for its exclusion . . . But where negligence is involved the tendency has been to apply principles analogous to those stated by Lord Atkin . . .'

And second, Lord Wilberforce said in *Anns v Merton London Borough* [1977] 2 All ER 492 at 498, [1978] AC 728 at 751–752:

> '. . . the position has now been reached that in order to establish that a duty of care arises in a particular situation, it is not necessary to bring the facts of that situation within those of previous situations in which a duty of care has been held to exist. Rather the question has to be approached in two stages. First one has to ask whether, as between the alleged wrongdoer and the person who has suffered damage there is a sufficient relationship of proximity or neighbourhood such that, in the reasonable contemplation of the former, carelessness on his part may be likely to cause damage to the latter, in which case a prima facie duty of care arises. Secondly, if the first question is answered affirmatively, it is necessary to consider whether there are any considerations which ought to negative, or to reduce or limit the scope of the duty or the class of person to whom it is owed or the damages to which a breach of it may give rise . . .'

Fully in conformity with these views, there are already in the books a number of cases of sub-bailment in which the owner of the goods has succeeded in an action against the sub-bailee (and be it noted, the sub-bailee alone) in negligence. These are *Lee Cooper Ltd v C H Jeakins & Sons Ltd* [1965] 1 All ER 280, [1967] 2 QB 1, *Morris v C W Martin & Sons Ltd* [1965] 2 All ER 725, [1966] 1 QB 716 and *Moukataff v British Overseas Airways Corp* [1967] 1 Lloyd's Rep 396. The explanation so far given of these cases, especially by Browne J in the last of these cases, and also by the Chancellor of Guyana in *Bart v British West Indian Airways Ltd* [1967] 1 Lloyd's Rep 239 (a case in which the plaintiff did not succeed, as his chattel, a pools coupon, was merely delayed in transmission, and not physically harmed in any way) has been that a sub-bailee is under a double duty, both to the bailee, and also to the bailor if he has the right to immediate possession or the goods are permanently injured or lost. This explanation appears also to be accepted by Professor G H L Fridman in his work *The Law of Agency* (5th edn, 1983), parts of which counsel for Mr Morris adopted in the course of his argument.

One incidental point which counsel made can, I think, be quickly got out of the way. He said that in the *Junior Books* case, which certainly extends the principle, whatever it be, from bailment to sub-contractors who carry out their work on the plaintiff's building negligently, so as to give the plaintiff a direct right against them, the sub-contractors knew that the plaintiffs were owners of the building. Here, Mr Morris had, at the stage at which he parted with the money, never heard of the plaintiff, and knew nothing of him. Hence, he submitted, there was no possibility of there being any privity between

Mr Morris and the plaintiff. I do not find this convincing. When Lord Roskill comes to
a list the essential matters giving rise to the cause of action, he nowhere suggests that
knowledge of the actual owner of the building (it would of course here be knowledge of
the principal) is a material ingredient (see [1982] 3 All ER 201 at 213–214, [1983] AC
520 at 546). Moreover, in *Morris v C W Martin & Sons Ltd* it is tolerably clear from the
report that the sub-bailee did not know of the identity of the owner of the chattel in
question.

b   In principle, I cannot see that knowledge of the precise owner can make any difference.
The duty, whatever it is, is owed to the true owner, because it must be apparent to the
sub-bailee that negligent actions by him in respect of the goods will cause loss to the true
owner.

Reverting to the main principle, and acknowledging that, in the light of the *Junior
Books* case, that principle, whatever it is, extends beyond bailment to embrace at any rate
c the negligent doing of work to a building by a sub-contractor, is it possible to extend the
principle without limit? Attractive though the prospect may be, I do not think it is. If
the principle does not have some certain limits, it will come perilously close to abrogating
completely the concept of privity of contract. A sub-bailee will be directly liable to the
bailor, and the sub-agent will be directly liable to the principal, for all negligent breaches
of whatever agreement he makes with the bailor or agent as the case may be, at any rate
d over a very wide field. I do not think the law has yet got to this point, if it ever will.

Therefore it seems to me that, in order to succeed in the present action in tort against
Mr Morris, the plaintiff must, as the starting point of his claim against him, allege that
the money in Mr Morris's hands was actually his money. If he can assert this, then I
would see no reason why the bailment cases already referred to should not apply, the
result being precisely the same as if Mr Morris had thrown away stamps or coins
e belonging to the plaintiff.

And that seems to me to be the precise point at which the claim against Mr Morris
breaks down in the present case. As I see it, there are really two routes, and only two
routes, by which the plaintiff could claim that the money given away by Mr Morris was
his money. First, if what he was seeking was some kind of tracing action. I do not need
to decide whether such an action would lie, although I incline to think that it would.
f The plaintiff would then trace the money through into the actual notes which Mrs
Morris negligently handed over to Mr Julian, and I can see no reason why the claim in
negligence should not then lie at the end of the 'tracing' chain.

Second, the plaintiff could ratify the action of Mr Medici in handing over the original
cheque from Mike Carter Auctions Ltd to Mr Morris, and then once again the same
result would follow. However, in both cases, it is clear that the plaintiff must, albeit
g incidentally, have waived any claim against Mr Medici. In the case of a 'tracing' claim, he
would have traced the money, completely bypassing Mr Medici, who himself never
actually had the money. In the case of ratification, he would have ratified Mr Medici's
action in putting the money into the hands of Mr Morris, and so would cease to have any
cause of action against Mr Medici.

Perhaps the matter can be put analytically in this manner. Can it be possible at one
h and the same time to say: 'A owes me £X and must pay that sum to me, but B has in fact
dissipated this very same sum, and must restore the same to me accordingly?' I do not
think it is, because unless the £X exists as an identifiable fund, B cannot have dissipated
the sum owed by A. And if it is sought to say that it exists as an identifiable fund, one is
in the realms of tracing. In truth and in short, nothing that Mr Morris can have done can
have affected in any way the plaintiff's property (the sole property of the plaintiff here in
j question), namely the right to be paid £13,062·50 by Mr Medici.

There is one final way of looking at the matter, which leads to precisely the same
result, but which perhaps throws up more exactly the reason why the right of direct
action in tort is, in the circumstances put, restricted to cases where what has been harmed
is the plaintiff's tangible property.

One may start by asking what, apart from the negligence of Mr Morris, the plaintiff's rights overall were. The answer is that the plaintiff has one right, and one right only, namely to require Mr Medici (and not Mr Morris) to account for the receipt of the money in question. One must then ask what, after the negligence of Mr Morris, the plaintiff's rights overall were. The answer is: precisely and exactly the same as they were before that negligence. Nothing whatsoever has been changed in any manner. From which it follows that, as is indeed the case, there can be no remedy in tort by the plaintiff as against Mr Morris.

This may be contrasted with the position where the sub-agent, sub-bailee or sub-contractor does some operation which he should not have done on physical property belonging to the plaintiff. Here the plaintiff's rights are clearly interfered with, and are different before and after the defendant's negligence; his very own property has been damaged in some way, and it is no answer to say that he may look to the bailee, agent or contractor to put it right. He may well be able to, but, even if so, his rights have been changed. He no longer gets back a perfect article, or an article perfectly repaired or worked on, which is his right; he can only get back the impaired article and damages. His rights have, clearly, to a more or less extent suffered a sea change as the result of the negligence. And that is why he has the direct action in tort against the person who has brought about that alteration.

Finally, by way of analysis, it must follow that, if the plaintiff did have a cause of action in negligence against Mr Morris in addition to a cause of action in account against Mr Medici, he must also logically have a cause of action in account against Mr Morris. This follows because, if Mr Morris was not accountable for the money, he could have chucked it out of the window as he did without any reference to the plaintiff. But I do not think that counsel for the plaintiff would for one moment submit that he could go as far as that; quite obviously, he cannot and has not attempted so to do as this would breach the fundamental principle that the action in account is one in contract, and there is no privity of contract.

I am very conscious that these are all ways of saying the same thing. Because of the difficulty and novelty of the points here in issue, I invited counsel for the plaintiff to tell me if he was aware of any case where there has been a judgment given against two persons in respect of the same alleged damage, one of those judgments being in contract and the other in tort. It seems to me that, as a matter of principle, there could not be such a case: for there to be a judgment of this general nature against two persons it appears to me that the defendants must either be co-contractors or joint tortfeasors.

Accordingly, for all the above reasons, I have come to the conclusion that the plaintiff has no case in tort against Mr Morris. I am conscious that this is, from an economic point of view, an unfortunate conclusion. For, if Mr Medici had appeared at the trial and had previously served a contribution notice, it appears to me quite clear that there would have been no answer thereto. And so, at the end of the day, the loss of the money would have fallen to have been made good by the person whose activities caused the loss, namely Mr Morris. As matters now stand, the plaintiff will have the difficulty of attempting to enforce the judgment against Mr Medici, who may not be able to meet it. It is possible, of course, that, as the result of bankruptcy proceedings against Mr Medici here, another action will be brought which will render Mr Morris liable; but none of these complicated steps would have been necessary if the course I have indicated had been adopted.

But, however tempting it is to proceed straight to an enforcement of Mr Morris's liability at the instance of the plaintiff, I am afraid that I must resist it. This is not an area where I am entitled to cut corners. Accordingly, at the end of the day it appears to me that I must dismiss the action as against Mr Morris.

Action against Mr Morris dismissed.

Solicitors: *Wray Smith & Co* (for the plaintiff); *Cullen & Co* (for Mr Morris).

Hazel Hartman   Barrister.

a

Re Malpass (deceased)

CHANCERY DIVISION

SIR ROBERT MEGARRY V-C

10, 13, 14 FEBRUARY 1984

b
Will – Option – Option to purchase realty – Option to purchase at agricultural value determined for probate purposes – Machinery under will for determining value defective – Court's power to remedy defect – Will directing executor to offer property to testator's son for purchase at agricultural value determined for probate purposes 'as agreed with District Valuer' – District valuer declining to take part in valuation – Whether court could provide alternative machinery for ascertaining value.

c
By his will the testator directed his executor and trustee to offer his son the opportunity to purchase the testator's freehold farm 'at the agricultural value thereof determined for probate purposes ... as agreed with the District Valuer'. After the testator's death it appeared that capital transfer tax would not be exigible on a transfer of the farm and therefore the district valuer declined to value the farm, even for the purpose of the option given to the son under the will. The trustee applied to the court for determination of the

d
questions whether on the true construction of the option clause in the will the option remained valid despite the district valuer's refusal to agree a valuation of the farm and whether the trustee remained under a duty to offer the farm to the son and, if so, on what terms. The testator's widow contended that the court had no jurisdiction to provide its own machinery for ascertaining the price if the machinery laid down by the option was ineffective, since the court was construing a will rather than attempting to give

e
business efficacy to a contract.

Held – A testamentary option framed in terms of offer and acceptance was contractual in nature and was, so far as possible, to be construed so as to make the option workable and effective, especially if the will contained elaborate and detailed provisions for giving effect to the option. Accordingly, where a testator's will provided ineffective machinery for ascertaining the value of property for the purposes of a testamentary option and the

f
machinery was merely a subsidiary and inessential part of the option, the court would if possible provide workable machinery to make the option effective. On the facts, the testator's will had prescribed the basis for determining the valuation for the purposes of the son's option, namely the agricultural value, and therefore the agreement of the district valuer was merely a subsidiary and inessential part of the option which the court could replace by other machinery. Since the purpose of requiring the district valuer's

g
agreement was to protect the other beneficiaries under the will by ensuring that the son paid a proper price for the farm, the court would direct an inquiry to determine the agricultural value of the farm, that value to be determined on the basis that the district valuer would have used, namely as if para 1(3)[a] of Sch 14 to the Finance Act 1981 applied and the farm were subject to a perpetual covenant preventing its use otherwise than as agricultural property (see p 317 *b* to *d* and *g* to p 318 *h* and p 319 *b c* to *g* and *j* to p 320 *a*,

h
post).

Talbot v Talbot [1967] 2 All ER 920 and *Sudbrook Trading Estate Ltd v Eggleton* [1982] 3 All ER 1 applied.

Notes
For testamentary option to purchase property forming part of testator's estate, see 50

j
Halsbury's Laws (4th edn) para 313, and for cases on the subject generally and on the price payable under such an option, see 50 Digest (Reissue) 71–76, 513–527, 544–550.
For the Finance Act 1981, Sch 14, para 1, see 51 Halsbury's Statutes (3rd edn) 1768.

Cases referred to in judgment
Bailey (decd), Re, Barrett v Hyder [1951] 1 All ER 391, [1951] Ch 407, CA.

a   Paragraph 1(3), so far as material, is set out at p 319 *c*, post

De Lisle, Re, White v De Lisle [1968] 1 All ER 492, [1968] 1 WLR 322.
Hayes's Will Trusts, Re, Pattinson v Hayes [1971] 2 All ER 341, [1971] 1 WLR 758.
Milnes v Gery (1807) 14 Ves 400, [1803–13] All ER Rep 369, 33 ER 574.
Sudbrook Trading Estate Ltd v Eggleton [1982] 3 All ER 1, [1983] 1 AC 444, [1982] 3 WLR
     315, HL; *rvsg* [1981] 3 All ER 105, [1983] 1 AC 444, [1981] 3 WLR 361, CA.
Talbot v Talbot [1967] 2 All ER 920, [1968] Ch 1, [1967] 3 WLR 438, CA.

Originating summons
By a summons dated 23 November 1983 the plaintiffs, Lloyds Bank plc (the bank), the
executor and trustee of the will of Edgar Percival Malpass deceased, applied for the
following relief: (1) that it be determined on the true construction of cl 4 of the testator's
will and in the events which had happened (i) whether the bank was under a duty to
make any offer to the first defendant to the summons, Anthony John Malpass (the son),
to sell Old Castle Farm, King's Stanley pursuant to cl 4 of the will, (ii) if so, whether such
offer should be an offer to sell the farm to the son (a) in accordance with and subject to
the provisions in cl 4 of the will, (b) at such price as was, in the opinion of an independent
valuer to be appointed by the bank, equal to the 'agricultural value' of the property
within para 1(3) of Sch 14 to the Finance Act 1981 and (c) on some other and if so what
terms, and (iii) if such offer should be in accordance with the provisions of cl 4, whether
the acceptance or purported acceptance of such offer by the son was capable of constituting
a valid contract for the sale and purchase of the property; (2) that directions be given as
to (i) the manner in which and the time at which any valuer was to be appointed for the
purposes of cl 4 of the will, (ii) the manner in which, the time at which and the basis on
which any necessary valuation of the property was to be made and (iii) the scale and
payment of the remuneration of any valuer so appointed; (3) that all further necessary
inquiries and directions be made or given; (4) further or other relief; (5) costs. The
testator's widow was the second defendant to the summons. The facts are set out in the
judgment.

Peter Crampin for the bank.
Christopher Gardner for the son.
P N D Pelham for the widow.

SIR ROBERT MEGARRY V-C. This is a case on a testamentary option which has
proved to be incapable of operation according to its literal terms. The testator had made
a previous will from which, I understand, the option was derived. At some time he lost
his testamentary capacity, and on 18 February 1983 Walton J, sitting in the Court of
Protection, made an order under the Mental Health Act 1959, as amended, requiring the
Official Solicitor to execute a will for the testator in the terms of a draft initialled by the
judge. On the same day the Official Solicitor duly executed the will. Six days later the
testator died; and on 26 May 1983 probate was granted. This showed the value of the
estate at nearly £150,000 gross and a little over £105,000 net. The major asset of the
estate is a farm. This has been valued at £105,000 as at the testator's death, on instructions
to value it as an agricultural unit. It is this farm which is the subject of the option in
dispute.
     The will appoints the bank as executor and trustee; and it is the bank which, on 23
November 1983, took out the originating summons now before me. Clause 3 of the will
gives all the testator's personal chattels to his widow. She is the second defendant. Clause
4 contains the disputed provision for an option in favour of a son of the testator; and he
is the first defendant. Clause 4(1) provides:

     'THE BANK shall by notice in writing offer my freehold property Old Castle Farm
     Kings Stanley aforesaid as more particularly specified in the Schedule hereto to my
     son Anthony John Malpass for the purchase of the same by him at the agricultural
     value thereof determined for probate purposes as at the date of my death as agreed
     with the District Valuer such offer to be made within twelve months of the date of

a
my death and to be accepted by my son within six months of receipt of the notice by him but notwithstanding anything herein contained the right of my son to exercise the option by accepting such offer shall absolutely cease on the expiration of eighteen months from the date of my death.'

In this provision, the main dispute relates to the words 'as agreed with the District Valuer', though the expressions 'the agricultural value', 'determined' and 'for probate purposes' have not been free from contention.

b
Clause 4(2) runs as follows:

'I FURTHER DECLARE as follows—(a) The option is personal to my son and shall be exercised by him during his lifetime and not by any person (including his personal representatives) after his death (b) The capital transfer tax payable in respect of the property on or by reason of my death including the tax (if any) payable by reason of the option price not being the full value of the property shall be paid out of my residuary estate (c) If in its absolute and uncontrolled discretion the Bank sees fit to do so it may accept from my son a mortgage upon the property for an amount not exceeding one half of the option price (d) Upon my son exercising the option he shall be entitled to conveyance of the fee simple of the property my son paying such costs as are paid by a purchaser for value. My son shall not be entitled to any abstract of title but shall accept without investigation such title as the Bank has at the time of the exercise of the option. Subject as hereinafter provided the property shall be vested in my son free from incumbrances capable of being discharged by money payment and such incumbrances (if any) together with the costs of discharging the same shall be discharged out of my residuary estate (e) Upon a sale or other transaction by the Bank in respect of or relating to the property after the expiration of eighteen months from the date of my death a statement in writing by the Bank that the option hereby given has not been exercised shall in favour of the purchaser or other person dealing with the Bank for money or money's worth be conclusive evidence of the facts so stated.'

Next, there is cl 4(3):

f
'PROVIDED ALWAYS that if and so long as my said wife desires to reside in Old Castle Farmhouse she shall be entitled to do so notwithstanding that my son has exercised the option.'

Clause 5 of the will then gives pecuniary legacies to two of the testator's grandchildren, and by cl 6 there is a gift of residue to the bank on trust for sale, and to stand possessed of the residue as thereinafter provided. Clause 7 then states:

g
'THE BANK shall pay the income of my residuary estate to my said wife during her life Provided Always that the Bank shall (if the option contained in clause 4 hereof shall not have been exercised by my said son) if my said wife so directs apply capital for the purpose of making Old Castle Farmhouse habitable and putting the same into good repair and condition or (whether or not such option shall be exercised) if she thinks fit in the purchase of another property selected by her as a residence and approved by the Bank as suitable for that purpose.'

Finally, there is cl 8:

'SUBJECT as aforesaid the Bank shall hold my residuary estate upon trust for such of my son Anthony John Malpass and my grandchildren Christopher Paul Malpass Susan Rachel Malpass Jane Malpass and Stephen David Malpass as shall survive me and if more than one in equal shares absolutely.'

I was told that no question arose about the remaining provisions of the will.

The four grandchildren who each take a share of residue were duly joined as defendants, though they have taken no part in the proceedings. Mr Crampin appeared for the bank, Mr Gardner for the first defendant, the son, and Mr Pelham for the second defendant, the widow. In broad terms, counsel for the son contended that the option was valid, and, *a* given suitable directions by the court, was enforceable, whereas counsel for the widow contended that it was void. At the centre of the dispute was the fact that the district valuer refused to play any part in the process of valuation, and so the words 'as agreed with the District Valuer' in cl 4(1) could not be satisfied.

This difficulty arose in the following way. On 22 June 1983 the bank wrote to the controller of the Capital Taxes Office to say that the district valuer had refused to agree anything in writing unless instructed to do so. After a telephone conversation and *b* another letter on 25 July 1983, the Capital Taxes Office replied in an undated letter, saying that the widow had a life interest in the farm under cl 4(3) of the will, and so the property was exempt under the Finance Act 1975, Sch 6, para 1(1). The district valuer would therefore not be instructed to consider the value of the farm. This seems plainly wrong, since all that cl 4(3) of the will did was to give the widow a right to occupy the farmhouse, not the entire farm. Accordingly, after taking advice, the bank wrote on 4 *c* January 1984 pointing this out, and saying that although the residuary gift gave the widow a life interest in the whole of the farm, this was subject to the son's option, so that to the extent that this was beneficial, liability to capital transfer tax could arise. Valuations in order to establish that the value of the benefit fell within the nil rate band would therefore have to be made. On 11 January 1984 the Capital Taxes Office replied, in effect agreeing with most of this view, with the important exception that as the prospects of *d* the nil rate band being exceeded was so small, no valuation would be made, even if the option was effective. Thus by another route the result was the same: the district valuer would not agree any valuation, and so the words 'as agreed with the District Valuer' could not be satisfied.

By this date, time was running out: the year in which the bank had to make the offer had not long to go. At 10 am on Tuesday last, 7 February, I heard an urgent application *e* for an expedited hearing of the originating summons. I was in fact able to offer counsel an immediate hearing that day, as events overnight had set a judge free. But this success on the application proved overwhelming, and not surprisingly counsel were unable to take immediate advantage of their good fortune. In the end, I heard the originating summons last Friday, 10 February. I delivered judgment that day; but in the discussions on the directions to be given a new point emerged, and my doubts grew about whether *f* all the authorities that might be helpful had been put before me. I accordingly withdrew my judgment and ordered the case to be reargued on the next working day, yesterday, 13 February; and this was done.

With that, I can return to cl 4(1) of the will, and in particular the words 'at the agricultural value thereof determined for probate purposes as at the date of my death as agreed with the District Valuer'. No question arises on the words 'as at the date of my *g* death', and as I have indicated the main question is on the words 'as agreed with the District Valuer' when it is known that the district valuer will not agree any value. Does this make the whole option void, as counsel for the widow contends? If not, what effect, if any, is to be given to those words?

Counsel for the widow's basic contentions were simple. The case was a case on the construction of a will, not a contract or lease, and the language was perfectly clear. Apart *h* from rectification, which has not been claimed, the court had no jurisdiction to vary or amend a will, especially when the difficulties are difficulties that have arisen as a result of events occurring after the testator's death. It was impossible to carry out the terms of the option as laid down by the will, and so the whole option failed.

Counsel for the son, on the other hand, relied on *Sudbrook Trading Estate Ltd v Eggleton* [1982] 3 All ER 1, [1983] 1 AC 444. That, as counsel for the widow emphasised, was a *j* decision on a lease, not a will. The lease gave the lessees an option to purchase the reversion—

'at such price not being less than twelve thousand pounds as may be agreed upon by two Valuers one to be nominated by the Lessor and the other by the Lessees or in default of such agreement by an Umpire appointed by the said Valuers . . .'

(See [1982] 3 All ER 1 at 3, [1983] 1 AC 444 at 474–475.)

a   The two main difficulties were, first, that no basis, whether open market value or anything else, was laid down for ascertaining the price, and, second, that the lessor refused to appoint a valuer, so that the machinery of the option would not work. The first difficulty was overcome by holding that the price was to be a 'fair valuation' (see [1982] 3 All ER 1 at 7, [1983] 1 AC 444 at 480) or 'a fair or reasonable value' or 'a fair price' (see [1982] 3 All ER 1 at 10, [1983] 1 AC 444 at 483) or 'a fair and reasonable price'

b   (see [1982] 3 All ER 1 at 13, [1983] 1 AC 444 at 487), as ascertained by objective standards. The second difficulty was overcome by overruling a doctrine stemming from *Milnes v Gery* (1807) 14 Ves 400, [1803–13] All ER Rep 369 to the effect that where an option had laid down a particular method of ascertaining the price, and this was ineffective, the court would not substitute its own machinery for ascertaining the price. This was in contrast with cases where no machinery of ascertainment had been laid down; in such

c   cases the court would provide its own machinery. The difference was between filling a void and evicting the ineffective to make way for an effective replacement.

The rule now laid down by the House of Lords, however, does not wholly dispose of the old doctrine. Only if the machinery laid down by the option which is ineffective is merely subsidiary and inessential will the court provide its own machinery; it will not do this if the machinery provided by the option constitutes an essential term of the

d   contract. Lord Fraser said ([1982] 3 All ER 1 at 10, [1983] 1 AC 444 at 483–484):

'. . . where an agreement is made to sell at a price to be fixed by a valuer who is named, or who, by reason of holding some office such as auditor of a company whose shares are to be valued, will have special knowledge relevant to the question of value, the prescribed mode may well be regarded as essential. Where, as here, the

e   machinery consists of valuers and an umpire, none of whom is named or identified, it is in my opinion unrealistic to regard it as an essential term. If it breaks down there is no reason why the court should not substitute other machinery to carry out the main purpose of ascertaining the price in order that the agreement may be carried out.'

f   Lord Fraser made it clear that his decision applied whatever the reason for the breakdown in the machinery, and not merely when it was caused by a refusal to appoint a valuer or other fault of one of the parties (see [1982] 3 All ER 1 at 10, [1983] 1 AC 444 at 484).

Counsel for the widow's primary contention was that this new doctrine had no application to a testamentary option. A will is a will, and must be construed as such, and not as a lease or a contract. The implication of terms in a contract, he said, such as those required to give it business efficacy, is subject to far less stringent requirements than the

g   implication of terms in a will, where nothing short of strict necessity would suffice; and he relied strongly on *Re Bailey (decd)* [1951] 1 All ER 391, [1951] Ch 407. Whatever force there is in such a contention for general purposes, I doubt its applicability to testamentary options. In *Talbot v Talbot* [1967] 2 All ER 920, [1968] Ch 1, a case which I found after I had withdrawn my first judgment, it was contended that a testamentary option was void for uncertainty, in that it provided for the purchase of property 'at a reasonable valuation'.

h   The option was in the form of a direct gift of the option, in contrast with the present case where the will provides for the bank making an offer which can be accepted. However, even in the case of a direct gift of an option, the nature of the option sounds in the field of contract. Speaking of a testamentary option, Harman LJ said ([1967] 2 All ER 920 at 921–922, [1968] Ch 1 at 10):

j   '. . . the principles of contract seem to me to apply to it, because the person getting a property under a testamentary option gets it by exercising the option and entering into a contract in that behalf with the executors.'

Where, as here, the option is framed in terms of offer and acceptance, its contractual nature seems to be a fortiori. Further, a provision in a will for establishing an option seems to me to be one which if possible ought to be construed as providing for an effective and workable option, especially when elaborate and detailed provisions for the purpose are set out in the will, as in the present case.

I should also observe that in the *Sudbrook* case, neither in the Court of Appeal nor in the House of Lords can I see anything to suggest that *Talbot v Talbot* is in any special position because it concerned a testamentary option as opposed to an option in a contract or a lease (see [1981] 3 All ER 105 at 113, [1982] 3 All ER 1 at 10, 12, [1983] 1 AC 444 at 458, 483, 486). If I may borrow a phrase from the dissenting speech of Lord Russell ([1982] 3 All ER 1 at 13, [1983] 1 AC 444 at 487), I should be sorry to think that whereas the court would ensure that in a lease or sale the main object 'is not stultified by a sidewind problem of valuation', it would allow this to happen in a will. Testators all too often have intentions which are not wholly self-consistent, and I hope that the courts will long ensure that the major will prevail over the minor. *Talbot v Talbot* gives clear authority for the court to provided workable machinery for a testamentary option which is devoid of machinery for ascertaining the value, as in the case of options in leases and contracts; the *Sudbrook* case provides clear authority for doing the same for a leasehold option where ineffective machinery for ascertaining the value has been provided but is merely subsidiary and inessential; why should not the same apply to a testamentary option?

The question, then, is whether in the present option the words 'as agreed with the District Valuer' amount to a merely subsidiary and inessential part of the machinery of the option, or whether they are of the essence. Counsel for the widow relies strongly on the words of Lord Fraser that I have quoted, referring to a named valuer, or an office-holder with a special knowledge relevant to the value. He spoke in glowing terms of the independence and official status of the district valuer, and on sources of local knowledge and past transactions which a district valuer had. Let all that be accepted, and there still remains the question whether it was of the essence of the valuation that the agreement of the district valuer should be obtained.

I cannot see that it was. The basis of valuation, that of agricultural value, had been prescribed, and I cannot see that the insertion of the district valuer into the process is anything more than a safeguard for the widow and those entitled to residue, to ensure that the son paid a proper price under the option. Probate valuations are commonly on the economical side, and they usually have to be revised upwards in discussions with the district valuer: see, for example, *Re Hayes's Will Trusts* [1971] 2 All ER 341 at 350, [1971] 1 WLR 758 at 768. Provided that there is some proper means of ensuring that the son pays a full and proper price on the basis laid down in the option, and not a mere 'probate value', as the popular phrase goes, I can see no grounds for thinking that the testator or anyone else can have been attaching any particular value to the participation of the district valuer in the process. If it was assumed that he would take part in the process in any case (an assumption that has proved unfounded), it was no burden to put him into the option.

In my judgment, therefore, the option falls within the doctrine laid down in the *Sudbrook* case. The machinery provided by the will is defective in a non-essential respect, and the court can and should make good the deficiency. The question is how.

In my judgment that I withdrew, I attached importance to the process of reaching agreement with the district valuer as a means of establishing a full value. With that in mind, I concluded that in place of the district valuer there should be another valuer, perhaps a retired district valuer, who would perform the functions of a district valuer in agreeing the agricultural value under cl 4(1) of the will. However, in the discussion of the directions to be given, emphasis for the first time was put on the word 'determined'; and this, among other matters, caused me to withdraw my judgment. The will contemplates a process of determination, and not merely making a valuation which is to be agreed; and a mere valuation could hardly be said to be a determination, even if it had been agreed with some substitute for a district valuer. The question, then, is what can fairly be said to be a determination for this purpose.

Again it seems to me that *Talbot v Talbot* is helpful. There, the court had directed an
a inquiry as to the reasonable price to be paid for the property in question; and the Court
of Appeal affirmed this decision. If in the present case there is an inquiry as to the
agricultural value for probate purposes, that would seem to me to produce something
that could be called a determination, as contemplated by the will; and the discussion on
such an inquiry must, it seems to me, be as efficacious in protecting all concerned as to
the propriety of the price as anything agreed with the district valuer. Accordingly I think
b that appropriate directions should be given as to an inquiry on this point.

There is then the question of the meaning of 'the agricultural value thereof'. The
existing valuation of the farm was made on instructions to value it 'as an Agricultural
Unit'. Under the Finance Act 1981, Sch 14, provision is made for relief for agricultural
property in relation to capital transfer tax. I need not go into the details of this relief, but
for the purposes of the schedule—

c   'the agricultural value of any agricultural property shall be taken to be the value
             which would be the value of the property if the property were subject to a perpetual
             covenant prohibiting its use otherwise than as agricultural property': see para 1(3).

The question is whether in the option the 'agricultural value' is to be ascertained on the
footing of the statutory definition, with the damping effect of the deemed perpetual
d covenant, or whether 'agricultural value' is to be given its ordinary meaning, with the
future prospects of the land unfettered by any perpetual covenant and so capable of
reflecting hopes of more valuable uses.

It seems plain to me that the words 'agricultural value thereof' must be construed in
their context. The question is one not of 'agricultural value thereof' simpliciter but of
'agricultural value thereof determined for probate purposes . . . as agreed with the District
e Valuer'. What 'agricultural value' would the district valuer agree for probate purposes?
His expected function must surely have been to agree a value for the purposes of the
Finance Act 1981, Sch 14. True, probate is usually granted before there is any process of
agreement with the district valuer; but as Pennycuick J pointed out in *Re De Lisle* [1968]
1 All ER 492 at 496, [1968] 1 WLR 322 at 328, the phrase 'valuation agreed for probate'
is capable of meaning 'valuation agreed in connection with obtaining probate', and so
f may mean the valuation agreed with the district valuer after probate has been obtained.
A value 'determined for probate purposes' is in my view even more readily to be
construed as referring to the value determined after probate has been granted as being
the proper value that would, if known, have been inserted in the affidavit used to obtain
probate. Accordingly, in my view 'agricultural value' in the option has the meaning set
out in the Finance Act 1981, Sch 14, para 1(3). This view seems to me to be supported by
g reference to capital transfer tax in cl 4(2)(b) of the will.

A further question is whether the option requires that the process of valuation should
be completed before the bank makes the offer to the son, so that the offer is made at a
stated price, or whether an offer made in terms of an unquantified price yet to be fixed
in accordance with the option as construed by the court will suffice. In other words, is
the option one which can be made before the price has been determined, so that the
h option could be exercised 'blind', or can it be made only at a stated price? I can see
nothing in the option to require the offer to state the price; and again *Talbot v Talbot* is of
value. It indicates that a direct testamentary option may be exercised 'blind' (see [1967] 2
All ER 920 at 925, [1968] Ch 1 at 16), and I think that this supports the view that a
testamentary requirement to make an offer can be construed as authorising the making
of a blind offer. The son, I may say, raises no objection to an unquantified offer being
j made to him; and the time for making the offer has now so nearly expired that no other
offer is practicable.

In the result my conclusions as regards cl 4(1) of the will are as follows:
(1) 'Agricultural value' means agricultural value as defined by the Finance Act 1981,
Sch 14, para 1(3).
(2) That value is to be determined as at 24 February 1983.

(3) An inquiry should be directed to determine that value.

(4) That inquiry must be held promptly, in view of the time limits laid down by the *a* will, so that the son may be assured of adequate time to consider whether to exercise the option, and I shall give directions for this purpose.

(5) The bank should forthwith, and in any event before 24 February next, give notice in writing offering the son the farm under the option clause in the will on the basis set out in paras (1) to (3) above.

Finally, I turn to the originating summons. Question 1(1) asks whether the bank is *b* under a duty to make any offer to the son pursuant to cl 4 of the will. To this I answer Yes. Question 1(2) in effect asks how the offer should be framed. Limbs (a) and (b) are not really appropriate, and the answer to limb (c), which reads, 'on some other, and if so what, terms', will have to be drafted in the light of the conclusions that I have just stated. Question 2 was left for consideration until after I had given judgment in respect of question 1, and I will therefore now hear what counsel have to say about it. Much of it *c* seems to be inappropriate.

Order accordingly.

Solicitors: *Collyer-Bristow*, agents for *Watterson Todman & Co*, Cheltenham (for the bank); *Sylvester & Mackett*, Trowbridge (for the son); *Nattrass & Co*, Gloucester (for the widow). *d*

Vivian Horvath Barrister.

e

Practice Direction

FAMILY DIVISION

Practice – Long vacation – Family Division – Business to be taken in long vacation – Estimated *f*
length – Certificate of fitness for vacation business.

Business which will be taken at the Royal Courts of Justice during the long vacation will be: (1) injunctions; (2) committals to, and release from, prison; (3) custody, access or any other application relating to a child's welfare when the estimated length of hearing does not exceed one day; (4) any other matter which has been certified by a registrar as being *g* fit for vacation business.

In any case falling within category (3) the estimate must be signed by the solicitor making the application or by counsel if instructed; it will only be in rare circumstances that a case, accepted for vacation hearing on the basis of an estimate of less than one day but which takes longer, will be continued to be heard during the vacation after the first day. *h*

In any case falling within category (4) a certificate signed by the solicitor making the application, or by counsel if instructed, must be supplied to the registrar that in his opinion (giving reasons) the matter is such that it must be dealt with during the vacation.

Whether the Clerk of the Rules lists an application within category (3), or a registrar accepts as vacation business an application within category (4), will be entirely a matter for his discretion. *j*

Issued with the approval of the President.

B P Tickle
Senior Registrar.

8 May 1984

Sport International Bussum BV and others v Inter-Footwear Ltd

HOUSE OF LORDS

LORD HAILSHAM OF ST MARYLEBONE LC, LORD ELWYN-JONES, LORD KEITH OF KINKEL, LORD BRIDGE OF HARWICH AND LORD TEMPLEMAN

9, 10, 11 APRIL, 17 MAY 1984

Equity – Forfeiture – Relief – Jurisdiction of court – Circumstances in which relief will be granted – Licence granted to defendant to use certain names and trade marks – Licence terminated on failure of defendant to provide guarantee for payment as provided by agreement – Whether court having jurisdiction to grant relief against forfeiture – Whether equitable relief applicable to contract unconnected with interest in land.

By an agreement embodied in the schedule to a Tomlin order following settlement of litigation between the parties the plaintiffs granted licences to the defendant to use certain names and trade marks and the defendant agreed to pay the plaintiffs £105,000 in three instalments. It was further agreed that the defendant would provide guarantees for the second and third instalments 'immediately upon payment' of each previous instalment and that if the defendant failed to pay either instalment on its due date or failed to furnish either guarantee the whole sum outstanding would become due and the licences would terminate forthwith. The defendant failed to provide the second guarantee guarantee until a fortnight after the payment of the second instalment. The plaintiffs sought judgment for the whole outstanding balance and a declaration that the licences had been terminated. The judge held (i) that the stipulation calling for the guarantee to be given immediately on payment was one in respect of which time was of the essence and (ii) that the court had no jurisdiction to grant relief from termination of the licences. The defendant's appeal to the Court of Appeal was dismissed. It appealed to the House of Lords, contending that the court could reinstate the licences under its equitable jurisdiction because (i) the provision stipulating termination of the licences for non-payment or failure to provide guarantees was only intended to secure payment, punctual or not, of each instalment and the second instalment although tardily guaranteed had in fact been paid, and (ii) the licences to use the trade marks and names created proprietory and possessory rights in intellectual property and fell within the court's jurisdiction to grant relief against forfeiture.

Held – The equitable jurisdiction to grant relief against forfeiture and penalties did not extend to an arm's length contract where time was of the essence or to a mere contractual licence. The Tomlin order constituted a contract between the plaintiffs and the defendant in the terms set forth in the schedule thereto, whereby the parties settled their litigation. The £105,000 paid by the defendant was accordingly not the purchase price of the licences but was part of the terms of the settlement of the litigation including the abandonment by the plaintiffs of all their claims against the defendant. Furthermore, the late tender of the second guarantee was a breach of the specific terms of the contract, under which time was of the essence, and accordingly the licences were terminated by the express terms of the contract. In the circumstances the sum of £105,000 was not a penalty. Accordingly, the dedendant had not established a case for equitable intervention and the appeal would be dismissed (see p 322 *f* to *j*, p 324 *d* to *j* and p 325 *a* and *d* to *h*, post).

Decision of the Court of Appeal [1984] 1 All ER 376 affirmed.

Notes

For relief against forfeiture, see 16 Halsbury's Laws (4th edn) paras 1447–1451, and for cases on the subject, see 20 Digest (Reissue) 898–899, 6695–6703.

Cases referred to in opinions

Bridge v Campbell Discount Co Ltd [1962] 1 All ER 385, [1962] AC 600, [1962] 2 WLR 439,   *a*
  HL; rvsg [1961] 2 All ER 97, [1961] 1 QB 445, [1961] 2 WLR 596, CA.
Cooden Engineering Co Ltd v Stanford [1952] 2 All ER 915, [1953] 1 QB 596, CA.
Dagenham (Thames) Dock Co, Re, ex p Hulse (1873) LR 8 Ch App 1022, LJJ.
Dunlop Pneumatic Tyre Co Ltd v New Garage and Motor Co Ltd [1915] AC 79, [1914–15] All
  ER Rep 739, HL.
Scandinavian Trading Tanker Co AB v Flota Petrolera Ecuatoriana, The Scaptrade [1983] 2   *b*
  All ER 763, [1982] 2 AC 694, [1983] 3 WLR 203, HL.
Shiloh Spinners Ltd v Harding [1973] 1 All ER 90, [1973] AC 691, [1973] 2 WLR 28, HL.
Stockloser v Johnson [1954] 1 All ER 630, [1954] 1 QB 476, [1954] 2 WLR 439, CA.

Interlocutory appeal

Inter-Footwear Ltd appealed against the judgment of the Court of Appeal (Ackner and   *c*
Oliver LJJ) ([1984] 1 All ER 376) given on 17 November 1983 affirming the decision of
Staughton J dated 12 October 1983 whereby he granted leave to the first respondent,
Sport International Bussum BV, to enter judgment for £35,000 against the appellant and
declared that a licence which had been granted by an agreement made between the
appellant on the one hand and the first respondent, the second respondent, Inter-Shoe
(Hong Kong) Ltd, and the third respondent, Heleen Margreet Alten-Van Zeggelaar (for   *d*
and on behalf of the estate of Frits Alten deceased), on the other hand, which agreement
was contained in the schedule to a consent order made on 18 June 1982, had been
terminated. The facts are set out in the opinion of Lord Templeman.

Alastair J D Wilson and Ian Wright for the appellant.
Colin Ross-Munro QC and Michael Burton for the respondents.
                                                                                    e

Their Lordships took time for consideration.

17 May. The following opinions were delivered.

LORD HAILSHAM OF ST MARYLEBONE LC. My Lords, having read in draft   *f*
the speech about to be delivered by my noble and learned friend Lord Templeman, I
need only say that I agree with him and consider that, for the reasons he gives, the appeal
should be dismissed.

LORD ELWYN-JONES. My Lords, I have had the advantage of reading in draft the
speech prepared by my noble and learned friend Lord Templeman. For the reasons given   *g*
by him I would dismiss this appeal.

LORD KEITH OF KINKEL. My Lords, I have had the benefit of reading in draft the
speech to be delivered by my noble and learned friend Lord Templeman. I agree with it,
and for the reasons he gives I too would dismiss the appeal.

LORD BRIDGE OF HARWICH. My Lords, for the reasons given in the speech of   *h*
my noble and learned friend Lord Templeman, with which I agree, I would dismiss the
appeal.

LORD TEMPLEMAN. My Lords, the appellant seeks equitable relief against
forfeiture. The respondents retort that equity will not resuscitate contractual rights   *j*
determined in accordance with express provisions in the contract.
  The first respondent, Sport International Bussum BV (which I shall call 'SI'), sold and
supplied sports shoes and leisure footwear manufactured in Taiwan by a subsidiary of SI.
In 1974 SI entered into an agreement with the appellant, Inter-Footwear Ltd, whereby
the appellant became the exclusive distributor in the United Kingdom of the goods of SI

for a period of ten years with the right to use the trade marks, registered designs and
names of SI and subject to payment to SI of a commission of 3% on the ultimate selling
prices. In 1981 SI and the appellant fell out and SI, supported by the other respondents,
instituted proceedings in the Queen's Bench Division of the High Court for alleged
breaches of the agreement and in particular for unpaid commission, damages for
purchasing goods other than the goods of SI, damages for selling the goods of SI outside
the United Kingdom and other relief. SI also instituted proceedings in the Chancery
Division of the High Court alleging that the appellant held certain registered trade marks
in trust for SI, seeking a transfer to SI of those trade marks, and claiming an injunction
restraining the appellant from using the trade marks on goods other than the goods of SI
and an account and payment of profits made from improperly using those trade marks.
The appellant denied that SI was entitled to any relief in the two actions and
counterclaimed in the Queen's Bench action for substantial damages for breach of an
alleged obligation on the part of SI to supply their goods at cost price.

By a consent order dated 18 June 1982 and made in the Queen's Bench action in the
Tomlin form (see *Practice Note* [1927] WN 290), SI and the appellant settled their
differences. By cl 3 of the schedule to the consent order the appellant agreed to pay SI
£105,000 in three instalments of £35,000 payable on the date of the consent order, 14
June 1983 and 14 June 1984, each instalment to be paid by banker's draft delivered to
SI's solicitors on or before the date for its payment. By cl 5 the appellant agreed to furnish
two guarantees issued by Nedbank Ltd, the first guarantee forthwith to secure the
payment of the second instalment and the second guarantee immediately on payment of
the second instalment to secure the payment of the third instalment. By cl 6 the appellant
acknowledged SI's absolutely proprietary right to the name and trade mark 'Inter' and to
the names and trade marks disputed in the Chancery action. By cl 8 SI granted the
appellant an exclusive licence for a period of two years from the date of the consent order
to use the specified names and trade marks for the sale of sports shoes, boots and leisure
footwear in the United Kingdom, North America, South Africa and other specified
countries. The appellant was also granted the right to use the names and trade marks
jointly with SI in Iceland, Spain and Gibraltar. By cl 12 the appellant was granted the
right for 18 months to purchase footwear manufactured under the names and trade
marks without paying any royalty or other sum to SI. Clause 13 was in these terms:

> 'If [the appellant] fails to pay any instalment on its due date (as provided in
> Paragraph 3) or duly to furnish either guarantee (as provided in Paragraph 5): (a) the
> full unpaid balance of the sum of £105,000 shall forthwith become due and payable,
> and [the respondents] may enter judgment and, so far as necessary, execute against
> [the appellant] for such balance, and (b) the licences referred to in Paragraph 8 and
> the right referred to in Paragraph 12 shall forthwith determine.'

Other provisions in the consent order provided for the termination of all litigation
between the appellant and SI without any order for costs, for the immediate termination
of the 1974 agreement and for the consent order to be accepted in full and final settlement
of all disputes known or unknown between the respondents and the appellant arising
out of any dealing prior to the date of the consent order.

The first instalment of £35,000 was duly paid and the first guarantee for the second
instalment was duly furnished. The second instalment was duly paid on 14 June 1983
but the second guarantee in respect of the third instalment was not furnished by Nedbank
Ltd on or before the due date, namely 14 June 1983, because Nedbank Ltd had not been
informed that its liability under the first guarantee had ceased as a result of the payment
of the second instalment. On 20 June 1983 SI claimed that the licence granted by cl 8
had been determined as a result of the failure of Nedbank to furnish the second guarantee
on or before 14 June 1983. On 23 June 1983 SI signed judgment for £35,000, the third
instalment, on the footing that by the failure of Nedbank to furnish the second guarantee
on or before 14 June 1983, cl 13 had come into operation. The second guarantee was
tendered on 27 June 1983. SI's judgment for £35,000 was subsequently set aside and on

7 October 1983 SI took out a summons in the Queen's Bench proceedings asking for a declaration that they were entitled to £35,000 and for a declaration that the licence *a* granted by cl 8 of the consent order had been determined pursuant to cl 13 of the order.

That summons came before Staughton J on 12 October 1983. Notwithstanding the absence of any proceedings claiming relief against forfeiture, the judge was persuaded to consider whether the court had power to grant relief against the forfeiture of the licence which had been incurred pursuant to cl 13 as a result of the failure of the appellant to comply with cl 8. Staughton J decided and the Court of Appeal ([1984] 1 All ER 376) *b* subsequently affirmed that no such power existed and the appellant now appeals.

My Lords, I regret that enthusiasm to debate the principle of relief against forfeiture blinded both parties to the necessity for constituting adequate proceedings claiming and resisting the grant by the court of relief against forfeiture. There was ample opportunity for these steps to be taken both before and after the misguided issue of the summons taken out by SI in the Queen's Bench action. In view of the costs which have been *c* incurred, your Lordships, while disapproving of the course which was adopted, were content to consider the appeal as though relief against forfeiture had in fact been claimed and denied.

The consent order constituted a contract between SI and the appellant in the terms set forth in the schedule. SI abandoned all their claims against the appellant, agreed to pay their own costs and granted the appellant the licences specified in cll 8 and 12 subject to *d* determination as provided by cl 13. The appellant abandoned all of its claims against SI, agreed to pay its own costs, and agreed to pay £105,000 and to procure the stipulated guarantees. It is impossible to equate the sum of £105,000 with a purchase price for the licence. The sum of £105,000 was part of the consideration offered by the appellant and accepted by SI. The licence, subject to determination, was part of the consideration offered by SI and accepted by the appellant for the consent order which settled all disputes *e* between the parties. At the date of the consent order the appellant was free to fight, to capitulate or to compromise on agreed terms. It chose to compromise on the terms set forth in the schedule to the consent order and SI chose to compromise on those terms and on no other terms. Clause 5 of the schedule which provided for the guarantee and cl 13 which provided for the determination of the licences are unambiguous. It is impossible to deduce and irrelevant to speculate whether SI attached less importance to *f* cl 13 than they attached to other provisions of the contract. The inclusion of cl 13 in the contract and the reliance of SI on that clause do not constitute conduct which can be stigmatised as oppressive or unconscionable.

The appellant claims relief against forfeiture. It admits that the late tender of the second guarantee was a breach of cl 5 of the schedule to the consent order, that time was of the essence in this respect, and that by the express terms of cl 13, the licences granted *g* by cll 8 and 12 were determined. But the appellant submits that equity has power to reinstate the licences because the provisions of cl 13 were only intended to secure the payment, punctual or not, of the sum of £35,000 which was tardily guaranteed and has now been paid.

Counsel who appeared for the appellant cited a number of authorities dealing with penalties, including *Dunlop Pneumatic Tyre Co Ltd v New Garage and Motor Co Ltd* [1915] *h* AC 79, [1914–15] All ER Rep 739, *Cooden Engineering Co Ltd v Stanford* [1952] 2 All ER 915, [1953] 1 QB 86 and *Bridge v Campbell Discount Co Ltd* [1961] 2 All ER 97, [1961] 1 QB 445, CA; *rvsd* [1962] 1 All ER 385, [1962] AC 600, HL. But in the present case the sum of £105,000 was not a penalty, nor was it the purchase price of the licences: it was a sum payable by the appellant in part consideration for all the benefits provided by SI as consideration for the consent order, including the abandonment of all claims for *j* injunctions, damages, interest and costs and a grant of two-year licences subject to termination under cl 13. Counsel also referred to authorities which, he suggested, shed a little doubt on the principle that equity will not grant specific performance where time is of the essence and default is made and not waived: see *Re Dagenham (Thames) Dock Co, ex p Hulse* (1873) LR 8 Ch App 1022 and *Stockloser v Johnson* [1954] 1 All ER 630, [1954]

1 QB 476. In my view these authorities do not justify rewriting the consent order in the present case so that time ceases to be of the essence.

Counsel ultimately relied on the observations of Lord Wilberforce in *Shiloh Spinners Ltd v Harding* [1973] 1 All ER 90 at 101, [1973] AC 691 at 723 that—

> 'we should reaffirm the right of courts of equity in appropriate and limited cases to relieve against forfeiture for breach of covenant or condition where the primary object of the bargain is to secure a stated result which can effectively be attained when the matter comes before the court, and where the forfeiture provision is added by way of security for the production of that result.'

That case concerned a right to forfeit leasehold property for failure to repair fences and maintain works for the protection of adjoining property. In *Scandinavian Trading Tanker Co AB v Flota Petrolera Ecuatoriana, The Scaptrade* [1983] 2 All ER 763, [1983] 2 AC 694, this House declined to apply the equitable doctrine of relief against forfeiture to a time charter. Lord Diplock confined that power to contracts concerning the transfer of proprietory or possessory rights (see [1983] 2 All ER 763 at 767, [1983] 2 AC 694 at 702). Counsel submitted that in the present case the licences to use the trade marks and names created proprietory and possessory rights in intellectual property. He admits, however, that so to hold would be to extend the boundaries of the authorities dealing with relief against forfeiture. I do not believe that the present is a suitable case in which to define the boundaries of the equitable doctrine of relief against forfeiture. It is sufficient that the appellant cannot bring itself within the recognised boundaries and cannot establish an arguable case for the intervention of equity. The recognised boundaries do not include mere contractual licences and I can see no reason for the intervention of equity. Your Lordships are concerned with an unusual contract bringing hostile litigation to an end and including a number of provisions which cannot be dissected so as to attribute different degrees of importance to different rights and obligations. I can see no reason for altering the rights of SI or the obligations of the appellant under cl 13 or any other clause. And I can see profound objections to the intervention of equity. In the Court of Appeal Oliver LJ indicated powerful reasons why in the present case the parties should be left to their bargain. He said ([1984] 1 All ER 376 at 384):

> 'Here were two commercial concerns, locked in litigation, advised by counsel and solicitors. They could not be more at arm's length. One can hardly conceive of a case in which certainty is more important than in a contract putting an end to litigation. The fact that part of the subject matter was the use of a trade mark underlines the need both for certainty and for the avoidance of delay, for, if a licence is determined, the licensor will wish to know at once, particularly in the case of an exclusive licence, whether he is entitled to preserve or build up his goodwill by entering on the territory himself or granting licences to others.'

It may be that none of these factors is decisive but in combination they lead me to the conclusion that this appeal ought to be dismissed.

Appeal dismissed.

Solicitors: *Lovell White & King* (for the appellant); *Baker & McKenzie* (for the respondents).

Mary Rose Plummer   Barrister.

Miramar Maritime Corp v Holborn Oil Trading Ltd
The Miramar

HOUSE OF LORDS

LORD DIPLOCK, LORD SCARMAN, LORD ROSKILL, LORD BRANDON OF OAKBROOK AND LORD BRIGHTMAN

11 APRIL, 24 MAY 1984

Shipping – Bill of lading – Incorporation of terms of charterparty – Terms relating to shipment, carriage or delivery of cargo and imposing obligations on 'charterer' – Whether incorporation rendering consignees of cargo as holders of bill of lading when cargo discharged personally liable for obligations of 'charterer'.

Where a bill of lading includes a clause which purports to incorporate the terms of a specified charterparty, there is no rule of construction that clauses in the charterparty which are directly germane to the shipment, carriage or delivery of goods and which impose obligations on the 'charterer' are presumed to be incorporated in the bill of lading with 'consignee of the cargo' or 'bill of lading holder' substituted for (where there is a cesser clause) or included in (where there is no cesser clause) the designation 'charterer'. Accordingly, a provision in a bill of lading which purports to incorporate the terms of the charterparty does not render the consignees of the cargo, as holders of the bill of lading when the cargo is discharged, personally liable to the shipowner for demurrage payable under the terms of the charterparty (see p 327 c d and p 331 j to p 332 d, post).

Adamastos Shipping Co Ltd v Anglo-Saxon Petroleum Co Ltd [1958] 1 All ER 725 distinguished.

Gray v Carr (1871) LR 6 QB 522, *Porteus v Watney* (1878) 3 QBD 534, dicta of Russell LJ in *The Merak* [1965] 1 All ER at 239 and of Lord Denning MR in *The Annefield* [1971] 1 All ER at 406 not followed.

Notes

For incorporation of the charterparty in a bill of lading, see 43 Halsbury's Laws (4th edn) paras 534–538, and for cases on the subject, see 43 Digest (Reissue) 267–272, 8438–8467.

Cases referred to in opinions

Adamastos Shipping Co Ltd v Anglo-Saxon Petroleum Co Ltd [1958] 1 All ER 725, [1959] AC 133, [1958] 2 WLR 688, HL.

Annefield, The, Annefield (owners) v Annefield (cargo owners) [1971] 1 All ER 394, [1971] 2 WLR 320, CA.

Gray v Carr (1871) LR 6 QB 522, Ex Ch.

Merak, The, T B & S Batchelor & Co Ltd v Merak (owners) [1965] 1 All ER 230, [1965] P 223, [1965] 2 WLR 250, CA.

Porteus v Watney (1878) 3 QBD 534, CA.

Appeal

Miramar Maritime Corp (the shipowners) appealed, with the leave of the Appeal Committee of the House of Lords granted on 19 January 1984, against the decision of the Court of Appeal (Sir John Donaldson MR, May and Dillon LJJ) on 28 October 1983 dismissing their appeal against the decision of Mustill J on 18 March 1983 in which he entered judgment for the shipowners for $US150,000 inclusive of interest in an action brought by them against Holborn Oil Trading Ltd (the consignees) claiming

$US279,795·68 being demurrage due under and pursuant to bills of lading signed on 5
June 1980. The facts are set out in the opinion of Lord Diplock.

Johan Steyn QC and Michael G Collins for the shipowners.
Gordon Pollock QC and Charles Macdonald for the consignees.

Their Lordships took time for consideration.

24 May. The following opinions were delivered.

LORD DIPLOCK. My Lords, the question before your Lordships' House in this appeal
is a short and, in my view, very simple question of construction of a bill of lading issued
pursuant to and in the form annexed to a tanker voyage charterparty in the standard
form known as 'Exxonvoy 1969' which is widely used in the tanker trade. More
specifically the question is whether the provision in the bill of lading which purports to
incorporate terms of the charterparty renders the respondents (the consignees), as holders
of the bill of lading when the cargo was discharged, personally liable to the appellants
(the shipowners) for demurrage payable under the terms of the charterparty to the
shipowners by SAE Petrochem Pte Ltd Singapore (the charterers), who are in liquidation
and insolvent.

At the trial of the action before Mustill J there were other issues between the parties
with which neither the Court of Appeal nor your Lordships have been concerned.
Although the amount of the demurrage in issue is of the order of $US250,000, the
principal purpose of the parties in pursuing the appeal from that part of Mustill J's
judgment that held that the consignees were not liable to the shipowners for demurrage
was to obtain an authoritative ruling on the question whether the holder of a bill of
lading in the form (the Exxonvoy bill of lading) annexed to a chartperparty in the
Exxonvoy 1969 standard form, if he were not himself the charterer, was nevertheless
personally liable to the shipowner for the full amount of demurrage payable by the
charterer under the terms of the charterparty. Neither party has contended either in the
Court of Appeal or in this House that the answer to this question depended on the
particular fact that in the instant case there was only one bill of lading and this covered a
complete cargo of petroleum products carried in the Miramar from Singapore to
Trincomalee in 1980. Exxonvoy 1969 contemplates that, at the charterer's option, there
may be more than one loading port and more than one discharging port and that separate
bills of lading may be issued, and must be issued if the charterer so requests, for shipments
forming parts of the complete cargo loaded, it may be, at different loading ports for
carriage to different discharging ports. The words in the Exxonvoy bill of lading on
which this appeal turns are the same irrespective of whether it is issued in respect of a
complete or a part of the cargo received on board at the first or any subsequent loading
port for carriage to and discharge at the last or any previous discharging port. There must
be ascribed to the words a meaning that would make good commercial sense if the
Exxonvoy bill of lading were issued in *any* of these situations, and not some meaning
that imposed on a transferee to whom the bill of lading for goods afloat was negotiated a
financial liability of unknown extent that no businessman in his senses would be willing
to incur.

The Court of Appeal, in a judgment delivered by Sir John Donaldson MR, upheld
Mustill J's rejection of the personal liability of the consignees to the shipowners for
demurrage although the reasons preferred by him for so doing differed somewhat, at any
rate in emphasis, from those of Mustill J.

Both judgments, however, took as their starting point what had been said by Russell
LJ in The Merak [1965] 1 All ER 230 at 239, [1965] P 223 at 260 and restated by Lord
Denning MR in The Annefield [1971] 1 All ER 394 at 406, [1971] P 168 at 184. Those two
cases were concerned with whether or not the presence of a clause expressed to incorporate
the terms of the charterparty in the bill of lading annexed, in The Merak to a charterparty

in the Nubaltwood standard form and in *The Annefield* in the Centrocon standard form, was effective to make the arbitration clause in the charterparty binding on a holder of the bill of lading other than the charterer himself. Although the incorporation clauses in the bills of lading used with the Nubaltwood, the Centrocon and the Exxonvoy 1969 charterparties respectively are not in identical words, there is no distinction to be drawn between them that is relevant to the instant appeal.

In strictness, what was said by Russell LJ and Lord Denning MR in *The Merak* and *The Annefield* was obiter as respects the correct approach to the extent to which incorporation clauses in bills of lading issued in standard forms annexed to charterparties are effective to impose on the bill of lading holder personal liability for non-performance of obligations undertaken by the charterer that are contained in clauses of the charterparty, other than an arbitration clause. Nevertheless, those dicta drew a clear distinction as respects incorporation in the bill of lading between an arbitration clause in the charterparty and a clause therein 'which is directly germane to the shipment, carriage and delivery of goods'. A clause that falls within this latter category, it was said, is to be treated as incorporated in the bill of lading even though it may involve a degree of 'manipulation' of the words in order to fit exactly a bill of lading.

The manipulation in the instant case for which the shipowners argued was of the word 'charterer' in the demurrage clause (cl 8) of Exxonvoy 1969, so as to substitute for it 'consignee' or 'bill of lading holder' when cl 8 was incorporated in the Exxonvoy bill of lading. Mustill J and Sir John Donaldson MR were able to find reasons for holding such substitution impermissible notwithstanding that a demurrage clause is one which is germane to the shipment, carriage and delivery of goods.

The shipowner's application for leave to appeal from the Court of Appeal's judgment was refused by that court, but was subsequently granted by an Appeal Committee of this House. As was explained to the petitioners at the hearing of the petition, leave was granted not because their Lordships had, at that stage, reached a state of prima facie doubt as to the correctness of the result reached by the Court of Appeal, but in order to give this House an opportunity of dealing with the extent, if any, to which it is permissible to indulge in what in the dicta to which I have referred was described as 'verbal manipulation' of clauses in charterparties in order, by means of an incorporation clause in a bill of lading, to impose on the holder of the bill of lading personal liability for non-performance of obligations which under the express terms of the charterparty are undertaken by 'the charterer' under that designation alone and are not therein referred to as being obligations of any other persons interested in the shipment.

The incorporation clause in the Exxonvoy bill of lading reads:

'THIS SHIPMENT IS CARRIED UNDER AND PURSUANT TO THE TERMS OF THE CHARTER DATED ... BETWEEN ... AND ... CHARTERER, AND ALL THE TERMS WHATSOEVER OF THE SAID CHARTER EXCEPT THE RATE AND PAYMENT OF FREIGHT SPECIFIED THEREIN APPLY TO AND GOVERN THE RIGHTS OF THE PARTIES CONCERNED IN THIS SHIPMENT.'

The effect of the clauses in Exxonvoy 1969, which deal with laytime, cl 5 (laydays), cl 6 (notice of readiness) and cl 7 (hours for loading and discharging), is to provide a combined total of 72 running hours of laytime for loading and discharge at loading and discharging port or ports, starting at each port six hours after receipt by the charterer or his agent of notice of readiness to load or to discharge, as the case may be. Clause 8 (demurrage) should be set out in full:

'Charterer shall pay demurrage per running hour and pro rata for a part thereof at the rate specified in Part I for all time that loading and discharging and used laytime as elsewhere herein provided exceeds the allowed laytime elsewhere herein specified. If, however, demurrage shall be incurred at ports of loading and/or discharge by reason of fire, explosion, storm or by a strike, lockout, stoppage or restraint of labor or by breakdown of machinery or equipment in or about the plant of the Charterer, supplier, shipper or consignee of the cargo, the rate of demurrage *a* shall be reduced one-half of the amount stated in Part I per running hour or pro rata for part of an hour for demurrage so incurred. The Charterer shall not be liable for any demurrage for delay caused by strike, lockout, stoppage or restraint of labor for Master, officers and crew of the Vessel or tugboat or pilots.'

The incorporation clause in the Exxonvoy bill of lading, it is argued for the shipowners, requires one to treat the bill of lading as if it included the provisions contained in cl 8 of *b* Exxonvoy 1969, not verbatim as they appear in that clause itself, but with the substitution by verbal manipulation of 'consignee under a bill of lading issued in respect of the whole or any part of the cargo' in the place of the word 'Charterer'.

My Lords, before I come to any refinements of semantics, I draw attention to the various combinations of circumstances affecting the using up of laytime and the accrual of liability to pay demurrage in which a bill of lading for some part of the cargo may be *c* issued by the master on behalf of the shipowners or after having been issued may be negotiated by the holder of the bill. Laytime may have been exhausted and the vessel may already be on demurrage before any cargo has been shipped at the first loading port, let alone subsequent loading ports if the charterparty gives an option for more than one. After completion of loading of the full cargo any unused laytime will start running again on arrival at the first discharging port and will continue to run until either (i) the cargo *d* has been completely discharged there or at subsequent discharging ports if there be more than one or (ii) the laytime is exhausted and liability for demurrage starts to accrue.

So, if the shipowners are right in their contention as to the construction of the incorporation clause in the Exxonvoy bill of lading, cl 8 read in conjunction with cll 5 to 7 of Exxonvoy 1969 has the effect that every consignee to whom a bill of lading covering any part of the cargo is negotiated is not only accepting personal liability to pay to the *e* shipowners freight, as stated in the bill of lading, but is also accepting blindfold a potential liability to pay an unknown and wholly unpredictable sum for demurrage which may, unknown to him, already have accrued or may subsequently accrue without any ability on his own part to prevent it, even though that sum may actually exceed the delivered value of the goods to which the bill of lading gives title.

My Lords, I venture to assert that no businessman who had not taken leave of his *f* senses would intentionally enter into a contract which exposed him to a potential liability of this kind; and this, in itself, I find to be an overwhelming reason for not indulging in verbal manipulation of the actual contractual words used in the charterparty so as to give to them this effect when they are treated as incorporated in the bill of lading. I may add that to do so would raise a whole host of questions as to how the liability is to operate as between different consignees of different parts of the cargo, to which questions no attempt has been made to vouchsafe any answer, let alone a plausible one. To give some *g* examples: is any personal liability for demurrage incurred by consignees of cargo which has been discharged before the expiry of laytime? If the discharge of a consignee's cargo takes place after the vessel is on demurrage is his liability to pay demurrage limited to the amount of demurrage accrued after the expiry of laytime and up to the time when the discharge of his part of the cargo is complete? Is each consignee liable for all *h* demurrage accrued while his cargo remains on board? Is the liability of each consignee to pay demurrage several? If the shipowner chooses to sue one consignee of part of the cargo for the full amount of demurrage has that consignee any right of contribution against consignees of other parts of the cargo and, if so, against which of them and on what basis?

My Lords, I bear in mind that in the nineteenth century case of *Gray v Carr* (1871) LR *j* 6 QB 522 the argument based on business common sense, although it appealed to those two outstanding nineteenth century jurists, Brett J (later Lord Esher) and Willes J, did not prevent the other members of the Court of Exchequer Chamber from concluding that, by the incorporation clause contained in a bill of lading issued for the complete cargo loaded under the particular form of charterparty in that case, there was incorporated in the bill of lading a clause appearing in the charterparty that provided for the payment of demurrage after expiry of agreed total laytime used at loading and discharging ports combined. The demurrage clause in the charterparty in question used the passive voice and thus did not expressly designate the person by whom such demurrage was to be paid; and the majority of the court (Kelly CB, Bramwell, Channell and Cleasby BB) held that by virtue of the incorporation clause in the bill of lading the consignee who was the holder of it was liable for demurrage that had accrued at the loading port before the cargo had been loaded and the bill of lading issued as well as demurrage that accrued at the discharging port thereafter.

The construction placed by the majority of the Court of Exchequer Chamber in *Gray v Carr* on the demurrage clause in the charterparty and the incorporation clause in the bill of lading was followed by the Court of Appeal in *Porteus v Watney* (1878) 3 QBD 534, where it was applied to a bill of lading for part of the cargo only. Brett LJ, who was a member of the court, regarded the reasoning of the majority in the earlier case from which he had dissented, as incapable of leading to a different conclusion where the bill of lading was for part of the cargo only.

These two cases, however, were decided by applying a literalist construction to the actual words appearing in particular clauses in a charterparty and a bill of lading which were in very different terms from those with which your Lordships are concerned in this appeal. No 'verbal manipulation' was called for, and your Lordships are not called on to decide whether these decisions ought to be treated as formally overruled; but, for my part, I have little doubt that both those cases and some other relatively old cases that followed them would, by the application of reasons based on commercial considerations to which I have already alluded, have been decided differently if they had been tried in the last two or three decades.

I turn now to the terms of Exxonvoy 1969 which it is provided by the incorporation clause in the Exxonvoy bill of lading are to 'apply to and govern the rights of the parties concerned in this shipment'. As there is no cesser clause in Exxonvoy 1969 such parties include the charterers until completion of discharge of the vessel, as well as the holders of the Exxonvoy bill of lading as consignees.

Exxonvoy 1969 comprises a preamble which states the parties, described as 'Owner' and 'Charterer' respectively, and the vessel's name. This is followed by Part I, in which particulars of the chartered voyage are to be inserted including, what is most directly relevant to the instant appeal, total laytime in running hours and the rate of demurrage. Part II, which is in standard printed form, consists of 26 numbered clauses to which there is annexed the Exxonvoy bill of lading.

The obligation on the master to sign bills of lading in this form is referred to in cl 1, and is expressly imposed by cl 20 (issuance and terms of bills of lading), which sets out in seven sub-paragraphs specific terms commonly included in bills of lading including the clause paramount. Clause 20 goes on to provide:

'(b) *The carriage of cargo under this Charter Party and under all Bills of Lading issued for the cargo* shall be subject to the statutory provisions and other terms set forth or specified in sub-paragraphs (i) through (vii) of this clause and such terms shall be incorporated verbatim or be deemed incorporated by reference in any such Bill of Lading . . .'

The seven sub-paragraphs comprise (i) a clause paramount, (ii) a Jason clause, (iii) a general average clause, (iv) a both to blame clause, (v) a limitation of liability clause, (vi) a war risks clause and (vii) a deviation clause. There is nothing here to impose on a consignee or bill of lading holder any personal liability for demurrage; and parenthetically I draw attention to the fact that the passage in para (b) of cl 20, for which I have myself supplied the emphasis, draws a distinction between carriage under the charterparty and carriage under bills of lading. It recognises the coexistence of a plurality of contracts for the carriage of the same goods in the vessel: the charterparty is one, a bill of lading issued for those goods after it has been negotiated is the other.

My Lords, in 22 of the 26 clauses in Part II there are express references to contractual *a* rights or obligations of 'the Charterer' under that designation. For my part, I can see no business reason for verbal manipulation of that designation in any of those clauses so as to substitute for the words 'the Charterer,' or to include within that expression 'the consignee' or 'holder of a bill of lading' even if the whole of Part II of Exxonvoy 1969 were set out verbatim in the Exxonvoy bill of lading issued pursuant to cl 20.

I see no justification for resort to the maxim of construction falsa demonstratio non nocet cum de corpore constat, such as induced this House in *Adamastos Shipping Co Ltd v*
b *Anglo-Saxon Petroleum Co Ltd* [1958] 1 All ER 725, [1959] AC 133 to treat the words 'This bill of lading' as if they were 'This charterparty'. This part of the *Adamastos* case, on which, unlike other issues in the same case, the House was unanimous, provided as good an elementary textbook example of the application of this Latin maxim as the classic one in which the intended corpus which is 'Blackacre' is, by an obvious mistake, described as 'Whiteacre'. In the instant case, however, every reference to 'the Charterer' by that
c designation in Exxonvoy 1969 although it would not necessarily affect directly legal obligations as between the shipowner and the consignee would nevertheless make perfectly good sense, when incorporated verbatim in the Exxonvoy bill of lading, if it meant the person designated as 'the Charterer' in the chartperparty and no one else.

If further reasons were needed (and for my part I do not think they are) for treating 'the Charterer' as meaning only the person referred to in the preamble to Exxonvoy 1969
d as the charterer and no one else, a good semantic reason may be found in the fact that in four clauses in Part II, of which one is cl 8, the demurrage clause itself, and the other three are cl 10 (pumping in and out), cl 14 (ice) and cl 19 (general exceptions clause), there are specific reference to 'consignee' under that express designation in the very same sentence as a separate reference to 'the Charterer'.

Mustill J's main reason for rejecting the argument that the word 'Charterer' in the first
e sentence of cl 8 should be read as incorporated in the Exxonvoy bill of lading as meaning or including 'bill of lading holders', an expression which he took from cl 21 of Exxonvoy 1969, the lien clause, was the presence in the charterparty of the lien clause itself, which is in the following terms:

f
> 'The Owner shall have an absolute lien on the cargo for all freight, deadfreight, demurrage and costs, including attorney fees, of recovering the same, which lien shall continue after delivery of the cargo into the possession of the Charterer, or of the holders of any Bills of Lading covering the same or of any storageman.'

This clause he regarded as providing the shipowners with a sufficient remedy against loss resulting from failure of the charterers to pay demurrage and so rendered unnecessary any verbal manipulation of the word 'Charterer' in the first sentence of cl 8.

g My Lords, I deliberately refrain from expressing any view on the effect of this curiously drafted lien clause, except to say that the time may be ripe for this House to re-examine this and other standard forms of lien clauses around which there seems to have accumulated a mystique which cries out for clarification and simplification. But the question of a lien for demurrage under the Exxonvoy bill of lading in the instant case, although it arose at the trial, is not the subject of appeal to the Court of Appeal or to your
h Lordships' House. So this does not afford the occasion for this House to embark on this topic.

In the Court of Appeal, Sir John Donaldson MR relied more particularly on the semantic argument based on the presence of the express reference to 'consignee' distinguishing him from 'Charterer' in the second sentence of cl 8 itself, under which the shipowners' claim for demurrage was brought, and he relied also on the inclusion of cl
j 20 (issuance and terms of bills of lading), to which I have referred in some detail earlier in this speech. I agree, with respect, that both of these are convincing reasons for rejecting the shipowners' argument based on the incorporation of cl 8 in the Exxonvoy bill of lading by means of the incorporation clause; I regard it, however, as more important that this House should take this opportunity of stating unequivocally that, where in a bill of lading there is included a clause which purports to incorporate the terms of a specified

charterparty, there is not any rule of construction that clauses in that charterparty which are directly germane to the shipment, carriage or delivery of goods and impose obligations on the 'charterer' under that designation are presumed to be incorporated in the bill of lading with the substitution of (where there is a cesser clause), or inclusion in (where there is no cesser clause) the designation 'charterer', the designation 'consignee of the cargo' or 'bill of lading holder'.

For the reasons that I have given I would dismiss this appeal.

LORD SCARMAN. My Lords, I have had the advantage of reading in draft the speech delivered by my noble and learned friend Lord Diplock. I agree with it and for the reasons he gives I would dismiss the appeal.

LORD ROSKILL. My Lords, I have had the advantage of reading in draft the speech delivered by my noble and learned friend Lord Diplock. For the reasons he gives I would dismiss this appeal.

LORD BRANDON OF OAKBROOK. My Lords, I have had the advantage of reading in draft the speech prepared by my noble and learned friend Lord Diplock. I agree with it, and for the reasons which he gives I would dismiss this appeal.

LORD BRIGHTMAN. My Lords, I agree that this appeal should be dismissed for the reasons given by my noble and learned friend Lord Diplock.

Appeal dismissed.

Solicitors: *Holman Fenwick & Willan* (for the shipowners); *Waltons & Morse* (for the consignees).

Mary Rose Plummer　　Barrister.

Stoke-on-Trent City Council v B & Q (Retail) Ltd

HOUSE OF LORDS

LORD DIPLOCK, LORD FRASER OF TULLYBELTON, LORD KEITH OF KINKEL, LORD ROSKILL AND LORD TEMPLEMAN

27, 28, 29 MARCH, 17 MAY 1984

Shop – Sunday closing – Enforcement by local authority – Promotion or protection of interests of inhabitants of its area – Trader in local authority's area deliberately and flagrantly flouting Sunday closing laws – Fines not acting as deterrent – Local authority applying for injunction to restrain trader from acting in contravention of law – Whether local authority proper plaintiff – Whether proceedings required to be brought by Attorney General – Whether local authority acting to protect interests of inhabitants – Shops Act 1950, ss 47, 71(1) – Local Government Act 1972, s 222(1)(a).

Practice – Parties – Local authority – Promotion or protection of interests of inhabitants of their area – Prevention of deliberate contravention of Sunday trading laws – Local authority seeking injunction to restrain trader from acting in contravention of law – Whether authority bound to sue on relation of Attorney General – Whether local authority entitled to obtain injunction in own name – Shops Act 1950, ss 47, 71(1) – Local Government Act 1972, s 222(1)(a).

The defendant company traded on Sunday at two shops in the area of the plaintiff local authority in breach of s 47[a] of the Shops Act 1950 despite warnings from the local authority not to do so. The local authority was concerned about the proliferation of

---

a　Section 47, so far as material, is set out at p 336 g, post

a   unauthorised Sunday trading in its area and had received complaints from other traders
of infringements of the Sunday trading legislation. Those traders intimated to the
authority that they themselves would feel obliged to open on Sundays unless the
authority acted to enforce observance of the Sunday trading law. By virtue of s 71(1)[b] of
the 1950 Act the authority was under a 'duty . . . to enforce within their district the
provisions of this Act'. The authority initiated, but did not pursue, criminal proceedings
which could at the time have resulted in the defendant company being fined up to £50
b   for a first offence and up to £200 for any subsequent offence. The authority also issued a
writ seeking an injunction restraining the defendants from continuing to trade in breach
of the 1950 Act and sought an interlocutory injunction in the same terms. In bringing
the action the authority purported to act under s 222(1)(a)[c] of the Local Government Act
1972, which conferred on local authorities power to institute civil proceedings 'in their
own name' where they considered it 'expedient for the promotion or protection of the
c   interests of the inhabitants of their area'. The judge granted the interlocutory injunction
sought and the Court of Appeal upheld his decision. The defendants appealed to the
House of Lords, contending that a local authority's power to claim injunctive relief under
s 222 of the 1972 Act to restrain anticipated offences was limited to circumstances where
the acts complained of were likely to cause a public nuisance and that otherwise an action
which sought to restrain a breach of the criminal law could only be brought by the
d   Attorney General and then only in exceptional circumstances. At the hearing of the
appeal the defendant company, on inquiry being made from the Woolsack, refused to
say whether it intended to resume trading on Sunday contrary to s 47 of the 1950 Act if
the injunction were lifted.

Held – The appeal would be dismissed for the following reasons—
e   (1) The effect of s 222(1) of the 1972 Act was to empower a local authority to institute
proceedings in its own name in a proper case to restrain anticipated criminal offences
without resort to the Attorney General. Such power was additional to, and did not
derogate from, the power to enforce obedience to the public law which the Attorney
General had arising out of his office or by means of a relator action. However, the power
of a local authority to act under s 222(1) was limited to the promotion or protection of
f   the interests of the inhabitants of its area and was subject to the well-established principles
relating to judicial review of the exercise of an executive power (see p 334 j to p 335 f,
p 339 j to p 340 e and j, p 341 d to g and p 342 j, post); *Gouriet v Union of Post Office
Workers* [1977] 3 All ER 70 distinguished.
        (2) Furthermore, when a local authority sought to use its power under s 222(1) of the
1970 Act to institute proceedings in its own name seeking an injunction in civil
g   proceedings as a means of preventing a breach of the criminal law, the authority had to
show not merely that the offender was infringing the law but that he was deliberately
and flagrantly flouting it, since breach of the injunction might lead to more onerous
penalties being imposed on the offender than those that would be imposed for the
criminal offence, and therefore the court would exercise its jurisdiction to grant an
injunction with caution. On the facts, the local authority was entitled to take the view
h   that the defendant company intended to continue to flout the law and would not be
deterred by the maximum fine that could be imposed, since such a fine would be
substantially less than the profits which could be made from illegal Sunday trading.
Accordingly, there was sufficient justification for the grant of an interlocutory injunction
(see p 334 j to p 335 f and p 341 h to p 342 e and h j, post); dictum of Bridge LJ in *Stafford
BC v Elkenford Ltd* [1977] 2 All ER at 528 applied.
j   Per curiam. In carrying out the duty imposed on it by s 71(1) of the 1950 Act 'to
enforce . . . the provisions of this Act' a local authority must first decide whether the
conduct prima facie constitutes a contravention of the Act and, if so, whether it is
necessary to institute and carry on proceedings in respect of that prima facie contravention
in order to secure observance of the Act. In so deciding the local authority is entitled to

---

b   Section 71(1), so far as material, is set out at p 336 h, post
c   Section 222(1) is set out at p 339 j, post

have regard to the financial consequences of a prosecution to the ratepayers and whether
a doubtful prosecution would cast an unduly heavy financial burden on them; but a local　*a*
authority cannot properly say that it will never carry out its statutory duty because of the
expense involved (see p 334 *j*, p 335 *c d* and p 336 *a* to *f* and *j*, post); dictum of Webster J
in *R v Braintree DC, ex p Willingham* (1982) 81 LGR at 79 approved.

Decision of the Court of Appeal [1983] 2 All ER 787 affirmed.

Notes
b

For the power of local authorities to prosecute or defend, see 28 Halsbury's Laws (4th
edn) para 1339, and for cases on the subject, see 16 Digest (Reissue) 274–276, 2611–2626.

For the Shops Act 1950, ss 47, 71, see 13 Halsbury's Statutes (3rd edn) 357, 371.

For the Local Government Act 1972, s 222, see 42 ibid 1053.

Cases referred to in opinions
c

A-G v Cockermouth Local Board (1874) LR 18 Eq 172.
A-G v Logan [1891] 2 QB 100.
Associated Provincial Picture Houses Ltd v Wednesbury Corp [1947] 2 All ER 680, [1948] 1
　KB 223, CA.
Gouriet v Union of Post Office Workers [1977] 3 All ER 70, [1978] AC 435, [1977] 3 WLR
　300, HL.
d
Hampshire CC v Shonleigh Nominees Ltd [1970] 2 All ER 144, [1970] 1 WLR 865.
Kent CC v Batchelor [1978] 3 All ER 980, [1979] 1 WLR 213.
Prestatyn UDC v Prestatyn Raceway Ltd [1969] 3 All ER 1573, [1970] 1 WLR 33.
R v Braintree DC, ex p Willingham (1982) 81 LGR 70, DC.
Solihull Metropolitan BC v Maxfern Ltd [1977] 2 All ER 177, [1977] 1 WLR 127.
Stafford BC v Elkenford Ltd [1977] 2 All ER 519, [1977] 1 WLR 324, CA.
e
Tottenham UDC v Williamson & Sons Ltd [1896] 2 QB 353, CA.

Interlocutory appeal

The defendants, B & Q (Retail) Ltd, appealed with leave of the Appeal Committee of the
House of Lords granted on 28 July 1983 against the decision of the Court of Appeal
(Lawton, Ackner and Oliver LJJ) ([1983] 2 All ER 787, [1984] Ch 1) on 26 April 1983　*f*
dismissing an appeal by the appellants from an order of Whitford J dated 25 June 1982
whereby he granted the plaintiffs, Stoke-on-Trent City Council (the respondents), an
injunction restraining the appellants until after judgment in the action or until further
order from trading at its premises at Waterloo Road, Burslem, Stoke-on-Trent and at
Leek Road, Hanley, Stoke-on-Trent in breach of the Shops Act 1950. The facts are set out
in the opinion of Lord Templeman.
g

Robert Alexander QC, John E A Samuels QC and *Nicholas Davidson* for the appellants.
Robert Reid QC and *Nicholas Patten* for the respondents.

Their Lordships took time for consideration.

h
17 May. The following opinions were delivered.

LORD DIPLOCK. My Lords, the facts of this case are set out in the judgment to be
delivered by my noble and learned friend Lord Templeman, which I have had the
advantage of reading in draft. I agree with his reasons for upholding the injunction in
this case and dismissing this appeal. I would associate myself with the comments made　*j*
by him and by my noble and learned friends Lord Fraser and Lord Roskill on the caution
with which a court should approach the grant of an injunction to prevent infringements
of the criminal law for which Parliament has enacted a maximum pecuniary penalty. I
also agree with Lord Roskill's observations on certain passages in the extempore judgment
of the Court of Appeal in *R v Braintree DC, ex p Willingham* (1982) 81 LGR 70 in reaching
what I do not doubt was a correct decision refusing judicial review in that case.

LORD FRASER OF TULLYBELTON. My Lords, I have had the advantage of
reading in draft the speech of my noble and learned friend Lord Templeman, and I agree
with it. I wish particularly to associate myself with his view that something more than
infringement of the criminal law must be shown before the assistance of civil proceedings,
by way of injunction, can be invoked by the local authority. That something more is
required in order to establish that the offender is not merely infringing the law but that
he is 'deliberately and flagrantly flouting it': see *Stafford BC v Elkenford Ltd* [1977] 2 All
ER 519 at 528, [1977] 1 WLR 324 at 330 per Bridge LJ. In the present case the judge was
satisfied that the intention of flouting the law had been brought home to the appellants
and I am not prepared to differ from his conclusion to that effect.

I agree also with Lord Roskill's observations on *R v Braintree DC, ex p Willingham* (1982)
81 LGR 70. I would dismiss the appeal.

LORD KEITH OF KINKEL. My Lords, I have had the benefit of reading in draft the
speech to be delivered by my noble and learned friend Lord Templeman. I agree with it,
and for the reasons he gives I too would dismiss the appeal.

LORD ROSKILL. My Lords, I have had the advantage of reading in draft the speech
of my noble and learned friend Lord Templeman. I agree with it and for the reasons he
gives I would dismiss this appeal. In agreement with both Whitford J and the Court of
Appeal (see [1983] 2 All ER 787, [1984] Ch 1), I am clearly of the opinion that an
injunction should issue for I see no reason to doubt that were that injunction now
discharged Sunday trading in defiance of the Shops Act 1950 might well be resumed in
the respondents' area. But I wish to record my particular agreement with the observations
of both my noble and learned friends Lord Fraser and Lord Templeman that something
more than infringement of the criminal law must be shown before it is proper for a local
authority to seek and the court to grant an injunction, thus enabling civil process to be
invoked in support of the criminal law with the consequence that more serious penalties
might be imposed for breach of an injunction than the 1950 Act allows for breach of the
relevant provisions of that statute.

The other matter to which I wish to advert is the decision of the Divisional Court
(Donaldson LJ and Webster J) in *R v Braintree DC, ex p Willingham* (1982) 81 LGR 70, a
decision discussed in argument before this House. The essential facts of that case were
simple. A group of shopkeepers in Witham within that district council's administrative
area sought and obtained an order of judicial review of the council's decision not to
prosecute certain persons for alleged Sunday trading in Witham. In his judgment
Donaldson LJ said (at 75):

> 'So there were two factors plainly operating on the committee's mind, in addition
> to the factor that this matter ought to be determined: that it was going to be
> expensive and it was going to be unpopular. Neither of those factors are legitimate
> factors to be taken into account in terms of the duty which is imposed upon the
> council under section 71 of the Act of 1950.'

Later in his judgment Donaldson LJ said (at 78–79):

> 'But in the present case it is quite clear that the council have taken account of the
> financial liabilities involved in performing the section 71 duty, which is not a
> permissible factor to be taken into account, save in the case where there are two
> ways of enforcing the provisions of the Act of 1950, and one is cheaper than the
> other. Then of course it is permissible to take it into account. But you cannot escape
> from the duty merely because it is expensive. That was the first error. The second
> error was to take account of the fact that the infringing activity (if infringing it is) is
> very popular in the locality. That, reasonably clearly, did influence the council,
> although I fully accept that they were advised that they should not allow it to
> influence them.'

My Lords, I do not doubt that, on the basis that the decision not to prosecute was
founded on the supposed popularity of Sunday trading in Witham, the council were at

fault and the judicial review was for that reason properly ordered. But if by his reference in the two passages I have quoted to 'expense' and 'taking account of financial liabilities' *a* Donaldson LJ meant that, in weighing all the factors before deciding whether or not to prosecute in a particular case or group of cases, a local authority must never take into account the possible financial consequences to their ratepayers of a prosecution, both in the event of its success and of its failure, I respectfully disagree. A local authority charged with the duty of enforcing the 1950 Act cannot of course properly say that it will never carry out its statutory duty because of the expense involved in so doing. Were it to adopt *b* that attitude, I do not doubt that its decision would be subject to judicial review on *Wednesbury* principles (see *Associated Provincial Picture Houses Ltd v Wednesday Corp*[1947] 2 All ER 680, [1948] 1 KB 223). If Donaldson LJ meant no more than that I would respectfully agree. But the passages quoted, albeit in an extempore judgment, are susceptible of a wider interpretation. I think the duty of a local authority is correctly summarised by Webster J in the concluding sentences of his judgment (81 LGR 70 at *c* 79):

'... the duty of that authority under section 71(1) is first of all to consider—and these matters may have to be done at the same time, but not necessarily—whether that conduct prima facie constitutes a contravention of the provisions of the Act. If so, then they have to consider whether it is necessary to institute and carry on proceedings in respect of that prima facie contravention in order to secure observance *d* of the provisions of the Act. If they decide that it is necessary to do so, then they have a duty to institute and carry on those proceedings.'

My Lords, I see no reason why when considering whether it is necessary to institute and carry on proceedings, the local authority are not entitled to have regard, in relation to the particular case or cases in question, to the financial consequences of any suggested action. If for example there is a serious or doubtful question of law involved which may *e* involve a series of appeals and thus cast a heavy financial burden on ratepayers, whatever the result but especially if the prosecution ultimately fails, I cannot think that the local authority after taking proper legal advice is debarred from taking that factor among others into account before reaching their final decision whether or not it is necessary to institute and carry on proceedings.

f

LORD TEMPLEMAN. My Lords, the appellants, B & Q (Retail) Ltd, challenge the right of the respondents, Stoke-on-Trent City Council, to bring proceedings to restrain the appellants from trading on Sundays from the appellants' shops in Stoke-on-Trent in breach of the Shops Act 1950.

Section 47 of the 1950 Act provides that, save for certain authorised transactions, every shop in England and Wales shall 'be closed for the service of customers on Sunday.' By *g* s 71(1):

'It shall be the duty of every local authority to enforce within their district the provisions of this Act ... and for that purpose to institute and to carry on such proceedings in respect of contraventions of the said provisions ... as may be necessary to secure observance thereof.'

h

Section 71(2) directs every local authority to appoint inspectors for the purposes of the Act and provides:

'... An inspector may, if so authorised by the local authority, institute and carry on any proceedings under this Act on behalf of the authority.'

I agree with the observations of my noble and learned friend Lord Roskill concerning *j* the duty of the local authority under s 71 of the Act.

The appellants' shops at Waterloo Road, Burslem and Leek Road, Hanley are within the district of the council. The appellants' shops traded in prohibited articles on Sunday, 11 April 1982, and after a warning from a council representative, again on 18 April. The appellants were warned of legal proceedings on 19 April and traded in prohibited articles on 25 April.

a By s 59 of the 1950 Act the occupier of a shop which trades on Sundays in breach of the 1950 Act was made liable to a fine of £5 for a first offence and £20 in the case of a second or subsequent offence. By s 31 of the Criminal Justice Act 1972 the penalties were increased to £50 and £200 respectively and those were the maximum penalties for offences up to 11 April 1983. By ss 35 to 48 of the Criminal Justice Act 1982 from 11 April 1983 an occupier of a shop trading in breach of the 1950 Act is liable to a maximum fine of £500 for any offence and the Home Secretary can by order, subject to a negative

b resolution by Parliament, increase the maximum penalty to an extent justified by any change in the value of money since July 1977.

In addition to initiating but not completing criminal proceedings which could have resulted in the imposition on the appellants of a fine of £50 for the first offence and £200 for every subsequent offence, the council on 5 May 1982 issued a writ in the Chancery Division of the High Court for an injunction to restrain the appellants from continuing

c to trade in breach of the 1950 Act. On 25 June 1982 Whitford J in those proceedings granted an interlocutory injunction restraining the appellants until trial of the action or further order from trading in breach of the 1950 Act. Against that order the appellants appealed unsuccessfully to the Court of Appeal (see [1983] 2 All ER 787, [1984] Ch 1) and now appeal to your Lordships' House.

By the common law of England, a plaintiff can only sue for interference with his

d private rights, or for interference with a public right whereby he suffers special damage, peculiar to himself. A breach of the 1950 Act does not interfere with the private rights of the council or cause the council special damage and accordingly the council could not at common law bring civil proceedings complaining of any breach of the 1950 Act. At common law the Attorney General may institute proceedings to enforce the terms of a public Act of Parliament and—

e 'It is not necessary for the Attorney-General to shew any injury at all. The Legislature is of opinion that certain acts will produce injury, and that is enough.'

(See *A-G v Cockermouth Local Board* (1874) LR 18 Eq 172 at 178 per Jessel MR.)

The Attorney General may institute proceedings himself ex officio, and in that event is liable to incur and possibly pay costs. In the alternative the Attorney General may

f authorise another person, called the relator, to institute proceedings in the name of the Attorney General and, in that event, the relator is liable for costs. But—

'There is, in fact, no difference between an information filed ex officio by the Attorney General and a proceeding by him at the relation of a third party, except as to costs . . .'

g (See *A-G v Logan* [1891] 2 QB 100 at 103 per Wills J.)

'. . . when the Attorney General proceeds at the relation of a private person or a corporation, he takes the proceeding as representing the Crown, and the Crown through the Attorney General is really a party to the litigation. It is quite true that when the proceeding is taken at the relation of a subject, the practice is to insert his

h name in the proceedings as the relator, and to make him responsible for the costs, but I do not think that this practice in any sense makes the relator a party to the proceedings, although he is responsible for the costs . . . the practice of making the relator responsible for the costs of the action had its origin not in the protection of the defendant but of the Crown.'

(See *A-G v Logan* [1891] 2 QB 100 at 106 per Williams J.)

j At common law therefore the council could not bring proceedings against the appellants to restrain breaches of the 1950 Act. The council could have asked the Attorney General to take such proceedings at the relation of the council: See *Gouriet v Union of Post Office Workers* [1977] 3 All ER 70 at 80, [1978] AC 435 at 477 per Lord Wilberforce:

'A relator action . . . is one in which the Attorney-General, on the relation of individuals (who may include local authorities or companies), brings an action to assert a public right. It can properly be said to be a fundamental principle of English law that private rights can be asserted by individuals, but that public rights can only be asserted by the Attorney-General as representing the public. In terms of constitutional law, the rights of the public are vested in the Crown, and the Attorney-General enforces them as an officer of the Crown. And just as the Attorney-General has in general no power to interfere with the assertion of private rights, so in general no private person has the right of representing the public in the assertion of public rights. If he tries to do so his action can be struck out.'

The power of the Attorney General to institute proceedings to uphold public rights and duties enables the Attorney General, whether acting ex officio or in relator actions, to invoke the assistance of civil courts in aid of the criminal law. This is an exceptional but well-recognised power: see *Gouriet v Union of Post Office Workers* [1977] 3 All ER 70 at 83, [1978] AC 435 at 481. Thus at common law the Attorney General, at the relation of the council, but only if the Attorney General in his absolute discretion thought fit, had power to seek an injunction restraining the appellants from committing breaches of the 1950 Act within the area of the council. No such proceedings were however instituted.

Thus far the common law. But Parliament may confer, and undoubtedly has in some instances conferred, limited powers on local authorities to institute and maintain proceedings to ensure compliance with public duties. For certain purposes Parliament has supplemented the power of the Attorney General to act in the national public interest with a power for a local authority to act in the interests of the public within the area administered by that authority.

Section 107 of the Public Health Act 1875 provided:

'Any local authority may, if in their opinion summary proceedings would afford an inadequate remedy, cause any proceedings to be taken against any person in any superior court of law or equity to enforce the abatement or prohibition of any nuisance under this Act, or for the recovery of any penalties from or for the punishment of any persons offending against the provisions of this Act relating to nuisances . . .'

In *Tottenham UDC v Williamson & Sons Ltd* [1896] 2 QB 353 the Court of Appeal decided that s 107 did not enable a local authority to bring proceedings in their own name instead of requesting the Attorney General to allow proceedings to be taken in his name at the relation of the local authority. Kay LJ said (at 354–355):

'The ordinary law is, that when anyone complains of a public nuisance he must obtain the fiat of the Attorney-General for proceedings by way of information, unless he can shew that the nuisance of which he complains is the cause of special damage to himself, and so ground for an action . . . The section relied on is s. 107; but that does not say that a local authority can take proceedings which no private person can take, and which are unknown to the law. Had that been the intention of the Act, I should have expected to find the new remedy, hitherto unknown to the law, stated in explicit terms.'

Section 107 of the Public Health Act 1875 was repealed and replaced in an altered form by s 100 of the Public Health Act 1936 in these terms:

'If in the case of any statutory nuisance the local authority are of opinion that summary proceedings would afford an inadequate remedy, they may *in their own name* take proceedings in the High Court for the purpose of securing the abatement or prohibition of that nuisance, *and such proceedings shall be maintainable notwithstanding that the authority have suffered no damage from the nuisance.*' (My emphasis.)

Thus Parliament reversed the effect of the decision in *Tottenham UDC v Williamson & Sons Ltd* by authorising the local authority, in explicit terms, to take proceedings in their

own name and by exempting the local authority from proving that the local authority
had suffered special damage from a statutory nuisance in which damage was the essence
of the wrongdoing.

By s 116(2) of the Highways Act 1959 a county council might 'assert and protect the
rights of the public to the use and enjoyment of' any county road in the county. By
s 116(5):

'Without prejudice to their powers under section 276 of the Local Government
Act 1933, a council may, in the performance of their functions under the foregoing
provisions of this section, institute or defend any legal proceedings and generally
take such steps as they deem expedient.'

By s 116(6) if a parish council alleged that a county road had been unlawfully stopped
up or obstructed then—

'it shall be the duty of the council of that district, unless satisfied that the
allegations are incorrect, to take proper proceedings accordingly.'

In *Hampshire CC v Shonleigh Nominees Ltd* [1970] 2 All ER 144, [1970] 1 WLR 865
Plowman J held that the terms of s 116 were not sufficiently explicit to enable a county
council to bring proceedings in their own name. Section 70(1) of the Highways Act 1971
then amended the Highways Act 1959 so that s 116(5) (now s 130(5) of the Highways
Act 1980) enables a county council to 'institute proceedings *in their own name*'. Similarly,
s 116(6) (now s 130(6) of the 1980 Act) directs the county council 'to take proper
proceedings accordingly *and they may do so in their own name*'.

Thus Parliament reversed the effect of the decision of Plowman J in *Hampshire CC v
Shonleigh Nominees Ltd* by authorising the county council to take proceedings in their own
name. This express power makes it impossible for any court to conclude after the 1971
amendments, as Plowman J concluded prior to those amendments, that the only relevant
power available to the county council is power to request the Attorney General to allow
proceedings to be taken in the name of the Attorney General at the relation of the county
council. In proceedings instituted under the Highways Act to assert and protect the
rights of the public to use and enjoy roads and highways, special damage is irrelevant and
was therefore not mentioned in the amendments to the Highways Act 1959 as it had
been mentioned in the alterations to the Public Health Act 1875 to which I have referred.

Section 276 of the Local Government Act 1933, to which reference was made in
s 116(5) of the Highways Act 1959, provided:

'Where a local authority deem it expedient for the promotion or protection of the
interests of the inhabitants of their area, they may prosecute or defend any legal
proceedings.'

In *Prestatyn UDC v Prestatyn Raceway Ltd* [1969] 3 All ER 1573, [1970] 1 WLR 33
Goff J applied the dictum of Kay LJ in *Tottenham UDC v Williamson & Sons Ltd* [1896] 2
QB 353 at 354–355 and decided that the terms of s 276 were not sufficiently explicit to
enable a local authority to bring proceedings in their own name.

Section 276 of the Local Government Act 1933 was replaced in an altered form by
s 222 of the Local Government Act 1972, which is in these terms:

'(1) When a local authority consider it expedient for the promotion or protection
of the interests of the inhabitants of their area—(a) they may prosecute or defend or
appear in any legal proceedings and, *in the case of civil proceedings, may institute them
in their own name*, and (b) they may *in their own name* make representations in the
interests of the inhabitants at any public inquiry held by or on behalf of any Minister
or public body under any enactment . . .'

Thus Parliament reversed the effect of the decision of Goff J in *Prestatyn UDC v Prestatyn
Raceway Ltd* by authorising a local authority to take proceedings in their own name. The

terms of s 222 are sufficiently explicit to enable a local authority to bring proceedings in
their own name and to contradict the view that the powers of the local authority under   *a*
s 222 are limited to requesting the Attorney General to allow proceedings to be instituted
in his name at the relation of the local authority. In proceedings instituted to promote or
protect the interests of inhabitants generally, special damage is irrelevant and was
therefore not mentioned in s 222.

Where Parliament conferred jurisdiction on a local authority in the Public Health
1875, the Highways Act 1959 and the Local Government Act 1933, the extent of that   *b*
jurisdiction was partially emasculated by judicial decision and then restored or extended
by the legislature. I can see no justification for emasculating s 222 and Oliver J declined
to do so in *Solihull Metropolitan BC v Maxfern Ltd* [1977] 2 All ER 177, [1977] 1 WLR 127.

In a powerful argument on behalf of the appellants counsel submitted that the
conferment on a local authority of power to institute civil proceedings in aid of public
law is a constitutional change which requires even more explicit language than that   *c*
which is to be found in s 222, presumably an explicit power to institute proceedings
otherwise than in the name and with the consent of the Attorney General. But when
Parliament authorised a local authority to institute proceedings 'in their own name'
Parliament cannot have intended that the local authority should continue to be debarred
from instituting proceedings 'in their own name' but should be obliged to institute
proceedings in the name and with the consent of the Attorney General. Section 222 does   *d*
not deprive the Attorney General of his power to enforce obedience to public law by
proceedings ex officio or by relator action. Section 222 confers an additional power on a
local authority which is charged with the administration of an area. When the present
proceedings were before the Court of Appeal the Attorney General advised the court that
in his view s 222—

> 'was clearly designed to confer a substantial measure of autonomy on local   *e*
> authorities in respect of law enforcement within their areas. The Attorney-General
> welcomes that autonomy in regard to the control of those activities generally
> associated with local authority jurisdiction.'

(See [1984] Ch 1 at 9.)

In *Kent CC v Batchelor* [1978] 3 All ER 980, [1979] 1 WLR 213, s 222 was invoked to   *f*
restrain a farmer who owned woodland subject to a tree preservation order made by a
local authority from damaging or destroying protected trees. This was a typical case in
which the local authority was in a better position than the Attorney General to judge
whether it was expedient for the promotion or protection of the interests of the
inhabitants of their area that proceedings for an injunction should issue.

Counsel for the appellants relied heavily on passages from the speeches in your   *g*
Lordships' House in *Gouriet v Union of Post Office Workers* [1977] 3 All ER 70, [1978] AC
435 which emphasised the important constitutional position of the Attorney General in
enforcing laws on behalf of the public generally and emphasised the unfettered discretion
of the Attorney General to give or withold his consent to the initiation of relator
proceedings. But in that case Viscount Dilhorne made the reservation with which no one
quarrelled that—   *h*

> 'it is the law, and a long established law, that save and insofar as the Local
> Government Act 1972, s 222, gives local authorities a limited power so to do, only
> the Attorney-General can sue on behalf of the public for the purposes of preventing
> public wrongs . . .'

(See [1977] 3 All ER 70 at 94, [1978] AC 435 at 494.)   *j*

The power of the local authorities is of course limited to the promotion or protection
of the interests of the inhabitants of their area.

Counsel for the appellants submitted that the effect and the only effect of s 222 was to
enable a London borough council to sue in their own name. For historical and esoteric
reasons, prior to s 222 of the Local Government Act 1972, a London borough council,
although a local authority, could only sue in the name of the corporation as the mayor

and burgesses of the borough. The result of s 222 is that a London borough council can
a   now sue in that name. This petty and immaterial alteration in nomenclature could not
in my view have been the sole or even an intended object of the differences between
s 276 of the Local Government Act 1933 and s 222 of the Local Government Act 1972.
A desire to change nomenclature could not in any event have been responsible for
inspiring the amendments to the Highways Act 1959 which were effected by the
Highways Act 1971 and which correspond to the amendments made to s 276 of the
b   Local Government Act 1933 by s 222 of the Local Government Act 1972.

Counsel for the appellants argued that the power conferred by s 222(1)(*b*) of the Local
Government Act 1972 for a local authority to make representations at a public inquiry
'in their own name' could not have been designed to remove the necessity for a relator
action. It is not clear what s 222(1)(*b*) was designed to achieve or whether it in fact created
any power which was not exercisable prior to 1972. It may well be that the express power
c   granted by s 222(1)(*b*) for a local authority to make representations in the interests of the
inhabitants at any public inquiry was inserted ex abundanti cautela or was designed to
emphasise that the local authority could make representations on behalf of the inhabitants
generally and not merely on its own behalf and were not obliged to support the views
expressed by those inhabitants who themselves appeared at the inquiry. Whatever the
reasons for s 222(1)(*b*) the provisions of that paragraph do not shed any light on the true
d   construction of s 222(1)(*a*) and do not contradict the meaning and effect of s 222(1)(*a*)
which I have indicated. I agree therefore with the Court of Appeal and Whitford J that
s 222 conferred on the council power in a proper case to institute proceedings in their
own name and without resort to the Attorney General against the appellants. It does not
of course follow that the council were justified in seeking or that Whitford J was justified
in granting an injunction in the present case and counsel for the appellants submitted
e   that the injunction ought now to be discharged.

Section 222 requires that a local authority shall only act if they 'consider it expedient
for the promotion or protection of the interests of the inhabitants of their area.' Any
exercise by the local authority of this statutory power is subject to the control of judicial
review and the application of the principles enunciated in *Associated Provincial Picture
Houses Ltd v Wednesbury Corp* [1947] 2 All ER 680, [1948] 1 KB 223. In considering the
f   exercise of their powers the local authority must take into account matters which they
ought to take into account, ignore matters which they ought not to take into account and
then reach a decision which is not so unreasonable that no reasonable local authority
could have come to it. Where the local authority seeks an injunction, the court will
consider whether the power was rightly exercised and whether in all the circumstances
at the date the application for an injunction is considered by the court, the equitable and
g   discretionary remedy of an injunction should be granted.

In the present case, when the council decided to institute proceedings and when
Whitford J decided to grant an interlocutory injunction, the appellants had committed
offences under the Shops Act 1950. The council invoked the assistance of the civil court
in aid of the criminal law in order to ensure that the appellants did not commit further
offences under the 1950 Act. The right to invoke the assistance of the civil court in aid of
h   the criminal law is a comparatively modern development. Where Parliament imposes a
penalty for an offence, Parliament must consider the penalty is adequate and Parliament
can increase the penalty if it proves to be inadequate. It follows that a local authority
should be reluctant to seek and the court should be reluctant to grant an injunction
which if disobeyed may involve the infringer in sanctions far more onerous than the
penalty imposed for the offence. In *Gouriet v Union of Post Office Workers* [1977] 3 All ER
j   70 at 83, [1978] AC 435 at 481 Lord Wilberforce said that the right to invoke the
assistance of civil courts in aid of the criminal law is 'an exceptional power confined, in
practice, to cases where an offence is frequently repeated in disregard of a, usually,
inadequate penalty . . . or to cases of emergency . . .' In my view there must certainly be
something more than infringement before the assistance of civil proceedings can be
invoked and accorded for the protection or promotion of the interests of the inhabitants
of the area. In the present case the council were concerned with what appeared to be a

proliferation of illegal Sunday trading. The council was by s 71 of the 1950 Act charged with the statutory duty of ensuring compliance with the 1950 Act. The council received letters from traders complaining of infringements of the Sunday trading legislation by other shops and intimating that the complainants would themselves feel obliged to open on Sundays in order to preserve their trade unless the 1950 Act was generally observed. The council could not treat some traders differently from others. The council wrote to warn infringing traders some of whom ceased to trade on Sundays as a result of the warnings. In one case where an ignored warning was followed by the issue of a writ the proceedings resulted in an undertaking to desist. In these circumstances there was ample justification for the council to take the view that it was expedient in the general interests of the inhabitants to take such steps as were necessary to ensure compliance by the appellants with the laws of Sunday trading.

It was said that the council should not have taken civil proceedings until criminal proceedings had failed to persuade the appellants to obey the law. As a general rule a local authority should try the effect of criminal proceedings before seeking the assistance of the civil courts. But the council were entitled to take the view that the appellants would not be deterred by a maximum fine which was substantially less than the profits which could be made from illegal Sunday trading. Delay while this was proved would have encouraged widespread breaches of the law by other traders, resentful of the continued activies of the appellants. The poor trader would be deterred by the threat of a fine; the rich trader would consider breaking the law each Sunday if illegal trading produced profit in excess of the maximum fine and costs. In *Stafford BC v Elkenford Ltd* [1977] 2 All ER 519 at 528, [1977] 1 WLR 324 at 330 Bridge LJ said:

> 'We have been urged to say that the court will only exercise its discretion to restrain by injunction the commission of offences in breach of statutory prohibitions if the plaintiff authority has first shown that it has exhausted the possibility of restraining those breaches by the exercise of the statutory remedies. Ordinarily no doubt that is a very salutory approach to the question whether or not the court will grant an injunction in the exercise of its discretion, but it is not in my judgment an inflexible rule. The reason why it is ordinarily proper to ask whether the authority seeking the injunction has first exhausted the statutory remedies is because in the ordinary case it is only because those remedies have been invoked and have proved inadequate that one can draw the inference, which is the essential foundation for the exercise of the court's discretion to grant an injunction, that the offender is . . . "deliberately and flagrantly flouting the law".'

In the present case any doubt about the attitude of the appellants has been resolved by their attitude to the proceedings themselves. Whitford J concluded that the appellants were proceeding—

> 'on the basis that if an interlocutory injunction be not granted now they would be free to trade . . . they hope, if they are successful in staying the grant of an interlocutory injunction, that they are going to be able to continue to trade in defiance of the provisions of s 47 of the Shops Act 1950.'

Immediately on the opening of the appeal of the appellants to your Lordships' House, my noble and learned friend Lord Diplock inquired whether if the injunction were discharged the appellants intended to resume trading in defiance of the provisions of s 47 of the 1950 Act. No answer has been vouchsafed. Whitford J and the Court of Appeal took the view that on the law and the facts an injunction should issue and I would dismiss this appeal.

Appeal dismissed.

Solicitors: *Clifford-Turner*, agents for *Hepherd Winstanley & Pugh*, Southampton (for the appellants); *Sharpe Pritchard & Co* (for the respondents).

Mary Rose Plummer   Barrister.

a Grand Champion Tankers Ltd v Norpipe A/S and others
The Marion

HOUSE OF LORDS
b LORD DIPLOCK, LORD SCARMAN, LORD ROSKILL, LORD BRANDON OF OAKBROOK AND LORD BRIGHTMAN
2, 3, 4, 5, 9 APRIL, 17 MAY 1984

Shipping – Limitation of liability – Actual fault or privity of owner – Damage caused by master's negligence in using obsolete chart – Ship's managers failing to ensure that master having up-to-date charts – Vessel damaging pipeline not shown on obsolete chart – Whether actual fault of owners – Whether owners under obligation to ensure efficient management of ship in return for benefits conferred by statutory right to limitation of liability – Whether owners entitled to leave navigation matters to discretion of master – Whether owners under duty to ensure master having up-to-date and corrected charts – Whether owners entitled to limitation of liability – Merchant Shipping Act 1894, s 503(1).

In March 1977 a Liberian tanker owned by the appellants left Hamburg on a voyage to Teesside. While waiting to berth at Teesside the master attempted to anchor the vessel and in doing so damaged an oil pipeline lying on the sea bed. The respondents, who were oil companies having an interest in the pipeline, brought an action against the appellants in the Admiralty Court alleging that the damage to the pipeline had been caused by the negligence of the appellants' servants or agents on board the vessel and claimed damages in excess of $US25m. The appellants admitted liability for the fouling of the pipeline and consequential damage done to it but commenced a limitation action of their own against the respondents seeking to have their total liability in respect of the damage limited to some £982,000 by virtue of the limitation provisions in the Merchant Shipping Acts 1894 to 1979. The respondents contended (i) that the immediate cause of the damage was the negligence of the master of the vessel in navigating by reference to an obsolete chart on which the pipeline was not shown and that if he had had an up-to-date chart he would have been aware of the existence of the pipeline, (ii) that, having regard to the express provisions of s 503(1)[a] of the Merchant Shipping Act 1894, the appellants were only entitled to limitation of liability if they could show that the damage to the pipeline had occurred 'without their actual fault or privity', the burden being on the appellants to prove (a) that there was no actual fault on their part and (b) if there was, that it did not contribute to the damage to the pipeline, and (iii) that, since the appellants had entirely delegated the management and operation of the vessel to an English company of ship managers, any fault on the managers' part constituted, as a matter of law, the actual fault of the appellants, and in fact the managers were at fault (a) in failing to provide a proper system for ensuring that charts and other nautical publications on board the vessel were not obsolete or superseded, or, if still current, were kept up to date at all times, and (b) in failing to ensure that a Liberian safety inspectorate report relating

---

a   Section 503(1), so far as material, provides: 'The owners of a ship, British or foreign, shall not, where all or any of the following occurrences take place without their actual fault or privity; (that is to say,) . . . (d) Where any loss or damage is caused to any property (other than any property [on board the ship]) . . . through the act or omission of any person (whether on board the ship or not) in the navigation or management of the ship . . . or through any other act or omission of any person on board the ship; be liable to damages beyond the following amounts; (that is to say,) . . . (ii) In respect of such loss, damage or infringement as is mentioned in paragraph . . . (d) of this subsection, whether there be in addition loss of life or personal injury or not, an aggregate amount not exceeding [an amount equivalent to 1,000 gold francs] for each ton of their ship's tonnage.'

to the omission of corrections to the vessel's navigational charts was brought to their
managing director's notice, which if it had been would have resulted in the corrections   *a*
being made. At the trial of the limitation action the judge held that, having regard to
evidence of the practice of other experienced shipowners and managers, the provision of
charts and their maintenance were the responsibility of the master, and the appellants
and their managers had quite properly left such matters to him. The judge accordingly
held that the damage to the pipeline had occurred without actual fault on the part of the
appellants and granted them a decree of limitation of liability. The respondents appealed   *b*
to the Court of Appeal, which allowed the appeal and held that the appellants were not
entitled to a decree of limitation. The appellants appealed to the House of Lords.

Held – As part of the obligation imposed on a shipowner to ensure efficient management
of his ship in return for the benefits conferred by the statutory right to limitation of
liability, the shipowner or his manager was required to exercise sufficient supervision   *c*
over the master of the ship in relation to the ship's charts to ensure (a) that the ship should
have on board and available for use the current versions of the charts necessary for the
ship's voyage, (b) that any obsolete or superseded charts which might formerly have been
proper for use on such a voyage should either be destroyed or at least be segregated from
the current charts in such a way as to avoid the possibility of confusion between them,
and (c) that either the current charts should be kept corrected up to date at all times, or at   *d*
least such corrections should be made prior to their possible use on any particular voyage.
In having no proper system for ensuring that the charts and other nautical publications
on board the vessel were not obsolete or superseded or if still current were kept up to
date and also in not ensuring that their managing director had given proper instructions
to ensure that the Liberian safety inspectorate report was brought to his notice, the
appellants' managers were at fault and that fault was, as a matter of law, the actual fault   *e*
of the appellants. Accordingly, it was impossible for the appellants to show that the
damage to the pipeline had not been caused 'without their actual fault' and therefore
they were not entitled to take advantage of the statutory limitation of liability. The
appeal would therefore be dismissed (see p 345 *d* to *f*, p 347 *j* to p 348 *c*, p 350 *f* to *j* and
p 352 *b* to *j*, post).

Northern Fishing Co (Hull) Ltd v Eddom, The Norman [1960] 1 Lloyd's Rep 1, The Lady   *f*
Gwendolen, Arthur Guinness Son & Co (Dublin) Ltd v Freshfield (owners) [1965] 2 All ER 283
and Rederij Erven H Groen and Groen v The England (owners) [1973] 1 Lloyd's Rep 373
applied.

Notes
For limitation of liability of shipowners and others, see 43 Halsbury's Laws (4th edn) para
1100, and for cases on the subject, see 43 Digest (Reissue) 630–633, 11413–11431.   *g*
For exclusion of limitation of liability for actual fault or privity, see 43 Halsbury's
Laws (4th edn) para 1108, and for cases on the subject, see 43 Digest (Reissue) 640,
11479–11482.
For the Merchant Shipping Act 1894, s 503, see 31 Halsbury's Statutes (3rd edn) 328.
As from a day to be appointed s 503 of the 1894 Act is to be repealed by the Merchant
Shipping Act 1979, s 50(4) and Sch 7 (subject to a saving in s 35 thereof) and fresh   *h*
provision for the limitation of liability of shipowners is made by s 17 of and Pt II of Sch
4 to the 1979 Act.

Cases referred to in opinions
Lady Gwendolen, The, Arthur Guinness Son & Co (Dublin) Ltd v Freshfield (owners) [1965] 2
    All ER 283, [1965] P 294, [1965] 3 WLR 91, CA.   *j*
Northern Fishing Co (Hull) Ltd v Eddom, The Norman [1960] 1 Lloyd's Rep 1, HL.
Rederij Erven H Groen and Groen v The England (owners) [1973] 1 Lloyd's Rep 373, CA.
Yuille v B & B Fisheries (Leigh) Ltd and Bates, The Radiant [1958] 2 Lloyd's Rep 596.

Appeal
Grand Champion Tankers Ltd appealed, with the leave of the Appeal Committee of the
House of Lords granted on 20 October 1983, against the decision of the Court of Appeal

(Sir John Donaldson MR, Dunn and Purchas LJJ) ([1983] 2 Lloyd's Rep 156) dated 20
a May 1983 allowing the appeal of the respondents, Norpipe A/S (a corporate body), the
Royal Ministry of Oil and Energy, Den Norske Stats Oljeselskap A/S (otherwise Statoil),
Phillips Petroleum Co Ltd, American Petrofina Exploration Co of Norway, Norske Fina
A/S, Norsk Agip A/S, Elf Aquitaine Norge A/S, Norsk Hydro A/S, Total Marine Norsk
A/S, Eurofrep Norge A/S, Coparex Norge A/S, Cofranord A/S, and all other persons
claiming or being entitled to claim damages by reason of or arising out of damage caused
b to the Tees-Ekofisk oil pipeline by the appellants' vessel Marion, from the judgment of
Sheen J ([1982] 2 Lloyd's Rep 52) dated 20 March 1982 whereby he held that the
appellants were entitled to limit their liability in respect of damages caused by the
appellants' vessel Marion to the oil pipeline. The facts are set out in the opinion of Lord
Brandon.

c   *Anthony Clarke QC* and *Jeremy Russell* for the appellants.
   Gordon Pollock QC and *David Steel QC* for the respondents.

Their Lordships took time for consideration.

17 May. The following opinions were delivered.
d
LORD DIPLOCK. My Lords, I have had the advantage of reading in draft the speech
of my noble and learned friend Lord Brandon. I agree with it, and for the reasons which
he gives I would dismiss this appeal.

LORD SCARMAN. My Lords, I have had the advantage of reading in draft the speech
e to be delivered by my noble and learned friend Lord Brandon. I agree with it, and for
the reasons he gives I would dismiss the appeal with costs.

LORD ROSKILL. My Lords, I have had the advantage of reading in draft the speech
to be delivered by my noble and learned friend Lord Brandon. I agree with it, and for
the reasons which he gives I would dismiss this appeal.
f
LORD BRANDON OF OAKBROOK. My Lords, on 12 March 1977 the Liberian
tanker Marion, owned by the appellants, left Hamburg for Teesside in order to load a
cargo there. On 14 March the Marion arrived near the entrance to the Teesside fairway,
but, because there was no loading berth immediately available for her, she was obliged
to come to anchor and wait. The place where her master, Captain Potenza, chose to
g anchor her was off Hartlepool about 2·7 miles east of The Heugh and about one mile
from the Tees fairway buoy. Four days later, on 18 March, a loading berth having
become available for her, the Marion tried to weigh anchor so as to enable her to proceed
inward to that berth. Her efforts to do so, however, failed because her anchor had fouled
a pipeline on the sea bed which carries oil from the Ekofisk Field through Tees Bay to
Teesside. As a result of the anchor of the Marion so fouling the pipeline, and of her efforts
h to haul it up after that had happened, the pipeline was severely damaged.
        On 27 September 1977 the 13 named respondents, all of whom are oil companies of
one kind or another, brought an action against the appellants in the Admiralty Court in
which they alleged that the fouling of the pipeline by the anchor of the Marion, and the
damage to the pipeline resulting from such fouling, had been caused by the negligence
of the servants or agents of the appellants on board that ship. The amount of the damages
j claimed in the action exceeded $US25m.
        On 23 July 1981 the appellants formally admitted liability for the fouling of the
pipeline and the consequential damage done to it. On the following day, 24 July, the
appellants began an action of their own in the Admiralty Court against the 13 named
respondents and all other persons having claims in respect of the damage to the pipeline,
in which they claimed a decree that they were entitled to have their total liability in
respect of such damage limited to the sum of £982,292·06, pursuant to the relevant
provisions of the Merchant Shipping Acts 1894 to 1979.

The limitation action was tried by Sheen J over a period of 32 days in January, February
and March 1982. On 30 March 1982 the judge, in a reserved judgment, decided the
action in favour of the appellants and granted them the decree of limitation of liability
which they sought (see [1982] 2 Lloyd's Rep 52).

By notice of appeal dated 10 May 1982 the 13 named respondents appealed to the
Court of Appeal against the decision of Sheen J. The appeal was heard by a division of the
Court of Appeal consisting of Sir John Donaldson MR, Dunn and Purchas LJJ over a
period of seven days in April and May 1983. On 20 May 1983 the Court of Appeal, in
reserved judgments, unanimously allowed the appeal, ordered that the appellants be
refused a decree of limitation of liability and refused them leave to appeal to your
Lordships' House (see [1983] 2 Lloyd's Rep 156). Leave for the appellants to do so was
later given by the Appeal Committee.

My Lords, the issues between the parties have fortunately been considerably narrowed
since the lengthy hearing of the action before Sheen J. The following matters of fact and
law, or of mixed fact and law, were common ground before your Lordships. Firstly, that,
if the appellants are entitled to limit their liability, the sum of £982,292·06 referred to
earlier is the correct amount of their limited liability. Secondly, that the immediate cause
of the damage to the pipeline was the negligence of the master of the Marion, Captain
Potenza, in navigating by reference to a long obsolete chart on which the pipeline was
not shown, leading him to let go his anchor in a place where, if he had been aware of the
presence of the pipeline, as he would have been if he had navigated by reference to an
up-to-date chart, he would never have done. Thirdly, that, having regard to the express
terms of s 503 of the Merchant Shipping Act 1894, as amended by the Merchant Shipping
(Liability of Shipowners and Others) Act 1958, the material parts of which are to be
found set out in full in the judgment of Sheen J (see [1982] 2 Lloyd's Rep 52 at 54), the
appellants are only entitled to have their liability limited if they can prove that the
damage to the pipeline occurred without actual fault on their part. Fourthly, that, on the
true construction of the statutory provisions referred to above, the burden of proving (a)
that there was no actual fault of the appellants and (b) that, if there was any such actual
fault, it did not contribute to the damage to the pipeline is in either case on the appellants.
Fifthly, that, since the appellants had delegated the management and operation of the
Marion wholly to an English company, Fairfield-Maxwell Services Ltd (FMSL), the person
whose fault would constitute, as a matter of law, the actual fault of the appellants is the
managing director of FMSL, Mr Downard. Sixthly, that, whereas FMSL employed three
other persons in a managerial capacity, namely Mr Lowry as operations manager, Mr
Graham as assistant operations manager and Mr Martinengo (an engineer) as
superintendent, no faults of theirs, if they occurred, could constitute, as a matter of law,
the actual fault of the appellants.

There were two main respects in which it was contended for the 13 named respondents
that the appellants had failed to discharge the burden of proving that there had been no
fault on the part of Mr Downard which contributed to the damage to the pipeline. First,
it was said that the appellants had not proved that Mr Downard had a proper system for
ensuring that the charts and other nautical publications on board the Marion (a) were not
obsolete or superseded or (b), if still current, were kept corrected up to date at all times.
Second, it was said that the appellants had not proved that there had been no fault of Mr
Downard in failing to ensure that there was brought to his notice a document received
by FMSL from the Liberian marine inspectorate on 28 April 1976 and known as a safety
inspection report, relating to an inspection of the Marion in February of that year. That
report stated among other things 'Nav. charts for trade of vessel corrections obmitted
[sic] for several years', and it was said that, if Mr Downard had seen that report and read
that statement, he would, on his own admission, have taken immediate and radical steps,
which his subordinates did not take, to put matters right.

It will be necessary later to examine the evidence, and the findings of the two courts
below, with regard to the two criticisms of Mr Downard referred to above. Before doing
that, however, it will, I think be helpful to indicate the approach which courts have in
recent years adopted to questions of actual fault on the part of shipowners or ship
managers in contested limitation actions.

a The question whether, where damage had been done by a ship, such damage occurred without the actual fault of her owners or managers is primarily one of fact, to be decided by reference to all the circumstances of any particular case. Such a question involves nevertheless an element of law, in that the answer to it must depend, in part at least, on what approach courts dealing with contested limitation actions adopt, in relation to safety of navigation, to the responsibilities of masters on the one hand and shipowners or ship managers on the other.

b There was a time when courts dealing with contested limitation actions considered that shipowners or ship managers sufficiently discharged their responsibilities if they appointed a competent master and thereafter left all questions of safe navigation, including the obtaining at their expense of all necessary charts and other nautical publications, entirely to him. That former approach of such courts has now been out of date for more than 20 years, as appears from the decision of the Court of Appeal in *Rederij Erven H Groen and Groen v The England (owners)* [1973] 1 Lloyd's Rep 373.

c The issue in that case was whether Mr Groen, the owner of a motor coaster which traded frequently to the Port of London without the assistance of a pilot, was guilty of actual fault contributing to a collision between his ship and another in the River Thames, in that he had failed to take any, or any proper, steps to ensure that the master of his ship had on board, and available for his use, a copy of the latest Port of London River Byelaws.

d It was held by the Court of Appeal, reversing the Admiralty judge, that Mr Groen had been guilty of actual fault in this respect, and that it had not been proved that such fault did not contribute to the collision.

In relation to that issue, Sir Gordon Willmer, who was the acknowledged master of Admiralty law in his time, said (at 383):

e 'It may be that 20 years ago what Mr. Groen did and did not do might have passed muster; but the decision of the House of Lords in the case of *The Norman* ([1960] 1 Lloyd's Rep 1) seems to me to have thrown quite a fresh light on the extent of the managerial duties of owners and managers, especially in relation to the supply of navigational information and publications to their vessels. It seems to me that it is no longer permissible for owners or managers to wash their hands so completely of

f all questions of navigation, or to leave everything to the unassisted discretion of their masters. This relatively new approach, as I think it is, was well illustrated by the decision of this court in *The Lady Gwendolen* ([1965] 2 All ER 283, [1965] P 294). I am not going to go into the details of that case, the facts of which were very different from those of the present case, but I venture to quote two sentences from the judgment which I myself delivered in that case ... I am reported as saying

g ([1965] 2 All ER 283 at 296, [1965] P 294 at 345): "... It seems to me that any company which embarks on the business of shipowning must accept the obligation to ensure efficient management of its ships if it is to enjoy the very considerable benefits conferred by the statutory right to limitation." Then, after referring to another case called *The Radiant* ([1958] 2 Lloyd's Rep 596) where again the facts were quite different from those of the present case, I proceeded to quote a sentence

h which I had used in delivering judgment in that case, and which again I think is appropriate to this case: "... The fundamental fault in respect of which I am disposed to blame Mr. B. [that is the manager] is that he never had any proper comprehension of what his duty as managing director of a fleet of this sort was ...". It appears to me that Mr. Hendrikus Groen was very much in the same position as the managing owner in that case.'

j My Lords, I am of the opinion that what Sir Gordon Willmer there described as 'This relatively new approach', begun by your Lordships' House in *The Norman* in 1960 and continued by the two subsequent decisions of the Court of Appeal in *The Lady Gwendolen* in 1965 and *The England* in 1973, should now be regarded as the correct approach in law to the problem of actual fault of shipowners or ship managers in contested limitation actions. It follows that I regard it as right to apply that approach to the facts of the present case.

I shall consider first the criticism of Mr Downard that he had no proper system for ensuring that the charts on board the Marion (a) were not obsolete or superseded or (b), if still current, were kept corrected up to date. It was not, and could not sensibly, have been disputed that, in order to ensure the safe navigation of a ship on the voyages undertaken by her, three requirements with regard to charts have to be fulfilled. The first requirement is that she should have on board, and available for use, the current versions of the charts necessary for such voyages. The second requirement is that any obsolete or superseded charts, which might formerly have been proper for use on such voyages, should either be destroyed, or, if not destroyed, at least segregated from the current charts in such a way as to avoid any possibility of confusion between them. The third requirement is that the current charts should either be kept corrected up to date at all times, or at least that such corrections should be made prior to their possible use on any particular voyage.

Mr Downard took over as managing director of FMSL in the summer of 1975, and he was assisted, as I have already indicated, by three subordinates with managerial responsibilities, Mr Lowry as operations manager, Mr Graham as assistant operations manager and Mr Martinengo as superintendent. His system with regard to charts was to make the master of the Marion solely responsible for ensuring, with the aid of one or more of his deck officers, that the three requirements referred to above were fulfilled. The master indented for the charts which he thought necessary and FMSL paid the bill for them. FMSL also continued a practice, which had been begun in December 1974, before Mr Downard took over as managing director, of sending to the Marion on a regular basis all weekly Admiralty notices to mariners and all chart correction traces relating to Admiralty charts. Mr Downard, deliberately and as a matter of considered policy, did not either himself, or through Mr Lowry or Mr Graham, exercise any supervision of any kind over the way in which the master of the Marion, who was ordinarily for many years Captain Potenza, performed the responsibilities with regard to charts which had been assigned to him. The criticism made of this system is that it provided no means by which Mr Downard could know whether those responsibilities were being discharged properly or not. In fact Captain Potenza had for years a curious propensity for using out-of-date or uncorrected charts in preference to current and corrected charts, of which, because of the absence of any supervision in this field, Mr Downard remained blissfully unaware.

In considering whether this lack of supervision was a fault on Mr Downard's part, the practices of other reputable shipowners at or about the same time is clearly relevant, although, unless the evidence of such practices is all one way, or nearly all one way, it cannot be decisive. The parties adduced before the judge at the trial a whole mass of evidence, both oral and written, with regard to the practices of other reputable shipowners. His judgment is reported (see [1982] 2 Lloyd's Rep 52), and he expressed his conclusions about this evidence in a paragraph which reads (at 64):

'The totality of the evidence has left me in no doubt that a large majority of shipowners of high reputation regard the provision of charts and their maintenance as matters which are quite properly left to the responsibility of the master. In the light of all the evidence which I have heard I am quite satisfied that a prudent shipowner is entitled to regard the provision of charts as the responsibility of the master unless he has good reason to think that the master is not carrying out his responsibility. In that event further action is required. It may even become necessary to relieve the master of his command.'

If the first sentence of this paragraph with regard to the totality of the evidence relating to practice had been justified, it would have represented a finding of fact by the trial judge which, though not in theory decisive in showing that Mr Downard was not in fault for using the system which he did use, would in practice have gone a long way in that direction. The Court of Appeal, however, did not accept that either the finding of fact or the conclusion drawn from it by Sheen J were justified by the evidence. The judgments of that court are also reported (see [1983] 2 Lloyd's Rep 156), from which it appears that the leading judgment was, at the request of Sir John Donaldson MR, delivered by Dunn LJ. Dunn LJ, after referring to the passage from the judgment of Sheen J set out above, said (at 164):

> 'I am bound to say, having been taken through the relevant transcripts of evidence of the expert witnesses, that I am very doubtful if I would have come to the same conclusion as the learned Judge.'

Although Dunn LJ does not there say in terms that he would, in the light of the evidence, have reached a conclusion about its overall effect contrary to that reached by Sheen J, I think it is clear from other parts of his judgment that that is indeed what he would have done.

Be that as it may, at the hearing of this appeal before your Lordships, you were, very sensibly, referred to only comparatively small parts of the vast mass of evidence on practice. Instead, counsel for the 13 named respondents placed before your Lordships, in the form of two schedules, the contents of which were not seriously challenged by counsel for the appellants, a summary of the essential evidence of practice adduced on either side. Those schedules show, as counsel for the appellants had no alternative but to admit, that the finding of Sheen J that, on the totality of the evidence, a large majority of shipowners of high reputation regard the provision of charts and their maintenance as matters which are quite properly left to the responsibility of the master, without any supervision by owners or their managerial representatives, cannot be supported.

The schedules instead are indicative of three main matters. The first matter indicated by them is that, while a substantial number of reputable shipowners do rely solely on their masters for obtaining and maintaining charts, without exercising any supervision over them in this respect, a majority of such shipowners are not content with such a system or lack of system. That majority, while relying primarily on their masters for obtaining and maintaining charts, exercise a degree of supervision over them in order to satisfy themselves that they are carrying out properly their duties in that field. The forms of supervision used vary considerably, depending no doubt on the size of the companies concerned, the number and types of ships which they operate and the trades in which such ships are employed. The forms of supervision used, however, include, first, regular or random checks by marine superintendents or other qualified managerial staff when ships are visited by such persons in port, second, the complete overhaul, in the form of inspection and checking of chart rooms and their contents, at regular or irregular intervals, and, third, the complete landing of the contents of chart rooms for inspection and checking, again at regular or irregular intervals.

The second main matter which the schedules indicate is that the practice of relying solely on the master, without exercising any supervision over him, is characteristic mainly of shipowners in the United States. It further appears, from some of the evidence, that one reason for this sole reliance is, as one witness very frankly put it, that some shipowners 'do not want to know'. That deliberate ignorance may well be attributable to the fear of the award of punitive damages by juries in the United States in the event of marine casualties caused by the use of obsolete or uncorrected charts of which, if shipowners did exercise supervision, they might be found to have been actually or constructively aware.

The third matter which the schedules indicate is that, during the last 20 years or so, an increasing number of shipowners have adopted a system involving at least some degree of supervision of their masters in relation to charts.

The Marion operated under the Panamanian flag until 1975, when, following her purchase by the appellants, she changed to operating under the Liberian flag. On that change it became the appellants' duty to pay regard to Liberian notices to mariners issued not only after, but also before, her change of flag.

In March 1972 the Bureau of Maritime Affairs of the Republic of Liberia had issued a marine notice, addressed to shipowners, masters and officers of merchant ships, informing them that an amendment adopted by the IMCO Assembly should from then onwards apply to all Liberian ships. That notice stated:

> 'All ships shall carry adequate and up-to-date charts, sailing directions, lists of

lights, notices to mariners, tide tables and all other nautical publications necessary for the intended voyage.'

In August 1972 a further marine notice was issued by the Liberian authorities. It was addressed to shipowners, masters and officers of merchant ships and it expressly described its subject matter as 'Navigational Charts, Publications and Notices to Mariners'. The full text of the notice is set out in the judgment of Dunn LJ ([1983] 2 Lloyd's Rep 156 at 163). For present purposes it is sufficient to say that it included the following significant passage:

'Reports on investigations of strandings and other navigational casualties continue to show an alarming increase in the number of such accidents wherein the direct or proximate cause has been attributed to failure to have on board up-to-date charts, publications, notices and similar navigational data.'

My Lords, I quoted earlier a passage from the judgment of Dunn LJ in the Court of Appeal dealing with the evidence of practice, and expressing a doubt, which the schedules placed before your Lordships amply justify, about the conclusion reached by Sheen J on that evidence. It now becomes apposite to set out a further passage from the judgment of Dunn LJ which follows immediately after the passage quoted earlier. The Lord Justice continued as follows (at 164):

'It seems to me, in the light of the Liberian Marine Notices, that the practice, if it be a practice, of leaving the correction of charts wholly to the master, without even knowing what if any system was in operation on board the vessel, and without any supervision of the master and his officers, was fraught with danger, and not consistent with the high standard of care the Judge held was owed by shipowners in relation to charts. If, as here, the master is grossly negligent and effectively operates no system at all for the correction of charts, that will not come to light unless and until there is a casualty. I cannot regard that as a satisfactory situation where the safety of lives and valuable property is concerned.'

What Dunn LJ was there saying about the correction of charts still basically current applies a fortiori to the destruction or effective segregation of charts which have become obsolete, and have on that account been superseded by other and more modern charts.

I stated earlier, after referring to what had been said by Sir Gordon Willmer in *Rederij Erven H Groen and Groen v The England (owners)* [1973] 1 Lloyd's Rep 373 at 383, that what he there described as 'This relatively new approach' should now be regarded as the correct approach in law to the problem of actual fault of shipowners or ship managers in contested limitation actions and that it would be right to apply that approach to the facts of the present case. Proceeding on that basis, I entirely agree with the strictures made by Dunn LJ on the system, or perhaps more correctly the lack of system, followed by FMSL in their management and operation of the Marion, so far as the obtaining and keeping up to date of charts are concerned. It was the duty of Mr Downard to ensure that an adequate degree of supervision of the master of the Marion in this field was exercised, either by himself or by his subordinate managerial staff, Mr Lowry or Mr Graham, each of whom was fully qualified to exercise such supervision. I am further of the opinion that, in so far as Mr Downard failed to perform his duty in this respect, such failure constituted in law actual fault of the appellants.

Having dealt with the first criticism of Mr Downard, that he had no proper system for ensuring that the charts and other nautical publications on board the Marion (a) were not obsolete or superseded or (b), if still current, were kept corrected up-to-date, and having held that that criticism was justified, I turn now to the second criticism made against him. That was that he failed to ensure that there was brought to his notice a document received by FMSL from the Liberian marine inspectorate on 26 April 1976, and in consequence failed to take proper steps to remedy the deplorable state of affairs with regard to navigational charts revealed by that report. In order to examine this second criticism properly, it is necessary to record some further facts as found by the trial judge.

Early in 1976 the Marion went to Genoa dockyard for repairs and maintenance. On 5

February 1976, while the ship was there, an inspection of her was carried out by or on behalf of the marine inspection division of the Liberian Bureau of Maritime Affairs. The report of that inspection was signed on 27 February 1976 by Captain Manca, who had been master of the Marion at the time of the inspection, but was superseded by Captain Potenza on 26 February 1976.

Part G of the report is entitled 'Navigational Charts, Publications and Records'. The report on the Marion contained in Part G, opposite the head of information 'd Navi. Charts', the devastating comment 'Nav. charts for trade of vessel corrections obmitted [sic] for several years'.

That report was sent to FMSL with a covering letter dated 20 April 1976, and was received by FMSL on 28 April 1976. It was read by Mr Lowry and Mr Graham. Mr Downard, however, was at that time absent in Greece on another assignment, and he was not informed about the receipt of the report, or the devastatingly adverse comment contained in it with regard to navigational charts. I shall consider later the reason why he was so left uninformed.

On 9 June 1976, more than six weeks after FMSL received the report, Mr Graham, in his capacity as assistant operations manager, wrote a letter to Captain Potenza about various aspects of the report, including the adverse comment relating to navigational charts. In this connection he stated that the action which FMSL required Captain Potenza to take was as follows:

'4. Ensure that all charts and navigational publications are regularly corrected in accordance with the information contained in the Weekly Admiralty Notices to Mariners which are sent to you. A careful record of the corrections are to be made and kept for future inspection.

5. Compile and mail to us soonest a requisition for Admiralty Charts and Navigational Publications which need to be replaced to ensure that your vessel has an adequate outfit of charts and publications which are corrected to the most recent information available. As soon as new editions are received by you, obsolete copies are to be destroyed.'

Mr Graham ended the letter with these requests:

'Please acknowledge receipt of this letter by returning a signed copy as provided. Also please advise progress made in rectifying deficiencies referred to in the report of Safety Inspection.'

Captain Potenza did not comply with the first of these requests, but Mr Graham reasonably inferred, from subsequent requisitions by him for a substantial number of new charts, that he must have received it. As to the second request, there were no progress reports from Captain Potenza in respect of the matters referred to as items 4 and 5 in the body of the letter quoted above, and no, or no effective, follow-up by Mr Graham or Mr Lowry.

Mr Downard agreed in evidence that the report disclosed an appalling situation in regard to the charts on board the Marion and was such as to destroy his confidence in the system for the provision and maintenance of charts, and his confidence in the master. He said that he should have been told of the report (he did not in fact become aware of it until after the fouling of the pipeline in March 1977), and that, if he had, he would have sent a representative of Potters (well-known chart suppliers) to make a thorough inspection of the charts, and, if the position was unsatisfactory, he would have considered dismissing the master. In short he would have taken prompt and effective action himself instead of the delayed and ineffective action taken by Mr Graham, under the direction of Mr Lowry.

With regard to this aspect of the case, Sheen J found that the action to be taken on the report was a matter which could quite properly be delegated by Mr Downard to Mr Graham, who was sufficiently qualified to deal with the matter. In the Court of Appeal, however, a different view was taken. Dunn LJ said (at 165):

'Mr. Lowry should never have been allowed to take the decision, and Captain Downard was at fault in permitting a situation to exist in which important

operational decisions affecting the safety of the vessel were taken by Mr. Lowry . . .
It is not for the Court to say what action should have been taken by Captain
Downard when he left for Greece in 1976. But he should at least have ensured that
operational matters, especially those relevant to the safety of the vessel, were left in
competent hands or, if he had any doubts about his subordinates (which he appears
to have had) he should have ensured that a matter as important as the Liberian
report was brought to his personal attention. In fact he failed to take any step at all
to deal with an adverse safety report by the Liberian authorities, although he must
have known that there was to be a safety inspection when the vessel was in dry dock
at Genoa.'

Once again I consider that the strictures made by Dunn LJ are fully justified.

It was strongly urged on your Lordships by counsel for the appellants that the only
fault in relation to Mr Downard not having the Liberian report brought to his notice was
that of Mr Lowry and Mr Graham. Their faults were not, as a matter of law, the actual
fault of the appellants. There was, accordingly, no actual fault of the appellants in this
respect.

My Lords, I am not prepared to accept this contention. Mr Downard, during the
prolonged periods when he was absent in Greece, was in frequent contact with FMSL,
presumably by telex or telephone, and there would have been no practical difficulty
about his being informed of the Liberian report and its contents. It is, in my view, an
inescapable inference from the fact that neither Mr Lowry nor Mr Graham told him of
the report and its contents that the instructions which he left behind him when he went
to Greece, with regard to the matters about which he required that he should be kept
informed, were insufficiently clear, or insufficiently precise, or insufficiently comprehensive. If that inference is drawn, as drawn I think it must be, it follows that it was at least
in part Mr Downard's own fault that he was not told about the report. In so far as it was
his own fault, it constituted, as a matter of law, actual fault of the appellants.

My Lords, in the result I conclude that there were two actual faults of the appellants:
first, in Mr Downard's failure to have a proper system of supervision in relation to charts;
and, second, in failing, when he departed for Greece, to give to Mr Lowry and Mr
Graham instructions with regard to the matters about which he required to be kept
informed which were sufficiently clear, precise and comprehensive.

There remains only the question of causation, which presents little difficulty, especially
having regard to the incidence of the burden of proof. The appellants could not, and did
not, prove that, if FMSL had had a proper system of supervision in relation to charts,
Captain Potenza would still in March 1977 have been navigating with a hopelessly
obsolete chart, even though a modern one showing the pipeline was on board and
available to him. Equally the appellants could not, and did not, prove that, if Mr
Downard had been informed promptly about the Liberian report and its contents, the
same events would still have taken place. The likelihood is, in either case, that Captain
Potenza would either have been persuaded by FMSL to abandon his propensity for
navigating with obsolete charts or, if he proved to be incapable of reform in that respect,
have been relieved of his command. In these circumstances it is impossible for the
appellants to establish that the two actual faults of the appellants which I have held were
committed did not contribute to the damage to the pipeline.

My Lords, for the reasons which I have given, I am of opinion that the Court of Appeal
was right to reverse the decision of Sheen J, and that this appeal should be dismissed with
costs accordingly.

LORD BRIGHTMAN. My Lords, I agree that the appeal should be dismissed for the
reasons given by my noble and learned friend Lord Brandon.

Appeal dismissed.

Solicitors: *Clyde & Co* (for the appellants); *Coward Chance* (for the respondents).

Mary Rose Plummer   Barrister.

The Antonis P Lemos

COURT OF APPEAL, CIVIL DIVISION
CUMMING-BRUCE AND PARKER LJJ
30, 31 JANUARY, 14 FEBRUARY 1984

Admiralty – Jurisdiction – Action in rem – Claim arising out of agreement relating to carriage of goods in a ship or to use or hire of a ship – Agreement – Whether 'agreement' must be agreement between plaintiff and defendant – Whether relevant that cause of action cannot be pleaded without reference to agreement – Whether fact that claim cannot be pleaded without reference to agreement conclusive that claim 'arising out of' agreement – Supreme Court Act 1981, s 20(1)(a)(2)(h).

In order for a plaintiff's claim to arise out of an 'agreement relating to the carriage of goods in a ship or to the use or hire of a ship', within s 20(2)(h)ª of the Supreme Court Act 1981, so as to found the Admiralty jurisdiction of the High Court under s 20(1)(a) of that Act, it is necessary for the plaintiff to establish merely that his claim arises out of an agreement of the relevant kind, ie an agreement relating to the carriage of goods in a ship or to the use or hire of a ship, and it is irrelevant that the agreement in question may not be an agreement between the plaintiff and the defendant. Moreover, if the cause of action cannot be pleaded without reference to a relevant agreement, that is a factor to be taken into consideration when determining whether the claim falls within the terms of s 20(2)(h); but the mere fact that the claim cannot be pleaded without reference to such an agreement is not conclusive that the claim is a claim 'arising out of' the agreement (see p 355 j to p 356 a and f g, p 357 e f and p 358 a, post).

Notes

For the Admiralty jurisdiction of the High Court, see 1 Halsbury's Laws (4th edn) paras 307–312, and for cases on the subject, see 1(1) Digest (Reissue) 219–223, 1240–1251.

For the Supreme Court Act 1981, s 20, see 51 Halsbury's Statutes (3rd edn) 612.

Cases referred to in judgments

Jade, The, The Eschersheim, Erkowit (owners) v Jade (owners), Erkowit (cargo owners) v Eschersheim (owners) [1976] 1 All ER 920, [1976] 1 WLR 430, HL.
Moschanthy, The [1971] 1 Lloyd's Rep 37.
Nuova Raffaelina, The (1871) LR 3 A & E 483.
Queen of the South, The, Corps (trading as Corps Bros) v Queen of the South (owners) (Port of London Authority intervening) [1968] 1 All ER 1163, [1968] P 449, [1968] 2 WLR 973.
St Elefterio, The, Schwarz & Co (Grain) Ltd v St Elefterio ex-Arion (owners) [1957] 2 All ER 374, [1957] P 179, [1957] 2 WLR 935.
Sennar, The [1983] 1 Lloyd's Rep 295.
Stag Line Ltd v Foscolo Mango & Co Ltd [1932] AC 328, [1931] All ER Rep 666, HL.

Cases also cited

Astro Vencedor Cia Naviera SA of Panama v Mabanaft GmbH [1971] 2 All ER 1301, [1971] 2 QB 588, CA.
Buchanan (James) & Co Ltd v Babco Forwarding and Shipping (UK) Ltd [1977] 3 All ER 1048, [1978] AC 141, HL.
Heyman v Darwins Ltd [1942] 1 All ER 337, [1942] AC 356.
I Congreso del Partido [1981] 2 All ER 1064, [1983] 1 AC 244, HL.
Union of India v E B Aaby's Rederi A/S [1974] 2 All ER 874, [1975] AC 797, HL.

---

a Section 20, so far as material, is set out at pp 355 c d, post

Interlocutory appeal

The plaintiffs, Samick Lines Co Ltd, appealed, pursuant to the leave of the judge, from   *a*
the order of Sheen J made on 27 May 1983 on an application by the defendants, the
owners of the ship Antonis P Lemos (the respondents), setting aside the writ in rem
issued on 20 May 1983 by the appellants against the ship and the warrant of arrest of the
ship they had obtained against the ship. In releasing the ship from arrest Sheen J imposed
certain conditions as to security and costs. The facts are set out in the judgment of Parker
LJ.   *b*

Bernard Rix QC and *Peter Hayward* for the appellants.
Mark O Saville QC and *Jonathan Gaisman* for the respondents.

Cur adv vult
c

14 February. The following judgments were delivered.

PARKER LJ (giving the first judgment at the invitation of Cumming-Bruce LJ). By a
charterparty dated 16 October 1981 between the appellants as charterers and Sammisa
Co Ltd of Seoul (Sammisa), described as owners, the appellants chartered the vessel
Antonis P Lemos, owned by the respondents, for one time-chartered trip. The   *d*
charterparty provided that the charterers were to have liberty to sublet the vessel but
were to advise owners of any subletting.

At the time the vessel was on time charter to Sammisa under a charterparty dated 22
February 1980 between Sammisa and a company called Containertank Corp (Containertank), who were described therein as disponent owners. That charterparty too contained
a liberty to sublet with an obligation to advise of any subletting.   *e*

All that is known of the relationship between Containertank and the respondents is
that the respondents had by agreement entrusted the operation of the vessel to them.

Shortly before the charterparty of 16 October, namely on 21 September, the appellants
had entered into a voyage charterparty with Agri Industries for the carriage of a cargo of
25,000 metric tons of heavy grains and/or sorghums and/or soybeans 10% more or less in
the appellants' option from America to one or two safe berths/anchorage Alexandria or   *f*
in charterer's option one or two safe berths/anchorages Port Said. By such charterparty
the appellants guaranteed the vessel's maximum arrival draught not to exceed 32 feet in
salt water. The charterparty did not name the vessel but provided that the performing
vessel was to be declared 'at least 10 days prior ETR loadport'.

The vessel Antonis P Lemos was duly declared under the voyage charter and on 20 and
21 October loaded a cargo at Houston. She arrived in Alexandria on 11 November but   *g*
her draught then exceeded 32 feet. As a result she was unable to berth until lightened
and delay was thereby caused.

As a result of the breach of the guarantee of maximum draught, the appellants had to
pay the costs of lightening and incurred certain other expenses and loss. In order to
recover such losses they issued on 20 May 1983 a writ in rem in the Admiralty Court
against the respondents, at the same time obtaining a warrant for the arrest of the vessel   *h*
pursuant to which she was duly arrested.

The indorsement on the writ is in the following terms:

'The Plaintiffs, as sub-charterers of the Defendants' ship ANTONIS P LEMOS under a
time charter dated 16 October 1981 made between Sammisa Co Ltd as Owners and
the Plaintiffs as charterers, claim damages for the loss suffered by them by reason of
the negligence of the Defendants, their servants or agents in causing permitting or   *i*
suffering the said ship to load a quantity of corn at Houston, Texas, USA on 20 and
21 October 1981 such that her draft on arrival at Alexandria, Egypt on 11 November
1981 exceeded 32 feet rendering her unable to berth without lightening.'

It will be observed that the claim is a straightforward claim in tort and that the

negligence alleged relates solely to the loading into the vessel of such a quantity of corn
a that her draught on arrival exceeded 32 feet.

By notice of motion dated 24 May 1983 the respondents sought an order that the writ
and warrant of arrest be set aside and the vessel released from arrest on the ground that
the High Court had no jurisdiction in respect of the appellants' claim and/or that such
claim did not fall within s 20(2) of the Supreme Court Act 1981.

The respondents' motion was heard by Sheen J on 26 May 1983. He made the order
b sought, giving his reasons for so doing on 7 June 1983. The appellants now appeal by
leave of the judge.

Subject to a new point raised by leave in this court, with which I shall deal briefly at
the end of this judgment, the sole question for determination is whether the appellants'
claim falls within s 20(2)(*h*) of the 1981 Act.

Section 20(1) of the 1981 Act, so far as presently material, provides:

c   'The Admiralty jurisdiction of the High Court shall be as follows, that is to say—
(*a*) jurisdiction to hear and determine any of the questions and claims mentioned in
subsection (2) . . . (*c*) any other Admiralty jurisdiction which it had immediately
before the commencement of this Act . . .'

By s 20(2) the questions and claims referred to in sub-s (1)(*a*) include:

d   '(*g*) any claim for loss of or damage to goods carried in a ship; (*h*) any claim arising
out of any agreement relating to the carriage of goods in a ship or to the use or hire
of a ship.'

The judge held that in order to fall within para (*h*) the claim must have its origin in an
agreement between the plaintiffs and the defendants and that, since there was no such
e agreement, the court had no jurisdiction. The appellants submit that the judge erred in
law and that it is sufficient to bring a claim within para (*h*) of s 20(2) if either: (i) there is
a general factual connection between the claim and an agreement of the relevant kind,
or (ii) such an agreement is a material fact for the purposes of pleading the claim, or (iii)
such an agreement is relevant to establish one or more of the three components of a claim
in negligence, namely duty of care, breach of that duty and resulting damage, or (iv)
f there is a commercial nexus between the claim and such an agreement.

The respondents submit that the judge was right and indeed, albeit faintly, that claims
within para (*h*) are limited to claims in contract between plaintiff and defendant.

Central to the appellants' argument was the proposition that Pt I of the Administration
of Justice Act 1956, and in particular s 1(1), was based on and intended to give effect to
the International Convention relating to the Arrest of Sea-going Ships (Brussels, 10 May
g 1952; TS 47 (1960); Cmnd 1128) and thus that it and its successor, s 20(2) of the 1981
Act, should be given a liberal and broad rather than a restricted construction, and so
construed, if reasonably possible, to conform to the language of the convention. That
proposition is well established by authority: see, for example, *Stag Line Ltd v Foscolo Mango
& Co Ltd* [1932] AC 328 at 350, [1931] All ER Rep 666 at 677, and *The Jade, The
Eschersheim, Erkowit (owners) v Jade (owners), Erkowit (cargo owners) v Eschersheim (owners)*
h [1976] 1 All ER 920 at 924–925, [1976] 1 WLR 430 at 435–436.

There were here unquestionably a number of agreements falling within para (*h*) of
s 20(2). Unless, therefore, that paragraph must be read as referring only to agreements
between the plaintiff and the defendant, the only question for consideration is whether
the appellants' claim is a claim arising out of any of those agreements.

The paragraph contains no words of limitation restricting the agreements mentioned
j to agreements between the plaintiff and the defendant. It would have been simple so to
limit them if any such limitation had been intended. The convention contains no words
of limitation either. I am unable to find any sufficient reason for importing such words,
and would only do so if compelled by authority. In the absence of such authority I would
accordingly hold that, if the plaintiff can establish that his claim arises out of an agreement
of the relevant kind, ie an agreement relating to the carriage of goods in a ship or to the

use or hire of a ship, then even if such agreement is not one between himself and the defendant, that claim falls within para (h).   *a*

The appellants here assert negligence in loading in America such a quantity of corn that the vessel's arrival draught exceeded 32 feet in salt water. If that claim is sustainable, a matter which does not presently arise, it can only be because (a) the appellants had under the voyage charter guaranteed the maximum draught on arrival, (b) the master or the defendants were aware of that guarantee, and, probably, (c) the charterparty of 16 October included provisions that the master should be under the orders and directions of   *b* the appellants as regards employment and that loading should be under the supervision of the master (which provisions were also in the headcharter). Again, in the absence of authority, I would hold that such a claim plainly arises out of the voyage charterparty, or the charterparty of 16 October, or both. I do so principally because, in the absence of the contractual guarantee and the master's or owner's awareness of it, it would, as it seems to me, be quite impossible to contend that there was a duty to load only such quantity as   *c* would enable the vessel to arrive at Alexandria with a maximum draught of 32 feet. This was not seriously disputed by the respondents.

Whether the plaintiff's claim will succeed or not is another matter. There may be one or more impregnable defences, but at this stage they do not arise: see *The St Elefterio, Schwarz & Co (Grain) Ltd v St Elefterio ex-Arion (owners)* [1957] 2 All ER 374, [1957] P 179.

There is no authority which compels me to reach a different conclusion. In the above   *d* case Willmer J held that the words were wide enough to cover claims in tort, and this was followed by Brandon J in *The Moschanthy* [1971] 1 Lloyd's Rep 37 and by Sheen J himself in *The Sennar* [1983] 1 Lloyd's Rep 295. None of these three cases afford in my view any real assistance on the question whether the relevant agreement must be between the plaintiff and defendant.

In the last of them, however, Sheen J tested the matter by considering whether the   *e* claim could be pleaded without reference to a relevant contract, in that case a bill of lading. In the present case he took the view that the appellants could plead their case without reference to the charterparty and that consequently the claim could not be said to arise out of it.

Since he did not in his judgment refer to the voyage charterparty, I take it that he was referring to the charterparty of 16 October. It may be that the claim could be pleaded   *f* without reference to that charterparty, although I doubt it, but reference to the voyage charterparty would, as I have said, be essential.

I accept that if a cause of action cannot be pleaded without reference to a relevant agreement it is a factor to be taken into consideration when determining whether a claim falls within the words of para (h), but I must not be taken as asserting that if a relevant agreement has to be referred to that is conclusive on the question whether the claim   *g* arises out of the agreement. I do not consider that it is either necessary or desirable to attempt to formulate any test, and I can readily envisage a case, for example, where a cause of action could be pleaded without reference to an agreement but where a particular head of damage would require such reference.

In reaching his conclusion the judge, apart from *The Sennar*, relied on a passage in the speech of Lord Diplock in *The Jade, The Eschersheim* [1976] 1 All ER 920, [1976] 1 WLR   *h* 430. There the question for decision was whether claims under a salvage agreement, made by the master on behalf of both the owners of the Erkowit and the owners of her cargo, fell within certain paras of s 1(1) of the 1956 Act. One of the paragraphs was para (h). As to this, the issue was whether the salvage agreement was an agreement relating to the use or hire of any ship.

In considering this question Lord Diplock said that the agreement was entered into on   *j* behalf of the cargo owners as well as the ship owners (see [1976] 1 All ER 920 at 925, [1976] 1 WLR 430 at 437). The judge said, in relation to this:

> 'That statement would have been unnecessary unless it was essential to show that a plaintiff must be a party to the agreement in order to establish that the claim "arises out of the agreement".'

I accept readily that Lord Diplock is most careful in the use of language but with

a respect to the judge it is, in my view, impossible to attribute to Lord Diplock's observation any intention to indicate that, for a claim to fall within para (*h*), the relevant agreement must be between plaintiffs and defendants. In the context Lord Diplock was, in my view, doing no more than rehearsing a fact. Counsel for the respondents did not seriously argue to the contrary. I gain no assistance from *The Jade, The Eschersheim* other than that already mentioned relating to the general approach to the construction of the paragraph.

b The judge also relied on *The Nuova Raffaelina* (1871) LR 3 A & E 483. In that case the plaintiffs were brokers and had negotiated a charterparty between owners and charterers which provided for them to be paid commission. The sole question was whether they could sue on the agreement, but Sir Robert Phillimore said (at 486):

c '... the appellants, who are brokers, cannot sue upon this instrument made between other parties, whatever use they might make of it as evidence in another action upon an implied contract for their services. As the jurisdiction of the Court of Passage must in this case be founded upon a claim growing out of the charterparty, a claim which I have said the appellants cannot maintain, I must ... dismiss the appeal ...'

d The words of the statute in that case were the same as in s 20(2) of the 1981 Act but the decision was no more than a decision that the brokers could not sue on a contract to which they were not parties. It is not authority that the words only cover claims arising out of agreements to which plaintiffs and defendants are parties and even if it were it is not binding.

None of the other cases cited in argument afforded any assistance.

e Whilst in my judgment the judge erred in holding that the claim did not fall within s 20(2)(*h*) of the 1981 Act, I should make it plain that I reject not only the respondents' contentions, but also the suggested tests advanced by counsel for the appellants. It is sufficient for the purposes of this appeal to say that on the ordinary meaning of the words the appellants' claim is, in my view, a claim arising out of a relevant agreement notwithstanding that such agreement is not between the appellants and the respondents,

f and on that simple ground I would allow this appeal.

This makes it unnecessary to deal with the new point raised in this court, which was that, even if the claim did not fall within s 20(2)(*h*) of the 1981 Act, there was still jurisdiction by virtue of the provisions of s 20(1)(*c*), which preserves any pre-existing Admiralty jurisdiction. By virtue of this and a similar preservation in s 1(1) of the 1956 Act, it was argued that the appellants could rely on the provision in the Supreme Court

g of Judicature (Consolidation) Act 1925, s 22(1)(*a*)(xii)(3), which conferred Admiralty jurisdiction in respect of any claim 'in tort in respect of goods carried in a ship'.

The point was raised as a result of observation made by Brandon J in *The Queen of the South, Corps (trading as Corps Bros) v Queen of the South (owners) (Port of London Authority intervening)* [1968] 1 All ER 1163 at 1168, [1968] P 449 at 455. It was not seriously pursued in this court and in view of that fact and the fact that it is not necessary to decide

h it, I say only that the appellants' claim does not appear to me to be a claim in tort in respect of the goods carried in the vessel and that, even if it is, it does not follow that the jurisdiction in rem, which is what matters here, goes with it. Section 21(1) of the 1981 Act permits actions in personam in *all* cases within the Admiralty jurisdiction. Actions in rem, however, may only be brought in certain cases which do not include cases falling within s 20(1)(*c*). Unless, therefore, s 20(1)(*c*) must be construed as preserving not only

j the Admiralty jurisdiction but also the power to exercise that jurisdiction in rem, the preserved jurisdiction would not avail the appellants,

Counsel for the respondents submitted that, since the 1981 Act did not provide for actions in rem in those cases in which there was Admiralty jurisdiction only by virtue of s 20(1)(*c*), that was an end of the matter. The point was not further argued. Counsel's argument appears at first sight to be a complete answer, for to construe s 20(1)(*c*) in the

manner necessary to circumvent it presents formidable difficulties. It is unnecessary to
say more than this.

a

CUMMING-BRUCE LJ. I agree.

Appeal allowed. Leave to appeal to the House of Lords granted.

Solicitors: *Holman Fenwick & Willan* (for the appellants); *Richards Butler & Co* (for the
respondents).

b

Patricia Hargrove   Barrister.

c

Pioneer Aggregates (UK) Ltd v Secretary of State for the Environment and others

HOUSE OF LORDS

d

LORD FRASER OF TULLYBELTON, LORD SCARMAN, LORD ROSKILL, LORD BRIDGE OF HARWICH AND
LORD BRANDON OF OAKBROOK

15, 19, 20, 21 MARCH, 24 MAY 1984

*Town and country planning – Duration of planning permission – Extent of duration – Whether
permission can be abandoned – Whether permission can be extinguished merely by conduct –*
e
*Whether commercial decision to terminate permitted operations on land extinguishing permission
in absence of term in permission to that effect – Town and Country Planning Act 1971, s 33(1).*

*Statute – Comprehensive statutory code – Power of court to go beyond provisions of code –
Application of principles of private law – Application of principles of private law permissible only
where statutory code makes no provision for problem before court.*
f

It is a general rule of town and country planning law that the duration of a valid planning
permission is governed by the provisions of the planning legislation. Since that legislation
makes no provision for the abandonment of planning permission but rather, by s 33(1)[a]
of the Town and Country Planning Act 1971, provides that any grant of planning
permission to develop is, except in so far as the permission otherwise provides, to enure
g
for the benefit of the land and of all persons for the time being interested therein (with
the clear implication that only the legislation or the terms of the permission itself can
stop the permission from so enuring), it follows that planning permission cannot be
extinguished by mere conduct alone (see p 359 *j*, p 362 *j* to p 363 *b* and *h j*, p 364 *e f*,
p 366 *g h* and p 367 *f* to *h*, post); *Ellis v Worcestershire CC* (1961) 12 P & CR 178, *Prosser v
Minister of Housing and Local Government* (1968) 67 LGR 109, *Hartley v Minister of Housing*
h
and Local Government [1969] 3 All ER 1658, *Petticoat Lane Rentals Ltd v Secretary of State
for the Environment* [1971] 2 All ER 793, *Pilkington v Secretary of State for the Environment*
[1974] 1 All ER 283, *Hoveringham Gravels Ltd v Chiltern DC* (1977) 76 LGR 533 and
Newbury DC v Secretary of State for the Environment [1980] 1 All ER 731 distinguished;
Slough Estates Ltd v Slough BC (No 2) [1970] 2 All ER 216 considered.

A commercial decision to terminate operations on land where there is a valid planning
j
permission for such operations cannot by itself extinguish that permission unless the
terms of the permission provide that that is to be the effect of the termination (see p 359 *j*
and p 367 *d* to *h*, post).

a   Section 33(1) is set out at p 363 *g h*, post

Where a field of law is governed by a comprehensive legislative code, it is an
a impermissible exercise of the judicial function to go beyond the statutory provision by
applying the principles of private law merely because they may appear to achieve a fairer
solution to the problem being considered than that covered by the statute law. Only
where the code is silent or ambiguous may the courts resort to the principles of private
law to resolve difficulties by the application of common law or equitable principles (see
p 359 j, p 363 b to d and p 367 f to h, post).

b

Notes
For permitted development, see 46 Halsbury's Laws (4th edn) para 106.
    For the Town and Country Planning Act 1971, s 33, see 41 Halsbury's Statutes (3rd
edn) 1624.

c ### Cases referred to in opinions
Ellis v Worcestershire CC (1961) 12 P & CR 178.
Hartley v Minister of Housing and Local Government [1969] 3 All ER 1658, [1970] 1 QB 413,
    [1970] 2 WLR 1, CA.
Hoveringham Gravels Ltd v Chiltern DC (1977) 76 LGR 533, CA.
Newbury DC v Secretary of State for the Environment [1980] 1 All ER 731, [1981] AC 578,
d   [1980] 2 WLR 379, HL.
Petticoat Lane Rentals Ltd v Secretary of State for the Environment [1971] 2 All ER 793, [1971]
    1 WLR 1112, DC.
Pilkington v Secretary of State for the Environment [1974] 1 All ER 283, [1973] 1 WLR 1527,
    DC.
Prosser v Minister of Housing and Local Government (1968) 67 LGR 109, DC.
e *Slough Estates Ltd v Slough BC (No 2)* [1970] 2 All ER 216, [1971] AC 958, [1970] 2 WLR
    1187, HL; *affg* [1969] 2 All ER 988, [1969] 2 Ch 305, [1969] 2 WLR 1157, CA; *affg*
    (1968) 19 P & CR 326.

Appeal
By an enforcement notice dated 25 February 1980 the Peak Park Joint Planning Board
f required Pioneer Aggregates (UK) Ltd (Pioneer) and Edmund Harry Mollatt, the owner
of land at Heathcote in Derbyshire known as Hartshead Quarry, to reinstate the materials
removed in the course of mining and other operations carried out on the appeal site on
the ground that there had been a breach of planning control within the period of four
years before the date of the service of the notice. Pioneer and the appeal site owner
appealed to the Secretary of State for the Environment, who dismissed the appeals.
g Pioneer appealed. On 19 February 1982 Glidewell J (46 P & CR 113) allowed the appeal
and remitted the matter to the Secretary of State for further consideration. The board
appealed to the Court of Appeal and Pioneer cross-appealed. On 15 June 1983 the Court
of Appeal (Eveleigh, O'Connor and Sir David Cairns) (46 P & CR 113) dismissed the
appeal and the cross-appeal and refused the board leave to appeal to the House of Lords.
The board appealed to the House of Lords with leave to the Appeal Committee granted
h on 20 October 1983. The facts are set out in the opinion of Lord Scarman.

Michael Barnes QC and *Harold Singer* for the board.
David Widdicombe QC and *Charles George* for Pioneer.

Their Lordships took time for consideration.

j
24 May. The following opinions were delivered.

LORD FRASER OF TULLYBELTON. My Lords, I have had the advantage of
reading in draft the speech of my noble and learned friend Lord Scarman. I agree with it
and, for the reasons stated in it, I would dismiss this appeal.

LORD SCARMAN. My Lords, in this appeal two questions fall to be considered by the House. The first is a question of legal principle: whether a planning permission for *a* the development of land can be abandoned by act of a party entitled to its benefit. Abandonment, it is said, has the effect that thereafter no person can lawfully resume the hitherto permitted development without obtaining a fresh planning permission. The local planning authority, appellant in this appeal, submits that abandonment effective to terminate a planning permission is recognised by law. The respondent, the owner of land to which the permission in dispute relates, submits that no such abandonment is *b* recognised by law.

If the answer to the question of principle be in the affirmative, it will become necessary to consider whether on the facts of the case the permission was abandoned. If it were, the appeal (on this premise) would succeed. But if the question of principle should be answered in the negative, the appeal must be dismissed unless the House is prepared to accept the appellant's alternative contention, which raises the second question: namely *c* has the development, which was permitted by the relevant planning permission, been completed? It is conceded, correctly, that, if what was then permitted has been completed, a resumption of the same type of operations would be not the resumption of the earlier development but a new development requiring a fresh planning permission. The first question is of importance in the planning law. If, however, the second question be answered in the affirmative, the appeal would have to be allowed irrespective of the *d* answer to the first. The second question depends on the proper construction of the terms of the relevant planning permission, and on their application to the facts of the case.

My Lords, I propose first to outline such of the facts as are necessary to determine the two main questions, and second, to consider those two questions. The subsidiary issue whether the permission has been abandoned will not arise unless in law it is possible to abandon it. *e*

The facts

For a full statement of the facts I would refer to the admirable judgment of Glidewell J before whom the appeal came from the enforcement notice after being dismissed by the Secretary of State.

The Peak Park Joint Planning Board, the appellant, is the local planning authority for *f* the part of Derbyshire which includes the area of land with which the appeal is concerned. Pioneer Aggregates (UK) Ltd, the respondent, is the owner of the land. By an enforcement notice dated 25 February 1980 the board required Pioneer to remedy what in the notice was alleged to be a breach of planning control, namely development of the land by certain mining operations. Pioneer admits the operations but contends that they constituted no breach of planning control. The case is really a test case. Pioneer is not *g* mining on the site. It knew that the local planning authority took the view that to resume mining on the site would be a breach of planning control. It fired one blast to remove some stone so as to bring the difference of opinion to a head. Pioneer has done nothing further save to exercise its rights of appeal against the enforcement notice.

The site to which the notice relates is an area of some 25 acres within the Peak District National Park. It is to the north of a lane leading to the hamlet of Heathcote. I shall refer *h* to this area as the northern or the appeal site. There is on the appeal site an existing limestone quarry and attendant plant and buildings. But until the test firing of February 1980 there had been no quarrying or other mining operations since 1966.

The history of mining on the appeal site, so far as presently relevant, can be shortly stated. On 31 October 1950 the then Minister of Town and Country Planning (to whom at the time application for planning permission to work minerals had to be made) *j* granted Hartshead Quarries Ltd permission for the mining and working of limestone on an area of land which included the appeal site. This area included, additionally to the appeal site, a larger piece of land on the south side of Heathcote Lane and separated from the appeal site by the lane. The permission allowed for the construction of a tunnel under the lane. The reason for the tunnel (which, however, was never constructed, though a

detailed permission was granted in 1955) becomes clear from a study of the conditions
imposed for the disposal of waste material. So long as mining was confined to the appeal
site, waste material was to be tipped on to a spoil bank. If and when mining was extended
to the area south of the lane, the waste material was to be brought across (or under) the
lane and tipped in the quarry made by the excavations on the northern site. Since they
bear on the second question, it will be convenient at this stage to quote in full two of the
conditions subject to which permission was granted:

> '3. On the completion of quarrying in the area north of the highway tipping of
> waste material on the said spoil bank shall cease and all waste material shall be
> deposited within the excavations formed by quarrying in that area to a level surface.
> 4. On the conclusion of quarrying in the area north of the road all mineral stocks
> shall be stored in that area.'

It is clear from these two conditions that quarrying on the land to the south of the lane
was envisaged as (allowably) continuing after conclusion of quarrying to the north, but
that, if it did, waste material should no longer be deposited on the spoil bank but in the
northern quarry and mineral stocks were to be stored on the northern site.

On 9 November 1962 a further permission was granted extending the area of
excavation and of tipping subject to conditions. Nothing turns on this permission, which
is to be read merely as an extension of the 1950 permission subject to certain conditions.

Hartshead extracted limestone from the appeal site from 1950 to 1966. On 15
September 1966 they wrote to the board a letter in which they gave notice that they
would cease quarrying not later than 31 December of that year. They had confined their
operations to the appeal site, although they had acquired the land, or, at the very least,
the mineral rights in the land to the south of the lane. Their letter dealt with all the land
covered by the planning permission, ie the land both to the south and the north of the
lane. It indicated clearly their intention to cease quarrying and to vacate all the land and
to remove their plant and buildings. The board relies on this letter and the subsequent
course of negotiations to establish their case that Hartshead, by electing to treat the 1950
permission (together with its 1962 extension) as at an end, abandoned it.

I pass over the negotiations which followed on Hartshead's ceasing from mining
operations save only to mention that they negotiated with the board a satisfactory
solution to the restoration problem. On 6 January 1967 the board wrote to Hartshead
informing them that the restoration conditions had been met to its satisfaction. The
board did not insist on a full compliance, probably because it believed that Hartshead's
departure marked the finish of mining operations on the land to which the permission
related.

In 1978 Pioneer became interested in the area covered by the permission of 31 October
1950 as extended by that of 9 November 1962. It asked whether planning permission to
quarry was needed. By letter dated 29 January 1979 the board took the two points which
now fall to be decided by the House. The board said:

> 'In relation to the entire quarry (one planning unit) for which planning permission
> was granted by letter dated 31st October, 1950, as extended by the permission of
> 9th November, 1962, planning permission for the site has been abandoned.'

The letter is ambiguous. It is not clear whether it refers to all the land covered by the
1950 permission or only to the land north of the lane (the appeal site). I read it as alleging
that planning permission in relation to all the land to which the 1950 permission related
had been abandoned. Whether that be right or wrong, the letter certainly did go on to
deal explicitly with the appeal site and in relation to that site made the second, alternative
point on which the appellant relies in the appeal. The board said:

> 'In addition and in the alternative, the North West area having been completed to
> the written satisfaction of the planning authority pursuant to the third condition
> [of the 1950 permission], cannot now be opened up without a new express
> permission.'

The first question: abandonment

If the board is right, a valid planning permission can be abandoned by the conduct of *a* landowner or occupier of land; and the effect of the party's conduct will be to bind all persons interested in the land now or hereafter whether or not they have notice of the abandonment. The planning permission would be entered in a public register; but not so its abandonment. Nor would it be possible by inspection of the land to discover whether the permission had been abandoned, for the absence of implementation of a planning permission is no evidence that a valid permission does not exist. It is perhaps *b* not surprising that no trace of any such rule can be found in the planning legislation. If there be such a rule, it has been imported into the planning law by judicial decision.

The case on which the appellant relies for the existence of such a rule is *Slough Estates Ltd v Slough BC (No 2)* (1968) 19 P & CR 326, Megarry J; *affd* [1969] 2 All ER 988, [1969] 2 Ch 305; *affd* [1970] 2 All ER 216, [1971] AC 958. It is the only reported case in which a rule of abandonment has been recognised as applicable to a planning permission. The *c* plaintiff owned a trading estate of some 500 acres. In January 1945, when about half the estate had been developed, the company sought permission to develop the remaining 240 acres. On 17 October 1945 the council wrote to the company permitting development for industrial purposes. But between 1945 and 1965 the company behaved as if the 1945 permission did not exist. The company sought and obtained fresh planning permissions for factory building covering about 150 of the 240 acres. In 1955, 90 acres remained *d* undeveloped. The company, in accordance with their post-1945 practice, applied for permission to develop the 90 acres for industrial buildings; but this time it was refused. The company then applied for and obtained £178,545 compensation for loss of development value.

In 1966 the company made a startling change of course: it applied to the High Court for a declaration, inter alia, that the permission of 17 October 1945 was still in force. The *e* trial judge, Megarry J, held that the terms of the letter of 17 October 1945 were so obscure that the planning permission was ineffective but embarked, obiter, on a lengthy discussion as to the possibility of abandonment, expressing the view that, if an owner or occupier of land evinced by his conduct an unequivocal intention to abandon planning permission, such permission would be extinguished by abandonment. The Court of Appeal ruled that the October 1945 letter on its true construction was a valid outline *f* planning permission but held that the company by claiming and obtaining compensation had elected to abandon its rights under the permission and could not now revive the permission. The company had made its election between inconsistent rights, the effect of which was to extinguish the permission. On appeal, this House held that the purported permission of 1945 was ineffective because it failed to identify the land to which it related. Lord Pearson, with whose speech the other members of the House agreed, *g* expressly reserved the question whether a planning permission could be abandoned.

The decision of the Court of Appeal was, of course, binding on Glidewell J and the Court of Appeal in the present case. Both courts refused, however, to accept that the *Slough* decision introduced into the planning law any general rule of abandonment, treating it as a limited exception to what they held was the general rule, namely that planning permission cannot be extinguished merely by conduct. They went on to find *h* that the facts of the present case did not fall within the *Slough* exception of election. Accordingly, Glidewell J allowed Pioneer's appeal from the minister (who had held that planning permission could be abandoned), and the Court of Appeal dismissed the board's appeal from his decision. Neither court dealt expressly with the second question raised in the appeal, though it was, the House was informed, raised. Impliedly, they must be considered to have rejected the board's contention. *j*

My Lords, on the question of abandonment I find myself in agreement with both courts below that there is no such general rule in the planning law. In certain exceptional situations not covered by legislation, to which I shall refer, the courts have held that a landowner by developing his land can play an important part in bringing to an end or making incapable of implementation a valid planning permission. But I am satisfied that a   the Court of Appeal in the *Slough* case erred in law in holding that the doctrine of election between inconsistent rights is to be incorporated into the planning law either as the basis of a general rule of abandonment or (which the courts below were constrained to accept) as an exception to the general rule that the duration of a valid planning permission is governed by the provisions of the planning legislation. I propose now to give my reasons for reaching this conclusion.

b   Planning control is the creature of statute. It is an imposition in the public interest of restrictions on private rights of ownership of land. The public character of the law relating to planning control has been recognised by the House in *Newbury DC v Secretary of State for the Environment* [1980] 1 All ER 731, [1981] AC 578. It is a field of law in which the courts should not introduce principles or rules derived from private law unless it be expressly authorised by Parliament or necessary in order to give effect to the purpose of the legislation. Planning law, though a comprehensive code imposed in the public

c   interest, is, of course, based on land law. Where the code is silent or ambiguous, resort to the principles of private law (especially property and contract law) may be necessary so that the courts may resolve difficulties by application of common law or equitable principles. But such cases will be exceptional. And, if the statute law covers the situation, it will be an impermissible exercise of the judicial function to go beyond the statutory provision by applying such principles merely because they may appear to achieve a fairer

d   solution to the problem being considered. As ever in the field of statute law it is the duty of the courts to give effect to the intention of Parliament as evinced by the statute, or statutory code, considered as a whole.

Parliament has provided a comprehensive code of planning control. It is currently to be found in the Town and Country Planning Act 1971, as subsequently amended. Part II (ss 6–21) of the 1971 Act imposes on local planning authorities the duty of preparing and

e   submitting to the minister development plans formulating their policy and their general proposals for the development and use of land in their area. Widespread publicity has to be given to the preparation or alteration of such plans. There is provision for local public inquiries in certain specified circumstances. Part III (ss 22–53) imposes general planning control. Section 23(1) declares the rule: subject to the provisions of the section, planning permission is required for the development of land. There are certain exceptions, of

f   which the most notable are rights in connection with the use of land existing prior to certain specified dates related to the introduction of planning control (commonly called 'existing use rights'): ss 23 and 94 of the 1971 Act. Section 29 deals with the grant of planning permission; note that the local planning authority must have regard to the provisions of the development plan. In determining an application for permission the authority must take into account 'any representations' made to them within the time

g   specified in the section. And there are extensive provisions for giving publicity to applications (s 26 to 28).

Section 33(1) is of crucial importance. It provides:

'Without prejudice to the provisions of this Part of this Act as to the duration, revocation or modification of planning permission, any grant of planning permission

h   to develop land shall (except in so far as the permission otherwise provides) enure for the benefit of the land and of all persons for the time being interested therein.'

The clear implication is that only the statute or the terms of the planning permission itself can stop the permission enuring for the benefit of the land and of all persons for the time being interested therein. I would comment, in passing, that the provision in s 33(1) was in the law as s 21 of the Town and Country Planning Act 1962, when the *Slough* case

j   [1969] 2 All ER 988, [1969] 2 Ch 305 was decided; but the Court of Appeal made no reference to it.

The provisions in the 1971 Act governing the duration, modification, revocation and termination of planning permission are extensive: see ss 41 to 46. It is unnecessary to analyse them in detail. Perhaps the most significant common feature of the various procedures is the involvement of public authority, local and central, when questions as to duration, modification, revocation or termination of planning permission arise. And, of course, the procedures involve notice to persons interested as well as to the applicant *a* and/or landowner.

Orders can also be made by a local planning authority for the discontinuance of a use of land or for the removal of buildings under s 51. The Secretary of State must confirm any such order made, and again there is provision for publicity.

Section 52 enables a local planning authority to enter into an agreement with a landowner restricting or regulating the development or use of land. The agreement is *b* registrable.

Indeed, the permissions and orders to which I have briefly referred are, with one exception, either registered in a register maintained under the planning legislation, or registrable as local land charges under the Local Land Charges Act 1975. The exception is a notice (a 'completion notice') under s 44 of the 1971 Act setting a time limit after which, subject to confirmation by the minister, a planning permission shall cease to have *c* effect. Such notices are, however, the subject of a specific, though optional, inquiry of the local authority contained in the officially approved form of inquiry used in connection with searches of the local land charges register.

Finally, it is necessary to refer to the recent amendment to the 1971 Act, namely the Town and Country Planning (Minerals) Act 1981. Section 7 provides that there shall be introduced into the 1971 Act a new s 44A setting a limit to the duration of a planning *d* permission to work minerals. Section 10 is directly in point. It introduces into the 1971 Act a new s 51A under which the mineral planning authority, if it appears that the working of minerals has permanently ceased on any land, may prohibit its resumption. If such a prohibition is contravened, a criminal offence is committed. These provisions are not yet in force. But they strongly reinforce the view of the law relating to planning control as being a comprehensive code, and they show clearly that the problem of the *e* future of planning permission for the working of minerals where mining operations have permanently ceased is left to public authority, and that subject to the usual safeguards such permission can be effectively terminated by order under the new s 51A.

Viewed as a question of principle, therefore, the introduction into the planning law of a doctrine of abandonment by election of the landowner (or occupier) cannot, in my judgment, be justified. It would lead to uncertainty and confusion in the law, and there *f* is no need for it. There is nothing in the legislation to encourage the view that the courts should import into the planning law such a rule, recognised though it is in many branches of the private law (eg the law of easements, the commercial law and the law of trade marks), as Megarry J in his learned, though obiter, discussion of the principle has shown in *Slough Estates Ltd v Slough BC (No 2)* (1968) 19 P & CR 326.

There are, however, quite apart from the *Slough* case a number of reported judicial *g* decisions which, on first sight and before analysis, might seem to suggest that there is room in the planning law for a principle, or an exception, allowing the extinguishment of a planning permission by abandonment.

Three classes of case can be identified. The first class is concerned not with planning permission but with existing use. In *Hartley v Minister of Housing and Local Government* [1969] 3 All ER 1658, [1970] 1 QB 413 the Court of Appeal (Lord Denning MR, Widgery *h* and Cross LJJ) held that the minister as the tribunal of fact was entitled to find on the evidence that the resumption of a car sales use on a site where previously there had been two uses, namely car sales and a petrol-filling station, was after a cessation of the car sales use for some four years a material change of use and so properly the subject of an enforcement notice. The minister, the court held, was entitled to find as a fact that the previous use had ceased, having been abandoned by the owner or occupier of the land. *j* This was not a case of abandoning a planning permission. There was in fact no existing use of the land for car sales because the use had ceased years ago. An existing use which has been deliberately ended before resumption arises is not existing at the date of resumption; accordingly, the resumption was a material change of use, and so required planning permission. The issue was one of fact, as Widgery LJ emphasised in his

judgment. And it had nothing whatever to do with the extinguishment of a planning
a permission. Widgery LJ in the course of his judgment made a significant comment
([1969] 3 All ER 1658 at 1661, [1970] 1 QB 413 at 422):

> 'When the car sales use ceased in 1961 there could be no question of a material
> change of use on which an enforcement notice could be founded in reliance on that
> fact alone.'

b The use no longer existing, the change back four years later was the material change of
use on which the notice could be founded.

The second class of case has been described as that of the 'new planning unit', a term
coined by Widgery LJ in *Petticoat Lane Rentals Ltd v Secretary of State for the Environment*
[1971] 2 All ER 793 at 796, [1971] 1 WLR 1112 at 1117. This line of cases was discussed
in *Newbury DC v Secretary of State for the Environment* [1980] 1 All ER 731 at 738–739,
c 752–753, [1981] AC 578 at 598–599, 616–617 by Viscount Dilhorne and myself. I will
not repeat what was then said. Two comments, however, should be made. First, the cases
are, without exception, cases where existing use rights were lost by reason of a new
development sanctioned by a planning permission. There is no case, so far as I am aware,
in which a previous planning permission has been lost by reason of subsequent
development save in circumstances giving rise to the third class of case, which I shall
d discuss in a moment. In the class of case now under discussion the existing use right
disappears because the character of the planning unit has been altered by the physical fact
of the new development. As Lord Parker CJ remarked in the first of the cases, *Prosser v
Minister of Housing and Local Government* (1968) 67 LGR 109 at 113:

> 'The planning history of this site, as it were, seems to me to begin afresh . . . with
> the grant of this permission . . . *which was taken up and used.* . .' (Emphasis supplied.)
e

Second, it is clear that where the evidence fails to establish the creation by development
actually carried out on the land of a new planning unit the grant of planning permission
does not preclude a landowner from relying on an existing use right. Indeed, as *Newbury's*
case itself shows, existing use rights are hardy beasts with a great capacity for survival.

The third class of case comes nearer to the facts and law of the present appeal. These
f cases are concerned not with existing use rights but with two planning permissions in
respect of the same land. It is, of course, trite law that any number of planning
permissions can validly co-exist for the development of the same land, even though they
be mutually inconsistent. In this respect planning permission reveals its true nature, a
permission that certain rights of ownership may be exercised but not a requirement that
they must be.

g But, what happens where there are mutually inconsistent permissions (as there may
well be) and one of them is taken up and developed? The answer is not to be found in
the legislation. The first reported case appears to have been *Ellis v Worcestershire CC*
(1961) 12 P & CR 178, a decision of Mr Erskine Simes QC to which Lord Widgery CJ
referred with approval in what must now be regarded as the leading case on the point,
Pilkington v Secretary of State for the Environment [1974] 1 All ER 283 at 289, [1973] 1 WLR
h 1527 at 1534.

Mr Erskine Simes QC said (12 P & CR 178 at 183), in a passage which Lord Widgery
CJ was later to describe as exactly illustrating the principle:

> 'If permission were granted for the erection of a dwelling house on a site showing
> one acre of land as that to be occupied with the dwelling house, and subsequently
j > permission were applied for and granted for a dwelling house on a different part of
> the same acre which was again shown as the area to be occupied with the dwelling
> house, it would, in my judgment, be impossible to construe these two permissions
> so as to permit the erection of two dwelling houses on the same acre of land. The
> owner of the land has permission to build on either of the sites, but wherever he
> places his house it must be occupied with the whole acre.'

Pilkington was a Divisional Court decision. It has been approved by the Court of Appeal in *Hoveringham Gravels Ltd v Chiltern DC* (1977) 76 LGR 533. Its facts were that the owner   *a* of land was granted planning permission to build a bungalow on part of the land, site 'B'. It was a condition of the permission that the bungalow should be the only house to be built on the land. He built the bungalow. Later the owner discovered the existence of an earlier permission to build a bungalow and garage on another part of the same land, site 'A'. That permission contemplated the use of the rest of the land as a smallholding. He began to build the second bungalow, when he was served with an enforcement notice   *b* alleging a breach of planning control. The Divisional Court held that the two permissions could not stand in respect of the same land, once the development sanctioned by the second permission had been carried out. The effect of building on site 'B' was to make the development authorised in the earlier permission incapable of implementation. The bungalow built on site 'B' had destroyed the smallholding; and the erection of two bungalows on the site had never been sanctioned. This was certainly a commonsense   *c* decision, and, in my judgment, correct in law. The *Pilkington* problem is not dealt with in the planning legislation. It was, therefore, necessary for the courts to formulate a rule which would strengthen and support the planning control imposed by the legislation. And this is exactly what the Divisional Court achieved. There is, or need be, no uncertainty arising from the application of the rule. Both planning permissions will be on a public register; examination of their terms combined with an inspection of the land   *d* will suffice to reveal whether development has been carried out which renders one or other of the planning permissions incapable of implementation.

My Lords, I find nothing in any of these cases to cast doubt on the view of principle to which a study of the legislation has led me. Indeed, *Pilkington's* case [1974] 1 All ER 283, [1973] 1 WLR 1527 may be contrasted with the *Slough* case [1970] 2 All ER 216, [1971] AC 958 in that it reveals the proper exercise of the judicial function in a field of codified   *e* law. It is a decision supporting and strengthening the planning control imposed by Parliament in contrast with the Court of Appeal's decision in the *Slough* case which renders control uncertain, is likely to cause confusion, and which to that extent works to undermine the intention of Parliament.

Strangely and ironically, it would appear that the *Slough* case could have been decided along *Pilkington* lines. For, assuming the validity of the 1945 planning permission in the   *f* *Slough* case, several acres of the estate which in the 1944–45 plan had been included as a car park were covered with factory buildings constructed pursuant to a subsequent planning permission. Under the *Pilkington* rule the subsequent development would have sufficed to make the outline plan approved in 1945 incapable of implementation. Lastly, it will be observed that the *Pilkington* situation resembles the 'new planning unit' class of case in that a permitted development which has been carried out has so altered the   *g* character of the land that its planning history now begins with the new development.

For these reasons I would answer the first question in the appeal in the negative. There is no principle in the planning law that a valid permission capable of being implemented according to its terms can be abandoned.

The second question: completion of permitted development   *h*

I turn now to the second of the two main questions in the appeal. The board submits that on the true construction of the terms of the 1950 permission as extended by the 1962 permission the permitted development to the north of Heathcote Lane has been completed and cannot be resumed without a fresh planning permission. It is recognised that the area of land to which the 1950 permission related comprised more than the appeal site in that the permission related to areas to the north and south respectively of   *j* Heathcote Lane and was drafted so as to grant permission to work minerals in both areas. It is said, however, that it was a permission for two separate developments and that, on the cesser by Hartshead of mining operations north of the lane together with the restoration of the land to the satisfaction of the board, the development was completed so that a resumption now in that area would be a new development requiring fresh

a planning permission. Particular reliance is placed on conditions 3 and 4 of the permission (the two conditions which I have earlier set out) whereby it was provided that on the completion of quarrying on the northern site waste material should be deposited in the quarry on the northern land and mineral stocks should be stored on the northern land. The suggestion is that these conditions indicate either a completion of the authorised development of the northern land before the commencement of a separate development south of the lane or, at the very least, two separate developments whether
b contemporaneous or successive.

My Lords, I do not so read the permission. In terms it relates to the whole area of land south and north of the lane. It is a permission to mine and work minerals in that area. It contains detailed conditions as to method of working and as to restoration work after quarrying. The permission plainly envisages the continued use of the northern land for mineral working even after quarrying in that area has ceased; for the nothern land is to
c be used at all times both during and after quarrying north of the lane for the deposit of waste material and for the processing and storage of minerals, from whatever part of the land to which the permission relates they are won. The permission, as I read its terms, contemplated an authorised development of the land south and north of the lane treated as one planning unit.

I reject, therefore, the submission that the permission was for two separate developments
d and that one of them was complete when Hartshead ceased operations in 1966. I suspect that in 1966 the board confused the commercial termination of Hartshead's operations with the completion of the development permitted by the 1950 permission as extended in 1962. A commercial decision to terminate operations on land where there is a valid planning permission for such operations cannot by itself extinguish the planning permission unless the terms of the permission provide that such shall be the effect of the
e termination. To give such effect to a commercial decision in the absence of terms to that effect in the planning permission would be to fly in the face of s 33(1) of the 1971 Act which lays down that, save where the permission so provides, the grant of planning permission enures for the benefit of the land and of all persons for the time being interested in the land.

For these reasons I would dismiss the appeal with costs.
f

LORD ROSKILL. My Lords, I have had the advantage of reading in draft the speech of my noble and learned friend Lord Scarman. For the reasons he gives I too would dismiss this appeal with costs.

LORD BRIDGE OF HARWICH. My Lords, for the reasons given in the speech of
g my noble and learned friend Lord Scarman, with which I agree, I would dismiss this appeal.

LORD BRANDON OF OAKBROOK. My Lords, I have had the advantage of reading in draft the speech prepared by my noble and learned friend Lord Scarman. I agree with it, and for the reasons which he gives I would dismiss the appeal.
h

Appeal dismissed.

Solicitors: *Theodore Goddard & Co* (for the appellants); *Coward Chance* (for the respondents).

Mary Rose Plummer   Barrister.

Procon (GB) Ltd v Provincial Building Co Ltd and others

COURT OF APPEAL, CIVIL DIVISION

CUMMING-BRUCE, GRIFFITHS AND STEPHEN BROWN LJJ

17, 18 JANUARY 1984

Costs – Security for costs – Amount of security – Principles for determining amount of security – Discretion – Exercise of discretion – Full indemnity or discounted estimate of party and party costs – Security normally to be on full indemnity basis – Discount to be made to allow for court's estimate of reduction by taxing officer – Relevance of possibility of settlement where application for security made early in proceedings – RSC Ord 23, r 1.

Costs – Security for costs – Appeal – Approach of Court of Appeal – Court of Appeal normally accepting judge's exercise of discretion unless satisfied he went wrong – RSC Ord 23, r 1.

The court's discretion under RSC Ord 23, r 1[a] to order a plaintiff to give such security for the defendant's costs of the action or other proceeding in the High Court as the court thinks just is, on the plain language of the rule, unrestricted, and there is no justification for any 'conventional approach' of fixing a sum of two-thirds of the estimated party and party costs rather then ordering security on a full indemnity basis. Nor should any distinction be made between actions in the commercial list and other proceedings in the Queen's Bench Division. The correct principle is that any security ordered should be such as the court thinks just in all the circumstances of the case. Normally a discount will be made to take account of the court's expectation of any reduction by the taxing officer of the fees particularised, but after making that discount the court should, if satisfied that the defendant has made an honest actual estimate of his costs and disbursements, order that amount to be incorporated in the order for security. Where security is sought at a very early stage in the proceedings it is relevant to take into account the possibility that the action may be settled, perhaps quite soon, in which case it may be appropriate to make an arbitrary discount of the estimated probable future costs, the amount of the discount (if any) depending on the court's view of all the circumstances. Where there is an appeal against the judge's decision, the Court of Appeal will normally accept the judge's exercise of his discretion unless it is satisfied that he went wrong (see p 373 j, p 375 j to p 376 j, p 378 c d, p 379 d to j and p 380 a to c, post).

Dicta of Lindley MR and Chitty LJ in *Dominion Brewery Ltd v Foster* (1897) 77 LT at

---

a Rule 1 provides:

'(1) Where, on the application of a defendant to an action or other proceeding in the High Court, it appears to the Court—(a) that the plaintiff is ordinarily resident out of the jurisdiction, or (b) that the plaintiff (not being a plaintiff who is suing in a representative capacity) is a nominal plaintiff who is suing for the benefit of some other person and that there is reason to believe that he will be unable to pay the costs of the defendant if ordered to do so, or (c) subject to paragraph (2), that the plaintiff's address is not stated in the writ or other originating process or is incorrectly stated therein, or (d) that the plaintiff has changed his address during the course of the proceedings with a view to evading the consequences of the litigation, then if, having regard to all the circumstances of the case, the Court thinks it just to do so, it may order the plaintiff to give such security for the defendant's costs of the action or other proceeding as it thinks just.

(2) The Court shall not require a plaintiff to give security by reason only of paragraph (1)(c) if he satisfies the Court that the failure to state his address or the mis-statement thereof was made innocently and without intention to deceive.

(3) The references in the foregoing paragraphs to a plaintiff and a defendant shall be construed as references to the person (howsoever described on the record) who is in the position of plaintiff or defendant, as the case may be, in the proceeding in question, including a proceeding on a counterclaim.'

507–508, of Mars-Jones J in *Sir Lindsay Parkinson & Co Ltd v Triplan Ltd* [1973] 2 All ER
a at 282, of Geoffrey Lane J in *T Sloyan & Sons (Builders) Ltd v Brothers of Christian Instruction*
[1974] 3 All ER at 720 and of Lord Diplock in *Birkett v James* [1977] 2 All ER at 804
applied.

Notes
For security for costs in general, see 37 Halsbury's Laws (4th edn) paras 298–309, and for
b cases on the subject, see 37(2) Digest (Reissue) 428–436, 2615–2673.

Cases referred to in judgments
Birkett v James [1977] 2 All ER 801, [1978] AC 297, [1977] 3 WLR 38, CA and HL.
Dominion Brewery Ltd v Foster (1897) 77 LT 507, CA.
Imperial Bank of China India and Japan v Bank of Hindustan China and Japan (1866) LR 1 Ch
App 437.
c *Parkinson (Sir Lindsay) & Co Ltd v Triplan Ltd* [1973] 2 All ER 273, [1973] QB 609, [1973]
2 WLR 632, CA.
Sloyan (T) & Sons (Builders) Ltd v Brothers of Christian Instruction [1974] 3 All ER 715.

Interlocutory appeal
d The first and second defendants, Provincial Building Co Ltd and Provincial Refining Co
Ltd, appealed with the leave of the judge against the order of Bingham J on 6 July 1983
whereby he ordered that their counterclaim against the plaintiffs, Procon (GB) Ltd, be
stayed unless within 28 days the first and second defendants provided, in a manner
acceptable to the plaintiffs or, in the event of any dispute over the form of the security,
to the satisfaction of the court, the sum of £6m as security for the plaintiffs' costs of
e defending the counterclaim. The facts are set out in the judgment of Cumming-Bruce
LJ.

Alexander Irvine QC and *Nicholas Dennys* for the first and second defendants.
Jonathan R Playford QC for the plaintiffs.

f **CUMMING-BRUCE LJ.** This appeal raises two issues. The first issue is a matter of
general importance. On what principle should security for costs be awarded? That is to
say, when it is decided that security should be ordered, on what principle should the
amount of that security be determined?
That second issue raises the question whether on the facts the security ordered by the
judge was too much, on the ground that he did not take a sufficiently cautious view in
order to protect the party against whom security was ordered from the oppression of
g meeting security likely or liable to exceed the costs which the party seeking security had
incurred or was likely to incur, when taxed on a party and party basis. That second
question has involved consideration of much detail. In order to decide whether that
ground of appeal was made out it was necessary for this court to take as much trouble as
the judge to appreciate the history and prospects in the legal proceedings, to identify the
issues with reasonable particularity and to consider the evidence relied on by the party
h seeking security as substantiating the costs which that party maintained had already been
incurred and which would be accepted by the taxing master on a party and party basis.
So this judgment first has to deal with the point of principle in order to determine
whether the judge was right when, having made his appreciation of the impact of costs
already incurred and his prognostication of the costs likely to be incurred between July
1983 and 11 January 1984, he decided to arrive at the amount of his order without
j deducting one-third as an arbitrary fraction from the sums that his apreciation of the
costs had led him to calculate.
The judge said in his judgment:

'I recognise that there is a difference in practice between various branches of this
court. In the Commercial Court it is generally accepted that, if we are presented

with applications for security for costs without an attempt to particularise, two-thirds is ordered, but, if there is a particularisation with facts and figures, then particularly in respect of past costs, and making an allowance for what might be taxed off, we give an indemnity. I am bound to say that I believe that this is the correct principle and I do not see why, if the costs have been incurred, there should not be security for all of them and not two-thirds. I think that this is a case where the Commercial Court practice should be adopted. It is a major piece of litigation which is at least quasi-commercial and accordingly I will not take the practice of two-thirds but grant an indemnity of whatever I consider to be the proper sum.'

It is important for a proper understanding of that passage in the judgment to bear in mind, as is clear from the preceding passage in the judgment, that when the judge used the phrase 'grant an indemnity' he meant an indemnity to protect the party seeking security in respect of party and party costs only, and nothing in his judgment is to be understood as meaning that he was intending to grant an indemnity for anything else, e g solicitor and client costs, solicitor and own client costs and so on.

Counsel for the first and second defendants has submitted that the judge was wrong in a number of respects. First, on a point of detail, counsel submits that this is not a commercial case within the meaning of those words for the purpose of listing commercial cases in the Commercial Court; the definition of commercial cases in RSC Ord 72, r 1(2) provides:

'In this Order "commercial action" includes any cause arising out of the ordinary transactions of merchants and traders and, without prejudice to the generality of the foregoing words, any cause relating to the construction of a mercantile document, the export or import of merchandise, affreightment, insurance, banking, mercantile agency and mercantile usage.'

This was, having regard to the pleadings, an action commenced by builders against the building owners. The claim was a simple claim for the balance of moneys due under the contract: nothing obscure, nothing uncertain and the kind of case that, if there is no defence, usually ends in judgment under RSC Ord 14. But it is not unknown, when builders try to recover their final payment, that they are confronted with a defence alleging by way of set-off that the work has not been properly done. That defence was pleaded by the first defendants in this action. They particularise, and further particularise, and they made a counterclaim in so far as their damage flowing from the plaintiffs' breaches of contract exceeded the amounts claimed by the plaintiffs in their statement of claim. By way of counterclaim the first, and thereafter the second, defendants sought to recover damages in the total sum, as it now is, of $Can230m-odd, a figure which vastly exceeds the amount claimed by the plaintiffs in respect of costs of work done. The action in consequence of the particulars of the allegations of bad work, negligence and delay in operation of the contract has become rather massive. The pleadings run into hundreds of pages. The pleadings are supplemented by a schedule of further particulars which runs into some 833 pages and that was the bare bones of the set-off and counterclaim because, as is right and proper, there has now come into existence a Scott Schedule which deals in appropriate columns with the allegations initially incorporated in the pleadings.

The action proceeded and the counterclaim proceeded. The counterclaim is not as simple as a mere elucidation and investigation of hundreds of alleged defects of engineering, draughting and construction, but also involves the statement and investigation of this gigantic claim for consequential loss which in the circumstances (and it is unnecessary for me to elaborate) is not, from the plaintiffs' point of view, a very easy exercise. When they built the refinery in Canada, purportedly pursuant to contract, the refinery reached the stage of mechanical completion and the second defendants operated the refinery until they went into liquidation. The first and second defendants say that their losses were proximately caused by the inefficiency of the plaintiffs' construction work. It is obvious that other factors contributed; there was a change in the

market situation for crude oil between the time when this enterprise was planned and
a the building contract formed, and the date when, many years afterwards, the refinery
began to operate.

There was another difficulty. At one stage during their operation of the refinery, the
directors, or some of them, of the second defendants ran off with $Can32m which the
company had relied on for working capital. So the investigation on the part of the
plaintiffs into the validity of the counterclaimants' claim for consequential loss does
b involve a protracted complex investigation of the financial causation of the collapse of
the refinery's operations. The first and second defendants are in liquidation but there are
assets: at one time the asset of the refinery and now, as I understand it, assets represented
by proceeds of sale of the refinery. That is not quite the end of the story because there are
massive claims in the liquidations by unsecured creditors and they sufficiently show that
it is now most unlikely that, if the plaintiffs obtain judgment, they will receive anything
c other than a slender dividend in the liquidation, if at all.

The action and the counterclaim have been proceeding for years and, when the
plaintiffs, as defendants to the counterclaim, launched their application for security for
costs, they supported that application by an affidavit of their solicitor, followed by further
evidence from him which included a statement of the costs already incurred by the
plaintiffs on the counterclaim, which costs had, at the date of the hearing before the
d judge, already been paid, and the plaintiffs, as defendants to the counterclaim, sought
security in respect of those costs already incurred and also asked for further security in
respect of future costs to be incurred.

The trial is at present fixed for 11 January 1985. The judge decided on the application
of the defendants to limit his gaze to the period that would elapse between 6 July 1983
(the hearing before the judge) and 11 January 1984. The judge tried to make an estimate
e of how the plaintiffs' costs in meeting the counterclaim would be building up during
that period. The judge decided not to look beyond that date of 11 January 1984.

Counsel for the first and second defendants in this court submitted that this was not a
commercial action: it is a building and engineering dispute of a very common kind
though of exceptionally massive proportions, and though there are financial inquiries
necessarily implicit in the analysis of the counterclaim for damages, and though there
f are other legal proceedings arising out of the collapse of the refinery enterprise and the
liquidation of the first and second defendants, in truth and in fact this is the kind of
action which occurs in the Queen's Bench Division every day of the week: three or four
official referees sit every day determining exactly this class of counterclaim. So, it is
submitted, the principles which govern the practice in connection with security for costs
in the Queen's Bench Division are the relevant principles and Bingham J was wrong in
g preferring the practice which, in his experience, he regarded as the practice of the
Commercial Court. Counsel for the first and second defendants supported that submission
by drawing our attention to the differences in the procedure for control of actions
proceeding in the commercial list as compared to other actions proceeding in the Queen's
Bench Division. When a case is assigned to the commercial list the commercial judge
takes control of the interlocutory procedure and that procedure is geared to the subject
h matter. Instead of the kind of pleadings which the rules require elsewhere in the Queen's
Bench Division, pleading is by points of claim and points of defence; everything is
required to be concise. The judge determines the interlocutory programme with a view
to achieving a great expedition and so, from the very beginning, the judge is introduced
progressively more and more intimately into the subject matter of the proceedings.
Contrast the background of interlocutory proceedings in the Queen's Bench Division
j which are not in the commercial list. The rules of pleading are followed and may, as in
this case, be voluminous. Interlocutory business is usually undertaken by the masters or
on appeal to the judge in chambers of the day. There is not usually any single judicial
figure in control of the whole case from the beginning. Therefore, it is submitted, the
judge was wrong in disregarding the practice in the Queen's Bench Division generally
and preferring the practice, as the judge recognised it to be, in the Commercial Court.

Counsel for the first and second defendants makes another respectful criticism of the passage in the judgment to which I have referred. Unable to find authority on this point, *a* he sought to investigate as best he could the experience of practitioners in the Commercial Court and as a result was able to inform this court that, if the judge thought there was a settled practice in the Commercial Court of the kind that he described, he was probably wrong because, though some practitioners in the Commercial Court do expect that security for costs which had been particularised will be granted on a 100% basis, sometimes, and indeed quite often, the order is not 100% of the particularised costs but *b* something much more like two-thirds. Counsel for the first and second defendants submits that the practice in the Queen's Bench Division is settled and is accurately summarised in a note to RSC Ord 23 in *The Supreme Court Practice 1982* vol 1, p 440, para 23/1–3/22. That note reads as follows:

'*Amount of Security.*—The amount of security awarded is in the discretion of the Court, which will fix such sum as it thinks just, having regard to all the circumstances *c* of the case. It is not the practice to order security on a full indemnity basis. The more conventional approach is to fix the sum at about two-thirds of the estimated party and party costs up to the stage of the proceedings for which security is ordered; but there is no hard-and-fast rule. It is a great convenience to the Court to be informed what are the estimated costs, and for this purpose a skeleton bill of costs usually affords a ready guide (cited with approval by Geoffrey Lane J. in *T. Sloyan &* *d* *Sons (Builders) Ltd.* v. *Brothers of Christian Instruction* ([1974] 3 All ER 715 at 720)).'

Counsel for the first and second defendants submits that that note is accurate, and that the effect that should be given to it (which he submits is the effect which is given by judges of the Queen's Bench Division) is that, unless there is some unusual feature, the judge, after ascertaining, as he must, the estimated party and party costs up to the stage *e* of the proceedings with which he is proposing to deal, must deduct an arbitrary fraction on one-third of those costs so that the party who has proved those costs will have to bear them himself without security; and if the plaintiff (in this case the defendants (as counterclaimants)) is a corporation outside the jurisdiction, who is in liquidation with negligible net assets (if any), the defendant to the counterclaim will have the privilege of this practice of fighting the counterclaim, paying the costs that are necessary and *f* reasonable in order to meet the claim, will then obtain security in respect of two-thirds of those costs but will incur the other third of the costs, pay them, and, at the end of the day, if successful on the counterclaim have the privilege of obtaining nothing in respect of those costs from the unsuccessful counterclaimant. This is a privilege which the plaintiffs in this case do not wish to enjoy. And their reluctance to reconcile themselves to the two-thirds' rule of practice can be appreciated when one looks at the figures which *g* the judge arrived at when trying to decide what costs had reasonably been incurred. I quote from the judgment:

'The plaintiffs' evidence is that, as of 1 May 1983, costs of approximately £5.5m have been incurred and the estimate to 11 January 1985 is a further £5m, and I suggest that a ratio in the correct proportion of continuing costs to January 1984 *h* would be £1·75m. That is not a precise estimate but it seems the best that we can do on the figures available.'

When the judge came to the passage in his judgment in which he stated the order he was making, he said:

'The bulk of the security being sought to 11 January 1984 has already been *j* incurred and . . . is on a party and party basis. An element in respect of future costs is more tenuous of course because it is speculation and I think it is also right to bear in mind that in very substantial taxations, such as this one will be, inevitably it will be taxed down and I have no doubt that the plaintiffs' solicitors would be astounded if their bill survived without any reduction. Inevitably, whatever figure I come to

a
will be unscientific. All that I can do is to choose a figure, bearing in mind the
principles I have just stated. The figure I have come to is £6m. This sum should be
given by way of security acceptable to the plaintiffs or, failing agreement, to the
satisfaction of the court.'

So where his calculations, on the view that he had formed of the plaintiffs' evidence, led
to a total up to 11 January amounting to £7·25m, the judge reduced that to the sum of
£6m, stating that he had in mind that the figures presented in the exhibit of particulars
b
would inevitably be taxed down. But that £6m was the judge's view of a just figure on
what has been described as an indemnity basis, meaning 100% of the costs actually
incurred, or probably to be incurred on a party and party basis up to 11 January.

The defendants say that that figure was anyway £2m too much because if the judge
had followed the practice described in the note to RSC Ord 23 in *The Supreme Court
Practice 1982* having arrived at his £6m, which allows for a reduction of the figures in
c
the exhibit on taxation, he should have ordered security in two-thirds of that amount
and so that part of the appeal, in terms of quantum, is about £2m. That is quite a lot of
money and explains why the builders are resisting the appeal.

We had the advantage of the researches of counsel for the plaintiffs into the history of
the note presently published under the heading 'Amount of Security' in the notes to RSC
Ord 23 in *The Supreme Court Practice 1982* and I express my gratitude to him for his
d
industry. It emerges therefrom that from 1910 until 1940 there was a note in *The Yearly
Practice of the Supreme Court* under RSC Ord 65, r 6 as follows:

'The amount of the security is in the discretion of the judge and depends on the
circumstances of each case. In the King's Bench Division the amount is fixed at the
discretion of the master according to the amount claimed and the nature of the
e
claim.'

Then from 1943 until 1960 in successive editions of *The Annual Practice* a note under RSC
Ord 65, r 6 read:

'The amount of security was usually in Ch. D. £100, as provided by C.O. 40, r. 6,
but is not now limited in amount.'
f
Then from 1961 to 1963 in *The Annual Practice* for those years a note under RSC Ord 65,
r 6 read as follows:

'The amount of security awarded is in the discretion of the judge, and depends on
the circumstances, it is not the practice to order security on a full indemnity basis.
Usually in Ch. D. £100 was ordered as provided by C.O. 40, r. 6, but the amount is
g
not now limited . . .'

Since 1964 the note has read as it reads today in *The Supreme Court Practice 1982*:

'. . . It is not the practice to order security on a full indemnity basis. The more
conventional approach is to fix the sum at about two-thirds of the estimated party
and party costs up to the stage . . . for which security is ordered; but there is no hard-
h
and-fast rule . . .'

Such is the history of the notes. The time has come to refer to the rule. RSC Ord 23,
r 1(1) provides:

'Where, on the application of a defendant to an action or other proceeding in the
High Court, it appears to the Court—(a) that the plaintiff is ordinarily resident out
j
of the jurisdiction . . . then if, having regard to all the circumstances of the case, the
Court thinks it just to do so, it may order the plaintiff to give such security for the
defendant's costs of the action or other proceeding as it thinks just.'

On the plain language of the rule there are no words restricting the generality of the
discretion to be exercised by the court. One asks oneself how comes it that since 1964 the

editors of *The Supreme Court Practice* have given the advice which appears in their note? And, if there is the conventional approach fixing the sum at about two-thirds of the estimated party and party costs, as the editors state, how is that conventional approach to be regarded as properly consistent with the terms of the rule?

Counsel for the first and second defendants correctly submitted that there are many statutory provsions, whether in Acts of Parliament, rules of court or otherwise, which, by their plain language, having regard to its grammatical effect, confer an unfettered discretion on the court, but it is not at all uncommon for the court itself, with its experience of the practical application of the discretion, to state guidelines which, to the extent that the guidelines require, have the effect of restricting within the stated principle the exercise of judicial discretion. He submits that that is exactly what judges of the Queen's Bench Division in their wisdom have done in relation to Ord 23 and that experience has satisfied them that the just and sensible approach to quantum of security is to restrict the security to about two-thirds of the estimated party and party costs.

What light, if any, is thrown on the history of this rule and the notes in *The Supreme Court Practice* by decided cases? Again, we are indebted to counsel for the plaintiffs for his concise review of the authorities. I start in 1897 with *Dominion Brewery Ltd v Foster* 77 LT 507. In that case the defendants alleged that the company was insolvent, and that the costs of the action would amount to a very large sum, owing to the fact that the evidence and documents involved in the case were very extensive. The amount, as computed by the defendants' solicitors, was upwards of £1,000, so they applied under s 69 of the Companies Act 1862 for an order that the plaintiffs should give sufficient security for costs. When counsel for the appellants was opening his appeal from the order of Kekewich J, he submitted that the words 'sufficient security' in s 69 of the 1862 Act must mean enough to satisfy the defendants' probable costs, which in that case were computed at £1,000. Lindley MR observed (at 507):

> 'We have to consider the possibility of a collapse of the action. The 1000*l*. estimate is based on the assumption that the case will be fought out . . . The principle to be applied is that the security ought not to be illusory nor oppressive—not too little nor too much.'

When he came to give judgment, Lindley MR said (at 508):

> 'It is obvious that, as to a question of *quantum* such as this, you cannot lay down any very accurate principle or rule. The only principle which, as it appears to me, can be said to apply to a case of the kind is this, that you must have regard, in deciding upon the amount of the security to be ordered, to the probable costs which the defendant will be put to so far as this can be ascertained. It would be absurd, of course, to take the estimate of the managing clerk to the defendant's solicitors and give him just what is asked for. You must look as fairly as you can at the whole case.'

Lindley MR proceeded to state that the court thought that the security ordered by the judge in the Chancery Division should be increased substantially, and continued:

> 'We must take into account the chance of the case collapsing without coming to trial. And on the whole we think that the sum of 600*l*. is a reasonable one, and is sufficient.'

Chitty LJ, after referring to s 69 of the 1862 Act, said (at 508):

> 'I really do not see how we can lay down any rule more useful than that, or any rule more precise. There must be some estimate made as to what expenses the defendant will be put to, and the court has to take a reasonable view of all the circumstances, the nature of the suit, or any other matters that may properly be brought in.'

He agreed with what had been said by Lindley MR.

There it is quite clear that the thinking of Lindley MR, as he stated, was influenced by the fact that the court had to consider the possibility of a collapse of the action; but the

a solicitors' clerk's estimate of £1,000 had been based on the assumption that the action would be fought out.

The next case to which I refer is *T Sloyan & Sons (Builders) Ltd v Brothers of Christian Instruction* [1974] 3 All ER 715. Most of the consideration given by the judge, Geoffrey Lane J, was concerned with an analysis of the degree to which the costs were likely to be treated as costs of the counterclaim to which the contractors were in the position of

b defendants and in respect of which they could not be ordered to give security. But the judge referred to the history of cases on security for costs and he began by referring to *Imperial Bank of China India and Japan v Bank of Hindustan China and Japan* (1866) LR 1 Ch App 437. He quoted a passage from Knight Bruce LJ in that appeal, where the Lord Justice had said (at 438):

c 'It appears to me the word "sufficient" must have been intended to have a meaning, and that if the practice of the Court was to be followed the Act would have said so. There is nothing to limit the amount of the security.'

The reference there was to the practice of the court limiting its order for security to £100.

Geoffrey Lane J then quoted from Lindley MR's judgment in *Dominion Brewery Ltd v*

d *Foster*, to which I have already referred. He went on to say ([1974] 3 All ER 715 at 720):

'The reference in the judgment to the chance of the case collapsing is relied on by counsel for the builders because as he informed me, without dissent from counsel for the Brothers, the probability is that after legal argument before the arbitrator in May, the unsuccessful party will appeal to the Court of Appeal and that thereafter,

e as he put it, "the situation will change". It seems to me that this is a possibility which can properly be considered when fixing security, particularly as a further application could always be made if necessary, although how far such consideration can be translated into arithmetical terms is problematical. I regard the relevant dictum of Lindley MR as meaning that the court should, or at any rate may, order somewhat less than if there seemed to be every prospect that the case would be

f fought to a finish.'

Finally one comes to the judgment of Mars-Jones J in *Sir Lindsay Parkinson & Co Ltd v Triplan Ltd* [1973] 2 All ER 273 at 282, [1973] QB 609 at 619–620, where he said:

'I gather it has become the practice to order something in the region of two-thirds of the best estimate the court can make of the probable costs in the normal run of

g cases. If that is so, then I would point out that building arbitrations of this kind are not the normal run of cases. The discount of two-thirds, or whatever proportion the court may decide, is made to cover the possibility that the whole of the probable costs would not be incurred because the case was settled or not proceeded with for some reason at some stage. Counsel for Parkinson has argued that the discount also takes into account the possibility that the plaintiff might succeed and that as the

h offer to settle includes an allowance for that possibility I should not make a further discount from my estimate of Parkinson's probable costs ... In my judgment, where some reasonable assessment of the plaintiff's chances of success can be made at this interlocutory stage, and that must be comparatively rare, that would be relevant to the question of whether security for costs should be made or not, but not to the issue of quantum of the security to be ordered except insofar as a further

j discount might be called for in addition to that made for the possibility that the whole of the estimated costs might not be incurred.'

I am satisfied that, having regard to the provisions of RSC Ord 23, r 1(1), which on their face confer an unfettered discretion on the court, there is no solid reason for a general and arbitrary practice whereby, after estimating party and party costs up to the

date of the proceedings for which security is ordered, an arbitrary fraction of one-third is
knocked off before the order for security is made. There is nothing, in my view, in the
authorities that have been cited to this court to justify the validity of what the editors of
The Supreme Court Practice 1982 describe as the more conventional approach of fixing the
sum of two-thirds of the estimated party and party costs. On the contrary, in the cases
which I have cited, the principle is this: the security should be such as the court thinks in
all the circumstances of the case is just. If security is sought, as it often is, at a very early
stage in the proceedings, the court ordering security will be faced with a situation in
which a solicitor or his clerk has made an estimate of the costs likely in the future to be
incurred; and probably the costs already incurred, or paid, will be a very small fraction
of the security that the applicant is seeking. At that stage one of the features of the future
of the action which is relevant is the possibility that the action may be settled, perhaps
quite soon. In such a situation it may well be sensible to make an arbitrary discount of
costs estimated as the probable future costs, but whether one-third is likely in any given
case to be a sensible discount, and whether any discount at all should be made, will
depend on the view of the court on consideration of all the circumstances. There are two
ways in which the court can deal with it. The court may, as the judge did here, form a
view on the amount of party and party costs which had already been incurred and then
make an estimate necessarily approximate of the costs that would be likely to build up
during the next six months; and there was nothing before the judge to give him the
slightest reason for expecting that this action would settle in the next six months.
Therefore, on the principles which in my view are to be derived from the language in
the rule, and the words of Lindley MR in *Dominion Brewery Ltd v Foster* (1897) 77 LT 507
at 508, there was no reason to think that it would be just to the plaintiffs to knock off an
arbitrary fraction of party and party costs which the judge was satisfied had, as to most of
them, already been incurred and paid, but as to others would necessarily be subject to an
informed appreciation and estimate. Indeed, had the judge in the circumstances adhered
to what was thought to be the conventional Queen's Bench Division approach, the result
would have been wholly unjust. It would have meant that the plaintiffs, in order to meet
the counterclaim, had or would incur £2m costs which they had no prospect of ever
recovering from anybody. That cannot possibly be just.

In my view, whatever the practice in the Commercial Court may be (as to which we
have heard varying accounts from the bar) as far as the position in this Queen's Bench
action is concerned, the words of the rule point to the order made by the judge; and there
was no occasion, having regard to all the circumstances, for making any fractional
deduction, whether one-third or otherwise. I take the view that the note under the
heading 'Amount of Security' which has been published in *The Supreme Court Practice* to
the notes to Ord 23 since 1964 is expressed in too dogmatic and inflexible terms and has
probably given rise to a misunderstanding by masters and judges of the principles to be
followed having regard to the words of the rule. In my view, I would respectfully suggest
to the editors of *The Supreme Court Practice* that they reconsider the words of their note.
As I have stated, where there is a prospect of settlement, that is a factor to be taken into
account by the court in deciding the quantum of security to be ordered. But in a case
such as the present, where millions of pounds of costs assessed on a party and party basis
have become the subject of fee notes and have in most cases already been paid, there is no
reason that I can see in justice or common sense for any conventional discount of the
kind described in the note. There will, of course, be a discount as the judge made, having
regard to his expectation that the fees which were particularised before him would be
reduced by the taxing master (that is a quite different matter), but when that discount
has been made, if the judge is satisfied that the solicitors have honestly attempted to
make, and have made, an actual estimated calculations of their costs and disbursements,
then, when the judge has arrived at what he thinks is the actual figure, he should order
that figure to be the figure incorporated into his order for security.

It is to be hoped that the editors of the *The Supreme Court Practice* will decide not to
advise practitioners of the existence of any conventional scale unless they are perfectly

a certain, on a scrutiny of the case law, that authoritative guidance has been given in the cases which explains the way in which the rule should be applied.

For those reasons, on the first issue raised in the appeal, I hold that the first and second defendants fail. I have dealt with the matter at some length because I regard it as a matter of some importance.

I come to the next point; that is particular to the circumstances and history of this case. Counsel for the first and second defendants has, with characteristic persuasiveness, sought
b to persuade us that when one looks at the schedule in which the plaintiffs' solicitor, Mr Pearl, set out the particularisation of the build up of costs to date, there are not less than three items which cry out aloud as inviting suspicion. The first is the enormous sum which has been paid by the plaintiffs for the purpose of using a computer company to control discovery in the action. The figure runs to £2,246,000. Counsel for the first and second defendants submits that, if the plaintiffs like to enjoy the facilities of silicon chips
c and expensive gadgets, then good luck to them, but they never consulted those defendants, as counterclaimants, before embarking on this enormous computer adventure. The plaintiffs' solicitor swears that, in his view, this has saved the plaintiffs money. The documents are over a million in number. Their analysis and classification was a gigantic task and if silicon chips are not to be used (the people called 'programmers' are very expensive in New York) then, according to Mr Pearl, he would have had to set a
d great team of solicitors and executives, assisted no doubt by engineering or financial experts, into slogging out the detail of the relevance of documents and the number of documents for which privilege could be claimed. Counsel for the first and second defendants submits that that is all very well and no doubt Mr Pearl believes every word he says, but the computer, as the plaintiffs' solicitor now knows, threw up an immense amount of duplication of paper and the computer is not proof against irrelevance by any
e means, so that the whole exercise, enormously expensive, really ought not to be taken without a great many pinches of salt when it comes to inviting the court to include it as an item in an order for security. Counsel for the first and second defendants points to the fees on a view of the refinery by the plaintiffs' legal advisers, a brace of leading counsel, a brace of junior counsel and solicitors and I know not what army of engineers to explain to the lawyers what they were looking at; it is an enormous sum of money. With
f politeness and moderation counsel for the first and second defendants submitted that perhaps on the other side of the Atlantic people do themselves rather better than we are used to doing ourselves, and, though he did not suggest that the whole thing was a major jollification of the sort that one associates with American conventions, he submits that a shrewd and reasonably cynical court should wonder a little whether it is sensible to make the defendants put up the security when they really have no idea whether the scale of
g those fees was as economical as it should have been. And there are other items. We have been taken through, and we tried before we came into court to read, enough of the uninviting bundle in order to gain some appreciation of the validity of the opinions expressed by Mr Pearl culminating in his table of fees.

The first and second defendants submit that there is enough here to justify this court taking the view that the assessment, or appreciation, of reasonable party and party costs
h should have been done by the judge in a more critical way and that he should have knocked quite a lot off the figures which he accepted too uncritically.

The answer I believe is to be found in words used by Lord Diplock in a very different context in the well-known case of *Birkett v James* [1977] 2 All ER 801 at 804, [1978] AC 297 at 317. At the beginning of his speech, dealing with the principles that apply in relation to dismissal for want of prosecution, Lord Diplock said:
j
> 'It is only very exceptionally that an appeal on an interlocutory order is allowed to come before this House. These are matters best left to the decision of the masters and, on appeal, the judges of the High Court whose daily experience and concern is with the trial of civil actions. They are decisions which involve balancing against one another a variety of relevant considerations on which opinions of individual

judges may reasonably differ as to their relative weight in a particular case. That is
why they are said to involve the exercise by the judge of his "discretion".'

The context of those observations is very different, but to my mind they apply exactly,
with only slight grammatical modification, to the situation posed by the applicant for
security for costs. In this case the application was made to Bingham J, a judge of great
experience particularly in the Commercial Court, but a judge whose personal and
professional qualifications are such that there is every reason to have complete confidence
in his capacity to form a view about what has, on the history of the costs already incurred,
been a reasonable build up of costs and perfectly qualified to form a view about what is
likely for the next six months, having regard to the history on the previous build up of
actual costs, to be a sensible estimate to arrive at. In spite of the invitation to us of counsel
for the first and second defendants to regard the figures accepted by the judge as reflecting
too great an innocence on the part of the judge and reflecting also absence not of cynicism
but of cautious criticism about the figures which the plaintiffs' solicitor is putting
forward, I take the view that the right approach in this court is that, unless we are satisfied
that the judge has gone wrong when he accepted this figure or that, we ought to begin
by trusting the judge on whom Parliament has conferred the exercise of discretion. If
the judge trusted the plaintiffs' solicitor and on examining his tables decided that the
expenses appeared reasonable so that Mr Pearl's judgment about it could be relied on, I
cannot see any reason why this court should take a different view of Mr Pearl from that
taken by the judge, and I would add (whether it was the case in the instant case or not I
know not) that very frequently judges in the Queen's Bench Division including the
Commercial Court have learnt a great deal over the years about the judgment and
reliability of solicitors who give evidence before them in matters of costs. That may or
may not be a factor present in this case (I do not think it matters) but it is an additional
reason why this court should be cautious merely out of an inborn sense of cynicism about
mistrusting the testimony of the solicitors to whom the plaintiffs have confided the
conduct of their defence to the counterclaim.

For those reasons, without going into more than the minimal detail in this judgment,
I reject the second submission of counsel for the first and second defendants.

As to the fifth ground of appeal, in which it is pleaded that—

> 'The Learned Judge was wrong to infer that the Plaintiffs' payment into Court
> was or was likely to have been made, not as an admission of liability, but as a
> prudent precaution against any risk in costs when: (a) the amount paid in is the
> equivalent of the sum which the Plaintiffs contend represents the limit of their
> liability under the contract: and (b) the Plaintiffs are claiming very substantial sums
> in the action'

it is, in my view, sufficient to say, first, that I see no reason in the material before us for
holding that the judge was wrong and, second, I see very good reasons for thinking that
the judge was right.

I would add one last matter. The first and second defendants are in liquidation. Their
assets are unlikely, as now understood, to equal their unsecured liabilities, quite apart
from these proceedings. The costs of preferring the counterclaim must be very great,
though I think it is most natural that the costs in making the complaints against the
builders and engineers are likely to be a great deal less, at any rate during the history to
date, than the costs of the plaintiffs in meeting the allegations. But the first and second
defendants' costs must be very great. Where has it all come from? The plaintiffs, for
years, tried to find out; nobody would tell them. It now appears that there is a perfectly
natural explanation and the Export Credits Guarantee Department may have a common
interest with the first and second defendants in the success of the counterclaim, at any
rate in relation to the defective work which the counterclaim has alleged. I cannot say
that there is no mystery about it now; there is much less mystery than there was, but it
adds nothing to any relevant issue that arises on this appeal, save in this way: it does give
a historical explanation of the situation in which the plaintiffs are building up costs

a which, without security, can never be recovered while the defendants have, we now know, been in the position in which, in spite of having no assets, have been able to continue the litigation to date and incur the costs. But, having said that, I cannot see that those matters have any relevance to any issue which arose in this appeal.

I would dismiss this appeal.

b **GRIFFITHS LJ.** I agree that this appeal should be dismissed and I only venture to add a few words of my own because a note in *The Supreme Court Practice* has stood unchallenged for 20 years.

This appeal requires the court to decide whether, on an application for security for costs under RSC Ord 23, r 1(1), the court is entitled to award security for costs in the sum which the court estimates the applicant would recover on taxation on a party and party basis, or whether, at least in the Queen's Bench Division, the court is limited by a long-c standing practice to awarding no more than two-thirds of that sum. The first and second defendants submit that the court is limited to awarding two-thirds of the estimate of the taxed costs. Their argument is largely founded on the note to Ord 23 in *The Supreme Court Practice 1982* vol 1, p 440, para 23/1–3/22, which has already been read by Cumming-Bruce LJ, and which has stood unaltered since 1964. No authority was cited in support of the note and, as Cumming-Bruce LJ's review of the authorities has d demonstrated, no support of the note can be derived from authority.

Having heard of the researches of counsel for the plaintiffs in the masters' corridor, I am not myself persuaded that a two-thirds fixed practice in fact exists, but if it does I am satisfied that it is time it stopped. I can see no sensible reason why the court should not order security in the sum which it considers the applicant would be likely to recover on taxation on a party and party basis if the court considers it just to do so. This, as I e understand it, is the practice of the judges in the Commercial Court and it is a practice that ought also to be followed in the rest of the Queen's Bench Division. It is, of course, for the party seeking an order for security to put before the court material that will enable the court to make an estimate of the costs of the litigation. In the normal course of things, it is to be expected that the court will, to some extent, discount the figure it is asked to award. Allowance will have to be made for the unquenchable fire of human f optimism and the likelihood that the figure of taxed costs put forward would not emerge unscathed after taxation. It is to be observed in the present case that it was this element that led Bingham J to make a substantial discount in the order of 19%. If the estimate includes future costs, these discounts may be large to allow for the possibility of the settlement of the litigation and this will be particularly so if application is made at the commencement of the litigation and costs are assessed on the assumption that the g litigation will proceed to a final trial. In such cases it may be sensible to discount by as much as one-third and I strongly suspect myself that, because some of the masters were doing this where they were asked to estimate security at a very early stage, the note in *The Supreme Court Practice* emerged in its present form.

Furthermore, if very little information is put before the court on which it can estimate costs, then again it will be reasonable to make a large discount, particularly when it is h borne in mind that, if the security proves inadequate as litigation progresses, it is always possible for a further application to be made for more security.

But, having said that, it would be quite wrong, in order to avoid the mental discipline involved in examining the particular facts of the case to determine what is a just figure, to apply a rule of thumb and just reduce every estimate by one-third to avoid trouble, and if any such practice has been insidiously developing it is, as I say, time that it was j stopped.

On the particular facts of the present case, the bulk of the costs for which security has been ordered had already been incurred and the judge had the opportunity of looking at the bills and had the affidavit of a highly reputable commercial solicitor to support the assertion that these costs had already been incurred. It seems to me in those circumstances that this was a case where justice demanded that the estimate of costs should be based on that which the applicants were already out of pocket.

I agree for the reasons given by Cumming-Bruce LJ that it was a matter for the discretion of the judge to consider the particular figures, bringing to them a lifetime of experience in this field of work. I see no reason for interfering with his discretion and, for the reasons I have given, in my view he was fully entitled to award costs on what he described as an 'indemnity basis', which was in fact on the basis of awarding costs equivalent to his best estimate of the taxed costs which had actually been incurred.

I would only add this, that £6m may seem a very daunting figure, but it is in fact only approximately 3% of the sum at stake in this vast litigation. I doubt if it would be considered an adequate basis for a contingency fee on the other side of the Atlantic.

I agree for these reasons and those given by Cumming-Bruce LJ that this appeal should be dismissed.

STEPHEN BROWN LJ. I agree that this appeal should be dismissed for the reasons given by Cumming-Bruce LJ. I also desire to associate myself with the observations of Griffiths LJ on the note in *The Supreme Court Practice 1982*. It is time that it was removed.

Appeal dismissed.

Solicitors: *Herbert Smith & Co* (for the first and second defendants); *Davies Arnold & Cooper* (for the plaintiffs).

Bebe Chua   Barrister.

R v Watts

COURT OF APPEAL, CRIMINAL DIVISION
PURCHAS LJ, KILNER BROWN AND RUSSELL JJ
12 JANUARY 1984

Drugs – Controlled drugs – Amphetamine – Amphetamine existing in two stereoisomeric forms – Amphetamine and one stereoisomeric form both included in list of controlled drugs – Other stereoisomeric form not included in list – Whether other stereoisomeric form not a controlled drug – Whether prosecution required to prove presence of both stereoisomeric forms where unlawful possession of 'amphetamine' is alleged – Misuse of Drugs Act 1971, Sch 2, Pt II, para 1.

On the true construction of the Misuse of Drugs Act 1971 the full generic meaning is to be given to the word 'Amphetamine' where it appears in para 1 of Pt II of Sch 2 to that Act, with the result that for the purposes of the Act 'Amphetamine' embraces both stereoisomeric forms of the substance, namely dexamphetamine and levoamphetamine, notwithstanding that the former also appears in the list in para 1 while the latter does not. It follows that in a prosecution alleging unlawful possession of amphetamine contrary to s 5 of the 1971 Act the prosecution is not bound to prove that the substance possessed by the accused contained both dexamphetamine and levoamphetamine (see p 382 *d* to *f* and p 384 *e* to *g*, post).

DPP v Goodchild [1978] 2 All ER 161 considered.

Notes

For possession of a controlled drug with intent to supply, see 11 Halsbury's Laws (4th edn) para 1093 and 30 ibid para 746, and for cases on the subject, see 15 Digest (Reissue) 1077–1078, 9170–9173.

For the Misuse of Drugs Act 1971, s 5, Sch 2, Pt II, para 1, see 41 Halsbury's Statutes (3rd edn) 884, 914.

Case referred to in judgment

DPP v Goodchild [1978] 2 All ER 161, [1978] 1 WLR 578, HL.

Case also cited
a *Muir v Smith* [1978] Crim LR 293, DC.

Application for leave to appeal
The appellant, Nigel Blair Watts, applied for leave to appeal against his conviction in the Crown Court at Shrewsbury before his Honour Judge Northcote and a jury on 21 September 1983 of possessing amphetamine with intent to supply it to another contrary

b to s 5(3) of the Misuse of Drugs Act 1971. The appellant also applied for leave to appeal against the sentence of 12 months' imprisonment, 6 months of which term was suspended, imposed on him for that offence. Leave to appeal against conviction was granted and the hearing of the application was treated as the hearing of the appeal. The facts are set out in the judgment of the court.

c *John Deacon Riley* for the appellant.
Nicholas Budgen for the Crown.

PURCHAS LJ delivered the following judgment of the court. On 21 September 1983 in the Crown Court at Shrewsbury the appellant, who applies for leave to appeal against conviction and sentence, was convicted of possessing a controlled drug with intent to

d supply and sentenced to 12 months' imprisonment, 6 months of the term being suspended. The other count in the indictment was of simple possession, and the jury was discharged from returning a verdict on it.

The matters with which this appeal is concerned arose out of an incident on 20 November 1982 when the appellant was discovered with a motor car in the glove compartment of which were were five envelopes containing a white powder. As far as

e this appeal is concerned the dispute has ranged over a very small area. At the trial a number of matters were contested, such as conversations between the appellant and the police and the appellant's intention in having this substance in his possession. The jury decided those matters adversely to the appellant, and there has been no criticism of the judge's summing up on those aspects.

The appeal has revolved round the question whether the white powder contained a

f drug which falls within the categories of drugs in Pt II of Sch 2 to the Misuse of Drugs Act 1971. Evidence was called by both sides about the drug known as amphetamine. For the purposes of this appeal there is common ground as to the chemistry of amphetamine. It has two forms which are relevant to the appeal, it not being wholly excluded that there may possibly be some other form. The two forms are levoamphetamine and dexamphetamine. They are two stereoisomeric forms of amphetamine, and, as will

g appear from their names, one form has a molecular structure in which the atoms are disposed in a left-handed rotary structure and the other has the same atoms disposed in a mirror-image or right-handed rotary structure. The chemical constitution of both forms is the same. They differ however in their pharmacological properties. Dexamphetamine is a much more powerful drug than levoamphetamine. Mr Boldock, a witness who gave evidence for the defence, purported to say that levoamphetamine, because it does not

h appear in the list of class B drugs in Sch 2, was not a controlled drug. That is correct to the extent that in the list of drugs in class B, which is comparatively shorter than the list in class A, amphetamine appears unqualified by any chemical adjective, and then later dexamphetamine, but levoamphetamine does not appear.

Expert evidence about which there is common ground also established that amphetamine is an artificially prepared drug, as opposed to a drug appearing in natural

j form, to be found in other parts of the schedule, such as poppy leaves, which were dealt with in the case to which we have been referred, *DPP v Goodchild* [1978] 2 All ER 161, [1978] 1 WLR 578. The evidence about which there is common ground also established that normally when amphetamine is prepared in a laboratory it contains in various proportions both dexamphetamine and levoamphetamine, but it may possibly consist wholly of one or the other, though that would involve a high degree of chemical separation or purification.

At one point in the expert evidence the mixture was described as a racemic mixture. 'Racemic' is variously defined in dictionaries. In the expert evidence it was described *a* merely as a 'mixture of the two forms'. The Concise Oxford Dictionary (7th edn, 1982) defines it as 'composed of equal numbers of dextrorotatory and laevorotatory molecules in a compound'.

The cross-examination of Mr Barclay, the expert witness called for the prosecution, disclosed that in his laboratory notes there was an entry to the effect that the powder appeared to be a mixture of 2:1 ephedrine and amphetamine, but 'he couldn't really say'. *b* I have probably inaccurately transposed those notes, but their effect was that the analysis certainly could not determine that there was present a specific amount of dexamphetamine, and that it was possible that the powder was wholly levoamphetamine, however unlikely in practice that would be.

In considering an appeal in a criminal matter, however, this court must view the question of conviction wholly in favour of the appellant where there is doubt as to the *c* evidence before the court; and, when we come at a later stage in this judgment to deal with questions of apparent omission, error or ambiguity, counsel for the appellant, who has presented this appeal with skill and clarity, makes the point that the citizen should not be at risk in his liberty if there is ambiguity in the statute. We have that very much in mind.

The appeal has therefore been considered on the basis that this white powder, apart *d* from the ephedrine content, was wholly levoamphetamine. On that basis it is necessary for us now to turn to the schedule itself. It is conceded that if amphetamine in the schedule includes levoamphetamine the appeal must fail. On the other hand, if the maxim expressio unius exclusio alterius can be applied to the category of drugs listed in Pt II of the shedule then the inclusion in the list of dexamphetamine as a separate item would exclude levoamphetamine and the appeal must succeed, because the possibility *e* cannot be excluded that the white powder was wholly levoamphetamine, however unlikely in practice that may be. We would further add that it is possible, by some analytical methods which require a comparatively large quantity of the substance, to determine the presence or absence of either of the two stereoisomeric forms of amphetamine.

In his directions to the jury the judge did not deal with the distinction between the *f* two forms of amphetamine. He fairly rehearsed the evidence and referred to the submission of the defence that the specific mention of dexamphetamine had the effect of excluding levoamphetamine. In the round he dealt with it these words:

'The offence under the Misuse of Drugs Act 1971 deals with a variety of drugs of different degrees. Class A drugs, which deal with the more dangerous variety, the *g* sort that mentions heroin and so on and its various derivatives, are the most serious type and most dangerous type of drug to be used. Next down the category, so far as Parliament has decided, we find other drugs such as cannabis, which I expect most of us have heard about if we have not actually seen it, and in the category of class B drugs is set out amphetamine, the drug alleged in this particular charge. There is also another drug, dexamphetamine, and about that Mr Barclay the chemist said: *h* "Well, it does not make a lot of sense to include dexamphetamine as a separate substance or drug because in fact it is one kind of amphetamine", just as, you remember, I suggested to him yesterday there may be varieties of whisky, but they are all really whisky. He said: "The only thing I can think is that at about the time this Act was drafted there was a common stimulant on the market in chemist shops called Dexadrine; that was its trade name." He said: "Probably the draftsman added *j* that as a way of ensuring that Dexadrine would no longer be available to those who wanted to misuse it." The Act goes on to say that those class B drugs are controlled and not merely in their pure or liquid form, but any sort made out of it or any preparation containing it. According to Mr Barclay, what he examined was amphetamine on an approximate 2:1 ratio, diluted with another mild but not controlled stimulant called ephedrine, because, he said, it is very powerful stuff and

in its concentrated form is rather difficult to handle ... He said he analysed the
powder in a number of ways. He said: "I have not the slightest doubt that it is
properly called amphetamine", because the first test is to discover whether, against
the control sample of amphetamine used in the machine he used, it had the same
properties, and he said it did. "There can be no doubt about it," he said. "It is
amphetamine." '

In dealing with the expert evidence called by the defence the judge said:

'As against that [the evidence of Mr Barclay] Mr Boldock, who has also been a
forensic science officer and is properly qualified as a chemist, said that in his view
(and this seems to be common ground) amphetamine is an isomer, is a mixture of
the two sub-groups that I have already mentioned, and he said that in his view it
would have to be proved that both of those were in the substance examined for it
properly to be called amphetamine. He did not in fact analyse it, and he was offering
his view as a matter of opinion.'

It is to that reference to the evidence of Mr Boldock that we made the comment during
the course of argument that the construction of the 1971 Act is of course a matter of law
for the court and not a question for the expert witnesses; but this appeal has proceeded
on the basis that the two forms of amphetamine are usually constituents of amphetamine
as a class.

The judge therefore left the matter to the jury on the basis that, if they were satisfied
that amphetamine, of whatever isomer it might be, was proved to be present in the
powder, then at least on the aspect of possession they should convict. For that reason we
have treated this appeal on the basis that the powder should be considered as being
wholly levoamphetamine, because of the omission by the judge specifically to mention
the significance of the distinction drawn by the two expert witnesses.

The construction of the schedule places before the court two alternatives. Parliament,
in drafting the categories in class B, has generally speaking referred to specific chemical
names, and in para 2 of Pt II of the schedule put in the extra definition, namely: 'Any
stereoisomeric form of a substance for the time being specified in paragraph 1 of this
Part of the Schedule.' Had the description dexamphetamine not been included in the
category of class B drugs, in our view it would not have been arguable but that
levoamphetamine, on the evidence agreed in this case being a stereoisomeric form,
together with dexamphetamine would both fall under the generic term 'amphetamine'.
But the question raised is whether para 2 is applicable when one of two stereoisomeric
forms is specifically mentioned in para 1.

Reliance was placed by counsel for the appellant on part of the speech of Lord Diplock
in DPP v Goodchild [1978] 2 All ER 161 at 164, [1978] 1 WLR 578 at 581:

'Following on the lists of controlled drugs specified by name in each of the three
classes are additional paragraphs designed to incorporate in the class closely related
chemical analogues of the listed drugs, such as stereoisomers, esters, ethers and salts.
In addition there is a paragraph which incorporates within the relevant class "Any
preparation or other product containing a substance or product for the time being
specified in [the list of drugs] above." '

Counsel for the appellant has submitted that he was entitled to rely on that extract from
the speech to support his contention that for a charge effectively to be brought in relation
to amphetamine the prosecution had to charge and prove the presence of dexamphetamine.

Lord Diplock further in his speech deals with the issue raised in that case of the various
descriptions of the forms of cannabis or cannabis derivative mentioned in the schedule
of class A and class B drugs. Counsel for the prosecution has referred us to the passage
which immediately follows ([1978] 2 All ER 161 at 164, [1978] 1 WLR 578 at 582):

'Most, though not all, of the listed drugs in the three classes, A, B and C, are
described by their precise chemical name and are synthetic substances which do not

occur in the natural state. In the case of these drugs there is no room or doubt for ambiguity. Either a substance is the described synthetic drug (or a preparation or other product containing the described synthetic drug) or it is not.'

The fine point of construction therefore is whether in including amphetamine Parliament intended that generic term to embrace both dexamphetamine and levoamphetamine. If this was not the case the inclusion of amphetamine in addition to dexamphetamine was otiose and surplusage in the category of drugs listed in Pt II. To put the question in another way, why did Parliament include dexamphetamine, when that particular stereoisomeric form of amphetamine was already embraced in the generic term 'amphetamine'? Counsel for the appellant has submitted that Parliament did so exclude levoamphetamine. But if that submission is correct there was no need for Parliament to include amphetamine as a generic term at all.

The alternative approach to this problem of construction, proposed by counsel for the Crown, is that the error was not one of the inclusion of amphetamine but of the inclusion of dexamphetamine, which was itself unnecessary. This was the approach recommended by Mr Barclay.

The court has therefore to look at this problem as a pure matter of construction. Just as it was not relevant for Mr Boldock to say that levoamphetamine was not a controlled drug, it was not admissible for Mr Barclay to say that Dexadrine was included because it had been abused, it not having been a controlled drug before the enactment of this statute. The court must therefore look at the inclusion of both amphetamine and dexamphetamine as two items in the same list of class B drugs and decide how that is properly to be construed.

After very careful consideration of the submissions of both counsel, we have come to the conclusion that greater effect will be given to the intention of Parliament, as disclosed by the content and context of the statute, by holding that amphetamine embraces both forms of it. The addition of dexamphetamine was unnecessary, and its inclusion is certainly not sufficiently strong to justify the application of the maxim already cited, which would have the startling effect that one of two stereoisomeric forms of amphetamine would be excluded from the category of drugs, quite apart from the fact that it would raise considerable practical difficulties in analysing the all too frequently small amount of the drug that is available.

Taking the question of construction in the round we have therefore come to the conclusion that the full generic meaning of the word 'Amphetamine', where it appears in para 1 of Pt II of the schedule, should be given to it, and that the appeal against conviction must fail.

There is also an application for leave to appeal against sentence. We can see absolutely nothing wrong with the sentence that was passed, and so that application will be refused.

Appeal against conviction and application for leave to appeal against sentence dismissed.

The court refused leave to appeal to the House of Lords but certified, under s 33(2) of the Criminal Appeal Act 1968, that the following point of law of general public importance was involved in the decision: whether on the correct construction of Sch 2 to the Misuse of Drugs Act 1971 in a prosecution alleging unlawful possession of amphetamine the presence of dexamphetamine as a separate controlled drug in the schedule imposed on the prosecution the burden of proving beyond reasonable doubt that the substance contained both levoamphetamine and dexamphetamine for the prosecution to succeed.

12 April. The Appeal Committee of the House of Lords (Lord Keith of Kinkel, Lord Bridge of Harwich and Lord Templeman) dismissed a petition by the appellant for leave to appeal.

Solicitors: *Thomas Andrews Humphrys & Co,* Wrexham (for the appellant); *Garrard Mitchell & Co,* Shrewsbury (for the Crown).

Dilys Tausz   Barrister.

a
Chief Constable of Hampshire v A and others

COURT OF APPEAL, CIVIL DIVISION
WALLER, OLIVER AND PURCHAS LJJ
20 FEBRUARY, 1 MARCH 1984

b
Injunction – Interlocutory – Preservation of proceeds of crime – Extent of court's powers to grant injunction in favour of police – Money in bank account – Money obtained through fraudulent trading – Money mixed with legitimately obtained money in bank account – Moneys incapable of separation into legitimate and illegitimate elements – Whether police entitled to injunction restraining dealings with bank account – Supreme Court Act 1981, s 37(1).

The defendants were alleged by the chief constable to be running a secondhand motor
c vehicle business based on fraud in that the vehicles in question were high-mileage police
cars which had been purchased at auction, then had their mileometers wound back and
were thereafter offered for sale with false representations about their mileage. It was also
alleged that the vehicles were sold to customers on hire purchase at inflated sale prices so
that the customers were credited with larger deposits than that actually paid and the
defendants accordingly received higher commissions from the hire-purchase companies
d than they had actually earned. The chief constable further alleged that when the
defendants started in business they had purchased two properties by means of substantial
bank loans which were subsequently paid off out of the proceeds of the fraudulent
trading. The properties had since been sold and there remained a sum of £117,000 either
in the defendants' trading bank accounts or in the hands of their solicitors. The chief
constable sought an injunction restraining the defendants from withdrawing, transferring
e or otherwise dealing with moneys in their trading bank accounts before their trial on
criminal charges of conspiring to defraud customers and the hire-purchase companies.

Held – Although (per Waller and Oliver LJJ) s 37(1)[a] of the Supreme Court Act 1981
conferred on the court power to grant an injunction to prevent the proceeds of crime
being dissipated, that power could only be exercised where the asset in respect of which
f the injunction was sought could be identified as being or representing property which
had been stolen or otherwise unlawfully obtained. On the facts (Purchas LJ concurring),
the most that could be said was that only some of the moneys paid into the defendants'
trading bank accounts had been obtained by unlawful means and since those moneys
had been mixed with other moneys properly obtained by untainted trading activities the
balance in the bank accounts was incapable of separation into legitimate and illegitimate
g elements. It followed that the chief constable was not entitled to the injunction sought
(see p 387 *h* to p 388 *b d e g* and *j* to p 389 *h* and p 390 *a b*, post).
Chief Constable of Kent v V [1982] 3 All ER 36 distinguished.

Notes
For the grant of interlocutory injunctions generally, see 24 Halsbury's Laws (4th edn)
h para 953, and for cases on the subject, see 28(2) Digest (Reissue) 968–989, 67–161.
   For the Supreme Court Act 1981, s 37, see 51 Halsbury's Statutes (3rd edn) 632.

Cases referred to in judgments
Chic Fashions (West Wales) Ltd v Jones [1968] 1 All ER 229, [1968] 2 QB 299, [1968] 2
   WLR 201, CA.
j *Chief Constable of Kent v V* [1982] 3 All ER 36, [1983] QB 34, [1982] 3 WLR 462, CA.

---

a   Section 37(1) provides: 'The High Court may by order (whether interlocutory or final) grant an
    injunction or appoint a receiver in all cases in which it appears to the court to be just and
    convenient to do so.'

Malone v Comr of Police of the Metropolis [1979] 1 All ER 256, [1980] QB 49, [1978] 3 WLR 936, CA.   *a*

Cases also cited
PCW (Underwriting Agencies) Ltd v Dixon [1983] 2 All ER 158; *on appeal* [1983] 2 All ER 697n, CA.
West Mercia Constabulary v Wagener [1981] 3 All ER 378, [1982] 1 WLR 127.

b

Interlocutory appeal
The plaintiff, the Chief Constable of Hampshire, appealed against the order of Sir Neil Lawson, sitting as a judge of the High Court on 11 November 1983 discharging an injunction granted by Nolan J on 11 August 1983 restraining the defendants A, B, R, V and D from withdrawing, transferring or otherwise transacting in respect of two sums of money held in accounts by a firm of solicitors and a bank. Execution of the order of Sir Neil Lawson was stayed pending the appeal. The facts are set out in the judgment of Waller LJ.

c

R N *Titheridge* QC and *Derwin Hope* for the chief constable.
W R H *Crowther* QC and *Alexander Layton* for the defendants.

Cur adv vult   *d*

1 March. The following judgments were delivered.

WALLER LJ. This is an appeal from Sir Neil Lawson sitting as a judge of the High Court in the Queen's Bench Division, when he refused to grant to the plaintiff chief   *e* constable an injunction restraining the defendants from withdrawing money from certain bank accounts. The first two defendants, who I shall call 'A' and 'B', were companies engaged in the buying and selling of secondhand motor vehicles, and the third, fourth and fifth defendants, whom I shall call 'R', 'V' and 'D', were directors of one or both of the two defendant companies and were concerned in the running of both of them.   *f*

The chief constable's case is that those defendants were running a business based on fraud in that the motor vehicles were high-mileage police cars which were purchased at auction and which then had the mileometer wound back either to zero or nearly zero, and thereafter the vehicles were offered for sale with false representations about the mileage. Furthermore, they were sold to customers who purchased on hire purchase and the sale price was inflated so that the purchaser was credited with a larger deposit than he   *g* had in fact made, and the defendants received higher commission from the hire-purchase companies than they had in fact earned. Furthermore, the basic sale price was very much more than the car was in fact worth.

The chief constable's case is that when the defendants started in business they purchased two properties by means of substantial loans from the bank, and that those loans were paid off out of the proceeds of fraudulent trading. Those two properties have now been   *h* sold and there is a sum of £117,000 either in the bank or in the hands of the defendants' solicitor which the chief constable claims should be frozen as being the proceeds of fraud.

The chief constable applied in the first instance to Nolan J ex parte, who granted a temporary injunction forbidding the withdrawal of any sums from the above-mentioned accounts and Sir Neil Lawson, having heard argument, refused to continue that injunction save that he provided that it should continue until the hearing of an appeal   *j* against his decision.

Before Sir Neil Lawson and before us the chief constable has relied on *Chief Constable of Kent v V* [1982] 3 All ER 36, [1983] QB 34. That was a decision where this court held (by a majority) that an injunction restraining the defendant from withdrawing money from two named bank accounts was properly made because it was said that the money in those

accounts was the proceeds of cheques forged by the defendant. It is not easy to discern
a the principle for which the case is authority. Lord Denning MR held that the provision
of s 37(1) of the Supreme Court Act 1981 conferred 'a new and extensive jurisdiction on
the High Court to grant an injunction' and that it was no longer necessary 'that the
injunction should be *ancillary* to an action claiming a legal or equitable right' (see [1982]
3 All ER 36 at 40, [1983] QB 34 at 42; Lord Denning MR's emphasis).

Lord Denning MR then turned to what he described as the crucial question in the case,
b and decided that the chief constable had a sufficient interest to apply for an injunction.
Donaldson LJ did not go so far as Lord Denning MR in describing the effects of s 37(1),
and said ([1982] 3 All ER 36 at 42, [1983] QB 34 at 45):

'These are wide words, but I am quite unable to see how it can appear to the court
to be just and convenient to make such an order, save in the enforcement or
protection of a legal or equitable right or interest.'
c

And Donaldson LJ, basing his conclusion on *Chic Fashions (West Wales) Ltd v Jones* [1968]
1 All ER 229, [1968] 2 QB 299, which dealt with the police right to seize goods, went on
([1982] 3 All ER 36 at 44, [1983] QB 34 at 47):

'... I consider that the common law can and should similarly invest the police
d with a right to "detain" moneys standing to the credit of a bank account if and to
the extent that they can be shown to have been obtained from another in breach of
the criminal law.'

In effect, Donaldson LJ was holding that this was a legal right within his earlier words.
Slade LJ held that 'The court would have no jurisdiction to grant the chief constable an
e injunctive relief save in the enforcement or protection of a legal or equitable right' (see
[1982] 3 All ER 36 at 45, [1983] QB 34 at 49). He was then broadly accepting the
formulation of Donaldson LJ. But Slade LJ rejected Donaldson LJ's reasoning in relation
to the chief constable, saying that only if it were possible to say that the chief constable
had a present or contingent legal or equitable right to demand that such moneys be
actually paid over to him would he have the right to injunctive relief (see [1982] 3 All
f ER 36 at 47, [1983] QB 34 at 51). Therefore, there is a fundamental difference in the
conclusion of Slade LJ compared with the conclusions of Lord Denning MR and
Donaldson LJ. They each take the view that, it being settled that the chief constable
would have the right to seize property believed to have been stolen found on the premises
of a defendant, it follows that he should have the right to injunctive relief to prevent the
proceeds of crime being dissipated: Lord Denning MR because of the change in the law
in 1981 enlarging the power of the court, and Donaldson LJ taking the view that it is a
g logical step from the *Chic Fashions* case. Neither Lord Denning MR nor Donaldson LJ
regarded it as essential that the chief constable should have the right to have the money
actually paid over to him, which is the view of Slade LJ.

Sir Neil Lawson preferred the judgment of Slade LJ, finding the reasoning of Lord
Denning MR difficult to follow. In my judgment, however, there was agreement
h between Lord Denning MR and Donaldson LJ that there is power to grant an injunction
to prevent the identified proceeds of crime being dissipated.

The next question is to consider whether, on the facts of this case, it is one where the
court ought to grant the injunction prayed for or some modification of it. In this case the
charges are charges of conspiracy to defraud, and so, even accepting that the trading
receipts of the companies would contain substantial proceeds of fraudulent transactions,
j these proceeds would not be specific sums, as in the case of forged cheques. In *Chief
Constable of Kent v V* there was one victim, and the relevant fraud was easily identifiable.
In this case the amount paid for a particular car would not be the amount repayable in
proceedings based on fraud, because the true value of the car would have to be brought
into account. And, while the payment would not necessarily have to be traced with the
same accuracy as equity would demand, nevertheless the difficulties in this case are very

great. Furthermore, there would appear to be a very large number of persons who have suffered loss, and the difficulties I envisage would be repeated in each case.

Finally, the fund with which we are concerned is the proceeds of the sale of the two properties which were purchased by means of loans from the bank which have been paid off from the trading accounts of the companies. But some of the cash flow must have been free from fraud, and it may well be that much of the fraudulent trading receipts have been spent on day-to-day living. In my judgment, therefore, on the particular facts of this case, I would not grant an injunction, and accordingly I would dismiss this appeal.

OLIVER LJ. I agree. As Waller LJ has said, and as counsel for the defendants has submitted, it is not easy to discern a single underlying ratio in the majority judgments in *Chief Constable of Kent v V* [1982] 3 All ER 36, [1983] QB 34, but for my part I am, with respect, unable to accept the basis on which the jurisdiction was put by Lord Denning MR, a basis which was rejected both by Donaldson LJ and by Slade LJ in his dissenting judgment. Both Lord Denning MR and Donaldson LJ were, however, agreed to this extent, that jurisdiction to grant an injunction on the application of the chief constable in that case existed only if he could be found to have sufficient interest in making the application, and they appear broadly to have been in agreement as to the foundation of the interest which they held to exist and to be sufficient. That was to be found in the duty of the chief constable to seize and detain goods stolen or unlawfully obtained and to restore them to their true owner, a similar duty being applied by analogy to intangible assets such as a credit in a bank account.

That must, however, rest in my judgment on an ability in the court to identify the asset in respect of which the injunction is sought as itself either being or representing property which has been stolen or otherwise unlawfully obtained, for it is clear from *Malone v Comr of Police of the Metropolis* [1979] 1 All ER 256, [1980] QB 49 that there is no right or duty of detention in the case of property which is the absolute property of an accused not the subject of any charge and that such property cannot be frozen in his hands merely because, if convicted, he may become subject to an order under the provisions of s 28 of the Theft Act 1968 or s 35 or s 43 of the Powers of Criminal Courts Act 1973. That the jurisdiction is so limited is, I think, implicit in the judgment of Lord Denning MR, but is express in that of Donaldson LJ, who observed ([1982] 3 All ER 36 at 44, [1983] QB 34 at 47):

> 'In the instant appeal I consider that the common law can and should similarly invest the police with a right to "detain" moneys standing to the credit of a bank account *if and to the extent* that they can be shown to have been obtained from another in breach of the criminal law.' (Emphasis supplied.)

In agreement with Waller LJ, I cannot see how such identification is possible in the instant case, or how there is anything here to be 'restored to the true owners'. Indeed, counsel for the chief constable was ultimately compelled to appeal to the desirability of preserving property for distribution to creditors generally in a criminal bankruptcy.

The injunction here is sought in order to freeze in the hands of the individual defendants' solicitors the proceeds of the sales of the properties which were held by them, or some one or more of them individually, and were acquired with loans made to them personally by banks. The overdrafts or loan accounts thus quite properly created were reduced or extinguished by payments from various sources, but certainly in part from moneys which were provided by regular transfer from the trading accounts of the two companies. Certainly, however, in the case of one of the properties, it is accepted that a substantial repayment was made by one of the individual defendants out of the proceeds of sale of his own dwelling house, as to which there is no suggestion in the evidence that it was obtained otherwise than lawfully.

Moreover, even in relation to such part of the indebtedness as was discharged by payments made to the individual defendants out of the companies' trading accounts, the highest that it is put (or, indeed, that it can be put) is that those moneys included 'at least in part' moneys obtained by fraud. When this is analysed, however, it becomes apparent

that, even if it is a permissible exercise to trace into a property acquired by means of a
a bank loan moneys which are subsequently applied in reduction of that loan, it is quite
impossible to identify in those moneys any particular sum or proportion which can be
said to represent money unlawfully obtained. Accepting for the purposes of this appeal
that the facts relied on by the chief constable can be substantiated in full, the most that
they show is that fraudulent representations were made in 'a large number' of the
transactions into which the companies entered, both with hire-purchase companies and
b with customers in the period covered by the charges of conspiracy in the criminal
proceedings. So far as the customers are concerned, the fraud alleged is the making of
false representations as to the quality or condition of the vehicles sold, but it is not alleged
that the contracts with customers have been rescinded, so that one is left with the position
that, as a result of fraud, many of the companies' customers (whose number is unspecified)
have claims in damages against the companies and the individual defendants, the precise
amount of which is, at the moment, quite incapable of quantification.
c   So far as the hire-purchase companies are concerned, the fraud consisted of the
overstatement of the true prices of the vehicles sold by attributing an excessive value to
the vehicles given in part exchange, with the result that excessive sums were paid for the
vehicles hired to customers and that the commission on transactions paid by the hire-
purchase companies was inflated. But here again, the amount of loss suffered by each
d hire-purchase company depends on the extent, if any, to which customers have defaulted,
and the resale value of vehicles repossessed. So that the highest that it can be put is that
some (possibly even the bulk) of the moneys paid into the trading accounts are moneys of
the companies which have been obtained by fraudulent misrepresentations giving rise to
claims for unliquidated damage. Those moneys having been mixed with other moneys
properly obtained by untainted trading activities, there remains, after payment of
e outgoings and expenses, a balance of trading profit, which is incapable of separation into
legitimate and illegitimate elements, out of which sums have been paid in reduction of
the individual loans, some of those sums being claimed to be directors' remuneration
which, it is said, was unauthorised by resolution in general meeting but which appears
in fact to have been paid with the agreement of all shareholders in the companies. No
part of those sums can be separately identified by any known principle of tracing as being
f exclusively 'the proceedings of fraud', or as having been 'obtained from another in breach
of the criminal law'.
         It is not, as I have said, easy to determine what are the ratio and the ambit of *Chief
Constable of Kent v V*, nor is it necessary for the decision of this appeal to determine its
precise limits. Whatever those may be, I am for my part quite satisfied that what counsel
for the chief constable is seeking to do in the circumstances which exist here is not to
apply *Chief Constable of Kent v V*, but to extend it, and I am unable to see the logical or
g rational basis on which it can be extended to cover the funds in respect of which the
jurisdiction is sought in this case.
         I too would dismiss the appeal.

PURCHAS LJ. I agree that on the particular facts of this case as already outlined by
h Waller and Oliver LJJ that this appeal must fail. On any view of the effect of s 37(1) of
the Supreme Court Act 1981, the chief constable has not sufficiently identified the funds
which he wishes to freeze as being the proceeds of the crime or crimes with which the
defendants have been charged.
         I wish to reserve my views on the broader issues which have been argued before us.
Doubtless it will be necessary at some time in the future to determine precisely where
j the line must be drawn between those circumstances which give rise to a legal or
equitable right or interest in a constable to have resort to the powers of the court granted
by s 37(1) and those which do not. The discharge by a constable of his common law duty
to pursue not only criminals but also in order to preserve evidence of the proceeds of
crime as part of his duty to protect the public clearly fall within the former category: see
Chic Fashions (West Wales) Ltd v Jones [1968] 1 All ER 229, [1968] 2 QB 299. On the other
hand, an attempt to exercise subrogated rights to claim compensation by the victims of

crime leading to an application to the court to achieve the preservation of funds with
which such claims could be met do not: see *Malone v Comr of Police of the Metropolis* [1979]   *a*
1 All ER 256, [1980] QB 49. In order to invoke the powers of the court under s 37(1) of
the 1981 Act, the subject matter must be identifiable with the proceeds of crime rather
than the civil claims of the victims of crime. Fortunately, for reasons given by Waller
and Oliver LJJ, it is not necessary to resolve this interesting question in this appeal.

I agree, for the reasons given by Waller and Oliver LJJ, that this appeal must be
dismissed.   *b*

Appeal and action dismissed. Leave to appeal to the House of Lords refused.

Solicitors: *Theodore Goddard & Co*, agents for *R A Leyland*, Winchester (for the chief
constable); *Hancock & Willis*, agents for *Faithfull & Bowker*, Winchester (for the defendants).

c

Sophie Craven   Barrister.

R v Secretary of State for the Home
Department, ex parte Kirkwood   *d*

QUEEN'S BENCH DIVISION (CROWN OFFICE LIST)
MANN J
10 FEBRUARY 1984

Crown proceedings – Nature of relief – Jurisdiction – No power in court to grant injunction   *e*
against officer of Crown – Whether power to stay order made by Secretary of State for surrender
of fugitive offender – Crown Proceedings Act 1947, s 21.

Extradition – Surrender – Person accused or convicted of extradition crime – Secretary of State's
power to order surrender – Fugitive contending that extradition would violate European
Convention on Human Rights – Fugitive applying to European Commission of Human Rights for   *f*
decision on matter – Secretary of State ordering surrender of fugitive while application pending
– Whether Secretary of State entitled to make the order – Whether Secretary of State bound to
consider articles of convention – Extradition Act 1870, s 11 – European Convention on Human
Rights, art 3.

In 1982 the applicant, who was wanted in the State of California on a murder charge, was   *g*
arrested in England. The United States government requested his extradition. On 11
May 1983, after considering the request, the metropolitan stipendiary magistrate
committed him to prison under s 10 of the Extradition Act 1870. The applicant made
no application for a writ of habeas corpus but he applied to the European Commission of
Human Rights, claiming that his extradition would be a violation of art 3 of the European
Convention on Human Rights on the ground that, if he were convicted in California, he   *h*
would be sentenced to death and the inordinate delay in carrying out the death penalty
in that state would amount to inhuman and degrading treatment. The commission
indicated, under r 36[a] of its rules of procedure, that he should not be extradited before
December 1983. It was the practice of the Secretary of State for the Home Department
to heed such an indication, so he took no action while it applied. The commission did
not renew the indication in December but intimated that it would consider the   *j*
admissibility of the applicant's application to it in March 1984. In February 1984 the
Secretary of State issued a warrant, under s 11[b] of the 1870 Act, ordering the applicant to

---

a   Rule 36 is set out at p 392 *e*, post
b   Section 11, so far as material, is set out at p 392 *g h*, post

be surrendered to the United States authorities. Before the warrant was executed, the
a applicant applied ex parte for leave to apply for judicial review of the order on the ground
that the Secretary of State should not have acted while the application to the commission
was extant and the question of whether there would be a breach of art 3 of the convention
was undecided. Leave to apply for judicial review was granted and an order was made
under RSC Ord 53, r 3(10), directing that the grant of leave should operate as a stay of
proceedings on the warrant until the application for judicial review was determined. The
b Secretary of State applied for the stay to be discharged, contending (i) that the court was
prevented by s 21ᶜ of the Crown Proceedings Act 1947 from ordering a stay and (ii) that,
even if it had power to grant a stay, it should not have exercised it in the circumstances.

Held – The stay would be discharged because the court was prohibited by s 21 of the
1947 Act from granting an injunction against an officer of the Crown and the stay was
c equivalent to an injunction restraining the Secretary of State from exercising his executive
function. In any event, when exercising his powers under the 1870 Act the Secretary of
State was not obliged to consider the provisions of the European Convention on Human
Rights since it was not part of the law of the United Kingdom; and accordingly, even if
there had been jurisdiction to grant the stay, the court would still have ordered it to be
removed because the applicant's chances of success by way of judicial review were
d negligible (see p 393 c d g h, p 394 b to e and p 395 f to h, post).

Notes
For restrictions on granting injunctions against an officer of the Crown, see 11 Halsbury's
Laws (4th edn) para 1435.
    For the surrender of a fugitive to a foreign state by warrant of the Secretary of State,
e see 18 ibid paras 203, 210, 238.
    For the Extradition Act 1870, ss 10, 11, see 13 Halsbury's Statutes (3rd edn) 257, 258.
    For the Crown Proceedings Act 1947, s 21, see 8 ibid 860.

Cases referred to in judgment
Associated Provincial Picture Houses v Wednesbury Corp [1947] 2 All ER 680, [1948] 1 KB
f 223, CA.
R v Chief Immigration Officer, Heathrow Airport, ex p Salamat Bibi [1976] 3 All ER 843,
    [1976] 1 WLR 979, CA.
R v Secretary of State for the Home Dept, ex p Fernandes (1980) Times, 21 November, CA.
Yaqoob v Secretary of State for the Home Dept (23 September 1983, CA Unbound Transcript
    1027).

g **Application for removal of stay**
Ernest Major Kirkwood applied for leave to challenge by way of judicial review an order
made, under s 11 of the Extradition Act 1870, on 5 February 1984 by the Secretary of
State for the Home Department directing that the applicant should be surrendered to the
United States authorities. On 7 February Mann J granted leave and, at the request of the
applicant, made an order under RSC Ord 53, r 3(10)(*a*), directing that the grant of leave
h should operate as a stay of proceedings in respect of the Secretary of State's order until
after the determination of the application for judicial review. On 10 February the
Secretary of State applied for the stay to be discharged. The facts are set out in the
judgment.

Simon D Brown for the Secretary of State.
j *Colin Nicholls QC* for the applicant.

MANN J. On 7 February counsel moved ex parte on behalf of Ernest Major Kirkwood
for leave to challenge an order dated 5 February 1984 made by the Secretary of State for

---

c   Section 21, so far as material, is set out at p 393 d to g, post the Home Department under s 11 of the Extradition Act 1870. I granted leave to move. I also granted interim relief under RSC Ord 53, r 3(10)(*a*). The effect of my grant was to *a* prevent the Secretary of State implementing his order until after the determination of the application for judicial review or until such time as this court otherwise ordered. There is before the court today an application on behalf of the Secretary of State to remove the stay which I imposed.

The background to the matter can be stated chronologically. On 24 July 1982 two persons were murdered and there was an attempt to murder another person in San *b* Francisco in the State of California. The State of California alleges that it was Ernest Major Kirkwood who committed the murders and the attempted murder. Ernest Major Kirkwood (whom I shall refer to as 'the applicant') came to this country in November 1982. He was arrested on a warrant granted by the metropolitan stipendiary magistrate pursuant to a request by the United States government. The procedure under the 1870 Act was undertaken. On 11 May 1983 the metropolitan stipendiary magistrate committed *c* the applicant into custody following his consideration of the request for extradition. There was no application for habeas corpus.

On 13 July 1983 the applicant made an application to the European Commission of Human Rights claiming that his extradition would be in breach of art III of the European Convention on Human Rights (Convention for the Protection of Human Rights and Fundamental Freedoms (Rome, 4 November 1950; TS 71 (1953); Cmd 8969)) on the *d* ground that the inordinate delay in carrying out the death penalty in California amounts to inhuman and degrading treatment and punishment. It is inherent in that application that the sentence or a sentence for murder in the State of California is death. Indeed, that is the case. On 14 July 1983 the commission applied r 36 of its rules of procedure. Rule 36 provides:

> 'The Commission, or where it is not in session, the President may indicate to the *e* parties any interim measure the adoption of which seems desirable in the interest of the parties or the proper conduct of the proceedings before it.'

The indication given was in the sense that extradition should not occur. The r 36 indication was renewed on 17 October and again on 14 November. It was not renewed on 15 December. No reason was given for the absence of renewal, but it was stated that *f* the admissibility of the application would be considered in the fortnight commencing 5 March 1984. To complete the chronology a further application was made on behalf of the applicant for a r 36 indication. That was refused on the evening of 7 February 1984 after the hearing in this court.

The practice of the Secretary of State is to heed indications under r 36. Hence, the Secretary of State stayed his hand while such indications were prevalent. The Secretary of *g* State is empowered under s 11 of the 1870 Act as follows:

> '... Upon the expiration of the said fifteen days, or, if a writ of Habeas corpus is issued, after the decision of the court upon the return to the writ, as the case may be, or after such further period as may be allowed in either case by a Secretary of State, it shall be lawful for a Secretary of State, by warrant under his hand and seal, to order the fugitive criminal (if not delivered on the decision of the court) to be *h* surrendered to such person as may in his opinion be duly authorized to receive the fugitive criminal by the foreign state from which the requisition for the surrender proceeded, and such fugitive criminal shall be surrendered accordingly ...'

A warrant dated 2 February is the order which the applicant seeks to impugn. It was to have been executed on 8 February, but has not yet been served. The grounds for the *j* application are in essence that the Secretary of State's decision to proceed under s 11 is a decision which no reasonable Secretary of State properly instructed could have made. Counsel in his grounds for the application asserts, first, that the Secretary of State has failed to consider the legal obligation of the United Kingdom to provide the applicant with an effective remedy in the event of a breach of art 3 of the European convention, a second, that he has failed to consider that if the applicant is returned to the United States of America before the European Commission of Human Rights has examined his case during its session commencing 5 March 1984 the applicant will be deprived of his remedy, third, by making the order at this stage rather than by waiting until the next session of the commission on 5 March he has concluded unreasonably and without proper foundation that the European Commission will find in favour of the United Kingdom, or alternatively he has decided that the applicant should be returned to the

b United States irrespective of any determination of the European Commission or Court.

Counsel for the applicant also asserted that, in all the circumstances of the case and in particular in that it involves the applicant's freedom from inhuman and degrading treatment whilst awaiting execution, the decision is one which no reasonable Secretary of State could have made. That attack was qualified in the course of the hearing on 7 February in the sense that it was reduced to an attack on the decision having been taken

c some few weeks before 5 March, when the commission commences the session in which the admissibility of the application will be considered.

Counsel for the Secretary of State put his case in two ways. He says, first, that I had no jurisdiction to grant the stay which I did and, second, even if I did have such jurisdiction on the merits it should not have been exercised. By 'on the merits' I understand him to say that this court in considering whether or not to grant interim relief must pay regard

d to the likely fate of the ultimate application when it is heard. I take first the jurisdiction point. He says that having regard to s 21 of the Crown Proceedings Act 1947 this court has no power to grant a stay. He drew my attention to sub-s (1), which provides:

'In any civil proceedings by or against the Crown the court shall, subject to the provisions of this Act, have power to make all such orders as it has power to make in proceedings between subjects, and otherwise to give such appropriate relief as the

e case may require: Provided that:—(a) where in any proceedings against the Crown any such relief is sought as might in proceedings between subjects be granted by way of injunction or specific performance, the court shall not grant an injunction or make an order for specific performance, but may in lieu thereof make an order declaratory of the rights of the parties . . .'

f I need not read proviso (b). Subsection (2) provides:

'The court shall not in any civil proceedings grant any injunction or make any order against an officer of the Crown if the effect of granting the injunction or making the order would be to give any relief against the Crown which could not have been obtained in proceedings against the Crown.'

g It is common ground between the parties that for this purpose proceedings by way of judicial review are civil proceedings.

Counsel for the Secretary of State said that there is no distinction between a stay and an injunction in the present context and he referred me to *Yaqoob v Secretary of State for the Home Dept* (23 September 1983, CA Unbound Transcript 1027), a decision of Dillon LJ sitting as a single judge in the Court of Appeal, Civil Division, where he said in

h relation to an immigration matter:

'It is, however, a matter for the Secretary of State and in view of the Crown Proceedings Act 1947 I do not think this court has any jurisdiction to make an order against the Secretary of State restraining him from removing Mr Yaqoob pending the hearing of the appeal. The appeal is concerned not with the steps for Mr Yaqoob's removal but with the propriety or otherwise of his refusal of admission last year.

j The stay sought of proceedings for removal is not a stay of the enforcement of an order of the court, it is an injunction to restrain the Secretary of State from exercising his executive functions and that the court cannot grant. Therefore, I do not feel able to grant any relief, especially as it is not appropriate to grant an interim declaration in lieu of the injunction since that would have no legal effect. Therefore, I must make no order on that part of the application which seeks a stay which I have mentioned.

a

Counsel for the applicant argued that there was before 1947 an inherent jurisdiction in the court to grant a stay, and that that inherent jurisdiction survived the 1947 Act in the sense that the words of s 21 which I have read do not exclude an inherent and anterior jurisdiction. I am not persuaded by anything that he said that there was such an inherent anterior jurisdiction. So far as the words of s 21 are concerned, I cannot attach any significance to the omission of the word 'civil' as prefatory to 'proceedings' where that word secondly occurs in sub-s (2). The omission seems to me to be simply an omission by way of drafting technique, a technique which is also employed in sub-s (1). I do not share his view that sub-s (2) can be read as concluding in effect with the words 'before the commencement of this Act'. In my judgment the sole purpose of sub-s (2) is to prevent the subject from achieving indirectly a result which he could not achieve directly by reason of the provisions of sub-s (1). I regard the observations of Dillon LJ as binding on me. Even if they were not binding on me, I find the argument of counsel for the Secretary of State quite irresistible. He conceded that the success of his argument would demonstrate that there is a lacuna in this court's power to control exercises of executive discretion. Whether it is right or wrong that there should be such a lacuna is not a matter it is appropriate to comment on this afternoon. I do, however, draw attention to the commentary in *Wade on Administrative Law* (5th edn, 1982) pp 517–518.

b

c

d

On that ground alone the stay would have to go, but it would be wrong of me to limit myself in that way and I should express a view on the merits of the matter, because if I was adverse to the Secretary of State on the likelihood of an application for judicial review ultimately succeeding he might wish to delay further the issue of the warrant. As I have indicated by reference to the grounds of counsel for the applicant's application, central to his case is the *Wednesbury* principle (see *Associated Provincial Picture Houses v Wednesbury Corp* [1947] 2 All ER 680, [1948] 1 KB 223) and the operation of that principle in relation to the application which has been made to the European Commission.

e

Counsel for the Secretary of State submits that the *Wednesbury* principle cannot have any operation in this case, because the Secretary of State is not under our law obliged to have any regard to the treaty provisions. He referred me to *R v Secretary of State for the Home Dept, ex p Fernandes* (1980) Times, 21 November, a decision of the Court of Appeal where that which was before the court was a challenge to a deportation order, when there was also an extant application to the European Commission. It was argued on behalf of Mrs Fernandes that the Secretary of State should not proceed, having regard to her application to the Commission. The first judgment was given by Waller LJ, who said:

f

'What I have said is on the assumption that it is right to take into account the provisions of the Convention on Human Rights, but there is in my view another ground on which this appeal should be dismissed, namely that the Secretary of State was not under any such legal obligation. In *R v Chief Immigration Officer, ex p Salamat Bibi* [1976] 3 All ER 843, [1976] 1 WLR 979 the relevance of the European Convention on Human Rights to the municipal law of this country was considered. Lord Denning MR said this in relation to the European Convention ([1976] 3 All ER 843 at 847, [1976] 1 WLR 979 at 984): "The position as I understand it is that if there is any ambiguity in our statutes, or uncertainty in our law, then these courts can look to the convention as an aid to clear up the ambiguity and uncertainty, seeking always to bring them into harmony with it. Furthermore, when Parliament is enacting a statute, or the Secretary of State is framing rules, the courts will assume that they had regard to the provisions of the convention, and intended to make the enactment accord with the convention, and will interpret them accordingly. But I would dispute altogether that the convention is part of our law. Treaties and declarations do not become part of our law until they are made law by Parliament." Roskill LJ said ([1976] 3 All ER 843, [1976] 1 WLR 979 at 985): "I would only add one word on the argument to which we have listened on the European Convention

g

h

j

a on Human Rights. Like Lord Denning MR, I am of the view that this convention is not part of the law of England. It is not necessary to go into elaborate reasons why that is so. Suffice it to say that a treaty does not become part of the municipal law of this country unless and until it is the subject of legislation in the ordinary way. That is axiomatic; it has been laid down for many years. What is said is that the immigration officers should, in exercising their powers under the rules which, as I have already said, are part of the law of this country, take into account the provisions

b of the convention, which is not. With respect, I am unable to agree."'

After further comment Waller LJ continued:

'In my judgment, there was no legal obligation on the Secretary of State to consider whether or not this was a contravention of articles of the convention. I have little doubt that the Secretary of State, in considering this application, did consider these facts as part of the general picture, but the question which this court

c has to ask itself is whether, when the letter was received, the Home Secretary was acting fairly, and can it be said, on the information before the court, that his decision was such that no reasonable man in his position could have made it? In my judgment that is quite impossible.'

d Ackner LJ said:

'I agree. It seems to me that there are three separate bases on which this appeal must fail. First, that the Secretary of State in exercising his statutory powers is not obliged to take into account the provisions of the convention which are not part of the law of this country. The convention is a treaty and may be resorted to in order to help to resolve some uncertainty or ambiguity in municipal law.'

e Counsel for the applicant sought to resist the reasoning in these passages by pointing out that the consequences for Mrs Fernandes were far less serious than the consequences for his client. That I accept. He said that the Secretary of State must be under an obligation to consider the treaty obligations where the consequence of not doing something is the probable consignment of the applicant to 'Death Row'. It would be wrong, unjust and oppressive, says counsel for the applicant, not to do so. Accepting as I

f do that the consequences for the applicant are more serious than the consequences for Mrs Fernandes, I am quite unable to distinguish the decision in *Ex p Fernandes* on that ground. Accordingly, as it seems to me, the chances of success by way of judicial review are negligible.

I should add this. Counsel for the Secretary of State said that the Secretary of State has in fact taken into account the treaty obligations and manifestly so. He points to the

g Secretary of State having stayed his hand whilst the r 36 indications were extant. Indeed, it is deposed to on his behalf that it is the practice of the United Kingdom to comply with the r 36 indications. That is a practice. It cannot be more, because the indications are mere indications and give rise to no obligation under public international law. They do not, of course, give rise to any obligation under our municipal law.

For those reasons, even if the jurisdiction point was not as I have decided it to be, I

h would have removed the stay. This application is accordingly successful.

Order for removal of stay.

Solicitors: *Treasury Solicitor*; *Maxwell & Gouldman* (for the applicant).

April Weiss   Barrister.

Re Mathew (deceased)   *a*

FAMILY DIVISION
ANTHONY LINCOLN J
21 DECEMBER 1983, 14 MARCH 1984

Executor and administrator – Administrator – Appointment in special circumstances – Grant   *b*
passing over prior claims – Limitation of grant – Whether grant may be made to agreed grantees
without excluding right of executors named in will to apply subsequently for probate – Supreme
Court Act 1981, s 116(2).

Administration of estates – Grant of administration – Jurisdiction – Registrar – Revocation of
grant – Whether registrar having jurisdiction to revoke grant of administration ordered by
another registrar on ground that latter registrar had no jurisdiction to make order made –   *c*
Supreme Court Act 1981, s 121(1) – Non-Contentious Probate Rules 1954, r 42.

In 1972 the testator made a will appointing his brother, T, and a solicitor, G, to be the
executors and trustees of his will. He died in 1983 and was survived by, inter alios, his
four brothers. After the testator's death there was a dispute between T and the other
three brothers as to the administration of the will. At that time G was practising abroad   *d*
and was unable to take up the executorship personally. Accordingly, G executed a power
of attorney appointing two solicitors within the jurisdiction as his agents to apply for and
obtain letters of administration with the will annexed. T, who opposed the appointment
of the attorneys, applied to the court under s 116[a] of the Supreme Court Act 1981 for an
order passing over G and his attorneys and granting administration to himself and
another named person. Before the application was heard, discussions were held between   *e*
all the parties concerned as to the future administration of the estate and it was then
agreed that there should be three administrators, namely a solicitor who had no previous
connection with the dispute or the estate, T's solicitor and one of G's attorneys. On 17
August 1983 the registrar made a consent order granting letters of administration of the
estate to the three agreed persons and reserving power to the executors to apply for a   *f*
grant of probate. T subsequently wished to obtain a grant of probate, and on 21
November another registrar made an order setting aside the first registrar's order and
revoking the grant of letters of administration on the ground that the first registrar had
had no jurisdiction, when granting letters of administration, to reserve power to the
executors to apply subsequently for a grant of probate. The other three brothers applied
to the court to set aside the second registrar's order and to restore the first registrar's
order. The questions arose (i) whether the first registrar had had power when granting   *g*
letters of administration to 'reserve power' to the executors named in the will and (ii)
whether the second registrar had had power to revoke the grant or set aside the first
registrar's order for lack of jurisdiction.

Held – (1) In view of the very wide terms of s 116(2) of the 1981 Act, which provided
for any grant of administration which passed over prior claims to grant to be limited 'in   *h*
any way the court thinks fit', the court could, if it was satisfied that there were special
circumstances making it necessary or expedient to do so, grant letters of administration
to agreed grantees without excluding the right of the executors named in the will to

a   Section 116 provides: *j*
    '(1) If by reason of any special circumstances it appears to the High Court to be necessary or
    expedient to appoint as administrator some person other than the person who, but for this section,
    would in accordance with probate rules have been entitled to the grant, the court may in its
    discretion appoint as administrator such person as it thinks expedient.
    (2) Any grant of administration under this section may be limited in any way the court thinks
    fit.'

apply subsequently for probate (which would not be a double probate). Since the first
a registrar had had power to make the order that she made, since that order gave effect to
the agreement of the parties and since there were none of the rare circumstances, such as
duress or mistake, which would justify the court in reopening a consent order, there
were no grounds for setting aside the order (see p 398 *h j*, p 400 *a* to *f* and *h j* and p 401
c d, post); dictum of Ewbank J in *Re Clore (decd)* [1982] Fam at 117 applied.

(2) Moreover, the power of a registrar to call in and revoke a grant of probate or
b administration under s 121(1)[b] of the 1981 Act or r 42[c] of the Non-Contentious Probate
Rules 1954 did not include jurisdiction to consider whether an earlier decision by another
registrar (which was a decision made by a co-ordinate tribunal) was made pursuant to
jurisdiction. Since there was no fresh evidence which would have enabled the subsequent
tribunal to review and vary the earlier order, it followed that the second registrar had no
jurisdiction to set aside the first registrar's order or to revoke the grant. The second
c registrar had, however, had power to look at the effect of the grant in the light of the
circumstances prevailing at the time of the hearing before him, the changed circumstances
being the desire of T to exercise the power preserved for him (as it had been for G or his
attorneys) under the first registrar's order to apply for a grant of probate. Accordingly,
since the first registrar's order had proved an obstacle to T's wish to obtain a grant of
probate, it was right for the court to make such an order as would avoid any doubt and
d would allow T to seek a grant of probate (see p 400 *j* to p 401 *e*, post).

Notes
For special circumstances enabling the court to pass over a person otherwise entitled to a
grant of administration, see 17 Halsbury's Laws (4th edn) para 955, and for cases on
subject, see 23 Digest (Reissue) 251–259, 3041–3122.

For the jurisdiction of a registrar to revoke a grant of probate or administration, see 17
e Halsbury's Laws (4th edn) paras 777, 1057, 1064.

For the Supreme Court Act 1981, ss 116, 121, see 51 Halsbury's Statutes (3rd edn) 858,
862.

For the Non-Contentious Probate Rules 1954, r 42, see 7 Halsbury's Statutory
Instruments (4th reissue) 343.

f **Case referred to in judgment**
Clore (decd), Re [1982] Fam 113, [1982] 2 WLR 314; *affd sub nom IRC v Stype Investments
(Jersey) Ltd, Re Clore (decd)* [1982] 3 All ER 419, [1982] Ch 456, [1982] 3 WLR 228,
CA.

Appeal
g Charles, Francis and Robert Mathew, three brothers of Theobald Mathew deceased,
appealed against the order of Mr Registrar Terian made on the application of the
respondent, Thomas Mathew, on 21 November 1983 setting aside an order of Mrs
Registrar Pearce on 17 August 1983 and revoking a grant of letters of administration to
Alec John Bateson, Jocelyn Timothy Henry Thomas and Riou Benson in respect of the
estate of the deceased. The appeal was heard in chambers but judgment was given by
h Anthony Lincoln J in open court. The facts are set out in the judgment.

Michael Hart for the appellants.
Peter Cowell for the respondent.
Timothy Lloyd for the grantees.

j   *Cur adv vult*

---

b   Section 121(1) provides: 'Where it appears to the High Court that a grant either ought not to have
     been made or contains an error, the court may call in the grant and, if satisfied that it would be
     revoked at the instance of a party interested, may revoke it.'
c   Rule 42, so far as material, provides: 'If a registrar is satisfied that a grant should be amended or
     revoked he may make an order accordingly . . .'

14 March. The following judgment was delivered.

ANTHONY LINCOLN J. This is an appeal by Charles, Francis and Robert Mathew, the three brothers of the deceased testator, against an order of Mr Registrar Terian made on 21 November 1983, setting aside an order made by Mrs Registrar Pearce dated 17 August 1983 and revoking a grant of letters of administration to Alec Bateson, Jocelyn Timothy Thomas and Riou Benson. The three brothers are, accordingly, in effect seeking to reinstate Mrs Registrar Pearce's order. A fourth brother, Thomas Mathew, is seeking to uphold Mr Registrar Terian's order so as to restore the state of affairs which existed before the grant of letters of administration was made. The appeal raises an unusual question largely arising out of the use in a court order of a phrase not normally to be found in such an order.

The late Theobald Mathew was a successful farmer whose estate near Market Harborough, Leicestershire largely consisted of agricultural land and buildings, the whole being of considerable value. On 27 March 1972 he made a will, appointing his brother Thomas and a solicitor (David Glynn) to be the executors and trustees of his will. The contents of the will are otherwise not material to the appeal, save to say that certain brothers were beneficiaries of a trust created by the will.

On 10 July 1983 the testator died. He was survived by the four brothers and six sisters who were left legacies. There is, unhappily, much friction and suspicion among the members of the family. In this very dispute the three brothers are to a greater or lesser extent in confrontation with Thomas. At the time of the death of the testator, the executor David Glynn was carrying on his professional practice in Hong Kong. Because he considered himself unable to take up the executorship personally, Mr Glynn executed a power of attorney in favour of two partners of the firm of Messrs Charles Russell & Co, Mr Riou Benson and Mr David Long, practising within the jurisdiction. The terms of the power of attorney reflected the terms of r 30(1) and (2) of the Non-Contentious Probate Rules 1954, SI 1954/796 as amended by SI 1967/748: it empowered the donees to apply for and obtain a grant of letters of administration (with the will annexed) of the estate for Mr Glynn's benefit and use and until the latter should apply for and obtain a grant of probate. This meant that the two London solicitors were the deputies or agents of Mr Glynn, equipped with such full powers as Mr Glynn could exercise as executor in administering the estate. They enjoyed these powers until they completed the administration or until such time as Mr Glynn, if he chose, took up a grant of probate. If he did that, their agency under the power of attorney would end. And so it can be said that under the power of attorney Mr Glynn's right to apply for and obtain a grant was preserved, if not reserved.

Now Mr Thomas Mathew was dissatisfied with this situation. He opposed the participation of both Mr Benson and Mr Long in the administration of the estate, for reasons which are the subject of considerable dispute and which it is not necessary for me to investigate. He applied under s 116 of the Supreme Court Act 1981 for the court to appoint as administrator some person other than the person who but for that selection would have been entitled to the grant. He invited the court to pass over the prior claims of the executor Mr Glynn and those whom he had deputed his attorneys (Mr Benson and Mr Long) and to grant letters of administration to a Mr Nicholas Sibley and himself. The reasons for and merits of such a grant do not require to be assessed by me.

In granting such an application the court has to be satisfied that there are special circumstances from which it appears necessary or expedient that such persons be administrators. I follow Ewbank J in Re Clore (decd) [1982] Fam 113 at 117 in giving an unrestricted interpretation to the words 'special circumstances'. By s 116(2) the court is equipped with a power, in exercising this discretion, which is without fetter: it may define the grant in any way it thinks fit, ordering an unlimited or limited grant. In the week leading up to the hearing before Mrs Registrar Pearce there were discussions between all those concerned about the future administration of this estate. A compromise emerged which was intended to give effect to the following plan. There were to be three

administrators: a solicitor who had no previous connection with the dispute or the estate,
a   Mr Alec Bateson of Messrs Trower Still & Keeling; along with him, Mr Jocelyn Timothy
Thomas, solicitor at the time for Mr Thomas Mathew was to be the second; Mr Benson,
the donee of Mr Glynn's power of appointment, would be the third. A consent order was
to be made by the registrar incorporating these sensible compromise proposals.

There was, however, a complicating factor. Shortly before the hearing it appears that
a bankruptcy notice was issued against Thomas Mathew. It is said (I emphasise that I am
b   specifically invited *not* to resolve issues of fact such as this, if it be an issue) that the parties
to the imminent consent order knew of this notice before coming before the registrar.
Thomas Mathew claims that in these circumstances he considered himself for the time
being disqualified from taking a grant of probate or letters of administration until he got
rid of the bankruptcy petition.

On 17 August the consent order was made by Mrs Registrar Pearce in these terms:

c
'IT IS ORDERED pursuant to Section 116 of the Supreme Court Act 1981 by consent
that Letters of Administration of the Estate of Theobald Mathew deceased be granted
to [the three agreed persons whose names are given] with the Will annexed . . .'

and then there follow the words:

d
'. . . power being reserved to the Executors named in the Will the said Thomas
Mathew and David Hardy Glynn but on terms that no application shall be made by
either of them without first giving thirty days Notice of intention so to do to the
solicitors of each of the parties who have consented to this Order.'

A question has arisen as to the effect of these words in the case of a grant of letters of
administration with the will annexed. In the case of a grant of probate no difficulty
e   would have arisen. They are commonly used in the latter connection. Thus, where a
grant of probate is made to one of several executors and at that time the remaining
executors have not as yet made an application for a grant, the latter are not shut out from
seeking entry into the administration of the estate. These words are used to preserve the
right of the remaining executors to make application subsequently. It is as much as to
say that the grant of probate is made by the court to one executor without prejudice to
f   the right of the others to apply and obtain a double grant of probate.

But can the words be used in the case of the grant of letters of administration with the
will annexed? Do things stand differently in this latter instance? Clearly no question of
double probate arises, for neither of the executors had applied for probate in the first
place. Mrs Registrar Pearce's order is attacked by counsel for Mr Charles Mathew for
including such words. They are said to be contrary to established practice; it is said that
g   they would result in the executors being empowered to come into the administration
subsequently to an earlier grant of letters of administration and obtain a grant of probate.
It is said that, if the powers were to be exercised, a grant of probate would then coexist
with a previous grant of letters: a procedural impossibility.

The terminology 'power reserved' is familiar to practitioners in probate matters. It is
discussed in *Tristram and Coote's Probate Practice* (26th edn, 1983) only in relation to a
h   grant of probate (at p 111). This reflects the practice at the Principal Registry. If one
executor is granted probate, any other executors (unless they have renounced) retain their
power to take up probate. In this way it is reserved. But the order of Mrs Registrar Pearce
was unusual. No executor had been granted probate. The grant was to administrators.
She was being asked, with the consent of all parties, to pass over the executors but, as I
see it, not for all time. The executors wanted to have the power subsequently to come in
j   as executors; they wanted to keep open that option. Mr Glynn's agents (Mr Benson and
Mr Long) took their grant subject to this qualification under the power of attorney; they
had no power under their power of attorney to agree to an unqualified, unlimited grant.
And Mr Thomas Mathew hoped to rid himself of his supposed bankruptcy disqualification
and wished to preserve his freedom to apply for probate. This was a pro tem agreement,
in my view, with each surrogate taking up a grant that was defeasible in the event that

his principal decided to go for probate. In the case of Mr Bateson, who was surrogate to no one, he consented to play a role no different from that of his co-grantees. Though he may not have realised it, his grant too was defeasible.

And so the intention of Mrs Registrar Pearce was to make an order that gave effect to the agreement of the parties. She intended that there should be a limited grant of letters of administration to the three agreed grantees without excluding the right of the executors to apply subsequently for probate (which I must emphasise would *not* be a double probate). Why else insert the unusual phrase more commonly found in another context, 'power . . . reserved'? In this context it would seem to mean 'without prejudice to the rights of subsequent applicants for probate or for letters of administration'; in other words, that the grant was to be limited until the executors or one of them shall apply for and obtain a grant of probate. The order was drawn up and none of the parties objected to the inclusion of the phrase or applied to correct the order under the slip rule: some indication that they considered the terms of the order to reflect what they had agreed. Mrs Registrar Pearce had exercised her discretion by making a limited grant, in circumstances which all parties agreed by implication were special and it was expedient and necessary to get on with the collection and distribution of the estate and end the arguments if only for the time being.

Furthermore this was a consent order. All the parties were fully advised. The circumstances in which a consent order of any kind can be reopened are rare. There is none to justify such a course here: not duress, nor mistake (except perhaps a mistake of law). As I see it, if the order of Mrs Registrar Pearce stands, the power of the executors to apply for probate remains unimpaired. They are free to make application themselves or by their attorneys in proper form for probate or letters of administration; but again this will not be a case of double probate.

Accordingly, while not wishing to encourage the unorthodox use of a term usually associated with double probate, I can see no reason, in the special circumstances of an agreed order, not to give effect to the whole of Mrs Registrar Pearce's order, including the words 'power . . . reserved', by interpreting it as an order that a limited and defeasible grant of letters be made to the three agreed parties.

The matter, however, does not stop there. This is an appeal not against Mrs Registrar Pearce's order but against Mr Registrar Terian's order setting it aside and revoking the limited grant, and so it is necessary to look at events subsequent to her grant.

On 31 August Thomas Mathew obtained an order rescinding a receiving order made against him. He was now free of the supposed disqualification and wished to apply for probate. His solicitor attended at the registry for the purpose of obtaining 'double probate', which he thought the order of Mrs Registrar Pearce envisaged. His client swore the oath appropriate to double probate which had to be modified to fit the unusual circumstances. The application for double probate was refused after reference to the Chief Probate Clerk. The latter stated that there was no authority to reserve power to executors on the appointment of administrators. He suggested the application that was in fact made to Mr Registrar Terian. Meanwhile a grant of letters issued to the three grantees on 22 September.

The first ground of the application took up the Chief Probate Clerk's suggestion: Mrs Registrar Pearce was said to have no jurisdiction, on the grant of letters, to reserve power to executors to apply for the like or any grant and therefore, it was said, her grant was null and void. I do not agree. The terms of her discretion under s 116(2) of the 1981 Act are very wide. She thought fit for good reason to order a limited grant. All the conditions of the provision as to expediency and the like were fulfilled. Lack of jurisdiction in my judgment was no ground for revoking the grant or setting aside her order. In any event it cannot be that a tribunal (in this case a registrar) has under r 42 of the 1954 rules or s 121(1) of the 1981 Act, the jurisdiction to consider whether an earlier decision by another registrar, a co-ordinate tribunal, herself had jurisdiction. And this is not a case where there was fresh evidence to enable the subsequent tribunal to review and vary the earlier order, or where the application was in the first instance ex parte. The remedy of a the aggrieved party was by way of appeal against Mrs Registrar Pearce to a judge in chambers, even if it were out of time.

The alternative stance in the application was to accept that the earlier order *was* made with jurisdiction (however unorthodox the terminology). On this footing a direction is sought against the Senior Probate Clerk to make a grant in such form as the court may determine.

b Mr Registrar Terian acceded to the application on the first ground. He set aside the order and revoked the grant. I have already stated that in my view Mr Registrar Terian had no jurisdiction to review Mrs Registrar Pearce's order on an appellate basis; but he has power to look at the effect of the grant in the light of the circumstances as they prevailed at the time of his hearing. The changed circumstance was the desire of Mr Thomas Mathew to exercise the power which had been preserved for him under Mrs Registrar Pearce's order to apply for a grant of probate, as it had been for the other c executor (Mr Glynn) or his attorneys. If as a matter of probate practice the existing grant has proved for some reason to be an obstacle in the path of such an application (and it appears to be so regarded) then it is right for the avoidance of doubt that the court should make a direction. I have held that the grant was limited by Mrs Registrar Pearce so as to end on the application by the executors or one of them for, and the obtaining of, a grant (whether of probate or letters of administration). In ordinary circumstances, probate d procedure does not appear to me to require court intervention in a case of this kind. The order pursuant to which the limited grant was made should take effect proprio motu. But to pre-empt further dispute and even litigation I will direct the Senior Probate Clerk in terms as to which I must invite the assistance of counsel, but such that they give effect to the tenor of this judgment. I would to this extent vary the order of Mr Registrar Terian.

e *Order accordingly.*

Solicitors: *Druces & Attlee* (for the appellants); *Goddens & Thickness* (for the respondent); *Charles Russell & Co* (for the grantees).

f   Bebe Chua   Barrister.

Re Billson's Settlement Trusts

g COURT OF APPEAL, CIVIL DIVISION
WALLER, WATKINS AND BROWNE-WILKINSON LJJ
14 NOVEMBER, 1 DECEMBER 1983

Legitimation – Right of legitimated persons to take interests in property – Disposition coming into operation after date of legitimation – Settlement made in 1934 including trust for 'any child' of
h *settlor's son – Plaintiff illegitimate child of settlor's son born in 1936 – Plaintiff subsequently legitimated by parents' marriage in 1937 – Whether plaintiff entitled to take under 1934 settlement – Whether plaintiff claiming under 'disposition coming into operation after date of legitimation' – Whether plaintiff's interest arising on date of his legitimation – Whether relevant disposition the instrument creating the trust or the trust itself – Legitimacy Act 1926, s 3(1)(b).*

j Under a settlement dated 5 December 1934 the settlor settled certain property on trusts which included a trust for 'any child' of his son G with a gift over for the benefit of G's nephews and niece. The plaintiff was G's only son and was born in 1936 when his parents were not married. His parents married in 1937, with the result that, by virtue of s 1(1)[a]

───────────────────────────────────

a Section 1(1) is set out at p 403 g h, post

of the Legitimacy Act 1926, the plaintiff was legitimated from the date of the marriage. The question arose whether the plaintiff, being an illegitimate child who was legitimated *a* after the date of the settlement, was entitled to take under a settlement which was executed after the 1926 Act came into force. The judge held that the plaintiff was not entitled to take because he was not claiming 'under any disposition coming into operation after the date of legitimation', within s 3(1)(b)[b] of the 1926 Act, since the relevant disposition was the 1934 settlement, which had been made before and not after the plaintiff's legitimation. The plaintiff appealed, contending that the relevant disposition *b* was the particular disposition affecting him under the settlement, which was the trust in his favour, which came into operation on his legitimation.

Held – On the true construction of s 3(1)(b) of the 1926 Act the relevant 'disposition' was the instrument or document creating the interest or trust rather than the interest or trust itself, since the Act distinguished between 'interests' and 'dispositions' and made it clear that legitimated children were not to be treated for all purposes as if they were born *c* legitimate but were only entitled to take an interest in property in those limited circumstances expressly provided for in the Act. Furthermore, even if the trust in favour of the plaintiff was the relevant 'disposition' it came into operation on the date of the settlement and not when the plaintiff became a potential beneficiary by his legitimation, because the trust came into operation when a binding obligation was imposed on the trustees to carry out the trust, notwithstanding that the object of the trust was not then *d* in existence. Accordingly, the plaintiff's claim was excluded by s 3(1)(b) because he was not legitimated until after the disposition under which he claimed an interest came into operation. The appeal would therefore be dismissed (see p 404 *e* to p 405 *b* and *e* to *j*, p 406 *d* and p 407 *b* to *d*, post).

Re Hepworth [1936] 2 All ER 1159 and dicta of Viscount Simonds in *Philipson-Stow v IRC* [1960] 3 All ER at 818-819 considered.   *e*

Notes
For rights to property of legitimated person, see 1 Halsbury's Laws (4th edn) para 670, and for cases on the subject, see 32 Digest (Reissue) 31–34, 208–227.

For the Legitimacy Act 1926, ss 1, 3, see 1 Halsbury's Statutes (3rd edn) 63, 64.

As from 1 January 1976 s 3 of the 1926 Act was replaced (with savings) by para 12 of *f* Sch 1 to the Children Act 1975, which made new provision with respect to the rights of, inter alios, legitimated persons to take interests under instruments containing dispositions of property. As from 22 August 1976 s 1(1) of the 1926 Act and para 12 of Sch 1 to the 1975 Act were replaced (with savings) by ss 2 and 5 of the Legitimacy Act 1976.

Cases referred to in judgments   *g*
Hepworth, Re, Rastall v Hepworth [1936] 2 All ER 1159, [1936] Ch 750.
Hoff, Re, Carnley v Hoff [1942] 1 All ER 547, [1942] Ch 298.
Philipson-Stow v IRC [1960] 3 All ER 814, [1961] AC 727, [1960] 3 WLR 1008, HL.
Wicks's Marriage Settlement, Re, Public Trustee v Wicks [1940] Ch 475.

Cases also cited   *h*
Brinkley's Will Trusts, Re, Westminster Bank Ltd v Brinkley [1967] 3 All ER 805, [1968] Ch 407.
C v C [1947] 2 All ER 50, sub nom *Colquitt v Colquitt* [1948] P 19, DC.
IRC v Dowdall O'Mahoney & Co Ltd [1952] 1 All ER 531, [1952] AC 401, HL.

Appeal   *j*
The plaintiff, Christopher John Billson, appealed against the decision of Leonard Hoffmann QC sitting as a deputy judge of the High Court on 15 July 1982 whereby he

---

b   Section 3(1) is set out at p 403 *j*, post

a held on an originating summons taken out by the plaintiff that the plaintiff was not entitled to any interest in a settlement made on 5 December 1934 by Edgar Leicester Billson. The defendants to the summons and the respondents on the appeal were Christopher Schofield Harley and Simon James Mosley, the trustees of the settlement, and Roger Dalrymple Billson, Hew Richard Dalrymple Billson, Kathleen Shirley Behrens and Sydney Arthur Woolven, the beneficiaries under the gift over contained in the settlement. The facts are set out in the judgment of Browne-Wilkinson LJ.

b *Leolin Price QC* and *Hubert Picarda* for the plaintiff.
Mark Herbert for the defendants.

Cur adv vult

c 1 December. The following judgments were delivered.

BROWNE-WILKINSON LJ (giving the first judgment at the invitation of Waller LJ). This appeal raises a question on the true construction of the Legitimacy Act 1926, which came into force on 1 January 1927.

d Under a settlement dated 5 December 1934 Edgar Leicester Billson settled certain property on trusts which can be shortly summarised as follows: (1) on protective trusts for his son Geoffrey for life; (2) Geoffrey was given power to appoint one-half of the income to his wife for life; (3) subject thereto, by cl 4, in trust for 'the children or remoter issue' of Geoffrey as he by deed or will should appoint and in default in trust for 'the children or any child' of Geoffrey who has attained the age of 21 years or being female attain that age or may marry; (4) the ultimate trust (in the events which have happened)
e was for the benefit of Geoffrey's nephews and niece (the third, fourth and fifth defendants).

The plaintiff, Christopher Billson, was Geoffrey's only son. He was born on 15 June 1936, his parents not being then married. They married on 14 July 1937. Under s 1 of the Legitimacy Act 1926 Christopher was legitimated from the date of the marriage.

f There is no doubt that, apart from the provisions of the 1926 Act, Christopher could take no interest under the settlement. Before the passing of the 1926 Act, an illegitimate child could not take any property interest as a 'child' of his parent, and legitimation by subsequent marriage was not recognised. The question in this appeal is how the 1926 Act affects a disposition made in a settlement executed after the Act came into operation conferring interests on a 'child', the illegitimate child being legitimated by virtue of the 1926 Act after the date of the settlement.

g The relevant provisions of the 1926 Act are the following:

'**1.**—(1) Subject to the provisions of this section, where the parents of an illegitimate person marry or have married one another, whether before or after the commencement of this Act, the marriage shall, if the father of the illegitimate person was or is at the date of the marriage domiciled in England or Wales, render
h that person, if living, legitimate from the commencement of this Act, or from the date of the marriage, whichever last happens . . .

(3) The legitimation of a person under this Act does not enable him or his spouse, children or remoter issue to take any interest in real or personal property save as is hereinafter in this Act expressly provided . . .

3.—(1) Subject to the provisions of this Act, a legitimated person and his spouse,
j children or more remote issue shall be entitled to take any interest—(*a*) in the estate of an intestate dying after the date of legitimation; (*b*) under any disposition coming into operation after the date of legitimation; (*c*) by descent under an entailed interest created after the date of legitimation; in like manner as if the legitimated person had been born legitimate . . .

10 . . . (2) Nothing in this Act shall affect the operation or construction of any disposition coming into operation before the commencement of this Act, or affect any rights under the intestacy of a person dying before the commencement of this *a* Act.

11. For the purposes of this Act, unless the context otherwise requires . . . The expression "disposition" means an assurance of any interest in property by any instrument whether inter vivos or by will . . .'

Mr Leonard Hoffmann QC, sitting as a deputy judge of the High Court in the Chancery Division, had no difficulty in holding that the plaintiff took no interest. He was *b* legitimated by the marriage of his parents only after the date of the settlement, which the judge assumed (apparently without argument to the contrary) to be the date on which the relevant disposition came into operation for the purposes of s 3(1)(*b*) of the 1926 Act. The plaintiff appeals against that decision.

Counsel for the plaintiff submits that on the true construction of s 3(1) of the 1926 Act the plaintiff is entitled to the fund as a 'child' of Geoffrey under a disposition which came *c* into operation after the date of his legitimation. He submits that the relevant disposition is not, as the judge assumed, the settlement of 1934, but the interests conferred by cl 4 of that settlement on Geoffrey's children and issue. That disposition did not come into operation, he submits, until there was an object of those trusts in existence, ie in this case until the legitimation of the plaintiff by the marriage of his parents on 14 July 1937. Therefore the relevant disposition came into operation on his legitimation and the case *d* falls within s 3(1)(*b*).

In support of these contentions he submits that s 10(2) of the 1926 Act shows that, in relation to any disposition coming into operation after commencement of the Act on 1 January 1927, the construction of the disposition must take into account the provisions and effect of the Act. I agree with this submission. But I am unable to take the next step urged by counsel that the intention of the Act (and therefore of documents construed by *e* reference to it) is so far as possible to treat legitimated children as though they were legitimate. In my judgment such a wide intention is neither to be gathered from the Act nor to be attributed to settlors or testators.

So far as the donors (whether testators or settlors) are concerned, the only general intention which it is possible to attribute to them is that their dispositions shall operate in accordance with the provisions of the 1926 Act. So far as Parliament is concerned, the *f* words of the Act make it clear that legitimated children are not to be treated for all purposes as though they were born legitimate. On the contrary, s 1(3) makes it clear that the legitimated child is not to take any interest in real or personal property save to the extent 'expressly' provided in the Act. Then, so far as relevant, s 3(1) expressly declares the limited circumstances in which the legitimated child is to be entitled to take an interest in property. *g*

I cannot extract from these provisions any general intention or rule of construction other than an intention, both of Parliament and of a donor, that a legitimated child should take an interest in the circumstances specified in s 3(1) of the 1926 Act. The only question is the true construction of s 3(1).

Counsel's submissions raise two separate but interrelated questions. (1) What was the relevant disposition? (2) When did that disposition come into operation within the *h* meaning of the 1926 Act?

What was the disposition?

In my judgment as a matter of first impression the 'disposition' referred to in the 1926 Act is the instrument under which the relevant interests are created (ie the 1934 *j* settlement), not the individual limitation under which the plaintiff claims. The word 'disposition' is defined by s 11 as meaning 'an assurance of any interest in property by any instrument whether inter vivos or by will'. To my mind this definition makes it clear that the disposition is the provision creating the interest, not the interest itself. This is reinforced by s 3(1), which refers to 'any interest . . . under any disposition'. The words a used are more appropriately read as a reference to the trust document than to the individual trusts.

This first impression is reinforced by other factors. It is to be noted that the 1926 Act does not refer to dispositions 'to' the legitimated child. In effect counsel is asking us to read the Act as if it did so provide. The Act refers only to the disposition under which the legitimated child's interest arises.

Next, the provisions of s 10(2) demonstrate that the disposition is the instrument as a
b whole. Section 10(2) is plainly directed to preventing the Act from having retrospective effect so as to alter the operation of trusts declared before the passing of the Act. If counsel's construction is correct, it would be ineffective for this purpose. Say that there was a settlement made in 1920 under which the fund was held on trust for A for life with remainder to B's children and, in default of such children, to C. B has one child who is legitimated after 1926, but before the death of A. If counsel's argument is correct, the
c relevant disposition is not the 1920 settlement but the separate limitation in favour of B's children which, he says, comes into operation on the legitimation of B's child after 1926. The result would be that B's claim would not be excluded and the Act would have retrospective operation so as to alter the operation of trusts established before it was passed. Thereby the interest vested in C before the Act was passed would be expropriated without compensation.

d Counsel for the plaintiff relied on certain dicta by Viscount Simonds in *Philipson-Stow v IRC* [1960] 3 All ER 814 at 818–819, [1961] AC 727 at 742. That case concerned s 28(2) of the Finance Act 1949, which required the House of Lords to determine what was the proper law regulating the 'disposition under or by virtue of which [property] passes'. Viscount Simonds's remarks certainly indicate that, for the purposes of that section, there may be separate 'dispositions' in the same instrument. I have some doubts whether
e Viscount Simonds's remarks were intended to apply to anything other that the construction of that section. But, even if separate trusts can, in certain cases, be treated as separate dispositions, the question remains in each case whether Parliament meant by using the word 'disposition' to refer to the instrument as a whole, rather than the individual limitations. For the reasons I have given, in my judgment, in the 1926 Act Parliament was treating the instrument as a whole as the disposition.

f For these reasons, in my judgment, the relevant 'disposition' in the present case was the 1934 settlement as a whole and not the individual limitations in cl 4 of the 1934 settlement.

When did the disposition come into operation?

If, as I think, the disposition was the 1934 settlement as a whole, there is no doubt it
g came into operation when it was executed.

If, contrary to my view, the trusts in cl 4 of the 1934 settlement are to be treated as the relevant disposition, counsel for the plaintiff submits that those trusts did not come into operation until, for the first time, there was an object of those trusts in existence, ie in this case on the legitimation of the plaintiff. It is to be noted that counsel is not contending that the cl 4 trusts came into operation only on the vesting or falling into
h possession of the interests under cl 4. His contention is that, for the purposes of the 1926 Act, a disposition comes into operation when a potential beneficiary first comes into existence, whether or not that beneficiary is the legitimated person or whether the interest is contingent, vested or in possession.

To an equity lawyer, this is a bold, not to say heretical, submission. A trust 'comes into operation' when a binding obligation is imposed on the trustees to carry out that trust.
j There are innumerable trusts for the benefit of unborn and unascertained persons. They have immediate effect. The fund cannot be dealt with so as to prejudice their interests. Arrangements are made under the Variation of Trusts Act 1958 varying their rights. To an equity lawyer those trusts are as much 'in operation' as any other trusts.

Moreover, as counsel for the defendants pointed out, if counsel for the plaintiff is right in saying that the disposition in cl 4 did not 'come into operation' until the legitimation of the plaintiff, the power of appointment could not validly have been exercised until that date. Yet there is nothing under the general law which prevents a power of appointment being exercised before an object of the power is in existence.

Counsel for the plaintiff relied on the contrast between the words used in the 1926 Act and another statute passed in the same year, the Adoption of Children Act 1926. Section 5(2) of that Act provides that the adoption order shall not deprive or confer on the adopted child any interest under any intestacy or disposition 'whether occurring or made before or after the making of the adoption order', and that the words 'child', 'children' or 'issue' in any 'disposition whether made before or after the making of an adoption order' are not to be given any different meaning. Counsel for the plaintiff suggested that the use of the word 'made' in the Adoption of Children Act 1926 showed that in the Legitimacy Act 1926 the words 'coming into operation' must refer to a different point in time from that on which the document was made. I do not agree. In the Adoption of Children Act 1926 the time at which a settlement or will operates is irrelevant since the Act did not change the adopted child's rights whenever the disposition was made. In contrast, under the Legitimacy Act 1926 the time at which the disposition operates is crucial, and the draftsman had to cover dispositions both by deed and by will. In the case of a will, the material date might be either the date of execution (for the purposes of construction) or the date of death. In my judgment the use of the words 'coming into operation' is attributable to the need to define the date of death as the relevant time. Therefore in my judgment the clear effect of s 3(1) of the Act is to exclude the plaintiff's claim since he was not legitimated until after the disposition under which he claims an interest came into operation.

This view is supported by authority. In *Re Hepworth* [1936] 2 All ER 1159, [1936] Ch 750 the question related to the trusts established by the will of a testator who died before 1927. The claimant was born before 1 January 1927 but was legitimated on that date by s 1 of the 1926 Act. The question was whether she could take an interest under the will as a 'child' of her father. It was argued that the relevant disposition did not come into operation on the death of the testator, but only when the gift to the children vested (which was after 1 January 1927). Farwell J rejected this submission, holding that the relevant disposition was the will, which came into operation on the death of the testator. Although, as counsel for the plaintiff points out, that case was concerned with a pre-1927 trust and his argument that the disposition did not come into operation until the legitimation of the child was not advanced, Farwell J's reason for his decision did not turn on those points. It is a clear decision that, for the purpose of the 1926 Act, the disposition comes into operation when the document containing the trust, be it a settlement or a will, comes into operation.

The other cases to which we were referred, *Re Wicks's Marriage Settlement* [1940] Ch 475 and *Re Hoff* [1942] 1 All ER 547, [1942] Ch 298, were both concerned with the exercise, after 1927, of powers of appointment conferred by documents coming into operation before 1 January 1927. They are therefore not directly in point since the question was whether, on the true construction of the trust instrument, the legitimated child to whom an appointment was made was an object of the power. But in *Re Hoff* [1942] 1 All ER 547 at 550, [1942] Ch 298 at 303 Farwell J again decided that the relevant disposition was the will of the testator which came into operation on his death.

Finally, if there was a doubt as to the true construction of the Act, there are two matters which could legitimately be taken into account. First, s 15(4)(*a*) of the Family Law Reform Act 1969, although obscure in some respects, is plainly drafted on the basis that a disposition for the purposes of s 3(1) of the 1926 Act comes into operation when it is 'made' and not at any later date. Although Parliament may, in 1969, have been mistaken as to the existing law, one should assume that it was not so mistaken; in the absence of clear words, one should seek to construe the earlier Act so as to accord with Parliament's understanding or its effect.

Second, counsel for the plaintiff accepts that his submission is a novel one and that, hitherto, trusts have been administered on the basis that a child legitimated after the date

of the settlement or the date of death was not entitled to any interest. It follows that, if
a we were to uphold counsel's arguments, a number of established titles would be upset.
Trust funds will have been distributed and trusts varied ignoring the rights of such
legitimated children, who would accordingly be entitled to sue for breach of trust or
trace the trusts assets. In a case of doubt I would lean against upsetting such established
titles.

For these reasons, although viewed through 1983 spectacles the plaintiff has a very
b strong moral claim to the fund and I would like to hold in his favour, I feel unable to do
so. The attitude to legitimation in 1926 was very different from the attitude today. I
must give effect to what, in my judgment, is the clear meaning of the 1926 Act.
Although this is no consolation to the plaintiff, it is reassuring that because of the passing
of the Family Law Reform Act 1969 similar hardships are unlikely to occur in the future.
I would dismiss the appeal.

c
WATKINS LJ. I have had the advantage of reading in draft the judgment of Browne-
Wilkinson LJ. I agree with it.

WALLER LJ. I have had the advantage of reading in draft the judgment of Browne-
Wilkinson LJ, and this has convinced me that it is right to reject the persuasive arguments
d of counsel for the plaintiff. I agree with the judgment which he has delivered.

Appeal dismissed. Leave to appeal to the House of Lords refused.

*7 February 1984. The Appeal Committee of the House of Lords (Lord Diplock, Lord Keith of
Kinkel and Lord Brightman) dismissed a petition by the plaintiff for leave to appeal.*

e
Solicitors: *Stanleys & Simpson North* (for the plaintiff); *Frere Cholmeley* (for the defendants).

Sophie Craven   Barrister.

f

Practice Direction

g FAMILY DIVISION

*Child – Removal from jurisdiction – Wardship and guardianship – Application for leave to
remove child normally to be made to judge – Cases where application may be made to registrar.*

The judges of the Family Division are of the opinion, and it is accordingly hereby
h directed, that an application for leave to remove a child out of England and Wales in
wardship and guardianship cases shall be made to a judge except in the following cases,
when it shall be made to the registrar, namely (a) where the application is unopposed or
(b) where the application is for the temporary removal of the child unless it is opposed
on the ground that the child may not be duly returned. The registrar may make such
order on the application as he thinks fit or may refer it or any question arising thereon to
j a judge.

Issued with the approval of the President.

B P TICKLE
14 May 1984   Senior Registrar.

Francome and another v Mirror Group Newspapers Ltd and others

COURT OF APPEAL, CIVIL DIVISION

SIR JOHN DONALDSON MR, FOX AND STEPHEN BROWN LJJ

13, 14, 16 MARCH 1984

Equity – Breach of confidence – Injunction – Information obtained by illegal telephone tapping – Defence – Public interest in disclosure – Defendant newspaper obtaining tapes of plaintiff's telephone conversation – Tapes obtained by illegal telephone tapping – Tapes alleged to show plaintiff committing criminal offences and breaches of rules of racing – Publication of tapes constituting criminal offence – Whether publication in public interest – Whether interlocutory injunction restraining publication pending trial of action should be granted – Whether defendant should disclose source of tapes before trial of action – Wireless Telegraphy Act 1949, s 5 – Contempt of Court Act 1981, s 10.

The defendants, the proprietors of a national newspaper, its editor and two of its reporters, obtained from an undisclosed source a number of taped telephone conversations made by the plaintiffs, a well-known and very successful jockey and his wife. The tapes had been made by illegal tapping of the plaintiffs' telephone in circumstances not involving the defendants but which constituted a criminal offence under s 5[a] of the Wireless Telegraphy Act 1949. Section 5 further provided that disclosure of any information obtained as a result of illegal telephone tapping was also an offence. The tapes allegedly revealed breaches by the first plaintiff of certain Jockey Club regulations and possibly the commission by him of criminal offences. The defendants intended to publish material from the tapes which would expose only the first plaintiff, and they told him of their existence. In consequence the plaintiffs brought an action against the defendants seeking damages for trespass or breach of confidence, an injunction restraining the defendants from publishing material based on the tapes or any transcript made therefrom, delivery up of the tapes and any transcript, and an order that the defendants disclose the source from which they had obtained the tapes. The defendants contended, inter alia, that the plaintiffs had no cause of action against them since (i) they had not been parties to the trespass, (ii) there was no right of action against them or their source for breach of confidence regarding telephone conversations since users had to accept the inherent risk of eavesdropping by reason of, inter alia, crossed lines and official telephone tapping, and (iii) s 5 did not confer any private right in respect of illegal telephone tapping. The defendants further contended by way of defence that they were entitled to rely on the 'iniquity rule' that publication was justified as being in the public interest because it would expose conduct which involved a breach of the law or was contrary to the public interest. They further asserted that the injunction sought by the plaintiffs restraining the defendants from committing a criminal offence under s 5 of the 1949 Act could only be granted on the motion of the Attorney General, that in reality the first plaintiff's claim would lie in defamation after publication, in defence of which they would plead justification, and that, just as publication of defamatory material would not be restrained where such a defence was intended to be raised, so the injunction should not be granted against the defendants. They also claimed that they were protected by s 10[b] of the Contempt of Court Act 1981 from disclosing their source. The judge granted an injunction restraining publication and ordering the defendants to disclose the source from which they had obtained the tapes. The defendants appealed.

Held – The plaintiffs were entitled to protect, by means of legal redress, confidential material uttered in their private telephone conversations and accordingly they had a good

---

a   Section 5, so far as material, is set out at p 412 *a* to *c*, post

b   Section 10 is set out at p 413 *e*, post

a   cause of action against the defendants in respect of illegal tapping of their telephone which breached their right to the confidentiality of their telephone conversations. The plaintiffs also had an arguable case that they had private rights under s 5 of the 1949 Act and therefore they were entitled to an injunction to preserve their rights pending trial. The fact that the plaintiffs' cause of action was for breach of confidence meant that the principles relating to justifiable publication of defamatory material did not apply. Furthermore, the defendants were not entitled to publish on the basis that the public

b   interest justified a breach of the criminal law (ie of s 5 of the 1949 Act) because any public interest could be served by making the tapes available to the police or the Jockey Club and in those circumstances publication before trial would only serve the defendants' interests rather than any public interest. Accordingly, in the exercise of its discretion to preserve the rights of the parties pending trial, the court would uphold the injunction restraining publication of the taped material, since the balance of justice or convenience

c   lay in the plaintiffs' favour. However, an order for the disclosure of the identity of the defendants' source was inappropriate at the interlocutory stage since once the source was disclosed there would be no point in having a trial on that issue. The injunction requiring disclosure of the source of the tapes would therefore be discharged and to that extent the appeal would be allowed (see p 412 *d e*, p 413 *c d* and *f* to p 414 *d*, p 415 *a* to *g* and *j* and p 416 *e* to *h*, post); *Malone v Comr of Police of the Metropolis (No 2)* [1979] 2 All ER 620

d   distinguished.

    Per Sir John Donaldson MR and Fox LJ. In a parliamentary democracy obedience to the law is not a question of choice, apart from the extremely rare exception of the moral imperative. The proposition that citizens are free to commit a criminal offence where they have formed the view that it will further what they believe to be the public interest is inimical to the rule of law and parliamentary democracy (see p 412 *h* to p 413 *b* and

e   p 415 *g* to *j*, post).

Notes

For unauthorised interception and disclosure of wireless telegraph messages, see 36 Halsbury's Laws (3rd edn) 685, para 1090.

    For the Wireless Telegraphy Act 1949, s 5, see 35 Halsbury's Statutes (3rd edn) para 98.

f   For the Contempt of Court Act 1981, s 10, see 51 ibid 505.

Cases referred to in judgments

A-G v Jonathan Cape Ltd, A-G v Times Newspapers Ltd [1975] 3 All ER 484, [1976] QB 752, [1975] 3 WLR 606.

British Steel Corp v Granada Television Ltd [1981] 1 All ER 417, [1981] AC 1096, [1980] 3 WLR 774, Ch D, CA and HL.

g   *Coco v A N Clark (Engineers) Ltd* [1969] RPC 41.

Gouriet v Union of Post Office Workers [1977] 3 All ER 70, sub nom *Gouriet v A-G* [1978] AC 435, [1977] 3 WLR 300, HL.

McCall v Abelesz [1976] 1 All ER 727, [1976] QB 585, [1976] 2 WLR 151, CA.

Malone v Comr of Police of the Metropolis (No 2) [1979] 2 All ER 620, [1979] Ch 344, [1979] 2 WLR 700.

h   *Saltman Engineering Co Ltd v Campbell Engineering Co Ltd* (1948) [1963] 3 All ER 413, CA.

Cases also cited

Hubbard v Vosper [1972] 1 All ER 1023, [1972] 2 QB 84, CA.

Initial Services Ltd v Putterill [1967] 3 All ER 145, [1968] 1 QB 396, CA.

RCA Corp v Pollard [1982] 3 All ER 771, [1983] Ch 135, CA.

j   *Schering Chemicals Ltd v Falkman* [1981] 2 All ER 321, [1982] QB 1, CA.

Woodward v Hutchins [1977] 2 All ER 751, [1977] 1 WLR 760, CA.

Interlocutory appeal

By a writ issued on 5 March 1984 the plaintiffs, John Francome and Miriam Francome, claimed against the defendants, Mirror Group Newspapers Ltd, Michael Molloy, Alister Martin and Roger Beam, (i) damages, including exemplary damages, for breach of confidence, (ii) damages, including exemplary damages, for trespass, (iii) an injunction restraining the defendants whether by themselves, their servants or agents or otherwise *a* from publishing or causing to be published any article based on or making use of the contents of telephone conversations made by the plaintiffs which had been taped without their knowledge or consent, (iv) an order that the defendants deliver up forthwith to the plaintiffs all tapes, transcripts and notes of such conversations. The plaintiffs further sought an order that the defendants reveal their source. On 8 March 1984 Park J granted the injunction sought and ordered (i) delivery up of the tapes etc to an agreed third party, *b* (ii) disclosure by the defendants to the plaintiffs of their source and (iii) a speedy trial of the action. The defendants appealed with leave of Park J. The facts are set out in the judgment of Sir John Donaldson MR.

Leonard Hoffmann QC and *Andrew Caldecott* for the defendants.
Richard L Hartley QC and *Thomas Shields* for the plaintiffs.

c

Cur adv vult.

16 March. The following judgments were delivered.

SIR JOHN DONALDSON MR. The plaintiffs are husband and wife, the husband being the champion National Hunt jockey. The defendants are the proprietors of the *d* Daily Mirror, its editor and two of its reporters.

Someone (and we do not know his identity or that of his assistants) saw fit to plant what is popularly known as a 'bug' with a view to eavesdropping on any telephone conversations which were made to or from the plaintiffs' home. This was not official telephone tapping. Indeed it may not have been tapping in the strict sense at all, since it is common ground that it involved the use of radio-telephony. It also had nothing to do *e* with the Daily Mirror. It is not clear for how long the 'bug' was in operation, but it was for not less than three months and may have been longer.

The Daily Mirror came into the story when the eavesdroppers offered to sell them 38 tapes of telephone conversations obtained by this means. In seeking to confirm the authenticity of the tapes, the reporter defendants approached Mr Francome and told him of their existence. *f*

The plaintiffs then began an action in which they claimed the following relief: (1) exemplary damages for breach of confidence; (2) exemplary damages for trespass; (3) an injunction restraining all the defendants from publishing or causing to be published any article which was based on or made use of the plaintiffs' telephone conversations; (4) an order for the delivery up of the tapes and transcripts from the tapes and notes of the conversations. Later the plaintiffs asked that the defendants should be ordered to identify *g* their source, ie the person or persons who offered to sell them the tapes.

Park J on 8 March made various orders. For present purposes it suffices to say that he (a) ordered a speedy trial, (b) granted the injunction which had been sought, (c) ordered the defendants to deliver the tapes, transcripts and any notes of telephone conversations to a third party, (d) ordered the defendants to reveal their source within 24 hours. The defendants now appeal. *h*

It is of paramount importance that everyone should understand the exercise on which the judge was, and we are, engaged. There is to be a speedy trial at which the rights of the parties will be determined. That has not yet happened. We are concerned, so far as we can, to preserve the rights of the parties meanwhile. It is not our function to decide questions of fact or law which will be in issue at the trial. If they are arguable, that is the time and the place when they should be argued. *j*

Let it be said at once that no one seeks to defend the action of those who 'bugged' the plaintiffs' telephone. This conduct was quite clearly a criminal offence under s 5 of the Wireless Telegraphy Act 1949, and may also have involved a trespass to the plaintiffs' property. This is not likely to be the issue at the trial. That issue is likely to be whether the defendants can make any, and if so what, use of the fruits of that criminal act.

The plaintiffs say that the defendants cannot be allowed to make any use of the tapes
a or of the conversations which they record. There is a twofold basis for this contention.
The first is that both the eavesdroppers and the defendants know full well that the
conversations were confidential. Although users of the telephone take the risk of crossed
lines and of official telephone tapping, they are entitled to regard their conversations as
confidential and anyone overhearing those conversations knows that that is the position.
It is therefore idle for an eavesdropper, and particularly a deliberate eavesdropper, to
b contend that he did not know that the conversations were confidential. The plaintiffs say
that, in the cicumstances revealed by the evidence, the defendants were in the same
position as the eavesdroppers. Both were under a duty to preserve the confidentially of
the plaintiffs' private conversations.

The second basis for this contention is that, as the defendants well knew, the tapes and
transcripts came into existence by means of acts which constituted criminal offences
c under the 1949 Act and, as the plaintiffs say, disclosure of, inter alia, the contents of the
messages contained in those conversations would also constitute such an offence.

The claim for an order requiring the defendants to identify their source was not
included in the writ, but arose in the course of the proceedings before Park J. It is based
on the decision of the House of Lords in *British Steel Corp v Granada Television Ltd* [1981]
1 All ER 417, [1981] AC 1096 and, whilst being advanced on behalf of both plaintiffs, is
d pressed particularly on behalf of Mrs Francome.

The defendants accept that the plaintiffs may have various causes of action against the
eavesdroppers, but rightly say that this is not directly relevant. They go on to say that the
plaintiffs have no right of action against them. So far as trespass is concerned, they were
not parties to it. This may well be right. They go on to say that there is no cause of action
against them or the eavesdroppers for breach of an obligation of confidentiality. The
e authority for this rather surprising proposition is said to be *Malone v Comr of Police of the
Metropolis (No 2)* [1979] 2 All ER 620, [1979] Ch 344. Suffice it to say that Sir Robert
Megarry V-C expressly stated that he was deciding nothing on the position when tapping
was effected for purposes other than the prevention, detection and discovery of crime
and criminals or by persons other than the police (see [1979] 2 All ER 620 at 651, [1979]
Ch 344 at 384). This is thus a live issue.

f The defendants then go on to submit that, whatever their obligations towards the
plaintiffs on grounds of confidentiality, they can rely on the classic, but ill-defined,
exception of what is quaintly called 'iniquity'. The basis of this exception is that, whilst
there is a public interest in maintaining confidentiality, there is a countervailing public
interest in exposing conduct which involves a breach of the law or which is 'anti-social'. I
use the term 'anti-social', without defining it, to describe activities which, whilst not in
g breach of the law, are seriously contrary to the public interest. In the defendants'
submission the tapes revealed breaches by Mr Francome of the rules of racing and,
bearing in mind the large sums of money which are staked on the results of the races,
this conduct they say is 'anti-social' within the meaning of the iniquity rule and may also
involve criminal offences. Let me say at once it is not for me to say whether the tapes
bear this interpretation and I express no view on that point. That will also be an issue.

h The defendants go on to say that they have no intention of writing or publishing
anything which is defamatory of Mrs Francome or of publishing any part of the tapes
which relate to conversations to which she was a party. However, so far as Mr Francome
is concerned, they say that they are prepared to justify anything which they may write
and publish about him and that in those circumstances it would be contrary to all
precedent for them to be forbidden to write and publish matter which, in the absence of
j justification, might be held to be defamatory. They submit that they should not be
restrained from publishing the transcripts of the tapes and extracts therefrom or a
summary by way of justifying any comments which, in the absence of such justification,
might constitute an actionable libel.

This leaves two matters: the plaintiffs' reliance on s 5 of the 1949 Act and the claim
that the defendants should reveal their source.

The 1949 Act

Section 5 is in the following terms:

'Any person who ... (*b*) otherwise than under the authority of the Postmaster General or in the course of his duty as a servant of the Crown, either (i) uses any wireless telegraphy apparatus with intent to obtain information as to the contents, sender or addressee of any message (whether sent by means of telegraphy or not) which neither the person using the apparatus nor any person on whose behalf he is acting is authorised by the Postmaster General to receive; or (ii) except in the course of legal proceedings or for the purpose of any report thereof, discloses any information as to the contents, sender or addressee of any such message, being information which would not have come to his knowledge but for the use of wireless telegraphy apparatus by him or by another person, shall be guilty of an offence under this Act.'

Section 14 is headed 'Penalties and legal proceedings'. It prescribes penalties for offences, including offences under s 5, and continues in sub-s (7) as follows:

'Nothing in the preceding provisions of this section shall limit any right of any person to bring civil proceedings in respect of the doing or apprehended doing of anything rendered unlawful by any provision of this Act . . .'

For the defendants it is submitted that this subsection shows that s 5 gives rise to no right enforceable by a private individual (see the judgment of Lord Denning MR in *McCall v Abelesz* [1976] 1 All ER 727, [1976] 1 QB 585). It would follow, so it is submitted, that the plaintiffs have no right to rely on s 5 of the 1949 Act.

Suffice it to say that I am far from sure that the plaintiffs do not have rights under the 1949 Act, if they have suffered damage by breach of the Act which is special to them (see *Gouriet v Union of Post Office Workers* [1977] 3 All ER 70, [1978] AC 435). This again will be an issue.

Mr Molloy, the editor of the Daily Mirror, adverted to the 1949 Act in his affidavit. He said in para 3:

'I have not yet finally decided whether to publish this story and its exact wording will depend upon further enquiries ... Any story will be carefully vetted by a barrister in the First Defendant's legal department and I shall also have to give careful consideration to the probability that publication would be an offence under Section 5(*b*) of the Wireless and Telegraphy Act, although I would not regard this fact as an absolute bar to publication if I considered that publication was justifiable in the public interest . . .'

I draw attention to the use of the word 'probability' which I regard as wholly accurate. Mr Molloy thus claims the right in what he judges to be the public interest to comply or not to comply with the law of the land made by Parliament by the constitutional processes. Furthermore his counsel submits that it is not for any civil court to restrain him or to make any order which might incidentally have this effect, although not couched in the terms of the statute.

I hope that Mr Molloy will acquit me of discourtesy if I say with all the emphasis at my command that I regard his assertion as arrogant and wholly unacceptable. Parliamentary democracy as we know it is based on the rule of law. That requires all citizens to obey the law, unless and until it can be changed by due process. There are no privileged classes to whom it does not apply. If Mr Molloy and the Daily Mirror can assert this right to act on the basis that the public interest, as he sees it, justifies breaches of the criminal law, so can any other citizen. This has only to be stated for it to be obvious that the result would be anarchy.

It is sometimes said, although to be fair to Mr Molloy he has not said it, that all are free to break the law if they are prepared to pay the penalty. This is pernicious nonsense. The right to disobey the law is not obtainable by the payment of a penalty or licence fee. It is not obtainable at all in a parliamentary democracy, although different considerations arise under a totalitarian regime.

In saying this I nevertheless recognise that, in very rare circumstances, a situation can

arise in which the citizen is faced with a conflict between what is, in effect, two
a inconsistent laws. The first law is the law of the land. The second is a moral imperative,
usually, but not always, religious in origin. An obvious example is the priest's obligation
of silence in relation to the confessional, but others can be given. In conducting the
business of the courts, judges seek to avoid any such conflict, but occasionally it is
unavoidable. Yielding to the moral imperative does not excuse a breach of the law of the
land, but it is understandable and in some circumstances may even be praiseworthy.

b   However, I cannot over-emphasise the rarity of the moral imperative. Furthermore, it
is almost unheard of for compliance with the moral imperative to be in the financial or
other best interests of the persons concerned. Anyone who conceives himself to be
morally obliged to break the law should also ask himself whether such a course furthers
his own interests. If it does, he would be well advised to re-examine his conscience.

The media, to use a term which comprises not only the newspapers but also television
c and radio, are an essential foundation of any democracy. In exposing crime, anti-social
behaviour and hypocrisy and in campaigning for reform and propagating the views of
minorities, they perform an invaluable function. However, they are peculiarly vulnerable
to the error of confusing the public interest with their own interest. Usually these
interests march hand in hand, but not always. In the instant case, pending a trial, it is
impossible to see what public interest would be served by publishing the contents of the
d tapes which would not equally be served by giving them to the police or to the Jockey
Club. Any wider publication could only serve the interests of the Daily Mirror.

The other remaining matter is the plaintiffs' claim for an order that the defendants
reveal their source. This claim is based on *British Steel Corp v Granada Television Ltd* [1981]
1 All ER 417, [1981] AC 1096. The most obvious answer is provided by s 10 of the
Contempt of Court Act 1981, which provides:

e
    'No court may require a person to disclose, nor is any person guilty of contempt
    of court for refusing to disclose, the source of information contained in a publication
    for which he is responsible, unless it be established to the satisfaction of the court
    that disclosure is necessary in the interests of justice or national security or for the
    prevention of disorder or crime.'

f   The plaintiffs say that this section has no application because there has as yet been no
publication and, anyway, disclosure is necessary in the interests of justice. This is very
debatable.

What then should we do? I stress, once again, that we are not at this stage concerned
to determine the final rights of the parties. Our duty is to make such orders, if any, as are
appropriate pending the trial of the action. It is sometimes said that this involves a
g weighing of the balance of convenience. This is an unfortunate expression. Our business
is justice, not convenience. We can and must disregard fanciful claims by either party.
Subject to that, we must contemplate the possibility that either party may succeed and
must do our best to ensure that nothing occurs pending the trial which will prejudice his
rights. Since the parties are usually asserting wholly inconsistent claims, this is difficult,
but we have to do our best. In so doing, we are seeking a balance of justice, not of
h convenience.

In the present case, assuming that the plaintiffs are entitled to an order that the
defendants reveal their source, I cannot see that they will be substantially prejudiced if
they have to wait until after the trial of the action, particularly as a speedy trial has been
ordered. On the other hand, if we allow the judge's order to stand, any argument by the
defendants at the trial that the plaintiffs are not entitled to seek an order would be wholly
j academic. I would therefore quash this part of the judge's order.

There remains the injunction concerning disclosure. Such disclosure as has taken place
in affidavits is authorised by the exception in s 5 of the 1949 Act as being a disclosure 'in
the course of legal proceedings'. For the injunction granted by the judge, I would
substitute an injunction restraining—

    'the defendants by themselves, their servants or agents from disclosing, otherwise
    than under the authority of the appropriate minister of the Crown as the successor

of the Postmaster General or in the course of legal proceedings, any information as
to the contents, sender or addressee of any telephone messages passing to or from
telephones at the home of the plaintiffs, being information which would not have
come to the knowledge of the defendant, but for the use of wireless telegraphy
apparatus by the defendants or any of them or by another person.'

The defendants have submitted that such an injunction can only be granted at the suit
of the Attorney General. I disagree. We have a complete discretion what order to make
in order best to preserve the rights of the parties. In my judgment an order forbidding
the defendants to commit what would probably constitute a criminal offence, but
otherwise leaving them free to pursue such course as they deem proper, will best achieve
this object.

Assuming that the tapes reveal evidence of the commission of a criminal offence or a
breach of the rules of racing, and I stress that this is an assumption, it may well be in the
public interest that the tapes and all the information to be gleaned there from be made
available to the police and to the Jockey Club. Accepting the defendants' expressed desire
to promote the public interest, it will be open for them to apply to the appropriate
minister of the Crown for authority to disclose all the information to one or other or
both of these authorities. Furthermore, if the defendants wish to publish statements
which are prima facie defamatory of Mr Francome, and they have disavowed any
intention of making such statements about Mrs Francome, the exception contained in
the injunction which I propose and in the section of the Act will leave them free to use
the tapes as evidence in support of a plea of justification.

I would allow the appeal accordingly.

FOX LJ. It is not the practice of the court to grant an interlocutory injunction
restraining the publication of a libel if the defendant intends to plead justification. In the
present case the Daily Mirror say that they will justify any material which they publish
about Mr Francome and that, so far as Mrs Francome is concerned, they have no intention
of publishing any part of the tapped conversations to which she was a party. Accordingly,
it is said that no injunction should be granted. In the present case, however, the plaintiffs'
claim is not based on defamation but, primarily, on the protection of confidential
material, namely private telephone conversations. They are also, I think, asserting private
rights under the Wireless Telegraphy Act 1949, but I need not examine that for present
purposes.

In *Malone v Comr of Police of the Metropolis (No 2)* [1979] 2 All ER 620 at 645, [1979] Ch
344 at 375 Sir Robert Megarry V-C said:

'The right of confidentiality accordingly falls to be considered apart from any
contractual right. In such a case, it has been said that three elements are normally
required if a case of breach of confidence is to succeed: "First, the information itself,
in the words of Lord Greene M.R. in [*Saltman Engineering Co Ltd v Campbell
Engineering Co Ltd* (1948) [1963] 3 All ER 413 at 415] must 'have the necessary
quality of confidence about it'. Secondly, that information must have been imparted
in circumstances importing an obligation of confidence. Thirdly, there must be an
unauthorised use of that information to the detriment of the party communicating
it": see *Coco v A N Clark (Engineers) Ltd* [1969] RPC 41 at 47, cited by Lord Widgery
CJ in *Attorney-General v Jonathan Cape Ltd* [1975] 3 All ER 484 at 494, [1976] QB 752
at 769. Of the second requirement, it was said in the *Coco* case that "However secret
and confidential the information, there can be no binding obligation of confidence
if that information is blurted out in public or is communicated in other
circumstances which negative any duty of holding it confidential".'

The Vice-Chancellor went on to say ([1979] 2 All ER 620 at 645, [1979] Ch 344 at
376):

'It seems to me that a person who utters confidential information must accept the
risk of any unknown overhearing that is inherent in the circumstances of
communication.'

It is said that this statement negatives the existence of any right to confidentiality in the
a present case. I do not agree. The Vice-Chancellor was only dealing with a case of
authorised tapping by the police and he makes that clear (see [1979] 2 All ER 620 at 651,
[1979] Ch 344 at 384). Illegal tapping by private persons is quite another matter, since it
must be questionable whether the user of a telephone can be regarded as accepting the
risk of that in the same way as, for example, he accepts the risk that his conversation may
be overheard in consequence of the accidents and imperfections of the telephone system
b itself. Accordingly, in my opinion, there is a serious issue to be tried on the matter of
confidentiality.

The Daily Mirror states that it will rely on iniquity and public interest as a defence to
any claim of confidentiality. The claim of confidentiality and the claim of iniquity raise
questions of law and fact which cannot be determined on an interlocutory application.
They require a full trial.

c If the Daily Mirror is permitted to publish the tapes now, the consequent harm to Mr
Francome might be such that he could not be adequately compensated in damages for
any wrong thereby done to him whatever the result of subsequent proceedings. Unless
Mr Francome is given protection until the trial, I think that a trial might be largely
worthless from his point of view even though he succeeded. In the circumstances I would
grant an injunction in the terms proposed by Sir John Donaldson MR. That is not in
d quite the same terms as that granted by the judge but, for the reasons indicated by Sir
John Donaldson MR, I think it is better suited to the requirements of the case.

It was the contention of the defendants that an injunction in this form was directed,
in effect, to preventing a breach of the provisions of the 1949 Act and could only be
granted on the motion of the Attorney General. I do not think that is correct. I am
satisfied that, having regard to the issue of confidentiality, the court is entitled to grant
e an interlocutory injunction to give such protection as it thinks fit to the plaintiffs pending
trial. That injunction is for the protection of the rights or possible rights of the plaintiffs
as individuals. In determining the form of that injunction, we must have proper regard
to the interests of both parties. I think that the proposed form is suitable for all these
purposes. The fact that it adopts the language of the 1949 Act or any other Act is not
material.

f As regards the order made by the judge for disclosure of the identity of the Daily
Mirror's informant, I think that order should be discharged. It is not appropriate to this
stage of the proceedings. Once the name is disclosed, there is no going back on it. There
would be no point in having a trial so far as that matter is concerned, and I think it is a
matter that needs fuller investigation than is possible on an interlocutory application. I
can see that, if the plaintiffs are entitled to disclosure of the name, the sooner they have it
g the better. But a speedy trial has been ordered and, to do justice to the defendants, it
would not, in the circumstances of this case, be right to compel disclosure now.

There is one further matter. Mr Molloy, in his affidavit, says that he would have to
give careful consideration to the probability that publication of the tapes would be an
offence under the 1949 Act. He goes on to say that he would not regard that fact as an
absolute bar to publication if he considered that publication was justifiable in the public
h interest. This suggests that Mr Molloy has a choice in the matter even though publication
would be unlawful. It must be said flatly that he has no choice. His duty is to obey the
law. Parliament by s 5(b) of the 1949 Act created a criminal offence. The proposition that
citizens are free to commit a criminal offence if they have formed the view that it will
further what they believe to be the public interest is quite baseless in our law and inimical
to parliamentary authority. I do not disregard the existence of what is called the moral
j imperative. But such cases are rare in the extreme. On the evidence before us, there is
nothing in the present case which approaches such a situation.

I would make the orders which I have indicated.

STEPHEN BROWN LJ. In this appeal the defendants seek to set aside two orders
made by Park J on 8 March 1984. The first is an order restraining until the trial of the
action the publication by the defendants of any article making use of the contents of

telephone conversations made by the plaintiffs or either of them which had been taped without their knowledge and consent and the second is an order requiring the defendants to disclose on affidavit the identity of the supplier of the tape recordings.

Counsel for the defendants has argued that the plaintiffs have no obvious cause of action against the defendants. Nevertheless he has conceded that they do have an arguable case for alleged breach of confidence and possibly also for relief based on a breach of s 5 of the Wireless Telegraphy Act 1949. He submits, however, that the balance of convenience is against restraining publication of the tape recordings by the defendants, who did not instigate the telephone tapping but only came into possession of the tapes. He argues that in any event the only damage likely to be suffered by the first named plaintiff would be that any publication would be defamatory and that the defendants would seek to justify this. Accordingly, he submits that an interlocutory injunction restraining publication would be contrary to the accepted principles of defamation proceedings. Furthermore, he urges that it is in the public interest that the defendant newspaper should publish material allegedly disclosing breaches of the rules of racing by Mr Francome.

The defendants do not dispute that the tape recordings in question have been obtained illegally and in breach of s 5 of the 1949 Act and that they were and are fully aware of this fact. They also accept that publication by them of information contained in them would be likely to constitute a breach of the criminal law on their part. Nevertheless they say that they should be allowed to exercise their discretion to 'publish and be damned'. Counsel for the defendants submits that it is not for the court in civil proceedings to seek to restrain by injunction a breach of the criminal law.

In this case the plaintiffs are seeking to enforce a private right. Serious questions arise as to what use, if any, may be made of tape recordings which are known to have been obtained illegally by unauthorised telephone tapping. In my judgment, publication by the defendants of the contents of the tape recordings in advance of the trial of the action and before the tape recordings have been authenticated would be likely to prejudice a fair trial of the plaintiffs' claim. So far as the defendants are concerned, it is open to them to serve the public interest, if they so wish, by seeking the appropriate authority to place the tapes in the hands of the police or the stewards of the Jockey Club. An order restraining publication by them until the trial of the action would merely postpone for a time the publication of a possibly sensational story. It will be unlikely to prejudice their position in the trial of the action.

The fact that coincidentally publication would be a criminal offence which the defendants say they are prepared to commit strongly reinforces the case for an injunction.

I am in no doubt that the balance of convenience lies in the plaintiffs' favour and that an injunction in the terms proposed by Sir John Donaldson MR should be granted.

So far as the order for the disclosure by the defendants of the identity of the supplier of the tape recordings is concerned, I agree with Sir John Donaldson MR and Fox LJ that such an order is inappropriate at this interlocutory stage, particularly in the light of an early trial of the action.

I am not satisfied on the evidence, despite the fears of further distribution of the tapes expressed by the plaintiffs, that any prejudice to them will result if this matter awaits full consideration at the trial.

I would accordingly allow the appeal to the extent that the order for disclosure should be discharged.

Appeal allowed in part. Leave to appeal to the House of Lords refused.

Solicitors: *Nicholson Graham & Jones* (for the defendants); *McCloy Day-Wilson & Co,* Newbury (for the plaintiffs).

Diana Procter   Barrister.

Lion Laboratories Ltd v Evans and others

COURT OF APPEAL, CIVIL DIVISION
STEPHENSON, O'CONNOR AND GRIFFITHS LJJ
20, 21, 22, 26 MARCH 1984

Equity – Breach of confidence – Injunction – Information obtained from confidential internal documents of plaintiff company – Defence – Public interest in disclosure – Defendant newspaper obtaining confidential internal documents from ex-employees of plaintiffs – Plaintiffs manufacturing instruments measuring level of intoxication by alcohol – Documents disclosing doubts on acccuracy and reliability of instruments – Whether disclosure of contents of documents in public interest – Whether interlocutory injunction restraining disclosure of contents of documents pending trial of action should be granted – Whether possible trade loss caused by disclosure a ground for refusing injunction.

The plaintiff company manufactured and marketed an electronic computerised instrument known as the Lion Intoximeter 3000 which was used for measuring levels of intoxication by alcohol. Sixty per cent of the plaintiffs' sales were in the United Kingdom. In April 1983 the Home Office approved the Intoximeter for use by the police and from May 1983 about 700 of the instruments were used as one of the two approved devices for testing the breath of drivers of motor vehicles suspected of driving with an alcoholic concentration above the limit prescribed by s 12 of the Road Traffic Act 1972. In 1984 two technicians who had worked on the instruments left the plaintiffs' employment and subsequently the plaintiffs learnt that the two ex-employees were trying to contact the national newspapers with copies of some of the plaintiffs' internal correspondence. The documents concerned were all confidential and indicated doubts as to the reliability and accuracy of the instruments. On 8 March 1984 the plaintiffs issued a writ against the two ex-employees and against the proprietors and the editor of a national newspaper seeking an injunction restraining the defendants from disclosing or making use of any confidential information belonging to the plaintiffs, and damages for breach of confidence and/or breach of copyright. The plaintiffs also applied for and were granted an ex parte interlocutory injunction in the terms of the writ. The following day the newspaper published an article stating that the plaintiffs' instruments were prone to serious error and that further information on the instruments had been withheld by a court order obtained by the plaintiffs. On an application by the defendants to have the ex parte injunction discharged the judge held that, although responsible newspapers had the right to investigate and publish material in the public interest even though it might be embarrassing to others, there was a strong prima facie case on the facts that the defendants had committed an inexcusable breach of confidentiality. The judge accordingly held that the documents did not fall within any exception to the general principle that confidential documents were to be protected and he continued the injunction. The defendants appealed, contending (i) that in weighing up the competing public interests the judge had failed to take into account the fact that what the newspaper had already been able to publish about the instruments was in itself sufficient to cause grave public disquiet and to generate a strong public interest in learning the evidence on which the allegations had been based, (ii) that it was in the public interest for there to be no secrecy about a device whose results were used as evidence against a person charged with a criminal offence and (iii) that just as an injunction would not be granted in an action for libel where the defence of justification was intended to be raised so also an injunction should not be granted in an action for breach of confidentiality where the defendant had a reasonable defence of public interest. The plaintiffs contended, inter alia, (i) that a defendant could not rely on the defence of public interest in an action for breach of confidentiality where the plaintiff had not been guilty of misconduct, (ii) that not only was it important to maintain confidentiality but also the court should be reluctant to countenance disloyalty or to lend its aid to breaches of trust, whatever the motives of the informer, and (iii) that publication of the documents would cause irreparable trade damage to the plaintiffs and the court should therefore maintain the status quo by upholding the judge's order.

Held – The appeal would be allowed for the following reasons—

(1) It was well established that there was a defence of public interest to actions of breach of confidence and breach of copyright if it could be shown that it was in the public interest to publish confidential information. Furthermore, such a defence was not limited to cases in which there had been any wrongdoing on the part of the plaintiff. In deciding whether a defence of public interest could be raised in the particular circumstances of a case, the court had to take into account, (a) the wide difference between what was interesting to the public and what it was in the public interest to make known, (b) the fact that the media had a private interest of their own in publishing what appealed to the public in order to increase circulation, (c) that the public interest might be best served by an informer who possessed confidential information giving that information to the police or some other responsible body rather than the press and (d) that the public interest did not only arise where there was iniquity to be disclosed and that a defendant ought not to be restrained solely because what he wished to publish did not show misconduct on the part of the plaintiff. If the court decided that the defence of public interest could be raised, it had to go on to weigh the competing interests of, on the one hand, the public interest in preserving the rights of organisations and of individuals to maintain the secrecy of confidential information against, on the other, the interest of the public to be informed of matters which were of real public concern (see p 422 *h* to p 423 *a* and *c* to p 424 *a* and *d* to *f*, p 430 *a b* and *j* to p 431 *d* and *f g* and p 432 *h* to p 433 *f*, post); dictum of Page Wood V-C in *Gartside v Outram* (1856) 26 LJ Ch at 114, *Initial Services Ltd v Putterill* [1967] 3 All ER 145, *Fraser v Evans* [1969] 1 All ER 8, *Hubbard v Vosper* [1972] 1 All ER 1023, *Woodward v Hutchins* [1977] 2 All ER 751, *British Steel Corp v Granada Television Ltd* [1981] 1 All ER 417 and *Francome v Mirror Group Newspapers Ltd* [1984] 2 All ER 408 applied.

(2) On the facts, the court had to weigh the public interest in maintaining the confidentiality of the plaintiffs' documents against the public interest in the accuracy and reliability of an approved device on which depended the liability of a person to disqualification, fine or even imprisonment for a drink-driving offence. The plaintiffs were the only manufacturer licensed by the Home Office to produce the instrument and owed a grave obligation to the public to ensure that it was manufactured and maintained to the highest standards, since failure to observe that obligation would mean the possibility of wrongful convictions and loss of liberty being imposed on members of the public. Accordingly it was unquestionably in the public interest that information which showed that such an instrument was not reliable should be made public. The defendants had made out a powerful case for publication in the public interest and in the circumstances it would be wrong to refuse leave to publish material that might lead to a reappraisal of a device that had the potential for causing a wrongful conviction of a serious criminal offence. Furthermore, any damage which the plaintiffs suffered because of loss of sales in the United Kingdom and overseas could be compensated for by an award of damages if the plaintiffs succeeded at the trial. Accordingly the ex parte interlocutory injunctions would be discharged (see p 424 *d* to *f* and *j* to p 425 *d*, p 427 *e* to *g*, p 428 *e* to *j*, p 429 *d* to p 430 *a* and *j*, p 431 *g h*, p 432 *c* to *f*, p 433 *c f g* and *j*, p 434 *a* and *c* and *g h* and p 435 *a* to *f*, post).

Per Stephenson LJ. There may be circumstances in which the public has a right to receive, and the media have a right or even a duty to publish, confidential information, even if the information has been unlawfully obtained in flagrant breach of confidence and irrespective of the motive of the informer (see p 422 *j*, post).

Per Griffiths LJ. Where the press raise the defence of public interest, the court must appraise it critically, but if the court is convinced that a strong case of public interest has been made out the press should be free to publish, leaving the plaintiff to his remedy in damages (see p 435 *d e*, post).

Notes

For equitable relief against breach of confidence, see 16 Halsbury's Laws (4th edn) para 1455.

For the Road Traffic Act 1972, s 12 (as substituted by the Transport Act 1981, Sch 8),
a see 51 Halsbury's Statutes (3rd edn) 1437.

Cases referred to in judgments
Beloff v Pressdram Ltd [1973] 1 All ER 241.
Birkett v James [1977] 2 All ER 801, [1978] AC 297, [1977] 3 WLR 38, CA and HL.
British Steel Corp v Granada Television Ltd [1981] 1 All ER 417, [1981] AC 1096, [1980] 3
b   WLR 774, CA and HL.
Evans v Bartlam [1937] 2 All ER 646, [1937] AC 473, HL.
Francome v Mirror Group Newspapers Ltd [1984] 2 All ER 408, CA.
Fraser v Evans [1969] 1 All ER 8, [1969] 1 QB 349, [1968] 3 WLR 1172, CA.
Gartside v Outram (1856) 26 LJ Ch 113.
Hadmor Productions Ltd v Hamilton [1982] 1 All ER 1042, [1983] 1 AC 191, [1982] 2 WLR
c   322, HL.
Hubbard v Vosper [1972] 1 All ER 1023, [1972] 2 QB 84, [1972] 2 WLR 389, CA.
Initial Services Ltd v Putterill [1967] 3 All ER 145, [1968] 1 QB 396, [1967] 3 WLR 1032,
     CA.
Khashoggi v Smith [1980] CA Transcript 58.
Osenton (Charles) & Co v Johnston [1941] 2 All ER 245, [1942] AC 130, HL.
d *Schering Chemicals Ltd v Falkman Ltd* [1981] 2 All ER 321, [1982] QB 1, [1981] 2 WLR
     848, CA.
Woodward v Hutchins [1977] 2 All ER 751, [1977] 1 WLR 760, CA.

Interlocutory appeal
The defendants, Philip Anthony Evans, Robert Tracey Smith, Sir Larry Lamb and Express
e Newspapers plc, appealed against the order of Leonard J made on 14 March 1984 whereby
he ordered, inter alia, (i) that the application of the third and fourth defendants to
discharge the injunction granted ex parte to the plaintiffs, Lion Laboratories Ltd, by
Leonard J on 8 March 1984 be refused, and (ii) that until trial or further order the
defendants and each of them be restrained from (a) disclosing or making use of any
confidential information being the property of the plaintiffs for any purpose whatsoever
f and (b) infringing the plaintiffs' copyright in their internal or other documents. The facts
are set out in the judgment of Stephenson LJ.

Michael Bloch for the first and second defendants.
Robert Alexander QC and *Geoffrey Shaw* for the third and fourth defendants.
Anthony Hoolahan QC and *Harry M Boggis-Rolfe* for the plaintiffs.

g
                                                             Cur adv vult

26 March. The following judgments were delivered.

STEPHENSON LJ. There are before the court appeals by four defendants from an
h injunction which Leonard J granted ex parte on 8 March 1984 and refused to discharge
on 14 March. The four defendants are, first and second, two former employees of the
plaintiff company and, third and fourth, the editor and publishers of the Daily Express.
The plaintiff company is a company incorporated in this country who, under licence
from a United States corporation, manufacture and market an electronic computerised
instrument known as the Lion Intoximeter 3000. They sell these Intoximeters to overseas
j customers, but 60% of their sales are in this country, for use by the police for measuring
intoxication by alcohol, as the name implies. On 18 April 1983 the Home Office
approved these Intoximeters for that use, and since May 1983 about 700 of them have
been in use, mainly as one of the two approved devices for testing the breath of drivers
of motor vehicles suspected of driving with an alcoholic concentration above the limit
prescribed by para 12 of Sch 8 to the Transport Act 1981. The Intoximeters were in
particularly extensive use at Christmas time 1983.

On 10 January 1984 the second defendant, Smith, left the plaintiffs' employment, followed on 13 February by the first defendant, Evans. Both men were technicians who *a* had worked on the Intoximeter. On 2 March the plaintiffs were informed by an informant that two ex-employees were trying to contact Fleet Street with copies of the plaintiffs' internal correspondence. On 7 March Mr Rees, a reporter employed by the fourth defendants, called on Dr King, who had been the plaintiffs' senior research chemist and head of the calibration laboratory until he left that post in December 1983, with internal memoranda of the plaintiffs. He also called on Dr Williams, who was, and still *b* is, the plaintiffs' marketing director, with four internal documents, with which this case is principally concerned. Two of those four documents were marked, in one description or another, confidential and all are conceded to have been confidential. Mr Rees's object in calling on Dr King and Dr Williams was to authenticate the documents, and there is no dispute as to their authenticity. On 8 March the plaintiffs issued a writ claiming an injunction and damages for breach of confidence and/or breach of copyright. On that *c* day Leonard J granted the plaintiffs an injunction ex parte, with leave to issue a summons returnable on 15 March. At that stage nothing confidential had been published.

I read the terms of the order made by the judge on 8 March:

> '(A) Until 15th day of March 1984 or further order the Defendants and each of them be restrained from:—(1) Disclosing or making use of any confidential information being the property of the Plaintiff for any purpose whatsoever. (2) *d* Infringing the Plaintiff's copyright in their internal or other documents. (B) The Defendants and each of them should within 14 days deliver up all documents or copies thereof containing such confidential information or being the subject of such copyright in the defendants' possession, power or control. (C) The Defendants and each of them should within 14 days disclose the identity of the supplier of any such confidential information or supplier of any such documents. (D) That the First and *e* Second Defendants should within 5 days disclose list verified by Affidavit all persons to whom they have supplied any such documents or confidential information . . .'

On 9 March, the next day, the Daily Express published a censored article. It was headed 'Exposed: The Great "Breath Test" Scandal', and it read:
f

> 'The Intoximeter 3000, the controversial breathtest machine which has convicted thousands of motorists has an unacceptably high failure rate. This is the conclusion reached after a Daily Express investigation into defects which have plagued the machine. The investigation has revealed that the Intoximeter is so prone to error that many of the drunk driving cases "proved" by the machine must now be suspect. Our inquiries show that:—The Intoximeter gave a disturbing percentage of faulty *g* performances during Home Office proving tests. It continued to behave erratically after being approved as an "evidential" instrument which began convicting drivers in May last year. The Home Office conducted its biggest ever blitz on drinking drivers over Christmas and New Year—at a time when it knew there was a problem with the 3000. Angry solicitors are currently challenging 500 cases where they fear that the Intoximeter is in danger of creating miscarriages of justice. An eminent *h* scientist claims that the 3000 appears to be subject to faulty design and should never have been introduced as an evidential instrument. There is a distressing history of the 3000 going wrong inside police stations. A calibration expert, employed to ensure the accuracy of the Intoximeter, left Lion Laboratories because he was unhappy with the situation over the Intoximeter. He told the Daily Express: "It is no secret that the machine presents serious problems in calibration". There is *j* evidence that the machine can be affected by weather conditions, lightning, power supply surges, cigarette smoke and the chemical used for fingerprinting in police stations. Professor Vincent Marks, Professor of Chemical Bio-Chemistry at Surrey University, said: "The assumption made in current legislation that machines cannot lie and are foolproof is unmitigated nonsense!". He is an expert witness on cases involving the Lion Intoximeter.'

a There were further pages of that issue of the Daily Express on which appear blanks, covered by the legend:

'BREATH TEST SCANDAL

Further information on the Intoximeter was scheduled for this space. It has been withheld because of a High Court order obtained by the manufacturer. This order will be contested.'

b

On 12 and 13 March the judge heard counsel in support of the third and fourth defendants' application to discharge that injunction and he prepared his judgment to be delivered on the next day. On the next day, 14 March, Mr Bloch of counsel appeared for the first and second defendants, who entered the lists for the first time, through no fault of their own or, I assume, of anybody else. The judge, after hearing counsel for the first c and second defendants and counsel for the third and fourth defendants, delivered the judgment which he had prepared in circumstances which he explained in giving judgment. He said:

'[Counsel for the first and second defendants] was content with an arrangement by which his two defendants would agree to be treated as being parties to the hearing which concluded last night, without their making any submissions or d placing any evidence before me. They would then be in a position where they would have a standing in the Court of Appeal and, subject to the discretion of that court, might address not only arguments in law to the Court of Appeal but also submit affidavit evidence on their behalf.'

After referring to the opposition of counsel for the third and fourth defendants to that e course, he said:

'I have come to the conclusion that there is substance in [counsel for the third and fourth defendants'] contention that the matter having effectively finished he is entitled to have a judgment which he may wish to make the subject of an appeal.'

f The judge then made an order slightly amending the terms of the ex parte injunction. Paragraph (A) of his order, against which this appeal is brought, is:

'Until trial or further order the Defendants and each of them be restrained from:—(1) Disclosing or making use of any confidential information being the property of the Plaintiff for any purpose whatsoever. (2) Infringing the Plaintiff's copyright in their internal or other documents.'

g

The orders in paras (B), (C) and (D) are not the subject of these appeals. Those orders still exist and, for all the court knows, have been complied with.

There is still in this action by the plaintiffs no claim for defamation. There could not, of course, have been such a claim in advance of publication when the writ was issued on 8 March, but there has been no amendment of the writ since that date.

h There is no dispute, first of all, that the documents which are the subject of this appeal are confidential, that they were taken by the first and second defendants without authority and handed over to the fourth defendants (whether for reward we do not know) and that publication would be a breach of confidence by all four defendants subject to a defence that it is in the public interest that they should be published now. Equally there is no dispute that the copyright of these documents is in the plaintiffs and j to publish them would infringe the plaintiffs' copyright, subject to the same public interest being a just cause or excuse for their publication. The defendants want to be allowed to publish other confidential documents as well as the principal four. I shall refer to all those documents later.

The judge considered the law laid down in several decisions of this court in the last 20 years. He set out the two conflicting interests raised by the parties and found that the scale tipped in favour of continuing his injunction.

He said:

'Of course, it is most important that the operation of a machine which is the a
provider of evidence which can lead to conviction should be subjected to careful
scrutiny. Nobody, and certainly not I, would doubt the right of the press to probe
and question the machine's validity. However, I would doubt that technical matters
of this kind are best investigated in the columns of a daily newspaper, however
distinguished it may be. There is the further aspect that uninformed reaction to b
scientific discussion might improperly undermine public confidence in the
operation of a machine which has been approved by the Home Secretary. I would
have thought that the Home Office was a more appropriate initial forum for
discussion of its merits or demerits. On the other hand, I am driven to the conclusion
that there is a strong public interest in maintaining the system by which free and
frank criticism of their own highly technical products should be permitted to the c
scientifically qualified employees of a company such as the plaintiff company.
However, if possibly disgruntled ex-employees were free to pass such criticism to
the press for publication, either in part or as a whole, it would inevitably be inhibited
or even cease altogether. In my judgment that would operate in the public harm. I
can find no exception to the general principle which protects confidential documents
in the facts of this case. In my judgment the scale tips clearly in favour of d
maintaining their confidentiality.'

The judge then considered submissions by the defendants on copyright and fair
dealing, and the submissions of counsel for the plaintiffs in support of the injunction,
and he stated his conclusions in this way:

'I wish to say that I recognise fully the right of responsible newspapers to e
investigate in the public interest and to publish material which may be embarrassing
to other people. In this case, however, I am satisfied that there is a strong prima facie
case of inexcusable breach of confidentiality and the clear danger of inexcusable
breach of copyright which requires me to maintain the injunction which I granted
ex parte...'
f

He was in my judgment right to make no difference between confidence and copyright
for the purposes of this case, and I shall not consider them separately.

This court has had the advantage of hearing much fuller argument than the judge
heard, not only from counsel for the third and fourth defendants but also from counsel
for the first and second defendants, who, in the circumstances already explained, had no
opportunity of arguing the case for the first and second defendants before the judge, but g
who has been of assistance to the court with his arguments in this case. We have also
heard fuller argument from counsel on behalf of the plaintiffs. It is furthermore right to
say that during the course of hearing this appeal the campaign against the plaintiffs'
Intoximeter, which does not appear to have started until 9 March, has gathered strength
from the daily publication of further critical material in the third and fourth defendants'
newspaper in particular, and it may be elsewhere. h

The problem before the judge and before this court is how best to resolve, before trial,
a conflict of two competing public interests. The first public interest is the preservation
of the right of organisations, as of individuals, to keep secret confidential information.
The courts will restrain breaches of confidence, and breaches of copyright, unless there is
just cause or excuse for breaking confidence or infringing copyright. The just cause or
excuse with which this case is concerned is the public interest in admittedly confidential j
information. There is confidential information which the public may have a right to
receive and others, in particular the press, now extended to the media, may have a right
and even a duty to publish, even if the information has been unlawfully obtained in
flagrant breach of confidence and irrespective of the motive of the informer. The duty of
confidence, the public interest in maintaining it, is a restriction on the freedom of the
press which is recognised by our law, as well as by art 10(2) of the European Convention

for the Protection of Human Rights and Fundamental Freedoms (Rome, 4 November
a 1950; TS 71 (1953); Cmd 8969); the duty to publish, the countervailing interest of the
public in being kept informed of matters which are of real public concern, is an inroad
on the privacy of confidential matters.

So much is settled by decisions of this court, and in particular by the illuminating
judgments of Lord Denning MR in *Initial Services Ltd v Putterill* [1967] 3 All ER 145,
[1968] 1 QB 396, *Fraser v Evans* [1969] 1 All ER 8, [1969] 1 QB 349, *Hubbard v Vosper*
b [1972] 1 All ER 1023, [1972] 2 QB 84, *Woodward v Hutchins* [1977] 2 All ER 751, [1977]
1 WLR 760 and (dissenting) *Schering Chemicals Ltd v Falkman Ltd* [1981] 2 All ER 321,
[1982] QB 1. I add to those the speeches of Lord Wilberforce, Lord Salmon and Lord
Fraser in *British Steel Corp v Granada Television Ltd* [1981] 1 All ER 417, [1981] AC 1096.

There are four further considerations. First, 'There is a wide difference between what
is interesting to the public and what it is in the public interest to make known': per Lord
c Wilberforce in *British Steel Corp v Granada Television Ltd* [1981] 1 All ER 417 at 455,
[1981] AC 1096 at 1168. The public are interested in many private matters which are no
real concern of theirs and which the public have no pressing need to know. Second, the
media have a private interest of their own in publishing what appeals to the public and
may increase their circulation or the numbers of their viewers or listeners; and (I quote
from the judgment of Sir John Donaldson MR in *Francome v Mirror Group Newspapers*
d *Ltd* [1984] 2 All ER 408 at 413) '... they are peculiarly vulnerable to the error of
confusing the public interest with their own interest'. Third, there are cases in which the
public interest is best served by an informer giving the confidential information not to
the press but to the police or some other responsible body, as was suggested by Lord
Denning MR in the *Initial Services* case and by Sir John Donaldson MR in the *Francome*
case. Fourth, it was said by Page Wood V-C in *Gartside v Outram* (1856) 26 LJ Ch 113 at
e 114, 'there is no confidence as to the disclosure of iniquity'; and though counsel concedes
on the plaintiffs' behalf that, as Salmon LJ said in *Initial Services v Putterill* [1967] 3 All ER
145 at 151, [1968] 1 QB 396 at 410, 'what was iniquity in 1856 may be too narrow, or
too wide, in 1967', and in 1984 extends to serious misdeeds or grave misconduct, he
submits that misconduct of that kind is necessary to destroy the duty of confidence or
excuse the breach of it, and nothing of that sort is alleged against the plaintiffs in the
f evidence now before the court.

Counsel for the third and fourth defendants and counsel for the first and second
defendants have not been able to find any case where a defendant has been able to rely on
on public interest in defence of a claim for breach of confidence and the plaintiff has not
also been guilty of such misconduct. And there are passages in the speeches of Lord
Wilberforce and Lord Fraser in *British Steel Corp v Granada Television Ltd* in which they
g appear to be satisfied with describing the 'public interest rule' as the 'iniquity rule'. But I
nowhere find any authority for the proposition, except perhaps in the judgment of
Ungoed-Thomas J in *Beloff v Pressdram Ltd* [1973] 1 All ER 241 at 260, that some modern
form of iniquity on the part of the plaintiffs is the only thing which can be disclosed in
the public interest; and I agree with the judge in rejecting the 'no iniquity, no public
interest' rule and in respectfully adopting what Lord Denning MR said in *Fraser v Evans*
h [1969] 1 All ER 8 at 11, [1969] 1 QB 349 at 362 that some things are required to be
disclosed in the public interest, in which case no confidence can be prayed in aid to keep
them secret, and '[iniquity] is merely an instance of a just cause and excuse for breaking
confidence'.

Griffiths LJ put this case in argument. Suppose the plaintiffs had informed the police
that their Intoximeter was not working accurately or safe to use, and the police had
j replied that they were nevertheless going to continue using it as breath test evidence.
Could there then be no defence of public interest if the defendants sought to publish that
confidential information, simply because the plaintiffs themselves had done nothing
wrong but the police had? There would be the same public interest in publication,
whichever was guilty of misconduct; and I cannot think the right to break confidence
would be lost, though the public interest remained the same.

Bearing this last consideration in mind, in my opinion we cannot say that the defendants must be restrained because what they want to publish does not show misconduct by the plaintiffs.

We have then, with the other three considerations in mind and remembering that confidentiality is admitted, to ask what the judge called the 'sole question', namely:

'... whether the defendants have shown that they have an arguable defence to the plaintiffs' claims in respect of breach of confidentiality and breach of copyright,'

and that means, as counsel for the third and fourth defendants ultimately expressed it, a serious defence of public interest which may succeed, not, of course, will succeed, at the trial. He had expressed it rather differently as a reasonable defence, taking the words from the judgment of Lord Denning MR in *Hubbard v Vosper* [1972] 1 All ER 1023, [1972] 2 QB 84, where it was treated like a plea of justification or fair comment in a libel suit. And there are statements in the judgments of Lord Denning MR in *Fraser v Evans* [1969] 1 All ER 8, [1969] 1 QB 349 and of Roskill LJ in the unreported case of *Khashoggi v Smith* [1980] CA Transcript 58, which indicate that a plaintiff should not be better off if he claims for breach of confidence than if he claims for defamation. But I respectfully agree with Sir David Cairns in *Khashoggi's* case 'that there is a fundamental distinction between the two types of action'. To be allowed to publish confidential information, the defendants must do more than raise a plea of public interest: they must show 'a legitimate ground for supposing it is in the public interest for it to be disclosed'. Then, as Lord Denning MR said in *Woodward v Hutchins* [1977] 2 All ER 751 at 755, [1977] 2 WLR 760 at 764, 'the courts should not restrain it by interlocutory injunction, but should leave the complainant to his remedy in damages', after (I will assume, though I am not sure that Lord Denning MR would have agreed) considering and weighing in the balance all relevant matters, such as whether damages would be an adequate remedy to compensate the plaintiffs if they succeeded at the trial.

We cannot of course at this stage decide whether the balance will come down on the side of confidentiality or of public interest. But, to see if there is a serious defence of public interest which may succeed at the trial, we have to look at the evidence and, if we decide that there is such a defence, to perform a balancing exercise, as indicated for instance in the judgment of Lord Denning MR in *Woodward v Hutchins* and in the speech of Lord Fraser in *British Steel Corp v Granada Television Ltd* [1981] 1 All ER 417 at 480, [1981] AC 1096 at 1202, which is so apt that I follow the judge in quoting it. In that case Lord Fraser said:

'The answer to the question therefore seems to me to involve weighing up the public interest for and against publication. The balance does not in my opinion depend on the use made of the leaked information by the appellants in this particular case. Anyone who hands over to the press a bundle of confidential documents belonging to someone else must surely expect, and intend, that, if they contain information of topical interest, it will be published in some form. The informer's motives are, in my opinion, irrelevant. It is said, and I am willing to accept, that in this case the informant neither asked for nor received any money, or other reward, but that he acted out of a keen sense of indignation about the dealings between BSC and the government before and during the strike. No doubt there is a public interest in maintaining the free flow of information to the press, and therefore against obstructing informers. But there is also I think a very strong public interest in preserving confidentiality within any organisation, in order that it can operate efficiently, and also be free from suspicion that it is harbouring disloyal employees. There is no difference in this respect between a public corporation like BSC and an ordinary company.'

The defendants' case for publication now is simple and does not, in my judgment, require any appreciation of highly technical matters to be understood. It is that the plaintiffs' Intoximeter, which they alone make and distribute in this country, is by law providing the sole evidence on which many members of the public have been, and are

being, prosecuted to conviction for road traffic offences, that its accuracy is therefore a
a matter of grave public concern and that the confidential documents purloined by the
first and second defendants, which the third and fourth defendants want to publish, and
the first and second defendants want to be free to use, increase already existing doubts
about the accuracy of the Intoximeter. The gravity of the issue raised by the defence of
public interest is underlined by the 'blitz' or 'crack-down' on drivers of motor vehicles
who had drunk alcohol, which police forces carried out around Christmas 1983, when
b many drivers were convicted and fined, and some imprisoned, for offences proved solely
by the uncorroborated evidence of the plaintiffs' Intoximeter. The defendants' case is that
the public should know, and the press should give them now, any material which may
indicate that the Intoximeter is either inherently defective or incorrectly operated,
contrary to the denials of the plaintiffs and the Home Office. Such material, say the
defendants, is to be found in the plaintiffs' own documents, abstracted and copied by the
c first and second defendants, but forbidden by the judge's injunction to be published by
the third and fourth defendants. What makes this case so special is that the plaintiffs'
right to keep inviolate the secrecy of the information which the defendants wish to
publish is undisputed, and the only question for interlocutory decision is whether that
right is outweighed by the public interest, not in exposing persons who may be guilty of
offences for which they have not been punished, but in disclosing the risk of the plaintiffs'
d being instrumental in punishing other people for offences which they may not have
committed.

Of the device, or instrument itself, it is only necessary to say that the motorist suspected
of driving with a concentration of alcohol above the prescribed limit blows twice into a
tube connected with an infra-red analyser which determines the alcohol concentration in
his breath, and that concentration is automatically recorded on a thermal printer. The
e test is controlled by a micro-computer and checked by a breath simulator providing
automatic calibration checks. A print-out of all relevant details, including the
concentration of alcohol in the breath, in microgrammes per 100 ml of breath is the
evidence tendered in the courts by police officers specially instructed and trained in the
operation of the machine.

The limit prescribed by the statute is 35 microgrammes of alcohol per 100 ml of
f breath. The 'de facto prosecution limit' is said to be a higher minimum of 40
microgrammes, but the statutory conviction limit is 35. The statute also provides that if
the breath test records a concentration of no more than 50 microgrammes, the suspect
may claim an old-fashioned blood or urine test in replacement of the breath test. We are
told that the suspect is in fact informed of that right on instructions to police forces, but
there is no statutory requirement that he must be so informed.

g It is plain from these facts that an error of a few microgrammes will make a serious
difference in two cases. If the Intoximeter reads 35 plus when it should read 35 minus
(or 40 plus when it should read 40 minus) the suspect will have to face a charge instead
of walking out of the police station a free man. If the Intoximeter reads 50 plus when it
should read 50 minus, he is deprived of his right to a test by other means than the
Intoximeter.

h There is one other danger if the Intoximeter is not working properly: it may not
record the breath of a suspect even when properly blown into the tube and that suspect
might in consequence risk being convicted of failing to provide a specimen of breath
without reasonable excuse.

One cause of error is recognised to require safeguards. That is the presence of acetone
in the breath, particularly of diabetics and persons on slimming diets. Concentrations of
j acetone in the breath would cause wrong readings of alcohol concentration unless
compensated by an acetone sensor built into the Intoximeter. To avoid these errors and
the possibility of unjust convictions resulting from them, the Home Office requires
compliance with British Calibration Standards by means of calibration tests for 7 days;
and the use of the Intoximeter is restricted to authorised police officers. The plaintiffs
have manufactured and sold about 700 of these Intoximeters, mainly, as I have said, for
use in this country, and more than that number of calibration certificates have been

issued by some of the plaintiffs' senior employees, certifying that they comply with the British Calibration Standards.

What the defendants want to publish are, first, four documents exhibited to the first affidavit sworn by Dr Jones, who is the chairman and managing director of the plaintiff company, and is one of those who have certified these Intoximeters, second, a number of reports exhibited to the affidavit of Mr Rees, a journalist employed by the fourth defendants, and, third, a report of Dr Williams, the plaintiffs' marketing director.

I need spend no time on the second and third of these categories, which generally speaking record faults in particular machines, except to say that I accept the submission of counsel for the plaintiffs that a report and certain documents exhibited to Mr Rees's affidavit are entitled to the protection of an injunction until trial. I need not refer further to one of the documents exhibited to Dr Jones's affidavit, namely a long report on 'Breath Acetone and the Lion Intoximeter 3000' by Dr Jones, because at the invitation of the court the defendants did not press for disclosure of that report.

I must, however, say more about three other documents exhibited to Dr Jones's affidavit. The first is entitled 'Giving Evidence in Court as an Expert Witness', and the advice comes from Dr Williams in that document, which is dated 30 October 1983. I need not read it, because, by itself, I would agree with the judge that it has little if any significance, but I think it has significance in conjunction with the two other documents exhibited to his affidavit. I find it necessary to refer in greater detail to those documents because they are the foundation of the defendants' case for discharging the injunction, and I have come to the conclusion that the defendants have made out their case in regard to those documents that they should no longer be restrained from disclosing them.

The second document is a memorandum of 20 December 1983 from Dr Jones to directors, who include Dr King and Dr Blyth, the other two scientists employed by the plaintiffs, who issued certificates for these Intoximeters.

It is headed:

'Re: IR 3000 AND ACETONE COMPENSATION;

PRELIMINARY NOTE—PENDING DETAILED INSTRUCTIONS FROM PMW [that is Dr Williams].

Recent tests by the Home Office on acetone compensation with a 10 mg% solution have shown that the great majority of instruments have little or no compensation. On checking back, it would appear that this has arisen because the instruments were not set up correctly, according to laid down procedures. Secondly, it would appear that the majority of the tests data on the acetone–alcohol mixture are not within BCS Specifications (i.e. the alcohol reading with acetone present should be less than the alcohol reading alone). In general, it would appear to be on average 2 µg higher. Failure to correctly compensate for acetone has caused us acute embarrassment and loss of confidence by the Home Office and Police. It has also resulted in a tremendous waste of Lion manpower and will continue to do so. It could still result in a withdrawal of all instruments as no one is prepared to stand up in court and testify to the acetone correction being exact. The Home Office now insist that all instruments be checked with a 45 µg acetone standard and compensated accordingly. The Home Office laboratories will assist with this and will attempt to visit all instruments during January and early February to test for acetone compensation and provide us with data to generate a new code. They will then key in the notified I.D. and test if the compensation works on acetone standard.'

I do not think I need read the rest of the document, which ends by referring to Dr Williams and Dr Blyth training forensic personnel in the first two weeks of January re procedures.

The third document is from Dr King to Dr Jones, Dr Williams and a number of others, I think 13 in all, including Dr Blyth. It is headed: 'Certification of IR 3000.' It then states that on Wednesday, 15 December (that is 1982) the majority of instruments in the certification area were performing adequately. There is then a reference to windy weather, and the third paragraph reads:

'In the past I have allowed instruments to be repaired, readjusted and reprogrammed during certification, on the understanding that it was merely a temporary measure which would soon be unnecessary once the instruments were functioning correctly. However, with more than 100 certificates issued, the situation shows no sign of improving. I can no longer write certificates for instruments which I know are not operating properly and I cannot ignore a failure on one day of 65%. In my opinion this renders the whole concept of certification pointless and worthless. The following points stand out clearly:—I have a moral duty to the BCS to adhere to the conditions laid down and agreed upon . . .'

I do not think I need read much more of the document, but I should read this:

'It is not unreasonable to ask that the machines perform properly for seven days. It should be used as a filter to remove rogues before they leave the building. By sending out instruments which are not 100% we are committing ourselves to completing them later. This means that I am not certifying a complete instrument. I am extremely concerned about the amount of repairs, adjustments and alterations made after they leave my hands and the effects this will have (both real and imagined) on the certified status of the instrument. The certificate and label implies some sort of confidence in the operation of the instrument. In view of the ease with which calibration can be lost, I would understand it if this confidence was also lost . . . today, a machine must function properly for 7 days without repair reprogramming or readjustment in order to gain a certificate.'

Public confidence in these Intoximeters has already been shaken by matters which the fourth defendants and other newspapers have already published without attempts to restrain them, or claims for libel, on the part of the plaintiffs. It may be that the damage which publication of these documents may do to the plaintiffs' reputation will add little to that already done. But it must, in my opinion, be right that the public should know also that the plaintiffs' senior research chemist and head of the calibration laboratory had apparently certified machines in 1982 as complying with Home Office requirements when they were imperfectly calibrated and was so critical of the practice that he then left the plaintiffs' employment, and that the plaintiffs' chairman and managing director was informing his own staff on the eve of the Christmas 1983 'crack-down' on drunken drivers that many of the plaintiffs' machines did not comply with Home Office standards and might have to be withdrawn after the 'crack-down' was over.

I know that Dr Jones has given explanations of why he wrote what he did on 20 December 1983, and why Dr King wrote what he did in December 1982, in two affidavits, the last sworn after counsel's criticism of his memorandum at the hearing before Leonard J. Counsel for the plaintiffs relied on those explanations as making disclosure of the unexplained document one-sided and misleading. I would read them if I thought they helped the plaintiffs' case; but the defendants have undertaken by counsel to publish them with the second and third documents exhibited to Dr Jones's affidavit which I have quoted if required by the plaintiffs to do so, and I do not read them. The only comments of Dr King himself are contained in Mr Rees's affidavit. Paragraph 8 of that affidavit says this:

'When I saw Dr. King on the morning of Wednesday March 7th 1984, I showed him the two memoranda from himself and Dr. Jones. Of the first he said "Oh yes, that was mine. I wrote that memorandum and received the other one. There were problems with calibration but any machine that left my hands after a week was calibrated and working—whether it continued to work is another matter". He used those or very similar words. In addition, as reported in Friday's Daily Express, he asked me whether this was what I would call "blowing the whistle", confirmed that he was unhappy with his situation about the Intoximeter, and that he had resigned; confirmed that there were difficulties with the machine; and he said "I have no doubt that the public will be disturbed by what you have uncovered".'

Dr King still acts as a consultant to the plaintiffs, but there is no affidavit from him
either explaining his own memorandum or challenging Mr Rees's evidence.

Now the judge summarised all three documents exhibited to Dr Jones's affidavit which
I have referred to, but all that he says about the public interest in disclosing them is
contained in two passages of his judgment. The first is:

> 'In more general terms [counsel for the third and fourth defendants] maintains
> there is a general public interest that there should be disclosure of the documents
> which outweighs the plaintiffs' claim of confidentiality. He emphasises the fact that
> the Intoximeter is a machine for providing evidence on which people are convicted
> of a criminal offence.'

The second passage is the passage which I have already read:

> 'Of course, it is most important that the operation of a machine which is the
> provider of evidence which can lead to conviction should be subjected to careful
> scrutiny.'

I appreciate what the judge said at the beginning of his judgment:

> 'Since it is a hearing in chambers, I do not propose to enter into a lengthy survey
> of the evidence all of which is available in the affidavits and accompanying exhibits.
> I shall confine myself to a summary of those parts which seem to me to be necessary
> for understanding.'

I hesitate to assume that the judge had not attended to, or understood, evidence which
he does not refer to simply because he does not refer to it. I read again what he said:

> 'I can find no exception to the general principle which protects confidential
> documents in the facts of this case. In my judgment the scale tips clearly in favour
> of maintaining their confidentiality.'

That is, I think, his answer to the question whether the defendants had shown an arguable
defence, and I cannot see how he could have found in the facts of this case no reasonable
defence of public interest if he had fully appreciated and properly evaluated the evidence
before him. If he did not mean that there was nothing in the defence, but only that,
although reasonable and serious, it was not serious enough to tip the scale in favour of
breaking confidentiality, his decision was, in my judgment, plainly wrong, wrong
because he misunderstood either the law or the evidence and gave too little weight to the
dangers of unjust convictions if the Intoximeter's printouts were inaccurate owing to the
machine's being inadequately calibrated or wrongly operated, and also to the need for a
reappraisal of the Intoximeter by the Home Office to allay mounting public disquiet. He
may, I think, have been influenced also in reaching that decision by giving too much
weight to his view that a daily newspaper was not the best forum for investigating
technical matters, and a less appropriate forum than the Home Office for the discussion
of the Intoximeter's merits and demerits. I have tried to explain that the public interest
in the confidential information which the fourth defendants' newspaper wants to publish
does not depend on understanding or misunderstanding technical matters, though the
result of the publication of that information may well be to apply pressure on the
authorities to conduct a scientific investigation and discussion of those matters (such as
appears to have been carried on already in the Law Society's Gazette). Furthermore, the
Home Office is publicly committed to supporting the machine and its continued use,
and, however strongly it might make plain its opposition to obtaining unjust convictions
by means of which it at present approves, it is associated in the public mind with the
machine, and the police use of it, as reliable evidence in courts of law.

I therefore consider that, in so far as the judge exercised his discretion in continuing
the injunction, this court is entitled, and indeed required, unless there are other factors
which plainly outweigh the public interest, to set aside his decision on principles which
have been laid down by the House of Lords in *Evans v Bartlam* [1937] 2 All ER 646,

[1937] AC 473, *Osenton v Johnston* [1941] 2 All ER 245, [1942] AC 130, *Birkett v James*
a [1977] 2 All ER 801, [1978] AC 297 and, most recently, *Hadmor Productions Ltd v Hamilton*
[1982] 1 All ER 1042, [1982] AC 191.

Counsel for the plaintiffs has submitted that there are such other factors. There is not
only the importance of preserving confidentiality, and any court must be reluctant to
countenance disloyalty, or to lend its aid to breach of trust, whether the servant turned
informer is disgruntled or greedy or eccentric or public-spirited. There is of course also
b the importance of uninhibited evaluations and criticisms by the plaintiffs of their own
Intoximeter and of any troubles it may have had in the early stages or developed later,
and that they should not be abused for the creation out of context of one-sided, ill-
informed and unjustified doubts. But there is also, he submits, the importance of not
weakening confidence in the machine if it is a reliable aid to protecting the public from
drunken driving. He further objects to the advantage that disclosure may give to trade
c competitors and the irreparable damage it may do to the plaintiffs; and, he says, it will
bring final ruin for the plaintiffs because there will be no trial if the documents are
disclosed, and therefore we should preserve the status quo by upholding the judge's
order.

If the defendants are restrained from publication of the report by Dr Jones entitled
'Breath Acetone and the Lion Intoximeter 3000' and those parts of the documents
d exhibited to Mr Rees's affidavit to which I have referred, the first objection will be met.
As to the second and third, I cannot see that any damage from consequent loss of sales in
this country and overseas cannot be compensated for by an award of damages if the
plaintiffs succeed at trial; and the damage cause by releasing these documents will not
add to the damage caused by what has already been published without objection, or
make it any more unlikely that the plaintiffs' action for breach of confidence and
e copyright will ever be tried.

The judge never referred to the damage already done to the reputation of the plaintiffs
and their Intoximeter by what had already been published and merely recorded the
arguments of counsel for the plaintiffs on the damage which would be done by further
publication without putting it in the scales, I think because he had already decided that
they tipped in the plaintiffs' favour for breach of confidence and also because the damage
f done by 14 March is not as great as the damage done by further publication since that
date. It may be distasteful to let damage done by a newspaper weigh in support of its
application to be allowed to do more damage by breaking confidence. Nevertheless, the
existing damage is, in my view, a matter which the court must now take into account,
and that is another factor which entitles us to differ from the judge.

I read again the judge's conclusion:

g   '. . . I am satisfied that there is a strong prima facie case of inexcusable breach of
confidentiality and the clear danger of inexcusable breach of copyright which
requires me to maintain the injunction which I granted, ex parte, on Thursday. The
application by the third and fourth defendants to discharge the injunctions is
accordingly refused.'

h If he had had the full argument that we have had on the evidence contained in these
documents and their implications, and had had less of his attention directed to questions
of copyright and fair dealing, he might well have come to the opposite conclusion and
found in public interest just cause and excuse for their disclosure. The issue raised by the
defendants is a serious question concerning a matter which affects the life, and even the
liberty, of an unascertainable number of Her Majesty's subjects, and though there is no
j proof that any of them has been wrongly convicted on the evidence of the plaintiffs'
Intoximeter, and we certainly cannot decide that any has, we must not restrain the
defendants from putting before the public this further information how the Lion
Intoximeter 3000 has worked, and how the plaintiffs regard and discharge their
responsibility for it, although the information is confidential and was unlawfully taken
in breach of confidence.

I would therefore allow the appeals and discharge the injunction, save as to the documents I have referred to.

a

O'CONNOR LJ. I agree that the appeal should be allowed and that the order proposed by Stephenson LJ should be made.

I agree for the reasons given by Stephenson LJ; I only add a few words of my own because of the importance of the case.

Section 8 of the Road Traffic Act 1972, as substituted by the Transport Act 1981, made   *b* a far-reaching change in the law requiring drivers of motor vehicles suspected of having consumed alcohol to provide specimens for analysis. The change was to introduce specimens of breath as the primary specimen. Section 8 provides:

'(1) In the course of an investigation whether a person has committed an offence under section 5 or section 6 of this Act a constable may, subject to the following provisions of this section and section 9 below, require him—(a) to provide two   *c* specimens of breath for analysis by means of a device of a type approved by the Secretary of State; or (b) to provide a specimen of blood or urine for a laboratory test . . .

(3) A requirement under this section to provide a specimen of blood or urine can only be made at a police station or at a hospital; and it cannot be made at a police station unless—(a) the constable making the requirement has reasonable cause to   *d* believe that for medical reasons a specimen of breath cannot be provided or should not be required; or (b) at the time the requirement is made a device or a reliable device of the type mentioned in subsection (1)(a) is not available at the police station or it is then for any other reason not practicable to use such a device there; or (c) the suspected offence is one under section 5 of this Act and the constable making the requirement has been advised by a medical practitioner that the condition of the   *e* person required to provide the specimen might be due to some drug; but may then be made notwithstanding that the person required to provide the specimen has already provided or been required to provide two specimens of breath . . .

(6) Of any two specimens of breath provided by any person in pursuance of this section that with the lower proportion of alcohol in the breath shall be used and the other shall be disregarded; but if the specimen with the lower proportion of alcohol   *f* contains no more than 50 microgrammes of alcohol in 100 millilitres of breath the person who provided it may claim that it should be replaced by such a specimen as may be required under subsection (4) [which enables him to substitute a specimen of urine or blood], and if he then provides such a specimen neither specimen of breath shall be used . . .'

g

Subsection (7) makes it an offence to fail to provide a specimen without reasonable excuse. Section 12, the interpretation section, defines the prescribed limit of 35 microgrammes of alcohol in 100 ml of breath, and 80 milligrammes of alcohol in 100 ml of urine, a well-known figure.

By the Breath Analysis Devices (Approval) Order 1983 (dated 18 April 1983) the Secretary of State approved two devices for the purposes of s 8, one of which was the   *h* Intoximeter 3000 manufactured by the plaintiffs. Evidence of the proportion of alcohol in a specimen of breath may be given by producing a document containing a statement which is automatically produced by the approved device: see s 10(3) of the 1972 Act as substituted by the 1981 Act.

I refer to these statutory provisions because in my judgment they make it clear that the accuracy and reliability of an approved device are matters of the utmost public   *j* interest, since the liability of a person accused of a drink-driving offence to disqualification, fine and even imprisonment may depend thereon.

The plaintiffs, like any other company or individual, are entitled to protect material in which they have copyright and to prevent the use of confidential information by persons who have obtained it in the course of their employment for purposes of their own. It is in the public interest that confidential information should remain confidential.

So, in the present case, we have a conflict between two public interests, for there is no
a dispute that the plaintiffs' documents, taken by the first and second defendants and
handed to the fourth defendants, contain confidential information, and some of that
information, in particular contained in the memoranda of December 1982 from Dr King
and 20 December 1983 from Dr Parry Jones, raises doubts about the device that at least
call for an explanation.

How are these conflicting interests to be resolved? I think one must start from the
b standpoint of the plaintiffs. The defendants are threatening to use and publish confidential
material. The plaintiffs may have causes of action for breach of copyright and conversion,
and after publication for libel or slander of goods; but the heart of the matter is the
unauthorised use of the confidential information, and that can be protected by the
equitable remedy of injunction. If the information is confidential, which is conceded in
the present case, then prima facie the plaintiffs are entitled to relief, but it must be
c remembered that the relief is discretionary, so that it can be tailored to the facts of any
particular case.

In cases where the plaintiff is also claiming damages for libel, the court may be
influenced by the practice of refusing an injunction to restrain further publication where
justification is pleaded: see *Woodward v Hutchins* [1977] 2 All ER 751, [1977] 1 WLR 760.
There is, however, a clear distinction between the two types of action, as was pointed out
d by Sir David Cairns in *Khashoggi v Smith* [1980] CA Transcript 58, where the plaintiff was
seeking to restrain publication of lurid details of her personal life betrayed by a servant.
Sir David Cairns said:

> 'It seems to me that there is a fundamental distinction between the two types of
> action, in that in the one case the plaintiff is saying "Untrue and defamatory
> statements have been made about me", and in the other case the plaintiff is saying
e > "Statements which are about to be published are statements about events which
> have happened and have been disclosed as a result of a breach of confidence".'

Counsel for the third and fourth defendants has submitted that just as a plea of
justification operates to block restraint by injunction in defamation, so too a plea that it
is in the public interest to publish should block relief in breach of confidence. I cannot
f accept this proposition. The generic defence to breach of confidence, that it is in the
public interest to publish, must be supported by evidence to show why the plaintiff
should not be given interlocutory relief. Everything depends on the facts of the case;
thus the court will not restrain the exposure of fraud, criminal conduct, iniquity; but
these are only examples of situations where the conflict will be resolved against the
plaintiff. I do not think that confidence can be overridden without good reason to support
g the contention that it is in the public interest to publish. The plaintiff will not necessarily
be seeking to prevent publication of matters derogatory to himself, but nevertheless
there may be circumstances that make it just not to restrain publication.

In my judgment this is such a case, at least so far as some of the information is
concerned. I think that the judge misunderstood the evidence before him, in that he
seems to have thought that an explanation of the matters raised in the two memoranda
h of December 1982 and 20 December 1983 had been put forward, whereas I do not think
it possible to come to that conclusion from the evidence. I do not think that para 8 of the
affidavit of Dr Williams is sufficient to fill the total lack of explanation given by Dr Parry
Jones as to the Home Office disquiet, particularly as he asserts that he drafted the note as
a result of a telephone conversation with Dr Williams. There is also no evidence from Dr
King to deal with the memorandum of December 1982.

j In his judgment the judge dealt with this matter in this way. He said:

> 'Exhibit 7 is a memorandum by Dr Parry Jones to his fellow directors with regard
> to the Intoximeter's capacity for compensating for acetone in its breath alcohol
> readings. In his second affidavit, Dr Jones refers to the memorandum in paras 19 to
> 23 inclusive, and explains that the memorandum contains a wrong assumption that
> his company was failing to comply with standards which had been laid down by the

British Calibration Society. On that basis, he wrote a memorandum to galvanise the company's employees and management into action. Exhibit 8 is a memorandum from Dr Walter King, who was a senior research chemist with the plaintiffs until late 1983, to Dr Jones and other employees of the company, on the subject of certification of the calibration of the Intoximeter machine. In that document, Dr King expresses strong criticism of the practice of certifying the accuracy of machines which were to be sent out from the company's factory.'

As I have said, the judge does not seem to have appreciated that Dr Parry Jones is silent on the fourth paragraph of the memorandum and does not deal with that allegation, and nor in my judgment does Dr Williams give any sufficient explanation, for interlocutory purposes, to displace the plain meaning of that memorandum.

It is in these circumstances that it seems to me the judge has failed to direct himself on, or to assimilate correctly, the evidence which was before him. In addition, he has nowhere dealt with the matter raised in Stephenson LJ's judgment, namely that, by the time the matter was before him on 12–13 March and the morning of 14 March, there was already a great clamour which had been raised by the Daily Express in their issues of 9 and 10 March, and there was, in the public arena, criticism of the machine which called for a reappraisal by the Home Office and the police of its use for prosecuting persons suspected of drink-driving offences. Whether that clamour is well founded or not remains to be seen: it is a matter for trial. But that there is a clamour there can be no doubt, and, once the public interest has been properly aroused and brought out in public, then it seems to me that material such as that contained in the documents which it is proposed to release from the bounds of the injunction should be before the public and not restrained from use.

I agree entirely with Stephenson LJ that this is an interlocutory application. We are not deciding one way or the other whether the Intoximeter is a good machine or whether the complaints that are made against it are justified. It may well be that nobody has been wrongly convicted by it; it may well be that it has sufficient safeguards built into it which will prevent that. But there is a public disquiet. In my judgment there are good grounds for disquiet, and for those reasons I agree that the appeal should be allowed.

GRIFFITHS LJ. The plaintiffs have obtained an interlocutory injunction which restrains the Daily Express from publishing the contents of a number of their internal documents. These documents were taken from the plaintiffs by two of their ex-employees without authority and given to the Daily Express in breach of the duty of confidence that they owed to the plaintiffs as their employers. The Daily Express concede that if they publish the plaintiffs' documents they will prima facie do so in breach of confidence and in breach of copyright. But in the particular circumstances of this case they submit that it is in the public interest that these documents, or the information they contain, should be published in their newspaper and that the judge was wrong to prevent their doing so.

The first question to be determined is whether there exists a defence of public interest to actions for breach of confidentiality and copyright, and, if so, whether it is limited to situations in which there has been serious wrongdoing by the plaintiffs, the so-called 'iniquity' rule.

I am quite satisfied that the defence of public interest is now well established in actions for breach of confidence and, although there is less authority on the point, that it also extends to breach of copyright: see by way of example *Fraser v Evans* [1969] 1 All ER 8, [1969] 1 QB 349, *Hubbard v Vosper* [1972] 1 All ER 1023, [1972] 2 QB 84, *Woodward v Hutchins* [1977] 2 All ER 751, [1977] 1 WLR 760 and *British Steel Corp v Granada Television Ltd* [1981] 1 All ER 417, [1981] AC 1096.

I can see no sensible reason why this defence should be limited to cases in which there has been wrongdoing on the part of the plaintiffs. I believe that the so-called iniquity rule evolved because in most cases where the facts justified a publication in breach of confidence the plaintiff had behaved so disgracefully or criminally that it was judged in

the public interest that his behaviour should be exposed. No doubt it is in such
a circumstances that the defence will usually arise, but it is not difficult to think of
instances where, although there has been no wrongdoing on the part of the plaintiff, it
may be vital in the public interest to publish a part of his confidential information.
Stephenson LJ has given such an example in the course of his judgment.

I therefore agree with Leonard J that it is not an essential ingredient of this defence
that the plaintiffs should have been guilty of iniquitous conduct.

b   I do not accept the submission that there is so close an analogy between an action for
libel or slander and an action for breach of confidence that the courts should adopt a
similar approach to a defence of justification and a defence of public interest. If a
newspaper says that it intends to plead justification, the court will not, as a general rule,
restrain publication. The court makes no attempt to evaluate the defence at the
interlocutory stage: it leaves the plaintiff to his remedy in damages if the newspaper fails
c to justify the libel. Any other rule would involve an unacceptable gag on the press, and,
if the press cannot justify, the plaintiff's reputation can be restored by verdict or apology
and he can be properly compensated in damages.

But if the same approach was adopted in actions for breach of confidence it would, to
use counsel for the plaintiffs' colourful phrase, indeed be a mole's charter. There is a
public interest of a high order in preserving confidentiality within an organisation.
d Employees must be entitled to discuss problems freely, raise their doubts and express
their disagreements without the fear that they may be used to discredit the company and
perhaps imperil the existence of the company and the livelihood of all those who work
for it. And I am old-fashioned enough to think that loyalty is a virtue that it is in the
public interest to encourage rather than to destroy by tempting disloyal employees to sell
confidential documents to the press, which I am sure would be the result of allowing the
e press to publish confidential documents under cover of a shadowy defence of public
interest.

When there is an admitted breach of confidence and breach of copyright, there will
usually be a powerful case for maintaining the status quo by the grant of an interlocutory
injunction to restrain publication until trial of the action. It will, I judge, be an
exceptional case in which a defence of public interest which does not involve iniquity on
f the part of the plaintiff will justify refusing the injunction. But I am bound to say that I
think this is such a case.

I am very conscious of the fact that in recent years the Court of Appeal may at times
have been too ready to interfere with the discretion of a High Court judge. Lord Diplock
in *Hadmor Productions Ltd v Hamilton* [1982] 1 All ER 1042, [1983] 1 AC 191 has recently
reminded us of our function in an appeal against the exercise of discretion, and that we
g are not to interfere with the discretion of the judge merely because we would have
exercised the discretion differently. Bearing this warning in mind, I am nevertheless
satisfied that this is a case in which it has been demonstrated that the judge erred in his
approach to the exercise of his discretion, and that it is permissible for this court to
intervene, applying the principles of which we have been reminded in *Hadmor*'s case.

As I understand the judgment, the judge was not satisfied that there was a serious issue
h to be tried on the defence of public interest. I think this must be so, because he says near
the start of his judgment:

'The sole question is whether the defendants have shown that they have an
arguable defence to the plaintiffs' claims . . .'

He answers this by saying:

j   'I can find no exception to the general principle which protects confidential
documents in the facts of this case.'

Bearing in mind the subject of this litigation, I find this a very surprising conclusion.

We are here dealing with a machine on the accuracy of which may depend a person's
livelihood, or even his liberty. In certain circumstances, namely a reading of over 50, an
accused person is given no right to challenge the machine by a blood or urine test; even

when there is a right to a blood or urine test between readings of 35 and 50, surprisingly
there is no statutory obligation to tell the accused of his right. The introduction of such a   *a*
machine into the criminal process in our country is unique; it was introduced in May
1983 and has naturally been a subject of public interest and debate ever since.

The plaintiffs are the only manufacturers licensed by the Home Office to produce this
machine. They owe a grave obligation to the public to ensure that the machine is
produced and maintained to the highest standards. If they do not honour this obligation,
with the result that the machine may give inaccurate readings, or fail to register a sample   *b*
of breath, people may be wrongly convicted and be powerless to do anything about it. In
these circumstances, if material comes into the hands of the press which on a fair reading
suggests that the manufacturers are not honouring their obligation, or that the machine
is not reliable, it seems to me that it is beyond question that it is in the public interest
that this disturbing information should be made known to the public.

I stress the words 'on a fair reading' because it would be very much against the public   *c*
interest to undermine confidence in a machine which, if it is reliable, is a very valuable
tool in the fight against drunken driving. The whole history of the drink and driving
laws shows the lengths to which drivers will go to escape conviction on any technicality
or bogus argument. There will always be those ready to latch onto any accusation against
this machine, however unfounded it may be. 'A fair reading' of the material involves
looking closely at the explanation of the documents given by the plaintiffs, because it is   *d*
obvious that, in the course of developing and servicing a machine such as this, documents
may come into existence which express doubts about the machine which later prove to
be unjustified or based on a misapprehension of the principles on which the machine
works, or some other mistake. To publish such documents out of context would be a
most mischievous action and wholly contrary to the public interest.

I have therefore looked closely at the two principal documents with which we are   *e*
concerned, namely the memoranda of December 1982 and 1983, and the explanations
contained in the plaintiffs' affidavits. I do not want at this stage to say more than I must,
because we are only at the interlocutory stage and I may be doing the plaintiffs an
injustice. However, I have no doubt that both memoranda, on the face of them, disclose
a very disturbing situation which, if true, gives grave cause for concern about both the
standards of the manufacturers and the operation of the machine.   *f*

The December 1982 memorandum appears to show that the machines were being
certified as correctly calibrated when they had not passed the prescribed test. No evidence
has been offered from the author of that document, although he is still employed as a
consultant by the plaintiffs.

The memorandum of December 1983 is, on its face, even more worrying, and I cannot
regard the affidavits from its author as providing either a complete or a convincing   *g*
explanation for its contents. As matters stand at present, it appears to me that there is
here a serious issue to be tried and that the defendants have a strongly arguable defence
of public interest.

How then did the judge come to the opposite conclusion? I believe, with all respect to
him, that he must have misapprehended the thrust of the criticism that can legitimately
be founded on the memoranda. He said: '. . . I would doubt that technical matters of this   *h*
kind are best investigated in the columns of a daily newspaper . . .' and that appears to be
his main reason for concluding that the defendants had not shown that they had an
arguable defence to the plaintiffs' claim or, if they had, that the balance came down
heavily on the side of the plaintiffs. But there is nothing technical in either of the
memoranda; they are both easily understood by the layman. The Daily Express do not
want to carry on a technical debate through their columns; that is clear from the material   *j*
which they took out of the paper as a result of the injunction. The Daily Express say that
it is legitimate to use this material to put pressure on the authorities to reappraise every
aspect of this machine and its manufacture, and that it is in the public interest that this
should be done, because it may not be as safe to rely on it as the Home Office believes. I
agree that it would be inappropriate to conduct a scientific reappraisal through the
columns of a daily newspaper, and it is for that reason that I agree that the highly

a technical and very confidential documents referred to by Stephenson LJ should remain
protected. But I believe that a campaign to put pressure on the authorities is from time
to time an essential function of a free press, and we would all be the worse for it if the
press were unduly inhibited in this field of their activity. Nor do I think it any answer to
say in this case that the Daily Express should have gone to the Home Office in the first
instance, rather than publish.

The public stance of the Home Office is that there is no risk of a false conviction as a
b result of the use of the machine. The Home Office are an interested and committed
party. Of course I do not suggest that the Home Office would deliberately shut their eyes
to evidence that the machine, or the manufacturers, might not be as reliable as they
thought; but civil servants are human, and beauty lies in the eye of the beholder. I think
in all the circumstances that the Daily Express are not to be criticised for thinking that
the impact of the revelations in their newspaper would be more likely to galvanise the
c authorities into action than a discreet behind-doors approach.

Because I am forced to the conclusion that the judge misapprehended the evidence
contained in the vital documents, I agree that this court is free to, and should, consider
how the discretion to grant an interlocutory injunction should be exercised.

The defendants have, in my view, made out a powerful case for publication in the
public interest. In these circumstances I can see no alternative but to permit publication.
d It would surely be wrong to refuse leave to publish material that may lead to a reappraisal
of a machine that has the potential for causing a wrongful conviction of a serious criminal
offence.

When the press raise the defence of public interest, the court must appraise it critically,
but, if convinced that a strong case has been made out, the press should be free to publish,
leaving the plaintiff to his remedy in damages.

e I end with one word of caution. There is a world of difference between what is in the
public interest and what is of interest to the public. This judgment is not intended to be
a mole's charter.

For these reasons I agree with the order proposed by Stephenson LJ.

Appeal allowed in part.

f
Solicitors: *John Bell & Co*, Cardiff (for the first and second defendants); *Lovell White & King*
(for the third and fourth defendants): *Phillips & Buck*, Cardiff (for the plaintiffs).

Diana Brahams   Barrister.

g

Kaitamaki v The Queen

PRIVY COUNCIL
LORD SCARMAN, LORD ELWYN-JONES, LORD BRANDON OF OAKBROOK, LORD BRIGHTMAN AND
h SIR GEORGE BAKER
28 MARCH, I MAY 1984

Criminal law – Rape – Sexual intercourse without consent – Defendant realising woman not
consenting after he had penetrated her – Whether rape complete on penetration – Whether
defendant guilty of rape by continuing intercourse – Crimes Act 1961 (NZ), ss 127, 128(1).
j

The appellant was charged in New Zealand with one offence of rape. By s 128(1)[a] of the
New Zealand Crimes Act 1961 rape was defined as 'the act of a male person having sexual
intercourse with a woman or girl . . . without her consent' and by s 127[b] of that Act it

---

a   Section 128(1), so far as material, is set out at p 437 g, post
b   Section 127 is set out at p 437 f, post

was provided that 'sexual intercourse is complete upon penetration'. The Crown's case
was that the appellant had broken into a dwelling house and then twice raped a young *a*
woman who was the occupier. It was not disputed that intercourse took place twice but
the defence was that the woman had consented or that the appellant had honestly
believed that she was consenting. At the trial in the Supreme Court of New Zealand the
appellant gave evidence that after he had penetrated the woman for the second time he
became aware that she was not consenting but that he did not desist from intercourse.
The judge directed the jury that, if the appellant continued the act of intercourse having *b*
realised that the woman was not willing, it then became rape. The jury convicted the
appellant. The appellant appealed to the Court of Appeal of New Zealand, contending
that for the purposes of the 1961 Act a man who penetrated a woman with her consent
could not become guilty of rape by continuing the intercourse after a stage when he
realised that the woman was no longer consenting because rape was penetration without
consent and once penetration was complete the act of rape was concluded. The Court of *c*
Appeal rejected that submission and dismissed the appeal. The appellant appealed to the
Privy Council.

Held – The purpose of s 127 of the 1961 Act was to remove any doubts as to the
minimum conduct required to prove the fact of sexual intercourse, and the word
'complete' in that section was used in the sense of having come into existence but not in *d*
the sense of having come to an end. Sexual intercourse was a continuing act which only
ended with withdrawal, because the offence of rape was defined by s 128(1) of the 1961
Act as 'having' intercourse without consent. It followed that the appellant had been
rightly convicted and the appeal would accordingly be dismissed (see p 437 *h j* and p 438
a b, post). *e*

Notes
For the offence of rape, see 11 Halsbury's Laws (4th edn) paras 1226, 1228, and for cases
on the subject, see 15 Digest (Reissue) 1209, 1211–1212, 10373–10378, 10383–10394.

Sections 127 and 128 of the New Zealand Crimes Act 1961 correspond to s 44 of the
Sexual Offences Act 1956 and s 1 of the Sexual Offences (Amendment) Act 1976. For s 44 *f*
of the 1956 Act, see 8 Halsbury's Statutes (3rd edn) 440 and for s 1 of the 1976 Act, see
46 ibid 322.

Cases referred to in judgment
R v Mayberry [1973] Qd R 211.
R v Salmon [1969] SASR 76. *g*
Richardson v R [1978] Tas SR 178.

Appeals
Tamaitirua Kaitamaki appealed, by special leave to appeal in forma pauperis granted on *h*
22 December 1982, against two decisions of the Court of Appeal of New Zealand. The
first appeal was against a decision of the Court of Appeal (Richmond P and Richardson J,
Woodhouse J dissenting) ([1980] 1 NZLR 59) on 19 March 1980 dismissing the appellant's
appeal against his conviction on 15 March 1979 in the Supreme Court of New Zealand
before Speight J and a jury on a charge of rape; the second appeal was against the refusal
of the Court of Appeal (Richardson, McMullin and Barker JJ) ([1981] 1 NZLR 527) on 23 *j*
October 1981 to grant him legal aid to prosecute the first appeal in the Judicial Committee
of the Privy Council. The case is reported on the issue in the first appeal only. The facts
are set out in the judgment of the Board.

B V MacLean (of the New Zealand Bar) for the appellant.
Peter Thornton and *Robert Fardell* (of the New Zealand Bar) for the Crown.

1 May. The following judgment of the Board was delivered.

a

LORD SCARMAN. This appeal is in truth two appeals. The appellant appeals, by special leave, against two decisions of the Court of Appeal of New Zealand. In the first he appeals against the decision by a majority of the court (Richmond P and Richardson J, Woodhouse J dissenting)([1980] 1 NZLR 59) dismissing his appeal from a conviction of rape. In the second he appeals against a refusal of the Court of Appeal (Richardson,

b McMullin and Barker JJ) ([1981] 1 NZLR 527) to grant him legal aid to prosecute his appeal to the Judicial Committee of the Privy Council in the rape case.

The rape appeal

 In the early hours of 19 November 1978 the appellant broke and entered a dwelling house. The Crown's case was that he then twice raped a young woman who was an

c occupier of the premises. There was no dispute that intercourse had taken place on the two occasions. The defence was that the woman consented (or that the appellant honestly believed that she was consenting).

 But, when the appellant came to give evidence, his case as to the second occasion was that after he had penetrated the woman for the second time he became aware that she was not consenting; he admitted, however, that he did not desist from intercourse. In

d summing up this part of the case the trial judge said to the jury:

  'I tell you, as a matter of law ... that if, having realised she is not willing, he continues with the act of intercourse, it then becomes rape ...'

 It is said that this direction was wrong in law. The appellant's counsel submits that by the criminal law of New Zealand if a man penetrates a woman with her consent he

e cannot become guilty of rape by continuing the intercourse after a stage when he realises that she is no longer consenting.

 The submission raises a question as to the true construction of ss 127 and 128 of the Crimes Act 1961. Section 127 defines sexual intercourse and is in these terms:

  'For the purposes of this Part of this Act, sexual intercourse is complete upon penetration; and there shall be no presumption of law that any person is by reason

f of his age incapable of such intercourse.'

Section 128 defines rape and, so far as is material, is in these terms:

  '*Rape.*—(1) Rape is the act of a male person having sexual intercourse with a woman or girl—(*a*) Without her consent ...'

g Counsel for the appellant took one point only; but he submitted that it was all he needed. He relied on the definition in s 127 to establish the proposition that rape is penetration without consent; once penetration is complete the act of rape is concluded. Intercourse, if it continues, is not rape, because for the purposes of the Act it is complete on penetration.

 The Court of Appeal by a majority rejected the submission, expressing the opinion

h that the purpose of s 127 was to remove any doubts as to the minimum conduct needed to prove the fact of sexual intercourse. 'Complete' is used in the statutory definition in the sense of having come into existence, but not in the sense of being at an end. Sexual intercourse is a continuing act which only ends with withdrawal. And the offence of rape is defined in s 128 as that of 'having' intercourse without consent.

 Their Lordships agree with the majority decision of the Court of Appeal, and with the

j reasons which they gave for rejecting the appellant's submission and for construing the two sections in the way in which they did. As Lord Brightman observed in the course of argument before the Board, s 127 says 'complete', not 'completed'. The Board was referred not only to the two Australian cases discussed by the Court of Appeal (*R v Salmon* [1969] SASR 76 and *R v Mayberry* [1973] Qd R 211) but to a third one, *Richardson v R* [1978] Tas SR 178. None of these cases is directly in point because each is concerned with statutory provisions which differ from the two sections of the New Zealand statute with which this appeal is concerned. Their Lordships rest their view on the true construction, as they see it, of the two sections already quoted of the Crimes Act 1961.

Their Lordships were, however, disturbed by the course taken by the Crown at the trial. The indictment charged one offence of rape. The prosecution case was that there were two rapes. In the event, as could have been anticipated, there developed two different defences. To the first allegation the defence was consent; to the second the defence was that she consented to penetration but not to the subsequent intercourse, which, however, was not sexual intercourse for the purposes of the 1961 Act (see s 127). The Crown well knew that its case was that there were two rapes. In fairness to the accused each should have been separately charged. The Board is, however, satisfied that in the present case there has been no miscarriage of justice. Their Lordships, therefore, will humbly advise Her Majesty that this appeal should be dismissed.

The legal aid appeal

The Court of Appeal rejected the appellant's application for legal aid to prosecute an appeal to the Judicial Committee of the Privy Council on the ground that the court had no jurisdiction under the Offenders Legal Aid Act 1954 to grant it. The Board, finding itself in complete agreement with the judgment of the Court of Appeal delivered by Richardson J, will deal with this appeal very briefly.

The statute law of New Zealand confers no right of appeal from the Court of Appeal in criminal proceedings. But Her Majesty can, by the exercise of her prerogative, grant special leave to appeal. The jurisdiction to grant legal aid in criminal proceedings is conferred by s 2(1) of the 1954 Act, which is in these terms:

'Any Court having jurisdiction in criminal proceedings may, in respect of any stage of any criminal proceedings and in accordance with this Act, direct that legal aid be granted to any person charged with or convicted of any offence, if in its opinion it is desirable in the interests of justice to do so.'

Section 3(1) provides as follows:

'The Governor-General may from time to time, by Order in Council, make such regulations as may in his opinion be necessary or expedient for giving full effect to the provisions of this Act.'

The appellant submits that s 2(1) is to be construed as empowering the Court of Appeal to grant legal aid so as to enable a person to petition for special leave and to prosecute an appeal to the Judicial Committee. Their Lordships reject the submission on two grounds. The first is that, having disposed finally of the criminal proceeding before it by dismissing the appeal, the court no longer has any jurisdiction in the matter of that criminal proceeding. The second is that the scheme of the 1954 Act is that such regulations are to be made as may in the opinion of the Governor General be necessary and expedient for giving full effect to the Act. Detailed regulations were made first in 1956; the current regulations were made in 1972. They make no provision for legal aid to prosecute an appeal to the Judicial Committee. Since it is clear from ss 2(1) and 3(1) that regulations are necessary for giving effect to the 1954 Act, the absence of any provision in the regulations dealing with legal aid in the Privy Council is fatal to the appellant's submission: for the power to grant legal aid has to be exercised 'in accordance with this Act'.

Their Lordships will, therefore, humbly advise Her Majesty that this appeal should be dismissed.

Each appeal being conducted on behalf of the appellant 'as a poor person', there will be no order as to costs.

Appeals dismissed.

Solicitors: *Wray Smith & Co* (for the appellant); *Allen & Overy* (for the Crown).

Mary Rose Plummer   Barrister.

a

Hart v Aga Khan Foundation (UK)

COURT OF APPEAL, CIVIL DIVISION
CUMMING-BRUCE LJ AND BUSH J
15, 16, 19 MARCH 1984

b

Costs – Taxation – Litigant appearing in person – Claim for costs for expenditure of time in appearing in court – Claim for costs for expenditure of time in preparing case – Litigant suffering pecuniary loss – Litigant allowed two-thirds of amount allowed to a solicitor for similar work – High Court proceedings – Whether litigant allowed notional costs of instructing counsel – Whether litigant allowed notional counsel's fees – Whether litigant can claim costs based on amount allowed to a solicitor if part of preparatory done in leisure time – Whether in calculating notional amount allowable to a solicitor taxation should proceed on basis of time a solicitor would spend or time actually spent by litigant – RSC Ord 62, r 28A(1)(2)(3).

c

The following principles are applicable in taxing the costs of a litigant in person under RSC Ord 62, r 28A[a]—

(1) where the litigant has suffered pecuniary loss and the costs allowable for time spent in court are, by virtue of r 28A(1) and (2), to be taxed on the basis of two-thirds of the amount that would have been allowable if a solicitor had been employed, the notional

d

costs of a solicitor in instructing counsel to appear in the High Court, including counsel's fees, are not allowable on the taxation, because (a) r 28A(1) and (2) refers only to the litigant being notionally represented by 'a solicitor' and not by a solicitor and counsel, (b) counsel's fees are technically a disbursement made by a solicitor rather than 'work' done by him and (c) r 28A(2) makes it clear that the only disbursements that a litigant in person may claim on taxation are such disbursements as he has actually made and which,

e

if made by a solicitor, would be regarded as necessarily and properly made for the purpose of the litigation. In determining the notional costs of a solicitor the taxing officer should postulate in relation to preparation for trial a solicitor doing all the work necessary and proper for the purpose of preparing a full brief to counsel with a concise review of the relevant facts, an identification of the issues of law and fact, an identification, where

f

appropriate, of issues on which expert evidence would be relevant and, where an expert is not engaged, the work the solicitor would himself need to do to acquire the necessary knowledge (see p 442 *j* to p 443 *b* and *d* to *f*, p 444 *a* to *d* and p 448 *d* to *j*, post); dictum of Lord Langdale MR in *Re Remnant* (1849) 11 Beav at 613 applied;

(2) in calculating, for the purposes of r 28A(2), two-thirds of the amount that would have been allowable if the litigant had been represented by a solicitor, the taxation should

g

proceed on the basis of the time a solicitor would have spent doing the work rather than on the basis of the time actually spent by the litigant (see p 444 *f* to p 445 *d*, p 446 *e f* and p 448 *h j*, post);

(3) where the litigant does part of the preparatory work for his case in his working time (and thereby loses wages or salary) and part of the preparatory work in his leisure time, he is entitled to recover up to two-thirds of what would have been allowed to a

h

solicitor for the preparatory work done in his working time and is restricted, by virtue of r 28A(3), to recovering £2 an hour for the preparatory work done in his leisure time. It is wrong, however, to take a narrow view of what is working time where the occupation of the litigant in person is such that the business of the litigation may disqualify him from accepting work which would otherwise have been available (as in the case of an actor, who may have had to refuse an engagement because the effect of the dislocation caused

j

by the litigation may continue after the determination of the particular engagement) (see p 446 *j*, p 447 *a* to *c* and *h j* and p 448 *h j*, post).

On a review of taxation, where a judge is sitting with assessors, it is open to the court to vary the opinion of the taxing officer only if it is shown that he had regard to irrelevant considerations or failed to take into account relevant considerations or if the court is

---

a Rule 28A is set out at p 442 *f* to *h*, post

satisfied that his decision on the facts was clearly wrong (see p 445 *h* to p 446 *a* and p 448
h j, post); *Associated Provincial Picture Houses Ltd v Wednesbury Corp* [1947] 2 All ER 680   ***a***
applied.

    The Supreme Court Rule Committee might well consider whether the figure of £2 an
hour in r 28A(3) is still appropriate for the amount allowed to a litigant in person who
has not suffered any pecuniary loss in doing any work to which the costs relate (see p 447
g h and p 448 *h j*, post).

    Decision of Lloyd J [1984] 1 All ER 239 affirmed.   ***b***

Notes
For a litigant in person's costs, see 37 Halsbury's Laws (4th edn) para 750.

Cases referred to in judgments
Associated Provincial Picture Houses Ltd v Wednesbury Corp [1947] 2 All ER 680, [1948] 1   ***c***
    KB 223, CA.
Parikh v Midland Bank Ltd [1982] CA Bound Transcript 101.
Remnant, Re (1849) 11 Beav 603, 50 ER 949.

Interlocutory appeal
On 13 June 1981 the plaintiff, Diane Lavinia Macleod-Johnstone Hart, a litigant in
person, obtained judgment in her action against the defendants, the Aga Khan Foundation   ***d***
(UK), for £750 damages. The defendants were ordered to pay the plaintiff's costs of the
action taxed on the High Court scale. On 24 June 1982 Master Berkeley taxed the
plaintiff's bill of costs. On 2 July the plaintiff lodged two objections to the taxation. Her
first objection related to item 8 in the bill, namely costs of attending court, for which
pursuant to RSC Ord 62, r 28A(2) the master had allowed £83 per day as being two-thirds
of what he would have allowed a solicitor on the notional basis that the plaintiff was   ***e***
represented by a solicitor. The plaintiff's objection was that the master should also have
allowed under r 28A(2) two-thirds of a solicitor's notional cost of briefing leading and
junior counsel to appear in court. The second objection related to item 10 in the bill,
namely costs of preparation for the hearing, for which the master had allowed £1,025
pursuant to r 28A(2) and (3). The plaintiff's objection was that the master should have
allowed the plaintiff £4,474 for the costs of the preparatory work. On 15 December 1982   ***f***
Master Berkeley gave his reasons for overruling the plaintiff's objections. By a summons
dated 23 December 1982 the plaintiff sought an order that her objections be allowed. On
7 July 1983 Lloyd J sitting with Master Clews and Mr J M Bradshaw as assessors ([1984]
1 All ER 239) dismissed the summons. The plaintiff appealed to the Court of Appeal
with the leave of Lloyd J. The facts are set out in the judgment of Cumming-Bruce LJ.
                                                                                              g
The plaintiff appeared in person.
John Marrin for the defendants.

CUMMING-BRUCE LJ. The background of this appeal, in which the plaintiff appeals
the order made by Lloyd J sitting with assessors ([1984] 1 All ER 239) on review of the
taxation of her costs by the master, is as follows. The plaintiff is an actress of distinction   ***h***
who at all material times was actively pursuing her profession. She lives at 18 Thurloe
Close, London. Immediately opposite her house there is now a building on an island site
known as the Ismaili Centre. Contractors set about preparing the site for the building
which now stands thereon. The course of that work, which involved pile-driving and, on
the allegations of the plaintiff, who succeeded in the action, involved a great deal of noise
and vibration, subjected her for a substantial period of time to nuisance. Having suffered   ***j***
the nuisance for as long as she could bear it she commenced an action on 21 November
1980 against the defendants claiming damages for nuisance arising out of the building
activities on the site. She also claimed an injunction.

    The chronology is as follows. On 21 November she issued her writ; on 13 January
1981 she applied for an interlocutory injunction (with success); there was an appeal

a against the judge's order on 12 February; the action came on for trial before Boreham J, beginning on 8 June, which lasted several days; judgment was delivered on 15 June when the judge awarded £750 damages and continued the injunction; on 24 June 1982 there was a taxation by the taxing master of the plaintiff's bill of costs; on 2 November the master heard and determined the plaintiff's objections to the taxation and on 2 December gave his reasons. The plaintiff sought review. On 23 June 1983 Lloyd J sat with two assessors and reviewed the taxation, and upheld it. Judgment was given on 7

b July. The plaintiff appeals against the order of the judge upholding the taxation of the taxing master.

In the bill that the plaintiff submitted for taxation there are two items with which this court is now particularly concerned. The first was her claim for attendance at the hearing (item 8). She claimed for the first day of the hearing £1,520 based on two-thirds of the notional fee of leading counsel, junior counsel and solicitor attending the hearing and for

c subsequent days she claimed £520 on five different days, claims which were founded on the same notional approach to the taxation of her costs. The master taxed down those claims substantially, taking the view that he should tax on the basis only of two-thirds of the work that a solicitor would have had to do by way of attendance and rejecting her claim for two-thirds of the notional fees that a solicitor would have obtained on taxation with disbursements for counsel.

d The other item of the bill which has been the subject of controversy is item 10 under the heading 'Preparation for the hearing', and her claim under item 10 alone is claimed at £4,474, which was taxed down by the master to £1,025.

It is quite clear that the plaintiff, for the purposes of preparing herself for the hearing of the interlocutory injunction and for the trial before the judge, did a great deal of work, extremely conscientiously, faced with formidable practical difficulties. By way of

e example of her difficulties, the defendants submitted expert reports which on perusal disclosed an attempt by the experts to apply a scientific analysis to problems of vibration and noise, a branch of the applied sciences which is still in an inchoate state, and, in order to understand the technical issues which the defendants wanted to raise at the trial, the plaintiff at first sought to instruct experts herself but was unable to obtain experts who would assist her. She is bitter about the response which she received from experts. She

f believes that they refused to act because it would not be personally in their interests to give evidence against a major building contractor. If she is right about that, it does not reflect well on the experts concerned, who, if those facts are well founded, had not got a proper understanding of their professional duty. In the result the plaintiff, with great determination, applied herself to trying to discover herself by reference to papers issued by authoritative bodies the material which would enable her to analyse and to take issue

g with experts relied on by the defendants.

It may well be, though as we have not seen the judgment of Boreham J we do not know, that the plaintiff was too apprehensive about the probable impact on the judge of expert evidence, because an experienced professional lawyer would know by experience that in nuisance cases judges pay far more attention to evidence that they find to be reliable about the actual effect of the building works than on theoretical opinions from

h experts. However that may be, there is no doubt, in my view, that over a period of nine months the plaintiff worked extremely hard. It was obviously a matter of very great difficulty for her, as it would be for anybody else, to put an accurate arithmetical figure on the hours that she actually worked. She thought that she was being moderate in asking the taxing master to accept the figure of some 250 hours as a perfectly reasonable figure without any element of exaggeration or greediness.

j The taxing master appears to have formed the view that the time that she had necessarily and properly worked was something of the order of 86 hours, and when he came to consider the solution of the statutory problem with which he was faced he decided that a solicitor, in preparation for the trial, would probably have taken 40 hours of professional time. The plaintiff is deeply aggrieved both by the approach and by the result of the taxing master's decision.

One of the matters, as she candidly told us, which has led to her sense of genuine *a*
grievance is a consideration of the disparity between the figure allowed to her on taxation
and the figure which the taxing master would probably have allowed had the defendants
succeeded and asked the taxing master to tax their costs. They were represented by
leading counsel, junior counsel and solicitors. They would have incumbered the case
with a wealth of expertise which they thought might have affected the judge's mind and
there would have been disbursements for the expenses of those experts, and experience
shows that the fees charged by experts are very considerable. I learnt without surprise *b*
that the plaintiff has a deep sense of grievance having regard to that disparity. She knows
that if she had lost the case she would have been faced with the most enormous bill of
costs, for which indeed she had made financial provision by putting herself into a position
in which she would have been able to sell real property if she was faced with that
misfortune.

But, having said that, the time has come to remind myself that the problem is a *c*
statutory problem and that the question falls for resolution with reference to the
provisions of the Litigants in Person (Costs and Expenses) Act 1975 and the rules made
thereunder. The title of that Act is 'An Act to make further provision as to the costs or
expenses recoverable by litigants in person in civil proceedings'. Section 1(1) provides:

> 'Where, in any proceedings to which this subsection applies, any costs of a litigant
> in person are ordered to be paid by any other party to the proceedings or in any *d*
> other way, there may, subject to rules of court, be allowed on the taxation or other
> determination of those costs sums in respect of any work done, and any expenses
> and losses incurred, by the litigant in or in connection with the proceedings to
> which the order relates.'

So the Act does not prescribe the factors to be taken into account by the taxing master *e*
on the taxation of costs, but enacts that the taxation of the sums to which the party in
person is entitled under s 1(1) shall be subject to rules of court. The relevant rule is RSC
Ord 62, r 28A, which provides:

> '(1) On a taxation of the costs of a litigant in person there may, subject to the
> provisions of this rule, be allowed such costs as would have been allowed if the work
> and disbursements to which the costs relate had been done by or made by a solicitor *f*
> on the litigant's behalf.
> (2) The amount allowed in respect of any item shall be such sum as the taxing
> officer thinks fit not exceeding, except in the case of a disbursement, two-thirds of
> the sum which in the opinion of the taxing officer would have been allowed in
> respect of that item if the litigant had been represented by a solicitor.
> (3) Where in the opinion of the taxing officer the litigant has not suffered any *g*
> pecuniary loss in doing any work to which the costs relate, he shall not be allowed
> in respect of the time reasonably spent by him on the work more than £2 an hour.
> (4) A litigant who is allowed costs in respect of attending court to conduct his
> own case shall not be entitled to a witness allowance in addition.
> (5) Nothing in Order 6, rule 2(1)(b), or rule 32(4) of this Order or Appendix 3
> shall apply to the costs of a litigant in person. *h*
> (6) For the purposes of this rule a litigant in person does not include a litigant
> who is a practising solicitor.'

The question, therefore, which had to be determined by the taxing master was how to
apply to the facts the provisions of the rule.

The first point taken by the plaintiff on this appeal is that, having regard to the terms *j*
of the rule, the taxing master should have allowed a notional figure, being two-thirds of
what would have been taxed as disbursement to counsel under the item 'attendance at
the hearing'.

When para (1) is considered, it appears that the taxing master may allow such costs as
would have been allowed if the work and disbursements to which the costs relate had

been done by or made by a solicitor on the litigant's behalf. A solicitor has not got a right
a of audience in the High Court. The exercise is a notional exercise under para (1). The
taxing master has to say to himself, 'She did not instruct a solicitor but I have to apply a
statutory fiction for the purposes of taxation and decide what costs would have been
allowed and what disbursements would have been allowed if the work had been done by
a solicitor.'

The plaintiff's submission is that the whole of that exercise was a statutory, imaginary
b exercise and there is nothing any more imaginary about imagining disbursements to
counsel than about imagining the work which a solicitor would himself have done on
the litigant's behalf; and as the solicitor would not have had a right of audience in the
High Court the plaintiff submits that, in order to make sense of the notional exercise, the
conclusion to which the court should arrive as a matter of construction is that, for
purposes of attendance, the notional exercise should contemplate the solicitor himself
c charging a fee for the work that he has done and should also include the disbursements,
themselves also notional, which the imaginary solicitor would necessarily have had to
make when he instructed counsel to attend at the hearing, and, I would think, also such
disbursements by way of retainer of experts as the solicitor would reasonably have made.

Having regard to the artificial nature of the exercise which has been imposed on the
taxing master by para (1), it is easy to see the force of the submission that the plaintiff
d unsuccessfully made to the judge, and has made to us. But para (1), as a matter of
construction, falls to be read with para (2), and para (2), which I have already recited,
distinguishes between the amount to be allowed in respect of any item, being such sum
as the taxing master thinks fit, not exceeding two-thirds of the sum which in his opinion
would have been allowed in respect of the item if the litigant had been represented by a
solicitor, as distinguished from the case of disbursements; because on a proper
e construction of para (2) it is quite plain that, in the case of a disbursement, there is no
deduction to be made of one-third of the amount of the disbursement. Disbursements
are to be allowed at 100%. That, in my view (which is the same view as that taken by the
master and the judge), points perfectly plainly to the inference that the draftsman of para
(2) was contemplating that disbursements would be actual disbursements as compared to
notional disbursements. There is no other rational explanation for the distinction
f between the provision that the notional work of a solicitor should be taxed down to two-
thirds in comparison with the 100% allowance to be made for disbursements.

There is another consideration which is relevant. The noun used by the Rule
Committee in paras (1) and (2) was 'disbursements', which may be compared with the
phrase in s 1 of the 1975 Act, which provides for allowing on taxation 'sums in respect of
work done, and any expenses and losses incurred'. The word 'disbursement' in the
g context of taxation was recognised as long ago as 1849 as having a particular meaning
limiting the generality of the word. In Re Remnant (1849) 11 Beav 603 at 613, 50 ER 949
at 954 Lord Langdale MR expressed it as follows:

'From this certificate, and from the inquiries which I have made [which he had
made after seeking the collective opinion of taxing masters], it appears to me, that it
is the practice of solicitors, who may have to pay or advance money on behalf of
h their clients, carefully to distinguish such professional disbursements as ought to be
entered in their bills of costs, from such other advances or payments, as ought to be
entered only in their cash accounts, as cash payments or advances. And it seems to
me a very reasonable and proper rule, that those payments only, which are made in
pursuance of the professional duty undertaken by the solicitor, and which he is
bound to perform, or which are sanctioned as professional payments, by the general
j and established custom and practice of the profession, ought to be entered or allowed
as professional disbursements in the bill of costs.'

That description of the proper ambit of disbursements when used in the context of
taxation of a solicitor's costs has undoubtedly prevailed ever since and there is to my
mind no doubt at all that when the Rule Committee, for the purposes of drafting RSC

Ord 62, r 28A, prescribed 'On a taxation of the costs of a litigant in person there may . . . be allowed such costs as would have been allowed if the work and disbursements . . . had *a* been done by or made by a solicitor . . .', they were using the noun 'disbursements' in the sense in which ever since (and indeed before) 1849 it has been used in the context of taxation of costs. When para (2) of r 28A is read with para (1) it is to my mind sufficiently clear as a matter of construction that the only disbursements that a litigant in person can claim on taxation are such disbursements as he has actually made and which, if made by a solicitor, would be regarded as necessarily and properly made for the purposes of the *b* litigation. If, in fact, no disbursement has been made, then on a proper construction of r 28A it would not be right for the taxing master to allow for a notional disbursement, such as, for example, a notional disbursement to counsel or a notional disbursement for any other purpose. There is no other meaning which can give a rational explanation of the distinction between the amounts to be allowed in respect of disbursements in para (2) and the amounts to be allowed in the case of work done by a notional solicitor.   *c*

For those reasons I have no doubt that those grounds of appeal by which the plaintiff challenges the determination of the master and of the judge in respect of the disallowance of notional disbursements must fail, and I say no more about it.

The second item which arises on the grounds of appeal arises in respect of the amount that the taxing master allowed for work done. The way in which it was put in the sixth ground of appeal is as follows: *d*

> 'That the learned judge was wrong in his under-estimation of the hours of preparation. In the approximate 7 month duration of this action, there was a possibility of 28 weeks at 6 hours a day; a possible 840 hours. Acquiring the expert knowledge in order to counter the Defendants expert witnesses and win the case, cannot even be estimated now. The learned judge misunderstood the Plaintiff in respect of the hours worked and referred to her mistake when she had tried to *e* submit earlier that if the notional counsel was not allowed, the hours for the solicitor would be greatly increased.'

In order to consider that ground of appeal it is necessary to consider carefully the provisions of r 28A(2): 'The amount allowed in respect of any item shall be such sum as the taxing officer thinks fit . . .'; so far so good. But the next words are of great *f* importance: '. . . not exceeding . . . two-thirds of the sum which in the opinion of the taxing officer would have been allowed in respect of that item if the litigant had been represented by a solicitor.' The exercise which is therein imposed on the taxing master is to apply his mind to all the problems which the preparation for the action, including in this case the preparation for the interlocutory injunction, would have imposed on a conscientious solicitor who is notionally regarded as doing the work. The work actually *g* done by the litigant in person, to a greater or lesser degree, may afford some guidance as to the work which a solicitor would have done. That would depend on the degree to which the litigant in person correctly appreciated the business involved. In many cases it is likely that the work actually done by a litigant in person will be of negligible assistance to the taxing master when considering what work a solicitor would have done on the case, but it is of course necessary for the taxing master to go carefully through the *h* business involved in preparation for every stage of the trial; thus, in the case of discovery of documents (and in this case there was heavy discovery of documents), the master would ask himself how much work a solicitor would have had to do in order to prepare the list of documents, to inspect the documents of the other side and to take any decisions that might be necessary as to the need for further discovery; and, in relation to preparation for trial after discovery is concluded, the amount of work a nuisance case would involve, *j* appreciation of all the relevant facts, noise, vibration and so on, and then consideration of the degree to which applied science was likely to be of any real assistance to the judge in deciding whether the work was such as to constitute a nuisance. Where, as in this case, the defendants submitted expert reports, the solicitor would have to peruse those reports to decide how far they were relevant, and to understand the reports, either by instructing *a* experts on his own side (which the plaintiff in person unsuccessfully tried to do in this case) or, failing that, qualifying himself by reading published reports of what, if anything, the relevant applied sciences were likely to produce on their application to the facts of the particular nuisance case before him.

Those are all matters which the taxing master has to consider when considering the material before him on taxation. He then has to form his independent judgment, based on his experience as to the time that a solicitor would reasonably, necessarily and properly

b have taken to do that work. Having done that, the taxing master has to decide the fees that a solicitor would be allowed on a party and party taxation and then to allow to the litigant in person two-thirds of that sum. As the exercise which the rule requires imposes on the taxing master the duty to allow two-thirds of the sum which would have been allowed in respect of each item if the litigant had been represented by a solicitor, it is likely that the work actually done by a litigant in person will have very little relation to

c the work that a solicitor would have to do, but that will depend entirely on the nature of the litigation and the practical problems of preparation that the litigation throws up. The rule evidently contemplates that the taxing master, from his experience, would be able to analyse the material put before him and arrive at a reasonable (though inevitably not precise) figure that he would have taxed if a solicitor had done the work.

In the instant case the taxing master, having considered the material, decided, for item

d 10 of the bill, to proceed on the basis that a solicitor would have taken 40 hours to do all the necessary and proper work on preparation of the case. That is a question of quantum, which is particularly within the expertise of taxing masters.

On review, the judge sat with two assessors, one of whom, we are told, was a taxing master. They examined the taxing master's decision as to the notional 40 hours. They heard the submissions of the plaintiff and by the decision which is expressed in the

e judgment of Lloyd J they evidently accepted the 40 hours which the taxing master had allowed. That is to be collected from one sentence in the judgment. But the conciseness of the conclusion whereby the 40 hours was accepted by the judge, which must in the context mean the judge sitting with his assessors, who were there particularly for the purpose of assisting the judge on questions of quantum, must mean that the judge with his assessors, having applied their minds to the criticisms made to them by the plaintiff

f in person, decided that 40 hours was a figure which the taxing master could arrive at in the course of the exercise imposed on him by r 28A(1) of forming his opinion about the amounts that would have been allowed to a solicitor. The relevant sentence of the judgment is ([1984] 1 All ER 239 at 243):

'The master allowed £1,025. He took the view that a solicitor would have taken no more than 40 hours for the work in question, giving a total under item 10,

g including mark-up, of £1,600 at the most. Two-thirds of that figure (which I accept) is the maximum which he could have allowed.'

In my view there is no material before this court which could entitle this court to interfere with the decision of the judge sitting with assessors on the quantum of the notional time that a solicitor would have taken in respect of the item for preparation for

h trial. As a matter of construction r 28A(2) proceeds on the basis that it is for the taxing master to form an opinion on what would have been allowed. On a review, where a judge is sitting with assessors, it is in my view clearly open to the court sitting with such assessors, on review of the opinion of the taxing master, to vary the opinion of the taxing master either as to the number of hours that a notional solicitor would have taken or as to the fee that a notional solicitor would have obtained on taxation. But it is clear from

j the terms of the judgment that there was in the opinion of the court, sitting with assessors, no sufficient ground shown for substituting a different opinion for the opinion of the taxing master. The approach, in my view, is the approach which is relevant whenever legislation confides to a court the determination of fact or opinion to a specified person or body. It is open to a court on review to reject the opinion of the taxing master only if it is shown on *Wednesbury* principles (see *Associated Provincial Picture Houses Ltd v*

Wednesbury Corp [1947] 2 All ER 680, [1968] 1 KB 223) that the taxing master had regard   *a*
to irrelevant considerations, or failed to take into account relevant considerations, or if
the court is satisfied that the opinion of the taxing master on the facts was clearly wrong.

I am not satisfied that it has been shown to this court that Lloyd J, sitting with assessors,
had material before him which should have led him to the view that the opinion of the
taxing master was clearly wrong. For that reason, in relation to the figure of 40 hours
(which, in the opinion of the taxing officer, he would have allowed if the litigant had
been represented by a solicitor) no ground has been shown in this court for interfering   *b*
with the opinion of the taxing master.

The next rule that falls for consideration is r 28A(3):

> 'Where in the opinion of the taxing officer the litigant has not suffered any
> pecuniary loss in doing any work to which the costs relate, he shall not be allowed
> in respect of the time reasonably spent by him on the work more than £2 an hour.'   *c*

The submission made to this court by the plaintiff is that, in the split of work between
work done in working time and work done outside working time, the taxing officer was
wrong and the court was wrong to uphold the taxing officer in the split of time which
the taxing officer made between the time which he attributed to her as the time that she
necessarily and properly spent on the work.   *d*

Before coming to an analysis of that submission made by the plaintiff, it is in my view
sensible to look back to r 28A(2). It is clear that that paragraph imposes an upper limit on
the amount in respect of work done that the taxing master may allow. The matter was
considered in this court in *Parikh v Midland Bank Ltd* [1982] CA Bound Transcript 101.
This court then decided that, having regard to the provisions of para (2), it provided an
upper limit beyond which the taxing master might not go, so that, however many hours   *e*
were reasonably spent by a litigant in person for the purposes of the exercise set out in
para (3), the upper limit that a litigant may recover cannot exceed two-thirds of the sum
which, in the taxing master's opinion, would have been allowed in respect of an item if
the litigant had been represented by a solicitor.

On the figures in the instant appeal the result is rather dramatic because the maximum
that the taxing master could have allowed on the basis of a solicitor undertaking the   *f*
work in 40 hours would be the sum of about £1,033. I say 'about' because the variable is
the difference between a mark up of 50% and a mark up of 60%, and the figure which I
have just stated splits the difference between the two. That being the upper limit, as the
order of the taxing master was £1,025, there can be no question of this court on a review
varying the taxing master's order on the basis that it should have been £8 more than it
actually was. The exercise is a notional exercise (there is not room for much precision)   *g*
and this court would be quite wrong if it contemplated tinkering with the taxing
master's order of £1,025 because it was £8 on the wrong side. The plaintiff, who has a
very clear and informed judgment in this matter, accepts that she would have never
dreamed of appealing to the judge, or to this court, if she had appreciated that the most
that she could have got, if she did make out her case other than on 40 hours, was a few
pounds more than the master in fact ordered. The gravamen of her case on item 10 is   *h*
that it is the 40 hours which is completely wrong.

I have expressed my reasons for rejecting that submission and therefore, when one
comes to the exercise of the split between working time and time spent on the case
outside working time, it turns out that that exercise is irrelevant on the facts before this
court because, if the whole of the amount had been allowed in working time, she could
not have been allowed more than about £1,033. I have no doubt that the rule   *j*
contemplates that the maximum amount under r 28A(2) is the upper limit, and, if a
litigant in person works reasonably for, say, 1,000 hours at £2 an hour outside working
time, under this rule the unfortunate litigant is not allowed to recover more than the
maximum under para (2).

For that reason it is of no practical assistance for the purpose of determining this appeal

to go into the whys and wherefores of the master's split when he split his figure of 86
a   hours as to 50% into hours done in working time and 50% done otherwise.

For myself I would hold that there is a great deal of force in the submission of the
plaintiff that, given the nature of her work, it is quite wrong to take a narrow view about
the period for which she was working in what would have been working time if she had
got the contract referred to in the bundle. I would have thought that it might have been
perfectly reasonable to say that the whole of the work that she did, on a sensible basis
b   having regard to an actress's professional commitments, should have been regarded as
having been done in working time, because I recognise the force of her case that, if she is
disqualified by the business of the litigation from accepting work in a play which is
going to take something like 15 weeks, the effect of that dislocation is likely to continue
after the determination of that particular contract. However, having said that, and
recognising that I have formed that view although the taxing master took a different
c   view, it can have no practical result by reason of the impact of the upper limit prescribed
by r 28A(2).

In my view this is a case in which the plaintiff, honest and conscientious, is a victim of
the terms of the rule. It has to be recognised that the Rule Committee had to devise a
rule that would apply to vast numbers of taxations of costs of litigants in person.
Sometimes, as the judge said, the effect of the rule may be to give a litigant in person
d   rather more than an actual loss; in other cases (of which I regard this as one) the rule only
enables the litigant in person to recover on taxation a sum substantially less than the sum
that she actually lost. That follows from the words of the 1975 Act, and it may well be
that in this unsatisfactory world it is impracticable for the Rule Committee to devise
anything which is likely to work more fairly than the present rule, which is liable to
work, in theory, upwards or downwards in any given case.

e   The plaintiff invites this court, irrespective of the outcome of the appeal, to make an
observation, if it thinks it right, for the consideration of the Rule Committee on the
figure of £2 an hour, which is the figure which is allowed for time when the litigant has
not suffered any pecuniary loss. That figure was prescribed in 1976 and has remained
unchanged ever since. It is, of course, a wholly artificial figure: it does not purport to be
linked to any particular calculus; it is not expressed as being related to the average
f   remuneration of any class of work person; it is plucked out of the air. The plaintiff has
submitted that it is a ludicrous figure today and that it is wrong that work that she has
reasonably done out of working time should qualify her for a payment of about £1 less
than she would pay a cleaner doing the simple menial work which she may employ a
cleaning lady to do.

One has to bear in mind that, when the Rule Committee determined to allow £2 an
g   hour, they appreciated that that was a figure that would not be revised year by year by
reference to changes in the average working remuneration of any class of citizens; they
expected their rule to last for some time. I would go so far as to say that it would be
useful for the Rule Committee to look at the figure in r 28A in the year 1984 and decide
whether, in their view, it is still the appropriate figure. It is for them then to decide
whether to seek a statutory rule varying the amount of £2 an hour.

h   As I thought it unnecessary to deal with the detail canvassed under r 28A(3), I would
only say that, as a matter of construction, I have no doubt that the view taken by the
judge as to the meaning of any pecuniary loss in doing any work was clearly right. It
cannot have been the intention of the draftsman or the Rule Committee that, if any
pecuniary loss was sustained, thereafter the approach of the taxing master to the work
done should continue to be on the basis of that pecuniary loss as compared to the taxing
i   master looking at the period when the work was done in the course of what would
otherwise have been remunerative work which the litigant would have been undertaking.

I have one other observation. The plaintiff rightly has drawn attention to the difficulty
of the notional exercise which the taxing master had to undertake, and the judge has
observed that, at any rate in relation to disbursements, taxing masters and judges have
differed in their approach. As far as disbursement goes there will be no difficulty now

because the matter has been determined as a matter of construction, but, in relation to the work done by the notional solicitor, that does not present an easy problem to a taxing   *a* master, however experienced he is, for this reason: for work in the High Court, a solicitor has not got a right of audience; had a solicitor been instructed he would have briefed counsel and would also have made disbursements on experts in order to qualify counsel to deal with any expert problem that arose in the case. What work does the rule contemplate as the work which the notional solicitor has undertaken and done? Had the solicitor been retained for county court proceedings in which he had a right of audience   *b* which he was going on instructions to exercise, then the solicitor would have had to do all the work himself which was necessary to qualify himself to argue the case, to make his submissions on the law, to make his submissions on the facts and to qualify himself where the opposite party is calling experts or relying on expert reports, to analyse those reports and to cross-examine the experts in order to demonstrate to the court the frailty of their reasoning and of the fallibility of the belief that their science could usefully aid   *c* the judge in the practical problem that he had to decide. However, as these were High Court proceedings and not county court proceedings, there is no set of rules which, by rule of thumb, enables the taxing master to decide exactly what a solicitor would have been allowed on taxation. He has to form his own view about it.

I certainly do not have any intention of tying taxing masters to an obligation to condescend in their reasoning or in published reasons to a degree of detail which is otiose   *d* or unnecessary. To do so will only add greatly to the expense of taxations and the time taken on them. But I would venture to suggest, recognising that I speak without any experience of taxation, that, having regard to the terms of r 28A(2), the exercise, necessarily imaginary, which the taxing master has to undertake is to postulate in relation to preparation for trial a solicitor doing all the work necessary and proper for the purpose of preparing a full brief to counsel with a concise review of the relevant facts, an   *e* identification of the issues of law and fact, an identification of issues on which expert evidence would be relevant and, where, as in this case, the litigant has not obtained any expert opinion so that she had to do all the work, learning the quasi science, herself, the solicitor would have had to do the same thing and would have had to qualify himself by obtaining published information of the kind that the litigant in person in this case succeeded in obtaining. I would think that, in order to undertake successfully the   *f* difficult exercise imposed on the taxing master under para (2), that is the kind of approach which would be sensible and reasonable in a case similar to the present, because how the taxing master sets about identifying the notional solicitor's work will vary in the case of the business concerned. I am speaking, having in my mind the kind of problems that were likely to arise in a case of nuisance such as the present, in which the defendants had sent expert reports for agreement and consideration. It would, I think,   *g* when the taxing master is asked to give reasons for his decision, be helpful for him to give such detail as is reasonable, indicating the heads of work which a solicitor would have had to undertake and the time which, in his opinion, a solicitor would have taken under each head of work. I make these observations with some diffidence, recognising that I am wholly ignorant of the expertise which is enjoyed by taxing masters.

For the reasons I have stated, I would dismiss the appeal.   *h*

BUSH J. I agree with what Cumming-Bruce LJ has said. For the reasons expressed by him, I, too, would dismiss the appeal.

Appeal dismissed. Leave to appeal to the House of Lords refused.

j

Solicitors: *Masons* (for the defendants).

Carolyn Toulmin   Barrister.

a

R v D

HOUSE OF LORDS
LORD HAILSHAM OF ST MARYLEBONE LC, LORD FRASER OF TULLYBELTON, LORD SCARMAN, LORD
BRIDGE OF HARWICH AND LORD BRANDON OF OAKBROOK
8, 9 MAY, 21 JUNE 1984

b

Criminal law – Kidnapping – Parent – Parent taking away unmarried child under 18 years –
Whether parent committing crime of kidnapping.

Criminal law – Kidnapping – Consent to being taken away – Child – Absence of consent to be
inferred in case of very young child – Absence of consent a question of fact for jury in case of older
c   child – Relevance of consent to defence of lawful excuse.

Child – Removal from jurisdiction – Removal in defiance of court order – Removal of child
normally to be dealt with as contempt of court rather than as subject of criminal prosecution –
Criminal prosecution only appropriate for exceptional cases – Private prosecution of parent for
kidnapping own child extremely undesirable.

d

The common law offence of kidnapping exists in the case of a child victim under the age
of 14 years and may be committed by a parent who takes and carries away by force or
fraud his own unmarried child under the age of majority, ie the age of 18 years, without
the consent of the child and without lawful excuse. In all cases it is the absence of the
child's consent which is material. In the case of a very young child the absence of consent
would be a necessary inference from its age, but in the case of an older child it is a
e   question of fact for the jury whether the child concerned has sufficient understanding
and intelligence to give its consent, and, if the jury considers that it has these qualities, it
must then consider whether it has been proved that the child did give its consent.
Although the absence of the consent of the person having custody or care and control is
not material to whether the child consented to being taken away, the giving of consent
by such a person may be relevant in supporting a defence of lawful excuse (see p 450 c to
f   e g, p 455 f h j and p 457 c d g to j, post); The People (A-G) v Edge [1943] IR 115 explained.
It is desirable, as a matter of policy, that the conduct of parents who snatch their own
children in defiance of a court order relating to their custody, care and control should be
dealt with as a contempt of court rather than as a subject of a criminal prosecution. The
latter method of dealing with the problem should only be used in exceptional cases,
where the conduct of the parent concerned is so bad that an ordinary right-thinking
g   person would immediately and without hesitation regard it as criminal in nature. It is
extremely undesirable that there should, in any circumstances, be any private prosecutions
for the kidnapping by a parent of his own child (see p 450 c to g, p 457 j to p 458 b, post).
Decision of the Court of Appeal [1984] 1 All ER 574 reversed.

h   **Notes**
For the offence of kidnapping, see 11 Halsbury's Laws (4th edn) para 1212, and for cases
on the subject, see 15 Digest (Reissue) 1109, 1240, 9312, 10583.

Cases referred to in opinions
Agar-Ellis, Re, Agar-Ellis v Lascelles (1883) 24 Ch D 317, CA.
i   People, The (A-G) v Edge [1943] IR 115, Eire SC.

Appeal
The Crown appealed with leave of the Appeal Committee of the House of Lords granted
on 26 January 1984 against the decision of the Court of Appeal, Criminal Division
(Watkins LJ, Mustill and Skinner JJ) ([1984] 1 All ER 574, [1984] 2 WLR 112) on 31

October 1983 allowing an appeal by the respondent, D, against his conviction in the
Central Criminal Court on 18 May 1982 before his Honour Judge Lymbery QC and a
jury of kidnapping his daughter, E, then aged five years. The Court of Appeal had
refused leave to appeal to the House of Lords but certified, on the application of the
prosecutor, that two points of law of general public importance (set out at p 451 c, post)
were involved in its decision. The facts are set out in the opinion of Lord Brandon.

Richard Du Cann QC, Ann Curnow and *Nicholas Purnell* for the Crown.
Neil Taylor QC and *Peter Ralls* for the respondent.

Their Lordships took time for consideration.

21 June. The following opinions were delivered.

LORD HAILSHAM OF ST MARYLEBONE LC. My Lords, having read in advance
the draft speech about to be delivered by my noble and learned friend Lord Brandon, I
need only say that I agree with him both on the questions directly raised on the appeal,
and on the two separate questions with which the speech concludes, namely his
observations on the Irish case of *The People (A-G) v Edge* [1943] IR 115, and his views as to
the undesirability of private prosecutions for this offence, and the complete propriety of
initiating criminal proceedings in the instant case.

LORD FRASER OF TULLYBELTON. I have had the advantage of reading in draft
the speech of my noble and learned friend Lord Brandon. I agree with it, and for the
reasons stated in it I would answer the certified questions in the affirmative and allow the
appeal.

LORD SCARMAN. My Lords, I have had the advantage of reading in draft the speech
to be delivered by my noble and learned friend Lord Brandon. I agree with it, and for
the reasons he gives I would allow the appeal.

My noble and learned friend expresses the view that private prosecution for the
kidnapping by a parent of his own child is extremely undesirable. I wholly agree. I
would suggest that the opportunity provided by the Child Abduction Bill being now
before Parliament might be used to introduce a provision into the law that the prosecution
of a parent requires the consent of the Director of Public Prosecutions.

LORD BRIDGE OF HARWICH. My Lords, for the reasons given in the speech of
my noble and learned friend Lord Brandon I would allow this appeal. Subject to one
reservation, I fully agree with that speech.

My reservation relates to the issue raised by the second certified question. My noble
and learned friend, with the concurrence of the rest of your Lordships, proposes to
answer that question with an unqualified affirmative. For my part, I should have
preferred to answer the question: 'Yes, when the parent acts in contravention of the order
of a court of competent jurisdiction restricting his or her parental rights.' It is unnecessary
to go further for the purpose of deciding the present appeal, since the respondent clearly
did so act.

I should make it clear that my proposed answer to the second question is by no means
intended to imply a concluded opinion that there are no other circumstances in which a
parent may be convicted of kidnapping his or her own child. Whether there may be
such other circumstances and, if so, whether they are capable of limitation or definition
are difficult questions, which were scarcely argued before your Lordships. In my
respectful opinion, it would be prudent to indicate expressly that the present decision of
your Lordships' House does not purport, even by way of obiter dictum, to pre-empt the
answer to either of those questions. They should be left for decision if and when they
arise.

LORD BRANDON OF OAKBROOK. My Lords, kidnapping is now, and has been
a since the seventeenth century and earlier, a criminal offence under English law. In this
appeal your Lordships are called on, for the first time, to examine the nature, ingredients
and scope of this offence as it exists in the conditions of today, and to give an authoritative
ruling on them. In particular, your Lordships are called on to decide whether the offence
can be committed by a father against his own child so long as that child is an unmarried
minor.

b   On 18 May 1982 at the Central Criminal Court the respondent was convicted before
his Honour Judge Lymbery QC and a jury of a number of offences, including that of
kidnapping his daughter, E, then five years of age. By an order dated 6 December 1983
the Court of Appeal, Criminal Division, consisting of Watkins LJ, Mustill and Skinner JJ
quashed that conviction, certified that two points of law of general importance were
involved in the decision, but refused the Crown leave to appeal to your Lordships' House.
c The two points of law so certified were as follows:

> '(a) Whether the common law offence of kidnapping exists in the case of a child
> victim under the age of fourteen years; (b) Whether in any circumstances a parent
> may be convicted of such an offence where the child victim is unmarried and under
> the age of majority.'

d   The Court of Appeal, in a judgment delivered by Watkins LJ, with which the other
two members of the court agreed, held that the answers to both these points should be in
the negative, and it was on that basis that the court quashed the respondent's conviction
(see [1984] 1 All ER 574, [1984] 2 WLR 112). Leave for the Crown to appeal to your
Lordships' House was later granted by the Appeal Committee.

        My Lords, the history of the events which led up to the prosecution of the respondent
e has been set out fully and clearly by Watkins LJ in his judgment, to which reference may
be made if necessary. For the purposes of the present appeal, however, I propose to give
only such an account of the material facts as appears to me to be necessary in order to
enable the two certified points of law to be examined and answered.

        The material facts concern in the main three persons: the respondent; his wife,
Audrey; and their daughter, E. I shall refer to these three persons as 'the father', 'the
f mother' and 'the child', respectively.

        The father, who is a New Zealander, and the mother, who is an Englishwoman, were
married in England on 28 July 1973. The mother then already had two children, a girl,
S, born in 1965 of a previous marriage which had ended in divorce, and a boy, J, born in
1969 of a long-standing association with another man. I shall refer to S and J as 'the other
children', and to S, J and E collectively as 'the children'.

g   In January 1974 the father and the mother, with the other children, went from
England to New Zealand. Their intention was to set up at least a temporary, and perhaps,
if they agreed about it, a permanent, home in that country. On 6 February 1976 a girl,
E, was born to them there.

        In April 1977 the other children returned from New Zealand to England, and went to
live for the time being with the mother's parents there. In September 1977 the father
h and the mother, with the child, also returned from New Zealand to England. The
marriage had by then run into serious difficulties, which led the mother, in order to
prevent the father from taking the child away with him to New Zealand without her
consent, to apply to the Family Division of the High Court for an order making the child
a ward of court. As a result the child became a ward as from 10 April 1978. The mother
and the father separated, the mother going to a new address which she thought was
j unknown to the father. Meanwhile, the order making the child a ward of court was
served on the father, who consulted a solicitor about it. He subsequently went back to
New Zealand for the time being.

        On 21 July 1978 there was an interlocutory hearing in the wardship proceedings
before a registrar of the Family Division, at which both the mother and the father were
legally represented. At the conclusion of that hearing an order was made by consent that

the child should continue to be a ward of court, that she should remain in the care and control of the mother until further order, and that there should be a report by a court welfare officer with regard to the father's wish to have access to her.

By December 1978 the mother had been living for some time with the children at a flat in Romford, Essex. On 13 December 1978 the father, who had earlier returned from New Zealand to England again, forced his way uninvited into the mother's flat. He had with him as accomplices two thugs, named Hunter and Aherne respectively, both of whom had knives or other sharp instruments, and one of whom wore a stocking mask. The mother was terrified and the father proceeded to remove the child by force and take her away with him. Hunter stayed behind in order, by the threat of using what the father had described to the mother as a gas bomb, to prevent the mother from informing the police or anyone else of what had happened until sufficient time had elapsed for the father to make good his escape from this country. This he did, travelling soon after with the child to New Zealand.

Subsequently, the mother followed the father to New Zealand and recovered the child, pursuant to a court order obtained by her there. On 6 February 1979 she arrived back in England with the child, and installed herself with the children at an address in Peterborough of which she did not inform the father.

In October 1981 the father came back from New Zealand to England once again. He found out the house in which the mother and the children were living, and began to keep a close watch on it. At 8 am on 6 November 1981 the father entered the house by fraud and demanded that the mother should hand over the child to him, which she refused to do. She fled into the street, carrying the child, who was wearing her pyjamas only. The father pursued the mother there, and, after a struggle, he took the child from the mother by force, and carried the child to a waiting car, in which he once again made good his escape with her. He then travelled with the child to the Republic of Ireland.

The mother followed the father to Ireland and recovered the child from him. The father himself was then arrested on a warrant, which had earlier been issued by the Havering Magistrates' Court, and brought back in custody to this country. There he was charged with a series of criminal offences relating, firstly, to his conduct in December 1978, and, secondly, to his conduct in November 1981.

My Lords, on 10 May 1982 the father appeared before Judge Lymbery and a jury at the Central Criminal Court to stand trial on an indictment containing nine counts. Of these nine counts only two are material to this appeal, namely counts 1 and 6, which were in these terms:

'FIRST COUNT

STATEMENT OF OFFENCE

KIDNAPPING

PARTICULARS OF OFFENCE

[D] on the 13th day of December 1978 stole and unlawfully carried away [E], a child aged two years, against her will.'

'SIXTH COUNT

STATEMENT OF OFFENCE

KIDNAPPING

PARTICULARS OF OFFENCE

[D] on the 6th day of November 1981 stole and unlawfully carried away [E], a child aged five years, against her will.'

At the trial a submission was made to the judge by Mr Taylor, as counsel for the father, that counts 1 and 6 above were bad and should be quashed. The ground, and the only ground, of that submission was that it was not possible at common law for a father to kidnap his own unmarried child, so long as that child was still a minor, and, accordingly, neither count 1 nor count 6 disclosed any criminal offence in respect of which the father could be tried or convicted.

a   Judge Lymbery, after hearing full argument from Mr Taylor on behalf of the father, and such argument as he considered necessary from Miss Curnow, counsel for the Crown, rejected the submission made by the former. He ruled that, by the common law of England, a father could commit the offence of kidnapping his own child, even though that child was still a minor. He went on to direct the jury accordingly.

In relation to count 1 the father had given evidence that he had a lawful excuse for taking the child from the mother and out of this country, in that he believed that the

b   child was an illegal immigrant and could therefore be lawfully removed. The judge left this excuse to the jury as a good defence to the charge, if they believed the father's evidence about it. He was, in my opinion, plainly wrong to do so because, assuming that a father can, in principle, kidnap his own minor child, a belief that the child is an illegal immigrant would not be a good defence to a count in respect of such kidnapping. To put it another way, the protection of the criminal law against kidnapping applies as much to

c   a person who is an illegal immigrant as it does to persons lawfully in this country. As I have said, however, the judge left this misconceived defence to the jury, as a result of which they unanimously acquitted him on count 1.

In relation to count 6 the father had not in his evidence put forward any similar excuse for his conduct. As a result the jury convicted the father on count 6, albeit only by a majority of 11 to 1.

d   During the course of the argument your Lordships were referred to a wide body of authority relating to the common law offence of kidnapping. This body of authority fell into three parts. First, there were extracts from 4 Bl Com (12th edn, 1795) 218–219, 1 East PC (1803) 428, 1 Hawk PC (8th edn, 1824) 119–120, Chitty *Criminal Law* (2nd edn, 1826) vol 4, p 92, Serjeant Stephen *Summary of the Criminal Law* (1834) p 156, Deacon *Digest of the Criminal Law* (1836) vol 1, pp 725–726 and *New Law Dictionary* (2nd edn,

e   1836) p 2. Second, there were the reports of certain cases of kidnapping decided in the seventeenth century. And, third, there were the reports of a series of modern cases of kidnapping, the first of which was decided in 1937 and the last in 1983.

From this wide body of authority six matters relating to the offence of kidnapping clearly emerge. First, the nature of the offence is an attack on, and infringement of, the personal liberty of an individual. Second, the offence contains four ingredients as follows:

f   (1) the taking or carrying away of one person by another, (2) by force or by fraud, (3) without the consent of the person so taken or carried away and (4) without lawful excuse. Third, until the comparatively recent abolition by statute of the division of criminal offences into the two categories of felonies and misdemeanours (see s 1 of the Criminal Law Act 1967), the offence of kidnapping was categorised by the common law as a misdemeanour only. Fourth, despite that, kidnapping was always regarded, by reason of

g   its nature, as a grave and (to use the language of an earlier age) heinous offence. Fifth, in earlier days the offence contained a further ingredient, namely that the taking or carrying away should be from a place within the jurisdiction to another place outside it; this further ingredient has, however, long been obsolete and forms no necessary part of the offence today. Sixth, the offence was in former days described not merely as taking or carrying away a person but further or alternatively as secreting him; this element of

h   secretion has, however, also become obsolete, so that, although it may be present in a particular case, it adds nothing to the basic ingredient of taking or carrying away.

The Court of Appeal, as will be apparent from what I said earlier, was of the opinion that, while in general the nature and the ingredients of the offence of kidnapping were as I have described them above, there were two limitations on the scope of such offence. The first limitation was that the offence could not be committed by anyone against a

j   child under the age of 14. The second limitation was that, in any case, the offence could not be committed by a parent against an unmarried child who was still a minor.

It must be said at once that these two limitations on the scope of the offence are not to be found anywhere in the wide body of authority to which I referred earlier. The opinion of the Court of Appeal on the matter appears to have been founded in the main on two considerations. The first consideration was the decision of the Irish Supreme Court in *The*

People (A-G) v Edge [1943] IR 115. The second consideration was the nature and form of successive English statutes passed during the nineteenth century in order to deter the commission of the crime of child stealing.

I shall consider *Edge's* case first. In that case the question for determination was whether a count in an indictment which charged the defendant with kidnapping a boy aged 14½ by unlawfully carrying him away and secreting him against the will of his lawful guardian disclosed any offence known to the law. It was not in dispute that the boy concerned was on friendly terms with the defendant and went away with him entirely voluntarily, without the use by the defendant of either force or fraud. The Dublin Circuit Criminal Court held that the count properly disclosed the common law offence of kidnapping, and the jury, having been so directed, convicted him on that count of that offence. The defendant appealed to the Court of Criminal Appeal, which upheld the conviction. The defendant brought a further appeal to the Supreme Court, which, by a majority, allowed the appeal and quashed the conviction. The ground of the majority's decision was that, once a child reached the age of discretion, which in the case of a boy was, as a matter of law, 14 years, he was free to choose where and with whom he should live, and that, in such a case, the consent or absence of consent of the child's lawful guardian was not relevant.

I consider next the successive English statutes which were passed during the nineteenth century in order to deter the commission of the crime of child stealing. The first statute was 54 Geo 3 c 101, passed on 18 July 1814 and described as 'An Act for the more effectual Prevention of Child Stealing'. That Act provided:

'Whereas the Practice of carrying away young Children, by forcible or fraudulent means, from their Parents or other Persons having the Care and Charge or Custody of them, commonly called Child Stealing, has of late much prevailed and increased: And Whereas no adequate Punishment is as yet provided by Law in *England* or *Ireland* for so heinous an Offence; Be it therefore enacted . . .

[I.] That if any Person or Persons, from and after the passing of this Act, shall maliciously, either by Force or Fraud, lead, take or carry away, or decoy or entice away, any Child under the Age of Ten Years, with Intent to deprive its Parent or Parents, or any other Person having the lawful Care or Charge of such Child of the Possession of such Child, by concealing and detaining such Child from such Parent or Parents, or other Person or Persons having the lawful Care or Charge of it . . . every such Person or Persons . . . shall be deemed guilty of Felony, and shall be subject and liable to all such Pains, Penalties, Punishments and Forfeitures, as by the Laws now in force may be inflicted upon, or are incurred by, Persons convicted of Grand Larceny.

2. Provided always, and be it further enacted, That nothing in this Act shall extend, or be construed to extend, to any Person who shall have claimed to be the Father of an illegitimate Child, or to have any Right or Title in Law to the Possession of such Child, on account of his getting Possession of such Child, or taking such Child out of the Possession of the Mother thereof, or other Person or Persons having the lawful Charge thereof . . .'

The second statute was 9 Geo 4 c 31, passed on 27 June 1828 and described as 'An Act for consolidating and amending the Statutes in *England* relative to Offences against the Person'. Section 21 of that Act re-enacted in substance, but with variations with regard to punishments, the primary provisions of the 1814 Act. It also preserved, although in somewhat different language, the proviso in favour of the father of an illegitimate child contained in s 2 of the 1814 Act.

The third statute was the Offences against the Person Act 1861, which by s 56 substantially re-enacted the offence of child stealing previously enacted by the 1814 and 1828 Acts, but with three differences. First, it increased the age of a child in respect of whom the offence could be committed from 10 to 14. Second, it provided that the protection which the two earlier Acts had afforded to the father of an illegitimate child

should apply also to the mother of such a child. And, third, it provided that the
maximum sentence for the offence should be imprisonment for seven years.

It is not apparent why the Court of Appeal, Criminal Division thought it necessary to
deal at all with what it held to be the first limitation on the scope of the common law
offence of kidnapping, namely that it could not be committed against a child under 14.
Your Lordships were informed by counsel on both sides that the existence of such a
limitation was not contended for by counsel for the father, and that the court heard no
argument by counsel on either side with regard to the point.

It is even less apparent why the Court of Appeal, having elected to deal with the point
when it was not necessary for it to do so, and without having had the benefit of hearing
argument from counsel on either side with regard to it, came to the conclusion on it
which it did, namely that there was no common law offence of kidnapping a child under
14 at all.

So far as *Edge's* case [1943] IR 115 is concerned, the Irish Supreme Court did not decide
that kidnapping a child under 14 was not an offence at common law. What it decided
was that, where a man is charged with the common law offence of kidnapping a child,
and it becomes necessary to consider whether the taking or carrying away of the child
was with or without consent, the relevant consent depended on the age of the child. If
the child was below the age of discretion, fixed by the law as 14, the relevant consent was
that of the parent or other lawful guardian of the child; but, if the child was above the
age of discretion, the relevant consent was that of the child himself. On the facts of the
case before it, the child whom the defendant was accused of kidnapping, being 14½, was
above the age of discretion, and, being above that age, had gone away voluntarily with
the defendant. The court held, accordingly, that the defendant's conviction could not
stand.

There is, in my view, nothing in *Edge's* case, to show that the Irish Supreme Court was
of the opinion that there did not exist any common law offence of kidnapping a child
under 14. On the contrary, it is implicit in its decision that it considered that such an
offence did exist, but that, in order to establish it, the taking or carrying away of such a
child would have to be shown to have been without the consent of the child's parent or
other lawful guardian, rather than without the consent of the child himself. It will be
necessary to consider later whether this distinction, between a child over 14 and one
under 14, accords with the English law of kidnapping.

Again there is, in my opinion, nothing in any of the three nineteenth century statutes
against child stealing, to which I have referred above, which supports the view that there
is no common law offence of kidnapping a child under 14. The 1814 Act was, as its terms
indicate, passed in order to provide a means of preventing child stealing, which would
be more effective than that which existed already. The means which existed already
consisted in the prosecution of child stealers for the common law misdemeanour of
kidnapping with the limited punishments attaching to that offence. The more effective
means which the 1814 Act provided consisted in the creation of a new statutory offence
of child stealing, and in the categorisation of that new offence as a felony punishable in
the same way as grand larceny, with the utmost severity of punishment which that
entailed. I can find nothing in the 1814 Act which indicates, either expressly or by
necessary implication, that Parliament intended by it to abolish, or detract in any way
from, the existing common law misdemeanour of kidnapping in relation to children
under 10. I hold the same opinion with regard to the subsequent 1828 and 1861 Acts.
They introduced some modifications into the statutory offence of child stealing, but in
no way impinged on the existing common law offence of kidnapping in relation to
children under 10 in the case of the 1828 Act or children under 14 in the case of the 1861
Act.

For these reasons I can find no support of any kind for the proposition laid down by
the Court of Appeal in the present case that there is no common law offence of kidnapping
a child who is under 14 years of age, and I wholly reject that proposition. It follows that
I would answer the first of the two certified points of law in the affirmative.

I turn now to the second limitation on the scope of the common law offence of kidnapping which the Court of Appeal considered existed, namely that the offence does not cover the case of a parent who takes or carries away his own child by force or fraud, so long as such child is an unmarried minor. It is right to observe, with regard to this second limitation, that the point was clearly taken by Mr Taylor for the father and argued fully by him before the Court of Appeal. Your Lordships were, however, informed both by Mr Taylor for the father and by Miss Curnow for the Crown that, because the court appeared, during the course of Miss Curnow's argument on the point, to have formed a view favourable to her on it, she did not develop that argument anything like so fully as she would otherwise have done. I do not suppose for one moment that the Court of Appeal intended to do anything other than give a full and fair hearing to counsel on both sides with regard to the point. It does seem, however, that the court may inadvertently have failed to carry out this intention in Miss Curnow's case. If so, it cannot be other than a matter of regret that this should have occurred.

In coming to its conclusion with regard to the second point, the Court of Appeal appears to have relied on two main considerations. The first consideration was that, if a father snatched a child contrary to an order of a court relating to its custody or care and control, such court had ample powers to punish him for contempt of court. That being so, it was not necessary that his conduct should be brought within the province of the criminal law; it was rather, by reason of the difficulties characteristic of disputes between parents about their children, much better that it should not. This consideration appears to me to be one of policy only, for which there is indeed much to be said, and about which it will be necessary to say something more at a later stage. In my opinion, however, it is not a consideration which can of itself have any bearing on the question whether the second limitation on the scope of the common law offence of kidnapping exists or not.

The second consideration was that, in all three of the nineteenth century statutes dealing with child stealing referred to earlier, the legislature thought it necessary to include an express provision for the protection of the father of an illegitimate child, and in the 1861 Act extended such protection to the mother of such a child as well. It was argued forcefully by counsel for the father that the inclusion of this express protection for the father of an illegitimate child, combined with the absence of any provision giving comparable protection to the father of a legitimate child, could only be explained on the basis that the legislature considered that it was impossible for a father of a legitimate child, who took or carried away such child by force or fraud, to be guilty of a criminal offence of any kind, including the common law offence of kidnapping.

My Lords, I think it very likely that, in the state of society and family law which existed in England in the nineteenth century, this opinion would indeed have been held by the legislature. This is because in those times both the generally accepted conventions of society and the courts by which such conventions were buttressed and enforced, regarded a father as having absolute and paramount authority, as against all the world, over any children of his who were still under the age of majority (then 21), except for a married daughter. The nature of this view of a father's rights appears clearly from various reported cases, including, as a typical example, *Re Agar-Ellis, Agar-Ellis v Lascelles* (1883) 24 Ch D 317. The common law, however, while generally immutable in its principles, unless different principles are laid down by statute, is not immutable in the way in which it adapts, develops and applies those principles in a radically changing world and against the background of radically changed social conventions and conditions.

I stated earlier that the fourth ingredient of the common law offence of kidnapping was that the taking and carrying away should be without lawful excuse. During the greater part of the nineteenth century I do not doubt that the position of paramountcy in the family accorded to a father, both by generally accepted social conventions and by courts which buttressed and enforced them, would, in most cases at any rate, have afforded a father, who took or carried away by force or by fraud an unmarried child of his under the age of 21 without the latter's consent, a lawful excuse for his conduct, and that, by reason of the existence of such lawful excuse, the prosecution of a father for the common law offence of kidnapping such child would have failed.

a Since the nineteenth century, however, the generally accepted social conventions relating to the paramountcy of a father's position in the family have been progressively whittled away, until now, in the second half of the twentieth century, they can be regarded as having disappeared altogether. Parents are treated as equals in at least most respects, and certainly in relation to their authority over their children. English law, both common law and statute law, has recognised this fundamental change in the position of a father in the family. The significance of these changes to the subject under

b discussion is clear and can be stated as follows. While a father who behaved in the way that the respondent did in snatching his own child in December 1978 and again in November 1981 might well, if he had behaved in the same way in the nineteenth century, have escaped conviction for kidnapping her on the ground that his paramount authority as a father afforded a lawful excuse for his conduct, that defence could not possibly avail him in the fact of the radically changed social and legal attitudes of today.

c For the reasons which I have given, I consider that the Court of Appeal was wrong in answering the second certified point of law in the way in which it did. I am of opinion that, having regard to the changed social conditions and legal attitudes existing today, it is possible for a father to commit the common law offence of kidnapping his own minor child. It follows that I would answer the second, as well as the first, of the two certified points of law in the affirmative.

d The result of answering both the certified points of law in the affirmative is that the appeal must be allowed, that the order of the Court of Appeal, Criminal Division dated 6 December 1983 must be set aside, and that the conviction of the father on count 6 of the indictment against him must be restored. He may consider himself fortunate not to have been convicted on count 1 also, particularly having regard to the fact that his two accomplices were tried and convicted for their part in the father's plot on that occasion,

e and each sentenced to two years' imprisonment.

My Lords, having reached that conclusion about the disposition of the appeal, I must now deal with two matters to which I said that I would return later. One of those matters is whether the doctrine laid down by the Irish Supreme Court in *Edge's* case [1943] IR 115 that the person the absence of whose consent is an essential ingredient of the common law offence of kidnapping is that of the child if it has reached an age of

f discretion fixed by law, but that of its father or other guardian if it has not, applies also under English law.

In my opinion, to accept that doctrine as applicable under English law would not be consistent with the formulation of the third ingredient of the common law offence of kidnapping which I made earlier on the basis of the wide body of authority to which your Lordships were referred. That third ingredient, as I formulated it earlier, consists of

g the absence of consent on the part of the person taken or carried away. I see no good reason why, in relation to the kidnapping of a child, it should not in all cases be the absence of the child's consent which is material, whatever its age may be. In the case of a very young child, it would not have the understanding or the intelligence to give its consent, so that absence of consent would be a necessary inference from its age. In the case of an older child, however, it must, I think, be a question of fact for a jury whether

h the child concerned has sufficient understanding and intelligence to give its consent; if, but only if, the jury considers that a child has these qualities, it must then go on to consider whether it has been proved that the child did not give its consent. While the matter will always be for the jury alone to decide, I should not expect a jury to find at all frequently that a child under 14 had sufficient understanding and intelligence to give its consent.

j I should add that, while the absence of the consent of the person having custody or care and control of a child is not material to what I have stated to be the third ingredient of the common law offence of kidnapping, the giving of consent by such a person may be very relevant to the fourth such ingredient, in that, depending on all the circumstances, it might well support a defence of lawful excuse.

The other matter to which I said that I would return is the desirability, as a matter of policy, of prosecuting for kidnapping parents who snatch their own children in defiance of a court order relating to their custody or care and control. With regard to this I accept fully that, in general, it is desirable, as a matter of policy, that the conduct of such parents *a* should be dealt with as a contempt of court, rather than as the subject matter of a criminal prosecution. The latter method of dealing with the problem should, in my view, only be used in exceptional cases, where the conduct of the parent concerned is so bad that an ordinary right-thinking person would immediately and without hesitation regard it as criminal in nature. In all other cases the problem will best be dealt with by the taking of appropriate proceedings for contempt of court. I would add that I would *b* regard it as extremely undesirable that there should, in any circumstances, be any private prosecutions for the kidnapping by a parent of his own child.

So far as the present case is concerned, I consider that there are four factors which amply justified the decision to prosecute the father for kidnapping the child on the two occasions when he snatched her from the mother. The first factor is the appalling nature of the father's conduct on the occasion of the first snatch in December 1978, when he *c* terrified the mother by having with him as accomplices the two thugs to whom I referred earlier. The second factor is the repetition by the father of his conduct, albeit without the assistance of similar accomplices, in November 1981. The third factor is that on each of the two occasions the child, who was a ward of court, was removed out of the jurisdiction. The fourth factor is that the father had, in connection with his two acts of snatching the child, committed a series of other offences, in respect of all of which it was right and *d* proper that he should be indicted and tried in a criminal court.

Appeal allowed. Order of Court of Appeal, Criminal Division set aside. Conviction on count 6 restored.

Solicitors: *Director of Public Prosecutions*; *Gary Jacobs & Co*, Romford (for the respondent). *e*

Mary Rose Plummer   Barrister.

R v Secretary of State for the Home Department, ex parte Fatima
R v Secretary of State for the Home Department, ex parte Bi

f

g

COURT OF APPEAL, CIVIL DIVISION
SIR JOHN DONALDSON MR, SLADE AND PARKER LJJ
16, 24 MAY 1984

Divorce – Foreign decree – Recognition by English court – Overseas divorce – Proceedings in country outside British Isles – Proceedings – Talaq divorce – Talaq pronounced by husband in *h* *United Kingdom – Husband a national of Pakistan – Wife resident in Pakistan – Notice of talaq served on Pakistani authorities and wife in accordance with Pakistani law – Talaq not revoked and marriage validly dissolved under Pakistani law – Whether pronouncement of talaq part of 'proceedings' by which divorce obtained – Whether divorce 'obtained by means of . . . proceedings' in Pakistan – Recognition of Divorces and Legal Separations Act 1971, ss 2(a), 3(1).*

j

A Pakistani Muslim living in England wished to divorce his wife, who was living in Pakistan. He pronounced talaq in England against her, and in accordance with Pakistani law sent written notice that he had done so to her and to the appropriate public authority in Pakistan. The talaq was not revoked and 90 days later the marriage was declared dissolved according to Pakistani law. In subsequent immigration proceedings the

a   question arose whether the talaq divorce should be recognised by the English courts
    under ss 2ᵃ and 3ᵇ of the Recognition of Divorces and Legal Separations Act 1971.

Held – (1) Since 'other proceedings' in s 2(a) of the 1971 Act were not limited to quasi-
judicial proceedings, the pronouncement of the talaq, as the first essential step in the
chain of events that had to take place before a talaq divorce was effective under Pakistani
b   law, could not be isolated from the other steps and accordingly it formed part of the
relevant 'proceedings'. It followed that the 'proceedings' by which the divorce had been
obtained had taken place partly in the United Kingdom and partly in Pakistan (see p 463
b c e g and p 464 e, post); dicta of Lord Fraser and Lord Scarman in *Quazi v Quazi* [1979] 3
All ER at 911, 918 applied.
    (2) When ss 2 and 3(1) of the 1971 Act were read together it was clear that the 'judicial
c   or other proceedings' by which an 'overseas divorce' was obtained were required, if the
divorce was to be recognised under the 1971 Act, to be (a) one set of proceedings only
and (b) a set of proceedings which had been instituted in the same country as that in
which the relevant divorce was ultimately obtained (see p 464 d e, post).
    (3) It followed therefore that the divorce was not an 'overseas divorce' within s 2(a)
because the entirety of the relevant proceedings had not taken place in Pakistan and,
d   moreover, the condition specified in s 3(1) was incapable of fulfilment since there was no
such date as 'the date of the institution of the proceedings in the country in which [the
divorce] was obtained' (see p 464 e to g, post).
    Decision of Taylor J sub nom *R v Immigration Appeal Tribunal, ex p Secretary of State for
the Home Dept* [1984] 1 All ER 488 affirmed.

e   **Notes**
For the recognition of overseas divorces, see 8 Halsbury's Laws (4th edn) paras 484–485,
and for cases on the subject, see 11 Digest (Reissue) 564–566, 1270–1279.
    For the Recognition of Divorces and Legal Separations Act 1971, ss 2, 3, see 41
Halsbury's Statutes (3rd edn) 219.

f   **Cases referred to in judgment**
Chaudhary v Chaudhary (1983) 13 Fam Law 177.
Manzoor v Allah Wasaya PLD 1973 BJ 36.
Quazi v Quazi [1979] 3 All ER 897, [1980] AC 744, [1979] 3 WLR 833, HL; *rvsg* [1979] 3
    All ER 424, [1980] AC 744, [1979] 3 WLR 402, CA; *rvsg* [1980] AC 744.
g   *Qureshi v Qureshi* [1971] 1 All ER 325, [1972] Fam 173, [1971] 2 WLR 518.
R v Registrar General of Births Deaths and Marriages, ex p Minhas [1976] 2 All ER 246,
    [1977] QB 1, [1976] 2 WLR 473, DC.
Sharif v Sharif (1980) 10 Fam Law 216.
Zaal v Zaal (1983) 4 FLR 284.

h   **Appeals**
Ghulam Fatima and Shafeena Bi appealed against the decision of Taylor J hearing the
Crown Office list on 11 July 1983 sub nom *R v Immigration Appeal Tribunal, ex p Secretary
of State for the Home Dept* [1984] 1 All ER 488, [1984] 2 WLR 36 whereby, on separate
applications for judicial review which were heard together, he refused orders of certiorari
to bring up and quash (1) the decision of an immigration officer made on 31 July 1982
j   whereby he refused Ghulam Fatima leave to enter the United Kingdom and (2) the
decision of an immigration officer made on 24 February 1983 whereby he refused
Shafeena Bi leave to enter the United Kingdom and a decision dated 26 May 1983 giving

---

a   Section 2, so far as material, is set out at p 461 f, post
b   Section 3, so far as material, is set out at p 461 g, post

directions for her removal to Pakistan. The Secretary of State for the Home Department was the respondent to both appeals. The facts are set out in the judgment of the court.

a

Sibghatullah Kadri and *Harjit Grewal* for the appellant Ghulam Fatima.
Owais Kadri for the appellant Shafeena Bi.
Simon D Brown for the Secretary of State.

Cur adv vult

b

24 May. The following judgment of the court was delivered.

SLADE LJ. This is the judgment of the court on two appeals from a judgment of Taylor J sub nom *R v Immigration Appeal Tribunal, ex p Secretary of State for the Home Dept* [1984] 1 All ER 488, [1984] 2 WLR 36 given on 11 July 1983 in immigration cases. Both appeals turn on the same point of law, that is to say the effect in English law of a talaq divorce pronounced in England but perfected in Pakistan. The appellant in the first case is Ghulam Fatima. The appellant in the second case is Shafeena Bi. They are both Pakistani nationals. The respondent in each case is the Secretary of State for the Home Department.

c

According to ancient Muslim law, a marriage between Muslims will be immediately dissolved if a husband pronounces talaq three times. This form of talaq (a bare talaq) is immediately effective for this purpose and does not even require notification to the wife.

d

In Pakistan, however, a bare talaq is no longer recognised as effective by itself to dissolve a marriage. In 1961 the Muslim Family Laws Ordinance was there enacted. Section 7(1) placed a fetter on the right of a husband to dissolve a marriage in this manner, by introducing four conditions which have to be satisfied if a talaq is to be effective under Pakistani law, that is to say (a) the talaq has first to be pronounced, either orally or in writing, (b) notice thereof has to be given to the chairman of the relevant local union council in Pakistan, (c) a copy of the notice has to be supplied to the wife, (d) 90 days have to expire following the delivery of the notice to the chairman.

e

Section 1(2) of the 1961 ordinance provides that it extends to the whole of Pakistan and applies to all Muslim citizens of Pakistan, wherever they may be. Section 7 reads:

'Talaq.—(1) Any man who wishes to divorce his wife shall, as soon as may be after the pronouncement of *talaq* in any form whatsoever, give the Chairman notice in writing of his having done so, and shall supply a copy thereof to the wife.

f

(2) Whoever contravenes the provisions of subsection (1) shall be punishable with simple imprisonment for a term which may extend to one year or with a fine which may extend to 5,000 rupees or with both.

(3) Save as provided in subsection (5), a *talaq* unless revoked earlier, expressly or otherwise, shall not be effective until the expiration of ninety days from the day on which notice under subsection (1) is delivered to the Chairman.

g

(4) Within thirty days of the receipt of notice under subsection (1), the Chairman shall constitute an Arbitration Council for the purpose of bringing about a reconciliation between the parties, and the Arbitration Council shall take all steps necessary to bring about such reconciliation.

(5) If the wife be pregnant at the time *talaq* is pronounced *talaq* shall not be effective until the period mentioned in subsection (3) or the pregnancy, whichever be later, ends.

h

(6) Nothing shall debar a wife whose marriage has been terminated by *talaq* effective under this section from remarrying the same husband, without an intervening marriage with a third person, unless such termination is for the third time so effective.'

The facts relating to Ghulam Fatima, as set out in the judge's judgment, are briefly as follows. She sought entry into the United Kingdom on 31 July 1982 as fiancée of her sponsor, Mohammed Afzal. He, like her, is a Pakistani national, and was married in January 1968 in Pakistan. In November 1968 he came to the United Kingdom. On 22

May 1978 he pronounced talaq against his wife and made a statutory declaration that he
a had done so before a solicitor in Bolton. Copies of that document were sent to the wife
and to the chairman of the relevant union council in Pakistan. No reconciliation having
been effected and 90 days having elapsed, the marriage was dissolved according to
Pakistani law. However, the immigration officer, not being satisfied that the marriage
was effectively dissolved according to English law, was not satisfied that the intended
marriage between the applicant and her sponsor could take place within a reasonable
b time. He therefore refused the applicant entry.

The facts relating to Shafeena Bi, as set out in the judge's judgment, are as follows. She
arrived at Heathrow on 24 February 1983 seeking entry as fiancée of her sponsor,
Mohammed Zamir. The sponsor, who is also a Pakistani national, had settled in England
in 1974, but had been married in 1970 in Pakistan, whilst on a visit there. He returned
to England alone after the marriage and his wife stayed in Pakistan. On 17 September
c 1981 he pronounced talaq against her and made a statutory declaration that he had done
so before a solicitor in Redditch, Worcestershire. Two copies of that declaration were sent
to Pakistan, one to the wife and one to the chairman of the relevant union council. No
reconciliation occurred and, after 90 days had elapsed, their divorce was effective under
Pakistani law. The immigration officer took the same view as the immigration officer in
Ghulam Fatima's case. He therefore refused entry. On 26 May 1983 amended directions
d were given for the applicant's removal following a decision by the Secretary of State to
remove her.

Having obtained the necessary leave each of Ghulam Fatima and Shafeena Bi sought
judicial review of the relevant decision of the immigration officer. The question for
Taylor J, who heard their applications, was whether the immigration officer in each case
was entitled to take the view that he could not be satisfied that the proposed marriage
e could take place within a reasonable time. This question in turn depended on whether
or not in each case the talaq divorce was by English law effective to dissolve the sponsor's
first marriage.

In 1971 the Recognition of Divorces and Legal Separations Act 1971 was passed to
amend the law relating to the recognition of divorces and legal separations in this
country. Section 2 defines 'overseas divorces' for the purpose of the Act. So far as material
f for present purposes, it reads as follows:

'Sections 3 to 5 of this Act shall have effect . . . as respects the recognition in the
United Kingdom of the validity of overseas divorces . . . that is to say, divorces . . .
which—(a) have been obtained by means of judicial or other proceedings in any
country outside the British Isles; and (b) are effective under the law of that country.'

g Section 3(1) provides:

'The validity of an overseas divorce or legal separation shall be recognised if, at
the date of the institution of the proceedings in the country in which it was
obtained—(a) either spouse was habitually resident in that country; or (b) either
spouse was a national of that country.'

h The Pakistani talaq divorces of the two sponsors satisfy those conditions essential to
their recognition in this country which are set out in ss 2(b) and 3(1)(b). The issue is
whether they also satisfy the further condition set out in s 2(a). This issue makes it
necessary to answer two questions. (A) Did the relevant 'proceedings' by means of which
the divorces were obtained take place wholly in Pakistan as the appellants contend? (If
Yes, the appellants must succeed.) (B) If the relevant 'proceedings' took place partly in
j England and partly in Pakistan, are the divorces capable of satisfying the conditions of
s 2(a)?

We shall first consider question (A). In Quazi v Quazi [1979] 3 All ER 897, [1980] AC
744 the House of Lords had to consider the effect of a talaq divorce where both parties to
a marriage were Muslims and Pakistani nationals. In 1974 the husband, having flown to
Pakistan, purported to divorce the wife by pronouncing the talaq and taking the other
steps made requisite by s 7 of the 1961 ordinance. The husband subsequently sought a

declaration from the English court that the marriage had been lawfully dissolved. The
Court of Appeal ([1979] 3 All ER 424, [1980] AC 744) allowed an appeal by the wife   *a*
from Wood J ([1980] AC 744), holding that the phrase 'judicial or other proceedings' in s
2(*a*) of the 1971 Act excluded from recognition a foreign decree which depended for its
legal efficacy solely on the acts of the parties to the marriage. The House of Lords
unanimously reversed this decision, holding that the words 'other proceedings' in s 2(*a*)
of the 1971 Act were not to be limited to quasi-judicial proceedings, by being construed
ejusdem generis with judicial proceedings, but referred to any proceedings other than   *b*
judicial proceedings which were officially recognised in the country in which they were
taken. It was accordingly held that validity of the husband's divorce was entitled to
recognition in this country under the 1971 Act.

Their Lordships in *Quazi v Quazi* did not have to decide whether the pronouncement
of the talaq itself formed part of the relevant 'proceedings', since this act itself, like all the
other relevant acts, had in that case been performed by the husband in Pakistan. Lord   *c*
Fraser, however, said ([1979] 3 All ER 897 at 911, [1980] AC 744 at 817):

> 'The proceedings are instituted by the talaq itself, which forms part of them. That
> must be so having regard to the provision in s 3(1) of the Act that the tempus
> inspiciendum for habitual residence and nationality is the date of the institution of
> the proceedings. The subsequent notice to the civil judge may or may not lead to
> arbitration proceedings actually taking place, but it at least gives an opportunity to   *d*
> the wife to make her views known to the arbitration council and it also invests the
> divorce with a certain formality which is essential in Pakistan to its effectiveness. I
> express no opinion whether a bare talaq pronounced in some country where, unlike
> Pakistan, it would be effective without any further procedure, should be recognised
> under the Recognition Act of 1971 as a valid divorce.'

Lord Scarman said ([1979] 3 All ER 897 at 918, [1980] AC 744 at 826):   *e*

> 'Under the law of Pakistan, therefore, talaq is the institution of proceedings
> officially recognised as leading to divorce and becomes an effective divorce only
> after the completion of the proceedings and the expiry of a period laid down by
> statute. The proceedings in this case were, therefore, officially recognised, and led to
> a divorce legally effective in Pakistan. Further, the trial judge was correct in holding   *f*
> that the effective divorce was obtained *by means of* these proceedings; for without
> them there would have been no effective divorce.' (Lord Scarman's emphasis.)

Lord Fraser and Lord Scarman thus plainly regarded the pronouncement of the talaq
itself as forming part of the relevant 'proceedings'.

Counsel for the appellant Ghulam Fatima relied on a passage in the speech of Lord   *g*
Diplock in which he said ([1979] 3 All ER 897 at 903, [1980] AC 744 at 808–809):

> 'It is rightly conceded on behalf of the wife that the divorce by talaq which was
> obtained in Pakistan followed on acts which though not judicial do fall within the
> description "other proceedings officially recognised" in that country. The
> pronouncement of the talaq was required by law to be notified to a public authority,
> the chairman of the union council; he in turn was required by law to constitute an   *h*
> arbitration council for the purposes of conciliation and to invite each spouse to
> nominate a representative. These are "proceedings"; none the less so because in the
> event neither spouse elects to take advantage of the opportunity for conciliation
> which the arbitration council presents. They are proceedings that are not merely
> officially recognised but are also enforced by penal sanctions under the Muslim
> Family Laws Ordinance 1961. Without such proceedings the divorce by talaq never   *j*
> becomes effective. The proceedings come first, the divorce follows them 90 days
> after they have been commenced.'

As counsel pointed out, it would appear that in his references to 'proceedings' in the
course of this passage Lord Diplock was not including the pronouncement of the talaq

a itself. Nevertheless, it was not necessary for him to consider whether the pronouncement also formed part of the 'proceedings' and it is by no means clear that he was directing his mind to this point. Nor do we read a passage in Lord Salmon's speech ([1979] 3 All ER 897 at 906, [1980] AC 744 at 812), in which he described the giving of notice of the talaq as a 'proceeding', as directed to the point. On the other hand, passages from the speeches of Lord Fraser and Lord Scarman, which we have cited, explicitly cover it and should, in our judgment, be followed.

b It is worthy of note that s 7(6) of the 1961 ordinance refers to a marriage which 'has been terminated by *talaq* effective under this section'. The ordinance itself thus seems to envisage that the talaq itself is part of the non-judicial proceedings which have the effect of terminating a marriage. Be that as it may, once one accepts, as the House of Lords has held, that the phrase 'other proceedings' in s 2(a) of the 1971 Act is not limited to quasi-judicial proceedings, we find it difficult to see how one can properly isolate the first

c essential step in the chain of events that has to take place before a talaq divorce is effective under Pakistani law (ie the pronouncement of the talaq) from the other steps and say that it does not itself form part of the relevant 'proceedings'.

Counsel for the appellant Ghulam Fatima referred us to a Pakistani decision, *Manzoor v Allah Wasaya* PLD 1973 BJ 36 at 39, in which, after quoting the terms of s 7 of the 1971 ordinance, Aftab Hussain J said:

d 'The pronouncement of divorce, therefore, does not operate as divorce. It is merely manifestation of wish to divorce.'

This passage, however, does not seem to us to assist in any way in refuting the argument that the pronouncement of the talaq is the first step in and part of the relevant 'proceedings' for the purpose of applying s 2 of the 1971 Act.

e We have been referred to three conflicting decisons of judges of first instance in which they have considered whether the single act of pronouncing a bare talaq three times can fall within the description of 'proceedings' for this purpose. In *Sharif v Sharif* (1980) 10 Fam Law 216 Wood J held that it could not. In *Zaal v Zaal* (1983) 4 FLR 284 Bush J held that it could. In *Chaudhary v Chaudhary* (1983) 13 Fam Law 177 Wood J adhered to his previous view that it could not. We do not think that it is necessary for this court to

f decide which of these two conflicting views is correct, and indeed it is preferable to express no opinion on the point, especially since we have been told that an appeal from the *Chaudhary* decision is shortly to come before this court.

In the present case, the pronouncement of the talaq was itself the institution of the proceedings which are officially recognised in Pakistan as leading to the relevant divorce: see *Quazi v Quazi* [1979] 3 All ER 897 at 918, [1980] AC 744 at 826 per Lord Scarman. In

g our judgment, Taylor J was right in deciding, as he did, that the pronouncement itself formed part of the relevant 'proceedings' for the purpose of s 2 of the 1971 Act and that those proceedings took place partly in England and partly in Pakistan.

We now turn to question (B) above.

A few months before the 1971 Act was passed, Simon P in *Qureshi v Qureshi* [1971] 1 All ER 324, [1972] Fam 173 had held that a talaq divorce obtained by a husband

h domiciled in England, following the pronouncement of a talaq in England, should be recognised by the English courts. The law, as declared in this decision, has since been affected, not only by the 1971 Act but also by s 16(1) of the Domicile and Matrimonial Proceedings Act 1973, which provides:

'No proceeding in the United Kingdom, the Channel Islands or the Isle of Man shall be regarded as validly dissolving a marriage unless instituted in the courts of

j law of one of those countries.'

Section 16(2)(b) of that Act makes it clear that the word 'proceeding' in this context is apt to include a proceeding other than a proceeding in a court of law.

The two divorces in the present cases have been aptly described in the course of argument as 'transnational' divorces because they have not been obtained either by means of proceedings which took place exclusively outside the United Kingdom (so as indisputably to fall within s 2(a) of the 1971 Act) or by means of proceedings which took place exclusively within the United Kingdom (so as indisputably to fall within s 16(1) of the 1973 Act).

The only authority to which we have been referred in which the applicability of ss 2 and 3 of the 1971 Act to a transnational divorce has been considered is the decision of the Divisional Court in *R v Registrar General of Births Deaths and Marriages, ex p Minhas* [1976] 2 All ER 246, [1977] QB 1. In that case, it was held that a talaq divorce obtained by a Pakistani, who had written the initiating notice of talaq in this country, could not be recognised under s 3, since it was not obtained in 'proceedings . . . outside the British Isles' as required by s 2(a). However, despite the close similarity on its facts, counsel for the Secretary of State though submitting that it was correctly decided, felt able to place little or no reliance on this decision. For, as Lord Fraser pointed out in *Quazi v Quazi* [1979] 3 All ER 897 at 910, [1980] AC 744 at 816, this decision was evidently based on a misunderstanding of the effect of the 1961 ordinance. And that misunderstanding clearly coloured the whole of the Divisional Court's conclusion.

Effectively, therefore, we have to answer question (B) above without the benefit of any authority, save the careful and lucid judgment of the judge in the court below.

We accept that the words of s 2(a) of the 1971 Act, if read in isolation, are capable of more than one construction. But they have to be read in the whole of their context. The wording of ss 2 and 3(1) when read together, in our judgment, make it clear that in using the phrase 'judicial or other proceedings', in the course of its definition of an 'overseas divorce', the legislature contemplated (a) one set of proceedings only, (b) a set of proceedings which had been instituted in the same country as that in which the relevant divorce was ultimately obtained. On any other footing the phrase 'at the date of the institution of the proceedings in the country in which it was obtained' in s 3(1) would be inept. That phrase in its context manifestly refers to proceedings of any nature mentioned in s 2(a), that is to say whether of a judicial or other nature.

It follows that, in our judgment, the judge was right in deciding that the requirement in s 2(a), that the overseas divorce must have been obtained by means of proceedings in a country outside the British Isles, means that the entirety of the relevant 'proceedings', whatever they may have been, must have taken place in the overseas country.

In the present cases, the entirety of the relevant 'proceedings' did not take place in Pakistan because the pronouncement of the talaq which instituted the proceedings took place in this country. The divorces accordingly were not, in our judgment, 'overseas divorces' within the definition contained in s 2(a). Furthermore, the condition specified in s 3(1) is incapable of fulfilment in either case, since there is no such date as 'the date of the institution of the proceedings *in the country in which* [*the divorce*] *was obtained*'.

Lord Diplock in *Quazi v Quazi* [1979] 3 All ER 897 at 900, [1980] AC 744 at 804 pointed out that the purpose of the 1971 Act was to enable the United Kingdom to give effect in its domestic law to the Hague Convention on the Recognition of Divorces and Legal Separations of 1970 (1 June 1970; TS 123 (1975); Cmnd 6248). He described the mischief which the convention was designed to cure as that of 'limping marriages', that is to say 'marriages that were recognised in some jurisdictions as having been validly dissolved, but in other jurisdictions as still subsisting'. Counsel for the appellant Ghulam Fatima strongly urged that this court should not by its decision in these cases leave the two sponsors with 'limping marriages' which are recognised in Pakistan, but not in this country, as having been dissolved.

We have some sympathy with this submission. Nevertheless we are far from certain that it would be the policy of the legislature to encourage the obtaining of 'divorces by post' by Pakistani nationals resident in this country by means of the talaq procedure. Section 16 of the 1973 Act seems to us to suggest otherwise. We can therefore see no obvious reasons of legislative policy sufficient to justify giving s 2(a) of the 1971 Act a meaning other than that which the wording of the subsection in its context appears to require.

a For the reasons which we have stated, which are much the same as his own, we agree with the judge that the Pakistani talaq divorces of the two sponsors do not satisfy the conditions of s 2(a) and that the immigration officer was in each case entitled to take the view that he could not be satisfied that the proposed marriages would take place within a reasonable time. The construction which we place on s 2(a) of the 1971 Act makes it unnecessary to consider whether the respective marriages of the sponsors were dissolved by a 'proceeding in the United Kingdom' within the meaning of s 16(1) of the 1973 Act.

b We accordingly dismiss these appeals.

Appeals dismissed. Application by Ghulam Fatima for leave to appeal to the House of Lords refused.

c Solicitors: *J Esner & Co*, Bolton (for the appellant Ghulam Fatima); *Wakefield & Co* (for the appellant Shafeena Bi); *Treasury Solicitor*.

Diana Procter   Barrister.

Etablissement Commercial Kamira v Schiazzano

COURT OF APPEAL, CIVIL DIVISION
CUMMING-BRUCE LJ AND SIR DENYS BUCKLEY
22 FEBRUARY 1984

e *Landlord and tenant – Long tenancy at low rent – Continuation as statutory tenancy – Terms of statutory tenancy – Determination of terms by court – Principles applicable in determining terms – Fairness and justice as between parties – Relevance of terms of contractual tenancy – Lease of maisonette – Tenancy limited to residential use for one household only – Whether prohibition on sharing maisonette justified as term of statutory tenancy – Landlord and Tenant*
f *Act 1954, s 7(1).*

By a lease made in 1957 the landlord let a maisonette to the tenant for a term of 24 years expiring in June 1981. The lease was a long lease at a low rent within Pt I of the Landlord and Tenant Act 1954 and contained covenants by the tenant not to use the maisonette otherwise than as a private residence in the occupation of one household only and not to
g assign, underlet or part with possession of the maisonette or any part of it without the landlord's written consent, which was not to be unreasonably withheld. The lease did not contain any covenant against the tenant sharing the maisonette. On the expiry of the lease in June 1981 the tenancy was continued by virtue of s 3 of the 1954 Act, and in October 1982 the landlord served a notice on the tenant under s 4 of that Act proposing a statutory tenancy of the maisonette. The parties agreed to a term in the proposed
h statutory tenancy under which the tenant was not to use the maisonette otherwise than as a private residential dwelling in the occupation of one household only. However, the landlord proposed a covenant prohibiting the tenant from assigning, sharing, underletting or parting with possession of the maisonette, which was revised by the tenant to one prohibiting him only from assigning or parting with possession without the landlord's consent, which was not to be unreasonably withheld. The parties being unable to agree
j that term, the landlord applied to the court to settle it under s 7(1)[a] of the 1954 Act. The judge determined that a term should be included in the statutory tenancy prohibiting the tenant not only from assigning, underletting or parting with possession of the maisonette but also from sharing it, on the ground that a term permitting the tenant to

---

a   Section 7(1) is set out at p 467 *f g*, post

do any of those things even with the landlord's consent would be inconsistent with the
term regarding the user of the maisonette. The tenant appealed.   *a*

Held – (1) The duty of the court in exercising its discretion under s 7(1) of the 1954 Act
to determine the terms of a statutory tenancy was to act fairly between the parties, and
that involved taking into account as a primary consideration the state of affairs which
existed between them at the date of the hearing, which in turn involved taking into
consideration the rights and obligations of the parties under the previous contractual   *b*
lease. The terms of the contractual lease were not, however, to be given priority over the
other material considerations but were only one of the matters to be considered in
determining the terms of the statutory tenancy; in particular, it would not necessarily be
just and fair as between the parties to incorporate into the statutory tenancy covenants
that were contained in the previous contractual lease, because covenants imposed at the
commencement of a long lease which was none the less for a limited period would not   *c*
necessarily be appropriate to a succeeding statutory tenancy, which might continue for
an unlimited period, and could pass on the tenant's death to members of his family,
without the landlord having any control over the term of the lease (see p 468 *e g*, p 470 *h*
to p 471 *c* and p 473 *d*, post); *Lagens Properties Ltd v Bandino* (1965) 193 EG 980 approved.
(2) There was no ground for interfering with the judge's decision to prohibit any
assignment, underletting or parting with possession of part of the maisonette, because   *d*
such a term had been contained in the previous contractual lease, was consistent with the
term to be included in the statutory tenancy regarding user of the maisonette as a private
residence occupied by one household only and was necessary to protect the landlord from
the rights of any subtenant on termination of the statutory tenancy. However, those
reasons were not material to the question whether the tenant should be prohibited from
sharing the maisonette (which in any event was not a precise concept and could cover   *e*
ordinary hospitality). Since the question of sharing did not appear to have been argued
before or considered by the judge, the court was entitled to exercise its own discretion in
that matter. On the facts, there was no reason in justice or fairness to include in the terms
of the statutory tenancy a prohibition on sharing which had not been contemplated by
the parties when they entered into the previous contractual lease. The appeal would
accordingly be allowed to the extent of removing the prohibition on sharing ordered by   *f*
the judge (see p 471 *c* to *e g j* to p 472 *c e h* to p 473 *h*, post).

Notes
For settlement of the terms of a statutory tenancy on termination of a contractual long
tenancy at a low rent, see 27 Halsbury's Laws (4th edn) paras 844–845.
For the Landlord and Tenant Act 1954, ss 3, 4, 7, see 18 Halsbury's Statutes (3rd edn)   *g*
730, 732, 735.

Cases referred to in judgments
Dobbs v Linford [1952] 2 All ER 827, [1953] 1 QB 48, CA.
Downie v Turner [1951] 1 All ER 416, [1951] 2 KB 112, CA.
Lagens Properties Ltd v Bandino (1965) 193 EG 980, Cty Ct.   *h*

Cases also cited
O'May v City of London Real Property Co Ltd [1982] 1 All ER 660, [1983] 2 AC 726, HL.
Segal Securities Ltd v Thoseby [1963] 1 All ER 500, [1963] 1 QB 887.

Appeal   *j*
By an originating application dated 14 February 1983 Etablissement Commercial Kamira,
of Vaduz, Liechtenstein (the landlord) applied for the settlement, pursuant to Pt I of the
Landlord and Tenant Act 1954, of the terms of a statutory tenancy of premises consisting
of a maisonette at 5 Green Street, London W1 on the expiration of the long tenancy at a
low rent of the premises held by the respondent, Vittorio Schiazzano (the tenant). On 10
August 1983 his Honour Judge McDonnell sitting in the Westminster County Court

ordered that the terms of the statutory tenancy should include, inter alia, a term that the
a tenant should not assign or share or underlet or part with possession of the premises or
any part thereof in any way whatsoever. The tenant appealed from that part of the order,
seeking the substitution of a term that the tenant should not share, underlet or part with
possession of any part of the premises without the landlord's previous written consent
such consent not to be unreasonably withheld, or alternatively that the judge's order in
relation to that term be set aside and the matter remitted to the county court for
b redetermination. The facts are set out in the judgment of Cumming-Bruce LJ.

John Male for the tenant.
Thomas Seymour for the landlord.

c **CUMMING-BRUCE LJ.** Etablissement Commercial Kamira (the landlord) is the
assignee of the reversion dependent on the term created by a sublease made on 28
October 1957, whereby the third- and fourth-floor maisonette, 5 Green Street, London
W1, was demised to the respondent, Dr Vittorio Schiazzano (the tenant), for a term of
years which expired by effluxion of time on 21 June 1981. As the lease was a long lease
at a low rent within the provisions of Pt I of the Landlord and Tenant Act 1954, the
d tenancy created thereby was continued by virtue of s 3, and on 25 October 1982 the
landlord served on the tenant a notice proposing a statutory tenancy and specifying 27
April 1983 as the date on which the long tenancy must come to an end.

The tenant notified the landlord that he was not going to give up possession and as the
parties were unable to agree the terms of the statutory tenancy, which was to come into
force with effect from 28 April 1983, the landlord issued an originating application
e asking the court to decide what the terms should be.

There were a number of issues between the parties on the terms for which one or the
other were contending, and in the usual way a travelling draft came into existence,
drafted initially by the landlord's solicitors, then amended by the tenant's solicitors in
order to show wherein they disagreed and what they wanted, followed by reamendment
in blue by the landlord's solicitors showing how much, if at all, they accepted the
f proposals proposed by amendment by the tenant's solicitors.

By s 7 of the 1954 Act, where the parties cannot agree on the terms of the statutory
tenancy which is to succeed the contractual tenancy, it is provided by sub-s (1):

> 'The terms on which the tenant and any successor to his statutory tenancy may
> retain possession of the dwelling-house during that period other than the amount of
> the rent shall be such as may be agreed between the landlord and the tenant or
g > determined by the court.'

It is to be observed that by the drafting of that subsection Parliament has not imposed
any clog or restraint on the discretion which the court has to exercise, when the court has
to determine the terms which are not agreed. There are no words in the subsection
which indicate the considerations which the court has to regard as material when
h determining how to exercise the discretion.

In that regard s 7(1) of the 1954 Act is to be contrasted with the provisions in s 35 of
the same Act. Section 7 appears in that bundle of sections collected in Pt I of the Act
whereby Parliament enacted security of tenure for certain residential tenants on
termination of long tenancies at low rents, which, prior to 1952, had been excluded from
the ambit of the successive Rent Acts and which began in 1917. Section 35 by contrast is
j in Pt II of the same Act. The subject matter thereof is to afford security of tenure for
business, professional and other tenants. So the subject matter of Pt I, which is concerned
with residential tenants, manifestly gives rise to quite different considerations from those
which Parliament is likely to consider relevant to the statutory security of tenure for
business, professional and other tenants. I do not doubt that that is the explanation of the
difference in language between s 35 in Pt II and s 7(1) in Pt I, because by s 35 it is
provided:

'The terms of a tenancy granted by order of the court under this Part of this Act (other than terms as to the duration thereof and as to the rent payable thereunder) shall be such as may be agreed between the landlord and the tenant or as, in default of such agreement, may be determined by the court; and in determining those terms the court shall have regard to the terms of the current tenancy and to all relevant circumstances.'

Contrast s 7(1): 'The terms . . . shall be such as may be agreed between the landlord and the tenant or determined by the court.'

His Honour Judge McDonnell had first to decide the terms relating to repairs. He made his orders in that regard. There is no appeal against that part of the judge's order. By his order he also dealt with the terms which should govern the occupation and right of possession of the tenant. It is with that part of the judge's order only with which this court is now concerned.

In the travelling draft document the landlord's solicitors had drafted sub-cl (v) of cl 6, being the tenant's covenants, in the following terms: 'Not assign or share or underlet or part with possession of the maisonette or any part thereof in any way . . .' On receipt of that proposed term the tenant's solicitors redrafted that clause to read as follows: 'Not assign or part with possession of the maisonette or any part thereof without the previous written consent of the landlord such consent not to be unreasonably withheld.' They sent their amended form of sub-cl (v) back to the landlord's solicitors.

The landlord's solicitors decided not to accept any of the tenant's proposed revision, and so, the parties not having agreed terms, the matter came before the county court judge to settle the terms in accordance with the powers conferred by s 7(1) of the 1954 Act on him.

It is clear, on consideration of the language in s 7(1), that the judge has a discretion, and the exercise of that discretion is a matter for judicial decision without any statutory guidance as to the considerations that are relevant, much less as to any considerations to which the court has to have regard. The county court has therefore to determine the terms so as to do what is fair and just to the best of the court's ability to both parties.

When the matter came before the judge, as it comes also before us, the considerations relevant to the exercise of the judicial discretion had not been considered in any reported authority, though we have the advantage of the judgment of his Honour Judge Herbert delivered in the Westminster County Court on 1 February 1965 in *Lagens Properties Ltd v Bandino* 193 EG 980. It appears from that extremely brief report that the way that the county court judge approached the exercise of his discretion was as follows. He held that neither statute nor authority (of which there was none) gave any direction with regard to terms as to use or the extent to which covenants contained in the long lease should be incorporated in the terms of the statutory tenancy. Whether such covenants should be incorporated was therefore a matter of judicial discretion to do what was fair between the parties and the state of affairs as they existed at the date of the hearing was of primary importance. The judge on the facts of that case continued:

'The house being at the material time occupied as a single family residence, the tenant's intention to use it in the distant future as a source of income should be disregarded, and the statutory tenancy should not incorporate any power to divide or sub-let.'

Judge Herbert so held in spite of the fact that, by the terms of the current lease, that long lease was of a substantial dwelling house with a right to divide and sublet as three separate dwellings. Shortly before the expiry of that lease the whole of the house was in fact converted to single family occupation.

When Judge McDonnell came to deal with the only issue with which this court is concerned, he expressed his decision in the following terms:

'Now I come to the next matter in dispute as to the terms, namely as to subletting or parting with possession of part of the maisonette and, as both counsel recognise, it may not be necessary to contain an express covenant against assigning or underletting the whole of the maisonette because of course if this is a statutory tenancy there is nothing to assign. And it may be that, if there were an underletting of the whole, then the tenant, the respondent, would have no defence to proceedings for possession on the grounds that he is no longer occupying the premises as his home.'

I interpolate, with respect, that there the judge was plainly right, because the statutory right of the tenant under the statutory tenancy is a personal right and if the tenant had unhanded himself of possession of the whole he would have lost any statutory right to be on the premises. The judge went on:

'But it has been urged on me that there should be included a provision entitling him to sublet or part with possession of part of the premises with the written consent of the landlord, such consent not to be unreasonably withheld. Now it seems to me that is not a desirable thing and might indeed be inconsistent with the term in no (iv) of the tenant's covenants not to use the maisonette otherwise than as a private residential dwelling in the occupation of one household only. But [counsel for the tenant] drew my attention to the fact that there was a similar restriction on user otherwise than as a private residential dwelling in the occupation of one household only in no (8) of the tenant's covenants in the old sublease and that the immediately following covenant was not to assign, under-let or part with possession of the maisonette or any part thereof nor to assign the benefit of or part with this underlease without the previous written consent of the landlords, such consent not to be unreasonably withheld in the case of a respectable and responsible tenant or assignee, and then a proviso that the landlords might as a condition of consent to an assignment require the assignee to enter into direct covenants with the landlords. Now it seemed to me that that argument although superficially attractive did not conclude the matter because if the two covenants were to stand together then the tenant might assign or underlet or part with the possession of the whole of the maisonette to someone who was a respectable and responsible person and who would use the maisonette as a private residential dwelling in the occupation of one household only. And I cannot envisage any subletting or parting with possession of part of the maisonette which would be consistent with compliance with the user covenant. And so I shall direct that the statutory tenancy shall contain the simple covenant not to assign or share or underlet or part with possession of the maisonette or part thereof in any way whatsoever.'

In the instant case the judge addressed his attention specifically to the terms of the contractual lease which set the contractual stage for the succeeding situation, namely the statutory tenancy coming into existence pursuant to the 1954 Act. The judge observed that, by the tenant's covenants in the underlease dated 28 October 1957, the lessee entered into a covenant by cl 2(8) not to use the maisonette otherwise than as a private residential dwelling in the occupation of one household only and not to use or permit the same to be used for any trade or business profession whatsoever. By sub-cl (9) of the same clause the tenant entered into a further covenant not to assign, underlet or part with possession of the maisonette or any part thereof nor to assign the benefit of or part with the underlease without the previous written consent of the landlords, such consent not to be unreasonably withheld in the case of a respectable and responsible tenant or assignee.

At first sight there appears to be an inconsistency between the covenants entered into by the lessee not to use the maisonette other than as a private residential dwelling in the occupation of one household only and the provisions of the immediately succeeding covenant which gave him the right to underlet or part with possession of the maisonette or part thereof with the written consent of the landlord, such consent not to be unreasonably withheld.

As a matter of construction it is clearly right to discover and determine the intention

of the parties by reading the covenant in sub-cl (8) together with the terms of the
covenant in the immediately succeeding sub-cl (9). As Harman J expressed it in this court   *a*
in *Dobbs v Linford* [1952] 2 All ER 827 at 830, [1953] 1 QB 48 at 53:

> 'The covenants in a lease must be construed by reference to the covenants which
> follow or precede them. Thus, where a covenant not to use otherwise than as a
> private dwelling-house is followed by a covenant against sub-letting a part without
> consent, one must construe the first by reference to the second, and that is all that
> JENKINS, L.J., was saying in *Downie* v. *Turner* ([1951] 1 All ER 416, [1951] 2 KB 112).   *b*
> It also follows, in my judgment, that, where the covenant to use as a private
> dwelling-house is followed by a covenant not to sub-let the whole, the inference is
> irresistible that there was no need in the second covenant to provide against sub-
> letting of a part, because that was already provided for in the covenant not to use
> otherwise than as a dwelling-house, scilicet, one single dwelling-house.'
>   *c*

The only passage in Judge McDonnell's judgment which the tenant respectfully
criticises is this passage: '. . . I cannot envisage any subletting or parting with possession
of part of the maisonette which would be consistent with compliance with the user
covenant.' Counsel for the tenant out of the wealth of his ingenuity has suggested a
hypothesis which in his submission would have enabled the judge to envisage a subletting
or parting with possession which was consistent with compliance with the user covenant.   *d*
More particularly, he invited the court to consider this hypothesis. Supposing that the
tenant invited a student to come to the premises where he would enjoy the occupation
of a bedroom, also to be used as a study, but to live with the tenant for practical purposes
as part of the family, sitting down at the dining table (or in modern conditions more
probably the kitchen table), and sharing the amenities of the living room, retiring to
sleep and to study to the room which he would solely occupy. That, it is submitted,   *e*
might be, according to the detailed effect, a situation in which the tenant would part
with part of the maisonette, namely the one room which the student used as a bed-sitter,
but it would be consistent with the use of the maisonette as a private residential dwelling
in the occupation of one householder, because the student would have become part of
the household of the tenant.

By such an illustration counsel for the tenant invited this court to take the view that   *f*
the judge was wrong when he said that he could not envisage any subletting or parting
with possession of part of the maisonette which would be consistent with compliance
with the user covenant. He went on to submit that, having regard to the terms of the
1957 lease which specifically prohibited the tenant wholly from parting with possession
of the maisonette or any part thereof without the previous written consent of the
landlords, that having been the state of affairs which regulated the relations between   *g*
landlord and tenant in the antecedent 21 years, as a matter of fairness the judge should
have decided to incorporate in the lease the term for which the tenant was contending in
the exchanges of the travelling draft.

For my part I approach the question of the way in which the statutory discretion
should be exercised very much in the way in which it was expressed by Judge Herbert in
1965 in the Westminster County Court: in the exercise of the judicial discretion the   *h*
court has to do what is fair between the parties and the state of affairs as they exist at the
date of the hearing is of primary importance. One of the obviously material factors in
that state of affairs is the bundle of rights and obligations enjoyed or imposed by landlord
and tenant by the terms of the current lease. But Parliament has deliberately decided, as
may be concluded from the contrast between the terms of s 35 and s 7(1), not to give the
terms of the existing lease any priority in the list of considerations which the court   *j*
should, as a matter of common fairness, take into account in order to determine how to
exercise its discretion.

In the case of a long lease entered into, as this one was in 1957, it does not appear
necessarily obvious that the terms that were appropriate on the grant of the lease in 1957
for a term of 24 years will be the terms that are just and fair between the parties when a

contractual lease comes to an end and is succeeded by a statutory lease granting to the
tenant security of tenure for an unlimited period, the limits of that period themselves
depending on the statutory prescriptions enacted by Parliament from time to time as to
the determination of the statutory tenancy. Thus, looking at the history of the Rent Acts,
at one time the statutory tenancy ended with the death of a tenant. In the later period
the statutory tenancy could be the subject of a succession from a statutory tenant to
specified members of the tenant's family. So from the landlord's point of view he has no
control, once the contractual term has been succeeded by a statutory tenancy, over the
term of the lease.

That is a relevant consideration in considering whether it is just or fair to incorporate
in the statutory terms word for word the terms of the obligations settled by the tenant in
the previous contractual engagement. I would hold that there is no ground for interfering
with the way in which the judge decided to prohibit any subtenancy or parting with
possession. The statutory tenancy is itself contemplated by Parliament as conferring
personal rights on the tenant. There may be situations in which fairness points to the
inclusion of a provision that the tenant may have the right to sublet or part with
possession of part of the premises with the consent of the landlord not to be unreasonably
withheld, but, having regard to the history of the previous relationship between the
parties and the fact that some 24 years later the court had to decide what was just and
fair, I see no reason to hold that the judge wrongly exercised his judicial discretion in
deciding to exclude from the terms of the lease any right to sublet or part with possession
of part of the premises.

As to the illustration that counsel for the tenant gave us of one situation which could
be contemplated as a situation which the judge should have taken into account, it is an
illustration which to my mind would be sufficiently exceptional, unusual and indeed
unlikely. It would be wrong to have regard to such a hypothesis when the parties came
either to attempt to agree the terms of the lease or for the judge to take that hypothesis
into account in determining the terms of the lease. For that reason I would uphold that
part of the judge's order in which he prohibited subletting or parting with possession of
any part of the premises.

Then I come to his decision to prohibit sharing of the premises. The situation seems
to me, with respect to the judge, to be rather different. The reasoning of the judge
appears to have been reasoning in which the judge focused his mind entirely on the
problem of user of a private residential dwelling in the occupation of one household
only. He contrasts the contractual right to underlet or part with possession with the
maisonette or any part thereof, or to assign. Nowhere in that, which is the only relevant
passage of the judge's judgment, is there any examination of the considerations relevant
to the question whether the tenant should have the right of or alternatively be prohibited
from sharing the premises with another or other persons. The explanation of that fact, at
first sight surprising, is I think sufficiently clear when one looks at the history of the
travelling draft.

The landlord's first proposals were 'Not assign or share or underlet or part with
possession of the maisonette or any part thereof . . .' The tenant's solicitors by revision
deleted the words 'or share or underlet' and added the words 'without the previous
written consent of the Landlord such consent not to be unreasonably withheld'. As far as
I can judge, when the judge decided to reject the proposed amendment proffered on
behalf of the tenant, and to prefer the draft first proffered by the landlord's solicitors, he
simply incorporated as the term which he determined in the exercise of his judicial
discretion the words first proposed by the landlord's solicitors, 'Not assign or share or
underlet or part with possession of the maisonette or any part thereof . . .'

But the considerations which moved the judge to decide to prohibit subletting or
parting with possession of part of the maisonette do not seem to me to be material to a
quite different question, which is whether the tenant should be prohibited from sharing
the maisonette. The strong reason against allowing the tenant to sublet or part with
possession of part of the premises, even with the consent of the landlord, is the obvious

risk that that is liable to involve the reversioner on the termination of the statutory
tenancy, because the Rent Acts themselves provide that in certain situations on the
determination of the tenancy a subtenant, where there is one, shall continue to enjoy the
subtenancy, but to do so in privity with the landlord, who had been the head landlord
and the grantor of the lease to the tenant. That seems to me, on the facts of this case, a
strong reason for the exercise of discretion in the way in which the judge exercised it in
relation to subletting or parting with possession with part of the premises.

But when one comes to consider the prohibition against sharing, the first question is:
what does it prohibit? Sharing is not a precise concept. What may begin as what is
regarded as ordinary hospitality to a guest may gradually and by indefinable stages be
recognised at a later date as something which ordinary reasonable people would regard
as sharing. If a tenant is prohibited from sharing, he may be in great difficulty in
deciding when it is safe for him to offer ordinary hospitality to friends or relations. He
may have reason to be anxious, if he has extended hospitality to friends or relations,
whether the time may not have come when a court might take the view that he was now
sharing his maisonette. His guest may be eager to share the expense of the maisonette.
The tenant who is otherwise anxious to accept might well be inhibited from doing so in
case the court might find on the facts that he has committed breach of covenant not to
share. If he is only allowed to share with the written consent of his landlord, a corporate
body in Liechtenstein, who at the moment, we are told, manage the maisonette through
a management agency in London, would he, before he invited anybody to stay in his
house, have to communicate with Liechtenstein or the managing agents and then await
their consent before extending the invitation to a friend or relation to enjoy his hospitality
for a determinate or indeterminate time? In the hands of a ruthless landlord eager to
recover possession, I have no difficulty in envisaging that a prohibition on sharing might
be used as a weapon undermining the security of tenure and the quiet enjoyment of the
tenant. From the tenant's point of view, I would have thought that fairness and justice
suggests that he should be free to share his maisonette with persons of his choice,
whatever those words may mean. From the point of view of the landlord, what is the
prejudice? It was submitted by counsel for the landlord that, if people other than the
tenant and his immediate family are allowed to stay in the maisonette, the landlord will
never know whether the tenant is abusing his position by secretly entering into a sublease
or parting with possession of part of the premises. That submission is fortified by the
concern of the landlord whether he would ever dare to accept rent if he knew that the
tenant was giving hospitality to someone who stayed in the maisonette, because there is
the risk that the tenant, once that situation was accepted, might raise it in court
proceedings for a waiver of a breach of covenant.

I am bound to say that I take the view that anxieties about waiver are far-fetched.
There is only a waiver if there is an acceptance of rent with full knowledge of the
subtenancy, parting of possession or whatever the breach of covenant alleged may be. It
seems to me that there would be no risk at all to the landlord in the court holding that
the acceptance of rent without knowledge of all the relevant facts constituted a breach of
covenant.

Counsel for the landlord also referred to dangers which the landlord might encounter,
having regard to the terms of the headlease which he had decided to negotiate in 1977. I
have considered that submission, but I am unmoved by it.

On a balance of the advantages and prejudices to be gained or suffered by landlord and
tenant respectively in relation to a prohibition on sharing, it seems to me that on the
material before the judge there was no good ground for prohibiting sharing of the
maisonette. No such covenant existed in the contractual lease which regulated the
relationship between landlord and tenant for 22 years. Prohibition on sharing only came
into the matter because it was included in the draft covenant proffered to the tenant by
the landlord's solicitors when the travelling draft started its journey.

I would hold on the facts of this case that there is no reason in justice and fairness to
incorporate in the terms of the statutory lease a prohibition on sharing which was not
contemplated by the parties to the contractual lease when that was entered into. For

those reasons I would hold that this court is entitled, on a review of the discretion of the
a judge, to review the exercise of his discretion when he decided to prohibit sharing, for
the reason that there is nothing in his ratio decidendi that is relevant to the introduction
into the terms of a prohibition on sharing. With respect to the judge it seems to me at
least doubtful whether he really addressed his mind systematically to the relevant
considerations.

Having decided that the court is entitled to review the discretion of the judge, and
b having decided that no good reason is shown by the judge for including the prohibition
on sharing, I would hold that the court should decide in that regard to exercise the
discretion itself and decide what term should be incorporated under s 7(1) in relation to
sharing. On the balance of the relevant considerations I would hold that justice and
fairness does not warrant a prohibition on sharing. I would add that justice and fairness
does not point either to a qualified prohibition on sharing, that is to say a prohibition on
c sharing save with the consent of the landlord, such consent not to be unreasonably
withheld, because of the practical inconveniences in which the tenant might be involved
if it became necessary to make up his mind when he was sharing and then to obtain
consent before the sharing began, and this would be too difficult to reconcile with a quiet
life.

For those reasons I would rule that the judge's order be varied by deleting from the
d relevant clause of the lease the words 'or share'.

SIR DENYS BUCKLEY. I entirely agree with everything that has fallen from the lips
of Cumming-Bruce LJ in the judgment just delivered and put my own position very
shortly.

I see no ground for interfering with the exercise by the trial judge of his discretion to
e omit from cl 6(v) of the terms of the statutory tenancy in this case any exception in
respect of assigning, underletting or parting with possession of the maisonette or any
part thereof with the written consent of the landlord, such consent not to be unreasonably
withheld. The reason stated by the judge in his judgment for so doing appears to me to
justify his exercising his discretion in this respect in the way in which he did.

That reason however seems to have no bearing on the question whether in cl 6(v) of
f the terms there should be included a prohibition against sharing the maisonette. No such
prohibition is to be found in the antecedent underlease dated 28 October 1957. No
argument about this aspect of the case seems to have taken place before the judge. It is
not apparent that he was ever asked to apply his mind to this topic at all.

The genesis of the words 'or share' in cl 6(v) was the draft proposed terms formulated
by the landlord's legal advisers. These words were, amongst others, struck out by the
g tenant's legal advisers, but reinserted by the landlord's advisers. It would seem that the
judge, having decided to exclude any reference to transactions with the landlord's written
consent, simply adopted the clause as originally drafted. The inclusion of the words 'or
share' in the terms of the statutory tenancy would impose a restriction on the tenant to
which he was not previously subject. It should, in my judgment, only be included in the
terms of the statutory tenancy if fairness to the landlord requires its inclusion. I have not
h been satisfied that there is any ground for saying that this prohibition should be included
in fairness to the landlord.

I agree that in these circumstances we should, in the exercise of our own discretion,
delete the words 'or share' from cl 6(v) of the terms, but in other respects we should
affirm the judge's decision.

j *Appeal allowed to limited extent of deleting words 'or share' from judge's order. Tenant's
application for leave to appeal refused.*

Solicitors: *Paisner & Co* (for the tenant); *Lawrence Jones & Co* (for the landlord).

Sophie Craven   Barrister.

Harrington v Roots   *a*

HOUSE OF LORDS
LORD FRASER OF TULLYBELTON, LORD ELWYN-JONES, LORD SCARMAN, LORD ROSKILL AND LORD BRIDGE OF HARWICH
2 MAY, 14 JUNE 1984

Magistrates – Proceedings – Control by judicial review – Magistrates dismissing charge without **b**
giving prosecution opportunity to present case – Magistrates dismissing information because date
of adjournment sought by prosecution not convenient for defence – Prosecutor applying for
certiorari to quash dismissal and mandamus directing justices to hear prosecution evidence against
defendant – Whether on application for judicial review court has power to interfere with
magistrates' dismissal of charge – Whether rehearing of information would place defendant in
double jeopardy – Whether relevant that magistrates acted in breach of rules of natural justice in **c**
acquitting defendant – Magistrates' Courts Act 1980, s 9(2).

The defendant was charged with assaulting a police constable and using threatening
behaviour likely to cause a breach of the peace. On 13 August 1982, the date fixed for
the hearing of the charges, he appeared in a magistrates' court. Both he and the prosecutor
were legally represented. At the start of the hearing the prosecutor applied for an   **d**
adjournment because the constable alleged to have been assaulted was away on holiday.
The defence raised no objection to an adjournment. The magistrates decided to adjourn
the case until 24 August. The defence then asked for an adjournment to another date
because the defendant would himself be away on holiday on 24 August. The magistrates
refused to allocate another date for the hearing of the case and instead, without asking
the prosecution if they were in a position to proceed forthwith, decided to dismiss the   **e**
charges. The prosecutor applied for judicial review of the magistrates' decision by way of
orders of certiorari to quash the decision to dismiss the informations and mandamus to
direct the magistrates to hear the evidence against the defendant. On the hearing of the
application the defendant conceded that the magistrates had acted in breach of natural
justice in dismissing the informations without giving the prosecution an opportunity to
present their case but submitted that the decision to dismiss the informations amounted   **f**
to an acquittal and accordingly was not open to judicial review since to order the charges
to be reheard would be to put the defendant in jeopardy a second time. The Divisional
Court upheld that contention and dismissed the application. The prosecutor appealed to
the House of Lords, where the defendant further contended that the proceedings had
been validly begun once his pleas of not guilty had been taken and that therefore
although the justices had acted improperly they had acted within their jurisdiction and   **g**
the acquittals which followed were not amenable to judicial review.

Held – By dismissing the information without first giving the prosecution an opportunity
to proceed on the basis of the evidence then available to them, the justices had been in
breach of their statutory duty under s 9(2)*[a]* of the Magistrates' Courts Act 1980 to hear
the evidence of the parties. It followed that the dismissal had been without jurisdiction   **h**
and was therefore a nullity. The Divisional Court accordingly had had power to issue
mandamus to remit the matter to the justices for a rehearing. However, since the
magistrates' decision was a nullity it would not have been appropriate to issue certiorari.
The appeal would therefore be allowed, but in the circumstances no other order would
be made (see p 475 *h j*, p 478 *b* to *e*, p 479 *j* to p 480 *a f* to *j*, post).
   Dicta of Lord Campbell CJ and Coleridge J in *R v Brown* (1857) 7 E & B at 761, *R v*   **j**
Marsham, ex p Pethick Lawrence [1911–13] All ER Rep 639 and *R v West* [1962] 2 All ER
624 applied.
   R v Simpson [1914] 1 KB 66 considered.

---

a   Section 9 is set out at p 477 *h j*, post

a Per curiam. (1) For the purposes of the rule against double jeopardy, jeopardy in the relevant sense only arises after a lawful acquittal or a lawful conviction (see p 475 h j, p 479 d e and p 480 h, post); dicta of Lord Sumner in *Crane v DPP* [1921] All ER Rep at 32 and of Lord Devlin in *DPP v Nasralla* [1967] 2 All ER at 166 applied.

(2) An acquittal by justices acting within their jurisdiction will not be susceptible to judicial review merely because the justices acted in breach of the rules of natural justice (see p 475 h j and p 480 e f h, post).

b Decision of the Divisional Court of the Queen's Bench Division sub nom *R v Dorking Justices, ex p Harrington* [1983] 3 All ER 29 reversed.

Notes

For control of justices' proceedings by judicial review, see 11 Halsbury's Laws (4th edn) para 1529 and 29 ibid para 474.

c For the Magistrates' Courts Act 1980, s 9, see 50(2) Halsbury's Statutes (3rd edn) 1451.

Cases referred to in opinions

Crane v DPP [1921] 2 AC 299, [1921] All ER Rep 19, HL.
DPP v Nasralla [1967] 2 All ER 161, [1967] 2 AC 238, [1967] 3 WLR 13, PC.
R v Brown (1857) 7 E & B 757, 119 ER 1427.
R v Marsham, ex p Pethick Lawrence [1912] 2 KB 362, [1911–13] All ER Rep 639, DC.
d *R v Middlesex Justices, ex p DPP* [1952] 2 All ER 312, [1952] 2 QB 758, DC.
R v Simpson [1914] 1 KB 66, DC.
R v West [1962] 2 All ER 624, [1964] 1 QB 15, [1962] 3 WLR 218, CCA.

Appeal

John Alfred Harrington, a police officer, applied, with the leave of McCullough J given e on 10 November 1982, for (1) an order of certiorari to quash an order made by the Dorking justices sitting at Dorking Magistrates' Court on 13 August 1982 that two informations laid against the respondent, Peter Arnold Roots, be dismissed and (2) an order of mandamus requiring the justices to hear the evidence against the respondent. On 20 May 1983 the Divisional Court of the Queen's Bench Division (Robert Goff LJ and Glidewell J) ([1983] 3 All ER 29, [1983] QB 1076) dismissed the application and on 2 f June 1983 refused leave to appeal to the House of Lords but certified, under s 1(2) of the Administration of Justice Act 1960, that a point of law of general public importance (set out at p 476 d, post) was involved in the decision. On 20 October 1983 the Appeal Committee of the House of Lords gave the appellant leave to appeal to the House of Lords. The facts are set out in the opinion of Lord Roskill.

g *Kenneth Zucker QC* and *Howard Vagg* for the appellant.
David Jeffreys QC and *Roger Bull* for the respondent.

Their Lordships took time for consideration.

14 June. The following opinions were delivered.

h **LORD FRASER OF TULLYBELTON.** My Lords, I have had the advantage of reading in draft the speech of my noble and learned friend Lord Roskill, and I agree with it. For the reasons given by him I would allow the appeal and answer the certified question (as amended) in the affirmative.

j **LORD ELWYN-JONES.** My Lords, I have had the advantage of reading in draft the speech prepared by my noble and learned friend Lord Roskill, and for the reasons he has given I would allow the appeal and answer the amended question in the affirmative.

LORD SCARMAN. My Lords, having read in draft the speech to be delivered by my noble and learned friend Lord Roskill, I would for the reasons he gives allow the appeal and answer the amended question in the affirmative.

LORD ROSKILL. My Lords, this appeal by the prosecution arises out of the refusal of the Divisional Court (Robert Goff LJ and Glidewell J) ([1983] 3 All ER 29, [1983] QB 1076) on 20 May 1983 to make an order for judicial review of a decision by the Dorking justices given on 13 August 1982. By that decision those justices purported to dismiss two informations against a man named Peter Arnold Roots. It is apparent from the terms of the leading judgment given by Robert Goff LJ that the Divisional Court reached its conclusion with marked reluctance and only because it felt constrained by authority and indeed to some extent by principle to hold that, notwithstanding that it was common ground that the justices had acted in what was described as a breach of the rules of natural justice, it was not open to the Divisional Court to grant judicial review of their decision in a case where the result of their action was the acquittal of the defendant. Robert Goff LJ said ([1983] 3 All ER 29 at 32, [1983] QB 1076 at 1082):

'We wish to record our disquiet at the anomaly which appears to us to be revealed by the present case in the procedure for reviewing decisions of justices ... It must appear strange to complainants that, when the basis of their case is so serious a matter as a breach of the rules of natural justice, they are bound to adopt a procedure under which, if there has been an acquittal, this court has no power to intervene ... However, that is, as we see it, the effect of the law as it now stands, which we have been bound to apply in the present case.'

The Divisional Court subsequently granted a certificate in the following terms:

'Whether upon the dismissal by Justices of an information as a result of a breach of the rules of natural Justice the Queen's Bench Divisional Court has power upon an application by the Prosecutor for Judicial Review to quash the acquittal and remit the Matter to the Justices for rehearing.'

Leave to appeal was refused by the Divisional Court but was later granted by your Lordships' House.

The relevant facts are simple and can be shortly stated. The first of the two informations charged Roots with assaulting a police office named Lane in the execution of Lane's duty, the alleged assault having taken place at Dorking on 2 July 1982. The second charged Roots with an offence against s 5 of the Public Order Act 1936. There were four other defendants similarly charged but seemingly only the case of Roots was dealt with on the occasion now complained of. Your Lordships were told by counsel that the other four defendants had in due course been convicted and sentenced.

The charges against Roots came on for hearing before the justices on 13 August 1982. There was thus no undue delay between the date of the alleged offences and their hearing. At the present time some five weeks' delay is by no means excessive. Both the prosecution and Roots were legally represented. At the outset of the proceedings counsel for the prosecution sought an adjournment since Lane was then on annual leave. Both Roots's counsel and the court had been previously told that such an application would be made. No objection was offered on Roots's behalf. The justices retired and then decided to adjourn the case against Roots until 24 August 1982. But Roots had already booked his holiday over a period which included that date and naturally did not wish to postpone it. The Divisional Court was informed that the justices had already been apprised of that fact before they retired. Counsel for Roots thereupon asked for another date. The justices refused this request. Counsel very properly pressed his submission on Roots's behalf, pointing out that Roots was entitled to the same treatment as had been accorded to the prosecution in respect of Lane's holiday. Counsel for the prosecution did not oppose this request.

The chairman of the justices apparently then said that the justices were in a difficult position 'and for that reason had decided the case should be dismissed'. Counsel for the prosecution then asked the justices to reconsider their decision. At no time did he tell the justices that he could not proceed then and there. Indeed, he had available another witness to the alleged assault. He pointed out, entirely correctly, that if the justices had

refused the adjournment sought it was their duty to inform the prosecution of that fact
and then let the prosecution decide what line the prosecution would take, whether to
proceed then and there on the available evidence or to offer no evidence.

The justices again retired and, after apparently seeking advice from a 'senior clerk' in
another court, returned to court to announce that their decision must stand. It was in
these circumstances that the prosecution not surprisingly sought judicial review of the
decision.

My Lords, no explanation has been vouchsafed of the reasons for what can only be
regarded as this remarkable action by the justices. No doubt they were not obliged to
give any explanation or to reveal what advice they had been given if they did not wish to
do so. But, in the absence of some explanation (none is readily apparent), it is clear that
their action was both wrong and unjudicial.

As I have already stated it was conceded below that the rules of natural justice had not
been complied with and indeed that phrase is used in the certificate which I have already
quoted. It would seem from the judgment of Robert Goff LJ that in the Divisional Court
the case was argued solely on the basis that a failure to comply with the rules of natural
justice was the relevant consideration. As will later emerge I am of the opinion that such
a failure is not the relevant consideration. It is however clear, and no one has suggested
otherwise, that the action of the justices cannot be supported.

The sole question for your Lordships' House now to determine is whether on the facts
I have summarised the Divisional Court had power to grant judicial review. It is apparent
that if it had felt able to do so it would have granted the relief sought. Counsel for the
appellant prosecutor made it plain that, if the House were to allow this appeal, the
prosecution would not, after the lapse of time since the alleged offences, now seek for the
case to be remitted to the Divisional Court for an order of mandamus to be issued to the
justices to hear and determine the informations according to law. He said that the matter
was brought to this House as one of principle only. No further proceedings against Roots
were contemplated.

My Lords, stated briefly, the argument which prevailed below was that the dimissal of
the informations amounted to acquittals on both charges, that an acquittal was not open
to judicial review since to order the charges to be reheard would be to put Roots in
jeopardy a second time and that to do so was contrary both to principle and to the
authorities cited in the judgment of Robert Goff LJ. Before your Lordships it was also
strongly urged for Roots that the procedings against him had been validly begun once
his pleas of not guilty had been taken, as they were, and that although the justices had
subsequently acted improperly it was within their jurisdiction to do that which they did,
that acquittals followed and that those acquittals were not now amenable to judicial
review.

My Lords, the jurisdiction of a magistrates' court is founded on statute. It is to the
relevant statutory provisions that I now turn in order to consider whether or not the
justices acted within or without their statutory duty. These provisions do not appear to
have been drawn to the attention of the Divisional Court: they are not referred to in the
judgment of Robert Goff LJ. They are to be found in the Magistrates' Courts Act 1980.
Section 9 appears under the cross-heading 'Summary trial of information' and reads:

'(1) On the summary trial of an information, the court shall, if the accused
appears, state to him the substance of the information and ask him whether he
pleads guilty or not guilty.

(2) The court, after hearing the evidence of the parties, shall convict the accused
or dismiss the information.

(3) If the accused pleads guilty, the court may convict him without hearing
evidence.'

Section 10(1) reads:

'A magistrates' court may at any time, whether before or after beginning to try an information, adjourn the trial, and may do so, notwithstanding anything in this Act, when composed of a single justice.'

Section 15(1) reads:

'Where at the time and place appointed for the trial or adjourned trial of an information the accused appears or is brought before the court and the prosecutor does not appear, the court may dismiss the information or, if evidence has been received on a previous occasion, proceed in the absence of the prosecutor.'

Identical provisions were respectively contained in ss 13(1), (2) and (3), 14(1) and 16(1) of the Magistrates' Courts Act 1952, the immediate precursor of the 1980 Act.

There is no doubt that the provisions of s 9(1) were complied with. But to my mind there is equally no doubt that the provisions of s 9(2) were not. Reading ss 9(2), 10(1) and 15(1) together it is clear that, when the prosecutor is present and has evidence available which he desires to call, the justices, if they refuse any application for an adjournment, must give the prosecutor the opportunity of calling that evidence if he so wishes, must then hear that evidence when called and of course also hear the parties and then adjudicate on all that evidence. They cannot dismiss any information until after they have heard the parties and whatever evidence the parties may properly lay before them, save of course where no evidence is tendered by the prosecution. In acting as they did these justices acted in breach of their statutory duty under s 9(2). Once they decided to refuse the adjournment, it was their duty to invite the prosecution to proceed on the basis of the evidence then available to them. Counsel for the prosecution was, as already stated, entirely right in inviting the justices to take that course. The justices were in grave error, first, in dismissing the information out of hand and, second, in adhering to that decision when invited to depart from it.

What then are the consequences of this failure to comply with their statutory duty? The problem is not novel, as many of the cases cited in argument before your Lordships, but seemingly not before the Divisional Court, show. I shall refer only to a few. In *R v Brown* (1857) 7 E & B 757, 119 ER 1427 a defendant was charged on an information alleging a colliery offence in his capacity as an owner and manager of a colliery. Before the justices the point was taken that as there were other owners and managers the defendant could not properly be charged unless those others were also charged. The justices accepted this submission and dismissed the information on this ground. The prosecution sought and obtained an order of mandamus against the justices to hear and determine the information. The matter was heard before the Court of Queen's Bench, consisting of Lord Campbell CJ, Coleridge, Erle and Crompton JJ. Lord Campbell CJ said (7 E & B 757 at 761, 119 ER 1427 at 1429):

'The objection taken was a preliminary objection, that the proper parties were not before the Court. To uphold that objection is not to exercise jurisdiction, but to decline it. The mandamus therefore should go.'

Coleridge J said: 'It appears to me that the duty of adjudging has been declined.' Thus mandamus was issued, notwithstanding that before the justices the defendant had been acquitted. It was never suggested that because the dismissal was an acquittal it was wrong to issue mandamus or that the effect of so doing was to place the defendant in jeopardy a second time following that acquittal.

My Lords, there are other cases where initial proceedings had been held to be nullities so as not to prevent further proceedings on the same charge. *R v Marsham, ex p Pethick Lawrence* [1912] 2 KB 362, [1911–13] All ER Rep 639 is such a case. The initial conviction was a nullity because the main prosecution witness had been inadvertently allowed to give his evidence unsworn. On the second hearing, a further conviction followed. It was sought to quash that conviction. The Divisional Court emphatically rejected the argument that the defendant had been in jeopardy on the first occasion since on that first occasion she had never been 'legally convicted or legally acquitted' (see [1912] 2 KB 362 at 365, [1911–13] All ER Rep 639 at 640–641 per Avory J). It is true that in the same case Lord Alverstone CJ said (obiter) that very different considerations would have arisen had

there been an acquittal on the first occasion. But the Lord Chief Justice did not state what
a those very different considerations were and in argument before your Lordships counsel
were unable to suggest any. Indeed, this statement is with respect inconsistent with the
passage in the judgment of Avory J to which I have referred.

R v West [1962] 2 All ER 624, [1964] 1 QB 15 is another such case. There justices had
tried summarily and dismissed an information which they had no jurisdiction to try
since the offence in question was not triable summarily but only on indictment. The
b defendant was later indicted for the same offence and convicted. His conviction was
upheld in the Court of Criminal Appeal on the ground that the initial acquittal had been
a nullity (see the judgment of the Court of Criminal Appeal delivered by Streatfeild J
[1962] 2 All ER 624 at 630–632, [1964] 1 QB 15 at 27–30). No doubt in some cases the
distinction between actions by justices which are without jurisdiction and thus a nullity
and actions which are an erroneous exercise of jurisdiction may be fine. Thus in *R v
c Simpson* [1914] 1 KB 66 the defendants were acquitted by two justices one of whom was
unqualified to sit in the absence of a consent which had been neither sought nor given.
The prosecution sought certiorari to quash the acquittal and this was refused by the
Divisional Court. But the decision appears to have proceeded on the basis that the
acquittal in question was not a nullity.

My Lords, in view of the observation regarding jeopardy in the judgment of Robert
d Goff LJ, it is necessary to point out, as is indeed plain from the judgment of Avory J
already cited, that an accused person is not, in the context of a plea of autrefois convict or
autrefois acquit, in jeopardy merely because that person is standing trial on a particular
charge and in a popular sense is in jeopardy as being in peril of conviction. Jeopardy in
the relevant sense only arises after a lawful acquittal or a lawful conviction. I cannot do
better than refer to the opinion of the Judicial Committee of the Privy Council delivered
e by Lord Devlin in *DPP v Nasralla* [1967] 2 All ER 161 at 166, [1967] 2 AC 238 at 249–
250 where he said:

> '... but if the rule against double jeopardy and the principles of autrefois are to
> produce the same result, the word "peril" must be given a more restricted meaning.
> It is true that the object of the plea of autrefois is to ensure that a man is not placed
> in double jeopardy. It is true also that as a general rule, i.e., whenever the trial of an
> *f* offence is concluded as it usually is, it is right to say that the accused must not be put
> in jeopardy again. But what is essential to the plea of autrefois is proof of a verdict
> of acquittal of the offence alleged—not proof that the accused was in peril of
> conviction for that offence ...'

Lord Sumner in *Crane v DPP* [1921] 2 AC 299 at 332, [1921] All ER Rep 19 at 32 said, in
g a venire de novo case:

> 'Acquittal implies that a true legal trial has been had. Here there has legally been
> none at all, but only the semblance of one, a mis-trial, which does not count.'

Finally, I refer to Short and Mellor *The Practice of the Crown Office* (2nd edn, 1908)
p 206. In the chapter dealing with mandamus the authors, after setting out the
h circumstances in which mandamus will not issue to justices, say:

> 'The applicant must clearly show that the justices have refused and declined
> jurisdiction. What amounts to a refusal of jurisdiction is often a difficult matter to
> decide ... Whether a magistrate has come to a right conclusion or not, either on the
> law or the facts, cannot be inquired into on mandamus, but only whether he has
> adjudicated; but it must be an adjudication within his jurisdiction and according to
> *j* law.'

My Lords, I am clearly of the view that what happened in the instant case was, to adapt
Lord Sumner's phrase, no trial at all. The dismissal of these informations was without
jurisdiction and was a nullity. To borrow the phrase of Coleridge J in *Brown's* case (1857)
7 E & B 757 at 761, 119 ER 1427 at 1429, the duty of adjudging was declined. Both on
principle and authority I see no reason why, had the prosecution sought to take the

matter further, mandamus should not have issued to the justices directing them to hear and determine these informations according to law. Since in my view their orders were a nullity I do not think that it would have been right to order certiorari to issue as well. But as the prosecution seek no more than that this appeal should be allowed I would propose that no other substantive order should now be made.

My Lords, I ought in conclusion to refer to *R v Middlesex Justices, ex p DPP* [1952] 2 All ER 312, [1952] 2 QB 758, a case much relied on in the court below. For my part, with great respect, I do not think that that decision of an exceptionally strong five-judge Divisional Court assists in deciding the present appeal. The trial there in question was on indictment at quarter sessions and not summary before justices. That trial had begun. Pleas had been taken. There was jurisdiction to try the offence charged. Prosecuting counsel had opened the case for the prosecution to the jury before the chairman most improperly intervened and directed the jury to return a verdict of not guilty. Quite apart from the fact that the trial was on indictment, I do not see how it could have been said that what happened was a nullity. It was a case of a chairman of quarter sessions acting within his jurisdiction giving a direction to a jury which was as improper as it was erroneous. But I do not find it necessary to consider that case further since the provisions of s 10 of the Courts Act 1971 (and now ss 28(1) and (2) and 29(3) of the Supreme Court Act 1981) make it impossible today for the High Court to review the jurisdiction of the Crown Court in matters relating to trials on indictment, whatever the precise limits of the supervisory jurisdiction of the High Court over courts of quarter sessions may have been before their abolition in 1971.

My Lords, I have already at the outset of this speech drawn attention to the use of the phrase 'breach of the rules of natural justice' in the judgment of Robert Goff LJ and in the certificate and I have already indicated that I did not think that such a breach was for present purposes the relevant consideration. My reasons for so thinking will now be apparent. It is not difficult to visualise a case, though I hope it would be extremely rare, where justices acting within their jurisdiction nevertheless acted so unfairly that they could properly be said to be acting in breach of the rules of natural justice. I would not wish it to be thought in such a case that, if an acquittal followed, that acquittal was for that reason alone necessarily susceptible to judicial review. In my view the test is not breach of the rules of natural justice but whether the decision of the justices to dismiss an information is a decision which they had no jurisdiction to take because they were declining to adjudicate on a matter on which it was their duty to adjudicate and thus was a nullity. On this basis, to raise the correct question the certificate should be treated as amended so that it reads: 'Whether, on the dismissal by the justices of an information after they have failed or refused to adjudicate thereupon by declining to receive the evidence desired to be led by the prosecution, the Queen's Bench Divisional Court has power on an application by the prosecutor for judicial review to quash the acquittal and remit the matter to the justices for rehearing.' My Lords, I would answer that amended question in the affirmative on the ground that that dismissal was a nullity (save that in most such cases I do not think it would be necessary for certiorari to issue as well as mandamus).

I would allow this appeal accordingly. I understand all your Lordships agree that the costs of both parties should be paid out of central funds.

LORD BRIDGE OF HARWICH. My Lords, for the reasons given in the speech of my noble and learned friend Lord Roskill, with which I agree, I would allow the appeal and answer the certified question (as amended) in the affirmative.

Appeal allowed.

Solicitors: *Wontner & Sons* (for the appellant); *Downs*, Dorking (for the respondent).

Mary Rose Plummer   Barrister.

R v Secretary of State for the Home Department, ex parte Dannenberg

COURT OF APPEAL, CIVIL DIVISION
DUNN, O'CONNOR AND PARKER LJJ
21 FEBRUARY, 6 MARCH 1984

Criminal law – Appeal – Criminal cause or matter – Decision of Divisional Court – Appeal to Court of Appeal – Appeal against refusal of Divisional Court to quash recommendation for deportation made by magistrates' court following conviction of criminal offence – Whether decision of Divisional Court a judgment in a 'criminal cause or matter' – Whether appeal lying to Court of Appeal – Immigration Act 1971, s 6 – Supreme Court Act 1981, s 18(1)(a).

European Economic Community – Freedom of movement – Restrictions justified on grounds of public policy, public security or public health – Expulsion of EEC national following conviction of criminal offence – Court imposing sentence recommending deportation of defendant – Validity of recommendation – Reasons for recommendation – Court recommending deportation required to give reasons – Mode of giving reasons – Crown Court – Magistrates' courts – EEC Council Directive 64/221, arts 6, 9(1).

A refusal by the Divisional Court to quash a recommendation made by a magistrates' court under s 6[a] of the Immigration Act 1971 for the deportation of a person who has been convicted of an offence constitutes a 'judgment of the High Court in [a] criminal cause or matter' within s 18(1)(a)[b] of the Supreme Court Act 1981 and accordingly no appeal lies to the Court of Appeal against such a refusal (see p 483 e f and p 484 a j to p 485 d, post); dictum of Lord Wright in *Amand v Secretary of State for Home Affairs* [1942] 2 All ER at 388 applied; *R v Southampton Justices, ex p Green* [1975] 2 All ER 1073, *R v Crown Court at Sheffield, ex p Brownlow* [1980] 2 All ER 444 and *R v Stipendiary Magistrate at Lambeth, ex p McComb* [1983] 1 All ER 321 distinguished.

The Crown Court or a magistrates' court, when recommending the deportation from England of a national of a member state of the EEC who has been convicted of an offence, must give its reasons in order to comply with arts 6[c] and 9(1)[d] of EEC Council Directive 64/221. In the case of a recommendation for deportation made by the Crown Court a copy of the transcript of the judge's sentencing remarks, including his reasons for making the recommendation, is sufficient to constitute a valid 'opinion' within art 9(1). In the case of a recommendation made by a magistrates' court a brief statement of the reasons will suffice; the statement need not necessarily be made in open court but it should be committed to writing and signed by the magistrates (see p 487 c to f and p 488 c to e, post); dicta of the Court of Justice of the European Communities and of Donaldson LJ in *R v Secretary of State for the Home Dept, ex p Santillo* [1981] 2 All ER at 911–912, 916 applied.

---

a   Section 6, so far as material, provides:
'(1) Where ... a person convicted of an offence is liable to deportation on the recommendation of a court, he may be recommended for deportation by any court having power to sentence him for the offence ...
(5) Where a court recommends or purports to recommend a person for deportation, the validity of the recommendation shall not be called in question except on an appeal against the recommendation or against the conviction on which is made; but—(a) ... the recommendation shall be treated as a sentence for the purpose of any enactment providing an appeal against sentence ...'

b   Section 18(1), so far as material, provides: 'No appeal shall lie to the Court of Appeal—(a) ... from any judgment of the High Court in any criminal cause or matter ...'

c   Article 6 is set out at p 485 j, post

d   Article 9(1) is set out at p 485 j to p 486 a, post

Notes

For appeals from the Divisional Court to the Court of Appeal, see 37 Halsbury's Laws *a*
(4th edn) paras 661, 681.

For what constitutes a criminal cause or matter, see 11 ibid para 1505, and for cases on
the subject, see 14(2) Digest (Reissue) 757–761, 6312–6346.

For the deportation of non-patrials, see 4 Halsbury's Laws (4th edn) para 1011, and for
cases on the subject, see 2 Digest (Reissue) 208–214, 1177–1224.

For the Immigration Act 1971, s 6, see 41 Halsbury's Statutes (3rd edn) 25.   *b*

For the Supreme Court Act 1981, s 18, see 51 ibid 608.

For EEC Council Directive 64/221, arts 6, 9, see 42A ibid 132.

Cases referred to in judgment

Amand v Secretary of State for Home Affairs [1942] 2 All ER 381, [1943] AC 147, HL.

R v Crown Court at Sheffield, ex p Brownlow [1980] 2 All ER 444, [1980] QB 530, [1980] 2   *c*
WLR 892, CA.

R v Nazari [1980] 3 All ER 880, [1980] 1 WLR 1366, CA.

R v Secretary of State for the Home Dept, ex p Santillo [1981] 2 All ER 897, [1981] QB 778,
[1981] 2 WLR 362, CJEC, DC and CA.

R v Southampton Justices, ex p Green [1975] 2 All ER 1073, [1976] QB 11, [1975] 3 WLR
277, CA.   *d*

R v Stipendiary Magistrate at Lambeth, ex p McComb [1983] 1 All ER 321, [1983] QB 551,
[1983] 2 WLR 259, DC and CA.

Appeal

The applicant, Henry Knull Dannenburg, appealed against the decision of the Divisional
Court of the Queen's Bench Division (McNeill and McCullough JJ) on 29 September   *e*
1983 dismissing his application for judicial review by way of orders of certiorari to
remove into the High Court and quash a recommendation for his deportation made on
19 May 1983 by the Mid-Sussex Magistrates' Court and a deportation order made on 30
June 1983 by the Secretary of State for the Home Department. The facts are set out in
the judgment of the court.

          f

Alan Newman for the applicant.
David Latham for the Secretary of State.

                                        Cur adv vult

6 March. The following judgment of the court was delivered.   *g*

DUNN LJ. This is an appeal from a judgment of the Divisional Court given on 29
September 1983 whereby the court dismissed applications for judicial review, made with
leave, for orders of certiorari to remove into the High Court and quash a deportation
order made by the Home Secretary on 30 June 1983 and a recommendation for
deportation made by the Mid-Sussex magistrates on 19 May 1983. The principal ground   *h*
of the application to the Divisional Court was that the magistrates, in making the
recommendation, did not give any reasons, contrary to the provisions of EEC Council
Directive 64/221 of 25 February 1964, as interpreted by the Court of Justice of the
European Communities in *R v Secretary of State for the Home Dept, ex Santillo* [1981] 2 All
ER 897, [1981] QB 778.

We take the facts from the judgment of the Divisional Court which was in the   *j*
following terms:

'The applicant is a citizen of the Federal Republic of Germany. He came to this
country in July 1981 and was given temporary permission to enter and stay. On a
date in 1982 he was given a resident's permit for a period of five years. On 29 April

a   1983 the applicant appeared before the Mid-Sussex Magistrates' Court, sitting at
Haywards Heath, charged with seven offences. Four of those offences required his
consent to summary trial. He gave that consent, and to those four offences and the
three other offences he entered pleas of guilty. The justices then adjourned the
matter. The matter next came before the justices on 19 May, 1983. By that time, in
addition to considering sentence, the justices had before them a notice which had
been given to the applicant not less than seven days previously, pursuant to s 6(2) of
b   the Immigration Act 1971, to the effect that they would be invited to consider
whether or not they should make a recommendation for the deportation of the
applicant. The justices sentenced the applicant in respect of the seven offences and
made a recommendation pursuant to s 6(1) of the 1971 Act. The applicant himself
was present at both hearings; he was represented by a solicitor. The material before
the justices, having regard to the fact that pleas of guilty had been entered, was as
c   follows: an outline of the relevant facts in relation to each charge by the prosecuting
solicitor; the applicant's antecedent history, including a list of his previous
convictions both in this country and in Germany; a social inquiry report on the
applicant; and the evidence of the immigration officer. The justices were addressed
by the applicants' solicitor, as he thought fit, in respect of those various matters
which the justices had to consider. The justices passed the sentence and made the
d   recommendation to which I have referred. Pursuant to that recommendation, the
applicant was ordered to be detained until the Secretary of State considered the
recommendation. In due course the Secretary of State did consider it and, on 30
June 1983, he made a deportation order under s 5(1) of the 1971 Act, the applicant
having become liable for that course by virtue of s 3(6). Thereafter, in pursuance of
the contents of that order, he was detained until removal.'

e   Neither the justices nor the Home Secretary gave any reasons for the recommendation
or the deportation order.
In this court counsel for the Secretary of State submitted that the court had no
jurisdiction to consider an appeal from the refusal of the Divisional Court to quash the
recommendation, because such a refusal constituted a judgment of the High Court in a
f   'criminal cause or matter', so that no appeal lay to this court by reason of s 18(1)(a) of the
Supreme Court Act 1981.
Section 6(5) of the Immigration Act 1971 provides that, where a court recommends a
person for deportation, the recommendation shall not be called in question except on an
appeal against the recommendation or against the conviction for which it is made, but
the recommendation shall be treated as a sentence for the purpose of any enactment
g   providing an appeal against sentence. Section 50(1) of the Criminal Appeal Act 1968
provides that the word 'sentence', in relation to an offence, includes a recommendation
for deportation. (See also s 47(7) of the 1981 Act.) Schedule 3 to the 1971 Act, as amended
by s 64 of and Sch 10 to the Criminal Justice Act 1982, gives power to detain a person
recommended for deportation pending the making of a deportation order.
For many years the test to be applied in deciding whether or not a judgment was given
h   in a criminal cause or matter was thought to have been settled by the House of Lords in
Amand v Secretary of State for Home Affairs [1942] 2 All ER 381, [1943] AC 147. Lord
Wright said ([1942] 2 All ER 381 at 388, [1943] AC 147 at 162):

i   'The principle which I deduce from the authorities which I have cited and the
other relevant authorities which I have considered, is that if the cause or matter is
one which, if carried to its conclusion, might result in the conviction of the person
charged and in a sentence of some punishment, such as imprisonment or fine, it is a
criminal cause or matter. The person charged is thus put in jeopardy. Every order
made in such a cause or matter by an English court, is an order in a criminal cause
or matter, even though the order, taken by itself, is neutral in character and might
equally have been made of a cause or matter which is not criminal.'

This test involves looking at the order under review, and if it was made in the course of criminal proceedings then it is a 'criminal cause or matter'. If that test is applied in this case, it is clear that the refusal to quash the recommendation was made in a criminal cause or matter. The recommendation was made in criminal proceedings following a conviction and, for the purpose of appeal, was to be treated as part of the sentence.

However, since *Amand's* case, there have been a number of decisions of this court which it is said suggest that the test is a different one. In *R v Southampton Justices, ex p Green* [1975] 2 All ER 1073, [1976] QB 11 this court held that an appeal from a decision of justices to estreat a recognisance was not a criminal cause or matter. In that case, although Lord Denning MR looked at the application to estreat and not at the order of the High Court, he applied the test suggested by Viscount Simon LC in *Amand's* case [1942] 2 All ER 381 at 385, [1943] AC 147 at 156, saying ([1975] 2 All ER 1073 at 1076, [1976] QB 11 at 15):

'If the matter is one the direct outcome of which may be trial of the applicant and his possible punishment for an alleged offence by a court claiming jurisdiction to do so, the matter is criminal.'

Lord Denning MR held that the outcome of the application to estreat was not a trial of the surety: there was no possible punishment, and he treated the application as being a civil proceeding separate from the criminal proceedings in which the recognisance had been given.

In *R v Crown Court at Sheffield, ex p Brownlow* [1980] 2 All ER 444, [1980] QB 530 this court held by a majority (Lord Denning MR dissenting) that the Divisional Court had no jurisdiction to consider an application to quash a judge's order in the Crown Court, that the chief constable be supplied with a copy of the panel of jurors and that he should supply to the solicitors for the defence and prosecution full particulars of any criminal convictions recorded against any member of the panel. The decision turned on s 10(1) and (5) of the Courts Act 1971, and the majority held that the judge's order was a matter in relation to a trial on indictment. Lord Denning MR held that this court had jurisdiction to entertain an appeal, since the judge's order was not made in a criminal cause or matter (see [1980] 2 All ER 444 at 449–450, [1980] QB 530 at 537). He once again went back to the order itself and, applying the same test as he had applied in *R v Southampton Justices, ex p Green*, treated the order as being a separate matter from the trial of the accused, the application not giving rise to a trial of the chief constable leading to punishment. Shaw LJ expressed the view that, while the order was ancillary and collateral to a criminal cause or matter, it might not fall within the scope of such matters (see [1980] 2 All ER 444 at 454, [1980] QB 530 at 543). Brandon LJ expressed no concluded view (see [1980] 2 All ER 444 at 456, [1980] QB 530 at 546).

In *R v Stipendiary Magistrate at Lambeth, ex p McComb* [1983] 1 All ER 321, [1983] QB 551 the Divisional Court refused an application for a declaration against the Director of Public Prosecutions with regard to the release of certain exhibits in committal proceedings pending against the applicant.

Sir John Donaldson MR followed *R v Southampton Justices, ex p Green* [1975] 2 All ER 1073, [1976] QB 11 and described the test as being 'whether the order sought to be reviewed was itself criminal in the sense that it was one which could lead to a trial or punishment' (see [1983] 1 All ER 321 at 329, [1983] QB 551 at 563). Applying that test, he held that this court had jurisdiction to entertain an appeal. May LJ also felt bound to apply the test in *R v Southampton Justices, ex p Green*, although doubting whether it was correct and preferring the approach of Lord Wright in *Amand's* case [1942] 2 All ER 381 at 387, [1943] AC 147 at 160 (see [1983] 1 All ER 321 at 332, [1983] QB 551 at 567.)

Counsel for the applicant submitted in this court that a recommendation for deportation could lead to a trial or punishment and so was not a criminal cause or matter. Its only consequences were that a deportation order might be made by the Home Secretary and the person concerned returned to his own country.

We cannot accept that submission. A recommendation for deportation falls squarely

within the principle enunciated by Lord Wright in *Amand*'s case. It cannot be regarded
a as separate from the criminal proceedings, as were the application to estreat the
recognisance in *R v Southampton Justices, ex p Green* [1975] 2 All ER 1073, [1976] QB 11,
or the judge's order against the chief constable in *R v Crown Court at Sheffield, ex p
Brownlow* [1980] 2 All ER 444, [1980] QB 530, and the instant case is distinguishable
from *R v Stipendiary Magistrate at Lambeth, ex p McComb* [1983] 1 All ER 321, [1983] QB
551 where there had been no order at all and the court was considering an application for
b a declaration as to the rights and duties of the Director of Public Prosecutions, which
were quite separate from the criminal proceedings themselves.

The statutory provisions to which we have referred show that a recommendation for
deportation forms an integral part of the criminal proceedings in which it is made and
may result in the detention of the person concerned pending the making of a deportation
order. It is not possible to separate the recommendation from the conviction which
c necessarily precedes it, the sentence of which it is to be treated as part for the purpose of
appeal, or the right of appeal to the Court of Appeal, Criminal Division. Moreover, the
validity of a recommendation cannot be called in question except on such an appeal. In
those circumstances we hold that the refusal of the Divisional Court to quash the
recommendation was made in a criminal cause or a matter, and that no appeal against
that refusal lies to this court. This ruling does not affect the substance of the appeal, since
d the applicant is still entitled to say that the deportation order was invalid because the
recommendation was made without reasons.

The merits of the appeal fall into a comparatively small compass. Article 48 of the
EEC Treaty provides that freedom of movement for workers shall be secured within the
Community and shall entail the right, subject to limitations justified on, inter alia,
grounds of public policy, to stay in a member state for the purpose of employment in
e accordance with the provisions governing the employment of nationals of that state.

EEC Council Directive 64/221 of 25 February 1964, the provisions of which are
enforceable by nationals of member states, provides for 'the co-ordination of special
measures concerning the movement and residence of foreign nationals which are justified
on grounds of public policy' etc. The relevant articles are as follows:

f 'Article 1
   1. The provisions of this Directive shall apply to any national of a Member State
   who resides in or travels to another Member State of the Community, either in
   order to pursue an activity as an employed or self-employed person, or as a recipient
   of services . . .

Article 2
   1. This Directive relates to all measures concerning entry into their territory,
g issue or renewal of residence permits, or expulsion from their territory, taken by
   Member States on grounds of public policy, public security or public health . . .

Article 3
   1. Measures taken on grounds of public policy or of public security shall be based
h exclusively on the personal conduct of the individual concerned.
   2. Previous criminal convictions shall not in themselves constitute grounds for
   the taking of such measures . . .

Article 6
   The person concerned shall be informed of the grounds of public policy, public
   security, or public health upon which the decision taken in his case is based, unless
i this is contrary to the interests of the security of the State involved . . .

Article 9
   1. Where there is no right of appeal to a court of law, or where such appeal may
   be only in respect of the legal validity of the decision, or where the appeal cannot
   have suspensory effect, a decision refusing renewal of a residence permit or ordering

the expulsion of the holder of a residence permit from the territory shall not be
taken by the administrative authority, save in cases of urgency, until an opinion has
been obtained from a competent authority of the host country before which the
person concerned enjoys such rights of defence and of assistance or representation as
the domestic law of that country provides for. This authority shall not be the same
as that empowered to take the decision refusing renewal of the residence permit or
ordering expulsion . . .'

The difficulty is to reconcile the procedure for the co-ordination of special measures
concerning the movement of foreign nationals on grounds of public policy provided by
EEC Council Directive 64/221, which, by reason of s 2 of the European Communities
Act 1972, is part of the law of this country with the procedure for the deportation of
aliens under the Immigration Act 1971. It was common ground in this court and in the
Divisional Court that an English court of competent jurisdiction, whether the Crown
Court or, as in this case, a magistrates' court, constituted a 'competent authority' within
the meaning of art 9 of the directive and that a recommendation for deportation may
constitute an 'opinion' obtained from such authority, although the applicant asserted that
the recommendation, to be a valid 'opinion' under art 9, must give reasons. The only
question in dispute, therefore, was whether and to what extent the recommending court
was required by the directive to give reasons for its recommendation.

The Divisional Court held that the magistrates were under no obligation to give any
reasons. They relied on the judgment of the Court of Justice of the European
Communities in *R v Secretary of State for the Home Dept, ex p Santillo* [1981] 2 All ER 897
esp at 911, where it said:

'The requirement contained in art 9(1) that any decision ordering expulsion must
be preceded by the opinion of a "competent authority" . . . can only constitute a real
safeguard . . . if both the administration and the person concerned are in a position
to take cognisance of the reasons which led the "competent authority" to give its
opinion . . .'

The Divisional Court held:

'In the present case, neither the Secretary of State nor the applicant could have
had the slightest doubt about the material on which the justices acted. They were
both, to use the European Court's words, "in a position to take cognisance of the
reasons which led the 'competent authority' to give its opinion". The facts were not
disputed. There was material relating to the applicant's conviction, his previous
record, the social inquiry report on him and such material as there was (we have no
information about this) arising out of any evidence given by the immigration
officer. In addition, there was the material supplied by the applicant's own solicitor
in such submissions as he thought fit to make to the justices. At the end of the day,
it is difficult to see, on uncontested material of that sort, what the justices could have
said beyond stating that they would make a recommendation. The simple question
for them was, "On the uncontested material before us, do we or do we not make a
recommendation?" and that is what they did.'

Accordingly, the Divisional Court dismissed the application.

We consider whether the conclusion of the Divisional Court was correct, firstly, by
looking at the EEC Council directive itself, without regard to the judgment of the
European Court in *R v Secretary of State for the Home Dept, ex p Santillo*. The directive,
taken as a whole, limits or restricts the rights of freedom of movement for workers
required to be secured by art 48 of the EEC Treaty. Such restriction can, by art 3 only, be
based on the personal conduct of the individual concerned. The procedure under art 9
envisages that, where, as in this country, the only recourse to the courts as to the validity
of a decision to expel is as to the legal validity of the decision, then no such decision shall
be taken by the administrative authority 'until an opinion has been obtained from a

competent authority'. The primary purpose of the 'opinion' appears to be to inform the

a administrative authority of the view of the competent authority. Taken on its own, the word 'opinion' could mean no more than 'conclusion', but art 6 provides that the person concerned shall be informed by the administrative authority of the grounds of public policy on which the decision to expel is based, and, if no reasons are given by the competent authority, the administrative authority will not know the grounds on which the opinion is given and will be obliged to consider its own grounds without reference

b to the views of the competent authority.

   This is not to say that the administrative authority is bound by the grounds given by the competent authority and may not base its decision on grounds of its own, but it would seem contrary to the intention of art 9 that the administrative authority should not have the opportunity of considering the grounds on which the competent authority based its decision. If no reasons are given, it will be impossible for the administrative

c authority to know whether the competent authority has taken the proper factors into consideration in reaching its opinion. For example, as the result of art 3(2), a decision to expel could be challenged in the courts on the ground that it was based wholly on the previous convictions of the person concerned. If the opinion of the competent authority was based solely on that consideration, the administrative authority should, it would appear, have an opportunity of considering the matter before adopting the opinion, and,

d if the person concerned knew that the opinion was based on that consideration only, he might have the opportunity of challenging the decision itself, even though the grounds for that decision contained no reference to previous convictions. Conversely, without such knowledge, it might be difficult for him to challenge the decision. Taking the directive on its own, therefore, in our judgment it envisages reasons being given by the competent authority as part of its opinion.

e   We turn then to consider the judgment of the European Court in *R v Secretary of State for the Home Dept, ex p Santillo* [1981] 2 All ER 897 at 912. The relevant paragraph, para 3(*a*), is, so far as material, in these terms: '... the person concerned [should be] in a position to take cognisance of the reasons which led the "competent authority" to give its opinion ...' In our judgment, with all respect to the Divisional Court, it is impossible to say that a person is in a position to take cognisance of reasons unless he is informed of those reasons. We cannot accept the view of the Divisional Court that in this case the

f reasons were obvious from the material provided to the applicant. It might have been that the magistrates made the recommendation simply because of the number and gravity of the applicant's previous convictions. That would have been acceptable under English law for a person who was not a Common Market citizen, but, if the decision had been based on that consideration alone, it would have been insufficient material on

g which to base a deportation order in respect of a Common Market citizen.

   A practical question then arises as to the form in which courts making recommendations for the deportation of Common Market citizens should state their reasons so as to comply with EEC Council Directive 64/221. When *R v Secretary of State for the Home Dept, ex p Santillo* came back to the English courts this question was not considered by the Court of Appeal (see [1981] 2 All ER 897 at 917, [1981] QB 778 at 792). In that case the

h recommendation had been made in the Crown Court, and the judge, in the course of his sentencing remarks, referred to the gravity of the offences, the lack of a medical recommendation and the position of Santillo's family, and concluded by saying that his duty required him to recommend deportation 'in the interests of the Community and the protection of the Community'. It was not suggested that the judge should have said more.

j   However, in the Divisional Court Donaldson LJ said obiter ([1981] 2 All ER 897 at 916, [1981] QB 778 at 786):

   'The second is the decision of the Court of Appeal in *R v Nazari* [1980] 3 All ER 880, [1980] 1 WLR 1366, which pointed out that no court should make an order recommending deportation without full inquiry into all the circumstances, gave some guidance on the principles involved and held that the court should give reasons for its decision if a recommendation is to be made. It would avoid subsequent argument if those reasons included some indication of the extent to which the current and previous criminal convictions of the accused have been taken into account and, in so far as this has been done, the light which, in the view of the court, such conviction or convictions throw on the likely nature of the accused's personal conduct in the future. The giving of reasons is not only in accordance with this decision, it is also consistent with the philosophy disclosed by art 6 of the directive which requires that the person concerned shall be informed of the grounds of public policy security or public health on which the decision taken by the Secretary of State in his case is based, unless it is contrary to the interests of the security of the state.'

R v Nazari was not an EEC case, but in EEC cases a short statement of the reasons for the recommendation should always be given on the lines suggested by Donaldson LJ. Copies of this statement should be sent both to the Home Secretary and to the prisoner. In the Crown Court this will present no difficulty. A copy of the transcript of the judge's sentencing remarks, including his reasons for making a recommendation for deportation, will be sufficient. In magistrates' courts, where there is no shorthand writer, different considerations apply. We are aware that it is not the usual practice for magistrates to give reasons for their sentences, and we do not encourage them to do so, save in cases where they make a recommendation for the deportation of an EEC citizen. In such cases a brief statement of the reasons must always be given on the lines suggested by Donaldson LJ. The statement need not necessarily be made in open court, but should in any event be committed to writing, no doubt on the advice of the clerk, and be signed by the magistrates. Copies of it should be sent, together with the recommendation itself, as soon as reasonably practicable to the Home Secretary and to the prisoner.

In an affidavit sworn by the chairman of the bench in this case he set out the reasons for which the recommendation was in fact made. They were in the following terms:

'12. We were unanimous in our opinion that there existed a sufficiently serious threat to society and that it would be wrong to allow the applicant to remain in this country having regard to his past conduct, the nature of the offences committed by him and his use of this country as a refuge from Justice. 13. We felt that if he were allowed to remain in this country there was a strong likelihood that he would continue to commit crime.'

If those reasons had been communicated to the Home Secretary and the applicant, together with the recommendation in this case, we can find no possible ground on which the recommendation could have been challenged.

The argument in the Divisional Court and this court was directly solely to the failure to comply with art 9 in relation to the recommendation. However, in the course of argument it was observed by the court that the deportation order itself did not contain information of the grounds on which the order was made, and was accordingly bad on its face having regard to the provisions of art 6. Counsel for the Secretary of State accepted this and accepted that the deportation order could not stand on that ground alone.

Accordingly the appeal is allowed and the deportation order will be quashed on the grounds that it fails to comply with art 6 of EEC Council Directive 64/221 of 25 February 1964 and that the recommendation of the magistrates on which it was based failed to comply with art 9 of the directive.

Appeal allowed. Order of certiorari quashing deportation order.

Solicitors: *Winstanley-Burgess* (for the applicant); *Treasury Solicitor*.

Bebe Chua   Barrister.

Saul v Norfolk County Council

COURT OF APPEAL, CIVIL DIVISION
LAWTON, SLADE AND BROWNE-WILKINSON LJJ
20, 21 FEBRUARY, 21 MARCH 1984

Agricultural holding – Tenancy – Death of tenant – Smallholding – Tenancy granted by smallholdings authority in 1965 pursuant to Agriculture Act 1947 – Application by survivor of tenant for grant of new tenancy – Whether tenancy granted 'in pursuance of' Agriculture Act 1970 – Whether tenancy an 'agreement' made under repealed statute having corresponding provisions in 1970 Act – Agriculture Act 1970, Sch 3, paras 3, 9 – Agriculture (Miscellaneous Provisions) Act 1976, ss 18(4)(f), 20(1).

In April 1965 a county council who were a smallholdings authority granted a tenancy of a smallholding to the applicant's father in pursuance of Pt IV of the Agriculture Act 1947, which was later replaced by Pt III of the Agriculture Act 1970. When his father died in January 1982 the applicant applied to an agricultural land tribunal for a direction under s 20(1)^a of the Agriculture (Miscellaneous Provisions) Act 1976 that he was entitled to a tenancy of the holding on the basis that he was a child of the tenant who was eligible to succeed to the tenancy. The council opposed the application on the ground that s 18(4)(f)^b of the 1976 Act applied, rendering the succession provisions in s 20 inapplicable because 'the holding consists of land held by a smallholdings authority . . . for the purposes of smallholdings within the meaning of Part III of the Agriculture Act 1970, and the tenancy was granted by them . . . in pursuance of the said Part III'. The applicant contended that the tenancy granted to his father in 1965 had not been granted 'in pursuance of' Pt III of the 1970 Act and therefore s 18(4)(f) did not apply. The tribunal held that s 18(4)(f) did apply and therefore they had no jurisdiction, because the tenancy granted to the applicant's father had effect under para 9^c of Sch 3 to the 1970 Act as if it had been made under Pt III of the 1970 Act, since it was an 'agreement made . . . by virtue of [a] repealed enactment [which] could have been made . . . by virtue of a corresponding provision of Part III of [the 1970] Act' and therefore had effect 'as if made' under the corresponding provision. On appeal by the applicant the judge held that s 18(4)(f) applied only to tenancies granted after the 1970 Act came into operation and not to tenancies granted prior to the 1970 Act, because pre-1970 tenancies were 'lettings' which were continued in effect by para 3^d of Sch 3 to the 1970 Act and were not affected by para 9. The council appealed.

Held – On its true construction s 18(4)(f) of the 1976 Act was restricted to tenancies granted under the 1970 Act and did not affect tenancies granted prior to the 1970 Act, since the ordinary and natural meaning of tenancies granted 'in pursuance of . . . Part III' was tenancies granted in the exercise of the authority conferred by Pt III of the 1970 Act. Furthermore, para 9 of Sch 3 to the 1970 Act did not apply to, and therefore did not require any other meaning to be given to, s 18(4)(f) because the tenancy of a smallholding was not an 'agreement' within the meaning of para 9, having regard to the fact that such tenancies were 'lettings', which were fully and adequately covered by para 3 of Sch 9. However, even if the tenancy of a smallholding was an 'agreement' for the purposes of para 9, a pre-1970 tenancy was not thereby deemed to have been made under the 1970 Act but merely had effect 'as if made' under that Act and therefore was not to be treated as having been granted 'in pursuance of' Pt III of the 1970 Act. Accordingly, the

---

a   Section 20(1), so far as material, is set out at p 490 *j*, post
b   Section 18(4), so far as material, is set out at p 491 *d*, post
c   Paragraph 9 is set out at p 492 *g*, post
d   Paragraph 3 is set out at p 492 *f*, post

agricultural land tribunal had been wrong to decide that they lacked jurisdiction to hear the application. The council's appeal would therefore be dismissed (see p 493 j, p 494 a to c j, p 495 e to g and p 496 d to h, post).

Notes

For provision for succession on the death of the tenant of an agricultural holding, see Supplement to 1 Halsbury's Laws (4th edn) para 1011A.

    For the Agriculture Act 1947, Pt IV, see 2 Halsbury's Statutes (3rd edn) 124.

    For the Agriculture Act 1970, Pt III, Sch 3, paras 3, 9, see 40 ibid 138, 161.

    For the Agriculture (Miscellaneous Provisions) Act 1976, ss 18, 20, see 46 ibid 31, 36.

Appeal

Norfolk County Council appealed against the judgment of McNeill J hearing the Crown Office list on 13 July 1983 whereby he allowed an appeal by the respondent, Richard John Saul, by way of case stated dated 10 March 1983 from a decision of the Agricultural Land Tribunal (Eastern Division) dated 16 November 1982 and held that such tribunal had jurisdiction to entertain Mr Saul's application for a direction under s 20(1) of the Agriculture (Miscellaneous Provisions) Act 1976 that he was entitled to a tenancy of an agricultural holding known as Clinks Farm, Toft Monks, Beccles, Suffolk, of which the council were the landlords. The facts are set out in the judgment of the court.

Konrad Schiemann QC and *Patrick Hamlin* for the council.
Derek Wood QC and *Seddon Cripps* for Mr Saul.

Cur adv vult

21 March. The following judgment of the court was delivered.

SLADE LJ. This is an appeal by the Norfolk County Council from a judgment of McNeill J given on 13 July 1983. It raises a question as to the applicability of the succession provisions contained in the Agriculture (Miscellaneous Provisions) Act 1976 to a tenancy of a smallholding. We have been told that its outcome will be of importance to a number of smallholding authorities throughout this country.

By his judgment the judge allowed the appeal of the respondent, Mr Saul, by way of case stated dated 10 March 1983 from a decision of the Agricultural Land Tribunal (East Area), and held that the tribunal had jurisdiction to entertain Mr Saul's application for a direction entitling him to a tenancy of an agricultural holding known as Clinks Farm, Toft Monks, Beccles, Suffolk, pursuant to s 20(1) of the 1976 Act. The judge also referred the matter back to the tribunal for their decision.

The facts can be shortly stated. Mr Saul's father became a tenant of the holding by virtue of a written agreement dated 9 April 1965. He died on 21 January 1982. The appellant council are, and have at all material times been, the landlords. As a smallholding authority, they have held the farm for the purposes of smallholdings within the meaning of the legislation relating to smallholdings. In May 1982 Mr Saul applied to the Agricultural Land Tribunal for a direction entitling him to a tenancy of the holding pursuant to s 20(1) of the 1976 Act. His claim was based on the provisions of s 18 and the succeeding sections contained in Pt II of that Act, which introduced a new scheme for family succession on the death of the tenant of an agricultural holding.

Section 20(1) of the 1976 Act gives any 'eligible person', as defined by the Act, the right within the relevant period to 'apply to the Tribunal for a direction entitling him to a tenancy of the holding'. So far as material, s 18(1) reads as follows:

> 'Where after the passing of this Act the sole (or sole surviving) tenant of an agricultural holding dies and is survived by any of the following persons ... (c) a child of the deceased ... the following sections of this Part of this Act (except

a   sections 20(14) and 23(8), which are of general application) shall apply unless excluded by subsection (4) below . . .'

Section 18(2) contains a definition of 'eligible person'. Under this definition a child of a deceased tenant of the holding will qualify if he satisfies a number of stated conditions, which are set out in paras (*a*), (*b*) and (*c*). The condition in para (*b*) is that—

b   'in the seven years ending with the date of death his only or principal source of livelihood throughout a continuous period of not less than five years, or two or more discontinuous periods together amounting to not less than five years, derived from his agricultural work on the holding or on an agricultural unit of which the holding forms part.'

Section 18(3) somewhat relaxes the condition in para (*b*) in a case where a survivor of the deceased during the relevant period has been attending a full-time course at an *c*   establishment of further education. However, s 18(4) contains provisions which have the effect of rendering the succession provisions of Pt II inapplicable in certain stated circumstances. So far as material for present purposes, it provides:

'The following sections of this Part of this Act shall not apply . . . (*f*) if the holding consists of land held by a smallholdings authority or the Minister for the purposes of smallholdings within the meaning of Part III of the Agriculture Act 1970, and *d*   the tenancy was granted by them or him in pursuance of the said Part III . . .'

After Mr Saul's application had been made, the matter came before the tribunal on a preliminary issue raised by the council whether or not the provisions of s 18(4)(*f*) disqualified Mr Saul from making an application under s 20(1).

Reverting to the words of s 18(4)(*f*), it is common ground that, on the facts, 'the *e*   holding consists of land held by a smallholdings authority . . . for the purposes of smallholdings within the meaning of Part III of the Agriculture Act 1970, and the tenancy [of 9 April 1965] was granted by them'. The whole issue on this appeal is whether that tenancy was granted 'in pursuance of the said Part III' within the meaning of that phrase as used in s 18(4)(*f*). The judge, reversing the decision of the tribunal, held that it was not, and accordingly Mr Saul is not disqualified from making his *f*   application. The council now appeal from his decision.

At this point it is necessary to refer to the legislation relating to smallholdings, which goes back to the last century. Its purpose has not been to create a special category of agricultural tenants: it is, we think, common ground that, broadly, its purpose has always been to increase the supply of smallholdings available for letting to suitable persons who wish to become farmers on their own account, but might not otherwise be in a financial *g*   position to do so. In this century there have been three principal batches of relevant legislation. The first was to be found in the Small Holdings and Allotments Acts 1908 to 1931, which gave local authorities certain powers to acquire land for the purpose of providing smallholdings and thereafter to let and sell it. The second was to be found in Pt IV of the Agriculture Act 1947, which, with certain savings and exceptions, repealed the 1908 to 1931 Acts. Section 47(1), for the express purpose of affording to persons with *h*   agricultural experience an opportunity of becoming farmers on their own account, imposed a duty on county councils to provide smallholdings for letting to such persons. Section 52(1) stated:

'Smallholdings provided by a smallholdings authority shall be let to the persons by whom the smallholdings are to be farmed in accordance with the following provisions of this Part of this Act: Provided that nothing in this section shall affect *j*   any letting in force at the commencement of this Part of this Act.'

The tenancy granted to Mr Saul's father in 1965 was granted in pursuance of Pt IV of the 1947 Act.

Once the tenant of a smallholding has acquired his tenancy, he is, with certain exceptions but in most respects, in the same position as any other tenant of agricultural

land. Thus, since the time when Pt III of the 1947 Act introduced provisions designed to
give security of tenure to the tenants of agricultural land and these provisions were   *a*
replaced by the Agricultural Holdings Act 1948, tenants of smallholdings have enjoyed
the benefit of the protection given by those Acts. However, neither of these two Acts
conferred general rights of succession on survivors of a deceased tenant.

There then followed the Agriculture Act 1970, which (by s 113(3) and Pt III of Sch 5)
repealed almost the whole of Pt IV of the 1947 Act and replaced it with a large number
of sections relating to smallholdings, which are contained in Pt III of the 1970 Act.   *b*
Though it is only necessary to refer to a few of its specific provisions, we think that the
council are correct in submitting that the 1970 Act set out a new and comprehensive
statutory scheme for the acquisition and management of smallholdings. Section 44
contained provisions empowering the letting of land held by a smallholdings authority
for the purposes of smallholdings. Section 64(1) provided that the transitional provisions
contained in Sch 3 to the Act should have effect.   *c*

Schedule 3, which was headed 'Transitional Provisions for Part III', so far as material,
read as follows. Paragraph 1 stated:

> 'In this Schedule "the repeal" means the repeal by this Act of the enactments
> specified in Part III of Schedule 5 thereto, and "the repealed enactments" means the
> enactments so specified.'
>   *d*

We pause to mention that 'the repealed enactments', with a very few exceptions, included
all those provisions of the 1908 to 1931 Acts and the 1947 Act relating to smallholdings
which were still in force.

Paragraph 2 stated:

> 'Any land which immediately before the commencement of Part III of this Act is
> held by a smallholdings authority for the purposes of smallholdings shall,   *e*
> notwithstanding the repeal, continue to be held by that authority for the purposes
> of smallholdings, subject to any power exercisable by the authority by virtue of any
> enactment to appropriate or dispose of it for other purposes.'

Paragraph 3, which echoed the proviso to s 52(1) of the 1947 Act, stated: 'The repeal
shall not affect the validity of any letting effected before the commencement of Part III   *f*
of this Act.'

Paragraph 9, which is of special significance for the purpose of the present appeal,
stated:

> 'Without prejudice to the preceding provisions of this Schedule, in so far as any
> agreement made, record, map or plan compiled and kept, or other thing done by
> virtue of any of the repealed enactments could have been made, compiled and kept   *g*
> or done by virtue of a corresponding provision of Part III of this Act, it shall not be
> invalidated by the repeal but shall have effect as if made, compiled and kept or done
> by virtue of that corresponding provision.'

In exercise of certain powers conferred by ss 44(6) and 63 of the 1970 Act, a statutory
instrument, namely the Smallholdings (Selection of Tenants) Regulations 1970, SI 1970/   *h*
1049, was made which, by reg 3(2), gave certain exemptions to the widow of a deceased
tenant from the general qualification, required by reg 3(1), of practical experience of
farm work. Otherwise, no special status of eligibility by succession was recognised by the
1970 Act.

There then followed the 1976 Act, Pt II of which has introduced an entirely new
scheme for succession on the death of a tenant of an agricultural holding, under which   *j*
the procedure is to be initiated by an application to an agricultural land tribunal made
by an 'eligible person' pursuant to s 20 for a direction entitling him to a tenancy of the
holding.

In the course of argument in this case, the council's counsel more than once referred
to the Act as having introduced 'statutory rights of succession'. With no disrespect to the

argument, we think that this phrase is somewhat misleading. Before a direction may be
a made under s 20 by the tribunal for the grant of a new tenancy to a particular applicant,
they have to satisfy themselves as to four matters, namely: (1) that the applicant is
eligible; (2) that he is suitable; (3) if there are two or more applicants, that the particular
applicant is the most suitable, or that the landlord assents to the grant of a joint tenancy;
and (4) that the tribunal have refused consent to the operation of the landlord's notice to
quit, if such notice has been served.

b   As to the first of these matters, the criteria as to eligibility are to be found in the first
three subsections, sub-ss (1) to (3), of s 18 of the 1976 Act. We have briefly referred to
some, but not all, of these criteria already. If the applicant establishes his eligibility, the
onus then falls on him to satisfy the tribunal that he is suitable. The criteria as to
suitability are to be found set out in s 20(8) of the 1976 Act, which includes as relevant
matters the applicant's training or practical experience in agriculture, his age, physical
c health and financial standing, and the landlord's views on the applicant's suitability. As
to the third of the matters mentioned above, s 20(6) and (9) contains provisions to cover
the procedure for the tribunal to apply when dealing with applications by more than one
person. Finally, quite apart from the three obstacles facing the applicant which we have
already mentioned, the tribunal must afford the landlord an opportunity to apply for
their consent under s 22 of the 1976 Act to the operation of the landlord's notice to quit.
d Sections 2 and 3 of the Agricultural Holdings (Notices to Quit) Act 1977 contain further
provisions restricting the operation of notices to quit agricultural holdings and governing
the giving or withholding of the tribunal's consent to the operation of notices to quit.

     Enough has been said to show that, even if an 'eligible' person applies to the tribunal
for a direction entitling him to a new tenancy, it is far from a foregone conclusion that
he will obtain the direction sought. Nevertheless, the legislature has thought it right, by
e s 18(4) of the 1976 Act, to specify certain circumstances in which the following sections
of Pt II shall not apply at all, with the consequence that a person who would otherwise be
'eligible' will be deprived of the right even to apply for a direction under s 20. For present
purposes, the only possibly relevant contingency mentioned in s 18(4) is that mentioned
in para (f), which, so far as material, we will repeat:

f   'if the holding consists of land held by a smallholdings authority ... for the
       purposes of smallholdings within the meaning of Part III of the Agriculture Act
       1970, and the tenancy was granted by them ... in pursuance of the said Part III.'

     At very first sight it might seem clear that the relevant tenancy in the present case,
having been granted in 1965, was not granted 'in pursuance of' an Act passed in 1970.
But the matter is not so simple as that. The tribunal in a very careful decision came to
g the conclusion that the wording of para 9 of Sch 3 to the 1970 Act was appropriate to
enable the reference in s 18(4)(f) to a 'tenancy granted in pursuance of the said Part III'
to apply to a tenancy such as the 1965 tenancy, granted in pursuance of Pt IV of the 1947
Act. On these grounds the tribunal considered that Mr Saul was not even eligible to apply
for a new tenancy. Furthermore, we have been told that agricultural land tribunals
generally have applied a similar construction of the 1976 Act in relation to tenancies of
h smallholdings granted under the 1947 Act.

     Their views are entitled to respect. As appears from para 14 of their decision, the
tribunal in the present case clearly considered that it was Parliament's intention that all
smallholdings should be wholly excluded from the succession provisions contained in Pt
II of the 1976 Act; they accordingly declined to give the relevant statutory provisions an
interpretation which would defeat that presumed intention. We have some sympathy
j with their attitude, but, like the judge, have come to the conclusion that the wording of
those statutory provisions too clearly bears a contrary sense to permit the construction
placed on them by the tribunal.

     No doubt, some such words as 'the tenancy was granted by them or him' had to be
included in s 18(4)(f), lest it should have effect of depriving an eligible survivor of a
deceased tenant of an agricultural holding of his rights under Pt II of the 1976 Act,

merely because the smallholdings authority had acquired the reversion and had thus become the landlords. The draftsman of s 18(4)(*f*), however, chose to add the words 'in pursuance of the said Part III'. These words cannot, in our judgment, be rejected as otiose. Some force must be given to them. If they are given their ordinary and natural meaning, s 18(4)(*f*) is not apt to include the tenancy granted to Mr Saul's father in 1965. The ordinary and natural meaning of the words 'in pursuance of the said Part III' is, in our judgment, 'in exercise of the authority conferred by Pt III of the 1970 Act'. The tenancy of 1965 was not granted in exercise of such authority. It was granted in exercise of the authority conferred by the Pt IV of the 1947 Act.

It follows that if the council are to succeed on this appeal, they must show that para 9 of Sch 3 to the 1970 Act, which is the linchpin of their argument, has the effect of obliging a meaning other than their ordinary and natural meaning to be attached to the words 'in pursuance of the said Part III' in s 18(4)(*f*).

On analysis, the essential stages in the council's submissions in this context are, we think, as follows. (1) The 1965 tenancy was an 'agreement' within the meaning of para 9 of Sch 3 to the 1970 Act. (2) Such agreement, though it was actually made by virtue of one of the repealed enactments (ie the 1947 Act), 'could have been made' by virtue of a corresponding provision of Pt III of the 1970 Act. (3) Under para 9, such agreement therefore is not invalidated by the repeal of the 1947 Act, but has effect as if made by virtue of that corresponding provision. (4) In applying s 18(4)(*f*) of the 1976 Act, one must therefore treat the 1965 tenancy as having been granted 'in pursuance of Part III of the 1970 Act'.

The judge considered that the council failed at the first of these four hurdles, and so do we. We accept that the grant of any tenancy must import an agreement between landlord and tenant, though the agreement need not necessarily precede the grant. Nevertheless, it is significant that, while we have been referred to a number of provisions of the 1970 Act which specifically refer to a 'letting' (eg ss 37, 44 and 45), we have been referred to no provision in the body of that Act which uses the word 'agreement' in a sense which includes a letting.

One then comes to Sch 3 and finds in para 3 a specific provision that the repeal of the repealed enactments 'shall not affect the validity of any letting effected before the commencement of Part III of this Act'. If it were correct to say that the word 'agreement' in para 9 includes a letting, it is difficult to see what purpose would have been served by including a provision in that paragraph to the effect that certain lettings should not be 'invalidated by the repeal'. In regard to lettings falling within paras 9 and 3, such a provision would have been mere surplusage, having regard to what had already been provided by para 3. In regard to other lettings *not* falling within both paragraphs, it would have been positively confusing. On the footing that the word 'agreement' in para 9 included a letting, that paragraph would not have exempted from invalidation *all* lettings effected by virtue of one of the repealed enactments; it would merely have exempted those pre-1970 Act lettings which 'could have been made by virtue of a corresponding provision' of Pt III of the 1970 Act. The provisions of the 1970 Act authorising the letting of smallholdings as smallholdings are in some respects significantly narrower than the provisions of the 1947 Act which they replaced (see particularly s 52). Furthermore, the definition of a 'smallholding' in s 66 of the 1947 Act was repealed and replaced by the 1970 Act (cf s 39(2) of that Act). No convincing reason has been suggested why the legislature should have intended to include certain classes of pre-1970 Act tenancies within para 9 of Sch 3 to that Act, but not others.

The conclusion that the word 'agreement' in para 9 is not apt to include a letting is reinforced when one discovers that there are a number of 'agreements', referred to by that description in the relevant legislation, which the word *is* manifestly apt to cover. Thus, by way of some examples, at least in many instances: (1) an 'agreement' of the nature referred to in s 49(1) of the 1947 Act could have been made by virtue of the equivalent s 46 of the 1970 Act; (2) an 'agreement' of the nature referred to in s 51(3)(*a*) or (*b*) of the 1947 Act could have been made by virtue of the equivalent s 47(3) or (4) (as the case may be) of the 1970 Act; (3) an 'agreement' of the nature contemplated by s 56(2)

of the 1947 Act could have been made by virtue of the equivalent s 54(2) and (3) of the
a 1970 Act.

As to 'records', the duty of a smallholdings authority to compile and keep records of
the nature referred to in s 58(2)(a) of the 1970 Act is similar to the duty previously
imposed by s 62(a) of the 1947 Act. As to 'maps or plans', their duty to compile and keep
maps or plans of the nature referred to in s 58(2)(b) of the 1970 Act is similar to the duty
previously imposed by s 62(b) of the 1947 Act. As to 'things done', their duty to keep
b accounts imposed on them by s 58(1) of the 1970 Act is similar to the duty previously
imposed on them by s 60(1) of the 1947 Act and the duty to send to the minister a report,
imposed by s 59(1) of the 1970 Act is similar to the duty previously imposed by s 63(1)
of the 1947 Act.

It was clearly necessary for the 1970 Act to contain some provision ensuring the
validity and continuing effect of all these various agreements, maps, records or plans or
c things which had been made, compiled, kept or done pursuant to any of the repealed
enactments, notwithstanding their repeal. Paragraph 9 was included with this purpose
in mind. There was some discussion in the course of argument as to the force of the
additional words 'but shall have effect as if made, compiled and kept or done by virtue of
that corresponding provision', bearing in mind the earlier words of the paragraph
preventing invalidation. We think that the correct explanation of the purpose of these
d additional words is that suggested by counsel for Mr Saul, namely that, where appropriate,
a discharge of a relevant obligation under one of the repealed enactments is to be treated
as discharging the equivalent obligation of the party concerned under Pt III of the 1970
Act. We do not think that any greater force than that can properly be attributed to these
additional words.

For all these reasons, we have reached the clear conclusion that the reference to
e 'agreement' in para 9 of Sch 3 is apt to include ancillary agreements relating to
smallholdings which are of the nature referred to in the 1947 Act, and require to be
preserved, but that it is not apt in its context to include existing lettings themselves,
which are already fully and adequately covered by para 3.

If this conclusion is correct, it must mean that para 9 is irrelevant to the present issues
and that this appeal must fail on this account alone. We should, however, refer to a
f submission made in the alternative on behalf of Mr Saul. The submission was that, even
if the word 'agreement' in para 9 includes a letting, para 9 is not on its true construction
a 'deeming provision'. Accordingly, it is submitted, in applying s 18(4)(f) of the 1976
Act to the facts of the present case, even on this hypothesis, it still would not be right to
treat the 1965 tenancy as having been granted 'in pursuance of the said Part III', within
the meaning of those words as used in the subsection. We think that this contention also
g is well founded.

In opposition to it, and in general support of this appeal, counsel for the council relied
strongly and eloquently on the supposed anomalies that would ensue if the words of
s 18(4)(f) were read and applied on their own, without full regard to para 9 of Sch 3 to
the 1970 Act, in the sense hitherto given to that paragraph by the agricultural land
tribunals. In their submission, there could be no good policy reason why in 1976 the
h legislature should have seen fit to give a 'right of succession' to the tenants under pre-
1970 Act tenancies of smallholdings, but not to tenants under any other such tenancies;
they pointed out that, if the judge's construction of the legislation is correct, this is likely
to lead to the freezing of substantial quantities of land which might otherwise be available
for sale or for letting as smallholdings to new tenants whom the authority considered
more deserving.

j We appreciate the concern of the council in this context and confess that we would
have felt happier in rejecting their arguments if some obvious reason of policy had been
suggested to explain this differentiation between categories of tenancies of smallholdings;
in our opinion, they have not. There are, however, three observations which we wish to
make in this context. First, the construction which the council place on s 18(4)(f) of the
1976 Act and para 9 of Sch 3 to the 1970 Act would itself give rise to apparent anomalies.
We have already pointed out that, even if the word 'agreement' in para 9 includes a

letting, the paragraph would still not have applied to *all* lettings effected by virtue of one of the repealed enactments: it would have applied only to those pre-1970 Act lettings which 'could have been made by virtue of a corresponding provision' of Pt III of the 1970 Act. Accordingly, even if the council's construction were right, s 18(4)(*f*) would not have disqualified the successors of tenants of smallholdings in cases where the letting was a pre-1970 Act letting and could *not* have been made by virtue of a corresponding provision of this nature. It is difficult to see any obvious reason of policy why persons in this category should be given any specially favourable treatment. Second, for reasons already explained, it is not, even on our construction of the 1976 Act, correct to regard it as having conferred a right of succession on eligible tenants under pre-1970 Act tenancies of smallholdings; all it does is to confer on such persons a right to *apply* for the relevant direction, which is not conferred on tenants under post-1970 Act tenancies. The point relating to the freezing of land supplies therefore has less force than might at first sight appear. Third, it would not, in our judgment, be right to conclude that, because no obvious reasons of policy suggest themselves, the legislature may not have deliberately made this differentiation for what it considered good and sufficient reasons. Simply, for example, it is conceivable (we put it no higher) that it considered that survivors of tenants holding their smallholdings under tenancies of longer standing deserved preferential treatment, at least to the extent of being permitted to apply for a direction; some slight support for this conjecture is possibly to be derived from s 18(2)(*b*) of the 1976 Act.

However, we think that any arguments based on the supposed intention of the legislature can avail the council only if the meaning of the wording of s 18(4)(*f*) is not clear. In our judgment, the meaning is clear and unequivocal. As counsel for Mr Saul pointed out, one has to attribute to Parliament in 1976 the knowledge that there were in existence at that date three categories of tenancies of smallholdings, namely (1) those granted pursuant to the 1908 to 1931 Acts, (2) those granted pursuant to the 1947 Act, (3) those granted pursuant to the 1970 Act. The only sense which we can make of the words 'in pursuance of the said Part III', as appearing in s 18(4)(*f*), is that they were deliberately intended to disqualify from any possible rights of succession the survivors of those tenants holding under category (3), but not those holding under categories (1) and (2). If the intention had been to disqualify tenants holding under all three categories, the words 'in pursuance of the said Part III' would have been otiose and misleading. We find it impossible to attribute to the legislature the intention to incorporate into the construction of s 18(4)(*f*) the provisions of para 9 of Sch 3 to the 1970 Act (however that paragraph should be construed) by a process of implication. It is not even as if the wording of the two provisions tallies. Paragraph 9 uses neither the word 'tenancy' nor the phrase 'in pursuance of'. The mere existence of para 9 cannot, in our judgment, justify the attribution of an artificial meaning to the words of s 18(4)(*f*) quite different from what those words naturally bear.

To sum up, we conclude that (a) the word 'agreement' in the context of para 9 of Sch 3 to the 1970 Act is not apt to include a 'tenancy', (b) even if that conclusion were wrong, the wording of s 18(4)(*f*) still would not be apt to refer to the tenancy of 1965, which was granted in pursuance of Pt IV of the 1947 Act. For these reasons, which are much the same as those of the judge, we think that he reached the correct conclusion and dismiss this appeal.

Appeal dismissed. Leave to appeal to the House of Lords refused.

14 June. The Appeal Committee of the House of Lords (Lord Diplock, Lord Roskill and Lord Brightman) dismissed a petition by the council for leave to appeal.

Solicitors: *Sharpe Pritchard & Co*, agents for *T D W Molander*, Norwich (for the council); *Nicholson Cadge & Gilbert*, Lowestoft (for Mr Saul).

Mary Rose Plummer   Barrister.

a
Lewis v Lewis and another

COURT OF APPEAL, CIVIL DIVISION
SIR JOHN ARNOLD P AND ANTHONY LINCOLN J
23, 24 FEBRUARY, 5 MARCH 1984

b
Divorce – Property – Protected or statutory tenancy – Transfer of protected or statutory tenancy on termination of marriage – Legislation giving court power to make transfer order 'on granting decree . . . or at any time thereafter' – Decree made absolute before legislation coming into force – Whether power to make transfer order exercisable retrospectively – Matrimonial Homes Act 1967, Sch 2.

c
On its true construction Sch 2[a] to the Matrimonial Homes Act 1967 (which was inserted in that Act by Sch 2 to the Matrimonial Homes and Property Act 1981 in place of the original provisions of s 7 of the 1967 Act) does not have retrospective effect. Accordingly, the power given to the court by Sch 2 to the 1967 Act to make an order for the transfer of a statutory tenancy from one spouse to another 'on granting a decree of divorce . . . or at any time thereafter' cannot be exercised in favour of a party who obtained a decree of divorce before the commencement of the 1981 Act. Such a party remains bound by the
d
original provisions of s 7 of the 1967 Act and cannot apply for a transfer of tenancy order after the decree has been made absolute (see p 500 *h j*, p 502 *c* to *e* and p 503 *c*, post).

Yew Bon Tew v Kenderaan Bas Mara [1982] 3 All ER 833 applied.

Powys v Powys [1971] 3 All ER 116 and *Chaterjee v Chaterjee* [1976] 1 All ER 719 distinguished.

e
Williams v Williams [1971] 2 All ER 764 considered.

Notes
For retrospective effect of statutes, see 44 Halsbury's Laws (4th edn) paras 921–926, and for cases on the subject, see 44 Digest (Repl) 284–291, 1132–1218.

For the court's powers in relation to protected or statutory tenancies following decrees
f
of divorce, see 13 Halsbury's Laws (4th edn) paras 1127–1128 and 22 ibid para 1057.

For the Matrimonial Homes Act 1967, s 7, see 17 Halsbury's Statutes (3rd edn) 146, and for Sch 2 to that Act (as inserted by the Matrimonial Homes and Property Act 1981, Sch 2), see 51 ibid 1038.

As from 9 August 1983 s 7 of and Sch 2 to the 1967 Act were replaced by s 7 of and Sch 1 to the Matrimonial Homes Act 1983.

g
Cases referred to in judgments
Boyer v Warbey [1952] 2 All ER 976, [1953] 1 QB 234, CA.
Carson v Carson and Stoyek [1964] 1 All ER 681, [1964] 1 WLR 511.
Chaterjee v Chaterjee [1976] 1 All ER 719, [1976] Fam 199, [1976] 2 WLR 397, CA.
Metropolitan Properties Co Ltd v Cronan (1982) 44 P & CR 1, CA.
Powys v Powys [1971] 3 All ER 116, [1971] P 340, [1971] 3 WLR 154.
h
Williams v Williams [1971] 2 All ER 764, [1971] P 271, [1971] 3 WLR 92.
Yew Bon Tew v Kenderaan Bas Mara [1982] 3 All ER 833, [1983] 1 AC 553, [1982] 3 WLR 1026, PC.

Interlocutory appeal
Metropolitan Properties Co Ltd, the landlords of a flat known as 10F Hyde Park Mansions,
j
Old Marylebone Road, London W2 and the second respondents to an application by Hazel Suzette Lewis (the wife) for an order under Sch 2 to the Matrimonial Homes Act 1967 (as inserted by s 6 of and Sch 2 to the Matrimonial Homes and Property Act 1981),

---

a   Schedule 2, so far as material, is set out at p 499 *d e*, post

appealed against an order of his Honour Judge Aron Owen sitting as a judge of the High Court on 18 November 1983 whereby he ordered that the first respondent, Geoffrey Elias Lewis (the husband), should cease to be entitled to occupy the flat with effect from 4 March 1978 and that with effect from that date the wife should be deemed to be the statutory tenant of the flat. The facts are set out in the judgment of Anthony Lincoln J.

David Neuberger for the landlords.
Daniel Pearce-Higgins for the wife.
The husband did not appear.

Cur adv vult

5 March. The following judgments were delivered.

ANTHONY LINCOLN J (giving the first judgment at the invitation of Sir John Arnold P). This is an appeal against an order of his Honour Judge Aron Owen, sitting as a High Court judge, made on 18 November 1983. He had before him an application by an ex-wife, Mrs Hazel Lewis, under the Matrimonial Homes and Property Act 1981, relating to a flat which she occupied at 10F Hyde Park Mansions, Old Marylebone Road, London W2. Her ex-husband did not oppose the application, but the landlords did. The judge directed that the ex-husband should cease to be entitled to occupy the flat and that the ex-wife should be deemed to be the statutory tenant. The direction was made under para 3(1) of Sch 2 to the Matrimonial Homes Act 1967, as inserted by Sch 2 to the 1981 Act. The landlords now appeal against that direction. The appeal raises the question whether the 1981 Act may properly be construed to have retroactive effect and, if so, the further question whether the order could be made in the circumstances of this case.

The material facts are that on 8 December 1970 the appellant landlords granted Mr Geoffrey Lewis (the husband) a renewal of his lease of the flat. It was a term certain to expire on 28 September 1975. At the time of the renewal he and his wife were still married and they lived at the flat with their children. It is not disputed that the renewed tenancy thus granted was a protected tenancy under s 1 of the Rent Act 1977, fulfilling all the required conditions of that Act. On the expiry of his tenancy the husband held over and thus became a statutory tenant. On 1 October 1975 he left his wife and the flat, never to return, but she continued to live there, herself paying the rent. On 3 March 1978 the wife obtained a decree nisi which became absolute on 4 August. Neither the husband nor the wife took legal advice or were represented in those divorce proceedings. It was no doubt for this reason that before obtaining her decree absolute the wife failed to make an application under s 7 of the Matrimonial Homes Act 1967 for a transfer of the husband's statutory tenancy. As the law then stood, under s 7(5) of the 1967 Act such an application ceased to be available to her on and after the issue of the decree absolute.

The husband's statutory tenancy survived his departure from the flat because the wife remained in residence there and he was deemed to be himself in residence. But the statutory tenancy did not survive the decree absolute: see *Metropolitan Properties Co Ltd v Cronan* (1982) 44 P & CR 1. The wife now became a person without any right to occupy the flat and subject to an eviction order. This state of affairs continued until March 1982. During the intervening period of 3½ years the wife paid and the landlords accepted the rent. The latter were until that date wholly unaware of the divorce and of the husband's departure from the flat.

When they became aware that the husband was no longer there and in the belief that he had died the landlords began proceedings against the wife. They soon learned that the husband was alive and joined him as second defendant. They claimed that the wife occupied as a trespasser and that the husband's statutory tenancy ended with the decree absolute. Judge Owen, in his capacity as county court judge, tried the claim and held that the wife was not the tenant.

Since this appeal raises a question of construction, the merits of the respective parties

play no part in the final determination. But it is to be observed that, if the wife had been
a advised during the divorce proceedings, it is probable that she would well before the
decree absolute have had her attention drawn to such claims as were available to her,
including an application for transfer of the husband's statutory tenancy under the 1967
Act, and the distressing situation in which she now finds herself would never have arisen.

As it is, she now applies under the 1981 Act and she has to show that that Act is
retrospective in its operation, in the sense that the powers given to the courts in that Act
b may be exercised in relation to a decree of divorce granted before the commencement of
the Act, and retroactive in its effect, in the sense that such powers when exercised will
transform an act which was unlawful under the then current law, namely her trespass in
the flat, into a lawful act, namely a deemed statutory tenancy under the 1981 Act. She
has to show, in effect, that the right to apply for a transfer which was extinguished under
the 1967 Act by the decree absolute is capable of being resurrected under the terms of
c the 1981 Act.

The terms of para 1(1) in Pt I of Sch 2 to the 1967 Act as inserted by Sch 2 to the 1981
Act are as follows:

> 'Where one spouse is entitled, either in his or her own right or jointly with the
> other spouse, to occupy a dwelling house by virtue of—(a) a protected tenancy or
> statutory tenancy within the meaning of the Rent Act 1977 . . . then, on granting a
> *d* decree of divorce . . . or at any time thereafter (whether, in the case of a decree of
> divorce . . . before or after the decree is made absolute), the court by which the
> decree is granted may make an order under Part II below.'

Paragraph 3(1), which is in Pt II, runs as follows:

> 'Where the spouse is entitled to occupy the dwelling house by virtue of a statutory
> *e* tenancy within the meaning of the Rent Act 1977, the court may by order direct
> that, as from such date as may be specified in the order, that spouse shall cease to be
> entitled to occupy the dwelling house and that the other spouse shall be deemed to
> be the tenant . . . under that statutory tenancy.'

It is necessary to consider the way in which this schedule is brought into effect in order
f to dispose of a very brief argument put forward on behalf of the wife. Section 6 of the
1981 Act, which came into force on 14 February 1983, substituted the schedule for the
previous time limit in s 7 of the 1967 Act. It was argued that this method of amending
the earlier section suggests that the later terms should take effect as if they were part of
the 1967 Act and therefore in force at the time. This was not argued in the court below
and no authority was cited to support the proposition. But in any case the argument
stands or falls with the larger proposition as to the schedule itself.
g
The general principles of statutory construction with regard to retrospectivity have
recently been reaffirmed in *Yew Bon Tew v Kenderaan Bas Mara* [1982] 3 All ER 833,
[1983] 1 AC 553. In that case a defendant had acquired an entitlement to plead a time
bar. Subsequent legislation had extended the limitation period. It was held that such
entitlement was an accrued right and that the later legislation providing for a longer
h limitation period was not to be construed retrospectively so as to deprive the defendant
of his defence unless such a construction was unavoidable on the language used. The
defendant had an accrued right to plead that the plaintiff's action was barred. Lord
Brightman said ([1982] 3 All ER 833 at 839, [1983] 1 AC 553 at 563):

> '. . . the proper approach to the construction of the [Public Authorities Protection
> *j* (Amendment) Act 1974 (Malaysia)] is not to decide what label to apply to it,
> procedural or otherwise, but to see whether the statute, if applied retrospectively to
> a particular type of case, would impair existing rights and obligations . . . an accrued
> right to plead a time bar, which is acquired after the lapse of the statutory period, is
> in every sense a right, even though it arises under an Act which is procedural. It is a
> right which is not to be taken away by conferring on the statute a retrospective

operation, unless such a construction is unavoidable . . . The plain purpose of the 1974 Act, read with the [Public Authorities Protection Ordinance 1948 (Malaysia)], was to give and not to deprive; it was to give to a potential defendant, who was not on 13 June 1974 possessed of an accrued limitation defence, a right to plead such a defence at the expiration of the new statutory period. The purpose was not to deprive a potential defendant of a limitation defence which he already possessed.'

So too in the instant case the purpose of the 1981 Act was to give spouses the right to apply 'on and after the decree absolute' for a transfer of interest. On the granting of the decree absolute and thereafter the husband and the landlords had acquired a vested right to defeat a transfer application under the 1967 Act. If the 1981 Act is to be applied retrospectively, it impairs and indeed defeats that existing right. If the decision in *Yew Bon Tew* is applicable, then it becomes necessary to see whether anything in the language of Sch 2, as inserted by the 1981 Act, points to such a retrospective construction as being unavoidable. However, counsel for the wife contends that the approach to matrimonial statutes should be different and within that difference broadly consistent. He draws attention to a number of decisions in the early 1970s where statutes creating similar powers to order the transfer of matrimonial property have been construed to have retrospective effect.

In *Williams v Williams* [1971] 2 All ER 764, [1971] P 271 Lord Simon P had to consider s 4 of the Matrimonial Proceedings and Property Act 1970. The terms of that section are similar to those in Sch 2 as inserted by the 1981 Act enacting that 'On granting a decree of divorce . . . or at any time thereafter (whether, in the case of decree of divorce . . . before or after the decree is made absolute)' the court may order various transfers.

Lord Simon P found that there were no express terms compelling a retrospective construction. He pointed out that the following words could have been employed ([1971] 2 All ER 764 at 771, [1971] P 271 at 279): 'on granting a decree of divorce (*whether before or after the coming into force of this Act*) or at any time thereafter . . .' It is a matter for surprise and regret that the draftsman of later Bills containing similar provisions appears to have disregarded this important recommendation, which, if implemented, would have given the quietus to such litigation as this. He has also disregarded a further passage where Lord Simon P said ([1971] 2 All ER 764 at 772, [1971] P 271 at 281):

'I hope that it will not be thought presumptuous if I suggest that it is desirable that wherever possible a statute should indicate in express and unmistakable terms whether (and, if so, how far) or not it is intended to be retrospective. The expenditure of much time and money would be thereby avoided.'

Lord Simon P went on to balance the various indications for and against an implication of retrospectivity. He considered the words 'or thereafter' and the argument as in the instant case that they were indications in favour of retrospectivity. He said ([1971] 2 All ER 764 at 772, [1971] P 271 at 280):

'. . . the words . . . seem to me to be entirely neutral; they make perfectly good sense if limited to proceedings instituted after the Act came into force; and there is certainly nothing in them to rebut the presumption against retrospection.'

Unless certain subsequent decisions to which I will advert in a moment have cast doubt on that finding, I would respectfully accept the reasoning as applicable to the same words in para 1(1) of Sch 2 as inserted in the 1981 Act. It follows that unless other considerations are present (such as the workability of the Act), the neutrality of the phrase 'on or after' leaves untouched the sovereignty of the presumption against retrospectivity. Lord Simon P in fact held the provision with which he was concerned to be retrospective. But he relied on very special reasons for doing so. By repealing an earlier Act, Parliament had created a vacuum, a total absence of judicial power to give ancillary relief in cases antecedent to the 1970 Act. At the time legislation of this type was in its infancy, and Lord Simon P regarded a retrospective construction as necessary to give reasonable

efficacy to the Act. It would not work properly otherwise. In the circumstances, an
erosion of the presumptive principle against retrospectivity was felt to be a necessary and
remedial measure. The same cannot be said of the 1981 Act. It works perfectly well
without such aids. It was passed after many years of experience in this field of legislation.
It is said that there would be many wives in the same unprotected position as this wife;
but there is no evidence for such an assertion and I find no reason to think that such
evidence exists.

It is argued for the wife that the guidance given by the decision in *Yew Bon Tew* is not
applicable to the construction of matrimonial decisions in that judgment. It does not
appear from a reading of *Williams v Williams* as a whole that Lord Simon P discerned any
distinctive feature in the principles and jurisprudence affecting the construction of
matrimonial statutes. It is clear that he saw the principles of construction as a single
comprehensive code irradiating over the whole statutory field without distinction. The
same view was taken by Scarman J in *Carson v Carson and Stoyek* [1964] 1 All ER 681,
[1964] 1 WLR 511. He adopted the classical approach by refusing to hold that a section
of the Matrimonial Causes Act 1963 was retrospective, on the ground that its effect would
be to impair accrued rights.

However, there are two decisions which, by encouraging reliance on the same phrase
'on granting a decree or thereafter' as one of a number of indicia of retrospectivity, appear
to cast doubt on Lord Simon P's attitude to the phrase. In *Powys v Powys* [1971] 3 All ER
116, [1971] P 340 Brandon J was engaged in construing s 2 of the Matrimonial
Proceedings and Property Act 1970, which created similarly phrased powers in relation
to financial orders. He arrived at the conclusion that the powers operated retrospectively.
To that extent the wife's reliance on the same phrase in the 1981 Act is in line with
Brandon J's decision.

In *Chaterjee v Chaterjee* [1976] 1 All ER 719 at 723, [1976] Fam 199 at 206 Ormrod LJ
adopted the same approach to the same phrase in ss 23 and 24 of the Matrimonial Causes
Act 1973, 'even if it involves the risk', he said, 'that some people may be exposed to
retrospective interference with their rights and obligations.' Ormrod LJ expressly
approved the decision in *Williams v Williams* notwithstanding Lord Simon P's view that
the phrase, far from being an indication of retrospectivity, was neutral in that regard. In
Williams, *Powys* and *Chaterjee* the common feature was the need to make the statutes
workable and the reforms effective at this period of their introduction. Thus, the
judgment of Sir John Pennycuick in *Chaterjee* emphasised the need to see these statutes
in their historical context. He arrived at a retrospective interpretation on the basis of the
'statutory and judicial background' of the Act (see [1976] 1 All ER 719 at 726, [1976]
Fam 199 at 209), a phrase which may embrace the deficiencies in the earlier legislation
and the need to make the reforms effective by judicial restriction on the presumption
against retrospectivity. The terms of Stamp LJ's assent do not suggest that he favoured
any one of the earlier decisions rather than another or the erosion of the presumption.
Lord Simon P's approach in *Williams* may in my view be said to remain unaffected by
the later decisions. If there be any apparent inconsistency between Lord Simon P's view
that 'On granting a decree . . . or at any time thereafter' was a phrase neutral in its effect
on the question whether a retrospective interpretation should be given to the power
already thus introduced and the view of Brandon J and Ormrod LJ that the use of that
phrase supported a retrospective construction, the latter view should, in my judgment,
be taken to be based on no more than a consideration that the phrase is entirely consistent
with the retrospective interpretation if there are other factors to justify that interpretation.

It was argued for the wife that the general principle in *Yew Bon Tew*, concerned as it
was with litigation between a plaintiff and defendant at arm's length, offers little or no
guidance in interpreting a statute primarily intended to resolve conflicts between
husbands and wives. The contest on the application under Sch 2 is normally one between
spouses. Landlords are given a right of hearing under para 8 (no rules have yet been
enacted). In the present case the husband did not contest the wife's claim for a transfer;
the real contest was with the landlords. It is true that in a case such as the present the

landlords can be described as collecting a windfall out of their tenant's matrimonial
difficulties. But it is equally true (in less emotive terms) that the landlords had a vested   *a*
right to possession of the flat in which the wife remained as a trespasser. They acquired
this because the wife's limitation period had expired at the date of the decree absolute. It
is difficulty to see any distinction between the quality of that right and the right of the
defendant in *Yew Bon Tew* to rely on the passage of time for immunity from claim.

The powers in Sch 2 are discretionary. It was argued on behalf of the wife that the
court in exercising such discretion would, indeed should, take into account any hardship   *b*
suffered by the parties to the application or by third parties, when giving effect to the
retrospective construction. If, however, all the conditions which give rise to the
presumption against such construction are fulfilled or, inversely, if no circumstances
exist which displace the presumption, as is the position here, the existence of the
discretion is a tenuous aid to construction.

It is a weighty consideration (and one which is favourable to the wife's contention)   *c*
that the three decisions, *Williams*, *Powys* and *Chaterjee*, all gave retrospective effect to
broadly similar provisions in matrimonial statutes. But against this has to be weighed
the need to prevent further and continuing erosion of an important principle of our
unwritten constitution: the presumption against retrospective operation. The earlier
statutes were in danger of leaving the mischief which brought them into existence
unremedied. By contrast the statutory and judicial background to the 1981 Act has   *d*
changed: there is the accumulated experience in enacting and exercising these transfer
powers. This Act was not designed to deal with an urgent reform or a substantial vacuum
arising from a new crop of matrimonial Acts conferring novel powers, as was the case in
the 1960s and 1970s. The 1981 Act enlarges the court's powers as envisaged by the Law
Commission and it does so effectively without creating any glaring lacuna. Accordingly,
I would apply the principle enunciated in *Yew Bon Tew* without qualification to the   *e*
present case, adopt the approach of Lord Simon P to the phrase 'on granting of a decree
of divorce . . . or . . . thereafter' and refuse to divest the landlords of their properly
acquired right.

If, contrary to my view, the 1981 Act ought to be given retrospective effect, the wife
has then to show that the appropriate subject matter exists on which the power of the
court, in retrospect, can act. Schedule 2 as inserted by the 1981 Act confers on the court   *f*
the jurisdiction and power to order transfers of protected and statutory tenants.
Paragraphs 1 and 3 of the schedule contain the words 'Where one spouse *is* entitled . . . to
occupy . . . the court . . . may . . . order'. There are four moments in time at which such
subject matter could be required in general principle to exist: the date of the decree of
divorce, nisi or absolute, the date of issue of proceedings for transfer under the Act or the
date of the hearing. Since on the grant of the decree (and therefore at the time of the   *g*
application and hearing) the husband ceased to be entitled to occupy the flat either
himself or by his wife as a statutory tenant, the wife has to establish that under the terms
of the 1981 Act the correct date is the date of one or other of the decrees. If the
determinant moment is the decree absolute, the applicant fails to qualify, for the
entitlement ceases at the very moment of the decree. The judge therefore went back to
the decree nisi as the point of reference. There are difficulties in such a choice. First,   *h*
there is nothing in the language of the provisions which points to this rather than any
later event. Second, the use of the present tense is inconsistent with a reference back to
the earlier decree. Nor is the language of the schedule subjected to any less strain if the
decree absolute is the point of reference. The decree is one of the events on which the
power may be exercised. It may also be exercised 'at any time thereafter'. If the power
were in any given case to be exercised substantially later than the decree, there is an   *j*
artificiality in taking the decree as the determinant event. The ordinary and natural
meaning and in particular the present tense point to the date of the application, ie the
moment that the claim, based on the postulate, is preferred. As a matter of language the
hearing might well be a determinant event but because its date is to some extent a matter
of chance, uncontrollable by the parties, I would reject it. It is true that the word 'spouse'

a is (after decree absolute) no longer an accurate description of the applicant, but in the context it can reasonably be considered a term identifying the applicant by reference to her former status, a term used throughout the Act and in particular in the schedule for such a purpose.

It was argued in the alternative that the wife's status after the decree absolute was in some way analogous to a statutory tenancy in that certain obligations and rights continue to be enforceable against and by her: see *Boyer v Warbey* [1952] 2 All ER 976, [1953] 1
b QB 234. But, even if this argument were open to the wife, it is unsustainable. The subject matter of the transfer power is defined in the schedule as being a statutory or protected tenancy. Rights and obligations may arise out of and posterior to a statutory tenancy; they do not themselves constitute such a relationship. Accordingly, in the circumstances of this case, there was no relevant subject matter on which the power could be exercised at the time of the hearing, and the wife fails in this respect too. The appeal should, in my
c view, be allowed.

SIR JOHN ARNOLD P. I agree.

Appeal allowed. Leave to appeal to the House of Lords granted.

d Solicitors: *Memery Crystal & Co* (for the landlords); *Max Bitel Greene & Co* (for the wife).

Bebe Chua   Barrister.

e # Gammon (Hong Kong) Ltd and others v Attorney General of Hong Kong

PRIVY COUNCIL
LORD FRASER OF TULLYBELTON, LORD SCARMAN, LORD BRIDGE OF HARWICH AND LORD
f BRIGHTMAN
28, 29 FEBRUARY, 1, 5 MARCH, 8 MAY 1984

Criminal law – Absolute liability – Statutory offence – Principles applicable in determining whether offence absolute – Acts prohibited by statute on ground of public safety – Regulation of building works – Offence for contractor to deviate in material way from approved building plans
g *– Offence for person responsible for carrying out works to carry out or permit works to be carried out in manner likely to cause risk of injury or damage – Heavy penalties imposed for offences – Whether offences of strict liability – Building Ordinance (HK) (revised edn 1981), s 40(2A)(b)(2B)(b).*

The appellants were, respectively, the registered contractor, the project manager and the site agent for building works on a site in Hong Kong, the second and third appellants
h being employees of the first. Following the collapse of part of a temporary lateral support system which was included in plans approved by the building authority, the contractor was charged with diverging or deviating in a material way from the work shown in the approved plans contrary to s 40(2A)(b)[a] of the Hong Kong Building Ordinance (revised edn 1981) and with carrying out the building works in a manner likely to cause risk of injury to any person or damage to any property contrary to s 40(2B)(b) of that ordinance,
j and the project manager was charged that, being the contractor's manager, he carried out the works, and the site agent that he permitted the works to be carried out, in a manner likely to cause risk of injury or damage contrary to s 40(2B)(b). At the trial, the magistrate ruled that mens rea of all the facts constituting the offences charged was a necessary

---

a   Section 40, so far as material, is set out at p 505 g to p 506 a, post

ingredient of the offences and he acquitted the appellants on the grounds that neither
knowledge of the materiality of the deviation from the plans under s 40(2A)(b) nor
knowledge of the risk of injury or damage under s 40(2B)(b) had been proved against the a
appellants. The Court of Appeal of Hong Kong allowed an appeal by the prosecutor on
the ground that the offences charged were offences of strict liability and that accordingly
mens rea of the materiality of the deviation from the plans under sub-s (2A)(b) and the
likelihood of risk of injury or damage under sub-s (2B)(b) were not required to be proved.
The appellants appealed to the Privy Council. Section 40 of the ordinance created a b
number of offences in addition to those created by sub-ss (2A)(b) and (2B)(b), the wording
of some of which expressly required full mens rea. The penalties for offences against sub-
ss (2A)(b) and (2B)(b) were heavy.

Held – (1) Although there was a presumption of law that mens rea was required before c
a person could be held guilty of a criminal offence, that presumption could, in relation
to a statutory offence, be displaced where the statute was concerned with an issue of social
concern, eg public safety. However, even where a statute was concerned with such an
issue, the presumption of mens rea would stand unless it could also be shown that the
creation of strict liability in regard to the offence in question would be effective to
promote the objects of the statute by encouraging greater vigilance to prevent the d
commission of the prohibited act (see p 508 f g, post); *Sherras v De Rutzen* [1895–9] All
ER Rep 1167, *Lim Chin Aik v R* [1963] 1 All ER 223 and *Sweet v Parsley* [1969] 1 All ER
347 applied.

(2) It was consistent with the purpose of the ordinance, which was to regulate building
works to which it applied, and thus to regulate an activity involving potential danger to
public safety, that some at least of the criminal offences created by the ordinance should e
be of strict liability, since strict liability would promote greater vigilance. Whether a
particular provision of the ordinance created an offence of strict liability depended on the
true meaning of the words of that provision construed with reference to its subject
matter and to whether strict liability in respect of all or any of the essential ingredients
of the offence would promote the object of the provision. Neither the fact that sub-ss
(2A)(b) and (2B)(b) of s 40 appeared in a section which created other offences which f
expressly required full mens rea nor the severity of the maximum penalties under those
subsections of themselves went to show that full mens rea was required in respect of
offences under the subsections. However, since the object of sub-s (2A)(b) was to prevent
material deviations from the approved plan by persons bearing responsibility for the
works, and since it would seriously weaken the effectiveness of the subsection if proof of
knowledge of such materiality were required, it followed that proof of such knowledge g
was not required and to that extent the offence under sub-s (2A)(b) was one of strict
liability. Likewise, since the purpose of sub-s (2B)(b) was to prevent persons who had the
power of decision from carrying out building works in a manner likely to cause risk of
injury or damage, it followed that proof of knowledge of the likelihood of such risk was
not required, and to that extent the offence under sub-s (2B)(b) was also one of strict
liability; the use of the word 'permits' in sub-s (2B)(b) did not by itself, however, indicate h
the necessity for mens rea but merely required that the defendant should have power to
control whether the actus reus (the carrying out of the works in the manner prohibited)
should be committed. The appeal would therefore be dismissed and the case remitted to
the magistrate (see p 508 h j, p 509 b c g to p 510 a d e j to p 511 c e to j and p 512 c to h,
post).

j

Notes
For the requirement of mens rea, see 11 Halsbury's Laws (4th edn) para 4, and for cases
on the subject, see 14(1) Digest (Reissue) 17–25, 36–72.

For offences of strict liability, see 11 Halsbury's Laws (4th edn) para 18.

Cases referred to in judgment

A-G v Chan Wing On [1964] HKLR 491.

Chung Yat v R [1978] HKLR 355.

James & Sons Ltd v Smee, Green v Burnett [1954] 3 All ER 273, [1955] 1 QB 78, [1954] 3 WLR 631, DC.

Lim Chin Aik v R [1963] 1 All ER 223, [1963] AC 160, [1963] 2 WLR 42, PC.

Sherras v De Rutzen [1895] 1 QB 918, [1895–9] All ER Rep 1167, DC.

Sweet v Parsley [1969] 1 All ER 347, [1970] AC 132, [1969] 2 WLR 470, HL.

Appeal

Gammon (Hong Kong) Ltd, Yee Chin Teo and Chak Shing Mak appealed against the judgment of the Court of Appeal of Hong Kong (Huggins V-P, Yang and Barker JJA) dated 11 February 1983 allowing the appeal of the respondent, the Attorney General of Hong Kong, by way of case stated, from the appellants' acquittals on 3 May 1982 in the Hong Kong Magistrates' Court (Mr S A M Clay) of offences under the Buildings Ordinance of Hong Kong, and remitting the matter to that court. The facts are set out in the judgment of the Board.

Robert Alexander QC, John Mathew QC and Anthony Hooper for the appellants.

The Crown Prosecutor for Hong Kong (M Lucas QC), The Senior Assistant Crown Prosecutor for Hong Kong (C W Reid) and D Fitzpatrick (of the Hong Kong Bar) for the respondent.

8 May. The following judgment of the Board was delivered.

LORD SCARMAN. This appeal is from a judgment of the Court of Appeal of Hong Kong allowing the appeal of the Attorney General from the decision of the magistrate, whereby he dismissed charges brought against the three appellants in respect of alleged contraventions of the Buildings Ordinance (revised edn 1981). The issue of the appeal is whether the offences charged are offences of strict liability or require proof of mens rea as to their essential facts.

The first appellant, Gammon (Hong Kong) Ltd (the company), is a contractor registered under the ordinance and was carrying out building works at a site known as Marine Lot 3, Queen's Road Central, Hong Kong. The second and third appellants were employees of the company, being respectively the project manager and site agent for the works.

The appellants were charged under s 40(2A) and (2B) of the ordinance. It is necessary to set out in full the two subsections:

> '(2A) Any person for whom any building works, street works, lift works or escalator works are being carried out and any authorized person, registered structural engineer, registered contractor, registered lift contractor or registered escalator contractor directly concerned with any such works who—(a) permits or authorizes to be incorporated in or used in the carrying out of any such works any materials which—(i) are defective or do not comply with the provisions of this Ordinance; (ii) have not been mixed, prepared, applied, used, erected, constructed, placed or fixed in the manner required for such materials under this Ordinance; (b) diverges or deviates in any material way from any work shown in a plan approved by the Building Authority under this Ordinance; or (c) knowingly misrepresents a material fact in any plan, certificate, form or notice given to the Building Authority under this Ordinance, shall be guilty of an offence and shall be liable on conviction to a fine of $250,000 and to imprisonment for 3 years.
>
> (2B) Any person (whether or not an authorized person, a registered structural engineer or a registered contractor) directly concerned with any site formation works, piling works, foundation works or other form of building works who—(a) carries out or has carried out such works, or authorizes or permits or has authorized or permitted such works to be carried out, in such manner that it causes injury to

any person or damage to any property; or (b) carries out or has carried out such works, or authorizes or permits or has authorized or permitted such works to be carried out, in such manner as is likely to cause risk of injury to any person or damage to any property, shall be guilty of an offence and shall be liable on conviction to a fine of $250,000 and to imprisonment for 3 years.'

The company was charged with a material deviation from an approved plan in contravention of sub-s (2A)(b) and with carrying out works in a manner likely to cause risk of injury or damage in contravention of sub-s (2B)(b). The second and third appellants were charged under sub-s (2B)(b); it was charged against the second appellant that, being the company's manager, he carried out the works, and against the third appellant that he permitted the works to be carried out, in a manner likely to cause risk of injury or damage.

The appeal is by way of case stated. There was not, however, a full trial of the case in the magistrate's court. At the conclusion of the prosecution case the magistrate ruled that mens rea (knowledge, or 'constructive knowledge') of all the facts was a necessary ingredient of the offences charged. The defence, thereafter, confined its evidence to the issue of knowledge, and did not develop its case on the other facts. Specifically, the defence led no evidence to counter the prosecution case that the deviation from the plan was a material deviation or that the manner in which the works were carried out did in truth create the likelihood of risk of injury or damage. Nor was the issue of 'constructive knowledge' (ie recklessness or mere negligence) fully explored.

As a result of the course taken at trial the case stated sets out only the facts and assumptions on which the magistrate, and later the Court of Appeal, decided one question of law, namely: are the offences charged offences of strict liability? Their Lordships think that the course taken at the magistrate's court was unfortunate, for it means that, whatever answer their Lordships give to the question of law, the case will have to go back to the magistrate for a full trial. The expense already incurred and the future expense of a second trial are too formidable to be viewed with equanimity even when the parties are as substantial as this company and the Crown.

The facts relevant to the issue can be very briefly summarised. The company had delegated the fulfilment of its obligations under the ordinance on the site to the second and third appellants; it is accepted, therefore, that the company is vicariously responsible if either of them contravened or failed to comply with the provisions of the ordinance. If either of them committed an offence in the course of his employment, the company has also offended and is liable to the penalties imposed by the ordinance.

The offending act, which is the basis of all the charges, was the removal of part of the lateral support system on the site, a system which was required in the interest of safety by plans approved by the building authority. The removal was 'a deviation of substance' from the plans; and it is to be assumed for the purpose of the appeal (for it is not admitted by the appellants) that the removal was likely to cause a risk of injury or damage. The magistrate was not satisfied on the evidence that either the second appellant or the third appellant (for whose acts and omissions the company would be criminally responsible) knew that the removal of part of the lateral support system constituted a material deviation from approved plans or that it was likely to cause a risk of any injury or damage. He therefore dismissed the charges. He stated the following questions of law for the opinion of the court:

'(1) Whether I was correct in law in holding that in relation to a prosecution under Section 40(2A)(b) of the Buildings Ordinance Cap. 123 it is necessary for the prosecution to prove that a defendant knowingly or intentionally deviated or diverged in a material way from plans approved by the Building Authority. (2) Whether I was correct in law in holding that in relation to a prosecution under Section 40(2B)(b) of the Buildings Ordinance Cap. 123 it is necessary for the prosecution to show that a defendant knowingly or intentionally caused the likelihood of risk of injury to any person or damage to property.'

a   The Court of Appeal answered both questions in the negative and remitted the case to the magistrate.

The general law

In *Sweet v Parsley* [1969] 1 All ER 347 at 350, [1970] AC 132 at 149 Lord Reid observed that—

b   'it is firmly established by a host of authorities that mens rea is an essential ingredient of every offence unless some reason can be found for holding that that is not necessary.'

The question in the appeal is whether the ordinance, correctly interpreted, provides a sound reason for holding that the offences created by sub-s (2A)(*b*) and (2B)(*b*) of s 40 of the ordinance are offences of strict liability. The Attorney General of Hong Kong contends that it does; the appellants contend that it does not.

c   Before, however, one considers the ordinance, it is necessary to have clearly in mind the applicable principles of the criminal law. Three cases, all of them well known, bear directly on the issue. In *Sherras v De Rutzen* [1895] 1 QB 918, [1895–9] All ER Rep 1167 the court had under consideration the prohibition contained in the Licensing Act 1872 on the supply by a licensee of liquor to a police constable while on duty. The appellant's

d   case was that he did not know and had no reason to believe that the constable was on duty. The court quashed the conviction. Wright J, in the course of his judgment, considered the classes of case in which the presumption of mens rea can be displaced in English law. He saw three principal classes of cases in which the presumption can be displaced; two of them are relevant to this appeal, namely (1) cases where the prohibited acts are not criminal in any real sense but are acts which in the public interest are

e   prohibited under a penalty, and (2) cases of public nuisance. He prefaced his judgment by a statement of general principle ([1895] 1 QB 918 at 921, [1895–9] All ER Rep 1167 at 1169):

          'There is a presumption that mens rea, an evil intention, or a knowledge of the wrongfulness of the act, is an essential ingredient in every offence; but that presumption is liable to be displaced either by the words of the statute creating the

f   offence or by the subject-matter with which it deals, and both must be considered.'

In *Lim Chin Aik v R* [1963] 1 All ER 223, [1963] AC 160 the Judicial Committee accepted Wright J's formulation of principle as correct. But the Board warned that the adoption of the principle does not dispose of the question whether the presumption is displaced (see [1963] 1 All ER 223 at 227–228, [1963] AC 160 at 172–173). For the

g   difficulty of applying the principle remains. What should be the proper inferences to be drawn from the language of the statute under review? And what are the inferences to be drawn from the subject matter with which the statute deals?

The Board went on to state an approach to these two questions which was later approved and accepted by the House of Lords in *Sweet v Parsley*. The Board said ([1963] 1 All ER 223 at 228, [1963] AC 160 at 174):

h   'Where the subject-matter of the statute is the regulation for the public welfare of a particular activity—statutes regulating the sale of food and drink are to be found among the earliest examples—it can be and frequently has been inferred that the legislature intended that such activities should be carried out under conditions of strict liability. The presumption is that the statute or statutory instrument can be effectively enforced only if those in charge of the relevant activities are made

j   responsible for seeing that they are complied with. When such a presumption is to be inferred, it displaces the ordinary presumption of mens rea.'

But the Board added ([1963] 1 All ER 223 at 229, [1963] AC 160 at 175):

          'Where it can be shown that the imposition of strict liability would result in the prosecution and conviction of a class of persons whose conduct could not in any way affect the observance of the law, their Lordships consider that, even where the statute is dealing with a grave social evil, strict liability is not likely to be intended.'

    a

However, in *Sweet v Parsley* [1969] 1 All ER 347 at 350, [1970] AC 132 at 149 Lord Reid refused to accept that in determining the question of mens rea or strict liability it is sufficient merely to have regard to the subject matter of the statute in construing the words of the provision creating the offence. Other considerations have to be borne in mind including the nature of the prohibited act; if it were 'truly criminal', it would be nesessary, for example, to consider whether the public interest really required that an   *b* innocent person should suffer in order that fewer guilty men might escape.

In the course of his speech in *Sweet v Parsley* [1969] 1 All ER 347 at 362, [1970] AC 132 at 163, Lord Diplock addressed himself directly to the question which their Lordships have to consider in this appeal. He said:

> 'But where the subject-matter of a statute is the regulation of a particular activity   *c* involving potential danger to public health, safety or morals in which citizens have a choice whether they participate or not, the court may feel driven to infer an intention of Parliament to impose, by penal sanctions, a higher duty of care on those who choose to participate and to place on them an obligation to take whatever measures may be necessary to prevent the prohibited act, without regard to those considerations of cost or business practicability which play a part in the determination   *d* of what would be required of them in order to fulfil the ordinary common law duty of care. But such an inference is not lightly to be drawn, nor is there any room for it unless there is something that the person on whom the obligation is imposed can do directly or indirectly, by supervision or inspection, by improvement of his business methods or by exhorting those whom he may be expected to influence or control, which will promote the observance of the obligation (see *Lim Chin Aik* v.   *e* *Reginam* ([1963] 1 All ER 223 at 228, [1963] AC 160 at 174)).'

In their Lordships' opinion, the law relevant to this appeal may be stated in the following propositions (the formulation of which follows closely the written submission of the appellants' counsel, which their Lordships gratefully acknowledge): (1) there is a presumption of law that mens rea is required before a person can be held guilty of a criminal offence; (2) the presumption is particularly strong where the offence is 'truly   *f* criminal' in character; (3) the presumption applies to statutory offences, and can be displaced only if this is clearly or by necessary implication the effect of the statute; (4) the only situation in which the presumption can be displaced is where the statute is concerned with an issue of social concern; public safety is such an issue; (5) even where a statute is concerned with such an issue, the presumption of mens rea stands unless it can also be shown that the creation of strict liability will be effective to promote the objects of the   *g* statute by encouraging greater vigilance to prevent the commission of the prohibited act.

The ordinance

Their Lordships turn to consider the purpose and subject matter of the ordinance. Its overall purpose is clearly to regulate the planning, design and construction of the building works to which it relates in the interests of safety. It covers a field of activity where there   *h* is, especially in Hong Kong, a potential danger to public safety. And the activity which the ordinance is intended to regulate is one in which citizens have a choice whether they participate or not. Part IV (s 40) of the ordinance makes it very clear that the legislature intended that criminal sanctions for contraventions of the ordinance should be a feature of its enforcement. But it is not to be supposed that the legislature intended that any of the offences created by the ordinance should be offences of strict liability unless it is plain,   *j* from a consideration of the subject matter of the ordinance and of the wording of the particular provision creating the offence, that an object of the ordinance, eg the promotion of greater vigilance by those having responsibility under the ordinance, would be served by the imposition of strict liability.

The appellants submit that there is no necessity for strict liability in respect of any of the offences charged. Their first submission is that strict liability would not promote

a greater vigilance. If the persons charged had no knowledge of an essential fact, what could they have done to avoid its occurrence? Their second submission is more comprehensive. They submit that strict liability in respect of any offence created by the ordinance would run counter to the structure and character of the ordinance. The ordinance, it is submitted, relies not on criminal liability but on the elaborate and stringent provisions for the registration of persons qualified to ensure that its requirements

b are met.

So far as the first submission is concerned, their Lordships are satisfied that strict liability would help to promote greater vigilance in the matters covered by the two offenders with which this appeal is concerned (the material deviation under sub-s (2A)(*b*) and the risk of injury or damage under sub-s (2B)(*b*)). The second submission is more formidable. Their Lordships, however, reject it also. Their Lordships agree with the

c view expressed by the Court of Appeal as to the purpose and subject matter of the ordinance. The Court of Appeal saw no injustice in the imposition of heavy penalties for offences under the ordinance 'whether resulting from intentional infringement of the law, negligence or incompetence'. They made this powerful comment:

> 'Any large scale building operation will almost inevitably produce circumstances
> in which a departure from the generally accepted standards (whether of work or
d > materials) will be likely to cause danger. Indeed, the extent of the danger and of the
> damage which may be done will frequently be enormous. It therefore behoves the
> incompetent to stay away and the competent to conduct themselves with proper
> care. A building contractor who delegates his legal responsibilities to an agent can
> fairly be held liable if he appoints an agent who is incompetent or careless: he should
> regulate his business in such a way as to avoid, on the one hand, the appointment of
e > incompetent agents and, on the other, the consequences of any carelessness by a
> competent agent. Only if he is made responsible for seeing that the statutory
> standards are maintained can the purpose of the legislation be attained and in such
> a case as this the presumption of strict liability displaces the ordinary presumption
> of mens rea: see *Lim Chin Aik v R* [1963] 1 All ER 223 at 228, [1963] AC 160 at 174.'

f   Important as are the provisions of the ordinance for the registration, disqualification and discipline of persons qualified, authorised and registered to perform the duties and obligations required by the ordinance, the legislature by enacting Pt IV (s 40) of the ordinance clearly took the view that criminal liability and punishment were needed as a deterrent against slipshod or incompetent supervision, control or execution of building works. The imposition of strict liability for some offences clearly would emphasise to those concerned the need for high standards of care in the supervision and execution of

g work. The view that their Lordships have reached, after the thorough review of the ordinance and its history which counsel undertook helpfully and with great assiduity in the course of their submissions, is that, where the ordinance provides for an offence in terms which are silent or ambiguous as to the need for full mens rea covering all its essential ingredients, the wording of the particular provision must be carefully examined

h against the background and in the context of the ordinance to determine whether it is necessary to interpret the silence or resolve the ambiguity in favour of mens rea or of strict liability.

Put in positive terms, the conclusion of the Board is that it is consistent with the purpose of the ordinance in its regulation of the works to which it applies that at least some of the criminal offences which it creates should be of strict liability. It is a statute

j the subject matter of which may properly be described as—

> 'the regulation of a particular activity involving potential danger to public health
> [and] safety . . . in which citizens have a choice whether they participate or not . . .'

(See [1969] 1 All ER 347 at 362, [1970] AC 132 at 163 per Lord Diplock.)

Whether, therefore, a particular provision of the statute creates an offence of full mens rea or of strict liability must depend on the true meaning of the words of the particular provision construed with reference to its subject matter and to the question whether strict liability in respect of all or any of the essential ingredients of the offence would promote the object of the provision.

Before leaving the consideration of the ordinance as a whole, their Lordships refer briefly to two decisions of the Hong Kong courts on which the appellants placed some reliance. The earlier in date was a decision of MacFee J on appeal from the magistrate. In *A-G v Chan Wing On* [1964] HKLR 491 MacFee J allowed an appeal by an architect against a conviction on a charge of using defective materials (s 27(5) of the 1955 ordinance, the predecessor of s 40(2A)(*a*)); the judge held that it was necessary to prove knowledge that defective materials were used. The second case was *Chung Yat v R* [1978] HKLR 355, in which it is clear that Leonard J assumed that to establish offences (under the statutory provisions which preceded sub-s (2A)(*a*) and (*b*)) of using defective materials and of deviation from plan it was necessary to prove knowledge that the materials were defective and that the deviations were material. It was, however, not contended otherwise by the Crown: all parties assumed that before a person could be convicted he 'must be fixed with the knowledge active or constructive that the defect existed and that the deviations were material' (at 359).

Their Lordships accept that these decisions support the view of the ordinance (and of the offences charged in this case) for which the appellants contend. They were not, however, binding on the Court of Appeal. In their Lordships' opinion the Court of Appeal was fully entitled to reject any guidance that there might be in these cases as to the true construction of the ordinance or its provisions. The Court of Appeal clearly preferred to base its decision on its own view as to the purpose of the ordinance and as to the meaning of the particular provisions which the court had to construe. Their Lordships have followed the same course. As will become clear, their Lordships agree with the Court of Appeal. To the extent (if at all) that these two cases point to a different conclusion from that reached by the Court of Appeal they must be held to be overruled.

Subsections (2A) and (2B)

Their Lordships now turn to consider the two subsections in detail and separately; for it does not follow that, if one subsection should create an offence of strict liability, the other must also do so. But first a few observations on certain features common to both.

The first common feature is that both subsections have a characteristic of which Lord Reid spoke in *Sweet v Parsley* [1969] 1 All ER 347 at 350, [1970] AC 132 at 149. The specific provisions sub-ss (2A)(*b*) and (2B)(*b*) belong to that:

> 'multitude of criminal enactments where the words of the Act simply make it an offence to do certain things but where everyone agrees that there cannot be a conviction without proof of mens rea in some form.'

Each provision clearly requires a degree of mens rea, but each is silent whether it is required in respect of all the facts which together constitute the offence created. The issue here is, therefore, a narrow one. Does sub-s (2A)(*b*) require knowledge of the materiality of the deviation? Does sub-s (2B)(*b*) require knowledge of the likelihood of risk of injury or damage?

The second common feature is that each provision appears in a section which creates many other offences, the wording of some, though not all, of which clearly requires full mens rea.

A third common feature is that the maximum penalties fror the offences which they create are heavy: a fine of $250,000 and imprisonment for three years. There is no doubt that the penalty indicates the seriousness with which the legislature viewed the offences.

The first of these features raises the determinative question in the appeal. Their Lordships will, therefore, consider it later in respect of each subsection.

The second feature, in their Lordships' opinion, proves nothing. One would expect a wide range of very different offences in a statute which establishes a comprehensive

system of supervision and control over a great range of complicated works in diverse
a circumstances. And it can be said with equal force that a feature of s 40 is that in many
cases where mens rea is required it expressly says so, and that, where a defence of
reasonable excuse or lack of knowledge is to be available, it makes express provision to
that end; examples may be seen in sub-ss (1B), (1C), (2A)(c), (2C), (6), (7) and (7A).

The severity of the maximum penalties is a more formidable point. But it has to be
considered in the light of the ordinance read as a whole. For reasons which their
b Lordships have already developed, there is nothing inconsistent with the purpose of the
ordinance in imposing severe penalties for offences of strict liability. The legislature
could reasonably have intended severity to be a significant deterrent, bearing in mind
the risks to public safety arising from some contraventions of the ordinance. Their
Lordships agree with the view on this point of the Court of Appeal. It must be crucially
important that those who participate in or bear responsibility for the carrying out of
c works in a manner which complies with the requirements of the ordinance should know
that severe penalties await them in the event of any contravention or non-compliance
with the ordinance by themselves or by anyone over whom they are required to exercise
supervision or control.

Subsection (2A)
d This provision applies to building owners, authorised persons (ie architects, surveyors,
structural engineers), registered structural engineers and registered contractors. It is thus
confined to persons bearing responsibility for the decision to undertake works and for
their supervision and control. There is plainly an element of mens rea in the offences it
creates: the wording of paras (a) and (b) does not make clear how far mens rea extends;
the wording of para (c) reveals an offence of full mens rea. The statutory predecessors to
e paras (a) and (b) were considered in the two Hong Kong cases, *A-G v Chan Wing On* and
Chung Yat v R, which neither the Court of Appeal nor their Lordships have found helpful
in determining this appeal.

The wording of para (b) clearly requires knowledge of the approved plan and of the
fact of deviation. But in their Lordships' view it would be of little use in promoting
public safety if it also required proof of knowledge of the materiality of the deviation. As
f it was put on behalf of the Attorney General, if the offence requires knowledge of the
materiality of the deviation to be proved, the defendant is virtually judge in his own
cause. The object of the provision is to assist in preventing material deviations from
occurring. If a building owner, an authorised person or a registered person is unaware of
the materiality of the deviation which he authorises (and knowledge of the deviation is
necessary), he plainly ought to be. He is made liable to criminal penalties because of the
g threat to public safety arising from material deviations from plans occurring within the
sphere of his responsibility. The effectiveness of the ordinance would be seriously
weakened if it were open to such a person to plead ignorance of what was material. In
the words already quoted of the Court of Appeal, '. . . it behoves the incompetent to stay
away and the competent to conduct themselves with proper care'.

Subsection (2B)
h The construction of sub-s (2B)(b) is more difficult, but their Lordships are satisfied that
it imposes strict liability for substantially the same reasons as those which have led them
to this conclusion in respect of sub-s (2A)(b). The offence created clearly requires a degree
of mens rea. A person cannot carry out works or authorise or permit them to be carried
out in a certain manner unless he knows the manner which he is employing, authorising
or permitting. The appellants laid great emphasis on the reference to 'permitting' as an
j indication of full mens rea. They referred their Lordships to *James & Son Ltd v Smee*
[1954] 3 All ER 273, [1955] 1 QB 78. But their Lordships agree with the answer of the
Court of Appeal to this point:

'We would therefore hold that the word "permitting" in s 40(2B)(b) does not by
itself import mens rea in the sense of intention to cause a likelihood of risk of injury

or knowledge that such likelihood would result but does require that the defendant shall have had a power to control whether the actus reus (the carrying out of the works in the manner which in fact causes a likelihood of risk of injury) shall be committed or not.'

Two further points were, however, developed by the appellants. The first was the wide range of the subsection. It covers any person (whether or not authorised or registered under the ordinance) who is directly concerned with the works. Thus an unskilled labourer engaged in carrying out works on the site would be, it is said, criminally liable if he did something which was dangerous without knowing it. Their Lordships are by no means certain that a labourer on site could be described as a person directly concerned with the manner in which works are carried out on site, for he has no control. But, if he is, it has to be shown under para (a) or para (b) that he bears (or shares) responsibility for determining the manner in which the works are carried out. The purpose of the provision is to prevent persons who have the power of decision, whoever they may be, from choosing and putting into effect a manner of carrying out the works which is likely to cause risk. If a workman should take it on himself to decide, for instance, to remove part of the necessary lateral support system of the site, there would be good reason for making him criminally responsible under the ordinance if what he chose to do was likely to cause risk, whether he knew it or not; but it would have to be proved that the removal was his choice. The offence is not merely 'carrying out works' but doing so in a certain manner. No offence can be committed save by one who bears (or shares) responsibility for deciding the manner in which the works are to be carried out.

Their Lordships find some support for their view that sub-s (2B)(b) is an offence of strict liability in the wording of the offence created by sub-s (2B)(a). The wording of para (a) points to strict liability, once injury or damage has in fact been caused. Anyone who has carried out, authorised or permitted work to be carried out in a manner which has in fact caused injury or damage is caught.

Conclusion

For these reasons their Lordships conclude that to the extent indicated the offences charged against the appellants are of strict liability. Their counsel did develop a detailed argument on the long history of the Buildings Ordinance, beginning with its enactment in 1955 and continuing through many amendments until the present day. But there is nothing in the history to suggest any view of the ordinance or the subsections under consideration other than that taken by the Court of Appeal and now adopted by their Lordships. The basic submission of the appellants was that the imposition of strict liability (to the extent analysed in the earlier part of this judgment) 'could not in any way affect the observance of the law . . .' (see *Lim Chin Aik v R* [1963] 1 All ER 223 at 229, [1963] AC 160 at 175). Their Lordships reject the submission for the reasons which they have given. Their Lordships will humbly advise Her Majesty that the appeal be dismissed. The order of the Court of Appeal that the case be remitted to the magistrate stands. The appellants must pay the respondents' costs in the Court of Appeal and before the Board. The costs in the magistrate's court must be for the magistrate to decide on conclusion of the further hearing in his court.

Appeal dismissed; case remitted to magistrate.

Solicitors: *Denton Hall & Burgin* (for the appellants); *Charles Russell & Co* (for the respondents).

Mary Rose Plummer   Barrister.

a

Thake and another v Maurice

QUEEN'S BENCH DIVISION
PETER PAIN J
27, 28, 29 FEBRUARY, 1, 2, 26 MARCH 1984

b   Contract – Surgery – Nature of contract – Vasectomy – Whether surgeon can contract to produce particular medical result when result depending on healing of human tissue.

Contract – Warranty – Collateral warranty – Breach – Surgery – Vasectomy – Patient told that vasectomy resulting in irreversible sterility – Patient thereby induced to have vasectomy – Patient not warned of risk that effect of vasectomy might be naturally reversed – Patient regaining fertility – Patient's wife becoming pregnant – Whether surgeon in breach of warranty.

c

Medical practitioner – Negligence – Surgery – Failure to warn of result of surgery – Failure to warn that result of surgery might be naturally reversed – Vasectomy – Failure to warn that patient might regain fertility – Patient's wife becoming pregnant – Wife not aware of pregnancy until too late for abortion – Whether failure to give warning of possible regaining of fertility a breach of surgeon's duty of care – Whether damage consisting of pregnancy or of not knowing of pregnancy until too late for abortion.

d

Damages – Unwanted pregnancy – Negligence – Assessment of damages – Public policy – Surgeon failing to warn that vasectomy could be followed by natural regaining of fertility – Patient's wife becoming pregnant – Whether damages recoverable for unwanted pregnancy.

e   The plaintiffs, a railway guard and his wife, lived in a three-bedroomed council house with their five children. They lived in straitened circumstances on the first plaintiff's income, which was supplemented by the second plaintiff doing domestic work when she did not have a child under school age. In order to prevent any further addition to the family, the plaintiffs consulted the defendant, a surgeon, to see whether the first plaintiff could be sterilised by vasectomy. The defendant discussed the nature of the operation *f*   with the plaintiffs and made it clear that a vasectomy was final and that the first plaintiff would become permanently sterile. The plaintiffs were asked to sign forms consenting to the operation. The first plaintiff signed a form stating that he consented to undergo the operation of vasectomy, that the nature of the operation had been explained to him by the defendant, that he had been told that the object of the operation was to render him sterile and incapable of parenthood and that he understood that the effect of the *g*   operation was irreversible. The second plaintiff signed a form stating that she agreed to the operation of vasectomy being carried out on the first plaintiff and that the nature and effect of the operation had been explained to her by the defendant. The operation was carried out by the defendant in October 1975 and tests a few months later showed his ejaculate to be sperm free. In 1977 the second plaintiff became pregnant but failed to recognise the symptoms until it was too late for an abortion. Tests on the first plaintiff *h*   proved that he was fertile. A healthy child was born April 1978. The plaintiffs brought an action against the defendant claiming that their contract with the defendant was not simply a contract to carry out a vasectomy but a contract to sterilise the first plaintiff and that that contract had been broken when he became fertile again, alternatively that they were induced to enter into the contract by a false warranty or innocent misrepresentation that the operation would render the first plaintiff permanently sterile, or in the further *i*   alternative that the defendant failed to warn them that there was a small risk that the first plaintiff might become fertile again. There was no suggestion that the defendant had not performed the operation properly, and at the time of the operation it was known in medical circles that very occasionally the effect of the operation could be reversed naturally. The questions arose (i) whether there had been a breach of contract, (ii) whether the defendant had advised the plaintiffs of the risk that the first plaintiff might become fertile again and whether there had been a breach of a collateral warranty or a misrepresentation, (iii) whether there had been any contractual negligence, (iv) whether public policy precluded an award of damages for the birth of a healthy child and, if it did not, (v) what the appropriate measure of damages was.

Held – (1) Although the defendant had not intended to enter into a contract which absolutely guaranteed sterility, the test of what the contract was did not depend on what the parties to it thought it meant but on what the court objectively determined that the words used meant. The consent form contained no warning that the operation might not succeed in its effect, and being the defendant's document any doubt about its meaning was to be construed against him. Although normally surgeons would not deliberately guarantee any result which depended on the healing of human tissue, there was no reason in law why a surgeon should not contract to produce such a result. On the facts and the evidence, the contract was not merely a contract to perform a vasectomy but was a contract to make the first plaintiff irreversibly sterile (see p 519 d e j to p 520 a, post).

(2) On the balance of probabilities the defendant either failed to give a warning of the risk that the first plaintiff might become fertile again or gave so vague a warning that the risk was not conveyed to the plaintiffs. The defendant described the effect of the operation as an established medical fact. That statement was not a promise as to the future; and, without a warning, it was a factual statement on a crucial factor which was made by a person who had special knowledge and skill, which was made with the intention of inducing the plaintiffs to enter into the contract for the vasectomy, and which in fact did induce the plaintiffs to enter into the contract. The defendant was accordingly in breach of a warranty that the first plaintiff would become irreversibly sterile. Damage resulted from the fact that the collateral warranty was broken rather than the fact that the plaintiffs were induced to enter the contract; the breach of warranty occurred when the first plaintiff became fertile and the damage occurred when the second plaintiff became pregnant (see p 519 b, p 520 c d and p 521 b to e, post); *Esso Petroleum Co Ltd v Mardon* [1976] 2 All ER 5 applied.

(3) Alternatively, since the warning was necessary not merely to enable the first plaintiff to decide whether to have the operation but to enable prompt steps to be taken (if the plaintiffs so wished) to seek an abortion to counteract his regained fertility, it followed that the failure to give the warning was a breach of the contractual duty of care. The damage caused by that failure was not that the second plaintiff conceived but that because of the lack of warning she failed to recognise promptly that she had conceived, with the result that the pregnancy continued without any steps being taken to terminate it until it was too late to do so (see p 522 e to g and p 523 g, post).

(4) Having regard to the policy of the state, as expressed in legislation and social provision (eg family planning was generally practised, abortion was legalised over a wide field, and vasectomy, as a method of family planning, was not only legal but available under the national health service), it could not be said that the birth of a healthy baby was always a blessing or that it was necessarily against public policy to award damages for the unwanted birth of a healthy child. The reasons put forward in the past to support public policy against such an award of damages could however be valid considerations in the assessment of damages in a particular case (see p 526 d to f and p 527 f, post); *Udale v Bloomsbury Area Health Authority* [1983] 2 All ER 522 not followed.

(5) In all the circumstances, there would be no award for the distress, pain and suffering undergone by the plaintiffs because that was cancelled out by the joy they had received from the child. They were entitled, however, to damages for the birth and upkeep of the child, but on a moderate basis in view of the humble household into which the child had been born (see p 527 a b g j, post).

Notes

For collateral contracts, see 9 Halsbury's Laws (4th edn) paras 334, 544.

For the standard of care required of doctors, see 34 ibid para 12, and for cases on the subject, see 33 Digest (Reissue) 262–288, 2162–2330.

For public policy and the measure of damages, see 12 Halsbury's Laws (4th edn) para
1133.

Cases referred to in judgment

Bain v Forthergill (1874) LR 7 HL 158, [1874–80] All ER Rep 83.
Bentley (Dick) Productions Ltd v Harold Smith (Motors) Ltd [1965] 2 All ER 65, [1965] 1 WLR
623, CA.
Bissett v Wilkinson [1927] AC 177, [1926] All ER Rep 324, PC.
Bolam v Friern Hospital Management Committee [1957] 2 All ER 118, [1957] 1 WLR 582.
Chatterton v Gerson [1981] 1 All ER 257, [1981] QB 432, [1980] 3 WLR 1003.
Esso Petroleum Co Ltd v Mardon [1976] 2 All ER 5, [1976] QB 801, [1976] 2 WLR 583, CA.
Gray v Barr (Prudential Assurance Co Ltd, third party) [1971] 2 All ER 949, [1971] 2 QB
554, [1971] 2 WLR 1334, CA; *affg* [1970] 2 All ER 702, [1970] 2 QB 626, [1970] 3
WLR 108.
Heilbut Symons & Co v Buckleton [1913] AC 30, [1911–13] All ER Rep 83, HL.
Hills v Potter [1983] 3 All ER 716.
Heron II, The, Koufos v C Czarnikow Ltd [1967] 3 All ER 686, [1969] 1 AC 350, [1967] 3
WLR 1491, HL.
Hunter v Hanley 1955 SLT 213.
McKay v Essex Area Health Authority [1982] 2 All ER 771, [1982] QB 1166, [1982] 2 WLR
890, CA.
Sciuriaga v Powell [1980] CA Transcript 597; *rvsg* (1979) 123 SJ 406.
Sherlock v Stillwater Clinic (1977) 260 NW 2d 169.
Sidaway v Bethlem Royal Hospital Governors [1984] 1 All ER 1018, [1984] 2 WLR 778, CA.
Sorenson v Cargill Inc (1968) 163 NW 2d 59.
Thill v Modern Erecting Co (1969) 170 NW 2d 265.
Udale v Bloomsbury Area Health Authority [1983] 2 All ER 522, [1983] 1 WLR 1098.
Whitehouse v Jordan [1980] 1 All ER 650, CA; *affd* [1981] 1 All ER 267, [1981] 1 WLR
246, HL.

Action

By a writ dated 16 July 1981 the plaintiffs, Donald Edward Thake and Patricia Ann
Thake, brought an action for damages for misrepresentation, breach of contract, breach
of warranty and negligence in respect of an agreement made with the defendant, B A
Maurice, in or about September 1975 to perform a vasectomy operation and in respect of
the performance by the defendant of that operation on the first plaintiff on or about 18
October 1975. The action was heard in London but judgment was given in Exeter. The
facts are set out in the judgment.

Roger Henderson QC and *Lawrence West* for the plaintiffs.
E A Machin QC and *Roderick Adams* for the defendant.

Cur adv vult

26 March. The following judgment was delivered.

PETER PAIN J. In 1975 the two plaintiffs were at their wits' end. They had four
children and a fifth was on the way. Mr Thake was a railway guard and they were having
the greatest difficulty in managing on his pay, so Mr Thake had a vasectomy which was
performed by the defendant. The operation appeared to be a success and both plaintiffs
were convinced that Mr Thake was now sterile. They resumed normal sexual intercourse
without any further contraceptive precaution.

In 1978 Mrs Thake began to miss her periods. She did not worry because she was
convinced that it was impossible for her to conceive. She put it down to an early onset of
the change of life. Eventually she went to her doctor and was shattered to find that she

was four months pregnant. Her husband was tested and it was found that he had become
fertile again. He was one of those rare cases in which nature had formed a bridge of scar   *a*
tissue between the cut ends of the vas through which the sperm could pass.

The two plaintiffs now claim damages against the defendant on three alternative
grounds. Firstly, they assert that the contract was not simply a contract to carry out a
vasectomy, but was a contract to sterilise Mr Thake which was broken when he became
fertile again. Secondly, they put their case on breach of collateral warranty or innocent
misrepresentation. They submit that they were induced to enter into the contract by a   *b*
false warranty or representation that the operation would render Mr Thake irreversibly
sterile. Thirdly, they allege contractual negligence in that the defendant failed to warn
them that there was a small risk that Mr Thake would become fertile again.

An interesting point also arises as to the assessment of damages, should the plaintiffs
succeed on liability. The defendant asserts that, as a matter of public policy, damages
may not be awarded for the birth of a healthy child.   *c*

I shall deal first with the facts, except for the one matter that is in dispute: whether
any, and if so what, warning was given by the defendant, when he first saw the plaintiffs,
that there was a small risk that Mr Thake might become fertile again. Then I shall deal
with the nature of vasectomy and the processes of early and late recanalisation by which
fertility may be restored. Against that background I shall deal with the need for a
warning and whether one was given in this case. That will provide sufficient material to   *d*
deal with the three ways in which the plaintiffs put their case. That will bring me to the
question of public policy and finally to the computation of damages.

The facts

Mr and Mrs Thake were married in 1961. They now have six children: Mark who is
21, Paul 19, Andrew 16, Kim 15, Lee 8, and Samantha 5. They all live at home in a three-   *e*
bedroomed council house. The three elder boys share one room; Kim (a girl) shares
another room with Lee (a boy) and Samantha.

Mr Thake is now a guard and has worked for British Rail for the last 30 years. Mrs
Thake ekes out the family income by doing domestic work when she has not got a child
under school age. Economically their life is not easy. Although the family is entitled to
free travel on British Rail, they have not had a holiday for many years. The problem of   *f*
clothing the family is solved by the use of jumble sales and a clothing club.

When Mrs Thake was pregnant with Kim, she saw Dr Pickles at Pembury Hospital
and asked for sterilisation, but the doctor was unwilling because she was then under 30.
Seven years later, Lee put in an appearance and this time Dr Pickles agreed that Mrs
Thake might be sterilised and put her on the national health service list but warned her
that it might be a very long wait for the operation. The Thakes could not afford to have   *g*
the operation done privately, so Mr Thake suggested that he should be sterilised by
vasectomy. Mrs Thake agreed and they consulted their general practitioner, Dr Lemerle.
She thought it was a good idea and arranged for the plaintiffs to see the defendant. They
went to see him and had a very sensible discussion about the nature of the operation. He
sought to dissuade them in order to make quite sure that they really understood what it
meant. He pointed out that, if Mrs Thake died, Mr Thake might want to remarry and   *h*
his new wife might want children. He also pointed out that one or more of the Thakes'
children might die and the Thakes might want to add to their family again. But the
plaintiffs firmly made up their minds. The defendant made it clear that they must regard
the decision as final and there would be no turning back. He said that there was a possible
operation for restoring fertility but he could not guarantee that it would succeed;
therefore, they must be clear that they desired Mr Thake to be permanently sterile.

Finance was discussed and it was arranged that the defendant would do the operation
for £20 only, under a local anaesthetic which was the cheapest possible method. The
defendant said that the Thakes must not have sexual intercourse without contraceptives
after the operation until two consecutive samples of Mr Thake's ejaculate proved to be
clear of sperm. The first sample would be taken about a month after the operation and

the next one about a month later. If one proved positive, further samples would be
required.

The defendant produced a form which husband and wife had to sign as consenting to
the operation and on which he entered various particulars. The wording of the form
was:

'CONSENT FOR PRIMARY STERILISATION.

I Donald Thake ... being over the age of twenty-one years hereby consent to
undergo the operation of Vasectomy, the nature of which has been explained to me
by Mr B. A. Maurice. I have been told that the object of the operation is to render
me sterile and incapable of parenthood. I understand that the effect of the operation
is irreversible. I also consent to the administration of a local or other anaesthetic.'

That is dated 25 September 1975 and signed by Mr Thake. Then:

'AGREEMENT BY SPOUSE.

I Patricia Thake the Wife of the above-named being over the age of twenty-one
years hereby agree to the operation of Vasectomy being carried out on my Husband,
the nature and effect of which has been explained to me by Mr B. A. Maurice. I have
read and understand the whole of this form and it has been signed by my Husband
in my presence.'

That has a similar date and is signed by Mrs Thake. Then:

'I confirm that I have explained the nature and effect of this operation to the
patient and his spouse.'

That has a similar date and is signed by the defendant.

There is an issue between the plaintiffs and the defendant whether the defendant gave
any warning as to the possibility of the operation failing to sterilise Mr Thake. The
plaintiffs both say he did not and the defendant says that he did. As this issue is central to
my decision I shall return to it later.

The operation was carried out in October 1975. Samples of Mr Thake's ejaculate were
found to be sperm free on 2 December 1975 and 13 January 1976. On 16 January 1976
the defendant wrote to Mr Thake:

'The result of your second analysis has just come through. Both of these tests
show that there are no sperms present in either specimen and this being so you may
reasonably take no further contraceptive precautions from now on.'

The Thakes then engaged in normal sexual relations without contraceptives. In 1978
Mrs Thake missed her period in August and again in September. This did not trouble
her: she thought it might be an early onset of the menopause, as her mother had had an
early menopause. She went apple picking in the autumn, which was fairly heavy work,
and she began to get backache. In addition, she began to put on a bit of weight. But she
tells me she did not associate any of these symptoms with pregnancy because she thought
that that was quite impossible. Eventually, in order to satisfy her mother, she went to see
Dr Lemerle, who said it was highly unlikely she was pregnant but that she would give
her a test. When the test proved positive Dr Lemerle was so astonished that she insisted
on another test. Then a specimen was taken from Mr Thake and it was found to contain
sperm. Mrs Thake discussed the matter with Dr Lemerle and asked if she could have an
abortion. Dr Lemerle said it was too late as by this time Mrs Thake was about five months
pregnant.

The defendant invited the two plaintiffs to visit him and they saw him on 28
November 1978. He asked about abortion and they told him that Dr Lemerle had said it
was too late, but they checked again with Dr Lemerle who confirmed this. The defendant
also suggested adoption but Mrs Thake flatly refused this, saying that if the child was to
be born it must be a member of the family.

The plaintiffs then passed through a very trying period. Their marriage had been a very happy one but they were so worried and sickened by what had occurred that they were under great strain. For a time this affected their relationship, but Samantha arrived on 5 April and thereafter things got better. Now she is a lovely little girl and they say they are both delighted with her and she is a blessing.

The nature of vasectomy

The sperm passes out of the testicle through a canal called the vas. It is not necessarily ejaculated immediately but may remain secreted in one of the vesicles for some time. A vasectomy is performed by removing a piece from the vas and tying back each end so that the ends are facing in opposite directions. The patient is not rendered immediately sterile because of the sperm secreted in the vesicles. This will be gradually flushed out of the system as ejaculation takes place. A patient is not regarded as sterile until two consecutive samples, as mentioned above, show no trace of sperm.

There were known in 1975 to be two ways in which, in rare cases, this operation might prove ineffective. They are referred to as early recanalisation and late recanalisation. Early recanalisation may take place in one of two ways. If a portion of the vas is not removed or the ends are not effectively tied back, the vas may reunite so that the canal is restored. Alternatively, pregnancy may take place because intercourse without contraceptives is engaged in before the sperm which has already passed through the vas has been flushed out of the system. As a matter of language, this latter alternative is not really recanalisation at all but the medical authorities use this term. Late recanalisation may take place long after the patient has been pronounced sterile. It is due to the formation of scar tissue around the cut ends of the vas which forms a bridge between the two ends and provides a channel through which the sperm can pass.

In this case there is no suggestion but that the defendant performed the operation properly. He removed 1·3 cm from one vas and 1·7 cm from the other and tied the ends back. It was common ground that what has taken place in this case is late recanalisation.

Was a warning given?

The defendant says that when advising on this particular operation he gives a warning in the terms set out in the further and better particulars in para 4 of the defence:

'I am not a plumber. One is dealing with healing tissues. Despite all the efforts one makes to separate the ends they have been known very occasionally to join up. Having said that just as there is a danger in being knocked down when one crosses the road, one does not stop crossing the road because of that.'

He does not pretend, after this lapse of time, to remember the exact words he used to the plaintiffs but he says that he is sure that he gave his normal warning. The plaintiffs flatly deny that any such warning was given. They say that the defendant did speak to them in these terms but this was at the interview in November 1978 when he was seeking to explain why the operation had proved ineffectual. They both insist that they left the defendant's surgery in 1975 convinced that if Mr Thake had the operation he would be permanently sterile from the time when two consecutive sperm tests had proved negative.

This is almost the only issue of fact in the case. I can get little help from the demeanour of the witnesses. Both the plaintiffs struck me as truthful people who told a simple story in a completely forthright manner. The defendant, too, appeared to me to be a completely reliable person, in addition to being a competent and caring surgeon. However, the circumstances point strongly to the absence of any warning or, at all events, any clear warning. It is plain that the plaintiffs were desperately anxious to avoid any addition to their family. I feel quite certain that, if they had had any inkling that there was even the slightest chance of Mr Thake becoming fertile once more, Mrs Thake would have been round to see her general practitioner as soon as a period was missed.

The Thakes struck me as intelligent people and I am quite satisfied that they genuinely

thought it was impossible that Mr Thake should make Mrs Thake pregnant again. I do
a not see how they could have been of this mind if they had been warned of the slightest
risk of late recanalisation. It has to be borne in mind that the major part of the discussion
was whether the Thakes were quite sure that they wanted this operation because there
was no going back. On the balance of probabilities I am satisfied that the defendant
either failed to give any warning of the risk of late recanalisation on this one occasion or
gave the warning in terms so vague that it did not convey the risk to the Thakes, although
b they were paying close attention to what he said.

Breach of contract
   This case differs from the ordinary 'medical negligence' case in that the plaintiffs put
their case boldly in contract. They do not complain of the way in which the defendant
carried out the operation. Their primary case is that he contracted to render the male
c plaintiff irreversibly sterile and that he failed to do so. They contend that there was a
breach of contract at the time when the male plaintiff again became fertile and that this
resulted in damage when Mrs Thake conceived.
   That there was a contract there can be no doubt. It is the content of the contract that is
in issue. The defendant's first line of defence is that he gave the necessary warning. I
have already found that this line will not hold; so one comes to the second line, which is
d that the contract was to perform a vasectomy skilfully and not to produce any guaranteed
result. I am left in little doubt that the defendant did not intend to enter into a contract
which absolutely guaranteed sterility; nor did he use any such word as 'guarantee'. But
the test as to what the contract in fact was does not depend on what the plaintiffs or the
defendant thought it meant, but on what the court objectively determines that the words
used meant.
e   In my opinion the contract was partly oral and partly in writing: it was contained in
the words used between the parties and the words of the consent form. I thought at first
that the defendant was right in contending that this was no more than a contract to
perform a vasectomy; but, in the light of my finding about absence of warning, this
contention will not stand up to close analysis. The defendant showed by gesture how he
explains this operation to his patients. He holds both arms horizontally with the clenched
f fists together; then he pulls them apart to indicate the gap that is formed when a piece of
vas is removed. Then he bends his wrists backwards to show how the ends of the vas are
tied back so that they face in opposite directions. The plaintiffs say, and the defendant
does not dispute, that when he was explaining the operation to them he also drew a
rough sketch. I am satisfied that this would convey to the ordinary layman that it would
be impossible for the sperm to pass again through the vas. Indeed, the defendant
g recognised that without his usual warning his demonstration would leave a patient with
the impression that he would become completely sterile.
   I look next to the wording of the consent form. By this, the plaintiffs both acknowledge
that the nature of the operation has been explained to them by the defendant. The male
plaintiff acknowledges that he has been told that the object of the operation is to render
him sterile and incapable of parenthood and that he understands that the effect of the
h operation is irreversible. Mrs Thake acknowledges that the nature and effect of the
operation has been explained to her by the defendant and that she has read and understood
the whole of the form. The defendant confirms that he has explained the nature and
effect of this operation to the plaintiffs.
   This language contains no warning that the operation may not succeed in its effect. It
is the defendant's document, and if there is any doubt about its meaning (and I do not
j think there is) then it is to be construed against the defendant on the contra proferentem
principle. It is subject only to the qualification which was explained orally: that there
must be two consecutive negative tests before the male plaintiff could be regarded as
sterile.
   I have hesitated before arriving at this conclusion. It is a decision which surgeons will
regard with alarm. I accept that they would not deliberately guarantee any result which

depended on the healing of human tissue; but there is no reason in law why a surgeon
should not contract to produce such a result. I have to ascertain what the terms of the   *a*
contract were on the unusual facts of this case. I have been driven by the logic of the
argument which counsel presented for the plaintiffs to the conclusion that the contract
was to make the male plaintiff irreversibly sterile.

Collateral warranty or misrepresentation
      It is not strictly necessary to deal with this in view of my decision as to the nature of   *b*
the contract, but I think it will be appropriate to deal with it shortly, as it has been argued
fully, and another court might take the view that the contract was for vasectomy only,
there being no agreement as to the result.
      In these circumstances it seems to me that the position would be governed by the
decision of the Court of Appeal in *Esso Petroleum Co Ltd v Mardon* [1976] 2 All ER 5,
[1976] QB 801. The statement as to the effect of the operation, without a warning, was a   *c*
factual statement on a crucial factor made by the defendant, who had special knowledge
and skill, with the intention of inducing the plaintiff to enter into the contract for
vasectomy. It did induce the plaintiff to enter into the contract and so the defendant was
in breach of warranty.
      I quote from Lord Denning MR's judgment ([1976] 2 All ER at 13–14, [1976] QB 801
at 817–818):   *d*

      'Ever since *Heilbut Symons & Co v Buckleton* [1913] AC 30, [1911–13] All ER Rep
      83 we have had to contend with the law as laid down by the House of Lords that an
      innocent misrepresentation gives no right to damages. In order to escape from that
      rule, the pleader used to allege—I often did it myself—that the misrepresentation
      was fraudulent, or alternatively a collateral warranty. At the trial we nearly always   *e*
      succeeded on collateral warranty. We had to reckon, of course, with the dictum of
      Lord Moulton ([1913] AC 30 at 47, [1911–13] All ER Rep 83 at 90) that "such
      collateral contracts must from their nature be rare". But more often than not the
      court elevated the innocent misrepresentation into a collateral warranty; and thereby
      did justice—in advance of the Misrepresentation Act 1967. I remember scores of
      cases of that kind, especially on the sale of a business. A representation as to the   *f*
      profits that had been made in the past was invariably held to be a warranty. Besides
      that experience, there have been many cases since I have sat in this court where we
      have readily held a representation—which induces a person to enter into a contract—
      to be a warranty sounding in damages. I summarised them in *Dick Bently Productions
      Ltd v Harold Smith (Motors) Ltd* [1965] 2 All ER 65 at 67, [1965] 1 WLR 623 at 627
      when I said: "Looking at the cases once more, as we have done so often, it seems to   *g*
      me that if a representation is made in the course of dealings for a contract for the
      very purpose of inducing the other party to act on it, and it actually induces him to
      act on it by entering into the contract, that is prima facie ground for inferring that
      the representation was intended as a warranty. It is not necessary to speak of it as
      being collateral. Suffice it that the representation was intended to be acted on and
      was in fact acted on." Counsel for Esso retaliated, however, by citing *Bisset v Wilkinson*   *h*
      [1927] AC 177, [1926] All ER Rep 343 where the Privy Council said that a statement
      by a New Zealand farmer that an area of land "would carry 2,000 sheep" was only
      an expression of opinion. He submitted that the forecast here of 200,000 gallons
      was an expression of opinion and not a statement of fact; and that it could not be
      interpreted as a warranty or promise. Now, I would quite agree with counsel for
      Esso that it was not a warranty—in this sense—that it did not *guarantee* that the   *j*
      throughput *would be* 200,000 gallons. But, nevertheless, it was a forecast made by a
      party, Esso, who had special knowledge and skill. It was a yardstick (the "eac") by
      which they measured the worth of a filling station. They knew the facts. They knew
      the traffic in the town. They knew the throughput of comparable stations. They
      had much experience and expertise at their disposal. They were in a much better

a position than Mr Mardon to make a forecast. It seems to me that if such a person makes a forecast—intending that the other should act on it and he does act on it—it can well be interpreted as a warranty that the forecast is sound and reliable in the sense that they made it with reasonable care and skill. It is just as if Esso said to Mr Mardon: "Our forecast of throughput is 200,000 gallons. You can rely on it as being a sound forecast of what the service station should do. The rent is calculated on that footing." If the forecast turned out to be an unsound forecast, such as no person of

b skill or experience should have made, there is a breach of warranty.'

As to the defendant's special knowledge and skill there can be no doubt. The defendant's description of the effect of the operation was factual: he was describing the effect of such an operation as an established medical fact. It was not a promise as to the future.

It was the defendant's case that the defendant had no interest in persuading the

c plaintiffs to enter into the contract. He was doing them a favour by arranging for the operation to be performed on the cheap. But he made his statements intending that the plaintiffs should act on them in deciding whether to have the operation or not; and the plaintiffs clearly did rely on them in deciding to enter into the contract.

Counsel for the plaintiffs pressed his case on this point mainly under s 2 of the Misrepresentation Act 1967. It may be that he could succeed under this head. But there

d are some difficulties because the damage resulted from the fact that the collateral warranty was broken rather than the fact that the plaintiffs were induced to enter into the contract of vasectomy.

The reamended statement of claim is wide enough for this to be treated as a breach of collateral warranty, and in my view the plaintiff would succeed under this head if he did not succeed from straightforward breach of contract. The damages would be the same.

e The breach of warranty occurred when the male plaintiff became fertile and the damage flowed when the female plaintiff became pregnant.

Contractual negligence

I ought also to state my conclusions under this head although they are not necessary to my decision.

f The defendant agreed that in 1975 he considered it necessary to give a warning, prior to vasectomy, of the risk of late recanalisation and that the warning had to be in sufficiently clear terms to be understood. On the face of it this must mean that a failure to give such a warning would be a breach of duty.

But it was argued for the defendant that there was a fatal gap in the plaintiffs' case. Reference was made to the classic passage in *Bolam v Friern Hospital Management Committee*

g [1957] 2 All ER 118 at 121, [1957] 1 WLR 582 at 587 where McNair J, charging the jury, referred with approval to the words of the Lord President (Clyde) in the Scottish case of *Hunter v Hanley* 1955 SLT 213 at 217:

'In the realm of diagnosis and treatment there is ample scope for genuine difference of opinion, and one man clearly is not negligent merely because his conclusion differs from that of other professional men, nor because he has displayed

h less skill or knowledge than others would have shown. The true test for establishing negligence in diagnosis or treatment on the part of a doctor is whether he has been proved to be guilty of such failure as no doctor of ordinary skill would be guilty of if acting with ordinary care.'

It was asserted that the plaintiffs must fail because they had not called expert evidence to show that no surgeon of ordinary skill would have failed to give a warning in all the circumstances. This seems to me to be an utterly artificial argument. I had the evidence of a thoroughly competent surgeon, namely the defendant, as to the need for a warning; there was no reason to suppose that there was any other school of thought. There was no suggestion of some reason why it might not be desirable to give such a warning. I cannot see why the plaintiffs should not be entitled to rely on the evidence of the defendant.

It was open to the defendant to call evidence to show that there was another view, if
he so wished. Counsel for the defendant applied to me to admit the evidence of a   *a*
urologist. I do not know what that evidence might have been. I was not prepared to
admit it because it seemed to me that the defendant was quite cynically flouting an order
of the court in order to gain a tactical advantage. The deputy registrar on 28 June 1982
ordered:

> '(a) If either party intends to place reliance at the trial on expert evidence, that   *b*
> party shall, within 10 weeks after setting down, disclose the substance of that
> evidence to the other party in the form of a written report, which shall be agreed if
> possible; (b) Unless such reports are agreed, the parties shall be at liberty to call as
> expert witnesses those witnesses, the substance of whose evidence has been disclosed
> in accordance with the preceding paragraph, and any other expert to support the
> substance of the disclosed report.'   *c*

The defendant appealed against this order and his appeal was dismissed by the judge
in chambers on 19 October 1982. The defendant did not disclose his report until the
Friday before the trial, which was fixed for the subsequent Monday.

I was referred to a number of authorities on the 'doctrine of informed consent', which
has found acceptance in the United States and Canada but has been rejected by the courts *d*
in this country. I refer to *Sidaway v Bethlem Royal Hospital Governors* [1984] 1 All ER 1018,
[1984] 2 WLR 778, *Chatterton v Gerson* [1981] 1 All ER 257, [1981] 1 QB 432 and *Hills v
Potter* [1983] 3 All ER 716.

I do not think that these decisions have much bearing on the present case. This is not
a case where there was some debate whether the patient should be told of the risk of the
operation itself going wrong. It was a case where there was a risk that nature might, after *e*
a considerable lapse of time, reverse the effect of an operation that was initially perfectly
satisfactory. The process of late recanalisation may occur in rare cases although the
operation has been effective. The warning is necessary not to enable the patient to
consider whether to have the operation or not, but to enable prompt steps to be taken (if
he and his wife so wish) to seek an abortion to counteract his regained fertility.

I take the view that this case on its facts stands on its own and the failure to give a   *f*
warning was plainly a breach of the contractual duty of care. But if the case is put in this
way the damage that flows is different from the damage under the previous two heads.
The breach of duty occurs when the defendant fails to warn the plaintiffs either at the
pre-operation interview or when he writes his letter of 16 January 1976 to Mr Thake
saying that 'you may reasonably take no further contraceptive precautions from now on'.
I do not think any warning can be imported into the use of the word 'reasonably' by   *g*
itself. The damage that this failure causes is not that Mrs Thake conceives but that she
does not know promptly that she has conceived. It flows from this that she continues her
pregnancy without taking any steps to have it terminated until such time as it is too late
to have that done.

Counsel for the defendant sought to advance two reasons why this damage did not
flow. In the first place he argued that it would not have been in the reasonable   *h*
contemplation of the defendant that Mrs Thake would not recognise the early signs of
pregnancy. She was an experienced mother and it is right that at one stage the defendant
said he would have thought that she would pick up the early signs of pregnancy, but he
added that conversely she was in a late age group and might have thought that the
menopause was starting and not have recognised the other signs of pregnancy. It follows
from that, coupled with his evidence that without a warning the parties would have left   *j*
his surgery with the impression that there would be complete sterility, that it must have
been in the contemplation of the defendant, as a reasonable surgeon, that Mrs Thake
might not recognise her pregnancy until it was too late. Counsel for the defendant
referred me at length to *The Heron II, Koufos v C Czarnikow Ltd* [1967] 3 All ER 686,
[1969] 1 AC 350 on this issue. Whether the risk be expressed as not likely to happen or
liable to happen or whether it be said that there was a serious possibility or a real danger

a of it happening, I am quite satisfied it must have been in the reasonable contemplation of the defendant.

Alternatively, counsel contends that the plaintiffs have not established that Mrs Thake would have been able to secure an abortion. He referred me to the terms of s 1 of the Abortion Act 1967:

b '(1) Subject to the provisions of this section, a person shall not be guilty of an offence under the law relating to abortion when a pregnancy is terminated by a registered medical practitioner if two registered medical practitioners are of the opinion, formed in good faith—(a) that the continuance of the pregnancy would involve risk to the life of the pregnant woman, or of injury to the physical or mental health of the pregnant woman or any existing children of her family, greater than if the pregnancy were terminated . . .

c (2) In determining whether the continuance of a pregnancy would involve such risk of injury to health as is mentioned in paragraph (a) of subsection (1) of this section, account may be taken of the pregnant woman's actual or reasonably foreseeable environment . . .'

The defendant had agreed that a letter from Dr Lemerle might be treated as evidence without calling the writer. The fourth paragraph reads:

d 'I did tell Mrs. Thake that she was too far advanced into pregnancy, and that 12–14 weeks was the stage beyond which obstetricians were unwilling to terminate a pregnancy unless there was a life threatening situation. I discussed with her the continuation of the pregnancy and she agreed to carry on to full term.'

The plaintiffs' advisers seemed to think that this concession by the defendant included a e concession that Mrs Thake could have had an abortion if she had gone to Dr Lemerle in time. I think it is plain that Dr Lemerle thought so; but the letter does not say so, so I have to look for other evidence.

The defendant was asked about this and he pointed out that he was a surgeon and not an obstetrician and would therefore not make any decision on this himself. But, to his credit, he freely agreed that Mrs Thake could probably have got an abortion in the first f 12 to 14 weeks of pregnancy. He was able to give this evidence as to the state of medical opinion in his locality, having been a consultant there since 1966, and he volunteered the information that there would have been no religious difficulty. In addition, there is the evidence that Dr Pickles, the obstetrician at Pembury Hospital, had put Mrs Thake on the national health service list for sterilisation when she was carrying Lee.

I only have to decide on the balance of probabilities whether Mrs Thake could have g got an abortion in the early period of pregnancy. I am satisfied she could and would have done, had she known she was pregnant.

I hope the defendant will not feel that any stigma attaches to him by reason of this finding, because I feel sure that he is an excellent surgeon who merely had a momentary lapse. May I quote the words of Donaldson LJ in *Whitehouse v Jordan* [1980] 1 All ER 650 at 666 in the Court of Appeal:

h 'There are very few professional men who will assert that they have never fallen below the high standards rightly expected of them. That they have never been negligent. If they do, it is unlikely that they should be believed. And this is as true of lawyers as of medical men. If the judge's conclusion is right, what distinguishes Mr Jordan from his professional colleagues is not that on one isolated occasion his acknowledged skill partially deserted him, but that damage resulted. Whether or j not damage results from a negligent act is almost always a matter of chance and it ill becomes anyone to adopt an attitude of superiority.'

Public policy

The question whether damages may be awarded in respect of the birth of a healthy child has been the subject of a number of decisions in the United States. These are

conveniently collected in a judgment of the Supreme Court of Minnesota sitting in banc
in *Sherlock v Stillwater Clinic* (1977) 260 NW 2d 169 and at 174–175:   *a*

> 'Pretermitting moral and theological considerations, we are not persuaded that
> public policy considerations can properly be used to deny recovery to parents of an
> unplanned, healthy child of all damages proximately caused by a negligently
> performed sterilization operation. Analytically, such an action is indistinguishable
> from an ordinary medical negligence action where a plaintiff alleges that a physician   *b*
> has breached a duty of care owed to him with resulting injurious consequences.
> Where the purpose of the physician's actions is to prevent conception or birth,
> elementary justice requires that he be held legally responsible for the consequences
> which have in fact occurred. While other courts have referred to a negligent
> sterilization case as a "wrongful birth" action, we believe that this type of case is
> more properly denominated an action for "wrongful conception," for it is at the   *c*
> point of conception that the injury claimed by the parents originates. It should be
> further emphasized that this cause of action is exclusively that of the parents, since
> it is they and not the unplanned child who have sustained both physical and
> financial injury by the physician's negligence. Viewed in this manner, the parents
> of an unplanned child should at least be entitled to recover all damages immediately
> incident to pregnancy and birth. The allowance of these damages, we believe, is   *d*
> wholly consistent with the elementary principle of compensatory damages which
> seeks to place injured plaintiffs in the position that they would have been in had no
> wrong occurred. See, *Sorenson v. Cargill, Inc.* ((1968) 163 NW 2d 59). Incidental
> damages include such items as prenatal and postnatal medical expenses, pain and
> suffering incurred by the child's mother, and loss of consortium to the extent that it
> can be proved under the guidelines set forth in *Thill v Modern Erecting Co.* ((1969)   *e*
> 170 NW 2d 865). Most troublesome is the matter of allowing recovery for the costs
> of rearing a normal, healthy child. Ethical and religious considerations aside, it
> must be recognized that such costs are a direct financial injury to the parents, no
> different in immediate effect than the medical expenses resulting from the wrongful
> conception and birth of the child. Although public sentiment may recognize that
> to the vast majority of parents the long-term and enduring benefits of parenthood   *f*
> outweigh the economic costs of rearing a healthy child, it would seem myopic to
> declare today that those benefits exceed the costs as a matter of law. The use of
> various birth control methods by millions of Americans demonstrates an acceptance
> of the family-planning concept as an integral aspect of the modern marital
> relationship, so that today it must be acknowledged that the time-honoured
> command to "be fruitful and multiply" has not only lost contemporary significance   *g*
> to a growing number of potential parents but is contrary to public policies embodied
> in the statutes encouraging family planning.'

That was, I should say in fairness to the Supreme Court of Minnesota, a majority decision.
   In England the matter has been considered only twice. In *Sciuriaga v Powell* (1979) 123
SJ 406 Watkins J had to consider damages where an attempt at abortion had been carried
out so unskilfully that a healthy child was born. He said (and I read from the transcript   *h*
of his judgment):

> 'The sole and effective causes were the defendant's breaches of contract from the
> consequences of which I cannot, despite a further resourceful attempt by [counsel]
> to persuade me to, allow him to escape. This attempt is founded on public policy. It
> is, he submits, repugnant to people's sensibilities and wholly wrong for damages to   *j*
> be awarded for breaches of contract which arise out of a failed operation for
> termination of pregnancy. In 12 Halsbury's Laws (4th edn) para 1133 the following
> statement appears: "A plaintiff may recover, or fail to recover, damages in a novel
> situation by reason of the view of public or social policy taken by the courts. Most
> of the developments have been in the law of negligence." The instant case has
> undoubtedly produced a novel situation. Does public policy demand that it shall be

one from which this plaintiff can gain no redress? During a study of various cases in which the notion that public policy shall cause the court to abstain from redressing a wrong by an award of damages, I have not found an instance of a court declaring that public policy demands that damages shall not be awarded for a breach of contract, the contract being to perform a legal act for proper reward. Abortion is legal in circumstances which Parliament has prescribed. The attempted abortion carried out by the defendant was in accordance with the law. But it is the law of the land. So if a woman wishes to be rid of a pregnancy and in a legal way causes herself to be operated on for that purpose I perceive no policy, public or other, why she should not recover such damages as she can prove she has sustained by the surgeon's negligent failure or other breach of duty to abort her. Surely no one in these days would argue to the contrary if the child subsequently born was deformed or diseased. The fact that the child born is healthy cannot give rise, I think, to a different conclusion save, of course, as to the measure of damages. So I hold that this plaintiff is entitled to recover such damages as have by the evidence been proved to flow directly from the defendant's breaches of contract.'

When this case went to the Court of Appeal ([1980] CA Transcript 597) counsel did not pursue the public policy point, but Waller LJ, having said that he had ignored policy considerations, said:

'In doing so, I must not be taken as assenting to the view that they would be irrelevant in every case ... I quite see that the incidence of pregnancy and the necessity for Caesarian birth would properly form items of damage for the failure of the operation and, indeed, in this case, one of the heads of damage covers this, but once a woman has given birth to a healthy child without harm to her and the fears of the doctors have been shown to be unfounded, I would not regard it as unarguable in another case that thereafter no more damage would arise.'

Jupp J considered the same point in *Udale v Bloomsbury Area Health Authority* [1983] 2 All ER 522 at 531, [1983] 1 WLR 1098 at 1109, where the birth was due to a negligently performed sterilisation operation. It appears from the report that he did not have Watkins J's decision before him. He said:

'Mrs Udale's claim does not match the claim which the Court of Appeal disallowed in [*McKay v Essex Area Health Authority* [1982] 2 All ER 771, [1982] QB 1166]. However, the considerations of public policy there put forward are impressive and are relevant to this case. Together with some of the submissions made by counsel for the defendants, they persuade me to the view that on the grounds of public policy the plaintiff's claim in this case, in so far as they are based on negligence which allowed David Udale to come into this world alive, should not be allowed. The considerations that particularly impress me are the following. (1) It is highly undesirable that any child should learn that a court has publicly declared his life or birth to be a mistake, a disaster even, and that he or she is unwanted or rejected. Such pronouncements would disrupt families and weaken the structure of society. (2) A plaintiff such as Mrs Udale would get little or no damages because her love and care for her child and her joy, ultimately, at his birth would be set off against and might cancel out the inconvenience and financial disadvantages which naturally accompany parenthood. By contrast, a plaintiff who nurtures bitterness in her heart and refuses to let her maternal instincts take over would be entitled to large damages. In short virtue would go unrewarded; unnatural rejection of womanhood and motherhood would be generously compensated. This, in my judgment, cannot be just. (3) Medical men would be under subconscious pressure to encourage abortions in order to avoid claims for medical negligence which would arise if the child were allowed to be born. (4) It has been the assumption of our culture from time immemorial that a child coming into the world, even if, as some say, "the world is a vale of tears", is a blessing and an occasion for rejoicing.'

In these circumstances I have to make up my mind on first principles.

In the first place this action sounds in contract. On the authorities generally public *a* policy has interfered with a claim for damages for breach of contract only where, but for the plaintiff's prior wrong, he would have suffered no damage from the defendant's breach of contract: *McGregor on Damages* (14th edn 1980) paras 202–203. For example, in *Gray v Barr (Prudential Assurance Co Ltd; third party)* [1971] 2 All ER 949, [1971] 2 QB 544 damages were refused on the ground that no man should be allowed to profit at another's expense for his own conscious and deliberate wrong. I need not consider the *b* exception to this general rule provided by *Bain v Forthergill* (1874) LR 7 HL 158, [1874–80] All ER Rep 83.

I therefore approach this matter with caution. There remains some doubt whether the categories of public policy are now closed: see *Cheshire and Fifoot on the Law of Contract* (10th edn, 1981) p 318. However that may be, I take the view that a judge of first instance should hesitate long before attempting to ride this unruly horse in a new *c* direction.

In approaching this problem I firmly put sentiment on one side. A healthy baby is so lovely a creature that I can well understand the reaction of one who asks: how could its birth possibly give rise to an action for damages? But every baby has a belly to be filled and a body to be clothed. The law relating to damages is concerned with reparation in money terms and this is what is needed for the maintenance of a baby. *d*

I have to have regard to the policy of the state as it expresses itself in legislation and in social provision. I must consider this in the light of modern developments. By 1975 family planning was generally practised. Abortion had been legalised over a wide field. Vasectomy was one of the methods of family planning which was not only legal but was available under the national health service. It seems to me to follow from this that it was generally recognised that the birth of a healthy baby is not always a blessing. It is a *e* blessing when the baby is to be born to the happy family life which we would all like a baby to have. Many people hold that that end can be best achieved by restricting natural fertility.

The policy of the state, as I see it, is to provide the widest freedom of choice. It makes available to the public the means of planning their families or planning to have no family. If plans go awry, it provides for the possibility of abortion. But there is no *f* pressure on couples either to have children or not to have children or to have only a limited number of children. Even the one-parent family, whether that exists through choice or through misfortune, is given substantial assistance.

Against that background I ask myself whether the reasons advanced by Jupp J are so compelling that I ought to follow his decision. I do not think they are and, in deference to his careful reasoning, I will consider them one by one. *g*

I do not think that if I award damages here it will lead little Samantha to feel rejection. She is surrounded by a happy, albeit somewhat poverty-stricken, family life. It is this that must make her feel wanted and not rejected. She may learn in years to come that her conception was unwanted. But there is nothing exceptional about this. What matters to a child is how it is received when it enters life. It so often happens that parents reconcile themselves to an unwelcome conception and accept the child with joy. If *h* Samantha is as bright as her father thinks, by the time she comes to consider this judgment (if she ever does) she will, I think, welcome it as a means of having made life somewhat easier for her family.

Next I have to consider the difficulty in setting off the joy of Samantha against the financial disadvantages that her parents would undergo. If I adopt the public policy which Jupp J favours then virtue will indeed go unrewarded. Every credit is due to the *j* plaintiffs for the way in which they have welcomed Samantha into the family. The method of set-off presents difficulties but, once again, I think it can be solved by looking at the hard cash involved and ignoring the intangibles. Both plaintiffs suffered great distress on learning of Mrs Thake's pregnancy. Mrs Thake underwent pain and discomfort in the course of her labour, although it was not particularly difficult. As a result of these

sufferings they had a healthy child. But the fact that she has been such a joy to them is
a   largely of their own making. If they had been reluctant to accept her and grudging in
the sacrifices they had to make for her support, then they might have had little joy. As I
see it, the birth of a healthy child should be set off against their disappointment and the
labour pains so that they cancel each other out. The joy they have for Samantha is largely
of their own making in the way they have met their difficulties. The claim for Samantha's
support and for the costs of the birth remain.

b   If the principle of public policy applies it should apply throughout and there should
be no award in respect of the birth. The injustice of this course was apparent to Jupp J
who said ([1983] 2 All ER 522 at 531–532, [1983] 1 WLR 1098 at 1109–1110):

>   'It seems to me that it is legitimate, without detracting from the above principles
>   of public policy, to have some regard to the disturbance to the family finances which
c   >   the unexpected pregnancy causes. One may look at the cost of the layette and the
>   sudden necessity of having to find more ample accommodation in assessing the
>   damages for the unwanted pregnancy, without regarding the child as unwanted.
>   One has to bear in mind here that the child has, up until the age of 4 years 2 months,
>   in fact lived in that house without the extension. It has not of course been built.
>   Accordingly, in my view, it is proper to increase the award of damages with this in
d   >   mind when awarding general damages for the pain, suffering, inconvenience,
>   anxiety and the like, mentioned at the beginning of this judgment.'

I do not see the logical basis of this approach.
The third reason advanced hardly applies here since there was no possiblity of an
abortion. But, in view of the divisions within the medical profession, I think it has little
force. The decision whether to abort or not will usually rest with an obstetrician, who
e   may well be quite independent of the medical man who faces a possible charge of
negligence.
As to the fourth ground, for the reasons I have already given I do not accept that it is
part of our culture that the birth of a healthy child is always a blessing. It may have been
the assumption in the past. I feel quite satisfied that it is not the assumption today.
I entirely accept that the reasons put forward by Jupp J may be valid considerations in
f   the assessment of damages in a particular case. But I feel that to erect them into a rule of
public policy applicable to all cases would work great injustice, as it would here. I
therefore prefer to follow Watkins J.

Damages

g   Applying what I have said, I make no award for the distress, pain and suffering
undergone by either of the plaintiffs. I confine myself to the costs of Samantha's birth
and upkeep. The plaintiffs have claimed for this on a moderate basis. They have made
their calculations on the basis of the supplementary benefit scales. This is right. Samantha
has been born into a humble household and the defendant should not be expected to do
more than to provide her with necessaries.
h   Happily, the net figures have been agreed between the parties, subject to liability. The
cost of the layette (Mrs Thake having optimistically disposed of all baby clothes) and
Samantha's upkeep to her first birthday is agreed at £717. From her first birthday to her
fourth birthday the agreed figure is £960. The claim from her fourth to her seventeenth
birthday has been substantially reduced to a compromise figure of £5,000. I understand
that these figures make due allowance for child and any other allowance. If I am wrong
j   about this I will be happy to hear further argument as to quantum.
As soon as Samantha goes to school Mrs Thake will resume her part-time domestic
work. It is not contended that she should have done so sooner. The agreed figure for her
loss from January 1980 to April 1984 is £2,000.
There will therefore be judgment for the plaintiffs for £6,677. I will divide this
between the plaintiffs as I am asked. In addition there will be judgment for the second

plaintiff for £2,000; and I gather, from the information given to me, that interest has
been agreed at £1,000.   *a*

Judgment for the plaintiffs for £9,677.

Solicitors: *F B Jevons Riley & Pope*, Tonbridge (for the plaintiffs); *Hempsons* (for the
defendant).

K Mydeen Esq   Barrister.   *b*

c

Shah v Swallow

HOUSE OF LORDS

LORD DIPLOCK, LORD FRASER OF TULLYBELTON, LORD ROSKILL, LORD BRIDGE OF HARWICH AND
LORD BRANDON OF OAKBROOK

17 MAY, 21 JUNE 1984   *d*

*Magistrates – Information – Statement of offence – Document commencing prosecution charging
more than one offence – Preamble containing particulars common to all offences and ensuing
paragraphs charging individual offences alleged to have been committed – Whether document
containing five informations or one information charging five offences – Whether document valid
– Magistrates' Courts Rules 1981, rr 12, 100.*   *e*

The respondent, who carried on a food business, was charged in one document with five
offences against various provisions of the Food Hygiene (General) Regulations 1970. The
first paragraph of the document set out allegations of fact common to all of the offences,
namely that the respondent on a specified date at a specified place being a person carrying
on a specified food business in the course of that business committed 'the five offences   *f*
hereunder specified' contrary to 'the several provisions hereunder specified of the [1970
regulations]'. The five subsequent numbered paragraphs separately identified each
offence alleged to have been committed, specifying in each case the particular provisions
of the 1970 regulations alleged to have been contravened. The magistrates convicted the
respondent of four of the offences. The respondent appealed, contending that the
document was a single information charging more than one offence and consequently   *g*
was invalid under rr 12(1)[a] and 100[b] of the Magistrates' Courts Rules 1981. The Divisional
Court of the Queen's Bench Division upheld that contention and quashed the convictions.
On appeal to the House of Lords,

Held – Where substantial factual material was common to a number of offences to be
charged and the offences were in contravention of various provisions of the same   *h*
legislative instrument, the setting out of the common factual and legal material in the
preamble to the document commencing the prosecution and the subsequent
incorporation of it by express or implied reference in each of the ensuing numbered
paragraphs charging the several offences alleged to have been committed fulfilled the
requirements of r 100 of the 1981 rules and constituted one document containing a
number of informations. The document was therefore valid under r 12 of the 1981 rules   *j*
and the appeal would accordingly be allowed (see p 529 *g h*, p 531 *e f* and p 532 *e g*, post).
  Edwards v Jones [1947] 1 All ER 830 distinguished.

---

a   Rule 12(1) is set out at p 530 *h*, post
b   Rule 100 is set out at p 530 *j* to p 531 *a*, post

Notes

a For the scope of information, see 29 Halsbury's Laws (4th edn) para 318, and for cases on the subject, see 33 Digest (Reissue) 116–117, 739–750.

For the Food Hygiene (General) Regulations 1970, see 9 Halsbury's Statutory Instruments (5th reissue) 209.

For the Magistrates' Courts Rules 1981, rr 12, 100, see 13 ibid (4th reissue) 60, 95.

b **Cases referred to in opinions**

Clayton v Chief Constable of Norfolk [1983] 1 All ER 984, [1983] 2 AC 473, [1983] 2 WLR 555, HL.

Edwards v Jones [1947] 1 All ER 830, [1947] KB 659, DC.

Appeal

c The Director of Public Prosecutions appealed, pursuant to his powers under the Prosecution of Offences Act 1979 and the Prosecution of Offences Regulations 1978, SI 1978/1357, and with leave of the Appeal Committee of the House of Lords granted on 26 January 1984, against the decision of the Divisional Court of the Queen's Bench Division (Watkins LJ and McCullough J) on 4 November 1983 whereby that court allowed an appeal by way of case stated by the respondent, Saiyad Shah, against his

d conviction by the justices for the petty sessional division of Croydon sitting at Croydon Magistrates' Court on 28 February 1983 of four offences against various provisions of the Food Hygiene (General) Regulations 1970, SI 1970/1172, on an information preferred by the prosecutor, Michael Andrew Swallow, against the respondent. The Divisional Court certified, under s 1(2) of the Administration of Justice Act 1960, that points of law of general public importance (set out at p 530 *a b*, post) were involved in its decision to

e allow the appeal, but refused leave to appeal to the House of Lords. The facts are set out in the opinion of Lord Bridge.

Anthony Arlidge QC and *Brian Jubb* for the Director of Public Prosecutions.
Nigel Ley and *Renée Calder* for the respondent.

f Their Lordships took time for consideration.

21 June. The following opinions were delivered.

LORD DIPLOCK. My Lords, I have had the advantage of reading in draft the speech of my noble and learned friend Lord Bridge. I agree with it, and for the reasons which
g he gives I would allow this appeal.

LORD FRASER OF TULLYBELTON. My Lords, I have had the advantage of reading in draft the speech of my noble and learned friend Lord Bridge. I agree with it, and for the reasons stated in it I would allow the appeal.

h **LORD ROSKILL.** My Lords, I have had the advantage of reading in draft the speech to be delivered by my noble and learned friend Lord Bridge. I agree with it, and for the reasons which he gives I would allow this appeal.

LORD BRIDGE OF HARWICH. My Lords, the respondent was convicted on 28 February 1983 by the Croydon justices of four offences in contravention of various
j provisions of the Food Hygiene (General) Regulations 1970, SI 1970/1172. He was fined £100 for each offence and ordered to pay £280 costs. He appealed by case stated to a Divisional Court (Watkins LJ and McCullough J), who felt reluctantly compelled by authority to allow his appeal on the ground that he had been tried on an information charging more than one offence. They certified the following questions as points of law of general public importance involved in their decision:

'(1) whether the document commencing the prosecution was an information charging five offences and therefore failing to comply with the Magistrates' Courts Rules 1981 and the Magistrates' Court (Forms) Rules 1981 or whether it was one document containing five informations and consequently valid within the meaning of the said Rules. (2) whether the document laying an information must state that it is an information. (3) whether a preamble containing particulars common to a number of otherwise separate allegations and which is contained in a single document connects them in such a way as to render them as charging a number of offences in one information.'

The Divisional Court refused leave to appeal but it was granted by your Lordships House.

The form of the information or informations is set out in para 1 of the case stated by the justices. It charged the respondent in the following terms:

'On the 12th May. 1982, at "Burnells" 92 High Street, Croydon in the London Borough of Croydon, being a person carrying on a food business namely the trade or business of retail confectioner, in the course of that business committed the five offences hereunder specified.

CONTRARY to the several provisions hereunder specified of the Food Hygiene (General) Regulations 1970 made under Section 13 of the Food and Drugs Act 1955, hereunder referred to as "the said regs."

1. The food business was being carried on at insanitary premises in that there was evidence of a heavy infestation of rodents and numerous boxes and packages of confectionery had been gnawed eaten or damaged by rodents and insect larvae.

CONTRARY to Regs. 6 and 29(2)(a) of the said regs.

2. While engaged in the handling of food did not take all steps reasonably necessary to protect the food from risk of contamination in that food which was unfit for human consumption was not kept apart from other food.

CONTRARY to Regs. 9 and 29(2)(a) of the said Regs.

3. All parts of the structure of every food room were not kept clean in that the floor and all surfaces in the basement were covered in dust which was inches thick in places.

CONTRARY to Regs. 25 and 29(2)(a) of the said Regs.

4. All parts of the structure of every food room were not kept clean in that the floor and all surfaces in the rear stockroom were covered in dust dirt and debris.

CONTRARY to Regs. 25 and 29(2)(a) of the said Regs.

5. All parts of the structure of every food room were not kept clean in that floor and shelving in the front shop area were filthy with thick black dust.

CONTRARY to Regs. 25 and 29(2)(a) of the said Regs.'

The relevant provisions of the Magistrates' Courts Rules 1981, SI 1981/552, are the following:

'12.—(1) Subject to any Act passed after 2nd October 1848, a magistrates' court shall not proceed to the trial of an information that charges more than one offence.

(2) Nothing in this rule shall prohibit 2 or more informations being set out in one document.'

'100.—(1) Every information, summons, warrant or other document laid, issued or made for the purposes of, or in connection with, any proceedings before a magistrates' court for an offence shall be sufficient if it describes the specific offence with which the accused is charged, or of which he is convicted, in ordinary language avoiding as far as possible the use of technical terms and without necessarily stating all the elements of the offence, and gives such particulars as may be necessary for giving reasonable information of the nature of the charge.

a
(2) If the offence charged is one created by or under any Act, the description of the offence shall contain a reference to the section of the Act, or, as the case may be, the rule, order, regulation, byelaw or other instrument creating the offence.'

The Magistrates' Courts (Forms) Rules 1981, SI 1981/553, to which the first certified question also refers, throw no light on the issue raised since they contain the following provision:

b
'2.—(1) The forms contained in Schedule 2 to these Rules or forms to the like effect may be used, with such variation as the circumstances may require, in connection with proceedings in magistrates' courts . . .'

c
The sole argument in support of the respondent's case that the five offences charged against him were contained in a single information rests on the proposition that the first paragraph of the relevant document embodied allegations of fact which it was necessary to allege in relation to each of the offences charged in accordance with r 100(1) and the second paragraph identified the regulations creating the several offences which it was necessary to specify in relation to each of the offences in accordance with r 100(2) of the Magistrates' Courts Rules 1981. Counsel for the respondent conceded at the outset of the argument, as he was bound to do, that if the common material contained in the two

d
opening paragraphs had been repeated in each of the five numbered paragraphs specifying the separate offences charged he would have had no case to argue. But this more prolix manner of alleging the five separate offences charged, apart from wasting time and paper, would have made no difference whatever to the substance of the document. It would still have conveyed precisely the same meaning to the mind of the reader. Where, as here, substantial factual material is common to a number of offences to be charged and the offences are in contravention of various provisions of the same legislative instrument,

e
it seems to me an eminently sensible economy that the common factual and legal material should be set out once at the beginning and then incorporated by express or implied reference in each of the ensuing numbered paragraphs charging the several offences alleged to have been committed. The argument that this manner of fulfilling the requirements of r 100 by way of the single document expressly permitted by r 12(2) turns the document into a single information charging more than one offence is quite

f
untenable. The document quoted in para 1 of the case stated plainly set out five separate informations charging five separate offences.

The Divisional Court felt constrained to allow the respondent's appeal against his convictions by the authority of *Edwards v Jones* [1947] 1 All ER 830, [1947] KB 659. I am, with all respect, unable to see that that case is of any relevance to the issue in this appeal. In *Edwards v Jones* a single information charged both dangerous driving and

g
driving without due care and attention. These were alternative charges arising out of a single driving incident. Objection was taken before the justices that this contravened s 10 of the Summary Jurisdiction Act 1848, the statutory predecessor of r 12(1) of the Magistrates' Courts Rules 1981. For the defendant it was submitted that it was for the prosecutor to elect on which charge to proceed. The prosecutor's reply was that it was for the justices, not for him, to decide, having heard the evidence, which of the two offences

h
had been committed. The justices accepted the prosecutor's submission and proceeded to convict the defendant of driving without due care and attention. It must be remembered that this was at a time before the decision of this House in *Clayton v Chief Constable of Norfolk* [1983] 1 All ER 984, [1983] 2 AC 473, when the law was thought to be that justices could not try two informations together without the consent of the defendant. This was an important part of the court's ratio decidendi in *Edwards v Jones* [1947] KB

j
659 at 662–663; cf [1947] 1 All ER 830 at 832, as the following passage from the judgment of Lord Goddard CJ shows:

'There is no ground for saying that if an information discloses two offences the magistrates can hear the two offences together and then say: "We will convict on one." That would be giving the go-by to the provisions of s. 10 of the Act, which makes it clear that in a magistrates' court a defendant can only be called upon to

answer one charge at a time. If there are two informations or summonses against a
defendant, in which the facts are very much the same, of course it is quite open to
the defendant to say that he will agree to their being heard at once. That is constantly
done and there is no reason why it should not be done. In this case the defendant
did not agree to anything of the sort. He took the objection that the information
was bad, and so it was. No agreement by the defendant would put that right. But
the information could have been amended by striking out one of the charges. A
charge could then have been preferred under the other section and the defendant
could have said: "I want one heard first and see what happens to that, and then I will
consider what I will do with regard to the second charge."'

But, in any event, *Edwards v Jones* was a classic case of a single information charging
alternative offences which was bad for duplicity. It arose from entirely different
circumstances and gave rise to an entirely different question from those with which the
instant case is concerned.

I should perhaps add that the Divisional Court took the unusual course here, when
hearing an appeal by case stated, of receiving affidavit evidence. Your Lordships do not
know the precise circumstances, so I refrain from criticism, save to say that the affidavit
evidence, when looked at, seems to add nothing to the material set out in the case stated
which was of any assistance in answering the only question of law requiring an answer
as posed in para 7(a) of the case stated in the following terms:

'Whether or not we were entitled to rule that the document reproduced in
paragraph 1 above constituted five valid informations.'

I would answer the certified questions (1) and (3) as follows. (1) The document
commencing the prosecution was one document containing five informations and
consequently valid under r 12 of the Magistrates' Courts Rules 1981. (3) No. I do not
understand how question (2) raises a point of law involved in the decision under appeal
and, accordingly, I would not answer it.

I would allow the appeal, set aside the orders of the Divisional Court, restore the order
of the justices and order the respondent to pay the costs of the London borough of
Croydon in the Divisional Court and of the Director of Public Prosecutions from the
time he took over the conduct of the case in the Divisional Court and in this House.

LORD BRANDON OF OAKBROOK. My Lords, I have had the advantage of
reading in draft the speech prepared by my noble and learned friend Lord Bridge. I agree
with it, and for the reasons which he gives I would allow the appeal and make the further
orders proposed by him.

Appeal allowed.

Solicitors: *Director of Public Prosecutions; Ouvry Goodman & Co*, Sutton (for the respondent).

Mary Rose Plummer   Barrister.

a

Insurance Officer v Hemmant

COURT OF APPEAL, CIVIL DIVISION
WALLER, OLIVER AND PURCHAS LJJ
1, 13 MARCH 1984

b

National insurance – Mobility allowance – Entitlement – Residence – Residence in Great Britain – Change of residence to outside Great Britain after decision to pay allowance given – Whether continued residence in Great Britain throughout period allowance payable a condition for payment of allowance – Whether power to review decision to pay allowance where change of residence after date of decision to pay allowance – Social Security Act 1975, ss 37A(1)(7), 104(1)(b).

c

On the true construction of s 37A(1)[a] of the Social Security Act 1975 it is a continuing condition of entitlement to mobility allowance that the applicant for the allowance continues to be ordinarily resident and present in Great Britain throughout the period for which the allowance is payable and it is not sufficient merely to satisfy a once-for-all condition of residence in Great Britain at the date when the application for mobility allowance is received. Furthermore, s 37A(7) of the 1975 Act simply indicates the date from which an entitlement to mobility allowance takes effect and does not preclude a review under s 104(1)(b)[b] of the decision to award mobility allowance where there is a change of circumstances regarding the applicant's place of residence after the decision to award the allowance is made. It follows, therefore, that where after the date of a decision to award mobility allowance the applicant permanently takes up residence outside Great Britain there is power, under s 104(1)(b), to review the decision to award him mobility allowance (see p 535 j to p 536 b d e and p 537 h to p 538 a, post).

d

e

Notes

For mobility allowance, see 33 Halsbury's Laws (4th edn) para 451.
   For review of decisions of insurance officers, see ibid para 622.
   For the Social Security Act 1975, ss 37A, 104, see 45 Halsbury's Statutes (3rd edn) 1124, 1201.

f

Appeal

The insurance officer appealed pursuant to the leave of the social security commissioner granted on 10 February 1983 from the commissioner's decision made on 15 November 1982 dismissing his appeal from the decision of a local tribunal given on 2 June 1981 reversing the insurance officer's decision made on 5 December 1980 whereby the insurance officer reviewed his original decision to award the respondent, Maurice George Edward Hemmant, mobility allowance under s 37A(1) of the Social Security Act 1975 from 29 July 1976 (the date the claim for the allowance was received) to 25 May 1993 (the date of his sixty-fifth birthday) because there had been a relevant change of circumstances in that on 20 September 1979 the respondent ceased to be ordinarily resident in Great Britain and went to live in the Irish Republic, and revised the original decision by disallowing payments of mobility allowance as from 21 September 1979 because from that date the respondent was no longer ordinarily resident in Great Britain. The facts are set out in the judgment of Oliver LJ.

g

h

Simon D Brown for the insurance officer.

j   *Richard Sheldon* for the respondent.

Cur adv vult

---

a   Section 37A, so far as material, is set out at p 534 h and p 535 b, post
b   Section 104(1), so far as material, is set out at p 535 d e, post

13 March. The following judgments were delivered.

a

OLIVER LJ (giving the first judgment at the invitation of Waller LJ). This is an appeal, with leave pursuant to s 14 of the Social Security Act 1980, from a decision of the social security commissioner given on 15 November 1982 upholding the respondent's claim to remain entitled to a mobility allowance pursuant to s 37A of the Social Security Act 1975 (which I shall call 'the Act'). The point raised by the appeal is a short point of construction of the legislation governing mobility allowances, and the salient facts can be shortly *b* stated.

The respondent, having become disabled to an extent which prevented him from walking, applied for a mobility allowance on 29 July 1976. Following a report from a medical board that he was likely to continue to be unable to walk until pensionable age, he was awarded a mobility allowance from 29 July 1976 (the date of his application) until 29 May 1993 (the date of his sixty-fifth birthday). On 20 September 1979 he went to live *c* in the Irish Republic. The insurance officer having been notified of this event, he reviewed the original award and issued a decision disallowing further payments of mobility allowance from 21 September 1979. The respondent appealed against that decision to a local tribunal, which allowed his appeal on 2 June 1981.

The point which was argued before the tribunal, and on which the appeal was determined, was the validity of a requirement of continued residence in the United *d* Kingdom, having regard to the provisions of art 51 of the EEC Treaty and the regulations adopted thereunder by the European Economic Community, the respondent having moved to, and taken up residence in, another member state.

From this decision, the insurance officer, the present appellant, appealed to the social security commissioner, and on the original hearing before him the matter was argued on the same ground as that argued before the local tribunal. After that hearing, however, *e* the commissioner himself raised the question with which this appeal is concerned, namely whether, on the true construction of the Act and the regulations made under it, the original decision to award a mobility allowance is reviewable at all by reason of a change of residence after the date from which the award takes effect. He therefore invited further submissions on this point and, after written submissions, determined the appeal in the respondent's favour on the ground that the statute conferred no power to review *f* the original decision; alternatively that, if there was a power to review, it was inapplicable in the case of a change of residence by reason of the provisions of s 37A(7).

Section 37A was introduced by s 22 of the Social Security Pensions Act 1975, and is in the following terms, so far as material:

> '(1) Subject to the provisions of this section, a person who satisfies prescribed *g* conditions as to residence or presence in Great Britain shall be entitled to a mobility allowance for any period throughout which he is suffering from physical disablement such that he is either unable to walk or virtually unable to do so.
> (2) Regulations may prescribe the circumstances in which a person is or is not to be treated for the purposes of this section as suffering from such physical disablement as is mentioned above; but a person qualifies for the allowance only if—(a) his *h* inability or virtual inability to walk is likely to persist for at least 12 months from the time when a claim for the allowance is received by the Secretary of State; and (b) during most of that period his condition will be such as permits him from time to time to benefit from enhanced facilities for locomotion.'

Subsections (3) and (4) deal with the rate of allowance and do not require consideration in the context of this appeal. Subsection (5) is of peripheral significance having regard to *j* the provisions of sub-s (7). So far as relevant, sub-s (5) provides:

> 'No person shall be entitled to a mobility allowance . . . (b) except in prescribed cases, for any week before that in which a claim for the allowance by or in respect of him is received by the Secretary of State.'

Subsection (6) provides for regulations to be made for reducing allowances in certain
cases where invalid carriages or other appliances are provided by the National Health
Service, and sub-s (6B) (added by the Social Security Act 1979) extends, until the age of
75, allowances previously made and ending on the attainment of the age of 65. Subsection
(7) is the critical provision in relation to the argument on this appeal. It provides:

> 'Except so far as may be provided by regulations, the question of a person's
> entitlement to a mobility allowance shall be determined as at the date when a claim
> for the allowance is received by the Secretary of State.'

Thus, to summarise the effect of the section, the applicant has to fulfil two
qualifications: that is to say he has to comply with the 'prescribed conditions' as to
residence or presence and he has to comply with the requirements of sub-s (2) and the
regulations made thereunder as regards the extent and duration of his disability. But the
question of his entitlement, certainly as regards his original claim for allowance, has to
be judged at the date when the claim is received by the Secretary of State.

Before considering the prescribed conditions and the regulations, it will be convenient
to refer to the power to review decisions. That is contained in s 104(1) of the Act which
is, so far as material, in the following terms:

> 'Any decision under this Act of an insurance officer, a local tribunal or a
> Commissioner may be reviewed at any time by an insurance officer, or on a
> reference from an insurance officer, by a local tribunal if—(a) the officer or tribunal
> is satisfied and, in the case of a decision of a Commissioner, satisfied by fresh
> evidence, that the decision was given in ignorance of, or was based on a mistake as
> to, some material fact; or (b) there has been any relevant change of circumstances
> since the decision was given . . .'

Turning back now to s 37A(1), the precondition of any entitlement at all to mobility
allowance is compliance with the 'prescribed conditions as to residence or presence in
Great Britain', and these are to be found in r 2 of the Mobility Allowance Regulations
1975, SI 1975/1573, which provide, so far as relevant to this appeal, as follows:

> 'ENTITLEMENT
> *Entitlement conditions as to residence and presence in Great Britain*
> 2.—(1) Subject to the following provisions of this regulation, the prescribed
> conditions as to residence or presence in Great Britain to be satisfied by any person
> in respect of any day for the purposes of section 37A shall be—(a) that he is ordinarily
> resident in Great Britain; and (b) that he is present in Great Britain; and (c) that he
> has been present in Great Britain for a period of, or periods amounting in the
> aggregate to, not less than 52 weeks in the 18 months immediately preceding that
> day . . .
> (3) For the purposes of paragraph (1)(b) and (1)(c), a person who is absent from
> Great Britain on any day shall be treated as being present in Great Britain—(a) if on
> that day he is—(i) a merchant seaman within the meaning of the Family Allowances
> (Qualifications) Regulations 1969; or (ii) a member of the forces within the meaning
> of those Regulations; or (iii) living with such a member of the forces and is that
> member's spouse, son, daughter, father, father-in-law, mother, or mother-in-law; or
> (b) if his absence is, and when it began was, for a temporary purpose and has not
> lasted for a continuous period exceeding 26 weeks; or (c) where his absence is
> temporary and for the specific purpose of his being treated for incapacity, or a
> disabling condition, which commenced before he left Great Britain, during such
> period as the Secretary of State may allow having regard to the circumstances of the
> case.'

Now leaving aside sub-s (7) of s 37A for the moment, there is nothing on the face of
the section or of the regulations which indicate that satisfying the prescribed conditions
as to residence and presence in Great Britain is a once-for-all condition which does not

have to endure throughout the period over which the allowance is payable. On the ordinary reading of sub-s (1) of s 37A the requirement of residence is one which continues to apply in just the same way as the requirement of continuing disability, and that is entirely consistent with reg 2(3), which refers to the conditions to be fulfilled 'on any day'. Indeed, this accords with common sense, for it is difficult to see why the legislature should have thought it either necessary or desirable to provide lifelong benefits at the expense of the British taxpayer for a person who may immediately leave the country and take up permanent residence elsewhere. Counsel for the respondent indeed accepts that it is a necessary consequence of his interpretation of the statutory provisions that a person who fulfils the prescribed conditions on the day on which the application is received by the Secretary of State is entitled and continues to be entitled to an allowance, even though he takes up permanent residence in a foreign country on the following day. Moreover, the concept of a continuing necessity to satisfy the prescribed conditions is one which is clearly reflected in the analogous provisions of the same chapter of the Act which provide for other non-contributory benefits. Thus attendance allowance (s 35), invalidity pension (s 36) and invalid care allowance (s 37) are all clearly expressed to be dependent on the prescribed conditions as to residence continuing to be satisfied and the regulations prescribing those conditions are in substance the same as reg 2(3) already referred to.

Now it is true that s 37A is somewhat differently expressed, but having regard to the fact that this is a section inserted by subsequent legislation, I do not, for my part, feel that too much significance ought to be attached to verbal differences. The obvious purpose of sub-s (1) of s 37A on its face, as it seems to me, is to apply to the payment of mobility allowance similar continuing conditions of residence to those applied to the other non-contributory benefits provided for by the immediately preceding sections. Equally, the obvious purpose of sub-s (7) of s 37A is, as it seems to me, simply to indicate the date from which an entitlement to allowance is to commence. Hence the necessity for sub-s (5)(b) of s 37A in order to cater for the possibility of cases in which it is desirable that an allowance should be backdated.

The argument to the contrary which found favour with the commissioner is put in two ways. First, it is said that sub-s (7) in terms precludes any application for any review at all under s 104(1)(b), except in cases where regulations otherwise provide. Second, and alternatively, it is said that if s 104(1)(b) applies at all, sub-s (7) takes a change of residence out of the category of 'relevant circumstances' since residence is relevant only at the date when the original claim is received. These alternative ways of putting the case seem to me on analysis to come to much the same thing. A number of indicia are prayed in aid in their support. First, it is said that if one looks at s 22 of the Social Security Pensions Act 1975, which introduced s 37A, one will observe that sub-s (3) provides expressly for a power to make regulations to review decisions where regulations have been made permitting claims to be treated as if made for a period beginning after the date of the claim and permitting, in such case, conditional awards to be made. This, it is argued, is inconsistent with the application of the general power of review under s 104. There is, as it seems to me, nothing in this point, for the powers of review in s 104 are limited in their grounds and not fully comprehensive.

Second, it is said that the non-continuous nature of the residence requirement is supported by reg 10A of the Social Security Benefit (Persons Abroad) Regulations 1975, SI 1975/563 (inserted by SI 1975/1573, reg 10), which provides that a person shall not be disqualified for receiving mobility allowance because of absence from Great Britain. Again, in my judgment, nothing turns on this. Section 82(5) of the Act provides:

'Except where regulations otherwise provide, a person shall be disqualified for receiving any benefit, and an increase of benefit shall not be payable in respect of any person as the beneficiary's wife or husband, for any period during which the person—(a) is absent from Great Britain . . .'

The effect of the regulation (and similar regulations have been made in relation to other non-contributory benefits provided for in the Act) is merely to disapply this section. It

does not affect the necessity to comply with the prescribed conditions for which the
a statute provides and does not, therefore, cast any light on whether those conditions are to
be regarded as continuing or once-for-all conditions.

Third, it is argued that there are two regulations, namely regs 5 and 20 of the Mobility
Allowance Regulations 1975, which would be unnecessary and otiose if the general
power of review in s 104 applied. Regulations 5, so far as relevant, provides as follows:

b
'(1) A claim for an allowance may be made, or treated as made, for a period
beginning on such date later than the date on which the claim is received, being a
date not more than 3 months after the date on which it is so received, as the Secretary
of State may determine . . .

(3) Where, in accordance with the foregoing provisions of this regulation, a claim
is made or treated as made, for a period beginning after the date on which it is
received—(a) the entitlement to an allowance of the person in respect of whom such
c claim is made shall be determined having regard to the physical disablement to
which that person may be expected to be subject at the beginning of the period for
which the claim is, or is treated as being, made; and (b) if it appears that the
conditions for entitlement to an allowance will be satisfied from the beginning of
such period, an award of an allowance, to be payable from that date, may be made
subject to the condition that, when the allowance becomes payable in accordance
d with such award, the person in respect of whom such claim is made satisfies the
requirements for entitlement to an allowance for which provision is made in section
37A or in these regulations; and if at any time during the period for which such an
award is made, any of those requirements are found not to have been satisfied, the
award shall be reviewed.'

e It is said that reg 5(3) is otiose if the general power of review applies. This is merely a
variant of the argument based on s 22(3) of the Social Security Pensions Act 1975, and I
cannot accept it. One of the possibilities which had to be provided for was that of a
conditional award and of a mistaken belief that the condition had been complied with.
The power of review in s 104(1)(a) would not indeed permit a review in such a case, since
the mistake would relate not to the decision but to something occurring (or not occurring)
f after the decision. Equally, a mistake as to fulfilment of the condition could hardly be a
'relevant change of circumstance' within s 104(1)(b).

Regulation 20 deals with the review of medical decisions and this in terms directs that
the question of continued compliance with the medical conditions for an allowance is to
be considered as at the date of the application for review. Thus, it is said, this is a case
where, as contemplated by sub-s (7) of s 37A, regulations do provide for a date for
g fulfilment of condition of entitlement other than the date of the receipt of the claim. The
fact that such an express provision was necessary demonstrates, it is said, that without
it there could be no review except as at the date of the claim and thus supports the
contention that s 104(1) is excluded. Again, I find myself unable to accept this. Section
104 is, in my judgment, not concerned with medical reviews. It is limited to reviews of
the decisions of insurance officers, local tribunals and commissioners, and even if one
h posits a general power of review in s 104 a specific power to review the medical condition
of the applicant for allowance is required.

Despite the very clear and helpful argument of counsel for the respondent, I cannot,
for my part, find anything in the legislation itself or in the regulations made thereunder
which leads to the conclusion that sub-s (7) of s 37A is dealing with anything but the
original claim for allowance or which, with respect to the commissioner, compels a
j construction which is not only out of line with the clearly expressed legislative intention
as regards other forms of non-contributory benefit, but which also produces results which
seem to me to be contrary to common sense.

In my judgment, s 104(1)(b) enables a review to be held on a permanent change of
residence, and I would therefore allow the appeal and remit the matter to the
commissioner for decision on the other points argued before him.

PURCHAS LJ. I agree.

WALLER LJ. I also agree.

Appeal allowed. Commissioner's decision set aside; matter remitted to commissioner for redetermination.

Solicitors: *Solicitor to the Department of Health and Social Security*; *Ralph Haring & Co* (for the respondent).

Sophie Craven   Barrister.

Mills v Anderson

QUEEN'S BENCH DIVISION AT NEWCASTLE UPON TYNE
BENET HYTNER QC SITTING AS A DEPUTY JUDGE OF THE HIGH COURT
16 FEBRUARY, 22 MARCH 1984

Executor and administrator – Administrator – Relation back of title – When relation back occurs – Whether approach in determining when relation back occurs subjective or objective.

Executor and administrator – Administrator – Estoppel against administrator – Estoppel in relation to agreements made or acts done before grant of administration – Whether administrator estopped from denying validity of agreements made or acts done by him before grant of administration.

In determining whether letters of administration should be allowed to relate back to the date of death of the deceased thus validating acts done by the administrator before letters of administration were obtained, the correct test is whether at the date of the grant it would, objectively speaking, be beneficial to the estate for the general rule against relation back not to apply. Accordingly, there can be no relation back in order to validate acts which were done before the grant of letters of administration with the subjective aim of benefiting the estate but which have not in fact benefited the estate at all (see p 543 *d* to *f*, post); *Waring v Dewberry* (1718) 1 Stra 97, *Morgan v Thomas* (1853) 8 Exch 302 and *Bodger v Arch* (1854) 10 Exch 333 applied.

An administrator is not estopped from denying the validity of an act done or an agreement entered into by him in relation to the estate before he was granted letters of administration since any representation made before letters of administration were granted could not have been made by him in his capacity as administrator (see p 544 *a*, post); *Metters v Brown* (1863) 1 H & C 686 applied.

Notes

For the doctrine of relation back and for estoppel against an administrator, see 17 Halsbury's Laws (4th edn) paras 735–737, and for cases on the subject, see 23 Digest (Reissue) 47–51, 542–576.

Cases referred to in judgment

Bodger v Arch (1854) 10 Exch 333, 156 ER 472.
Doe d Hornby v Glenn (1834) 1 Ad & El 49, 110 ER 1126.

a   *Gammell v Wilson* [1981] 1 All ER 578, [1982] AC 27, [1981] 2 WLR 248, HL; *affg* [1980]
        2 All ER 557, [1982] AC 27, [1980] 3 WLR 591, CA.
    Metters v Brown (1863) 1 H & C 686, 158 ER 1060.
    Morgan v Thomas (1853) 8 Exch 302, 155 ER 1362.
    Waring v Dewberry (1718) 1 Stra 97, 93 ER 408.

Preliminary issue

b   By a writ issued on 15 July 1982 the plaintiff, James William Mills, the father and
    administrator of the estate of Gary Wilfred Mills deceased, letters of administration
    having been granted to the plaintiff on 7 May 1982, brought an action for the benefit of
    the estate against the defendant, John Edward Anderson, claiming damages under the
    Law Reform (Miscellaneous Provisions) Act 1934. The defendant denied liability, and in
    para 7 of his defence pleaded further or in the alternative that on or about 2 May 1980,
c   after the plaintiff's cause of action, if any, had accrued to him, it was agreed between the
    plaintiff's solicitor and the defendant's insurers that the insurers should pay to the
    plaintiff the sum of £375 plus the actual funeral expenses in respect of the deceased and
    costs in discharge of his cause of action, and that the sum paid under that agreement to
    the plaintiff on 20 June 1980 was accepted by him in discharge of the alleged cause of
    action. By a reply the plaintiff admitted the agreement but denied that at the date thereof
d   any cause of action had then accrued to him or that it was or could be made by or be
    binding on the deceased's estate. By an order dated 30 March 1983 it was ordered that
    there should be a separate trial of the issue raised in para 7 of the defendant's defence.
    The issue was heard in Newcastle upon Tyne, but judgment was given in Liverpool. The
    facts are set out in the judgment.

e   *Humphrey Potts QC* and *David R Wood* for the plaintiff.
    Peter Fox for the defendant.

Cur adv vult

f   22 March. The following judgment was delivered.

    BENET HYTNER QC. The plaintiff is the father and administrator of the estate of
    his deceased son Gary Wilfred Mills who was tragically killed in a road accident on 28
    September 1979. He was then only 16 years of age. The deceased had been riding a
    moped along a public road during the hours of darkness when he collided with a
g   stationary unlit tractor owned by and in the charge of the defendant.
        The statement of claim alleges negligence and claims damages from the defendant
    under the Law Reform (Miscellaneous Provisions) Act 1934 for the benefit of the estate.
    The defence denies negligence, alleges contributory negligence and in para 7 avers that
    there has been accord and satisfaction in that—

h   'On or about 2nd May 1980, after the Plaintiff's cause of action, if any, had
        accrued to him, it was agreed between the Plaintiff's Solicitor acting on behalf of the
        Plaintiff, and the Defendant's Insurers acting on his behalf that the said insurers
        should pay the Plaintiff the sum of £375 plus actual funeral expenses and costs and
        that the Plaintiff should accept the same in discharge of his said cause of action, and
        that such agreement should be and the same accordingly was accepted in discharge
        of the alleged cause of action.'

j   By para 8 of the defence it is averred that 'On 20th June 1980 the said insurers paid the
    Plaintiff's Solicitor the said sum as agreed'.
        By his reply the plaintiff admits that on 2 May 1980 a letter was written by the
    plaintiff's solicitor agreeing to accept an offer of £375 and funeral expenses in full
    settlement, but it continues:

'The Plaintiff does not admit that any cause of action had then accrued to him or that the said offer was or could be made by, or be binding upon, the Estate of Gary Wilfred Mills deceased.'

The plaintiff further admits that the defendant's insurers tendered a cheque for the said sum but avers that this was refused and that the moneys are held on deposit.

It is this issue of accord and satisfaction that I am now asked to decide by way of preliminary issue.

Evidence was given to me by Mr John Dodgson, a claims inspector with the defendant's insurers, NFU Mutual, and on behalf of the plaintiff by Mr Norman Peacock, a partner in the firm of Allan Henderson Beecham & Peacock, the plaintiff's solicitors. It is a pleasure to record that these two pleasant young men gave their evidence with such candour that there is virtually no conflict of fact and that the only difficulty facing me is to determine the law which should be applied to the facts.

Mr Peacock was initially instructed by the present plaintiff in October 1979. However, at that date the plaintiff was not the administrator of the estate since letters of administration had not then been taken out; nor as we shall see were letters taken out until long after the events with which I am concerned in this judgment. In January 1980 Mr Peacock attended the inquest and on 24 January wrote a letter before action to the defendant. The letter was in common form claiming 'Law Reform damages' but it began with the words 'We have been consulted on behalf of the estate of the late Master Mills . . .'

The defendant duly passed that letter to his insurers and in reply to a query from him the head office of the insurers instructed Mr Dodgson to 'try a compromise first. If they will not concede or only very little then get a police report'. On 14 March Mr Dodgson called on Mr Peacock. A report of that meeting was made by Mr Dodgson, and Mr Peacock's recollection of what occurred conforms to that report. The material part of the discussion was an offer by Mr Dodgson to pay 50% of the Law Reform Act damages and reasonable funeral expenses. It is clear that both regarded the Law Reform Act damages as being confined to damages for loss of expectation of life (and which they both appear to have undervalued at £750). It is also clear that there was no meeting of minds because Mr Dodgson was offering 50% of the aggregate of the two figures whereas Mr Peacock understood him to be offering the funeral expenses plus 50% of the Law Reform Act damages. Mr Peacock was not happy with this offer and no agreement was reached at that meeting. Despite his dissatisfaction with the offer Mr Peacock took instructions from the plaintiff and his wife on 26 March, and as a result on May 1980 he wrote a letter saying, 'Our clients [sic] will accept an offer of £375 and the funeral expenses in the sum of £231·15 in full settlement to conclude this distressing matter'. After intimating the amount of his legal charges Mr Peacock continued, 'we assume you do not wish us to extract Letters of Administration but will accept the parents' discharge'.

I pause here to observe that if the opening words of the letter before action had caused the insurers to suppose that letters of administration had been taken out this letter openly corrected any such impression.

As I have already indicated Mr Peacock was in effect accepting an offer which had never been made and this was pointed out by Mr Dodgson to his head office in a memorandum dated 6 May 1980. However, Mr Dodgson also pointed out that 'in the light of the recent circular on the "lost years" it might be as well to settle without more ado. If you agree we will tie it up'. Mr Dodgson told me that the circular to which he referred in his memorandum was a note circulated through the offices of the insurance company warning them of the recently reported decision of the Court of Appeal in *Gammell v Wilson* [1980] 2 All ER 557, [1982] AC 27 affirming, by a majority, a decision of my own at first instance and in effect giving the plaintiff a claim for damages under the Law Reform (Miscellaneous Provisions) Act 1934 far in excess of the claim for loss of expectation of life and funeral expenses.

It is therefore no surprise that the immediate reply of the head office was 'settle at this

as soon as you can and do not raise any query on costs'. Mr Dodgson wasted little time.
a He telephoned Mr Peacock telling him that the insurers would pay the whole of the
funeral expenses together with the costs and £375, being half the loss of expectation of
life figure. During that telephone conversation he jotted down on a pad the various
figures and the full name of the plaintiff's wife so that he could prepare the necessary
form of discharge.

On 2 June, having not heard from Mr Peacock, he wrote:

b
> 'We note that we still await the full Christian names of Mrs. Mills to enable us to
> prepare the necessary agreement form and settlement cheque. We look forward to
> hearing from you as quickly as possible.'

On 17 June, however, Mr Peacock replied:

c
> 'We are sorry about the delays but you will doubtless have read the recent case of
> *Gammell v Wilson and another* reported in the Weekly Law Reports which clearly
> does alter the framework of this case and any settlement to be concluded by the
> parents or administrator. It remains to be seen whether an appeal is pursued and we
> invite your comments.'

Mr Dodgson's predictable comments were contained in his reply dated 20 June.
d Enclosing a cheque for £850·90 made payable to Mr Peacock's firm and which was stated
to be in full and final settlement 'of all present and future claims by or on behalf of the
parents or administrators of the estate of Gary Wilfred Mills deceased against John
Edward Anderson . . .' Mr Dodgson continued:

> 'Whilst we note what you say in your letter dated 17th June, 1980 we would draw
> your attention to your open letter dated 2nd May, 1980 from which it is perfectly
e > clear that there has been offer and acceptance.'

After taking some time to consider the matter Mr Peacock replied on 15 July 1980:

> 'Our clients instruct us to defer settlement pending the outcome of any appeal in
> the *Gammell v Wilson* case and accordingly we have to return your cheque for
f > £850·90. Only an administrator in the estate of the late Master Mills can give an
> unqualified acceptance and discharge. This has not occurred and therefore we
> consider there has been no formal settlement.'

On 21 July Mr Dodgson returned the cheque to Mr Peacock and reaffirmed his view
that there had been offer and acceptance and finally on 24 July Mr Peacock retorted:

> 'It may be there has been an offer and acceptance but the relevant consideration is
g > whether such agreement is legally binding, given the deceased died intestate and
> the acceptance was by someone other than the administrator.'

He indicated that the cheque would be held to the insurers' immediate order.

Both witnesses were completely frank about their motives and intentions. Mr Dodgson
had frequently settled cases before March 1980 where a claim had been made by parents
h of a deceased infant but no letters of administration had been taken out. He was aware of
the legal requirement for a discharge by an executor or administrator and his office used
a set form of discharge and indemnity by the parents. Similarly, where a live infant
made a claim for damages and this was settled for a modest amount the insurers did not
always go to the trouble and expense of obtaining an approval of the court for the
settlement but again used a form of discharge and indemnity, a sample of which was
j produced.

Since on an intestacy the estate would be divided between both parents it was necessary
for the protection of the insurers where no letters of administration were taken out to
pay the cheque to both and to receive an indemnity from both.

Mr Dodgson was completely frank about his state of knowledge. He knew that letters
of administration had not been taken out and on 2 May he assumed that letters would

not be taken out. He knew furthermore that the discharge and indemnity were required to protect his company in the event of a subsequent action on behalf of the estate in relation to the death. Similarly, he knew in the case of an injured infant that if he accepted the parents' discharge on a settlement without the approval of the court the defendant would be liable to be sued by the infant when he attained his majority; the indemnity would then in theory protect his company.

In these circumstances it is plain that had he given thought to the matter. Mr Dodgson must have concluded that the agreement reached between himself and Mr Peacock was not legally binding on the estate.

Mr Peacock for his part conceded readily that he had reached an agreement with Mr Dodgson but regarded it as his duty not to advise his clients to implement it if it was not in their interests so to do and if it was not legally binding.

It merely remains to record that letters of administration were granted to the plaintiff out of the Newcastle upon Tyne District Registry on 7 May 1982.

These being the facts, counsel for the plaintiff made a number of submissions of law based on statements in two textbooks, *Williams, Mortimer and Sunnucks on Executors, Administrators and Probate* (16th edn, 1982) (to which I shall refer as '*Williams*') and Spencer Bower and Turner's *Estoppel by Representation* (3rd edn, 1977) (to which I shall refer as '*Spencer Bower*'). These textbook statements were supported by footnotes referring to old cases none of which was or could have been available to counsel, and with the consent of both counsel I have subsequently read the cases concerned to ensure that they do indeed support the textbook statements.

In essence counsel for the plaintiff submitted that letters of administration do not in general relate back to the date of death nor can estoppel operate against a party who has changed his legal personality but that letters may relate back where this would operate for the benefit of the estate. The agreement concluded between the parties in the instant case not being of benefit to the estate, since the decision of the Court of Appeal in *Gammell v Wilson* was indeed upheld by the House of Lords (see [1981] 1 All ER 578, [1982] AC 27) the exceptions to the general rule do not apply and consequently the agreement between Mr Dodgson and Mr Peacock was not binding on a subsequent administrator.

Williams states (at p 91):

> 'Cases may, however, be found where the letters of administration have been held to relate back to the death of the intestate so as to give a validity to the acts done before the letters were obtained.'

But it also says (at p 92):

> 'Such relation back exists only in those cases where the act done is for the benefit of the estate.'

This statement is supported by a reference to *Morgan v Thomas* (1853) 8 Exch 302, 155 ER 1362, and I am satisfied that this decision does indeed support that statement which appears to be taken almost verbatim from the judgment of Parke B (8 Exch 302 at 307, 155 ER 1362 at 1364):

> 'An act done by a party who afterwards becomes administrator, to the prejudice of the estate, is not made good by the subsequent administration. It is only in those cases where the act is for the benefit of the estate that the relation back exists, by virtue of which relation the administrator is enabled to recover against such persons as have interfered with the estate, and thereby to prevent it from being prejudiced and despoiled.'

The fact that relation back does exist in certain cases as an exception to the general rule that it does not is supported by three further statements in *Williams* (at pp 428–429):

> 'It is clear that the title of an administrator, though it does not exist until the grant of administration, relates back to the time of the death of the intestate; and

a that he may recover against a wrongdoer who has seized or converted the goods of
the intestate after his death in an action of trespass or trover . . . It would also seem
that whenever anyone acting on behalf of the intestate's estate, and not on his own
account, makes a contract with another before any grant of administration, the
administration will have relation back, so that the benefit of the contract is not lost
and the administrator may sue upon it, as made with himself.'

b The latter statement is supported by *Bodger v Arch* (1854) 10 Exch 333, 156 ER 472,
which I am satisfied does justify it.

I pause here to observe that it is clear from that statement that although letters may
not have been granted a person may act 'on behalf of the intestate's estate' and it was
therefore perfectly proper for Mr Peacock to write the letter before action 'on behalf of
the estate' even though he knew that there was no administrator.

c The third statement in *Williams* is as follows (at p 430):

'The doctrine of "relation back" must be applied only to protect the estate from
wrongful injury occurring in the interval before grant.'

This statement is said to be supported by *Waring v Dewberry* (1718) 1 Stra 97, 93 ER 408,
and again I am satisfied that it is a statement supported by the ratio in that case.

d Subject to a submission by counsel for the defendant to which I shall refer below and
subject to one possible ambiguity these statements seem to me to support the submissions
of counsel for the plaintiff. I have, however, to consider whether an act done for the
benefit of the estate means an act which looking back objectively is of benefit to the estate
or whether it may include acts which were done subjectively for the benefit of the estate
even though looking back they have not benefited the estate at all. It is perfectly clear
that, in arriving at his decision to conclude an agreement with Mr Dodgson, Mr Peacock
e believed that he was acting for the benefit of the estate. Indeed, had the House of Lords
in *Gammell v Wilson* decided that damages for loss of expectation of life should be a token
figure never intended to rise with inflation at all and consequently should have reverted
to £250, the agreement would have been of considerable benefit to the estate.

I am satisfied, looking at all the cases as a whole, that relation back only occurs when it
f would be beneficial to the estate for the general doctrine not to operate. The exception
applies to prevent injury to the estate, and, in my judgment, the approach should be a
purely objective one.

Before turning to the submission of counsel for the defendant and for the sake of
completeness I turn to consider whether the doctrine of estoppel can apply. Counsel for
the plaintiff relied on *Spencer Bower* (p 125, para 127):

g 'Just as, for the purposes of estoppel by representation, amongst other purposes,
there may be a unity of *persona* (in the strict juridicial sense of the word) between
two physically distinct individuals, *e.g.* principal and agent, as has already been
pointed out, so, conversely, one and the same person in the physical sense may in
contemplation of law occupy two *personae* or characters, one private, and the other
official, in which case, when litigating in the latter capacity, he is not estopped by
h any representation made by him in the former, and *vice versa*.'

Again the footnote case, *Metters v Brown* (1863) 1 H & C 686 at 693, 158 ER 1060 at
1063, fully supports that statement:

'In *Doe d Hornby v. Glenn* ((1834) 1 Ad & El 49, 110 ER 1126), which was cited on
j the argument it was held that an agreement entered into by an executor de son tort
did not bind him after he had become rightful administrator. In our opinion the
plaintiff, who sues as an administrator of his mother, must be considered in the
position of a stranger, and therefore the rule as to estoppel does not apply; for
whenever a person sues, not in his own right, but in the right of another, he must
for the purposes of estoppel be deemed a stranger.'

I am consequently quite satisfied that the plaintiff in this case cannot be estopped from denying the validity of an act done by him in relation to the estate before he became administrator.

This latter doctrine was not challenged in principle by counsel for the defendant, who nevertheless submitted that in the circumstances of this case the doctrine did not apply; nor did he challenge the general validity of the submissions made by counsel. In an ingenious argument, however, he submitted that where there was an agreement concluded between parties one of whom later became an administrator and where the agreement was such as would permit the administrator to sue on it, the contract could then be used by the other party as a shield even though he could never use it as a sword.

There is no doubt in my mind that the first premise of counsel for the defendant is justified. Let us supppose that, before any act were done by the plaintiff, subsequent to letters of administration, to deny the validity of the contract, a witness had been discovered who wholly exonerated the defendant from all blame for the death of the deceased, the plaintiff could successfully have sued on the agreement. So, submits counsel, it would be wholly anomalous if in such circumstances the defendant cannot, in answer to a claim, set up the same agreement as a defence.

This argument merits careful consideration but I can find nothing in the two textbooks or in the cases which supports it. In the light of the decision in *Gammell v Wilson* the agreement concluded by both parents purportedly on behalf of the estate was not of benefit to it. The judgment at first instance in *Gammell v Wilson* which the House of Lords later affirmed as good law was given on 27 July 1979, which not only preceded the agreement but also the death itself. The judgments in the Court of Appeal were delivered on 1 April 1980, which also predated the agreement. It cannot be said therefore that even at the date of the agreement it was of benefit to the estate. I do not therefore have to consider the position which might arise if the act done was, at the time of its performance, of benefit to the estate but as a result of supervening events, including decisions of the courts, had later become injurious to the estate.

In these circumstances I have reached the conclusions, first, that this agreement was not concluded on behalf of the estate by the administrator, second, that the doctrine of relation back does not operate to bind him as administrator, and third, that as administrator he is not estopped from denying the validity of an agreement entered into by him on behalf of himself and his wife; and I consequently hold on the preliminary issue that the defendant has not made out the averment of accord and satisfaction.

The costs of the hearing before me and any other costs relating solely to the issue of accord and satisfaction will be the plaintiff's in any event.

I would like to express my gratitude to both counsel for their very considerable assistance in what has been an interesting but by no means easy case.

Determination accordingly.

Solicitors: *Allan Henderson Beecham & Peacock*, Newcastle upon Tyne (for the plaintiff); *Sinton & Co*, Newcastle upon Tyne (for the defendant).

K Mydeen Esq   Barrister.

The Tuyuti

COURT OF APPEAL, CIVIL DIVISION
ACKNER AND ROBERT GOFF LJJ
5, 6 APRIL 1984

Admiralty – Jurisdiction – Action in rem – Arrest of ship – Stay of proceedings – Arbitration agreement – Court bound to grant stay – Whether court permitted to order arrest of ship or to continue arrest already obtained – Whether security obtained by arrest constituting security in arbitration or in possible future action in rem – Arbitration Act 1975, s 1(1).

Arbitration – Stay of court proceedings – Power of court to order stay – Whether power limited to cases where court seised of matter after arbitration agreement made – Arbitration Act 1975, s 1(1).

The plaintiffs were the owners of cargo shipped on the defendants' ship under bills of lading which included a London arbitration clause. Part of the cargo was off-loaded in Spain and the remainder was discharged at Rotterdam. The cargo owners complained that the cargo was discharged in a damaged condition. In January 1984 they issued a writ in rem in the Admiralty Court claiming damages for breach of the contract of carriage for the cargo, and on the same day they obtained a warrant for the arrest of the ship. The ship was not in the jurisdiction and the writ was not served nor was the ship arrested. On 17 February, in order to protect themselves under the time provisions in the arbitration clause, the cargo owners nominated an arbitrator. On 27 February the shipowners nominated an arbitrator and on 2 March they applied under s 1(1)[a] of the Arbitration Act 1975 for a stay of the cargo owners' action in rem and an order setting aside the warrant of arrest. The judge granted the stay of action and ordered a stay of execution of the warrant of arrest. The cargo owners appealed against the order staying execution of the warrant of arrest. On the appeal the shipowners contended that when the court stayed proceedings under s 1(1) of the 1975 Act it was required to stay the whole proceedings, including execution of any warrant of arrest. They also contended that the effect of permitting the security which would be obtained by the arrest of the ship to be retained in case the arbitration foundered if an award in favour of the cargo owners was not satisfied would be to permit the security to be obtained for the purpose of the arbitration, which was an impermissible exercise of the court's jurisdiction in rem.

Held – Where a defendant to an action in rem applied to the court to stay the action under s 1(1) of the 1975 Act pending submission to arbitration the court was entitled, when granting the stay, to order the arrest of the defendant's ship or to continue any arrest already obtained if it was shown by the plaintiff that any arbitration award in his favour was unlikely to be satisfied by the defendant. In arresting or continuing the arrest of the ship as security, the security was being administered not in relation to the arbitration proceedings but in relation to a possible judgment in the action in rem. Since there was clear evidence that the shipowners might well be unable to satisfy any arbitration award in favour of the cargo owners, the appeal would be allowed and the judge's order reversed in so far as it imposed a stay on the execution of the warrant of arrest (see p 549 *e f*, p 552 *g* to *j*, p 553 *g* to *j*, p 554 *h j* and p 555 *h j*, post).

The Rena K [1979] 1 All ER 397 applied.

The Andria [1984] 1 All ER 1126 considered.

Per curiam. The court's power to order a stay of legal proceedings under s 1(1) of the 1975 Act pending arbitration is not limited to cases where the court becomes seised of the action or matter only after the parties have made an arbitration agreement (see p 555 *c d* and *g* to *j*, post).

---

a   Section 1(1) is set out at p 547 *h j*, post

Notes

For stay of court proceedings pending arbitration, see 2 Halsbury's Laws (4th edn) para
555 and 37 ibid para 440, and for cases on the subject, see 3 Digest (Reissue) 70–76, 360–
390.

For the jurisdiction in rem, see 1 Halsbury's Laws (4th edn) paras 305, 311, and for
cases on the subject, see 1(1) Digest (Reissue) 219–223, 1240–1251.

For warrant of arrest of a ship, see 1 Halsbury's Laws (4th edn) paras 366–368, and for
cases on the subject, see 1(1) Digest (Reissue) 294–295, 1759–1770.

For the Arbitration Act 1975, s 1, see 45 Halsbury's Statutes (3rd edn) 33.

As from a day to be appointed s 26 of the Civil Jurisdiction and Judgments Act 1982
will enable the court on staying or dismissing Admiralty proceedings on the ground,
inter alia, that the dispute should be submitted to arbitration to retain an arrested ship
(or any bail or security given instead) as security for the satisfaction of any award given
in the arbitration.

Cases referred to in judgments

Andria, The [1984] 1 All ER 1126, [1984] 2 WLR 570, CA.
Cap Bon, The [1967] 1 Lloyd's Rep 543.
Golden Trader, The, Danemar Scheepvaart Maatschappij BV v Golden Trader (owners) [1974]
    2 All ER 686, [1975] QB 348, [1974] 3 WLR 16.
*Jade, The, The Eschersheim, Erkowit (owners) v Jade (owners), Erkowit (cargo owners) v
    Eschersheim (owners)* [1976] 1 All ER 920, [1976] 1 WLR 430, HL.
Paczy v Haendler & Natermann GmbH [1981] 1 Lloyd's Rep 302, CA.
Rena K, The [1979] 1 All ER 397, [1979] QB 377, [1978] 3 WLR 431.

Application and interlocutory appeal

The plaintiffs, the owners of cargo lately laden on board the ship Tuyuti, applied for leave
to appeal and if granted appealed against the order of Sheen J on 29 March 1984 whereby
he ordered that all further proceedings in the cargo owners' action in rem against the
Tuyuti be stayed pursuant to s 1 of the Arbitration Act 1975 and that there be a stay of
execution of the warrant of arrest of the Tuyuti. The facts are set out in the judgment of
Robert Goff LJ.

Richard Aikens for the cargo owners.
Nigel Teare for the shipowners.

ROBERT GOFF LJ (delivering the first judgment at the invitation of Ackner LJ).
There is before the court a renewed application by the plaintiffs for leave to appeal from
an order by Sheen J dated 20 March 1984 under which, on the defendants' application,
he stayed all further proceedings in the action pursuant to s 1 of the Arbitration Act 1975
and further ordered that there be a stay of execution of the warrant of arrest issued in the
action until further order. He refused leave to appeal.

For reasons which I shall explain in a moment, the plaintiffs' application for leave to
appeal against the order of a stay under s 1 of the 1975 Act is restricted to one limited
point. It is against the order staying the execution of the warrant of arrest that their
application is primarily directed. They appeared before Ackner LJ a day or two ago and
he then adjourned the matter for consideration by this court. We heard submissions
yesterday, for which we are much indebted, and we decided to give judgment
immediately because the relevant vessel is due to enter the jurisdiction of the court in
the next few days, and so the question whether the warrant of arrest should be subject to
a stay of execution has assumed some urgency.

The matter arises as follows. The plaintiffs were the owners of cargo shipped on the
defendants' ship Tuyuti (which I shall refer to as 'the vessel') at Montevideo, in Uruguay,
in December 1982. I shall refer to the plaintiffs as 'the cargo owners' and to the defendants
as 'the shipowners'. The cargo was a general cargo. We are concerned in the present case
quantity of screws loaded in two containers shipped under a single bill of lading, destined
with a quantity of wool shipped under 38 bills of lading destined for Liverpool, and a

a for Rotterdam. The cargo owners claim that the wool, part of which was off-loaded in Spain and the remainder discharged at Rotterdam, was discharged in a damaged condition, and that this damage was due to the unseaworthiness of the vessel, arising from the state of the hatch covers and the adjacent stowage in the holds of other cargo which was spontaneously combustible. The containers of screws were lost overboard in a storm.

b The cargo owners' claim in respect of the damage to the wool amounts to about $US450,000 and for the loss of the screws to about $US40,000. Each of the bills of lading under which the wool was shipped was in the same form and contained a clause paramount (cl 2) and a so-called jurisdiction clause (cl 3) which provided that the bill of lading should be governed by English law and included a London arbitration clause. The bill of lading under which the screws were shipped contained no arbitration clause, but contained an exclusive jurisdiction clause under which disputes were to be referred to a court in the country where the carrier had his principal place of business, which was

c Uruguay, and that the proper law of the contract was the law of Uruguay.

The wool cargo was discharged in January 1983. The one-year time limit, with extensions, was due to expire on 17 February 1984. On 31 January 1984 the cargo owners issued their writ in the action, and on the same day the cargo owners' solicitors obtained a warrant for the arrest of the vessel. She has not yet come within the jurisdiction of the Admiralty Court, and so the writ has not been served, nor has the vessel been arrested.

d However, solicitors acting on behalf of the shipowners discovered that the writ had been issued. They then voluntarily filed an acknowledgment of service on behalf of the shipowners, although no writ had been served. Their purpose in so doing I shall explain in a moment.

On 17 February 1984, in order to protect the time position having regard to the

e arbitration clause in the wool bills of lading, the cargo owners' solicitors nominated an arbitrator. The appointment was expressed to be in respect of both the wool bills of lading and the screws bill of lading, and was also expressed to be without prejudice to, inter alia, cargo claimant's rights to arrest any of the shipowners' vessels. On 27 February the shipowners' solicitors responded, nominating an arbitrator both under the wool bills of lading and under the screws bill of lading.

f On 2 March the shipowners issued a notice of motion, asking for a stay of proceedings. This was served on 13 March. Argument took place before Sheen J on 20–23 March and, as I have recorded, he delivered his judgment on 29 March. The shipowners applied for a stay of proceedings under s 1 of the Arbitration Act 1975 and, if necessary, an order setting aside the warrant of arrest. It is common ground between the parties that the wool bills of lading contained a non-domestic arbitration agreement, to which s 1 of the 1975 Act applied. The screws bill of lading contained no such agreement. Even so, by

g virtue of the nomination of the parties' arbitrators, there has come into existence an ad hoc arbitration agreement in respect of the dispute which has arisen under the screws bill of lading, though there is a dispute whether s 1 of the 1975 Act applies in the circumstances of the present case.

It will, I think, be helpful if at this stage I set out the provisions of s 1(1) and (2) of the

h 1975 Act:

'Staying court proceedings where party proves arbitration agreements.—(1) If any party to an arbitration agreement to which this section applies, or any person claiming through or under him, commences any legal proceedings in any court against any other party to the agreement, or any person claiming through or under him, in

j respect of any matter agreed to be referred, any party to the proceedings may at any time after appearance, and before delivering any pleadings or taking any other steps in the proceedings, apply to the court to stay the proceedings; and the court, unless satisfied that the arbitration agreement is null and void, inoperative or incapable of being performed or that there is not in fact any dispute between the parties with regard to the matter agreed to be referred, shall make an order staying the proceedings.

(2) This section applies to any arbitration agreement which is not a domestic arbitration agreement; and neither section 4(1) of the Arbitration Act 1950 nor section 4 of the Arbitration Act (Northern Ireland) 1937 shall apply to an arbitration agreement to which this section applies.'

I need not refer to sub-ss (3) and (4).

The shipowners' application for a stay was made under that section. I must now explain the purpose of the shipowners in entering a voluntary acknowledgment of service. This was to make what has been called a 'pre-emptive strike'. Their purpose was to put themselves in a position to make an application for a stay of proceedings under s 1 of the 1975 Act before their vessel arrived within the jurisdiction of the court, so that they could obtain an order which would effectively freeze the warrant of arrest before the vessel was arrested. For the cargo owners counsel has conceded, rightly in my opinion, that the effect of the Rules of the Supreme Court (in particular Ord 20, r 10, Ord 10, r 1(5) and Ord 75, rr 1, 3 and 8) is that the shipowners did by this step put themselves in the position of defendants to an action in personam in which proceedings are deemed to have been served, and so they did, by acknowledging service, enable themselves to make an application under s 1 of the 1975 Act.

Moreover, if the decision of the judge is right, the shipowners' pre-emptive strike has been successful. Before the judge the following issues arose. The first issue was whether he should grant a mandatory stay of the proceedings. As to that, counsel for the cargo owners submitted to the judge, first, that no stay should be granted in respect of the claim under the wool bills of lading because on the evidence the shipowners were in such financial difficulty that they were unable to satisfy any arbitration award which might be made against them, with the effect that the arbitration agreement was incapable of being performed within those words in s 1 of the 1975 Act and, second, that, as regards the screws bill of lading, s 1 of the 1975 Act was not applicable because proceedings were commenced before the parties entered into the ad hoc arbitration agreement. The judge rejected the first of these submissions and counsel has not sought to pursue the point before this court. The judge also rejected the second submission on the ground that on the form of indorsement on this particular writ it was not possible to distinguish the claim of one plaintiff from the claim of another. So the result was that the judge granted a stay of proceedings in respect of all claims under s 1 of the 1975 Act.

He then proceeded to consider the position as regards the warrant of arrest. The judge rejected an argument of the shipowners that the effect of an order for a stay of proceedings was that the warrant could not be executed, and so the question then arose whether an order should be made staying the execution of the warrant. For the cargo owners counsel advanced two reasons why no such order should be made. His first submission was that the court has power under s 12(6)(*f*) of the Arbitration Act 1950 to permit or order the arrest of a ship for the purpose of obtaining security in an arbitration. His second submission was that the court has power to permit or order the arrest of the ship on the evidence before it to secure a judgment in the action on the principles stated by Brandon J in *The Rena K* [1979] 1 All ER 397, [1979] QB 377, because it appeared that the shipowners might well be unable to satisfy an arbitration award and, in that event, the cargo owners might find it necessary to invoke the residual jurisdiction of the Admiralty Court to lift the stay and allow the action in rem to proceed. The judge rejected both these submissions, and so ordered a stay of execution of the warrant of arrest. The pre-emptive strike, therefore, succeeded.

The cargo owners, in seeking leave to appeal, submit that the judge was wrong in rejecting each of these two submission. The first of the two submissions I can deal with briefly. Section 12(6) of the 1950 Act provides, so far as material, as follows:

'The High Court shall have, for the purpose of and in relation to a reference, the same power of making orders in respect of . . . (*f*) securing the amount in dispute in the reference . . . as it has for the purpose of and in relation to an action or matter in the High Court . . .'

The submission of counsel for the cargo owners before the judge, which he repeated
a before us, was that the power to issue a warrant of arrest under which the Admiralty
Marshal is commanded to execute the warrant by arresting the ship constitutes a power
of the High Court of making an order securing the amount in dispute within this
subsection. A similar submission was considered on two occasions by Brandon J, first in
The Golden Trader, Danemar Scheepvaart Maatschappij BV v Golden Trader (owners) [1974]
2 All ER 686 at 695, [1975] QB 348 at 358 and second in *The Rena K* [1979] 1 All ER 397
b at 418, [1979] QB 377 at 408. On each occasion the submission was rejected by him.
I turn straight to *The Rena K*, where Brandon J had this to say:

'I was unable to accept the basic argument with regard to s 12(6)(*f*) put forward
for the charterers in *The Golden Trader*, because it appeared to me that, on the true
construction of that provision, it did not cover the arresting of a ship, or the keeping
of a ship under arrest, in the exercise of the court's jurisdiction in rem at all. The
c provision refers to the power of "making orders in respect of . . . securing the
amount in dispute". This did not seem to me to be appropriate language to describe
the process of arrest in an action in rem, because such arrest does not result from the
making of any order by the court, but from the party concerned himself causing a
warrant of arrest to be issued under RSC Ord 75, r 5, subject to the requirements of
that rule. The matters to which I thought the provision did relate were the court's
d powers of securing amounts in dispute in various other ways, for instance by
making orders under RSC Ord 29, rr 2(3) and 6. I still think that s 12(6)(*f*) does not
cover the arresting of a ship, or the keeping of a ship under arrest, in the exercise of
the court's jurisdiction in rem. It follows that I am equally unable to accept the
extended argument as to the effect of that provision put forward for the cargo
owners in the present case. The point involved in the extension itself, however, is a
e separate one, and I shall return to it shortly,'

This reasoning was followed and applied by the judge in the present case, and I find
myself to be in agreement with him. I must confess that it would not have occurred to
me to describe the jurisdiction to issue a warrant of arrest as a power of the court of
making an order securing the amount in dispute. I would describe it as a power to issue
f a warrant, the warrant being rather an instruction to the marshal than an order in the
sense in which the latter word is usually used in interlocutory orders of the court,
especially having regard to the orders listed in paras (*a*) to (*h*) of s 12(6), relating to such
matters as security for costs, discovery and so on. I agree with Brandon J that s 12(6)(*f*)
relates to the court's powers under such rules as Ord 29, rr 2(3) and 6, and that it does
not, on its true construction, refer to the jurisdiction to issue a warrant of arrest. I can see
g no ground for interfering with the judge's decision on this point.
I turn then to the central point in the case, which is concerned with the principle
enunciated by Brandon J in *The Rena K*. The question of the Admiralty Court's jurisdiction
to arrest a ship or to continue such an arrest in relation to arbitration proceedings was
recently considered by this court in *The Andria* [1984] 1 All ER 1126, [1984] 2 WLR 570.
It may help to put the principle in *The Rena K* in its context if I first refer to the judgment
h in *The Andria*. In that case it was held that, although the only prerequisite to the court's
jurisdiction to issue a warrant for arrest is that a writ must have been issued in an action
in rem, nevertheless the court should not exercise that jurisdiction for the purpose of
providing security for an award which may be made in arbitration proceedings. The
relevant passage in the judgment of the court in *The Andria* [1984] 1 All ER 1126 at
1134–1135, [1984] 2 WLR 570 at 579–580 reads as follows:

j 'The mere fact that the dispute between the parties falls within the scope of an
arbitration agreement entered into between them does not of itself generally
preclude one of them from bringing an action. Accordingly, the mere existence of
an arbitration agreement will not of itself prevent a party from issuing a writ, or
serving the writ and (in the case of an action in rem), procuring the arrest of the
ship, or otherwise proceeding with the action. But the arbitration agreement can, of
course, have certain consequences. For example, if an action is begun, the other

party may apply for a stay of proceedings. Generally speaking, the court's power to grant a stay in such a case is discretionary; though of course in cases falling within s 1 of the Arbitration Act 1975 the court is bound to grant a stay. Again, if a party actively pursues proceedings in respect of the same claim both in the court and in arbitration, his so proceeding may be regarded as vexatious and an abuse of the process of the court; if so, the court may, in the exercise of its inherent power, require him to elect in which forum he will pursue his claim: see *The Cap Bon* [1967] 1 Lloyd's Rep 543. Next, let it be supposed that, before the court has granted a stay of proceedings under the Arbitration Acts, the plaintiff has obtained security by the arrest of a ship in an action in rem. If the stay is granted in the exercise of its discretionary power under s 4 of the Arbitration Act 1950, the court may require, as a condition of granting a stay, that alternative security should be made available to secure an award made in the arbitration proceedings: see *The Golden Trader*. If a mandatory stay is granted under s 1 of the Arbitration Act 1975, no such term can be imposed. But it has been held by Brandon J that, where it is shown by the plaintiff that an arbitration award in his favour is unlikely to be satisfied by the defendant, the security available in the action in rem may be ordered to stand so that, if the plaintiff may have thereafter to pursue the action in rem (possibly using an unsatisfied arbitration award for the purpose of an issue estoppel) the security will remain available in that action: see *The Rena K*. (We have not had to consider the principle in that case, and we have not heard arguments on the point; however, we proceed on the basis that that principle is sound.) However, on the law as it stands at present, the court's jurisdiction to arrest a ship in an action in rem should not be exercised for the purpose of providing security for an award which may be made in arbitration proceedings. That is simply because the purpose of the exercise of the jurisdiction is to provide security in respect of the action in rem, and not to provide security in some other proceedings, eg arbitration proceedings. The time may well come when the law on this point may be changed: see s 26 of the Civil Jurisdiction and Judgments Act 1982, which has however not yet been brought into force. But that is not yet the law. It follows that, if a plaintiff invokes the jurisdiction of the court to obtain the arrest of a ship as security for an award in arbitration proceedings, the court should not issue a warrant of arrest.'

It is the principle in *The Rena K*, summarised in the passage I have just read, which the cargo owners have invoked in the present case. In *The Andria* this court declined to express any opinion on the soundness of that principle, which had not been considered in argument before it. It is necessary to turn to *The Rena K* itself to find a statement of that principle, and the basis on which it was formulated. Brandon J there drew a distinction between the choice of forum for the determination of the merits of the dispute and the right to security in respect of maritime claims under the Admiralty law of this country, and pointed out that this distinction had been recognised and given effect to by the way in which the court had exercised its jurisdiction in relation to foreign jurisdiction clauses and in vexation cases. He continued ([1979] 1 All ER 397 at 415, [1979] QB 377 at 404–405):

'If this distinction between choice of forum on the one hand and right to security on the other is recognised and given effect to in foreign jurisdiction clause cases and vexation cases, I cannot see any good reason why it should not equally be recognised and given effect to in arbitration cases, whether the grant of a stay is discretionary under s 4(1) of the 1950 Act, or, as in the present case, mandatory under s 1(1) of the 1975 Act. I would stress again in this connection also that the distinction in question is clearly recognised and given effect to by the Brussels Arrest Convention (TS 47 (1960); Cmnd 1128). The process by which property, which has been lawfully arrested in an action in rem, can be released at the instance of the party interested in it, is the making by the court of an order for the issue of a release under RSC Ord 75, r 13(4). That rule provides, so far as material: "A release may be issued at the instance of a party interested in the property under arrest if the court so orders . . ."

That rule, as I understand it, gives the court a discretion, when an application for an order for the issue of a release is made, whether to make such order or not. The discretion so given is, so far as the terms of the rule go, unfettered, but it must, like any other discretion, be exercised judicially. There is nothing in s 1(1) of the 1975 Act which obliges the court, whenever it grants a stay of an action in rem in which security has been obtained, to make an order for the unconditional release of such security. Nor did s 4(2) of the 1950 Act, now repealed, impose any such obligation. That being so, I think that it is a matter for the discretion of the court, acting under the rule referred to above, what order it should make with regard to such security, and that the way in which it exercises that discretion must depend on the circumstances of each particular case. If, on the one hand, the case is one where in all probability the stay will be final and there will therefore never be any judgment in the action to be satisfied, the court should exercise its discretion by releasing the security unconditionally, as was done in *The Golden Trader*. If, on the other hand, the case is one where the stay may well not be final and there may well therefore still be a judgment in the action to be satisfied, the court should exercise its discretion either by refusing to release the security at all or by only releasing it subject to a term that the defendants shall provide alternative security for payment of any award in the arbitration. On this view of the law it is necessary to consider, in relation to the facts of this particular case, whether in all probability the stay will be final and there will therefore never be any judgment in the action to be satisfied or whether the stay may well not be final and there may well therefore still be a judgment in the action to be satisfied.'

Brandon J then proceeded to consider and reject an argument that the power to lift the stay of the action could not be exercised once an arbitration award had been made because, once an award was made, the cause of action would become merged in the award and, therefore, would no longer be available for prosecution in the action. He concluded, however, that no such merger would take place where the cause of action was in rem. He then concluded the relevant passage in his judgment as follows, addressing himself to the facts of the case before him ([1979] 1 All ER 397 at 417, [1979] QB 377 at 406):

'The result is that I accept the argument of counsel for the cargo owners that, if an award should be made against the shipowners and they should be unable to satisfy it, the cargo owners would be entitled to have the stay of the action removed and to proceed to a judgment in rem in it. I examined earlier . . . the financial situation of the shipowners and the position of the club in the matter. As a result of that examination I have no hesitation in concluding that this is a case in which, if the cargo owners should obtain an award in respect of the full amount of their claim, the shipowners might well be unable to satisfy it, either themselves or through the medium of the club. It follows, on my view, that a cause of action in rem does not, as a matter of law, become merged in an arbitral award, that this is a case where the stay might well not be final and that there might well therefore still be a judgment in the action to be satisfied. In these circumstances, applying the principles for the exercise of the court's discretion which I concluded earlier were the right principles to apply, I consider that the court ought in this case to have exercised its discretion, as at 28th July 1977, by either keeping the ship under arrest or by only releasing her subject to a term for the provision of alternative security.'

On the basis of that principle, counsel for the cargo owners submitted to the judge in the present case that, having regard to the evidence before the court relating to the financial situation of the shipowners, they might well be unable to satisfy an award in the pending arbitration and, therefore, it would not be appropriate for the judge, in the exercise of his discretion, to stay the execution of the warrant of arrest, so that the vessel could be arrested to provide security to enable a judgment in the action to be satisfied, if the stay of the proceedings were thereafter to be lifted and the cargo owners were to obtain such a judgment in the action. The judge's reaction to that submission was as

follows. He quoted a passage from this court's judgment in *The Andria* [1984] 1 All ER
1126 at 1134–1135, [1984] 2 WLR 570 at 579–580 which I have already set out in this   *a*
judgment, and he then continued:

> 'In *The Rena K* Brandon J pointed out that a claimant who obtains an award in an
> arbitration is not prevented from pursuing his remedy in an action in rem. It was
> for this reason that the judge found it possible to hold that the security obtained by
> the arrest of *The Rena K* could be retained in case the plaintiffs' award in the
> arbitration remained unsatisfied. In that event the plaintiffs would seek to persuade   *b*
> the court to lift the stay in the action. In *The Andria* the Court of Appeal did not
> have to consider whether the course taken by Brandon J in *The Rena K* was justified
> in principle. Mr Macdonald [counsel for the shipowners] invited me to say that I
> would not follow that decision because it was wrong in principle. I do not have to
> decide that point because in the light of the passage quoted above from the judgment
> of the Court of Appeal in *The Andria* there can be no doubt that the court's   *c*
> jurisdiction to arrest a ship in an action in rem will not be exercised for the purpose
> of providing security for an award in arbitration proceedings until s 26 of the Civil
> Jurisdiction and Judgments Act 1982 is brought into force. I can only express the
> hope that that section will soon come into force. For these reasons I order that this
> action be stayed and that there be a stay of execution of the warrant of arrest until
> further order.'   *d*

With all respect to the judge, however, it was not being suggested to him by the cargo
owners at this stage of their argument that it would be appropriate, on the principle in
The Rena K, for the court's jurisdiction to arrest to be exercised for the purpose of
providing security for an award in arbitration proceedings. That had been their
submission based on s 12(6)(*f*) of the 1950 Act, but the whole point of the principle of   *e*
The Rena K invoked by the cargo owners was that security is provided not for an
arbitration award but for judgment in the action in rem itself, if the stay of the action
should subsequently be lifted after failure by the shipowners to satisfy an award in the
arbitration.

Before the court, counsel for the shipowners repeated the submission made before the
judge by Mr Macdonald that the principle in *The Rena K* was wrong and ought not to be   *f*
followed. But he put in the forefront of his argument a submission that the decision of
the judge should be supported on a different ground. This submission was founded on
the wording of s 1(1) of the 1975 Act. Under that subsection in the circumstances there
specified it is provided that the court 'shall make an order staying the proceedings'. This
meant, submitted counsel, the whole proceedings. The warrant of arrest is the creature
of the action itself. If the proceedings have to be stayed, there can be no further steps   *g*
taken in those proceedings, and in particular no further steps can be taken to execute the
warrant of arrest.

This argument I am unable to accept. I do not consider that counsel can, so to speak,
pre-empt the position in this way. The function of a stay of proceedings under s 1(1) is to
give effect to the arbitration agreement; only in so far as it is necessary for that purpose
should the proceedings be stayed. To take a simple example, let it be supposed that in   *h*
certain proceedings two claims are advanced, one of which is within the relevant
arbitration agreement and the other is not. In such a case it would be entirely consistent
with s 1(1) to order a stay of the proceedings only in so far as they are related to the claim
within the arbitration agreement, allowing the proceedings to continue as to the other
claim. Likewise, in my judgment, if the principle in *The Rena K* is well founded, it
presupposes that the security will stand for the purpose of a judgment in the action in   *j*
rem in the event, which on the evidence might well occur, of the arbitration foundering
because an award is not satisfied and the stay then being lifted. To permit security to be
retained for that purpose is, on the principle as stated in *The Rena K*, consistent with
giving effect to the arbitration agreement, and so the security is not caught by a stay
which has effect only so far as is necessary to give effect to the arbitration agreement.

It is necessary, therefore, to proceed to consider whether the principle in *The Rena K* is well founded. Counsel for the shipowners advanced four reasons why in his submission

a it was not. He first submitted that it ignored the reality of the situation. In reality, he said, if a stay of the action in rem is lifted after an arbitration award has been made but has not been honoured, the action is being used for the purpose of enforcing the award. All that will happen is that the award will be invoked as an issue estoppel, and a judgment will be given which has in practice the effect of enforcing the award. The Admiralty jurisdiction, he pointed out, is a jurisdiction to hear and determine claims within the

b categories specified in s 20 of the Supreme Court Act 1981. In a *Rena K* type of case there would be no hearing or determination at all. I cannot accept this submission. At the very least, as counsel for the cargo owners pointed out, there will be a determination whether to give effect to an issue estoppel, and so the award and the basis on which the award is said to create an issue estoppel will have to be the subject of evidence before the court if not admitted. There will, therefore, be a hearing and a determination, though it may

c well be brief. Moreover, it will not in law be an action in which the award is itself enforced. The action is not an action on the award, but an action founded on the original cause of action identified in the writ. The result may be that a judgment will be obtained in a sum equal to the sum awarded by arbitration, and in respect of the same cause of action, but it does not follow that the award itself is being enforced in the action.

Counsel for the shipowners next submitted that to give effect to the principle in *The*

d *Rena K* is really to order a stay of proceedings on terms, which is not permissible under a statute requiring a mandatory stay of proceedings. I do not agree. A stay of proceedings on terms occurs where a stay would only be effective if a certain condition is fulfilled, e g the provision of security in a certain sum. But on the principle in *The Rena K* there is an unconditional stay of proceedings. All that happens is that it leaves the warrant of arrest unaffected.

e Next, counsel for the shipowners referred to a decision of this court in *Paczy v Haendler & Natermann GmbH* [1981] 1 Lloyd's Rep 302. That case has, however, no bearing on the principle in *The Rena K*, which was apparently not cited to the court, being concerned not with that principle but with the effect of the words 'incapable of being performed' in s 1(1) of the 1975 Act.

Finally, counsel for the shipowners submitted that under the principle in *The Rena K*

f the effect is that, despite a stay of proceedings, a vessel can be arrested or detained under arrest, and all sorts of steps will be taken in consequence, e g the vessel will be in the custody of the marshal, he may have to seek directions from the court and the parties may have to appear before the court on applications for directions, all of which, he submitted, were inconsistent with a stay of proceedings. I do not, however, find this argument persuasive, because the vessel is arrested or retained as security, and the security

g is being administered not in relation to the arbitration proceedings but in relation to a possible judgment in the action in the event of the stay of the proceedings being lifted.

It follows that I am unable to accept any of counsel's criticisms of *The Rena K* principle. I for my part find the reasoning of Brandon J in *The Rena K* persuasive, and, for the reasons set out by him in his judgment in that case, I respectfully accept the principle as stated by him as being well founded.

h It is, of course, true that in *The Rena K* the question was whether it was possible in the event of a stay of proceedings to retain security that had already been obtained, whereas in the present case the question is whether, if a stay of proceedings is ordered, the warrant of arrest shall stand unaffected so that it can be executed by the marshal in the event of the vessel coming within the jurisdiction of the court. I can, however, see no relevant distinction between the two cases. If the principle in *The Rena K* is well founded, it is in

j my judgment equally applicable in both cases. If it is applicable the effect must be that a warrant of arrest already issued but not executed will not be stayed and that security already obtained by the execution of the warrant of arrest or otherwise will not be released.

Before I turn to consider whether on the evidence this is a case where *The Rena K* principle should be applied, I should briefly mention one other argument advanced by counsel for the shipowners. This was that, since the affidavit sworn to lead the warrant

of arrest did not disclose the fact that there was an arbitration clause in the wool bill of
lading, there had not been the full and frank disclosure which is required on ex parte *a*
applications of this kind, and on that ground also the arrest should be set aside: see *The
Andria*. In my judgment, this argument is without substance, as appears from the
judgment in that case. There an arrest was set aside because the affidavit to lead the
warrant failed to disclose that at the date of the affidavit the parties had entered into an
ad hoc arbitration agreement for the resolution of the very dispute which was the subject
matter of the action in rem and that the parties were actively pursuing arbitration *b*
proceedings under that agreement. In such circumstances the court would, had it been
aware of those facts, have declined to exercise its jurisdiction to issue a warrant, unless
facts were also deposed to (which they were not) bringing the case within the principle
in *The Rena K*. The present case is, however, not such a case. It does not follow that,
because there is an arbitration agreement, eg (as here) an arbitration clause in a bill of
lading, that agreement will be invoked for the purpose of deciding a dispute which has *c*
arisen under it, and so, as is pointed out in the judgment in *The Andria* [1984] 1 All ER
1126 at 1135–1136, [1984] 2 WLR 570 at 580–581, the mere fact that there is an
arbitration agreement does not of itself generally preclude a party of the agreement from
bringing an action or, in the case of an action in rem, procuring the arrest of a ship. I can
discern no lack of disclosure in the affidavit to lead the warrant in the present case.

I turn then to the question whether, on the evidence, this is an appropriate case for the *d*
application of *The Rena K* principle. The evidence discloses the following state of affairs.
First, the shipowners can obtain no assistance from their P & I Club, because that club,
the Oceanus, is in severe financial difficulty and indeed is at present the subject of
winding-up proceedings in Bermuda. So the possibility of club support, assuming that
that factor would in any event be relevant, can be rejected as out of the question in the
present case. So far as the shipowners themselves are concerned, it appears from the *e*
evidence that they own two ships. The Tuyuti herself is stated by the shipowners'
solicitors to have a sound, open market value of about $US700,000 but she is subject to
two mortgages: on the first, over 8m French francs are still outstanding, and the second
appears to be for a sum of about $US720,000. The other ship, the Yaguari, was purchased
at some unspecified date for $US1,500,000, but it appears that $US840,000 of her
purchase price is still outstanding, presumably on mortgage. In addition, $US270,000 is *f*
owed by the shipowners in respect of bunkers; Oceanus has unpaid calls in the sum of
$US413,000 in respect of the shipowners' fleet, of which $US117,000 relates to the Tuyuti
herself, though we are told that these calls are the subject matter of a dispute between
the shipowners and the club; and there are cargo claims which have to be directly
attended to by the shipowners owing to the failure of Oceanus. It is scarcely surprising
that in these circumstances the shipowners have stated that they recognise that the cargo *g*
owners will not find the position encouraging, although they have expressed hopes as to
the payment of these debts and as to the future when they emerge from the most difficult
times in which the shipping industry now finds itself.

As counsel for the shipowners pointed out, this is not the case of a one-ship company,
where the single ship is likely to be disposed of to defeat the claim. But the applicable
test is whether, if the plaintiff should obtain an award in respect of the full amount of *h*
that claim, the defendants might well be unable to satisfy it. I feel bound to conclude
that, on the evidence now before us, that test is indeed fulfilled. I should add that in
reaching that conclusion I have taken into account a limitation fund established, I believe
in Antwerp, by means of an AFIA bond.

It follows, in my judgment, that on the evidence in this case the *Rena K* principle is
applicable and that the warrant of arrest should not be stayed but should be allowed to *j*
stand to be executed as appropriate. For these reasons I would give leave to appeal and,
treating the hearing of the renewed application for leave as the hearing of the appeal, I
would allow the appeal and reverse the judge's order in so far as it imposed a stay on the
execution of the warrant.

I should before concluding this judgment refer to one other argument advanced by
counsel for the cargo owners, both before the judge and before this court, relating to the

screws bill of lading. So far as the claim under that bill of lading is concerned, the writ and the warrant were issued first, and the ad hoc submission to arbitration came later. In his argument on this point counsel focused on the opening words of s 1(1) of the 1975 Act, which reads: 'If any party to an arbitration agreement to which this section applies ... commences any legal proceedings ...' It follows, submitted counsel, that the subsection only applies where, at the time of the commencement of the proceedings, that party was already a party to the relevant arbitration agreement. This was not so in

respect of the screws bill of lading. Accordingly, s 1(1) had no application to the claim under that bill of lading and there should have been no stay of proceedings in respect of it. This submission raises the question of the meaning to be given to the word 'commences' in the subsection. Ought that word to be read as relating only to commencement of proceedings by a person who is then party to the relevant arbitration proceedings? Or ought it to be read as referring to commencement at any time, including

commencement before the arbitration agreement has been made? An absolutely literal construction favours the first approach, but regard to the purpose of the subsection would appear to favour the second approach, because it is not apparent why the court's duty to stay proceedings should not equally apply where an arbitration has been entered into after proceedings have been commenced. I am inclined to prefer the latter approach. There is however here an ambiguity, and since the 1975 Act was passed to give effect to

the New York Convention on the Recognition and Enforcement of Foreign Arbitral Awards (TS 20 (1976); Cmnd 6419), it is legitimate in such circumstances to have regard to the treaty: see *The Jade, The Eschersheim, Erkowit (owners) v Jade (owners), Erkowit (cargo owners) v Eschersheim (owners)* [1976] 1 All ER 920, [1976] 1 WLR 430. Article II of the treaty provides as follows;

'1. Each Contracting State shall recognize an agreement in writing under which the parties undertake to submit to arbitration all or any differences which have arisen or which may arise between them in respect of a defined legal relationship, whether contractual or not, concerning a subject matter capable of settlement by arbitration.

2. The term "agreement in writing" shall include an arbitral clause in a contract or an arbitration agreement, signed by the parties or contained an exchange of

letters or telegrams.

3. The court of a Contracting State, when seized of an action in a matter in respect of which the parties have made an agreement within the meaning of this article, shall, at the request of one of the parties, refer the parties to arbitration ...'

That article shows that under the treaty the court's duty to refer the parties to arbitration

arises when seized of an action in a matter in respect of which the parties have made an arbitration agreement. It is not limited to cases where after the parties have made such an agreement the court becomes seized of the action or matter. Recourse to the treaty therefore favours the second approach, which I myself have felt inclined to accept as a matter of construction. In these circumstances, I would reject the literal approach, and it follows that I would, therefore, reject the argument of counsel for the cargo owners on

this point.

For these reasons I would not interfere with the judge's order staying the proceedings in relation to the screws bill of lading as well as the wool bill of lading. I would only allow the appeal so far as it relates to the stay of execution of the warrant of arrest.

ACKNER LJ. I agree, and there is nothing that I can usefully add.

Leave to appeal granted. Appeal allowed so far as relates to stay of execution of warrant of arrest. Leave to appeal to House of Lords refused.

Solicitors: *Clyde & Co*, Guildford (for the cargo owners): *Ince & Co* (for the shipowners).

Carolyn Toulmin   Barrister.

R v Secretary of State for the Environment and others, ex parte Ward

a

QUEEN'S BENCH DIVISION (CROWN OFFICE LIST)

WOOLF J

25, 26, 27, 28 JULY, 5 OCTOBER 1983

b

Local authority – Caravan sites – Provision of caravan sites – Duty of local authority – Judicial review of authority's decision – Authority providing site in accordance with duty – Site provided proving unsuitable for human habitation – Authority deciding to cease to provide site and not providing alternative site – Secretary of State refusing to direct authority to comply with duty to provide site – Whether gipsy living on existing site having sufficient interest to apply for judicial review of local authority's and Secretary of State's decisions – Whether relevant that authority's *c* *area designated as area in which unauthorised camping prohibited – Whether court should grant relief – Caravan Sites Act 1968, ss 6(1), 9, 12(1) – Supreme Court Act 1981, s 31(3) – RSC Ord 53, r 3(7).*

A London borough leased an area of land from the Greater London Council for a term of seven years from 9 February 1976 in order to discharge the duty imposed on it by s 6(1)ᵃ *d* of the Caravan Sites Act 1968 to provide caravan sites for gipsies residing in or resorting to the borough's area. The Secretary of State then made a designation under s 12(1)ᵇ of the 1968 Act that the borough's area was an area in which unauthorised camping was prohibited. Despite substantial expenditure by the borough the caravan site proved to be unsuitable for human habitation because of pollution. The borough therefore resolved to close the site on the expiry of a one-year extension of the lease and further resolved not *e* to provide an alternative site, but made it clear that no action would be taken to evict gipsies then living on the existing site or to cut off essential services to the site such as water and electricity while they remained there. The applicant, a gipsy living on the site, applied to the Secretary of State to exercise his powers under s 9ᶜ of the 1968 Act to direct the borough to comply with its duty under s 6(1) to make adequate provision for a caravan site for gipsies. There being no immediate danger of the gipsies being evicted *f* from the existing site or of services to the site being cut off, the Secretary of State declined to give directions under s 9, on the ground that at that stage there was no urgent need for him to do so, but he stated that he would keep the situation under review. The applicant applied under RSC Ord 53 for judicial review of the Secretary of State's failure to give directions under s 9 and of the borough's decision to cease to provide the existing site without providing an alternative site. *g*

Held – (1) The applicant had 'a sufficient interest', within s 31(3)ᵈ of the Supreme Court Act 1981 and RSC Ord 53, r 3(7)ᵉ, to apply under Ord 53 for judicial review of the borough's decision to discontinue providing the existing site and not to provide any alternative site for his use because (a) he was personally and directly affected by that decision, (b) the Secretary of State's designation under s 12(1) of the 1968 Act of the local *h* authority's area as an area where unauthorised camping was prohibited did not release the authority from its duty under s 6(1) to provide camping sites for gipsies, and (c) the

---

a   Section 6(1), so far as material, is set out at p 563 *a b*, post

b   Section 12(1) provides: 'Subject to subsection (3) below, the Minister may by order made on the application of a county council or London borough council designate the area of that council as an *j* area to which section 10 of this Act applies [ie as an area in which unauthorised camping is unlawful].'

c   Section 9 is set out at p 563 *d*, post

d   Section 31(3) is set out at p 564 *e*, post

e   Rule 3(7) is set out at p 564 *d*, post

existence of an alternative remedy under s 9 of the 1968 Act by which the Secretary of
a State could give directions to a local authority to provide camping sites did not prevent
the applicant from applying, pursuant to public law, for relief under Ord 53 in regard to
the borough's failure to comply with its duty under s 6(1) (see p 564 e f, p 565 f g, p 566
b c, p 567 a b and p 569 c d, post); IRC v National Federation of Self-Employed and Small
Businesses Ltd [1981] 2 All ER 93 applied; Pasmore v Oswaldtwistle UDC [1895–9] All ER
Rep 191, Bradbury v Enfield London Borough [1967] 3 All ER 434, Kensington and Chelsea
b London BC v Wells (1973) 72 LGR 289 and Meade v Haringey London Borough [1979] 2 All
ER 1016 distinguished.

(2) Since the Secretary of State was only required to give a direction under s 9 of the
1968 Act if he concluded that it was 'necessary' to do so, and since it had been reasonable
for the Secretary of State to conclude that it was unnecessary to give such a direction to
the borough, it was premature for the court to consider interfering with the Secretary of
c State's exercise of his discretion under s 9. Accordingly, the application for judicial review
of the Secretary of State's decision would be dismissed (see p 567 c f g, post).

(3) In performing its duty under s 6(1) of the 1968 Act a local authority was under a
positive obligation to give proper consideration to the accommodation to be provided for
gipsies in its area. Since the evidence showed that when the borough took the decision to
cease to provide the site it did not appreciate the true nature or consequences of its
d decision, it was appropriate for the court to issue an order of certiorari to quash its
decision so that the matter could be reconsidered in a proper manner and, in particular,
with due regard to the fact that it was required by s 6 to provide adequate accommodation
for gipsies residing in its area irrespective of whether or not the Secretary of State had
exercised his power under s 9 to give directions (see p 568 b to h, post).

Per curiam. Although as a matter of general principle there is jurisdiction to grant
e relief under Ord 53 regarding the provision by a local authority of camping sites for
gipsies, if the matter can also be dealt with under s 9 of the 1968 Act the court, in the
exercise of its discretion under Ord 53, will normally refuse to grant relief, so as to avoid
any conflict between the Secretary of State's view of what is adequate, necessary or
expedient in all the circumstances and the court's view of the matter. Where, however,
s 9 does not provide a convenient remedy, as in a complaint of failure by the Secretary of
f State properly to exercise his powers under the 1968 Act or in an application seeking
review of the manner in which a local authority has reached its decision under s 6(1), the
court in the exercise of its discretion under Ord 53 would not normally refuse relief (see
p 565 j to p 566 c and p 569 g, post).

Notes

g For the powers of local authorities with respect to the provision of caravan sites, see 29
Halsbury's Laws (4th edn) para 118.

For the Caravan Sites Act 1968, s 6, see 24 Halsbury's Statutes (3rd edn) 230, and for
ss 9, 12 of that Act (as substituted by the Local Government, Planning and Land Act
1980, ss 1(3), 175, Sch 3, para 13), see 50(2) ibid 1393, 1839.

For the Supreme Court Act 1981, s 31, see 51 ibid 625.

h

Cases referred to in judgment

Bradbury v Enfield London Borough [1967] 3 All ER 434, [1967] 1 WLR 1311, CA.
Cutler v Wandsworth Stadium Ltd [1949] 1 All ER 544, [1949] AC 398, HL.
Glossop v Heston and Isleworth Local Board (1879) 12 Ch D 102, [1874–80] All ER Rep 836,
CA.
i IRC v National Federation of Self-Employed and Small Businesses Ltd [1981] 2 All ER 93,
[1982] AC 617, [1981] 2 WLR 722, HL.
Kensington and Chelsea London BC v Wells (1973) 72 LGR 289, CA.
Meade v Haringey London Borough [1979] 2 All ER 1016, [1979] 1 WLR 637, CA.
Pasmore v Oswaldtwistle UDC [1898] AC 387, [1895–9] All ER Rep 191, HL.
R v Secretary of State for Wales, ex p Price (7 February 1983, unreported), QBD.

Cases also cited

Annison v District Auditor for St Pancras Metropolitan Borough [1961] 3 All ER 914, [1962] a
1 QB 489, DC.
Chief Constable of Kent v V [1982] 3 All ER 36, [1983] QB 34, CA.
Cumings v Birkenhead Corp [1971] 2 All ER 881, [1972] Ch 12, CA.
Greater London Council v Jones (1973) 72 LGR 320.
Laker Airways Ltd v Dept of Trade [1977] 2 All ER 182, [1977] QB 643, CA.
Leigh v National Union of Railwaymen [1969] 3 All ER 1249, [1970] Ch 326. b
Lonrho Ltd v Shell Petroleum Co Ltd [1981] 2 All ER 456, [1982] AC 173, HL.
Nottingham Corp v Newton [1974] 2 All ER 760, [1974] 1 WLR 923, DC.
Padfield v Minister of Agriculture Fisheries and Food [1968] 1 All ER 694, [1968] AC 997,
HL.
Secretary of State for Education and Science v Tameside Metropolitan Borough [1976] 3 All ER
665, [1977] AC 1014, HL. c
Wilford v West Riding of Yorkshire CC [1908] 1 KB 685.

Application for judicial review

Martin Ward, a gipsy who was a licensee of a caravan site on a site known as the Westway
Travellers site, applied, with the leave of McNeill J granted on 22 June 1983, for judicial
review of the following decisions or other proceedings: (1) the decision of the Secretary d
of State for the Environment made on 24 June 1984 not to give directions to the London
Borough of Hammersmith and Fulham (Hammersmith) (who leased the Westway
Travellers site from the Greater London Council (the GLC)) and the Royal Borough of
Kensington and Chelsea (Kensington) (who contributed to the cost of the site) pursuant
to s 9 of the Caravan Sites Act 1968 requiring them to provide pursuant to s 6 of the 1968
Act a site for the accommodation of the caravans on the Westway Travellers site; (2) the e
decision of Hammersmith to relinquish on 24 June 1983 its interest in the Westway
Travellers site; and (3) the failure of Hammersmith and Kensington to make provision
after 24 June 1983 of adequate accommodation for gipsies residing in or resorting to
their areas. The relief sought by the applicant was (i) an order of mandamus directing
the Secretary of State to give directions to Hammersmith and Kensington requiring
them after 24 June 1983 to provide pursuant to s 6 of the 1968 Act such sites for the f
accommodation of such numbers of gipsies' caravans as the Secretary of State might
specify; (ii) alternatively a declaration that the Secretary of State was required by law to
give such directions; (iii) an injunction restraining Hammersmith from relinquishing its
interest in the Westway Travellers site until such time as it had made provision of
adequate accommodation for a like number of gipsies as those presently accommodated
on the site; (iv) an order of mandamus directed to Hammersmith and Kensington g
requiring them to discharge their statutory duty under s 6 of the 1968 Act; and (v) such
further or other relief as might be just and equitable in the circumstances. The facts are
set out in the judgment.

Stephen Sedley QC and David Altaras for the applicant.
John Laws for the Secretary of State. h
Alexander Irvine QC and Alan Wilkie for Hammersmith.
Roger Gray QC and Oliver Wise for Kensington.
Derek Wood QC and David Halpern for the GLC.

Cur adv vult

j

5 October. The following judgment was delivered.

WOOLF J. The applicant is a gipsy within the meaning of that term in the Caravan
Sites Act 1968. He brings the application in order to ensure that he will have a site on
which to park his two caravans so that he can live in those caravans with his wife and
nine children. He brings the proceedings against the Secretary of State because the

Secretary of State has power to direct local authorities to provide sites for gipsies' caravans
a   under the 1968 Act. He has also brought these proceedings against the two borough
councils because, at the present time, he is licensee of a caravan pitch on a site known as
the Westway Travellers site, which is jointly provided by the boroughs, who were
proposing to cease to provide the site and would in fact have already ceased to provide it
but for the commencement of these proceedings and the interim relief granted by the
court. The Greater London Council (the GLC) has also taken part in these proceedings
b   and has been represented before me because it is the owner of the site, but there is no
duty on the GLC to provide sites for gipsies, and the applicant claims no relief in relation
to the GLC.

The Secretary of State and the two boroughs dispute that they are in breach of their
statutory duties under the 1968 Act, and that they have acted in any other way which is
unlawful. In addition, they raise general points whether or not the applicant is a person
c   who is entitled to seek relief from the courts, and dispute that the court has jurisdiction
to grant the applicant any relief, assuming that he has the necessary standing to seek such
relief, and that he would otherwise be entitled to it.

The facts

There is some dispute on the evidence how long gipsies have been residing within the
d   two boroughs. The applicant's evidence suggests that they have resorted to the area since
the nineteenth century and that they have certainly been coming to the boroughs since
1966. It is accepted, however, that early in 1973 gipsies moved onto a site in Wood Lane,
Hammersmith and, by May 1973, there was talk of the gipsies moving into the Royal
Borough of Kensington and Chelsea as well.

In 1973 the borough of Kensington sought orders for possession against a number of
e   gipsies in respect of land situated under the Westway motorway. Those proceedings
went to the Court of Appeal and resulted in the decision of that court, to which I will
have to refer later, namely *Kensington and Chelsea London BC v Wells* (1973) 72 LGR 289.

The respondent boroughs decided in about 1975 to jointly provide the site around
which these proceedings revolved.

The site was leased to the Borough of Hammersmith and Fulham by the GLC under a
f   lease made on 9 February 1976 for the term of seven years from 24 June 1975. By that
lease the borough convenanted to keep the site in a good state of repair and condition
and free from rubbish and litter, at the end or other sooner termination of the term to
leave and yield up the demised premises in proper state of repair and condition, to move
any buildings erected on the site and not to use the site for any purpose other than that
of a gipsy caravan site for not more than 20 caravans at a time.

By a separate agreement made between the two boroughs on 15 April 1976 (which
g   recited that the boroughs were required to provide adequate accommodation for gipsies
residing in or resorting to their respective areas) the two boroughs agreed to share equally
the cost of providing that site. They were influenced into taking the action of providing
the site by their desire to have the boroughs designated under the 1968 Act. I will deal
with the effect of designation later, but designation orders were made by the Secretary of
h   State in respect of Kensington and Chelsea on 17 April 1975 (SI 1975/647), on the ground
that it was not expedient to make any provision in the borough for accommodation of
gipsies residing in or resorting to that area and, on 1 July 1975 in respect of the borough
of Hammersmith (SI 1975/1082), on the ground that adequate provision was made in
the borough for the accommodation of gipsies residing in or resorting to that area. The
accommodation referred to was the accommodation on the Westway site.

j   The applicant and his family were among the original inhabitants of the site in 1975.
The site, according to a report before me, dated 10 February 1983, is now fully occupied,
all the bays being let. There is even said to be a squatter problem, which is detrimental
to the bona fide residents. The site has main services and arrangements are made for
refuse disposal. Buildings providing wash-house and toilet facilities have been erected on
the site and electricity is supplied to the site in a manner which enables the caravans to
be connected to power points. The charges on the site differ between winter and summer,

but the current licence fees of £15·50 and £19·50 per family, including all services, are nothing like sufficient to cover the cost of providing the site.

Notwithstanding this substantial expenditure, the site is far from being a desirable place in which to reside. It is in the shadow of the elevated section of the Westway, where it intersects with the Westcross Route. There is a railway nearby and considerable pollution. All the parties were agreed that it was a thoroughly unsuitable place for a caravan site, particularly one occupied by families with children. Counsel for the applicant agreed a new location was desperately needed, but said the existing site was better than nowhere.

Because of the state of the site, the applicant made a complaint against both boroughs for failing to abate the statutory nuisance under ss 99 and 92(1)(a) of the Public Health Act 1936. A stipendiary magistrate initially dismissed the complaint, but the applicant then appealed to the Divisional Court and on 2 November 1982 that court remitted the matter to the stipendiary magistrate so that he could find the complaint proved and make the necessary abatement order. This the stipendiary magistrate did on 10 February 1983. Under the order, the boroughs had to carry out a substantial amount of work, including ensuring that 'the mean lead level on the site does not exceed two thousand parts per million and to monitor lead pollution on the site by taking at least fourteen samples at three monthly intervals'. A further appeal to the Crown Court by the boroughs against the order has been adjourned pending the outcome of these proceedings.

It is a matter of serious complaint by counsel for the applicant that, in the public health proceedings, the attitude of the boroughs was far from frank. The boroughs strongly disputed that they were guilty of creating a nuisance before the stipendiary magistrate. They disputed that the expert evidence called on the applicant's behalf was accurate as to the dangers to health from pollution, whereas it is now apparent from the papers disclosed in these proceedings that the boroughs recognised that there was a health problem throughout.

Whether or not counsel's complaints are justified, there is no doubt that on 3 November 1982 the leader's co-ordinating committee of the borough of Hammersmith resolved that the Westway site was totally unsuitable for human habitation and should close on the expiry of the current one-year extension of the lease, subject to the concurrence of the borough of Kensington. This decision of the co-ordinating committee on behalf of the borough is one of the decisions the lawfulness of which is challenged in these proceedings.

The one-year extension of the lease referred to in the resolution referred back to a letter from the GLC of 29 June 1982 written to the borough of Hammersmith recording a resolution of a committee of the GLC that the borough be informed—

> 'that in view of the unsuitability of the site for its present use this Council is not willing to offer them a new lease of the land in Latimer Road for use as a gipsy site, but is prepared to allow them to remain as tenants of the land holding over on the terms and conditions of the current lease for a maximum period of one year.'

The precise basis on which the borough has retained the site since 24 June 1982 is in dispute, but it is not necessary for me to determine the issues involved for the purpose of the present application, as the GLC does not require possession and is quite content to allow the borough councils to make use of the site for the purpose of providing facilities for the gipsies.

The dispute did, however, affect the attitude of the borough of Hammersmith as to what was to happen after June 1983. There was a meeting between the GLC and the two boroughs concerned on 11 March 1983 and, according to the minutes of that meeting, Hammersmith was taking the view that it was impossible for the borough to meet the requirements of the order of the stipendiary magistrate, that it would not renew the lease from June 1983 and that the site would then become the GLC's responsibility. The borough also made it clear that, having considered all alternative sites, it did not consider that there was any alternative appropriate site within the borough of Hammersmith.

The reasons for the borough taking the view that the site could not be operated lawfully
a are expanded in the evidence filed on behalf of the borough.

The order made by the stipendiary magistrate required the borough to ensure that the
mean lead level on the site did not exceed 2,000 parts per million. However, readings
taken by the borough at the site between the beginning of March and the end of May
1983 showed a mean level of 4,020 parts per million, excluding the two highest readings
which were obtained. It is the borough's contention that there were no steps which were
b open to it which could ensure that the site would not exceed the requirements of the
stipendiary magistrate's order. The borough also points out that during the year 1982–
83 the net expenditure for the site after deducting the income was £66,374 and
considerable further expenditure would be involved in complying with those parts of
the order which were capable of being complied with.

The conclusions of the borough were the subject of a formal resolution made on 27
c April 1983. On that date, the leader's co-ordinating committee resolved, inter alia—

> 'that no suitable land is available in the Borough for use as a Travellers Site,
> whether as a single large site or as a number of sites each of less than one acre; to
> hand back the site to the Greater London Council in an uncleared state in June 1983,
> when the period of one year for which the GLC allowed the Council to continue to
> occupy the site on expiry of the original lease in June 1982 will come to an end; to
d > support the London Borough of Ealing in pressing for a longer term solution to the
> problem by securing provision for Travellers by the GLC on a regional basis; to
> inform the GLC of this Council's decision, and to seek GLC support for any
> approaches to the government on regional provision as a longer term solution; [and]
> to make immediate and urgent representation to the appropriate Minister to clarify
> this Council's position when the site has been handed back to the GLC, and to seek
e > to retain designation with nil provision.'

This is the second resolution of the borough attacked by the applicant.

On 5 May 1983 the borough of Hammersmith informed the GLC of the effect of the
resolution and went on in the letter to point out that the borough 'is nevertheless anxious
to avoid causing unnecessary hardship to the gipsies presently living on the site' and that,
f having regard to the policy expressed by the GLC, the borough did not propose—

> 'to obtain vacant possession of the site or to destroy the existing facilities before
> terminating its interest in June. In addition, the London Electricity Board and the
> Thames Water Authority have been advised that, with effect from 24th June 1983,
> your Council will be responsible for the charges for their respective services.'

g It is quite clear that by the date of the letter of 5 May the borough of Hammersmith
had come to the conclusion that it was not in a position to make any provision for the
gipsies on the Westway site, that it was not going to retain responsibility for that site and
that, while it was not going to take any action to evict the gipsies, it was not proposing to
take any further responsibility for them, but to leave it to the GLC to accept responsibility
for the site.

h Although the GLC was sympathetic towards the position of the gipsies, it did not feel
in a position to take over this responsibility and, being faced with a situation where three
local authorities were surrendering responsibility, the gipsies turned their attention to
the Secretary of State.

By letter dated 12 May 1983 the first application was made to the Secretary of State,
who has certain powers to intervene under s 9 of the 1968 Act. This was followed up by
j a further application dated 26 May 1983, which was accompanied by various documents.
By letter dated 3 June 1983 the minister promised a decision as soon as possible and,
although consideration of the matter was delayed by the general election, the Department
of the Environment on behalf of the minister communicated with the various parties
involved and investigated the situation.

On 21 June 1983 the borough of Hammersmith wrote to the minister, pointing out

that the borough was only seeking to vacate the site after the most strenuous efforts both
to manage the site and to seek an alternative location had been made. The letter also   *a*
pointed out that the statutory undertakers had been informed that they should not
terminate the water or electricity services.

On 15 June 1983 the borough wrote to the department, confirming the situation and
its contention that all it was doing was 'returning this site to its owners, the GLC'. It is,
however, also made clear that the borough was not to be responsible for the charges and
services provided by the statutory undertakers, though the 'service should remain   *b*
available whilst the site is occupied'.

The borough of Kensington made its position clear to the department in a letter of 21
June 1983, the relevant part of the letter reading as follows:

'As you will know, the Council is exempted by its designation order from the
requirement to provide a gipsy site within the Royal Borough and indeed no suitable
sites exist. Whilst the Royal Borough has, over the past seven years, been prepared   *c*
to share with Hammersmith and Fulham the very high cost of maintaining the
Westway site, the Council now considers that it must be recognised (as it already is
for Westminster, Camden and Islington), that Central London is not an appropriate
place for gipsy sites and that the Council should rely on its designation order.'

On the information available to him, the minister came to the conclusion that there   *d*
was no danger of services being cut off from the site and he therefore gave what appears
to be an interim decision on 24 June 1983 in the following terms:

'We have now heard from the London Borough of Hammersmith & Fulham,
who assure us that, when the site is returned on 24 June to the GLC, the services to
the site will not be cut off and there is no question of gipsies being evicted either by
them or by the GLC. As there appears to be no immediate danger of eviction or   *e*
withdrawal of services to the gipsies on the Westway site, the Secretary of State does
not consider that there is an urgent need for him to use his powers of direction
under Section 9 of the Caravan Sites Act 1968 but he will keep the situation under
review.'

I would underline the words 'urgent need' and 'he will keep the situation under review'   *f*
in that last sentence.

On the evidence before me, it does appear that the view of the minister about the
continuation of the provision of services was over-sanguine and that there was in fact a
real danger that the services would have been cut off. The applicant forestalled this by
applying for leave to apply for judicial review, with the assistance of the North Kensington
Law Centre, on 21 June 1983, and on 24 June 1983, the day the borough of Hammersmith   *g*
was proposing to give up responsibility for the site, McNeill J ordered that the borough
be restrained from parting with possession of the site and that the borough should
continue to discharge the costs of providing services to the site. With the co-operation of
the borough, that position has continued up to the date of this judgment.

The relevant statutory provisions   *h*

The first statute which has to be considered is the Caravan Sites and Control of
Development Act 1960. Section 23 of that Act gave to local authorities the power to
prohibit the stationing of caravans on commons. That power, according to counsel for
the applicant, enabled local authorities to take away from gipsies all their traditional
stopping places. However, s 24 gave the local authorities power within their area to
provide sites where caravans may be brought and to do anything appearing to them   *j*
desirable in connection with the provisions of such sites, in particular to acquire land for
that purpose and to provide services or facilities for the health or convenience of those
occupying the sites. The power to acquire land includes a power to acquire land
compulsorily.

According to its long title, the Caravan Sites Act 1968, was an Act to make provision
for the benefit of occupiers of caravan sites, to secure the establishment of such sites by

a   local authorities for the use of gipsies and other persons of nomadic habit and control in certain areas the unauthorised occupation of land by such persons.

Section 6(1) placed a duty on local authorities to provide sites for gipsies. It provides, so far as relevant:

b
> '... it shall be the duty of every local authority being the council of a county, county borough or London borough to exercise their powers under section 24 of [the 1960 Act] so far as may be necessary to provide adequate accommodation for gipsies residing in or resorting to their area.'

Section 7(1) sets out the extent of the duty under s 6(1) by specifying that it 'shall extend only to determining what sites are to be provided and acquiring or appropriating the necessary land'. The subsection also lays down that 'it shall be the duty of the council of the district in which any such site is located to exercise all other powers under section
c   24 [of the 1960 Act] in relation to the site'.

Section 9 deals with the powers of the Secretary of State. Like ss 10, 11 and 12, to which I must also refer, s 9 has been amended by the Local Government, Planning and Land Act 1980, and I refer to its provisions and the provisions of the other sections in their amended form.

Section 9 (as substituted by s 1(3) of and para 13 of Sch 3 to the 1980 Act) provides:

d
> 'The Secretary of State may, if at any time it appears to him to be necessary so to do, give directions to any local authority to which subsection (1) of section 6 of this Act applies requiring them to provide, pursuant to that section, such sites or additional sites, for the accommodation of such numbers of caravans, as may be specified in the directions; and any such directions shall be enforceable, on the application of the Secretary of State, by mandamus.'

e
It is convenient to refer next to s 12 (which was substituted by s 175(1) of the 1980 Act), which gives the minister power to make an order on the application of a council designating the area of that council as an area to which s 10 of the Act applies. However, that power is subject to s 12(3) which provides:

f
> 'The Minister shall not make an order ... in respect of any area unless it appears to him either that adequate provision is made in the area for the accommodation of gipsies residing in or resorting to the area, or that in all the circumstances it is not necessary or expedient to make any such provision.'

Section 10(1) made it an offence in any area designated for—

g
> 'any person being a gipsy to station a caravan for the purpose of residing for any period—(*a*) on any land situated within the boundaries of a highway; or (*b*) on any other unoccupied land; or (*c*) on any occupied land without the consent of the occupier.'

Finally, s 11 (which was substituted by s 174 of the 1980 Act) enables a magistrates' court to make an order for the removal of any caravan, together with any person residing
h   in it, which is in a designated area in contravention of s 10. On an order being made under that section, the local authority had what counsel for the applicant properly described as 'swingeing powers' to give effect to the order.

It was pursuant to these provisions that the boroughs were designated in the circumstances to which I have previously referred. There can be no doubt that this designation was linked to the provision of the Westway site for the use of gipsies.

j   Having regard to these facts and the foregoing statutory provisions, the relief which is sought by the applicant is as follows: first, an order of mandamus directing the Secretary of State to give directions to the boroughs to provide sites for the accommodation of such numbers of gipsy caravans as the Secretary of State may specify; second and alternatively, a declaration that the Secretary of State is bound by law to give directions; third, an order of certiorari to quash the decision of the Secretary of State given in the letter of 24 June 1983 not to exercise his powers of direction under s 9, and an order of mandamus requiring him to consider according to law whether the boroughs are providing adequate accommodation pursuant to s 6; fourth, an order of certiorari to quash the resolution of 3 November 1982 of the borough of Hammersmith's leader's co-ordinating committee, and the resolution of 27 April 1983 of the same committee to hand back the site to the GLC; fifth, an injunction restraining the borough of Hammersmith from parting with possession of the Westway site and an order directing the borough to continue to discharge the cost of providing electricity and water to the site and to continue to provide for disposal of domestic refuse in conjunction with the borough of Kensington, and an order restraining the borough of Kensington from resiling from the agreement of 15 April 1976; and, sixth, an order of mandamus requiring the boroughs to discharge their statutory duty under s 6 of the 1968 Act.

In relation to these claims for relief, the various respondents have advanced different arguments, but it is convenient to consider first of all the submission of counsel for Hammersmith that the applicant has no right to seek relief from the court against his client.

The right of the applicant to seek relief by way of judicial review

RSC Ord 53, r 3(7) provides:

'The Court shall not grant leave unless it considers that the applicant has a sufficient interest in the matter to which the application relates.'

The Supreme Court Act 1981, by s 31(3), provides:

'No application for judicial review shall be made unless the leave of the High Court has been obtained in accordance with rules of court; and the court shall not grant leave to make such an application unless it considers that the applicant has a sufficient interest in the matter to which the application relates.'

In the absence of authority, I would have no hesitation in saying that clearly the present applicant has a sufficient interest. He is personally and directly affected by the decision of the borough of Hammersmith not to continue to provide the Westway site or any alternative site for his use.

Counsel for Hammersmith relied on the recent decision of the House of Lords in *IRC v National Federation of Self-Employed and Small Businesses Ltd* [1981] 2 All ER 93, [1982] AC 617, but I do not find anything in the speeches of their Lordships in that case inconsistent with the view I have indicated. On the contrary, I consider that the passages in the speeches relied on by counsel appear to be in accord with that view. However, I should refer shortly to two passages from the speech of Lord Wilberforce and the speech of Lord Fraser. Lord Wilberforce said ([1981] 2 All ER 93 at 97, [1982] AC 617 at 631):

'In the present case we are in the area of mandamus, an alleged failure to perform a duty. It was submitted by the Lord Advocate that in such cases we should be guided by the definition of the duty, in this case statutory, and inquire whether expressly, or by implication, this definition indicates, or the contrary, that the complaining applicant is within the scope or ambit of the duty. I think that this is at least a good working rule though perhaps not an exhaustive one.'

Lord Fraser said ([1981] 2 All ER 93 at 108, [1982] AC 617 at 646):

'There is also general agreement that a mere busybody does not have a sufficient interest. The difficulty is, in between those extremes, to distinguish between the desire of the busybody to interfere in other people's affairs and the interest of the person affected by or having a reasonable concern with the matter to which the application relates. In the present case that matter is an alleged failure by the Revenue to perform the duty imposed on them by statute.'

So far as this case is concerned, I would have difficulty in categorizing the applicant as a 'busybody'.

However, counsel for Hammersmith contends that, even if normally the applicant *a*   would be regarded as complying with the locus standi requirements of Ord 53, the right of the applicant to apply to the court is excluded by the fact that the 1968 Act provides a specific remedy which therefore deprives the applicant of any other form of remedy than that given by the statute, in accordance with the principle laid down by the House of Lords in *Pasmore v Oswaldtwistle UDC* [1898] AC 387, [1895–9] All ER Rep 191.

In his carefully developed argument, counsel for Hammersmith stressed the relationship between ss 6 and 9 and ss 10 and 12. He submitted that the duty which is
b   owed pursuant to s 6 is of such a nature that it is not available to gipsies as a class or, a fortiori, to a particular gipsy and, therefore, the applicant has no cause of action against the local authority and no sufficient interest to enable him to obtain relief.

Counsel for the applicant submitted that, as the designation orders in this case had been made on the basis that the site would be provided by Hammersmith, Hammersmith was under an implied obligation not to cease to provide the site and, in ceasing to provide
c   the site, Hammersmith was guilty of misfeasance. Counsel sought to establish misfeasance because this was recognised as creating an exception to the principle laid down in *Pasmore's* case.

In *Bradbury v Enfield London Borough* [1967] 3 All ER 434, [1967] 1 WLR 1311 an exception (which was extended by the Court of Appeal in *Meade v Haringey London Borough* [1979] 2 All ER 1016, [1979] 1 WLR 637) was also made for situations where a
d   plaintiff has suffered special damage, or there has been a use of powers for improper purposes: see *Meade's* case [1979] 2 All ER 1016 at 1023–1025, 1027, [1979] 1 WLR 637 at 645–647, 649–650 per Lord Denning MR and Eveleigh LJ.

Both these cases were cases where private rights were being sought to be enforced, and I regard it as inappropriate to extend the exceptions generally to the public law field with which Ord 53 is normally concerned. However, in respect of the relief by way of
e   injunction and declaration sought in the present application, the exceptions could have relevance since, even though the injunctions and declaration are sought under Ord 53, such relief can only be obtained if it could be obtained by way of ordinary action and this involves establishing the infringement of a private right.

The 1968 Act does not create any such right. But, in any event, I am not satisfied that it would be right to imply any prohibition of the sort relied on by counsel for the
f   applicant, the breach of which is said to amount to misfeasance, from the relationship between ss 12 and 6. Nor, on the other hand, do I accept, as counsel contends on behalf of the borough of Kensington, that designation under s 12, even on the ground that it is not expedient to make provision, puts an end to the duty of a borough under s 6.

The way I understand Parliament intended the provisions contained in ss 6 to 12 to work is as follows: first, designation under s 12 does not in any circumstances entirely
g   release a local authority from its duty under s 6 (even though a designation order has been made under s 12, it is still possible for an application to be made to the Secretary of State to make directions under that section); second, the application could bring to his attention facts which had previously not been known to the Secretary of State, which could alter the situation and therefore make it appropriate for him to give a direction, though if he did so no doubt he would revoke the designation which had previously
h   been made under s 12 (an express power to do this is provided by s 12(4)); third, however, where a designation is in existence, a local authority can act on the assumption that normally, unless there has been a change of circumstances since the making of the designation order, the Secretary of State will come to the same conclusion as he had on the application by the local authority for designation; and, fourth, in normal circumstances it is clearly intended by Parliament that it is the minister who shall have the responsibility
j   for overseeing whether adequate provision is being made or whether it is not necessary or expedient for it to be made, and he should give effect to his views not only by making a designation order where appropriate, but also by taking the existence of designation into account in deciding whether or not it is proper for him to exercise his discretion under s 9 and make a direction.

The effect of this approach to these sections is that, as a matter of general principle, even though there is jurisdiction to grant relief under Ord 53, if the application could

also have been dealt with under s 9, the courts should not grant relief so as to avoid a
possible conflict between the minister's view of what is adequate, necessary or expedient
and that of the court. However, the court will normally only exercise its discretion to
refuse relief where it would otherwise be granted in those cases in respect of which s 9
provides a convenient remedy. Section 9 does not, for example, cover a situation where
what is complained of is a failure by the Secretary of State himself to properly exercise
his power under the 1968 Act; nor does it apply where what is being sought is not a
direction of the sort that can be made and enforced under s 9, but a review of the manner
in which the local authority has reached its decision. Irrespective of whether or not the
Secretary of State would make a direction under s 9, the local authority is still required
by law to properly consider how it will exercise its discretion in respect of the duty placed
on it by s 6 of the 1968 Act and the powers which it is given by s 24 of the 1960 Act.

Counsel for Hammersmith contends that it is not open to me to come to these
conclusions as to the power of the court to intervene on judicial review because of the
decision of the Court of Appeal in *Kensington and Chelsea London BC v Wells* (1973) 72 LGR
289. That case not only involved one of the respondents to the present application, but
also required the Court of Appeal to consider the very same provisions which I have been
considering. Roskill LJ, giving the leading judgment, clearly came to the view that,
because of the remedy provided by s 9, there is no right of 'redress available in the courts
at the hands of the individual gipsy'. However, on examining the reasoning of the Lord
Justice, it is clear that he was dealing with the question of whether or not an individual
gipsy has a personal right which he can enforce in the courts, and was not dealing with
applications under Ord 53 pursuant to public law. This is apparent from the reference
which was made to *Cutler v Wandsworth Stadium Ltd* [1949] 1 All ER 544, [1949] AC 398
and the fact that Roskill LJ said (72 LGR 289 at 297):

> 'But, as Cairns L.J. pointed out in the course of the argument, one has to have
> regard to what the duty is which it is sought to enforce. That duty is not a duty in
> favour of each individual gipsy to have an individual caravan site; the duty in the
> case of the council of a county borough or London borough is to provide
> accommodation for not more than 15 caravans at a time . . . But it would be curious,
> to say the least, if, where the obligation is of a general kind . . . it should give rise to
> an individual right at the suit of an individual who is by no means certain . . . to be
> the beneficiary . . .'

I have not lost sight of the fact that in their cross-applications against the Kensington
and Chelsea London Borough Council in *Wells's* case a mandatory injunction or an order
of mandamus was sought. No doubt the applicant in *Wells's* case was encouraged to seek
an order of mandamus because that was the order made by the judge at first instance in
Pasmore's case. However, in neither case was the order of mandamus being sought except
as a means of enforcing an alleged private right in an ordinary inter parties civil action
and, although an order of mandamus was sought, the proceedings were not prerogative
proceedings.

This was a distinction which Lord Macnaghten at any rate had in mind in *Pasmore's*
case [1898] AC 387 at 398, [1895–9] All ER Rep 191 at 195, because he referred to the
judgment of James LJ in *Glossop v Heston and Isleworth Local Board* (1879) 12 Ch D 102,
[1874–80] All ER Rep 836, which was a judgment which made this distinction clear,
and, although Lord Macnaghten did indicate that the evils of litigation would be much
the same in one case as in another, he did not go so far as to suggest there was no
distinction between the two types of proceedings. The distinction had not only been
drawn by James LJ in that case, but it had been particularly emphasised by Brett LJ as
well. Brett LJ said (12 Ch D 102 at 122, [1874–80] All ER Rep 836 at 844):

> 'Now, supposing they had neglected or refused to do their duty, then I think they
> would have been liable to a mandamus, but not to a mandamus to be granted by
> the Chancery Division. It would have been a prerogative mandamus, as it is called,

a
to them as a public body to enter upon and do their duty. That, as it seems to me, under the *Judicature Act* as it was before, is a remedy that can be granted only in the Court of Queen's Bench.'

I do not, however, regard *Wells's* case as requiring me to come to the conclusion that, irrespective of the merits and any question of discretion, the alternative remedy under s 9 prevents the applicant applying for judicial review. Indeed, in *Wells's* case 72 LGR
b
289 at 299 Roskill LJ was careful to leave open the possibility that there could be circumstances when proceedings could be brought before the court.

The position of the minister
Although counsel for the Secretary of State very helpfully made general submissions to me as to the proper construction of the 1968 Act, the conclusion which I have come to as to the Secretary of State's position is based on my view of the facts. It is clear from s 9
c
that before the Secretary of State can give directions he has to come to the conclusion that it is 'necessary' to do so. If he does come to that conclusion then, notwithstanding that s 9 uses the word 'may', there is little room for the exercise of discretion.

Here, the Secretary of State was not directly involved until the letter of 12 May 1983 was sent to him. The letter made it clear that the position was one of urgency, but the
d
urgency was based on the fact that it was suggested that Hammersmith had let it be known that it would cease to be responsible for water and electricity services after 24 June. On 16 June 1983 the borough of Hammersmith had written to the department indicating that, whilst the borough could not be responsible for the charges, services should be available whilst the site is occupied, and contending that the GLC has power to provide services to the site. Apparently, there was also a discussion on the same day between the representative of the department and the representative of the North
e
Kensington Law Centre. There is a conflict between the notes as to what precisely was said during this conversation, but the department could reasonably be of the view that there was 'no immediate danger of eviction or withdrawal of services'.

The situation was extremely complicated as to what the alternatives were and, on the information before the Secretary of State, it cannot be said, in my view, that he was acting in any way improperly or unreasonably in coming to the conclusion not to make
f
directions at that stage, because there was no urgent need for him to do so, but to keep the situation under review.

These proceedings then supervened, though it appears from the department's evidence, sworn on 14 July 1983, that at that time the department was still arranging meetings to discuss the provision of accommodation for the gipsies in the boroughs.

I therefore agree with counsel for the Secretary of State that it would be premature for
g
the court to consider interfering with the minister's exercise of his discretion at this stage. The boroughs are contending that there are no suitable alternative sites and, even if the Secretary of State comes to the conclusion that directions are necessary, considerable investigations are going to have to be made on behalf of the minister before satisfactory directions can be given.

h
The position of the borough of Hammersmith
Quite apart from his arguments as to lack of standing, counsel contended on behalf of the borough that the duty under s 6 could only be breached when content had been given to it by a s 9 direction.

At first sight, support is given to such an approach by the judgment of Roskill LJ in
j
Wells's case 72 LGR 289 at 298, where he said:

'The position is clear under section 6. The duty under section 6(1) is a duty imposed subject to the provisions of section 6(2). When one looks at that duty as so qualified, it is clearly a duty which, in relation to a county borough or a London borough, cannot in any event exceed an obligation to provide more than 15 caravan sites, and then only if the Minister does not give an exempting direction. One has great sympathy with the argument that this inaction has been allowed to go on for three and a half years and nothing has yet happened. "How long," say the defendants, *a* rhetorically, "have we to wait to know what our position is? How long is it going to be before the Minister, if he ever does, invokes his powers under section 9(2) or 9(3)?" The answer to that, as I think, is that, unless and until the machinery under section 9(1) or 9(2) is operated, the councils are not in breach.'

For my part, I would underline and emphasise the words 'unless and until the machinery *b* . . . is operated'.

That approach by Roskill LJ is explained by the fact that he was considering s 6 in its unamended form, and sub-s (2) at that time gave the minister power to give directions exempting the local authority from the duty imposed by s 6(1). That power to exempt was expressly repealed by s 173(a) of the Local Government, Planning and Land Act 1980, and the express repealing of the power to exempt does justify my taking a different *c* view of the duty from that expressed in *Wells's* case.

However, on the assumption that I am bound by what Roskill LJ said in *Wells's* case, with which the other members of the court agreed, this does not detract from the obligation on the borough to properly consider what sites it is going to provide and what sites it was proposing to cease to provide. The decision which the borough took, as counsel for the applicant pointed out, is similar to the decision in *Meade v Haringey* *d* *London Borough* [1979] 2 All ER 1016 at 1028, [1979] 1 WLR 637 at 651, which Eveleigh LJ described as 'not a simple failure . . . [but] a decision positively to stop production, as it were'.

When the local authority is under an express duty of the nature provided by s 6, a decision to this effect should only be taken after proper consideration of the position. The approach of the council can be ascertained from the documents to which I referred *e* at the beginning of this judgment, in particular the letter to the department of 16 June 1983. There it is suggested that all the borough is doing is returning a site to its owners on the expiry of the tenancy. This is a wholly unrealistic description of what was happening. The borough, in truth and in fact, was giving up its duty under s 6 of the 1968 Act to provide a site. This could not be excused by suggesting that the GLC would then be responsible. As counsel pointed out in argument on behalf of the GLC, there are *f* considerable impediments in the way of the GLC providing a site. The GLC is not a local authority for the purposes of s 24 of the 1960 Act. It is not licensed to provide the site, so its permitting of the land to be used as a caravan site would be prohibited under s 1 of the 1960 Act, and it is at least highly doubtful whether the residual power under s 137 of the Local Government Act 1972 would enable the GLC to provide services as apparently the borough was advised. *g*

The indications from the evidence are that when the local authority took the decisions to cease to provide the site, it did not appreciate the true nature of its decisions or what would or would not be the consequences. I, therefore, take the view that its decisions should be quashed by this court so that the matter can be reconsidered by the authority in the proper manner, in particular with due regard to the fact that s 6 of the 1968 Act requires it to provide adequate accommodation for gipsies residing in its area, irrespective *h* of whether or not the Secretary of State has exercised his power under s 9 to give directions.

The order of certiorari will relate both to the decision of 3 November 1982 and to that of 27 April 1983.

I am not, however, of the view that it would be appropriate to give any further relief to the applicant against the borough. As the borough perfectly properly points out, there *j* are great difficulties in its meeting the terms of the order made by the stipendiary magistrate and, even if it would be right to make an order of mandamus or grant an injunction, having regard to the powers of the Secretary of State and the absence of any private right, I would not have been minded to make such an order or to grant an injunction because complying with the order or injunction could require the borough to *a* do something which is unlawful. It is much better to leave the manner in which it will perform its duty to the borough in the first instance, and to the Secretary of State if he considers that it is not performing its duty.

The position of the borough of Kensington

The decision of the borough of Hammersmith was reached in collaboration with the borough of Kensington, and, having come to the conclusion which I have with regard to
b the borough of Hammersmith, the same reasoning applies to the borough of Kensington. No specific relief by way of certiorari is sought against this borough and so I do not grant any such relief. I do not regard it as appropriate or necessary to enforce the agreement of 15 April 1976. I have no doubt that, while the borough of Hammersmith continues to provide the site, the borough of Kensington will continue to honour the agreement of 15 April 1976.

c There remain two further matters with which I must deal. It was argued on behalf of the borough of Kensington that the fact of designation under s 12 had the result as a matter of law that it was no longer under a duty under s 6. I do not accept that submission. It may not be expedient or necessary for the borough to make provision under s 12 because adequate provision is being provided for gipsies residing in or resorting to its area by a neighbouring borough. This does not mean that there is not a
d duty; it merely means that the duty is being complied with without the borough itself providing the accommodation. If circumstances changed, the borough could be in breach of its duty, although in practice the duty is not likely to be enforced until the designation is revoked.

The final matter to which I should refer is the decision of McCullough J in *R v Secretary of State for Wales, ex parte Price* (7 February 1983, unreported), of which I have been
e supplied with a transcript. That judgment was relied on by both borough authorities. It was a decision in relation to an application to challenge the refusal of the Secretary of State to make a direction under s 9. I suspect that McCullough J did not have the advantage that I have had of having my attention drawn to the legislature history to which I have already referred.

However, McCullough J came to the conclusion that there must be implied into s 6 a
f qualification that the duty of the council is limited to that which is 'practicable or reasonably practicable or reasonable or that it must use its best endeavours'.

The duty is not, in my view, qualified precisely in this way. It is qualified by the fact that what is or is not adequate accommodation is a question in the first instance for the authority concerned, which has to make a value judgment, taking into account all the circumstances. It is also qualified by the fact that, except in exceptional circumstances,
g the court will not seek to enforce that duty, but leave the matter to the Secretary of State, who can be expected to only exercise his powers when it is appropriate to do so.

Order of certiorari accordingly.

Solicitors: *Michael O'Dwyer* (for the applicant); *Treasury Solicitor*; *C T Mahoney* (for Hammersmith); *A J Colvin* (for Kensington); *R A Lanham* (for the GLC).

N P Metcalfe Esq   Barrister.

United States Government and others v McCaffery

a

HOUSE OF LORDS

LORD DIPLOCK, LORD FRASER OF TULLYBELTON, LORD ROSKILL, LORD BRIDGE OF HARWICH AND LORD BRANDON OF OAKBROOK

14 MAY, 14 JUNE 1984

b

Extradition – Evidence – Duty of magistrate – Magistrate to consider whether conduct of accused would, if committed in England, constitute an extradition crime – Whether question of double criminality to be considered – Extradition Act 1870, s 10, Sch 1 – Extradition Act 1873, s 3.

Habeas corpus – Habeas corpus ad subjiciendum – Criminal matter – Appeal to House of Lords – c
Appeal against grant of habeas corpus by Divisional Court – Duty of Divisional Court pending appeal – Appeal by requisitioning state in extradition proceedings – Divisional Court making unqualified order releasing fugitive from custody – Divisional Court not to release fugitive except on bail pending appeal – Administration of Justice Act 1960, ss 5, 15.

The respondent was charged in the United States of America with federal offences d
consisting of using wire, radio or television to transmit communications for fraudulent purposes in interstate or foreign commerce and of transporting in interstate or foreign commerce a valuable security knowing it to have been converted or taken by fraud. The United States government sought the extradition from the United Kingdom of the respondent. The respondent was arrested and brought before a metropolitan stipendiary magistrate, who made an order under s 10[a] of the Extradition Act 1870 committing him e
to prison pending his surrender to the United States government to answer charges which were described in the Secretary of State's order to the magistrate to proceed as 'theft, obtaining property by deception and securing the execution of a valuable security by deception'. The conduct of the respondent and his confederates on which those crimes were based and in which use was made of interstate means of communication or transportation involved an elaborate international fraud whereby persons in various f
states in America were induced to transmit to the respondent's confederates in the State of Georgia large sums in commission for bogus undertakings given by an English company controlled by the respondent to procure from prime international banks millions of dollars by way of loan in order to finance projects in which the victims of the fraud were interested. Although the respondent's part in the fraud took place in England he was liable to be extradited as an accessory by virtue of s 3[b] of the Extradition Act 1873. g
The respondent applied to the Divisional Court for a writ of habeas corpus to obtain his release from custody. The Divisional Court granted his application on the grounds (i) that he was not liable to be surrendered because the underlying crimes of which he was accused were crimes against state laws and not against federal laws and (ii) that whether a fugitive criminal should be surrendered depended on whether the offence of which he was accused was a crime not only in the foreign state but also under English law and that h

---

a Section 10, so far as material provides: 'In the case of a fugitive criminal accused of an extradition crime, if the foreign warrant authorising the arrest of such criminal is duly authenticated, and such evidence is produced as (subject to the provisions of this Act) would, according to the law of England, justify the committal for trial of the prisoner if the crime of which he is accused had been committed in England, the police magistrate shall commit him to prison but otherwise shall order him to be discharged . . .'
j

b Section 3 provides: 'Every person who is accused or convicted of having counselled, procured, commanded, aided, or abetted the commission of any extradition crime, or of being accessory before or after the fact to any extradition crime, shall be deemed, for the purposes of the principal Act and this Act, to be accused or convicted of having committed such crime, and shall be liable to be apprehended and surrendered accordingly.'

there was no English equivalent to the fraud by wire or interstate transportation offences

a with which the respondent was charged. The Divisional Court made an unqualified order for the discharge of the respondent from custody. The United States government, the Secretary of State and the prison governor appealed to the House of Lords.

Held – (1) Under the Constitution of the United States criminal law in general was a subject that fell within the legislative competence of the individual constituent states of

b the federation and within the exclusive jurisdiction of the state courts unless there was an interstate or foreign element in the offence that had been committed or some question of legal rights conferred by the Constitution was involved, in which case jurisdiction was conferred on a federal court instead of a state court. The underlying crimes of which the respondent was accused were crimes against state laws and were covered by the extradition treaty with the United States (see p 574 *d e*, p 575 *f g* and p 576 *d* to *f*, post); *Jennings v US*

c *Government* [1982] 3 All ER 104 applied.

(2) The duty of the magistrate in considering an application for extradition of a fugitive under s 10 of the 1870 Act was to determine on the evidence whether the conduct of the accused, if it had been committed in England, would have constituted a crime falling within one or other of the descriptions included in the list of offences described in Sch 1 to the 1870 Act, as amended, and was not whether the double

d criminality test applied based on a comparison with the offence specified in the foreign warrant of arrest. Since the conduct of the respondent's confederates in committing the underlying fraud would have amounted to a crime in England, the committal order had been rightly made. Accordingly the appeal would be allowed and the orders of the Divisional Court set aside (see p 572 *j* to p 573 *b*, p 575 *h j* and p 576 *d* to *f*, post); *Government of Denmark v Nielsen* [1984] 2 All ER 81 applied.

e Per curiam. The warning given by the House of Lords in 1972 in relation to appeals under the Criminal Appeal Act 1968 that, where the Court of Appeal allows an appeal against conviction by a defendant who would, but for that decision, be liable to be detained and the prosecutor is granted, or gives notice that he intends to apply for, leave to appeal to the House of Lords, the defendant should not be released except on bail while the appeal is pending to the House of Lords applies equally to appeals to the House of

f Lords from the Divisional Court in proceedings on application for habeas corpus in criminal matters under ss 5^c and 15^d of the Administration of Justice Act 1960, since by virtue of those sections the defendant if released unconditionally by the Divisional Court is not liable to be detained again if the appeal is allowed (see p 575 *j* to p 576 *a* and *c* to *f*, post); *DPP v Merriman* [1972] 3 All ER 42 applied.

---

g c Section 5, so far as material, provides:

'(1) Where the defendant in any proceedings from which an appeal lies under section one of this Act would, but for the decision of the court below, be liable to be detained, and immediately after that decision the prosecutor is granted, or gives notice that he intends to apply for, leave to appeal, the court may make an order providing for the detention of the defendant, or directing that he shall not be released except on bail . . . so long as any appeal under section one of this Act is pending . . .

h (5) Where the court below has power to make an order under subsection (1) of this section, and either no such order is made or the defendant is released or discharged . . . before the appeal is disposed of, the defendant shall not be liable to be again detained as the result of the decision of the House of Lords on the appeal.'

d Section 15, so far as material, provides:

'(1) Subject to the provisions of this section, an appeal shall lie, in any proceedings upon application for habeas corpus, whether civil or criminal, against an order for the release of the

j person restrained as well as against the refusal of such an order . . .

(4) Except as provided by section five of this Act in the case of an appeal against an order of a Divisional Court on a criminal application, an appeal brought by virtue of this section shall not affect the right of the person restrained to be discharged in pursuance of the order under appeal and (unless an order under subsection (1) of that section is in force at the determination of the appeal) to remain at large regardless of the decision on appeal.'

Notes

For extradition to a foreign state, see 18 Halsbury's Laws (4th edn) paras 223–229, and *a* for cases on the subject, see 24 Digest (Reissue) 1118–1142, *11910–12158*.

For bail pending appeal to the House of Lords from the Divisional Court, see 11 Halsbury's Laws (4th edn) para 722.

For the Extradition Act 1870, s 10, Sch 1, see 13 Halsbury's Statutes (3rd edn) 257, 266. For the Extradition Act 1873, s 3, see ibid 270.

For the Administration of Justice Act 1960, ss 5, 15, see 8 ibid 492 and 7 ibid 724 *b* respectively.

For the Criminal Appeal Act 1968, see 8 ibid 687.

Cases referred to in opinions

DPP v Merriman [1972] 3 All ER 42, [1973] AC 584, [1972] 3 WLR 545, HL.
Government of Denmark v Nielsen [1984] 2 All ER 81, [1984] 2 WLR 737, HL. *c*
Jennings v US Government [1982] 3 All ER 104, [1983] 1 AC 624, [1982] 3 WLR 450, HL.

Appeal

On 8 September 1983 the respondent, John Horsburgh McCaffery, applied to the Divisional Court of the Queen's Bench Division for an order that a writ of habeas corpus ad subjiciendum should issue directed to the governor of HM Prison Pentonville, to the *d* United States government and to the Director of Public Prosecutions to have discharged a committal order made by W E C Robins, a metropolitan stipendiary magistrate sitting at Bow Street Magistrates' Court on 26 August 1983, committing the respondent into the custody of the governor of HM Prison Pentonville pursuant to s 10 of the Extradition Act 1870. On 20 October 1983 the Divisional Court (McNeill and McCullough JJ), for reasons delivered on 28 November 1983, allowed the application and ordered that the *e* respondent be discharged out of custody. The United States government, the Secretary of State for Home Affairs and the governor of HM Prison Pentonville appealed to the House of Lords with leave of the Divisional Court granted on 28 November 1983. The facts are set out in the opinion of Lord Diplock.

Clive Nicholls QC and *David Paget* for the appellants. *f*
The respondent did not appear.

Their Lordships took time for consideration.

14 June. The following opinions were delivered.

LORD DIPLOCK. My Lords, this appeal is an extradition case in which the state *g* requesting the surrender of a fugitive criminal accused of an extradition crime is the United States of America. The appeal follows hotfoot on the decision of this House in another extradition case, *Government of Denmark v Nielsen* [1984] 2 All ER 81, [1984] 2 WLR 737, in which this House upheld the judgment delivered on 12 May 1983 by a Divisional Court composed of Robert Goff LJ and Mann J. It was known to the differently *h* constituted Divisional Court which heard the instant case (McNeill and McCullough JJ) that *Nielsen's* case, which they declined to follow, was the subject of an appeal then pending to this House.

What the Divisional Court had held in *Nielsen's* case, which had come before that court in the form of an application for judicial review of a magistrate's order discharging Nielsen from custody, was that on the true construction of the Extradition Acts 1870 to *j* 1935, and in particular the 1870 principal Act, the test whether a person in respect of whom a warrant for his arrest had been issued in a foreign state for an offence alleged to have been committed in that state was liable to be surrendered as a fugitive criminal was *not* whether the offence specified in the foreign warrant of arrest as that for which it had been issued was substantially similar to a crime under English law falling within the list

of offences described in the Sch 1 to the Extradition Act 1870, as currently amended (ie
a the so-called 'double criminality' test). The right test, as stated by the Divisional Court in
Nielsen's case, was whether the *conduct* of the accused, if it had been committed in
England, would have constituted a crime falling within one or more of the descriptions
included in that list.

The judgment of the Divisional Court in *Nielsen's* case, which had been given by
Robert Goff LJ has received the express approval of this House on appeal. In my own
b speech, with which the four other members of the Appellate Committee expressed their
agreement, occasion was taken to point out that, when surrender of a fugitive criminal
was sought under the principal extradition treaty with Denmark or under extradition
treaties with other states that followed a similar form, evidence of a foreign law that
defined the particular offence for which the warrant of arrest had been issued in that state
was irrelevant to any question that fell to be considered by the magistrate or by the
c Divisional Court on any subsequent application for habeas corpus. Accordingly, the
practice that appeared to have been followed since the turn of the century at Bow Street
of adducing such evidence of foreign law in all cases of persons accused of an extradition
crime was mistaken. It was pointed out, however, in my speech that in what, for
convenient brevity, I called 'exceptional accusation cases', an extradition treaty with a
particular state might contain provisions that would make it necessary for evidence on
d some matter of foreign law to be adduced on the part of the requesting state in extradition
proceedings. The precise matter on which evidence of foreign law would be necessary
would depend on the terms of the particular extradition treaty.

The extradition treaty with the United States concluded on 8 June 1972 and scheduled
to the United States of America (Extradition) Order 1976, SI 1976/2144 made under s 2
of the 1870 Act, does contain, in art III, a provision of this kind which brings extradition
e proceedings for the surrender of a fugitive criminal from the United States of America
into the category of exceptional accusation cases. Article III reads:

'(1) Extradition shall be granted for an act or omission the facts of which disclose
an offence within any of the descriptions listed in the Schedule annexed to this
Treaty, which is an integral part of the Treaty, or any other offence, if: (*a*) the offence
is punishable under the laws of both Parties by imprisonment or other form of
f detention for more than one year or by the death penalty; (*b*) the offence is
extraditable under the relevant law, being the law of the United Kingdom or other
territory to which this Treaty applies by virtue of sub-paragraph (1)(*a*) of Article II;
and (*c*) the offence constitutes a felony under the law of the United States of America.

(2) Extradition shall also be granted for any attempt or conspiracy to commit an
offence within paragraph (1) of this Article if such attempt or conspiracy is one for
g which extradition may be granted under the laws of both Parties and is punishable
under the laws of both Parties by imprisonment or other form of detention for
more than one year or by the death penalty.

(3) Extradition shall also be granted for the offence of impeding the arrest or
prosecution of a person who has committed an offence for which extradition may
be granted under this Article and which is punishable under the laws of both Parties
h by imprisonment or other form of detention for a period of five years or more.

(4) A person convicted of and sentenced for an offence shall not be extradited
therefor unless he was sentenced to imprisonment or other form of detention for a
period of four months or more or, subject to the provisions of Article IV, to the
death penalty.'

j   As was held by this House in *Jennings v US Government* [1982] 3 All ER 104 at 113,
[1983] 1 AC 624 at 639, on the true construction of this article, the requirements of para
(1)(*a*) and (*c*) must be satisfied as respects offences of the descriptions listed in the schedule
to the treaty as well as as respects any other offence. By virtue of s 2 of the 1870 Act, this
imposes a restriction on the operation of the Act as respects extradition to the United
States of America. So evidence is required that, under the criminal law in force in that

part of the United States of America where the conduct took place that is relied on as
constituting the criminal offence for which the extradition of the accused is requested,   *a*
that conduct (i) amounts to an offence that is punishable by a custodial sentence of more
than one year or by the death penalty and (ii) constitutes a felony. Uncontradicted
affidavit evidence by qualified United States lawyers that these two requirements were
satisfied as respects the offences for which a warrant for the arrest of McCaffery had been
issued by the United States District Court for the Northern District of Georgia was
adduced before the metropolitan magistrate in the proceedings in the instant case; so   *b*
nothing turns on this, nor is there any reference to this matter in either of the judgments
in the Divisional Court.

The offences with which McCaffery was charged that were relied on in the United
States ambassador's request for McCaffery's extradition were offences against federal laws
of the United States of America, specifically §§ 1343 and 2314 of Title 18 of the United
States Code. Put broadly, but sufficiently for present purposes, these offences consist of   *c*
using wire, radio or television to transmit communications for fraudulent purposes in
interstate or foreign commerce (§ 1343) and of transporting in interstate or foreign
commerce a valuable security knowing it to have been converted or taken by fraud
(§ 2314).

Under the Constitution of the United States of America, criminal law is in general a
subject that falls within the legislative competence of the individual constituent states of   *d*
the federation and within the exclusive jurisdiction of state courts unless there is an
interstate or foreign element in the offence that has been committed or some question of
legal rights conferred by the Constitution of the United States is involved. The presence
of an interstate or foreign element in the offence that is the subject of a criminal charge
is sufficient to confer jurisdiction to try the offence in a United States federal court instead
of a state court. A device that is not uncommonly employed for the purpose of founding   *e*
such federal criminal jurisdiction is to charge the accused not with the underlying fraud
itself but with the use of interstate transport or interstate means of communication for
the purpose of carrying out the fraud. Reference to this practice which on first
encountering it strikes an English or Scots lawyer as strange, not to say disingenuous, is
made in what is called a 'Protocol of Signature' to the extradition treaty, which is in the
following terms: *f*

> 'At the time of signing this day the Extradition Treaty between the Government
> of the United Kingdom of Great Britain and Northern Ireland and the Government
> of the United States of America (hereinafter referred to as "the Treaty"), the
> undersigned have agreed as follows: (1) Article III of the Treaty shall permit the
> Government of the United States of America to obtain the extradition of a person
> for an offence to which the Treaty relates when United States Federal jurisdiction is   *g*
> based upon interstate transport or transportation or the use of the mails or of
> interstate facilities, these aspects being jurisdictional only. (2) This Protocol of
> Signature shall form an integral part of the Treaty.'

My Lords, I do not find it necessary for the purpose of disposing of the instant appeal
to describe in any detail the conduct of McCaffery and his confederates that gave rise to   *h*
the requisition by the government of the United States of America for his surrender.
Suffice it to say that it involved an elaborate international fraud whereby persons in
various other states in the United States of America were induced to transmit to
McCaffery's confederates in the State of Georgia large sums in commission for bogus
undertakings by an English company controlled by McCaffery to procure from prime
international banks millions of dollars by way of loan in order to finance projects in   *j*
which the victims of the fraud were interested. McCaffery's individual part in this
fraudulent scheme was played in London. He does not appear to have been personally
present in the United States at any time during the period that it was successfully
operating but his role involved him in executing and transmitting to his confederates in
the State of Georgia the bogus undertakings addressed to intended victims of the fraud.

To those confederates, moneys for commission, obtained by their and McCaffery's
a fraudulent misrepresentations, were transmitted by their victims, who for this purpose
made use of interstate means of communication or transportation.

The reason why McCaffery, despite the fact that it appears that all the physical acts that
he did personally in furtherance of this international fraud were being done by him in
England, is nevertheless liable to be extradited to the United States of America is to be
found in s 3 of the Extradition Act 1873. This section provides that persons accused of
b having been accessories to an extradition crime shall be deemed for the purposes of the
1870 and 1873 Acts to be accused of having committed such crime and shall be liable to
be apprehended and surrendered accordingly. So McCaffery is to be treated, for the
purposes of his extradition, as if everything that was done by his confederates in the State
of Georgia in furtherance of the fraudulent scheme had been done in that state by
McCaffery personally. No point as to the applicability of this section to McCaffery was
c taken in the judgment of the Divisional Court.

The Secretary of State's order to the magistrate to proceed described the crimes of
which McCaffery was accused of committing in the United States of America, as 'theft,
obtaining property by deception and securing the execution of a valuable security by
deception'. These are extradition crimes under the Extradition Acts 1870 to 1935, as
currently amended, and also fall within one or other of items 13 and 17 of the list of
d offences in the schedule referred to in art III of the Extradition Treaty. They are based on
acts done by McCaffery's confederates in the United States in the course of carrying out
the underlying fraud in which use was made by those confederates of interstate means of
communication or transportation. For convenience, I will call these acts 'the underlying
crimes'. The Divisional Court did not accept the suggestion that there was not adduced
before the magistrate evidence that would have been sufficient to justify the committal
e for trial of McCaffery for the underlying crimes, if what he and his confederates had
done had been done by them in England. The order to proceed does not include the
offences under § 1343 or § 2314 of Title 18 of the United States Code for the obvious
reason that these are not extradition crimes.

In his judgment McNeill J held that there were two grounds on which McCaffery was
entitled to be discharged from custody. The first, which I confess to finding astonishing,
f was that the extradition treaty with the United States does not provide for extradition to
the United States of persons accused of crimes against state laws, but only of persons
accused of crimes against federal laws. I have already pointed out that under the
Constitution of the United States of America criminal law in general is a state and not a
federal subject. That crimes against state laws are covered by the extradition treaty is also
evident from the recent judgment of this House in *Jennings v US Government*, to which I
g have already referred. The extradition crime for which surrender was ordered in that
case was not a crime under federal law at all but one under the law of the State of
California alone.

This first ground of McNeill J was not expressly relied on by McCullough J. He joined
with McNeill J in relying and elaborating in his own language on the latter's second
ground, viz that *Nielsen's* case was wrongly decided, that what both the magistrate and
h the Secretary of State were concerned with was *not* whether the conduct of the accused
(or in the instant case his confederates in the underlying fraud) would have amounted to
an extradition crime if that conduct had taken place in England, but *was* whether the
double criminality test was satisfied. The reasons why both judges were wrong in so
holding were dealt with so fully and recently in the decision of this House dismissing the
appeal in *Nielsen's* case that there is no need to repeat them here.

j I would accordingly allow this appeal and would set aside the order of the Divisional
Court of 20 October and 28 November 1983. But, so far as its effect on McCaffery is
concerned, to set aside these orders is no more than a brutum fulmen. This is because the
Divisional Court either overlooked or disregarded the fact that the warning given by this
House in *DPP v Merriman* [1972] 3 All ER 42, [1973] AC 584 in relation to the Criminal
Appeal Act 1968 was equally applicable to the importance of making an order under s 5

of the Administration of Justice Act 1960 (which, by s 15, is made applicable to appeals to the House of Lords in proceedings on application for habeas corpus in criminal matters), directing that the person restrained shall not be released except on bail so long as the appeal to the House of Lords is pending.

If ever there was a case which called for an order of this kind instead of an unqualified order for discharge of the person awaiting surrender for an extradition crime, the instant case provides a prime example. The Divisional Court, for reasons that I have not found easy to follow in the judgments, regarded itself as entitled to decline to follow the recent judgment of another Divisional Court in *Nielsen's* case which not only was prima facie binding on it but to its knowledge was under appeal to this House. To make matters worse the court made an unqualified order for McCaffery's discharge on 20 October 1983 when it announced its decision to allow the appeal, but adjourned to a later date the expression of its reasons for doing so and also the question whether or not to grant leave to appeal to the House of Lords. The second order by which leave to appeal to this House was granted was not made until 28 November 1983. By then it was too late. By virtue of ss 5 and 15 of the Administration of Justice Act 1960 McCaffery is not liable to be detained again. The procedure which the court chose to follow in relation to McCaffery's discharge is, in my view, inexplicable.

LORD FRASER OF TULLYBELTON. My Lords, I have had the advantage of reading in draft the speech of my noble and learned friend on the Woolsack. I agree with it and for the reasons stated in it I would allow the appeal.

LORD ROSKILL. My Lords, I have had the advantage of reading in draft the speech to be delivered by my noble and learned friend Lord Diplock. I agree with it and for the reasons which he gives I would allow this appeal.

LORD BRIDGE OF HARWICH. My Lords, for the reasons given in the speech of my noble and learned friend Lord Diplock, with which I agree, I would allow this appeal.

LORD BRANDON OF OAKBROOK. My Lords, I have had the advantage of reading in draft the speech prepared by my noble and learned friend Lord Diplock. I agree with it, and for the reasons which he gives I would allow the appeal.

Appeal allowed.

Solicitors: *Director of Public Prosecutions.*

Mary Rose Plummer　　Barrister.

a
Harman v Glencross and another

FAMILY DIVISION
EWBANK J
15, 16 FEBRUARY 1984

b
Execution – Charging order – Land – Interest in land – Joint tenancy – Wife commencing divorce proceedings and serving notice of severance in relation to joint tenancy – Creditor obtaining judgment against husband and obtaining charging order on husband's interest in matrimonial home – Wife seeking to vary charging order or for it not to be enforced until hearing of her application for ancillary relief – Whether wife entitled to apply for variation of charging order – Whether court should consider wife's position when making charging order on matrimonial home – Whether interest of wife and children to be balanced against interest of creditor – Charging Orders Act 1979, ss 1, 3(5).

c

In 1970 the husband and wife purchased a house which was transferred into their joint names. In 1980 the marriage broke down and on 12 January 1981 the wife petitioned for divorce. Meanwhile the husband's business affairs had run into difficulties and on 15 January the husband's solicitor informed a creditor that divorce proceedings were imminent and that it was likely that the house would be sold and the proceeds shared equally between the husband and the wife. In March the wife commenced ancillary proceedings for property adjustment and other financial relief. On 9 May the wife served notice of severance of the joint tenancy and on 20 May she obtained a decree nisi. On 22 May the creditor issued a writ for moneys owed to him by the husband and in due course entered summary judgment. The creditor then obtained a charging order absolute under s 1[a] of the Charging Orders Act 1979 in respect of the husband's interest in the matrimonial home but without serving the application for a charging order on the wife or giving her notice of it. When the wife discovered the existence of the charging order, she applied under s 3(5)[b] of the 1979 Act for it to be discharged, or in any event not enforced until the hearing of her application for ancillary relief. The registrar ordered that the charging order was to be subject to any order made in the ancillary proceedings and further ordered, in the ancillary proceedings, that the husband's interest in the matrimonial home was to be transferred to the wife. The creditor appealed against the variation of the charging order made by the registrar. The questions arose (i) when, if at all, it was appropriate for the court to consider the wife's position when deciding whether to make a charging order in respect of a matrimonial home, and (ii) if it was appropriate, how the interests of the wife and children were to be balanced against the interests of a creditor. The creditor contended that the wife was not a 'person interested in any property to which the order relates' within the meaning of s 3(5) of the 1979 Act because (i) the wife only had a claim in the matrimonial home and not an 'interest' and (ii) that the wife's interest was not in the land but in the proceeds of sale, and therefore because of her lack of locus standi she was not entitled to apply under s 3(5) for the charging

h
_____

a   Section 1, so far as material, provides:
    '(1) Where, under a judgment or order of the High Court or a county court, a person (the "debtor") is required to pay a sum of money to another person (the "creditor") then, for the purpose of enforcing that judgment or order, the appropriate court may make an order in accordance with the provisions of the Act imposing on any such property of the debtor as may be specified in the order a charge for securing the payment of any money due or to become due under the judgment or order.
    (5) In deciding whether to make a charging order the court shall consider all the circumstances of the case and, in particular, any evidence before it as to—(a) the personal circumstances of the debtor, and (b) whether any other creditor of the debtor would be likely to be unduly prejudiced by the making of the order.'
b   Section 3(5) is set out at p 581 f, post

order to be varied but had to seek relief when the creditor applied under s 30 of the Law
of Property Act 1925 for an order for sale.

a

Held – The appeal would be dismissed for the following reasons—

(1) A wife who was the joint owner of a matrimonial home was entitled to be heard
on an application by a creditor of her husband to obtain a charging order absolute under
s 1 of the 1979 Act over her husband's interest in the matrimonial home, because of her
interest in the property and because the court had a duty at least to consider whether she
ought not to be given notice of the hearing so that she could be heard (see p 581 *b* to *e*,
post).

b

(2) Similarly a wife who was the joint owner of a matrimonial home was entitled to
apply under s 3(5) of the 1979 Act for the variation or discharge of a charging order on
her husband's interest in the home, because the 'interest' required to support such an
application was not restricted to an interest in land or an interest on which the charge
was imposed, but extended to the wife's joint interest in the matrimonial home. It
followed that the wife was entitled to apply under s 3(5) to vary the order (see p 581 *g h*
and p 582 *e* to *g*, post); *Taylor v Taylor* [1968] 1 All ER 843 and *Whittingham v Whittingham
(National Westminster Bank Ltd intervening)* [1978] 3 All ER 805 considered.

c

(3) In deciding whether to make a charging order the court had to consider all the
circumstances of the case and weigh the interests of the creditor against the interests of
the wife, with no presumption either way. In particular the fact that a refusal to make a
charging order absolute would not thereby deprive the creditor of his debt and it might
still be open to him to recover it by other means and the fact that the making of a
charging order absolute might make the family homeless were both matters to be taken
into account. In all the circumstances there were overwhelming reasons for making the
charging order subject to the order made in the ancillary proceedings (see p 583 *a b* and *h*
to p 584 *b* and *h* to p 585 *a*, post).

d

e

Notes

For equitable charges and mortgages, see 28 Halsbury's Laws (4th edn) paras 509–512,
515, and for cases on the subject, see 35 Digest (Reissue) 54–57, 355–381.

For severance of joint tenancies, see 39 Halsbury's Laws (4th edn) paras 534–541, and
for cases on the subject, see 38 Digest (Reissue) 606–612, 5071–5137.

f

For the power to impose charging orders on land, see 17 Halsbury's Laws (4th edn)
paras 547–554, and for cases on the subject, see 21 Digest (Reissue) 49, 4004–4006.

For the Law of Property Act 1925, s 30, see 27 Halsbury's Statutes (3rd edn) 385.

For the Charging Orders Act 1979, ss 1, 3, see 49 ibid 767, 771.

Cases referred to in judgment

g

First National Securities Ltd v Hegerty [1984] 1 All ER 139.

Holliday (a bankrupt), Re, ex p trustee of the bankrupt v The bankrupt [1980] 3 All ER 385,
[1981] Ch 405, [1981] 2 WLR 996, CA.

Irani Finance Ltd v Singh [1970] 3 All ER 199, [1971] Ch 59, [1970] 3 WLR 330, CA.

Lowrie (a bankrupt), Re, ex p trustee of the bankrupt v The bankrupt [1981] 3 All ER 353, DC.

h

Mesher v Mesher and Hall (1973) [1980] 1 All ER 126, CA.

Mullard v Mullard (1981) 3 FLR 330, CA.

Roberts Petroleum Ltd v Bernard Kenny Ltd (in liq) [1982] 1 All ER 685, [1982] 1 WLR 301,
CA.

Taylor v Taylor [1968] 1 All ER 843, [1968] 1 WLR 378, CA.

Whittingham v Whittingham (National Westminster Bank Ltd intervening) [1978] 3 All ER
805, [1979] Fam 9, [1978] 2 WLR 936, CA.

j

Appeal

The plaintiff, Martin Alexander Harman (the creditor), appealed against the decision of
Mr Registrar Angel on 9 May 1983 ordering that the charging order absolute made on 7
September 1981 by Master Elton be varied to provide that the interest of the defendant,

a Roy Leslie Glencross (the husband), in the asset specified in the schedule to the order, namely the freehold property known as 155 Daneland, East Barnet, Hertfordshire, stand charged subject to any order of the court on the application of Mrs Maureen Glencross (the wife) for ancillary relief in divorce proceedings against the husband with payment of £9,351·83, the amount due from the husband to the creditor on a judgment of the High Court dated 21 July 1981 and interest. The facts are set out in the judgment.

b *Peter Wright* for the creditor.
Walter Aylen QC and *David Martineau* for the wife.
Barry Green QC and *John Harwood-Stevenson* for the husband.

EWBANK J. This appeal concerns a former matrimonial home. The wife has divorced her husband and she has been seeking a transfer of her husband's interest in the matrimonial home to her. The husband is in debt and his creditor has been seeking a
c charging order on the house. The two cases to begin with were proceeding independently, but at a late stage they were brought together. Some of the problems that are facing me would have been solved if the cases had been brought together earlier.

On 9 May 1983 the matter came before Mr Registrar Angel and he preferred the claims of the wife. The creditor now appeals to this court.

d The house concerned was bought on 23 March 1970, before the husband and wife married. It was bought on mortgage and it was transferred into joint names of the husband and wife-to-be. They were married on 30 May 1970. They have two children, Sarah who is nine and Emma who is seven. There are three charges on the house. These charges were executed by the husband and the wife and registered. The first charge is the mortgage and the second and third are bank loans. They take priority to the interests
e of the husband and wife, but otherwise they are of no direct relevance to this case.

In May 1979 the husband started in partnership with Martin Harman (the creditor). In August 1980 the husband left the wife and children at the matrimonial home. On 12 January 1981 the wife filed a petition for dissolution of her marriage. This petition is on a printed form and contains the usual prayer for ancillary relief including a property adjustment order. The petition is under s 1(2)(b) of the Matrimonial Causes Act 1973,
f and asserts that the respondent has behaved in such a way that the petitioner cannot reasonably be expected to live with him. It alleges desertion from August 1980. It alleges adultery from October 1980 and, amongst other things, it alleges that the husband asked the wife to sign the charge in favour of the bank against the security of the matrimonial home on an assurance that the loan would not exceed £2,000 and it goes on to assert that contrary to that assurance the husband allowed the loan to go up to £4,500.

g The partnership between the husband and the creditor was in trouble and by early 1981 solicitors' letters were being written. On 8 January 1981 the creditor's solicitors wrote to the husband saying that the situation in relation to the partnership was serious, their liabilities now totalled £33,000 and of that £22,000 was owed to a company belonging to the creditor in respect of advances made by that company to the partnership. The husband's solicitors replied on 15 January. The petition for divorce had been served
h on the husband the previous day. The letter from the husband's solicitors said that it appeared that there were to be divorce proceedings and said that they had written to the wife's solicitors suggesting that as the property was in joint names it was likely that he and the wife would share the proceeds of sale on a fifty-fifty basis. The significance of this letter is that it indicates that the creditor was told at this stage that the wife had an interest in the house, if he did not know already, and that divorce proceedings were
i imminent.

On 23 March the wife filed a notice of application to proceed with her application for property adjustment and financial relief. This is the step initiating the wife's claim in the divorce proceedings. On 9 May the wife served notice of severence in relation to the joint tenancy. On 20 May the wife obtained a decree nisi of dissolution of marriage. On 22 May the creditor issued his writ in the Queen's Bench Division. The writ was for £9,250-odd, being half the money expended by the creditor on behalf of the partnership and the creditor asserted that he was entitled to look to the husband for contribution. The husband did not defend this writ and judgment was entered for £9,250 plus costs on 21 July. In August application was made for a charging order. The creditor's solicitors swore an affidavit in which it was said that the house was in the joint ownership of the husband and the wife and asking for a charge on the husband's interest in the property. The application to the master was made ex parte, as is normal, and a charging order nisi was made on 17 August. On 7 September 1981, the application was made for a charging order absolute and that application was granted.

The wife was not served with the application for a charging order, nor given notice of the application. In due course, she found out about it and on 30 December she made an application to vary the charging order. She asked that the charging order should be discharged or not enforced until the hearing of her application for ancillary relief. The decree absolute was made on 1 February 1982. The wife's application to vary the charging order came before the master on 18 May, and he made an order, subject to the wife having her divorce proceedings transferred to the High Court, that her application for variation should be transferred to the Family Division with the intention that that application should be heard by the court hearing the wife's application for ancillary relief.

The two applications eventually came before Mr Registrar Angel on 9 May 1983. He made an order that the charge should be subject to any order made by the court in the application by the wife in the divorce proceedings. On the following day the registrar had to consider the wife's application in the divorce proceedings for ancillary relief and property adjustment. The creditor did not attend on that day, although he had attended the previous day on the question of variation of the charging order. The creditor took the view, as I understand it, that the registrar had already made up his mind that he was going to transfer the husband's interest to the wife and that there was no point in attending, although he could have attended and he could have been heard. The registrar made an order as expected that the husband's interest, subject to the mortgage and two charges, should be transferred to the wife. He dismissed all other claims for relief.

The house is said to be worth £31,500. The three charges (that is the mortgage and the two bank charges) amount to £9,100. The equity in the house accordingly is £22,400. A half interest would accordingly be £11,200. The amount of the judgment debt owing to the creditor with interest is now over £13,000. Accordingly, a charge on the husband's half interest in the house would exhaust that half interest completely.

Two main points arise in this appeal. The first is when, if at all, it is appropriate to consider the wife's position in relation to a charging order being made on a matrimonial home; and second, if it is appropriate to consider it, how do you balance the interests of the wife and the children against the interests of a creditor? The creditor says that, although a wife can be heard on an application for a charging order absolute where she is a joint owner of the matrimonial home, in this case she was not heard. He goes on to say that she is not entitled to apply for a variation and that once the order has been made it is too late. She must take her chance on an application made by the creditor under s 30 of the Law of Property Act 1925. On the face of it this is an unattractive argument, but the creditor insists that it is correct in law although it was not a point that was, in fact, taken before the registrar. Until the Charging Orders Act 1979 it was not possible for a creditor to obtain a charging order in relation to a jointly owned home. This is because the charging order could only be obtained against land and the interest in a jointly owned home is not an interest in land but an interest in the proceeds of sale. The 1979 Act extended the scope of charging orders to apply to interests held under trust. This was done by s 2(1)(a)(ii) of the 1979 Act. Since 1979, accordingly, a jointly owned home has been available as an object of a charging order. However, by the 1979 Act it was provided that in deciding whether to make a charging order the court should consider all the circumstances of the case, in particular any evidence before it as to the personal circumstances of the debtor and whether any other creditor of the debtor will be likely to be unduly prejudiced by the making of the order. That is s 1(5) of the Act.

The 1979 Act followed a report by the Law Commission (Report on Charging Orders

(Law Com no 74; Cmnd 6412)) which was presented to Parliament in March 1976. I
a have been referred, by agreement, to para 43, which reads:

> 'At present there is a tendency for the Court to accede almost automatically to a
> judgment creditor's request for a charging order. We think that this should not be
> so, not only because it makes priority gaining too easy, but also because it may result
> in charging orders being made in cases where they are really unfair to the debtor.'

b And they proposed that the court should have a full discretion in deciding whether or
not to accede to an application.

Now, if the court has, as the statute provides, to consider all the circumstances and has
a discretion to decide whether a charging order should be made, it seems to me clear that
the court ought to allow the wife to be heard in circumstances such as these before
coming to any decision. Charging orders are dealt with in RSC Ord 50, and in the note
c to Ord 50, in *The Supreme Court Practice 1982* vol 1, p 828, para 50/1–9/15 there is this
passage:

> '... the court has power on making the order *nisi*, to direct service of copies of the
> order and of the affidavit in support, on any other creditor of the judgment debtor
> or indeed on any other interested person as may be appropriate in the circumstances.
> Presumably such other creditor or other interested person would be allowed, and
d   indeed would be entitled, to attend and to be heard on the hearing of the further
> consideration of the matter, when the court will be considering whether or not to
> make the order absolute.'

I would say that not only has the court the power to direct service and notice to an
interested person, but in a case of this sort, where the wife is a joint owner of a
e matrimonial home on which a charging order is sought, the court has a duty at least to
consider whether she ought not to be given notice of the hearing so that she can be heard
and so that, in accordance with the statute, all the circumstances of the case can be
considered.

Here, as I have mentioned, no notice was given to the wife and the charging order was
made absolute without her being heard. When she found out she made an application to
f vary. That application was made under s 3(5) of the 1979 Act. This section provides:

> 'The court by which a charging order was made may at any time, on the
> application of the debtor or of any person interested in any property to which the
> order relates, make an order discharging or varying the charging order.'

The property, using wide terms, to which this order relates is the matrimonial home and
g at first sight it would appear that the wife was a person interested in the property and
accordingly entitled to apply. She would appear to have two interests. She is the applicant
for an order transferring the husband's interest in the home to her. And, secondly, she is
a tenant in common and the occupier of the home. But, on behalf of the creditor, it is
said that in truth she has no interest and has no locus standi. It is also said that, although
under s 1(5) the court has a discretion and has to consider all the circumstances of the
h case, there is no such discretion in s 3(5) on an application to vary. It is difficult to see
how the court can decide whether to discharge or vary an order without considering the
circumstances and I am not impressed with that second point.

The main thrust of the creditor's argument is that the wife has no interest in the
property to which the order relates. In the first instance the creditor relies on *Whittingham
v Whittingham (National Westminster Bank Ltd intervening)* [1973] 3 All ER 805, [1979] Fam
j 9. This was a case where the wife was applying for an order to transfer property. It was
not, however, the former matrimonial home. Stamp LJ said ([1978] 3 All ER 805 at 814,
[1979] Fam 9 at 21): '... an applicant under that section [that is s 24 of the 1973 Act] has
clearly not got an interest in or a proprietary right to land ... until an order has been
made in his or her favour.' And it is said that merely making a claim does not give an
interest in the land. But Stamp LJ, in that sentence, in parenthesis said in terms: 'I am

not speaking of a matrimonial home.' So that so far as he was concerned the matrimonial home was being excluded from his consideration. Speaking in general terms Stamp LJ was saying that a wife could have a claim, but not an interest, until the claim had crystallised into an order.

Secondly, the creditor says that the wife's interest is not in the land but in the proceeds of sale. The creditor refers to *Taylor v Taylor* [1968] 1 All ER 483, [1968] 1 WLR 378. This was a case where the wife was making a claim under s 17 of the Married Women's Property Act 1882 for a share in the home. The husband contracted to sell the home, the wife registered a lis pendens and accordingly prevented completion and the husband applied to the court for her lis pendens to be removed. Danckwerts LJ said ([1968] 1 All ER 483 at 487, [1968] 1 WLR 378 at 383):

'... the wife's interest at the most was a share in the proceeds of sale of the property, and ... there was, therefore, no interest which she possessed in the land at all, but merely in the proceeds of the sale ...'

And he decided that in those circumstances a lis pendens was not an appropriate charge to be registered.

I am also referred to *Irani Finance Ltd v Singh* [1970] 3 All ER 199 at 203, [1971] 1 Ch 59 at 79, where Cross LJ said:

'The words "interest in land" are no doubt capable in an appropriate context of including interests under trusts for sale of land ... but for one hundred years before 1956 the words, or equivalent words, have been held in this field not to include interests arising under trusts for sale.'

And it is asserted on behalf of the creditor that both those cases indicate that where the expression 'land' is used an interest in the proceeds of sale is not included.

The section which provides for variation, however, relates not to interests in land, but to interests in any property to which the order relates. It does not, as it might have done, refer to interests on which the charge is imposed. If it did, that might limit the wife's application because the charge is imposed on the husband's share and not on hers. The charging order itself provides that the defendant's interest in the land shall stand charged. The land is specified in the schedule. The schedule reads: 'The freehold property known as 155, Daneland, East Barnet,' which is the matrimonial home. The question under s 3(5) of the 1979 Act is: what property does the order relate to? The answer, quite clearly in my judgment, is: 155 Daneland, East Barnet.

So I find that the wife was entitled to make an application under s 3(5). If she had been given the opportunity of being heard on the original application for the charging order absolute, it would not, of course, be necessary for her to apply under s 3(5) and probably any application she made would be unsuccessful.

The question then arises how it is possible to balance the interests of the creditor and the wife in deciding whether a charging order should be made. Here I have been much assisted by a recent case called *First National Securities Ltd v Hegerty* [1984] 1 All ER 139. This was a case where the husband forged his wife's signature on a legal charge in order to get a loan and the lenders were under the impression that husband and wife had given them a legal charge over property. The judge held that the wife could not be bound by the husband's forgery, but that for his part he had given a valid equitable charge in favour of the lenders in relation to his beneficial interest. The judge (at 142) recited a submission made on behalf of the lenders which he approved. The submission was that the lenders should ordinarily be granted a charging order absolute unless the judgment debtor established some good reason why the order should not be made. And he referred in that context to the statement of principles made by Lord Brandon in *Roberts Petroleum Ltd v Bernard Kenny Ltd (in liq)* [1982] 1 All ER 685 at 690, [1982] 1 WLR 301 at 307. The second proposition enunciated by Lord Brandon was that the burden of showing cause why a charging order nisi should not be made absolute is on the judgment debtor. Now, *Roberts Petroleum Ltd v Kenny* was a case about a petrol station. The question of a home

did not arise, nor did the question of the interests of a person other than the judgment
a debtor arise. And it is clear that Lord Brandon was not considering the sort of question
that is posed in this case.

So far as this case is concerned, I am dealing with a wife who is a person interested in
the matrimonial home and, in my judgment, I have to consider in deciding whether
there should be a charging order all the circumstances of the case. That means I have to
consider the circumstances of the wife and the circumstances of the creditor. I have a
b discretion whether a charging order should be made, having regard to all the
circumstances. In the type of circumstances which exist in this case, I do not think I am
helped by considering whether there is any presumption one way or another, particularly
having regard to the wording of s 1(5).

The most important distinction between this case and *Hegerty's* case is that in *Hegerty's*
case the husband had created a valid equitable charge of his beneficial interests in the
c home in favour of the creditor. It was because of the charge on the home which the
creditor thought he had that the money was lent. This, in my judgment, was a
compelling consideration which does not exist in this case. Bingham J was also swayed
by the prospect that in an application under s 30 of the Law of Property Act 1925, by the
creditor for the possession of the house, the wife would be given an opportunity for her
personal and family position to be investigated.

d   I have been referred to *Re Holliday (a bankrupt), ex p trustee of the bankrupt v The bankrupt*
[1980] 3 All ER 385 at 397, [1981] 1 Ch 405 at 424, where Buckley LJ said:

> 'Balancing the interest of the creditors and the interest of the wife, burdened, as I
> say, with the obligation to provide a home for the three children of the marriage, in
> my view the right attitude for the court to adopt is that the house should not be sold
> at the present juncture.'

e
This case might give ground for thinking that under s 30 an order might ordinarily be
made postponing a creditor until circumstances were such that the wife could reasonably
be expected to give up her home. This is a type of order which is familiar in the Family
Division, although it is often criticised for difficulties that arise in the future. It is known
as a Mesher v Mesher order and provides for the wife to keep the home as a home for
f herself and the children until the children are grown up and the home then to be sold
and the proceeds divided in whatever proportion is appropriate: see *Mesher v Mesher and
Hall* (1973) [1980] 1 All ER 126.

However, in a later case of *Re Lowrie (a bankrupt), ex p trustee of the bankrupt v The
bankrupt* [1981] 3 All ER 353 the Divisional court of the Chancery Division made it quite
clear that *Holliday's* case was an exceptional case and Walton J said (at 356): 'One can
g scarcely, I think, imagine a more exceptional set of facts, and the court gave effect to
those exceptional facts.' And in *Lowrie's* case the wife was given three months to find
another home and to leave.

If it is right, in accordance with s 1(5) of the 1979 Act, that all the circumstances of the
case are to be taken into account before a charging order is made, I cannot help feeling
that leaving a decision until an application under s 30 of the 1925 Act is made is failing
h to do justice to a wife. After all, under s 30 the only real question which the court is
concerned with is how long is the wife to continue to have possession and not whether
there should be a sale at all.

In considering the circumstances in the case, one has to consider what are the wife's
rights and how they compare with the creditor's rights. At common law a wife had a
right to be maintained and housed during the marriage. This was subject to certain
j exceptions. This right is probably now a mutual right, but the right still exists and in
certain circumstances can be enforced. It arises from the status of marriage itself. After
divorce the wife has a right to be provided for in relation to capital and income in
accordance with an order of the court. The question is: how are these rights to be
balanced against the rights of a creditor to be paid his debt? The statute itself gives the
answer: the answer is that all the circumstances of the case have to be taken into account

and the judge has to come to a conclusion as to what is just in the circumstances. It has to be remembered that refusing to make a charging order absolute does not discharge the debt owed by the debtor. The creditor may have other ways open to him. On the other hand the granting of a charging order absolute may mean the family losing their home and not being able to rehouse themselves. This may, in some cases, be a factor which has to be taken into account.

The registrar, on hearing this application, referred to a case in the Court of Appeal, *Mullard v Mullard* (1981) 3 FLR 330. The registrar, having referred to *Mullard*'s case, drew this conclusion:

'If, on the other hand, a creditor is simply owed money and is not formally before the court and, in particular, where the husband does not ask to be preferred, the court will prefer the wife and children to the creditor as in *Mullard*.'

I have to say that I do not agree with the conclusion drawn by the registrar. Nor do I think that it can be derived from reading *Mullard*'s case. What Balcombe J said in giving the leading judgment in the Court of Appeal was (at 332): '. . . it does not seem to me right that the court, exercising this particular jurisdiction, should necessarily prefer the claims of the creditors to those of the wife and children . . .' In my judgment the decision in *Mullard v Mullard* is quite neutral in relation to the claims of the wife and the creditor and leaves the discretion which is granted under s 1(5) of the 1979 Act undisturbed.

The registrar, having come to the conclusion he did, did not go on to consider all the circumstances of the case as he might otherwise have done. It accordingly falls to me to deal with that aspect.

The creditor has not filed evidence concerning his circumstances, although they are referred to in particular in the 1979 Act. He has had an opportunity during the course of the proceedings before me to file evidence, but has not done so. The factors of importance in coming to a decision seem to me to be these. In favour of the creditor: first, he is owed a debt and he ought to be able to enforce it against any asset of the husband; second, if the partnership had prospered the wife and children would have benefited, and, it is said on his behalf, if the opposite happens and the business fails the wife must bear the loss as well as everybody else. In support of the wife's case the following points are made. First, she has been cheated once already by her husband in relation to the charge to the bank. Second, she was not a party to the debt incurred by her husband and never agreed to the debt being incurred. Third, the creditor could, if he had wished, have asked for the debt to be made a charge on the house before he advanced the money. He would then be in the same position as the bank is now. Fourth, the creditor was the partner of the husband and knew of the husband's wife and children and home. Fifth, the creditor had notice of the divorce petition on 15 January 1981, before he served his writ in the Queen's Bench Division. Sixth, the wife filed her notice of application for transfer of property before the writ. Seventh, it is said that if the wife had been able to register her claim for a transfer of property as lis pendens on the land charges register it would have taken priority. The land concerned in this case, however, is registered land and it is not open to her to make any entry on the register as she is a joint owner. This point seems to me to have very little substance, but I mention it only because it has been made. Eighth, the effect of a charging order absolute will be to transfer the whole of the husband's interest in the home to the creditor, leaving the wife with nothing to claim against in the divorce proceedings. The creditor, on the other hand, if the charging order absolute is discharged, still has his debt. The creditor, it is said, could if he wished have applied in the s 24 proceedings. He chose not to. He could have asked in the s 24 proceedings that only part of the husband's interests should be transferred to the wife. He could have asked, alternatively, that some form of settlement which might protect his interest should be made, e g a Mesher v Mesher type of order, as I have already indicated. And, last, it is said on behalf of the wife that the figures indicate that if the charging order absolute stands she will not have enough money left to rehouse herself and the children.

In the circumstances of this case I have come to the conclusion that the case for a postponing the charging order in favour of any order the wife might get in the divorce proceedings was overwhelming and I have come to the conclusion that the registrar made the right order. I accordingly dismiss this appeal.

Appeal dismissed.

b Solicitors: *Cecil Altman & Co* (for the creditor); *E W Parkes & Wilshire*, Barnet (for the wife); *Pollards*, Radlett (for the husband).

Bebe Chua   Barrister.

---

c # Thames Guaranty Ltd v Campbell and others

COURT OF APPEAL, CIVIL DIVISION
STEPHENSON, MAY AND SLADE LJJ
2, 3, 6, 23 FEBRUARY 1984

d *Equity – Charge – Creation of equitable charge – Joint tenancy – Borrower agreeing to create charge over property as security for loan – Borrower joint tenant of property – Other joint tenant not consenting to creation of charge – Lender making advance on assumption that borrower sole proprietor of property – Borrower depositing title documents with lender as security without other joint tenant's consent – Whether equitable charge created over borrower's beneficial interest in the property – Whether other joint tenant entitled to recover title documents from lender.*

e In January 1973 the husband and the wife jointly purchased a home but before registration of the transfer to them as joint tenants was complete the plaintiff company agreed with the husband by letter to grant him a loan. The letter stated that 'This facility is to be secured by a first charge on your property'. At that time the company did not know and could not have known that the transfer of the property was to be to the f husband and the wife as joint tenants. On 1 June 1973, after registration was completed, the documents of title were sent to the company by the husband's solicitors on his instructions. The wife did not consent either to the charging of the property or to the deposit of the title documents with the company. On two further occasions in 1975 the company agreed to renew the loan and increase the principal sum. On each occasion the letter offering the loan to the husband stated that it would 'continue to be secured by a g first charge on the property' and the letters acknowledged that the husband and wife were the joint owners. The husband subsequently became bankrupt and the company claimed against him for unpaid principal and interest, contending that it was a secured creditor by virtue of an equitable charge granted in its favour over the husband's interest in the property. The wife counterclaimed for the return of the title documents and contended that the company did not have a valid charge. The judge held (i) that the court h would not exercise its discretion by ordering the husband to partly perform his promise by creating an equitable charge over his beneficial interest, even though that promise had been supported by consideration moving from the company, because to do so would prejudice the wife as a third party by making her vulnerable to an order for the sale of the property on the company's application under s 30[a] of the Law of Property Act 1925, and (ii) that no equitable charge had been created by the husband over his beneficial

j _____

a Section 30 provides: 'If the trustees for sale refuse to sell or to exercise any of the powers conferred by either of the last two sections, or any requisite consent cannot be obtained, any person interested may apply to the court for a vesting order or other order for giving effect to the proposed transaction or for an order directing the trustees for sale to give effect thereto, and the court may make such order as it thinks fit.'

interest. Accordingly the judge ordered on the wife's counterclaim that the company deliver up to the husband and the wife the land certificate and that the charges register *a* be rectified by the cancellation of the notice of deposit. The company appealed.

Held – The appeal would be dismissed for the following reasons—

(1) Although it was a well-established principle of equity that where a person represented in the course of concluding a contract that he could grant title to a certain property, or was entitled to a certain interest in that property, the other party could *b* obtain an order compelling him to grant that title or interest which in fact he had, when considering whether to make an order for partial performance the court was required to have regard to the interests of third parties. However, the mere fact that such an order would give the chargee a locus standi to apply for a sale of the property under s 30 of the 1925 Act would not of itself necessarily deprive an innocent chargee of the remedy of partial performance. On the facts, an order for partial performance was not the *c* appropriate remedy because, in particular, (a) the effect of an order for partial performance in favour of the company would clearly cause real and substantial prejudice to the wife because there was a real possibility that the company could then intervene in the third party proceedings and successfully resist the order for rectification to which the wife was otherwise entitled, thereby defeating her claim to the entire beneficial interest in the property (as opposed to a severed one-half interest), and (b) on the evidence the wife had *d* not been made aware that the company had been granted rights in the property until about 1976 whereas by that date, as the facility letters of 1976 showed, the company had acquired full knowledge that the wife was at least a joint owner of the property but had taken no effective steps to make her aware of the transactions with her husband concerning the property. It followed that the judge was right to refuse to exercise his discretion ordering the husband to partly perform his promise by creating an equitable *e* charge over his own beneficial interest (see p 595 *j* to p 596 *a*, p 598 *h j* and p 599 *c* to p 600 *b* and *h j*, post); dictum of Lord Langdale MR in *Thomas v Dering* [1835–42] All ER Rep at 717 and *Cedar Holdings Ltd v Green* [1979] 3 All ER 117 applied.

(2) Furthermore, even if the husband had had a beneficial interest in the property, he would not have been entitled to part with the land certificate without the consent of the wife as joint owner of the legal estate. Accordingly, the wife had at all times been entitled *f* to request the return of the land certificate to the joint custody of herself and the husband (see p 600 *c* to *e* and *h j*, post).

Decision of Mann J [1984] 1 All ER 144 affirmed.

Notes

For equitable charges and mortgages, see 28 Halsbury's Laws (4th edn) paras 509–512, *g* 515, and for cases on the subject, see 35 Digest (Reissue) 54–57, 355–381.

For severance of joint tenancies, see 39 Halsbury's Laws (4th edn) paras 534–541, and for cases on the subject, see 38 Digest (Reissue) 606–612, 5071–5137.

For cases on joint tenancies, see 38 Digest (Reissue) 596–606, 4940–5067.

For the Law of Property Act 1925, s 30, see 27 Halsbury's Statutes (3rd edn) 385.

h

Cases referred to in judgment

Bailey (a bankrupt), Re, ex p the trustee of the bankrupt v Bailey [1977] 2 All ER 26, [1977] 1 WLR 278, DC.
Cedar Holdings Ltd v Green [1979] 3 All ER 117, [1981] Ch 129, [1979] 3 WLR 31, CA.
Colebrook's Conveyances, Re, Taylor v Taylor [1973] 1 All ER 132, [1972] 1 WLR 1397.
Craddock Bros Ltd v Hunt [1923] 2 Ch 136, [1923] All ER Rep 394, CA.   *j*
Debtor, Re a, ex p the trustee v Solomon [1966] 3 All ER 255, [1967] Ch 573, [1967] 2 WLR 172.
Elias v Mitchell [1972] 2 All ER 153, [1972] Ch 652, [1972] 2 WLR 740.
First National Securities Ltd v Hegerty [1984] 1 All ER 139.
Harman v Glencross [1984] 2 All ER 577.

a *Holliday (a bankrupt), Re, ex p the trustee of the bankrupt v The bankrupt* [1980] 3 All ER 385, [1981] Ch 405, [1981] 2 WLR 996, CA.

Shaw v Foster (1872) LR 5 HL 321.

Thomas v Dering (1837) 1 Keen 729, [1835–42] All ER Rep 711, 48 ER 488.

Turner (a bankrupt), Re, ex p the trustee of the bankrupt v Turner [1975] 1 All ER 5, [1974] 1 WLR 1556.

Wallis v Simmonds (Builders) Ltd, Re [1974] 1 All ER 561, [1974] 1 WLR 391.

b *Williams & Glyn's Bank Ltd v Boland, Williams & Glyn's Bank Ltd v Brown* [1980] 2 All ER 408, [1981] AC 487, [1980] 3 WLR 138, HL.

Wilson v Wilson [1969] 3 All ER 945, [1969] 1 WLR 1470.

Appeal

By a writ dated 26 October 1976 the plaintiffs, Thames Guaranty Ltd, a company in
c liquidation, brought an action against the first defendant, Theophillus Count Campbell, claiming repayment of principal and interest amounting to £10,451·83 on a loan made by the plaintiffs, which loan was guaranteed by the second defendant, Likemarts Ltd, on the authority of the third defendant, Michael Jonathan Gillis, a director of the second defendant. By an order dated 13 April 1981 Laurel May Campbell was added as fourth defendant and given leave to counterclaim against the plaintiffs for delivery up to her of
d the certificate of title relating to a property at 10 Holmewood Gardens, London SW2, purchased by Mr and Mrs Campbell and for cancellation of a charge in favour of the plaintiffs registered against the title. The second and third defendants settled the claim against them and took no part in the proceedings. By a third party notice dated 13 May 1982 directed to the fifth defendant, the Official Receiver, as trustee in bankruptcy of the estate of Mr Campbell, Mrs Campbell sought the following questions to be determined
e as between either the plaintiffs or herself and the Official Receiver, namely (i) whether the transfer of the freehold of the property ought to be rectified by deleting the declaration of beneficial interest therein contained, and (ii) the extent of her beneficial interest in the property. By an order dated 12 May 1983 Mann J ([1984] 1 All ER 144) ordered (i) that Mr Campbell pay to the plaintiffs £34,362·44, (ii) on Mrs Campbell's counterclaim that the plaintiffs deliver up to Mrs Campbell the land certificate of the
f title to the property and (iii) that the charges register be rectified by the cancellation of the notice of deposit of the certificate registered on 30 April 1974. The plaintiffs appealed against so much of the judge's order as ordered the plaintiffs to deliver up to Mrs Campbell the land certificate and as ordered the charges register to be rectified. Mrs Campbell and the Official Receiver took no part in the appeal. The facts are set out in the judgment of the court.

g *J G Boggis* for the plaintiffs.
A V B Bartlett for Mrs Campbell.

Cur adv vult

h 23 February. The following judgment of the court was delivered.

SLADE LJ. This is the judgment of the court on an appeal by the plaintiffs in an action, Thames Guaranty Ltd, which is now in liquidation, from part of an order of Mann J ([1984] 1 All ER 144) made on 12 May 1983. There are five persons named as defendants to the action, namely Mr Theophillus Count Campbell, Likemarts Ltd, Mr Michael
j Jonathan Gillis, Mrs Laurel May Campbell (the fourth defendant), who is the wife of the first defendant, and the Official Receiver as his trustee in bankruptcy.

The procedural history of the case is a somewhat tangled one. Though this might not appear clearly from the documentation, the real issue on this appeal, in the events which have happened, is whether the plaintiffs are entitled to an equitable charge on the beneficial interest, if any, of Mr Campbell under the statutory trust for sale affecting a property known as 10 Holmewood Gardens, London SW2. This is the matrimonial home of Mr and Mrs Campbell and the freehold title to it has since 1973 been registered in their joint names at HM Land Registry.

The plaintiffs formerly carried on business as bankers. Between August 1972 and March 1976 they granted four overdraft facilities to Mr Campbell. These arrangements involved, inter alia, the deposit by Mr Campbell of the land certificate for 10 Holmewood Gardens with the plaintiffs in June 1973. This deposit was made without the consent of Mrs Campbell, the co-proprietor, and she did not even become aware of it until some years later. The plaintiffs, however, assert that the arrangements have created a charge in equity on the beneficial interest (if any) of Mr Campbell in the property.

On 30 April 1974 the plaintiffs registered a notice of deposit of land certificate at HM Land Registry. The plaintiffs also obtained security for Mr Campbell's borrowing by two guarantees given by Likemarts in 1975, both of which were signed on its behalf by Mr Gillis.

On 22 March 1976 the plaintiffs went into liquidation and a liquidator was appointed. By that date Mr Campbell's indebtedness to the plaintiffs had risen to about £9,500.

The pleadings

In November 1976 the plaintiffs instituted procedings against Mr Campbell and Likemarts, claiming recovery of the sum said to be due to them. Mr Campbell, in his defence to the action, pleaded, inter alia, that, in depositing the deeds to the property with the plaintiffs, he did so merely for safe keeping, and further had no authority to bind his wife. He counterclaimed for the return of the deeds. Likemarts, in its defence, pleaded, inter alia, that he had no authority to give the guarantees. The result of these claims and cross-claims was that in 1977 Mr Gillis was joined as a third defendant, and the plaintiffs sought damages against him for breach of warranty of authority.

On 16 February 1977 a receiving order was made against Mr Campbell. On 13 July 1977 he was adjudicated bankrupt, and, as we have said, the Official Receiver is his trustee in bankruptcy. In April 1981 an order was made for the amendment of the writ by adding the name of Mrs Campbell as fourth defendant and giving her liberty to counterclaim against the plaintiffs. In June 1981 she served a counterclaim alleging, inter alia, that the purchase of the property had been effected with funds entirely provided by her, and that she and Mr Campbell held it as legal joint tenants on a resulting trust in her favour. Alternatively, she asserted that if, contrary to her contention, Mr Campbell shared the beneficial interest with her, he had no authority from her to deposit the land certificate with the plaintiffs. The only relief sought by the prayer to this counterclaim was (1) an order that the plaintiffs should deliver up to Mrs Campbell the land certificate of the property and (2) an order that the charges register of the relevant title should be rectified by the cancellation of the notice of deposit of land certificate registered on 30 April 1974.

In October 1981 the plaintiffs served a defence to Mrs Campbell's counterclaim. In this pleading, inter alia, they denied the alleged resulting trust in favour of Mrs Campbell. They further alleged that Mr Campbell had the requisite authority to deposit the land certificate with them. Further or alternatively they also pleaded:

> '. . . by the deposit of the Land Certificate with the Plaintiffs on or about the 5th day of June 1973, the 1st Defendants [sic] mortgaged and/or charged his interest in the said property. In the premises the Plaintiffs are entitled to retain the said Land Certificate.'

This plea, as will appear, in our judgment involved a non sequitur.

In May 1982, Mrs Campbell was given leave to issue a third party notice to the Official Receiver, as trustee in bankruptcy of Mr Campbell. It was ordered that this notice should stand as a statement of claim against the Official Receiver, who became the fifth defendant to the action. By this notice, Mrs Campbell required that—

> 'the following questions or issues, viz:—(1) whether the transfer of the freehold

a   of the said property ought to be rectified by deleting the declaration of beneficial interest therein contained, and (2) the extent of the Fourth Defendant's beneficial interest in the said property, should be determined not only as between the Plaintiffs and the Fourth Defendant, but also as between either or both of them and yourself.'

This reference to rectification requires explanation. The transfer of the freehold to Mr and Mrs Campbell made on 2 February 1973 was thereby expressed to be made to them as 'joint tenants in law and equity'. The claim to rectification thus sought deletion of the
b   words 'and equity'.

The hearings before Mann J and his judgments
    On 9 May 1983 the hearing of the action began before Mann J. It is common ground that, in opening the case on behalf of the plaintiffs, their counsel told the judge that there were three main issues to be decided in the proceedings, namely, first, the plaintiffs'
c   claim against Mr Campbell, second, Mrs Campbell's claims against the plaintiffs and, third, Mrs Campbell's claims against the Official Receiver. He told the judge that the principal issue had become whether the plaintiffs had acquired an equitable charge on Mr Campbell's beneficial interest in the property, and that, while the Official Receiver had written a letter saying that he would not contest the claims of the plaintiffs to be secured creditors to this extent, such claims would be resisted by Mrs Campbell. He
d   further explained to the judge that the issues involved in Mrs Campbell's claims against the Official Receiver were of importance to the plaintiffs, because, even if Mrs Campbell succeeded in her contention that no charge had already been created in favour of the plaintiffs, this would not prevent the plaintiffs from obtaining a charging order over any beneficial interest in the property to which Mr Campbell might be entitled. The trial then proceeded against Mr Campbell and Mrs Campbell, with none of the other
e   defendants taking part in the proceedings. The claims against Likemarts and Mr Gillis had been disposed of by way of compromise.

    The judge heard, first, evidence relating to the first two of the three issues to which the plaintiffs' counsel had referred. The hearing of this evidence concluded on 10 May 1983. On 12 May 1983 he gave judgment on the two issues. As to the plaintiffs' claim against Mr Campbell, he found that Mr Campbell's indebtedness as at 9 May 1983, when
f   the hearing began, had risen to £34,362·44. He accordingly gave judgment for the plaintiffs against Mr Campbell for this sum. No appeal from this part of the judgment is before us.

    The judge in his judgment then proceeded to consider Mrs Campbell's counterclaim against the plaintiffs. He explained that this counterclaim and the plaintiffs' defence to it had caused an argument whether the plaintiffs had an equitable charge over Mr
g   Campbell's beneficial interest in the property. Most of the rest of his judgment was devoted to considering this issue. His eventual conclusion was that no equitable charge had been created by Mr Campbell over his beneficial interest ([1984] 1 All ER 144 at 152–153):

        'Mrs Campbell is therefore successful on the issue with the plaintiff ... The
h   delivery up [of the land certificate] to [Mr and Mrs Campbell] as trustees must follow from what I have said.'

Accordingly, on Mrs Campbell's counterclaim, he ordered that the plaintiffs should deliver up to Mr and Mrs Campbell the land certificate and that the charges register should be rectified by the cancellation of the notice of deposit. He concluded this part of his judgment with these words:
j

        'The notice of deposit of the land certificate seems in any event to have been misconceived as the plaintiff does not now rely on s 66 of the Land Registration Act 1925. I would, however, welcome [counsel for Mrs Campbell's] observations as to my powers under s 82. After hearing those observations I shall hear [Mrs Campbell's] claim against [the Official Receiver]. Those proceedings relate to the extent of [Mrs

Campbell's] beneficial interest in 10 Holmewood Gardens. It must be a consequence of my decision that the plaintiff is not entitled to intervene in those proceedings.' *a*

There then followed a colloquy between the judge and counsel, in the course of which submissions were made in relation to s 82 and the form of the order. Before it had ended, the plaintiffs' counsel had asked for a stay of the order pending appeal. In due course this matter was dealt with by Mrs Campbell's solicitors giving certain undertakings.

The plaintiffs' counsel then withdrew and took no further part in the proceedings. He did not specifically request the judge, in the light of the contemplated appeal by the *b* plaintiffs, to reconsider his decision that they were not entitled to intervene in the third party proceedings. In the plaintiffs' absence the judge accordingly went on to hear evidence and argument in the third party proceedings. At their conclusion on the same day, 12 May 1983, he gave judgment in those proceedings. Counsel for Mrs Campbell has helpfully supplied us with his notes of this judgment. Though these have not been seen or corrected by the judge, we know of no reason to doubt their substantial accuracy. *c* From them it appears that the judge expressed himself as satisfied that he had the jurisdiction to make the order for rectification of the transfer sought by Mrs Campbell, on the authority of *Wilson v Wilson* [1969] 3 All ER 945, [1969] 1 WLR 1470 and *Re Colebrook's Conveyances, Taylor v Taylor* [1973] 1 All ER 132, [1972] 1 WLR 1397. He accepted Mrs Campbell's evidence that she had provided the entire purchase price of the property. He inferred that, while Mr and Mrs Campbell had agreed that the property *d* should belong to her, the solicitors who dealt with the transfer on their behalf had been instructed to put it into their joint names, as a matter of courtesy to Mr Campbell, but had been told nothing about the beneficial interests. The solicitors, in the judge's view, probably assumed that they were to be joint tenants in equity, as well as in law, and this was how the words 'in equity' came to be erroneously inserted in the transfer. The judge accordingly ordered that the transfer of the property into the joint names of Mr and Mrs *e* Campbell should be rectified by the deletion of the words 'and equity', and further declared that the whole beneficial interest in the property was, and had been since the date of the transfer, vested in Mrs Campbell.

The estoppel point

The plaintiffs now appeal from the judgment in the main action. It would appear that *f* unless and until the order for rectification of the transfer were set aside they would not be entitled to rely on the words 'and equity' which appeared in the original form of transfer for the purpose of supporting their claim that Mr Campbell had a beneficial interest in the property, which he was at liberty to charge. For, once an order has been made for rectification of a written instrument, 'it is to be read as if it had been originally drawn in its rectified form': see *Craddock Bros Ltd v Hunt* [1923] 2 Ch 136 at 151, 160, *g* [1923] All ER Rep 394 at 402, 405 per Lord Sterndale MR and Warrington LJ.

Nevertheless, prima facie, the plaintiffs, if they succeed on the present appeal, will still be free to establish, if they can, by evidence other than the (now neutral) wording of the transfer itself, that Mr Campbell had a beneficial interest in the property which he could effectively charge to them. Prima facie, at least, the declaration made by the judge, having been made in proceedings in which they were not permitted to intervene, is not *h* binding on them.

Counsel Mrs Campbell, however, has submitted that, in view of the course which the proceedings took in the court below, the plaintiffs by their counsel implicitly agreed to be bound by the decision of the judge in the third party proceedings, and by virtue of that decision are accordingly estopped from asserting that Mr Campbell ever had a beneficial interest in the property which he could charge in their favour. This was one of *j* his alternative grounds for submitting that the plaintiffs can have no charge of the nature which they assert. It is convenient to deal with this particular submission straight away.

With the wisdom of hindsight, we think that before the plaintiffs' counsel retired from the court at the conclusion of the judgment in the main action it might have been better if everyone concerned had paused to consider the practical consequences (for

example the risk of duplicated hearings) which might have ensued in the event of a
a successful appeal by the plaintiffs in the main action, if the third party proceedings were
heard and determined in the plaintiffs' absence. Nevertheless, we think that the plaintiffs
can be estopped in the manner now suggested only if their counsel by his conduct
represented to the judge and the other parties that, *whether or not any* appeal by them on
the issue of the charge was successful, the plaintiffs would be content to abide by his
decision on the questions of the beneficial ownership and rectification after a hearing
b conducted in their absence. It is not suggested that any explicit representation of this
nature was made; and, having heard counsel for the plaintiffs, we have no doubt whatever
that he did not intend to make any implicit representation of this nature. He and counsel
for Mrs Campbell, who also appeared in the court below, have given us the benefit of
their recollections as to the course of the proceedings. Having heard them, we do not on
the whole think that the plaintiffs' counsel could reasonably have been understood as
c committing his clients to this extent; and, at the time, counsel for Mrs Campbell himself
clearly did not so understand him, since he has very frankly told us that the estoppel
point occurred to him only some time after the judge had disposed of the case.

In the circumstances, though counsel for Mrs Campbell was quite entitled to raise it in
the interests of his client, we think that the argument based on estoppel is ill-founded,
and does not dispose of this appeal.

d
The other issues on this appeal

By their notice of appeal in its original form, the plaintiffs sought, inter alia, orders—

'(a) that the fourth Defendant's [Mrs Campbell's] counterclaim be dismissed and
(b) that insofar as the same may be necessary it be declared that the first Defendants
[Mr Campbell's] beneficial interest in the property situate and known as 10
e   Holmewood Gardens, London SW2 is validly charged to secure the first Defendants
indebtedness to the Plaintiff . . .'

However, at a very early stage in his opening of the appeal, counsel for the plaintiffs
accepted that on any footing he would have great difficulties in asking for dismissal of
Mrs Campbell's counterclaim. Even if the plaintiffs have an equitable charge on Mr
Campbell's beneficial interest (if any) in the property, this seems to us, for reasons which
f we will elaborate later in this judgment, to be no answer to her claim that she is entitled
to have the title deeds transferred into the joint names of herself and her husband and to
rectification of the charges register by the cancellation of the notice of deposit.

Accordingly, in our judgment it could be said that, in proceeding to decide the
question whether or not the plaintiffs have a charge of this nature, the judge was deciding
more than the parties were strictly entitled to ask him to decide, having regard to the
g form of the relief sought by their pleadings. Nevertheless, this question was clearly a
highly relevant one for the parties. For if Mr Campbell had a beneficial interest in the
property, and the plaintiffs were correct in asserting that they had taken an effective
charge on that beneficial interest, they would have the right, as 'persons interested', to
apply to the court for an order for sale of the property under s 30 of the Law of Property
h Act 1925.

At the start of this appeal, counsel on both sides expressed the hope that, despite any
procedural irregularities, we should proceed to determine the question whether or not
the plaintiffs are entitled to the alleged charge, as did the judge. In these circumstances
we permitted amendment of the statement of claim so as to include a new head of relief
claimed by the prayer, namely—

j   'a declaration that the liabilities of the first Defendant [Mr Campbell] to the
Plaintiff are secured by way of equitable charge over the first Defendant's beneficial
interest, if any, in [the property],'

and equivalent amendment to the body of the statement of claim. We also permitted
amendment of the notice of appeal so as to include a request that the judge's order be
varied, inter alia, by the inclusion of a declaration of this nature.

Thus, the substantial question at issue before this court, as before the judge, is whether the plaintiffs have any charge on Mr Campbell's beneficial interest, *if any*. Subsequent references in this judgment to such beneficial interest must accordingly be read as if the words 'if any' were added, where the context so requires.   *a*

The history of the overdraft facilities

At this point it is necessary to set out in somewhat greater detail the history of the overdraft facilities and the various facts on which the plaintiffs rely in support of their   *b* claim to a charge on Mr Campbell's beneficial interest in the property. We will take them largely verbatim from the judge's very careful judgment.

On 24 August 1972 the plaintiffs granted their first overdraft facility to Mr Campbell, but its terms are not material. On 11 October 1972 Mr and Mrs Campbell purchased a leasehold interest in the house for £4,000; that purchase was completed on 15 November and the transfer was to Mr and Mrs Campbell jointly. Shortly thereafter the ground landlord was approached with a view to his selling the freehold reversion. He was willing   *c* to do so for the sum of £975 and contracts were exchanged on or about 19 December.

The solicitors acting for Mr and Mrs Campbell were a firm called Osmond Gaunt & Rose who, on 12 January 1973, received a cheque from Mr Campbell. On presentation that cheque was not met. On 22 January Osmond Gaunt & Rose had a telephone conversation with the plaintiffs. The terms of that conversation are unknown but, in   *d* consequence of it, the solicitors wrote to the plaintiffs in the following terms, on 23 January 1973:

'Dear Sirs,

Re: 10 Holmewood Gardens, S.W.2.

Theophillus Count Campbell   *e*

We refer to our telephone conversation of the 22nd January when you informed us that on presentation of Mr. Campbell's cheque for £900, this cheque would be met subject to our confirming that we will hold the Title Deeds of the above property to your order. We confirm that we have instructions from our client to hold the Title Deeds relating to the Freehold and Leasehold interests of the above property to your order, and you may accept this letter as our undertaking so to do.'   *f*

A cheque was duly met and the purchase was completed on 2 February.

The transfer was to Mr and Mrs Campbell as 'Joint tenants in law and equity' and in that transfer they declared that the leasehold interest vested in them should merge and be extinguished in the freehold title. Shortly thereafter the documents of title were sent to the Land Registry for a first registration. The title number is SGL 157598 and the proprietors are Mr and Mrs Campbell.   *g*

On 3 April 1974 the plaintiffs wrote to Osmond Gaunt & Rose in these terms:

'Dear Sirs,

Re: 10 Holmewood Gardens, S.W.2.

Theophillus Count Campbell   *h*

In a recent discussion with our mutual client we have agreed to provide him with a temporary advance facility secured by a first charge on his property at the above address. Accordingly we would appreciate receiving the Title Deeds relating to this property in order that our interest may be properly registered. Perhaps you would be good enough to contact Mr. Campbell regarding the contents of this letter a copy of which has been sent to him.'   *j*

The reply from Osmond Gaunt & Rose was in these terms:

'We are in receipt of your letter of the 3rd April. We are awaiting completion of Registration of the Title by the Land Registry. We are hoping to receive Land Certificate shortly and this will be forwarded to you immediately on receipt.'

On the same day, that is on 9 April 1973, the solicitors wrote to Mr Campbell in these
a terms:

'Dear Mr. Campbell,
Re: 10 *Holmewood Gardens, S.W.2.*
Further to my telephone conversation with you of the 6th April when you
confirmed to me that the Title Deeds of the above property were to be sent to
Thames Guaranty Limited, I enclose herewith a copy of a letter which I have today
b written to them.'

On 24 May 1973 the plaintiffs granted to Mr Campbell a second overdraft facility
which, so far as material, was in these terms:

'Dear Mr Campbell,
In order to place your facility at this office on a regular basis this writing indicates
c the terms of the accommodation granted. Amount: £5,000. Term: Not to exceed 3
months from date of this letter . . . Interest Rate . . . Security: This facility is to be
secured by a first charge on your property at 10, Holmewood Gardens, London,
S.W.2, registered in favour of Thames Guaranty Limited. To complete our
documentation on this transaction I wonder if you would be good enough to sign
the attached copy of this letter and return it to me as soon as possible . . .'

d
That letter was signed by Mr Campbell.
As at May 1973 the plaintiffs were clearly under the impression that Mr Campbell was
the sole owner of the property (which in their letter of 24 May 1973 they described as
'your property') and indeed, by signing that letter, Mr Campbell implicitly represented
that he was its sole owner. In our judgment the proper inference from the correspondence
is that the plaintiffs envisaged that the contemplated first charge on the property could
e and would be created pursuant to s 66 of the Land Registration Act 1925 by a deposit of
the land certificate, and that this deposit would be protected by an entry in the register
of a notice of deposit. Furthermore, Mr Campbell's solicitors, in our opinion, encouraged
them in this belief by the form of their correspondence.
Section 66 of the Land Registration Act 1925 provides:

f 'The proprietor of any registered land or charge may, subject to the overriding
interests, if any, to any entry to the contrary on the register, and to any estates,
interests, charges, or rights registered or protected on the register at the date of the
deposit, create a lien on the registered land or charge by deposit of the land certificate
or charge certificate; and such lien shall, subject as aforesaid, be equivalent to a lien
created in the case of unregistered land by the deposit of documents of title or of the
g mortgage deed by an owner entitled for his own benefit to the registered estate, or a
mortgagee beneficially entitled to the mortgage, as the case may be.'

The nature of a lien created by the deposit of title deeds is described thus in *Coote on
Mortgages* (9th edn, 1927) vol 1, p 86 in a passage cited by Templeman J in *Re Wallis &
Simmonds (Builders) Ltd* [1974] 1 All ER 561 at 564, [1974] 1 WLR 391 at 395 and by the
h judge in the present case ([1984] 1 All ER 144 at 152):

'A deposit of title deeds by the owner of freeholds or leaseholds with his creditor
for the purpose of securing either a debt antecedently due, or a sum of money
advanced at the time of the deposit, operates as an equitable mortgage or charge, by
virtue of which the depositee acquires, not merely the right of holding the deeds
until the debt is paid, but also an equitable interest in the land itself. A mere delivery
j of the deeds will have this operation without any express agreement, whether in
writing or oral, as to the conditions or purpose of the delivery, as the Court would
infer the intent and agreement to create a security from the relation of debtor and
creditor subsisting between the parties, unless the contrary were shown; and the
delivery would be sufficient part performance of such agreement to take the case
out of the statute [ie out of s 40 of the Law of Property Act 1925].'

We might add that in the case of registered land provision is made by the Land Registration Rules 1925, SR & O 1925/1093, r 239 for entry on the register of a notice of *a* a deposit, which will operate as a caution.

In writing their letters of 3 April and 24 May 1973, the plaintiffs plainly contemplated that Mr Campbell was to be the sole proprietor of the land within the meaning of s 66, and, we think, that the charge would be created by means of the convenient machinery made available by s 66.

On 1 June 1973, in accordance with their undertakings, Osmond Gaunt & Rose sent *b* the land certificate and the preregistration deeds to the plaintiffs, and informed Mr Campbell of it on the same day.

If the plaintiffs, or their legal advisers, had been diligent in the protection of their interests, they would, on receipt of the land certificate, have appreciated, first, that Mr Campbell was not the sole proprietor of the land, but that he and Mrs Campbell were joint proprietors, and, second, that Mrs Campbell's concurrence was necessary if an *c* effective charge on the property was to be created by the combined operation of the deposit of the land certificate and s 66 of the Land Registration Act 1925. It seems, however, that the plaintiffs did not appreciate either of these points until much later. Nearly eleven months later, on 29 April 1974, a solicitor acting on their behalf gave notice of deposit of land certificate to the Land Registry on the footing that an effective charge on the property itself had been created under s 66, and this notice, as we have *d* said, was registered in the charges register on 30 April 1974.

As the judge found, there is no doubt that Mr Campbell himself authorised deposit of the documents of title with the Land Registry. However, the plaintiffs concede that Mrs Campbell neither consented to the deposit nor even knew of it until some years later. She asked for the documents to be sent to her on 17 April 1976, but that request was refused. *e*

Meantime, on 13 January 1975, the plaintiffs granted to Mr Campbell a third facility, which, so far as material, was in these terms:

'Dear Mr. Campbell,
    In order to regularize the facility originally granted on 24 May, 1973 and subsequently renewed, we write to indicate the terms on which we are willing to renew this facility. Amount: £6,062·31. Term: To be repaid in full, together with *f* all interest accrued, by 31st December 1975. Interest Rate . . . Security: This facility will continue to be secured by a first charge on the property owned by you and your wife at 10, Holmewood Gardens, London S.W.2, registered in favour of ourselves. Please be good enough to sign and return the attached duplicate of this letter as confirmation of your agreement to the terms contained therein.'

That facility was indorsed 'Accepted' and signed by Mr Campbell. *g*

By 13 January 1975, as is indicated by the use of the phrase 'owned by you and your wife', the plaintiffs had become aware that Mrs Campbell was a joint proprietor with Mr Campbell. Nevertheless, they took no effective steps to ensure that she joined or concurred in the charge.

The final facility was dated 27 November 1975, and, so far as material, was in these *h* terms:

'Dear Mr Campbell,
    We set out below the terms and conditions on which we are prepared to renew your overdraft facility to include an increase in the principal sum due, of £3500:—
Amount: £9794·61 *Purpose* . . . *Term:* To be repaid in full by the 31st May 1976.
Interest Rate . . . *Security:* This facility will continue to be secured by the first charge *j* given by yourself on the property at 10 Holmewood Gardens, London SW2, which is owned jointly by your wife and yourself.' [There is then a reference to a guarantee, to which we need not refer, and it continues:] If the foregoing terms and conditions are acceptable to you, kindly sign and return the duplicate of this letter as your confirmation thereof.'

a That was indorsed 'Agreed' and signed by Mr Campbell, but the plaintiffs still took no effective steps to ensure that Mrs Campbell joined or concurred in the charge.

The submissions of law

On this appeal, as we have already indicated, we are not concerned with the indebtedness of Mr Campbell resulting from these arrangements, but with the plaintiffs' claim that the arrangements have given rise to an equitable charge on his beneficial
b interest in the property.

In support of this claim, the argument of counsel for the plaintiffs has been essentially based on two propositions, namely (1) that the facility letters agreed to by Mr Campbell gave rise to specifically enforceable contracts, each of which created an immediate equitable charge over his beneficial interest, and (2) that in any event the deposit of the land certificate had the same effect.

c We turn to consider the first of these two propositions. The facility letter of 24 May 1973 did not, in our opinion, purport to create an immediate charge on anything. As the judge pointed out, this is made clear by the use of the words of futurity 'is to be secured'. The letter has to be read against the background that Mr Campbell's solicitors had already undertaken to forward to the plaintiffs the land certificate when received. In our opinion, in its context, the signature by Mr Campbell of the letter amounted to a promise by him
d that the plaintiffs should be given an equitable charge on the freehold title to the property, which would be effected by virtue of the contemplated deposit of the land certificate. The words 'to complete our documentation on this transaction' support the conclusion that the parties contemplated that no further documentation would be required to complete the grant of his equitable charge, but that completion would be effected by the mere deposit of the title deeds with the plaintiffs.

e If, therefore, Mr Campbell had been the sole proprietor of the land at the time when the title deeds were sent to them on 1 June 1973, we could have seen no possible answer to a claim by the plaintiffs that, at least as from that date, an effective equitable charge on the freehold title was created in their favour.

On 1 June 1973, however, Mr Campbell, who had misled the plaintiffs as to his entitlement, had not obtained the consent of his co-proprietor to the creation of any
f charge. There is, therefore, no possibility that the facility letter of 24 May 1973 gave rise to an equitable charge on the *freehold title*, even after the deposit of the land certificate had been made.

Nevertheless, as at May 1973, Mr Campbell did have the power, without his wife's concurrence, to sever the beneficial joint tenancy in the property (which for present purposes we assume existed on that date) and to dispose of his severed beneficial interest
g in such manner as he thought fit. If, on 24 May 1973, he had signed a written assignment of his beneficial interest in the property in favour of the plaintiffs to secure the proposed advances, this would, in our opinion, unquestionably have amounted to a course of dealing sufficient to sever the beneficial joint tenancy and to create a charge on such beneficial interest, not a mere agreement to charge. But, the letter of 24 May 1973 was couched in executory terms as a mere agreement to charge. The judge likewise found
h nothing in the wording of the two facility letters of 13 January and 27 November 1975 which indicated the immediate creation of a charge as opposed to an agreement for a charge. His conclusion in this respect has not been challenged. What then was the effect of these agreements by which Mr Campbell promised to charge more than he had power to charge?

It is a well-established principle of equity that where, in the course of concluding a
j contract, a person has represented that he can grant a certain property, or is entitled to a certain interest in that property, and it later appears that there is a deficiency in his title or interest, the other party can obtain an order compelling him to grant what he has got and, in an appropriate case, to submit to a reduction of the consideration for the grant: (see *Fry on Specific Performance* (6th edn, 1921) paras 1257–1258 and the cases there cited). We will call this 'the doctrine of partial performance'. Prima facie the doctrine applies to

the agreement by Mr Campbell contained in the facility letter of 24 May 1973, and the
judge so accepted. As he put it ([1984] 1 All ER 144 at 150):

> 'There is no reason why an innocent person who gives consideration for the
> promise of a charge on the whole should not be in a position equivalent to that of a
> purchaser and thus secure an order for partial performance. In this case any order
> would be for the creation of a charge on the husband's beneficial interest in the
> property.'

The judge, however, having recognised the existence of the doctrine of partial
performance, found himself unable to apply it in favour of the plaintiffs, because of an
exception to the general principle, which will be referred to in this judgment as 'the
hardship exception', and is expressed thus in *Fry* at para 1270 as follows:

> 'The principle [ie the principle of partial performance] will not, it seems, be
> applied where the alienation of the partial interest of the vendor might prejudice
> the rights of third persons interested in the estate. Thus where a tenant for life
> without impeachment of waste under a strict settlement had contracted for the sale
> of the fee, the Court refused to compel him to alienate his life interest, on the
> ground that a stranger would be likely to use his liberty to commit waste in a
> manner different from a father, and more prejudical to the rights of those in
> remainder.'

The authority referred to in the last sentence is *Thomas v Dering* (1837) 1 Keen 729,
[1835–42] All ER Rep 711. Lord Langdale MR pointed out in that case that in a case
where it applies the doctrine of partial performance the court is effectively executing the
contract 'cy près'. He said (1 Keen 729 at 746, [1835–42] All ER Rep 711 at 717): 'Though
the vendor cannot be heard to suggest the difficulties which he has occasioned the Court
cannot avoid them.' This, we understand, is the basis on which the court regards itself as
bound to have regard to the interests of third parties when asked to apply the doctrine.

In the present case, the judge regarded the hardship exception as presenting the only
obstacle in the plaintiffs' path when they asserted that they were entitled to an equitable
charge on Mr Campbell's beneficial interest in the property by virtue of the doctrine of
partial performance. But he considered it an insuperable obstacle. He accepted the
submission made on behalf of Mrs Campbell that if an order for partial performance
were made in the plaintiffs' favour, so as to confirm the existence of the asserted charge,
this would prejudice Mrs Campbell's right as a joint tenant to the occupation of the
matrimonial home. For she would be exposed to the risk of proceedings by the plaintiffs
as persons interested under s 30 of the Law of Property Act 1925, and such proceedings,
the judge said, would be very likely to result in an order for sale. A sale, he observed,
would be very serious for her since, at the age of 61, she resided in the property with Mr
Campbell, also her youngest son aged 22, and on occasion her three young grandchildren.
Neither Mr Campbell nor Mrs Campbell had any income apart from the state retirement
pension, and she had virtually no capital assets other than her share in the house.

In these circumstances, the judge considered that potential hardship to Mrs Campbell
prevented the plaintiffs from successfully invoking the general doctrine of partial
performance. He regarded himself as impelled to reach this conclusion by the decision
of this court in *Cedar Holdings Ltd v Green* [1979] 3 All ER 117, [1981] Ch 129. The facts
of that case bore at least a strong superficial similarity to those of the present case. We
take them from the headnote ([1981] Ch 129):

> 'The defendants were joint beneficial owners of their former matrimonial home,
> which was registered in their joint names. Following the grant of a decree nisi of
> divorce to the second defendant, the first defendant and a woman posing as the
> second defendant executed a legal charge by way of mortgage on the house in favour
> of the plaintiffs. The deception by the first defendant having been discovered, the
> plaintiffs brought proceedings for, inter alia, a declaration that by executing the
> legal charge the first defendant had charged to the plaintiffs all his beneficial interest

in the house under the statutory trusts for sale and an order for the sale of the house. The second defendant, by way of counterclaim, sought a declaration that the house was not subject to any charge in favour of the plaintiffs.'

Whitford J held that the legal charge was ineffective to sever the joint beneficial ownership of the defendants or to effect any charge on the first defendant's beneficial interest. On appeal the plaintiffs put their case in two ways. First, they relied on the effect of the legal charge itself. The definition of 'a conveyance' in s 205(1)(ii) of the Law of Property Act 1925 includes 'mortgage or charge'. Section 63(1) provides that—

> 'Every conveyance is effectual to pass all the estate, right, title, interest, claim, and demand which the conveying parties respectively have, in, to, or on the property conveyed, or expressed or intended so to be, or which they respectively have power to convey in, to, or on the same.'

It was argued that by virtue of s 63 the legal charge created an equitable charge over the husband's equitable interest under the statutory trusts affecting the property. The Court of Appeal rejected this argument on the ground that a beneficial interest in the proceeds of sale of land held on the statutory trusts was not an interest in that land within the meaning of s 63(1). As their second, alternative, argument, the plaintiffs in *Cedar Holdings Ltd v Green* relied on the effect of the contract by the husband to give security for the advance, in pursuance of which the legal charge was executed. They submitted that the husband, having contracted to charge the whole legal estate and being unable to do so, could be compelled at the plaintiffs' election to charge his beneficial interest by virtue of the doctrine of partial performance. The Court of Appeal rejected this alternative argument likewise. The reason why Buckley LJ rejected it was simply that the subject matter for which the plaintiffs had contracted was an estate or interest in the house and that the doctrine of partial performance did not avail them. As he put it ([1979] 3 All ER 117 at 124, [1981] Ch 129 at 142):

> 'The doctrine in accordance with which those cases were decided is, in my opinion, directed to ensuring that the grantee shall obtain, if he so elects, as much of the subject-matter contracted to be granted as the grantor can convey, whether the deficiency be in respect of the physical extent of the subject-matter or of the estate or interest of the grantor in the subject-matter. It does not enable the grantee to demand a grant of some different subject-matter in lieu of that contracted for.'

In rejecting the argument based on the doctrine of partial performance on the grounds just stated, Buckley LJ did not rely on, or advert to, the hardship exception. Goff LJ, delivering the second judgment in that case, expressly agreed with all that Buckley LJ had said on the plaintiffs' second argument (see [1979] 3 All ER 117 at 127, [1981] Ch 129 at 146). Having expressed such agreement, however, he added that the plaintiffs' case must also fail on another ground ([1979] 3 All ER 117 at 127, [1981] Ch 129 at 147):

> '. . . namely that even in the straightforward case where the purchaser has some estate or interest in the land, albeit less than he contracted to give, the court will not order specific performance to the extent of his true estate or interest "where the alienation of the partial interest of the vendor might prejudice the rights of third persons interested in the estate" . . .'

He then referred to *Fry* at para 1270 and Lord Langdale MR's judgment in *Thomas v Dering* (1837) 1 Keen 729 at 747–748, [1835–42] All ER Rep 711 at 718. He said that partial performance would prejudice the other co-owner, the second defendant, in two ways. The first has no materiality to the present case. The second was stated by him thus ([1979] 3 All ER 117 at 128, [1981] Ch 129 at 147):

> 'In any case whether or not the court would ultimately order a sale under s 30 of the Law of Property Act 1925, such specific performance must be prejudicial to her position in proceedings against her under that section.'

Goff LJ said that in the circumstances the questions raised under s 30 did not call for a
decision. Shaw LJ agreed with both the judgments which had been delivered.

The decision in *Cedar Holdings Ltd v Green* subsequently fell to be considered by the
House of Lords in *Williams & Glyn's Bank Ltd v Boland* [1980] 2 All ER 408, [1981] AC
487. There, in each of two actions for possession of certain registered land, the
matrimonial home stood in the sole name of a married man as registered proprietor. His
wife had contributed a substantial sum of her own money towards its purchase or
towards paying off a mortgage on it, thus becoming an equitable tenant in common to
the extent of her contribution. Later each husband mortgaged the house by legal
mortgage to the appellant bank, which made no inquiries of the wife. On default of the
mortgagor, the bank brought proceedings for possession. The question then arose
whether the wife had an 'overriding interest', within the meaning of s 70(1)(g) of the
Land Registration Act 1925, which was binding on the bank and entitled her to resist its
claim to possession. In this context it had to be considered whether the interests of co-
owners under the statutory trusts are interests 'subsisting in reference to land', so as to
satisfy the opening and governing words of s 70. If *Cedar Holdings Ltd v Green* was correct,
they did not. However, Lord Wilberforce, with whose speech Viscount Dilhorne, Lord
Salmon and Lord Roskill agreed, had this to say ([1980] 2 All ER 408 at 414–415, [1981]
AC 487 at 507):

'. . . I find it easy to accept that they satisfy the opening, and governing, words of
s 70, namely, interests subsisting in reference to the land. As Lord Denning MR
points out, to describe the interests of spouses in a house jointly bought to be lived
in as a matrimonial home as merely an interest in the proceeds of sale, or rents and
profits until sale, is just a little unreal; see also *Elias v Mitchell* [1972] 2 All ER 153,
[1972] Ch 652 per Pennycuick V-C, with whose analysis I agree, and contrast *Cedar
Holdings Ltd v Green* (which I consider to have been wrongly decided).'

Counsel for the plaintiffs submitted that this disapproval of *Cedar Holdings Ltd v Green*
destroyed its authority, not merely for the main ground on which all members of the
court there relied, but also in respect of the second ground relied on by Goff LJ with the
concurrence of Shaw LJ. Accordingly, in his submission, the judge erred in considering
that their judgments obliged him to hold that the mere fact that a decision in favour of
the plaintiffs would give them a locus standi to apply for an order for sale of the property
under s 30 of the Law of Property Act 1925 must necessarily constitute prejudice to Mrs
Campbell sufficient to disentitle the plaintiffs from obtaining the remedy of specific
performance. He pointed out that s 30 does not give a 'person interested' the unqualified
right to an order for sale. Where an application is made under the section by one person
interested but is opposed by another such person, the court has a wide discretion in
deciding whose voice is to prevail. We have been referred to three cases in each of which,
as it happened, the court in the exercise of its discretion made orders for sale of a
matrimonial home or former matrimonial home at the instance of a husband's trustee in
bankruptcy, in the face of opposition from the wife: *Re a debtor, ex p the trustee v Solomon*
[1966] 3 All ER 225, [1967] Ch 573, *Re Turner (a bankrupt), ex p the trustee of the bankrupt
v Turner* [1975] 1 All ER 5, [1974] 1 WLR 1556, *Re Bailey (a bankrupt), ex p the trustee of
the bankrupt v Bailey* [1977] 2 All ER 26, [1977] 1 WLR 278. Nevertheless, as the recent
decision of this court *Re Holliday (a bankrupt), ex p the trustee of the bankrupt v The bankrupt*
[1980] 3 All ER 385, [1981] Ch 405 illustrates, such a result in a contest of this nature is
by no means a foregone conclusion. The discretion of the court is a real one and, in
considering whether or not to order a sale, it must weigh the conflicting legal and moral
claims of the creditors on the one hand and those of the wife on the other, taking all
relevant facts, including the existence of children, into account (see [1980] 3 All ER 385
at 395, [1981] Ch 405 at 421 per Buckley LJ).

Mrs Campbell's occupation of the property cannot be disturbed by the plaintiffs until
an application has been made under s 30 of the Law of Property Act 1925. In the
submission of counsel for the plaintiffs that would be the appropriate stage to consider

a   which of the competing equities are entitled to prevail, in the light of full evidence as to Mrs Campbell's personal and family position. This would appear to accord with the views of Bingham J as expressed in *First National Securities Ltd v Hegerty* [1984] 1 All ER 139 esp at 143, a decision which has still more recently been considered by Ewbank J in *Harman v Glencross* [1984] 2 All ER 577. Meantime, he submitted, there are no sufficient grounds for declining to treat the plaintiffs as entitled to specific performance of the agreement for a charge.

b   We are inclined to think that Lord Wilberforce, in expressing the view that *Cedar Holdings Ltd v Green* was wrongly decided, was, in the context of his speech in *Williams & Glyn's Bank Ltd v Boland*, doing no more than accepting the argument of the appellants' counsel (see [1981] AC 487 at 494) to the effect that the Court of Appeal in *Cedar Holdings Ltd v Green* had erred in rejecting the first of the two main arguments put before it, based on the effect of the legal charge itself. We therefore incline to the view that the judgments of Goff and Shaw LJJ in *Cedar Holdings Ltd v Green* remain good authority for what they

c   actually decided in relation to the second ground relied on by them. Nevertheless, we are doubtful whether Goff LJ in his judgment in *Cedar Holdings Ltd v Green* can have intended to lay down any general principle applicable beyond the facts of that particular case. We do not read the judgment of Lord Langdale MR in *Thomas v Dering* (1837) 1 Keen 729, [1835–42] All ER Rep 711, on which Goff LJ relied, as doing more than establishing that,

d   when an order for partial performance is sought, the court must consider and give due weight to the interests of third parties alongside the interests of the parties to the dispute. We see much force in the submission that the mere fact that an order for partial performance in cases such as the present would give the chargee a locus standi to apply for a sale under s 30 and should not, by itself, necessarily deprive an innocent chargee of the remedy of partial performance.

e   Nevertheless, even assuming (without deciding) in favour of the plaintiffs that this submission is well founded and that the *Cedar Holdings Ltd v Green* does not compel a contrary view, we have reached the clear conclusion that the judge was right to conclude that an order for partial performance would not be an appropriate remedy to afford to the plaintiffs on the particular facts of the present case. Quite apart from the s 30 point on which he relied in this context, there are, in our judgment, three further significant points to which he did not specifically refer. (1) The effect of making an order for partial

f   performance in favour of the plaintiffs would have been to give them a clear locus standi to intervene in the hearing of the rectification issue and other issues raised by the third party proceedings. (2) The additional prejudice to Mrs Campbell resulting from such intervention could have been real and substantial. For, as appears from *Snell's Equity* (28th edn, 1982) p 618, rectification will not be granted to the prejudice of a bona fide

g   purchaser for value without notice who has taken an interest under the instrument in its unrectified form. At least, at the time of the agreement for a charge contained in the facility letter of 24 May 1973, the plaintiffs apparently had no such notice. Their position at the time of the agreements for a charge contained in the two later facility letters is more doubtful. It might depend on whether the actual knowledge (which they had acquired by that time) that Mrs Campbell had a beneficial interest in the property

h   operated to give them constructive knowledge of her rights to rectification. Nevertheless, there is at least a live possibility that they could have successfully resisted the order for rectification to which Mrs Campbell has shown herself otherwise entitled, and thus could have defeated her claim to the entire beneficial interest (as opposed to a severed one-half interest) in the property. (3) So far as the evidence shows, Mrs Campbell was not made aware that the plaintiffs might have been granted rights in the property until about April

j   1976. The plaintiffs, however, by the date of the facility letter of 13 January 1975, had full knowledge that she was at least a joint owner of the property. But they took no effective steps to make her aware of the transactions with her husband which concerned the house. They were content to continue dealing solely with her husband.

In all the circumstances, we are satisfied that when the competing equities are considered, the hardship that Mrs Campbell, as an innocent third party, would suffer if an order were made for partial performance of the agreements for a charge would far outweigh the hardship that the plaintiffs would suffer if such an order were refused. They have largely been the architects of their own misfortune, in failing to require Mr Campbell to perfect the charge which he had agreed to give them, after they had acquired full knowledge of his wife's interest. As Goff LJ said in *Cedar Holdings Ltd v Green* [1979] 3 All ER 117 at 128, [1981] Ch 129 at 147, it might be different if he had made a contract to charge his share; but his only contract was to charge the entirety, and the court by an order for specific performance would be carrying into execution a new contract. For the reasons which we have given, we think that on the facts of the present case the judge was right to refuse to make an order which would have had this effect.

Finally, we turn briefly to consider the alternative argument of counsel for the plaintiffs, based on the deposit with the plaintiffs of the land certificate on behalf of Mr Campbell. Even if Mr Campbell had had a beneficial interest in the property, he would not have been entitled to part with the land certificate without the consent of Mrs Campbell as joint owner of the legal estate. As the judge put it ([1984] 1 All ER 144 at 152):

> 'The two are trustees of the deeds no less than they are of the legal estate. Trustees can act only with unanimity. One cannot part with custody of the deeds without consent of the other. That custody is not a thing which either can by himself effectively surrender for the purpose of dealing with his own beneficial interest.'

In agreement with the judge, we therefore consider that Mrs Campbell has at all times been entitled to request the return of the land certificate to the joint custody of herself and Mr Campbell.

Counsel for the plaintiffs more or less accepted that for these reasons there is no answer to Mrs Campbell's counterclaim. Nevertheless, he submitted that the initial deposit of the land certificate by itself evidenced an intention to create a charge and, while it could not operate to create a charge on the legal estate, it raised a presumption that a charge was being created in equity on that which Mr Campbell had the power to charge, namely his beneficial interest. However, we think that this point does not avail the plaintiffs. As Lord Cairns said in *Shaw v Foster* (1872) LR 5 HL 321 at 339–340:

> '. . . although it is a well-established rule of Equity that a deposit of a document of title without more, without writing, or without word of mouth, will create in Equity a charge upon the property referred to, I apprehend that that general rule will not apply where you have a deposit accompanied by an actual written charge. In that case you must refer to the terms of the written document, and any implication that might be raised, supposing there were no document, is put out of the case and reduced to silence by the document by which alone you must be governed.'

In our judgment the existence of the facility letters in the present case, with their express references to an agreement for, or a continuation of, a charge, leave no room for any implication that might have been raised by the deposit of the land certificate unaccompanied by any document.

Conclusion

For these reasons, we are not persuaded by either of the two alternative lines of argument ably presented by counsel for the plaintiffs. We think that the judge reached the correct decision and accordingly dismiss this appeal.

Appeal dismissed. Leave to appeal to House of Lords refused.

Solicitors: *Lieberman Leigh & Co* (for the plaintiffs); *Howard Thomas & Petrou* (for Mrs Campbell).

Diana Brahams   Barrister.

Colchester Estates (Cardiff) v Carlton Industries plc

CHANCERY DIVISION
NOURSE J
28, 29, 30 MARCH 1984

Precedent – Co-ordinate courts – Conflicting decisions – Stare decisis – Conflicting decisions of High Court – Earlier decision fully considered but not followed in later decision – Later decision normally to be considered as settling law at first instance – Exception where third judge convinced second judge wrong not to follow first.

Since it is desirable that the law, at whatever level it is decided, should generally be certain, it follows that, when a decision of a judge of the High Court has been fully considered, but not followed, by another judge of the High Court, the second decision should normally be considered as having settled the point at first instance, except only in the rare case where a third judge is convinced that the second judge was wrong not to follow the first (as where some binding or persuasive authority was not cited in either of the first two cases). On that basis, unless the party interested seriously intends to submit that it falls within that exception, the hearing at first instance in the third case will, so far as the point in question is concerned, be a formality, with any argument on it reserved to the Court of Appeal (see p 604 *h* to p 605 *b*, post).

Dictum of Denning J in *Minister of Pensions v Higham* [1948] 1 All ER at 865 applied.

Notes

For the effect of conflicting decisions of co-ordinate courts, see 26 Halsbury's Laws (4th edn) para 580, and for cases on the subject, see 30 Digest (Reissue) 276–280, 830–879.

Cases referred to in judgment

Bader Properties Ltd v Linley Property Investments Ltd (1968) 19 P & CR 620.
Hamilton v Martell Securities Ltd [1984] 1 All ER 665, [1984] 2 WLR 699.
Huddersfield Police Authority v Watson [1947] 2 All ER 193, [1947] KB 842, DC.
Middlegate Properties Ltd v Gidlow-Jackson (1977) 34 P & CR 4, CA.
Minister of Pensions v Higham [1948] 1 All ER 863, [1948] 2 KB 153.
SEDAC Investments Ltd v Tanner [1982] 3 All ER 646, [1982] 1 WLR 1342.
Sidnell v Wilson [1966] 1 All ER 681, [1966] 2 QB 67, [1966] 2 WLR 560, CA.
Swallow Securities Ltd v Brand (1983) 45 P & CR 328.

Cases also cited

Finchbourne Ltd v Rodrigues [1976] 3 All ER 581, CA.
Helby v Matthews [1895] AC 471, [1895–9] All ER Rep 821, HL.
Land Securities plc v Receiver for the Metropolitan Police District [1983] 2 All ER 254, [1983] 1 WLR 439.
Lock v Pearce [1893] 2 Ch 271, CA.
Moschi v Lep Air Services Ltd [1972] 2 All ER 393, [1973] AC 331, HL.
Moss' Empires Ltd v Olympia (Liverpool) Ltd [1939] 3 All ER 460, [1939] AC 544, HL.
Photo Production Ltd v Securicor Transport Ltd [1980] 1 All ER 556, [1980] AC 827, HL.
Plummer v Ramsey (1934) 78 SJ 175.
Skinners' Co v Knight [1891] 2 QB 542, CA.
Starrokate Ltd v Burry (1982) 265 EG 871, CA.

Originating summons

By a summons dated 22 December 1983 as amended the plaintiff, Colchester Estates (Cardiff), an unlimited company, sought an order giving the plaintiff leave to take proceedings for damages for breach by the defendant, Carlton Industries plc, of certain covenants to repair contained in a lease of certain premises for a term of 27 years from 1 December 1963 made on 13 April 1964 between the plaintiff and the defendant's predecessor in title, which assigned the lease to the defendant on 25 June 1980, (2) a direction under s 2 of the Leasehold Property (Repairs) Act 1938 that the plaintiff have the benefit of s 146(3) of the Law of Property Act 1925 in relation to the costs and expenses incurred in reference to the breaches of covenant, (2A) alternatively to (1) and (2) a declaration that the leave of the court was not required by the plaintiff to commence proceedings for the recovery of the costs incurred by the plaintiff of making good defects, decays and wants of repair under cl 2(1) of the lease and (3) costs. The facts are set out in the judgment.

Christopher Bathurst QC and *Michael Brindle* for the plaintiff.
Michael Barnes QC and *Patrick Talbot* for the defendant.

NOURSE J. This case is concerned with a provision in a lease which empowers the landlord to enter and make good at his own cost wants of repair for which the tenant is liable and then to claim repayment of the cost from the tenant. Provisions of that kind have commonly been included in leases since the early part of this century, if not before. The primary question here is whether, before the landlord can take proceedings for the recovery of the cost, the leave of the court is required pursuant to s 1(3) of the Leasehold Property (Repairs) Act 1938. The outcome of that question depends on whether the proceedings are properly to be regarded as proceedings for damages for breach of a covenant to repair, in which case leave is required, or as proceedings for recovery of a debt, in which case it is not.

The plaintiff is an unlimited company called Colchester Estates (Cardiff). The defendant, Carlton Industries plc, is the tenant of certain leasehold factory premises on the Colchester trading estate in Cardiff which it holds of the plaintiff under a lease dated 13 April 1964 made between the plaintiff of the first part, the defendant's predecessor in title of the second part and a guarantor of the third part. That lease was for a term of 27 years from 1 December 1963 at a rent which is currently £25,000 pa. The term will therefore expire at the end of 1990 and still has more than six years to run. The tenant's covenants are contained in cl 2 of the lease. Sub-paragraphs (c) and (d) contain covenants to paint the exterior and the interior respectively of the demised premises. Sub-paragraph (f) contains a full repairing covenant (damage by fire, storm or tempest excepted). Sub-paragraph (i), which contains the provision with which this case is concerned, is in these terms:

> 'To permit the Lessors or their agents at all reasonable and convenient times by appointment to enter the demised premises and examine the state of repair and condition thereof and to check and take inventories of the Lessors' fixtures therein and that the Lessees will repair and make good all defects decays and wants of repair thereto of which notice in writing shall be given by the Lessors to the Lessees and for which the Lessees may be liable hereunder within three months after the giving of such notice Provided that in case of default by the Lessees the Lessors may make good such defects decays and wants of repair and the cost of the same shall be repayable by the Lessees to the Lessors on demand.'

Sub-paragraph (s) contains a covenant to pay all reasonable and proper costs and charges and expenses incurred by the landlord in relation to any notice under s 146 of the Law of Property Act 1925.

The assignment of the lease to the defendant was made on 25 June 1980. Between October of that year and the summer of 1983 various notices under cl 2(i) or s 146 were given to the defendant by the plaintiff in respect of alleged wants of repair. There were various meetings and negotiations which do not seem to have led to much work being done. In any event the plaintiff was not satisfied. Accordingly, on 19 August 1983 it

served two further alternative notices, the first of which was intended to take effect under
cl 2(i) of the lease if s 146 and the 1938 Act do not apply, and the second of which was
intended to take effect if they do. Those notices related to what the plaintiff says are
wants of repair which have now become urgent and of which the aggregate cost is put at
£173,000. On 1 September the defendant served a counter-notice under s 1(2) of the
1938 Act. By its originating summons issued on 22 December 1983 the plaintiff
effectively seeks leave under s 1(3) to commence proceedings for the recovery of the cost
of the work in accordance with cl 2(i) of the lease, but without prejudice to its claim that
leave is not required. That claim has been raised by an amendment which seeks a
declaration that the leave of the court—

> 'is not required by the Plaintiff to commence proceedings for the recovery of the
> costs incurred by the Plaintiff of making good defects, decays and wants of repair
> under clause 2(i) of the said Lease.'

On the primary question the plaintiff contends that leave to commence proceedings
for the recovery of the cost of the work is not required and the defendant contends that
it is. If that question is determined in favour of the plaintiff, that will be an end of the
matter. If, on the other hand, it is determined in favour of the defendant, then the
defendant contends that the court has no power to grant leave to commence the
proceedings, first, because the plaintiff has not yet incurred any cost which is recoverable
under cl 2(i) and, second, because the notice served by it under s 146 is in any event
defective in a particular respect. If both those contentions fail, then it is agreed that the
application for leave will have to be heard on its merits, but it is also agreed that that
exercise cannot be embarked on today.

I turn therefore to the primary question, which is by no means free from authority.
In *Swallow Securities Ltd v Brand* (1983) 45 P & CR 328 McNeill J held that a right
conferred on a landlord by a provision comparable with cl 2(i) was a right to recover
damages for breach of a covenant to repair and that the leave of the court to commence
proceedings for the enforcement of that right was accordingly required. However, in
Hamilton v Martell Securities Ltd [1984] 1 All ER 665, [1984] 2 WLR 699 Vinelott J
declined to follow the decision of McNeill J and held the opposite. In the later case the
material provision was nearer in form to cl 2(i) than that in the earlier one, but it is
agreed that that is not a distinction of any importance. What may be of importance is
that Vinelott J was referred to certain authorities which were not cited to McNeill J. Of
these the one to which Vinelott J attached the greatest weight was the decision of the
Court of Appeal in *Middlegate Properties Ltd v Gidlow-Jackson* (1977) 34 P & CR 4 in which
the earlier decision of Roskill J in *Bader Properties Ltd v Linley Property Investments Ltd*
(1968) 19 P & CR 620 was approved. In each of those cases it was held that the right
conferred on a landlord by a covenant on the part of his tenant to pay all expenses
incurred by him in relation to any s 146 notice or the like was a right to recover not
damages but a debt due from the tenant. Accordingly, the 1938 Act did not apply and
the leave of the court to take proceedings for the recovery of the amount of the expenses
was not required.

In *Hamilton v Martell Securities Ltd* [1984] 1 All ER 665 at 674, [1984] 2 WLR 699 at
711 Vinelott J, having said that the decision of the Court of Appeal in *Middlegate
Properties Ltd v Gidlow-Jackson* was binding on him, expressed the view that it compelled
the conclusion that in the case before him the landlord's right to recover the costs of the
repairs was not a right to recover damages for breach of a covenant to repair within s 1(1)
and (2) of the 1938 Act. He then said that neither that decision nor the decision of
Roskill J in the *Bader Properties Ltd* case nor the decision of the Court of Appeal in *Sidnell
v Wilson* [1966] 1 All ER 681, [1966] 2 QB 67 had been cited to McNeill J in *Swallow
Securities Ltd v Brand*. In *Sidnell v Wilson* [1966] 1 All ER 681 at 683, 685, [1966] 2 QB 67
at 76, 79 both Lord Denning MR and Harman LJ had described the mischief which the
1938 Act was intended to defeat. Earlier in his judgment Vinelott J had gone into that
matter in some detail with a view of showing that it was at the least doubtful whether

the 1938 Act was intended to operate on a case of this kind (see [1984] 1 All ER 665 at 672–673, [1984] 2 WLR 699 at 708–709. Finally, Vinelott J pointed out that the attention of McNeill J was also not drawn to the difficulties which later emerged as a result of the decision of Mr Michael Wheeler QC in *SEDAC Investments Ltd v Tanner* [1982] 3 All ER 646, [1982] 1 WLR 1342 in applying s 1(5) to a case where a want of repair has actually been remedied by the landlord, or to the difficulties which would seem equally to confront a landlord who sought leave to bring proceedings to recover the cost of carrying out repairs before he had actually carried them out.

On this state of the authorities both counsel for the plaintiff and counsel for the defendant submitted that the existence of two conflicting decisions of judges of co-ordinate jurisdiction meant that I was entirely free to choose between them and should not start with any preference for one over the other. While I readily accepted that that would be the position where the second decision was given, for example, in ignorance of the first, I was troubled at the suggestion that it would necessarily be the same where the second was given after a full consideration of the first. Since this is a question on which the court has an interest of its own, I thought it right to make an independent research. That led me to the decision of Denning J in *Minister of Pensions v Higham* [1948] 1 All ER 863, [1948] 2 KB 153. I put that case to counsel during the course of argument yesterday afternoon and I hope and believe that they both had an opportunity of saying what they wanted to say about it.

Minister of Pensions v Higham was a case where Denning J, who was then the judge nominated to hear appeals from the pensions appeal tribunals in England, was faced with a conflict between a dictum in an earlier case of his own and a decision of the Court of Session on an appeal from one of the pensions appeal tribunals in Scotland. In the later case the Court of Session, having considered the dictum in the earlier one and having no doubt considered it fully, said that it was unable to agree with it. Denning J, having stated the special position in which he was there placed, said ([1948] 1 All ER 863 at 865, [1948] 2 KB 153 at 155):

'I lay down for myself, therefore, the rule that, where the Court of Session have felt compelled to depart from a previous decision of this court, that is a strong reason for my reconsidering the matter, and if, on reconsideration, I am left in doubt of the correctness of my own decision, then I shall be prepared to follow the decision of the Court of Session, at any rate in those cases when it is in favour of the claimant because he should be given the benefit of the doubt.'

Had the judge stopped there, I might well have agreed with counsel that the case could not, by reason of its special features, be treated as being of any general value. However, he went on to say this:

'In this respect I follow the general rule that where there are conflicting decisions of courts of co-ordinate jurisdiction, the later decision is to be preferred if it is reached after full consideration of the earlier decision.'

That unqualified statement of a general rule comes from a source to which the greatest possible respect is due. It is fortuitous that my own instinct should have coincided with it. However diffident I might have been in relying on instinct alone, the coincidence encourages me to suggest a reason for the rule. It is that it is desirable that the law, at whatever level it is declared, should generally be certain. If a decision of this court, reached after full consideration of an earlier one which went the other way, is normally to be open to review on a third occasion when the same point arises for decision at the same level, there will be no end of it. Why not in a fourth, fifth or sixth case as well? Counsel for the defendant had to face that prospect with equanimity or, perhaps to be fairer to him, with resignation. I decline to join him, especially in times when the cost of litigation and the pressure of work on the courts are so great. There must come a time when a point is normally to be treated as having been settled at first instance. I think that that should be when the earlier decision has been fully considered, but not followed, in a *a* later one. Consistently with the modern approach of the judges of this court to an earlier decision of one of their number (see e g *Huddersfield Police Authority v Watson* [1947] 2 All ER 193 at 196, [1947] KB 842 at 848 per Lord Goddard CJ), I would make an exception only in the case, which must be rare, where the third judge is convinced that the second was wrong in not following the first. An obvious example is where some binding or persuasive authority has not been cited in either of the first two cases. If that is the rule then, unless the party interested seriously intends to submit that it falls within the

b exception, the hearing at first instance in the third case will, so far as the point in question is concerned, be a formality, with any argument on it reserved to the Court of Appeal.

Applying the rule to the present case, first, I am satisfied that the decision of Vinelott J was reached after full consideration of the decision of McNeill J. Second, I am not convinced that Vinelott J was wrong in not following McNeill J. I have had full and careful arguments on both sides, each of which was almost certainly fuller than the

c argument on the same side in either of the earlier cases. I think it inappropriate either that I should examine those arguments or express any further view of my own. That implies no disrespect or ingratitude to counsel. Indeed, the contrary is the case. Whatever may be thought appropriate on any other occasion, this is a question on which it is in my judgment inappropriate that there should be any further debate or expression of judicial view below the level of the Court of Appeal. In the circumstances I need say only that I

d propose to follow and apply the decision of Vinelott J in *Hamilton v Martell Securities Ltd*.

The plaintiff therefore succeeds on the primary question. I will grant it a declaration in the form sought in para 2A of the amended originating summons.

Order accordingly.

Solicitors: *Ward Bowie*, agents for *Phoenix Walters & Co*, Cardiff (for the plaintiff); *Stones Porter & Co* (for the defendant).

Evelyn M C Budd   Barrister.

White v Brunton

a

COURT OF APPEAL, CIVIL DIVISION
SIR JOHN DONALDSON MR, FOX AND STEPHEN BROWN LJJ
12 MARCH 1984

Court of Appeal – Leave to appeal – Requirement of leave – Interlocutory or final order or judgment – Test whether order or judgment interlocutory or final – Nature of application or nature of order or judgment – Preliminary issue – Whether order or judgment made on preliminary issue final or interlocutory – Whether parties may waive requirements as to leave by agreement – Supreme Court Act 1981, s 18(1).

b

In determining whether an order or judgment is interlocutory or final for the purposes of leave to appeal under s 18(1)[a] of the Supreme Court Act 1981, regard must be had to the nature of the application or proceedings giving rise to the order or judgment and not to the nature of the order or judgment itself. Accordingly, where an order made or judgment given on an application would finally determine the matters in litigation, the order or judgment is final, thereby giving rise to an unfettered right of appeal. Since a preliminary issue, on a true analysis, is the first part of a final hearing, and not an issue preliminary to a final hearing, it follows that any party may appeal without leave against an order or judgment made on the preliminary issue if he could have appealed without leave against the order or judgment if that issue had been heard as part of the final hearing and the order or judgment on the preliminary issue had been made at the end of the complete hearing. To hold otherwise would, by depriving parties on a preliminary issue of an unfettered right of appeal, indirectly fetter the ability of the court to order such split hearings in cases where it was plainly in the interests of the more efficient administration of justice to do so (see p 607 f g and p 608 b to g, post); *Salaman v Warner* [1891] 1 QB 734 and *Salter Rex & Co v Ghosh* [1971] 2 All ER 865 followed; *Bozson v Altrincham UDC* [1903] 1 KB 547 disapproved.

Although the parties may take the view that they can by agreement waive the requirements as to leave, it is for the court to decide whether leave is required since that goes to jurisdiction (see p 608 h j, post).

c

d

e

f

Notes

For final and interlocutory judgments, see 26 Halsbury's Laws (4th edn) paras 504–507.

For the Supreme Court Act 1981, s 18, see 51 Halsbury's Statutes (3rd edn) 608–609.

Cases referred to in judgments

g

Bozson v Altrincham UDC [1903] 1 KB 547, CA.
Page, Re, Hill v Fladgate [1910] 1 Ch 489, CA.
Salaman v Warner [1891] 1 QB 734, CA.
Salter Rex & Co v Ghosh [1971] 2 All ER 865, [1971] 2 QB 597, [1971] 3 WLR 31, CA.
Shubrook v Tufnell (1882) 9 QBD 621, [1881–8] All ER Rep 180, CA.
Steinway & Sons v Broadhurst-Clegg (1983) Times, 25 February, CA.

h

Application

By a writ issued on 3 March 1978 the plaintiff, George Malcolm James White, brought an action against the defendant, John Greville Brunton, for damages for breach of contract and for a declaration that, by an agreement in writing dated 19 March 1970 and made between the defendant and the plaintiff, the defendant was bound to contribute to the

j

---

a   Section 18(1), so far as material, provides: 'No appeal shall lie to the Court of Appeal . . . (c) from any order, judgment or decision of the High Court or any other court or tribunal which, by virtue of any provision (however expressed) of this or any other Act, is final . . . (h) without the leave of the court or tribunal in question or of the Court of Appeal, from any interlocutory order or interlocutory judgment made or given by the High Court or any other court or tribunal, except in [certain specified cases].'

costs and expenses of the works effected by the plaintiff to the access road at South Ryehill, Nunthorpe Village, Cleveland. On 2 December 1981 the district registrar in the Middlesbrough District Registry ordered that a preliminary issue be tried, namely (i) whether on the true construction of the contract dated 19 March 1970 the defendant was under any liability for construction costs of, or maintenance expenses for, the access road having regard to the admitted fact that no re-excavation pursuant to cl 3(i)(a) of the contract had been done, and (ii) whether the defendant was under any liability for maintenance expenses incurred by the plaintiff before the access road was laid. By an order made on 29 March 1983 McCullough J determined the first preliminary issue in favour of the defendant. The plaintiff sought leave to appeal. The case is only reported on the question of whether leave to appeal was required.

Robert Reid QC and *John Fryer-Spedding* for the plaintiff.
Robin Stewart QC and *Brian Sommerville* for the defendant.

SIR JOHN DONALDSON MR. This is an appeal from a decision of McCullough J on a preliminary point. It has itself given rise to a preliminary point in this court, namely whether leave to appeal is required.

The starting point is clear enough. By s 18(1)(*h*) of the Supreme Court Act 1981, subject to certain immaterial exceptions,

> 'No appeal shall lie to the Court of Appeal . . . (*h*) without the leave of the court or tribunal in question or of the Court of Appeal, from any interlocutory order or interlocutory judgment . . .'

But, as is well known, this clarity conceals the obscurity of what is and is not an interlocutory order or judgment.

In *Shubrook v Tufnell* (1882) 9 QBD 621, [1881–8] All ER Rep 180 Jessel MR and Lindley LJ held, in effect, that an order is final if it finally determines the matter in litigation. Thus the issue of final or interlocutory depended on the nature and effect of the order as made. I refer to this as the 'order approach'.

In *Salaman v Warner* [1891] 1 QB 734, in which *Shubrook's* case does not appear to have been cited, a Court of Appeal consisting of Lord Esher MR, Fry and Lopes LJJ held that a final order is one made on such an application or proceeding that, for whichever side the decision is given, it will, if it stands, finally determine the matter in litigation. Thus the issue of final or interlocutory depended on the nature of the application or proceedings giving rise to the order and not on the order itself. I refer to this as the 'application approach'.

In *Bozson v Altrincham UDC* [1903] 1 KB 547 a Court of Appeal consisting of the Earl of Halsbury LC, Lord Alverstone CJ and Jeune P reverted to the order approach.

In *Re Page, Hill v Fladgate* [1910] 1 Ch 489 a Court of Appeal consisting of Cozens-Hardy MR, Fletcher Moulton and Buckley LJJ refused to apply the order approach to a case of striking out the proceedings, but declined to propound any rule of general application.

The next occasion on which the problem was looked at on broad lines of principle was in *Salter Rex & Co v Ghosh* [1971] 2 All ER 865, [1971] 2 QB 597, where Lord Denning MR, with the agreement of Edmund Davies and Stamp LJJ, considered and contrasted the judgment of Lord Alverstone CJ in *Bozson's* case with that of Lord Esher MR in *Salaman v Warner*. Lord Denning MR said ([1971] 2 All ER 865 at 866, [1971] 2 QB 597 at 601):

> 'Lord Alverstone CJ was right in logic but Lord Esher MR was right in experience. Lord Esher MR's test has always been applied in practice . . . I would apply Lord Esher MR's test to an order refusing a new trial. I look to the application for a new trial and not to the order made. If the application for a new trial were granted, it would clearly be interlocutory. So equally when it is refused, it is interlocutory . . . This question of "final" or "interlocutory" is so uncertain, that the only thing for practitioners to do is to look up the practice books and see what has been decided on

the point. Most orders have now been the subject of decision. If a new case should arise, we must do the best we can with it. There is no other way.'

More recently in *Steinway & Sons v Broadhurst-Clegg* (1983) Times, 25 February, this court followed *Salter Rex & Co v Ghosh* and, applying the application approach to a judgment in default of defence, held that it was an interlocutory judgment.

I know that at the present time a great deal of thought is being devoted to how this problem can best be resolved by making rules of court pursuant to the power conferred by s 60 of the 1981 Act, but, having made some vain attempts to produce a simple draft, I do not under estimate the difficulties. Meanwhile the plaintiff needs to know whether he has to obtain leave to appeal.

The court is now clearly committed to the application approach as a general rule and *Bozson*'s case can no longer be regarded as any authority for applying the order approach. However, the decision in *Bozson*'s case, as distinct from the reasoning, can be upheld on a different ground as an exception to the general rule. It was a case of a 'split trial', all questions of liability and breach of contract being tried before and separately from any issue as to damages. If the two parts of the final hearing of the case had been tried together, there would have been an unfettered right of appeal, even if the judgment had been that there was no liability and that accordingly no question arose as to damages. It is plainly in the interests of the more efficient administration of justice that there should be split trials in appropriate cases, as even where the decision on the first part of a split trial is such that there will have to be a second part, it may be desirable that the decision shall be appealed before incurring the possibly unnecessary expense of the second part. If we were to hold that the division of a final hearing into parts deprived the parties of an unfettered right of appeal, we should be placing an indirect fetter on the ability of the court to order split trials. I would therefore hold that, where there is a split trial or more accurately, in relation to a non-jury case, a split hearing, any party may appeal without leave against an order made at the end of one part if he could have appealed against such an order without leave if both parts had been heard together and the order had been made at the end of the complete hearing.

In effect that is the position in the present case, for in directing a preliminary issue on a point of construction the district registrar was seeking to divide the final hearing into two parts in the justified belief that it was possible that by adopting this course the expense of part of the hearing might be avoided. That the division may not have run exactly along the line dividing liability from quantum is, I think, immaterial. The decisive feature is that the 'preliminary issue' was not, when analysed, an issue preliminary to a final hearing, but the first part of a final hearing.

Accordingly I would hold that the plaintiff does not need leave to appeal.

FOX LJ. I agree.

STEPHEN BROWN LJ. I agree.

SIR JOHN DONALDSON MR. The registrar invites me to add, and I do add (and I hope my brethren will agree), that we ought to make it clear that the court in the form of the Civil Appeals Office and the registrar does take points on whether leave to appeal is needed, and occasionally there has been a protest from the parties, 'If my opponent does not mind, why should this point be taken?' The answer is that it goes to jurisdiction and the point has to be taken.

FOX LJ. I agree.

STEPHEN BROWN LJ. I agree.

The court then heard argument from counsel on the appeal.

Solicitors: *Freeman Daly & Jacks*, Darlington (for the plaintiff); *Latimer Hinks Marsham & Little*, Darlington (for the defendant).

Diana Procter　Barrister.

Walsh v Governor of Brixton Prison
and another

HOUSE OF LORDS

LORD FRASER OF TULLYBELTON, LORD ELWYN-JONES, LORD KEITH OF KINKEL, LORD SCARMAN AND LORD BRANDON OF OAKBROOK

21, 22 MAY, 28 JUNE 1984

Criminal law – Bail – Magistrates' court – Defendant in prison on remand in custody when due to appear in court to which he had been remanded on bail – Duty of prison governor to produce him to court – Whether governor in breach of duty in failing to produce prisoner to court – Whether Secretary of State under duty to produce or procure production of prisoner in court – Criminal Justice Act 1961, s 29(1) – Magistrates' Courts Act 1980, s 128(1)(b).

The appellant was remanded on bail by a magistrates' court, pursuant to an order made under s 128(1)(b)[a] of the Magistrates' Courts Act 1980, in connection with certain criminal charges, but before he was due to appear before the court he was remanded in custody by another magistrates' court in connection with other criminal charges. On the day on which he was due to appear before the first magistrates' court to answer to his bail the governor of the prison to which he had been remanded in custody was unable to produce him because staff shortages at the prison prevented the governor from supplying the necessary escort for the appellant. The appellant applied for judicial review of the governor's failure to produce him to the court, submitting that the governor and/or the Home Secretary were under a duty to produce him or procure his production to the court to which he had been remanded to appear on bail. The appellant also sought an order directing the governor to produce him to that court on the date on which he was required to appear and a declaration that the governor and the Home Secretary were under a duty to produce him to that court. The appellant further applied for a writ of habeas corpus ad respondendum directing the governor to bring him before yet another magistrates' court which had remanded him to appear on bail in relation to further criminal charges. The Divisional Court refused the applications. The appellant appealed to the House of Lords.

Held – Neither the Home Secretary nor the governor of a prison who held in his custody prisoners remanded on bail by a magistrates' court in accordance with s 128 of the 1980 Act was under an unconditional duty to produce them in court in accordance with the terms of their remand on duly notified dates. The duty of the Home Secretary, or of the governor acting under powers delegated to him, was merely to consider, in accordance with the Criminal Justice Act 1961, s 29(1)[b], whether he was satisfied that it was desirable in the interests of justice that such prisoners should be so produced and, if he was so satisfied, then not unreasonably to refuse to produce them. On the facts, it had not been unreasonable for the governor not to produce the appellant in court, and the appeal would accordingly be dismissed (see p 613 c d and p 614 b to d and h to p 615 b, post).

Decision of the Divisional Court of the Queen's Bench Division sub nom *R v Governor of Brixton Prison, ex p Walsh* [1984] 1 All ER 344 affirmed.

Notes

For the production in court of a prisoner, see 37 Halsbury's Laws (4th edn) para 1180.

For the Magistrates' Courts Act 1980, s 128, see 50(2) Halsbury's Statutes (3rd edn) 1554.

For the Criminal Justice Act 1961, s 29, see 25 ibid 868.

---

a   Section 128(1), so far as material, is set out at p 612 d, post
b   Section 29(1), so far as material, is set out at p 613 b, post

Case referred to in opinions

Raymond v Honey [1982] 1 All ER 756, [1983] 1 AC 1, [1982] 2 WLR 465, HL.   *a*

Appeal

Patrick John Walsh applied, with the leave of McCullough J granted on 16 September 1983, for (1) judicial review of the failure or refusal of the Governor of Brixton Prison and/or the Secretary of State for Home Affairs to produce the applicant to the South Western, Horseferry Road and Highbury Corner Magistrates' Courts on the dates he was   *b* remanded on bail to appear at those courts, by way of (a) an order directing the governor to bring the applicant before those courts on the dates on which he had been remanded to appear at those courts and (b) a declaration that the governor and the Secretary of State were under a duty to bring the applicant before the courts before whom he had been remanded to appear on bail, and (2) a writ of habeas corpus ad respondendum directed to the Governor of Brixton Prison to bring up the applicant before the South Western   *c* Magistrates' Court for trial and examination. On 27 October 1983 the Divisional Court of the Queen's Bench Division (Kerr LJ and Webster J) ([1984] 1 All ER 344, [1984] 2 WLR 217) dismissed his application. On 23 November 1983 the Divisional Court refused the applicant leave to appeal to the House of Lords but certified, pursuant to s 1(2) of the Administration of Justice Act 1960, that the following point of law of general public importance was involved in the decision: whether the Secretary of State for the Home   *d* Department and/or the governor of a prison who held in his or her custody prisoners remanded on bail in accordance with the provisions of the Magistrates' Courts Act 1980 was under a duty to produce them in court in accordance with the terms of their remand on duly notified dates. On 8 December 1983 the Appeal Committee of the House of Lords granted the applicant leave to appeal. The facts are set out in the opinion of Lord Fraser.   *e*

Ian A Macdonald and *Nicholas Blake* for the appellant.
Simon D Brown and *Christopher Symons* for the prison governor and the Secretary of State.

Their Lordships took time for consideration.   *f*

28 June. The following opinions were delivered.

LORD FRASER OF TULLYBELTON. My Lords, on 8 August 1983 the appellant, who had been arrested on the previous day, appeared in the South Western Magistrates' Court, London on charges of burglary and assault. He was remanded in custody to   *g* Brixton prison until 15 August. Since then he has been repeatedly remanded in custody, and he is still in Brixton prison awaiting trial on those charges, to which I shall refer for short as 'the South Western court charges'. At the time of his arrest, on 7 August, he was on bail, having been remanded on bail on no less than three other separate charges, or sets of charges. Two of these have now been disposed of. One of them was dismissed, and it need not be further considered. On the other the appellant was convicted and   *h* sentenced to three months' imprisonment, which he has now served. I shall have to refer briefly to this set of charges later.

The third set, which was for theft, criminal damage and assault, is still pending and on it arises the issue in this appeal. I shall refer to this set as 'the Horseferry Road charges'. This set of charges resulted from an incident which had led to the arrest of the appellant on 18 June 1983, and to his appearance in Horseferry Road Magistrates' Court on 19   *j* June. He was then remanded on bail until 9 August 1983. By 9 August he was in Brixton prison, having been remanded in custody on the South Western court charges, and he was not produced to the Horseferry Road court. The appellant does not blame the respondents for not having produced him on 9 August, because he had only been admitted to the prison on the previous day and he recognises that the governor did not

know until too late that he was due to appear at Horseferry Road court on 9 August. The
a subsequent history of the Horseferry Road charges is as follows. On 9 August the
magistrates enlarged the appellant's bail until 9 September, and in due course the police
applied to the governor of Brixton Prison, under s 29 of the Criminal Justice Act 1961,
for him to be produced on that date. The application was received at the prison on
7 September, but the appellant was not produced on 9 September because of staff shortage
at the prison. On 9 September the magistrates further enlarged bail until 16 September,
b and they instructed their clerk to write to the governor of the prison asking him to
arrange for the appellant's production at the court on 16 September. The clerk wrote as
instructed, and her letter was received at the prison on 15 September. The police also
requested the governor, by telephone on 12 September, to produce the appellant on 16
September at the Horseferry Road court. But on 16 September he was again not produced
and the magistrates, apparently losing patience, issued a bench warant for his arrest. The
c warrant has never been served on the appellant because of his being in prison. Meantime
the Horseferry Road charges are still pending and no progress has been made towards
bringing the appellant to trial on them.

The appellant alleges that there was a duty incumbent on the respondents to produce
him, or to arrange for his production, at Horseferry Road magistrates' court on 9 and 16
September, and that they failed to perform that duty although the governor of the prison
d had proper notice that his production was required in order to answer the Horseferry
Road charges. The governor has sworn an affidavit in which he states that the reason
why the appellant was not produced on 9 and 16 September was shortage of staff in that
insufficient prison officers were available to act as escorts. Further details of the history
of the various charges against the appellant are set out in the judgment of Webster J in
the Divisional Court and it is unnecessary for me to repeat them here (see [1984] 1 All
ER 344, [1984] 2 WLR 217). Part of the relief sought by the appellant in the Divisional
e Court was a writ of habeas corpus ad respondendum to bring up the appellant for trial
and to be examined at various magistrates' courts on dates on which he had been
remanded to appear at those courts. By the time that the appeal reached your Lordships'
House an order for habeas corpus ad respondendum would no longer have been
appropriate, because there was no future date until which the appellant had been
remanded on bail. But the question of principle remains whether the Secretary of State
f or the governor of a prison who holds in his custody prisoners remanded on bail by a
magistrates' court in accordance with the provisions of the Magistrates' Court Act 1980 is
under a duty to produce them at court in accordance with the terms of their remand on
duly notified dates.

Before the Divisional Court counsel for the appellant based his argument largely on
g various statutory provisions which he said imposed a duty on the governor to produce
the appellant to the Horseferry Road court. Before this House he no longer relied on the
statutory provisions for his primary argument, but relied entirely on a duty which he
said was imposed on the respondents at common law. Counsel accepted that it was not
an absolute duty; he accepted that if, for example, there was an acute shortage of staff
due to some emergency, such as a riot in the prison, on the date when a prisoner who
h had been remanded on bail on other charges was due to appear in court on those charges
the governor would not be under a duty to divert prison officers from dealing with the
emergency to escort the prisoner to court. But, in the absence of exeptional circumstances,
counsel said, the duty was incumbent on the governor as part of a more general duty to
obey orders of the court, and not to prevent other persons from obeying orders of the
court, or to obstruct or interfere with the course of justice. The authority on which
j counsel mainly relied for this part of the argument was *Raymond v Honey* [1982] 1 All ER
756, [1983] 1 AC 1, where a prison governor was held to have acted in contempt of court
by stopping a letter and enclosed documents which a prisoner had entrusted to the prison
authorities to be forwarded to the Crown Office at the Royal Courts of Justice. In that
case Lord Wilberforce referred to two basic principles from which he started and said
([1982] 1 All ER 756 at 758–759, [1983] 1 AC 1 at 10):

'First, any act done which is calculated to obstruct or interfere with the due course of justice, or the lawful process of the courts, is a contempt of court . . . Second, *a* under English law, a convicted prisoner, in spite of his imprisonment, retains all civil rights which are not taken away expressly or by necessary implication . . .'

In that case the House held that a prisoner's right 'to have unimpeded access to a court' (see [1982] 1 All ER 756 at 760, [1983] 1 AC 1 at 12 per Lord Wilberforce) had not been taken away or affected by reason of his imprisonment. But the form of access in question in that case was access by written communication. In the present case the appellant is *b* claiming a right to unimpeded access in the form not merely of being personally present in court, but by being taken there and produced to the court by the governor. That argument raises quite different issues from those raised in *Raymond v Honey*.

The duty of the governor of the prison into whose custody a person has been committed on remand by magistrates is imposed primarily by the Magistrates' Court Act 1980, s 128(1)(a). It is instructive to compare the provisions of para (a) (which deal with *c* remands in custody) with those of para (b) (which deal with remands on bail). These provisions are:

'Where a magistrates' court has power to remand any person, then, subject to section 4 of the Bail Act 1976 and to any other enactment modifying that power, the court may—(a) remand him in custody, that is to say, commit him to custody *to* *d* *be brought* before the court at the end of the period of remand or at such earlier time as the court may require; or (b) where it is inquiring into or trying an offence alleged to have been committed by that person or has convicted him of an offence, remand him on bail in accordance with the Bail Act 1976, that is to say, by *directing him to appear* as provided in subsection (4) below . . .' (Emphasis added.)

I have omitted amendments made by the Criminal Justice Act 1982, s 59 and Sch 9, as *e* they are not relevant for the present purpose. The duty of the governor of the prison to which a person remanded in custody has been committed is spelt out in further detail by the commitment order. An example is seen in the order made by the South Western Magistrates' Court on 15 August 1983, committing the appellant to Brixton prison on remand. It was addressed to the constables of the Metropolitan Police Force and to the governor of Brixton prison, and it directed the governor in these terms: *f*

'. . . and you, the Governor, [are hereby required] to receive the accused into your custody and, unless the accused is released on bail or you are otherwise ordered in the meantime, to keep the accused until the above date [22 August 1983] and then convey the accused to the said Magistrates' Court at the above time [10 am].'

g

But no similar duty to convey the accused to the court is imposed on the governor when a person is remanded on bail, and para (b) of s 128(1) quoted above clearly proceeds on the assumption that the person who had been remanded on bail will be at liberty, and it imposes the duty to appear on the person himself. So does s 3(1) of the Bail Act 1976.

Apart from their duty under the Magistrates' Courts Act 1980 the respondents are bound to obey the Habeas Corpus Act 1679 so far as it is applicable, and in particular to *h* obey s 8, which imposes a prohibition against removal of prisoners from the prisons to which they had been committed, except in certain circumstances specified in that section. I do not pause now to examine the archaic language of the 1679 Act, except to say that I assume for the purposes of this appeal that the appellant falls within the class of persons referred to in s 8 as 'subject of this realme' and that the reference to committal 'for any criminall *or supposed* criminall matter' (emphasis added) applies to committal on remand. *j* The provisions of s 8 have been modified to some extent by the provisions of later statutes. For example, under the Habeas Corpus Acts 1803 and 1804 power was given to the courts to award writs of habeas corpus for bringing prisoners before courts-martial and certain other bodies, and under the Criminal Law Amendment Act 1867, s 10 power was given to order a prisoner to be produced in certain circumstances without a writ of

habeas corpus. The statutory provision which appears to me relevant to the present
question (and which would modify the Habeas Corpus Act 1679 in so far as the latter
would otherwise apply to the circumstances of this case) is the Criminal Justice Act 1961,
s 29(1) of which provides:

'If the responsible Minister is satisfied, in the case of a person detained in any part
of the United Kingdom in a prison . . . that the attendance of that person at any
place in that or any other part of the United Kingdom or in any of the Channel
Islands or the Isle of Man is desirable in the interests of justice or for the purposes of
any public inquiry, the responsible Minister may direct that person to be taken to
that place.'

The discretionary power conferred by that provision on 'the responsible Minister' (the
Home Secretary) has been delegated by him to the governors of prisons for certain
purposes, one of which is to order the production of prisoners, at the request of the
police, to answer another charge: see Circular Instruction no 81/1971 issued by the Prison
Department of the Home Office and referred to in an affidavit by a Mr Hayzelden. So
the effect of s 29(1) of the 1961 Act, and of the circular, is that the governor of a prison
may direct a prisoner to be taken to a court if he is satisfied that his attendance at the
court is desirable in the interests of justice. That gives the governor a discretionary
power, but does not impose on him a duty, to have the prisoner brought to the court.
His only relevant duty is, in my opinion, first, to consider any request from the police
for the attendance of a prisoner in court, and, second, not to refuse unreasonably to
permit such attendance. It may be that after a request for attendance has been made by
the police, if a police escort were to attend at the prison to take the prisoner to court at
the end of his period of remand on bail, the governor might be under a duty to hand
him over to the police for that purpose, and a refusal to do so might, in some
circumstances, amount to obstructing the course of justice. But it is unnecessary to
consider the matter, as it does not arise on the facts of this case.

In this case, as I have already mentioned, requests for production of the appellant on
9 and 16 September were made by the police, and a further request was made for his
production on 16 September by the clerk of the Horseferry Road Magistrates' Court. On
16 September the governor replied to the clerk of the court apologising for not having
produced the appellant and giving the following explanation:

'Because of severe staff shortages I am not able to escort prisoners outside the
prison for further court appearances using prison officers. Under the provision of
Prison Rule 38(2) a prisoner required to be taken in custody outside a prison may be
taken by a police officer. Should the court so direct it would be possible to release
[the appellant] to the Police at the prison.'

That reply shows that the governor was not refusing to allow the appellant to be
produced to the court, but was merely explaining that he was unable to provide an escort
for the purpose. It has not been alleged that that was not his real reason, and in these
circumstances it would be out of the question to hold that he had acted unreasonably.
Counsel for the appellant submitted that the governor should have 'called on' the police
to take the appellant to the court, but the argument fails because the governor had no
power to give orders to the police.

It is a matter for regret that there was not closer co-operation between the prison
authorities and the police in this case. Mr Hayzelden explains in his affidavit that under
the Prison Rules 1964, SI 1964/388, r 38(2) a prisoner who is required to be taken in
custody anywhere outside a prison has to be kept in the custody either of a officer
appointed under s 3 of the Prison Act 1952 or of a police officer. An arrangement exists
in London whereby prisoners who have been remanded in custody to appear on a later
date in the magistrates' court are normally taken to court by the police. They operate a
system of collection and distribution of prisoners to London magistrates' courts. Where
prisoners have been remanded in custody to appear in the Crown Court in London, they

are conveyed by prison officers from Brixton prison, which is responsible for providing prison officers for the Crown Court throughout London. But the prison is not always able to provide the necessary escorts, and the usual procedure is for the prison authorities to review the applications for production 24 hours before they are due. If they cannot provide the necessary number of prison officers, the police are invited to collect some of the prisoners for production. Unfortunately this system broke down so far as the appellant was concerned on 9 and 16 September 1983. That is to be regretted but it has not been shown to have been due to the fault of either of the respondents.

The result is that in my opinion the Divisional Court reached the correct conclusion. The certified question should be answered as follows: 'Neither the Secretary of State nor the governor of a prison who holds in his custody prisoners remanded on bail by a magistrates' court in accordance with the provisions of the Magistrates' Court Act 1980 is under an unconditional duty to produce them at court in accordance with the terms of their remand on duly notified dates. The duty of the Secretary of State, or of the governor acting under powers delegated to him, is to consider, in accordance with the Criminal Justice Act 1961, s 29, whether he is satisfied that it is desirable in the interests of justice that such prisoners should be so produced and, if he is so satisfied, not unreasonably to refuse to produce them.'

While the certified question should in my opinion be answered in the way that I have proposed, I must draw attention to the state of affairs which has been disclosed in this appeal and which was rightly described by the Divisional Court as 'highly unsatisfactory' (see [1984] 1 All ER 344 at 351, [1984] 2 WLR 217 at 225). It appears to me to be little short of scandalous. The appellant has been in prison on remand since 9 August 1983, that is for more than nine months by the time the appeal was heard in your Lordships' House, awaiting trial on the South Western court charges. It is fair to recall that for part of that time he was serving the sentence of three months' imprisonment, on other charges which I have already mentioned. But he has not been brought to trial on the South Western court charges, or on the Horseferry Road charges on which he was originally remanded on bail on 19 June 1983. In respect of the later charges there appears to be a deadlock. The bench warrant for his arrest on those charges cannot be served on the appellant so long as he is in prison on remand, or while serving a sentence, if he is convicted and sentenced on the South Western court charges. The Horseferry Road charges may therefore continue to hang over his head indefinitely. We were informed by counsel for the respondents that the Secretary of State was well aware of the serious shortage of staff at Brixton prison and that he was taking energetic measures to remedy the shortage. I do not doubt that that is correct, but meanwhile the appellant's predicament urgently demands solution. Two things seem to be required. First, he must be brought to trial on the South Western court charges with the minimum possible further delay. Second, the deadlock which has arisen with regard to the Horseferry Road charges should be brought to the notice of the magistrates in that court in order that they can take suitable measures to bring it to an end. They might think it right to consider recalling for cancellation the bench warrant granted on 16 September 1983, which has been the main cause of the deadlock, and replacing it by an order that the appellant be brought before the court on a date which is early, but which will leave enough time for an arangement to be made between the police and the governor of the prison for an escort to be provided. It is intolerable that that present deadlock be allowed to continue.

I would answer the certified question as I have proposed, and dismiss the appeal.

LORD ELWYN-JONES. My Lords, I have had the advantage of reading in draft the speech prepared by my noble and learned friend Lord Fraser, and for the reasons he has given I would dismiss the appeal and answer the certified question as he has proposed.

LORD KEITH OF KINKEL. My Lords, for the reasons given in the speech of my noble and learned friend Lord Fraser, with which I agree, I too would dismiss the appeal.

LORD SCARMAN. My Lords, for the reasons given in the speech of my noble and
a learned friend Lord Fraser, with which I agree, I too would dismiss the appeal.

LORD BRANDON OF OAKBROOK. My Lords, I have had the advantage of
reading in advance the speech proposed by my noble and learned friend Lord Fraser. I
agree with it, and for the reasons which he gives I would answer the certified question in
the way which he proposes and dismiss the appeal.

b   *Appeal dismissed.*

Solicitors: *Hallmark Carter & Atkinson* (for the appellant); *Treasury Solicitor.*

Mary Rose Plummer   Barrister.

c

Haste v Sandell Perkins Ltd

QUEEN'S BENCH DIVISION
HIRST J
d 13, 14 DECEMBER 1983

*Damages – Personal injury – Loss of earnings – Deduction of social security benefits accruing to
injured person – One-half of value of benefits accruing for five years after accrual of cause of
action to be deducted from damages – Whether value of benefits accruing after expiry of five-year
period deductible from damages – Law Reform (Personal Injuries) Act 1948, s 2(1).*

e
An employee brought an action against his employers claiming damages for personal
injuries sustained in an accident which occurred in the course of his employment. The
employers were found to have been negligent and in calculating the special damages in
respect of the employee's loss of earnings the judge, as required by s 2(1)[a] of the Law
Reform (Personal Injuries) Act 1948, deducted one-half of the amount of industrial
f injury benefit which the employee had received for the five years following the accrual
of his cause of action. The question arose whether industrial injury, sickness, disablement
or invalidity benefit which accrued to him after the five-year period had expired could
be set off in full against his loss of earnings.

Held – On its true construction s 2(1) of the 1948 Act exhaustively defined the extent to
g which industrial injury, sickness, disablement or invalidity benefit could be deducted
when assessing damages for loss of earnings or profits in an action for personal injuries.
Accordingly, any such benefits accruing to the plaintiff after the five-year period
prescribed by s 2(1) had elapsed could not be taken into account in assessing the damages
(see p 167 *d e* and p 619 *h* to p 620 *a* and *f*, post).
    Hultquist v Universal Pattern and Precision Engineering Co Ltd [1960] 2 All ER 266 applied.
h   *Stott v Sir William Arrol & Co Ltd* [1953] 2 All ER 416, *Parsons v BNM Laboratories Ltd*
[1963] 2 All ER 658, *Parry v Cleaver* [1969] 1 All ER 555 and *Lincoln v Hayman* [1982] 2
All ER 819 considered.

Notes
For deduction of benefits received or receivable in assessing damages in tort, see 12
j Halsbury's Laws (4th edn) para 1152, and for cases on the principles of compensation
generally, see 17 Digest (Reissue) 87–90, 32–46.
    For the Law Reform (Personal Injuries) Act 1948, s 2, see 35 Halsbury's Statutes (3rd
edn) 548.

---

a Section 2(1), so far as material, is set out at p 617 *c*, post

Cases referred to in judgment

Barnes v Bromley London BC (1983) Times, 16 November.

British Transport Commission v Gourley [1955] 3 All ER 796, [1956] AC 185, [1956] 2 WLR 41, HL.

Hultquist v Universal Pattern and Precision Engineering Co Ltd [1960] 2 All ER 266, [1960] 2 QB 467, [1960] 2 WLR 886, CA.

Lincoln v Hayman [1982] 2 All ER 819, [1982] 1 WLR 488, CA.

Nabi v British Leyland (UK) Ltd [1980] 1 All ER 667, [1980] 1 WLR 529, CA.

Parry v Cleaver [1969] 1 All ER 555, [1970] AC 1, [1969] 2 WLR 821, HL.

Parsons v BNM Laboratories Ltd [1963] 2 All ER 658, [1964] 1 QB 95, [1963] 2 WLR 1273, CA.

Stott v Sir William Arrol & Co Ltd [1953] 2 All ER 416, [1953] 2 QB 92, [1953] 3 WLR 166.

Action

By a writ issued on 13 February 1981 the plaintiff, William George Haste, brought an action against the defendants, Sandell Perkins Ltd, his employers, claiming damages for personal injuries which he sustained in the course of his employment on 3 July 1978 as a result of the defendants' negligence and/or breach of statutory duty. The trial judge found that the defendants were 100% liable in negligence for the plaintiff's injuries. He awarded him £12,500 by way of general damages for pain, suffering etc and £5,992·05 by way of special damages for his past loss of earnings. The case is reported solely on the question whether the defendants were entitled to set off in full against his future loss of earnings industrial injury benefits etc accruing to him five years or more after the accident. The facts are set out in the judgment.

Alexander Dawson for the plaintiff.
Christopher Critchlow for the defendants.

HIRST J. In this case, the plaintiff claims damages for personal injuries against his employers on the basis of both breach of statutory duty and negligence.

The accident occurred on 3 July 1978 at the defendants' premises where the plaintiff was employed, that is at a timber yard at Wallington in Surrey. The plaintiff was in the course of unloading or about to unload some chipboard from a forklift truck when the top pieces of chipboard slipped forward and trapped his left leg causing him serious injuries. He was then aged 56. There were only two employees working manually at this yard and the plaintiff was the junior of the two. He was called the under-foreman and the other man, Mr Allison, who was also a witness, was the foreman. The reason why the yard appeared to be all non-commissioned officers and no private soldiers was because there had previously been other rank and file workers at the premises but for reasons which have not been gone into and do not matter these two men, the plaintiff and Mr Allison, were at the material time the only two people involved.

[His Lordship reviewed the evidence and found (i) that the defendants had been negligent and were 100% to blame for the plaintiff's injuries, and (ii) that the plaintiff had become unemployed as a result of their negligence. His Lordship awarded the plaintiff £12,500 by way of general damages for pain, suffering etc, and then considered the special damages in respect of his past loss of earnings. He found that the plaintiff's injuries and age were such that he could not obtain any employment and that he had been paid, under the Social Security Act 1975, industrial injury benefit since the date of the accident. In accordance with s 2(1) of the Law Reform (Personal Injuries) Act 1948, his Lordship deducted one-half of the amount of the industrial injury benefit received by the plaintiff up to the fifth anniversary of the accident and awarded him £5,992·05 in respect of his past loss of earnings. His Lordship continued:]

I now turn to deal with the question of future loss of earnings. Again, the figures are agreed mathematically, but this raises a point of major principle which is of some considerable importance.

a It has been very well argued, if I may be permitted to say so, by both sides, and has involved a quite extensive citation of authorities. Let me give the raw figures first, which vividly illustrate the nature of the problem. The continuing wages loss net after July 1983 is £70·96 a week. The total benefits, industrial injury benefits and the like, being received by the plaintiff amount to £72·57 a week. Consequently the plaintiff is already receiving in benefit £1·60 or so per week in excess of his continuing wages loss.

b The vital question at issue is: is this deductible? Because if it is it wipes out or substantially wipes out any future loss. Counsel for the plaintiff relies on the provisions of the statute in force, that is the Law Reform (Personal Injuries) Act 1948, which as amended by the Social Security (Consequential Provisions) Act 1975, Sch 2, reads as follows, and I am reading from s 2(1):

c 'In an action for damages for personal injuries (including any such action arising out of a contract), there shall in assessing those damages be taken into account, against any loss of earnings or profits which has accrued or probably will accrue to the injured person from the injuries, one half of the value of any rights which have accrued or probably will accrue to him therefrom in respect of any of the following benefits under the Social Security Act 1975 [and then the various types of benefit are listed] for the five years beginning with the time when the cause of action accrued . . .'

d Counsel for the plaintiff submits that that is a statutory code which concludes the matter in favour of the plaintiff. He submits that this section delimits the whole of the deduction which is permissible, namely half of five years' worth of those benefits whatever the duration of the past or future disability. In other words, he submits that it sets bounds as to both the minimum and the maximum amount which has to be taken into account.

e He cites in support of that argument three authorities. The first, which is a first-instance decision, is *Stott v Sir William Arrol & Co Ltd* [1953] 2 All ER 416, [1953] 2 QB 92, where Slade J held that, under this section, one-half of the benefit to be taken into account against the loss of earnings was not to be restricted to the period during which the loss was suffered, and that the court was entitled in its discretion to take into account f rights which had accrued after that period so as to reduce or extinguish the loss of earnings suffered.

Counsel for the plaintiff also relied on *Hultquist v Universal Pattern and Precision Engineering Co Ltd* [1960] 2 All ER 266, [1960] 2 QB 467, a decision of the Court of Appeal. There the plaintiff, who had suffered injury as a result of a breach of duty by his employers, the defendants, had his disability assessed 13 weeks after the injury under the National Insurance (Industrial Injuries) Act 1946 at 14% for life and he received a lump g sum gratuity of £210. He was then aged 36. His expectation of life was agreed at 35 years. The trial judge deducted from the agreed special damages one-half of this lump sum.

In the Court of Appeal, however, it was held that the amount of disablement gratuity for life which the court had to take into account under s 2(1) of the 1948 Act was one-h half of (and I emphasise these words) 'such proportion of the gratuity as the five-year period (or the unexpired portion [of that period]) bore to the injured person's expectation of life . . . or to any less period specified for the duration of the gratuity' (see [1960] 2 All ER 266 at 271, [1960] 2 QB 467 at 480). Accordingly, on the agreed expectation of 35 years' life, the deduction from the gratuity of £210 was assessed at one-half of £30, ie the court apportioned one-seventh of the gratuity, five years being one-seventh of the 35 j years.

Counsel for the plaintiff argued that, if there was no restriction to five years, and if all future benefits under this head however long they lasted had to be deducted, then it is quite obvious that the correct sum to deduct in the *Hultquist* case would have been half £210 and not half £30.

Counsel for the plaintiff cited the very recent case of *Barnes v Bromley London BC* (1983) Times, 16 November, in which his Honour Judge Smout QC, sitting as a High Court

judge in the Queen's Bench Division, rejected a submission for the defendant that the
plaintiff who had given credit for half his invalidity and industrial disablement benefits *a*
received for five years after the accident should in addition give credit for the whole of
those benefits which he had thereafter continued to receive. The judge said, as reported
in The Times:

'The submission [of the defendant] was founded on the general common law
principle that the plaintiff should not recover in damages more than he had lost by
the accident. But by section 2(1) of the 1948 Act Parliament had made specific *b*
provisions in relation, inter alia, to invalidity and industrial disablement benefits
and had thus abrogated the common law principle so far as it related to them.'

Finally, counsel for the plaintiff relied on the statement in the current edition of the
well-known textbook, *Munkman on Damages for Personal Injuries and Death* (1980, 6th edn)
p 85, where the editor says: *c*

'. . . the court can only take into account the benefit which will accrue within five
years from the time when the cause of action accrued . . .'

and cites the *Hultquist* case in support of that proposition. In a word, counsel for the
plaintiff's submission is that the question is settled in his favour by the words of the
statute. *d*
Counsel for the defendants' submission was that s 2(1) only applies to the period of
five years after the accrual of the cause of accident, on its proper construction, and that it
has no applicability whatever to any period thereafter. Consequently, submits counsel
for the defendants, the court is left to decide on general principle what should be
deducted for any period after the five years without any statutory constraint. On that
footing, he submits that as a matter of general principle double recovery should not be *e*
allowed and that the plaintiff should only be compensated once for the loss he actually
suffered.
Counsel for the defendants submitted that the trend of the law over recent years has
been towards rather than against deducting benefits, and he cited in support of that
argument s 5 of the Administration of Justice Act 1982, which provides that in personal
injuries actions any saving to the injured person attributable to his maintenance wholly *f*
or partially at public expense in a hospital or similar institution should be set off against
any income lost by him as a result of his injuries, reversing earlier decisions of the courts
to the contrary.
Counsel for the defendants cited a recent Court of Appeal case, *Nabi v British Leyland
(UK) Ltd* [1980] 1 All ER 667, [1980] 1 WLR 529, where the Court of Appeal held that
unemployment benefit was deductible, although I think it is fair to say that it reached *g*
that conclusion reluctantly and only because it was bound by an earlier decision of the
Court of Appeal in *Parsons v BNM Laboratories Ltd* [1963] 2 All ER 658, [1964] 1 QB 95.
Next counsel for the defendants relied on *Lincoln v Hayman* [1982] 2 All ER 819, [1982]
1 WLR 488, in which the Court of Appeal held that supplementary benefit was
deductible. Counsel for the defendants particularly relied on a passage in Dunn LJ's
judgment, the leading judgment, first of all where, having referred to conflicting *h*
decisions, he said he agreed with Latey J in one of those cases that there is no difference
in principle between unemployment benefit and supplementary benefit, and—

'Since therefore *Parsons v BNM Laboratories Ltd* is binding on us I would hold that
the supplementary benefit received is deductible from the plaintiff's damages.'

(See [1982] 2 All ER 819 at 821, [1982] 1 WLR 488 at 491.) *j*
Then Dunn LJ said ([1982] 2 All ER 819 at 822, [1982] 1 WLR 488 at 492):

'The question is therefore: when the right to supplementary benefit was conferred,
did Parliament intend that a plaintiff should enjoy it in addition to payment of his
damages? In some statutes Parliament has expressly provided that certain benefits
or a proportion thereof shall be disregarded in assessing damages.'

a   Next Dunn LJ cited the present section with which we are concerned, s 2 of the Law Reform (Personal Injuries) Act 1948, and also s 2 of the Fatal Accidents Act 1959. Then he proceeds:

> 'The principle is clear. A plaintiff is entitled to compensation for the loss he has suffered by reason of a tort. No more and no less. A plaintiff cannot recover more than he has lost. On the other hand completely collateral benefits are to be left out
b   > of account ... Where as here there is no indication in the statute as to the intention of Parliament I ask myself whether the payment of supplementary benefit is so remote from the damage caused in the accident that it should not be taken into account?'

and he holds that it should be deducted. Sir David Cairns and Waller LJ, who were the other two members of the court, agreed.

c   Finally, counsel for the defendants relied on the House of Lords case of *Parry v Cleaver* [1969] 1 All ER 555, [1970] AC 1, where the House of Lords by a majority of three to two held that a police constable's entitlement under the police pension fund to which he had contributed was not deductible. Lord Morris, who was one of the dissenters, said ([1969] 1 All ER 555 at 565, [1970] AC 1 at 22):

> 'In my view, the general principle and the general approach in calculating
d   > monetary loss in a case such as the present is that an injured person should receive such an amount of money as will put him in the same position as he would have been in if he had not received the injuries (see *British Transport Commission* v. *Gourley* ([1955] 3 All ER 796, [1956] AC 185)). A plaintiff should get such a sum in money as will represent the actual loss which has resulted to him in consequence of the defendant's negligence.'

e   Counsel for the defendants relied on a similar passage in Lord Pearson's speech (he was the other member of the minority) ([1969] 1 All ER 555 at 585, [1970] AC 1 at 46) and on a passage in Lord Pearce's speech ([1969] 1 All ER 555 at 575, [1970] AC 1 at 34):

> 'A man should be put financially in the position in which he would have been but for the accident.'

f   Earlier Lord Pearce said ([1969] 1 All ER 555 at 574–575, [1970] AC 1 at 34):

> 'Strict causation seems to provide no satisfactory line of demarcation. It would only lead one to a compromise like that contained in the National Insurance Act 1948, whereby both a plaintiff and a defendant were given some advantage from National Insurance benefits. This was quite a sensible compromise, but it is difficult
g   > . to find any legal principle to justify it.'

Lord Wilberforce also referred to this section with which we are concerned here as 'a compromise solution' (see [1969] 1 All ER 555 at 579, [1970] AC 1 at 39).

Counsel for the defendants submitted the *Hultquist* case [1960] 2 All ER 266, [1960] 2 QB 467 was distinguishable on the footing that it turned not on the construction of s 2(1)
h   but of s 2(6)(c) of the 1948 Act and was based on different facts, because in the *Hultquist* case the five years was still running whereas in the present case the five years has expired.

Counsel for the defendants' argument was an extremely attractive and impressive one if, and this is a big if, I am free from statutory constraint here. But in my judgment the plaintiff's arguments are right in relation to the benefit due in this case. My reasoning in favour of that conclusion is as follows.

j   I hold that s 2(1) of the 1948 Act on its proper construction covers the whole period past and future from the date the cause of action arose, and not merely the first five years. I support that conclusion by noting that it contains the mandatory word 'shall' and that 'loss of earnings or profits' comprises money which has accrued or probably will accrue to the injured person, ie with no limitation of time. In other words, the five-year limitation only applies to the benefit, but does not apply to the expectation of earnings or profits.

If the defendants' approach was correct, I think Parliament would have expressly applied the five years' restriction not only to the benefits but also to the profits and earnings. But Parliament has not done that. They have left the earnings and profits side at large and applied the five-year restriction only to the benefits. I therefore reject the defendants' construction which limits the whole application of the section to five years.

I consider this is fully in line with the *Hultquist* case, which, though not specifically and directly dealing with the very point at issue here, is none the less of great assistance. In my judgment the ratio decidendi of the *Hultquist* case did not turn just on s 2(6)(c) of the 1948 Act but was of general application.

If the defendant was right in his construction of the section, I cannot see how it would have been possible for the court to do other than deduct half of the £210 in the *Hultquist* case, but what it did was to make an apportionment limiting the deduction to half of five years' worth of the lump sum benefit, namely half of £30.

I think that *Barnes*'s case (1983) Times, 16 November was correct, and I respectfully follow it. I think *Munkman*'s statement is right, and I adopt it. I question whether counsel for the defendants is right that the trend is all one way in favour of extending deduction of benefits of this kind. He may be right in discerning a trend in *Lincoln*'s case [1982] 2 All ER 819, [1982] 1 WLR 488, but *Nabi*'s case [1980] 1 All ER 667, [1980] 1 WLR 529 points the other way, since it is quite clear the Court of Appeal was reluctant to deduct the unemployment benefit but felt constrained to do so by the authority of *Parsons*'s case [1963] 2 All ER 658, [1964] 1 QB 95. Even if counsel for the defendants is right about the trend, it cannot apply to a statutory case where the statute itself has laid down the limit of deductions. As Dunn LJ said in *Lincoln*'s case [1982] 2 All ER 819 at 822, [1982] 1 WLR 488 at 492, the general approach only applies when there is no indication in the statute as to the intention of Parliament. Here I hold that there is clear indication of the parliamentary intention in s 2(1) itself.

My decision is fully consistent with the dicta of Lord Pearce and Lord Wilberforce in *Parry*'s case [1969] 1 All ER 555 at 574–575, 579, [1970] AC 1 at 34, 39, referring to a statutory compromise: it seems to me that this is just exactly what s 2(1) of the 1948 Act provides. These benefits are partly contributory and what the 1948 Act is saying is that there will be a deduction over a limited period of five years of half those contributions, but not otherwise. It is a judgment of Solomon, a statutory compromise, and it is one I have to apply.

As a result, I hold that the plaintiff's benefits are not to be taken into account, and consequently under this heading I award him on the agreed three-year multiplier, three times his loss of £3,689·92 per year totalling £11,069·76.

In the result, I award £12,500 general damages, £5,992·05 for past loss of earnings, £11,069·76 for future loss of earnings and £197 in respect of the small miscellaneous items, making a grand total subject to interest of £29,758·81.

Judgment for the plaintiff accordingly.

Solicitors: *William J Stoffel & Co*, Beckenham (for the plaintiff); *Edward Lewis & Co* (for the defendants).

K Mydeen Esq   Barrister.

a

Denman v Essex Area Health Authority

QUEEN'S BENCH DIVISION
PETER PAIN J
8, 9, 10, 11 NOVEMBER 1983, 11 JANUARY 1984

b
Damages – Personal injury – Loss of earnings – Deduction of social security benefits accruing to injured person – One-half of value of benefits accruing for five years after accrual of cause of action to be deducted from damages – Whether value of benefits accruing after expiry of five-year period deductible from damages – Law Reform (Personal Injuries) Act 1948, s 2(1).

Section 2(1)[a] of the Law Reform (Personal Injuries) Act 1948 (which provides that when assessing the damages payable in an action for damages for personal injuries the court
c must take into account one-half of the value of specified social security benefits which accrue to him in the five years following the accrual of the cause of action) exhaustively defines the extent to which such benefits can be set off against his loss of earnings. Accordingly, once the five-year period prescribed by s 2(1) has elapsed, no deduction for benefits subsequently accruing to him can be made in assessing the damages (see p 625 *h*, post).

d
Hultquist v Universal Pattern and Precision Engineering Co Ltd [1960] 2 All ER 266 applied.
Parsons v BNM Laboratories Ltd [1963] 2 All ER 658, *Foxley v Olton* [1964] 3 All ER 248, *Eley v Bedford* [1971] 3 All ER 285, *Nabi v British Leyland (UK) Ltd* [1980] 1 All ER 667 and *Lincoln v Hayman* [1982] 2 All ER 819 considered.

Notes
e For deduction for benefits received or receivable in assessing damages in tort, see 12 Halsbury's Laws (4th edn) para 1152, and for cases on the principles of compensation generally, see 17 Digest (Reissue) 87–90, 32–46.
For the Law Reform (Personal Injuries) Act 1948, s 2, see 35 Halsbury's Statutes (3rd edn) 548.

f
Cases referred to in judgment
Barnes v Bromley London BC (1983) Times, 16 November.
Bradburn v Great Western Rly Co (1874) LR 10 Exch 1, [1874–80] All ER Rep 195.
British Transport Commission v Gourley [1955] 3 All ER 796, [1956] AC 185, [1956] 2 WLR 41, HL.
Eley v Bedford [1971] 3 All ER 285, [1972] 1 QB 155, [1971] 3 WLR 563.
g *Foxley v Olton* [1964] 3 All ER 248, [1965] 2 QB 306, [1964] 3 WLR 1155.
Hultquist v Universal Pattern and Precision Engineering Co Ltd [1960] 2 All ER 266, [1960] 2 QB 467, [1960] 2 WLR 886, CA.
Lincoln v Hayman [1982] 2 All ER 819, [1982] 1 WLR 488, CA.
Nabi v British Leyland (UK) Ltd [1980] 1 All ER 667, [1980] 1 WLR 529, CA.
Parsons v BNM Laboratories Ltd [1963] 2 All ER 658, [1964] 1 QB 95, [1963] 2 WLR 1273,
h CA.

Action
By a writ issued on 19 January 1979 the plaintiff, George Edward Frederick Denman, brought an action against the defendants, Essex Area Health Authority, claiming damages for personal injuries suffered and losses and expenses incurred as a result of an accident
j which occurred on or about 23 September 1973 at Victory House Corner, Thundersley, Essex, through the negligent driving, management and/or control of a motor vehicle owned by the defendants and driven by their servant or agent. The trial judge found that

---

a   Section 2(1), so far as material, is set out at p 623 *e f*, post

the defendants were liable for the plaintiff's injuries and that his claim was not statute-
barred. The case is reported solely on the question of whether the defendants were
entitled to set off against his past or future loss of earnings social security benefits received
five years or more after the accident. The facts are set out in the judgment.

Michael Brent QC for the plaintiff.
Timothy Stow for the defendants.

Cur adv vult

11 January. The following judgment was delivered.

PETER PAIN J. In this action, the plaintiff claims damages for personal injuries
sustained by reason of the negligence of the defendants by whom he was employed in
their ambulance service on 23 September 1973. The history is a curious one and it gives
rise to more extensive problems than one normally meets in a personal injury claim.

The plaintiff began to suffer back trouble in 1970. It did not respond to treatment, and
in 1972 he underwent a bone graft operation. It was apparently successful, and his
surgeon allowed him to return to light duties in June and then to full duties in February
1973. His work was heavy work. It involved the lifting of bodies, often in very awkward
positions.

The plaintiff resumed his work and all went well until September 1973, when the
ambulance in which he was riding overturned and the plaintiff was severely shaken.
However, after a short absence he returned to full duty. In October 1975 he strained his
back lifting and was off work for six weeks. Again he returned to full duties. In 1976 he
was again injured in a road accident while on duty and returned to work after four
weeks. By now his back was becoming increasingly troublesome. In April 1978 he went
sick and at long last he was referred back to the surgeon who had performed the 1972
operation, Mr Broadhurst. It was Mr Broadhurst who expressed the view that the 1973
accident had caused the repair effected in the 1972 operation to break down. The plaintiff
then took prompt steps to make a claim, which was rejected, and the writ was issued on
19 January 1979.

[His Lordship reviewed the evidence and found (i) that the accident in September
1973 reversed the effect of the operation in 1972, (ii) that the defendants were liable in
negligence for the accident, (iii) that the plaintiff's claim was not statute-barred but was
covered by s 2A of the Limitation Act 1975 because he did not know until May 1978 that
his injury from the accident was 'significant', (iv) that he had been invalided out of the
ambulance service in 1978 at the age of 44 and had not worked since and (v) that, but for
the accident, he would probably have been able to continue working in the ambulance
service until he was 55. His Lordship continued:]

The set off of social security benefits

It is agreed that, subject to liability, and subject to the issue I shall now deal with, the
correct figure for net special damage to date is £27,965. On the assumption that the
plaintiff continues to be unemployed by reason of the accident, the net continuing loss is
£6,670 per annum.

It is also agreed the plaintiff has received for the period beginning five years after the
accident up to trial, the following benefits:

	£
Sickness benefit	193·55
Invalidity benefit	18,231·15
Disablement benefit	1,773·56
Special hardship allowance	4,154·88
	24,353·14

It is further agreed that the plaintiff is receiving the following continuing benefits:

	£
Invalidity benefit	3,250 per annum
Disablement benefit	500 per annum
Special hardship allowance	1,000 per annum
	£4,750 per annum

Sickness benefit is payable under s 14 of the Social Security Act 1975, the condition of payment being incapacity for work. Invalidity benefit is payable under s 15 of the 1975 Act, and is payable where there is incapacity from work after sickness benefit has been paid for 168 days. Disablement benefit is payable under s 57 of the 1975 Act where an employed earner, by reason of personal injury arising by accident out of or in the course of his employment, suffers a loss of physical or mental faculty of more than 1%. The assessment of loss of faculty by virtue of Sch 8, para 1(c) is to be made without reference to the particular circumstances of the claimant other than age, sex and physical and mental condition. Incapacity for his particular work is, therefore, not relevant. Special hardship allowance is payable under s 60 of the 1975 Act where, as a result of the loss of faculty, the beneficiary is incapable and likely to remain permanently incapable, of following his regular employment and is incapable of following an occupation of equivalent standard which is suitable in his case.

Counsel for the defendants' argument is that sums received by way of benefits after the end of the five-year period should be set off in full against the plaintiff's loss of earnings. If this were done, the effect would be to reduce net special damage to £3,612 and continuing loss to £1,920 per annum.

Counsel for the defendants referred first to s 2(1) of the Law Reform (Personal Injuries) Act 1948, which provides:

'In an action for damages for personal injuries (including any such action arising out of a contract), there shall in assessing those damages be taken into account, against any loss of earnings or profits which has accrued or probably will accrue to the injured person from the injuries, one half of the value of any rights which have accrued or probably will accrue to him therefrom in respect of any of the following benefits... sickness benefit, invalidity benefit, non-contributory invalidity pension, injury benefit, disablement benefit for the five years beginning with the time when the cause of action accrued...'

He points out that the 1948 Act is silent as to what is to be done as to the specified benefits when they accrue more than five years after the accident, and that if they were to be ignored the Act could well have said so.

He asserts that at the time the 1948 Act was passed it was assumed that the common law would not require credit to be given for these benefits. But he further asserts that the common law was changed by the decision of the House of Lords in *British Transport Commission v Gourley* [1955] 3 All ER 796, [1956] AC 185. The basis of that decision was that, in assessing damages for loss of earnings, a judge must take the tax position into account. That was a claim in respect of personal injury.

In *Parsons v BNM Laboratories Ltd* [1963] 2 All ER 658, [1964] 1 QB 95, in a claim for damages for wrongful dismissal, the same principle was applied to unemployment benefit and the plaintiff was required to give credit for it in full against lost wages.

This decision was followed in *Foxley v Olton* [1964] 3 All ER 248, [1965] 2 QB 306, so far as unemployment benefit was concerned; but national assistance grants were not brought into account as being too remote because of their discretionary nature.

The same principle was applied to supplementary benefit in *Lincoln v Hayman* [1982] 2 All ER 819, [1982] 1 WLR 488. *Foxley v Olton* was distinguished because the right to supplementary benefit had by then become statutory and no longer involved any discretionary element.

Counsel for the defendants contends that there is no logic in distinguishing between the benefits set out in s 2(1) of the 1948 Act from unemployment benefit or supplementary benefit. Therefore he says that, apart from the exception created by that section, credit must be given in full for benefits received.

He recognises that this flies in the face of the practice since the 1948 Act was passed, but he boldly asserts that the practice followed for the past 35 years is wrong. I accept that, if his argument be sound, the fact that a wrong practice has been followed is no reason for rejecting his argument.

But it seems to me that his argument starts from a fallacy. *Gourley's* case did not alter the common law, it merely applied it to a given set of circumstances. The common law does not alter: it develops. Sometimes it develops in a way that surprises, but it always proceeds by the application of principle tinged with pragmatism to new circumstances. So it was here. The implementation of the Beveridge Plan provided a new scheme of benefits, which had to be adjusted to the existing law of damages for personal injuries. To the best of my recollection, there was no certainty what the answer at common law would be and Parliament stepped in to provide a statutory answer.

One is, therefore, driven to search for the intention of Parliament in passing s 2(1) of the 1948 Act. Was the intention to provide for those who were less seriously injured, so that the effect of their injuries would have passed away within five years, while leaving the long-term injured to the uncertainties of the common law? Or was the intention to strike a compromise, by virtue of which half the benefits received should be taken into account for the first five years, and the seriously injured should be left to the enjoyment of their benefits in full thereafter?

Save for *Barnes v Bromley London BC* (1983) Times, 17 November, which is a short note of a decision by his Honour Judge Smout QC sitting as a judge of the High Court, there is no direct authority on the point. He decided that, by s 2(1), Parliament had made specific provision in relation to invalidity and industrial disablement benefits and that had abrogated the common law principle in so far as it related to them.

In *Eley v Bedford* [1971] 3 All ER 285 at 288, [1972] 1 QB 155 at 158 MacKenna J considered whether a plaintiff had to give credit for benefits which she would have received had she claimed them timeously:

'I regard s 2 as an exhaustive statement of the circumstances in which a plaintiff's damages may be reduced by reason of national insurance benefits. If the case does not fall within the section, there is no ground for any reduction. On the principle laid down in *Bradburn v Great Western Railway* (1874) LR 10 Exch 1, [1874–80] All ER Rep 195, the plaintiff, but for s 2, would not have had to give credit for benefits received. The section alters this position, but only in respect of benefits which have been received at the date of judgment or which will probably be received thereafter. It does not alter the position in respect of benefits which have not been, and never can be, received.'

Counsel for the plaintiff referred me to two passages in the Court of Appeal decisions which seemed to take the same line as MacKenna J. In *Nabi v British Leyland (UK) Ltd* [1980] 1 All ER 667 at 669, [1980] 1 WLR 529 at 531 Brightman LJ in the course of reaffirming that employment benefit must be set off against loss of earnings said:

'As regards some of the contributory benefits described in s 12, the sort of issue which arises in the instant case has been resolved by statute. Section 2 of the Law Reform (Personal Injuries) Act 1948 (as amended by the National Insurance Act 1971) provides that in assessing damages for personal injuries, one half of sickness benefit and invalidity benefit shall be taken into account against loss of earnings. Widow's benefit and death grant are to be left wholly out of account under s 2 of the Fatal Accidents Act 1959 (as amended by the Social Security Act 1973). Unemployment benefit and retirement pensions are however untouched by statute in this context.'

a   In *Lincoln v Hayman* [1982] 2 All ER 819 at 822, [1982] 1 WLR 448 at 492 Dunn LJ
    said:

> 'The question is therefore: when the right to supplementary benefit was conferred,
> did Parliament intend that a plaintiff should enjoy it in addition to payment of his
> damages? In some statutes Parliament has expressly provided that certain benefits
> or a proportion thereof shall be disregarded in assessing damages. So s 2 of the Law
b > Reform (Personal Injuries) Act 1948 provides that one-half of any sickness benefit,
> invalidity benefit, non-contributory invalidity pension, injury benefit or disablement
> benefit for five years after the accident shall be taken into account. Section 4 of the
> Fatal Accidents Act 1976 (re-enacting s 2 of the Fatal Accidents Act 1959) provides
> that in assessing damages in respect of a person's death, there shall not be taken into
> account any insurance money, benefit, pension, or gratuity, which has been or will
> or may be paid as a result of the death. But there is no statutory provision in respect
c > of supplementary benefit paid to a person who has been injured in an accident, and
> Parliament must therefore be assumed to have left the question to the judges to be
> decided on principle.'

Both passages read as if the Lords Justices regarded s 2(1) as exhaustive, but, of course,
their minds were not specifically directed to the point I have to decide.

d   I derive most help from the decision of the Court of Appeal in *Hultquist v Universal
Pattern and Precision Engineering Co Ltd* [1960] 2 All ER 266, [1960] 2 QB 467. In that case
the issue was how much credit a plaintiff must give for a disablement gratuity. This is a
lump sum which is payable where disability caused by an accident arising out of or in
the course of employment is assessed at less than 20%. The plaintiff had been assessed at
14% for life and the Court of Appeal decided that the amount to be taken into account
e   was one-half of such proportion of the gratuity as the five-year period following the
accident bore to the injured person's expectation of life. It follows from this that the
proportion after the five-year period was not to be taken into account.

The issue that was argued related to the proportion of the gratuity to be taken into
account. The defendants argued that the amount of the gratuity was calculated under
the National Insurance (Industrial Injuries) Act 1946 at seven years' purchase, and that
f   therefore five-sevenths of the gratuity should be taken into account. They did not seek to
persuade the Court of Appeal, as counsel for the defendants would have done, that the
whole of the gratuity attributable for the post five-year period should be taken into
account.

The Social Security (Consequential Provisions) Act 1975, Sch 2, para 8, amended s 2 of
the 1948 Act so that sub-s (6) now reads:

g   > 'for the purposes of this section disablement benefit in the form of a gratuity is to
> be treated as benefit for the period taken into account by the assessment of the
> extent of the disablement in respect of which it is payable.'

Parliament thus gave its blessing to the decision in *Hultquist v Universal Pattern and
Precision Engineering Co Ltd*. This subsection can only be meaningful on the basis that
h   s 2(1) is exhaustive in defining how much of the benefits specified are to be taken into
account against loss of earnings.

Accordingly, I hold that the plaintiff is entitled to recover £27,965 by way of special
damages and a further sum for loss of future earnings calculated on a continuing loss of
£6,670 per annum.

j   *Quantum*
It follows from what I have said that the plaintiff is entitled to recover his net special
damage of £27,965.

He is also entitled to a sum for his loss of future earnings. I have held that as things are
he would probably have served until 55, that is for another 5½ years, but it has to be
remembered that the congenital weakness of his back has rendered him very vulnerable,

and that ambulance work is heavy work. I do not think that I should allow more than three years' purchase of the continuing loss of £6,670. In round figures this is £20,000.

There remains only the matter of pain and suffering and loss of amenity. It is very difficult to say how much of his present plight is due to the accident, and how much to congenital weakness. Immediately after the accident a very high proportion could be attributed to the accident, but the proportion has declined as the years go by and as he grows older an increasing proportion will, in my view, be attributable to nature.

In these circumstances, I think the best approach is to assess his condition as a whole and then take the proportion which is attributable to the accident. Mr Broadhurst put it at 50% as at today in his report, and increased this to 75% in his evidence. I think this is a good deal too favourable to the plaintiff, in the light of my finding that the plaintiff would have been wholly disabled for work, even without the accident, at 55. I have to look at the whole of his life from the date of the accident until death. I assess damages under this head at £25,000, and I attribute one-third of this to the accident and its effects. Damages under this head will, therefore, be £8,700.

There will, therefore, be judgment for the plaintiff for £56,665.

Judgment for the plaintiff accordingly.

Solicitors: *Robin Thompson & Partners*, Ilford (for the plaintiff); *Barlow Lyde & Gilbert* (for the defendants).

K Mydeen Esq   Barrister.

Griffiths v Griffiths

COURT OF APPEAL, CIVIL DIVISION
DUNN, WATKINS AND PARKER LJJ
27, 28 FEBRUARY 1984

Divorce – Financial provision – Lump sum order – Lump sum for children – Order for lump sum payment for benefit of children out of husband's share of proceeds of sale of matrimonial home – Husband on low income and in receipt of supplementary benefit – Wife not in receipt of supplementary benefit – Husband not intending to use proceeds of sale to provide accommodation for himself – Whether court entitled to order lump sum payment out of husband's share of proceeds of sale of matrimonial home – Matrimonial Causes Act 1973, ss 23(1)(f), 25(1).

On the divorce of the husband and wife, in April 1981, the wife was given custody of the two children of the marriage. The wife then applied for periodical payments and a lump sum payment for herself and the children and for a property adjustment order. In September the parties reached agreement to sell the matrimonial home and divide the net proceeds equally between them. The husband had paid the deposit and mortgage repayments on the matrimonial home out of his earnings. After the divorce the husband's earnings were low and he was in receipt of supplementary benefit but he was living with a woman, whom he intended to marry, in a house which she rented. The wife was living with another man, who was supporting her and the children of the marriage, and was not in receipt of supplementary benefit. When the wife's application for periodical payments and a lump sum payment came before the registrar, he made only a nominal order against the husband for periodical payments, having regard to the husband's means, but ordered, pursuant to s 23(1)(f)[a] of the Matrimonial Causes Act 1973, that on

---

a   Section 23(1), so far as material, provides: 'On granting a decree of divorce ... or at any time thereafter ... the court may make any one or more of the following orders, that is to say ... (f) an order that a party to the marriage shall pay to such person as may be so specified for the benefit of such a child, or to such a child, such lump sum as may be so specified ...'

the sale of the matrimonial home the husband should pay to the wife for the benefit of
a the children a lump sum payment of £4,000 or one-half of his share of the proceeds of
sale of the home, whichever was the lesser. The home was sold in September 1982,
leaving (after expenses) £7,682 payable to each of the parties. The wife received her share
of the proceeds but, in accordance with the registrar's order, half of the husband's share,
ie £3,841, was retained by the wife's solicitors. The husband appealed from the registrar's
order. The judge, having found that the husband did not intend to use any part of his
b share of the proceeds of sale for the purpose of providing accommodation for himself
and the woman he intended to marry, upheld in principle the registrar's decision that
the husband should make a lump sum payment to the wife for the benefit of the children
but reduced that amount to £2,750. The husband appealed from the judge's order,
submitting that, in the circumstances, where the wife could apply for supplementary
benefit if she was seriously in need and unable to support the children, it was wrong in
c principle for the court to use as a substitute for periodical payments a capital sum to
which the husband was entitled when he himself was on supplementary benefit. The
wife cross-appealed for an order restoring the registrar's order.

Held – It was not wrong in principle to regard a husband's share in the proceeds of sale
of the former matrimonial home as being part of his 'financial resources' which were
d available to meet his 'obligations', within s 25(1)(a) and (b) and (2)ᵇ of the 1973 Act,
provided that his share of the proceeds was not required for his own accommodation.
Since the husband was under an obligation, within s 25(1)(b), to support his children, and
since there was no ground for interfering with the judge's finding that the husband did
not intend to use any part of his share of the proceeds of sale to provide himself with
accommodation, it followed that, notwithstanding that the husband could not be
e required under s 18ᶜ of the Supplementary Benefits Act 1976 to contribute towards the
children's maintenance (because the wife was not receiving supplementary benefit for
them), it was an appropriate case in which to order the husband to make a lump sum
payment to the wife for the benefit of the children. In the circumstances, however, the

---

f *b* Section 25, so far as material, provides:

'(1) It shall be the duty of the court in deciding whether to exercise its powers under section
23(1)(a), (b) or (c) . . . in relation to a party to the marriage and, if so, in what manner, to have
regard to all the circumstances of the case including the following matters, that is to say—(a) the
income, earning capacity, property and other financial resources which each of the parties to the
marriage has or is likely to have in the foreseeable future; (b) the financial needs, obligations and
responsibilities which each of the parties to the marriage has or is likely to have in the foreseeable
future . . .

g (2) . . . it shall be the duty of the court in deciding whether to exercise its powers under section
23(1) . . . (f) . . . in relation to a child of the family and, if so, in what manner, to have regard to all
the circumstances of the case . . . and so to exercise those powers as to place the child, so far as it is
practicable and, having regard to the considerations mentioned in relation to the parties to the
marriage in paragraph (a) and (b) of subsection (1) above, just to do so, in the financial position in
which the child would have been if the marriage had not broken down and each of those parties
had properly discharged his or her financial obligations and responsibilities towards him . . .'

h *c* Section 18, so far as material, provides:

'(1) Where supplementary benefit is paid or claimed to meet requirements which are, or
include, those of a person whom another person is, for the purposes of this Act, liable to maintain
(in this section referred to respectively as "the dependant" and "the liable persons") the Secretary of
State may make a complaint against the liable person to a magistrates' court for an order under
this section . . .

j (3) On the hearing of a complaint under subsection (1) above the court shall have regard to all
the circumstances and, in particular, to the resources of the liable person, and may order him to
pay such sum, weekly or otherwise, as it may consider appropriate . . .

(5) Any payments ordered to be made under this section shall be made—(a) to the Secretary of
State in so far as they are attributable to any supplementary benefit (whether paid before or after
the making of the order); (b) to the person claiming supplementary benefit or (if different) the
dependant; or (c) to such other person as appears to the court expedient in the interests of the
dependant . . .'

judge had properly exercised his discretion in reducing the amount of the lump sum payment to £2,750. Accordingly both the appeal and the cross-appeal would be dismissed   *a*
(see p 632 *h* to p 633 *c* and *j* to p 634 *a* and *f* to *j*, post).

Dicta of Scarman LJ in *Chamberlain v Chamberlain* [1974] 1 All ER at 38 and of Finer J in *Williams (L A) v Williams (E M)* [1974] 3 All ER at 382 considered.

Per Watkins LJ. (1) Where on an application for periodical payments for the children of a broken marriage the father is ordered instead to make a lump sum payment to the mother for the benefit of the children, then, unless the lump sum is too small, it is   *b*
preferable that it should be secured so that the income from it will be used for the children's maintenance and the capital preserved so that in due course it will revert to the father or be given to the children (see p 634 *d* to *f*, post).

(2) It is doubtful whether the doctrine of the clean break can apply to an application for periodical payments in respect of children since their legal rights to be maintained by their father cannot be bought off or compromised (see p 634 *g*, post).   *c*

Notes
For lump sum payments following divorce, see 13 Halsbury's Laws (4th edn) paras 1105–1115.

For the Matrimonial Causes Act 1973, ss 23, 25, see 43 Halsbury's Statutes (3rd edn) 564, 567.   *d*

For the Supplementary Benefits Act 1976, s 18, see 46 ibid 1061.

Cases referred to in judgment
Chamberlain v Chamberlain [1974] 1 All ER 33, [1973] 1 WLR 1557, CA.
Chase v Chase (1982) Times, 23 October.
Hulley v Thompson [1981] 1 All ER 1128, [1981] 1 WLR 159, DC.   *e*
Minton v Minton [1979] 1 All ER 79, [1979] AC 593, [1979] 2 WLR 31, HL.
Williams (L A) v Williams (E M) [1974] 3 All ER 377, [1974] Fam 55, [1974] 3 WLR 379, DC.

Interlocutory appeal and cross-appeal
John Griffiths (the husband) appealed against the judgment of his Honour Judge Binns   *f*
given in the Norwich County Court on 29 November 1982 whereby, on the husband's appeal from an order of the deputy registrar dated 5 May 1982 ordering him on the sale of the matrimonial home to pay to Patricia Doris Griffiths (the wife) a lump sum of £4,000 or half his share of the net proceeds of the sale, whichever was the smaller, for the benefit of the two children of the marriage, the judge ordered that the appeal should be allowed to the extent that the husband should pay to the wife for the benefit of the   *g*
children a lump sum of £1,375 for each child, being a total lump sum payment of £2,750. The wife cross-appealed, seeking restoration of the registrar's order. On 12 July 1983 the Court of Appeal (Cumming-Bruce LJ and Sir George Baker) adjourned the hearing of the appeal to allow the husband and the wife to adduce further evidence, ordered that the Law Society be represented at the hearing of the appeal and ordered that the appeal be heard by a Court of Appeal consisting of three judges. The facts are set out   *h*
in the judgment of Dunn LJ.

Philip Sapsford for the husband.
John Holt for the wife.
Duncan Matheson for the Law Society.

j

DUNN LJ. This is an appeal from an order of his Honour Judge Binns sitting in the Norwich County Court on 29 November 1982 when he ordered a lump sum payment under s 23(1)(*f*) of the Matrimonial Causes Act 1973 for the benefit of the two children of the family. The main ground of the appeal is that the judge erred in principle in ordering a capital sum to be paid for the benefit of the children when the children's father, the husband, was in receipt of social security and, having regard to his means, was

not in a in position to meet any order for periodical payments. It was said that it was
a wrong in principle in those circumstances to deprive him of part of his only capital asset,
namely his share in the former matrimonial home.

The history of the matter is that the parties were married in 1967. There are two
children: Paul, born in 1969, and Nicola, born in 1972. The matrimonial home, which
was in the joint names of the parties, was at Watton in Norfolk. The husband left in
August 1980 and went to live with a Mrs Williamson in Ashford in Kent. Mrs
b Williamson, who is a widow, has three children, the eldest of whom is working and
makes some contribution to the family finances. Her two younger children are aged 14
and 7. She lives in a rented council house near Ashford which she is desirous of
purchasing. The wife remained with the two children of the family in the matrimonial
home. For the first six months after their separation she received supplementary benefits
for herself and the children, but she then met a Tech Sgt Capes of the United States Air
c Force who went to live with her in the matrimonial home and who took on himself the
support both of the wife and of the children of the family. The wife now has a child by
Sgt Capes born in April 1983, and they intend to get married, as do the husband and Mrs
Williamson.

On 28 October 1980 the wife filed a petition under s 1(2)(b) of the 1973 Act in which
she claimed all possible financial relief under both ss 23 and 24. There was a decree nisi
d on 2 March 1981. The custody of the children was committed to the wife, and the decree
was made absolute on 16 April 1981. On 21 August 1981 the wife gave notice of an
application for periodical payments and a lump sum for herself and the children and for
a property adjustment order.

In September 1981 there was correspondence between the solicitors, starting by the
wife's solicitors writing to say that the wife would be agreeable for the matrimonial
e home to be sold and, after deduction of the mortgage and expenses of sale and so on, that
the net balance should be divided equally between the parties. The husband's solicitors
replied to that letter agreeing that the house should be sold and the proceeds divided
equally on the basis that the wife would not herself be claiming periodical payments.
They went on to say:

f   'As to the claim for periodical payments for the children . . . until such time as he
    [ie the husband] is in receipt of a better income, it is for all practical purposes
    impossible for him to make any payments to speak of at all.'

They suggested that the application should stand over until the husband was able to
make progress towards securing a livelihood for himself.

The wife's solicitors wrote back on 29 September saying that she would require a
g nominal order for herself, and then, dealing with the periodical payments for the
children, they said: '. . . our instructions are not to let the application stand over. We will
deal with the matter further in due course.'

The application came before the registrar on 5 May 1982. He made a nominal order
for periodical payments in favour of the wife and ordered that, on the sale of the former
matrimonial home, the husband should—

h   'pay or cause to be paid for the benefit of the children . . . a lump sum payment
    of £4,000 or one half of his share in the net proceeds of sale whichever shall be the
    smaller.'

On 29 September 1982 the sale was completed and the completion statement shows
j that the total purchase price was £21,000. Then there are deductions in respect of the
mortgage, expenses of the transaction and solicitors' charges, leaving £7,682, being the
half share of the equity, payable to each of the parties. The £7,682, the wife's share, was
paid to her. In accordance with the registrar's order, half of the husband's share, namely,
£3,841, was retained by the wife's solicitors for the benefit of the children and the other
half was shown as being due to the husband. In fact he has, in the events which have
occurred, received some £2,500.

The husband appealed to the judge and on 29 November 1982 the judge made the order to which I have referred. He upheld the principle that the husband should pay a lump sum for the benefit of the children, but he reduced it to a total of £2,750, being £1,375 for each child. It is against that order that the husband now appeals, and, as I have said, the principal ground of appeal was that the judge was wrong to order a lump sum payment in the circumstances of this case.

The appeal first came into the list on 15 June 1983 before a differently constituted court. It was adjourned and the court ordered that there should be further evidence, in particular as to the husband's prospects of employment, and also that evidence should be put before the court as to the intentions of the Department of Health and Social Security with regard to the payment of benefits to the husband having regard to his capital assets, and also having regard to the proposal of Mrs Williamson to buy her council house. The court also ordered that the husband was to obtain for the benefit of the court the views of the Law Society as to the enforcement or otherwise of its charge in relation to the husband's costs in various alternative circumstances, depending on whether or not the judge's or registrar's order was upheld or whether the court ordered that there should be no lump sum payment at all. Following that order there was correspondence with the department which is before the court. The effect of it is that if the husband has more than £3,000 by way of capital he will not be eligible for supplementary benefits save that, if any of that capital is used for the purchase of a home for the husband, the commission has a discretion whether or not, and to what extent, to pay supplementary benefit. So far as family income supplement is concerned, the department points out that allotments for family income supplement are normally made for 52-week periods. The husband is in receipt of family income supplement at the moment. The present period ends on 15 March and, if there is any further application for family income supplement, he will be obliged to make a disclosure of any capital and effectively the same rules would apply as for supplementary benefit, and there is a rather complicated provision about interest which is contained in the letter. What I have said is intended to summarise the letter of 7 July 1983.

At the conclusion of the letter the department pointed out that, in the event of either of the children receiving supplementary benefit, the husband would be liable, as a liable relative, to make a reasonable contribution. That would be a matter in which the Supplementary Benefits Commission would have the power to make application to the magistrates. It would be a matter for the discretion of the magistrates whether to make any and, if so, what order against the husband, and, in exercising that discretion, following *Hulley v Thompson* [1981] 1 All ER 1128, [1981] 1 WLR 159, the magistrates would be entitled to take into account the terms of any order against the husband made in the county court.

So far as the Law Society charge was concerned, the Law Society took the provisional position in correspondence that the charge would bite on at any rate part of the husband's half share in the matrimonial home, because in the events that have occurred he would have preserved that, the wife's application for a lump sum having been specifically directed to his half share in the matrimonial home. But, as counsel for the Law Society, who appeared for the assistance of the court and for whose assistance we are grateful, indicated, that is a matter which would not be finally decided by the Law Society until the order of this court was made and the Law Society would have had an opportunity of considering the order and deciding whether or not the charge did apply. It would then of course be open to either party, if they were so advised, to challenge that determination of the Law Society in the courts, but it is a matter which at this stage does not arise for decision.

The court in July further adjourned the matter to a three-judge Court of Appeal, and it is on that basis that it has come before us.

I now turn to consider the financial resources and obligations of the parties as required by s 25 of the 1973 Act. The wife is wholly dependent on Sgt Capes, who supports her and the two children. According to an affidavit which we have, he has a net income of some £125 a week. He is liable under a court order to pay £25 a week maintenance for his wife and the two children of his marriage, who are 15 and 2 years old respectively.

The wife's only income is the family allowance, which is now £11·70 a week. They live
a in Brandon in Suffolk in a house which was bought partly with the wife's share of the
proceeds of sale of the former matrimonial home and, so far as the evidence goes, that is
the only capital asset which the wife has.

The husband, until about a year before the breakdown of the marriage, was in good
employment. He then ran into difficulties with his job. It is said that he had a nervous
breakdown, but in any event from the date of the separation in 1980 he was unemployed
b until February 1983, during which period he was receiving unemployment benefit and
supplementary benefit, a total of some £54 a week.

Mrs Williamson works part-time as a cleaner. She only earns a very modest amount,
put in one affidavit at £6 a week and in another at £3 a week. We are told that she is
now earning about £6 a week as a cleaner and she also receives the family allowance
which is now, £11·70. Her eldest child contributes £12 a week to the family and lives at
c home.

In February 1983 the husband started work at the modest wage of some £60 a week
gross, and pays his own stamp. We were told that he has had an increase in pay so that he
is now earning something over £80 a week, but it is still a modest sum by present-day
standards, and that is recognised by the department, because he is in receipt of family
income supplement in the sum of £16·20 a week. Now that he is in work and even with
d the assistance of the family income supplement, there is still a shortfall in the family
income compared with their expenditure.

So far as capital is concerned, the husband has already spent practically all of the £2,500
which was released to him, being his share in the proceeds of sale of the matrimonial
home. He has spent part of that on a new motor car, a washing-machine, a carpet and, he
says, miscellaneous items for the kitchen, which he has been modernising. Mrs
e Williamson is in a position to buy her council house for £11,850. We have the papers
from the Ashford Borough Council. That of course represents a substantial discount of
43% from the assessed value of the house, and she will no doubt be in a position to obtain
a mortgage in respect of that, or part of it any rate. According to the husband's affidavit,
it is anticipated that a substantial part of any deposit which she has to pay in respect of
that purchase will be provided by an interest-free loan from her brother, but he says in
f his affidavit that he would be expected, presumably by Mrs Williamson and her family,
to contribute about £4,000 to the purchase of that house. The intention of the husband
to contribute to the purchase of Mrs Williamson's council house was in dispute in the
county court. The judge made a finding about it. He said: 'I am not satisfied with [the
husband's] account that he is going to spend it on a council house and I don't find that
established.' That is a finding of fact which this court has not been seriously asked to go
g behind, and indeed is not a finding of fact that we could go behind.

Counsel for the husband in the course of his able address to us made a number of
submissions in support of the husband's case. He submitted, first of all, that the judge
was wrong to take a broad view of the case. He criticised in particular the judge's basic
approach to the case when the judge said: '. . . one has to do justice in the round, not with
the finesse and skill of a mathematician. The court must do the best it can. It profits one
h not to stray into byways.'

The first submission of counsel for the husband was that the judge failed to take into
account the husband's position vis-à-vis the Department of Health and Social Security
and also the potential right of the wife to claim supplementary benefits for the children.
He referred to a judgment of the Divisional Court in *Williams (L A) v Williams (E M)*
[1974] 3 All ER 377 esp at 381–382, [1974] Fam D 55 esp at 61 per Finer J, when the
i judge was describing what he called 'the dual system' of maintenance, that is to say by
way of applications to the magistrates' court on the one hand and to the Supplementary
Benefits Commission on the other. The judge referred especially to this sentence, where
Finer J said:

'But even within the dual system as it exists it is not, in my judgment, correct to
say that the courts must exclude from their consideration what is taking place on
the social security side of the same case . . .'

an observation which was repeated in different words by Heilbron J in *Chase v Chase* (1982) Times, 23 October. Counsel for the husband submitted that the judge was wrong *a* in this case to regard the husband as being in a position, because of his small sum of capital, to provide maintenance for his children when there would be no question of his being obliged to contribute towards their maintenance under any of the powers contained in the Supplementary Benefits Act 1976. Counsel submitted that, if the wife was seriously in need and was unable to maintain the children, she could always apply for supplementary benefit, and he submitted that it was wrong in principle in a situation of *b* this kind for the court to use a capital sum in the hands of a husband on supplementary benefit as a substitute for periodical payments. He said that it was not only wrong in principle but unjust in this case because of the agreement between the solicitors whereby the proceeds of sale of the matrimonial home had been agreed to be divided equally between the parties.

Counsel for the husband drew our attention to *Minton v Minton* [1979] 1 All ER 79, *c* [1979] AC 593, which is a decision of the House of Lords which approves of there being a clean break so far as that can be achieved in any particular case. He referred in particular to the well-known passage in the speech of Lord Scarman (see [1979] 1 All ER 79 at 87–88, [1979] AC 593 at 608), and submitted that in the instant case it was plain that, as far as capital was concerned, the intention of the parties had been that there should be a clean break and that capital should be regarded differently from income. He pointed out that *d* in this case if the marriage had continued there would have been no capital payment in respect of the children, and in support of his submissions that capital and income should be looked at separately he referred us to *Chamberlain v Chamberlain* [1974] 1 All ER 33 esp at 38, [1973] 1 WLR 1557 esp at 1564–1565 where Scarman LJ said:

'There are no circumstances in this case to suggest that any of these children had special circumstances that required them to make demands on their parents after *e* the conclusion of their full-time education. The capital asset, the house, was acquired by the work and by the resources of their parents, and, provided that the parents meet their responsibilities to their children as long as their children are dependent on them, this seems to me an asset that should revert then to the parents.'

Counsel for the husband submitted that that principle applied to this case. The asset *f* under consideration in this case is the husband's half share of the matrimonial home. He provided such down payment as there was. He made the mortgage repayments while he was working, accepting that the wife contributed indirectly by looking after the house, the husband and the children. None the less, this capital asset had been acquired by the work and resource of the parents. Counsel for the husband submitted that it was wrong in principle now for part of that asset to be paid to the children by way of a lump sum *g* payment. In considering that submission I observe that Scarman LJ added the important proviso that the parents meet their responsibilities to their children, and what is said on behalf of the wife in this case is that the husband has not met his responsibilities towards his children, because he has neither paid nor offered to pay any sum at all to the children or for their benefit since he left the matrimonial home. I agree that that statement of Scarman LJ must be read subject to the important qualification which he himself made, *h* and which is not fulfilled in the circumstances of this case.

I prefer to start considering the matter by looking at s 25 of the 1973 Act, which requires the court to have regard to all the circumstances of the case including, first, the income, earning capacity, property and other financial resources which each of the parties to the marriage has, or is likely to have in the foreseeable future, and second, the financial needs, obligations and responsibilities which each of the parties has, or is likely to have *j* in the foreseeable future. In this case the husband has an obligation to provide for the support of his own children, and included in his financial resources is a sum of cash which represents his share in the matrimonial home.

As counsel for the wife pointed out in argument, the court is reluctant to order payment of moneys which may be used for the purpose of the provision of accommodation, and, if it had been the intention of the husband to use this money for

the purpose of providing accommodation for himself and Mrs Williamson, the situation
a might have been different. But that is not this case, because there is the very specific
finding of the judge that he did not accept that that is the husband's intention. As I have
said, that is not a finding with which this court can interfere; indeed, it seems to me,
having regard to the probabilities and the surrounding circumstances, to be a finding
which is fully justified. The husband has already spent practically all of the money that
he has received on the purchase of what are nowadays known as consumer durables. He
b has secure accommodation with Mrs Williamson in her council house where she has
lived for many years and, although no doubt it would be to her advantage to buy the
house outright, the purchase of the house does not affect her security of tenure. It seems
to me that the judge was right to regard the husband's share in the proceeds of sale of the
matrimonial home as part of his financial resources, which is available to him to meet
his obligations to support his children so far as his resources allow. It is said with force
c that a situation may arise in the future when the wife will have spent the lump sum
(because the judge clearly envisaged that it was to be used for the day-to-day maintenance
of the children) and the husband might by then have improved his income position by
obtaining a better job, and she might then apply for a variation of the nominal order
which was made in favour of the children for an order of substance. That is admittedly a
possibility. Whether or not such an order is made will of course depend on the
d circumstances before the court at the time of any future application. At present, having
regard to the husband's modest income and his responsibilities towards Mrs Williamson
and her family, I would be surprised if any such order were made. On such an application,
no doubt the court would look carefully at the way in which the wife had spent the lump
sum to see whether it had been frittered away or whether it had been genuinely spent
for the benefit of the children. But, if the husband's position improved to the extent that
e the court on some future occasion thought it right to increase the order for periodical
payments above 5p a year, I myself would not regard that as an undesirable situation,
having regard to his obligation to maintain his children in accordance with his means,
whatever they may be from time to time.

There is obviously concern that the wife has the total control now of this modest
capital sum, and that has exercised the mind of the court and we put to counsel various
f suggestions, including a suggestion that there might be an order for secured periodical
payments for the children, but any such attempts to tie up the money would plainly be
difficult and cumbersome and probably inappropriate to the comparatively small amount
of money involved.

The judge saw the wife in the witness box. He formed a good view of her. He said:
'She is a sensible woman who will seek to do the best for her children.' Once again, that
is a finding of fact which has not been, and could not be, challenged and it justified the
g judge in my view in making the order which he made.

There is a cross-appeal that the order of the registrar should be restored. Counsel for
the wife has kept that open. He has scarcely argued it, but the judge came to the
conclusion that it was necessary to do, as he described it, 'justice in the round to the
children and to the husband'. He continued:

h   'One is entitled to have regard to the future, including the maintenance of these
        children. They are under 16. It is difficult to know if they will go on to further
        education. This figure awarded [ie the figure awarded by the registrar] was on the
        high side.'

And he reduced it to the figure of £2,750. I cannot possibly say that, exercising his
i discretion in that way, the judge erred. Accordingly, I would dismiss this appeal and the
cross-appeal.

WATKINS LJ. The judge, as has been said, was not satisfied that the husband was
going to use some or the whole of the remainder of the equity in his hands for the
purpose of purchasing in part the council house in which he nowadays lives with Mrs
Williamson, whom it is said he intends one day to marry. That was an unfortunate

finding for the husband. It has in my judgment provided an insuperable obstacle to his succeeding in his appeal to this court.

It is desirable, I think, when a marriage breaks down and two homes take the place of one that, generally speaking, the moneys which are available as a result of the breakdown are used as far as possible satisfactorily to create decent living conditions in both new homes, for the benefit not only of the parties who have joined together, but what is more important, for all the children affected by the upheaval.

If the judge had not come to the conclusion to which I have referred and had instead been confident that the husband would use the money as he professed he intends to for the purpose of helping to purchase a council house, I should have found the greatest difficulty in coming to the conclusion that this appeal should fail.

The next point to which I wish very briefly to refer is the advisability on an application for periodical payments of ordering a father to make a lump sum payment to a mother in the hope that she will faithfully discharge the trust thereby imposed on her to use the whole of it sensibly for the purpose of maintaining the children of the broken marriage. True it is that the judge found that this mother is a sensible woman. Nevertheless, she may be confronted with some kind of compelling reason for dipping into that fund for a purpose or purposes wholly unconnected with the maintenance of the children, and so dissipate, in whole or in part, such remainder as there is of it at that time. That is a risk which in most circumstances I would not be prepared to take. I think that usually the grant of a lump sum without the precautions being taken to which I shall refer in a moment is an undesirable order to make.

I should prefer that any lump sum which is ordered to be paid by a father to a mother for this purpose should be secured in some way, so that the income from it will be used for the maintenance of the children and the capital preserved so that eventually it will revert to the father's use or be given to the children when they reach their majority or thereabouts.

The problem here is, however, that the sum of money involved is so small. It will produce very little income, no matter how it is invested. It must not possibly be speculated with. The maximum income which could arise from sensible investment of the capital sum ordered to be paid in this case from the husband to the wife would be no more than about £7 or £8 a week. That is a wholly inadequate sum with which to maintain two children properly.

So I am compelled to come to the conclusion that the order of the judge should stand as it is.

I would add, finally, that I doubt very much whether the doctrine of clean break, so called, can ever apply to applications for periodical payments in respect of children. Their legal rights to be maintained by their father can be neither bought off nor compromised away. One can easily foresee that when this sum of money has been spent there will be further applications for periodical payments from the father. It may be he cannot complain about that; after all, he has the obligation, and a clear one, to maintain his own children until they are of a certain age. It should be clearly recognised here that the order made for the children's benefit will only suffice for a limited period of time.

For these reasons and with the reservations I have explained, I too would dismiss this appeal.

PARKER LJ. I agree that this appeal should be dismissed and also the cross-appeal, and I have nothing to add.

Appeal and cross-appeal dismissed.

Solicitors: *Hallett & Co*, Ashford, Kent (for the husband); *Fowell Thorold & Prentice*, Diss (for the wife); *David Edwards*, Secretary, Legal Aid (for the Law Society).

Bebe Chua   Barrister.

Cobstone Investments Ltd v Maxim

COURT OF APPEAL, CIVIL DIVISION
DUNN LJ AND WOOD J
11 APRIL 1984

Rent restriction – Possession – Nuisance or annoyance to adjoining occupiers – Adjoining – Whether neighbouring occupiers whose premises are not physically contiguous to tenant's premises are 'adjoining' occupiers – Rent Act 1977, s 98(1), Sch 15, Case 2.

On the true construction of Case 2[a] of Sch 15 to the Rent Act 1977 (which, by virtue of s 98(1)[b] of that Act, enables the court, where it considers it reasonable to do so, to make an order for possession of a dwelling let on a protected tenancy or subject to a statutory tenancy where the tenant has been guilty of conduct which is a nuisance or an annoyance to 'adjoining occupiers') the word 'adjoining' is used not in the narrow sense of 'contiguous' but in the wider sense of 'neighbouring'. Accordingly, an order for possession may be made under s 98 and Case 2 of Sch 15 against a statutory tenant who is guilty of conduct which is a nuisance or an annoyance to the occupiers of premises which are not physically contiguous to, or even (in the case of a multi-storey building) on the same floor as, his own but which are sufficiently close to his own to be affected by his conduct (see p 639 g to j, p 641 b and p 642 e and h to p 643 b, post).

Lightbound v Higher Bebington Local Board (1885) 16 QBD 577, *Cave v Horsell* [1912] 3 KB 533 and *Norton v Charles Deane Productions Ltd* (1969) 214 EG 559 applied.

Metropolitan Rly Land Corp v Burfitt [1960] CLY 2749 approved.

Marquess of Northampton Estate Trustees v Bond (1949) 155 EG 412 disapproved.

Notes

For orders for possession of premises where the tenant has been guilty of conduct which is a nuisance or annoyance to adjoining occupiers, see 27 Halsbury's Laws (4th edn) para 667, and for cases on the subject, see 31(2) Digest (Reissue) 1084–1085, 8463, 8469-8470.

For the Rent Act 1977, s 98, Sch 15, Case 2, see 47 Halsbury's Statutes (3rd edn) 504, 600.

Cases referred to in judgments

Cave v Horsell [1912] 3 KB 533, CA.
Grey v Pearson (1857) 6 HL Cas 61, [1843–60] All ER Rep 21, 10 ER 1216.
Lightbound v Higher Bebington Local Board (1885) 16 QBD 577, CA.
Metropolitan Rly Land Corp v Burfitt [1960] CLY 2749, Cty Ct.
New Plymouth BC v Taranaki Electric-Power Board [1933] AC 680, PC.
Northampton (Marquess) Estate Trustees v Bond (1949) 155 EG 412, Cty Ct.
Norton v Charles Deane Productions Ltd (1969) 214 EG 559.
Spillers Ltd v Cardiff (Borough) Assessment Committee [1931] 2 KB 21, [1931] All ER Rep 524, DC.
Wakefield Local Board v Lee (1876) 1 Ex D 336, DC.

Cases also cited

Ind Coope & Co Ltd v Hamblin (1900) 84 LT 168, CA.
Smith v Baker & Sons [1891] AC 325, [1891–4] All ER Rep 69, HL.
United Dominions Trust Ltd v Bycroft [1954] 3 All ER 455, [1954] 1 WLR 1345, CA.
Vale & Sons v Morgate-Street and Broad-Street Buildings Ltd and Albert Baker & Co Ltd (1899) 80 LT 487.
White v Harrow (1902) 86 LT 4, CA.

---

a   Case 2, so far as material, is set out at p 641 d, post
b   Section 98(1), so far as material, is set out at p 641 c, post

Appeal

The defendant, Pearl Maxim (the tenant), appealed against that part of an order of Mr   *a*
Seddon Cripps sitting as an assistant recorder in the West London County Court on
1 February 1984 whereby he ordered that the plaintiffs, Cobstone Investments Ltd (the
landlords), should recover against the tenant possession of the premises known as flat 2,
12 Queen's Gate, London SW7. The facts are set out in the judgment of Dunn LJ.

Michael Pearson for the tenant.	*b*
Mark West for the landlords.

DUNN LJ. This is an appeal from the order of Mr Seddon Cripps sitting as an assistant
recorder in the West London County Court on 1 February 1984, when he ordered that
the plaintiff landlords should recover against the defendant tenant possession of flat 2,
12 Queen's Gate, London SW7. He postponed the operation of the order for ten weeks,	*c*
which expires today.

The landlords, Cobstone Investments Ltd, are the owners of the whole of the premises
(no 12) and they also own the next door premises (no 11). They bought those premises
from Crofton Hotel Ltd, which occupies no 13, in 1980. The defendant was a sitting
tenant of flat 2. She had occupied that flat certainly from 1976 and before that she had
occupied a flat in no 11.	*d*

The tenant, under the terms of her lease with the Crofton Hotel, was entitled to central
heating in the flat and that central heating ceased to be available at the end of 1981. The
judge found that down to late 1981, when the landlords had completed the acquisition
of no 11, there was no difficulty between them and the tenant. The tenant's tenancy had
been duly determined by notice to quit, so that she was holding as a statutory tenant.

The landlords sought possession of the flat under Cases 1 and 2 of Sch 15 to the Rent	*e*
Act 1977. So far as Case 1 was concerned, although there had been substantial arrears of
rent at the date of issue of the proceedings, the arrears had been paid off and by the end
of the hearing the tenant had paid all the arrears of rent which were due. But the recorder
made his order under Case 2 on the ground that the tenant had been guilty of conduct
which was a nuisance or annoyance to adjoining occupiers.

The allegations of annoyance extended over a period from August 1982 to May 1983.	*f*
The conduct complained of was essentially verbal abuse and the use of obscene language
to effectively the landlord (although the company, in law, owned the premises; the
company was itself owned by Dr Al Shalabi) and there were also allegations of a similar
nature in respect of three other tenants of no 12, Mr Hosford, Mr Burgess and Miss
Barton. The case lasted ten working days in the county court. The recorder reserved his
judgment. He gave a full judgment in which he reviewed the whole of the voluminous	*g*
evidence which had been before him and he found eleven incidents proved, five relating
to Dr Al Shalabi, four to the other tenants of no 12, one related to a maintenance man
whose name was John, and the final incident involved the attachment to the door of the
tenant's flat of an abusive notice, which it was accepted had been written by the tenant
but actually attached to the door by somebody else.

The occupancy of the various flats at nos 11 and 12 is of some importance. Each house	*h*
consists of a basement, a ground floor and three upper storeys. In no 11 Dr Al Shalabi
uses the ground floor as an office. Although he does not live there, it was accepted that
he was in occupation of that flat. He was the only person from no 11 who made
complaint. As far as no 12 was concerned, there were no complaints from the occupier
of the basement. The tenant herself occupied flat 2 on the ground floor. The first floor
flat was occupied by some employees from the Iraqi Embassy. There was no complaint	*j*
from them. The second floor was occupied by Mr Burgess and Miss Barton, who were
complaining, and the third and top floor by Mr Hosford, who was also complaining.

Counsel for the tenant in this court realistically made no attack on the judge's findings
of fact, nor on his finding that the tenant had been guilty of conduct which constituted
an annoyance. His primary ground of appeal was that the three tenants of no 12 who did

complain were not adjoining occupiers within the meaning of the Act. He submitted
that the word 'adjoining' in Case 2 of Sch 15 to the 1977 Act means that the premises
must be contiguous in the sense of physically joining, or being coterminous with the
premises of the tenant of whose conduct complaint is being made. Counsel for the tenant
submitted that, in the context, the word 'adjoining' does not mean 'neighbouring'.

In support of that basic submission counsel referred us first of all to the Rent Act 1915
(which was the first of the Rent Acts) and the relevant provision is in s 1(3) where a
ground for ordering possession is if the tenant has been guilty of conduct which is a
nuisance or annoyance to adjoining or neighbouring occupiers. He pointed out that the
word 'neighbouring' had been deleted from the relevant statutory provision in the 1920
Act and does not appear in any subsequent Act or in the 1977 Act, and so (he submits)
that is an indication that Parliament intended to limit the category of persons who are
entitled to complain of nuisance and on whose complaints the court can order possession.

As far as the researches of counsel have been able to ascertain, there are only two
decisions of the courts which are directly in point on the construction of the word
'adjoining' in the Acts, and they are conflicting decisions of two very experienced county
court judges. The first is *Marquess of Northampton Estate Trustees v Bond* (1949) 155 EG
412, which is a decision of his Honour Judge Blagden when he adopted the restrictive
meaning of the word, which is contended for by counsel for the tenant, and held that the
tenants of a second-floor flat were not adjoining occupiers to the tenant of the ground-
floor flat, whose conduct was relied on as constituting a nuisance, and accordingly he
dismissed the claim for possession founded on complaints by the tenants.

The case the other way is *Metropolitan Rly Land Corp v Burfitt* [1960] CLY 2749, a
decision of his Honour Judge Harold Brown, in which the landlord claimed possession of
two rooms on the ground that—

> 'the defendant . . . was a nuisance and annoyance to adjoining occupiers. The
> defendant occupied rooms on the first floor. Evidence of annoyance to themselves
> was given by the occupiers of rooms above those of the defendant and on the second
> floor, and also by the occupier of rooms on the first floor, next to those of the
> defendant.'

The report is not clear. It would appear from the short extract from the report which I
have just read that some of the premises may have been physically touching but I do not
think that can have been the position because the judge made an order for possession.
He—

> '*held* (1) that the meaning of "adjoining" . . . has not been finally adjudicated and
> that a rather narrow construction had been placed on it; (2) that the statement in
> Megarry's *Rent Acts* ((8th edn, 1955) p 251) was the correct view, namely that the
> meaning "contiguous" was too strict; and (3) that where there was a building in
> small flats where bathrooms and lavatories had to be shared it was of the utmost
> importance that the tenants should live in harmony and that the landlord ought to
> have a right to claim possession even though the persons annoyed occupied rooms
> not physically adjoining those of the defendant.'

Counsel for the tenant then went on to cite a number of nineteenth century and early
twentieth century decisions based on restrictive covenants, where the covenants had
sought to restrain occupiers of adjoining premises from certain activities. In those cases
the word had been strictly construed as meaning absolutely contiguous, without anything
in between, or in physical contact with one another, or touching one another in some
part. The word had only been given a wider meaning where that could be deduced from
the context of the covenant itself. However, in *Norton v Charles Deane Productions Ltd*
(1969) 214 EG 559 at 560 Swanwick J put a wider construction on a restrictive covenant
in the following terms:

> 'that the lessee should not do or permit to be done on the demised premises or

any part thereof anything which might be, or grow to be, a source of nuisance, damage, inconvenience or annoyance to the lessors, or the owners or occupiers of any adjoining premises.'

The judge held that that covenant, as he put it, 'was not really intended to have anything to do with physical contact between the houses, but was intended to protect neighbouring properties'. The complainants in that case were occupiers of premises which were opposite the premises in question and three doors away from it.

Counsel for the tenant submitted that, in the context of the Rent Acts, which protect the right of occupation of tenants, the word 'adjoining' should be given a narrow or restricted meaning and that, if that meaning was accepted, then none of the three tenants of no 12 were adjoining occupiers because their premises did not physically touch flat 2. He conceded that, as there was a party wall between the tenant's flat and the flat occupied by Dr Al Shalabi at no 11, Dr Al Shalabi was an adjoining occupier and conduct relating to him could be taken into account; but he submitted that, if the complaints of the three tenants of no 12 were disregarded and only the complaints of Dr Al Shalabi were considered, then it was not reasonable for the judge to have made an order. It was said that the trouble started between the tenant and Dr Al Shalabi in December 1981 when the central heating was cut off, but until then there had been no difficulties between them.

I should say, in fairness to all the parties, that the absence of central heating was only one of a number of complaints which the defendant made to Dr Al Shalabi after he took over the premises, all of which the judge rejected except the complaint about central heating. It is unclear why the central heating was turned off. The fact is that the boiler from which the heating for no 12 came was physically in no 13, which of course remained in the ownership of the Crofton Hotel, and there is no finding in the judgment that Mr Al Shalabi deliberately cut the central heating off, although it may be that the absence of central heating was something which the tenant especially in the winter found annoying and unpleasant.

Counsel for the landlords submitted that the word 'adjoining' has more than one meaning: it is not confined to physically touching but it can also include 'neighbouring'. He submitted that in this case there was a close relationship between all the tenants in no 12. They all occupy the same building; they all share the same entrance; they all share the same common doorway; and the flat of each of them was connected by the stairs and hallway. He submitted that, in those circumstances, a wider meaning should be given to the word 'adjoining' than the narrow meaning sought to be put by counsel for the tenant. He pointed out, first of all, some of the anomalies which would arise in practice if the narrow meaning was given. To take this very case, it was accepted that Dr Al Shalabi's flat at no 11 adjoined the tenant's flat at no 12, but it might be that conduct by the tenant in her flat would be far more annoying to other occupiers of the same building than it would be to somebody like Dr Al Shalabi who lived next door, separated by a thick and possibly soundproof party wall and with a separate entrance. He also pointed out that, if counsel for the tenant's meaning was right, it would mean that you could have two tenants of flats on the same floor separated by a narrow passage or hallway and, because the flats were not touching one another, neither tenant would have any remedy against the other in respect of a nuisance or annoyance, and the landlord could not take proceedings for possession because one of those tenants was causing annoyance to the other. He also pointed out that all the first five cases in Sch 15 to the 1977 Act, which set out the grounds on which a landlord is entitled to possession from a statutory tenant, involve cases where the landlord's interest is being adversely affected, and he submitted that the purpose of Sch 15 was to protect the landlord's interest, and that a narrow interpretation of the word 'adjoining' would be wholly inconsistent with that. He added that, if the landlord was not able to take proceedings for possession on the ground of nuisance on the complaints of other occupiers of a building which was divided into flats, his interest might be seriously affected because he would be unable to let the other flats in the building at reasonable rents.

He drew our attention to *Lightbound v Higher Bebington Local Board* (1885) 16 QBD 577
a esp at 584 per Bowen LJ, where the court was concerned to define the meaning of
premises 'fronting', 'adjoining' or 'abutting' on the street within the meaning of a section
of the Public Health Act 1875. He referred to the passage in the judgment of Bowen LJ
in which he indicated that it was necessary to look at the subject matter of the section
and see what was its scope and object in construing the individual words which appear
in the section. That approach was also adopted in *New Plymouth BC v Taranaki Electric-*
b *Power Board* [1933] AC 680, a decision of the Privy Council, where again the Board was
concerned to construe the meaning of the word 'adjoining'. Lord Macmillan, giving the
advice of the Board, said (at 682):

> 'Their Lordships agree with the learned judges of the Court of Appeal that the
> primary and exact meaning of "adjoining" is "conterminous." At the same time it
> cannot be disputed that the word is also used in a looser sense as meaning "near" or
c > "neighbouring." But, as Lord Hewart C.J. said in a recent case, where the question
> was as to the meaning of the word "contiguous": "It ought to be the rule, and we are
> glad to think that it is the rule, that words are used in an Act of Parliament correctly
> and exactly, and not loosely or inexactly. Upon those who assert that that rule has
> been broken the burden of establishing their proposition lies heavily. And they can
> discharge it only by pointing to something in the context which goes to show that
d > the loose and inexact meaning must be preferred": *Spillers, Ld. v. Cardiff (Borough)*
> *Assessment Committee* ([1931] 2 KB 21 at 43, [1931] All ER Rep 524 at 528–529).'

Counsel for the landlords submitted that, when one looks at the scope and purpose of
the 1977 Act, the broad meaning (which is admittedly a secondary meaning of that
word) must strongly be preferred because of the anomalies involved in adopting the
e literal meaning.

This point has never previously been decided by the Court of Appeal. It is possible that
that is because of a short passage in the present Vice-Chancellor's classic work, *The Rent
Acts* (10th edn, 1967) p 27, which I cite, although, as we know from the judgment of
Judge Harold Brown it was certainly in the 8th edition which was published in 1955 and
very likely earlier still. The passage is in the following terms:

f > 'The words "adjoining" has been construed as meaning "contiguous", so that the
> occupants of a second floor flat have been held not to be "adjoining occupiers" to the
> ground floor flat beneath them.'

Then he cites *Marquess of Northampton Estate Trustee v Bond* (1949) 155 EG 412. The text
continues:

g > 'But this seems too strict a view; for one meaning of the word is "neighbouring"
> and all that the context seems to require is that the premises of the adjoining
> occupiers should be near enough to be affected by the tenant's conduct on the
> demised premises.'

I accept that statement as an accurate statement of the law. The premises here, which
h were occupied by the complainants, were in the same building as that occupied by the
tenant. They were sharing the common parts, including the common entrance, with the
tenant, and in my judgment they were near enough to be affected by her conduct on the
premises. And that was the view that was taken by the recorder, who did not have the
advantage of the citations from authority which we have had, but did have various
textbooks cited to him; and he expressed the view that 'not only the occupiers within
j no 12 upstairs, be they tenants or other persons lawfully on the premises, were adjoining
within the meaning and spirit of Case 2 but also the occupiers of flat 3 in no 11 were
adjoining'. I agree with the view that the recorder took on that point of law, so that
counsel for the tenant's primary ground of appeal fails.

There were essentially two other grounds of appeal. The first was that the recorder
failed to consider the exercise of his discretion under s 100(2) of the 1977 Act to suspend

the execution of the order for possession indefinitely so long as the tenant did not commit any conduct which was a reason for annoyance to adjoining occupiers.

Section 100(2) is in the following terms:

'On the making of an order for possession of such a dwelling-house, or at any time before the execution of such an order (whether made before or after the commencement of this Act), the court . . . may—(a) stay or suspend execution of the order, or (b) postpone the date of possession . . .'

We were told that there was no application before the court that the order should be stayed or suspended, but that the recorder did postpone possession for 10 weeks. His reason for not staying or suspending the order altogether was this:

'I know that her behaviour appears to have improved since May 1983 when the police were called and when [the landlords'] solicitors again threatened to take immediate action to apply to the court to prevent [the tenant] doing something. I assume at that stage [the tenant] received positive and strong advice that has caused her to behave pending the outcome of this action. I have no doubt that if I were not to grant an order for possession her behaviour would rapidly deteriorate and once again she would be accosting the other occupiers accusing them of whatever occurred to her and using foul language to them and others.'

The recorder had the advantage, which we have not had, of seeing the tenant in the witness box and the other occupiers over a period of ten working days. There is no ground on which we could interfere with the judge's discretion in respect of that matter, the word in the subsection being 'may', which imports a discretion in the judge.

The final ground of appeal is that the recorder, when considering the question whether it was reasonable to make an order for possession, misdirected himself, and particulars are given of five matters in respect of which the recorder is said to have misdirected himself.

The recorder dealt with the question of reasonableness in the following terms:

'I turn to consider whether it be reasonable to grant an order for possession against this tenant. Apart from those matters that I have found proved I bear in mind that [the tenant] withheld rent from July 1982 and made no apparent attempt to pay it until July 1983. I bear in mind that in my opinion [the tenant's] case has been grossly magnified and has substantially failed and in my opinion the nature of the magnification of [the tenant's] case is such as could not occur by accident. She and her advisers must have known what Mr Purdue and Mr Salmon would say when they were called and yet not only did they persist in their inflated counterclaim but indeed the very inflated figures were not included until 18 or 19 October 1983, that is some two or three days after this hearing commenced. When for example one sees the specific pleading additional heating £300 and sees that the sole support for that is a schedule that does not support a round figure let alone any other figure I am afraid I am driven to the conclusion that this is a [tenant] who with her advisers is prepared to put forward any case to cause difficulty to the landlord. [The tenant] has lied in my view. [The tenant] continued her nuisance and annoyance to adjoining occupiers after issue of the proceedings. On the other hand, I bear in mind that [the tenant] was complaining of lack of central heating in January 1982 and no steps have been taken to provide her with that heating and, once it had been pointed out to her, from September 1982 she was complaining about the lack of a rent book. However, as against those two matters and in particular [the landlords'] unfortunate reliance on [their] solicitors' advice as typified in para 5 of their letter of 28 September 1982 she did not in fact receive a rent book. I take into account all the criticisms made by [the tenant's] counsel of [the landlords'] conduct and the criticisms mainly unfounded made by her in her evidence. However, having heard [the tenant] at length and having seen a procession of witnesses give evidence of her a conduct I am driven to the conclusion that it is reasonable in this case to make an order for possession.'

The question of reasonableness is a matter for the discretion of the trial judge. The recorder in this case properly applied his mind to all the relevant circumstances relating to reasonableness and it would be quite impossible for this court to interfere with that finding. Accordingly I would dismiss this appeal.

b **WOOD J.** I agree. The plaintiff landlords in this action are claiming possession of flat 2, 12 Queen's Gate, London SW7. The defendant tenant is a statutory tenant and therefore the landlords can only obtain an order for possession if they can bring the case within s 98 of the Rent Act 1977 and the terms of Sch 15. The relevant wording of s 98 reads:

c '(1) Subject to this Part of this Act, a court shall not make an order for possession of a dwelling-house which is for the time being let on a protected tenancy or subject to a statutory tenancy unless the court considers it reasonable to make such an order and either . . . (b) the circumstances are as specified in any of the Cases in Part I of Schedule 15 to this Act . . .'

The landlords, therefore, have to prove that it is reasonable and also have to establish a situation under one of the cases in Sch 15. In this case the landlords sought to rely on
d Cases 1 and 2. Case 1 refers to non-payment of rent and Case 2, which has formed the major argument in this appeal, is reliance on acts which are 'a nuisance or annoyance to adjoining occupiers'.

I do not wish to add anything to what Dunn LJ has said about the discretion of the recorder as to reasonableness, or as to the point which was raised on the appeal on the postponement of the order under s 100.
e The main point taken by counsel for the tenant was that, when construing the words in Case 2 of Sch 15 'nuisance or annoyance to adjoining occupiers', 'adjoining' should be given a restricted meaning, namely 'contiguous', and it falls, therefore, to this court to interpret that phrase in this particular statute. He helpfully referred us to a number of authorities, but they are distinguishable on their facts and do not provide great assistance. However, there are two passages in the earlier authorities to which I would refer and
f from which I derive help in construing this statute. The first is in *Cave v Horsell* [1912] 3 KB 533 at 543–544. The passage to which I would refer is where Buckley LJ, dealing with matters of principle before dealing with the facts, said:

'There are few words, if indeed there be any, which bear a meaning so exact as that the reader can disregard the surrounding circumstances and the context in ascertaining the sense in which the word is employed. Not even words expressive of
g number escape the ordeal. There are trades in which a dozen does not mean twelve nor a hundred five score. There are words upon whose primary meaning there is no room for doubt. I may instance again the word "dozen." But this is not true of all words. Many are not of fixed, but of flexible, meaning. Such a word may have many primary meanings. It is for the reader, looking at the context, to say in which of those meanings it is employed. In making that determination, he must look at
h the subject-matter dealt with by the language in which the word occurs and see what is the scope and object of the instrument in which he finds it. Much discussion has passed before us upon Lord Wensleydale's language in *Grey v. Pearson* ((1857) 6 HL Cas 61 at 106, [1843–60] All ER Rep 21 at 36). He is not speaking of the meaning of a single word. A single word may have a primary or a derivational or a conventional or an ordinary or a precise meaning. But it is impossible to say that a
j single word has a grammatical meaning. Lord Wensleydale is speaking, not of a word, but of a sentence, of a series of limitations in a will, and his words are that the grammatical and ordinary sense of the words is to be adhered to, unless, &c. There are three words, "adjoining," "adjacent," and "contiguous," which lie not far apart in the meaning which they convey. But of no one of them can its meaning be stated

with exactitude and without exception. As to "adjoining," the expression "next adjoining" or "immediately adjoining" is common and legitimate. This expression at once conveys that two things may adjoin which are not next to each other. "Adjacent" conveys that which lies "near to" rather than that which lies "next to." "Contiguous" is perhaps of all three the least exact. Any one of the three may by its context be shewn to convey "neighbouring" without the necessity of physical contact. The cases which have been referred to serve as guides but not as authorities binding me in determining the meaning of the word "adjoining" in this lease. I must read the lease, and determine what is the meaning of the whole of this covenant containing, as it does, this word.'

If for 'lease' one reads 'statute' in that last paragraph, that is the function which I would seek to perform.

The other passage is in the case already referred to, *Lightbound v Higher Bebington Local Board* (1885) 16 QBD 577 at 584, where Bowen LJ said:

'In construing such words as "front," "abut," and "adjoin," in this Act of Parliament, actual contiguity is not necessary in order that the terms should be fulfilled. The case of *Wakefield Local Board* v. *Lee* ((1876) 1 Ex D 336) shews that. We have to go further and ascertain what is the true statutory meaning of this term as used in this section; and there is a broad rule of construction, of which the present case, so far as there is any law involved in it (which is very little), is to my mind an illustration. It is that in construing the words you must look at the subject matter of the section and see what is its scope and object.'

Thus, I must look at this Act, bearing in mind that the word 'adjoining' is capable of a secondary meaning, namely 'neighbouring'.

The scope and purpose of the Rent Acts, in one of its forms, is to give protection of occupation to the tenant, which protection would not be available at common law. The landlord's right to obtain possession is strictly limited but, at the same time, the interests of the landlord must be protected. As counsel for the landlords has pointed out in his submission, when one looks at the wording of Cases 1 to 5 of Sch 15 to the 1977 Act, it can clearly be seen that in each of those cases protection is intended for the interest of the landlord.

Turning to Case 2, and when considering the true meaning of the word 'adjoining', it is right to look at the sort of evidence which might be available or alleged to support the allegation of nuisance and annoyance. It might be drunkenness, abuse, noise, obstruction or violence, and one can think of others; but, if the restricted meaning for which counsel for the tenant argues is given to the word 'adjoining', then the interests of the landlord would clearly not be protected. It is possible to argue that, if the landlord owned only one flat in a block of flats or a subdivided house, then it might only be necessary to give the 'restricted' meaning; but even in that case, if the behaviour of his tenant was such as to fall within Case 2, he would be besieged with complaints and that would necessarily aggravate his relationship with the neighbours.

In my judgment if one did not give the wider meaning to the word 'adjoining' there would be many cases which would amount to anomalies or total absurdities. One instance has been given as an illustration by Dunn LJ, namely in the present case, where Dr Al Shalabi is next door entering his flat by a different front door and a different door to his flat, he would be within the phrase; on the other hand those persons using the same front door and the same staircase as the tenant would not be. Likewise, one could envisage a situation where the door of one flat opened onto a narrow landing and immediately opposite there was the door to another flat which would not be adjoining in the restricted sense. Thirdly, one could envisage those cases, which his Honour Judge Harold Brown had in mind in *Metropolitan Rly Land Corp v Burfitt* [1960] CLY 2749, where there was a common use of a bathroom, lavatory or other facilities.

In my judgment the meaning of the word 'adjoining' is not restricted to the meaning

of 'contiguous'. Each case must depend on the facts as found by the judge trying the
a action. It is a question of degree. There may be other ways of approaching the issue, but
it may be useful to consider it in this way: namely whether the relevant premises are
sufficiently close or related, so that the behaviour or conduct of the tenant of the one
affects the access to, or occupation or enjoyment of, that other by its occupiers.

With those few words, I agree that this appeal should be dismissed.

b *Appeal dismissed.*

Solicitors: *Oliver O Fisher & Co* (for the tenant); *Tucker Turner & Co* (for the landlords).

Bebe Chua   Barrister.

c

Graham and another v Philcox and another

d COURT OF APPEAL, CIVIL DIVISION
MAY AND PURCHAS LJJ
3, 4, 18 APRIL 1984

*Easement – Right of way – Conveyance – Inclusion in conveyance of land – Principles applicable
to determine if conveyance deemed to include right of way – Occupier under statutory tenancy of*
e *part of conveyed land enjoying right of way at date of conveyance – Transferor owning servient
tenement – Whether sufficient that right of way is enjoyed with or appertaining to land at date of
conveyance – Whether inclusion of right of way in conveyance depending on transferor's right of
occupation – Whether right of way appertaining to part of land enuring for benefit of whole of
land on transfer of whole of land by servient owner – Law of Property Act 1925, s 62(2).*

f *Easement – Right of way – Dominant tenement – Alteration to dominant tenement – Enlargement
of dominant tenement – Dominant tenement consisting of first-floor flat in house – Right of way
over adjoining property granted with lease of flat – House and right of way conveyed to plaintiff
– Plaintiff converting house to single residence – Whether alteration of dominant tenement
extinguishing right of way.*

g Land consisting of a big house and garden together with a coach house at the rear was
originally in single ownership. A drive running along the side of the garden gave access
to the coach house. The owner converted the coach house into two self-contained flats,
one on the ground floor and the other on the first floor. In December 1960 the owner of
the land let the first-floor flat in the coach house for a term of five years under a lease
which expressly granted a right of way over the drive for all purposes. In September
h 1963 the residue of the term of the lease was assigned to D. In November 1963 the owner
let the ground-floor flat in the coach house to W. The lease of the first-floor flat expired
in December 1965 and D held over as a statutory tenant. In November 1975, after the
death of the owner, his executors conveyed the freehold of the whole of the coach house
to W, subject to D's statutory tenancy of the first-floor flat. In June 1977 the executors
conveyed to the defendants the freehold of one of two semi-detached houses into which
j the big house had been divided, together with the land over which the right of way
granted by the 1960 lease ran, the conveyance being made subject to the right of way. In
November 1977 W's successors in title conveyed the freehold of the coach house to the
plaintiffs subject to D's statutory tenancy. In April 1982 D gave up his statutory tenancy
and the plaintiffs converted the coach house into a single dwelling. After the plaintiffs
had been using the right of way for some time, the defendants refused to allow them to

continue to use it. The plaintiffs sought a declaration as against the defendants that they
were entitled to use the right of way. The plaintiffs contended that at the date of the
1975 conveyance to W the right of way was an easement appertaining to the coach house *a*
which was enjoyed with part of the coach house and that that conveyance therefore
operated, by virtue of s 62(2)[*a*] of the Law of Property Act 1925, to convey the right of
way to W and thus to his successors, including the plaintiffs. The judge dismissed the
action, holding that s 62(2) did not have the effect of including a conveyance of the right
of way in the 1975 conveyance because the right of way was solely the subject matter of *b*
the 1960 lease and came to an end on the termination of D's statutory tenancy in 1982.
The plaintiffs appealed. On the appeal the defendants submitted that, even if the right of
way survived the termination of the statutory tenancy in 1982, the subsequent conversion
of the coach house by the plaintiffs into a single dwelling was a substantial alteration of
the dominant tenement, ie the first-floor flat, for the benefit of which alone the right of
way had been granted, which increased the burden of use of the right of way on the
defendants as servient owners, with the result that the right of way was extinguished. *c*
Alternatively, the defendants submitted that, if the right of way still subsisted, it did so
only for the benefit of the first floor of the coach house and not for the benefit of the
whole of the coach house.

d

Held – The appeal would be allowed, and the court would declare that the plaintiffs
were entitled to a right of way over the drive, for the following reasons—

(1) Whether an easement was included in a conveyance of land by virtue of s 62(2) of
the 1925 Act depended on whether the easement was enjoyed with or appertained to the
land or at least part of it at the date of the conveyance, and not on the transferor's right of
occupation of that land. Moreover, where a transferor of land was the same person as the *e*
owner of an adjoining servient tenement over which part of the land transferred enjoyed
a right of way at the time of the transfer, the effect of s 62(2) was to enlarge the right of
way so that thereafter it enured for the benefit of the whole of the land transferred and
not just for the part comprising the original dominant tenement (see p 649 *j* to p 650 *c*,
p 651 *g h* , p 652 *f* to *h* and p 655 *d* to *f*, post); dicta of Farwell J in *International Tea Stores*
Co v Hobbs [1900–3] All ER Rep at 306, of Neville J in *Lewis v Meredith* [1913] 1 Ch at 579 *f*
and *Wright v Macadam* [1949] 2 All ER 565 applied.

(2) The mere alteration to the extent of premises comprising a dominant tenement to
which a right of way was appurtenant was not of itself sufficient to extinguish the right
of way, or even to affect the entitlement to its use unless as a result of the alteration the
extent of the user of the right would be increased. Furthermore, excessive user of a
discontinuous easement could not of itself extinguish or even suspend such an easement. *g*
Where there was excessive user the servient owner was entitled to have that excessive
user restrained, but provided the dominant owner reverted to lawful user of the easement
his prior excessive user was irrelevant (see p 649 *b c e f*, p 650 *c*, p 651 *g h* and p 655 *d* to
g, post); *Milner's Safe Co Ltd v Great Northern and City Rly Co* [1907] 1 Ch 229 distinguished;
dicta of James LJ in *Wimbledon and Putney Commons Conservators v Dixon* [1874–80] All
ER Rep at 1220 and of Romer LJ in *Harris v Flower & Sons* (1904) 91 LT at 819 considered. *h*

(3) It followed that the 1975 conveyance of the coach house to W had operated to
convey the right of way over the drive then enjoyed by D, as tenant of the first-floor flat,
and that thereafter the right of way enured for the benefit of the whole of the coach
house and not just for the first-floor flat. That right of way therefore passed to the
plaintiffs on the conveyance to them of the coach house in 1977. Moreover the mere *j*
alteration of the coach house by the plaintiffs by converting it from two self-contained
flats into one dwelling could not have any effect on the existence of the right of way (see
p 649 *f g*, p 650 *c*, p 651 *f* to *h* and p 655 *h j*, post).

---

a   Section 62(2), so far as material, is set out at p 647 *b c*, post

Notes

a   For the effect of the Law of Property Act 1925 on easements enjoyed with or appertaining to land which is conveyed, see 14 Halsbury's Laws (4th edn) para 55, and for cases on the subject, see 19 Digest (Reissue) 42–49, 300–326.

For alterations of the dominant tenement, see 14 Halsbury's Laws (4th edn) paras 124–126, and for cases on the subject, see 19 Digest (Reissue) 109, 152–154, 723–733, 1083–1098.

b   For the Law of Property Act 1925, s 62, see 27 Halsbury's Statutes (3rd edn) 438.

Cases referred to in judgments

Allan v Gomme (1840) 11 Ad & El 759, 113 ER 602.
Ankerson v Connelly [1906] 2 Ch 544; *affd* [1907] 1 Ch 678, CA.
Darby v Thorner [1983] CA Bound Transcript 490.
c   *Garritt v Sharp* (1835) 3 Ad & El 325, 111 ER 437.
Harris v Flower & Sons (1904) 91 LT 816, CA.
International Tea Stores Co v Hobbs [1903] 2 Ch 165, [1900–3] All ER Rep 303.
Lewis v Meredith [1913] 1 Ch 571.
Luttrel's Case (1601) 4 Co Rep 86a, 76 ER 1065.
Milner's Safe Co Ltd v Great Northern and City Rly Co [1907] 1 Ch 208; *varied* [1907] 1 Ch
d   229, CA.
Wigginton & Milner Ltd v Winster Engineering Ltd [1978] 3 All ER 436, [1978] 1 WLR
1462, CA.
Wimbledon and Putney Commons Conservators v Dixon (1875) 1 Ch D 362, [1874–80] All
ER Rep 1218, CA.
Wright v Macadam [1949] 2 All ER 565, [1949] 2 KB 744, CA.

e
Cases also cited

Finch v Great Western Rly Co (1879) 5 Ex D 254.
Gregg v Richards [1926] 1 Ch 521, CA.
Grigsby v Melville [1973] 3 All ER 455, [1974] 1 WLR 80, CA.
Westwood v Heywood [1921] 2 Ch 130, [1921] All ER Rep 721.
f   *Miller v Tipling* (1918) 43 DLR 469, Ont SC.

Appeal

By particulars of claim the plaintiffs, Dr Finlay MacKenzie Graham and Mrs Sandra Johnston Graham, of the Coach House, High Rocks Lane, Tunbridge Wells, Kent, sought as against the defendant, Robert Philcox, of 6A Hungershall Park, Tunbridge Wells, Kent
g   (1) a declaration that the plaintiffs were entitled to a right of way over and along the drive forming part of the defendant's property at 6A Hungershall Park for themselves, their servants and licensees at all times and for all purposes with or without motor vehicles, (2) a declaration that the plaintiffs, their servants or licensees were entitled to park motor vehicles on the drive between the points marked A and B on the plan annexed to the particulars of claim, (3) an injunction restraining the defendant, his servants or agents
h   from doing or permitting any act or thing which would restrict, prevent or otherwise interfere with the plaintiffs' exercise of the right of way and the right to park motor vehicles on the drive, (4) damages for nuisance limited to £5,000 with interest thereon, (5) a declaration that the steps and porch hatched black on the plan annexed to the particulars of claim formed part of the Coach House and (6) so far as might be necessary (a) an injunction restraining the defendant from removing or otherwise interfering with
j   the steps and porch and (b) rectification of the registers of title to the Coach House and 6A Hungershall Park. By an order dated 19 October 1983 his Honour Judge Hammerton sitting at the Tunbridge Wells County Court ordered, by consent, that Mrs Pamela Mary Philcox be joined as second defendant to the action, and further ordered that there be judgment for the defendants on the claim on the ground that the plaintiffs were not entitled to any subsisting right of way over the drive for the benefit of their property, the Coach House, or any part thereof. The plaintiffs appealed. By a respondent's notice the

defendants contended that the judge's order should be affirmed on grounds additional to those contained in the judge's judgment. The facts are set out in the judgment of May LJ.   *a*

Robert Reid QC and *David Hodge* for the plaintiffs.
Gerald Godfrey QC and *Stephen Bickford-Smith* for the defendants.

Cur adv vult

18 April. The following judgments were delivered.   *b*

MAY LJ. This is an appeal by the plaintiffs against a judgment of his Honour Judge Hammerton in the Tunbridge Wells County Court of 19 October 1983. The judge had before him a claim by the plaintiffs as the freehold owners of premises known as the Coach House, High Rocks Lane, Tunbridge Wells, to the unobstructed use of a right of way from those premises over the defendants' adjoining land known as 6A Hungershall   *c* Park, Tunbridge Wells, to that road (Hungershall Park) itself. The judge dismissed the plaintiffs' claim and made a declaration on the defendants' counterclaim that there was no subsisting right of way over their land for the benefit of the plaintiffs' property or any part of it. The plaintiffs now appeal against that judgment.

The relevant land in this case was at one time all in one ownership. It was known as 6 Hungershall Park and comprised a large house with a garden, together with a coach   *d* house with a courtyard at the rear, that is to the south, and abutting what is now called High Rocks Lane (whether this is in law a highway is not entirely clear).

In so far as is material for present purposes, by a lease dated 10 December 1960 the freehold owner of the whole of the relevant land, one C J Maples, let the flat comprising the first upper floor of the Coach House to one Braithwaite for five years from 1 December 1960. By the terms of the parcels clause in that lease, the flat was let 'together   *e* with a right of way for all purposes over the entrance drive to Number 6 Hungershall Park and thence along the West side of the garden as far as the premises hereby demised'. On 1 September 1963 Braithwaite assigned his interest in the residue of the term granted by the lease to one Devaney.

By an agreement dated 4 November 1963 Mr Maples let the ground-floor flat in the Coach House to one Wilcox for a term of three years from 6 July 1963. That agreement   *f* also granted Wilcox a similar right of way to that granted to Braithwaite, but on the other, eastern, side of the relevant land.

Mr Maples died on 4 December 1973. At some time, whether before or after Maples's death does not matter, the big house was converted into two semi-detached houses, namely 6A and 6B Hungershall Park, and the garden was itself divided into two. 6A was the western half of the property, 6B the remaining eastern half.   *g*

By a conveyance of 5 November 1975 Maples's executors conveyed to Wilcox the land on which the Coach House was built together with that building 'at present occupied as two self-contained flats erected thereon and known as [The Coach House] High Rocks Lane Tunbridge Wells'.

Next, by a conveyance of 27 June 1977, the executors conveyed to the present respondents, the defendants Mr and Mrs Philcox, the freehold of 6A Hungershall Park,   *h* subject to the right in the tenant of the first-floor flat of the Coach House to use, inter alia, the right of way to Hungershall Park originally granted by the lease of that flat in the Coach House to Braithwaite of 10 December 1960.

By a lease and conveyance each of 16 November 1977 the successors in title to Wilcox conveyed the Coach House to the present appellants, the plaintiffs Dr and Mrs Graham, subject to Devaney's continuing statutory tenancy of the upper flat. Subsequently   *j* Devaney was persuaded to give this flat up. The plaintiffs then took it over and have thereafter occupied the whole of the Coach House as a residence. For some time the plaintiffs and the defendants were on friendly terms and the plaintiffs continued to use the right of way over the defendants' property, that is to say 6A Hungershall Park, as had been enjoyed by Devaney. However, at some stage relations between the two families deteriorated; the defendants locked a gate across part of the right of way and refused to allow the plaintiffs to continue to use it. As a result, the plaintiffs issued these proceedings

in the county court, claiming the right to use the right of way, together with an
injunction restraining the defendants from preventing them doing so and other
consequential relief. Two other less important points arise in this litigation, both of
which are largely dependent on the result of the plaintiffs' main claim, and I will deal
with them separately at the end of this judgment.

The plaintiffs' claim was based below and before us on the provisions of s 62(2) of the
Law of Property Act 1925. In so far as is material for present purposes, this subsection
reads:

> 'A conveyance of land, having houses or other buildings thereon, shall be deemed
> to include and shall by virtue of this Act operate to convey, with the land, houses, or
> other buildings, all . . . ways . . . easements, rights, and advantages whatsoever,
> appertaining or reputed to appertain to the land, houses, or other buildings
> conveyed, or any of them, or any part thereof, or, at the time of the conveyance . . .
> enjoyed with . . . the land, houses, or other buildings conveyed, or any of them, or
> any part thereof.'

The plaintiffs' case is that the right of way in dispute was an easement enjoyed and
used by Devaney at the time of the conveyance of the Coach House to Wilcox. By virtue
of s 62(2) that conveyance operated to convey that right of way to Wilcox, who conveyed
it to the plaintiffs' predecessors in title, who in turn conveyed it to the plaintiffs. Counsel
for the plaintiffs submitted that this result flowed from the operation of the clear
meaning of the subsection and it was what the judge described at any rate at first sight as
a logical and simple approach. However, in the result, he rejected the argument. In
relation to the conveyance by Maples's executors to Wilcox he said:

> 'The land was sold by personal representatives. The right of way was not enjoyed
> by them and it was not part of the property that they were enjoying. The right of
> way was totally the subject matter of the lease. So far as the purchaser was concerned
> he also was not enjoying the right of way and he had no right over the right of way
> as long as the lease continued. Neither the transferor nor the transferee were actually
> enjoying the easement.'

A little later in his judgment he summarised his view in this way:

> 'On the general proposition I have come to the conclusion that so far as the right
> of way is concerned this was granted by the lease and came to an end on Devaney's
> departure. Thereafter the right of way did not subsist independently of the lease or
> dependently on s 62 of the Law of Property Act 1925.'

It was on these grounds that the judge dismissed the plaintiffs' claim in the action.

In this court, counsel for the plaintiffs again relied on what he submitted was the clear
meaning of s 62(2). He contended that as the result of that statutory provision the
conveyance operated to pass to Wilcox and thus to his successors in title the easement
over 6A Hungershall Park which I have described. Counsel submitted that the judge's
approach started from a consideration of the user of the way *by the vendor*, which was
incorrect, and thus he reached the wrong conclusion at the end; what the judge ought to
have considered under s 62(2) was the use of the relevant way *with the land*.

In support of his submission, counsel for the plaintiffs referred us to a number of
authorities, among them *International Tea Stores Co v Hobbs* [1903] 2 Ch 165 at 172,
[1900–3] All ER Rep 303 at 306, where Farwell J said:

> 'The real truth is that you do not consider the question of title to use, but the
> question of fact of user; you have to inquire whether the way has in fact been used,
> not under what title it has been used, although you must of course take into
> consideration all the circumstances of the case . . .'

In addition, in *Lewis v Meredith* [1913] 1 Ch 571 at 579 Neville J was considering the
predecessor of s 62(2), namely s 6 of the Conveyancing Act 1881, and said:

> 'Easement or right in the strict sense there could not be, for the common
> ownership precluded the acquisition of any right or easement by the occupiers, but

International Tea Stores Co. v. *Hobbs* shews that "a right" permissive at the date of the grant may become a legal right upon the grant by force of the general words in s. 6 of the Conveyancing Act, 1881. From this point of view the circumstances under which the quasi right was enjoyed become immaterial so long as it was actually enjoyed and was of a nature which could be granted, that is to say, a right known to the law . . .'

Both these cases were cited with approval in the judgments in this court in the later case of *Wright v Macadam* [1949] 2 All ER 565, [1949] 2 KB 744. In relation to the instant appeal, the facts of that decided case are of some interest. The defendant landlord let a flat comprising two rooms and the usual offices to Mrs Wright, one of the plaintiffs, for one week. She remained in occupation thereafter under the provisions of the Rent Restriction Acts and some two or three months later the landlord gave her permission to use a garden shed at the premises to store her coal. This state of affairs continued for about 2½ years and then the landlord granted a new tenancy for one year of the flat with an additional room to Mrs Wright and her daughter. The agreement creating the tenancy, which was under hand only, made no reference to the coal shed, but Mrs Wright and her daughter continued to use it for another four years until the defendant asked them to pay a small extra amount for its use. It seems from the report that Mrs Wright herself would have been prepared to do so, but her daughter was strenuously opposed to any such arrangement. When the defendant in consequence tried to stop Mrs Wright and her daughter from using the coal shed they brought the proceedings which ultimately came before the Court of Appeal. On the particular question which is material in the present case, this court there held that Mrs Wright and her daughter were entitled to continue to use the coal shed because when the new tenancy was granted, which was a 'conveyance' for the purposes of s 62(2), the use of the coal shed was then being enjoyed with the original flat, which was part of the three rooms the subject of the fresh demise. Consequently s 62(2) applied so that the new tenancy operated to pass to the tenant not only the three rooms but also the right to use the coal shed.

Counsel for the defendants sought to support the judge's judgment principally on a basis which for my part I do not think was argued below; at least it finds little or no reference in the judgment. At the outset of the hearing of this appeal counsel for the defendants sought leave to file a respondent's notice out of time, which we granted. His principal submission was that, as the dominant tenement for the benefit of which the way is now claimed, namely the Coach House, is not the same as and is indeed greater than the dominant tenement for the benefit of which the way was originally granted, namely only the upper flat in the Coach House, therefore the plaintiffs cannot use that way now when the Coach House, is now one dwelling and the original two flats which it comprised have been combined into one. He referred us to the quotation from the judgment of Romer LJ in *Harris v Flower & Sons* (1904) 91 LT 816 at 819, which is quoted in *Gale on Easements* (14th edn, 1972) p 282 and which is in these terms:

'If a right of way be granted for the enjoyment of close A, the grantee, because he owns or acquires close B, cannot use the way in substance for passing over close A to close B.'

There are similar passages in the judgments of Vaughan Williams and Cozens-Hardy LJJ in the same case. Counsel for the defendants also relied on the decisions of Warrington J in *Ankerson v Connelly* [1906] 2 Ch 544 and Kekewich J in *Milner's Safe Co Ltd v Great Northern and City Rly Co* [1907] 1 Ch 208. Counsel for the defendants submitted further that, if one substantially alters a dominant tenement, an easement theretofore enjoyed with it can no longer be used, because by the alterations one has increased the burden of the use on the servient tenement. The easement is consequently lost, or at least suspended temporarily; thus in the present case the plaintiffs must accept that they cannot enforce their use of the disputed right of way for so long as the Coach House remains one dwelling. Counsel for the defendants also referred us to *Allan v Gomme* (1840) 11 Ad & El 759, 113 ER 602 and submitted that alterations which in truth destroy the identity of

the original dominant tenement, or which so affect its character as to make it no longer a
a tenement of the nature for the purpose of which the original easement was granted,
create a situation in which the continued user of the way is either excessive in quantity
or excessive as an activity not covered by the terms of the original grant, and the result is
thus the extinguishment or at least the suspension of the easement.

However, I doubt whether any excessive user, at least of a discontinuous easement, in
whatever respect the user may be excessive, will ever of itself bring to an end or indeed
b suspend such an easement (see *Gale on Easements* (14th edn, 1972) pp 346–347). The
owner of the servient tenement on which, ex hypothesi, the excessive burden is placed is
entitled to have that excessive user restrained. The fact that a court may grant an
appropriate injunction or make a declaration to this end does not in my judgment either
extinguish or suspend the easement. Provided that the owner of the dominant tenement
subsequently reverts to lawful use of the easement, his prior excessive use of it is then
c irrelevant.

In my opinion the statement of Romer LJ in *Harris v Flower & Sons* 91 LT 816 at 819
of the relevant principle of law which I have quoted must be considered in the context of
the facts of that particular case. Having stated the proposition, Romer LJ then went on
to say:

d   'The question is whether what the defendants do, or claim the right to do, comes
             within the proposition I have stated.'

He then went on to discuss the intended new user of the way in that case and concluded:

             'That would substantially enlarge the grant of the right of way. The servient
             tenement is not obliged to submit to the carrying of building materials for that
             purpose; and other instances might easily be given which would result in the user
e   of the right of way for the purposes of the land coloured blue, and not for the due
             and proper enjoyment of the land to which the way was appurtenant.'

In none of the judgments in any of the cases to which counsel for the defendants
referred us is there any suggestion that a mere alteration of a dominant tenement to
which a right of way may be appurtenant is sufficient to extinguish it, or indeed to affect
f the entitlement to its use unless as the result of that alteration the extent of the user is
thereby increased.

In my opinion, therefore, the mere alteration of the Coach House into one dwelling
cannot have had any effect on the existence of the right of way. It should be borne in
mind that there was no evidence whatever before the judge that the actual or anticipated
user by the plaintiffs of the way was in any way excessive, either in quantity or quality.

g Further, I do not think that on this issue any real distinction can be drawn between
the instant case on the one hand and *Wright v Macadam* [1949] 2 All ER 565, [1949] 2 KB
744 on the other. In that case also the right for which the plaintiffs contended had, at the
date of the conveyance relied on for the purposes of s 62(2), been enjoyed by the occupier
of only part of the whole premises in respect of which the continued enjoyment of the
right was claimed in the action.

h Counsel for the defendants then pointed to and compared some parts of some of the
conveyancing documents to which I have referred in an attempt to support an argument
based on s 62(4) of the 1925 Act, that an intention appeared, either expressly or by
necessary implication, in the conveyance to Wilcox of 12 November 1975 that s 62(2)
should not apply to it. I intend no disrespect to counsel for the defendants when I say
that I am satisfied that this point is really unarguable on the facts and documents in this
j case and I do not propose to deal with it in any further detail.

Finally, counsel for the defendants submitted that if, contrary to his primary
submission, the right of way still subsisted, then it did so only for the benefit of the first
floor of the Coach House. For the reasons I have already given and in the light again of
the decision in *Wright v Macadam* [1949] 2 All ER 565, [1949] 2 KB 744, I disagree.

In my judgment the judge was, with respect, wrong in law in the approach that he
adopted. The fundamental issue in this case was whether the right of way in dispute 'was

enjoyed with' at least part of the land and buildings conveyed to Wilcox in 1975. Where a transferor of land is the same person as the owner of an adjoining servient tenement over which part of the land transferred enjoys a right of way at the time of the transfer, then in my opinion the effect of s 62(2) is indeed to enlarge the right in the sense that it thereafter enures for the benefit of the whole of the land transferred. If one makes appropriate substitutions for some of the words in s 62(2) and omits immaterial parts, then for the purposes of the present case the subsection can be rewritten in this way:

> 'The conveyance (dated 5 November 1975) of the Coach House operated to convey with the Coach House the way over 6 Hungershall Park (still the property of the transferors in the conveyance) then enjoyed with the upper of the two flats (being part of the land and house, the Coach House, transferred by the conveyance).'

For these reasons I think that on the principal issue in this case this appeal must be allowed.

In addition to the right of way to which I have been referring, the plaintiffs contended that they were also entitled to a right of parking on the way in the area marked AB on the rough plan annexed to the particulars of claim. In the course of the argument of this appeal, counsel for the defendants conceded that, if the plaintiffs were held to be entitled to the right of way, then he would not contend that they were not also entitled to the right to park on the area to which I have referred. I need not, therefore, deal any further with the question of parking.

Finally, as the level of the land falls substantially from Hungershall Park, southwards across the defendants' property and down to High Rocks Lane, the level of the first floor of the Coach House is in fact below the level of the defendants' garden. To enable the occupiers of that first floor to obtain access to the way which I have been discussing there has at all material times been a porch attached to the Coach House, with a door giving access to steps which themselves lead up and onto the way proper at the level of the rear of the defendants' garden. It was argued below that on the proper construction of the conveyance of 5 November 1975 it had not transferred either the porch or the steps to Wilcox, the plaintiffs' predecessor in title. The judge held that the steps were not conveyed; he made no finding with regard to the porch. By their notice of appeal the plaintiffs contend that on this question the judge also erred and that both porch and steps are part of the Coach House.

In so far as material, the parcels clause in the conveyance was in these terms:

> 'ALL THAT plot of land situate at Tunbridge Wells in the County of Kent being part of a larger plot of land known as Number 6 Hungershall Park and for the purpose of identification only shown edged in red on the plan annexed hereto TOGETHER with the building at present occupied as two self-contained flats erected thereon and known as The Stable Flats [ie the Coach House] High Rocks Lane Tunbridge Wells.'

The plan referred to was drawn on a very small scale and the boundary between the land conveyed and that retained by the transferors is shown on it as a straight line which, if given effect to precisely, would I think mean that both porch and steps were indeed excluded from the land conveyed.

On this point our attention was drawn to the decision of this court in *Wigginton & Milner Ltd v Winster Engineering Ltd* [1978] 3 All ER 436, [1978] 1 WLR 1462, recently applied also in this court in the unreported case of *Darby v Thorner* [1983] CA Bound Transcript 490. In *Wigginton's* case [1978] 3 All ER 436 at 445, [1978] 1 WLR 1462 at 1473 Buckley LJ said:

> 'When a court is required to decide what property passed under a particular conveyance, it must have regard to the conveyance as a whole, including any plan which forms part of it. It is from the conveyance as a whole that that intention must be ascertained. To the extent that the conveyance stipulates that one part of it shall prevail over another part of it in the event of there being any contradiction between them in the ascertainment of the parties' intention, the court must of course give

effect to that stipulation. So if the conveyance stipulates that the plan shall not
a   control the description of the parcels, the court must have due regard to that
stipulation; but insofar as the plan does not conflict with the parcels I can see no
reason why, because it is described as being "for identification only", it should not
be looked at to assist in understanding the description of the parcels. The process of
identification is in fact the process of discovering what land was intended to pass
under the conveyance, and that is the precise purpose which the plan is said to serve.
b   Accordingly, so long as the plan does not come into conflict with anything which is
explicit in the description of the parcels, the fact that it is said to be "for the purpose
of identification only" does not appear to me to exclude it from consideration in
solving problems which are left undecided by what is explicit in the description of
any parcel.'

Bridge LJ agreed with Buckley LJ and said ([1978] 3 All ER 436 at 447, [1978] 1 WLR
c   1462 at 1475):

'I desire to add only a few words of my own as to the effect of the phrase "for the
purpose of identification only" and other similar phrases, when applied to a
conveyance plan. When a conveyance plan which is said to be for the purpose of
identification only shows a boundary line which differs in detail from some physical
d   feature on the ground which the conveyance otherwise indicates as the intended
boundary line, it is clear that the latter prevails over the former.'

I do not think that this final point in this appeal admits of any detailed analysis.
Directing myself in accordance with the dicta from the judgments of Buckley and
Bridge LJJ which I have quoted, I respectfully agree with the judge below at least in so
far as the steps are concerned. As the porch was physically a part of the building expressed
e   to be conveyed in the parcels clause in the 1975 conveyance, I think that on a proper
construction of that clause the porch was conveyed to Wilcox with the rest of the Coach
House. The steps on the other hand were not so part of the fabric of the Coach House,
they merely led to or were part of the claimed right of way, and clearly lay on the
transferors' side of the straight boundary line drawn on the plan, albeit that this was for
identification only. In my opinion, therefore, the steps were not conveyed with the
f   Coach House in 1975 and form no part of it. Such a view creates no practical difficulty
because the steps are clearly part of the way, to the enjoyment of which I have already
held the plaintiffs to be entitled.

Both counsel agreed that if this court were to allow this appeal on the right of way
issue then, in the first instance at any rate, it would be sufficient if we merely set aside
the order of the judge below and made appropriate declarations in accordance with our
g   views of the parties' respective rights. I would therefore wish to hear briefly from counsel
about the precise term of such declarations, but subject to this, for the reasons and in the
respects I have indicated, I would allow this appeal.

PURCHAS LJ. I agree that this appeal succeeds. As it raises a short but important point
on which, surprisingly, there is little direct authority, I propose to add a few words of my
h   own. The issue is to determine the impact of s 62(2) of the Law of Property Act 1925 in
a case of a conveyance of land described as 'The Stable Block', 6 Hungershall Park, part of
which was conveyed in the form of the reversion on the determination of a lease or
consequential statutory occupation of the first-floor flat, which was itself being enjoyed
together with the 'easements, rights, and advantages' subject to the section.

The background to the appeal has already been fully described in the judgment just
j   delivered by May LJ and it is necessary only for me to refer in detail to parts of some of
the documents, namely: the lease made on 10 December 1960 between Charles John
Maples, the landlord, and Matthew Braithwaite, the tenant; the assignment of the lease
made 1 September 1963 between Matthew Braithwaite and Laurence Devaney; and the
conveyance made 5 November 1975 between the executors of Charles John Maples and
Geoffrey Charles Wilcox through whom the appellant plaintiffs derive title.

The lease demised—

'ALL THAT tenement or flat on the first floor of the stable block at the rear of
Number 6 Hungershall Park . . . TOGETHER with the use of such part of the garden   *a*
of Number 6 Hungershall Park . . . AND TOGETHER with a right of way for all
purposes over the entrance drive to Number 6 Hungershall Park and thence along
the West side of the garden as far as the premises hereby demised TO HOLD the same
unto the Tenant for the term of five years from the First day of December One
thousand nine hundred and sixty.'

The assignment was made after three years of the lease had run and although the   *b*
consent of the landlord is not recited he was a witness to the deed. The assignment
assigned the residue of the term 'together with certain rights therein mentioned'. During
his occupation Devaney regularly used the right of way. As has already been described,
the ground floor of the stable block, or the Coach House as it came to be called, had been
let to Wilcox on 4 November 1963. Subsequently by the conveyance of 5 November
1975 the executors conveyed the whole of the freehold of the building to Wilcox: *c*

'Subject to the Tenancy of Mr. L.E. Devaney of the First Floor Flat created by a
Lease dated the 10th day of October 1960 . . . so far as the same is still subsisting but
with full right to and benefit of an apportioned part of the rent thereby reserved
attributable to the said Flat and the covenants on the part of the Tenant and
conditions therein contained so far as they relate to the said Flat.'
                                                                                          d
The question that arises is whether the right of way in fact being enjoyed by the tenant
Mr Devaney of the first-floor flat holding over some ten years after the termination of
the lease is an easement, right or advantage *appertaining to any part of the land conveyed*
within the meaning of s 62(2) of the 1925 Act when that right had at no time been
enjoyed by the late Charles John Maples, or the executors of his estate. This was a point
relied on by counsel for the respondent defendants. The county court judge concluded   *e*
that the easement created by the lease of 10 December 1960 came to an end at the
termination of the lease. This is the bald statement with which the judge commenced
his judgment, but as it stands it is ambiguous whether he refers to the easement as
formally created by the lease or whether he includes the use of the right of way preserved
by the Rent Restriction Acts. Subsequently in his judgment the judge refers to the fact
that at 5 November 1975, the date of the conveyance, Mr Devaney was a statutory tenant.   *f*
He was undoubtedly using the right of way at that time. It was certainly an easement,
right or advantage *reputed to appertain to the first-floor flat* and was enjoyed with that part
of the land, houses or other buildings conveyed. I can find nothing in the wording of
s 62(2) of the 1925 Act to indicate that the 'land conveyed' cannot include land subject to
a lease or an adverse right of occupation by a tenant protected by statute. The easement,
right or advantage is enjoyed with and appertains to the land, not to the statutory right   *g*
of occupation. The grant by which the right of way was originally created was a term of
five years; but there were no specific limitations to that grant. I agree with what has
already been said by May LJ in relation to the submissions of counsel for the plaintiffs
that the judge erred in considering the user of the way by the vendor rather than the user
of the right of way with the land (see the quotations from the judgments in *International
Tea Stores Co v Hobbs* [1903] 2 Ch 165 at 172, [1900–3] All ER Rep 303 at 306 and *Lewis v*   *h*
Meredith [1913] 1 Ch 571 at 579 in his judgment).

Although counsel for the defendants supported the decision of the judge based on his
conclusion that the duration of the easement was coterminous with the lease or right of
occupation as extended by statute, he also sought to support the judgment on wider
grounds, which, as May LJ has already commented, may have been argued but which do
not find mention in the judgment. The submission that the duration of the easement or   *j*
right was in some way coterminous to or linked with the tenancy created by the lease as
extended by a statutory right of occupation could only be supportable if there were
specific provisions qualifying the original grant of the easement to be found in the deed
by which the original term was created, or by a contrary intention being expressed in the
conveyance to which s 62(2) of the 1925 Act would otherwise apply (see s 62(4)). Such
specific qualifications are absent from the original lease and certainly would not be

imported by statute. It is, therefore, necessary to look for other grounds on which to
a support the decision of the judge as proposed in the respondent's notice.

In an admirably lucid and attractive argument counsel for the defendants submitted
that for any easement, right or advantage to continue in favour of the dominant tenement
the nature and extent of the dominant tenement must be retained, otherwise the
easement may be destroyed or possibly suspended, e g until the Coach House was again
used as two independent flats. Alternatively, he submitted that even if the easement was
b retained for part of a newly constituted dominant tenement it could only be enforced if
the use could be restricted in a realistic manner to that part of the newly constituted
dominant tenement representing the original dominant tenement in respect of which
the easement was either granted or translated by s 62 of the 1925 Act. He submitted that
on assuming occupation of the whole of the Coach House when Devaney surrendered
his occupation of the first-floor flat the plaintiffs' predecessor in title destroyed the
c identity of the dominant tenement and with it the easement attached to it. In the
alternative, he submitted that as the upper and lower flats were now in one single
occupation it would be quite impractical to restrict the enjoyment of the easement to the
first-floor flat. For these propositions he relied on the reference to *Harris v Flower & Sons*
(1904) 91 LT 816 at 819 in *Gale on Easements* (14th edn, 1972) p 282. *Harris v Flower &*
Sons was a case that turned essentially on excessive user although a considerable amount
d of the judgment relates to the use of buildings partly on the dominant tenement and
partly on another tenement in common ownership. In his judgment Vaughan Williams
LJ said:

> 'A right of way of this sort restricts the owner of the dominant tenement to the
> legitimate user of his right, and the court will not allow that which is in its nature a
> burden on the owner of the servient tenement to be increased without his consent
e > and beyond the terms of the grant. I do not think that it makes any difference
> whether the right of way arises by prescription or grant. The burden imposed on
> the servient tenement must not be increased by allowing the owner of the dominant
> tenement to make a use of the way in excess of the grant. There can be no doubt in
> the present case that, if this building is used as a factory, a heavy and frequent traffic
> will arise which has not arisen before. This particular burden could not have arisen
f > without the user of the blue land as well as of the pink. It is not a mere case of user
> of the pink land for a building, with some of the usual offices on the blue land
> connected with the buildings on the pink land.'

Counsel for the defendants also relied on the judgment of Kekewich J in *Milner's Safe
Co Ltd v Great Northern and City Rly Co* [1907] 1 Ch 208, but this case again depended on
g the change in the user of the dominant tenement rather than the change in nature,
destruction, or enlargement of the area of the dominant tenement. In that case the
owners of the dominant tenement built a railway station and then sought to use a right
of way for the purposes of the users of the railway as opposed to those coming on the
land in the ordinary way. Perhaps the important passage from the judgment is a
quotation (see [1907] 1 Ch 208 at 226) from the judgment of James LJ in *Wimbledon and
h Putney Commons Conservators v Dixon* (1875) 1 Ch D 362 at 368, [1874–80] All ER Rep
1218 at 1220:

> '. . . I am satisfied that the true principle is the principle laid down in these cases,
> that you cannot from evidence of user of a privilege connected with the enjoyment
> of property in its original state, infer a right to use it, into whatsoever form or for
> whatever purpose that property may be changed, that is to say, if a right of way to a
j > field be proved by evidence of user, however general, for whatever purpose, qua
> field, the person who is the owner of that field cannot from that say, I have a right
> to turn that field into a manufactory, or into a town, and then use the way for the
> purposes of the manufactory or town so built.'

In the event on appeal the case was compromised on the basis that the railway company
should be restrained from using the right of way by licensing or inviting any person

using their railway station as travellers to pass along it but that the restraint should not
extend to the railway company using the passage for the purposes of access by their *a*
officers, clerks or servants or by any person not being a traveller or intending traveller
reasonably visiting the premises. *Ankerson v Connelly* [1906] 2 Ch 544; *affd* [1907] 1 Ch
678, CA, with great respect to counsel for the defendants, does not assist his argument.
In that case the circumstances were so different from the instant case and, as was said by
Cozens-Hardy MR in the Court of Appeal, the case did not lay down any important point
of principle (see [1907] 1 Ch 678 at 682). *b*

By way of introduction to his submissions that the easement had been lost by the
change in user of the Coach House when it came into single occupation, counsel for the
defendants referred us to *Gale on Easements* (14th edn, 1972) pp 317–325. In particular he
relied on the paragraphs under the heading 'Extinguishment of easement by
encroachment' (at pp 324–325). The two main authorities referred to are *Garritt v Sharp*
(1835) 3 Ad & El 325, 111 ER 437 and *Luttrel's Case* (1601) 4 Co Rep 86a, 76 ER 1065. *c*
Garritt's case concerned the question whether, by converting a barn into a malthouse, the
plaintiff had lost his easement of light, and the rule for a new trial was made absolute on
the basis that the jury had not been required by the judge to consider whether the
plaintiff had essentially varied the manner in which the light was enjoyed (3 Ad & El 325
at 330, 111 ER 437 at 439):

> 'Under all these circumstances, we think the defendant entitled to a new trial. It *d*
> is enough to say that a party may so alter the mode in which he has been permitted
> to enjoy this kind of easement, as to lose the right altogether . . .'

Luttrel's Case concerned a plaintiff who pulled down two ancient fulling mills and erected
two mills to grind corn, relying on an easement for his supply of water enjoyed by the
ancient fulling mills. The case contains a long and detailed consideration of the *e*
preservation of easements in spite of alterations to the dominant tenement but it would
not help to burden this judgment by a detailed analysis. It is sufficient to quote from the
headnote:

> 'If the plaintiff, in an action on the case for disturbing his water-course, prescribe
> to have the water-course to his mills generally, it is sufficient. If a man has estovers
> by prescription to his house, although he alters the rooms and chambers of it, as to *f*
> make a parlour where there was a hall, or a hall where the parlour was, and the like
> alteration of the qualities, not of the house itself, by which no prejudice accrues to
> the owner of the wood; it is not any destruction of the prescription. Although he
> builds new chimnies, or makes an addition to the old house, he shall not lose his
> prescription: but he cannot employ any of his estovers in the new chimnies, nor in
> the part newly added.' *g*

These authorities are in line with *Allan v Gomme* (1840) 11 Ad & El 759, 113 ER 602, on
which counsel for the defendants relies, although it was held in *Allan v Gomme* that by
erecting a cottage under a shelter previously described as a woodhouse the defendant was
not entitled to make excessive user of his right of access resulting from the use of the
land as a cottage but that his original right was not destroyed. The right to use it in the *h*
manner and to the extent that it would have been used were it open ground was not
destroyed. Much of the judgment in that case was concerned with whether the words 'a
woodhouse' were merely descriptive of its position or were effective to limit its use and,
therefore, the use of the access. This part of the case does not assist in the instant appeal.

With reference to the particular facts of this case, in my judgment the distinction can *j*
be made by considering the sort of use made in fact. When the grant was made in the
lease the intention was to afford a right of access over the driveway and garden to the
first-floor flat, convenient access to which could be had in no other way. As has been
described by May LJ, the physical state of the land was unusual in that the steps down to
the entrance to the first-floor flat were at the level of that flat. In fact the whole of the
downstairs flat was below the level of the ground adjoining 6 Hungershall Park. The
circumstances were, therefore, almost those of an easement of necessity but not quite,

and certainly that consideration is not relevant here. The user contemplated, however, was that appropriate to a dominant tenement consisting of one dwelling unit housed in the first-floor flat. That having been said, nature being what it is, the range of 'de facto' user might vary immensely depending on the nature and intensity of activities on which the occupier might be engaged. Within this wide spectrum it would be difficult for the occupier of the servient tenement to challenge any normal social use as being excessive.

The only change that has now been made is that one dwelling unit is now housed where two dwelling units were previously housed. It does not follow of necessity that the 'de facto' user of the right of way made by the members of the unit now occupying both parts of the Coach House would be more than the user of that right to which the occupier personally and/or by his servants, invitees and licensees would have been entitled as occupier of the dominant tenement confined to the first floor. Indeed, it is not difficult to conceive of circumstances in which it might be a good deal less. This change is entirely different from the dramatic structural changes, changes of use considered in the cases to which reference has already been made, and falls far more within the concept of the alteration to the dominant tenement which was held not to have prejudiced the right to use the coalshed in *Wright v Macadam* [1949] 2 All ER 565, [1949] 2 KB 744, to which May LJ has already referred and on which counsel for the plaintiffs relied in support of his submission that mere alteration to the extent of the dominant tenement was not effective to destroy an easement or right. For the reasons already apparent in this judgment, I agree that counsel for the plaintiffs' submissions succeed.

With great respect to the judge, I think that he was wrong in deciding that the easement and right created in the first instance in the lease was coterminous with it or even with any further occupation by the grantee under statutory protection. The right of way having been created by direct grant and its use continuing even though under statutory protection at the time of the conveyance, the use and enjoyment of that easement fell within the terms of s 62 of the 1925 Act and the judge was in error in holding that it did not. Nor, for the reasons I have already given, can I accept the submissions made by counsel for the defendants that by enlarging the physical dimensions or indeed altering the nature of the dominant tenement from two individual flats to one dwelling house has the easement, right or advantage been destroyed. The occupier of the dominant tenement, however, will be and will remain subject to the rules requiring that the character and extent of the burden imposed on the servient tenement must not be enlarged. For want of a better definition, this burden must be said to be commensurate with the reasonable user of the means of access by the occupier, his servants, agents, invitees or licensees occupying a single dwelling unit. If by any change in the nature of his enjoyment of the dominant tenement the occupier thereof increases the burden on the servient tenement beyond this, then he will be liable to the consequences of excessive user which may be imposed on any person enjoying an easement, right or benefit of this kind.

Turning to the two subsidiary issues raised in the appeal, I agree that the porch formed part of the land conveyed, but that the steps were not included in the conveyance. There is nothing that I can usefully add to what has already been said by May LJ. As he has also said, counsel for the defendants conceded that if the plaintiffs were held to be entitled to the right of way he would not contend that this would not extend to a right to park on the area described. There is, therefore, no need to refer further to this matter.

For these reasons I agree that this appeal should succeed and that an appropriate declaration in the terms suggested by May LJ should be granted.

Appeal allowed. Declarations to the plaintiffs accordingly. Leave to appeal to the House of Lords refused.

Solicitors: *Thomson Snell & Passmore*, Tonbridge (for the plaintiffs); *John Pearson*, New Malden (for the defendants).

Frances Rustin   Barrister.

Re Besterman (deceased) *a*

COURT OF APPEAL, CIVIL DIVISION
OLIVER, FOX AND ROBERT GOFF LJJ
14, 15, 18 OCTOBER 1982

Family provision – Widow – Reasonable financial provision – Large estate – Husband leaving *b*
estate worth £1½m but making inadequate provision for wife – Bulk of estate left to university –
Marriage lasting 18 years and widow wholly blameless – Widow enjoying very high standard of
living during marriage – Widow without assets of her own – Widow left substantially less than
she would have received on divorce – What constitutes 'reasonable financial provision' –
Inheritance (Provision for Family and Dependants) Act 1975, ss 1(1)(2), 3(2).

c
The deceased and his wife were married in 1958, when he was aged 54 and she was 42.
They lived together amicably until his death in 1976. The deceased was a very wealthy
man and he left an estate worth about £1½m. During the 18 years of marriage the wife
enjoyed an extremely high standard of living appropriate to their financial position. By
his will the deceased left his wife personal chattels and a life interest in War Stock
producing an income of £3,500 a year, which was approximately equal to the *d*
housekeeping allowance which he had been accustomed to give her. The principal
beneficiary under his will was Oxford University. The deceased owed no obligation to
anyone other than his wife, who had no financial resources apart from the provision
made for her in the will and a state widow's pension of £400 a year. The wife applied for
an order under s 1(1)ᵃ of the Inheritance (Provision for Family and Dependants) Act 1975
that further provision be made for her out of the estate. Pending the hearing of the *e*
application an interim order was made for the payment to her of a capital sum of £75,000
to enable her to purchase a smaller house and vacate the matrimonial home, which was a
large, luxurious and fully staffed house worth £350,000, and for the payment of income
totalling £15,000 a year. The judge increased that provision so as to produce aggregate
capital of £259,000, amounting to one-sixth of the value of the estate. He did so by
enlarging the life interest in the War Stock to an absolute interest (worth £28,000), by *f*
ordering the payment out of the estate of £110,000 (to be increased to £120,000 by
agreement), which was the cost of an annuity, by ordering the payment of £15,000
additional capital and by leaving the £75,000 undistributed. The wife appealed, contending
that that provision was too low since it was considerably less than what she might
reasonably have expected to receive under s 25ᵇ of the Matrimonial Causes Act 1973 if
the marriage had ended in divorce, which was a factor s 3(2)ᶜ of the 1975 Act required *g*
the court to have regard to in calculating what was 'reasonable financial provision' under
s 1(2) for an applicant, and that in so far as the judge did have regard to that factor he
misdirected himself since he adopted as a criterion of reasonable financial provision the
obligation of maintenance. The principal beneficiary contended that the provision made
should not be such that the funds would ultimately pass to someone else on the applicant's
death. *h*

Held – In an application under the 1975 Act the amount required to satisfy the

a Section 1, so far as material, provides:
  '(1) Where after the commencement of this Act a person dies domiciled in England and Wales
  and is survived by ... (a) the wife or husband of the deceased ... that person may apply to the
  court for an order under section 2 of this Act on the ground that the disposition of the deceased's *j*
  estate effected by his will or the law relating to intestacy, or the combination of his will and that
  law, is not such as to make reasonable financial provision for the applicant.
  (2) In this Act 'reasonable financial provision'—(a) in the case of an application made by virtue
  of subsection (1)(a) above by the husband or wife of the deceased ... means such financial provision
  as it would be reasonable in all the circumstances of the case for a husband or wife to receive,
  whether or not that provision is required for his or her maintenance ...'
b Section 25, so far as material, is set out at p 662 g to j, post
c Section 3(2) is set out at p 662 a to c, post

requirements of s 25 of the 1973 Act was, by s 3(2) of the 1975 Act, merely one of the
a matters to which the court was to have regard and the overriding consideration was what
was reasonable in all the circumstances. Although at first sight the judge's award was not
palpably too low to satisfy the criterion of reasonable provision, he had adopted the
wrong approach in the circumstances of the case since he had equated what the wife's
financial position would have been if the marriage had broken down with her financial
needs and the amount required for her maintenance, which was only one of the matters
b to be taken into account under s 25 of the 1973 Act. In so doing he had adopted as the
basis for calculation the cost of the provision of an annuity to cover present income
requirements, and that took no account of possible future contingencies and was not
appropriate in the case of an application by a surviving spouse since s 1(2) of the 1975 Act
did not restrict reasonable provision to what was required for the maintenance of the
applicant. In the case of a very large estate where the testator's only obligation was to his
c widow who was wholly blameless and incapable of supporting herself, reasonable
provision required that she should have access to a sufficient lump sum to ensure beyond
any reasonable doubt that she was relieved of any anxiety for the future. On the particular
facts of the case, an overall sum of £378,000 was not excessive, since it constituted,
adding the value of the new house at £75,000, approximately a quarter of the available
assets. Accordingly, the capital sum ordered by the judge would be increased to £378,000,
d made up of the house, £75,000, the War Loan, £28,000, and capital, £275,000 (see p 659
b c, p 663 *j* to p 664 *c* and *f* to *h*, p 665 *e* and p 668 *g* to p 669 *e* and *j* to p 670 *b* and *e* to
p 671 *d* and *h j*, post).

Dictum of Greene MR in *Egerton v Jones* [1939] 3 All ER at 891–892 applied.

Wachtel v Wachtel [1973] 1 All ER 829 and *Preston v Preston* [1982] 1 All ER 41
considered.

e Per curiam. The absence of an opportunity to return to the court inherent in a lump
sum order made under s 2(1)(*b*) of the 1975 Act means that in assessing the lump sum
the court should take rather greater account of contingencies and inflation than it would
in the case of an order for periodical payments made under s 2(1)(*a*) (see p 669 *d* to *f*,
p 670 *g* and p 671 *j*, post); dictum of Ormrod LJ in *Robinson v Robinson* [1982] 2 All ER at
700 applied.

f
Notes

For matters to which the court is to have regard on an application for financial provision
from a deceased's estate, see 17 Halsbury's Laws (4th edn) para 1337.

For the Matrimonial Causes Act 1973, s 25, see 43 Halsbury's Statutes (3rd edn) 567.

For the Inheritance (Provision for Family and Dependants) Act 1975, ss 1, 2, 3, see 45
g ibid 496, 498, 501.

Cases referred to in judgments
Bellenden (formerly Satterthwaite) v Satterthwaite [1948] 1 All ER 343, CA.
Egerton v Jones [1939] 3 All ER 889, [1939] 2 KB 702, CA.
J v J [1955] 2 All ER 617, [1955] P 215, [1955] 3 WLR 72, CA.
h *N v N* (1928) 44 TLR 324, [1928] All ER Rep 462.
Page v Page (1981) Times, 30 January, CA.
Preston v Preston [1982] 1 All ER 41, [1982] Fam 17, [1981] 3 WLR 619, CA.
Robinson v Robinson [1982] 2 All ER 699n, [1982] 1 WLR 786n, CA.
Sharpe v Sharpe (1981) Times, 17 February, CA.
Wachtel v Wachtel [1973] 1 All ER 829, [1973] Fam 72, [1973] 2 WLR 366, CA.

j
Cases also cited
Coventry (decd), Re [1979] 3 All ER 815, [1980] Ch 461, CA; *affg* [1979] 2 All ER 408,
    [1980] Ch 461.
Inns, Re, Inns v Wallace [1947] 2 All ER 308, [1947] Ch 576.

Appeal
The plaintiff, Marie Louise Besterman, the widow of the testator, Theodore Deodatus

Nathaniel Besterman, who died on 10 November 1976, appealed against the judgment
of his Honour Judge Mervyn Davies QC, sitting as a judge of the High Court in the   *a*
Chancery Division, given on 31 July 1981, whereby on an application by the plaintiff for
an order under the Inheritance (Provision for Family and Dependants) Act 1975 that
reasonable provision be made for her out of the testator's estate, valued at 8 October 1982
at £1,436,280, he ordered the first three defendants, Gerald Grusin, Hugh Travers
Morgan and Hugh Redwald Trevor-Roper, Baron Dacre of Glanton, the executors of the
will and codicil of the testator, to transfer out of his estate to the plaintiff absolutely War   *b*
Loan Stock to the nominal value of £100,000, pay to the plaintiff a lump sum of
£125,000 and pay on behalf of or reimburse to the plaintiff the amount of any income
tax for which she might be assessed in respect of moneys advanced to her out of the estate
under an interim order made by Master Gowers on 21 July 1980. The fourth defendants
were the Chancellor, masters and scholars of the University of Oxford, the beneficiaries
under the testator's will. The plaintiff asked for an order that the lump sum ordered to   *c*
be paid under the judge's order be increased by such amount as the Court of Appeal
should deem fit. The facts are set out in the judgment of Oliver LJ.

Robert L Johnson QC and *Dirik Jackson* for the plaintiff.
C A Brodie QC and *Spencer G Maurice* for the university.
The first, second and third defendants did not appear.   *d*

OLIVER LJ. This is an appeal by the plaintiff from an order of his Honour Judge
Mervyn Davies QC sitting as a judge of the High Court in the Chancery Division, in
proceedings under the Inheritance (Provision for Family and Dependants) Act 1975. The
plaintiff, now aged 66, is the widow of the late Dr Theodore Besterman. He married her
on 29 December 1958, when he was 54 and she was 42, he having been then twice   *e*
previously married. Thereafter they lived together, first in Switzerland and then in
London and at Thorpe Mandeville in Oxfordshire, until his death at the age of 71 on 10
November 1976.
    There is a conflict of evidence about whether the marriage was altogether happy: he
was, on any showing, an extremely difficult man to live with; but happily it is
unnecessary to say anything more about that, since both sides accept that this is not to be   *f*
treated as a case depending on matrimonial conduct at all and that there is no reason for
assuming anything other than that the marriage was a contented one and that the
plaintiff was a faithful and dutiful wife to whom the deceased owed all the duties
ordinarily arising from the married state.
    The deceased left a will dated 29 July 1973 and that was proved (together with a
codicil) on 7 September 1977. The codicil merely altered the appointment of executors   *g*
and it does not matter for present purposes. The defendants are the three executors (who
do not appear in this court) and the University of Oxford (which, as we shall see, was the
major beneficiary under the will).
    The deceased's primary and absorbing interest was in eighteenth century French
literature and in particular the writings of Voltaire and Rousseau and the philosophy
known as the Enlightenment. It was to that study that he devoted the major part of what   *h*
has proved to be a very extensive estate and he made very little provision for the plaintiff.
    The following are, in summary, the dispositive provisions of the will. First of all, there
was a bequest to the widow of what I may call ordinary domestic and personal ornamental
chattels. Then there was a bequest to the British Museum of working copies of his own
writings, a bequest which, I should add, has been disclaimed. Then there was a bequest
of £100,000 nominal of War Stock to his executors on trust for the plaintiff for life with   *j*
the remainder on the trusts of the residue. That, of course, produces an income of about
£3,500. Then there was recited an agreement with the Taylor Institute of Oxford to
accept the testator's collection of art books on trust to offer them to the Ashmolean
Museum at half the agreed value for probate. That was followed by a bequest to Oxford
University of the collection on trust to let the plaintiff have the use of any 12 drawings

a   for her life and, subject thereto, either to retain the collection or to sell it to the museum, and if that sale was not completed within an agreed period to sell it for the best price obtainable and to hold the proceeds on the trusts of the residue. Finally, there was a residuary bequest to the university on trust to be used to complete the research on Voltaire and Rousseau and other authors of the Enlightenment 'and for such other relevant purposes as the Governing Body of the Taylor Institute shall think fit'. It should be mentioned that in construction proceedings in the Chancery Division that residuary
b   bequest has been held to create a valid charitable trust. That was done by an order of Slade J on 21 January 1980.

The deceased was not just a wealthy man. He was a very wealthy man and that is an important factor to be borne in mind in considering what is a reasonable provision for his widow. His estate was well over £1m. Even after allowing for a massive back duty claim and moneys paid under an interim order it amounts to only a little under £1½m,
c   which, owing to the charitable nature of the ultimate beneficiary, is happily not liable to be eroded by the payment of capital transfer tax.

On 21 July 1980 Master Gowers made an interim order in these proceedings for payment to the widow of a capital sum of £75,000 and of income pending the hearing at the rate of £11,500 a year in addition to the War Loan income, plus an order for payment by the executors of a sum of £3,500 per annum for the upkeep of the Thorpe
d   Mandeville house until sale. The purpose of that capital provision was to enable the widow to buy a house of her own and to vacate the Thorpe Mandeville house so that it could be sold. She, as might be expected, is accustomed to a higher than ordinary standard of living and it is not, I think, to be held against her that she in fact chose to purchase, and expresses herself as quite content with, what is, in fact, a very modest house for someone in her position.

e   The net assets of the estate are set out in the judge's judgment and were at that time as follows. They amounted to £1·37m made up of three elements: the Thorpe Mandeville house, £350,000; chattels, £787,000; and investments, £266,000. The judge continued: 'The chattels element comprises the books, writings etc, intended in cash or kind for the Taylor Institute. So taking that element from the global sum leaves £583,000.'

An updated valuation at 8 October 1982 puts the assets at £1,436,280, of which
f   £700,000 is in the form of liquid assets, quite apart from the valuable art books referred to in the will which, if sold, would provide over another £430,000.

It is unnecessary to dwell in any detail on the married life of the plaintiff and her husband. At the date of their marriage he was the honorary director of the Voltaire Institute Museum in Geneva and they lived in Voltaire's former residence, where they were in the centre of a good deal of social activity. In 1964 he took up a second residence
g   in what appears to have been a very luxurious flat in Pall Mall. In 1970, however, he fell out with the city authorities in Geneva, who were defraying the running costs of the institute, and he then transferred his activities to Oxford, buying a large and luxuriously appointed house at Thorpe Mandeville which constituted the matrimonial home up to the date of his death. There was evidence which suggested that the plaintiff was kept on a fairly tight rein so far as housekeeping money was concerned but a full domestic staff
h   were kept and she obviously enjoyed an extremely high standard of life and engaged in a good deal of social activity.

She had and has, however, very little money of her own; apart from such provision as is made for her out of the deceased's estate she has only a few personal chattels and her state widow's pension amounting to about £400 a year (that is much below the normal level because of the couple's relatively short period of residence in the United Kingdom).
j   For the widow of a millionaire, accustomed to the sort of standard of living that I have described, the testamentary provision of personal chattels and an income for life of £3,500 was clearly not a reasonable provision and the university has very properly acknowledged this throughout. The question which had to be determined by the judge, therefore, was not *whether* further provision should be made but *what* should be the extent of it and what form it should take.

Before I turn to the terms of the order which he made and which is now appealed from it will be convenient to state a little of what has occurred since the testator's death. *a* The house at Thorpe Mandeville was, as I have said, large and luxurious and fully staffed and you cannot simply close such a place down in a matter of a few days or weeks. The plaintiff was, in a figurative sense, locked in there because she had no money of her own to provide a home for herself and she continued to live there, the executors paying the outgoings and continuing her housekeeping allowance of £60 per week. Altogether there was expended in this way, out of the estate (but including the income to which the *b* plaintiff was entitled under the will), a sum of £31,000-odd between the deceased's death and June 1980 when the interim order was made. Some of this consists of moneys paid out of capital (because the estate was then unrealised) to supplement the obviously inadequate income which the plaintiff was receiving under the will and some consists of moneys paid either out of capital or out of income in discharge of servants' wages and other outgoings of the house. *c*

After the interim order the plaintiff applied the capital made available to her in purchasing the much smaller and more modest residence where she now lives. She has given evidence, which is not challenged, of her present living expenditure at present-day prices. For someone in her station in life and accustomed to the standard of living that I have described it is not excessive. Indeed, I would describe it as modest, but, of course, what she was deposing to was not what she would *like* to be able to spend but what she *d* was actually expending, a figure which was necessarily geared to the income available to her under the interim order and the will, for she has nothing else. It amounts to a little over £15,000 per annum but without making any provision for contingencies. So that is the position with which the judge had to deal: a lady of 66, with no means of her own save for a small pension of £400 and an income of £3,500 to which she was entitled for life under the will but with the use of a fairly modest freehold house purchased with an *e* advance from the estate and a current annual budget for necessities in that house of some £15,000. That was the position but with this further important factor (which counsel for the plaintiff submits that the judge tended to overlook) that this lady was the widow of a millionaire and had spent the last 18 years of her life, and might be thought reasonably to be entitled to expect to spend her widowhood, in the standard of life appropriate to that financial position. *f*

There is another factor which ought to be mentioned. The deceased had no obligations under his previous marriages. They were childless but there was an adopted son of full age who does not figure in the will and who has made no claim under the 1975 Act. Dr Besterman had devoted his life of scholarship to the literature of the Enlightenment and he had formed a close association with Oxford University (he received an honorary doctorate there in 1964), but, save in the sense that he would, no doubt, have considered *g* that he owed a duty to himself and to posterity to provide for and complete the work of scholarship in which he was passionately interested, it could not be said that he owed the university any duty, much less a duty which could reasonably be thought to override the very real obligations which he owed to his wife. Indeed, he himself recognised these obligations. When the plaintiff learned that he had made a new will in 1973 she was (as it turned out, with reason) concerned about what her position would be in the event of *h* his death. He got his solicitors to write to her assuring her that he had made an 'ample' provision for her. There is no reason to believe that he, much less his solicitors, could possibly have entertained any idea of misleading her and it can only be assumed that it was, indeed, his intention to provide for her 'amply', an intention borne out by a subsequent direction to his executors to treat her as generously as possible, but that he had so far lost touch with the real value of money as not to appreciate the reality of her *j* needs. That is a phenomenon not uncommonly associated with advancing age, particularly in an era of rapidly changing money values. The income which he left her was approximately equal to the housekeeping allowance which he had been accustomed to give her and it looks, though this is pure speculation, as if he may have assumed that she would simply go on living at Thorpe Mandeville during her widowhood in exactly the same style and manner as she had during his lifetime, but without appreciating that he had left her no endowment to enable her to do so.

Turning now to the statutory provisions, there has to be borne in mind that the 1975 Act contains rather special provisions as regards an application by a surviving spouse (as opposed to any other qualified applicant). Section 1(2) defines 'reasonable provision' for the purposes of the Act. I read now from s 1(2)(a), which is in these terms:

'In this Act "reasonable financial provision"—(a) in the case of an application made by virtue of subsection (1)(a) above by the husband or wife of the deceased [that is this case] . . . means such financial provision as it would be reasonable in all the circumstances of the case for a husband or wife to receive, whether or not that provision is required for his or her maintenance . . .'

It then goes on in para (b) to deal with the case of other applications:

'in the case of any other application made by virtue of subsection (1) above, means such financial provision as it would be reasonable in all the circumstances of the case for the applicant to receive for his maintenance.'

This is a subsection of particular importance in the present context. The Inheritance (Family Provision) Act 1938, which first introduced the concept of reasonable testamentary provision into English law, was an Act to provide for the *maintenance* of dependants. The present Act remains such an Act in relation to dependants other than surviving spouses, but this section expressly provides that in the case of a surviving spouse the governing criterion is to be what the court considers to be 'reasonable' provision unqualified by any such consideration. There may, of course, be cases where that reasonable provision in all the circumstances might be restricted to maintenance, but the subsection makes it clear that the court, in making such reasonable provision, is not to be inhibited by what I may call 'the 1938 Act concept' that maintenance is the only criterion or, indeed, even that that is the dominant consideration. I emphasise this because of the submission of counsel for the plaintiff that the judge, in approaching (as he did) the provision which he was called on to make on the basis of purchasing an annuity sufficient to meet what he regarded as the widow's immediately foreseeable income needs, was treating her maintenance as, if not the sole, at least the dominant criterion by which he was governed. Reverting to the 1975 Act, s 2(1) sets out the range of orders which the court may make and it is again important to bear in mind that it authorises a combination of different orders: payment of income, payment of a lump sum or the out and out transfer of property forming part of the estate. I mention that only because there seemed to be a suggestion in the submissions of counsel for the university that, because what the court is seeking to do is to make provision for the applicant, it ought to start with some sort of bias against making a provision which may, ultimately, have the effect of enabling the applicant to make provision for somebody else who is not an applicant. That, however, is something which is inherent in a lump sum order.

The key provisions are in s 3(1), (2), (5) and (6). Those provisions are as follows:

'(1) Where an application is made for an order under section 2 of this Act, the court shall, in determining whether the disposition of the deceased's estate effected by his will or the law relating to intestacy, or the combination of his will and that law, is such as to make reasonable financial provision for the applicant and, if the court considers that reasonable financial provision has not been made, in determining whether and in what manner it shall exercise its powers under that section, have regard to the following matters, that is to say—(a) the financial resources and financial needs which the applicant has or is likely to have in the foreseeable future . . . (c) the financial resources and financial needs which any beneficiary of the estate of the deceased has or is likely to have in the foreseeable future; (d) any obligations and responsibilities which the deceased had towards any applicant for an order under the said section 2 or towards any beneficiary of the estate of the deceased; (e) the size and nature of the net estate of the deceased . . . (g) any other matter, including the conduct of the applicant or any other person, which in the circumstances of the case the court may consider relevant.

(2) Without prejudice to the generality of paragraph (g) of subsection (1) above, where an application for an order under section 2 of this Act is made by virtue of section 1(1)(a) or 1(1)(b) of this Act [I pause to note that those are applications by surviving spouses], the court shall, in addition to the matters specifically mentioned in paragraphs (a) to (f) of that subsection, have regard to—(a) the age of the applicant and the duration of the marriage; (b) the contribution made by the applicant to the welfare of the family of the deceased, including any contribution made by looking after the home or caring for the family; and [and this is important], in the case of an application by the wife or husband of the deceased, the court shall also, unless at the date of death a decree of judicial separation was in force and the separation was continuing, have regard to the provision which the applicant might reasonably have expected to receive if on the day on which the deceased died the marriage, instead of being terminated by death, had been terminated by a decree of divorce . . .

(5) In considering the matters to which the court is required to have regard under this section, the court shall take into account the facts as known to the court at the date of the hearing.

(6) In considering the financial resources of any person for the purposes of this section the court shall take into account his earning capacity and in considering the financial needs of any person for the purposes of this section the court shall take into account his financial obligations and responsibilities.'

These then are the factors to which the court is directed to pay regard and of particular importance in this case are, first, the plaintiff's resources (she has none apart from the will), second, the principal beneficiary's needs (there are none save those connected with the carrying out of the purposes described by the bequest), third, the obligations owed to the plaintiff as his widow, fourth, the fact that this is an exceptionally large estate of a testator who owed no obligation to anyone other than his widow, fifth, the plaintiff's age (she is clearly unable to fend for herself but nevertheless has a fair expectation of life), and, finally and very importantly, what she might reasonably have expected to receive if the marriage had terminated, not by death, but by divorce.

Now the last factor is, of course, a further imponderable added to a list of imponderables, but it must bring into the calculation a consideration of the provisions of s 25 of the Matrimonial Causes Act 1973.

Sections 23 and 24 of that Act set out the range of orders which the court may make on granting a decree and s 25(1) provides:

'It shall be the duty of the court in deciding whether to exercise its powers under section 23(1)(a), (b) or (c) or 24 above in relation to a party to the marriage and, if so, in what manner, to have regard to all the circumstances of the case including the following matters, that is to say . . . (b) the financial needs, obligations and responsibilities which each of the parties to the marriage has or is likely to have in the foreseeable future . . .'

The important provision for present purposes is the end of the subsection which is in these terms:

'and so to exercise those powers as to place the parties, so far as it is practicable and, having regard to their conduct, just to do so, in the financial position in which they would have been if the marriage had not broken down and each had properly discharged his or her financial obligations and responsibilities towards the other.'

What the judge did (in, I should say, a most clear and careful judgment) was this. He first considered what assets were available and he found that, even segregating out of the estate of £1·4m the art books and other assets left to the university for the purposes of the charitable trusts, there were ample liquid funds available for making a lump sum

provision, it being agreed on both sides that a lump sum provision was the appropriate
a way of dealing with the plaintiff's claim. There were the proceeds of the Thorpe
Mandeville house amounting to some £350,000 and there were investments of something
over £260,000. The plaintiff had had £75,000 and that, he held, must be left undisturbed.
It gave her a secure roof over her head and one with which she, in evidence, had expressed
herself content. He thought, and I respectfully agree, that her life interest in the War
Loan ought clearly to be enlarged to an absolute interest to give her access to some capital
b over and above her home and he so ordered. This provided her with some £28,000, but,
of course, £28,000 which could only be drawn on at the expense of reducing her income.
He then calculated what income she would require to meet the expenditure to which she
had testified as her current expenditure in connection with her modest new home and
he concluded that she ought to have a gross income which would leave her with a net
spendable income of £17,000 per annum so as to have a small margin of income in hand
c for inflation. (There was a slight miscalculation in the figures here because everyone had
overlooked investment income surcharge, but the university has agreed that that ought
to be catered for and, accordingly, in any event the provision ordered should be increased
by £10,000 to compensate for this.) That, the judge considered, adequately catered for
her needs and the way to provide it was to calculate the capital cost of an annuity which
would produce the correct amount. To that he added a further capital sum of £15,000 as
d a sort of precautionary reserve. Thus the provision that he ordered in effect (though not
precisely so expressed in the order) was this: first, the enlargement of the plaintiff's life
interest in the War Stock; second, payment out of the estate of a sum of £110,000 (to be
increased by agreement to £120,000), the cost of an annuity; third, the payment of an
additional £15,000 free capital; and, fourth, the retention of the dwelling house and any
surplus of the sum of £75,000 paid under the interim order.
e   In arriving at this provision, he appears to have treated (I am bound to say, I think
erroneously) the £31,000-odd paid to the plaintiff or for the upkeep of the Thorpe
Mandeville house as if it were some additional *capital* provision made for her, whereas it
was in truth (at any rate in her hands) merely an advance against the income on the scale
which he considered that she needed between the death and the making of the interim
order. He therefore treated this as an addition to the sums referred to in the order and on
f that basis calculated that she would have received from the estate, on the implementation
of the order, an aggregate lump sum of £259,000 made up as follows: War Loan capital,
£28,000; house, £75,000; lump sum ordered, £125,000; plus previously advanced,
£31,000.
      Now, bearing in mind that the plaintiff is the only person to whom it could be said
that the deceased owed any duty to make provision and that he left an estate of about
g £1½m, that is by no means a generous figure. It amounts to a little over one-sixth of the
estate and so far as one can judge from those reported cases in the Family Division where
very wealthy spouses have been involved it appears to bear very little relation to the
provision which she would have been likely to have achieved if the marriage had ended
in divorce. Counsel for the plaintiff submits that it is so plainly too low that this court
ought to interfere, even though he accepts (as he must) that he is asking the court to
h interfere with the exercise of a judicial discretion. It would, he suggests, be a curious
result that a party to a happy and contented marriage who has behaved impeccably
should be thought to be entitled to a lesser provision from her husband than one who
has, perhaps, behaved quite improperly and whose marriage has, in consequence, ended
in divorce and dissension. I confess to some sympathy with this submission, though it
may be an inevitable consequence of the two different exercises which the court is
j directed to carry out. In an application under s 25 of the 1973 Act the court is directed,
so far as it is practicable and is just to do so, to put the parties in the same financial
position as they would have been if the marriage had not broken down. In that
calculation, the concept of what is 'reasonable' is nowhere mentioned, although the
parties' financial needs, which have been construed to mean 'reasonable requirements',
constitute one element to be considered. In an application under the 1975 Act, however,

the figure resulting from the s 25 exercise is merely *one* of the factors to which the court is to 'have regard' and the overriding consideration is what is 'reasonable' in all the *a* circumstances. It is, however, obviously a very important consideration and one which the statute goes out of its way to bring to the court's attention. If, therefore, the provision which the court finds to be reasonable under the 1975 Act turns out to be very widely at variance with the figure which might be expected to be achieved on a divorce, one is immediately driven to ask what regard the trial judge did in fact pay to it, and counsel for the plaintiff submits that in so far as the judge paid any regard to it he misdirected *b* himself by, in effect, equating what the plaintiff's financial position would have been if the marriage had continued with what he described as her 'needs', whereas that is, in fact, only one of the factors which the court is directed to take into account under s 25. That led him to the further step of adopting as his basis for calculation the cost of the provision of an annuity to cover present income needs and that, counsel for the plaintiff submits, is the wrong approach in the circumstances of this case, whatever may be said about it in *c* other cases where the size of the estate is necessarily a limiting factor.

Counsel for the university submits that the annuity calculation, whilst not the only possible approach, is certainly a permissible approach and is, in fact, the right one in the instant case for two reasons: first because the plaintiff has been good enough to make known her present income requirements, which give one a basis for a capital commutation, but second and more importantly because the Act is an Act to provide for *d* applicants and for nobody else and this is the method best suited to producing the result that the applicant will be looked after during her lifetime only and without the risk of funds passing ultimately to somebody other than the applicant.

This submission, which the judge accepted as the basis of his assessment of what was reasonable provision, is thus summarised in his judgment:

> '[Counsel for the university] made the point that any financial provision to be *e* made ought to be made for the applicant and not for others. From this it was argued that any lump sum awarded in such a case as this ought to be such a sum as, with a house and a reasonable amount of capital, will enable the applicant to buy a life annuity sufficient to cover her expenses of living.'

If I may venture to say so with respect, this seems to me to be perfectly right in a case *f* where the court is considering a lump sum provision for an applicant other than a surviving spouse, where maintenance is, in terms, a limiting factor. In the case of a surviving spouse, however, the argument appears to me to amount simply to an indirect way of nullifying the express provisions of s 1(2) of the 1975 Act. It amounts to saying that, although by that section the reasonable provision is one which is, by definition, not restricted to maintenance, nevertheless because it is a provision for the applicant and for *g* nobody else it is effectively limited to what is required for maintenance of the applicant. But first and fundamentally counsel for the university submits that the jurisdiction is a discretionary jurisdiction and that, on well-known principles, this court ought not to interfere with it unless either the judge was so wildly wrong as to make it clear that his decision cannot be supported or the plaintiff can point to some error in principle in arriving at the conclusion at which he in fact arrived. Where one is dealing with a very *h* large estate there is a very wide difference between what any two judges may consider reasonable and the larger the sums the wider becomes the area within which different conclusions may be reached without it being possible to say that either is wrong; and it is certainly not open to this court to interfere simply because, on the same facts, it thinks that it would have made a more generous provision.

Both counsel have referred to and relied on the recent decision of this court in *Preston* *j* *v Preston* [1982] 1 All ER 41, [1982] Fam 17, where the majority, although taking the view that they would have made a lesser provision for the wife under s 25 than that which was actually made by the judge in that case, nevertheless declined to interfere with his decision. Ormrod LJ said ([1982] 1 All ER 41 at 50, [1982] Fam 17 at 29):

> 'On the facts of the present case, my own view is that the provision made for the

a   wife by Ewbank J was too much, in the sense that I would not have awarded so large a sum. On the other hand, in this court, we have to bear in mind Asquith LJ's warning in *Bellenden* (*formerly Satterthwaite*) *v Satterthwaite* [1948] 1 All ER 343 at 345: "We are here concerned with a judicial discretion, and it is of the essence of such a discretion that on the same evidence two different minds might reach widely different decisions without either being appealable. It is only where the decision exceeds the generous ambit within which reasonable disagreement is possible, and

b   is, in fact, plainly wrong, that an appellate body is entitled to interfere." Where the court is dealing with very large resources the ambit of reasonable disagreement is very wide; it narrows progressively as the scale of resources diminishes and the options which will properly fulfil the requirements of s 25(1) become increasingly restricted.'

c   He had earlier referred to the submission of counsel for the husband, and said ([1982] 1 All ER 41 at 50, [1982] Fam 17 at 28):

'I think that on the true construction of s 25 there does come a point, in cases where the available resources are very large, as counsel for the husband submitted, when the amount required to fulfil its terms "levels off", and redistribution of capital as such, in some unspecified ratio begins, which is outside the section. The

d   problem, however, remains to determine where the levelling off point lies . . .'

Both sides, of course, accept this as a proper statement of the law. Where they differ is in its application to the facts of this case, counsel for the plaintiff submitting that the reaonable ambit in which disagreement is possible has been exceeded and counsel for the university submitting the contrary. Speaking for myself, I do not feel able to accept the submission of counsel for the plaintiff that the judge's award was so low as to be palpably

e   wrong in the sense that one looks at it and says straight away as a matter almost of instinct, 'That can't be right,' although I entirely accept that if one views the matter through the eyes of a judge of the Family Division and assumes that the jurisdiction is to be exercised on precisely similar lines to those applicable to an application under s 25 in divorce proceedings the submission may not be altogether misplaced. To that extent, therefore, I think that counsel for the university is right. But the matter does not, in my

f   judgment, end there and I bear in mind the following passage from the judgment of Greene MR in *Egerton v Jones* [1939] 3 All ER 889 at 891–892, [1939] 2 KB 702 at 705–706:

'. . . when a matter involving discretion comes before a judge, there must be in every case a number of considerations which he ought to have in mind for the purpose of enabling him to exercise his discretion. If it appears that he has taken

g   into consideration something which he ought not to have taken into consideration, or has omitted to take into consideration something which he ought to have taken into consideration, or if on all the facts the court is satisfied and convinced that the discretion has been wrongly exercised, it is the duty of this court to interfere.'

h   Counsel for the university submits that, the judge having referred in terms to the provisions of s 3(1) and (2) of the 1975 Act and to s 25 of the 1973 Act, it is evident that he did consider and have in mind all the relevant material. That does not seem to me to follow. Recitation and consideration are not necessarily the same and it is therefore necessary to consider with some care the judge's stated reasons for the decision at which he arrived.

j   Counsel for the plaintiff submits that, even if the final result was not palpably too low to satisfy the criterion of 'reasonable' provision, nevertheless there were several matters of principle in respect of which the judge misdirected himself. First and foremost, he says, the judge did not properly have regard to that which s 3(2) of the 1975 Act directs him to have regard to, viz the provision which the plaintiff might reasonably have expected to receive if the marriage had been dissolved on the day of the deceased's death, or, if he had regard to it, he fundamentally miscalculated what it was likely to be.

I therefore turn to the judge's judgment to see how he dealt with this point, which he certainly clearly had in mind. At the outset the judge found, obviously correctly, that **a** the plaintiff had no financial resources, a matter which he had to consider under s 3(1)(a). He also had to consider her financial needs and it is here, as I think, that there first creeps in a fallacy which, to my mind, underlies the judge's whole approach to the problem with which he was faced. What he said was this: 'The applicant has no special "financial needs" unless it be said that, having regard to her marriage over 18 years with her husband, her need is that some reasonable provision be made for her', and he goes on to **b** refer to *Preston v Preston* where Ormrod LJ equated 'needs' in s 25 of the 1973 Act with 'reasonable requirements'. I have spoken, with respect to the judge, of a fallacy because, whilst the proposition may not be fallacious in itself, it carries within it the seeds of a reasoning with which, speaking for myself, I am unable to agree. It is this. Reasonable provision is equivalent to 'financial need'. Financial need means reasonable requirements. 'Reasonable requirements' means reasonable annual expenditure out of income as found **c** by the judge or deposed to by the applicant. Therefore that which meets reasonable annual expenditure is reasonable provision. I hope that I am not doing an injustice to the judge, who obviously took a great deal of trouble over a difficult case where he had few guidelines in precedent to help him, but as I read his judgment this was essentially his reasoning and it is what led him to adopt the approach, which counsel for the plaintiff criticises, of adopting the price of an annuity as the appropriate basis for calculation in **d** this case. To put it another way, it led him to adopt, as the criterion for reasonable provision, the requirements for the maintenance of the plaintiff, to which s 1(2) of the 1975 Act makes it plain that he was not restricted. This is reflected in his approach to s 3(1)(d) of the 1975 Act, that is 'any obligations and responsibilities which the deceased had towards any applicant for an order'. What the judge said was this:

> 'Among the "obligations and responsibilities" referred to in s 3(1)(d), there was, in **e** my view, a plain obligation and responsibility on the deceased to see that his wife, so far as the estate allows, may maintain herself on a scale of living having some semblance [I think that must be a misprint for 'resemblance'] to the scale that was adopted during the marriage.'

Now it is true that the judge introduces the sentence with the words '*among the* **f** "obligations and responsibilities"' but it is tolerably plain, I think, from the remainder of his judgment that it was that obligation of *maintenance* which dominated his approach. It is also, I think, a fair criticism of the provision finally made by the order appealed from that the scale of maintenance which it permits bears, in fact, very little real resemblance to the scale of living adopted by the couple during their marriage.

It is the aspect of maintenance which again, I think, dominated the judge's approach **g** to s 3(2). He was referred to *Wachtel v Wachtel* [1973] 1 All ER 829, [1973] Fam 72 as an authority for the proposition that a lump sum payment following divorce may well amount to a third or even a half of the family assets, although it is accepted that this can now be considered as no more than a possible guideline or cross-check, and he reviewed the not very numerous cases available in the reports or elsewhere where very substantial assets were involved and *Wachtel* was referred to. In particular he was referred to *Preston* **h** *v Preston* (which I have mentioned above) which indicates the approach of the court to provision under s 25 of the 1973 Act where very large sums are involved. Since this really lies at the heart of the submissions of counsel for the plaintiff, I ought, I think, to refer briefly to the judgment of Ormrod LJ in that case where he says ([1982] 1 All ER 41 at 48, [1982] Fam 17 at 25–26):

> '[Section 25(1)] requires the court to make a hypothetical assessment of the future **j** financial position on two assumptions, (a) that the marriage had continued and (b) that each party had behaved "properly" to the other in financial matters, and then express the assessment in terms of a lump sum or its equivalent. The logical difficulties inherent in this process are so great that only a very approximate result can be achieved. The financial position before and after divorce is so fundamentally

different, especially on capital account, that it amounts to a difference in kind rather than degree, so comparison is impossible, except in the roughest terms. The larger the sums involved, the cruder the comparison will be. Had this marriage continued the wife would have been a de facto joint beneficiary in a very large fund over which she would have had no control; after divorce there will be two separate funds, one of which will belong absolutely to the wife and will be under her sole control, with all that that implies. This problem is not entirely new. Under the old law the courts had from time to time to deal with the financial affairs, after divorce, of the very rich, though, of course, in terms of income only, without the difficulties which are peculiar to capital provisions.'

Then he refers to a dictum of Lord Merrivale P in *N v N* (1928) 44 TLR 324 at 328, [1928] All ER Rep 462 at 466–467 which is in these terms:

'I conceive that I must take into consideration the position in which they were and the position in which she was entitled to expect herself to be and would have been, if her husband had properly discharged his marital obligation.'

Ormrod LJ goes on:

'These passages were cited with approval by Hodson LJ in *J v J* [1955] 2 All ER 617 at 620, [1955] P 215 at 242. He went on to say, speaking of the husband's standard of living: "The standard here is, in my opinion, a proper and, indeed, the only guide to be followed by the court in making provision for the maintenance of the wife", and he approved the course taken by the judge in that case who had made an analysis of the husband's non-business expenditure as the basis of his assessment, of the husband's standard of living ... In this case, the wife is entitled to expect a very high standard of living which would include a home in a house or flat at the top end of the market, and probably a second home in the country or abroad, together with a very high spending power. This means a very high after-tax income, but account must be taken of her ability to spend or invest capital so as to reduce the impact of taxation. To determine the scale on which these requirements should be provided, regard can be had to the husband's post-divorce way of life. His very high spending in recent years (which he has agreed was of the order of £60,000 to £70,000 pa net) can be taken as some measure of his standard of living, and properly reflected in the lump sum payable to the wife. The value of her claim to periodical payments, which she has offered to forgo, must also be taken into account, but discounted for the advantages of immediate payment of capital.'

After referring to *Preston v Preston*, the judge referred to *Page v Page* (1981) Times, 30 January in these terms:

'There Ormrod LJ equates a wife's "needs" in s 25 with "reasonable requirements" and regarded long years of marriage as a "contribution". But he drew attention to the fact that in that case the wife had not been actively engaged in the husband's business either by working or providing capital. £90,000 was ordered out of the husband's assets of £360,000. The wife already owned £29,000 of her own.'

I pause to mention that that amounted to one-quarter of the husband's total assets in that case.

Now, having reviewed the authorities, the judge referred to the rival submissions on both sides. (I mention in parenthesis that counsel for the plaintiff was contending that a figure of £350,000 would have been appropriate in the case of divorce and that by a fortiori reasoning £450,000 was appropriate in the case of death.) But the judge never in fact expressed any conclusion about what he thought would be the hypothetical s 25 provision to which s 3(2) of the 1975 Act obliged him to have regard, and one can only infer from the later part of his judgment that he rejected the submissions of counsel for the plaintiff and regarded the likely provision as being simply that which would meet the wife's reasonable income needs and provide her with a roof over her head. What he said was this:

> 'Looking back at the statutory provisions I have mentioned and the cases and arguments put before me, I must now decide what is in my view reasonable financial provision for the applicant. My first step is to say that [the plaintiff] should be confirmed in her ownership of her house. In her evidence [the plaintiff] says she is very happy there; so there is no occasion to provide any money to enable [her] to move to any other house. The house was bought out of the interim order authorising a payment of £75,000. That sum is confirmed to [the plaintiff]. With a house to live in, [the plaintiff's] financial needs otherwise must be considered in all the circumstances of the case. "Needs" is the word used in s 3(1)(a) as explained in s 3(6). I take "needs" to mean reasonable requirements, just as "needs" was similarly construed in s 25 of the Matrimonial Causes Act 1973 in *Page v Page*. To my way of thinking, bearing in mind [the plaintiff's] past style of life, her requirements of £15,325 a year as set out in her affidavit are not extravagant. I think it reasonable to enable [the plaintiff] to receive an income somewhat in excess of that sum, as well as some capital of her own. The capital should be provided by enlarging [the plaintiff's] life interest in the War Loan stock. See in this connection s 2(1)(c). Its current value is £28,250 and it brings in an income of £3,500 a year. Then [the plaintiff] should be provided with the means of bringing her income up to and beyond the net £15,325 a year that are her present expenses. That can be done by ordering a payment which will enable her to buy a life annuity if she so chooses. In my view, if [the plaintiff] is afforded the means of enabling her to meet her own estimate of her expenses in a house in which she is happy, with a little over to allow for some inflation, then "reasonable financial provision" will be made for her.'

What this amounts to as I read it is an equation of the reasonable provision to be made under the 1975 Act with the plaintiff's financial needs, that is to say her need for a roof over her head and her reasonable requirements for maintaining herself in the house in which she is in fact residing. There are two criticisms to which it is open. In the first place, it assumes that because the plaintiff has professed herself as presently content with the house which she was able to purchase that must be treated as fixing the scale of what she can reasonably be entitled to expect. That ignores the fact that that scale was, of course, itself dictated not by the plaintiff's totally free choice or her accustomed standard of living but by the amount of the interim award which the court was prepared to make. Indeed, the evidence makes it clear that at that stage the defendants were contending that she ought to be content with very much more modest living standards. But more importantly it really pays no regard at all to the provision which the plaintiff might reasonably expect on divorce, in which her needs or reasonable requirements constitute only one of the factors to be taken into account in assessing what her position would have been if the marriage had continued and the deceased had properly fulfilled his financial obligations to her. Now in thus placing the emphasis on what he conceived to be her present income requirements the judge laid the foundation for the calculation which he ultimately made by reference to the cost of an appropriate annuity and in my judgment he thus misdirected himself.

There was also another consideration which, in my judgment, should have commanded considerable weight but to which the judge attached very little importance. Although he made provision for what he described as 'a little over to allow for some inflation' he appears to have taken no real account of possible future contingencies. None was provided for in the plaintiff's own statement of her present income expenditure, but, of course, houses decay, circumstances change, the cost of living increases and the value of money falls, or certainly the history of the past ten years leads us so to believe. Furthermore, although, happily, the plaintiff appears to be in good health, there is an inevitable health hazard with advancing age and, having regard to the fact that this lady is the widow of a more than ordinarily wealthy man, reasonable provision would in my judgment require that she should have access to a sufficient sum to ensure beyond any

a reasonable doubt that she is relieved of any anxiety for the future. It is a criticism of the annuity purchase approach to the problem that the income which it is intended to provide is provided only if an annuity is actually purchased, which is not, in general, a course which a prudent adviser would advise in an age of inflation, and that postulates that there can be no resort to capital in the event of emergency. The answer of counsel for the university would be that she has access to capital in the form of the War Loan

b (£28,000) and the £15,000 awarded in addition to the annuity cost. But that, having regard to her age and the standard to which she is entitled to feel accustomed is less than adequate to leave her with complete security and moreover could only be realised at the expense of income, for it is clear that the notional income from these funds has to be brought into account in finding the £17,000 net spendable income which the judge thought that she ought to have.

c   In the case of a provision by means of periodical payments, the 1975 Act contains in s 6 provisions for the applicant to apply to the court for a variation of the order and an order can be made for further provision out of the sums set aside to meet the periodical payments. The order made in this case is, in effect, based on the hypothesis that the capital producing the income will not remain intact, for a very much larger sum would have to be set aside if one assumes that the income required is provided otherwise than

d by way of lump sum payment necessarily involves the plaintiff forgoing any right to come back to the court for further provision and counsel for the plaintiff argues that this is an important factor to be taken into account in assessing the amount of the lump sum, particularly in a case such as the present where there is a very large estate and there are no practical impediments to making a provision of an amount sufficient to cover all reasonable future contingencies.

e I think that this must be right. It is no answer, in my judgment, to say, as counsel for the university does, that the lump sum method of dealing with the matter is something that both sides wanted. So it was, but that is irrelevant. The relevant consideration is the extent of the lump sum and that ought (at any rate where, as here, the estate is ample for the purpose and scarcity of funds is not an inhibiting factor) to take account of the fact that the plaintiff is (whether or not of her own volition) giving up the right to return to

f the court for a variation of the provision in the event of unforeseen contingencies. The importance of this consideration in relation to provision under s 25 of the 1973 Act has been referred to recently by Ormrod LJ in *Robinson v Robinson* [1982] 2 All ER 699 at 700, [1982] 1 WLR 786 at 787 and in my judgment it equally applies in this jurisdiction. It is not clear that the judge gave any weight at all to it. That he had it in mind is clear but what he said was this:

g   '[Counsel for the plaintiff] said that, if a lump sum were awarded, then one should bear in mind that the award was once and for all whereas a periodic payment order could be the subject of an application to vary under s 6. So in asking for a lump sum award, [the plaintiff] was in some sense giving up an advantage she might have had had she sought a periodic payment. This, in days of inflation, was said to be a concession by [the plaintiff]. So it may be, but I do not feel able to take

h   much account of that consideration in determining an order in [the plaintiff's] favour.'

Counsel for the university says that 'not taking much account' is not the same as taking no account and he reminds us again that this is a discretionary jurisdiction. Whilst I see the force of that, I am bound to say that looking at the judgment as a whole I think that

j the judge really accorded no weight at all to this factor and I would, speaking for myself, be prepared to say that in this respect too he misdirected himself.

However, what, as it appears to me, is the fundamental flaw in the judge's calculation appears from the following passage from the judgment which, I think, demonstrates his view that even in the case of the surviving spouse his or her needs for maintenance are the limiting factor or at least the paramount factor. He should I think have looked at the position as a whole for the purpose of assessing what a reasonable provision would be in all the circumstances for the widow of a millionaire with no obligations to anyone else, and, indeed, a millionaire who had expressed himself as desirous of making very ample *a* provision for her. What he did in fact, as appears from the passage which I am about to quote, was to start from the position that particularly in the case of a large estate (and I am not quite clear why the size of the estate should be of particular relevance for this purpose) the court should start from the position that the provisions of the will must be upheld except to the extent that they are displaced by the obligation to maintain the widow during her lifetime. It was that which led him to adopt as the basis for his *b* calculation the price of what he considered an adequate annuity and which led him to provide a figure which, for my part, I think was, in all the circumstances of this case, a good deal too low.

What he said was this:

'I do not think that reasonable financial provision for [the plaintiff] within the 1975 Act requires the provision of so large a sum as [counsel for the plaintiff] *c* suggested. The effect of that would be to make provision for [the plaintiff] and as well to enable her to benefit those who come after her. The 1975 Act requires no more than that provision be made for the applicant alone. In such a case as this, where a large estate is concerned and both sides desire a once and for all lump sum payment, the order made should ensure, if possible, that provision be made in a way that will interfere as little as possible with the deceased's testamentary dispositions. *d* That means that in this case the applicant should be provided with a sum sufficient to enable her to purchase an appropriate annuity.'

In my judgment, therefore, the judge misdirected himself and this is, therefore, a case in which it is open to this court to review the exercise of his discretion and to form its own conclusion. *e*

What then is to be done? In the first place, I think that we must give much greater weight than did the judge to the provision which the plaintiff might have expected to get if the marriage had ended in divorce. What that is is a matter of speculation, but I would not seriously quarrel with the suggestion of counsel for the plaintiff that an overall sum of £350,000 could not be considered excessive. At the same time I do not think that I can accept that because the marriage did not terminate by divorce in fact, therefore and *f* a fortiori, she must be entitled to more; counsel for the plaintiff puts it (perhaps rather arbitrarily) at £100,000 more. As I have pointed out, however odd the result may be, the two Acts are not necessarily directed to achieving the same result and under this Act the overall criterion is what is reasonable.

I also think that the absence, which is inherent in a lump sum order, of an opportunity to return to the court does mean that, in assessing the lump sum, the court must take *g* rather greater account than might otherwise be the case of contingencies and inflation. I accept the submission of junior counsel for the plaintiff that reasonable provision, in the case of a very large estate such as this and a wholly blameless widow who is incapable of supporting herself, should be such as to relieve her of anxiety for the future. I say 'in the case of a very large estate' not because there is any difference in principle but simply because the existence of a large estate makes that which is desirable also practically *h* possible. It has been pointed out more than once that the calculation in cases of this sort is, of necessity, not one where any precision is possible, but for my part I take the view that reasonable provision in this case would dictate that, in addition to the secure roof over her head, the widow should have available to her a capital sum of sufficient size not simply to enable her to purchase an adequate annuity according to present day needs, but to provide her with the income which she needs and a cushion in the form of available *j* capital which will enable her to meet all reasonably foreseeable contingencies. What that sum is is a matter of judgment but I think that in assessing it we are entitled to take into account that, though the plaintiff is quite content with her present residence, it is in fact somewhat more modest than she might be thought to be entitled to expect to be provided for her by a husband in the financial position of the deceased. In confirming the title to the house and enlarging the life interest in the War Loan stock the judge was plainly right. It was also plainly right for the executors to forgo any claim to recover the £31,000 expended between the death and the interim order, for this is, in effect, merely interim maintenance, although the judge should not, in my judgment, have brought this in to his calculation of the overall capital provision. In addition to that part of his order, however, which I would allow to stand, I would direct the payment of a capital sum which, on a broad calculation, will when invested produce a gross income broadly sufficient to meet the widow's likely needs, a sum which will leave it open to her, if she wishes to increase her income, to do so by an annuity purchase if she is so advised, but which will also enable her to have a substantial and safe fund of capital with which to supplement her income if need arises. One hopes that it will not be necessary for her to do so to any great extent, but she is not a young woman and one bears in mind that in case of prolonged illness or other emergency very substantial capital expenditure might well become necessary. I would accordingly increase the capital sum ordered by the judge from £125,000 to £275,000, thus making an overall provision for the plaintiff of £378,000 made up as follows: house, £75,000; War Loan, £28,000; capital, £275,000. In arriving at this figure I have not taken as a starting point the *Wachtel* proportion but it has been suggested that this is a useful cross-check. Adding back the value of the house to the present value of the estate this provision constitutes approximately a quarter of the available total and confirms me in the belief that it is not excessive.

That then is the order that I would propose and I would only wish to add one thing. This is a very 'pure' case in the sense that it is virtually free from any complicating factors such as conflicting obligations, legal or moral, relevant conduct or substantial means of the applicant or other extraneous considerations. It equally makes it a very unusual case, a feature which is accentuated by the very substantial size of the estate. I have ventured to criticise the judge's annuity approach but I wish to emphasise that I do so only in the context of these particular facts. There may well be circumstances where it is not only a right approach but it is the only right approach. Again, it is a case of a surviving spouse where, under the 1975 Act, very special considerations apply and where the obligations owed by the deceased may be thought to be paramount over his testamentary intentions. I desire to emphasise what has been said, no doubt, many times before, that each case in this jurisdiction depends on its own particular facts and I think that it would be a pity if this case should be used as a basis for drawing general deductions of principle to be applied in other and probably quite different cases, whether of large or small estates. The fact that an estate is very large may of course reflect on what is reasonable, but it also relieves the court of some, at least, of the inhibiting practical considerations which affect the form of relief which may be appropriate and cannot properly, therefore, be used as a precedent for cases where those considerations exist. Our attention was drawn during the course of the argument to a decision of this court in *Sharpe v Sharpe* (1981) Times, 17 February where Ormrod LJ is reported as observing in relation to a s 25 application that there was no need to look at the reported cases. I read from the report:

> 'His Lordship said that it was often said that the Court of Appeal was inconsistent when considering family finances. Each family was unique, and often decisions decided on different facts or even similar facts, were not always helpful.'

I desire to sound the same note of caution in relation to the jurisdiction under this Act and to the instant case. For the reasons which I have given I would allow this appeal to the extent that I have indicated.

FOX LJ. I agree that this appeal should be allowed to the extent and for the reasons which Oliver LJ has given.

ROBERT GOFF LJ. I also agree.

Appeal allowed. Order below varied. Leave to appeal to House of Lords refused.

Solicitors: *Gouldens* (for the plaintiff); *Morrell Peel & Gamlen*, Oxford (for the university).

Mary Rose Plummer   Barrister.

Practice Direction

a

QUEEN'S BENCH DIVISION

County court – Transfer of action – Transfer from High Court – Actions suitable for transfer – Personal injury actions – Personal injury actions to which automatic directions apply – Procedure for transfer – County Courts Act 1959, s 75A – RSC Ord 25, r 8(3).

b

Notes

For the transfer of actions from the High Court to a county court, see 37 Halsbury's Laws (4th edn) para 66.

For the County Courts Act 1959, s 75A (as inserted by the Supreme Court Act 1981, s 149(1), Sch 3, para 8), see 51 Halsbury's Statutes (3rd edn) 525.

As from 1 August 1984 s 75A of the 1959 Act was replaced by s 40 of the County *c* Courts Act 1984.

1. (a) Provision has been made by s 75A of the County Courts Act 1959 for the transfer to a county court of High Court proceedings which are likely to be within the monetary limit of the jurisdiction of the county court or which are not likely to raise any important question of law or fact and are suitable for determination by the county court (see *d* s 75A(1)(b) and (d)).

(b) The jurisdiction to transfer may be exercised by the High Court either of its own motion or on the application of a party.

(c) Where proceedings have been so transferred, the county court may award any amount of damages which could have been awarded by the High Court (see s 75A(10)).

e

2. A party to a personal injury action to which automatic directions apply and which may be suitable for transfer should apply for directions as to the mode of trial before the action is set down (see RSC Ord 25, r 8(3)).

3. Where no such directions have been given, every action set down under automatic directions will be forthwith examined by a master. If it appears to him that the question of transfer to a county court ought to be considered, he will direct the court to give notice *f* to the parties to attend at a given date and time for such consideration and for such other directions as may be just. Any such notice will ordinarily be given within seven days of setting down.

4. If on such consideration the proceedings are transferred to a county court, the setting down will be set aside and an allowance authorised of the setting down fee. *g*

This direction is issued with the authority of the Lord Chief Justice and will have effect from 1 October 1984.

J R BICKFORD SMITH

4 July 1984   Senior Master. *h*

Explanatory note. This direction is intended to reconcile automatic directions with the provisions of s 75A of the County Courts Act 1959 and, by encouraging the transfer of suitable cases to county courts, to free High Court judges for other work, and to expedite hearings. As far as possible transfer will be to a county court which is convenient to the parties and which is organised for trials from day to day.

j

Weight v MacKay and another

HOUSE OF LORDS

LORD DIPLOCK, LORD FRASER OF TULLYBELTON, LORD KEITH OF KINKEL, LORD SCARMAN AND
LORD BRIGHTMAN

20 JUNE, 12 JULY 1984

*Certiorari – Jurisdiction – Crown Court – Certiorari quashing Crown Court decision –
Defendants convicted by magistrates and appealing to Crown Court against convictions – Crown
Court quashing convictions – Irregularity in Crown Court procedure – Crown Court failing to
hear case on merits by declining to receive all admissible evidence desired to be called by prosecutor
– Power of Divisional Court to order Crown Court to rehear appeal – Whether further rehearing
would put defendants in jeopardy a second time.*

The appellants were convicted by a magistrates' court of offences of obstructing a police
officer in the execution of his duty. They appealed against their convictions to the Crown
Court. At the hearing the Crown Court judge made an erroneous ruling on a preliminary
point of law as a result of which he stopped the proceedings before the main prosecution
witness had completed his evidence-in-chief and then allowed the appeals. The prosecutor
applied to the Divisional Court for judicial review of the Crown Court decision. The
Divisional Court issued an order of certiorari quashing the order of the Crown Court and
an order of mandamus to the Crown Court to rehear the appeals before a court presided
over by another judge. The appellants appealed to the House of Lords, contending that
although the Crown Court judge had been in error in his view of the law, so that from
the prosecutor's point of view there had been a breach of the rules of natural justice, the
Divisional Court had had no power to quash the order or to order a rehearing because to
do so would have the effect of putting the appellants in jeopardy for a second time and
would thus contravene the rule against double jeopardy. The appellants contended that
they had already been tried before a court (ie the Crown Court) which had had
jurisdiction to try them, which had accepted jurisdiction so as to put them in jeopardy,
which had embarked on a hearing on the merits and which had unambiguously acquitted
them.

Held – Although an appeal to the Crown Court from a magistrates' court was by way of
a rehearing on the evidence, it was still an appeal and not a trial by a court of first
instance. It followed that, where the Crown Court failed to hear an appeal against
conviction and sentence on the merits of the case by declining to receive all the admissible
evidence desired to be called by the prosecutor, there was no decision on the merits, and
the Divisional Court therefore had power to quash the Crown Court's decision and order
it to rehear and determine the appeal. In those circumstances a further rehearing would
not put the defendant in jeopardy for a second time because if the Crown Court decision
was quashed the defendant would remain convicted as a result of the original conviction
against him in the magistrates' court, given on the only occasion when he was put in
peril; that conviction would stand unless it was quashed, and if the defendant chose to
pursue his appeal to the Crown Court he would not be in peril of any other conviction
for the offence. The appellants' appeal would accordingly be dismissed (see p 674 *g*, p 675
j and p 676 *a b* and *e* to p 677 *c* and *f* to p 678 *b*, post).

R v Ridgway (1822) 1 Dow & Ry KB 132 and *R v Clare Justices* [1905] 2 IR 510 applied.

Dicta of Donaldson LJ in *R v Crown Court at Wolverhampton, ex p Crofts* [1982] 3 All
ER at 704 approved.

Notes

For certiorari to quash orders of inferior courts, see 11 Halsbury's Laws (4th edn) paras
1529–1530, and for cases on the subject, see 16 Digest (Reissue) 402–409, 4442–4724.

For autrefois convict and autrefois acquit, see 11 Halsbury's Laws (4th edn) paras 241–244, and for cases on the subject, see 14(1) Digest (Reissue) 440–441, 3774–3786.   *a*

Cases referred to in opinions

Harrington v Roots [1984] 2 All ER 474, [1984] 3 WLR 142, HL.
R v Clare Justices [1905] 2 IR 510.
R v Crown Court at Wolverhampton, ex p Crofts [1982] 3 All ER 702, [1983] 1 WLR 204, DC.   *b*
R v Middlesex Justices, ex p DPP [1952] 2 All ER 312, [1952] 2 QB 758, DC.
R v Ridgway (1822) 1 Dow & Ry KB 132.

Appeals

Robert MacKay and Gillian Hausamann appealed with leave of the Appeal Committee of   *c*
the House of Lords granted on 15 March 1984 against the decision of the Divisional
Court of the Queen's Bench Division (Ackner LJ and Taylor J) on 27 January 1984
granting an application by the respondent, Brian Weight, the Chief Constable of Dorset,
for judicial review (1) by way of an order of certiorari to quash an order made by his
Honour Judge Macdonald sitting at the Crown Court in Bournemouth on 21 January
1983 allowing the appeals of the appellants against their convictions by the Bournemouth   *d*
magistrates on 11 June and 14 May 1982 respectively of offences of obstructing a police
officer in the execution of his duty contrary to s 51(3) of the Police Act 1964, and (2) by
way of an order of mandamus directed to the Crown Court at Bournemouth to rehear
the appeals, before a court presided over by another circuit judge. The Divisional Court
had refused leave to appeal to the House of Lords but certified, under s 1(2) of the
Administration of Justice Act 1960, that a point of law of general public importance (set   *e*
out at p 675 *a*, post) was involved in the decision. The facts are set out in the opinion of
Lord Fraser.

John Spokes QC and *John Aspinall* for the appellants.
Anthony Scrivener QC and *Steven Whitaker* for the respondent.

                                                                                    f

Their Lordships took time for consideration.

12 July. The following opinions were delivered.

LORD DIPLOCK. My Lords, I have had the advantage of reading in draft the speech
of my noble and learned friend Lord Fraser. I agree with it, and for the reasons which he   *g*
gives I would dismiss this appeal.

LORD FRASER OF TULLYBELTON. My Lords, the appellants were convicted by
a magistrates' court of offences of obstructing a police officer in the execution of his duty.
They appealed to the Crown Court, which allowed their appeals. But the procedure in
the Crown Court was irregular and, on an application by the respondent (the prosecutor)   *h*
for judicial review, the Queen's Bench Divisional Court made an order of certiorari
quashing the order of the Crown Court, and of mandamus to the Crown Court to rehear
the appeal before a court presided over by another circuit judge. The Divisional Court
certified a question as raising a point of law of general importance, but refused leave to
appeal to your Lordships' House. Leave to appeal was subsequently given by the House.
The issue in the appeals is whether the Divisional Court had power to quash the order of   *j*
the Crown Court and to order a rehearing, or whether it did not have power to make
such orders because they would have the effect of putting the appellants in jeopardy for
a second time and would thus contravene the rule against double jeopardy.
    The Divisional Court certified the following question as raising a point of law of
general importance:

'Whether and in what circumstances it is open to a Divisional Court of the Queen's Bench by orders of Certiorari and Mandamus, on an application for Judicial Review pursuant to section 31 of the Supreme Court Act 1981 and Order 53 of the Rules of the Supreme Court to quash an order of the Crown Court allowing an appeal from Justices and to order the Crown Court to rehear and determine the Appeal.'

The irregularity which led to the quashing of the order of the Crown Court was that the judge prematurely stopped the proceedings before the main prosecution witness had completed his evidence-in-chief, and allowed the appeals. There is no dispute about what occurred in the Crown Court because, as it happens, the proceedings were recorded in shorthand on the application of counsel for the appellants, who had apparently anticipated that the appeal might go further, though not on the point which has in fact arisen. The first and main prosecution witness was the police officer whom the appellants were charged with obstructing. His evidence, putting it briefly, was that he had seen the appellants walking along a street in Bournemouth on the date mentioned in the charge sheet, and had noticed what he thought was a record or records tucked down inside the trousers of the appellant MacKay. He asked MacKay what it was. MacKay denied that there was anything there and tried to run away. A struggle followed, during which the police officer dropped a briefcase which he was carrying, and the appellant Hausamann, on the instructions of MacKay, picked up the briefcase and tried to run away with it. The police officer, with the help of some members of the public, succeeded in detaining both the accused, and as soon as he had done so he said to them: 'You are being arrested on suspicion of theft.' The judge thought, quite wrongly, that in order to constitute an arrest it was necessary for the person concerned to be told in words that he was being arrested. As Ackner LJ said in the Divisional Court:

'The learned judge appears to have been confusing that which [is] required to constitute an arrest with that which is required to constitute a *lawful* arrest.' (Ackner LJ's emphasis.)

For the latter purpose the person arrested must normally be told the reason for his arrest at the time of the arrest, or as soon as possible thereafter. But the arrest itself can be effected without any words being spoken. Acting on his view of the law, the judge cross-examined the police officer, in somewhat offensive terms, as to why he had not told the appellants before or during the struggle that they were being arrested. He heard submissions from counsel, in the course of which counsel for the respondent said that he might wish to ask the police officer what was in his briefcase, in order to show why he was anxious about the possibility of losing it. After a short retirement, the judge ruled that no arrest had been made before the struggle took place and that the appeal must be allowed. Counsel for the appellants concedes that the judge was in error in his view of the law, and that, from the point of view of the prosecutor, there had been a breach of the rules of natural justice.

On these facts counsel for the appellants submitted that the appellants had been tried before a court (the Crown Court) which had jurisdiction to try them, which had accepted jurisdiction so as to put them in jeopardy, which had embarked on hearing the case on its merits and which had unambiguously acquitted them. Against an acquittal in such circumstances, said counsel, there was a well-established principle that the prosecutor had no right of appeal, except under certain statutory exceptions none of which applied here, and he referred to the maxim nemo debit bis vexari pro una et eadem causa.

My Lords, there are in my opinion two answers to the argument so persuasively advanced by counsel for the appellants. Both depend essentially on the fact that the procedure in the Crown Court was not a trial by a court of first instance but an appeal. That is of course perfectly clear, but I shall refer briefly to the relevant statutory provisions to show the nature of the procedure in the Crown Court. The Magistrates' Courts Act 1980 provides by s 108(1) that a person convicted by a magistrates' court has a right of

appeal to the Crown Court. By s 110 it provides further that after the determination by
the Crown Court of an appeal from a magistrates' court 'the decision of the Crown Court   *a*
shall have effect as if it had been made by the magistrates' court against whose decision
the appeal is brought'. Counsel submitted that the effect of those words was to put the
decision of the Crown Court in exactly the same position as that of the magistrates' court
from which the appeal had come. For some purposes that is no doubt correct but it does
not affect the position that the decision of the Crown Court is that of an appellate tribunal
and not of a court of first instance.   *b*

The Supreme Court Act 1981 provides in s 45 for the general jurisdiction of the Crown
Court, and in s 48 it provides for its appellate jurisdiction. The only parts of s 48 which I
need quote are sub-ss (2) and (4). They are in the following terms respectively:

> '(2) On the termination of the hearing of an appeal the Crown Court—(*a*) may
> confirm, reverse or vary the decision appealed against; or (*b*) may remit the matter   *c*
> with its opinion thereon to the authority whose decision is appealed against; or (*c*)
> may make such other order in the matter as the court thinks just, and by such order
> exercise any power which the said authority might have exercised.
>
> (4) If the appeal is against a conviction or a sentence, the preceding provisions of
> this section shall be construed as including power to award any punishment,
> whether more or less severe than that awarded by the magistrates' court whose   *d*
> decision is appealed against, if that is a punishment which that magistrates' court
> might have awarded.'

Section 79(3) of the 1981 Act provides as follows:

> 'The customary practice and procedure with respect to appeals to the Crown
> Court, and in particular any practice as to the extent to which an appeal is by way of   *e*
> rehearing of the case, shall continue to be observed.'

The fact that an appeal to the Crown Court is by way of rehearing of the case, and that it
is a rehearing on the evidence, does not distinguish it in any relevant respect from the
more usual procedure of rehearing on documents, which is followed in ordinary civil
appeals: see RSC Ord 59, r 3.

The first answer to the argument of counsel for the appellants is that, although the   *f*
Crown Court embarked on a rehearing on the merits, it never completed the rehearing.
Its decision was made on an erroneous view of the law which misled the judge into
stopping the rehearing before the evidence was complete, and the consequence is that
there was no decision on the merits. Accordingly, it falls into the same class as *R v
Ridgway* (1822) Dow & Ry KB 132, where quarter sessions on appeal had quashed a
conviction on a point of form, and it was held that the order quashing the conviction   *g*
might itself be quashed. Bayley J said (at 139):

> '. . . I am of opinion, that the conviction in this case was improperly quashed, and
> that it is our duty to send the appeal back to the court of quarter sessions, in order
> that it may be heard there upon the merits.'

That statement is in principle applicable in the circumstances of the present case. See also   *h*
R v Clare Justices [1905] 2 IR 510, which was a decision to the same effect. Counsel for the
appellants submitted that once the court, being properly constituted, has started to hear
the evidence the proceedings cannot be a nullity, with the consequence that the accused
is in jeopardy and a decision for acquittal cannot be quashed. He relied on *R v Middlesex
Justices, ex p DPP* [1952] 2 All ER 312, [1952] 2 QB 758. But that case was concerned, as
Lord Roskill pointed out in this House recently in *Harrington v Roots* [1984] 2 All ER 474   *j*
at 480, [1984] 3 WLR 142 at 149, with a trial on indictment at quarter sessions, that is
with a trial in a court of first instance, and not with procedure at quarter sessions, sitting
as an appellate tribunal. It is my opinion of no assistance in the present appeal. In the
Middlesex Justices case the jury had returned a *verdict* of 'not guilty by direction' and it
was held that that verdict could not be quashed. In the present case the court of first
instance found the appellants guilty and an appeal against that decision was allowed by

the Crown Court, but there has never been a decision or finding of acquittal by any court. Whatever the position may be at a trial before a court of first instance, when it comes to procedure before quarter sessions sitting as an appeal court there is a clear distinction of principle between allowing an appeal against conviction after proceedings in which all the available evidence, so far as it is in the opinion of quarter sessions admissible, has been heard and allowing it after proceedings which have been prematurely aborted, without all the available and admissible evidence having been heard, because of a ruling by the court on a preliminary point. The former is not liable to be quashed. The latter, which is this case, is liable to be quashed on the grounds stated in *R v Ridgway* and *R v Clare Justices*.

The second answer to the argument for the appellants is that the appellants will not be put in jeopardy, in the relevant sense, by a further rehearing by the Crown Court. The reason was explained by Donaldson LJ in *R v Crown Court at Wolverhampton, ex p Crofts* [1982] 3 All ER 702 at 704, [1983] 1 WLR 204 at 207, where, after referring to the 'overriding principle of English law that no one should be put in peril of conviction twice in respect of the same offence', Donaldson LJ went on to say:

> 'For my part I accept that that principle is one of the most important principles of English criminal law and that if there is a conflict between that principle and the principle that courts will intervene in order to quash the decisions of inferior courts which are obtained by fraud, it is the former principle (that no one should be put in peril twice) which should prevail. But in my judgment that does not apply where a court is concerned with an acquittal by the Crown Court on appeal from magistrates, for this reason. If the Crown Court decision is quashed, and this will only occur when it is the beneficiary of the Crown Court decision who has been guilty of the fraud, the result will be not that the defendant is twice put in peril, but that he remains convicted as a result of the first and only occasion on which he was put in peril.'

Donaldson LJ referred to decisions obtained by fraud no doubt because on the facts of that case the appellants had succeeded in obtaining a decision of the Crown Court in their favour by perjury. But his reasoning seems to me to be equally applicable to decisions which are quashed on other grounds. Moreover, as my noble and learned friend Lord Brightman pointed out during the argument, there would be no question of double jeopardy if the Divisional Court's orders of certiorari and mandamus take effect, because the appellants are under no obligation to pursue their appeal before the reconstituted Crown Court. Whether they choose to do so or not, the only conviction against them for this offence will be the original conviction in the magistrates' court, given on the only occasion when they were put in peril. That conviction will stand unless it is quashed, and, if the appellants choose to pursue their appeal to the reconstituted Crown Court, they will not be in peril of any other conviction on this offence.

The question as certified is stated in terms too general to permit of a simple answer. The point which is intended to be raised in the appeal could I think be more appropriately stated by a question in the following form:

> 'Whether on the allowing by the Crown Court of an appeal from the justices against conviction and sentence, after the Crown Court has failed to hear such appeal on the merits by declining to receive all the admissible evidence desired to be led by the respondent, the Queen's Bench Divisional Court has power on an application by the respondent for judicial review to quash the order of the Crown Court and to order such court to rehear and determine the appeal.'

I would answer the question in that substituted form in the affirmative and would dismiss this appeal.

LORD KEITH OF KINKEL. My Lords, for the reasons given in the speech of my noble and learned friend Lord Fraser, with which I agree, I too would dismiss the appeal.

LORD SCARMAN. My Lords, I have had the advantage of reading in draft the speech delivered by my noble and learned friend Lord Fraser. I agree with it, and for the reasons he gives I would dismiss the appeal.

LORD BRIGHTMAN. My Lords, I respectfully agree that the certified question, in the substituted form proposed by my noble and learned friend Lord Fraser, should be answered in the affirmative, and that the appeal should be dismissed, for the reasons given by him.

Appeal dismissed

Solicitors: *Bower Cotton & Bower*, agents for *Andrews McQueen & Co*, Bournemouth (for the appellants); *Sharpe Pritchard & Co*, agents for M J *Davies*, Dorchester (for the respondent).

Mary Rose Plummer   Barrister.

Practice Note

CHANCERY DIVISION (COMPANIES COURT)
VINELOTT J
9 JULY 1984

Company – Compulsory winding up – Procedure – Attendance before registrar – Attendance on appointed day – Delay – Late attendance only allowed where good reason shown – Companies (Winding-up) Rules 1949, r 33.

VINELOTT J made the following statement at the sitting of the court. Under r 33 of the Companies (Winding-up) Rules 1949, SI 1949/330, the petitioner or his solicitor is required to attend before the registrar on the day appointed in the memorandum issued when a petition is presented. That day is invariably the Monday before the petition is due to be heard. It has been the practice to allow a petitioner or his solicitor to attend and lodge the papers after the day so appointed but not later than 1 pm on the Thursday preceding the day on which the petition is due to be heard. In recent months there has been a tendency on the part of some firms of solicitors to take advantage of this indulgence and to attend at the Companies Office with large numbers of petitions on the Wednesday, or even the Thursday morning. That, together with a continued increase in the number of petitions presented, has made it very difficult for the Companies Registry properly to check the papers presented.

The purpose of this statement is to remind all concerned that the proper time for attending before the registrar is the day appointed when a petition is presented, and that attendance after that day, not being later than 1 pm on the Thursday before the day the petition is due to be heard, will only be allowed if some good reason is shown for the delay in attending.

Jacqueline Metcalfe   Barrister.

R v Foster

COURT OF APPEAL, CRIMINAL DIVISION
WATKINS, MAY LJJ AND BUTLER-SLOSS J
27, 29 MARCH 1984

Crown – Prerogative – Pardon – Effect of grant of pardon – Whether pardon eliminates conviction in respect of which pardon granted.

Since the Crown no longer has a prerogative of justice but only a prerogative of mercy, it can only pardon the effects of a conviction and cannot remove the conviction itself. The only body which has power to quash a conviction is the Court of Appeal, Criminal Division. It follows that a free pardon in respect of a conviction does not eliminate the conviction, which continues to exist, and that the effect of the pardon is simply to remove from the subject of the pardon all the pains, penalties and punishments that ensue from the conviction (see p 684 *j*, p 685 *a* and p 687 *a* to *c*, post).

Cuddington v Wilkins (1615) Hob 81, *Hay v London (Tower Division) Justices* (1890) 24 QBD 561 and *R v Cosgrove* [1949] Tas SR 99 considered.

Notes

For pardons granted under royal perogative, see 8 Halsbury's Laws (4th edn) paras 949–952, and for cases on the subject, see 11 Digest (Reissue) 684–687, *179–243*.

Cases referred to in judgment

Cuddington v Wilkins (1615) Hob 81, 80 ER 231.
Hay v London (Tower Division) Justices (1890) 24 QBD 561, DC.
Prohibitions Del Roy (1607) 12 Co Rep 63, 77 ER 1342.
R v Cosgrove [1949] Tas SR 99.
R v Lee [1984] 1 All ER 1080, [1984] 1 WLR 578, CA.
Royal Commission on Thomas Case, Re [1980] 1 NZLR 602, HC Full Ct.
Searle v Williams (1618) Hob 288, 80 ER 433.

Appeal against conviction

On 21 February 1978 in the Crown Court at Nottingham before Stephen Brown J and a jury the appellant, Barry Arthur Foster who stood charged in an indictment containing four counts with rape (count 1), attempted buggery (count 2), indecent assault (count 3) and attempted rape (count 4), pleaded guilty to counts 1 and 4 and in respect of those counts was sentenced to be detained in hospital under ss 60 and 65 of the Mental Health Act 1959. He pleaded not guilty to counts 2 and 3 and those counts were ordered to remain on the file. Subsequent to the convictions another man confessed to having committed the offences charged in the indictment and in consequence the appellant, on 11 March 1982, was granted a free pardon in respect of the rape offence charged in count 1. The pardon did not affect count 4 and he remained in hospital under the order made under the 1959 Act. The appellant applied to the full court for leave to appeal out of time against his conviction and sentence on count 4 and also against his conviction on count 1 and the court granted leave. The grounds of the appeal against the convictions were (a) that in the light of new evidence not available at the time of the appellant's trial the convictions were unsafe and unsatisfactory and, in accordance with s 2(1)(*a*) of the Criminal Appeal Act 1968, should be quashed and (b) in regard to the conviction on count 1, that the free pardon did not have the effect of quashing that conviction and therefore the conviction on count 1 continued to exist and in all the circumstances should

be quashed as being unsafe and unsatisfactory. The facts are set out in the judgment of
the court.   *a*

J Melville Williams QC and *Oliver Thorold* for the appellant.
Anthony Arlidge QC and *R Horwood-Smart* for the Crown.

At the conclusion of the hearing of the appeal the court announced that the appeal against
conviction would be allowed for reasons to be given later.   *b*

29 March. The following judgment of the court was delivered.

WATKINS LJ. This is, fortunately for the good name of justice, a very unusual story
we have to tell. The leading figures in it are two men, namely the appellant, who is 37   *c*
years of age, a single man and a native of Nottingham, and Denzil Pearce, who is 35 years
of age, a married man and a native of Llanelly in South Wales.

Until 1977 the appellant was a man of good character who lived with his mother. He
is of low intelligence. Pearce, who has an appallingly bad criminal record, lived until late
in 1977 with his wife and two children in Hareholme, Rossendale, Lancashire. His
criminal career, for he seems to have had none other, began as long ago as 1958. He has   *d*
been convicted on many occasions for breaking into houses, offices and schools. He has
been to a detention centre, to Borstal and to prison for terms as long as 27 months. On
15 March 1976 he was convicted at Oldham Magistrates' Court of an indecent assault on
a girl under the age of 13 years. He was sent to prison for six months for that. On 8 June
1981 at Rossendale Magistrates' Court he was convicted of indecent exposure. For that
he received a sentence of one month's imprisonment suspended for two years. Little did   *e*
those magistrates know what lay beneath this dismal surface.

Not very long afterwards three small girls were playing together in an open space in
Accrington. Along came a man who indecently assaulted every one of them. Inquiries
were widespread. They led police to the home of Pearce. He was told he was suspected of
having attacked these girls in that way. He first of all denied that he had. Then he
admitted having done so. Gradually an astonishing tale unfolded of the commission by   *f*
him of a vast number of offences against very young girls in many places in Lancashire
and elsewhere, Nottingham included, to where he was taken by the police so that he
could show them where some of the offences he had committed had occurred.

Consequently he appeared at the Crown Court in Preston on 7 December 1981 where
he pleaded guilty to three offences of indecent assault, one of having sexual intercourse
with a girl under the age of 13 years and two attempts at committing that offence. He   *g*
asked for over 70 similar offences to be taken into consideration. In a medical report by
the well-known Dr Lawson from Risley Remand Centre he was described as a fetishist
and a menace to young children. Most of the other offences which he asked to be taken
into consideration consisted of indecent assaults on little girls. All the offences were
committed over a protracted period between 1975 and 1981. McNeill J sentenced him
to life imprisonment.   *h*

Among the offences of which he was convicted on indictment on his own confession
were two of particular interest to the police and subsequently to many others. They were
count 2, having sexual intercourse on 18 February 1977 at Nottingham with M, a girl of
the age of 10 years, and count 3, attempting to have sexual intercourse on 8 April 1977
at Nottingham with B, a girl of the age of 10 years.

The interest of the police sprang from the following events. On 7 November 1977   *j*
before the Crown Court at Nottingham, presided over by Stephen Brown J, the appellant
Barry Arthur Foster faced an indictment containing four counts. All the offences were
alleged to have taken place in Nottingham. By the first count he was charged with rape,
the particulars being that on 18 February 1977 he had sexual intercourse with M, a girl
of the age of 10, without her consent. By the second count he was charged that on 8 April

1977 he attempted to commit buggery on B, a girl of the age of 10 years. By the third
a count he was charged with indecently assaulting that young girl and by the fourth count
he was charged with attempting to rape a girl, T. He pleaded guilty to the first and fourth
counts on the indictment. He pleaded not guilty to the second and third. They were
ordered by the judge to lie on the file, not to be proceeded with further without the leave
of that court or the Court of Appeal, Criminal Division.

The appellant was sentenced in respect of counts 1 and 4 to hospital orders under ss 60
b and 65 of the Mental Health Act 1959.

The facts which require to be examined in a little detail on which the Crown relied to
secure the conviction of the appellant on those two counts were that on 18 February 1977
M was walking her dog in Bulwell, which is a part of Nottingham. She met a man who
invited her to accompany him. He took her to a disused railway bridge where he savagely
raped her. He then told her to go and tell her father what had happened. She went home.
c She was admitted to hospital where she remained for treatment for as long as 2½ weeks.
The psychological harm done by that rape could not at the time of the trial of the
appellant be properly assessed.

As for the matters with which counts 2 and 3 were concerned what was alleged was
that on 8 April 1977 at Colwick, Nottingham, B was going through some woods when a
man grabbed hold of her, pulled down her undergarments, indecently assaulted her and
d endeavoured unsuccessfully to commit buggery.

As to count 4, what is alleged to have taken place is that on the afternoon of 29 April
1977 two sisters, T, the subject of the charge, 10 years of age, and her elder sister, Y, who
was 13, went to a deserted factory near a local golf course. While they were in an old
house nearby a man approached them. He was described as about 5 ft 7 in tall, talked
rather slowly and was 'dozy'. The older girl thought he was 'not all there'. He was
e wearing, so she said, a square checked suit. He led these girls to some old buildings. The
older one ran away. The man kept hold of the younger girl's hand. She became frightened
and started to scream. None the less he exposed himself to her, pulled down her
underclothes, pushed her to the ground, lay on top of her and tried to have sexual
intercourse with her. She managed to escape eventually.

Following this attack, the police asked the public for help by advertising some at least
f of the details of the offence and a description of a man as provided by the two girls. A Mr
Warsop came forward and said that a man had tried to lure his 11 year old daughter into
an old building two days before in the same area. On the day this happened she had
pointed out the man to him. He tried to hit him, but the man ran off. The following day
Mr Warsop claimed to have seen this man again in company with a stoutish woman. He
described him as being slightly backward.

g What happened afterwards provided the only evidence on which the Crown could rely
for the conviction of the appellant. There was a series of interviews between him and the
police which commenced on 30 April 1977 at his home. It is pertinent to say of those
interviews that on occasions the appellant was alone with the police while they took
place, on others his mother was present and on still further occasions a social worker was
in attendance. In the course of those interviews he is recorded as having admitted
h committing the offences which I have outlined. There was no forensic evidence linking
him with any one of the offences. There was found on him however some cards
belonging to a company which had previously used the disused factory premises to
which count 4 related. There was no confirmation from any other source of anything
which he told the police on any one of the occasions when the interviews took place.

So much then for how it was that the appellant came to trial and pleaded guilty.

j He was examined before he appeared before Stephen Brown J by at least two consultant
psychiatrists. That was inevitable seeing that hospital orders were to be made. It is of
relevance to record in this judgment that one of the psychiatrists stated in his report on
27 October 1977 that although he had some reservations about the appellant's
involvement in the charge concerning the assault in Colwick woods, he would now take
the view that the appellant from what he had told him had committed that offence. In

his report he said: 'I had never, of course, had any doubt about his part in the other two offences'. Another consultant psychiatrist stated in his report:

'Barry Foster is a young man of subnormal intelligence with an abnormal appearance and with a speech defect. As yet there is much we do not know about him. He informs me that he committed the offence as he was upset that his sister was going on holiday without him.'

In a third report made by the consultant psychiatrist to whom I first referred it is recorded that the appellant was admitted to a local hospital for the mentally subnormal when he was ten years of age. He spent ten years in that hospital before being discharged home to live with his mother. This attempt at allowing him to live outside a hospital regime was unsuccessful and he was readmitted to hospital quite soon. Eighteen months before that report was made another attempt was made to rehabilitate him in the community following his discharge from hospital. He had by this time apparently spent two-thirds of his time under close institutional supervision. On examination it was discovered that he functioned at a level of subnormality of a person with an IQ level of 63. In the recommendation to the court for the making of the hospital orders this same consultant psychiatrist offered this opinion:

'In my opinion he [ie the appellant] is urgently in need of treatment under conditions of maximum security and it is my recommendation that this could best be provided in a special hospital such as Rampton Hospital.'

It was there that he went after the hospital orders were made. The judge on the evidence before him clearly had no alternative but to make those orders. It needs to be said, so we think, as clearly as possible that at the time they were made the pleas of guilty offered to the court by this appellant had all the appearance of being genuine and they were made seemingly without any equivocation whatsoever. It may be that it will be thought that the confessions which he is said to have made to the police were to some extent enticed from him by suggestions made by the police. Whatever criticism which is sought to be made of the police (we do not know whether they are open to criticism) has to be looked at in the light of the impression which this appellant made on two consultant psychiatrists by his confessions to them to the commission of the offences which we are now exploring.

Be that as it may, the confessions of Pearce and the detail in which he made those confessions casts a very different light on the confessions of the appellant. Consequent on Pearce's confessions senior police officers both in Lancashire and in Nottinghamshire considered this extraordinary state of affairs. The Director of Public Prosecutions was consulted. A report was sent to the Home Secretary. The conclusion of everyone concerned was that it was Pearce and not the appellant, his confession notwithstanding, who had attacked M and B. The appellant was not as has been said convicted of the attack on B. Those charges remained outstanding at the commencement of this appeal. The Home Secretary, being persuaded of the innocence of the appellant on the charge of rape, recommended to Her Majesty the Queen that the appellant be pardoned. So it was that on 11 March 1982 a free pardon was granted by Her Majesty to the appellant in respect of his conviction for rape. But he remained in Rampton because he was still subject to the hospital order made on count 4 of the indictment. The free pardon did not affect that count.

On 23 August 1983 on the appellant's application for release from Rampton the Home Secretary referred his case to a mental health review tribunal in these terms. (I read from a letter of 256 August 1983 addressed to the clerk to the mental health review tribunal for the Trent Regional Health Authority Area):

'The Home Secretary has decided to exercise his powers under section 66(6) of the Mental Health Act 1959 to refer the case of the above-named patient to a mental health review tribunal. The purpose of this reference is to anticipate the provisions of paragraph 3(2) of Schedule 1 to the Mental Health (Amendment) Act 1982, under which the patient would otherwise become eligible for obligatory reference to a *a* tribunal on 30th September 1983, in order to avoid the need to refer a large number of cases on that date.'

With the letter the Home Secretary sent a statement of the case. It is in some respects inaccurate. It was important for the tribunal not only to have an accurate statement of events but also to be sure when they came to hear the application of the appellant that they knew whether he remained convicted despite the pardon of the offence under count

b 1 (rape) and whether or not there was any prospect of his escaping in some way or another from the conviction on count 4. A solicitor was consulted about the matter and he assumed control of the appellant's affairs. Having studied all that had gone on and having been advised by counsel, he came to the conclusion that it would be proper to seek leave to appeal to this court, notwithstanding that the time for making the application had long since expired. Legal aid was obtained. The proceedings before the

c mental health review tribunal were adjourned. They still stand adjourned. Grounds of appeal were drafted by counsel and application was made to this court. The necessary extension of time was sought and granted and likewise leave to appeal against conviction, and if need be against sentence under count 4, was granted.

The grounds relied on are expressed very cogently. First it is contended that in the light of new evidence not available at the time of the appellant's trial his convictions on counts 1 and 4 are unsafe and unsatisfactory. So in accordance with the provisions of

d s 2(1)(a) of the Criminal Appeal Act 1968 those convictions should be quashed. It is asserted that new evidence is available. That new evidence consists in the main of the conviction of Pearce on the two counts already referred to in respect of the girls M and B. Moreover, the appellant has made an affidavit in which he now states positively that he did not commit any offence against either one of those two girls or the girl mentioned in count 4. It is further contended in the grounds of appeal that no matter how the evidence

e going to support the conviction under count 4 is viewed, it really hinges on the confession made to the police. Seeing that the confession made to the police under count 1 was obviously untruthful, it passes belief that the confession under count 4 is truthful.

An application for bail was made on 8 February 1984. It was granted by the single judge who made a condition of residence at a hostel. There the appellant remains at the

f present time. In a report provided to us dated 3 February 1984 one of the consultants to whom I have already referred states that the appellant's behaviour continues to be reasonable save for occasional words of violence. There is apparently no actual physical violence manifested. He says that the appellant relates well to the high staff/patient ratio plus considerable support and guidance. The consultant psychiatrist goes on: 'All members of staff feel that this should be maintained when he leaves Rampton Hospital and if this does occur his prospects will be reasonable.' It is obvious from the further

g contents of that report that the opinion of doctors and others who have cared for the appellant is to the effect that there are reasonable prospects that the appellant will quite soon be able to live in protected circumstances within the community again.

We must now look at the powers we have to deal with this unusual situation. The power of the court to quash convictions arises out of s 2(1) of the Criminal Appeal Act 1968, as amended by s 44 of the Criminal Law Act 1977. The effect of those provisions

h was considered very recently in *R v Lee* [1984] 1 All ER 1080, [1984] 1 WLR 578. The judgment of the court in that case was given by Ackner LJ on 21 November 1983. The conclusion of that court was that even though the appeal against conviction is in respect of a conviction brought about by a plea of guilty, this court is in the position none the less to quash it. In the judgment Ackner LJ said ([1984] 1 All ER 1080 at 1084, [1984] 1 WLR 578 at 583):

j 'The fact that the applicant was fit to plead, knew what he was doing, intended to make the pleas he did, pleaded guilty without equivocation after receiving expert advice [which incidentally seems to be the position here], although factors highly relevant to whether the convictions on any of them were either unsafe or unsatisfactory, cannot of themselves deprive the court of the jurisdiction to hear the applications.'

We agree with that and do not for one moment doubt that we have power to deal with this case on the basis that, providing the grounds are sufficiently compelling, we can *a* quash the conviction on count 1 of the indictment on the basis that it is either unsafe or unsatisfactory or both.

Second, we have to be satisfied that we have power to admit the new evidence which we are invited to examine. The power which we have in that respect is derived from s 23(1) of the 1968 Act. We need not recite the terms of that section. They are well known. It is equally unnecessary to say any more than that we deemed it necessary and *b* expedient to admit the new evidence. It is rare of course to allow fresh evidence to be heard after a plea of guilty has been made. The circumstances must be exceptional. We regard this case as undoubtedly exceptional and one in which we feel entitled to admit the fresh evidence even though it comes after plea and even though in the main it relates to events which occurred after that plea was made.

The evidence which we allowed in consisted of (though this was immaterial in the *c* event) a photograph of the appellant and an Identikit photograph of Pearce, papers in respect of the convictions of Pearce, which included the committal documents (properly certified) used in the Crown Court, likewise the indictment to which Pearce pleaded, his certificate of conviction and sentence and copies of the statements of offences taken into consideration. Moreover, counsel for the Crown has very helpfully set out for us, in a document composed by him, a series of admissions which he makes with the authority *d* of the Director of Public Prosecutions. These admissions go to the following facts. Firstly, that Pearce was convicted in the circumstances which I have outlined and of the two essential offences which matter, namely the attack on M and that on B. It is admitted too that it is inconceivable in the circumstances that the appellant could have made the attack on either one of those two girls and that Pearce must have been responsible for those attacks. The facts relied on in both cases are identical. On the basis of those admissions *e* we are invited by the Director of Public Prosecutions through counsel for the Crown to quash the conviction of the appellant on count 1. Before we could adequately consider whether or not it was open to us to take that course, we had to decide whether there was a conviction on count 1 to quash, seeing that a free pardon had been granted to the appellant by Her Majesty the Queen in respect of it.

It seems, so we were told, generally to be thought that the effect of a free pardon is to *f* wipe away the stain of conviction, or put in a more legalistic way, to quash it. Counsel for the Crown informed us that there had been many pardons given over the decade between 1973 and 1983. There have been 12 persons in prison at the time they were pardoned in respect of offences of which they were convicted and 2,284 persons pardoned who were not in prison, the vast majority of whom had been convicted of some kind of road traffic offence. To this deeply interesting issue both counsel for the appellant and *g* counsel for the Crown have devoted a vast amount of research, one effect of which has been the production of scholarly skeleton arguments which are fascinating in their tracing of the origins and history over many centuries of a free pardon. We are greatly indebted to both of them for their endeavours. From what they inform us, it is beyond doubt, so we think, that the effect of a free pardon on the continuing existence of a conviction has not been considered by our courts for very many years. *h*

The words of the pardon are instructive in themselves:

> 'Now know ye that We in consideration of some circumstances humbly represented unto Us, are Graciously pleased to extend Our Grace and Mercy unto the said Barry Arthur Foster and to grant him Our Free Pardon in respect of the said conviction, thereby pardoning, remitting and releasing unto him all pains penalties and punishments whatsoever that from the said conviction may ensue.' *j*

It would seem from those words that the beneficiary of the pardon is pardoned in respect of all pains, penalties and punishments ensuing from the conviction, but not pardoned in respect of the conviction itself.

The definition in law of a pardon, according to the Oxford English Dictionary, is

declared to be: 'A remission, either free or conditional, of the legal consequences of
a crime'. Many of the extracts we have been shown from textbooks and articles, some of
them written centuries ago, tend to support the proposition that a pardon leaves the
existence of a conviction untouched. These extracts include the works of Bracton and
Blackstone, *Hawkins' Pleas of the Crown* (1824) and *Holdsworth's History of English Law.* We
have been referred also to a number of English cases. In *Prohibitions Del Roy* (1607) 12 Co
Rep 63 at 64, 77 ER 1342 at 1343 James I was firmly, if not severely, advised his powers
b by the judges of the day. In the report it is stated:

> 'And the Judges informed the King, that no King after the Conquest assumed to
> himself to give any judgment in any cause whatsoever, which concerned the
> administration of justice within this realm, but these were solely determined in the
> Courts of Justice . . .'

c Statements to the like effect appear in many of the works to which we have been referred.
In cases decided later on, a contrary opinion seems to be expressed, for example in *Hay
v London (Tower Division) Justices* (1890) 24 QBD 561. In that case reliance was placed on
Cuddington v Wilkins (1615) Hob 81 at 82, 80 ER 231 at 232, where it was stated: '. . . the
King's pardon doth not only clear the offence it self, but all the dependencies, penalties
and disabilities incident unto it . . .' It is submitted, however, especially by counsel for
d the appellant, that on a full reading of both of those cases, *Cuddington's* case in particular,
it is doubtful whether they really do support the proposition that a conviction is done
away with by a free pardon. We agree with that.
In *Searle v Williams* (1618) Hob 288, 80 ER 433 it was stated that a pardon 'affirms the
verdict and dis-affirms it not as the purgation doth. So that to take it for both is to imply
contradictories'.
Although the courts in this country have not considered the position of pardon vis-à-
e vis conviction, Commonwealth countries have not been idle in the matter. Not for the
first time this court is grateful for the research of counsel and judges of the
Commonwealth and for the decisions appearing in reported cases. We refer above all in
this context to *R v Cosgrove* [1949] Tas SR 99, in which judgment was given by the
Supreme Court of Tasmania. In that case a pardon had been granted. It was a case which
involved corruption. It was held that the pardon granted was not the equivalent of an
f acquittal. From the report it is quite obvious that the court had been referred to many of
the past authorities, to some of which we have already referred. In the course of giving
judgment Morris CJ said (at 105–106):

> '[Counsel for the accused] contends that if a conspirator is pardoned he is in the
> position of one who has never committed the crime and another person can no
g > more be convicted of having conspired with him than of having conspired with one
> who has been acquitted or discharged. The gist of his contention is that a pardon
> wipes out the crime *ab initio*. I have examined the passages in *Hawkins' Pleas of the
> Crown* to which he referred and I think they do not go as far as he contends. At
> p. 538 the learned author is really illustrating the fact that sometimes you may have
> the offence of one so far dependent upon the offence of the other that one falls with
h > the other, and he instances the state of the law in England at the time as to
> accessories. The authorities on libel and slander in my opinion do not establish that
> a pardon wipes out the crime *ab initio*. They are based on a special policy which the
> law has seen fit to adopt in relation to defamatory words. *Blackstone* (vol 4, p 402)
> states the effect of a pardon as follows: "4, Lastly, the effect of such pardon by the
> King, is to make the offender a new man; to acquit him of all corporal penalties and
j > forfeitures annexed to that offence for which he obtains his pardon; and not so
> much to restore his former, as to give him a new, credit and capacity". That passage
> is entirely consistent with what *Hawkins* says. Accordingly, a pardon is in no sense
> equivalent to an acquittal. It contains no notion that the man to whom the pardon
> is extended never did in fact commit the crime, but merely from the date of the
> pardon gives him a new credit and capacity. The plea in my opinion is not sustained.'

Finally, so far as quotation from authority is concerned, we refer to *Re Royal Commission on Thomas Case* [1980] 1 NZLR 602. In 1979 Thomas was granted a free pardon in respect *a* of his conviction for the murders of David and Jeanette Crewe. Later a Royal Commission was set up to inquire into and to report on the circumstances of Thomas's conviction. The commission began its work and while it was sitting the New Zealand police association and others applied for a judicial review of certain decisions of the commission, for a writ of prohibition to prevent the commission from continuing to consider the matters referred to it under the terms of reference, or an order declaring that the *b* commission be disqualified from continuing to consider those matters. It is quite obvious from the judgment in the case that much of the argument presented to the court by counsel was devoted to the question of the impact of a free pardon on conviction. The High Court (Full Court) held, among other things:

> 'The effect of the pardon was to remove the criminal element of the offence *c* named in the pardon, but not to create any factual fiction, or to raise the inference that the person pardoned had not in fact committed the crime for which the pardon was granted. Thomas, by reason of the pardon, was deemed to have been wrongly convicted, and he could not again be charged with the murders of the Crewes.'

Many of the authorities shown to us are referred to in the judgment. The judgment of the court states (at 616); *d*

> 'Having dealt with the preliminary matters that were argued before us, we consider that we should immediately decide this question: "What is the true meaning and effect of the pardon?" We say this because the principal complaint made by the applicants is that the Commission has misconstrued that meaning and effect, and, by reason of this initial error, has misconceived the scope of its inquiries. *e* In New Zealand the source of the power to grant pardons is, and always has been, the Royal prerogative of mercy delegated initially to the Governor of the country, and, latterly, to the Governor-General.'

The court went on (at 619) to deal with the effect of a free pardon under one of the New Zealand statutes and later referred to this extract from 8 Halsbury's Laws (4th edn) para *f* 952:

> 'The effect of a pardon under the Great Seal is to clear the person from all infamy, *and from all consequences of the offence for which it is granted, and from all statutory or other disqualifications following upon conviction.* It makes him, as it were, a new man, so as to enable him to maintain an action against any person afterwards defaming him in respect of the offence for which he was convicted. The authorities suggest that *g* this statement may be an accurate one of the present position in England; but, to the extent of the passage that we have italicised, it probably overstates the effect of a pardon in some Commonwealth countries, and would have overstated it in New Zealand prior to the passage of s 407. The same authorities also indicate that pardons were strictly construed according to their terms, and that the "consequential effect" of a pardon on inheritance and other rights of the person pardoned made construction *h* of it a matter of importance.'

After referring to the situation as it obtained in the reigns of Charles I and Charles II the court stated (at 620):

> 'There are other instances of statutes being passed to obtain special results, but the pardon under the Great Seal was limited according to its terms and by the Act of *j* Settlement, and at no stage appears to have done more than is indicated by the statement in *Halsbury* that we have cited. In other words, its effect was to remove the criminal element of the offence named in the pardon, but not to create any factual fiction, or to raise the inference that the person pardoned had not in fact committed the crime for which the pardon was granted.'

We respectively agree that the effect of a free pardon is as stated in the judgments in
a the Tasmanian and New Zealand cases. In other words, the effect of a free pardon is such
as, in the words of the pardon itself, to remove from the subject of the pardon, 'all pains
penalties and punishments whatsoever that from the said conviction may ensue', but not
to eliminate the conviction itself.

Counsel for the Crown suggests that a person pardoned, rather than having his
conviction quashed, may be under the practical disadvantage that if he is called as a
b witness his conviction may be put to him; it could not be if it is quashed. We express no
opinion as to that. He has reminded us that constitutionally the Crown no longer has a
prerogative of justice, but only a prerogative of mercy. It cannot, therefore, he submits,
remove a conviction but only pardon its effects. The Court of Appeal, Criminal Division
is the only body which has statutory power to quash a conviction. With that we entirely
agree.

c Our conclusion is that the conviction of the appellant on count 1 of the indictment is
outstanding. It still survives. The appeal against it is therefore properly brought. Having
regard to the fresh evidence which we have admitted, we have no doubt that we should
quash that conviction although it resulted from a plea of guilty. In all the circumstances
the conviction is obviously unsafe and, if it be necessary to say it, unsatisfactory. It
remains finally to be said of that conviction that the Home Secretary wishes this court to
d know, and counsel for the Crown is instructed by the Director of Public Prosecutions to
state, that in his opinion the appellant is innocent of that charge.

We turn to counts 2 and 3. They can be dealt with briefly. It is most important from
many points of view that they be disposed of if they can be by verdicts of not guilty
being recorded. The machinery for that purpose was set in motion and adopted by this
court. We had no doubt whatsoever on the basis of the fresh evidence that if leave was
e given to proceed further with these two counts that very serious consideration had to be
given whether or not they could be sustained by the evidence now available. What
therefore happened in between arguments addressed to us and this judgment was that,
authority having been forthcoming to turn this court temporarily into a Crown Court,
and moreover for a transfer of the matter from Nottingham Crown Court to the Royal
Courts of Justice, one of us, Butler-Sloss J, sat as a judge of the Crown Court. Permission
f was granted by this court to proceed with counts 2 and 3 on the indictment. Butler-Sloss
J, having heard both counsel on the matter, ordered that verdicts of not guilty be recorded
in respect of counts 2 and 3.

There remains therefore for consideration count 4. The arguments which have been
addressed to us by both counsel on this count have led us to believe that our duty lies in
only one direction. What they say about that matter is this. Firstly, counsel for the
g appellant has submitted that it cannot be doubted now that the confession made by the
appellant on count 1 was untrue. Therefore it cannot be doubted that if he was capable
as he was of making such an untrue confession in respect of one matter, he was equally
capable of making a false confession in respect of another. He is a man of sub-normal
intelligence. No jury could possibly trust the word of a man who is obviously capable of
telling an appalling lie about himself. If a jury were to be confronted with all these facts
h they would inevitably, so it is submitted, come to the conclusion that it would be totally
unsafe to convict him on count 4. It is of course true that there was found on him pieces
of paper which could have come from the scene of the crime; but he was a local man, apt
to wander about the place and he could have picked up those pieces of paper at any time.
It is also true that he made his confession in respect of count 4 only the day after that
offence was committed. Those two factors are but two of very many which would have
j to be considered in relation to count 4, the outstanding one of which is the confession
itself and the circumstances in which it came to be made. Counsel for the Crown wholly
supports the submissions made by counsel for the appellant in this regard. He has the
instructions of the Director of Public Prosecutions to invite this court to quash the
conviction on count 4. We bear very carefully in mind an invitation of that nature,
which could only have been made after the most careful consideration had been given

by the Director to so important a matter as this. However, on the facts themselves this court has concluded that no jury properly directed could safely come to the conclusion that this appellant was guilty of count 4. Accordingly, we quash that conviction too.

The appeal therefore is allowed in respect of all counts on the indictment, save for those on which there has been a direction, namely counts 2 and 3.

Appeal allowed ; convictions quashed.

Solicitors: *Bryan & Armstrong*, Mansfield (for the appellant); *Director of Public Prosecutions*.

Dilys Tausz   Barrister.

R v Birmingham Juvenile Court, ex parte N (an infant)

QUEEN'S BENCH DIVISION (CROWN OFFICE LIST)
SIR JOHN ARNOLD P
15 MARCH 1984

Children and young persons – Care – Proceedings in juvenile court – Conditions to be satisfied before making order – Probability of neglect etc having regard to fact that court has found neglect or ill-treatment of another child belonging to same 'household' – Household – Child belonging to same household as another child in respect of whom care order made – Care order made in respect of older child – Parents divorcing and mother going to live with another man – Mother having younger child by that man – Whether both children belonging to same 'household' – Whether juvenile court entitled to make care order in respect of younger child because care order had already been made in respect of another child in same household – Children and Young Persons Act 1969, s 1(2)(a)(b).

In 1978 a care order was made in respect of a child who was then living with its parents. The care order was made under s 1(2)(a)[a] of the Children and Young Persons Act 1969 on the ground that the child was being ill-treated or its development or health was being affected. The parents were subsequently divorced and the mother went to live with another man by whom she had another child (the younger child). In 1983 the local authority applied to a juvenile court under s 1(2)(b) for a care order to be made in respect of the younger child on the ground that it was probable that the younger child would be ill-treated or its development or health affected, having regard to the fact that a court had already made a care order on those grounds in respect of another child (ie the elder child) who was 'a member of the household' to which the younger child belonged. The question arose whether both children belonged to the same 'household' for the purposes of s 1(2)(b), notwithstanding the divorce of the elder child's parents and the mother's subsequent association with the younger child's father. The juvenile court held that the children did belong to the same household and accordingly made a care order in respect of the younger child. The younger child appealed.

Held – Except where the primary facts dictated a particular result or conclusion in the light of the applicable law, the question of who was or was not a member of a household was a matter of fact and degree depending on all the circumstances; and in the context of

---

a   Section 1(2), so far as material, is set out at p 689 j, post

s 1(2) of the 1969 Act, which was concerned with the care and welfare of a child, it was

a the membership of the household to which a child belonged rather than the place where the household was located as a matter of residence that was relevant. In most cases the dominant person regarding the care and welfare of a child was its mother, and accordingly a mother's continued presence in a household was the relevant consideration in deciding whether there was a continuing household. Since the mother had been a member of the household to which each child belonged, it followed that the elder child and the younger

b child belonged to the same 'household' for the purposes of s 1(2)(b). The juvenile court had therefore been entitled to make a care order in respect of the younger child on the basis that a care order had already been made in respect of another child in the same household. The appeal would therefore be dismissed (see p 691 b to p 692 c, post).

Dictum of Woolf J in *England v Secretary of State for Social Services* (1981) 3 FLR at 224 applied.

c
Notes
For care proceedings in the juvenile court, see 24 Halsbury's Laws (4th edn) paras 729–732.

For the Children and Young Persons Act 1969, s 1, see 40 Halsbury's Statutes (3rd edn) 849.

d
Cases referred to in judgment
England v Secretary of State for Social Services (1981) 3 FLR 222.
Hornal v Neuberger Products Ltd [1956] 3 All ER 970, [1957] 1 QB 247, [1956] 3 WLR 1034, CA.
Simmons v Pizzey [1977] 2 All ER 432, [1979] AC 37, [1977] 3 WLR 1, HL.

e
Case stated
An infant, proceeding by his mother and next friend, appealed by way of case stated by the justices for the West Midlands Metropolitan County acting in and for the petty sessional division of Birmingham in respect of their determination that the appellant was a member of the same household as another child in respect of whom the condition for

f making a care order specified in s 1(2)(a) of the Children and Young Persons Act 1969 had been satisfied, within s 1(2)(b) of that Act, and in respect of whom a care order in favour of the respondent, the City of Birmingham District Council, had been made. The question for the opinion of the High Court was whether the juvenile court erred in law in holding that the term 'household' in s 1(2)(b) of the 1969 Act was satisfied notwithstanding that there had been a change in the family group. The facts are set out

g in the judgment.

Richard Woodhouse and *John Harvey* for the appellant.
R M K Gray QC for the respondent.

SIR JOHN ARNOLD P. This is a case in which the infant appellant appeals to this

h court by way of case stated from a determination of the Birmingham justices sitting in their juvenile court in relation to an issue which arose under s 1 of the Children and Young Persons Act 1969. The relevant paragraph of s 1(2) is para (b), which prescribes, as one of the conditions which has to be satisfied to bring a case within that section, that—

> 'it is probable that the condition set out in the preceding paragraph [ie para (a)]
> will be satisfied in his case, having regard to the fact that the court or another court
j > has found that that condition [ie the condition set out in para (a)] is or was satisfied
> in the case of another child or young person who is or was a member of the
> household to which he [ie the subject child] belongs.'

The magistrates came to the conclusion that that condition was satisfied to the extent that there existed the fact that the condition set out in para (a) was satisfied in the case of another child who was a member of the household to which the appellant belongs. The

condition in para (a) which is relevant is that the 'proper development [of the child] is
being avoidably prevented or neglected or [the child's] health is being avoidably impaired   *a*
or neglected or [the child] is being ill-treated'.

The mother, the next friend of the appellant child, had a child in 1976. On 1 September
1978 there was a finding in the Birmingham Juvenile Court that that child's proper
development was being avoidably prevented or neglected or the health of that child was
being avoidably impaired or that that child was being ill-treated. So there is no shadow
of a doubt here: a court had decided in relation to the earlier, older child of the mother   *b*
that the condition set out in para (a) was satisfied. But a lot of things have happened since
that child was born and that child was taken into care as a result of the proceedings in
which the relevant finding was made. At that time the mother was living with her
husband and the child who was then taken into care in a household (just the three of
them) and the first thing that happened (the exact date is not established, but it does not
matter) was that a separation took place between the mother and her husband. There   *c*
was subsequently a divorce. She moved house and became pregnant by another man
with whom she was at the time of conception not cohabiting (at least not in a permanently
structured way), but with whom she subsequently began to cohabit and is still cohabiting
on a quasi-permanent basis. That man was the father of the child in respect of whom the
order or determination appealed from was made.

It is therefore true to say that the circumstances in which the mother was living at the   *d*
relevant time when the case came before the juvenile court which made that
determination were quite remarkably different. The question which arises and which is
posed by the appeal is whether that change of circumstances causes the question posed
by para (b) of s 2(1) to be answered in the sense that the older child was not a member of
the household to which the subject child belonged. On that interesting question there is
no authority at all, so that one has to consider the matter, as I have done, in the light of   *e*
two factors. One is: what is the perceived purpose of the subsection? The second is, in
the light of what one thinks that is, to answer the question as best one may with the
assistance of such collateral, helpful authority or other learning as there may be.

There is a good deal of authority about the meaning which ought to be given in
varying circumstances to the word 'household' and from that one can obtain a good deal
of help. The matter perhaps might be looked at first in the light of the most recent of   *f*
these collateral authorities, because that contains some learning, namely a recent
judgment in April 1981 of Woolf J which contains an analysis which both sides accept
(as indeed I do) and which is helpful in approaching the present case. That case is *England
v Secretary of State for Social Services* 32 FLR 222. The question in that case arose under
the Family Income Supplement Act 1970. The question was: what was a household for
the purpose of the phrase 'a family shall consist of the following members of a household'.   *g*
That was a slight distinction in terms, but that is not in my view a matter of great
importance.

The important matter is this. In the course of the judgment Woolf J, after citing
among other authorities *Simmons v Pizzey* [1977] 2 All ER 432, [1979] AC 37, said (3 FLR
222 at 224):
                                                                                              h
'Although the speeches in the House of Lords to which I have made reference
make it clear that in the majority of cases the question as to who is or is not a
member of the household will not involve any question of law, there are a minority
of cases which will still give rise to questions of law. Indeed in *Simmons v Pizzey* itself
the House of Lords dismissed an appeal from the decision of the Divisional Court
overruling the decision of the justices. The position as I see it is as follows: there are   *j*
three categories of situation which can arise before the tribunal of fact. The first
category are those where the only decision which the tribunal can, as a matter of
law, come to is that the persons concerned are members of the household. The
second category of cases are those where the only decision which the tribunal of fact
can come to is that the persons concerned are not members of the household. The
third category of cases, which in practice will be the largest, are those where it is

a proper to regard the persons concerned either as being members or not being members of the household, depending on the view which the fact-finding tribunal takes of all the circumstances as a matter of fact and degree.'

There are two things to be said about that passage, which I find extremely helpful and informative, and they are these. First, in coming to that conclusion the judge derived support equally from cases like *Simmons v Pizzey* which arose in the context of a criminal b decision, that being a matter of overcrowding, and civil cases and applied them to his case, which was purely civil. The second is that when the judge used the words 'can come to' he meant either because the primary facts themselves dictated a particular result or because it is the only result which the fact-finding tribunal can legitimately reach on the application of the relevant principles as a conclusion from the primary facts, which must of course be a reasonable conclusion. It is quite apparent, as it seems to me, that at least c where the result is not dictated by one or other of those techniques then in every case the question falls to be answered on the basis, of course, of a foundation of legal interpretation, but thereafter on a consideration of all the circumstances as a matter of fact and degree. That is precisely in line with what was said in all the other cases which have been cited to me irrespective of whether they arose in a criminal or a civil context. Indeed this case, in spite of the anomalies in the ingredients of the subsection, is a civil matter, but d nevertheless it is one which permits an interference with the family, a removal of a child from its natural parent into the care of a local authority, and I would approach such a case always on the basis, to quote from *Hornal v Neuberger Products Ltd* [1956] 3 All ER 970 at 973, [1957] 1 QB 247 at 258, that 'a high . . . degree of probability . . . is required'.

The context of s 2(1), leaving out para (*f*), which has nothing to do with the rest of the relevant legislation, is a context of the care and welfare of the child. That is a circumstance e as relevant in my judgment to the question of what is a household to which the one child and the other must both belong or be members of as it is to any other consideration which arises under the subsection.

The argument of the local authority is careful to include at every stage the phrase 'the mother's household'. Obviously looked at in that way one observes a semantic emphasis on the continued presence of the mother, but I think that that really is an important f matter, in most cases at least, in considering whether there is a continuing household in the context of a section like this which deals with the upbringing of children in relation to which it must obviously be one of the principal factors which one has to take into account. The cases are all (and I think relevantly) cases in which the emphasis has been placed on the personal content of the household under consideration, not the topographical framework in which the households are to be found. I do think that that is the ultimate g factor that one has to consider in each case. It is of course quite true that, if there is a complete severance of locality between the household one has to consider at one stage and that which has to be considered at a later stage, it is more obvious perhaps, in a case in which there has been a real change of household, that that is the fact, if the households are differently located. But at the heart of the concept it is the persons who comprise the household which have to be considered I think and not the place where the household is h located as a matter of residence.

The context then is that of the magistrates in 1978 looking at the situation of a child just two years old whose development or treatment was alleged to be less than satisfactory. She lived in a group of persons consisting of the mother in the present case, the mother's husband and the child. It seems to me in relation to the question which had to be considered there that it was entirely reasonable to think that the mother was a person j whose presence in the household was of the very first importance. In the present circumstances of the new child (who is now just a year old and was at the date of the magistrates' hearing three months old) the household there consisted of the mother, her resident lover (the father of the child) and the child. At that stage again it seems to me that the dominant personality in terms of what constituted a household could reasonably be regarded as the caring mother. All that may be wrong in fact, but there is no fact which has emerged in the course of the case or which emerged before the magistrates

which rendered that, which at first sight is a reasonable method of considering the
question, unreasonable. I have no doubt at all in those circumstances that the facts were	*a*
such as to make it essential that the magistrates should conclude or could reasonably
conclude only that there was the same household of which the older child was a member
and to which the younger child belonged. I do not therefore think that the facts were
such that the magistrates were compelled to or could only reasonably reach the opposite
conclusion.

This seems to me to be a case which falls within what Woolf J in *England v Secretary of*	*b*
State for Social Services described as the third category, one in which the proper conclusion
had to be on the basis of those circumstances which constituted the fact and degree of the
particular case. I do not think that the magistrates' determination was reached otherwise
than reasonably in the sense that it cannot convincingly be said that no reasonable bench
of magistrates directing themselves properly on the facts known to them and the law
could have reached that conclusion. That analysis it seems to me makes it necessary for	*c*
me to dismiss the appeal by case stated and I so do.

There remains a question which, although not important, is not easy. The magistrates'
determination, having been timeously made the subject of an application for a case stated
with total propriety by the next friend (the mother) through her solicitors, came back
before the magistrates, who had, I am told in the case stated, at the stage at which they
made their determination adjourned it to a date in July 1983 to enable the situation to be	*d*
reviewed. I do not entirely understand what that means, but at all events it involved a
new appointment. Some difficulties arose (I think in relation to legal aid), so that at the
stage at which the case came back in July the future looked rather uncertain and therefore
the magistrates fixed a date in August for the hearing of the case. I do not know any
more detail than that and perhaps it does not very much matter. What the mother did
was to apply for judicial review in the form of a prohibition to stop the magistrates	*e*
trying the case in August on the date which had been appointed to deal with the matter
on the merits and that matter is done, in the way that these things are done these days,
under the appropriate judicial review order and that received the accolade of the single
judge and the matter is therefore still alive. He stayed any further proceedings, which
was obviously the sensible thing to do, and the object of the mother was achieved, which
was to prevent the magistrates proceeding to hear the case further on the basis of their	*f*
initial examination until the question whether their initial determination was right or
wrong had been decided.

The case is of course by no means concluded. There are two matters still to be
considered: first of all, whether it is probable in the terms of para (*b*) of s 1(2) that the
relevant conclusions will be reached having regard to the fact which I have now found in
common with the magistrates to exist; even if that probability is established, there still	*g*
remains the question posed by the end of the subsection whether the child was in need
of care or control which is unlikely in the absence of an order. All those matters still have
to be decided.

What should one then do in relation to the application for judicial review? My
inclination is simply to make no order on that, it now being of no practical consequence,
but of course if there were to be a successful appeal from my order that would result in a	*h*
rather different conclusion. Accordingly I am minded simply to prolong the stay for a
brief period leaving it to the Court of Appeal to prolong the stay further if it is so minded.

Appeal dismissed; case remitted to magistrates for further consideration. Leave to appeal to the
Court of Appeal granted.

j

Solicitors: *Mandleberg Rosenberg & Co*, Birmingham (for the appellant); *Sharpe Pritchard*
& Co, agents for *G W T Pitt*, Birmingham (for the respondent).

Bebe Chua   Barrister.

a

Pamplin v Fraser (No 2)

QUEEN'S BENCH DIVISION
PARKER J SITTING WITH MASTER CLEWS AND MR COLIN JAQUE AS ASSESSORS
1 1 OCTOBER, 4 NOVEMBER 1983

b
Costs – Taxation – Delay – Delay in commencing taxation proceedings – Delay of more than a year – Whether order for costs to be taxed interlocutory – Whether notice of intention to proceed required after delay of more than a year – Whether application for extension of time must be made before taxation – Whether taxation after delay of more than a year where notice of intention to proceed not given should be set aside for irregularity – RSC Ord 3, r 6, Ord 62, rr 16, 21.

c
Costs – Taxation – Time limit – Application for taxation out of time – Extension of time – Whether prejudice relevant when considering whether to grant extension – RSC Ord 62, r 16.

Costs – Taxation – Delay – Delay in commencing taxation proceedings – Delay of more than a year – No justification for delay – No notice of intention to proceed given – Master granting extension of time but disallowing costs of taxation proceedings – No particular prejudice shown –
d
Whether mere delay amounting to prejudice – Whether inconsistent to grant extension of time and then disallow costs of taxation – Whether on review court should interfere with master's decision – Whether only nominal sum for costs should be allowed – RSC Ord 62, rr 7(5), 8(6), 16, 35.

Costs – Taxation – Taxation referred to senior executive officer – Delay – Prejudicial delay or delay where notice of intention to proceed required but not given – Matter to be adjourned to taxing master if opposing party applying for order for nominal costs only or for whole of costs to
e
be disallowed – RSC Ord 62, rr 7(5), 13.

In September and October 1980 the appellant was convicted by magistrates of three minor offences in respect of which fines of £40, £20 and £5 were imposed. He appealed to the Divisional Court, which on 14 April 1981 affirmed the magistrates' decision,
f
dismissed the appeal and ordered that the costs be paid by the appellant to the respondent, such costs to be taxed by a taxing master. Although the respondent was required by RSC Ord 62, r 21 to commence proceedings for the taxation by lodging the relevant documents at the Supreme Court Taxing Office within three months from 14 April 1981, he did not do so until 20 May 1982, when he was some ten months out of time and over a year had elapsed from the date of the Divisional Court's order. An appointment was given for 15 June 1982. The bill was then duly taxed, and of the £550 claimed some
g
£500 including the costs of taxation was allowed. The appellant applied for a review by a taxing master under Ord 62, r 34 and lodged, inter alia, an objection to the whole bill, contending that because more than a year had elapsed since the date of the Divisional Court's order the respondent had been obliged by Ord 3, r 6[a] to give one month's notice of intention to proceed before beginning proceedings for taxation and that, not having done so, the taxation was invalid and the bill should have been wholly disallowed. The
h
appellant further contended (a) that although there was power under Ord 62, r 16[b] to

---

a   Rule 6, so far as material, provides: 'Where a year or more has elapsed since the last proceeding in a cause or matter, the party who desires to proceed must give to every other party not less than one month's notice of his intention to proceed . . .'

j

b   Rule 16, so far as material, provides:
    '(1) A taxing officer may—(a) extend the period within which a party is required by or under this Order to begin proceedings for taxation or to do anything in or in connection with proceedings before that officer . . .
    (3) A taxing officer may extend any such period as is referred to in the foregoing provisions of this rule although the application for extension is not made until after the expiration of that period.'

extend the time allowed for beginning taxation proceedings, which could be exercised
notwithstanding that time had expired, that power could not be exercised where notice   *a*
was required by Ord 3, r 6 but not given or where the matter was a criminal one in the
sense that it arose in criminal proceedings and where non-payment of costs could result
in imprisonment, and (b) that even if the power could be exercised in such cases it should
not be exercised where there was no excuse for the delay. The taxing master held that
the appellant had not shown that he had been prejudiced by the respondent's delay and
accordingly, although that delay was reprehensible and unexplained, it did not justify   *b*
depriving the respondent of all his costs. The taxing master therefore exercised his
discretion to grant an extension of time under Ord 62, r 16, but disallowed the costs of
the taxation under Ord 62, r 8(6)*c*. The appellant applied for a review by the judge under
Ord 62, r 35 of the taxing master's decision.

Held – (1) Although taxation of a bill of costs in a case took place after judgment in the   *c*
case had been given, the amount of the bill potentially remained in controversy until the
taxation was finished, whether the amount claimed was small or large and preparation
for assessment simple or complex. It followed therefore that a judgment for costs to be
taxed was interlocutory, and accordingly notice of intention to proceed to taxation after
a year's delay was required under RSC Ord 3, r 6 (see p 696 *j* to p 697 *c*, post); dictum of
Lord Ellenborough CJ in *May v Wooding* (1815) 3 M & S at 500 applied.   *d*
    (2) The consequence of failure to give notice to proceed to taxation after a year's delay
was not that the taxation would be set aside for irregularity but that the matter fell to be
dealt with under Ord 62, r 7(5)*d*, under which, in order to avoid prejudice to other
parties, a nominal or other sum for costs could be allowed or the whole bill disallowed
and the costs awarded to the other parties (see p 697 *f* to *h*, post).
    (3) Although on a review under Ord 62, r 35 the court would not lightly interfere   *e*
with the exercise by the taxing master of his discretion, there was in the circumstances
ample justification for doing so, because (a) the master had exercised his discretion on the
basis that Ord 3, r 6 did not apply and (b) when considering whether to grant an extension
of time under Ord 62, r 16 prejudice was not a governing consideration. Since extensions
of time were not to be granted lightly and since no justification for the delay had been
shown, the master had been wrong to grant an extension of time for beginning taxation   *f*
proceedings. Furthermore, there was an inconsistency between extending time and then
disallowing the fee for drawing the bill and attending the taxation: once the time had
been extended the bill was in time (see p 698 *b* to *d*, post).
    (4) Although no particular prejudice had been shown, it was clear that mere delay
could amount to prejudice, and where, with no possible excuse, the effect of the delay
had been to keep hanging over the appellant's head an unquantified debt which could   *g*
have been enforced by imprisonment and which because of the delay he could justifiably
have considered that the respondent regarded it to be too small to be worth proceeding
with, there could be sufficient prejudice to the appellant if the debt were then to be
quantified and made enforceable to warrant the court exercising its power under Ord 62,
r 7(5) to allow only a nominal sum for costs. The objection accordingly succeeded to the

h

c Rule 8(6) provides: 'Where in any proceedings before a taxing officer the solicitor representing any
    party is guilty of neglect or delay or puts any other party to any unnecessary expense in relation to
    those proceedings, the taxing officer may direct the solicitor to pay costs personally to any of the
    parties to those proceedings; and where any solicitor fails to leave his bill of costs (with the
    documents required by this Order) for taxation within the time fixed by or under this Order or
    otherwise delays or impedes the taxation, then, unless the taxing officer otherwise directs, the
    solicitor shall not be allowed the fees to which he would otherwise be entitled for drawing his bill   *j*
    of costs and for attending the taxation.'
d Rule 7(5) provides: 'Where a party entitled to costs fails to procure or fails to proceed with taxation,
    the taxing officer in order to prevent any other parties being prejudiced by that failure, may allow
    the party so entitled a nominal or other sum for costs or may certify the failure and the costs of the
    other parties.'

extent that the respondent would be allowed only £5 in respect of his entire bill (see
a p 698 *d* to *f*, post).

Per curiam. (1) Where it is found difficult or impossible to lodge a bill of costs within
the three months provided by Ord 62, r 21, it is not essential that an application for
extension of time be made prior to the hearing of the taxation; it may be made at the
hearing, and on proper justification the time may be extended notwithstanding that it
has expired. If, however, the time is not extended, the fee for drawing the bill and
b attending the taxation will, in the absence of a contrary direction, be disallowed under
Ord 62, r 8(6), and, where the delay has been inordinate and inexcusable and either
specific prejudice is established or the delay is so long that prejudice can be inferred, only
a nominal or other sum for costs may be allowed or the whole bill may be disallowed
under Ord 62, r 7(5) (see p 698 *j* to p 699 *b*, post).

(2) If, on the taxation of a bill of costs which has been referred to a senior executive
c officer under Ord 62, r 13, it appears that notice of intention to proceed after a year's
delay was required under Ord 3, r 6 but has not been given, or if there is such a delay as
might justify the exercise of the powers under Ord 62, r 7(5), notwithstanding that such
a notice has been given, the matter should be adjourned to a taxing master if the opposing
party submits that such powers should be exercised (see p 699 *b c*, post).

d Notes
For the requirement of notice of intention to proceed after a year's delay, see 37 Halsbury's
Laws (4th edn) para 34, and for cases on the subject, see 37(2) Digest (Reissue) 203–205,
1345–1354.

For the powers and discretion of taxing officers, see 37 Halsbury's Laws (4th edn) paras
731–732, and for cases on the subject, see 37(3) Digest (Reissue) 293–296, 4666–4680.
e For the time for beginning taxation proceedings, see 37 Halsbury's Laws (4th edn) para
733.

Cases referred to in judgment
Deighton v Cockle [1912] 1 KB 206, [1911–13] All ER Rep 133, CA.
Drake & Fletcher Ltd v Clark (1968) 112 SJ 95, CA.
f *May v Wooding* (1815) 3 M & S 500, 105 ER 698.
Suedeclub Co Ltd v Occasions Textiles Ltd [1981] 3 All ER 671, [1981] 1 WLR 1245.

Summons to review taxation
Barry Francis Pamplin appealed against the order of Master Hurst on 26 November 1982
whereby, on objection taken by the appellant to the taxation by the principal clerk, the
g master allowed in part and disallowed the remainder of the costs of the respondent,
Donald Fraser, consequent on the dismissal of the appellant's appeal to the Divisional
Court (Ackner LJ and McNeill J) ([1981] RTR 494) on 14 April 1981 following his
conviction in Preston Magistrates' Court on 9 October 1980 of obstructing a police officer
in the execution of his duty, failing to provide a specimen of breath and driving a vehicle
with defective lights, for which he was fined £40, £20 and £5 respectively. The
h summons was heard in chambers but judgment was given by Parker J in open court.
The facts are set out in the judgment.

Nigel Ley for the appellant.
Martin Strutt for the respondent.

Cur adv vult
j

4 November. The following judgment was delivered.

PARKER J. On 26 September and 9 October 1980 the appellant was convicted by a
magistrates' court sitting at Preston in Lancashire of three minor offences in respect of
which fines of £40, £20 and £5 were imposed.

He appealed by way of case stated to a Divisional Court of the Queen's Bench Division. That court, on 14 April 1981, affirmed the decision of the magistrates' court, dismissed the appeal and ordered that the costs be paid by the appellant to the respondent's solicitors, such costs to be taxed by a taxing master (see [1981] RTR 494).

Pursuant to RSC Ord 62, r 21(1) to (3), the respondent was accordingly required, within three months from 14 April, to commence proceedings for the taxation by producing the Divisional Court order and leaving a copy thereof at the appropriate office, which, in the present case, was the Supreme Court Taxing Office. By r 21(5) he was further required at the same time to lodge a simple statement as to other parties and, unless the taxing officer otherwise directed, his bills of costs, together with all necessary papers and vouchers. He did not take these steps within the time limited but he did so on 20 May 1982, when he was out of time by some ten months and when over a year had elapsed from the date of the order of the Divisional Court.

An appointment was given for 15 June 1982 and the bill was then duly taxed. It was a short bill occupying only three pages. The total amount claimed was £550·15. The amount allowed including costs of taxation was just over £500.

The appellant applied for review under Ord 62, r 34, and duly lodged objections. These numbered six, of which no 6 succeeded, nos 1 to 4 failed and no 5 was not pursued. On this review under r 35 objections nos 1 to 4 are repeated. I deal with them in turn.

Objection 1

This objection goes to the whole of the bill. The appellant contends (i) that, as, by 15 April 1982, more than a year had elapsed since the judgment of the Divisional Court, the respondent was obliged under Ord 3, r 6 to give one month's notice of intention to proceed before beginning proceedings for taxation, (ii) that, not having done so, the taxation was invalid and (iii) that the bill should be disallowed in toto. The appellant further submits that, although under Ord 62, r 16 there is power to extend the time allowed under r 21 for beginning taxation proceedings and although such power can be exercised on a taxation notwithstanding that time has expired, such power cannot be exercised where a notice is required by Ord 3, r 6 but not given or where, as here, the matter is a criminal one in the sense that it arose in criminal proceedings and where non-payment of the costs when taxed could result in the appellant's imprisonment. Further, even if in such cases the power could be exercised, it should, it is submitted, not be exercised where there was no excuse for the delay.

The first question for determination is whether a notice under Ord 3, r 6 was required at all. On the original taxation the principal clerk held that it was in any event too late to take the point and on review the master held that the rule related merely to the interlocutory stages of a case and had no application to proceedings after judgment, relying in support of his decision on *Deighton v Cockle* [1912] 1 KB 206, [1911–13] All ER Rep 133. In that case there had been an order giving leave to sign judgment but judgment was not in fact signed until more than a year later. On an application to set aside for irregularity on the ground that notice to proceed had not been given, the master refused the application. He was reversed by Scrutton J, who was in turn reversed by the Court of Appeal.

The judgments of the Court of Appeal contain passages which support the view that the rule has no application to proceedings after judgment, but the principle acted on was that stated by Lord Ellenborough CJ in *May v Wooding* (1815) 3 M & S 500, 105 ER 698 in these terms:

'The reason for the rule is this, that while the matter is still in controversy, the party should, after so long a lapse as four terms without any proceedings, have notice, that he may prepare himself, but when the matter has passed in rem judicatam by the verdict, the same reason does not apply. The rule of this Court therefore relates merely to interlocutory stages of the cause.'

If that principle is applied to an order for costs to be taxed a notice would be required.

a
Within its own area a judgment for costs to be taxed is as much interlocutory as a judgment for damages to be assessed. Much may and often will be in controversy. Before the party in whose favour the order for costs is made can enforce his order, he has to take the proper steps and the opposite party may resist. There are many cases where, as a result of opposition, large sums are taxed off the bill. In my judgment the principle stated by Lord Ellenborough CJ strongly supports the view that a notice must be given under Ord 3, r 6 where more than a year has elapsed after the judgment or order for costs

b
without any steps having been taken. In the present case it may well be that the bill was so short and simple that the appellant needed little time to prepare himself, but in many cases this will not be so and, if a party is entitled, as he is, to notice of intention to proceed in the case of an interlocutory judgment for damages to be assessed notwithstanding that the amount claimed is small and preparation for the assessment simple, I can see no reason in principle why after a lapse of a year he should not be entitled to a notice of an

c
intention to proceed to taxation of even a very complex bill of costs running to many many thousands of pounds. In my judgment such a notice is required.

The taxation of costs is however a process of its own. This is simply shown by reference to Ord 1, r 4. By that rule a 'master' does not include a master of the Supreme Court (Taxing Office). Hence, although by the same rule 'the Court' includes any master, it does not include a taxing master. Where, therefore, in the rules, powers are expressed to

d
be exercisable by the court or a master, such powers are not exercisable by a taxing master. The latter must find his powers under Ord 62, as for example in Ord 62, r 16 to extend time. In the context of delay or omission in connection with taxation the powers of the taxing masters are to be found in Ord 62, rr 7(4) and (5) and 8(6). These powers are extensive. Under r 7(5), where a party entitled to costs fails to procure or fails to proceed with taxation the taxing master, in order to prevent any other parties being

e
prejudiced by that failure, may allow the party so entitled a nominal or other sum for costs or may certify the failure and the costs of the other parties. Under r 8(6) there is a power to order a solicitor to pay the costs personally in the event of neglect or delay in taxation proceedings and, for failure to lodge a bill of costs within the time fixed by or under the order, fees for drawing the bill and attending on taxation are automatically disallowed unless the taxing master otherwise directs.

f
In *Suedeclub Co Ltd v Occasions Textiles Ltd* [1981] 3 All ER 671, [1981] 1 WLR 1245 a judgment in default of defence was set aside for irregularity on the ground that no notice of intention to proceed had been given and it is submitted that it follows that this is the course to be taken in the present case and that the taxation should be set aside. In my judgment this is not so. The consequences of failure to give the notice must depend on the powers of the taxing master, both when the matter is before him and when it is

g
before a judge on review under r 35.

On review before the taxing master the costs of taxation were disallowed under Ord 62, r 8(6). In my view the consequences of a failure to give notice under Ord 3, r 6 fall to be dealt with under Ord 62, 7(5), under which, in order to avoid prejudice to other parties, a nominal or other sum may be allowed or, in effect, the whole bill may be disallowed and the costs awarded to the other party or parties.

h
There was here no possible excuse for the delay which remained unexplained, but the taxing master on review said:

j
'[Counsel for the appellant] has told me nothing of any prejudice to his client save to say that the order for costs was in the nature of a penalty (pursuant to his argument that these were criminal proceedings) and that therefore his client was entitled to know the amount of the penalty. I reject that contention: the appellant's penalty for his misdemeanour had already been fixed by the magistrates' court. He voluntarily chose to proceed with an appeal by way of case stated and the price of failure is that he should pay the costs. In the light of the above I cannot be satisfied that the appellant has been prejudiced by the respondent's failure to lodge his bill within three months and I exercise my discretion under Ord 62, r 16 to extend the

period accordingly. Whilst the delay of 13 months is reprehensible and remains
unexplained, I do not find it so reprehensible as to call for the extreme penalty of
depriving the respondent of all his costs.'

a

It is to be observed that the master was there dealing with the question whether to
extend time under Ord 62, r 16, not the effect of failure to comply with Ord 3, r 6, which
he had held did not apply, that he extended the time and that he rejected the exercise of
the power under r 7(5) apparently on the ground that, although the delay was
unexplained, no particular prejudice to the appellant had been shown to his satisfaction.

b

In taking this course he was clearly influenced by the specific mention of prejudice in
r 7(5) and by the approach of the Court of Appeal in *Drake & Fletcher Ltd v Clark* (1968)
112 SJ 95. On a review under r 35 the court does not lightly interfere with the exercise
by the taxing master of his discretion, but in the present case there is ample justification
for doing so in that (i) it was exercised on the basis that Ord 3, r 6 did not apply and (ii)
when considering whether an extension of time should be granted prejudice is not the
governing consideration. There is ample authority that extensions should not be lightly
granted and in the present case no justification for the delay was shown. Indeed it is
specifically found that no adequate reason for the delay was shown. In those circumstances
no extension should have been granted. Furthermore there is an inconsistency between
extending the time and then disallowing the fee for taxation under r 8(6). Once the time
was extended the bill was in time.

c

d

No particular prejudice was shown, but it is clear that mere delay can amount to
prejudice and, where, with no possible excuse, the effect of the delay is to keep hanging
over the appellant's head an unquantified debt which may be enforced by imprisonment
and which by the delay he could justifiably consider was regarded by the respondent to
be too small to be worth proceeding with, I am of the clear view that there could be
sufficient prejudice to the appellant if the debt is now quantified and thus made
enforceable to warrant the exercise of the power under r 7(5) and to allow only a nominal
sum for costs. Accordingly objection 1 succeeds to the extent that there is allowed to the
respondent in respect of the entire bill the sum of £5 only.

e

In the light of the foregoing, objections 2, 3 and 4 do not strictly arise, but I nevertheless
express my views on them shortly.

f

Objection 2

This was to the sum of £4 for attending in conference with counsel. It was not pressed.
It was plainly rightly disallowed by the master.

Objection 3

The substance of this objection was that a sum of £35 allowed for a day's attendance
in court should be reduced to £21 (the maximum scale fee) on the ground that there was
no basis for the exercising of the master's discretion to exceed the scale in special cases.
The master refers to the importance of the case. It was no doubt important to the client
but so is every case. Neither I nor my assessors can discern any special feature of the case
which would justify exceeding the maximum scale fee. Accordingly had the matter
arisen the objection would have been allowed to the extent of reducing the sum allowed
from £35 to £21.

g

h

Objection 4

This was to the allowance of three and a half hours out of five hours claimed for
perusing papers and consideration. This was plainly a matter of assessment. Neither I
nor my assessors can see any ground for interfering with such assessment. The decision
of the taxing master to disallow this objection was entirely justified.

j

Reverting finally to the matter of delay, nothing in this judgment should be taken as
indicating that in all cases where it is found difficult or impossible to lodge a bill within
the three months provided for by Ord 62, r 21, and in many cases such a position will

arise, an application for an extension of time must be made prior to the hearing of the
a reference. It can be made then and the time may on proper justification be extended
notwithstanding that it has expired. If, however, it is not extended, then, in the absence
of a contrary direction, the fees for drawing the bill and attending the taxation will be
disallowed under r 8(6) and in appropriate cases there may be an exercise of the power
under r 7(5). Appropriate cases will however normally only be those where the delay has
been inordinate and inexcusable and where either specific prejudice is established or the
b delay is so long that prejudice can be inferred.

There is one further matter which requires to be mentioned. The powers under Ord
62, r 7(5) can only be exercised by a taxing master, but in the case of bills under £3,000
the taxation will under r 13 be referred to a senior executive officer. If, therefore, on
taxation of such a bill it appears that a notice under Ord 3, r 6 was required but has not
been given or if there is, albeit such a notice has been given, such a delay as might justify
c the exercise of the powers under r 7(5), the matter should, if the opposing party or parties
submit that such powers should be exercised, be adjourned to a taxing master.

Order accordingly.

Solicitors: *J S Siergant & Co*, Chorley (for the appellant); *Allan Jay & Co*, agents for
d *J V Bates*, Preston (for the respondent).

K Mydeen Esq   Barrister.

e

Drummond (Inspector of Taxes) v Brown

COURT OF APPEAL, CIVIL DIVISION
f SIR JOHN DONALDSON MR, FOX AND STEPHEN BROWN LJJ
12, 14, 15 MARCH, 6 APRIL 1984

*Capital gains tax – Disposal of assets – Capital sum derived from asset notwithstanding no asset
acquired by person paying sum – Capital sum received for loss of asset – Termination of tenancy
– Statutory compensation for termination of business tenancy – Tenant not able in law to prevent
g landlord from taking back premises – Whether compensation a capital sum derived from an asset
– Whether compensation a capital sum received for loss of an asset – Landlord and Tenant Act
1954, s 37(1)(2)(a) – Finance Act 1965, s 22(3).*

The taxpayer had been for many years a tenant of business premises. In September 1977
his landlord, a bank, served on him a notice under s 25 of the Landlord and Tenant Act
h 1954 terminating his tenancy. The notice stated that any application to the court by the
taxpayer for a new tenancy of the premises under Pt II of the 1954 Act would be opposed
by the landlord on the ground that the landlord intended to occupy the premises for its
own business. The taxpayer gave up possession of the premises on 1 April 1978 and on
the same day received from the landlord £31,384 as compensation under s 37(1)[a] of the
1954 Act, that sum being twice the rateable value of the premises and payable pursuant
j to s 37(2)(a). The taxpayer was assessed to capital gains tax under s 22(3)[b] of the Finance
Act 1965 on the footing that the payment constituted a capital sum 'derived' from an

_____

a   Section 37, so far as material, is set out at p 702 *c* to *e*, post
b   Section 22(3), so far as material, is set out at p 702 *h*, post

asset (ie the lease) or, alternatively, that it was a compensation for the loss of an asset (ie the lease or the taxpayer's security of tenure). The taxpayer appealed, contending that *a* s 22(3) did not apply since the right to the payment was derived from the 1954 Act itself and not from the tenancy or any other asset. The Special Commissioners allowed the appeal and the judge affirmed their determination. The Crown appealed to the Court of Appeal.

Held – The taxpayer's right to compensation on the termination of the lease was not *b* derived from his lease but from the provisions of the 1954 Act alone, and, because that Act, in creating that right where otherwise none would have existed, did not require any provisions to be written into the lease, it could not be said that the lease was the source of the taxpayer's entitlement to the compensation. Furthermore, the payment had not been made as compensation to the taxpayer for the loss of his lease because the lease had come to an end by the effluxion of time, and nor had it been made as compensation for his loss *c* of security of tenure because the landlord having established the ground in s 30(1)(g) of the 1954 Act, namely that it intended to occupy the premises for the purposes of its business, the taxpayer had not been entitled to any security of tenure. It followed therefore that the sum paid to the taxpayer was not a capital sum derived from an asset or compensation for the loss of an asset within s 22(3) of the 1965 Act. The appeal would therefore be dismissed (see p 702 j to p 703 b e f and p 704 a to f and h, post). *d*

　　Davis (Inspector of Taxes) v Powell [1977] 1 All ER 471 approved.

Notes

For capital gains tax chargeable on the disposal of assets, see 5 Halsbury's Laws (4th edn) paras 31–44.

　　For compensation for quitting business premises, see 27 ibid paras 518–519. *e*

　　For the Landlord and Tenant Act 1954, ss 25, 30, 37, see 18 Halsbury's Statutes (3rd edn) 559, 565, 576.

　　For the Finance Act 1965, s 22, see 34 ibid 877.

　　As from 6 April 1979 s 22(3) of the 1965 Act was replaced by s 20(1) of the Capital Gains Tax Act 1979.

f

Cases referred to in judgment

Cramas Properties Ltd v Connaught Fur Trimmings Ltd [1965] 2 All ER 382, [1965] 1 WLR 892, HL.

Davis (Inspector of Taxes) v Powell [1977] 1 All ER 471, [1977] 1 WLR 258.

Edicron Ltd v William Whiteley Ltd [1984] 1 All ER 219, [1984] 1 WLR 59, CA.

Grafton Street (14) London W1, Re, De Havilland (Antiques) Ltd v Centrovincial Estates *g* *(Mayfair) Ltd* [1971] 2 All ER 1, [1971] Ch 935, [1971] 2 WLR 159.

Cases also cited

Bayley (Inspector of Taxes) v Rogers [1980] STC 544.

Cardshops Ltd v John Lewis Properties Ltd [1982] 3 All ER 746, [1983] QB 161, CA.

Davenport (Inspector of Taxes) v Chilver [1983] Ch 293. *h*

International Military Services Ltd v Capital and Counties plc [1982] 2 All ER 20, [1982] 1 WLR 575.

IRC v Montgomery [1975] 1 All ER 664, [1975] Ch 266.

Marren (Inspector of Taxes) v Ingles [1980] 3 All ER 95, [1980] 1 WLR 983, HL.

O'Brien (Inspector of Taxes) v Benson's Hosiery (Holdings) Ltd [1979] 3 All ER 652, [1980] AC 562, HL. *j*

Appeal

The Crown appealed against the decision of Walton J ([1983] STC 506) on 9 May 1983 dismissing the Crown's appeal by way of case stated (set out at [1983] STC 507–511) from a decision of the Commissioners for the Special Purposes of the Income Tax Acts allowing a an appeal by the taxpayer, J Austin Brown, against an assessment to capital gains tax. The facts are set out in the judgment of the court.

John L Knox QC and *Robert Carnwath* for the Crown.
Peter Millett QC and *David C Milne* for the taxpayer.

Cur adv vult

b 6 April. The following judgment of the court was delivered.

FOX LJ. This is the judgment of the court. In this case the Crown claims that compensation payable to an outgoing tenant of business premises under s 37 of the Landlord and Tenant Act 1954, as amended by the Law of Property Act 1969, s 11, is c assessable to capital gains tax.

In 1959 the taxpayer was practising as a solicitor in London, in partnership with Mr A G Clerk, under the name of Murray Hutchins & Co. On 31 August 1959 the Union of London & Smith's Bank Ltd granted to the taxpayer and Mr Clerk as joint tenants a lease of a suite of rooms on the first floor of 49–50 Cornhill, London, for 14 years from 29 September 1959 and on 24 October 1960 the Union of London & Smith's Bank Ltd d granted to the taxpayer and Mr Clerk as joint tenants a lease of rooms on the second and third floors of the same building for 14 years from 29 September 1959.

Mr Clerk died in 1968. On 30 January 1973 the National Westminster Bank Ltd (the bank), which had acquired the reversions immediately expectant on the leases, granted to the taxpayer a further lease of the same premises for two years from 29 September 1973 and on 27 January 1975 the bank granted to the taxpayer a further lease of the same e premises for 15 months from 29 September 1974 to 25 December 1976. No further leases were granted after 26 December 1976 but the taxpayer continued to occupy the premises.

In September 1977 the bank served on the taxpayer a notice under s 25 of the 1954 Act terminating the tenancy as from 1 April 1978. The notice stated that the bank would oppose an application to the court for a new tenancy of the premises under Pt II of the f 1954 Act on the ground that it intended to occupy the premises for its own business.

The taxpayer did not challenge the bank's assertion that it required the premises for the purposes of its own business and, therefore, he had no grounds for contesting the notice. He had no choice but to give up possession.

Accordingly, the taxpayer gave up possession of the premises on 31 March or 1 April 1978 and, on the same day, he received from the bank £31,384 in respect of his right to g compensation under the 1954 Act.

The material provisions of the 1954 Act are as follows.

Section 23(1): Pt II of the Act 'applies to any tenancy where the property comprised in the tenancy is or includes premises which are occupied by the tenant and are so occupied for the purposes of a business carried on by him or for those and other purposes'.

Section 24(1):

h
'A tenancy to which [Pt II of the Act] applies shall not come to an end unless terminated in accordance with the provisions of [Pt II of the Act]; and . . . the tenant . . . may apply . . . for a new tenancy—(a) if the landlord has given notice under [the Act] to terminate the tenancy, or (b) if the tenant has made a request [under the Act] for a new tenancy . . .'

j Section 29(1): on application for a new tenancy and subject to sections 30 and 31 'the court shall make an order for the grant of a tenancy comprising such property, at such rent and on such other terms,' as are provided by the Act.

Section 30: this sets out the grounds on which the landlord may oppose the application for a new tenancy. These are broadly as follows: disrepair of premises, rent unpaid and substantial breaches of covenant by the tenant respectively (paras (a), (b) and (c)); the

landlord has offered and can provide suitable alternative accommodation (para (d));
premises are part of larger premises which the landlord could let at a higher rent as a
whole (para (e)); demolition or reconstruction (para (f)); '. . . that on the termination of
the current tenancy the landlord intends to occupy the holding for the purposes . . . of a
business to be carried on by him therein . . .' (para (g)).

It was because the ground in para (g) was applicable that the taxpayer accepted that he
must vacate the premises.

Section 31(1): this forbids the grant of a new tenancy by the court if the landlord
establishes any of the grounds on which he is entitled to oppose the application under
s 30.

Section 37: this deals with compensation and, so far as material, in relation to the
relevant date in this case, provides as follows:

> '(1) Where on the making of an application under section twenty-four of this Act
> the court is precluded . . . from making an order for the grant of a new tenancy by
> reason of any of the grounds specified in paragraphs (e), (f) and (g) of subsection (1) of
> section thirty of this Act . . . or where no other ground is specified in the landlord's
> notice under section 25 of this Act . . . and either no application under the said section
> 24 is made or such an application is withdrawn, then, subject to the provisions of this
> Act, the tenant shall be entitled on quitting the holding to recover from the landlord
> by way of compensation an amount determined in accordance with the following
> provisions of this section.
>
> (2) The said amount shall be as follows, that is to say,—(a) where the conditions
> specified in the next following subsection are satisfied it shall be twice the rateable
> value of the holding, (b) in any other case it shall be the rateable value of the holding.
>
> (3) The said conditions are—(a) that, during the whole of the fourteen years
> immediately preceding the termination of the current tenancy, premises being or
> comprised in the holding have been occupied for the purposes of a business carried on
> by the occupier or for those and other purposes; (b) that, if during those fourteen years
> there was a change in the occupier of the premises, the person who was the occupier
> immediately after the change was the successor to the business carried on by the
> person who was the occupier immediately before the change . . .'

The sum of £31,384 paid to the taxpayer by the bank was twice the rateable value of the
premises and was the sum payable pursuant to s 37(2)(a). The taxpayer was assessed to
capital gains tax on the £31,384. He appealed to the Special Commissioners, who allowed
the appeal. The Crown's appeal to the High Court was dismissed by Walton J ([1983] STC
506), and from that decision the Crown now appeals.

The matter is governed by the Finance Act 1965. Section 22(1) provides that 'All forms
of property shall be assets for the purposes of this Part of this Act . . .' Section 22(3) is as
follows:

> 'Subject to subsection (6) of this section, and to the exceptions in this Part of this
> Act, there is for the purposes of this Part of this Act a disposal of assets by their owner
> where any capital sum is derived from assets notwithstanding that no asset is acquired
> by a person paying the capital sum, and this subsection applies in particular to—(a)
> capital sums received by way of compensation for any kind of damage or injury to
> assets or for the loss, destruction or dissipation of assets or for any depreciation or risk
> of depreciation of an asset . . .'

The Crown advances the following contentions: (i) that the £31,384 was a capital sum
derived from an asset, namely the lease of 27 January 1975; (ii) in the alternative, that the
£31,384 was compensation for the loss of an asset.

In our opinion the £31,384 was not derived from the lease. The word 'derive' suggests a
source. The right to the payment was, in our view, from one source only, namely the 1954
Act. The lease itself gives no right to such a payment. It was the statute, and the statute
alone, which created the right to the payment. The statute simply created an entitlement

a where none would otherwise have existed. And in creating that entitlement it did not require that any provisions were to be written into the lease. Thus, there is no deeming provision which would in any way require one to treat the lease as being the source of the entitlement.

We do not think the sum can be said to be derived from any asset. It was, as Templeman J said in *Davis (Inspector of Taxes) v Powell* [1977] 1 All ER 471 at 474, [1977] 1 WLR 258 at 260 (a case in which he rejected the Crown's claim to capital gains tax on the compensation

b payable to an outgoing tenant under the Agricultural Holdings Act 1948), simply a sum which Parliament said should be paid. Further, Parliament has not said that the tenant is to be entitled to the payment just by proving the lease. He must also prove that the premises were occupied by him and were so occupied for the purposes of a business carried on by him or for those and other purposes and the right to the double compensation payable in the present case depended also on the fact that the tenant and his predecessors

c in the business had between them occupied the premises for business purposes for the previous 14 years. Thus, compensation is not the inevitable result of the lease. No doubt the right to compensation impinges on the landlord and the tenant. And no doubt the provisions of Pt II of the 1954 Act apply to all tenancies within s 23(1). But the right to compensation is still only a right given by Parliament. If Parliament chose to take it away, the lease by itself would not have conferred it. We do not think that it is accurately

d described as an 'incident' of the lease. It does not attach to the estate as such. It is a right given by statute to certain tenants in certain circumstances and the lease by itself did not confer a right to it. It was, as Brightman J said in *Re 14 Grafton Street, London W 1, De Havilland (Antiques) Ltd v Centrovincial Estates (Mayfair) Ltd* [1971] 2 All ER 1 at 5, [1971] Ch 935 at 942, 'a debt created by statute, on which the tenant may sue in other proceedings if necessary'.

e On the termination of his current lease the tenant of business premises may get one of three benefits. Thus he may get either (i) a new lease, or (ii) alternative accommodation, or (iii) compensation. Neither of the first two of these seems to us to derive from the lease any more than does the compensation. The alternative accommodation will be provided by a new lease, negotiated between the parties, of different premises. Similarly a new lease granted by the court is quite distinct from the old. It need not be of exactly the same

f premises or at the same rent or subject to the same provisions. It is true that the tenant would not have the opportunity of getting either if he had not obtained the original lease. But any right to get them, and the legal right to get compensation, comes wholly from the statute.

There are two further matters to which we should refer on this aspect of the case.

First, our attention was drawn, on behalf of the Crown, to s 39(2) of the 1954 Act, which

g provides as follows:

'If the amount of the compensation which would have been payable under section thirty-seven of this Act if the tenancy had come to an end in circumstances giving rise to compensation under that section and the date at which the acquiring authority obtained possession had been the termination of the current tenancy exceeds the amount of the compensation payable under section 121 of the Lands Clauses

h Consolidation Act 1845 or section 20 of the Compulsory Purchase Act 1965 in the case of a tenancy to which this Part of this Act applies, that compensation shall be increased by the amount of the excess.'

We do not think that this advances the Crown's case. If a landlord cannot get possession of the premises without an obligation to pay the compensation, it is difficult to see why

j the acquiring authority should. The provision throws no light on the question of derivation.

Second, it is said that if a tenant, shortly before the end of the lease, surrenders the fag-end of the lease for a cash sum which, inevitably, would take into account the amount of any compensation payable under the 1954 Act, the whole of the cash sum would be assessable to capital gains tax. That seems to us to be a wholly different situation. It is a plain case of a disposal of an asset, ie the residue, however short, of the term of the lease. If the parties choose to deal with the matter in that way, the tenant must take the consequences. He can avoid the result by insisting on the service of a notice under s 25 of *a* the 1954 Act and claiming his compensation under the Act on quitting the holding.

For the reasons which we have given, we are unable to accept that the compensation derived from the lease. We come to the alternative contention, namely that the sum was paid as compensation for the loss of an asset.

There was certainly no 'loss' of the lease. The lease came to an end by the effluxion of time. That was inherent in the nature of the estate. It was given a limited extension by the *b* statute, but that was never 'lost'. It determined under the statutory provisions.

It is said, however, that what was lost was security of tenure. We do not accept that. The taxpayer was never entitled to a security of tenure in the events which happened (i e that the bank required the premises for its own occupation). The scheme of the 1954 Act is that it provides for a tenant to make an application for a new tenancy but also provides, in s 30, for grounds on which the landlord may object. Those grounds fall into two categories. *c* Even if the ground in para (*a*) or (*b*) or (*c*) is established, the court retains a discretion in that it must consider whether the tenant ought not to be granted a new tenancy. There is no such discretion in relation to the other grounds. In the present case, the landlord having established the ground in para (*g*), the court could not have made an order for a new tenancy.

And it does not seem to us to be justifiable to assume that the compensation was given *d* for loss of security of tenure. We do not know for precisely what purpose Parliament gave the compensation. The sidenote (if that be admissable at all) to s 37 merely says: 'Compensation where order for new tenancy precluded on certain grounds.' It might be for 'disturbance' (see *Cramas Properties Ltd v Connaught Fur Trimmings Ltd* [1965] 2 All ER 382 at 385, [1965] 1 WLR 892 at 898 per Lord Reid) or for loss of goodwill (see *Edicron v William Whiteley Ltd* [1984] 1 All ER 219 at 224, [1984] 1 WLR 59 at 66 per Slade LJ) or for *e* the expenses of removal (as under the Agricultural Holdings Act 1948) or for a combination of reasons. All we know for certain is that it is a sum which Parliament, for whatever reasons, has directed to be paid.

In the circumstances we do not accept that it is established that the compensation was for the loss of any asset.

The result in our view is that Walton J's decision in the present case was right, as was the *f* decision in *Davis (Inspector of Taxes) v Powell* [1977] 1 All ER 471, [1977] 1 WLR 258, and the Crown's claim fails.

We can see nothing in any wider aspect of the matter to lead us to any different conclusion. In the present case we are dealing with a lease of a solicitor's office in the City of London. The compensation was substantial. But in many cases of shop premises the compensation is more modest. It is nevertheless of considerable importance to the outgoing *g* tenant. There are many cases in which he would need to spend all or most of it on costs incurred in relation to leaving the premises and installing himself in new ones. That it should be liable to reduction by a charge to capital gains tax reduces its effectiveness as a compensation payment. And it has to be remembered that leases of 50 years or less are wasting assets for capital gains tax purposes and their base cost is written down as their life progresses. A charge to the tax could, therefore, be a serious impost. *h*

We dismiss the appeal.

Appeal dismissed. No order as to costs. Leave to appeal to the House of Lords refused.

14 June. The Appeal Committee of the House of Lords (Lord Diplock, Lord Roskill and Lord Brightman) dismissed a petition by the Crown for leave to appeal.

Solicitors: *Solicitor of Inland Revenue ; Hunters* (for the taxpayer).

Gnana Mott   Barrister.

a # R v Cripps, ex parte Muldoon and others

COURT OF APPEAL, CIVIL DIVISION
SIR JOHN DONALDSON MR, FOX AND STEPHEN BROWN LJJ
21 MARCH, 3 APRIL 1984

b *Judgment – Order – Correction – Accidental slip or omission – Election court for local election – Correction of order for costs – Whether correction permissible – RSC Ord 20, r 11.*

Elections – Election court – Election court for local election – Decision of court – Order for costs – Variation or correction – Slip rule – Whether slip rule may be used to clarify order for costs once order perfected – Representation of the People Act 1949, ss 110(2), 115(6) – RSC Ord 20, r 11.

c
After the respondent had been elected as a councillor at a local government election, the petitioners presented a petition under the Representation of the People Act 1949 alleging that the respondent had been guilty of certain illegal practices in respect of the election, namely overspending and making an untrue return and declaration of expenses. In accordance with s 115(1)[a] of the 1949 Act, the petition was tried by an election court
d consisting of a barrister (the commissioner) who for the purposes of the trial had, by virtue of ss 115(6) and 110(2)[b], the same powers and privileges as a High Court judge on the trial of a parliamentary election petition. The commissioner held that the respondent had been substantially responsible for the petition being brought and ordered the respondent to pay to the petitioners 'three quarters (75%) of their costs properly incurred in relation to the Petition'. The petitioners and the respondent failed to agree on the
e meaning of the order and the respondent asked the commissioner to clarify it. The commissioner sat again and stated that he had intended to include in the order only those costs relevant to the two matters on which the petitioners had succeeded and that he had not intended to include the whole of the petitioners' costs. He issued a direction to that effect. The petitioners applied to the High Court for an order of certiorari to quash the direction on the ground that it was ultra vires because the commissioner was functus
f officio once the trial of the petition had been concluded and that therefore he had had no jurisdiction to vary the order for costs. The court granted an order of certiorari quashing the commissioner's direction. The respondent appealed, contending, inter alia, (i) that the commissioner had been entitled to give the direction on costs by virtue of the 'slip rule' contained in RSC Ord 20, r 11[c], which applied to the election court by virtue of s 115(6) of the 1949 Act, and (ii) that, notwithstanding that the trial of the petition ended
g when the commissioner had fulfilled his duties under the 1949 Act, he had continuing authority to exercise those powers.

Held – The appeal would be dismissed for the following reasons—
(1) The power to amend under the slip rule contained in RSC Ord 20, r 11 was not a power granted to the particular trial judge, but was one of the powers of the court
h generally, exercisable by a judge of the court, who may or may not have been the trial

---

a   Section 115, so far as material, provides:
     '(1) A petition questioning an election in England or Wales under the local government Act shall be tried by an election court consisting of a barrister qualified and appointed as provided by
j   this section . . .
     (6) The election court shall for the purposes of the trial have the same powers and privileges as a judge on the trial of a parliamentary election petition . . .'
b   Section 110(2), so far as material, provides: 'The election court shall, subject to the provisions of this Act, have the same powers, jurisdiction and authority as a judge of the High Court . . . and shall be a court of record.'
c   Rule 11 is set out at p 710 e, post

judge. Furthermore, the exercise of the slip rule was limited to correcting ambiguity in expression of an unambiguous decision. Since the formal order accurately reflected the commissioner's decision as to costs there was no room for the exercise of the slip rule (see p 710 *d e*, p 711 *b* to *f* and p 712 *j*, post).

(2) An election court, or a court concerned with a petition questioning a local election, was brought into existence by the appointment of a barrister to constitute that court and the trial of that petition was the life-work of the court. When that trial was concluded in accordance with the 1949 Act, not only was the barrister functus officio but the court ceased to exist. Furthermore, although it was well established that a judge was fully entitled, without recourse to the slip rule, to reconsider and vary any decision at any time before the order embodying, or based on, that decision was perfected, once the order was perfected the trial judge was functus officio and had no further power in his capacity as trial judge to reconsider or vary his decision, whether under the authority of the slip rule or otherwise (see p 710 *a* to *d g h* and p 712 *j*, post).

(3) It followed that although by s 115(6) of the 1949 Act a local election court had for the purposes of the trial the same powers and privileges as a judge on the trial of a parliamentary election petition, and thus had power to amend under the slip rule, those powers were inapplicable once the trial had been concluded by the formalities prescribed by the 1949 Act. Thereafter any slips had to be corrected by the High Court under its powers. Accordingly, since the commissioner was functus officio when he made the direction, he would not have been entitled to use the slip rule power to clarify his order even if it had been ambiguous. It followed that the court had been right to grant an order of certiorari to quash the commissioner's direction (see p 712 *c* to *j*, post).

Decision of the Divisional Court of the Queen's Bench Division [1983] 3 All ER 72 affirmed.

Notes

For the jurisdiction, status and practice of the election court, see 15 Halsbury's Laws (4th edn) paras 834, 855.

For the Representation of the People Act 1949, ss 110, 115, see 11 Halsbury's Statutes (3rd edn) 648, 653.

As from 15 March 1983, ss 110 and 115 of the 1949 Act were replaced by ss 123 and 130 of the Representation of the People Act 1983.

Cases referred to in judgment

Adam & Harvey Ltd v International Maritime Supplies Co Ltd [1967] 1 All ER 533, [1967] 1 WLR 445, CA.

Inchcape, Re, Craigmyle v Inchcape [1942] 2 All ER 157, [1942] Ch 394.

Preston Banking Co v William Allsup & Sons [1895] 1 Ch 141, [1891–4] All ER Rep 688, CA.

Suffield and Watts, Re, ex p Brown (1888) 20 QBD 693, [1886–90] All ER Rep 276, CA.

Tak Ming Co Ltd v Yee Sang Metal Supplies Co [1973] 1 All ER 569, [1973] 1 WLR 300, PC.

Cases also cited

Chessum & Sons v Gordon [1901] 1 KB 694, [1900–3] All ER Rep 260, CA.

R v Maidenhead Corp (1882) 9 QBD 494, CA.

Appeal

The respondent, Adrian Carnegie Slade, appealed against the judgment of the Divisional Court of the Queen's Bench Division (Robert Goff LJ and Mann J) ([1983] 3 All ER 72, [1984] QB 68) on 27 May 1983 whereby the petitioners, Denis Muldoon, Christopher Nigel Pearson Lewis, Richard Martin Cantor and Solomon Jacques Green, were granted judicial review by way of an order of certiorari quashing a direction as to costs given on

3 November 1982 by Mr Anthony Cripps QC sitting as an election commissioner. The
facts are set out in the judgment of the court.

a

Timothy Barnes for the respondent.
M G Tugendhat for the petitioners.

Cur adv vult

b

3 April. The following judgment of the court was delivered.

SIR JOHN DONALDSON MR. This appeal concerns the aftermath of an election
petition by Mr Muldoon and others questioning the election of Mr Slade to the Greater
London Council as a representative of the Richmond-on-Thames area. The petition has
c   proved a disaster for all concerned and the aftermath is, if possible, something worse.
    The election took place on 7 May 1981. The petitioners alleged that the respondents,
Mr Slade and his agent, Mrs Wainwright, had been guilty of corrupt or illegal practices
under no less than 15 different headings. Mr Anthony Cripps QC was appointed, under
s 115 of the Representation of the People Act 1949, to constitute an election court charged
with the duty of trying the petition and this he did over 13 days between 1 and 19 March
d   1982.
    On 23 March 1982 the commissioner delivered a long and detailed judgment in which
he rejected all the allegations of corrupt practices and all, save two, of the allegations of
illegal practices. These exceptions consisted of (1) expending £1,993·64 on the election,
when the maximum permissible amount was £1,992·98, an overspending of £0·66, and
(2), which was more serious, the making of an untrue return. He granted the respondents
e   relief from the consequences of these illegal practices, on their paying the petitioners'
costs relating to the application for relief.
    That left the question of who should pay the costs of the petitioners and of Mr Slade in
relation to the petition itself, including the trial of that petition. As the trial had lasted
13 days, those costs were bound to be heavy and in the event the petitioners say that their
costs alone amounted to £42,000.
f   The commissioner heard argument on this issue. Counsel for the respondents
submitted that Mr Slade should recover at least part of his costs from the petitioners. The
basis of this submission was that the petitioners had failed in 13 of the 15 issues and that
these occupied the greater part of the trial. On the other hand, Mr Peter Bowsher QC,
then appearing for the petitioners, submitted that the petitioners should have all the
costs. For present purposes it is only necessary to record that counsel for the respondents
g   referred the commissioner to 15 Halsbury's Laws (4th edn) paras 958–961. Paragraph
961 is in the following terms:

> 'General rule as to costs. The general rule is that costs follow the event, but the rule
> may be displaced by special circumstances, in which case the court will make a
> special order. The practice is that if the petitioner is successful and is awarded costs
h   > the respondent will nevertheless be awarded costs in respect of charges in which the
> petitioner was not successful and which involved the respondent in extra expense.
> The practice used to be to leave the question as to what extra expense has been so
> caused to be decided by the taxing master, but this practice no longer obtains, and
> the court settles the question of what costs should be allowed.'

The commissioner announced his decision in the following terms:

j
> 'It is clear to me that the respondent ought not to have any costs. The respondent
> has really brought the case on himself in the manner I have indicated. Therefore,
> there will be no order for any costs to be paid to the respondent. As far as the
> petition is concerned, I also bear that in mind and I bear in mind the fact that the
> petitioner has succeeded and has succeeded on matters which were raised and were

important, but in my judgment the petitioner has certainly taken up more time than was necessary, even in view of the way in which the respondent has refused at earlier stages to co-operate what appears to be reasonably in producing the documents. The order, therefore, is that the respondent has to pay three-quarters of the petitioners' costs, including the reamendment, to be taxed if not agreed.'

This was translated into a formal order, reading:

'IT IS FURTHER ORDERED that i the Respondent Adrian Carnegie Slade do pay to the Petitioners three quarters (75%) of their costs properly incurred in relation to the Petition including the costs reserved by this Court on 8 March, 1982 in dealing with the Petitioners' application to re-amend their petition and that such costs be taxed by a Taxing Master if not agreed . . .'

There matters rested until October 1982, when Mr Slade's solicitors received the petitioners' bill of costs. He then sought and obtained an adjournment of the appointment for taxation. In a letter to the chief taxing master, his solicitors said:

'. . . the principal Bill of Costs presented by the solicitors representing the Petitioners in this matter does not, in our view, conform with the Order for costs made by Commissioner Cripps QC. Briefly, the Election Petition sought to establish that the Respondent was guilty of a number of corrupt and illegal practices on a variety of grounds. In the end, the Petitioners failed to succeed on a number of such grounds, although they did succeed on others. However, the Court granted the Respondent relief in respect of the grounds on which the Petitioners did succeed. The principal Bill of Costs seeks to include the costs incurred by the Petitioner in respect of grounds on which they did not succeed, presumably on the basis that such costs were "properly incurred in relation to the Petition" as provided for in Commissioner Cripps QC's Order for costs. In our view the Petitioners should not be entitled to costs in respect of grounds on which they did not succeed and accordingly in order to avoid a lengthy dispute on taxation as to the interpretation of Commissioner Cripps QC's Costs Order and in particular the expression "properly incurred", we wish to have the opportunity on behalf of the Respondent to make an application to Commissioner Cripps QC for a clarification of his Costs Order.'

The application to the commissioner was made on 3 November 1982 and he said:

'The application before me raises a point under the order made at the end of the local government election petition heard earlier this year. The point concerns costs. The actual order . . . was "IT IS FURTHER ORDERED that i the Respondent . . . do pay to the Petitioners three quarters (75%) of their costs properly incurred in relation to the Petition including the costs reserved by this Court on 8 March, 1982 in dealing with the Petitioners' application to re-amend their petition and that such costs be taxed by a Taxing Master if not agreed . . ." I am certainly not going to seek to usurp any of the functions of a taxing master, for which I would be unqualified, nor am I going to seek in any way to vary the order which was made but merely to seek to clarify it. The main points about this lengthy matter were, first, that on the petition itself the respondents succeeded technically in the sense that there were illegal but not corrupt practices found. On the subsequent application the petitioners succeeded and it was clear that on any probable result of the evidence as it came out that there would be relief to the respondents on all the matters on which the petitioners succeeded. I therefore regarded the petitioners' result as being a success of what one might call to some extent a technical kind. It was for that reason that the 75% was imported into the order. That was one restriction on the costs to be paid. But there was also a completely separate restriction on the costs to be paid, namely those "properly incurred". In those properly incurred I intended to be included the costs relevant to the two matters on which the petitioners were successful, namely in relation to the return itself and in relation to the Young Liberals' letter, items 1 and

6 of the 15 headings mentioned in the judgment. I did not intend to be included any costs referable to any of the other items in those 15 headings, 2, 3, 4, 5, 7, 8, 9, 10, 11, 12, 13, 14 and 15, because it seems to me that on those matters, bearing in mind that there had only been as it were a technical success, on the other matters there was not even a technical success, but complete failure. Therefore what the order means is that the taxing master as best he can is to tax the costs which were incurred in relation to the two matters I have mentioned, the return itself and the Young Liberals' letter, and in addition to that the costs of the petitioners in relation to the application to reamend the petition. Having arrived at that total sum the order requires 75% only of that to be paid. In other words there were two restrictions: (i) as regards the percentage of the amount and (ii) as regards what headings should be included in the amount. The order itself does have as an appendix to it the dates and times on which the matter occupied the time of the court, and it might be possible from those to arrive at some proportion of time to satisfy the taxing master, or it might be possible to satisfy the taxing master by considering the issues. But in whatever way that is done, it is a matter for the taxing master. As far as this court is concerned it is quite clear that there are in the order two restrictions: (i) "properly incurred", which refers to the issues on which there was success and no others, and of course to the reamendment; and, (ii) to the 75%, which is the grading down of the total amount arrived at at the first stage on account of the fact that the petitioners' success was, as I have said, virtually of a technical type.'

The petitioners then applied for judicial review, seeking (a) an order of certiorari to move into the High Court and to quash a purported direction or judgment given on 3 November 1982 by Mr Anthony Cripps QC, (b) judicial review by way of a declaration that the taxing master is bound to proceed with the taxation of the costs of the petitioners pursuant to the order of the election court dated 26 March 1982 without regard to the directions or judgment given on 3 November 1982 and (c) judicial review by way of a declaration that on the true construction of the order dated 26 March 1982 the petitioners' costs are to be taxed on a party and party basis in accordance with RSC Ord 62, r 28 and the petitioners are to be paid three-quarters of their costs so taxed in accordance with Ord 62, r 9(4)(a).

The Divisional Court, consisting of Robert Goff LJ and Mann J ([1983] 3 All ER 72, [1984] QB 68), quashed what was described as 'a direction as to costs given on the 3rd day of November, 1982, by Mr. Anthony Cripps Q.C.' In reaching this decision the court held that (i) the commissioner became functus officio, and thenceforward had no power to correct his decision, under any 'slip rule' or otherwise, once he had concluded the trial of the petition in accordance with s 149 of the 1949 Act, and this occurred long before 3 November 1982, (ii) the commissioner was not purporting to exercise powers under any 'slip rule' and (iii) an election court concerned with local elections is to be regarded as an inferior court in the sense that its decisions can be the subject of judicial review on the basis that it has exceeded its jurisdiction.

Mr Slade now appeals and counsel on his behalf advanced four submissions: (i) the commissioner was entitled to give the direction on costs of 3 November 1982 by virtue of the powers conferred on the High Court by RSC Ord 20, r 11, and applied to the election court by s 115(6) of the 1949 Act; (ii) notwithstanding that the trial of the petition ended when the commissioner had fulfilled his duties under s 125 of the 1949 Act and was, in general, functus officio, he had continuing authority to exercise powers under RSC Ord 20, r 11 and s 115(6) of the 1949 Act; (iii) an election court concerned with a local election is not amenable to the judicial review jurisdiction of the High Court; (iv) if the High Court has a judicial review jurisdiction, it cannot, or should not, be exercised where the complaint relates solely to an order as to costs. It is sufficient for the purposes of disposing of this appeal to consider the first two of these submissions and accordingly the argument was confined to them.

Some passing confusion occurred during the course of the argument as a result of the use of the phrase 'functus officio' in two rather different contexts. Most courts continue *a* in existence over a period of time and deal with many different and separate proceedings. Questions arise on whether and to what extent the court has finally disposed of each proceeding or issue arising in such a proceeding. When it has, the judge who presided is said to have become functus officio, quoad that issue or those proceedings. An election court, or at least one concerned with a petition questioning a local election, is somewhat different. It is brought into existence by the appointment of a barrister to constitute that *b* court and the trial of that petition is the life-work of the court. When that trial has been concluded in accordance with s 125 of the 1949 Act, not only is the barrister functus officio but the court ceases to exist. The confusion, which was purely transient, arose out of references to the court itself being functus. We propose to use the term solely in the sense of describing the status of a judge who has finally disposed of proceedings before him or of particular issues in those proceedings. *c*

It is well settled that any judge is fully entitled to reconsider and vary any decision at any time before the order embodying or based on that decision has been perfected (see *Re Suffield and Watts, ex p Brown* (1888) 20 QBD 693 at 697, [1886–90] All ER Rep 276 at 278 per Fry LJ), although in some circumstances he may be under an obligation to give the parties a further opportunity to be heard. At that stage no 'slip rule' power is needed. However, once the order has been perfected, the trial judge is functus officio and, in his *d* capacity as the trial judge, has no further power to reconsider or vary his decisions, whether under the authority of the 'slip rule' or otherwise. The 'slip rule' power is not a power granted to the trial judge as such. It is one of the powers of the court, exercisable by a judge of the court who may or may not be the judge who was in fact the trial judge.

In the case of the High Court, the 'slip rule' power is contained in Ord 20, r 11, which is in the following terms: *e*

'Clerical mistakes in judgments or orders, or errors arising therein from any accidental slip or omission, may at any time be corrected by the Court on motion or summons without an appeal.'

It is surprisingly wide in its scope. Its primary purpose is akin to rectification, namely to allow the court to amend a formal order which by accident or error does not reflect the *f* actual decision of the judge: see *Preston Banking Co v William Allsup & Sons* [1895] 1 Ch 141, [1891–4] All ER Rep 688. But it also authorises the court to make an order which it failed to make as a result of the accidental omission of counsel to ask for it: see *Re Inchcape, Craigmyle v Inchcape* [1942] 2 All ER 157, [1942] 1 Ch 394, approved by the Judicial Committee of the Privy Council in *Tak Ming Co Ltd v Yee Sang Metal Supplies Co* [1973] 1 All ER 569 at 573, [1973] 1 WLR 300 at 304. It even authorises the court to vary an *g* order which accurately reflects the oral decision of the court, if it is clear that the court inadvertently failed to express the decision which it intended: see *Adam & Harvey Ltd v International Maritime Supplies Co Ltd* [1967] 1 All ER 533, [1967] 1 WLR 455. However, it cannot be overemphasised that the 'slip rule' power can never entitle the trial judge or a court to reconsider a final and regular decision once it has been perfected, even if it has been obtained by fraud: see per Lord Halsbury in the *Preston Banking Co* case [1895] 1 Ch *h* 141 at 143, [1891–4] All ER Rep 688 at 689. We say 'final' decision, because different considerations apply in the case of orders which are provisional, because, for example, they were obtained ex parte, and we say 'regular' because again different considerations arise where the order may be said to be irregular for any of a variety of reasons.

We therefore proceed to consider whether the proceedings before Mr Cripps on 3 November 1982 constituted a purported reconsideration and variation of the decision on *j* costs which he had made seven months before on 23 March 1982 or whether it constituted the correction of a mistake in a judgment or order or of an error therein arising from an accidental slip or omission. The latter would be permissible, subject to the special position of a local election court. The former would not.

It is interesting to note that Mr Slade's solicitors, when writing to the chief taxing

master, did not suggest that the order as drawn up did other than reflect the decision of
a the commissioner. Their contention was that the words 'properly incurred in relation to
the Petition' entitled the petitioners to no more than the costs in respect of grounds of
complaint on which they succeeded. The solicitors were giving notice that they intended
to apply to the commissioner for 'a clarification of his Costs Order'.

For our part we would accept that, if a court has reached a decision which is
ambiguously expressed either in the reasoned judgment or in the formal order giving
b effect to the decision, the ambiguity of expression can be removed in the exercise of 'slip
rule' powers. But the exercise must be limited to correcting ambiguity in expression of
an unambiguous decision. An ambiguous decision is no decision at all and any attempt
to turn it into an unambiguous decision is at least a variation and probably a new
decision. It would not, therefore, be necessarily fatal to counsel's submission on behalf of
Mr Slade that he was seeking a clarification of the commissioner's order, provided always
c that the commissioner's decision had been unambiguous and the ambiguity lay in the
order giving effect to that decision.

We therefore turn first to the commissioner's own words uttered on 23 March 1982.
He said: '. . . the respondent has to pay three-quarters of the petitioners' costs, including
the reamendment, to be taxed if not agreed.' Whether this was just, fair or reasonable is
beside the point. It was quite unambiguous. Then we turn to the formal order. This
d order required Mr Slade to—

> 'pay to the Petitioners three quarters (75%) of their costs properly incurred in
> relation to the Petition including the costs reserved by this Court on 8 March, 1982
> in dealing with the Petitioners' application to re-amend their petition and that such
> costs be taxed by a Taxing Master if not agreed . . .'

e Again this is quite unambiguous. It differed from the commissioner's words only in that
it spelt out that the order related to the costs incurred in relation to the petition, which is
admittedly correct, and in that it included the words 'properly incurred'. These words
are apparently almost always included in orders of election courts, although not in orders
of the High Court. However, if not expressed, they are implicit in any High Court order
since RSC Ord 62, r 28(2) defines party and party costs as those which were necessary or
f proper for the attainment of justice or for enforcing or defending the rights of the party
whose costs are being taxed. Accordingly we consider that the formal order accurately
reflected the commissioner's orally expressed decision as to costs.

That leaves only Mr Cripps's remarks on 3 November. He said in terms that he was
not going to seek in any way to vary the order which he had made in March. He then
proceeded to construe that order as providing two limitations on the costs recoverable by
g the petitioners, namely (a) a limitation to costs incurred in relation to items 1 and 6, on
which the petitioners had succeeded, and (b) a 75% limitation applied to costs falling
within this category. Now we regret that two things must be said about these remarks.
The first is that it was for the taxing master and not for Mr Cripps to construe his order.
If his construction was right, it added nothing to the court's order. If it was wrong, he
was purporting to vary that order. The second thing which must be said is that there is
h not the slightest trace in Mr Cripps's judgment of 23 March 1982 of any intention that
the recoverable costs should be limited to those incurred in relation to items 1 and 6 or
any obvious justification for a 75% limitation if they were so limited.

Appreciating, as we do, the sense of injustice experienced by Mr Slade in the light of
the course which these proceedings have taken, we have considered whether it would be
just and proper to extend the ambit of the 'slip rule'. The high-water mark thus far is
j provided by *Adam & Harvey Ltd v International Maritime Supplies Co Ltd* [1967] 1 All ER
533, [1967] 1 WLR 445, in which three Lords Justices ordered A to pay the costs of B in
the belief, which we confess that we shared until recently, that this did not carry with it
any right to immediate taxation and payment, unless the court expressly added words to
that effect. Harman LJ had in an interlocutory observation said 'No immediate taxation'
and, in the light of that circumstance, the court felt entitled to apply the 'slip rule'. It was

thus a case in which the court said one thing, but demonstrably meant another. A more common example is where a judge refers to 'the plaintiff' meaning thereby 'the defendant' or vice versa. But to apply the 'slip rule' in the present case would involve correcting an order, not on the basis that in the light of contemporary events or evidence it could be shown to have failed to express the judge's decision, but on the basis that seven months later the judge thought that he intended, or must have intended, something which he certainly did not express formally or informally at the time of decision. To admit of such an extension would be to invite judges to succumb to the very human failing of regretting a decision and then convincing themselves that they cannot ever have intended it. Judges are both human and fallible, but such an extension of the 'slip rule' is not the solution to the problems created thereby. The solution is a right of appeal, which does not exist in the circumstances of this case because there is no direct right of appeal on an order as to costs made by a local election court and, even if there were a remedy by way of judicial review, the order actually made did not involve any excess of jurisdiction, however broadly that concept may be applied.

In our judgment the commissioner's remarks on 3 November 1982 were wholly without effect. He had no power to construe or clarify his own order. He had no power to vary it and did not purport to do so. He had no power to rectify it under the 'slip rule', and again did not purport to do so. It is not therefore necessary to consider whether on that day he was sitting as 'Mr Commissioner Cripps QC' in or as a local election court or whether his remarks were those of 'Mr Anthony Cripps QC' speaking under a misapprehension as to his capacity. Suffice it to say that although by s 115(6) of the 1949 Act a local election court has 'for *the purposes of the trial* the same powers and privileges as a judge on the trial of a parliamentary election petition', which would import the High Court 'slip rule' power, it is probable that these powers are inapplicable once the trial has been concluded by the formalities prescribed by s 125 of the 1949 Act and that thereafter slips must be corrected by the High Court under the powers contained in s 137(3) of the 1949 Act. However, even if Mr Cripps had been appointed a deputy High Court judge and invited to exercise the powers of the High Court, for the reasons which we have given, he could not properly have 'corrected' the order which he had made in a wholly different capacity.

This disposes of the substance of the appeal, but we should explain why we consider it to be unnecessary to reach any decision on the jurisdiction of the Divisional Court in relation to the work of a local election court. That jurisdiction depends on the local election court being an 'inferior court' and not a 'superior court of record'. Assuming that a local election court is an inferior court in this sense, the Divisional Court was right to quash Mr Cripps's decision, if it was a decision at all, and would, in any event, have been right to grant a declaration that his remarks were of no effect in clarifying or varying the order of the election court. If, however, a local election court is not an inferior court, nevertheless the High Court has jurisdiction to declare and order that its own taxing master should tax the costs in accordance with the formal order of the election court and that he should have no regard to Mr Cripps's decision or remarks on 3 November 1982, those being made without jurisdiction. It is true that no such application has been made to the High Court, but it could be made and the result, if we are right in the views which we have expressed, is a foregone conclusion. It follows that there is no way in which Mr Slade can escape from the position created by the order of the Divisional Court, namely that the formal order of the election court as to costs takes effect according to its terms, and, whatever the technicalities, justice will best be served and costs saved if the appeal is dismissed.

We would therefore dismiss the appeal.

Appeal dismissed.

Solicitors: *Frere Cholmeley* (for the respondent); *Penningtons* (for the petitioners).

Frances Rustin   Barrister.

a   **Cresswell and others v Board of Inland Revenue**

CHANCERY DIVISION
WALTON J
23, 24, 25, 26, 27, 30 JANUARY, 1 FEBRUARY 1984

b   *Master and servant – Contract of service – Duties of employee – Change in method of work – Computerisation – Inland Revenue introducing computerisation of PAYE scheme to replace manual method of work of tax officers – Whether computerisation changing nature of tax officers' jobs.*

c   *Employment – Suspension – Employees refusing to operate new system of work – Employer refusing to pay wages while employees refusing to operate new system – Whether employer's refusal to pay wages amounting to suspension of employees.*

The Board of Inland Revenue wished to introduce a system of computer operation of the PAYE scheme. Computerisation would have the effect that calculations formerly done
d   manually by tax officers would be done by computer, all necessary documentation following an individual change of coding would be sent out automatically and where there was a universal review of coding, eg following a Finance Act, all necessary alterations and notifications would be done automatically. The effect for those grades of Inland Revenue staff involved, namely clerical assistants and tax officers, was that they would be required to enter relevant information into the computer via a visual display
e   unit rather than onto individual cards. The plaintiffs, a number of clerical assistants and tax officers, objected to the introduction of the scheme for computerisation on the ground that it would be a breach of their terms of service to introduce it without their consent. The board informed the plaintiffs that it was not prepared to continue with the old manual methods and that it would not pay them while they refused to operate the computerised system. The board also made it clear that it was not putting an end to the
f   plaintiffs' contracts of employment or seeking to take disciplinary action against them and that they would be paid if they returned to full-time work using the computerised system. The plaintiffs brought an action against the board seeking a declaration that the board was in breach of its contracts of employment with the plaintiffs in requiring them to operate or use the system and in suspending them without pay while they refused to operate the system. The plaintiffs contended that the introduction of the computerised
g   system would be such a change in the method of performing the tasks for which they had been recruited as to amount to a change in the nature of their jobs and that the plaintiffs were therefore being asked to perform work under wholly different contracts without their consent. The plaintiffs further contended that the board's action in refusing to pay them until they used the computerised system amounted to their suspension without complying with the appropriate disciplinary procedures and that the board was
h   therefore required to pay them until the proper suspension procedures had been carried out.

Held – The plaintiffs' action would be dismissed for the following reasons—
          (1) An employee did not have a vested right to preserve his working obligations completely unchanged as from the moment he first began work, but was expected to
j   adapt himself to new methods and techniques introduced in the course of his employment. The effect of the board's computerised system was not that the plaintiffs would be doing a different job but merely that they would be doing recognisably the same job in a different way. Although the content of some of the jobs might be considerably affected it would not be altered sufficiently to fall outside the original description of the plaintiffs' proper functions, since it could not be said that staff using the computerised system would be anything other than tax officers working the PAYE

scheme. The board was therefore entitled to introduce the computerised system and to require the plaintiffs to operate it under their existing contracts of employment (see p 720 d, p 721 c and j to p 722 j and p 725 g h, post); *North Riding Garages Ltd v Butterwick* [1967] 1 All ER 644 and *O'Neill v Merseyside Plumbing Co Ltd* [1973] ICR 96 applied.

(2) When the plaintiffs deliberately abstained from working the board was entitled, as a matter of contract, to rely on the principle of 'no work no pay' and was free of any obligation to pay them wages without being obliged to resort to suspension by the appropriate disciplinary procedures (see p 723 h j, p 724 e and p 725 f to h, post); *Gorse v Durham CC* [1971] 2 All ER 666 distinguished.

Notes

For payment of remuneration under a contract of employment, see 16 Halsbury's Laws (4th edn) para 552, and for cases on the subject, see 20 Digest (Reissue) 290–295, 2645–2659.

Cases referred to in judgment

Denmark Productions Ltd v Boscobel Productions Ltd [1968] 3 All ER 513, [1969] 1 QB 699, [1968] 3 WLR 841, CA.
Gorse v Durham CC [1971] 2 All ER 666, [1971] 1 WLR 775.
Laurie v British Steel Corp (23 February 1978, unreported), Ct of Sess.
North Riding Garages Ltd v Butterwick [1967] 1 All ER 644, [1967] 2 QB 56, [1967] 2 WLR 571, DC.
O'Neill v Merseyside Plumbing Co Ltd [1973] ICR 96, NIRC.
Secretary of State for Employment v ASLEF (No 2) [1972] 2 All ER 949, [1972] 2 QB 455, [1972] 2 WLR 1370, CA.

Cases also cited

Amos v Max-Arc Ltd [1973] ICR 46, NIRC.
Carnie (Peter) & Sons Ltd v Paton [1979] IRLR 260, EAT.
Coleman v Baldwin [1977] IRLR 342, EAT.
Henthorn v Central Electricity Generating Board [1980] IRLR 361, CA.
Kodeeswaran v A-G of Ceylon [1970] AC 1111, PC.
Mears v Safecar Security Ltd [1982] 2 All ER 865, [1983] QB 54, CA.
Robinson v British Island Airways Ltd [1978] ICR 304, EAT.

Action

By writ dated 6 January 1984 and an amended statement of claim served on 1 February 1984 the plaintiffs, Michael Barry Cresswell, Christine Jones, Gregory Robert Victor Lawrence, Linda Sharon Mason, Margaret Patricia Morris, Paul Leonard Roche, Kathryn Eveline Sidebotham and James Martin McElhone, sought, inter alia, as against the defendant, the Board of Inland Revenue, declarations (1) that the plaintiffs were not bound in order to perform their contracts of employment to operate and/or use computer systems or related equipment in connection with the administration of PAYE, (2) that the defendant was in breach of the plaintiffs' contracts of employment in instructing and/or requiring the plaintiffs to operate and/or use such computer systems and related equipment, (3) that the defendant was in breach of the plaintiffs' contracts of employment or alternatively their terms and conditions of service in suspending the plaintiffs without pay by reason of their refusal to operate and/or use such computer systems and related equipment without their consent, and (4) that the defendant was in breach of the plaintiffs' contracts of employment or alternatively their terms and conditions of service in suspending the plaintiffs without complying with the appropriate disciplinary procedures. The facts are set out in the judgment.

Eldred Tabachnik QC, James Goudie and Patrick Elias for the plaintiffs.
Peter Millett QC, John Mummery and P I F Vallance for the board.

Cur adv vult

1 February. The following judgment was delivered.

a

WALTON J. This case concerns the introduction by the defendant, the Board of the Inland Revenue, of a system of computer operation designed to assist in the administration of the well-known PAYE scheme. Critics of the Revenue (and on many matters I acknowledge I have been a critic) will, on learning of the move, add 'and about time too'. Here they will be wrong. The Revenue is already using computers to assist in this work in a number of districts, although the present proposed scheme is on rather a different basis from any scheme which has hitherto been implemented.

b

To the introduction of this new scheme, designated 'COP' (standing for nothing more sinister than computerisation of PAYE), the plaintiffs, members of the staff of the defendants, object, maintaining that it cannot be introduced, consistently with their respective terms of service, without their consent. Realistically, it is not the individual plaintiffs, who are merely representatives of the grades complaining (namely higher grade tax officers, tax officers and clerical assistants), who are responsible for this litigation: it is very much a union matter, the union concerned being the Inland Revenue Staff Federation.

c

It is, I think, right that the stance of the union in this matter should be appreciated. It is not really a Luddite stance seeking to delay the march of progress. On the contrary, as regards all schemes which have hitherto been put into operation using computers, the union has always co-operated with the board. And it is really ready to co-operate with the board (and indeed up to a point has already done so) in the introduction of COP.

d

I think there are two main reasons: first, it recognises that quite clearly it cannot stand indefinitely in the path of progress and, second, it recognises quite clearly that the introduction of COP will, when the system has lost its unfamiliarity, provide for its operators a job which will be free from much of the drudgery at present associated with it.

e

But therein lies the catch. However much it will (whatever they now think) benefit its operators, it will certainly lead to a diminution in the number of staff required to operate the new system. Naturally, the union does not relish the loss of membership or, as a fallback position, if there is to be such a loss it would wish this to come about by normal retirement and voluntary retirement, not by compulsory retirement. And so the union has sought a pledge from the board that there will be no compulsory retirements involved in the system being put into operation. It has also asked that the benefits of computerisation should be shared with the workforce, but inasmuch as the board will be spending a very considerable sum of money on COP, the effect of which will be both to improve the service to the public and to benefit the operators of that system, I take it that this was merely a negotiating ploy.

f

g

Down to 21 December 1983 the union was hopeful of being able to reach a satisfactory arrangement with the board in relation to redundancy. But on that date it was informed by the board that no guarantee could be given that there would be no compulsory redundancies as a result of COP. Hence these proceedings, based on the theory that in requiring the plaintiffs to operate COP the board is in breach of the terms of the contract of employment with each plaintiff.

h

In order to understand the plaintiffs' submissions it is necessary for me to give a brief and, it must be understood, totally superficial outline of how the PAYE system works at present and how it will work under COP. The whole basis of the system lies in the code which is allotted to each taxpayer subject to the system, which code informs his employer of the deductions which the employer must make from that employee's salary and, thereafter, account for to the Revenue.

j

The heart of the system lies in two control cards. There is a control card for the employer and then the cards for the employees ranged, in physical filing terms, behind that of the employer. An employee's control card is called a 'concard'. Obviously, from time to time there will be changes in the coding of an employee or of a person in receipt of social security pensions and other benefits to whom a special colour of card is allocated. When a change is made, the employee or other person will be sent a revised notice of coding. The employer or Department of Health and Social Security must also be notified of the change.

There are, of course, many reasons for alterations, e g alterations in the rate of personal allowances caused as the result of a Finance Act, the successful claiming by a taxpayer of an allowance which has not hitherto been granted to him, and, conversely, the application to the taxpayer of legislation taxing car and car fuel or other benefits. When this happens otherwise than at the commencement of a tax year there will be questions of underpayment of tax which, if the taxpayer is either a higher-rate taxpayer or has other income which has to be taken into charge to tax, may involve difficult decisions how, precisely, the matter is to be dealt with and whether it is possible to absorb the additional tax due in the current year or whether some should be left outstanding and dealt with by a variation in the coding for the subsequent year. There may be questions of the payment of tax. There will then be cases of employees commencing work in the tax district concerned and cases of employees leaving the tax district for work in other areas. The problems to which all these matters give rise can easily be imagined.

Throughout all these problems the crucial document is the employee's concard on which all the relevant information as to his current coding will be contained.

Hitherto all this work has been carried out manually at the offices of the tax district concerned. A great deal of this will be changed as a result of COP. It is here necessary to observe that until now only a proportion, albeit a large proportion, of the full programme has been set up and is ready to go into action and was, indeed, being operated at the end of last year. This part of the full programme is known as COP 1. COP 2 is promised, or threatened, depending on one's point of view, but is not yet something which has been set up or which any of the plaintiffs have been required to operate by the board. I shall have to consider the effect of this later but, for the moment, I confine myself to those activities which the board has asked some of its employees, including the plaintiffs, to undertake.

COP 1 has not been introduced universally; at the moment it is a programme confined to a number of tax districts in the West Midlands. Its essential feature, around which everything else revolves, is that the key to the whole system, the concard, is replaced by an entry on the computer called up on a visual display unit (VDU) by keying in, as the crucial matter, the employee's national insurance number (NINO). For the time being, at any rate, the concard is being retained as an index to enable this number to be ascertained; but apart from this function the concard ceases to matter. Attention is now throughout focused on the screen of the VDU displaying the same information as has hitherto been found on the concard. Thus, if an alteration is made to the employee's coding, this will now be effected by calling up the relevant display on the VDU and making the necessary alterations thereon.

Thereafter there are manifold benefits. In the first place the employee of the board concerned is no longer required to perform any arithmetic of any description; this will be done, as required, by the computer. I have no doubt that the vast majority of calculations made by tax officers are, and always have been, correct, but like the rest of humanity they are fallible. I have equally no doubt but that from time to time mistakes are made. It is no use telling the irate taxpayer that statistically the number of mistakes is insignificant. This does not assist him and he will have to spend time, and possibly money in various forms, in getting the matter put right.

Secondly, all the necessary documentation following a change of coding will be sent out automatically, no longer from the tax district concerned but from the central organisation controlling the computer. When the tax officer is satisfied that the correct figures have been entered on the VDU, he will press a button marked 'Send' and the rest will follow automatically. This procedure must, overall, be more accurate and quicker, and in some cases much quicker, than the present system.

Thirdly, in all cases where there is a universal review of coding as, for example, in consequence of changes effected by a Finance Act, the computer will make the necessary alterations, as directed to do so by central control, and send out the necessary documentation automatically. This will obviously be much quicker than the present manual system of alteration.

It is, however, of interest, and for present purposes I do not think it is more than that,
a to note that the system has been set up in such a way that, notwithstanding all the
advantages of automation, the tax officer always has the last word. If, for example, he
feels it is essential for a letter explaining the changes in coding which he has initiated to
be sent together with the notice of the change of coding and not, as will now normally
be the case, separately from it, he can indicate this by pressing the designated key and he
will then still be able to effect all the necessary documentation manually.

b The system was set up in all the 14 districts concerned between 3 October 1983 and
various dates in November and December 1983. It was set up with union co-operation
because, at that time, the union was convinced that it could negotiate a no job loss or, at
any rate, no compulsory redundancy agreement with the board, which has now proved
impossible. I fully accept that the co-operation was conditional and nothing can be made
of such co-operation by the board. Similarly, I accept that I ought not to attach any
c weight to the absence of any protests from the plaintiffs or anybody else in the same
grades in the 14 districts about such introduction; doubtless as loyal members of a trade
union they were following its instructions to co-operate.

During this time, of course, the necessary training on the use of the computer was
effected; a very limited number of half days being all that was required. The first part of
the system, COP 1, was thus in full operation, all the necessary records having transferred
d to the computer, by the end of 1983 and, as far as the evidence goes, in full and successful
operation. It had originally been intended to operate both parts of the system as one, but
early in 1983 the decision was taken to split it into two parts, the parts which thus
became COP 1 representing all the elements of the system except for the assessing and
repayment functions, and COP 2 representing the assessing and repayment functions.

Doubtless following union instructions, the plaintiffs have, since 3 January 1984,
e refused to use and operate COP 1 whilst making it perfectly clear that they were willing
to continue with the previous manual operation. Equally the board made it perfectly
clear that it would not countenance the plaintiffs using manual methods of operation,
nor would it pay any of the plaintiffs whilst they were refusing to work COP 1, but that
so far as the board was concerned it was not putting an end to the plaintiffs' contracts and
was ready and willing to pay the plaintiffs if they returned to full-time work operating
f COP 1. The board made it abundantly clear that it was not in any way seeking to use the
machinery of suspension or to take any other disciplinary action against the plaintiffs or
any of them.

This action was commenced by writ on 6 January 1984. It was amended by the
addition of the eighth plaintiff on 23 January 1984. The plaintiffs are, of course, all civil
servants; they hold grades as clerical assistants, tax officer and higher grade tax officer.
g The statement of claim (which is commendably short) reads, in part, as follows:

'3. The work which the Plaintiffs were employed and/or engaged to perform
and/or the work which they have habitually carried out in each case involves to a
considerable extent dealing manually with files and/or records and with
correspondence and inquiries arising therefrom. Further, save in the case of the
h Third Plaintiff, the said work involves making mental arithmetical calculations and,
in certain contexts, the independent exercise of discretion.

4. It is an implied term of the said contract alternatively terms of service that the
Plaintiffs cannot be required to perform tasks and/or carry out functions other than
those expressly stipulated in the said contracts of employment alternatively terms
of service, and/or such as are habitually carried out by custom and practice, together
j with such other tasks and/or functions necessarily and/or reasonably incidental
thereto.

5. Further, and in the alternative, it is an implied term of the said contracts
alternatively terms of service that the Plaintiffs cannot be required to change and/or
alter the manner and/or mode in which the said tasks and/or functions have been
habitually performed either at all or in such a manner as to make the tasks and/or

functions performed different in nature and/or in kind from those performed hitherto.

    6. In breach of the implied terms pleaded in paragraphs 4 and/or 5 herein, on or about 3rd January 1984 the Defendants instructed and/or required the Plaintiffs to operate and/or utilise computer systems and related equipment. [I am reading the statement of claim as originally delivered.] The use and operation of the said systems and/or equipment severely reduces the manual element in the performance of the said tasks and/or functions, and largely eliminates the need for mental calculations and the independent exercise of discretion.

    7. At all material times the Plaintiffs and each of them have been, and remain, ready and willing to carry out their contracts of employment alternatively to comply with their terms of service. They refused without their consent to operate and/or utilise the said computer systems and/or related equipment as instructed and/or required by the Defendants.'

The relief claimed is a declaration—

    '(1) That the Plaintiffs and each of them are not bound in order to perform their several contracts of employment alternatively terms and conditions of service with the Defendants to operate and/or utilise computer systems and/or related equipment in connection with the administration of PAYE.

    (2) That the Defendants are in breach of the said contracts of employment alternatively terms and conditions of service, in instructing and/or requiring the Plaintiffs and each of them to operate and/or utilise the computer systems and related equipment in connection with the administration of PAYE.

    (3) That the Defendants are in breach of the said contracts of employment alternatively terms and conditions of service in suspending the Plaintiffs and each of them without pay or at all . . .'

The quite astonishing thing about this pleading is that, although the whole of the allegations made are in relation to the nature of the work which the plaintiffs carry out (and, since they are civil servants, there can be but little dispute what that work is), there is not a single allegation of any nature whatsoever bearing directly on that matter. Yet, of course, as the result of, in the happy phrase used by counsel for the plaintiffs, documents flying about 'like confetti' in the middle of the hearing, I now know precisely the terms on which each of the plaintiffs was engaged. I can well understand that the plaintiffs themselves never realised or paid any attention to what, perhaps, for present purposes might well have been the most vital of such terms; what is surprising is that they do not, any of them, seem to have realised that there were any such terms of any nature whatsoever. What is surprising in the extreme in relation to the personal plaintiffs becomes quite incredible when one realises that in effect the plaintiffs in the present case represent the union. That the precise terms and conditions of service should be unknown by or, worse, unappreciated by the union ventures on the preposterous.

    However that may be, on the same day as the issue of the writ a notice of motion was launched, returnable before Nourse J on 11 January 1984. That notice was in the following terms:

    'The Plaintiffs' claim is for

    1. An order restraining the Defendant from requiring the Plaintiffs and each of them to perform their several contracts of employment or conditions of service with the Defendant otherwise than in accordance with the terms thereof and in particular restraining the Defendant from requiring the Plaintiffs and each of them to use or operate or utilise visual display terminals on line to a computer and/or the keyboards associated therewith in connection with the administration of PAYE.

    2. An order restraining the Defendant from suspending the Plaintiffs and each of them without pay by reason of their refusing without their consent to use, operate or utilise visual display terminals on line to a computer and/or the key-boards associated therewith in connection with the administration of PAYE.

a
3. An order restraining the Defendant from suspending the Plaintiffs and each of them without pay and/or taking any other disciplinary action against any of them unless and until the Defendant have complied with the procedures prescribed . . .'

The relief claimed never stood the slightest chance of being granted. In the first place, damages and not an injunction is the proper remedy in virtually every case of breach of contract, especially one relating to master and servant. Secondly, inasmuch as the relief

b claimed under paras 1 and 2 was claimed without limit of time, it ceased to be interlocutory relief and amounted, in effect, to the whole of the relief claimed in the action. The motion was thus one for judgment. But the crunch point was, of course, that no injunction will lie against the Crown.

However, all parties were anxious to obtain a speedy hearing of the matter and so it was agreed that the motion should be stood over to come on as a motion by order, both

c sides agreeing that the hearing of the motion should be treated as the trial of the action.

I fear that this was a total misconception of procedure. As the motion was, from the first, doomed to fail on the three separate grounds already indicated, the only effect of an agreement to treat the hearing of the motion as the trial of the action, ie to treat the motion as a motion for judgment, would have been to ensure an inevitable failure of the action. This, I am quite sure, was never intended by anybody. What, therefore, has taken

d place before me has been not the hearing of a motion but the full scale trial of the action with proper pleadings and duly set down, albeit heard, by consent of both parties, basically on affidavit evidence tested by cross-examination and with no full discovery.

Further, and I think that this was not due to any deficiencies in the learned pleader, in the events which happened, namely that the plaintiffs were never, at any stage, asked by the board to implement COP 2 but only COP 1, the statement of claim related only, on

e its true construction, to COP 1. It would clearly have been most unsatisfactory if I had had to decide what was the position as regards COP 1, possibly coming to a conclusion adverse to the plaintiffs, but leaving the position under COP 2 undecided.

Accordingly, at a late stage of the proceedings, I gave the plaintiffs leave, with the concurrence of Mr Mummery for the board, to amend the statement of claim so as to include a claim, strictly quia timet but none the less valid, in relation to the threatened

f introduction of COP 2.

During the hearing of the action I have had a large number of affidavits read to me on both sides, I have seen many of the plaintiffs' and the board's witnesses cross-examined and I have attended the showing of films on computerisation in the Revenue. I have also seen demonstrations of two transactions as effected manually and via the computer. I do not, however, think it necessary to go at all deeply into the evidence. Each of the

g witnesses who were cross-examined was clearly a person of integrity and, in many cases, distinction. And I have no doubt at all but that each was trying to assist the court to the best of his or her not inconsiderable ability. But it is really unnecessary to probe the minutiae of the evidence because there is no real dispute as to the facts: it is as to the interpretation of the fact of computerisation that the dispute lies and herein all that the plaintiffs, and those who gave evidence on behalf of the plaintiffs, could really do was to

h explain their own personal reaction to computerisation.

It is not very surprising that, on the whole, this is unfavourable. Even when one takes delivery of a new car there is always a period of tension before one has got to know it inside out, however long one has been driving. But some of the complaints made by the plaintiffs are, in my judgment, on any view wholly misconceived. They, or some of them, complain of the loss of 'discretion' and 'judgment' caused by computerisation.

j There is extremely little scope for 'discretion', properly so-called, in the taxing system. Similarly, the cases where any of the plaintiffs are required to exercise 'judgment' of any description are extremely few. Their function is basically to apply a very well defined rule book to the circumstances before them.

I can well understand that it is possible that some personal contact with taxpayers may be lost since the taxing officer will no longer write out the name and address of taxpayers and their reference number on communications. This was a specific complaint made to me in the witness box by the sixth plaintiff, who was an extremely articulate young man. But, however much any of the plaintiffs may revel in such matters of communication, it is quite clear that such complaints, and many others of like ilk, although numerous, amount to little more than saying that the person concerned does not like the new method of working and feels that his or her job satisfaction will be less. So be it; a loss of job satisfaction is always regrettable but by itself provides no cause of action.

I now turn straight away to a consideration of the main point on which counsel for the plaintiffs relied. He put his case in this way, that although it is undoubtedly correct that an employer may, within limits, change the manner in which his employees perform the work which they are employed to do, there may be such a change in the method of performing the task which the employee was recruited to perform proposed by the employer as to amount to a change in the nature of the job. This would mean that the employee was being asked to perform work under a wholly different contract and this cannot be done without his consent. That, submitted counsel, was what had happened here very clearly in the case of those plaintiffs who were clerical assistants, clearly in the case of such as are tax officers and, as regards higher-grade tax officers (although possibly not much affected by COP 1, certainly with the implementation of COP 2) similarly so affected.

It is a very fine line from counsel's submissions to the submission that employees have a vested right to preserve their working obligations completely unchanged as from the moment when they first begin work. This cannot surely, by any stretch of the imagination, be correct. That it is not so is very clearly shown by *O'Neill v Merseyside Plumbing Co Ltd* [1973] ICR 96. In that case the employee had entered the services of his employers in 1947 and remained (apart from absence for national service) in their employment until 1972. Throughout all that time he worked as a gas fitter, ie for something approaching a quarter of a century. Then his employers directed him to work at a hospital site as a general plumber and he refused on the ground that he was incompetent to perform the plumbing work required. He submitted that the purported transfer to work of a different kind from that to which he was accustomed made him redundant. He claimed redundancy and the hearing in the National Industrial Relations Court was on an appeal by him from an industrial tribunal. The court held that the crucial question to be asked was whether he was employed as a plumber or as a specialist gas fitter; in other words, what were his terms of employment? What was it that he was employed to do? For if he was employed as a general plumber then, although he had always previously worked as a gas fitter, 'the employers were plainly entitled to require him to do other forms of plumbing work, and the cause of his dismissal was quite simply that he refused to do that which he was required to do under his contract of employment' (see [1973] ICR 96 at 99).

The position in the present case is that the plaintiffs are, of course, all civil servants. Some little time was taken up during the course of the trial in ascertaining precisely what their terms of employment were, but, being civil servants, their employment is regulated by the Civil Service Order in Council 1982, which provides that (so far as here material) the qualifications of a person proposed to be appointed must be approved by the Civil Service Commissioners and no person can be appointed to any situation until they have issued a certificate of qualification. The order then contains a list of the grades applicable. For the purposes of the present case the grades are 'Clerical Assistant' and 'Tax Officer'. 'Higher grade tax officer' appears to be purely a departmental grade and, from the point of view of the Civil Service as a whole, it appears to me that they are merely 'Tax Officers'. This is also consistent with common sense: a higher-grade tax officer merely does the higher type of work required of a tax officer. In no sense is the precise nature of his work any different. Of course, a grade is not strictly a job description. The description of the job of a tax officer is like the description of the job of any other grade, namely 'the general duties appropriate to the grade concerned'. Bearing this in mind, it will be convenient, as a form of shorthand, to refer to the jobs as those of clerical assistant, tax officer or higher-grade tax officer as the case may be.

Granted that down to the present the work of each of these three grades has been done
a manually, with pen, paper and pocket calculator, if the employer changes this so as
largely to remove the necessity to use pen and paper but requires the person concerned
to use a computer instead or, in some cases, in addition, is the nature of the job thereby
fundamentally changed? I do not think that the drawing of parallels with other situations
really assists because, at the end of the day, it is the precise impact which is made by the
computerisation programme on the day-to-day work of these three grades which is in
b question. However there is, I think, one important point. When dealing with other
examples counsel for the plaintiffs made the point that the requirements of the employer
might be such that the employee was genuinely unable to comply therewith. He
instanced, for example, a typist engaged on audio typing who might be unable, with the
best will in the world, to readapt to a word processor. What then?

That kind of case can be left to be dealt with when it arises, although O'Neill's case
c would certainly not suggest that if the employee had been originally engaged as a typist
simpliciter there would really be much doubt about the matter.

But there can really be no doubt as to the fact that an employee is expected to adapt
himself to new methods and techniques introduced in the course of his employment (cf
North Riding Garages Ltd v Butterwick [1967] 1 All ER 644, [1967] 2 QB 560). Of course,
in a proper case the employer must provide any necessary training or retraining. I think
d the probable answer to counsel's point is simply that it will, in all cases, be a question of
pure fact whether the retraining involved the acquisition of such esoteric skills that it
would not be reasonable to expect the employee to acquire them. In an age when the
computer has forced its way into the schoolroom and where electronic games are played
by schoolchildren in their own homes as a matter of everyday occurrence, it can hardly
be considered that to ask an employee to acquire basic skills as to retrieving information
e from a computer or feeding such information into a computer is something in the
slightest esoteric or, even nowadays, unusual.

In any event in the present case one remarkable feature, comparable to that of the dog
which did not bark in the night, is that from first to last in all the voluminous evidence
put in by the plaintiffs, there is no suggestion whatsoever that the plaintiffs themselves,
or anybody else in any similar category in all the 14 districts covered by the present
f scheme, found any real difficulty in accepting the necessary instruction in the use of
COP 1 and putting it into practice as they had been doing for some little time at the end
of last year.

Whatever the change in working methods may be, it is one which, of course with
proper instruction (which I think the employer must be under a duty to provide and
which has, of course, been provided in the present case), the three grades concerned have,
g one and all, taken in their stride. However, I do not think that any such case as the
present is one which can be dealt with by a consideration of generalities.

[His Lordship then considered in detail how each grade was affected by COP 1 and
might be affected by the introduction of COP 2. In particular, his Lordship considered
an affidavit, filed on behalf of the plaintiffs, by Mr Miller, a professional job evaluator, in
which Mr Miller detailed for each grade the specific changes which would be made to
h each job as a result of the introduction of COP. His Lordship concluded that Mr Miller's
study showed that the effect of COP would be that (a) clerical assistants would be required
to enter details on the computer via the VDU in addition to functions which had hitherto
been carried out manually and (b) both grades of tax officer would be required to enter
the results of calculations or relevant information into the computer system instead of
entering it on the concard although there would be no additional responsibility imposed
j on the tax officer. His Lordship continued:]

All these changes having been effected to the working methods of each of the grades
concerned, is it possible to maintain that the job of clerical assistant and tax officer
remains the same, or have those jobs suffered a sea change into something rich and
strange? There was an interesting exchange between Mr Miller and myself just before
he was cross-examined by counsel for board. His own words were (when talking of the

job of a tax officer): 'I have been . . . conservative in assessing the proportion of the job which would be done in a different way.' So it was clear that he thought that after the introduction of COP it would still be the same job. When I put this to him he said that, yes, 'it was recognisably the same job but done in a different way'.

In this I think he was absolutely correct. It appears to me that each of the three jobs post-COP (and here I mean both COP 1 and COP 2) will be the same jobs as they were pre-COP, though in part done in a different way, that is to say the clerical assistants will still be clerical assistants. They will, of course, now have to enter certain information into the computer, but it must be remembered that a clerk is defined in the Shorter Oxford Dictionary as 'An officer who has charge of the records, correspondence etc., and conducts the business of any department'. A clerical assistant is one who assists, therefore, among other matters, in keeping the records and, depending on precisely how these records are kept, so will his duties vary.

One of the main functions of a computer is to store records and so it is well within the scope of the clerical assistant's job to help in keeping the necessary records by entering the information on a computer. This does not, pace some of the wilder suggestions that have been made in this case, make him a 'computer operator' any more than a customer who draws cash from a service-till facility afforded by his bank is a computer operator because he is required to feed certain information into the service-till as a prerequisite to drawing the cash he requires. Of course, the transaction here is one way, but it is no more outside the scope of the duties of a clerical assistant than filing the details desired to be recorded on a card; the essential step is the same in both cases.

And when one comes to consider the tax officer and the higher-grade tax officer, the matter is, if anything, even clearer. Here, although I think also the words 'computer operator' or, more picturesquely, 'slave to the machine' were bandied about during the course of the trial, it is extremely difficult to think that, if an entirely unprejudiced observer were to sit in the offices of any of the 14 districts for any length of time, observing intelligently all that went on, and was then asked what job these people have got, he would in all conscience be able to say that they were anything other than tax officers, that is to say officers working the PAYE tax system in all its manifold aspects.

Of course the changes in working methods and practices which COP brings in its train are great, although I think that the evidence has tended to exaggerate them. But that, as it seems to me, is not the point. COP merely introduces up-to-date modern methods for dealing with bulk problems; it leaves the jobs done by those who operate the new methodology precisely the same as before, although the content of some of the jobs, most notably that of the grade of clerical assistant, will have been considerably altered, but in no case altered anything like sufficiently to fall outside the original description of the proper functions of the grade concerned.

Moreover, the contrary conclusion would fly in the face of common sense. Although doubtless all of us, being conservative (with a small 'c') by nature, desire nothing better than to be left to deepen our accustomed ruts, and hate change, a tax officer has no right to remain in perpetuity doing one defined type of tax work in one particular way. At any moment he may be required to switch, for example, to Schedule D work, or, I assume, to some type of taxation work entirely outside the Income and Corporation Taxes Act 1970. It seems to me that if it is perfectly legitimate for the board to effect such changes, which would affect every single aspect of the working life of a tax officer, and not merely the way he is required to carry out one set of functions, it would be surprising in the extreme if it could not say that he was to carry out what he was doing, precisely and exactly what he was doing, but to come out of the horse and buggy age and use the computer to assist him to do it.

The foregoing is really the end of the plaintiffs' main case. But I must note a special point raised by counsel for the board. When, thanks to the 'shower of confetti', the letters of appointment and signed schedules were obtained in respect of each of the plaintiffs, it transpired that the following was one of the 'Main Conditions of Service' of each of them, namely:

a 'You will understand that the Crown, in consequence of its constitutional position, has the right to change its officers' conditions of service at any time, and that officers hold their appointments at the pleasure of the Crown and cannot therefore demand a period of notice as of right when their appointments are terminated. Nevertheless a period of notice will normally be given as specified below.'

b Counsel did not seek to rely on the Crown's constitutional rights in relation to employment, but did rely on this provision (so far as it goes) as a contractual term of the employment. To this counsel for the plaintiffs retorted that, whatever it was, it was not a contractual term, being a mere statement of what, rightly or wrongly, the Crown said its constitutional position was, and that, as a matter of fact, it was an incorrect statement of the position. I see the force of the contention of counsel for the plaintiffs, but the difficulty I feel is that this clause is expressly stated to be one of the 'Main c Conditions of Service', although the way in which the clauses are set out in the schedule applying to the appointment of the fourth plaintiff makes this particular point less clear. However, doing the best I can, I think that, even if this is to be taken merely as a statement of what the Crown erroneously supposes is the position, this was intended to be a binding provision of the terms of employment.

I can well see the necessity of such a clause, for the reason that, since all civil servants' d duties are defined by the grade which they occupy, it must be appropriate that from time to time the duties appropriate to particular grades should be varied. I do not think that it would be practicable to run the Civil Service as a whole if the duties were fixed and immutable. However, like counsel for the board, I do not really think that, at the end of the day, this clause is of major importance here. Counsel did not claim that the Crown could revise the duties appropriate to the grade of a taxing officer so as, in effect, to e include that of maintaining the hothouse at Kew. Whatever, therefore, be the limits on the Crown's power in this regard, it is accepted that there are limits. And for present purposes it is quite sufficient to rely on the ordinary duties of a taxing officer, for example, as confined to the implementation of the machinery for the recovery of tax through Schedule E by any appropriate method, and those of a clerical assistant as assisting in the clerkly duties of the office.

f I now have to deal with a quite different matter, but one with which I can deal very shortly. As soon as the plaintiffs made it clear that they were unwilling to work COP 1 and would not do so, the board made it clear that (i) it would not allow the plaintiffs to continue to work manually, as they desired, and (ii) that it would not pay the plaintiffs so long as they refused to work COP 1.

At the same time, the board also made it perfectly clear that it was not dismissing the g plaintiffs, and that the plaintiffs were free to return to work at any moment they chose, provided, of course, that they were willing to comply with the requirement to operate COP 1.

The plaintiffs' case on this is that that action, whatever name may be given to it, is properly 'suspension', and that, under their terms of service, it is not possible for the board to suspend them unless and until certain well laid down disciplinary procedures h have been carried out.

On this part of the case, which, if the plaintiffs were correct, would mean that the board would have to go on paying them all during the time they were refusing to carry out the perfectly lawful requirements of their employer, counsel for the board rested his case on the very simple ground that, so far as an employer and an employee are concerned, the promises of pay and work are mutually dependent. No work (or, at any rate, readiness j to perform whatever work it is the employee ought to be willing to perform if physically able to do so) no pay. This is such an obvious principle, founded on the simplest consideration of what the plaintiff would have to prove in any action for recovery of pay in respect of any period where he was deliberately absent from work of his own accord, that direct authority is slight, slight but sufficient. See e g *Denmark Productions Ltd v Boscobel Productions Ltd* [1968] 3 All ER 513 at 527–528, [1969] 1 QB 699 at 731–732 per

Winn LJ, *Secretary of State for Employment v ASLEF (No 2)* [1972] 2 All ER 949 at 966–
967, [1972] 2 QB 455 at 491–492 per Lord Denning MR, and in particular the unreported *a*
Scottish case of *Laurie v British Steel Corp* (23 February 1978), a decision of Lord Cowie. I
am certain that on this aspect of the law there is no difference between that of Scotland
and that of England, and what Lord Cowie said is as follows:

> 'It seems to me that, assuming that the pursuers were in material breach of their
> contracts in June 1976, there were certain remedies open to the defenders, and they
> could have exercised them if they had so desired. It does not follow, however, that, *b*
> because the defenders did not exercise their remedies, the pursuers have the right to
> demand performance of the defenders' part of the contract when they have not
> carried out their own part. In principle it does not seem to me to matter that the
> defenders have not taken the formal step of rescinding the contract. If the pursuers
> have not carried out their obligations, they cannot sue for performance by the
> defenders of their obligations. No reference is made in any of the cases to the *c*
> necessity of rescinding the contract before putting forward the defence that the
> other party cannot sue for performance because he has not fulfilled his own
> obligations. In my opinion it is not necessary to do so, and in these circumstances, if
> the defenders can establish a material breach of contract by the pursuers in June
> 1976, the latter would have no right of action to enforce payment by the defenders
> of their salaries or indeed to obtain the declarator sought.' *d*

He then stated that, apart from certain authorities he had already referred to, this
approach seemed to be consistent with various Scottish cases which he then quoted and
he concluded by repelling the pursuers' first plea-in-law.

Accordingly, there is nothing at all in any suggestion that the board was somehow
obliged to resort to suspension through disciplinary procedures before it was free of any *e*
obligation to pay the plaintiffs' wages. I think that any suggestion to the contrary is really
shocking to common sense.

With none of these cases, or the law as therein stated, did counsel for the plaintiffs
quarrel. He took an entirely different point. Granted that the law was as so stated,
nevertheless it was possible, he submitted, and I agree with this submission, for the board
to have contracted itself out of the right to refuse to pay for periods when the employee *f*
is unwilling to do the work for which he is being paid.

For this proposition he relied first on paras 47 and 49 of the Handbook for Information
and Guidance of the Staff of the Inland Revenue Department, which procedures were
asserted by the statement of claim to form part of the terms and conditions of the
plaintiffs' contract of service and, despite a formal denial in the defence, this was not
really controverted by the board. Those paragraphs, so far as material, read: *g*

> '47. The Board have power to suspend any officer from duty and they will use
> this power where serious misconduct is alleged or where an officer is arrested on
> any charge. In a case requiring immediate action an officer may be suspended by
> the Head of his Office or, in a local office, by the officer in charge. Suspension from
> duty carries with it suspension of pay for the time being, which may, in a case
> involving the possibility of loss of Crown moneys, extend to pay due, but not issued, *h*
> for the period prior to suspension. In arriving at their final decision in the case of an
> officer under suspension, the Board will determine whether or not pay shall be
> granted for the actual period of suspension or any part thereof . . .
>
> 49. Except in cases which may give rise to criminal proceedings, any charge of
> misconduct which is brought against an officer will be communicated to him in
> writing and he will be required to submit a written reply thereto which will be *j*
> considered before disciplinary action is taken. Suspension in appropriate cases . . .
> will not be delayed pending such representations. If the officer makes a request to
> that effect in his written reply to the charge he will be given an opportunity to
> represent his case orally before a senior officer other than his immediate superior
> and may be assisted in his representations by a friend or Association representative
> . . .'

a   Now the crucial point in the present case is that the board did not suspend any of the plaintiffs from duty, as it undoubtedly might have done. Indeed, from first to last the board made it perfectly clear that so far as the board was concerned the plaintiffs were free to return to work at any moment, provided that they carried out their duties in accordance with the board's requirements, which I have held to be perfectly lawful. But that, submitted counsel for the plaintiffs, did not matter, and in support he cited *Gorse v Durham CC* [1971] 2 All ER 666, [1971] 1 WLR 775 for the proposition that it did not

b   matter what label the board might give to what it had done: what it had in fact effected was a suspension. This would not directly assist him on the question of pay, but he then submitted that that suspension was an illegal one, since the correct procedures had not been carried out. Accordingly, the board could not rely on the suspension in any way.

   However, I do not think that *Gorse's* case, on analysis, avails him in the slightest. What happened in that case was that teachers refused to continue to supervise school meals,

c   which was a proper part of their duties. The relevant education committee passed a recommendation which included the words 'Any teacher refusing to undertake the supervision of school meals be suspended and no salary accrue to the teacher as from the date of suspension'. However, the relevant provisions in the terms of service provided that there should be no loss of salary if reinstatement followed suspension. In order to obviate this possibility, the employers attempted to devise an alternative form of wording

d   to disguise the fact of suspension. In these circumstances the judge concluded ([1971] 2 All ER 666 at 675, [1971] 1 WLR 775 at 785): 'The fact is that it was suspension, but the suspension procedure was not used.' And that, if I may say so, on the facts of that case, and the conduct of the employers, was an inescapable conclusion.

   What is further interesting about that case is the manner in which it was argued on behalf of the employers. No such argument as that which counsel acknowledges to be

e   clearly correct, no work no pay, was ever placed before the court. Not only were the cases dealing with this point not cited, but the wholly different argument was presented that the plaintiffs had repudiated their contracts (which was correct), that the county council had accepted that repudiation (which it most clearly had not), and that in consequence for the three and a half days in question there was no contract between the parties at all. No contract, therefore no pay due under it.

f   Whatever might be the merits of such an argument, it was an impossible one on the facts of the case. In this case it seems to me that from the first the board went out of its way to ensure that there should be no suspension, and there never was any. It may be unfortunate that, since there are many matters affecting an employee which depend on the precise length of service which he has had overall, obviously the time during which he has been absent from work through his own choice will not count towards any of

g   such periods. It is of course true that the same result is achieved as a result of suspension. But that is neither here nor there. Why anybody should imagine that periods of deliberate abstention from work should count as if the service had continued during that period escapes me. It is quite plain that as a matter of equity they should not.

   In the result, therefore, this action falls to be dismissed.

h   *Action dismissed.*

Solicitors: *Russell Jones & Walker* (for the plaintiffs); *Solicitor of Inland Revenue*.

Hazel Hartman   Barrister.

Beacon Carpets Ltd v Kirby and another   *a*

COURT OF APPEAL, CIVIL DIVISION
LAWTON, SLADE AND BROWNE-WILKINSON LJJ
7, 8, 9 MARCH, 4 APRIL 1984

Landlord and tenant – Covenant – Insurance – Fire – Landlord covenanting to insure in full value – Tenant covenanting to pay additional rent to cover premiums – Landlord covenanting in ***b*** *case of destruction or damage to premises to apply insurance moneys received in reinstating premises – Policy naming insured as landlord and tenant 'for their respective rights and interests' – Premises destroyed by fire – Premises underinsured – Tenant not wishing to occupy premises if rebuilt – Landlord deciding not to rebuild – Tenant surrendering lease to landlord – Right of tenant to damages for landlord's breach of covenant to insure in full value – Rights of landlord and tenant to insurance moneys.*   ***c***

In 1972 the landlords let a warehouse to the tenants for a term of 14 years. The lease provided that in addition to the ordinary rent the tenants were to pay a sum of money equal to the amount which the landlords might expend in insuring the demised premises against fire and other perils, and the landlords covenanted to keep the premises fully insured against loss or damage by fire and other perils and in the case of destruction of or ***d*** damage to the premises to expend or lay out with all convenient speed all insurance moneys received in rebuilding or reinstating the premises. The landlords insured the premises for £30,000 plus £3,000 to cover two years' rent and architects' and surveyors' fees. The policy named the insured as being the landlords and the tenants 'for their respective rights and interests'. The premises were substantially underinsured, the proper sum necessary to reinstate them in the event of total loss being about £50,000. In July ***e*** 1977 the premises were destroyed by fire, and of the total sum paid by the insurance company £26,484 was available for reconstruction. In November 1978 the tenants made it clear that they would not wish to occupy the building even if it were to be reconstructed and the landlords thereupon ceased to take any further step to reconstruct the building. On 5 October 1979 the tenants brought an action against the landlords claiming damages for breach of covenant by the landlords to keep the premises fully insured and to rebuild ***f*** with all convenient speed after the fire. The writ in the action was subsequently amended to include a claim for the whole of the insurance moneys. On 29 October the insurance company paid over the balance of the insurance moneys, amounting to £26,484, which was put into a joint account in the names of the parties' solicitors. In December the tenants unconditionally released half that sum to the landlords, and in March 1980 they surrendered the lease to the landlords. Under the surrender the parties mutually released ***g*** each other from all liability, claims and demands in respect of all breaches of any of the covenants in the lease 'save insofar as the same are the subject of the Action'. In 1981 the landlords resold the premises for £20,000 without having reconstructed the building on the site. The trial judge awarded the plaintiffs £2 nominal damages for breach of the covenant to insure to the full value but dismissed their claim for breach by the landlords of their covenant to reinstate the premises and their claim to the insurance moneys. The ***h*** tenants appealed.

Held – (1) The conduct of the parties was consistent with a tacit assumption by both sides that there was to be no rebuilding and that the parties were expecting either to agree terms of surrender or to establish claims in the insurance moneys. Moreover, the *j* unconditional release to the landlords of half the insurance moneys was wholly inconsistent with a continuing claim by the tenants for the application of those moneys in rebuilding and constituted an implied release of such claim. It followed therefore that the tenants' claim to damages for breach of covenant failed, save as to nominal damages for breach of the covenant to insure in the full value (see p 731 *g* to *j*, p 734 *e* to *g*, p 735 *h j* and p 736 *b*, post).

(2) With respect to the tenants' claim to the insurance moneys, the basic right of both the landlords and the tenants was to have the moneys applied in rebuilding for their respective benefit. However, because the parties had by their own acts released that right without agreeing how the moneys were to be dealt with, it could only be inferred that, in default of agreement, they were treating the insurance moneys as standing in the place of the building which would otherwise have been replaced. It followed that the insurance moneys belonged to the parties in shares proportionate to their respective interests in the property insured. Since their interests in the policy moneys came into existence at the date of the fire, when the right to the policy moneys arose, the respective interests would be valued as at that date. Accordingly, to that extent the appeal would be allowed and a declaration to that effect substituted (see p 732 *d* to *g* and *j* to p 733 *e*, p 734 *b* and *e* to *h*, p 735 *c* to *g* and p 736 *a b*, post); *Re King (decd), Robinson v Gray* [1963] 1 All ER 781 considered.

Notes

For application of insurance money under a covenant to insure, see 27 Halsbury's Laws (4th edn) para 349, and for cases on the subject, see 31(2) Digest (Reissue) 673–674, 5514–5530.

Cases referred to in judgment

King (decd), Re, Robinson v Gray [1963] 1 All ER 781, [1963] Ch 459, [1963] 2 WLR 629, CA; *rvsg* [1962] 2 All ER 66, [1962] 1 WLR 632.
Mumford Hotels Ltd v Wheler [1963] 3 All ER 250, [1964] Ch 117, [1963] 3 WLR 735.

Cases also cited

Brikom Investments Ltd v Carr [1979] 2 All ER 753, [1979] QB 467, CA.
Gleniffer Finance Corp Ltd v Bamar Wood and Products Ltd [1978] 2 Lloyd's Rep 49.
Hamer v Drummond (1939) 187 LT Jo 156.

Appeal

The plaintiffs, Beacon Carpets Ltd (the tenants), appealed against the decision of Russell J given on 10 November 1982 whereby he ordered that judgment be entered for the tenants for the sum of £2 nominal damages on their claim for breach of the covenant by the defendants, Malcolm Batsford Kirby and Hugh Montagu Butterworth (the landlords), to insure the premises demised by a lease dated 24 June 1972 against fire in their full reinstatement value, and rejected their claim for damages for breach by the landlords of their duty to rebuild the premises after they had been destroyed by fire with all convenient speed and also their claim to the insurance fund. The facts are set out in the judgment of Browne-Wilkinson LJ.

J Melville Williams QC and *Toby Kempster* for the tenants.
Jonathan Fulthorpe and *Martin Rose* for the landlords.

Cur adv vult

4 April. The following judgments were delivered.

BROWNE-WILKINSON LJ (giving the first judgment at the invitation of Lawton LJ). This is an appeal from Russell J who dismissed a claim by the former tenants of a warehouse in Bournemouth relating to the landlords' failure to reinstate those premises after they were destroyed by fire and the destination of the insurance moneys.

Under a lease dated 24 June 1972 Mr Kirby and Mr Butterworth (the landlords) let the premises to Beacon Carpets Ltd (the tenants) for a term of 14 years from 1 June 1972. The original rent was £1,500 per annum with provision for rent reviews. Clause 1 of the lease provided that in addition to the ordinary rent the tenants would pay—

'by way of further or additional rent from time to time a sum or sums of money equal to the amount which the Lessors may expend in effecting or maintaining the insurance of the demised premises against loss or damage by fire explosion and other perils together with a sum sufficient to cover two years rent thereof and architects' and surveyors fees to be incurred in connection with the reinstatement of any loss or damage as hereinafter mentioned . . .'

By cl 2(3) of the lease the tenants covenanted to keep the premises in repair. By cl 3(2) the landlords covenanted as follows:

'That the Lessors will at all times during the said term unless such insurance shall be vitiated by the act of the Lessee insure and keep insured the premises against loss or damage by fire explosion and other perils together with a sum sufficient to cover two years' rent thereof and architects' and surveyors' fees to be incurred in connection with the reinstatement of any loss or damage in some insurance office of repute in the full value thereof at the least in the joint names of the Lessors and the Lessee and will whenever required produce to the Lessee the policy or policies of such insurance and receipt for the last premium and FURTHER that in case of destruction of or damage to the demised premises or any part thereof the Lessors will with all convenient speed expend or lay out all moneys received in respect of such insurance in rebuilding or reinstating in a good and substantial manner the demised premises so destroyed or damaged.'

Clause 4(2) provided that if the premises were destroyed by fire the obligation to pay rent should be suspended until the premises should again be rendered fit for habitation and use.

The landlords insured the premises in the sum of £30,000 plus £3,000 to cover two years' rent and architects' and surveyors' fees. The policy named 'the insured' as the landlords and the tenants 'for their respective rights and interests'. It was common ground at the hearing that the premises had been substantially underinsured, the proper sum necessary to reinstate the premises in the event of total loss being a little over £50,000.

The premises were destroyed by fire on 16 July 1977. The total sum paid by the insurance company at a later date was £31,484, of which £2,000 was paid and applied in demolishing the shell of the building, £3,000 was on account of loss of rent and the balance of £26,484 was the sum available for reconstruction.

The landlords instructed architects in August 1977. The architects made an application for planning permission, which, to the surprise of all parties, was refused on 5 December 1977 on the grounds that the premises might be needed for road widening. A fresh application was made for planning permission for a smaller building and on 22 May 1978 planning permission for that building was granted, but only until 2 February 1986. Following receipt of that planning permission, a quotation for reconstruction was sought from a builder, who in September 1978 quoted what was thought to be an excessive figure. There ensued negotiations between the landlords' quantity surveyors and the builders, which led to the tender being reduced to a figure of £52,000 in October 1978, which figure was acceptable to the landlords.

The architects' plans for the building to be constructed included certain special features requested by the tenants. The landlords felt that the tenants should bear part of the cost of reconstruction to reflect this factor. In October 1978 they raised the question with the tenants in rather obscure terms and suggested a meeting to discuss the matter. On 31 October Mr Cross (the chairman of the tenants) wrote to Mr Kirby suggesting the possibility that the tenants might surrender their lease and agree with the landlords reasonable compensation. The proposed meeting took place on 7 November; Mr Cross made it clear that the tenants would no longer wish to occupy the building even if it were reconstructed, since it would be too small. There were preliminary discussions as to the possibility of the tenants surrendering the lease.

On 9 November Mr Cross wrote to Mr Kirby setting out the proposed terms of surrender. He pointed out that there was a substantial shortfall between the insurance

moneys and the cost of erecting the new building, which shortfall would have to be
a made good by the landlords (who were trustees of a trust) from some source. He pointed
out that the building which was to be erected was, in certain respects, tailored to the
special needs of the tenants, and if the lease were to be surrendered a cheaper building
could be put up which might command a profit rental. He suggested that, if there were
to be a surrender, the trustees would be free to put up such building as they wished and
could afford and let it at a much higher figure than would be payable under the existing
b lease. He confirmed that the proposed building would be too small and too restricting
for the business needs of the tenants. Bearing those matters in mind he offered to
surrender the lease to the landlords on payment of a sum of £15,000 to the tenants.

In a letter dated 13 November Mr Kirby rejected the suggestion for a surrender on
terms that the landlords should pay the tenants compensation and suggested that the
surrender should be on the terms that the tenants should pay the landlords compensation.
c He said that the landlords were holding the tenants to the terms of their lease and called
on the tenants to deal with the question of 'fixtures and fittings', which was the confusing
terminology applied to describe that part of the cost of reconstruction attributable to the
special needs of the tenants. Mr Cross replied on 17 November saying that, if the
landlords did not wish to take a surrender on reasonable terms, the tenants would start at
once looking for a suitable assignee of the lease; he pointed out that such assignee would
d be taking a purpose-built building primarily suitable to the tenants' business rather than
for general industrial purposes.

The correspondence as to surrender ceased at that point. However, the judge held that,
Mr Cross having made it unequivocally clear that the tenants did not wish to occupy any
building, the landlords thereupon ceased to take any further step to reconstruct the
building. In fact at no stage thereafter did the tenants call on the landlords to reconstruct;
e the site remained vacant.

Immediately after the fire the tenants had been temporarily housed in accommodation
provided by the local authority. They stayed in that temporary accommodation until
they found permanent alternative premises in June 1979.

Negotiations with the insurers had been taking place and they continued down to
October 1979. Apart from a sum of £2,000 used on demolition and £3,000 on account
f of rent, no insurance moneys had been paid over prior to 5 October 1979 when the writ
and statement of claim were served. The balance of the insurance moneys amounting to
£26,484 were paid over by the insurance company on 29 October 1979 and put into a
joint account in the names of the parties' solicitors. There was no agreement as to the
basis on which the moneys in the joint account were to be held, save that it was 'entirely
without prejudice to any of the issues involved in this dispute'.

g Shortly after 29 October the landlords' solicitors wrote to the tenants' solicitors
complaining of the tenants' refusal to release the insurance moneys; as a result, it was
alleged, the life tenant under the trust of which they were trustees had been deprived of
income and they claimed that the landlords were entitled to claim damages on that
account. On 6 December the tenants' solicitors wrote saying that the tenants had
reconsidered their attitude regarding moneys on deposit in their joint names and
h informed them that the tenants were now 'prepared to release such monies to your clients
subject to retention on deposit in joint names of the sum of £13,000 representing
approximately one half of the funds'. Following that letter £13,000 plus the appropriate
interest was retained and the balance of the moneys plus interest was released to the
landlords.

On 20 March 1980 the tenants surrendered the lease to the landlords. The surrender
j took the form of an assignment and surrender to the landlords of the premises demised
by the lease 'to the intent that the term of years granted by the said Lease may merge and
be extinguished in the reversion immediately expectant thereon'. By cl 2 of the surrender
the landlords released the tenants from—

> 'all liability claims and demands in respect of all breaches of any of the covenants
> contained in or otherwise arising out of the said Lease, save insofar as the same are

the subject of the Action between the [landlords] and the [tenants] in the High
Court of Justice 1979 B. No. 4762.'   *a*

By cl 3 the tenants released the landlords from all such liability in the same terms mutatis
mutandis.

In 1981 the landlords sold the premises for £20,000 without ever having reconstructed
the building on the site.

By the statement of claim served on 5 October 1979 the tenants allege breach by the
landlords of the covenant to keep the premises insured in the full reinstatement value   *b*
thereof and that by reason of that breach the landlords did not receive sufficient moneys
to rebuild or reinstate the premises. They further allege that the landlords had failed to
expend or lay out all moneys received in rebuilding or reinstating the premises. They
then allege that the tenants had—

> 'lost the benefit of the said Lease from the date upon which the [landlords] could   *c*
> and should have completed the rebuilding of the premises if they had complied
> with the said covenants until the end of their said term.'

They then plead that the tenants had suffered loss or damage. Such damage was
particularised as the value of the unexpired term of the lease and consequential loss,
being loss of profit caused by enforced occupation of inadequate premises from 16 July
1978 until 1 June 1979. They also claimed certain special damages. It is to be noted that   *d*
the statement of claim is framed as a general claim of failure to reconstruct; it is not in
terms limited to a failure to reconstruct 'with all convenient speed'. It is also to be noted
that the statement of claim as originally served contained no claim to the insurance
moneys as such; it will be recalled that the insurance moneys were not paid over until
after 5 October 1979.

A complicated defence and counterclaim was served. Nothing turns on its exact   *e*
wording. However, it is important to note that in the counterclaim the landlords claim
the following relief: 'An order that the Plaintiff do take all necessary steps to effect an
absolute and unqualified release of the insurance monies into the hands of the Defendants
forthwith.' The defence and counterclaim was served on 14 December 1979, ie well
before the date of the surrender of the lease.

On 14 September 1981 (ie long after the date of the surrender) the tenants reamended   *f*
their statement of claim to include the following:

> 'If, as is contended by the Defendants and denied by the Plaintiffs the Defendants
> were not obliged to rebuild or reinstate the demised premises, the Plaintiffs are
> entitled to the insurance moneys received, totalling £28,484 or alternatively to a
> proportion thereof and further to the sum of £13,516 or a proportion thereof, being   *g*
> the amount by which the insurance moneys received fell short of the estimated re-
> building costs of £42,000.'

That was the first occasion on which the tenants' claims in the pleadings included a claim
to the insurance moneys as opposed to claims for damages for breach of covenant.

It was in that state of the pleadings that the matter came on for trial before Russell J.
The trial lasted many days and we were told by counsel on the appeal that little attention   *h*
was paid to the complicated pleadings in the case. It is clear that, despite the width of the
pleadings, the tenants' claim for damages for breach of covenant before the judge was
not that the landlords had failed to reconstruct at all, but that they had failed to do so
'with all convenient speed'. The judge said that the case made by counsel for the tenants
was that the landlords should have erected the building by the end of October 1978 and
that the failure so to do gave rise to damages being, inter alia, loss of profits from that   *j*
date until the tenants obtained their new permanent accommodation in June 1979. The
judge said that the question he had to answer was whether the building should have been
erected at some date before June 1979. In those circumstances, there seems to have been
no investigation of the question whether the failure to re-erect the building at any time
constituted a breach of the covenant. Many days of the trial were taken up with detailed

evidence on this narrow issue and on the issue of loss of profits during the period ending
a in June 1979. The tenants claimed, in the alternative, that they were entitled to the
whole of the insurance moneys in reliance on the decision of the Court of Appeal in *Re
King (decd), Robinson v Gray* [1963] 1 All ER 781, [1963] Ch 459.

The judge, in a long and detailed judgment, found that the landlords had not been
guilty of the delay alleged. For reasons which will appear, it is not necessary for me to set
out his reasons. It is enough to say that the judge formed the view (1) that there was no
b actionable delay down to the meeting on 7 November 1979, (2) that the reason why the
building was not reconstructed thereafter was because Mr Cross had made it clear that
the tenants did not want to occupy the building if re-erected, (3) that, had it not been for
Mr Cross's attitude, the landlords would have reconstructed the building by June 1979.
As to the claim to the insurance moneys, the judge held that the landlords were entitled
to retain them. The judge held that the admitted failure to insure in the full value was a
c breach of covenant, but awarded only £2 nominal damages.

Damages for breach of covenant
The notice of appeal (and counsel for the tenants in opening the appeal) continued to
present the claim to damages for breach of covenant on the same basis as that advanced
before the judge. It was pointed out at an early stage of the hearing of the appeal that the
d covenant in cl 2(3) was to expend and lay out all moneys 'received' in respect of the
insurance, which covenant could not be broken until the insurance moneys had in fact
been received: see *Re King (decd)* [1962] 2 All ER 66 at 77, [1962] 1 WLR 632 at 644. The
insurance moneys were not received until 29 October 1979 and no breach of covenant
could have occurred before that date. Accordingly, the main question decided by the
judge relating to the delay prior to June 1979 was irrelevant, since no claim to loss of
e profit down to June 1979 could be maintained.

Faced with this difficulty, counsel for the tenants sought to put his case on a different
basis not argued below, viz that the landlords were in breach of covenant, since, even
after receipt of the insurance moneys, the landlords never applied the moneys in
rebuilding. He submitted that, if the landlords had rebuilt, the tenants could have sold
the residue of their term with the building on the site and that accordingly they lost the
f value of the residue of the term. Since this point was not argued below, there is little
evidence relating to it. But in my judgment there is sufficient to demonstrate that the
submission is not correct.

The judge found that, had it not been for Mr Cross's statement that the tenants no
longer required the building for their own occupation, it would have been rebuilt by
June 1979. The attitude adopted by the tenants did not in itself amount to a release by
g the tenants of their right to have the premises rebuilt; indeed, Mr Cross in the letter of
17 November 1968 plainly indicated that if there was no surrender the tenants would
look for an assignee of the term. But thereafter the tenants never suggested that the
landlords should in fact rebuild; to my mind the conduct of the parties is only consistent
with a tacit assumption by both sides that there was to be no rebuilding and that the
parties were expecting either to agree terms of surrender or to establish claims in the
h insurance moneys. The position is put beyond doubt by the agreement of the tenants to
the unconditional release to the landlords of half the insurance moneys; this was wholly
inconsistent with a continuing claim by the tenants that the insurance moneys should be
applied in rebuilding and must have constituted an implied release of such right.

Counsel for the tenants further submitted that the landlord had committed an
anticipatory breach of covenant by refusing to rebuild. This argument lacks any factual
j basis. There is no evidence that the landlords ever told the tenants that they would not
rebuild. On the contrary, as late as October 1979 the landlords were saying that they
wanted the insurance moneys to be held in the joint names earmarked 'for reinstatement
or compensation'.

Therefore in my judgment the tenants' claim to damages for breach of covenant fails,
save as to nominal damages for breach of the covenant to insure in the full value.

The insurance moneys

Before dealing with the substance of this issue, I must first mention one point, namely *a* the suggestion that the surrender of the lease operated to surrender any right of the tenants in the insurance moneys. Although I find it extraordinary that the surrender does not deal expressly with the insurance moneys, in my judgment the surrender did not in any way affect the parties' rights in these moneys. First, the surrender contained mutual releases from liability; if it was intended to affect the insurance moneys at all, it would have operated to extinguish not only the tenants' but also the landlords' interests, *b* leaving the moneys in the joint names without a beneficial owner. This would be a remarkable result. I am satisfied that this is not the result because the words in cll 2 and 3 of the surrender, 'save insofar as the same are the subject of the Action', operate to prevent the surrender of any claim which was in issue in the action. Although at the date of the surrender the statement of claim put forward no claim to the insurance moneys, the defence and counterclaim did. Therefore, there being a claim in the action relating *c* to the insurance moneys, on the true construction of the surrender, such claims were excluded from the mutual releases in the surrender and the parties' rights in those moneys (whatever they were) remained unaffected.

What were those rights? The basic right of both the landlords and the tenants was to have the insurance moneys applied in rebuilding for their respective benefit: see *Mumford Hotels Ltd v Wheler* [1963] 3 All ER 250, [1964] Ch 117 and *Re King (decd)* [1963] 1 All *d* ER 781 at 795, [1963] Ch 459 at 492 per Upjohn LJ. Due to the unusual way in which the parties have dealt with the matter, they have managed to reach a position where they have by their own acts released the right to have the moneys applied in rebuilding without agreeing how the moneys are to be dealt with. In the circumstances, it is perhaps not surprising that the legal result of their unusual actions is uncertain.

Not without hesitation, I have come to the conclusion that the moneys belonged to *e* the landlords and the tenants in shares proportionate to their respective interests in the property insured. It seems to me that the only explanation for the parties' conduct is that, once it was clear that the tenants did not want to occupy the building if rebuilt, both parties assumed that it would not be rebuilt and were, in default of agreement, treating the insurance moneys as standing in the place of the building which would otherwise have been replaced. If this analysis is correct, the tenants would have had the value of *f* their term of years and the freeholders would have had the rent. On this approach, the decision in *Re King* is irrelevant, since that case deals only with rights in insurance moneys once the prime purpose of rebuilding has been wholly frustrated by the actions of a third party and does not affect the case where the parties are treating the insurance moneys as standing in the place of the building.

If, on the other hand, the principle in *Re King* applies, I reach the same conclusion. In *g* *Re King* the lessee had covenanted (a) to keep the premises in repair, (b) at her own expense to insure the premises against fire in the joint names of the lessor and lessee, and (c) to apply the insurance moneys in rebuilding. Accordingly, all the obligations as to repair and insurance fell on the lessee. The premises were destroyed by fire and the insurance moneys paid into the joint names. Rebuilding was prevented by the compulsory purchase of the premises. The Court of Appeal (Lord Denning MR *h* dissenting) held that the lessee was entitled to the whole of the insurance moneys. Upjohn LJ held that the lessor's only interest in the policy moneys was as security for the performance by the lessee of her obligations to repair and reinstate, and that, the premiums on the policy having been paid by the lessee to meet the expense of performing the lessee's obligations, the policy moneys belonged to her. Diplock LJ held that the only interest insured by the policy was the lessee's interest and therefore the moneys belonged *j* to the lessee.

Applying those principles to the present case, it is impossible to hold that the insurance moneys belonged wholly to the landlords or to the tenants. Although the tenants, indirectly, paid the premiums, it was the landlords' obligation to apply the insurance moneys in reinstatement; therefore the policy was directly in support of discharging the a landlords' obligations and they must have an interest. On the other hand, the tenants indirectly paid the premiums and the basic duty to repair lay on the tenants. Therefore, in my judgment, the tenants must also have an interest. The apportionment of obligations between landlord and tenant in this case is quite different from that in *Re King* and adopting the approach of Upjohn LJ leads to the conclusion that both have an interest in the insurance moneys. The policy was effected in the joint names of the landlords and the tenants 'for their respective rights and interests', reflecting the fact that both did

b indeed have an insurable interest. Therefore the approach of Diplock LJ leads to the same result.

If both the landlords and the tenants have an interest in the policy moneys, in my judgment those interests can only be quantified by reference to their respective interests in the property, the subject matter of the insurance. The interests in the policy moneys came into existence at the date of the fire, when the right to the policy moneys arose.

c Therefore the respective interests should be valued as at that date. Counsel for the tenants suggested that, as there was only temporary planning permission for the building which expired at approximately the same date as the lease, it was right to hold that the interests in the building (and therefore the insurance moneys) were equal. I do not accept this: it is common knowledge that temporary planning permissions are very frequently extended and it is impossible to forecast how long the building would have stood for.

d I would therefore allow the appeal on this aspect of the case and substitute a declaration that the sum of £26,484 representing the insurance moneys belongs to the landlords and the tenants in shares proportionate to their respective interests in the demised premises (land and buildings) immediately before the fire. In default of agreement, this will involve (i) a valuation of the freehold with vacant possession on that date (£X) and (ii) a valuation of the leasehold on that date (£Y), both valuations being on the basis that there

e was unconditional planning permission. The sum of £26,484 will then be divisible by paying Y/Xths thereof to the tenants (plus interest actually received on the sum so paid) and paying the balance to the landlords to the extent that they have not already received them.

LAWTON LJ. During his submissions in this case counsel for the landlords said that at

f the trial counsel by mutual consent had released themselves from the pleadings. As the pleadings had not adequately defined the issues, this was not surprising; nevertheless this was an irregularity which should not have occurred, and which the trial judge should not have allowed to occur. In my opinion the departure added to the length of the trial and the proceedings in this court. Pleadings should identify the issues. If they do not, the parties may explore irrelevant issues. This is what happened in this case. The issue

g investigated over about seven days before the trial judge was misconceived as to both its legal and factual basis. At a trial departures from the pleadings should be identified to the judge and leave obtained for them to be made. If the justice of the case requires them to be allowed, they will be; and, when they are, the appropriate amendments to the pleadings should be made and a copy handed to the associate.

In this court counsel for the tenants, after some discussion, accepted that the tenants'

h case as put before the judge was founded on a misconstruction of the lease and a wrong view of the credibility of one of the two landlords. The judge's findings of fact and rulings on law as the case was then put were justified. But, when the legal consequences of his findings of fact, the admitted facts and the documents were considered in this court, a different case altogether appeared.

In my judgment the provisions of the lease relating to insurance were for the benefit

j of both the tenants and the landlords. The tenants had covenanted 'throughout the term to keep the premises . . . in good and substantial repair'. There was no term in the repairing covenant to excuse them from this obligation if the premises were destroyed or damaged by fire. Provision, however, was made by way of insurance to provide a fund out of which the cost of rebuilding could be met. The landlords were to take out insurance at the expense of the tenants and in the event of a fire 'with all convenient speed to expend or lay out all moneys received in respect of such insurance in rebuilding or reinstating . . .' The lease did not require the landlords to rebuild or reinstate; but *a* under it they were to expend or lay out the money received. In the event the landlords did start to make arrangements for rebuilding. Once the demised premises had been rebuilt rent, which under the lease was suspended pending rebuilding, would once again be payable and at the end of the term the landlords would have a building which could be let with vacant possession.

When the fire occurred on 16 July 1977 both the tenants and landlords acquired *b* interests in the money which the insurers were liable to pay, but it was not an interest which could be quantified then in terms of money. It was an interest to see that the money was used for the agreed purpose.

By the end of November 1978 the tenants had no intention of reoccupying the premises if they were rebuilt and the landlords did not intend to rebuild unless they had to. Both parties hoped the lease would be surrendered on terms which were mutually *c* acceptable. No such terms were agreed until 30 March 1980. By letter dated 17 November 1978 the tenants told the landlords that if their suggested terms of surrender were not accepted they would exercise their right to assign their interest under the lease. After this the lease continued to take effect as to rights and obligations; but it was understood and accepted that the tenants would not for the time being insist on the landlords continuing with the rebuilding plans. *d*

In October 1978 the insurers paid the insurance money in respect of the fire. It was held on joint account by the parties' solicitors. At that time the legal rights and obligations of the parties were as follows: the tenants could have insisted that the rebuilding should go on (some preliminary work had already been done), and if they had done so the landlords would have had to expend or lay out the money in respect of rebuilding. Shortly afterwards, by letter dated 4 December 1979, the tenants' solicitors agreed *e* unconditionally to release half the money to the landlords. The legal consequence of this was that the tenants released the landlords from their obligation to expend or lay out the money in respect of rebuilding. What had been a fund in which both parties had an interest how it was to be expended for their mutual benefit become a fund to which the landlords were entitled to at least half. Since the fund had been created for the purpose of protecting the interests of both parties, and one of them had asked and received money *f* for what had been no more than an interest how the whole fund was to be expended, what they were doing was impliedly agreeing to look to the fund as a source of money for themselves in proportion to the values of their respective interests, not as a source of money to be expended on rebuilding. In my judgment their interests should be valued in the way suggested by Browne-Wilkinson LJ in his judgment. I too would allow the appeal. *g*

SLADE LJ. I have had the advantage of reading in draft the judgments of Lawton and Browne-Wilkinson LJJ. I agree with them and only wish to add some observations regarding the tenants' claim to share in the insurance moneys.

The decision of this court in *Re King (decd), Robinson v Gray* [1963] 1 All ER 781, [1963] Ch 459 establishes no universally applicable principle governing the beneficial ownership *h* of a policy of insurance effected in joint names by a landlord or tenant, pursuant to a covenant contained in a lease. In determining this question in any given case, the first task of the court is, in my opinion, to ascertain the parties' intentions by reference to the relevant provisions of the lease in question and to any relevant provisions of the policy itself.

In his dissenting judgment in *Re King* [1963] 1 All ER 781 at 790, [1963] Ch 459 at *j* 484 Lord Denning MR rejected the tenant's submission that the only reason for placing the policy in joint names was to provide security for the performance by the tenant of his covenant to rebuild and reinstate. With reference to this argument, he said:

'The reason for [joint names] seems to me obvious. It was to ensure that both landlord and tenant were insured under the policy, each in respect of his interest in

the property. The tenant was insured in respect of his interest as leaseholder. The
a landlord was insured in respect of his interest as freeholder.'

On the particular facts in *Re King* the majority of the court drew a different inference
from that drawn by Lord Denning MR as to the parties' intentions from the reading of
the lease in question. They themselves accepted the tenant's submission to which I have
referred (see [1963] 1 All ER 781 at 795, 799, [1963] Ch 459 at 492–493, 498 per Upjohn
and Diplock LJJ). Nevertheless, Upjohn LJ in that case expressly accepted that 'The lessor
b and lessee could, of course, agree to enter into an insurance policy which would insure
their respective interests in the property' (see [1963] 1 All ER 781 at 795, [1963] Ch 459
at 492). This is what, I think, the parties in the present case agreed as between themselves,
though the insurer's obligation was to pay the policy moneys to them jointly.

The provisions of this lease are very different from those under consideration in *Re
King*. On reading it, I think it clear that it was contemplated that the policy was to be
c effected partly for the benefit of the landlords and that they would have an interest in it.
I say this for two reasons. First, the landlords were entitled, and, in default of the tenants'
agreement to the contrary, were bound, to use the policy moneys in reinstating a building
on land of which they themselves were the freeholders. Second, cl 4(2) of the lease
absolved the tenants from paying rent after the destruction of the premises by fire until
they should be rendered fit for habitation again, while the policy provided for by cl 1 of
d the lease had to include a sum sufficient to cover two years' loss of rent. On the other
hand, I think it no less clear from a reading of this lease that the tenants themselves were
intended to have an interest in the policy, for they were the persons who had the primary
obligation to repair the premises (under cl 2(3) of the lease) and who would be indirectly
providing the money for the payment of the premiums by way of additional rent. On
the proper view of this particular transaction, I feel no doubt that the reason for joint
e names was, to quote the words of Lord Denning MR in *Re King*, 'to ensure that both
landlord and tenant were insured under the policy, each in respect of his interest in the
property'. And this conclusion is entirely borne out by the terms of the policy itself,
which named the landlords and the tenants as the insured persons 'for their respective
rights and interests'. It is not suggested that the tenants failed in their obligations to pay
the appropriate additional rent to enable the policy to be maintained.
f In all the circumstances, I think it clear that if, without fault of either party,
supervening circumstances had made it impossible for the landlords and the tenants in
the present case to use the insurance moneys for the purpose contemplated by the lease,
namely the reinstatement of the premises, the moneys would have belonged to them
proportionately according to their interests. As Lord Denning MR put it in *Re King*
[1963] 1 All ER 781 at 791, [1963] Ch 459 at 486:
g
'If the covenant had been performed, the benefit of these moneys would have
come to both landlord and tenant in the shape of the rebuilt factory, and they would
both have benefited proportionately to their interests. So also when, owing to an
unforeseen event, the covenant is not performed, the moneys should be divided in
like proportions.'

h As things turned out, supervening events did not make it impossible for the insurance
moneys to be laid out in the reinstatement of the premises. Instead, I think the inevitable
inference from the arrangements made between the parties from December 1979 to
March 1980, in particular those relating to the unconditional release of one-half of the
insurance moneys to the landlords in December 1979 and the surrender of the lease, is
that the parties tacitly agreed that the insurance moneys then standing in their joint
j names would not be used for this purpose. There was, therefore, a mutually agreed
frustration of the original purpose of the policy.

With a casualness which is hard to understand, the landlords and the tenants never
even attempted to reach any explicit agreement as to the ultimate destination of the
balance of the policy moneys not paid over to the landlords, either at the time of the
payment in in December 1979 or when the negotiations for the surrender of the lease

were finally concluded in March 1980. However, with Lawton and Browne-
Wilkinson LJJ, I think that the only inference which can be drawn from the parties'   *a*
conduct over the period December 1979 to March 1980 is that, having abandoned all
thought of reinstatement, they were implicitly agreeing to look to the fund, still standing
in their joint names, as a source of money for themselves in proportion to the values of
their respective interests. If the landlords' intentions were in truth different from this,
they would have only themselves to blame for not saying so before the surrender was
finally agreed.   *b*
    For these reasons, and the further reasons given by Lawton and Browne-Wilkinson LJJ,
I too would allow this appeal and make a declaration in the terms indicated by Browne-
Wilkinson LJ.

*Appeal allowed; case remitted to a master of the Queen's Bench Division to evaluate the tenants'
interest in the insurance fund along the lines set out in Browne-Wilkinson LJ's judgment.*   *c*

Solicitors: *Atkins Walter & Locke,* Dorking (for the tenants): *J M B Turner & Co,*
Bournemouth (for the landlords).

Mary Rose Plummer   Barrister.

d

e

Practice Direction

COMPANIES COURT

f

*Practice – Companies Court – Chambers – Orders – Orders drafted in chambers normally to be
engrossed without reference to parties' solicitors – Orders dismissing winding-up petitions not
normally to be drawn up.*

1. The Practice Direction dated 15 October 1979 ([1979] 3 All ER 602, [1979] 1 WLR
1413) provided in para 6 thereof, inter alia, that all orders would be drafted in the   *g*
chambers of the registrar and that a copy of the draft would be sent to the solicitors for
the parties with an appointment to settle the same. This practice has been found to be
time-consuming and unnecessary in that solicitors almost invariably approve the order
as drafted and the appointment is vacated. It has therefore been decided that in future
the normal course will be for orders drafted in the chambers of the registrar to be
engrossed and a sealed copy sent to the party having carriage of the order without any   *h*
reference to the solicitors for the parties. If, however, the draftsman considers that an
order is unusually complicated or that for any other reason an appointment to settle it is
necessary or desirable, or if any party specifically requests an appointment to settle, then
drafts will be sent in accordance with the present practice.
    2. Orders dismissing winding-up petitions will not in future be drawn up at all unless
the order contains a direction for the taxation or payment of costs or unless any party   *j*
requests that a particular order be drawn.

    By direction of the Vice-Chancellor.

11 July 1984

R v Cain

HOUSE OF LORDS

LORD FRASER OF TULLYBELTON, LORD ELWYN-JONES, LORD KEITH OF KINKEL, LORD SCARMAN AND LORD BRANDON OF OAKBROOK

23 MAY, 19 JULY 1984

Criminal law – Bankruptcy order – Appeal against order – Circumstances in which appeal lies against making of criminal bankruptcy order – Powers of Criminal Courts Act 1973, s 40(1).

Criminal law – Bankruptcy order – Jurisdiction to make order – Defendant charged and convicted of conspiracy – Defendant not charged with or admitting participation in crimes constituting overt acts of the conspiracy – Whether question of defendant's participation in crimes which were immediate cause of loss resulting from conspiracy a matter for jury to establish by verdict or for judge to determine at sentencing stage – Powers of Criminal Courts Act 1973, s 39(1)(a)(2).

The appellant was convicted on two counts of an indictment which charged him with conspiracy to steal and conspiracy to commit robbery. The indictment was a multiple indictment containing 15 counts and charging six defendants but the appellant was charged only on the two counts on which he was convicted. Although the evidence at the trial, if believed, implicated the appellant as a participant in 25 burglaries, two robberies and one attempted robbery, all of which were in pursuance of the two conspiracies of which he was convicted, he was not charged with any of them and did not ask for any of them to be taken into consideration on sentence. However, after conviction the judge expressed himself as satisfied that the appellant had participated in those crimes, that the burglaries had caused losses to the victims to a total value of £150,000 and the robberies had caused losses to a total value of £630, and the judge was able to identify a number of victims, whose loss he was able to ascertain at £98,837. The judge then made a criminal bankruptcy order against the appellant. The appellant appealed against conviction and sentence to the Court of Appeal, which dismissed his appeal and upheld the criminal bankruptcy order. The appellant appealed to the House of Lords against the criminal bankruptcy order, contending (i) that the trial judge had had no power to make the order because the appellant had never admitted committing any of the crimes alleged to have been committed in furtherance of the conspiracies nor had he admitted the loss or damage arising therefrom and (ii) that it was for the jury at trial to establish by verdict the appellant's participation in those crimes. The Crown contended that, by virtue of s 40(1)[a] of the Powers of Criminal Courts Act 1973, no appeal lay from the making of a criminal bankruptcy order.

Held – (1) A criminal bankruptcy order was, by virtue of s 50(1)[b] of the Criminal Appeal Act 1968, a 'sentence' for the purposes of that Act, and the prohibition of appeals from the making of such orders contained in s 40(1) of the 1973 Act was therefore to be construed by reference to the provisions of the 1968 Act dealing with appeals against sentence. Since the right of appeal against sentence was of fundamental importance to the subject, it was to be inferred that where Parliament prohibited such an appeal it was dealing with the discretionary power of the court to make the order and not with orders defective in law. Accordingly, the statutory prohibition of appeal in s 40(1) of the 1973 Act was to be construed as being subject to an implied limitation so that no appeal lay, save where the issue was whether the court in making the order had exceeded its statutory power. It followed that the appellant had a right of appeal (see p 738 j to p 739 b, p 741 f to j and p 742 a b and g to j, post); R v Downing (1980) 71 Cr App R 316 and R v Reilly [1982] 3 All ER 27 approved.

(2) The Crown Court had not exceeded its powers in making the criminal bankruptcy order and the appeal would be dismissed because—

---

a   Section 40(1) is set out at p 740 d, post

b   Section 50(1), so far as material, provides: 'In this Act, "sentence", in relation to an offence, includes any order made by a court when dealing with an offender . . .'

(a) it was open to the Crown Court to find that a conspiracy had resulted in loss or damage to others in circumstances where the immediate cause of the loss was a crime *a* which constituted an overt act of the conspiracy (see p 738 *j* to p 739 *b* and p 742 *b c* and g to *j*, post); *R v Reilly* [1982] 3 All ER 27 applied.

(b) since the offences which were the immediate cause of the loss or damage suffered by others were linked with the two conspiracies of which the appellant had been convicted, the judge had been entitled to find under s 39(1)(*a*)*ᶜ* of the 1973 Act that the loss suffered was the result of the two offences of which the appellant had been convicted, *b* and in the circumstances s 39(2) was irrelevant (see p 738 *j* to p 739 *b* and p 742 *d e* and g to *j*, post); *DPP v Anderson* [1978] 2 All ER 512 distinguished.

(c) s 39(1) made it clear that the process of establishing whether the loss was the result of an offence only began after the defendant had been convicted of the offence and therefore the question whether the appellant's participation in the crimes which were the immediate cause of the loss resulting from the conspiracies of which they were the *c* overt acts was a question for the judge to determine when he turned to consider sentence and not for the jury at the trial to establish by verdict. Accordingly, a criminal bankruptcy order could properly be made if it appeared to the court at that stage that the losses suffered by others were the result of any conspiracy of which the defendant had been convicted (see p 738 *j* to p 739 *b* and p 742 *f* to *j*, post).

d

Notes

For criminal bankruptcy orders, see 11 Halsbury's Laws (4th edn) para 803, and for the effect of a criminal bankruptcy order, see 3 ibid paras 1055–1100.

For the Criminal Appeal Act 1968, s 50, see 8 Halsbury's Statutes (3rd edn) 719.

For the Powers of Criminal Courts Act 1973, ss 39, 40, see 43 ibid 334, 335.

e

Cases referred to in opinions

DPP v Anderson [1978] 2 All ER 512, [1978] AC 964, [1978] 2 WLR 994, HL; *rvsg* [1978] 2 All ER 8, [1978] AC 964, [1978] 2 WLR 798, CA.

R v Downing (1980) 71 Cr App R 316, CA.

R v Reilly [1982] 3 All ER 27, [1982] QB 1208, [1982] 3 WLR 149, CA.

R v Wehner [1977] 3 All ER 553, [1977] 1 WLR 1143, CA.

f

Appeal

Douglas Roy Cain appealed with leave of the Appeal Committee of the House of Lords granted on 24 November 1983 against the decision of the Court of Appeal, Criminal Division (Lord Lane CJ, Bingham and Taylor JJ) on 28 July 1983 dismissing his appeal against the criminal bankruptcy order made against him by his Honour Judge Stable QC *g* in the Crown Court at Snaresbrook on 26 May 1982 following his conviction on indictment for the offences of conspiracy to commit burglary and conspiracy to commit robbery. The Court of Appeal refused leave to appeal but certified, under s 33(2) of the Criminal Appeal Act 1968, that a point of law of general public importance (set out at p 739g, post) was involved in the decision. The facts are set out in the opinion of Lord Scarman.

h

Robin Grey QC and *William Boyce* for the appellant.
Anthony Arlidge QC and *Christopher Ball* for the Crown.

Their Lordships took time for consideration.

j

19 July. The following opinions were delivered.

LORD FRASER OF TULLYBELTON. My Lords, I have had the advantage of reading in draft the speech of my noble and learned friend Lord Scarman. I agree with it, and for the reasons stated in it, I would dismiss the appeal.

---

c   Section 39, so far as material, is set out at p 740 *a* to *c*, post

LORD ELWYN-JONES. My Lords, I have had the advantage of reading in draft the
a speech prepared by my noble and learned friend Lord Scarman. I agree with it, and for
the reasons which he gives I would dismiss the appeal.

LORD KEITH OF KINKEL. My Lords, for the reasons given in the speech of my
noble and learned friend Lord Scarman, with which I agree, I too would dismiss the
b appeal.

LORD SCARMAN. My Lords, Douglas Roy Cain appeals, with the leave of the House,
from the dismissal by the Court of Appeal, Criminal Division, of his appeal from the
criminal bankruptcy order made against him by the Crown Court sitting at Snaresbrook.
The appellant had been convicted on indictment of two offences, conspiracy to steal and
c conspiracy to rob. It was a multiple indictment containing 15 counts and charging six
defendants. The appellant, however, was charged only on the two counts on which he
was convicted. Although the evidence at trial, if believed, implicated the appellant as a
participant in 25 burglaries, two robberies and one attempted robbery, all of which were
in pursuance of the two conspiracies of which he was convicted, he was not charged with
any of them; nor did he ask for any of them to be taken into consideration on sentence.
d   After conviction and before imposing the criminal bankruptcy order the trial judge
expressed himself as being satisfied of the following facts: (1) that the conspiracy to steal
involved a total of 29 burglaries; (2) that the conspiracy to rob involved a total of four
robberies and one attempted robbery; (3) that the appellant took part in 25 of the
burglaries, in two of the robberies and in the attempted robbery; (4) that the burglaries
in which the appellant participated caused losses to the victims of money and chattels to
e a total value of over £150,000; (5) that the robberies in which he participated caused
losses to the victims of £630. The trial judge also identified a number of the victims
whose loss he was able to ascertain and stated: 'The total of their losses was a sum of
£98,837.' A 'Schedule of offences on which convictions were returned and persons
suffering loss or damage thereby' was annexed to the order. Although the schedule is at
first sight a little difficult to follow, it is in truth perfectly clear. It states that the persons
f named therein had suffered the loss or damage specified as a result of one or other of the
two conspiracies of which the appellant had been convicted.
The appellant appealed against his convictions and sentence. The appeal against the
convictions was dismissed; the sentence (which included an eight-year term of
imprisonment) was, subject to one modification, affirmed. The only appeal which
survives into your Lordships' House is against the criminal bankruptcy order, in respect
g of which the Court of Appeal has certified a point of law of general public importance,
namely:

'Whether or not a criminal bankruptcy order can be made on a conviction for
conspiracy to steal, in relation to individual burglaries alleged to have been
committed in furtherance of the conspiracy when the defendant has never admitted
any particular burglary either by plea or other admission nor even admitted the loss
h or damage alleged to have resulted therefrom.'

The certified point faithfully reflects the course of argument in the Court of Appeal.
No question was then raised as to the jurisdiction of the Court of Appeal to hear the
appeal. The court answered in the affirmative the question now raised by its certificate,
following *R v Reilly* [1982] 3 All ER 27, [1982] QB 1208, and upheld the order.
j   Only two issues have been raised in your Lordships' House. The first is the question:
does an appeal lie at all? This is the 'appellate jurisdiction point', and the answer has to be
found in the true construction of s 40(1) of the Powers of Criminal Courts Act 1973.
Secondly, if an appeal does lie, did the trial judge exceed his powers in making the
criminal bankruptcy order? This is the 'excess of power point' and the answer is to be
found in the true construction of s 39(1) of the 1973 Act.
The statutory provisions regulating the making of a criminal bankruptcy order are
ss 39 to 41 of and Sch 2 to the 1973 Act. Section 39(1) and (2) are as follows:

'(1) Where a person is convicted of an offence before the Crown Court and it appears to the court that—(a) as a result of the offence, or of that offence taken together with any other relevant offence or offences, loss or damage (not attributable to personal injury) has been suffered by one or more persons whose identity is known to the court; and (b) the amount, or aggregate amount, of the loss or damage exceeds £15,000; the court may, in addition to dealing with the offender in any other way (but not if it makes a compensation order against him), make a criminal bankruptcy order against him in respect of the offence or, as the case may be, that offence and the other relevant offence or offences.

(2) In subsection (1) above "other relevant offence or offences" means an offence or offences of which the person in question is convicted in the same proceedings or which the court takes into consideration in determining his sentence.'

The essential precondition to the making of an order is that a person has been convicted of an offence before the Crown Court. Where this has happened, the court (represented at this stage by the sentencing judge) may proceed to make an order provided it is satisfied of the matters specified in the section, of which those relevant to this appeal are: (1) that as a result of the offence (or offences) of which the person has been convicted loss or damage has been suffered by other persons known to the court; and (2) that the amount or aggregate of their loss resulting from the offence exceeds £15,000. By s 40(1): 'No appeal shall lie against the making of a criminal bankruptcy order.' Section 41 provides for an Official Petitioner who is to exercise the functions assigned to him by Sch 2; the Director of Public Prosecutions is to be the Official Petitioner.

Schedule 2 is the bridge between the powers of the Crown Court and the bankruptcy law. Paragraph 1 applies the bankruptcy law by providing that a criminal bankruptcy order is to be treated as an act of bankruptcy commited on the date on which the order was made. The offender against whom it is made is not thereby made bankrupt. Indeed, he may never be made bankrupt. Whether he is or is not depends first on whether a bankruptcy petition is presented against him If it is, bankruptcy proceedings will begin, in which event, subject to Sch 2, he will have all the rights afforded by the law to a debtor against whom a petition is presented. These rights include the rights of appeal under s 108 of the Bankruptcy Act 1914. Specifically he can resist the proof of debt; and Sch 2 itself, by para 9, provides him with the opportunity to challenge the amount of the loss or damage which it appeared to the Crown Court others had suffered as a result of his offence. Indeed, he is given the opportunity of showing that the loss did not in fact result from his offence.

The appellate jurisdiction point

The Crown submits, relying on s 40(1), that no appeal lies from the making of a criminal bankruptcy order. The sketch which I have offered of the consequences of an order affords an obvious explanation for Parliament's prohibition of appeal. The offender has the rights of a debtor (subject to Sch 2) under the bankruptcy laws, including a civil right of appeal. Parliament may reasonably have concluded that there is no need for a criminal appeal to protect the offender. Why then should the courts think it necessary to imply into s 40(1) a limitation on the generality of its prohibition?

There is a line of cases in which the Court of Appeal has implied a limitation. The court has construed the subsection as prohibiting only an appeal 'on the merits'. The judges have drawn a distinction between 'merits' and 'jurisdiction'. If the appeal is on the merits, a term which is used (unhappily) to describe an appeal against the exercise of the court's discretion, no appeal lies. If it be to the 'jurisdiction', a term which is used (unhappily) to describe the statutory requirements to be met before the power can be exercised, an appeal, it has been held, does lie. This distinction has been recognised and acted on in *R v Downing* (1980) 71 Cr App R 316 and *R v Reilly* [1982] 3 All ER 27, [1982] QB 1208.

The point reached your Lordships' House in *DPP v Anderson* [1978] 2 All ER 512, [1978] AC 964. It was dealt with briefly by Ormrod LJ when the case was in the Court of Appeal (see [1978] 2 All ER 8, [1978] AC 964), but was not, it would seem, the subject of

any argument in the House, where it was assumed that appellate jurisdiction exists where
a the question raised by the appeal is whether or not the sentencing judge has exceeded his
power in making the order. Ormrod LJ, in the course of delivering the judgment of the
Court of Appeal, made a comment which succinctly summarises the attitude to the
statutory prohibition of appeal developed by the Court of Appeal. The significant feature
of his comment is that it shows him to have seen the problem of the true construction of
s 40(1) as having to be solved in the light of the wider context of the general law relating
b to criminal appeals. Ormrod LJ said ([1978] 2 All ER 8 at 10, [1978] AC 964 at 967):

> '. . . it is plain that where the suggestion is that the order is a nullity, this court
> can adjudicate on that matter as has been held in relation to other similar problems.'

The 'other similar problems' have arisen in respect of probation orders, orders of absolute
discharge and orders of conditional discharge. The Court of Appeal has adopted the same
c line in dealing with the right of criminal appeal in these cases as in the case of the
criminal bankruptcy order.

These orders, like the criminal bankruptcy order, are by statute unappealable. But the
court has adopted the distinction between 'merits' and 'jurisdiction', allowing appeal to
lie for want of jurisdiction. The cases, which it is unnecessary to cite, are summarised in
R v Wehner [1977] 3 All ER 553 at 556, [1977] 1 WLR 1143 at 1146.
d The terms used to formulate the law by the judges of the Court of Appeal (which
include myself in *R v Wehner*) have not been happy. They have spoken of orders being
void or null for lack of jurisdiction in the court to make them. But you cannot describe
as a nullity an order made by a superior court of record, which is what the Crown Court
is: see s 4(1) of the Courts Act 1971 (now s 45(1) of the Supreme Court Act 1981). Nor is
the question really one of jurisdiction: it is a question whether the court has exceeded its
e power. An order of the Crown Court, once made, may be in excess of its statutory power
or otherwise irregular. But it is not a nullity. And it would undermine the authority of
the criminal law if orders made by the highest court of trial in criminal matters could be
disregarded as nullities. The order of the Crown Court stands unless and until set aside
by the court itself on application or, if appeal lies, by the appellate tribunal to which the
appeal is taken. But the terms used by the courts do not vitiate their reasoning. As
f I understand the ratio of the cases in which an appeal against an 'unappealable' order has
been allowed, it is that the statutory prohibition of appeal must be construed by reference
to the provisions in the Criminal Appeal Act 1968 dealing with appeal against sentence.

My Lords, I think this is the correct approach. A criminal bankruptcy order is a
sentence for the purposes of the 1968 Act: see s 50(1). By s 9 a person convicted on
indictment (ie after trial in the Crown Court) may appeal to the Court of Appeal against
g sentence. The Act imposes no conditions on this right save that it may be exercised only
with the leave of the Court of Appeal (s 11(1)); and, of course, no appeal lies against a
sentence fixed by law.

I think that the courts have been right to maintain in full the right of appeal against
sentence and to construe statutory prohibitions of appeal as not applicable to sentences
not authorised by law. The right of appeal against sentence is of fundamental importance
h to the subject: it is his protection against sentences not authorised by law as well as against
the sentence which is too severe or is inappropriate. It is a reasonable inference not to be
gainsaid save by specific statutory provision that where Parliament prohibits an appeal
against sentence it is dealing with the discretionary power of the court to make the order
and not addressing its prohibition to orders defective in law. In the absence of express
indication of the contrary, it would be unthinkable that Parliament could intend to
j deprive the subject of his right to appeal against a sentence which the court had no power
to pass. Further, there are very good, though differing, reasons for excluding an appeal
on the merits none of which apply to exclusion of appeal for lack of power to make the
order. In the case of a criminal bankruptcy order the offender-debtor, if bankruptcy
proceedings are brought against him, has the rights of a debtor under the bankruptcy
law, which include rights of appeal. In the case of probation and discharge orders, the
sooner an end is put to the criminal litigation the more likely is the chance of their

success. But, if an order is made which the court has no power to make, the court is imposing a sentence in circumstances in which Parliament has enacted that no such order may lawfully be made. In my view, therefore, appeal lies when the question is whether the Crown Court has exceeded its power. I would construe s 40(1) of the 1973 Act as subject to an implied limitation to the effect that no appeal lies save where the issue is that the court in making the order has exceeded the power conferred on it by Parliament.

The excess of power point

This has become a very short point. First, it is now admitted, indeed it seems to me beyond argument, that it is open to the Crown Court to find that a conspiracy has resulted in loss or damage to others in circumstances where the immediate cause of the loss is a crime which constitutes an overt act of the conspiracy. *R v Reilly* [1982] 3 All ER 27, [1982] QB 1208, which the Court of Appeal followed in this case, was in my view correctly decided.

Second, in the present case no offences were taken into consideration under s 39(2). On this ground alone *DPP v Anderson* [1978] 2 All ER 512, [1978] AC 964 is to be distinguished. In that case the House held that the offences in respect of which the defendant had not been convicted but which the judge treated as relevant under s 39(2) were not covered by the subsection in that the defendant had not agreed that they should be taken into consideration in determining sentence. A very different situation exists where there is a conspiracy offence of which the defendant has been convicted. There is no need to invoke s 39(2). In the present case the offences which were the immediate cause of the loss or damage suffered by others were linked with the two conspiracies of which the appellant was convicted in that they were overt acts committed in pursuance of one or other of them. Thus the judge found under s 39(1)(a) that the loss suffered was the result of the two offences of which the appellant was convicted.

There remains the third point taken by the appellant. It was submitted that it was for the jury at trial to establish by verdict the appellant's participation in the crimes which were the immediate cause of the loss resulting from the conspiracies of which they were the overt acts. The 1973 Act does not say so. Indeed, s 39(1) makes it clear that the process of establishing whether the loss was the result of an offence only begins after the defendant has been convicted of the offence. The jury has finished its task before the court turns to consider sentence. It is at the sentencing stage that the court has to make up its mind whether the facts exist which enable a criminal bankruptcy order to be made and whether it should exercise its power to make the order. An order can properly be made if it appears to the court at this stage that the losses suffered by others were the result of any conspiracy of which the defendant has been convicted. And this is what was done in the present case.

To conclude, I am satisfied that an appeal lies. I am equally satisfied that the appeal should be dismissed. I would answer the certified question in the affirmative, adding only that the question whether the loss or damage did in fact result from the conspiracy is a matter of fact for the sentencing judge to determine.

For these reasons I would dismiss the appeal.

LORD BRANDON OF OAKBROOK. My Lords, I have had the advantage of reading in draft the speech prepared by my noble and learned friend Lord Scarman. I agree with it, and for the reasons which he gives I would dismiss the appeal.

Appeal dismissed.

Solicitors: *Gordon James Morton* (for the appellant); *Director of Public Prosecutions.*

Mary Rose Plummer   Barrister.

Greater London Council v Holmes

QUEEN'S BENCH DIVISION

HIS HONOUR JUDGE SIR WILLIAM STABB QC SITTING AS A JUDGE OF THE HIGH COURT

16, 17 FEBRUARY 1984

Compensation – Displacement from land – Home loss payment – Displacement from dwelling – Land acquired by local authority and held by local authority for purpose for which it was acquired – Displacement of person from dwelling on land in consequence of carrying out of redevelopment on the land – Land acquired by local authority for development – Local authority subsequently selling land to third party for development – Sale necessitating clearance of land and displacement of occupier from dwelling on land – Whether occupier entitled to home loss payment – Whether displacement in consequence of 'redevelopment of land' or sale by local authority – Whether at time of displacement local authority holding land for purpose for which it was acquired – Land Compensation Act 1973, s 29(1)(c).

In November 1963 a local authority compulsorily acquired land for the purpose of clearing it and redeveloping it. In April 1967 the defendant became the tenant of a dwelling on the land. The local authority commenced clearance work on the land but in February 1980 resolved to sell the land as a cleared site to a third party for development. The local authority then completed the clearance of the site with the result that the defendant was displaced from his dwelling and housed elsewhere. The question arose whether he was entitled to a home loss payment under s 29(1)(c)[a] of the Land Compensation Act 1973 because he had been displaced from a dwelling 'in consequence of . . . the carrying out of . . . redevelopment on . . . land' which had been acquired by the authority and which was 'being held by the authority for the purposes for which it was acquired'. The defendant contended that the authority's resolution to sell the land for development by the third party and the clearance of the land for the purpose of effecting the sale, which gave rise to the defendant's displacement, were merely steps in the process of 'redevelopment on the land' by the local authority, which was the purpose for which it had been acquired, and that he had been displaced in consequence of the carrying out of that redevelopment.

Held – The purpose for which the local authority had acquired the land was for redevelopment by the authority itself and therefore by resolving to sell the land to a third party the authority had abandoned, and thereafter no longer held the land for, 'the purposes for which it was acquired', within s 29(1)(c) of the 1973 Act. Furthermore, the 'carrying out of . . . redevelopment' under s 29(1)(c) meant putting up new buildings on the land and accordingly clearance of the land for the purpose of effecting a sale to a third party was not 'redevelopment' but merely a step in connection with the sale. It followed that the defendant was not entitled to a home loss payment because at the time of his displacement the local authority no longer held the land for the purpose for which it had been acquired and the displacement had not occurred in consequence of the local authority carrying out redevelopment on the land (see p 745 f to p 746 a, post).

Dictum of Lord Widgery CJ in *R v Corby DC, ex p McLean* [1975] 2 All ER at 571 applied.

Notes

For home loss payments, see 8 Halsbury's Laws (4th edn) paras 335–337.

For the Land Compensation Act 1973, s 29, see 43 Halsbury's Statutes (3rd edn) 193.

Cases referred to in judgment

Follows v Peabody Trust (1983) 10 HLR 65, CA.

R v Corby DC, ex p McLean [1975] 2 All ER 568, [1975] 1 WLR 735, DC.

---

a   Section 29(1), so far as material, is set out at p 744 j, post

Application

By an originating summons dated 21 February 1983 the Greater London Council, the *a*
plaintiff, sought the court's determination on the following questions: (1) whether the
defendant, Leonard Thomas Holmes, was entitled to receive a home loss payment under
s 29(1)(c) of the Land Compensation Act 1973, as being a person who was displaced by
the council from a mobile home on land at 37 Clark Street, London, E1 in consequence of
the carrying out of redevelopment on the land, and (2) whether the displacement, in
consequence of the council's decision to clear the land and sell it with benefit of vacant   *b*
possession was displacement from a dwelling on land in consequence of the carrying out
of redevelopment on the land, within s 29(1)(c) of the 1973 Act. The facts are set out in
the judgment.

Guy Anthony for the council.
David Watkinson for the defendant.   *c*

HIS HONOUR JUDGE SIR WILLIAM STABB QC. By this originating summons
the plaintiffs, the Greater London Council, invite the court to provide the answer to the
following two questions:

> '(i) Whether the Defendant is entitled to receive payment of a "home loss
> payment" under the terms of Section 29(1)(c) of the Land Compensation Act 1973   *d*
> as being a person who has been displaced by the Greater London Council from a
> mobile home situate on land at 37 Clark Street, London, E1 in consequence of the
> carrying out of redevelopment on the said land.
> (ii) Whether the displacement from a dwelling in consequence of a decision by a
> Local Authority to clear the land on which the dwelling is situated and sell the land
> with benefit of vacant possession is "displacement from a dwelling on land in   *e*
> consequence of the carrying out of the redevelopment on the land" within the
> meaning of Section 29(1)(c) of the Land Compensation Act 1973.'

The short and interesting point raised by this summons falls to be resolved by interpreting
the true meaning of the provisions of s 29(1) of the Land Compensation Act 1973 in so
far as they apply to the circumstances of this case.   *f*

Those circumstances can be summarised from the agreed statement of facts as follows.
On 15 November 1963 the Greater London Council acquired what is known as 'the
Ashfield Street site', under their power of compulsory purchase, with the intention in
due course of redeveloping it by clearance and rebuilding. On 24 April 1967 the
defendant became the tenant of a mobile home at 37 Clark Street on that site and
continued to occupy it as his sole address until displaced in the circumstances described   *g*
below. On 16 July 1979 the council ordered all work on the project to be stopped, and
on 11 February 1980 its appropriate committee resolved that the site should be sold on
the open market for housing for sale. For this purpose it was necessary to clear the site by
demolishing existing houses and rehousing the occupants. As a result the defendant was
required to vacate his mobile home, which he did on 12 April 1980, and he was duly
rehoused by the council at his present address.   *h*

Section 29(1) of the Land Compensation Act 1973 (as amended by the Housing Act
1974 and the Rent Act 1977), so far as it is relevant to these circumstances, can be recited
as follows:

> '(1) Where a person is displaced from a dwelling on any land in consequence of
> ... (c) where the land has been previously acquired by an authority possessing   *j*
> compulsory purchase powers or appropriated by a local authority and is for the time
> being held by the authority for the purposes for which it was acquired or
> appropriated, the carrying out of ... redevelopment on the land ... he shall ... be
> entitled to receive a payment (hereafter referred to as a "home loss payment") from
> ... (iii) ... the authority carrying out the improvement or redevelopment ...'

It is accepted that, if the provisions of s 29(1) can properly be said to apply to the

a circumstances of this case, the defendant would otherwise fulfil the conditions which entitle him to receive the payment.

Counsel for the council contends that s 29 does not apply in these circumstances for two reasons. First, he contends that displacement did not occur from land which was for the time being held by the council for the purposes for which it was acquired. At the time of displacement, in April 1980, the council, having acquired the site with the

b intention of redevelopment, had abandoned its original intention and had resolved to sell the site for housing for sale. Second, he contends that the displacement was not in consequence of the carrying out of the redevelopment of the land. The demolition, or clearance, which gave rise to the need to displace the defendant from his dwelling was for the purpose of the sale of the land to another and not for its redevelopment by the council.

c Counsel for the defendant submits that what the council were doing by selling the site for the purpose of housing amounted to a step in its original intention that the land should be redeveloped, and that it matters not whether the actual redevelopment is to be carried out by the council or the purchaser of the land from the council. The land was acquired by the council for the purpose of redevelopment and so remains branded, so to speak, with that purpose. The demolition necessary for the proposed sale, so his argument

d goes, which gave rise to the displacement was simply a step in the process of achieving that purpose, and it can properly be said, therefore, that the displacement was in consequence of the carrying out of the redevelopment and that the land, at that time, was still being held by the council for its original purpose.

I was referred to two authorities in neither of which did the precise issue in this case arise. The first case was *R v Corby DC, ex p McLean* [1975] 2 All ER 568, [1975] 1 WLR

e 735 in which it was decided that redevelopment included the act of demolition which preceded the substitution of new buildings under a redevelopment scheme. The second was *Follows v Peabody Trust* (1983) 10 HLR 65 which was concerned with whether the demolition which caused the displacement was or was not part of the process of redevelopment. I confess that I derived little assistance from these two authorities. In each of them the all-important issues of the effect of a sale of the land by the authority to

f a third person and the actual redevelopment of that land by that third person did not arise.

It seems to me that the council by abandoning its original intention to redevelop the land, and by resolving that the land should be sold to a purchaser for the purpose of that purchaser building houses, was divorcing itself from the whole original concept. The council no longer could be said to be holding the land for the purpose for which it was

g acquired, which I hold to be for the purpose of redevelopment by the council itself. Furthermore, in my judgment, a step in connection with or for the purpose of the sale cannot properly be said to be part of a process of redevelopment; it is part of the process of the sale and not of the redevelopment, which, as I have said, must be a redevelopment carried out by the authority who make the payment, as the concluding words of s 29(1) make clear.

h If the words 'the carrying out of ... redevelopment' are to be given their ordinary meaning, as it was said that they should be by Lord Widgery CJ in *R v Corby DC* [1975] 2 All ER 568 at 571, [1975] 1 WLR 735 at 738, then I would consider those words to mean, or at least to include, the putting up of new buildings. Here the council are not to put up any new buildings, and therefore cannot be said to be carrying out any redevelopment. Any other construction, with all respect to the able and closely reasoned argument of

j counsel for the defendant, would in my view be putting an unjustifiable strain on the words of the section.

Accordingly, my answer to each of the two questions posed in the summons is in the negative because I do not consider that the defendant was a person who was displaced in consequence of the carrying out by the council of redevelopment of the land, or that the sale of the land by the council could in any way be regarded as part of the process of

redevelopment by the council, if having by that time abandoned its original intention so
to do.

a

Order accordingly.

Solicitors: *R A Lanham* (for the council); *Alison Scott* (for the defendant).

K Mydeen Esq   Barrister.   *b*

Freeman v Wansbeck District Council

COURT OF APPEAL, CIVIL DIVISION
SIR JOHN ARNOLD P AND LATEY J
19 JULY 1983

c

*Housing – Local authority houses – Tenant's right to buy – Exclusion of right – Dwelling having
substantially different features from those of ordinary dwellings – Different features designed to
make house suitable for occupation by physically disabled person – Substantially different features
– Designed – Whether comparison to be made with all ordinary dwellings or merely similar*   *d*
*dwellings in same locality – Whether dwelling 'designed' for occupation by disabled person only if
house built for such occupation – Housing Act 1980, Sch 1, Pt 1, para 3.*

Paragraph 3[a] of Pt 1 of Sch 1 to the Housing Act 1980, which excludes from the right to
buy council houses under s 1 any dwelling which has 'features . . . substantially different
from those of ordinary dwelling-houses and which are designed to make it suitable for   *e*
occupation by physically disabled persons', contemplates substantially different features
which are not to be found in an ordinary dwelling, such as a ramp instead of a staircase,
special doors, a lift, or cooking surfaces at a special height, and not features, such as an
additional downstairs lavatory, which might be found in an ordinary dwelling. A
dwelling has features 'designed' to make it suitable for occupation by a disabled person,
within para 3, only where the dwelling is built with such features for occupation by a   *f*
disabled person and not where an ordinary dwelling is merely 'intended', by reason of
the addition of special features, for occupation by a disabled person. Furthermore, in
comparing the dwelling in question with ordinary dwellings, the relevant comparison is
with all ordinary dwellings and not merely similar dwellings in the locality of the
dwelling in question (see p 748 *b* to *e* and *g* to *j*, p 749 *c d* and *f* to *j* and p 750 *a b*, post).

g

Notes
For the right to buy council houses, see Supplement to 22 Halsbury's Laws (4th edn) para
569A.
    For the Housing Act 1980, Sch 1, see 50(1) Halsbury's Statutes (3rd edn) 992.

Appeal   *h*
The defendant, Wansbeck District Council (the local authority), appealed against the
judgment of his Honour Judge Percy, given on 6 December 1982 in the Morpeth County
Court, whereby he declared that the plaintiffs, Mr Joseph Freeman and his wife Mrs
Margaret Freeman, were entitled to exercise the right given by s 1 of the Housing Act
1980 to buy the freehold of their council house at 27 Haydon Road, Ashington,
Northumberland, of which they were joint tenants. The facts are set out in the judgment   *j*
of Latey J.

James Chadwin QC and *Paul Benfield* for the local authority.
Frederick Such for the plaintiffs.

---

a   Paragraph 3 is set out at p 747 *d*, post

LATEY J (delivering the first judgment at the invitation of Sir John Arnold P). Mr
a Freeman was granted a tenancy of 27 Haydon Road, Ashington, Northumberland in
February 1970 and later that tenancy was converted into a joint tenancy for himself and
his wife, Mrs Freeman. They have a daughter, Jacqueline, who suffers from spina bifida.
The evidence is that she is not immobilised by any means. She can walk, but not too far,
and she can get up stairs, but with more difficulty than someone who is wholly fit. On 8
July 1975 the council converted for the Freemans a larder under the stairs into a
b downstairs, ground floor lavatory, and it did that pursuant to its powers under the
Chronically Sick and Disabled Persons Act 1970. This lavatory under the stairs has a
sloping roof and, in so far as it is relevant to mention it, the roof does slope to its lowest,
or at any rate is reduced to, 4 ft 6 in in height at the point where the lavatory pedestal is
situated.

To continue the history of the matter, a small wash-hand basin was added later in
c 1975, but nothing turns on that. Then on 13 October 1980 the Freemans put in an
application to exercise their right to buy the freehold of the house under the Housing
Act 1980. The local authority rejected that application, and it did so claiming that this
house fell within para 3 of Pt I of Sch 1 to the 1980 Act. That part of the schedule deals
with the circumstances in which the right to buy is excluded. Paragraph 3 reads:

d   'The dwelling-house has features which are substantially different from those of
     ordinary dwelling-houses and which are designed to make it suitable for occupation
     by physically disabled persons.'

So Mr and Mrs Freeman, whose principal aim, according to the evidence, in buying the
house if they could was to provide their disadvantaged child with security, were stopped
from buying. If they wished to go on they had to have recourse to the county court,
e which they did. They applied to that court. Their application did not come on for
hearing until 6 December 1982. Counsel for the local authority tells us that the reason
for that gross delay was, at any rate mainly, because there was some confusion in the
county court itself as to the proper procedure to be adopted.

At any rate it did come on for hearing before his Honour Judge Percy on 6 December
1982, and the judge rejected the contentions of the local authority and held that Mr and
f Mrs Freeman were entitled to exercise their right to buy the house. There was a full
hearing before the judge but, not content with his finding and decision, the local
authority appealed from that decision and the appeal comes before this court today.

There are two limbs in para 3 of Pt I of the schedule. The first question is whether the
dwelling house concerned has features which are substantially different from those of
ordinary dwelling houses; and the second question is whether, if such features exist, they
g are designed to make it suitable for occupation by physically disabled persons. The local
authority contended before the judge that there were features in this house which fall
within the ambit of para 3 as being substantially different from those of ordinary
dwelling houses; and it says that the word 'designed' means 'intended' and that the
downstairs lavatory, which it accepts is the only feature which could qualify under this
paragraph, was intended to make the house suitable for occupation by physically disabled
h persons.

Counsel for the local authority mounted an argument derived from the rather unusual
shape of the lavatory. Speaking for myself, I find it very difficult to see how para 3 in its
language about features which are substantially different from those of ordinary dwelling
houses ever contemplated such matters as shape and size, unless shape and size are linked
with a need of a handicapped person. Nobody suggests that that could be so in this case,
j because the shape and size were most unsuitable for a handicapped person. But the other
reason why I am bound to say this argument has caused me discomfort, if not indeed
distaste, is that although shape and size were mentioned before the judge it was never
the authority's case before the judge that they had got anything to do with what had to
be decided.

The authority's case depended on the evidence of its chief housing officer. His evidence,
summarising it, was this. On this particular estate houses were not built with and do not

have inside downstairs lavatories, but they have an outside lavatory. If any had downstairs lavatories, then those lavatories were put there especially. Therefore a downstairs lavatory is not typical. He went on to say:

> 'In my view, [if] any of our houses on North Seaton Estate . . . has a downstairs inside toilet, I would consider it to be a special feature, suitable [evidently he regarded suitability as the test] for disabled persons. I would resist its sale. I look at each estate in isolation, when deciding if there is any special feature in a particular house when compared with the rest of houses on that estate.'

In my view the argument advanced based on the shape of this particular lavatory, which, as can happen in many houses, is fitted in where it could be, fails, and it fails not merely because it was not put before the judge or contended for before the judge; not because there is not a word of mention of it in the notice of appeal, which incidentally is in such broad terms that it really tells us nothing in advance of this appeal, but because it itself is an argument without foundation. This lavatory, in my opinion, was not, to use the words of the paragraph again, a feature substantially different from the features of ordinary dwelling houses.

The other argument which was mounted was this. In deciding whether or not the dwelling house in question has features which are substantially different from those of ordinary dwelling houses, the local authority, as I understand it, is not only entitled to, but should in fact look at the matter locally. I cannot find in para 3 of Pt I of Sch 1 anything to justify an approach of limiting the question whether or not a house has special features which are substantially different from those of ordinary dwelling houses or to entitle the authority or, for that matter, any court which has to consider it, to draw comparisons merely with other houses locally. I do not believe that that is either the natural meaning of para 3 or was in any way intended by Parliament when one looks at the language which it has chosen.

If in fact there are no such features, as the judge rightly found in my opinion, then of course that is the end of the case. But we have been asked to consider also the second limb, and that means what is meant by the word 'designed'?

Counsel for the local authority asks us to say that that word 'designed' means intended—that and nothing more. Counsel for Mr and Mrs Freeman submits that the word 'designed' means formed in the architectural sense of the word. Of course the word 'designed' is an ambiguous word. It is possible to put either of those meanings on it, but I think that light is thrown on its real meaning in this context when one looks at para 5(a) of Pt I of Sch 1. Paragraph 5(a) reads as follows:

> '. . . he shall so determine if satisfied—(a) that the dwelling-house is designed or specially adapted for occupation by persons of pensionable age . . .'

I find it very difficult to accept the contention of counsel for the local authority that 'designed' means 'intended' there when you read it in conjunction with the following words 'or specially adapted'. It seems to me that, using one's common sense, the meaning of that phrase is that the dwelling house was either built for occupation by persons of pensionable age or, if it was not so built, has been specially adapted, and that surely is talking in terms of structure.

In a clear and, as I think, admirably succinct judgment the judge rejected both the contentions of the authority, and I think all becomes plain in this matter of interpretation if one exercises one's ordinary, everyday knowledge and regards the intention of the Act when it refers to features substantially different from those in ordinary dwelling houses as the sort of features we are all familiar with, such as ramps, specially widened doors, lifts, cooking surfaces at special heights for people who cannot stand up and do their cooking sitting down, and the like. At the end of it all one asks oneself this question: how (and I hope I do not put it too highly) in the name of common sense does the installation of one, small, rather cramped downstairs lavatory wholly incapable of accommodating a wheelchair fit in with what the Act envisages? The answer, in my judgment, is that it does not by any stretch of the imagination.

a We were told by counsel for the local authority that this is the first case under para 3 of Pt I of Sch 1 to the 1980 Act which has come to the Court of Appeal, that so far as those instructing him have been able to find out all over the country there are only three such cases which have appeared before the county courts, but that there are a number in the pipeline which are awaiting the decision of this court. In the light of that I had perhaps better say nothing about my initial feelings about this appeal and about the way these two plaintiffs have been kept out of buying their house for getting on for three years,

b beyond urging, so far as I can and as strongly as I can, this authority now to give this application all the priority it possibly can. In the light of what counsel has said, I accept that there was, or at any rate the authority thought there was, a really substantial question to be decided on the interpretation and application of para 3 of Pt I of Sch 1 to the 1980 Act, and therefore this particular pair of applicants had to suffer for the general good. I hope that from now onwards they will be given every possible help in their application

c and in speeding up the conveyance.

I would dismiss this appeal.

SIR JOHN ARNOLD P. I agree. One of the purposes of the Housing Act 1980 was to entitle what are called secure tenants to buy their houses from local authorities who were their landlords. But the power was not universal and unqualified. There were reservations

d and restrictions designed to leave in the hands of local authorities a housing stock which was regarded by Parliament as being proper so to be left, and part of the machinery of that restriction was the exclusion of the categories mentioned in Sch 1 from the right to buy. It is in the light of that overall intention that one must sensibly try to construe the statute.

The particular exclusion is one which, if it is to be effective to exclude, must relate to

e houses in respect of which both limbs of the restriction are satisfied. The excluded dwelling house must be shown to have features which are substantially different from those of ordinary dwelling houses and these features must also be shown to be designed to make it suitable for occupation by physically disabled persons. As regards the first of those limbs, the local authority puts the matter in two ways. First, it says that the possession by the house of a downstairs lavatory is of itself a feature which is substantially

f different from those of ordinary dwelling houses, and it reaches that conclusion by confining the ordinary dwelling houses with which the comparison has to be made to a particular class of dwelling houses, namely those situated in a socially similar area of the local authority's district and of a similar size to the house with which the comparison has to be made. Like Latey J, I can find no justification for that confinement. It seems to me that what is being contemplated in the relevant paragraph in Pt I of Sch 1 is a dwelling

g house exhibiting non-dwelling-house features or those at least which are not to be found in ordinary dwelling houses. One can think of many examples of domestic features which are not to be found in ordinary dwelling houses, wherever situated, such as Latey J has instanced: a ramp instead of a staircase, perhaps a lift or other mechanical contrivance instead of a staircase, and one can think of a number of other such features.

The second way it is put is that this feature, even if all ordinary dwelling houses are to

h be regarded for comparative purposes, is different, and substantially different, from any comparable features in such other houses in that this particular downstairs lavatory, though not as such substantially different from the features to be found elsewhere, is substantially different because instead of being, as it would have been if building conditions had permitted, a downstairs lavatory with an overall height from the floor to the ceiling of 6 ft 5 in, it has at one end an overall height of 4 ft 6 in and a sloping roof

j between the two. That is a difference, but, in my judgment, it is not a substantial difference.

Those conclusions are sufficient to decide the fate of this appeal.

As to the matter of design, I agree with everything which Latey J has said. Most particularly it seems to me to be right to construe the word 'design' in para 3 of Pt I of Sch 1 in the same way as the similar word 'design' ought to be construed in para 5 of that part of the schedule, there being no reason whatsoever in this case that I can discern to

abandon the ordinary rule of the interpretation of statutes, which is that, unless the
context otherwise indicates, a similar word should have a similar meaning wherever it
appears in the same part of the Act. It seems to me that when one looks at the word
'designed' in para 5(a) it must be construed in a manner similar to the words
'architecturally formed', not only by reason, as Latey J has pointed out, of its association
with the words 'specially adapted', but also because if it were there to be construed as
meaning 'intended' it would make para 5(b) wholly, or very nearly wholly, tautologous,
because if it were intended to be occupied by persons of pensionable age it would
necessarily, or almost necessarily, follow that it was the practice of the landlord to let it
only for occupation by such persons.

Apart from that, I come back to what I started with: the purpose of the exclusion is to
leave the local authority with a suitable housing stock, and it is far more relevant to view
a house in terms of its inclusion or exclusion from that residual stock by reference to its
character than by reference to the intention which historically lay behind the affording
to it of that character.

I agree that the appeal should be dismissed.

Appeal dismissed.

Solicitors: *Sharpe Pritchard & Co*, agents for *C D Occomore,* Ashington (for the local
authority); *Tocher Auld & Co*, Bedlington (for Mr and Mrs Freeman).

Bebe Chua   Barrister.

Cowan and others v Scargill and others

CHANCERY DIVISION
SIR ROBERT MEGARRY V-C
26, 27, 28, 29, 30 MARCH, 2, 3, 4, 5, 13 APRIL 1984

*Trust and trustee – Duty of trustee – Duty towards beneficiary – Investments – Power of
investment – Pension fund – Mineworkers' pension scheme – Scheme authorising overseas
investment and investment in energy resources competing with coal – Trustees appointed by
mineworkers seeking to restrict investments to investments in Britain and in industries not
competing with coal – Whether trustees of pension fund subject to general law relating to trustees
– Whether trustees entitled to prohibit particular investment for social or political reasons.*

A pension scheme for mineworkers provided for the payment of pensions and lump
sums to all industrial employees of the National Coal Board on retirement, injury and on
contracting certain diseases and also for payments to their widows and children. The
funds of the scheme were provided by contributions from mineworkers and by payments
made by the board. There were ten trustees of the scheme, five appointed by the board
and five by the mineworkers' union. The trustees' wide powers of investment under the
scheme entitled them to invest overseas and in energy industries other than coal. In 1982
the defendants, the five trustees appointed by the union, refused to approve an annual
investment plan for the scheme unless it was amended to prohibit any increase in
overseas investment, to provide for withdrawal from existing overseas investments at an
opportune time, and to prohibit investment in energy industries which were in direct
competition with coal. The defendants sought those restrictions on investment because
it was the union's policy that the scheme's funds should be invested in Britain rather than
overseas and should not be invested in energy industries which were in competition with
coal. The plaintiffs, the five trustees appointed by the board, applied to the court for
directions that the defendants were in breach of their fiduciary duties as trustees of the
scheme in refusing to concur in the adoption of the investment plan.

Held – (1) The trusts of a pension fund were in general governed by the ordinary law
a relating to trusts, subject to any contrary provision in the rules or other provisions which
governed the trust. In particular, the trustees of a pension fund were subject to the
overriding duty of trustees to do the best they could for the beneficiaries, the more so in
the case of a pension fund, where many of the beneficiaries were those who, as members
of the pension scheme, had contributed to the fund out of which their pensions were
paid. Moreover, the trustees were under a general duty, in the interests of the
b beneficiaries, to take advantage of the full range of investments authorised by the terms
of the trust, rather than narrowing that range, and pursuant to s 6(1)[a] of the Trustee
Investments Act 1961 they were required to consider the need for diversification of the
trust investments, which was even more important in the case of a large pension fund.
Accordingly, trustees of a pension fund could not refuse for social or political reasons to
make a particular investment if to make that investment would be more beneficial
c financially to the beneficiaries of the fund (see p 760 f to h, p 761 b to d, p 762 a b e, p 763
c to f, p 764 f to h and p 766 f, post); *Blankenship v Boyle* (1971) 329 F Supp 1089 and
Withers v Teachers' Retirement System of the City of New York (1978) 447 F Supp 1248
applied.

(2) On the facts, an investment policy in relation to the mineworkers' pension scheme
that was designed to further the union's policy of ensuring the general prosperity of the
d coal industry regardless of financial benefit to the beneficiaries under the scheme could
not be regarded as being a policy that was directed to obtaining the best possible results
for the beneficiaries, particularly when most of the beneficiaries were retired from the
coal industry and some of them, such as widows and children of deceased miners, had
never been engaged in the industry. Moreover, any possible economic benefit to the coal
industry that would accrue to the beneficiaries, as distinct from the general public, from
e imposing the restrictions on investment sought by the defendants was far too speculative
and remote. It followed that, by refusing to approve the investment plan unless the
restrictions on investment they sought were adopted, the defendants were in breach of
their fiduciary duties as trustees to do the best they could for the beneficiaries and to
invest in the full range of investments permitted under the terms of the scheme. In all
the circumstances the appropriate relief to grant was to make declarations regarding the
f defendants' duties as trustees of the scheme rather than to give directions (see p 764 j,
p 766 e f, p 767 c d f g and p 769 d, post).

Notes

For the exercise of the powers of trustees generally, see 38 Halsbury's Laws (3rd edn)
979–981, paras 1693–1696, and for the power of trustees to invest, see ibid 987–1009,
g paras 1710–1738, and for cases on the subject, see 47 Digest (Repl) 356, 371–373, 377–
383, 3213, 3325–3346, 3377–3426.

Cases referred to in judgment

Balls v Strutt (1841) 1 Hare 146, 66 ER 984.
h *Billes, Re* (1983) 148 DLR (3d) 512, Ont HC.
Blankenship v Boyle (1971) 329 F Supp 1089.
Buttle v Saunders [1950] 2 All ER 193.
C L, Re [1968] 1 All ER 1104, [1969] 1 Ch 587, [1968] 2 WLR 1275.
Evans v London Co-op Society Ltd (1976) Times, 6 July.
Harrison-Broadley v Smith [1964] 1 All ER 867, [1964] 1 WLR 456, CA.
j *Portland (Duke) v Topham* (1864) 11 HL Cas 32, [1861–73] All ER Rep 980, 11 ER 1242.
Towler's Settlement Trusts, Re [1963] 3 All ER 759, [1964] Ch 158, [1963] 3 WLR 987.
Whiteley, Re, Whiteley v Learoyd (1886) 33 Ch D 347, CA; *affd* (1887) 12 App Cas 727, HL.
Withers v Teachers' Retirement System of the City of New York (1978) 447 F Supp 1248.
Wyvern Developments Ltd, Re [1974] 2 All ER 535, [1974] 1 WLR 1097.

---

a   Section 6(1) is set out at p 762 e f, post

Cases also cited
British Museum (Trustees) v A-G [1984] 1 All ER 337, [1984] 1 WLR 418.
Klug v Klug [1918] 2 Ch 67.
Tempest v Lord Camoys (1882) 21 Ch D 571, CA.

Originating summons
By an originating summons dated 1 December 1983 the plaintiffs, James Robertson
Cowan, Fred Brian Harrison, Edward Smith, Philip Gordon Weekes and Peter William
Stafford, the present members appointed by the National Coal Board to the Committee
of Management of the Mineworkers' Pension Scheme sought as against the defendants,
Arthur Scargill, Lawrence Daly, Michael McGahey, Emlyn Williams and Raymond
Chadburn, the present members of the committee appointed by the National Union of
Mineworkers, the following relief pursuant to RSC Ord 85, r 2: (1) directions whether
the defendants were in breach of their fiduciary duties as members of the committee and
trustees of the scheme's money and investments in refusing to concur in the adoption of
the Investment Strategy and Business Plan 1982 unless amended to provide that (a) there
be no increase in the percentage of overseas investment, (b) overseas investment already
made be withdrawn at the most opportune time and (c) the committee adopt a proposal
not to invest in energy industries which were in direct competition with coal; (2)
directions whether the 1982 plan should be adopted by the committee and implemented;
(3) directions for the completion of the accounts of the scheme for the year to 30
September 1982; (4) all necessary and consequential directions and orders; (5) an order
for the costs of the proceedings; and (6) further or other relief. The facts are set out in the
judgment.

S A Stamler QC and *Patrick Howell* for the plaintiffs.
Mr Scargill appeared in person.

Cur adv vult

13 April. The following judgment was delivered.

SIR ROBERT MEGARRY V-C. I have before me an originating summons, issued
on 1 December 1983, which raises certain questions on the exercise of the powers and
duties of investment of the trustees of an employees' pension scheme, together with
certain other questions. The parties to the originating summons are the ten trustees of
the Mineworkers' Pension Scheme. The five plaintiffs are the trustees appointed by the
National Coal Board ('the board' or 'the NCB'). The five defendants are the trustees
appointed by the National Union of Mineworkers ('the union', or 'the NUM'). Mr Stamler
appeared on behalf of the plaintiffs, and the first defendant, Mr Arthur Scargill, appeared
in person. He had, I think, dispensed with the services of a Chancery silk and junior
some days before the case began, but he had retained the services of a solicitor, who was
able to sit with him in court and assist him. The other four defendants took no part in
the argument, but Mr Scargill told me that he was presenting his argument on behalf of
them as well as on his own behalf. I should say at the outset that Mr Scargill argued his
case throughout with both courtesy and competence. I wish to emphasise this, particularly
in view of the number of occasions on which I found it necessary to interrupt his
submissions, usually because he was going too fast for coherent note-taking, or because I
wished to be sure that I had correctly understood his submission, or that he was not
overlooking some point which tended against him.
    The main issue (and I put it very shortly) is whether the defendants are in breach of
their fiduciary duties in refusing approval of an investment plan for the scheme unless it
is amended so as to prohibit any increase in overseas investment, to provide for the
withdrawal of existing overseas investments at the most opportune time, and to prohibit
investment in energies which are in direct competition with coal. The investment plan
in question is the 'Investment Strategy and Business Plan 1982', which I shall call the

'1982 plan'. The 1982 plan was first presented to a meeting of the trustees on 9 June 1982
a as a replacement for a similar plan approved in 1980 (the '1980 plan'), and it has never
been approved. The 1980 plan replaced a plan made in 1976, the first of its kind.

Before I go any further, I must say something about the Mineworkers' Pension Scheme.
This was established under the Coal Industry Nationalisation (Superannuation)
Regulations 1950, SI 1950/376, made under the Coal Industry Nationalisation Act 1946,
s 37; and I shall call it 'the scheme'. It has been amended from time to time under the
b powers conferred by cl 37 of the scheme. This allows amendments to be made by
agreement between the board and the union, with a provision in cl 38 for resolving
matters in default of agreement. Both the scheme and the rules made under it are of
considerable complexity, but I need not explore these. Provision is made for the payment
of pensions and lump sums on retirement, injury and certain diseases, and for payments
to widows and children of members. The funds of the scheme are provided by
c contributions from members and by payments made by the board.

The scheme covers all industrial employees of the board, and there is a parallel scheme
for the board's non-industrial staff, called the NCB Staff Superannuation Scheme (the
'staff scheme'). The two schemes work together in various ways. There is a joint
investment sub-committee (the 'JISC') composed of representatives of the committees of
each of the schemes, some being representatives of both committees; and the JISC deals
d with much of the detail of the investment of the funds of the two schemes, with some
investments being made with moneys provided by both schemes. The funds of each
scheme are large, each being worth something in the region of £3,000m, with some
£200m being available for investment each year under the scheme. An advisory panel
of investment experts assists the JISC, and Mr H R Jenkins, the board's director-general
of investments, is the secretary of the JISC. He heads a large staff which carries out most
e of the work of managing the funds. The practical operation of this organisation for some
years now has been that the trustees have approved the general strategy for investment
in the form of the 1976 and 1980 plans, while the JISC, which meets more frequently,
has dealt with problems that arose when some proposed investment was very large, or
did not fall within the guidelines laid down by the plan, or were in some other way a
matter that should be discussed. Apart from that, Mr Jenkins and his staff have a wide
f discretion in making investments in accordance with the plan, and they do all the
detailed work.

As I have mentioned, there are ten trustees under the scheme. They form a committee
of management (the 'committee') which is in control of the fund. Five of the ten are
appointed and removable by the board and five are appointed and removable by the
union, with provision in each case for alternates. From the members of the committee
g appointed by the board, the board appoints a chairman and a joint deputy chairman, and
from the members appointed by the union, the union appoints the other joint deputy
chairman. At all material times Mr J R Cowan, the deputy chairman of the board, has
been chairman of the committee, and Mr F B Harrison the joint deputy chairman
appointed by the board. He is also chairman of the JISC. Until April 1982, Mr (now
Lord) Gormley was the joint deputy chairman appointed by the union; but when he
h retired as president of the union, Mr Scargill became president in his place, and he also
became the union's joint deputy chairman of the committee. The members of the
committee are expressly made trustees of the funds of the scheme, though they are given
power to act by a majority; but there is also an express provision that the chairman of a
meeting of the committee is not to have a second or casting vote. The powers of
investment are very wide, and there are also very wide provisions for appointing agents
j and for delegation. The scheme is fully funded. Members and the board make basic
contributions which are very approximately the same total amount, and the board also
makes deficiency payments in accordance with actuarial valuations. In addition, the
board has been making further voluntary contributions so that pensions may keep pace
with inflation. The net result, I understand, is that something of the order of two-thirds
of the payments come from the board and one-third from the members.

In earlier years, no formal plans or schemes for investment were made. However, in

1976 a four years' business plan was approved by the JISC and the committee, and in May 1980 this was replaced by the 1980 plan. Investment has been made since then on the basis of this plan. Under this, there were three main categories of investment, namely marketable securities (both gilts and equities); land; and 'industrial finance', which includes equities in small quoted companies, project finance for industry, and investment in agricultural operations. All three heads include overseas investment, and the first two include oil and gas. 'Targets', in the form of percentages, were set for various categories of investment.

The 1982 plan was a revised plan that was intended to replace the 1980 plan. It was submitted to the JISC on 11 May 1982, and was approved as being a very satisfactory plan for the next two years, 'provided good use was made of the flexibility which it afforded for further overseas equity investment'. The JISC accordingly submitted it to the committees of management of the two schemes with a recommendation for approval. The committee of the staff scheme approved it at its meeting on 8 June 1982; but it met a different fate at the forty-fifth meeting of the committee for the mineworkers' scheme held the next day, 9 June.

Apart from the replacement of Mr Gormley by Mr Scargill, the composition of the committee had remained unchanged for some years; and for many years the members had worked together with little dissension. There had been a sharp division about the way in which the scheme's shares should be voted at an annual general meeting of one company, but, subject to that, a consensus had always emerged after discussion. At the meeting on 9 June 1982 Mr Scargill, almost at the outset, said that an important principle had to be discussed, and that he was concerned about the rights of trustees to determine where the fund's resources were invested. This arose on a question of unionisation in a company in which the fund had a minority shareholding. It was agreed that there should be a special meeting to consider this and other matters of policy affecting the investments of the fund.

After certain other items had been considered, Mr Jenkins presented the 1982 plan, and went through it in detail. Mr Scargill then raised objections to the plan. He subsequently, in a letter of 19 August 1982, questioned the accuracy of the draft minutes of that meeting, and put forward his own versions of certain parts of those minutes; and it is from Mr Scargill's versions that I shall quote. His opening objection was to say that—

'while he approved of the remainder of the proposals, his organisation raised objections to investments in oil, investments overseas and the acquisition of land overseas.'

He said that there should not be any future investment in these three areas, and moved reference back of the business plan for 1982. He also said that in the long term all investments 'should be withdrawn from these areas'. When Mr Cowan suggested that the plan should stand until the next meeting of the JISC and that the alterations should be raised then, Mr Scargill said that he—

'could not accept Mr. Cowan's recommendation as he considered it would negate the meeting and would mean the Committee of Management was no more than a reporting body. He said that the three areas of investment were in direct conflict with the policy decision of N.U.M. Conference, and he suggested that investments in these three areas should not take place. He proposed that a special separate meeting should be held to discuss the principles, and again moved a reference back to that part of the Plan dealing with these three items.'

The upshot was that the meeting was adjourned so that the discussion could be resumed at an early date.

I pause there to say that although there have been minor variations in the wording of Mr Scargill's objections, they have remained substantially in this form throughout. 'Oil' has been replaced so as to become 'energies which are in direct competition with coal', so as to exclude, for instance, petrol and lubricating oil. Further, a distinction seems to have emerged between overseas investments, where not only must there be no increase in the a percentage but also the existing investments are to be disposed of as is opportune, and, on the other hand, competing energies, where no new investments are to be made, but there is no requirement to dispose of existing investments. However, I do not think that these variations matter much.

Immediately after the meeting of 9 June, Mr Cowles, the legal adviser to the board, who had been in attendance at the meeting, wrote to all members of the committee, summarising the oral advice that he had given at the meeting. The thrust of this was that the suitability of investments was to be judged almost exclusively by reference to financial criteria rather than their acceptability for political or other extraneous reasons, and that it was improper to place an embargo on certain classes of investments regardless of the financial consequences. On 17 June Mr Scargill wrote to Mr Cowan about the letter from Mr Cowles, saying that the union had taken legal advice, and that it was 'on the basis of this advice that we raised our objection' to the investments in oil and overseas investment. (For brevity, I shall use 'oil' as referring to energy industries in competition with the British coal industry.) The letter referred to Mr Cowles's statement that the suitability of investments was to be judged 'almost exclusively by reference to financial criteria rather than their acceptability for political or other extraneous reasons', and continued 'My colleagues and I do not accept that this interpretation is correct'. The letter quoted a sentence from the legal advice that the union had obtained; it now appears that this sentence came from an 18-page memorandum by a well-known firm of London solicitors dated 29 April 1982, as, indeed, Mr Scargill made plain in addressing me. I shall return to this later. At this stage I need only say that Mr Scargill had from time to time refused various requests to produce this memorandum. However, on day 4 of the hearing it was pointed out to him that if he asserted that he was supported by a legal opinion but he still refused to produce it, questions might then arise about how far the opinion did in fact support him; and he thereupon said that he would put the opinion in evidence, which he did a few days later. At no stage has there been any suggestion that the defendants had relied on any other legal advice.

On 25 June 1982 Mr Cowles addressed another note to all members of the committee. He pointed out that the legal advice mentioned in Mr Scargill's letter was concerned with the right of trustees to opt for one particular investment as against a viable alternative (a view that was not questioned), and said that this was not the issue under discussion. The committee's duty, he said, was to manage the funds in the best interests of the beneficiaries; and he then said:

> 'What is improper is for the Committee of Management to fetter the way they exercise their discretionary powers as trustees in the future by imposing an embargo on a wide range of investments regardless of the financial consequences.'

Mr Scargill's reply, on 30 June, was to state that the legal opinion obtained by the NUM covered all aspects of the scheme and the trustees' responsibilities, so that it was incorrect to draw the conclusion that the advice was not directed to the issue under discussion. He went on:

> 'We are advised that we can refuse to invest abroad or in oil and other energy industries, and it may be that, in the final analysis, the difference of opinion between you and ourselves will have to be resolved elsewhere!'

This was in substance repeated in subsequent letters to others.

On 5 July Mr Cowles wrote to Mr Scargill, seeking to discuss the difference of opinion with the solicitors who had advised the union; and he said that he assumed that they had seen the opinion obtained from two Chancery silks on the obligations of the committee in relation to the scheme's investments, and his own recent advice. He also said that it was difficult to comment on the union's request for legal advice and on the advice itself without seeing them, and said that it would be helpful to be supplied with copies. Mr Scargill's reply was that 'we ourselves have been counselled that it is wiser not to supply you with copies of the legal advice given us at this point'.

Then, on 21 September, Mr Scargill wrote to Mr Cowan, reiterating the 'total opposition' of the NUM trustees to investment overseas and in oil, seeking agreement to withdraw overseas investments, and seeking other changes in the operation of the scheme. These included making future investments require the approval of the 'Chairman and Vice-Chairman', and providing for the chairmanship to alternate between Mr Cowan and the president of the NUM. The adjourned forty-fifth meeting of the committee had not yet been held: on 15 June Mr Cowan had proposed three dates in June and July before the holiday season, but Mr Scargill had promptly replied that he was committed on all three dates, and he suggested no alternatives. Mr Cowan then became gravely ill, and did not return until early in January 1983. He then wrote to Mr M McGahey, one of the union trustees, to suggest that he and Mr Scargill should meet him (Mr Cowan) and Mr Harrison to discuss the fund's problems. The meeting was held on 25 January 1983, and a letter from Mr Scargill sets out the changes sought by him and Mr McGahey. A number of further changes were added to those that had already been sought. Instead of alternating chairmen, there were to be joint chairmen; there were to be quarterly meetings of the committee; the JISC was to be composed of trustees only; there was to be an investigation of all expenses paid for the past two years; there were to be fortnightly meetings of the two joint chairmen with Mr Jenkins so that the trustees could be involved in the actual decision-taking; and no investments above a certain level (e g £2m) should be made without agreement between the two joint chairmen and the professional fund managers. The letter stated that 'our legal advisers are satisfied that we are acting within the law'.

On 28 February 1983 two meetings of the committee took place. In the morning there was the forty-sixth meeting, and in the afternoon there was a resumption of the adjourned forty-fifth meeting. At the morning meeting, the minutes of the original forty-fifth meeting on 9 June 1982 were considered. They had been revised in the light of Mr Scargill's proposed corrections, but the joint secretary, after consulting his and his assistants' notes, had been unable to agree all of Mr Scargill's corrections. At the meeting, the committee, after discussion, accepted that no agreement could be reached on the minutes. After certain other points, the committee turned to the minutes of the scheme's investment sub-committee. The practice was for the JISC to meet as a body and reach its conclusions, and then for the meeting to split into two investment sub-committees, one for the mineworkers' scheme and the other for the staff scheme, and then for each sub-committee to adopt the decisions of the JISC. The committee had before it the minutes of its investment sub-committee for 17 August 1982 (mistakenly stated to be for 24 August), 24 November 1982 and 24 February 1983. Mr Scargill moved the rejection of the minutes on the ground that they contained points about investments which were contrary to the union's position as raised at the meeting of the committee on 9 June 1982. Mr Cowan pointed out that the meetings had taken place and the minutes had been agreed as a true record. (The minutes of the meeting of 17 August, I may say, had been duly signed at the meeting of the JISC on 24 November, and similarly on 24 February 1983 the minutes for 24 November had been duly signed.) Mr Scargill, however, said that the committee, as trustees of the scheme, were entitled to reject any minutes put before them; and in the event it was accepted that no agreement could be reached on the acceptance or rejection of the minutes in question.

After certain other matters, the committee turned to the draft report and accounts for the year ended 30 September 1982. There was a substantial discussion of various items, and then Mr Scargill said that he was 'not prepared to accept the Report and Accounts since they contained items which were contrary to Union policy'; and he then referred to a particular item. After Mr Cowan had said that the accounts stated what had been done, and that trustees could not reject the facts because they did not agree with the policy, Mr Chadburn, one of the union trustees, said that they could not agree to something which they had disagreed with for nine months. A vote was taken on the acceptance of the report and accounts, and five voted for and five against, the board's nominees voting for and the union's nominees against. I am glad to say that the minutes of this meeting were duly accepted and signed at the forty-seventh meeting on 14 November 1983.

In that state of affairs, the resumed forty-fifth meeting was held that afternoon, on 28
a February; and I am glad to say that the minutes of this meeting too were duly accepted
and signed on 14 November 1983. Mr Cowan said that the board had an interest in
investment strategy because they were responsible for two-thirds of the contributions,
and if the committee became at cross-purposes in that strategy, and investment income
was impaired, the board might find it impossible to continue to pay additional
contributions in order to finance cost-of-living increases to pensions. This referred to the
b voluntary payments that the board made without being required to do so by the scheme.
Mr McGahey replied that it was the members who provided the wealth which allowed
the board to pay contributions, and 'as such the Union had a unilateral right of disposal
of these resources'.

Mr Jenkins then introduced the 1982 plan. This is set out in a document some 30
pages long. After Mr Jenkins's introduction, Mr Cowles reminded the trustees that the
c investment power must be exercised solely for the benefit of the trust. Mr Scargill said
that there was no difference in the arguments from those presented in June. 'They
rejected the legal opinion that had been given and they also rejected the investment plan
presented by Mr. Jenkins.' He said that one investment 'raised moral questions about
investment in private health care and proposals should not be merely based on commerce'.
Continued investment abroad and in oil 'would be to the detriment of coal and would be
d against the interests of the Scheme's beneficiaries'. He then put forward his proposals for
change, and asserted that the legal advice received by the NUM trustees 'was contrary to
what had been received that day'. Mr Cowan said that he could not understand why the
NUM trustees were determined that money should not be invested overseas. This had
not been the case until the previous June, and he wondered what had happened to change
the situation. Mr Scargill then said that he believed that all the money available for
e investment could be invested in Britain. 'The policy of the N.U.M. was being carried out,
although before June it was not.' After enumerating his proposals, he said that lawyers
advising the NUM said that trustees could not be criticised for not investing in certain
areas. The position of the NUM trustees 'was not negotiable and their objection to these
three areas of investment were matters of principle'. There was then another vote on the
approval of the 1982 plan, with a five to five decision as before. The 1982 plan was
f therefore not approved. Finally, it was agreed that there should be a meeting between
senior representatives of the board and the union to discuss investment overseas and in
oil and gas, with a committee meeting as soon as possible thereafter.

There then followed a number of discussions and a series of resultant memoranda
which Mr Scargill and Mr Cowan in turn put forward. These set out different forms of
wording for some or all of the changes which Mr Scargill sought. Mr Scargill began, with
g his memorandum dated 10 May 1983; and this became known as memorandum A, with
the others in sequence. In view of Mr Scargill's sustained criticisms of Mr Jenkins, I think
I ought to read the last paragraph of his memorandum. It runs:

> 'We wish to place on record our deep appreciation of our Investment Fund
> Manager, Mr Hugh Jenkins, and his staff for all the work they have done and
> continue to do on behalf of the Mineworkers' Pension Scheme.'

h

Mr Cowan replied with memorandum B on 5 July, and memorandum C on 17 August.
18 August saw Mr Cowan's memorandum D and Mr Scargill's memorandum E. Then
there came, also on 18 August, memorandum F, which became a matter of controversy. It
stated most, if not all, of the points that Mr Scargill wished to have established. He
relied on it as showing that agreement had been reached between Mr Cowan and Mr
j Harrison on the one hand, and Mr Scargill and Mr McGahey on the other. However, the
covering letter and Mr Cowan's evidence make it clear that memorandum F was intended
not for the committee but as the basis for a presentation to the board for alterations in
the scheme which some (but not all) of the provisions of the memorandum would
require. Mr Scargill strongly contended that in some way this memorandum bound the
committee as regards the parts which did not require the board's approval, because, he
said, if there had been a meeting of the committee, Mr Cowan and Mr Harrison would

have voted with the five NUM members, and so the memorandum would have been carried by seven votes to three, or by six to four, if only Mr Cowan felt bound. Mr Scargill *a* did not explain how a binding decision could be produced by a meeting which had not been held merely because a note had been prepared after discussion by four of the ten members; and in any case Mr Cowan's covering letter stated that the document is 'not to be read as an agreement binding or in any way restricting the present Trustees in the discharge of their duties'. Plainly the document decided nothing. In addition, Mr Scargill wrote on 5 September with a further document, memorandum G, which differed in *b* certain minor respects from memorandum F. His letter stated that memorandum F had departed in some degree from the document prepared by him and Mr McGahey. Clearly he was not accepting memorandum F.

In October 1983 Mr Cowan wrote to Mr Scargill to say that there ought to be a meeting of the committee as Mr Jenkins had said that it shortly would be practicable no longer to invest on the basis of the 1980 plan; and he sought agreement to proceeding on the basis *c* of the 1982 plan pending the committee meeting. Mr Scargill replied, agreeing that there should be a meeting, but refusing to agree to any investments being made on the basis of the 1982 plan, bearing in mind his 'total opposition' to investments overseas and in energy in direct competition with coal. On 14 November there was the forty-seventh meeting of the committee. This time a shorthand writer was present in order to avoid any difficulty about minutes. The result is some 45 pages long. *d*

At an early stage Mr Cowan told the committee that the board had decided that it would no longer make up any deficiency in the income from the fund if that income did not suffice for increasing pensions in line with the rate of inflation. He had given warning of this possibility at the afternoon meeting of the previous 24 February. The reason, he said, was that the board was concerned at the delays in implementing the 1982 plan, and was also of the opinion that this might well diminish the income from the *e* fund. To this statement Mr Scargill took 'the strongest possible exception', and rejected the criticism that the scheme had suffered in any way. Before me, Mr Scargill was critical of Mr Cowan's statement as showing that Mr Cowan was speaking not as a trustee but as a representative of the board, and also that it was an attempt to put pressure on the trustees. I can see nothing wrong in Mr Cowan informing his fellow trustees of the decision of the board, a decision which might reduce the benefits of the scheme; and I *f* see no merit in requiring the board instead to write to the committee, as Mr Scargill suggested. A trustee who informs his fellows of some impending disadvantage to the trust does not cease to act as a trustee by so doing: indeed, it would almost certainly be a breach of his duty to remain silent.

I shall not quote from the minutes of the meeting at any length. Mr Scargill and others of the NUM trustees made it perfectly clear that they would not agree to any further *g* investment overseas or in energies competing with coal in any circumstances. Thus, when Mr Scargill was asked whether he would still say 'No' if a better financial result could be obtained by investing abroad, he said:

'The answer to that question has already been put fairly in this meeting previously. The National Union of Mineworkers unanimously at its Conference, in its individual branches, in its areas, and by representation of the trustees to this meeting, have *h* declared unequivocally that they are opposed to any investment overseas.'

The NUM trustees were then asked, 'Do you regard yourself as within the trust law of this country to be mandated?', and Mr Scargill replied, 'We regard ourselves to be acting within the law and we have been so legally advised.' It was then put to him that under the law you could not be mandated by someone outside to do what you did not think *j* right in terms of the financial returns, and Mr Scargill replied:

'I made it perfectly clear that the position of the N.U.M., determined by its Conference, its branches and its areas, was totally and unequivocally against overseas investment. That has also been reflected to this meeting by the trustees. There is no *a* ambiguity about the statement that I made and we are so advised legally that we are acting within the law.'

A little later he added:

'People representing the National Union of Mineworkers as trustees have reflected their views quite clearly that they are against overseas investments in any circumstances.'

b Subsequently he said:

'The National Union of Mineworkers' trustees are opposed in all circumstances to the investment of monies in the Mineworkers' Pension Scheme overseas.'

Mr Vincent, one of the NUM trustees, then said that this was not a mandate: 'it is N.U.M. policy'; and Mr Williams, another NUM trustee, said that the NEC decision was *c* unanimous, and that the policy went through the annual conference 'without any opposition—unanimous'.

After further discussion, Mr Cowles said that trustees must not fetter their discretion to invest, whereat Mr Scargill asserted that 'the proposals on principles which we have advanced are, in our legal advisers' view, quite within the law'. Mr Cowles then said that he had asked Mr Scargill to show him a copy of his opinion, but he had not done so, to *d* which Mr Scargill replied that 'if this action subsequently comes before another authority, at that stage no doubt you will be presented with our advice'. On being asked whether 'overseas' included EEC countries and the Third World, Mr Scargill said that it certainly did:

'I am speaking about investment in the United Kingdom—let there be no ambiguity about that. That is the policy of my Union and it is a principle decision.'
e

Towards the end of the meeting, Mr Scargill moved an amendment that the 1982 plan should not be implemented unless it incorporated a proposal, inter alia, 'to have no further increase in overseas investment over the 1980 Plan'. A page later he said that he had made his amendment 'very, very clear'; and he then stated it as being that the 1982 plan be adopted subject to three amendments, the first of which was 'that there be no *f* increase in the percentage of overseas investment'. 'No further increase' and 'no further increase in the percentage' do not, of course, produce the same result. Where the amount of the fund is steadily increasing, as is the case here, the first prohibits any purchase, whereas the second permits it within limits. I do not think that the difference matters much, as the issue is not how much restriction there should be, but whether there should be any. In the end, the meeting was adjourned.

g On 24 November 1983 the adjourned forty-seventh meeting was held. At an early stage, Mr Scargill said that—

'In order that the record be absolutely straight, at no time have the trustees of the N.U.M. had any other consideration than the benefit of the beneficiaries and it is towards that end that all our actions have been directed.'

h Not surprisingly, Mr Cowan pointed to the conflict between principles which sought to diversify the fund so as to maximise the return for beneficiaries by investing at home and abroad if necessary, and principles which placed an embargo on decisions by the investment managers which they might consider to be in the best interests of the beneficiaries. Mr Scargill asserted that his proposal was a perfectly reasonable proposal that was in the interests of the beneficiaries; and he said that the line being taken by the *j* NUM trustees was no different from the line taken when the 1982 plan was first presented. There were various references to the matter having to be resolved in the courts, and then, after Mr Scargill had said that they 'would not dream of coming to this meeting mandated or with a fixed policy', the meeting turned to other matters, some of which I shall have to refer to later. As I have mentioned, the originating summons was issued on 1 December 1983.

By the originating summons the plaintiffs seek directions under three heads. First, they seek—

'Directions whether the Defendants are in breach of their fiduciary duties as members of the Committee of Management of the Scheme and trustees of its money and investments in refusing to concur in the adoption of the Investment Strategy and Business Plan 1982 (initially presented to a meeting of the Committee on 9 June 1982) unless amended so that (1) there is to be no increase in the percentage of overseas investment; and (2) overseas investment already made is to be withdrawn at the most opportune time; and (3) the Committee adopts a proposal within the Business Plan of not investing in energies which are in direct competition with coal.'

Second, they seek—

'Directions whether the Investment Strategy and Business Plan 1982 should now be adopted by the Committee and implemented.'

Third, they seek—

'Directions for the completion of the accounts of the Scheme for the year to 30 September 1982.'

There is also a request for various consequential and other relief.

I can dispose of the third head quickly. At the outset of day 1 I asked Mr Scargill why it would not be possible for him and the other NUM trustees to sign the 1982 accounts with the addition of some words which showed that they did not question the accuracy of the accounts but dissociated themselves from certain matters disclosed in them. Mr Scargill then said that this had never been suggested by the plaintiffs, but that it was certainly a matter that could be considered. Towards the end of day 9 Mr Scargill referred to the point again, and said that if some such words could be inserted in the accounts, the defendants would have no objection to signing them. The matter was then left for discussion between the parties. Counsel for the plaintiffs did not think such words would produce any obstacles from his point of view, and so I shall say no more about question 3 unless I am asked to do so.

I turn to the law. The starting point is the duty of trustees to exercise their powers in the best interests of the present and future beneficiaries of the trust, holding the scales impartially between different classes of beneficiaries. This duty of the trustees towards their beneficiaries is paramount. They must, of course, obey the law; but subject to that, they must put the interests of their beneficiaries first. When the purpose of the trust is to provide financial benefits for the beneficiaries, as is usually the case, the best interests of the beneficiaries are normally their best financial interests. In the case of a power of investment, as in the present case, the power must be exercised so as to yield the best return for the beneficiaries, judged in relation to the risks of the investments in question; and the prospects of the yield of income and capital appreciation both have to be considered in judging the return from the investment.

The legal memorandum that the union obtained from their solicitors is generally in accord with these views. In considering the possibility of investment for 'socially beneficial reasons which may result in lower returns to the fund', the memorandum states that 'the trustees' only concern is to ensure that the return is the maximum possible consistent with security'; and then it refers to the need for diversification. However, it continues by saying that:

'Trustees cannot be criticised for failing to make a particular investment for social or political reasons, such as in South African stock for example, but may be held liable for investing in assets which yield a poor return or for disinvesting in stock at inappropriate times for non-financial criteria.'

This last sentence must be considered in the light of subsequent passages in the memorandum which indicate that the sale of South African securities by trustees might be justified on the ground of doubts about political stability in South Africa and the long-term financial soundness of its economy, whereas trustees could not properly support

a motions at a company meeting dealing with pay levels in South Africa, work accidents, pollution control, employment conditions for minorities, military contracting and consumer protection. The assertion that trustees could not be criticised for failing to make a particular investment for social or political reasons is one that I would not accept in its full width. If the investment in fact made is equally beneficial to the beneficiaries, then criticism would be difficult to sustain in practice, whatever the position in theory.

b But if the investment in fact made is less beneficial, then both in theory and in practice the trustees would normally be open to criticism.

This leads me to the second point, which is a corollary of the first. In considering what investments to make trustees must put on one side their own personal interests and views. Trustees may have strongly held social or political views. They may be firmly opposed to any investment in South Africa or other countries, or they may object to any

c form of investment in companies concerned with alcohol, tobacco, armaments or many other things. In the conduct of their own affairs, of course, they are free to abstain from making any such investments. Yet under a trust, if investments of this type would be more beneficial to the beneficiaries than other investments, the trustees must not refrain from making the investments by reasons of the views that they hold.

Trustees may even have to act dishonourably (though not illegally) if the interests of

d their beneficiaries require it. Thus where trustees for sale had struck a bargain for the sale of trust property but had not bound themselves by a legally enforceable contract, they were held to be under a duty to consider and explore a better offer that they received, and not to carry through the bargain to which they felt in honour bound: see *Buttle v Saunders* [1950] 2 All ER 193. In other words, the duty of trustees to their beneficiaries may include a duty to 'gazump', however honourable the trustees. As Wynn-Parry J said

e (at 195), trustees 'have an overriding duty to obtain the best price which they can for their beneficiaries'. In applying this to an Official Receiver, Templeman J said in *Re Wyvern Developments Ltd* [1974] 2 All ER 535 at 544, [1974] 1 WLR 1097 at 1106 that he—

'must do his best by his creditors and contributories. He is in a fiduciary capacity and cannot make moral gestures, nor can the court authorise him to do so.'

f In the words of Wigram V-C in *Balls v Strutt* (1841) 1 Hare 146 at 149, 66 ER 984 at 985:

'It is a principle in this Court that a trustee shall not be permitted to use the powers which the trust may confer upon him at law, except for the legitimate purposes of his trust.'

g Powers must be exercised fairly and honestly for the purposes for which they are given and not so as to accomplish any ulterior purpose, whether for the benefit of the trustees or otherwise: see *Duke of Portland v Topham* (1864) 11 HL Cas 32, [1861–73] All ER Rep 980, a case on a power of appointment that must apply a fortiori to a power given to trustees as such.

Third, by way of caveat I should say that I am not asserting that the benefit of the

h beneficiaries which a trustee must make his paramount concern inevitably and solely means their financial benefit, even if the only object of the trust is to provide financial benefits. Thus if the only actual or potential beneficiaries of a trust are all adults with very strict views on moral and social matters, condemning all forms of alcohol, tobacco and popular entertainment, as well as armaments, I can well understand that it might not be for the 'benefit' of such beneficiaries to know that they are obtaining rather larger financial returns under the trust by reason of investments in those activities than they

j would have received if the trustees had invested the trust funds in other investments. The beneficiaries might well consider that it was far better to receive less than to receive more money from what they consider to be evil and tainted sources. 'Benefit' is a word with a very wide meaning, and there are circumstances in which arrangements which work to the financial disadvantage of a beneficiary may yet be for his benefit: see, for example, *Re Towler's Settlement Trusts* [1963] 3 All ER 759, [1964] Ch 158; *Re C L* [1968]

1 All ER 1104, [1969] 1 Ch 587. But I would emphasise that such cases are likely to be very rare, and in any case I think that under a trust for the provision of financial benefits the burden would rest, and rest heavy, on him who asserts that it is for the benefit of the beneficiaries as a whole to receive less by reason of the exclusion of some of the possibly more profitable forms of investment. Plainly the present case is not one of this rare type of case. Subject to such matters, under a trust for the provision of financial benefits, the paramount duty of the trustees is to provide the greatest financial benefits for the present and future beneficiaries.

Fourth, the standard required of a trustee in exercising his powers of investment is that he must—

'take such care as an ordinary prudent man would take if he were minded to make an investment for the benefit of other people for whom he felt morally bound to provide.'

See *Re Whiteley, Whiteley v Learoyd* (1886) 33 Ch D 347 at 355 per Lindley LJ, and see also at 350, 358; *Learoyd v Whiteley* (1887) 12 App Cas 727. That duty includes the duty to seek advice on matters which the trustee does not understand, such as the making of investments, and on receiving that advice to act with the same degree of prudence. This requirement is not discharged merely by showing that the trustee has acted in good faith and with sincerity. Honesty and sincerity are not the same as prudence and reasonableness. Some of the most sincere people are the most unreasonable; and Mr Scargill told me that he had met quite a few of them. Accordingly, although a trustee who takes advice on investments is not bound to accept and act on that advice, he is not entitled to reject it merely because he sincerely disagrees with it, unless in addition to being sincere he is acting as an ordinary prudent man would act.

Fifth, trustees have a duty to consider the need for diversification of investments. By s 6(1) of the Trustee Investments Act 1961:

'In the exercise of his powers of investment a trustee shall have regard—(a) to the need for diversification of investments of the trust, in so far as is appropriate to the circumstances of the trust; (b) to the suitability to the trust of investments of the description of investment proposed and of the investment proposed as an investment of that description.'

The reference to the 'circumstances of the trust' plainly includes matters such as the size of the trust funds: the degree of diversification that is practicable and desirable for a large fund may plainly be impracticable or undesirable (or both) in the case of a small fund.

In the case before me, it is not in issue that there ought to be diversification of the investments held by the fund. The contention of the defendants, put very shortly, is that there can be a sufficient degree of diversification without any investment overseas or in oil, and that in any case there is no need to increase the level of overseas investments beyond the existing level. Other pension funds got on well enough without overseas investments, it was said, and in particular the NUM's own scheme had, in 1982, produced better results than the scheme here in question. This was not so, said Mr Jenkins, if you compared like with like, and excluded investments in property, which figure substantially in the mineworkers' scheme but not at all in the NUM scheme: and in any case the latter scheme was much smaller, being of the order of £7m.

I shall not pursue this matter. Even if other funds in one particular year, or in many years, had done better than the scheme which is before me, that does not begin to show that it is beneficial to this scheme to be shorn of the ability to invest overseas. The main difference between the 1980 and the 1982 plans, I may say, is that although the target for overseas investments remains at 15%, the 1982 plan increases the percentage of the cash flow that can be invested in overseas realty from 7½% to 10%, and relaxes the overall limit of 15% in this respect. It should be added that, in addition, something like 10% of the assets of British companies in which the fund has invested consist of overseas holdings, so that there is this additional foreign element. As for oil, the 1982 plan made no real difference: the existing holdings of just under 12% could have been maintained if that

a plan had been implemented.

Sixth, there is the question whether the principles that I have been stating apply, with or without modification, to trusts of pension funds. Counsel for the plaintiffs asserted that they applied without modification, and that it made no difference that some of the funds came from the members of the pension scheme, or that the funds were often of a very substantial size. Mr Scargill did not in terms assert the contrary. He merely said that

b this was one of the questions to be decided, and that pension funds may be subject to different rules. I was somewhat unsuccessful in my attempts to find out from him why this was so, and what the differences were. What it came down to, I think, was that the rules for trusts had been laid down for private and family trusts and wills a long time ago; that pension funds were very large and affected large numbers of people; that in the present case the well-being of all within the coal industry was affected; and that there

c was no authority on the point except *Evans v London Co-op Society Ltd* (1976) Times, 6 July and certain overseas cases.

I shall refer to the authorities in a moment, and consider the question of principle first. I can see no reason for holding that different principles apply to pension fund trusts from those which apply to other trusts. Of course, there are many provisions in pension schemes which are not to be found in private trusts, and to these the general law of trusts

d will be subordinated. But subject to that, I think that the trusts of pension funds are subject to the same rules as other trusts. The large size of pension funds emphasises the need for diversification, rather than lessening it, and the fact that much of the fund has been contributed by members of the scheme seems to me to make it even more important that the trustees should exercise their powers in the best interests of the beneficiaries. In a private trust, most, if not all, of the beneficiaries are the recipients of

e the bounty of the settlor, whereas under the trusts of a pension fund many (though not all) of the beneficiaries are those who, as members, contributed to the funds so that in due time they would receive pensions. It is thus all the more important that the interests of the beneficiaries should be paramount, so that they may receive the benefits which in part they have paid for. I can see no justification for holding that the benefits to them should run the risk of being lessened because the trustees were pursuing an investment

f policy intended to assist the industry that the pensioners have left, or their union.

I turn to the authorities. *Evans v London Co-op Society Ltd* (1976) Times, 6 July is a decision of Brightman J which has apparently achieved a considerable measure of renown among those concerned with pension funds as being the only English authority on the subject. I do not think that I need discuss the details of the case, because it seems to me to be perfectly clear that it is a decision on a particular rule of the pension fund there in

g question, r 7, and not on the general law. Rule 7 provided for the pensions committee to make loans on certain terms to the co-operative society in question, and the pension fund had been receiving from the society less than the market rate of interest on such loans. The substance of the decision was that the terms of r 7 permitted not only the self-investment of the pension funds but also the payment of less than the market rate of interest on such loans, even though the society was the trustee of the fund and so was

h profiting from its trust. I find it impossible to read pp 17–20 of the full transcript without reaching the conclusion that the judge was deciding the case on the extent to which r 7 took the case out of the ordinary law of trusts, and that but for r 7 the ordinary law of trusts would have been applied to the case. In my judgment, the case does nothing to support the contentions of the defendants. Instead, I think it provides some support for the plaintiffs.

j *Blankenship v Boyle* (1971) 329 F Supp 1089 was a case heard in the US district court for the District of Columbia by Judge Gesell. The trustees of a pension fund had allowed large sums of money to remain in bank accounts bearing no interest at a bank controlled by the union. Over an 18-year period, varying sums between $14m and $75m, representing between 14% and 44% of the fund's total resources, had been left in this way. The fund was established for the benefit of employees of coal operators, their families and dependants, and over 95% of the members of the fund were also members of the union. It was contended that the trustees could properly consider not only the interests of the beneficiaries but also collateral matters such as increasing the tonnage of union-mined coal; but this was rejected. The court reaffirmed the duty of undivided loyalty to the beneficiaries that a trustee owes, and did not accept that regard should also be paid to the union or its members who generated some of the income of the fund, or to the industry as a whole. That seems to me to be plainly right.

Withers v Teachers' Retirement System of the City of New York (1978) 447 F Supp 1248 arose out of the impending insolvency of the City of New York in 1975. The Teachers' Retirement System (TRS) and four other New York pension funds agreed to purchase $2,530m unmarketable and highly speculative New York City bonds over the next 2½ years in an attempt to stave off the imminent bankruptcy of the city; the share contributed by TRS was $860m. TRS was an unfunded scheme, and the evidence was that if the city ceased to make its massive contributions to the scheme, the reserves would be exhausted in some eight to ten years, even if the contributions by employees continued and there was a constant rate of retirement of teachers. In the US District Court for the Southern District of New York, Judge Conner considered and accepted *Blankenship v Boyle* and the traditional rules of equity, but held that the trustees had been justified in purchasing the bonds since they had done so in the best interests of the beneficiaries, and not out of concern for the general public welfare or the protection of the jobs of city teachers. The object of the trustees, who had imposed stringent conditions in an attempt to protect the TRS, had been to ensure the continuance of the city's major contributions to the scheme, and preserve the city's position as the ultimate guarantor of the payment of pension benefits; and this was in the best interests of the beneficiaries. This differed from the position in *Blankenship v Boyle*, where—

> 'the trustees pursued policies which may incidentally have aided the beneficiaries of the fund but which were intended, primarily, to enhance the position of the Union and the welfare of its members, presumably, through the creation and/or preservation of jobs in the coal industry.'

(See 447 F Supp 1248 at 1256.) Apart from the expression 'and/or', I would agree.

The American cases do not, of course, bind me; but they seem, if I may say so, to be soundly based on equitable principles which are common to England and most jurisdictions in the United States, and they accord with the conclusion that I would have reached in the absence of authority. Accordingly, on principle, on the *Evans* case, and on the two American cases, I reach the unhesitating conclusion that the trusts of pension funds are in general governed by the ordinary law of trusts, subject to any contrary provision in the rules or other provisions which govern the trust. In particular, the trustees of a pension fund are subject to the overriding duty to do the best that they can for the beneficiaries, the duty that in the United States is known as 'the duty of undivided loyalty to the beneficiaries' (see *Blankenship v Boyle* 329 F Supp 1089 at 1095).

In considering that duty, it must be remembered that very many of the beneficiaries will not in any way be directly affected by the prosperity of the mining industry or the union. Miners who have retired, and the widows and children of deceased miners, will continue to receive their benefits from the fund even if the mining industry shrinks: for the scheme is fully funded, and the fund does not depend on further contributions to it being made. If the board fell on hard times, it might be unable to continue its voluntary payments to meet cost-of-living increases, quite apart from the statement about this made by Mr Cowan at the forty-seventh committee meeting on 14 November 1983. The impact of that remote possibility falls far short of the imminent disaster facing the City of New York and TRS in the *Withers* case; and I cannot regard any policy designed to ensure the general prosperity of coal mining as being a policy which is directed to obtaining the best possible results for the beneficiaries, most of whom are no longer engaged in the industry, and some of whom never were. The connection is far too remote and insubstantial. Further, the assets of even so large a pension fund as this are nowhere near the size at which there could be expected to be any perceptible impact from the adoption of the policies for which Mr Scargill contends.

I turn to consider the grounds on which the prohibitions put forward by the defendants have been supported. First, there are the reasons put forward during the discussions by the trustees. I have already quoted a number of these. Put shortly, these were that the prohibitions were NUM policy: the union, as a matter of principle, was totally and unequivocally opposed to investment overseas. These views were put forward in various ways on various occasions, but the substance was unvarying. However, as I have mentioned, early in the meeting on 24 November 1983, nearly 18 months after the dispute had broken out, Mr Scargill asserted that at no time had the NUM trustees had 'any other consideration than the benefit of the beneficiaries and it is towards that end that all our actions have been directed'. At no stage did he explain how or why it was for the benefit of the beneficiaries to put union policy into force under the scheme by imposing the prohibitions. Nor did he attempt to reconcile his statement at the same meeting that he would not dream of coming to it 'mandated or with a fixed policy' with his consistent attitude of total opposition to overseas investment, as a matter of principle that was not negotiable. From time to time Mr Scargill made other assertions of this nature, again unexplained.

I can see no escape from the conclusion that the NUM trustees were attempting to impose the prohibitions in order to carry out union policy; and mere assertions that their sole consideration was the benefit of the beneficiaries do not alter that conclusion. If the NUM trustees were thinking only of the benefit of the beneficiaries, why all the references to union policy instead of proper explanations of how and why the prohibitions would bring benefits to the beneficiaries? No doubt some trustees with strong feelings find it irksome to be forced to submerge those feelings and genuinely put the interests of the beneficiaries first. Indeed, there are some who are temperamentally unsuited to being trustees, and are more fitted for campaigning for changes in the law. This, of course, they are free to do; but if they choose to become trustees they must accept it that the rules of equity will bind them in all that they do as trustees.

I must also refer once more to the legal advice which the union obtained from the solicitors. Mr Scargill repeatedly asserted that their legal advisers had taken the view that the proposals of the NUM trustees (namely the prohibitions) were within the law. He also rejected Mr Cowles's advice on the obligation to exercise the investment power solely for the benefit of the trust, and said that this was contrary to the legal advice that the union had received. Unlike Mr Cowles, Mr Scargill plainly had access to the whole of that legal advice. When at last he produced the memorandum containing that advice, after his previous refusals to do so, it could be seen that the advice in fact provided no support whatever for the prohibitions that the union trustees sought to impose, and that it accorded with Mr Cowles's advice, rather than contradicting it. The distinction that Mr Cowles made in his note of 25 June 1982 between opting for one particular investment as against a viable alternative and, on the other hand, imposing an embargo on a wide range of investments, does not require a lawyer to understand it; yet Mr Scargill continued to claim that the advice obtained by the union supported his views. The solicitors' memorandum also discussed proposals for a Pension Scheme Act, referring to the 1980 report of the Committee to Review the Functioning of Financial Institutions (the Wilson Report (Cmnd 7937)) and comments on it, and saying that any such Act was some years away. The memorandum thus clearly distinguished the law as it was from the law that there may be.

I do not know what were the instructions that were given to the solicitors, or what questions they were asked; but judging from the memorandum, at least one question seems to have been how far pension fund trustees could give effect to their social views in making investments, and how far they would be at risk if they did so. For the most part, if I may say so, the advice seemed to me to be sound, practicable, and readily intelligible to a layman of ordinary intelligence; but it certainly does not provide any support for the prohibitions proposed by the defendants.

I therefore reject any contention that the defendants' attempts to impose the prohibitions were supported by the legal advice that they had obtained or that it supported their rejection of the advice given by Mr Cowles. Mr Scargill's assertions of such support are simply untrue, and obviously so. I also reject any assertion that prior to

the commencement of these proceedings the benefit of the beneficiaries was the sole
consideration that the union trustees had: that also is untrue. The union trustees were   *a*
mainly, if not solely, actuated by a desire to pursue union policy, and they were not
putting the interests of the beneficiaries first, as they ought to have done. They were
doing so deliberately and in the teeth of proper legal advice from both sides of the table
as to the duties of trustees, and there has been no suggestion that at any time they
obtained further legal advice, as trustees who had genuinely intended to carry out their
fiduciary duties would have done when the serious conflict of views had become plain.   *b*
They were adamant in their determination to impose the restrictions, whether or not
they harmed their beneficiaries. In this respect I can see no difference between Mr
Scargill, who vehemently opposed investment overseas and in oil as soon as he became a
trustee, and the other four union trustees, who for years before the advent of Mr Scargill
had been operating under a policy of substantial investment overseas and in oil. As soon
as Mr Scargill arrived, they promptly abandoned their previous attitude and fell in beside   *c*
him.

This conclusion, however, does not end the matter. If trustees make a decision on
wholly wrong grounds, and yet it subsequently appears, from matters which they did
not express or refer to, that there are in fact good and sufficient reasons for supporting
their decision, then I do not think that they would incur any liability for having decided
the matter on erroneous grounds; for the decision itself was right. I must therefore turn   *d*
to the 30 or 35 affidavits which, with their voluminous exhibits, made up the eight large
volumes that were before me.

Some of the evidence filed by the defendants tended to show that the prohibitions
would not be harmful to the beneficiaries, or jeopardise the aims of the fund, and that
some pension funds get along well enough without any overseas investments. Such
evidence misses the point. Trustees must do the best they can for the benefit of their   *e*
beneficiaries, and not merely avoid harming them. I find it impossible to see how it will
assist trustees to do the best they can for their beneficiaries by prohibiting a wide range
of investments that are authorised by the terms of the trust. Whatever the position today,
nobody can say that conditions tomorrow cannot possibly make it advantageous to invest
in one of the prohibited investments. It is the duty of trustees, in the interests of their
beneficiaries, to take advantage of the full range of investments authorised by the terms   *f*
of the trust, instead of resolving to narrow that range.

There was other evidence filed by the defendants which was more to the point; and it
was met by countervailing evidence of the plaintiffs. This evidence was directed to
economics and investment strategy. At the outset I must say that I found the plaintiffs'
evidence the more cogent and practical, and more directly related to what was in issue.
The general thrust of the defendants' evidence in support of the restrictions that they   *g*
seek to impose was along the following lines. Pensions funds in Britain have enormous
assets. If all, or nearly all, of these assets were invested in Britain, and none, or few, were
invested overseas, this would do much to revive this country's economy and so benefit
all workers, especially if the investments were in the form not of purchasing established
stocks and shares but of 'real' investment in physical assets and new ventures. For the
mineworkers' scheme, the prosperity of the coal industry would aid the prosperity of the   *h*
scheme, and so lead to benefits for the beneficiaries under the scheme. This point was
put in various ways, and a short summary necessarily omits many facets; but in the end
the approach seems to me to have been along these general lines.

I readily accept that a case, and perhaps a strong case, can be made for legislation or
other provisions that in the general public interest would restrict the outflow of large
funds from this country and put the money to work here. I have already mentioned the   *j*
Wilson Report; and in July 1983 the TUC issued a report, some 35 pages long, called
'Pension Fund Investment and Trusteeship', which went into such matters in considerable
detail, dealing with many other points as well. Apart from legislation, the report
recommends the introduction of guidelines to restrict overseas investment by pension
funds; and of course the investment clauses in schemes may include such restrictions, or
may be altered to include them. It is only in the last five years that the abolition of
exchange control has made it easy to invest abroad, and the full effect of this restored

liberty has perhaps not yet been fully felt and evaluated in the investment world. It may

a well be, too, that a strong case could be made for the opposing view, precluding any restriction on overseas investment by pension funds. But I am not concerned with changes in the law or in the scheme for any pension fund, whether this fund or any other. I have to deal with this fund under the scheme as it now stands. I am concerned with a fund under which there are many beneficiaries who no longer have any financial interest in the welfare of the coal industry. They may well be 'interested' in it in the sense

b that they remember the years that they spent in it with affection or the reverse, and they may well find it 'interesting' to know what is going on in it, in the sense of gratifying a natural curiosity and concern about the industry and the people in it. But apart from such matters, they are not affected by the industry and its success.

In my view, therefore, the broad economic arguments of the defendants provide no justification for the restrictions that they wish to impose. Any possible benefits from

c imposing the restrictions that would accrue to the beneficiaries under the scheme (as distinct from the general public) are far too speculative and remote. Large though the fund is, I cannot see how the adoption of the restrictions can make any material impact on the national economy, or bring any appreciable benefit to the beneficiaries under the scheme. There is nothing whatever to suggest that the board will be in any difficulty in making its payments under the scheme unless the restrictions are adopted. There is not

d a shred of evidence to suggest that the board is in a state of imminent disaster like that which faced the City of New York in the *Withers* case, or that even if it were the imposition of the restrictions would save it; and in any case the scheme, unlike that in the *Withers* case, is fully funded. As for diversification, I can see that the risks inherent in an individual investment can be met by a modest degree of diversification; but where the risks are not merely for one particular investment but for a whole sector of the

e market, such as mining or tea, a wider degree of diversification will be needed. In any case, the question is one of excluding a very large sector of the market, and preventing diversification into investments in other countries which may do well at a time when the whole British market is depressed; and I can see no possible benefit in such an exclusion, especially in the case of a very large fund with highly skilled investment expertise.

f Accordingly, on the case as a whole, in my judgment the plaintiffs are right and the defendants are wrong. The question, then, is what order should be made. The summons is cast in the form of asking the court to give directions; but I doubt whether this is the most appropriate remedy. I think that at this stage it would be more appropriate for me to make declarations, and leave it to the defendants to carry out their duties as trustees in accordance with those declarations. I am ready to assume that they will comply with the

g law once the court has declared what it is. My only hesitation arises from a letter dated 3 January 1984 from Mr Scargill in which he answered a request to sign a document by saying that he had 'no intention of signing *anything* in connection with this investment'; and he suggested getting the signature of Vinelott J 'who apparently appointed himself a Trustee for the purposes of this investment'. This refers to a motion before Vinelott J some two weeks earlier in which he had authorised making a particular overseas

h investment, the RAMPAC investment. Against this, however, must be set Mr Scargill's proper attitude in this court on the signing of the accounts; and so, despite his regrettable letter, I shall not assume that the defendants intend to demonstrate their unfitness to continue as trustees by refusing to comply with the law as declared by the court. Accordingly, subject to what may be said when I have concluded this judgment, I propose to make suitable declarations, and to give liberty to apply for directions or other

j appropriate relief if the declarations are not duly acted on. It is important to get this large trust back on the rails; and it may help to do this if at this stage the court refrains from giving directions or making any coercive orders, whether under the inherent jurisdiction or otherwise, and remains in the background while the normal operation of the scheme is being re-established. It is very much to be hoped that there will be no need to consider the exercise of the court's inherent power to remove trustees. I should add that it is clear that the court can make declarations even though they have not been claimed in the proceedings (see *Harrison-Broadly v Smith* [1964] 1 All ER 867, [1964] 1 WLR 456).

Before I part with the case, there are certain other matters that I should mention. They do not affect what I have to decide, but they have plainly been bones of contention that have disturbed the smooth running of the scheme, and I do not think that I should pass over them in silence. First, there is the general question of deadlock. Mr Scargill placed much emphasis on the provisions of the scheme which established five trustees from each side and no casting vote: the concept of deadlock was built into the scheme, and ought not to be disturbed by the court. Initially he appeared to be arguing that the court had no jurisdiction to resolve any deadlock unless it was so complete that the affairs of the trust had been brought to a standstill; but by the end of the hearing he had accepted that the court had jurisdiction to resolve any deadlock. I therefore need not discuss *Re Billes* (1983) 148 DLR (3d) 512, which supports this view in relation to investment by trustees.

Despite Mr Scargill's emphatic submissions, I can see no particular significance in the so-called deadlock provisions. In an ordinary trust, the trustees can do nothing unless they are unanimous: a majority cannot prevail over a minority, and so the opportunities of a deadlock are even greater than under the scheme, where a majority suffices. Certainly I can see nothing in the so-called deadlock concept to affect the jurisdiction of the court. Nor, despite what Mr Scargill said, can I see anything significant in the fact that at the forty-fifth meeting of the committee, on 9 June 1982, when Mr Scargill first raised his objections to the 1982 plan, Mr Cowan adjourned the meeting without taking a vote, although there were only four NUM trustees at the meeting and so the 1982 plan could presumably have been approved by five votes to four. The adjournment seemed to me to be no more than the entirely proper conduct of a chairman at a meeting when an important point has arisen which has been strenuously debated and one side in the debate has not been fully represented. Although Mr Scargill stressed the adjournment, I could not discover any real relevance in it.

Second, there is the RAMPAC affair. This was the American investment which, as I have mentioned, was authorised by Vinelott J on 21 December 1983 on motion. The complaint is that the matter was put before the committee and the judge as a matter of urgency, whereas it has now emerged that in fact considerably more time was available. Nothing that I have to decide turns on this, and I shall not discuss it. But I think that I should say that I can well understand Mr Scargill having had feelings of suspicion in the matter, although in the end I think that his complaint really comes down to that of a failure by Mr Jenkins to discover more about the proposals than he in fact had found out at the time; and it has now been shown that there were difficulties in obtaining that information.

Third, there was a complaint that Mr Scargill and the other NUM trustees were being treated as second-class trustees, in that they were not given information about proposed investments when some of the NCB trustees were given it. Again, I can understand the complaint; but it is at least in part due to the structure under the scheme. One of the NCB trustees, Mr Cowan, is chairman of the committee. Another, Mr Harrison, is both a joint deputy chairman of the committee and the chairman of the JISC. It is therefore not at all surprising that Mr Jenkins should from time to time consult Mr Harrison or Mr Cowan, or both, on points that arise on investments. Yet Mr Scargill, who is also a joint deputy chairman of the committee, is not normally consulted in this way, and so he feels aggrieved at the difference in treatment between one joint deputy chairman and another. The explanation that Mr Harrison was consulted not qua joint deputy chairman of the committee but qua chairman of the JISC plainly did not satisfy Mr Scargill, who in cross-examining Mr Jenkins asked him whether he did not regard him, Mr Scargill, as a second-class trustee. As I have said, I can understand Mr Scargill's complaint; but it is nothing that arises under the originating summons that is before me. It is a matter for discussion when any changes in the constitution and operation of the scheme are under consideration. The same applies to what I think is Mr Scargill's more fundamental grievance, namely that the trustees, though responsible for general policy, have too little control over individual investments.

Fourth, I think that I should say something about certain other matters. Mr Scargill was critical of Mr Jenkins as being lacking in independence of the board, which paid his a salary; as disregarding Mr Scargill's views and failing to give proper consideration to his suggestions for investment; and in failing to provide various items of information. I shall not go into the details; I merely say that it seemed to me that after these matters had been examined there was little, if anything, that supported the criticism. Counsel for the plaintiffs pointed out that Mr Scargill had said at the resumed forty-fifth meeting of the committee on 28 February 1983 that he was not suggesting that Mr Jenkins was doing anything other than carrying out the existing policy decisions of the trustees; it

b was the policy decisions and the principles that were wrong. On 10 May 1983, too, there was the 'deep appreciation' of Mr Jenkins and his staff for all the work that they had done and were continuing to do that Mr Scargill chose to express in his memorandum A. That, of course, was before the RAMPAC affair, and this and other matters have fed the suspicions that Mr Scargill has been harbouring. If it has done no more, I hope that the course of not preventing these matters from being explored during the hearing will have

c contributed towards allaying those suspicions.

I shall say nothing about various other matters that emerged during the hearing, such as the ill-fated Centre Video venture. I have read through my notes and I have referred to many passages in the transcripts; and at the end of the day I have reached the conclusion that there is no need to lengthen any further this already too lengthy judgment.

d For the reasons that I have given, and subject to any submissions that there may be on the form of relief, I propose to make declarations along the lines that I have stated. I shall retain the matter.

Declarations accordingly.

e Solicitors: *Freshfields* (for the plaintiffs).

Vivian Horvath   Barrister.

Herbage v Pressdram Ltd and others

f

COURT OF APPEAL, CIVIL DIVISION
GRIFFITHS AND KERR LJJ
1 MAY 1984

Conviction – Spent conviction – Rehabilitation of offenders – Publication referring to spent
g *convictions – Grant of injunction restraining publication if publication is malicious – Rehabilitation*
of Offenders Act 1974, s 1(1).

Injunction – Interlocutory – Jurisdiction – Libel – Plaintiff seeking injunction restraining defendant
from publication – Publication referring to spent convictions – Grant of injunction restraining
publication if publication is malicious – Rehabilitation of Offenders Act 1974, s 1(1).

h

A person whose convictions are to be treated as spent by virtue of s 1(1)[a] of the Rehabilitation of Offenders Act 1974 can recover damages for libel provided he is able to show that publication of those convictions was malicious. The real issue to be tried is one of malice and the court will therefore apply the same principles as it would apply in a case where a defendant relies on a defence of qualified privilege, and will only intervene

j to grant an interlocutory injunction restraining publication where the evidence of malice is overwhelming (see p 772 *e* to *j*, post).

William Coulson & Sons v James Coulson & Co (1887) 3 TLR 846 applied.

---

a Section 1(1), so far as material, provides: '... where an individual has been convicted ... of any offence or offences, and the following conditions are satisfied ... then, after the end of the rehabilitation period so applicable ... that individual shall for the purposes of this Act be treated as a rehabilitated person ... and [the] conviction shall for those purposes be treated as spent.'

Notes

For spent convictions, see 11 Halsbury's Laws (4th edn) paras 584–585.   a

For the principles governing the grant of interlocutory injunctions, see 24 ibid paras 953–956, and for cases on the subject, see 28(2) Digest (Reissue) 968–980, 67–161.

For defamation actions by rehabilitated offenders and defences thereto, see 28 Halsbury's Laws (4th edn) para 93.

For the Rehabilitation of Offenders Act 1974, s 1, see 44 Halsbury's Statutes (3rd edn) 149.   b

Cases referred to in judgments

American Cyanamid Co v Ethicon Ltd [1975] 1 All ER 504, [1975] AC 396, [1975] 2 WLR 316, HL.

Bonnard v Perryman [1891] 2 Ch 269, [1891–4] All ER Rep 965, CA.

Coulson (William) & Sons v James Coulson & Co (1887) 3 TLR 846, CA.   c

Trevor (J) & Sons v Solomon (1977) 248 EG 779, CA.

Cases also cited

Armstrong v Armit (1886) 2 TLR 887, DC.

Bestobell Paints Ltd v Bigg [1975] FSR 421.

Cayne v Global Natural Resources plc [1984] 1 All ER 225, CA.   d

Collard v Marshall [1982] 1 Ch 571.

Harakas v Baltic Mercantile and Shipping Exchange Ltd [1982] 2 All ER 701, [1982] 1 WLR 955, CA.

Horrocks v Lowe [1974] 1 All ER 662, [1975] AC 135, HL.

Quartz Hill Consolidated Gold Mining Co v Beall (1882) 20 Ch D 501, CA.

Webb v Times Publishing Co Ltd [1960] 2 All ER 789, [1960] 2 QB 535.   e

Interlocutory appeal

The plaintiff, Alex William Herbage, appealed against the order of Webster J dated 10 February 1983 whereby he refused the plaintiff's application for an interlocutory injunction against the defendants, Pressdram Ltd, Feb Edge Litho (1979) Ltd, Private Eye Distribution (a firm) and Richard Ingrams, restraining them from publishing any   f
reference to the plaintiff's former convictions because they were to be regarded as spent by virtue of the provisions of the Rehabilitation of Offenders Act 1974. The facts are set out in the judgment of Griffiths LJ.

Richard Slowe for the plaintiff.

Desmond Browne for the defendants.   g

GRIFFITHS LJ. This is an appeal by Mr Herbage (the plaintiff) from the order of Webster J given on 10 November 1983 in which he dismissed the plaintiff's application for an injunction to restrain the defendants from further publication of the fact of his conviction of certain offences which are to be regarded as 'spent' offences for the purposes   h
of the Rehabilitation of Offenders Act 1974.

The plaintiff carries on business as an investment adviser. On 8 September 1966 he pleaded guilty to two offences under the Companies Act 1948 for which he received two sentences of six months' imprisonment to run concurrently. By virtue of the provisions of the 1974 Act those convictions were 'spent' after a period of seven years, and for the purposes of the 1974 Act the plaintiff is entitled to be treated as a rehabilitated person.   j
The magazine Private Eye has published a number of articles about the plaintiff's business activities. They are not complimentary, and in each they refer to the fact of the plaintiff's convictions. They also draw attention to various business failures with which they allege the plaintiff has been associated. They are clearly calculated to deter the investing public from reposing confidence in the plaintiff as an investment adviser.

By a writ dated 2 November 1983, the plaintiff started a libel action against the

a defendants, complaining of libels contained in four editions of Private Eye published
between January and November 1983. In these proceedings he seeks to restrain Private
Eye and the other defendants from publishing any further reference to his convictions.
Private Eye, through the affidavit of their editor Mr Ingrams, say they will justify the
contents of their articles and deny that they published them maliciously. Webster J
refused the injunction. He did so because he was not satisfied that on the material before
him it would be right to impute malice to the defendants. The case as argued before the
b judge proceeded on the basis that it was only in a wholly exceptional case that an
injunction would be granted in a libel action where the defendant pleaded justification
or that the words were published on a privileged occasion, so that the burden was on the
plaintiff to destroy the privilege by establishing malice; and, applying this principle,
there was ample material to justify the exercise of the discretion to refuse the injunction.
If the judge applied the right principle, counsel for the plaintiff does not seek to challenge
c this exercise of the judge's discretion. Counsel for the plaintiff has, however, by way of
an amended notice of appeal challenged the principles which he concedes are well
established in the general run of defamation actions and submits that the discretion
should be exercised differently where the defendant publishes a 'spent' conviction within
the meaning of the 1974 Act.

     The principles which it is conceded generally apply to the grant of interim injunctions
d in defamation actions are helpfully summarised in counsel for the plaintiff's skeleton
argument: first, no injunction will be granted if the defendant raises the defence of
justification. This is a rule so well established that no elaborate citation of authority is
necessary. It can be traced back to the leading case of Bonnard v Perryman [1891] 2 Ch
269, [1891–4] All ER Rep 965. Secondly, no injunction will be granted if the defence
raises privilege, unless the evidence of malice is so overwhelming that the judge is driven
to the conclusion that no reasonable jury could find otherwise; that is, that it would be
e perverse to acquit the defendant of malice. Thirdly, that in the face of this long-
established practice in defamation actions, the principles enunciated by the House of
Lords in American Cyanamid Co v Ethicon Ltd [1975] 1 All ER 504, [1975] AC 396 relating
to interim injunctions are not applicable in actions for defamation: see J Trevor & Sons v
Solomon (1977) 248 EG 779. These principles have evolved because of the value the court
has placed on freedom of speech and I think also on the freedom of the press, when
f balancing it against the reputation of a single individual who, if wrong, can be
compensated in damages. But now, says counsel for the plaintiff, a new factor is
introduced into the equation to which the court must give weight and which justifies a
radical departure from its practice in other defamation actions. The manifest overall
purpose of the 1974 Act, he says, is to allow a man to live down his past and put it behind
g him, and now the court must throw into the balance on the side of the individual that
intention of Parliament when balancing it against the value of free speech or of a free
press. This so tips the scale, he submits, that the court should in such cases apply the
approach for which guidance is found in the American Cyanamid case, rather than to apply
its present practice in other defamation actions. If the court were to accept this argument,
the practical effect would I believe be that in very many cases the plaintiff would obtain
h an injunction, for on the American Cyanamid principles he would often show a serious
issue to be tried, that damages would not be realistic compensation, and that the balance
of convenience favoured restraining repetition of the alleged libel until trial of the action.
It would thus be a very considerable incursion into the present rule which is based on
freedom of speech.

     With counsel for the plaintiff's argument in mind I now turn to the 1974 Act itself.
j Section 4 deals with the effect of rehabilitation, and I read part of sub-s (1):

     'Subject to sections 7 and 8 below, a person who has become a rehabilitated person
     for the purposes of this Act in respect of a conviction shall be treated for all purposes
     in law as a person who has not committed or been charged with or prosecuted for
     or convicted of or sentenced for the offence or offences which were the subject of
     that conviction . . .'

It is on those words that counsel for the plaintiff has primarily focused as exemplifying the overall intention of Parliament in passing the 1974 Act.

Counsel for the defendants responded by pointing out that the whole of s 4(1) is qualified by the opening words, which are 'Subject to sections 7 and 8 below'. Section 8 is a section which specifically deals with defamation actions. The two relevant parts of that section for the purposes of this appeal are sub-ss (3) and (5). Sub-s (3) reads:

> 'Subject to subsections (5) and (6) below, nothing in section 4(1) . . . shall prevent the defendant in an action to which this section applies from relying on any defence of justification or fair comment or of absolute or qualified privilege which is available to him, or restrict the matters he may establish in support of any such defence.'

Then sub-s (5) provides:

> 'A defendant in any such action shall not by virtue of subsection (3) above be entitled to rely upon the defence of justification if the publication is proved to have been made with malice.'

Counsel for the defendants submits that Parliament has specifically provided for the manner in which the scales should be held between on the one hand a rehabilitated person and on the other a person who is minded to publish about him information relating to a 'spent' conviction. The effect of these two subsections is to place a person who has rehabilitated himself in a more advantageous position than a person who has been convicted and has not rehabilitated himself by avoiding further conviction for the requisite period required under the 1974 Act. If a man has rehabilitated himself and his conviction is to be regarded as 'spent' and that conviction is published of him, he can recover damages if he is able to show that it was maliciously published. I take 'malice' in this subsection to mean published with some irrelevant, spiteful or improper motive. If it is so published, even though it is true that he has a 'spent' conviction, that conviction is to be disregarded. He is to be treated as though no such conviction had taken place and accordingly the publication is libellous. That is a great advantage over another man who may have had a conviction a number of years ago, but who has not yet fulfilled the qualifying period, and of whom, no matter how maliciously, it may be published that he has been convicted, since the defendant will have an absolute defence of justification. The rehabilitated person, for the purposes of the law of libel, is placed at a real advantage by virtue of the fact that he has kept clear of crime for the requisite period. It seems to me that this very closely equates the position with the case where a defendant relies on a defence of qualified privilege. In such a case, the law is now well settled. Only if, at the interlocutory stage, the evidence of malice is absolutely overwhelming will the court intervene to restrain publication by way of an interlocutory injunction: see *William Coulson & Sons v James Coulson & Co* (1887) 3 TLR 846.

Parliament having so provided, I can see no reason why this court should approach the resolution of the problem in this case in any different manner to that in which it would in any other defamation action where the real issue to be tried is one of malice. That is the issue in this case exactly in the same way as it is in every case where qualified privilege is pleaded as a defence.

Accordingly, I am not persuaded by counsel for the plaintiff's argument that this court should depart from a well-established practice. That being the basis on which Webster J approached this case, I would for my part dismiss this appeal.

KERR LJ. I agree. There is nothing I wish to add.

Appeal dismissed with costs. Leave to appeal to the House of Lords refused.

Solicitors: *Slowes* (for the plaintiff); *Bindman & Partners* (for the defendants).

Carolyn Toulmin   Barrister.

President of India v La Pintada Cia Navegacion SA

HOUSE OF LORDS

LORD FRASER OF TULLYBELTON, LORD SCARMAN, LORD ROSKILL, LORD BRIDGE OF HARWICH AND LORD BRANDON OF OAKBROOK

12, 13, 14, 15 MARCH, 24 MAY 1984

Interest – Debt – Late payment of debt – Power to award interest by way of general damages – Debt paid late but before proceedings for recovery commenced – Whether court having power to award interest by way of general damages – Law Reform (Miscellaneous Provisions) Act 1934, s 3(1) – Supreme Court Act 1981, s 35A

Arbitration – Award – Interest – Damages – Power of arbitrator to award interest – Claim for interest on payments made late but before commencement of arbitration – Whether interest can be awarded by way of damages at common law – Whether interest can be awarded by way of damages under Admiralty jurisdiction – Whether interest on interest can be awarded.

By a voyage charter dated 28 January 1975 the sub-charterer chartered the owners' vessel for a voyage from Europe to India. In May 1977 a dispute between the parties regarding unpaid freight and demurrage was referred to arbitration in England under the voyage charterparty. On 30 January 1981, before the arbitration took place, the owners after first refusing offers made by the sub-charterer then accepted in settlement amounts which the parties agreed represented the principal due to the owners for freight and demurrage. Following payment of the amounts offered the owners limited their claims against the sub-charterer in the arbitration to interest and costs. When the claim was arbitrated the umpire made an award on 20 May 1982 to the effect (a) that demurrage became payable on 1 September 1975 and therefore the owners were entitled to compound interest from that date until payment of demurrage by the sub-charterer in January 1981, (b) that freight became payable on 12 December 1978 but because previous offers had been rejected the owners could not complain of late payment until 1 February 1979 and therefore the owners were entitled to compound interest from the latter date until the payment in January 1981, and (c) that compound interest on both sums was payable from the date of payment until the date of the award. The sub-charterer appealed by way of special case stated against the umpire's award. The questions arose (i) whether the owners were entitled to an award of interest because of the late payment of freight and demurrage, (ii) whether the umpire had a discretion to award interest, and (iii) if so, whether he was justified in exercising that discretion. The judge held that he was bound by authority to uphold the umpire's award of compound interest because of the late payment of the debt owing to the owners, notwithstanding that payment had been made prior to the award. The sub-charterer appealed direct to the House of Lords.

Held – (1) In the absence of agreement between the parties regarding payment of interest on a debt due, a creditor had no remedy by way of a claim for general damages in respect of interest if the debt was paid late but before proceedings for its recovery were commenced, since the judicial award of interest as of right when proceedings had not been commenced would cause anomalies and conflict with the statutory remedy under s 35A[a] of the Supreme Court Act 1981 of the discretionary award of interest to a creditor who had commenced proceedings before the debt was paid. Furthermore, although there was obvious injustice if a creditor who had received late payment prior to his commencing proceedings was not entitled to interest, it would be an apparent usurpation of the legislative function if the court were to provide a remedy when Parliament had

---

a   Section 35A, so far as material, is set out at p 788 *a* to *e*, post.

not seen fit to do so when enacting s 35A. Accordingly, in the absence of agreement or statutory provision for the payment of interest the common law rule applied to a creditor who had not commenced proceedings before the debt was paid late, namely the court had no power to award interest, either simple or compound, by way of general damages for the late payment of a debt. That rule applied also to arbitrators since the reference of a dispute to arbitration in England implied that the arbitration was to be conducted in accordance with English law in all respects (see p 775 g to j, p 776 e to h, p 778 j, p 781 d, p 789 e to g and p 790 d to g, post); *London Chatham and Dover Rly Co v South Eastern Rly Co* [1893] AC 429 and *Chandris v Isbrandtsen Moller Co Inc* [1950] 2 All ER 618 applied; *Tehno-Impex v Gebr Van Weelde Scheepvarkantoor BV* [1981] 2 All ER 669 overruled.

(2) Where, however, a creditor was able to prove that he had suffered special damage (e g by himself having to pay interest on say an overdraft) as a result of the debtor's late payment of a debt the creditor was entitled to claim such special damage, notwithstanding that the debt was paid prior to the creditor commencing proceedings for its recovery (see p 775 g to j, p 776 e to h and p 787 d to g, post); *Wadsworth v Lydall* [1981] 2 All ER 401 approved.

(3) On the facts, at the date of making his award in May 1982 the umpire had no jurisdiction to award interest to the owners because the acceptance by the owners prior to the conclusion of the arbitration precluded him from making such an award either under the common law, or under the predecessor of s 35A of the 1981 Act, namely s 3(1)ᵇ of the Law Reform (Miscellaneous Provisions) Act 1934 (since that section did not empower a court to award interest on principal sums already paid), or under the Admiralty jurisdiction (within which the owners' claim fell) since that jurisdiction did not include power to award interest on debts already paid or the award of compound interest. It followed that the sub-charterer was not liable to pay interest and that its appeal would be allowed (see p 775 g to j, p 776 e to h, p 779 e f and p 782 f g, p 785 e f and p 790 h j, post); *The Medina Princess* [1962] 2 Lloyd's Rep 17 approved; *The Aldora* [1975] 2 All ER 69 explained.

Per curiam. The equitable power of the Admiralty Court to award interest on a debt or damages applies to all claims declared by s 20(2)ᶜ of the 1981 Act to be within the Admiralty jurisdiction of the High Court (see p 775 g to j, p 776 e to h and p 783 c to e, post).

Per Lord Scarman and Lord Roskill. It is to be hoped that a legislative solution will be found promptly to remedy the injustice caused to creditors who are deprived of interest on late payment of a debt merely because payment is accepted before proceedings are commenced for its recovery (see p 775 h and p 776 d e, post).

Notes

For claims for interest, see 32 Halsbury's Laws (4th edn) paras 106–109, and for cases on the subject, see 34 Digest (Reissue) 541–550, 4308–4410.

For the power of an arbitrator to award interest, see 2 Halsbury's Laws (4th edn) para 580, and for cases on the subject, see 3 Digest (Reissue) 201–203, *1235–1243*.

For the Law Reform (Miscellaneous Provisions) Act 1934, s 3, see 25 Halsbury's Statutes (3rd edn) 752.

For the Supreme Court Act 1981, s 20, see 51 ibid 612, and for s 35A, see 52 ibid 511.

As from 1 April 1983, s 3 of the 1934 Act was replaced by s 35A of the Supreme Court Act 1981.

Cases referred to in opinions

Addie (Robert) & Sons (Collieries) Ltd v Dumbreck [1929] AC 358, [1929] All ER Rep 1, HL.
Aldora, The, Tyne Tugs Ltd v M/V Aldora (owners) [1975] 2 All ER 69, [1975] QB 784, [1975] 2 WLR 791.
Amalia, The (1864) 5 NR 164n.

---

b   Section 3(1) is set out at p 779 d e, post.
c   Section 20(2) sets out the questions and claims which the High Court may hear and determine under its Admiralty jurisdiction.

Arnott v Redfern (1826) 3 Bing 353, 130 ER 549.

Badger, Re (1819) 2 B & Ald 691, 106 ER 517.

British Rlys Board v Herrington [1972] 1 All ER 749, [1972] AC 877, [1972] 2 WLR 537, HL.

Chandris v Isbrandtsen Moller Co Inc [1950] 2 All ER 618, [1951] 1 KB 240, CA.

Codelfa Construction Pty Ltd v State Rail Authority of New South Wales (1982) 56 ALJR 459 (Aust HC).

Government Insurance Office of New South Wales v Atkinson-Leighton Joint Venture (1980) 31 ALR 193 (Aust HC).

Hadley v Baxendale (1854) 9 Exch 341, [1843–60] All ER Rep 461, 156 ER 145.

London Chatham and Dover Rly Co v South Eastern Rly Co [1893] AC 429, HL.

Medina Princess, The [1962] 2 Lloyd's Rep 17.

Northumbria, The (1869) LR 3 A & E 6.

Page v Newman (1829) 9 B & C 378, 109 ER 140.

Tehno-Impex v Gebr Van Weelde Scheepvartkantoor BV [1981] 2 All 669, [1981] QB 648, [1981] 2 WLR 821, CA.

Trans Trust SPRL v Danubian Trading Co Ltd [1952] 1 All ER 970, [1952] 2 QB 297, CA.

Wadsworth v Lydall [1981] 2 All ER 401, [1981] 1 WLR 598, CA.

Appeal

The President of India (the sub-charterer) appealed against two judgments of Staughton J dated 26 October 1982 and 1 July 1983 by which he upheld an award in the form of a special case of Mr Bruce Harris as umpire dated 20 May 1982 and a further award by Mr Harris dated 30 December 1982 arising out of an arbitration in which the respondents, La Pintada Cia Navegacion SA, the owners of the vessel La Pintada, claimed as assignees to recover from the sub-charterer sums due by way of freight and demurrage under a charterparty in Ferticon form dated 28 July 1975 between the sub-charterer and North Atlantic Oil Ltd. On 1 November 1983 the Appeal Committee of the House of Lords granted the sub-charterer leave to appeal direct to the House, Staughton J having granted a certificate under s 12(3)(b) of the Administration of Justice Act 1969. The facts are set out in the opinion of Lord Brandon.

Nicholas Phillips QC and *Peregrine Simon* for the sub-charterer.
Mark O Saville QC and *Martin Moore-Bick* for the shipowners.

Their Lordships took time for consideration.

24 May. The following opinions were delivered.

LORD FRASER OF TULLYBELTON. My Lords, I have had the advantage of reading in draft the speech of my noble and learned friend Lord Brandon. His reasoning seem to me irresistible and I feel myself driven, though with reluctance, to agree that this appeal must be allowed, with the consequence that the arbitrator's alternative award will be upheld.

LORD SCARMAN. My Lords, I agree with the speech to be delivered by my noble and learned friend Lord Brandon, a draft of which I have had the opportunity of studying. But I wish to associate myself with the comments made by my noble and learned friend Lord Roskill. I also reach with regret and reluctance the conclusion that the appeal must be allowed. The sooner there is legislation along the lines proposed by the Law Commission (or some other solution achieving the same end) the better.

LORD ROSKILL. My Lords, I have had the advantage of reading in draft the speech of my noble and learned friend Lord Brandon. If I may respectfully say so I find his reasoning, leading to the consequence that this appeal must be allowed and the alternative award of the umpire upheld, compelling. But I freely confess that I have arrived at this conclusion, though without doubt, nevertheless with both regret and reluctance. It has long been recognised that *London Chatham and Dover Rly Co v South Eastern Rly Co* [1893]

AC 429 left creditors with a legitimate sense of grievance and an obvious injustice without remedy. I think the House in 1893 recognised those consequences of the decision, but then felt compelled for historical reasons to leave that injustice uncorrected. Since 1893 Parliament has intervened twice, first to remedy what Lord Brandon has called case 3 and secondly to remedy case 2. On the latter occasion Parliament, with the Law Commission's report before it, had the opportunity also to remedy the injustice to creditors to which case 1 (a debt paid late but before proceedings for its recovery have been begun) can so often give rise. But Parliament neither accepted the Law Commission's proffered solution to case 1 nor provided any substitute solution of its own. It must, I think, therefore be accepted that this inaction was deliberate. If so it cannot be right for this House in its judicial capacity by departing from the *London Chatham and Dover Rly* case to proffer a remedy which if applicable at all must apply to all three cases and not only to case 1 with the consequence that as regards cases 2 and 3 there would be concurrent and inconsistent remedies, one statutory and discretionary, the other at common law and as of right since once a breach of contract and damage caused by that breach are proved a court has no discretion but must award the damages claimed in full.

My Lords it would be idle to affect ignorance of the fact that the present state of the law in relation to case 1 places the small creditor at a grave disadvantage vis-à-vis his substantial and influential debtor. The former may fear to offend the latter by instituting legal proceedings either swiftly or indeed at all and it is notorious that some substantial and influential debtors are not slow to take advantage of this tactical strength, especially in times of financial stringency. It has taken two pieces of legislation, one some 50 years after 1893 and the other almost another half-century later, to remedy the injustice in cases 2 and 3. I venture to hope that whatever solution be ultimately adopted in case 1, whether the Law Commission's somewhat complicated solution or something simpler, that solution will be found promptly and the remaining injustice in this branch of the law finally removed.

LORD BRIDGE OF HARWICH. My Lords, I have read with admiration the comprehensive analysis and resolution of the issues arising in this appeal in the speech of my noble and learned friend Lord Brandon. I fully agree with his reasoning. I have only two observations to add in support of the conclusion that it would be a wholly inappropriate exercise of the judicial function for your Lordships' House now to depart from the rule laid down in *London Chatham and Dover Rly Co v South Eastern Rly Co* [1893] AC 429 that the common law does not award general damages for delay in payment of a debt beyond the date when it is contractually due.

First, if your Lordships were to reverse that rule, the alternative rule which must of necessity take its place could only be that in all cases of late payments general damages would be recoverable as of right calculated in accordance with the same common law principles that govern the award of general damages in the case of any other breach of contract. Such a sweeping provision would not merely be inconsistent with, but would, it seems to me, effectively override the carefully defined and restricted statutory provisions for the discretionary award of interest in certain cases so as to render them a dead letter.

Second, such a broad rule could make no provision, such as suggested by the Law Commission, for special cases where, even under the Law Commission's scheme for 'statutory interest' which Parliament did not adopt, the award of interest would be unjust, nor could it incorporate the many detailed qualifications and refinements which the Law Commission recommended as necessary to the working of the scheme which the Law Commission proposed: see the Law Commission's Report on Interest 1978 (Law Com no 88) paras 45–102.

I would allow the appeal.

LORD BRANDON OF OAKBROOK. My Lords, your Lordships have before you a combined appeal from two orders made by Staughton J in the Commercial Court on 29

October 1982 and 1 July 1983 respectively, which comes to you direct under the leapfrog
a procedure introduced by s 12 of the Administration of Justice Act 1969.

There are two questions which the facts of the present case require your Lordships to
decide. The first question is whether an umpire, in a London arbitration between
shipowners and charterers, has power to award to the former against the latter interest
on moneys due in respect of freight and demurrage, payment of which was made and
accepted after the arbitration had begun but before it had been concluded. The second
b question is, if so, whether such power extends to the award of compound, as distinct
from simple, interest.

While these are the two questions which the facts of the present case require your
Lordships to decide, they raise by necessary implication wider questions of far-reaching
general importance. The first such wider question is what remedies your Lordships
should hold, at this stage of English legal history, are available to a creditor for delay in
c the payment of a debt due to him. The second such wider question is whether an
arbitrator or umpire has power to award to a creditor against his debtor more extensive
remedies than those to which such creditor would be entitled if, instead of bringing
arbitration proceedings against his debtor, he brought an action against him in a court of
law.

My Lords, the facts giving rise to the appeal are these. By a time charterparty dated 2
d October 1973 the respondent company (the owners) chartered their ship, La Pintada (the
ship) to North Atlantic Oil Co Ltd (North Atlantic) for a specified period. By a voyage
sub-charter dated 28 January 1975 (the voyage charter) North Atlantic sub-chartered the
ship to the appellant (the sub-charterer) for a laden voyage from north west Europe to
India. Under the voyage charter, which contained a London arbitration clause, freight
was to be calculated in US dollars but paid in sterling, while demurrage was to be both
e calculated and paid in US dollars. On 31 December 1976 North Atlantic assigned all their
rights under the voyage charter to the owners.

In May 1977 the owners, as assignees of North Atlantic, began arbitration proceedings
against the sub-charterer in London, claiming substantial amounts for unpaid freight
and demurrage. On 30 January 1981, after previous offers by the sub-charterer to pay to
the owners the same amounts had not been accepted, the sub-charterer paid and the
f owners accepted £22,199·89 and $US58,017·35 in settlement of the latters' claims for
freight and demurrage respectively. It was later agreed that the two sums so paid and
accepted correctly represented the principal sums due from the sub-charterer to the
owners under the two heads of claim concerned. It was further held in the arbitration
that the sum for freight should have been paid on 12 December 1978 and that for
demurrage on 1 September 1975. Following the payment and acceptance of those two
g sums, the owners limited any further claims against the sub-charterer in the arbitration
to interest and costs.

The arbitrators appointed by the parties having disagreed, the umpire entered into the
arbitration, and by consent made an award dated 20 May 1982 in the form of a special
case for the opinion of the court. By that award he awarded, subject to the opinion of the
court on three questions of law stated by him, that the sub-charterer should pay to the
h owners, by way of compound interest, £8,035·46 in respect of freight unpaid from 1
February 1979 to 31 January 1981, and $US43,320·55 in respect of demurrage unpaid
for 1 September 1975 to 31 January 1981. The umpire further awarded that interest on
the principal sums concerned should continue to be compounded from 1 February 1981
to the date of his award. He awarded such interest, not merely single but compound, on
the principal sums previously owed in respect of freight and demurrage, even though, as
j I indicated earlier, those sums had been paid by the sub-charterer and accepted by the
owners on 30 January 1981 during the pendency of the arbitration proceedings.

The three questions of law stated by the umpire for the opinion of the court were to
the following effect: whether, on the facts found and the true construction of the voyage
charter, (1) the owners were entitled to an award of any sums in respect of the late
payment of freight or demurrage due under such charter, and, if so, what sums should

be awarded under that head; (2) he, the umpire, had jurisdiction to exercise any discretion to make an award of interest in respect of the late payment of freight and demurrage; *a* and (3) to the extent that his award was made following the exercise of his discretion, such exercise was justified in law.

The umpire's award of compound interest referred to above was made on the basis, which he held to be correct, that the answers to the first part of question (1) and to the whole of questions (2) and (3) were in each case 'Yes'. He went on to make an alternative award to take effect in the event of the court answering the first part of question (1) and *b* the whole of question (2) 'No', in which case the second part of question (1) and the whole of question (3) would not arise. By that alternative award he awarded that nothing was due from the sub-charterer to the owners, and gave certain directions with regard to costs, differing from those given in his primary award, which it is not necessary to set out in detail.

The umpire's award in the form of a special case came before Staughton J in the *c* Commercial Court on two occasions, the first on 25 October 1982 and the second on 1 July 1983. The reason for two separate hearings was that the judge thought that the umpire might not, in exercising his discretion in relation to interest, have taken into account what the judge regarded as a relevant factor, namely the conduct of the owners in not accepting the earlier offers of payment made by the sub-charterer. Because of this the judge thought it necessary to remit the award in order that the umpire, if he had not *d* taken that matter into account, might reconsider his award in the light of it. Following such remission the umpire, by a further award dated 30 December 1982, having considered the matter remitted to him, in effect affirmed his original award.

Two orders were made by Staughton J, one after the first hearing dated 29 October 1982, and the other after the second hearing dated 1 July 1983. Apart from the question of remission, the upshot of these two orders taken together was that Staughton J answered *e* the three questions of law stated by the umpire: (1) 'Yes, in the sums awarded by the umpire', (2) 'Yes' and (3) 'Yes', and upheld the further award of the umpire dated 31 December 1982, by which he had affirmed his original award. The judge went on to certify that a point of law of general importance was involved in respect of which he was bound by a decision of the Court of Appeal in previous proceedings and was fully considered in those previous proceedings, and granted the sub-charterer's application for *f* a certificate for leave to present a petition of appeal to your Lordships' House. The Appeal Committee subsequently gave leave for a combined leapfrog appeal from both orders.

My Lords, the previous proceedings in the Court of Appeal referred to by Staughton J in his certificate were those in *Tehno-Impex v Gebr Van Weelde Scheepvartkantoor BV* [1981] 2 All ER 669, [1981] QB 648 (which I shall refer to as *Tehno-Impex*). It follows that this appeal, although in form an appeal against the two orders of Staughton J referred to *g* above, is in substance an appeal against the decision in *Tehno-Impex*.

Before examining *Tehno-Impex* it will, I think, be helpful to summarise the law relating to the award of interest as it stood, or at any rate was generally understood to stand, at the date, 12 March 1981, when that case was decided. Later it will be necessary to examine part of the history of that matter in greater detail; but for the moment a summary will suffice in order that the background against which *Tehno-Impex* was decided can be *h* understood.

In making such a summary four areas of the law have to be looked at: first, the area of the common law; second, the area of Admiralty law; third, the area of equity; and, fourth, the area of statutory law.

First, the area of the common law. It had been decided by your Lordships' House in *London Chatham and Dover Rly Co v South Eastern Rly Co* [1893] AC 429 that at common *j* law, in the absence of any agreement or statutory provisions for the payment of interest, a court had no power to award interest, simple or compound, by way of damages for the detention (ie the late payment) of a debt. That decision was regarded as applying to any form of damages, and it was not until long afterwards, in cases to which I shall refer later, that the question whether it applied to special, as well as general, damages came to be considered.

Second, the area of Admiralty law. Here a different rule prevailed from that at
a common law. Under Admiralty law simple interest had for more than a century been
awarded, as a matter of course, on damages recovered in a damage action. Later, in 1975,
it was held that simple interest could be awarded on a sum recovered in a salvage action.
The situation with regard to the award of interest on sums recovered in an action for a
contractual debt had not been the subject matter of actual decision, but it was assumed,
following a dictum to which I shall refer later, that the rule applied to claims in contract
b as well as in tort.

Third, the area of equity. The Chancery courts, again differing from the common law
courts, had regularly awarded simple interest as ancillary relief in respect of equitable
remedies, such as specific performance, rescission and the taking of an account. Chancery
courts had further regularly awarded interest, including not only simple interest but also
compound interest, when they thought that justice so demanded, that is to say in cases
c where money had been obtained and retained by fraud, or where it had been withheld
or misapplied by a trustee or anyone else in a fiduciary position.

Fourth, the area of statutory law. The relevant statutory provision in force in 1981,
when *Tehno-Impex* was decided, was s 3(1) of the Law Reform (Miscellaneous Provisions)
Act 1934. That subsection provided:

d '(1) In any proceedings tried in any court of record for the recovery of any debt or
damages, the court may, if it thinks fit, order that there shall be included in the sum
for which judgment is given interest at such rate as it thinks fit on the whole or any
part of the debt or damages for the whole or any part of the period between the date
when the cause of action arose and the date of the judgment: Provided that nothing
in this section—(a) shall authorise the giving of interest upon interest; or (b) shall
apply in relation to any debt upon which interest is payable as of right whether by
e virtue of any agreement or otherwise; or (c) shall affect the damages recoverable for
the dishonour of a bill of exchange.'

Two points of importance are to be observed about the law relating to the award of
interest by courts of law at the time of the decision in *Tehno-Impex* as summarised above.
The first point is that neither the Admiralty Court, nor Chancery courts, awarded interest,
f except in respect of moneys for which they were giving judgment. The second point is
that the Admiralty Court never, and Chancery courts only in two special classes of case,
awarded compound, as distinct from simple, interest.

My Lords, it is against that background of the law relating to the award of interest
which prevailed at the time of the decision in *Tehno-Impex* that I turn to examine that
decision. The facts in that case were these. By a freight contract, which incorporated an
g amended Gencon charterparty and provided for disputes to be referred to arbitration in
London, shipowners agreed with charterers to carry on their vessels for an agreed freight
about 350,000 tons of cement from Split in Yugoslavia to Lagos or Port Harcourt. The
contract was suspended after 12 voyages and disputes between the parties as to demurrage
in respect of the 12 voyages were referred to arbitration. In his interim award the
arbitrator held that the charterers were entitled to a refund of $US30,000 with interest
h from 1 January 1977 for overpaid demurrage on the last voyage; but that, although the
charterers had delayed in making their demurrage payments on all voyages for periods
ranging from a few days to over 200 days, he had no jurisdiction to make any award on
the shipowners' claim for interest on such delayed payments or for interest on that
interest.

The shipowners applied by motion to the Commercial Court (Parker J) to set aside or
j remit the award for error of law on the face of it. Parker J dismissed the motion, holding
that the arbitrator had no power to award interest at common law, that the claim for
interest on interest was barred by para (a) of the proviso to s 3(1) of the 1934 Act, and
that, in so far as reliance was placed on the proposition that the shipowners' claim for
demurrage was within the Admiralty jurisdiction of the High Court under s 1(1)(h) of
the Administration of Justice Act 1956, the power of the Admiralty Court would have
been to award interest on damages and not interest simpliciter.

The shipowners appealed against the decision of Parker J, and their appeal came before a division of the Court of Appeal consisting of Lord Denning MR, Oliver and Watkins LJJ. The appeal was allowed by a majority, Oliver LJ dissenting; but, while a common ratio decidendi can be found in the judgments of the majority, it will be seen that Watkins LJ agreed only with a subsidiary ground, and not with the main ground, on which Lord Denning MR considered that the appeal should be allowed.

I shall examine the judgments of the majority first, and then the dissenting judgment of Oliver LJ. The main grounds on which Lord Denning MR would have allowed the appeal appear from two passages in his judgment: see [1981] 2 All ER 669 at 678, [1981] QB 648 at 666, 667. They were these: first, that arbitrators in the City of London were not bound by the common law rule against the award of interest at all, as understood to have been laid down in the *London Chatham and Dover Rly* case because that was not a rule of substantive law but one of practice only; and, second, that arbitrators were not bound by the prohibition against awarding compound interest contained in para (*a*) of the proviso to s 3(1) of the 1934 Act, because the Act did not apply to arbitrators but only to courts of record. In the result arbitrators had a discretionary power to award interest, either simple or compound, not only in respect of principal sums awarded at the same time, but also in respect of principal sums already paid, whether before or after the commencement of the arbitration.

While these were the main grounds on which Lord Denning MR would have allowed the appeal he relied also, in the alternative, on a subsidiary ground, the nature of which appears from an earlier passage in his judgment: see [1981] 2 All ER 669 at 674–675, [1981] QB 648 at 662. This subsidiary ground was that the cross-claims in the case were within the Admiralty jurisdiction of the High Court under s 1(1)(*h*) of the 1956 Act, which refers to 'any claim arising out of any agreement relating to the carriage of goods in a ship or to the use or hire of a ship'; that the cross-claims could have been pursued by action in the Admiralty Court; that, if they had been so pursued, the Admiralty Court would have awarded interest on both sides of the account; and that an arbitrator could therefore do the same.

Watkins LJ rightly considered himself bound by the common law rule against the award of any interest at all, as it was understood to have been laid down in the *London Chatham and Dover Rly* case, and it is clear that he did not agree with the view of Lord Denning MR, that the rule concerned was not one of substantive law but one of practice only, so that arbitrators were free to award interest in disregard of it. He considered, however, that the appeal should be allowed on the subsidiary ground relied on in the alternative by Lord Denning MR, that the case was one within the Admiralty jurisdiction of the High Court; that the rule of the Admiralty Court was to award interest on debts; and that that rule could legitimately be extended to the award of interest on principal sums already paid, and, so far as I can gather, to the award of compound, as well as simple, interest.

Oliver LJ, like Watkins LJ, rightly considered himself bound by the common law rule against the award of any interest at all as it was understood to have been laid down in the *London Chatham and Dover Rly* case, and did not agree with the view of Lord Denning MR that the rule was not one of substantive law but one of practice only, so that arbitrators were free to award interest in disregard of it. With regard to the common view of Lord Denning MR and Watkins LJ that the arbitrator in the case concerned had power to award interest because the claims and cross-claims were within the Admiralty jurisdiction of the High Court under s 1(1)(*h*) of the 1956 Act, Oliver LJ appears to have been willing to accept that, so far as claims which were within the jurisdiction of the High Court of Admiralty before the passing of the Judicature Acts 1873–75 were concerned, the High Court of Admiralty might have had power to award interest, including compound interest, on sums already paid. He considered, however, that the equitable power of the Admiralty Court to award interest at all, whether along with principal sums for which judgment was given, or on a claim for interest simpliciter in respect of principal sums already paid but paid later, did not extend to new categories of claims brought within the Admiralty jurisdiction of the High Court by Acts passed after the Judicature Acts 1873–75. The category of claim referred to in s 1(1)(h) of the 1956 Act had only been brought within the Admiralty jurisdiction of the High Court for the first time by an Act of 1920. It followed, therefore, in his view, that the equitable power of the Admiralty Court to award interest at all did not extend to the award of interest in respect of that category of claim.

All three members of the Court of Appeal rightly recognised that s 3(1) of the 1934 Act itself did not, by reason of its express terms, empower a court to award interest on principal sums already paid, or to award compound interest in any case.

My Lords, the main grounds on which Lord Denning MR would have wished to allow the appeal, namely that arbitrators in the City of London are free, so far as the award of interest are concerned, from the shackles which bind the High Court, and so have power to award interest, either simple or compound, on principal sums, whether payable under their award or already paid before their award, as they may in their discretion think just, was not, as I have already indicated, supported by either Oliver LJ or Watkins LJ. What is perhaps even more significant is that it was not supported by counsel for the owners at the hearing of this appeal in your Lordships' House.

The true position in law is, in my opinion, not in doubt. It is this. Where parties refer a dispute between them to arbitration in England, they impliedly agree that the arbitration is to be conducted in accordance in all respects with the law of England, unless, which seldom occurs, the agreement of reference provides otherwise. It is on this basis that it was held by the Court of Appeal in *Chandris v Isbrandtsen Moller Co Inc* [1950] 2 All ER 618, [1951] 1 KB 240 that, although s 3(1) of the 1934 Act, by its terms, empowered only courts of record to include interest in sums for which judgment was given for damages or debt, arbitrators were nevertheless empowered, by the agreement of reference, to apply English law, including so much of that law as is to be found in s 3(1) of the 1934 Act.

It is not without interest that the same approach has been adopted by the High Court of Australia in relation to s 94 of the Supreme Court Act 1970 (NSW), which is in terms similar to those of s 3(1) of the 1934 Act: see *Government Insurance Office of New South Wales v Atkinson-Leighton Joint Venture* (1980) 31 ALR 193, and *Codelfa Construction Pty Ltd v State Rail Authority of New South Wales* (1982) 56 ALJR 459. In the latter case, Mason J put the matter succinctly in a short passage in his judgment (at 472):

'The arbitrator's power to award interest in the present case, as *Atkinson-Leighton* decided, is referable to section 94. As such it is circumscribed by section 94(2)(a) and it does not extend to the making of an award for compound interest.'

It is clear, as a matter of both principle and authority, that the primary grounds on which Lord Denning MR would have wished to allow the appeal in *Tehno-Impex* [1981] 2 All ER 669, [1981] QB 648 cannot be supported. Counsel for the owners recognised this, and, as I have indicated earlier, wisely did not seek to support those grounds.

I turn to consider the only common ratio decidendi of the majority in the Court of Appeal, namely that since the claims and cross-claims which were before the umpire were of such a character as to be within the Admiralty jurisdiction of the High Court by virtue of s 1(1)(h) of the 1956 Act, the umpire was entitled to give the parties the same remedies as the Admiralty Court could have given them if the proceedings had taken the form of an action before it; and that, since the Admiralty Court would have had power to award compound interest on debts payment of which had been made and accepted before judgment, the umpire had power to do the same.

My Lords, this common ratio decidendi of the majority in the Court of Appeal was, in my opinion, based on two fundamental misconceptions about the power which a court exercising Admiralty jurisdiction then had to award interest. The first misconception was that an Admiralty Court then had power to award interest on debts already paid. The second misconception was that an Admiralty Court had power to award compound interest in any case at all.

With regard to these two misconceptions, the practice of the High Court of Admiralty
before the Judicature Acts 1873–75 was to award interest on such sums as it gave   *a*
judgment for in damage actions: see *The Amalia* (1864) 5 NR 164n, and *The Northumbria*
(1869) LR 3 A & E 6. There is further a dictum by Sir Robert Phillimore in *The
Northumbria* (at 10), that the practice applied equally to claims in contract and in tort.
This practice was followed by the Probate, Divorce and Admiralty Division of the High
Court after the Judicature Acts 1873–75, and by the Admiralty Court after its creation
by the Administration of Justice Act 1970. In *The Aldora, Tyne Tugs Ltd v Aldora (owners)*   *b*
[1975] 2 All ER 69, [1975] QB 748 I decided, sitting as a judge of the Admiralty Court,
that the practice of awarding interest in damage actions could and should be extended to
salvage actions by the award of interest on sums for which judgment was given in such
actions. The principal argument addressed to me against such extension was that neither
the Admiralty Court, nor its predecessors, had ever awarded interest on sums for which
judgment was given in salvage actions before. In relation to that argument I said ([1975]   *c*
2 All ER 69 at 74, [1975] QB 748 at 753):

> 'Having considered the matter carefully I do not see any reason why the principle
> on which the Admiralty Court proceeded in awarding interest in damage actions
> should not be applied also to salvage actions. The principle is stated to be an
> equitable one, and, so far as equity is concerned, I should have thought that a person
> claiming salvage was no less entitled to interest on his claim than a person claiming   *d*
> for damage. Indeed it might be thought that he was even more entitled. The main
> argument against applying the principle to salvage actions is that it does not appear
> to have been done before. When what is involved is no more than applying an
> equitable principle, long established in one class of case, to another class of case in
> which it is equally or even more appropriate, I do not think that this argument
> should prevail.'   *e*

At this point it is necessary to emphasise two matters. The first matter is that the
equitable principle of awarding interest in damage actions to which I there referred, and
which I held could and should be extended to salvage actions, involves, and involves
only, the award of interest on principal sums for which judgment is given. It does not
involve, and has never involved, awarding interest on principal sums already paid, and   *f*
there is no authority in any reported Admiralty case for the award of interest in such
cases.

The second matter is that the equitable principle of awarding interest in damage
actions to which I was there referring involves, and involves only, the award of simple
interest. It does not involve, and never has involved, the award of compound interest,
and again there is no authority in any reported Admiralty case for the award of interest   *g*
of that kind.

Watkins LJ, in his judgment in the *Tehno-Impex* case [1981] 2 All ER 669 at 689–690,
[1981] QB 648 at 682, cited the passage from my judgment in *The Aldora* [1975] 2 All
ER 69 at 74, [1975] QB 748 at 753, which I have myself set out above. He appears,
however, to have treated it as laying down some principle far wider than the terms of the
passage warrant, or than I intended them to convey.   *h*

I was not saying that the law and practice of the Admiralty Court allowed it to award
interest of any kind in any case in which it might feel that it would be just and equitable
to do so. In particular, I was not referring in any way either to the question of awarding
interest on sums already paid, or to the question of awarding compound interest. I was
not doing so for two very good reasons: first, that such questions never arose for decision
and, second, that it would never have occurred to those taking part in that case, all well   *j*
experienced in Admiralty law and practice, that any equitable principle of such width as
to encompass the award of interest on debts already paid, or the award of compound
interest in any case, did, or could ever, have existed.

I said that there was no authority for the proposition that the Admiralty Court could
award interest on debts already paid. There is, however, an authority against such a

a proposition: that is *The Medina Princess* [1962] 2 Lloyd's Rep 17, in which Hewson J held, in a wages action, that he had no jurisdiction to award interest on wages which, by the time he came to give judgment, had already been paid, albeit much later than they should have been paid. That decision was criticised, and its authority discounted, by Oliver and Watkins LJJ in their judgments in the *Tehno-Impex* case [1981] 2 All ER 669 at 684–685, 689, [1981] QB 648 at 675–676, 681. In my opinion, however, *The Medina Princess* was, as the law then stood, correctly decided, and your Lordships should take this

b opportunity of giving it your approval.

My Lords, on the footing that the common ratio decidendi of the majority of the Court of Appeal in this case was, for the reasons which I have given, based on two fundamental misconceptions about the scope of the powers which a court exercising Admiralty jurisdiction then had to award interest, it follows that the decision of that majority cannot be supported on the grounds on which it was reached.

c On the view which I take on the matters discussed above, it is not necessary to decide whether the equitable power of the Admiralty Court to award interest on a debt or damages applies to all such claims as were formerly by s 1(1)(h) of the 1956 Act, and are now by s 20(2) of the Supreme Court Act 1981, declared to be within the Admiralty jurisdiction of the High Court; or whether, as Oliver LJ considered, such power was limited to claims which were within the jurisdiction of the High Court of Admiralty

d immediately before the passing of the Judicature Acts 1873–75. Since the matter has been raised, however, I think it right to say that, in my opinion, the former view is the correct one, and that preferred by Oliver LJ is the wrong one. I reach this conclusion on the basis that, once a statute has declared that any particular claim is within the Admiralty jurisdiction of the High Court, all the characteristics of that jurisdiction, including the equitable power to award interest, apply to such claim.

e My Lords, if the owners had confined themselves to seeking to support the decision of the Court of Appeal in the present case on the grounds on which it was given, it would follow from what I have said so far that, since those grounds were misconceived, the appeal would be bound to succeed.

Counsel for the owners did not, however, seek to support the decision of the Court of Appeal solely on those grounds. On the contrary, he raised for the first time in your

f Lordships' House a fresh contention which, by reason of its nature, was not open to the owners either in the Commercial Court or the Court of Appeal. This fresh contention was that your Lordships' House should take advantage of the 1966 Practice Statement [1966] 3 All ER 77, [1966] 1 WLR 1234 to depart from its previous decision in *London Chatham and Dover Rly Co v South Eastern Rly Co* [1893] AC 429. The ground on which he invited such a departure was that the decision concerned produced manifest injustice, in

g that it deprived a creditor, who suffered damage or loss by reason of the late payment of a debt, of any common law remedy for such damage or loss, except where there was an agreement, express or implied, for the payment of interest in the event of repayment of the debt being delayed.

There are three cases in which the absence of any common law remedy for damage or loss caused by the late payment of a debt may arise, cases which I shall in what follows

h describe for convenience as case 1, case 2 and case 3. Case 1 is where a debt is paid late, before any proceedings for its recovery have been begun. Case 2 is where a debt is paid late, after proceedings for its recovery have been begun, but before they have been concluded. Case 3 is where a debt remains unpaid until, as a result of proceedings for its recovery being brought and prosecuted to a conclusion, a money judgment is given in which the original debt becomes merged.

j Counsel for the owners urged your Lordships, by departing from the previous decision of your Lordships' House in the *London Chatham and Dover Rly* case, to provide a common law remedy which would meet all three cases, 1, 2 and 3. The remedy would be to hold that a creditor can recover damages, in the form of simple or compound interest, for a breach of contract by his debtor in failing to repay the principal sum for which he was liable in due time.

My Lords, it is impossible to weigh the merits of the submission that you should depart from the earlier decision of your Lordships' House in the *London Chatham and Dover Rly* case, without first examining the history and origins of the common law rule there laid down; the history of the various interventions by the legislature in relation to that rule; and an important qualification of that rule made, rightly or wrongly (your Lordships will have to decide which) by the Court of Appeal.

The authorities on the award of interest in respect of debts paid late are concerned principally, if not entirely, with case 3, namely where a creditor sues his debtor to judgment, and the question is whether the sum for which judgment is given should include interest in respect of the late payment of the debt. Before 1829 the law with regard to the award of such interest was in doubt. Some authorities, such as *Re Badger* (1819) 2 B & Ald 691, 106 ER 517 and *Arnott v Redfern* (1826) 3 Bing 353, 130 ER 549 supported the award of interest; other authorities were against it. In 1829 the matter was considered by a strong Court of King's Bench presided over by Lord Tenterden CJ in *Page v Newman* (1829) 9 B & C 378, 109 ER 140. Having referred to what had been said by Best CJ in *Arnott v Redfern*, he said (9 B & C 378 at 380–381, 109 ER 140 at 141):

'If we were to adopt as a general rule that which some of the expressions attributed to the Lord Chief Justice of the Common Pleas in *Arnott v. Redfern* would seem to warrant, viz. that interest is due wherever the debt has been wrongfully withheld after the plaintiff has endeavoured to obtain payment of it, it might frequently be made a question at Nisi Prius whether proper means had been used to obtain payment of the debt, and such as the party ought to have used. That would be productive of great inconvenience. I think that we ought not to depart from the long-established rule, that interest is not due on money secured by a written instrument, unless it appears on the face of the instrument that interest was intended to be paid, or unless it be implied from the usage of trade, as in the case of mercantile instruments.'

Four years later, in 1833, the legislature intervened in the matter by passing the statute 3 & 4 Will 4, c 42 (the Civil Procedure Act 1833), of which Lord Tenterden himself was the author, and which has in consequence ever since been known as Lord Tenterden's Act. Section 28 of that Act provided:

'. . . That upon all Debts or Sums certain, payable at a certain Time or otherwise, the Jury on the Trial of any Issue, or on any Inquisition of Damages, may, if they shall think fit, allow Interest to the Creditor at a Rate not exceeding the current Rate of Interest from the Time when such Debts or Sums certain were payable, if such Debts or Sums be payable by virtue of some written Instrument at a certain Time, or if payable otherwise, then from the Time when Demand of Payment shall have been made in Writing, so as such Demand shall give Notice to the Debtor that Interest will be claimed from the Date of such Demand until the Term of Payment; provided that Interest shall be payable in all Cases in which it is now payable by Law.'

This provision did not in practice go very far to solve the problem at which it was directed. The courts took very strict views about the various conditions which had to be fulfilled, and the requirements which had to be complied with, before a jury could, if they thought fit, award interest.

London Chatham and Dover Rly Co v South Eastern Rly Co [1893] AC 429 was decided no fewer than 60 years after the passing of Lord Tenterden's Act. It was a case in which railway company A, being in an accounting situation with railway company B, sued to recover the balance of account due to it with interest. The claim for interest was put forward on two grounds. The first ground was that the case came within s 28 of Lord Tenterden's Act. The second and alternative ground was that railway company A had a common law right to recover interest by way of damages for the breach of contract by railway company B in delaying payment of the debt.

The leading speech in your Lordships' House was that of Lord Herschell LC, with
a whom Lord Watson, Lord Morris and Lord Shand all concurred. With regard to the
claim under Lord Tenterden's Act, Lord Herschell LC said (at 434–437) that the claim
failed on two grounds. The first ground was that there was no debt or sum certain
payable by virtue of a written instrument, as required by s 28 of that Act. The second
ground was that no demand for payment claiming interest had been made in writing, as
also required by that section.

b   With regard to the second and alternative claim for interest by way of damages for
breach of contract in paying the debt late, Lord Herschell LC (at 437) expressed strong
sympathy with the claim, going so far as to say that he would be inclined to give effect to
it if the law permitted him to do so. Having, however, examined the authorities
culminating in *Page v Newman* (1829) 9 B & C 378, 109 ER 140, to which I referred
earlier, he expressed the view that the reason given by Lord Tenterden for the rule laid
c down by him in that case seemed unconvincing, and having referred to the subsequent
passing by Parliament of Lord Tenterden's Act, with what he regarded as excessive
restrictions on the power to award interest contained in it, he concluded that he was, for
three reasons, bound to hold that it was not open, even to your Lordships' House, to
allow a claim for interest on this alternative basis.

Those three reasons, as they appear from the speech of Lord Herschell LC ([1893] AC
d 429 at 440–441) were these. First, the unanimous view of the Court of King's Bench in
Page v Newman; second, the restricted form of Lord Tenterden's Act, which Parliament
had passed in 1833 with obvious reference to that decision; and, third, the absence of any
challenge, or at all events any effective challenge, in the courts to the rule laid down in
Page v Newman after that case had been decided in 1829.

My Lords, following the decision, albeit the reluctant decision, of your Lordships'
e House in the *London Chatham and Dover Rly* case, the law in this field remained unchanged
until the passing by Parliament of the 1934 Act, s 3 of which I set out earlier in full.
Three points are to be observed with regard to that provision. First, like Lord Tenterden's
Act, it only dealt with case 3, that is to say, the inclusion of interest in the sum for which
judgment in respect of a debt (or damages) is given; second, again like Lord Tenterden's
Act, it made the award of interest a matter of discretion, not of right; and, third, it
f expressly forbade the award of interest on interest, ie of compound interest. The effect
of the first of these three points is that, while some further remedy for an unpaid creditor
was given in case 3, no remedy was given for a creditor paid late in cases 1 and 2.

In 1951 the first tentative judicial inroad into the previously accepted understanding
of the scope of the decision of your Lordships' House in the *London Chatham and Dover
Rly* case was made by Denning and Romer LJJ in *Trans Trust SPRL v Danubian Trading Co
g Ltd* [1952] 1 All ER 970, [1952] 2 QB 297. The case was concerned with breach of a
contract to provide a confirmed credit, and it is only significant in the present context
because of certain observations made in it by the two Lords Justices referred to above.
Denning LJ said ([1952] 1 All ER 970 at 977, [1952] 2 QB 297 at 306):

'It was said that the breach here was a failure to pay money and that the law has
never allowed any damages on that account. I do not think that the law has ever
h   taken up such a rigid standpoint. It did undoubtedly refuse to award interest until
the introduction of the Law Reform (Miscellaneous Provisions) Act, 1934, s. 3 (1):
see *London, Chatham & Dover Ry. Co. v. South Eastern Ry. Co.*, but the ground was that
interest was "generally presumed not to be within the contemplation of the parties";
see BULLEN & LEAKE, 3rd ed., p. 51, note (*a*). That is, I think, the only real ground on
which damages can be refused for non-payment of money. It is because the
j   consequences are as a rule too remote. But when the circumstances are such that
there is a special loss foreseeable at the time of the contract as the consequence of
non-payment, then I think such loss may well be recoverable. It is not necessary,
however, to come to a firm conclusion on this point, because I regard the provision
of a credit as different from the payment of money and not subject to the special
rules, if any there are, relating thereto.'

Romer LJ said ([1952] 1 All ER 970 at 978, [1952] 2 QB 297 at 307):

> '. . . I am not, as at present advised, prepared to subscribe to the view that in no *a* case can damages be recovered for non-payment of money. I agree with DENNING, L.J., that in certain circumstances such damages might well be recoverable provided that the loss occasioned to the plaintiff by the defendant's default was reasonably within the contemplation of the parties when the bargain between them was made.'

As appears from what Denning LJ himself said, these observations made by him and *b* Romer LJ were not necessary to the decison of the case before them, and must therefore be categorised as no more than obiter dicta. It will be seen, however, that they were the foundations on which other judges were later to build.

On 21 December 1974 Lord Elwyn-Jones LC requested the Law Commission, pursuant to s 3(1) of the Law Commissions Act 1965—

> 'To consider the law and practice relating to interest on debt (where interest has *c* not been provided for by contract) and on damages, and to make recommendations.'

On 7 April 1978 the Law Commission made its report to the Lord Chancellor, which was presented by him to Parliament by command of Her Majesty (Law Com no 88). That report contained recommendations for alterations in the relevant law and a draft Bill which, if they were to be adopted as a whole, would remedy the injustices to unpaid *d* creditors, not only in case 3 (as had been done earlier by the 1934 Act), but also in cases 1 and 2.

No legislative action was taken as a result of the Law Commission's report until the passing by Parliament of the Administration of Justice Act 1982, to the relevant provisions of which I shall come back later, observing only for the time being that the Act had not yet been passed at the date, 12 March 1981, when *Tehno-Impex* [1981] 2 All *e* ER 669, [1981] QB 648 was decided.

Meanwhile there intervened a second and more important judicial inroad into the previously accepted understanding of the scope of the decision of your Lordships' House in *London Chatham and Dover Rly Co v South Eastern Rly Co* [1893] AC 429. That inroad was made by the Court of Appeal (Ormrod and Brightman LJJ and Reeve J) in *Wadsworth v Lydall* [1981] 1 All ER 401, [1981] 1 WLR 598. The facts of the case, as summarised in *f* the headnote of the report (see [1981] 1 WLR 598) were these. The defendant, the owner of a dairy farm, entered into an informal partnership agreement with the plaintiff under which the partnership was granted an agricultural tenancy, and the plaintiff lived in the farm house and ran the farm. On the dissolution of the partnership, an agreement was made which provided, inter alia, that the plaintiff would give up possession of the farm on or before 15 May 1976, and in that event would receive £10,000 from the defendant. *g* On 10 May 1976 the plaintiff, expecting to receive £10,000 in five days' time and having no other capital, entered into an agreement for the purchase of a property from G, by which £10,000 of the purchase price was to be paid on completion. On 15 May 1976 the plaintiff gave up possession of the farm, but the defendant did not pay him £10,000. On 21 July 1976 G's solicitors served a 28-day notice to complete. In October 1976 the defendant paid the plaintiff £7,200. The plaintiff passed that sum on to G and raised the *h* balance of the sum due on completion by taking out a mortgage from G on which he had to pay the legal costs. In an action brought against the defendant the plaintiff claimed as special damages £335 in respect of interest that he had to pay G for late completion and £16·20 in respect of the mortgage costs. The action was tried by Smith J, who awarded the plaintiff damages, but disallowed the two items of special damage referred to above on the ground that they were too remote. *j*

The plaintiff appealed to the Court of Appeal, and before that court the defendant sought to rely on the *London Chatham and Dover Rly* case as precluding the recovery of damages for a breach of contract consisting only in the late payment of a debt. He further contended that the only remedy available to the plaintiff was an award of interest under

the 1934 Act. These contentions were not accepted by the Court of Appeal. Brightman
LJ, who gave the principal judgment, with which the other two members of the court
agreed, said ([1981] 2 All ER 401 at 405–406, [1981] 1 WLR 598 at 603):

> 'In my view the court is not so constrained by the decision of the House of Lords.
> In *London Chatham and Dover Railway Co v South Eastern Railway Co* the House of
> Lords was not concerned with a claim for special damages. The action was an action
> for an account. The House was concerned only with a claim for interest by way of
> general damages. If a plaintiff pleads and can prove that he has suffered special
> damage as a result of the defendant's failure to perform his obligation under a
> contract, and such damage is not too remote on the principle of *Hadley v Baxendale*
> (1854) 9 Exch 341, [1843–60] All ER Rep 461, I can see no logical reason why such
> special damages should be irrecoverable merely because the obligation on which the
> defendant defaulted was an obligation to pay money and not some other type of
> obligation.'

Brightman LJ went on to refer to, and place reliance on, the observations of Denning and
Romer LJJ in *Trans Trust SPRL v Danubian Trading Co Ltd* [1952] 1 All ER 970, [1952] 2
QB 297 which I cited earlier.

The distinction which Brightman LJ was there drawing between general and special
damages is the difference between damages recoverable under the first part of the rule in
Hadley v Baxendale (1854) 9 Exch 341, [1843–60] All ER Rep 461 (general damages) and
damages recoverable under the second part of that rule (special damages). On the facts of
the case before him Brightman LJ found that, by reason of special matters known to both
parties at the time of contracting, the two items of special damages claimed by the
plaintiff came within the second part of that rule. Accordingly, treating the *London
Chatham and Dover Rly* case as applying only to damages falling within the first part of
the rule in *Hadley v Baxendale* (general damages), he saw no reason why the plaintiff
should not recover the two disputed items of special damages under the second part of
that rule.

In my opinion the ratio decidendi of *Wadsworth v Lydall* [1981] 2 All ER 401, [1981] 1
WLR 598, that the *London Chatham and Dover Rly* case applied only to claims for interest
by way of general damages, and did not extend to claims for special damages, in the sense
in which it is clear that Brightman LJ was using those two expressions, was correct and
should be approved by your Lordships. On the assumption that your Lordships give
such approval, the effect will be to reduce considerably the scope of the *London Chatham
and Dover Rly* case by comparison with what it had in general previously been understood
to be.

The final stage of this strange but hardly uneventful history comes with the passing
by Parliament of the Administration of Justice Act 1982. Part III of the 1982 Act, which
first came into operation in 1983, has the cross-heading 'Powers of Courts to Award
Interest'. Section 15, which is the first section under that heading, provides:

> '(1) The section set out in Part I of Schedule 1 to this Act shall be inserted after
> section 35 of the Supreme Court Act 1981.
> (2) The section set out in Part II of that Schedule shall be inserted after section 97
> of the County Courts Act 1959 . . .
> (4) The provisions mentioned in subsection (5) below (which this section
> supersedes so far as they apply to the High Court and county courts) shall cease to
> have effect in relation to those courts.
> (5) The provisions are—(a) section 3 of the Law Reform (Miscellaneous Provisions)
> Act 1934; and (b) in the Administration of Justice Act 1969—(i) section 22 . . .
> (6) The section set out in Part IV of Schedule 1 to this Act shall be inserted after
> section 19 of the Arbitration Act 1950.'

Schedule 1 of the 1982 Act, referred to in s 15(1) and (2) of that Act, is in these terms:

'SCHEDULE 1

INTEREST ON DEBTS AND DAMAGES

PART I

SECTION INSERTED IN SUPREME COURT ACT 1981

35A. (1) Subject to rules of court, in proceedings (whenever instituted) before the High Court for the recovery of a debt or damages there may be included in any sum for which judgment is given simple interest, at such rate as the court thinks fit or as rules of court may provide, on all or any part of the debt or damages in respect of which judgment is given, or payment is made before judgment, for all or any part of the period between the date when the cause of action arose and—(a) in the case of any sum paid before judgment, the date of the payment; and (b) in the case of the sum for which judgment is given, the date of the judgment . . .

(3) Subject to rules of court, where—(a) there are proceedings (whenever instituted) before the High Court for the recovery of a debt; and (b) the defendant pays the whole debt to the plaintiff (otherwise than in pursuance of a judgment in the proceedings), the defendant shall be liable to pay the plaintiff simple interest at such rate as the court thinks fit or as rules of court may provide on all or any part of the debt for all or any part of the period between the date when the cause of action arose and the date of the payment.

(4) Interest in respect of a debt shall not be awarded under this section for a period during which, for whatever reason, interest on the debt already runs . . .

(6) Interest under this section may be calculated at different rates in respect of different periods . . .

(8) Nothing in this section affects the damages recoverable for the dishonour of a bill of exchange.

PART II

SECTION INSERTED IN COUNTY COURTS ACT 1959

[Here there follow provisions applicable to county courts of the same kind as those applicable to the High Court by virtue of Part I] . . .

PART IV

SECTION INSERTED IN ARBITRATION ACT 1950

19A. (1) Unless a contrary intention is expressed therein, every arbitration agreement shall, where such a provision is applicable to the reference, be deemed to contain a provision that the arbitrator or umpire may, if he thinks fit, award simple interest at such rate as he thinks fit—(a) on any sum which is the subject of the reference but which is paid before the award, for such period ending not later than the date of the payment as he thinks fit; and (b) on any sum which he awards, for such period ending not later than the date of the award as he thinks fit.

(2) The power to award interest conferred on an arbitrator or umpire by subsection (1) above is without prejudice to any other power of an arbitrator or umpire to award interest.'

When one compares these provisions of the 1982 Act with the corresponding provisions of s 3 of the 1934 Act, which by s 15(5)(a) of the 1982 Act they repeal and replace, the following points become apparent. First, whereas s 3 of the 1934 Act covered only the award of interest in case 3 (debts not paid before judgment in proceedings for their recovery has been given), the 1982 Act, by the insertion, by s 15(1) and Part I of Sch 1, of a new s 35A into the Supreme Court Act 1981, covers both case 3 and case 2 (late payments of debts after proceedings have been begun but before they have been concluded). In this respect the new provisions give substantial effect to the recommendations of the Law Commission. Second, while the new provisions cover both case 3 and case 2, they do not extend so far as to cover case 1 (late payment of debts before any proceedings for their recovery have been begun). In this respect the new provisions do not give effect to the recommendations of the Law Commission. Third, whereas s 3 of the 1934 Act, by its express terms, conferred powers to award interest on courts of record only, the 1981 Act, by s 15(6) and Part IV of Sch 1, confers similar powers on

a arbitrators and umpires as well. Fourth, while s 3 of the 1934 Act has been repealed, the prohibition against the award of anything but simple interest has been expressly preserved, both in the case of courts and in the case of arbitrators and umpires: see sub-ss (1) and (4) of the new s 35A inserted into the Supreme Court Act 1981, and sub-s (1) of the new s 19A inserted into the Arbitration Act 1950.

My Lords, I indicated earlier the matters which your Lordships would need to take

b into account in deciding whether or not to accede to the submission for the owners that you should depart from the earlier decision of your Lordships' House in *London Chatham and Dover Rly Co v South Eastern Rly Co* case [1893] AC 429.

These matters were, first, the history and origins of the common law rule laid down in that case; second, the history of interventions by the legislature in relation to that rule; and, third, the important qualification of that rule recently made by the Court of Appeal.

c Having examined all these three matters, I have reached the following conclusions with regard to the submission for the owners. First, an ideal system of justice would ensure that a creditor should be able to recover interest both on unpaid debts in case 1, and also in respect of debts paid late or remaining unpaid in cases 2 and 3. Second, if the legislature had not intervened twice in this field since the *London Chatham and Dover Rly* case, first by the 1934 Act and more recently by the 1982 Act, and if the Court of Appeal

d had not limited the scope of that case by its decision in *Wadsworth v Lydall* [1981] 2 All ER 401, [1981] 1 WLR 598, I should have thought that a strong, if not an overwhelming, case would have been made out for your Lordships' House, in order to do justice to creditors in all three cases 1, 2 and 3, to depart from the decision in the *London Chatham and Dover Rly* case. But, third, since the legislature has made the two interventions in this field to which I have referred, and since the scope of the *London Chatham and Dover*

e *Rly* case has been qualified to a significant extent by *Wadsworth v Lydall*, I am of the opinion, for three main reasons, that the departure sought by the owners would not now be justified.

My first main reason is that the greater part of the injustice to creditors which resulted from the *London Chatham and Dover Rly* case has now been removed, to a large extent by legislative intervention, and to a lesser extent by judicial qualification of the scope of the

f decision itself. My second main reason is that, when Parliament has given effect by legislation to some recommendations of the Law Commission in a particular field, but has taken what appears to be a policy decision not to give effect to a further such recommendation, any decision of your Lordships' House which would have the result of giving effect, by another route, to the very recommendation which Parliament appears to have taken that policy decision to reject, could well be regarded as an unjustifiable

g usurpation by your Lordships' House of the functions which belong properly to Parliament, rather than as a judicial exercise in departing from an earlier decision on the ground that it has become obsolete and could still, in a limited class of cases, continue to cause some degree of injustice.

In relation to this second consideration your Lordships were referred by counsel for the owners to the decision of your Lordships' House in *British Rlys Board v Herrington*

h [1972] 1 All ER 749, [1972] AC 877. That case has some analogies with the present case in the following respects. The Third Report of the Law Reform Committee (Cmd 9305), presented to Parliament in November 1954, had made recommendations for the clarification of, and alterations to, the law relating to the liability of occupiers to invitees, licensees and trespassers. In particular, it had recommended changes in the law relating to child trespassers. Following that report, Parliament passed the Occupiers' Liability Act

j 1957. That Act dealt with the recommendations in the report with regard to the liability of occupiers to invitees and licensees, but omitted to deal with the recommendations made in it with regard to the liability of occupiers to child trespassers. It was contended that, in those circumstances, your Lordships' House should not seek to fill the gap by laying down principles relating to the liability of occupiers to child trespassers, which involved, to some extent at least, a departure from an earlier decision of your Lordships' House in *Robert Addie & Sons (Collieries) Ltd v Dumbreck* [1929] AC 358, [1929] All ER Rep

1. Your Lordships' House, however, rejected that contention and did make a decision which involved at least some degree of departure from *Addie's* case.

    While there are, as I have said, some analogies between the present case and *British Rlys Board v Herrington* in the respects to which I have adverted, I do not think that it is justifiable to argue that, because your Lordships' House acted in the way it did in *Herrington's* case, it should act in a similar way in the present case. The question of the law relating to child trespassers was a matter of serious importance which needed to be dealt with without further delay. It was further the view of Lord Reid that the silence of Parliament with regard to child trespassers in the Occupiers' Liability Act 1957 might be attributable, not to a rejection by Parliament of the recommendations of the Law Reform Committee on the subject, but rather to Parliament being unable to make up its mind what to put in the place of the existing law, and leaving it to the courts to work out a solution to the problem concerned (see [1972] 1 All ER 749 at 757, [1972] AC 877 at 897). I doubt very much whether that explanation can account for Parliament's decision not to give effect in the 1982 Act to the recommendations of the Law Commission relating to case 1. In any event the only remaining loophole of injustice to creditors paid late is small, has existed for many years and does not seem to require closing urgently.

    My third reason is this. Suppose that your Lordships were to depart from the *London Chatham and Dover Rly* case in such a way as to give all creditors, whose debts either remained unpaid or were paid late, whether before or after action brought, a cause of action for interest by way of general damages for breach of contract, what would be the result? The result, as it seems to me, would be that such cause of action would be available to a creditor not only in case 1, in respect of which he still has no remedy except where he can prove special damages, but also in cases 2 and 3, in respect of both of which, since the coming into force of the 1982 Act, he already has a statutory remedy. What is more, the new cause of action so applicable to cases 2 and 3 would constitute a remedy as of right for a creditor, whereas the statutory remedy would remain discretionary only. There would accordingly exist, in relation to cases 2 and 3, two parallel remedies, one as of right and the other discretionary; and the likelihood would be that creditors would, because of this difference, come to rely mainly on the former, rather than the latter, right. It is, in my view, plainly to be inferred, from the form of the relevant provisions in the 1934 and 1982 Acts, that Parliament has consistently regarded the award of interest on debts as a remedy to which creditors should not be entitled as of right, but only as a matter of discretion. That being the manifest policy of the legislature, I do not consider that your Lordships should create, in relation to cases 2 and 3, a rival system of remedies which, because they would be remedies as of right, would be inconsistent with that manifest policy.

    My Lords, for the reasons which I have given I am of the opinion that no sufficient case has been made out for a departure by your Lordships' House from its earlier decision in the *London Chatham and Dover Rly* case, and that your Lordships should therefore decline to make any such departure.

    On the footing that the decision of the Court of Appeal in *Tehno-Impex* [1981] 2 All ER 669, [1981] QB 648 cannot be supported on the grounds on which it was made, and on the further footing that your Lordships' House would not, in all the circumstances of the case, be justified in departing from its earlier decision in the *London Chatham and Dover Rly* case, it follows that this appeal succeeds and must be allowed with costs both in this House and the Commercial Court. The consequence of the appeal being allowed is that the primary award of the umpire will be set aside and his alternative award in favour of the sub-charterer upheld.

Appeal allowed.

Solicitors: *Zaiwalla & Co* (for the sub-charterer); *Richards Butler & Co* (for the owners).

                                Mary Rose Plummer   Barrister.

_a # Trawnik and another v Ministry of Defence

CHANCERY DIVISION

SIR ROBERT MEGARRY V-C

12, 13, 28 MARCH, 2, 16 APRIL 1984

_b *Crown – Proceedings against – Liability of Crown – Liability arising 'otherwise than in respect of Her Majesty's government in the United Kingdom' – German plaintiffs suing in England in respect of damage threatened by British military authorities in Berlin – Plaintiffs relying on Crown Proceedings Act 1947 to bring action against Ministry of Defence – Whether plaintiffs bringing action 'under or in accordance with [the 1947] Act' – Whether Crown's liability arising 'otherwise than in respect of Her Majesty's government in the United Kingdom' – Crown Proceedings Act* _c *1947, ss 2, 17, 40(2)(b).*

Declaration – Availability of remedy – Declaration of plaintiff's rights – Plaintiff suffering as result of defendant's acts – Defendant immune from liability in tort – Whether open to plaintiff to seek declaration of his rights as against defendant.

_d The plaintiffs were West German residents who owned houses adjoining a military airfield occupied by the Ministry of Defence in the British sector of Berlin. They wished to prevent the ministry constructing a shooting range on part of the airfield close to the plaintiffs' houses for use by members of the British armed forces stationed in Berlin, on the ground that noise from the range would be a nuisance and would damage the plaintiffs' health. However the plaintiffs were unable to bring proceedings in Berlin because there was no court there which possessed jurisdiction to try a civil action in _e which the British military authorities were a party without the authority of the Allied Kommandatura, which had been refused. The plaintiffs therefore issued a writ and statement of claim in England against the Ministry of Defence as defendant, relying on the fact that the ministry was a government department listed under s 17^a of the Crown Proceedings Act 1947 as a department against which civil proceedings against the Crown could be brought. The plaintiffs sought a declaration that the ministry should not use _f the airfield so as to cause a nuisance to the plaintiffs by noise. The ministry applied under RSC Ord 18, r 19 and under the court's inherent jurisdiction for the action to be struck out as disclosing no cause of action against the ministry and as being an abuse of the process of the court, contending that the plaintiffs' reliance on s 17 meant that their action was an action 'under or in accordance with [the 1947] Act' within s 40(2)(b)^b, of that Act and was therefore barred if the Secretary of State certified, as he had, that any _g liability of the Crown arose 'otherwise than in respect of Her Majesty's Government in the United Kingdom'. The plaintiffs contended (i) that, although they had to rely on s 17 to bring their action because the ministry was not a separate legal entity, their claim against the Crown was in tort generally and was not a claim 'under or in accordance with [the 1947] Act' so that the restriction in s 40(2)(b) did not apply, and (ii) that in any event the plaintiffs were not suing in tort but merely seeking a declaration as to their rights. _h Subsequently the plaintiffs applied under Ord 15, r 6 to add the British military commandant in Berlin and the Attorney General as defendants if the proceedings against the Ministry of Defence were struck out.

_a Section 17, so far as material, provides:

_j   '(1) The Minister for the Civil Service shall publish a list specifying the several Government departments which are authorised departments for the purposes of this Act . . .

        (3) Civil proceedings against the Crown shall be instituted against the appropriate authorised Government department, or, if none of the authorised Government departments is appropriate or the person instituting the proceedings has any reasonable doubt whether any and if so which of those departments is appropriate, against the Attorney General . . .'

_b Section 40(2), so far as material, is set out at p 794 *h*, post

Held – (1) The plaintiffs' claim against the Ministry of Defence would be struck out because any proceedings taken in reliance on s 17 of the 1947 Act were necessarily proceedings 'under or in accordance with [the 1947] Act' for the purposes of s 40(2)(b) of that Act and therefore barred by the Secretary of State's certificate that any liability of the Crown alleged in the action arose 'otherwise than in respect of Her Majesty's Government in the United Kingdom' (see p 795 c d, p 798 f g and p 799 a, post).

(2) The plaintiffs would however be allowed to join the Attorney General and the British military commandant in Berlin as defendants, because although it was by no means clear that the plaintiffs were entitled to bring an action in tort against the Crown or a Crown servant outside the framework of the 1947 Act, thereby escaping the restriction on bringing proceedings imposed by s 40(2)(b) and the Secretary of State's certificate, the point was at least arguable and as a matter of discretion the joinder would be allowed to enable the plaintiffs to test their claim in a court (see p 800 e to j, post).

Per curiam. If a prospective defendant is immune from liability in tort it is not open to a plaintiff who will suffer from his acts to avoid that immunity by the device of framing the proceedings as a claim for a declaration of the plaintiff's rights instead of as a direct claim in tort (see p 797 c to e, post); Kynaston v A-G (1933) 49 TLR 300 followed.

Quaere. Whether proceedings against the Crown in tort that are pursued outside the framework of the 1947 Act, relying nevertheless on the exposure of the Crown by s 2ᶜ of that Act to actions in tort, can be said not to be proceedings 'under or in accordance with [the 1947] Act' even though it is only by virtue of that Act that the proceedings can be brought at all (see p 798 g to j, post).

Notes

For legal proceedings against the Crown and procedure under the Crown Proceedings Act 1947, see 11 Halsbury's Laws (4th edn) paras 1410–1450, and for cases on the subject, see 16 Digest (Reissue) 263–267, 2521–2536.

For the Crown Proceedings Act 1947, ss 2, 17, 40, see 8 Halsbury's Statutes (3rd edn) 846, 858, 871.

Cases referred to in judgments

Buck v A-G [1965] 1 All ER 882, [1965] Ch 745, [1965] 2 WLR 1053, CA; affg [1964] 2 All ER 663, [1965] Ch 745, [1964] 3 WLR 850.

Dyson v A-G [1911] 1 KB 410, CA.

Hubbuck & Sons Ltd v Wilkinson Heywood & Clark Ltd [1899] 1 QB 86, [1895–9] All ER Rep 244, CA.

Kynaston v A-G (1933) 49 TLR 300, CA; affg 49 TLR 114.

Manuel v A-G [1982] 3 All ER 786, [1983] Ch 77, [1982] 3 WLR 821; affd [1982] 3 All ER 822, [1983] Ch 77, [1982] 3 WLR 821, CA.

Summons

By summons dated 10 November 1983 the defendant, the Ministry of Defence, applied under RSC Ord 18, r 19 and the inherent jurisdiction of the court to strike out the writ and statement of claim in an action brought by the plaintiffs, Gunter Trawnik and Luise Reimelt, seeking declarations (i) that it was not lawful to use Gatow Airport in Berlin so as to cause a nuisance by noise to the plaintiffs, (ii) that the ministry should not use or permit others to use Gatow Airport so as to cause a nuisance by noise to the plaintiffs, and (iii) that members of Her Majesty's armed forces under the command of Major-General Gordon Lennox should not use Gatow Airport so as to cause a nuisance by noise to the plaintiffs. The grounds of the ministry's application were that the writ and statement of claim disclosed no cause of action in respect of which proceedings against the Crown were authorised by the Crown Proceedings Act 1947 and were an abuse of the process of the court because the alleged liability of the Crown arose otherwise than in respect of Her

---

c   Section 2, so far as material, is set out at p 795 e, post

Majesty's government in the United Kingdom. At the hearing of the summons the
plaintiffs sought to add Major-General Gordon Lennox, the British military commandant
in Berlin, and the Attorney General as defendants if the proceedings against the ministry
were struck out. The facts are set out in the judgment.

John R Macdonald QC and *Owen Davies* for the plaintiffs.
John Mummery for the ministry.

Cur adv vult

28 March. The following judgment was delivered.

SIR ROBERT MEGARRY V-C. I have before me a summons by the defendant, the
Ministry of Defence, to strike out the writ and statement of claim in a somewhat unusual
action by two plaintiffs. The application is made under RSC Ord 18, r 19 and the inherent
jurisdiction; and it alleges that the writ and statement of claim disclose no cause of action
against the ministry and that they constitute an abuse of the process of the court. For the
purposes of this application I have to take the facts to be as alleged in the amended
statement of claim. With some additions from the affidavit evidence, those facts may be
summarised as follows. Each plaintiff owns and occupies a house adjoining Gatow
Airfield in the British sector of Berlin. The ministry occupies that airfield. The ministry
has recently begun to construct a shooting range on part of the airfield close to the
plaintiffs' houses. If this shooting range is operated in accordance with the ministry's
stated intention, it will cause such an excessive noise that it will constitute a nuisance to
the plaintiffs' houses and injure their health. That nuisance is not justifiable by the law
of Berlin. The plaintiffs therefore claim three declarations: first, that it is not lawful to
use the airfield so as to cause a nuisance to the plaintiffs by noise; second, that the ministry
'should not use nor permit others to use' the airfield so as to cause a nuisance to the
plaintiffs by noise; and third, that members of Her Majesty's armed forces under the
command of a named major-general, who is the British military commandant of Berlin
and in command of Her Majesty's armed forces there, 'should not use' the airfield so as to
cause a nuisance to the plaintiffs by noise.

Last July the plaintiffs applied to the Administrative Court in Berlin for an injunction
to restrain the construction of the firing range. Under Law No 7 of the Allied
Kommandatura in Berlin, the German courts have no jurisdiction to hear any civil case
to which the allied forces are parties without the authority of the Allied Kommandatura
or the appropriate sector commandant. The Allied Kommandatura was duly asked to
authorise these proceedings, but refused to do so, whereupon the court dismissed the
application for want of jurisdiction. An appeal to the Administrative Court of Appeal
was dismissed on 24 November 1983 on the same ground. Ordinance No 68 of the Berlin
Military Government provides for the establishment of a High Court in the British sector
with criminal and civil jurisdiction, as well as summary courts; and these courts are
called Military Government Courts. These courts have such civil jurisdiction as the
commandant from time to time directs. However, no such courts appear to be in
operation; and there is no office for them, and no way of approaching any authority
connected with any such court in Berlin. The practical result is that there seems to be no
court in Berlin with any jurisdiction to hear the plaintiffs' application. The question is
whether this court has any jurisdiction. Counsel for the ministry says No, and counsel
for the plaintiffs says Yes. As might be expected, the Crown Proceedings Act 1947 is at
the centre of the dispute. This Act, which I shall call 'the 1947 Act' or 'the Act', is by no
means simple, and the argument lasted for most of two days.

At the outset I can dispose of one point with brevity. It was accepted that no difficulty
was caused by the land in question being outside this country. By s 30(1) of the Civil
Jurisdiction and Judgments Act 1982 the jurisdiction of this court in cases of tort affecting
immovable property extends to cases where the property is situated outside England and

Wales 'unless the proceedings are principally concerned with a question of the title to, or
the right to possession of, that property'. Neither title nor the right to possession is in
issue in this case, and so there is no territorial objection to this court exercising
jurisdiction.

With that, I can turn to the issues between the parties as they finally emerged. I say
that, because the lines of battle at the outset were not in the same places as they were
during the later stages of the argument; indeed, at times during the argument I found it
difficult to perceive just where they were drawn. In particular, during the argument
counsel for the plaintiffs made it plain that his contentions were founded on the plaintiffs
having a right to relief outside the 1947 Act, and that their claim was not based on any
cause of action conferred by that Act, though he did rely on certain provisions of the Act
as applying to proceedings which stood outside the Act, a process which counsel for the
ministry criticised as being an attempt to take the benefit of the Act without accepting
its burdens or restrictions. This approach differed from the attitude which, in opening,
counsel for the ministry had assumed that the plaintiffs were adopting, so that for a time
the rival contentions did not meet head on. Counsel for the plaintiffs also initially said
that he could succeed even if his case fell within the Act. I shall not spend any time on
how the arguments evolved; instead, I shall consider the arguments in what appeared to
be their final form.

The first question that I shall consider is essentially procedural. The Ministry of
Defence is not a corporate entity and so prima facie cannot be sued. However, the
plaintiffs say that the action is nevertheless properly constituted by virtue of s 17 of the
Act. Section 17(1) requires the Treasury to publish a list specifying the several government
departments 'which are authorised departments for the purposes of this Act', with names
and addresses and so on. Such a list has been published, and it includes the Ministry of
Defence. Section 17(3) provides that 'Civil proceedings against the Crown shall be
instituted against the appropriate authorised Government department', with provision
for cases where no such department is appropriate or there is some reasonable doubt
about this.

There appears to be nothing in these provisions to confine this procedural point to
proceedings taken under the Act, as distinct from those taken outside the Act; and s 23(2)
confirms this. That subsection provides that any reference in Pt II of the Act (and s 17 is
in Pt II) to 'civil proceedings against the Crown' is to be construed as a reference 'to the
following proceedings only'. Three heads are then set out. The first, put shortly, consists
of proceedings which, if the Act had not been passed, could have been brought by
petition of right. The second consists of proceedings which, if the Act had not been
passed, could have been brought by an action 'against the Attorney General, any
Government department, or any officer of the Crown as such'. The third consists of
proceedings which a person is entitled to bring against the Crown 'by virtue of this Act'.
Thus far, I think that the Act enables the plaintiffs to sue 'the Ministry of Defence' under
that name even if the proceedings are brought not under the Act but outside it.

Counsel for the ministry, however, points to s 40(2)(b). That reads as follows:

'Except as therein otherwise expressly provided, nothing in this Act shall . . . (b)
authorise proceedings to be taken against the Crown under or in accordance with
this Act in respect of any alleged liability of the Crown arising otherwise than in
respect of His Majesty's Government in the United Kingdom, or affect proceedings
against the Crown in respect of any such alleged liability as aforesaid . . .'

Then by s 40(3) a certificate of a Secretary of State to the effect that any alleged liability of
the Crown arises otherwise than in respect of His Majesty's government in the United
Kingdom 'shall, for the purposes of this Act, be conclusive as to the matter so certified'. I
have before me a certificate of Sir Geoffrey Howe, a Secretary of State, that any liability
of the Crown alleged in this action arises otherwise than in respect of Her Majesty's
government in the United Kingdom. Therefore, says counsel for the ministry, nothing
in the Act authorises proceedings to be taken against the Crown in accordance with the

Act, and so the plaintiffs in this action cannot rely on s 17. Not so, says counsel for the
a plaintiffs, since by ss 17 and 23, when read together, it is 'otherwise expressly provided',
so that s 40(2)(b) does not apply.

I do not think that the contention of counsel for the plaintiffs on this point can be
right. Section 40(2)(b) is concerned to exclude the liabilities of the Crown in right of its
many other territories; the Act is to apply only to its liabilities in right of the United
Kingdom. Sections 17 and 23 are not directed to such matters at all. There is no reference,
b either express or implied, to the right in which the Crown is alleged to be liable.
Furthermore, the draftsman of the Act has demonstrated perfectly clearly that he is
capable of making an explicit provision which otherwise expressly provides. Section 8(2)
relates to salvage services rendered by or on behalf of His Majesty, 'whether in right of
His Government in the United Kingdom or otherwise'. This section was not mentioned
during the argument and so I shall say little about it; but it does seem to me to reinforce
c the conclusion that I had reached without its aid.

It therefore seems to me that the plaintiffs are unable to rely on the 1947 Act, and
especially s 17, as enabling them to sue 'the Ministry of Defence'. As there is no legal
person of that name, and no statutory authority which enables the plaintiffs to bring an
action against a defendant by that name, the plaintiffs' claim must fail. However, these
are proceedings for striking out the action, and, as such, a high degree of assurance is
d required before such proceedings can succeed. I shall therefore consider this matter
further after I have examined the other contentions.

I turn next to the Crown's liability in tort. In its ultimate brevity, the point taken by
counsel for the ministry is that these are proceedings in tort, and that s 40(2)(b), coupled
with the Secretary of State's certificate, provides a complete bar to the proceedings.
Counsel for the plaintiffs denied that, contending that s 2 enabled the plaintiffs to sue the
e Crown in tort without being barred by s 40(2)(b). Section 2 provides that—

'(1) Subject to the provisions of this Act, the Crown shall be subject to all those
liabilities in tort to which, if it were a private person of full age and capacity, it
would be subject . . .'

though only in the cases specified. These cases are set out in sub-s (1)(a), (b) and (c), and
f also in sub-s (2), which is worded a little differently. The only case that I need mention is
the case in sub-s (1)(c):

'in respect of any breach of the duties attaching at common law to the ownership,
occupation, possession or control of property.'

That, said counsel for the ministry, for the first time enabled actions in tort to be brought
g against the Crown; and the Crown's liability was under the Act alone. Not so, said
counsel for the plaintiffs. True, the Crown had previously been immune from actions in
tort; but in the specified cases the Act made the Crown generally liable in tort, and there
was nothing to limit this liability to proceedings taken under the Act. The liability would
apply equally to proceedings pursued outside the Act. But, said counsel for the ministry,
the opening words of s 2(1) (namely 'Subject to the provisions of this Act') brought in
h s 40(2)(b) with its exclusion of liability. Even if that is right, said counsel for the plaintiffs,
look at the language of s 40(2)(b). He accepted that in this case the effect of s 40(2)(b) was
to provide a bar to any proceedings taken under the Act; but it did not, he said, provide
any bar to proceedings pursued outside the Act. Section 40(2)(b) prevented the Act from
authorising proceedings to be taken against the Crown 'under or in accordance with' the
Act, but that language plainly did not apply to proceedings pursued outside the Act to
j enforce the change in the general law made by s 2.

If that is right, said counsel for the ministry, the result would be remarkable. If a claim
were made against the Crown otherwise than in respect of the government in the United
Kingdom, everything would depend on how the proceedings were framed: if they were
framed under the Act, s 40(2)(b) would bar them, whereas if they were framed as being
brought outside the Act, s 40(2)(b) would be no bar, however little the claim had to do

with the government in the United Kingdom. The court should be very slow to attribute
such a capricious intent to Parliament, despite the fact that the phrase in s 40(2)(b) was　*a*
'under or in accordance with' the Act, without the addition of 'or by virtue of', a phrase
that might well have concluded the point. I should add that during the argument little
was said about the nature of proceedings against the Crown that were brought under the
Act as contrasted with the nature of such proceedings if they fall outside the Act. It was
simply accepted that there were proceedings of each class that could be brought.

Before I say any more about this, I shall turn to a related point taken by counsel for the　*b*
plaintiffs. Put broadly, he contended that the plaintiffs were not suing in tort at all. All
that they sought were certain declarations as to their rights. A declaration that the Crown
is liable to the plaintiffs in tort would be one thing, and a declaration that the plaintiffs
have a right not to be subjected to a nuisance by noise by the ministry is another; and the
latter form of declaration can be made even if the right is wholly unenforceable. He
stressed the width of the remedy by way of declaratory relief, and the absence of any　*c*
need to show that there is any cause of action (points which were not controverted), and
said that the essence of a declaratory judgment was that it stated the rights or legal
positions of the parties as they stood, without changing them: see Wade *Administrative
Law* (5th edn, 1982) p 522. I do not think that the declarations at present claimed by the
plaintiffs fit very well into that mould, with the use of the words 'should not' in two of
them; but that does not seem to be a matter of any great significance, for in granting　*d*
declarations it is common enough to revise the language so as to trim off any excess, and
to make the declaration fit the substance of the decision.

Counsel for the ministry contended that this argument was wrong. The declarations
sought, he said, plainly sounded in tort. In substance and effect, they were declarations as
to Crown wrongs, not declarations of the plaintiffs' rights, and they therefore fell within
the former inability to sue the Crown in tort and the present ability to sue the Crown in　*e*
tort in cases within s 2 of the Act. Neither the width of the remedy by way of declaratory
relief nor the absence of any need to show that there was a cause of action affected the
fact that the declarations were claims in tort, albeit quia timet.

Counsel for the ministry supported his contention by citing an authority on which he
strongly relied, namely, *Kynaston v A-G* (1933) 49 TLR 300. This was a decision of the
Court of Appeal which affirmed the decision of Farwell J (49 TLR 114). The claim there　*f*
was a claim for declaratory relief made by a retired officer in the Medical Corps who had
been recalled to service on the outbreak of war in 1914. Some of his complaints were
contractual in nature, but one of the declarations that he sought was that the Army
Council had exceeded their legal powers in depriving him of his seniority as a major and
in retaining him with the military forces after his name had been removed from the
active list. The case was argued on points of law raised by the defence which had been　*g*
ordered to be argued as preliminary issues. All I need say about the contractual issues is
that it was held that employment in the armed forces was not a matter of contract; but
the plaintiff's claim for a declaration as to his overlong retention on service was treated as
a claim in tort. On this, Lord Hanworth MR said (at 301):

> 'The last declaration asked for raised the point that the plaintiff had been retained　*h*
> on service for longer than he ought to have been retained. In other words, the
> plaintiff claimed that he had suffered a wrong at the hands of some one who detained
> him beyond his period of service. The action was brought for a declaration against
> the Attorney-General, as in *Dyson v. Attorney-General* ([1911] 1 KB 410). It was well
> to recall that the precedent then laid down was in respect of the construction of an
> Act of Parliament involving the rights of the King's subjects. It was not a question　*j*
> with regard to the service of any person to H.M. the King in any of the forces. Such
> a declaration as was asked for in *Dyson's* case bore no analogy to that asked for in the
> present proceedings, and it did not seem possible by means of the declaration sought
> in this case to obtain a decision on the merits or demerits of the Army Council. But
> another objection to this mode of proceeding was that it was a leading principle that
> the King could do no wrong, and the Courts could not deviate from it. If a wrong

had been done to the plaintiff that was a tort executed against him by some person or persons for whom there was no responsibility in the heads of departments. The action being for a tort must be against the person who had committed it, whether he did so in the service of the Crown or not. The Attorney-General was not the person who had done the act, nor was he responsible for it. On that ground also the action was misconceived, and the appeal must be dismissed.'

The report then states that Lawrence and Romer LJJ 'also gave judgment dismissing the appeal', without any other indication being given as to the nature of their judgments. I was told that there appears to be no better report of the case; and counsel for the plaintiffs not surprisingly pointed to the brevity with which the leading judgment had been reported, saying that it was a special case which should be confined to its own facts. He also reserved the right to contend in a higher court that it was wrongly decided.

The decision plainly binds me. The decision also seems to me, if I may say so, plainly right. If a prospective defendant is immune from liability in tort, I do not think that it is open to a plaintiff who will suffer from his acts to avoid that immunity by the simple device of framing the proceedings as a claim for declarations instead of as a direct claim in tort. The immunity is in tort, and no alteration in the mode of proceeding will alter that. It seems to me to be improbable in the extreme that, apart from the 1947 Act, the position could be that the Crown is immune from all proceedings in tort save that a declaration can be made that certain conduct by the Crown is tortious and wrong, and should not take place or be continued. I do not think that it would make any difference even if the declarations sought were to be reworded so as to speak of the rights of the plaintiffs rather than the wrong of the defendant. You do not prevent a claim for a declaration from being a claim in tort by saying that what you seek is not a declaration that the acts of the defendant are unlawful or tortious, but a declaration that you have a right not to be injured by the defendant's unlawful acts or torts.

I shall not expatiate on the exercise of the jurisdiction to strike out pleadings under RSC Ord 18, r 19 or the inherent jurisdiction. It is well settled that a claim should be struck out only if it is obvious and clear beyond doubt that the claim cannot possibly succeed. A plaintiff is not to be driven from the judgment seat merely because his claim is weak. The question is whether in the present case the plaintiffs' claim is so plainly bad that it should be struck out. One difficulty is that the case turns on the effect of the far from simple provisions of the 1947 Act on somewhat unusual facts. In delivering the judgment of the Court of Appeal in *Hubbuck & Sons Ltd v Wilkinson Heywood & Clark Ltd* [1899] 1 QB 86 at 91, [1895–9] All ER Rep 244 at 247, Lindley MR said that the summary procedure for striking out a statement of claim 'is only appropriate to cases which are plain and obvious, so that any master or judge can say at once that the statement of claim as it stands is insufficient'.

If one takes that statement at its full width, this does not appear to be a case for striking out. I doubt whether any master or judge could look at this case and 'say at once' that the statement of claim is insufficient. If the other party objects to the matter being dealt with on a summons to strike out, and contends that the question should instead be resolved by the trial of a question or issue under RSC Ord 33, r 3, then the *Hubbuck* case may well support the objection. That, however, has not happened in this case; and if instead the parties concur in seeking to have the point resolved on a summons to strike out, as they have done before me, I do not see why they should not do so, even if the point is one that initially is not plain and obvious, and does not enable the master or judge to say at once that the statement of claim is insufficient. But even if it takes some time to get there, the question at the end of the hearing must be whether it has then become obvious and clear beyond doubt that the claim cannot possibly succeed. I think that the court—

'must beware of any assumption that because a case takes a long time to argue, the points at issue must be doubtful. Arguments must be assessed on their quality rather than on their duration, and sometimes the weaker the case the greater the profusion of ingenuity in supporting it.'

(See *Manuel v A-G* [1982] 3 All ER 786 at 790, [1983] Ch 77 at 82.)

Counsel for the plaintiffs contended that in reaching my conclusion I should if possible
give effect to the opening sentence of art 6(1) of the European Convention on Human
Rights (Convention for the Protection of Human Rights and Fundamental Freedoms
(Rome, 4 November 1950; TS (1953); (Cmd 8969)). This states:

> 'In the determination of his civil rights and obligations . . . everyone is entitled to
> a fair and public hearing within a reasonable time by an independent and impartial
> tribunal established by law . . .'

If the statement of claim is struck out, the plaintiffs would be left without any lawful
means of preventing the nuisance from being created or of testing whether they were
entitled to do so, without having had the hearing which the convention requires. There
might be compensation for them once the nuisance had actually arisen, but that was far
from being the same as preventing it from arising. Therefore, the argument went, the
court should be especially slow to strike out the statement of claim.

It seems to me that the plaintiffs have a very real and substantial grievance. First, they
sued in the German courts in Berlin, and were stopped by the Allied Kommandatura.
Second, they found themselves unable to sue in the High Court in the British sector of
Berlin because the provisions in the ordinance for establishing that court had not been
carried out. Third, they sued here, and, if counsel for the ministry is right, the issue of
the Secretary of State's certificate requires these proceedings to be struck out. I do not
need the European Convention on Human Rights to tell me that it is deplorable that, as
counsel for the ministry accepts and asserts, there is no court with power to decide
whether the plaintiffs are entitled to the remedy that they seek. If heard, their claim
might fail, or the court might reach the conclusion that in all the circumstances of the
case (including the special position of Berlin) it would not be right to grant the
discretionary remedy of declaratory relief; but at least the plaintiffs would have had their
day in court, and would have had their claim considered on its merits. That would have
been their right if their houses and the shooting range had been in England; but because
they are in the British sector of Berlin, they are to be driven away, with no hearing on
the merits. I have heard no justification for what seems to me to be the plain injustice of
this. The convention is not, of course, law, though it is legitimate to consider its
provisions in interpreting the law; and naturally I give it full weight for this purpose.

In the end, I have to come back to the question whether the plaintiffs' claim in these
proceedings is so plainly bad that it should be struck out. On the procedural point, I
cannot see that there is any way round for the plaintiffs. The right to sue 'the Ministry of
Defence' depends on the 1947 Act, and the certificate of the Secretary of State plainly
precludes bringing these proceedings against that defendant, since they are necessarily
proceedings 'under or in accordance with this Act'. Nothing that counsel for the plaintiffs
has said seems to me to offer any prospect of escape from this.

On the other hand, the point of substance does not appear to me to be altogether
beyond argument. Proceedings for tort that are pursued outside the Act, relying on the
exposure of the Crown to actions in tort by s 2, can be said not to be proceedings 'under
or in accordance with this Act', even though it is only by virtue of the Act that they can
be brought at all. I am not sure that the somewhat remarkable distinction that this
produces is enough to make the words 'under or in accordance with' embrace words such
as 'by virtue of'. In the modern climate of statutory construction I am inclined to think
that it would; but the point, though mentioned in argument, was far from being fully
explored. No authorities were cited on the point, although in fact words and phrases
such as 'by virtue of', 'under or by virtue of', 'in accordance with' and 'under' have been
considered in a number of authorities. I am not sure how far these authorities help. I can
only say that quite apart from them I am not sure enough on the point to hold that the
action should be struck out, and the existence of some unexplored authorities adds to
that uncertainty; and in so far as the matter is one of discretion, I would not exercise that
discretion so as to strike out the action. In the result, I would not strike out the statement
of claim if this ground stood alone.

a   In the end, however, I am reluctantly compelled to the conclusion that, on the procedural point, the statement of claim must be struck out. But before I make any order to that effect, I must consider an application by counsel for the plaintiff that he made midway through the first day of the hearing. This was for leave to amend the statement of claim by adding the major-general who is the British military commandant of Berlin as the second defendant. Counsel for the ministry objected to this amendment being made, both generally and also at that stage, as he had not been informed of the proposed
b   application until earlier that day. I adjourned the application until the conclusion of the argument; and when that point was reached, it was agreed that it would be more convenient to hear the application after I had given judgment but before I made any order. I shall therefore hear that application.

Application for claim against the Ministry to be struck out granted.

c   **Application to join parties**
The plaintiffs applied to add Major-General Gordon Lennox and the Attorney General as defendants.

John R Macdonald QC and *Owen Davies* for the plaintiffs.
d   *John Mummery* for the Attorney General.
Major-General Gordon Lennox did not appear.

At the conclusion of the argument Sir Robert Megarry V-C granted the plaintiffs leave to add the Attorney General as a defendant but directed that the order was not to be perfected until his Lordship gave his reasons, which he would do later.

e   16 April. The following judgment was delivered.

SIR ROBERT MEGARRY V-C. This is an application by the plaintiffs under RSC Ord 15, r 6 for Major-General Gordon Lennox and the Attorney General to be added as defendants in place of the Ministry of Defence, against which I have already decided that the proceedings should be struck out. Various other amendments to the statement of
f   claim were sought, though these are mainly consequential; but I should mention that General Gordon Lennox, the British military commandant of Berlin, is to be sued both in his personal capacity and on behalf of the Crown. Mr Mummery now appears on behalf of the Attorney General, though he did not represent General Gordon Lennox, who is not represented; and Mr Macdonald again appears on behalf of the plaintiffs.
The case of counsel for the plaintiffs is very simple. The only reason why the
g   proceedings against the Ministry of Defence are to be struck out is that the ministry is not incorporated and so cannot be sued except by virtue of s 17 of the Crown Proceedings Act 1947; and the certificate of the Secretary of State precludes the plaintiffs from relying on that section. That, however, does not preclude the plaintiffs from suing those who are legal persons; and although the claim is in tort, s 2 of the Act has removed any inability
h   of a plaintiff to sue the Crown or any Crown servant in tort. Section 21(2) of the Act does not apply to such proceedings, and in any case a declaration against either of the proposed defendants would not constitute relief against the Crown which could not have been obtained in proceedings against the Crown.
The submissions of counsel for the Attorney General, which he helpfully supported by tendering a summary of his argument, was in effect that any claim against the Attorney General was bound to fail, and so it would be wrong to allow the plaintiffs to
j   add him as a defendant. True, the plaintiffs could have sued him initially; but if they had done this, an application by him to have the proceedings struck out as against him would have been bound to succeed. Under the Act 'civil proceedings against the Crown' must be brought against the appropriate authorised government department, here the Ministry of Defence: see s 17(3). This was a mandatory provision, and not a matter of option or discretion. The expression 'civil proceedings against the Crown' includes

proceedings against the Attorney General in tort for the purposes of Pts II, III and IV of
the Act (which include ss 17 and 40); for s 23(2)(c) makes the expression, for the purposes
of Pt II, include 'all such proceedings as any person is entitled to bring against the Crown
by virtue of this Act'; and for the purposes of Pts III and IV, s 38(4) makes the expression
include 'civil proceedings to which the Attorney General . . . as such is a party'.

The riposte of counsel for the plaintiffs was that s 17(3) had no application to this
action. By virtue of s 40(2)(b) and the Secretary of State's certificate, which counsel for the
Attorney General had relied on as preventing the plaintiffs from suing the Ministry of
Defence, nothing in the Act was to 'authorise proceedings to be taken against the Crown
under or in accordance with this Act'. The plaintiffs' claim, said counsel for the plaintiffs,
was a claim that was being made outside the Act, and not 'under or in accordance' with
it. Although by s 23(2)(c) any proceedings which a person was entitled to bring against
the Crown 'by virtue of this Act' were 'civil proceedings against the Crown' for the
purposes of Pt II of the Act, and so were brought within s 17(3), that could not override
the effect of s 40(2)(b) in preventing the claim from falling within s 17 at all. The case
was not one in which there was some overseas dominion, colony or other territory of the
Crown in which there was some minister or other person or body that could be sued as
representing the Crown, as had been the case in *Buck v A-G* [1964] 2 All ER 663, [1965]
Ch 745; *affd* [1965] 1 All ER 882, [1965] Ch 745. The governmental responsibility for
the British sector of Berlin was a matter of some obscurity, and the plaintiffs ought to be
allowed to sue the Attorney General in addition to the commandant, lest on suing the
commandant alone it should emerge that he was the wrong defendant.

The argument of counsel for the Attorney General is plainly cogent, and I am far from
being sure that the answer of counsel for the plaintiffs will hold water. At the same time,
I must remember that it is for the plaintiffs to decide initially who the defendants are to
be; and if they join a defendant who ought not to be joined, the defendant's course is to
apply to have the claim struck out as against him. As I said in my judgment on 28 March,
the 1947 Act is by no means simple, and I do not feel sufficiently sure of the inevitability
of success of the argument of counsel on behalf of the Attorney General to say that the
claim against him should be struck out. Nor am I at all clear about the status of the
commandant or the government of the British sector of Berlin; and it would be
lamentable if the claim proceeded against the commandant alone, and then the plaintiffs
were to be met by a contention that he was the wrong defendant, and that they ought to
have sued some general representative of the Crown instead.

The plaintiffs most certainly ought to be able to have their claim tested in some court
somewhere. They have been thwarted in Berlin by being prevented by the Allied
Kommandatura from suing in the German courts, and by the failure to set up a High
Court in the British sector, despite the provisions of Ordinance No 68; and now they are
faced once more with procedural difficulties, this time by the complexities of the 1947
Act. If I were satisfied that proceedings against the Attorney General would fail, I would
refuse leave to join him; but although I have serious doubts whether they will succeed, I
am certainly not satisfied that they will fail. In so far as the matter rests in my discretion,
I would unhesitatingly exercise it in favour of allowing the joinder. It was for these
reasons that on 2 April I gave leave to join the Attorney General, though at the request of
his counsel I directed that the order should not be perfected until I had stated the reasons
for my decision, as I have now done. I also give leave to join General Lennox.

*Application to join Major-General Gordon Lennox and the Attorney General as defendants
granted.*

Solicitors: *Seifert Sedley & Co* (for the plaintiffs); *Treasury Solicitor.*

                                                    Vivian Horvath   Barrister.

                              End of Volume 2